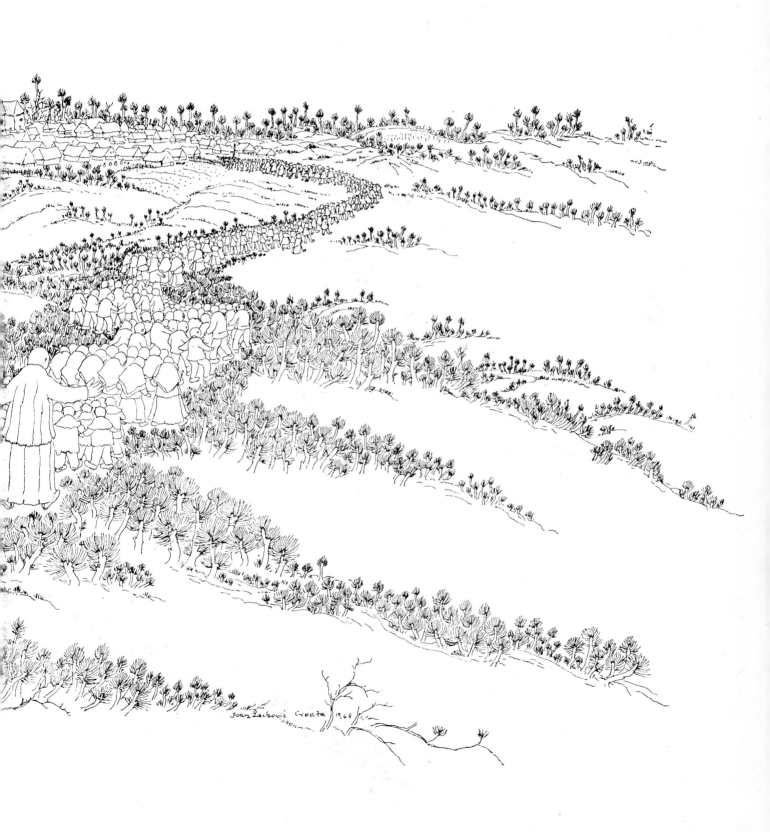

Joan Lachowic Croata 1968

KT-145-920

WORLD ENCYCLOPEDIA OF NAIVE ART

A Hundred Years of Naive Art

OTO BIHALJI-MERIN
NEBOJŠA-BATO TOMAŠEVIĆ

WORLD
ENCYCLOPEDIA
OF
NAIVE
ART
A Hundred Years of
Naive Art

Frederick Muller
London

WORLD ENCYCLOPEDIA
OF NAIVE ART

Editors
Oto BIHALJI-MERIN
Nebojša-Bato TOMAŠEVIĆ

Publication Adviser
Ljubivoje STEFANOVIĆ

Design
Miodrag VARTABEDIJAN

Senior Editor
Emilija PAVKOVIĆ

Translators
Kordija KVEDER
Madge PHILLIPS
Karolina UDOVIČKI
Arthur SHKAROVSKY-RAFFÉ
W. E. YUILL

First published in Great Britain in 1984 by Frederick Muller

Frederick Muller is an imprint of Muller, Blond & White Limited, 55/57 Great Ormond Street, London, WCIN 3HZ.

Copyright © 1984, Jugoslovenska Revija, Belgrade

All rights reserved. No part of this publication may be reproduced, stored in a retrieval system, or transmitted in any form or by any means, electronic, mechanical, photocopying, recording or otherwise, without the prior consent of Muller, Blond & White Limited.

British Library Cataloguing in Publication Data

Bihalji-Merin, Oto
  World encyclopaedia of naive art
  1. Primitivism in art
  I. Title   II. Tomasevic, Nebojsa
  759.05'3   ND1482.P7

  ISBN 0-584-95062-4

Printed and bound in Yugoslavia by Gorenjski Tisk, Kranj

Rousseau, Henri: I Myself — Portrait-Landscape

CONTRIBUTORS

Oto BIHALJI-MERIN
Art historian and art critic, Yugoslavia

Ernesto CARDENAL
Writer, painter and Minister of Culture, Nicaragua

Gert CLAUSSNITZER
Editor-in-chief of *Verlag der Kunst*, Dresden, Germany (GDR)

Jacques COLLARD
Writer and art critic, Belgium

Ruth DEBEL
Art critic and gallery-owner, Israel

Aleksandar DEMAJO
Yugoslav Ambassador, Bolivia

M. T. SOLÁ DE DANDOLO
Art critic, Argentina

Nico van der ENDT
Art critic, Netherlands

John FOWLER
Art critic and gallery-owner, USA

José GÓMEZ-SICRE
Director of Modern Art Museum of Latin America, Washington, USA

Prof. Thomas GROCHOWIAK
Professor of art history, art critic, Germany (FRG)

Mircea-Petru ILIESCU
Art critic, Romania

Aleksander JACKOWSKI
Director of the Institute for Non-professional Art of the Polish Academy
of Science, Poland

Georges KASPER
Editor of *Gazette pro Arte* and gallery-owner, Switzerland

Boris KELEMEN
Director of Zagreb City Museum, Yugoslavia

Sumio KUWABARA
Professor of the Musashino Academy of Art, Japan

Thomas LACKEY
Associate of the National Museum, Canada

Bianca McCULLOUGH
Art critic, Australia

Dino MENOZZI
Art critic, editor-in-chief of *L'Arte Naive*, Italy

Ida F. MIHÁLY
Associate of the National Gallery of Budapest, art critic, Hungary

Modest MORARIU
Art critic, editor-in-chief of *Meridiane*, Romania

Prof. Fritz NOVOTNY
Architect and writer of *Naive Art*, Germany (FRG)

Ma. Dolores BARAJAS PALOMO
Cultural Attaché of the Mexican Embassy, Belgrade

Dr. Dimitrios PAPASTAMOS
Director of National Art Museum, Greece

Prof. Arsen POHRIBNY
Professor of art history and art critic, Germany (FRG)

Tony RUSSELL
Associate of Museo de Arte Popular *Salvador Valero*, Venezuela

Charles SCHAETTEL
Curator of *Musée du Vieux Château*, Musées de Laval, France

Gerhard SCHOENBERNER
Art critic and writer, Berlin

Natalia SHKAROVSKAYA
Art historian and art critic, USSR

Angela TAMVAKI
Art critic, Greece

Stefan TKAČ
Art critic, Czechoslovakia

Nebojša-Bato TOMAŠEVIĆ
Art critic and publisher, Yugoslavia

Julia WEISSMAN
Writer and art critic, USA

Sheldon WILLIAMS
Art critic and painter, Great Britain

Naive artists from the following countries are included:

Argentina
Australia
Austria

Belgium
Bolivia
Brazil

Canada
Chile
China
Cuba
Cyprus
Czechoslovakia

France

East Germany
West Germany
Ghana
Great Britain
Greece

Haiti
Honduras
Hungary

Iceland
Indonesia
Ireland
Israel
Italy

Jamaica
Japan

Kenya

Mexico

Netherlands
New Zealand
Nicaragua
Nigeria

Palau
Panama
Poland
Portugal

Romania

Spain
Switzerland

Uganda
Upper Volta
USA
USSR

Venezuela

Yugoslavia

Zaire

Smajić, Petar: Adam and Eve

CONTENTS

Benassi, Enrico: A Muse of Ancient Rome

Oto Bihalji-Merin
A Hundred Years
of Naive Art

DISCOVERY OF A TIMELESS ART

Rousseau, Henri: A Hungry Lion Rends an Antelope

The work of naive artists is as old as man's need for artistic activity. All art is naive to begin with. From the end of the 19th century onwards, ever since the advent of Henri Rousseau on the artistic scene, and throughout the 20th century so far, naive art has outlasted the ever-changing variety of aesthetic styles. Although subject to its own laws, naive art remains nevertheless an essential part of the artistic scene in any period.

The growing attraction of naive art at the present time has profound roots and is not a mere fashionable craze.

Our civilization has entered a critical phase in its scientific and technical development. The more the world expands within our consciousness, the more acutely the individual feels alienated from it. The professional artist is involved in exploration and experiment, and his attention is focussed on newly discovered mysteries in the material world. In such circumstances it may seem something of a paradox to suggest withdrawal into the purest and most childlike province of human vision, the art of the naives. The 20th century, however, has taught us to look at things in a new way. The irresistible march of technical progress, paid for by an increasing depletion of our psychic capital, has directed the eye of the artist once more towards elemental images. In their search for comprehensive links and affinities, artists and connoisseurs are turning not only towards the archaic experiences of sensibility but also toward the later forms of naive and primitive art.

Idol of South Sea, New Ireland

Stanisavljević, Milan: Human Machine

*Wooden Mask, Itumba Region
(between Gabon and Congo)*

*Picasso, Pablo:
Les Demoiselles d'Avignon*

This upsurge of the naive and the primitive within the sphere of our civilization, initiated by Paul Gauguin's journey to Tahiti, is the final recourse of modern European art to the resources of energy embodied in nature. Naive painters form no particular "trend" within modern art. Their artlessly eccentric structures stand outside the intellectual concerns of professional artists. Their work stems from an unforced and carefree impulse of the heart. But in the abundance and variety of those works which are classified as neo-primitive or naive art, not everything can be ascribed to modes of artistic expression. For as authentic naivety is rooted in the profoundest recesses of our existence, decorative artlessness and rudimentary storytelling are not the sole features of naive art; there is also delight in discovery and in the use of imaginative pictorial statement.

The character of naive art flourishes in a psychic landscape of simplicity and ingenuousness. If the naive artist relinquishes these qualities, then he is liable to jeopardize the specific climate in which his art thrives. Normally, it is impossible to detect any sign of chronological development in the career of a naive painter, although over the years he may well perfect his technique and handle the material of his compositions with increasing ease. But if feeling and sensibility begin to flag, then he starts repeating himself and produces work of a purely routine kind, so that originality and spontaneity are soon lost. As his paintings or sculptures become technically more accomplished, their tension and radiance decline.

Those artists who are sufficiently talented to achieve a certain mastery are not the only ones worth studying. There are many other people seeking relaxation from the demands of their work in artistic creation who are also able, by originality of observation and by directness of narrative approach, to make their contribution to the restoration of a pictorial language that would otherwise have been lost. Such people devote their evenings, weekends and holidays to artistic pursuits. It is not surprising that a number of leading naive painters did not embark on their artistic careers until they were well advanced in years, for it is in later life that people have most leisure. Henri Rousseau himself was not able

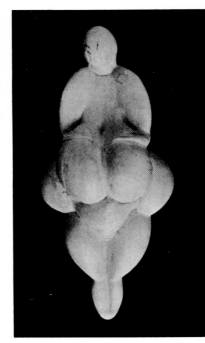

The Venus of Lespugue,
Haute Garonne

Bombois, Camille: Woman Bather and Water Lilies

The Venus of Willendorf

to pursue his art until he was a pensioner, and this was also the case with Louis Vivin, a post office employee, and Morris Hirshfield, a slipper manufacturer. And it was not until Grandma Moses found work in the fields too arduous that she took up her paint-brush in order to find a meaning in life through this new form of activity. I am not suggesting that all naive artists are capable of creating works of enduring value. But many of these people who have actively turned to naive forms of expression constitute a leaven for the art of the future.

More and more creative individuals are seeking refuge in naive art from the hectic and denatured world in which they live. It is the infinite variety, as much as the character of this propensity for artistic creativity, almost tantamount to a mass movement, that attracts our sympathetic interest.

However, the size of the movement now makes it necessary to turn a critical spotlight on the phenomenon of naive art, to identify its lasting values and to distinguish them from artistic products of a meretricious kind. We must also ask ourselves whether it will be possible, in a world of mass media and rapid, radical change, to preserve intact a form of artistic expression which we ourselves recognize as a survival from a more natural and spontaneous mode of existence, or whether these preserves of the naive will also be swept away by the passage of time.

In the early years of the century it was sufficient, for purposes of definition, to compare the works of the few naive artists then known with those of professional painters. When professional artists abandoned their academic style, the distinction was drawn between professional and amateur work. But this division, too, was in turn to be rendered obsolete by subsequent developments. For the increasing scale and intensity of their activity turned many of the naive artists into professionals. Port-au-Prince and Hlebine are no longer the only places where naive artists live who can be regarded as full-time professionals.

The problems that arise when we look more closely at naive art are no easier to resolve than those in other areas of art. The many facets of the phenomenon to which we apply the term naive art make it necessary to define all its varieties with the greatest possible precision: primitive art, folk art, popular painting, rural and urban amateurism, the pseudo-naive, self-conscious naivety and naive art. There are hardly any hard and fast categories, dividing lines are vague and any kind of strict differentiation is questionable. Classification here does not imply aesthetic judgement, but is merely intended to guide and clarify.

In my book, *The Naive Image of the World*, (1959), naive artists were defined for the first time as individuals practising their art world-wide but outside historical and stylistic categories. The naive artist is less concerned to grapple with the form of things than with the things themselves. As with children and primitive peoples, pictorial representation and reality constitute a single identity. This definition is firmly established: it has been incorporated in the *Sachwörterbuch der Kunst der 20. Jahrhunderts* and in most publications concerned with naive art.

The present work of reference attempts to explain and summarize our theoretical and practical knowledge of naive art, to offer definitions and, in its main section, to provide biographical entries on the individual artists in alphabetical order.

The Term "Naive" and its Definition

Naive artists have been designated in many ways: painters of instinct, Painters of the Sacred Heart, Maîtres Populaires de la Réalité, Neo-primitives, Sunday painters and "insite" artists. All these terms contain an element of truth, but none of them is entirely satisfactory.

If we employ the term "naive", then this is because it is more suitable than others to characterize this type of art. The concept of "untrained painter" is too broad, embracing as it does all those practitioners without professional training, from folk art and regional art down to dilettantes and amateurs from various social strata. The term "Sunday painter", on the other hand, seems to be too restrictive, since it suggests a mere hobby, an occasional preoccupation.

The flowery expression "Painters of the Sacred Heart", with its poetically sentimental overtones, refers solely to the first group of painters formed by Wilhelm Uhde; they have now come to be regarded as classics of the naive.

The term "Maîtres Populaires de la Réalité" is applicable to only a proportion of naive artists, for naive painters and sculptors are frequently unrealistic dreamers and visionaries. "Painters of instinct" includes not only naive painters but also the graphic artists of primitive peoples. Naive artists might, then, perhaps be called "Twentieth-century Primitives", and this is sometimes done. Whereas primitive art, however, emerges from a total cultural complex at a particular stage in its evolution, and has a cultural function, the art of the neo-primitives, the naive artists, is based on individuality.

The founders of the Triennial Festival of Naive Art in Bratislava have suggested the term "Insite Art". They suggested that the word "naive" has, at least in the Slavonic languages, a faintly derogatory association. The term "insitus", borrowed from Latin and meaning "native, ingenuous" was, however, neutral. But terms change. Half a century after the death of Douanier Rousseau the expression "naive art" still sounds sufficiently convincing. It is certain that naive artists no more consider their works naive than the creators of the many-armed Shiva figures would term their work fantastic. Things themselves are never fantastic, but their essence, seen from some other point of view, may well be so.

Archaic Art and the Art of Primitive Peoples

A certain element of the naive exists wherever observation of nature does not entirely coincide with the processes of intellectual comprehension. Art was obliged initially to discover or devise both the world and the means of its representation.

In the process of artistic formation and materialization certain invisible forces made their appearance alongside the visible features of reality. Once given artistic form, they persisted. Early huntsmen tried to determine the fortunes of the chase by means of magic ritual. The power of magic was for them as real as the power of the stone axe which they invented. Art revolved around the form of the animal. In so far as the female figure made its appearance, it was in terms of fertility symbols. Representations of the male figure were less frequent and showed man in his role as huntsman. Man did not look beyond the horizon of his practical existence. Magic preceded the loss of innocence entailed in the acquisition of knowledge.

Prehistoric man, abandoning the mode of life of the hunter and food-gatherer, devised abbreviations and pictographic signs that were no longer illustrations but mental images, reflections of the transition from his existence as a herdsman to the settled life of the early tiller of the soil.

The formal vocabulary of primeval and archaic art has something in common with the representations of primitive peoples in our own age: in both cases it is a matter of communication and conjuration. Graven images, idols, ancestral totems are designed to facilitate a dialogue with supernatural powers. The conception of space is governed by the restricted field of view, being perceived and shaped as a single entity. This is pre-perspectival art, marked in painting by the exclusive use of the full frontal or the profile aspect. Sculpture is characterized by economy of forms and simplified stylization.

The artists of so-called primitive peoples belong to pre-industrial cultures. They have their roots in ideas derived from religious myths. These anonymous artists feel themselves to be links in an endless chain of generations and to be identical with their work. The sculptor is less concerned to give form to what he sees around him than to embody its inner meaning. The art of primitive people is a formal language governed by instinct, a ritual rather than an aesthetic activity. It is the perfection of its form which charges the work with the magic that endows it with special powers.

As the mythical interpretation of the world is supplanted by a conceptual view an art develops in which objective criteria of reality and the natural laws of optics come into their own. The primeval pictorial qualities of the naive fade away.

Folk Art: Art by and for the People

The term "folk art" is linked to the cultural landscape of an agrarian community: folk art implies a cultural heritage and historical sequence; it is not based on individual taste but on an observed world of custom and tradition. It persists as long as a socially and psychologically stable community survives. In modern civilization old social structures are in process of disintegration. Folk art and peasant art are losing their original inner significance and turning into the decorative trappings of a lost tradition.

The Horse of Lascaux

Hirshfield, Morris: The Tiger

Industrial mechanization, modern means of communication, new materials and substances, new colours are beginning to oust the objects and forms of folk art. They are disrupting the contemplative and patriarchal mode of life and changing the relationship of the artisan to the consumer. A popular art of little value in itself, adapted to the needs of fashion and the market-place, has begun to make its appearance as a kind of substitute folk art.

The anonymous forces that were once manifested in folk art live on underground, and as the community disintegrates they begin to seek an individual rebirth. Disintegrating folk art merges into an amateur art which combines the last traces of the collective with the ageless urge to play and man's perpetual childish desire to impart shape to things: hence the art of the naive.

24

Painting of a schoolboy (named Ivan Stoilović)

Children's Art

The predilection for archaic and primitive art also awakened a deeper interest in the nature and significance of children's art. It was the insights offered by depth psychology and the modern view of art which made it possible to detect authentic creative values in the awkward spontaneity, the honest clumsiness and the inept instinctiveness that are characteristic of children's art.

Somewhere between speech and the skill of writing there takes place the discovery of signs that are equivalent to a perception of the world. From the somnambulist lines scribbled by a child there develops the pictorial symbol of his earliest act of perception. As with the invention of writing, these pictorial signs of children's art are a form of communication. Both the child and the naive painter are striving to elucidate their experience of the world and to transmute it into pictorial terms. Defective anatomy and lack of perspective are not the expression of a deliberate stylistic design but of a rationally undeveloped stage of consciousness.

The educational process diverts the intensely pictorial imagination in the direction of rational comprehension and abstract thought. Perceptions that were initially total are dissected and replaced by logical imitation. A child's drawing thus ceases to express a spontaneous experience and is adapted to the visual and intellectual norm of the adult.

Since the introduction of children's programmes on television, which can reach many more individuals than the cinema ever could, the brilliant cartoon films of Walt Disney and his successors have exerted a considerable influence on the receptive function of the childish imagination: classic figures like Mickey Mouse and Donald Duck, as well as characters from Sesame Street and the Muppet Show, have become archetypes for the visual imagery of young people. They represent a break between the early exploratory children's drawing and the type of drawing which has been inundated with optical impressions, modified and adapted and which has consequently forfeited its naive quality.

Comparison of works by children with those by naive artists often displays profound affinities; in the subsequent development of children's drawing and that of naive artists, however, an increasing divergence may be observed, to the point where they become entirely distinct. The child's pictures are the product of a transitional phase; as he develops, his instinctive impulses are reduced and the creative act is, as a rule, increasingly replaced by a deliberate and rational conception. The naive artist's work has the power of survival; the child's art perishes as he develops.

The Artistic Expression of the Mentally Ill

Works of art by mental patients, like children's art, stand outside the historical course of human evolution. They, too, run counter to the logical terms of reference, deny the reservations imposed by civilization and erase all the conventional relationships between the individual and the object. Again, like children's art, the art of the mentally ill is incapable of achieving any kind of continuity, since the calligraphy of mental anxiety and neurosis derives its impulse from a pathological condition which is liable to disrupt the process of artistic creation.

The precise distinction between normality and mental instability, sickness and health, has always been difficult to draw. In modern art it is no longer capable of clear definition. Unlike the Renaissance artist, the present-day artist no longer thinks of himself as *homo universalis*, in tune with the natural order of the world and the cosmos. He employs the language of the absurd and the grotesque to express the nightmares and hallucinations that haunt him: visions of terror, insecurity and isolation are his themes.

In the case of the mentally sick, native talent is just as decisive a factor as with normal, healthy artists. Mental illness cannot turn anyone into a genius,

César, drawing of a patient named Aloyse

but it can liberate existing talents, which, freed from conventions, stylistic and otherwise, can create works of aesthetic merit.

Pictures of this kind are not conceived in a spirit of deliberate premeditation. The mental patient does not go looking for his themes, but projects from within the vision which torments him; it bursts forth, borne on the irresistible torrent of the unconscious, and develops with a spontaneity of the kind that we may observe in the painting of the 20th century in the forms of serial painting and the informel idiom.

Spare-time Painters and Amateurs

In most European countries amateur art has been dominated by the influence of prevailing artistic styles. The artists called themselves "dilettanti" and often produced, with less adequate means, the same kind of work as professionally trained artists — but to a lower standard of accomplishment.

The forerunners of naive painting in North America, untrained painters of humble origins, did not form their image of the world in contrast to the general trend of artistic development, as was the case in France. They belonged within the same community as the pioneers whose houses they decorated, whose portraits they painted and whose tastes they shared.

Any attempt to distinguish precisely between folk art, amateur painting and naive art must be made in the context of the relevant historical and cultural background.

Movements aiming to emancipate peoples and tribes in Africa and Oceania are introducing fresh elements into amateur art. Africa's strongly traditional tribal art, which exerted a great deal of influence on naive artists as in Central and South America, is vanishing on its home ground in the face of an advancing industrial civilization. In its place, a popular amateur art is growing up there which stands in distinct contrast to tradition.

Turning to the sphere of Oriental culture, we find it difficult to distinguish between folk art and naive art. In Asia and the Far East traditional art has been less affected by the dissociation of consciousness. The peasant amateur painters of present-day China are the bearers both of a strictly defined formal tradition and a revolutionary social ethos.

Let us try to define the points of similarity and contrast as between amateur art and naive art. The amateur painter tries to reproduce the appearance of visible reality and achieves his effects less by the study of anatomy and perspective than by borrowing self-contained components from the work of established professional artists. Even in the case of naive painters we can detect a desire to assimilate the work of professionally trained artists. But their approach to the phenomena of nature is emotionally coloured and guided by instinct. Amateurs follow in the wake of professional art and feel that they somehow belong in the same context. For this reason they also follow the stylistic changes of high art, albeit cautiously and hesitantly, imparting to their works a taste of Classicism, Impressionism, Expressionism, elements of the Surreal or the Abstract.

Whereas the naive painter endeavours to represent the inner nature of things and appearances from his own experience, without regard to the limitations of his knowledge or potential, the amateur artist tries to adopt traditional techniques and even stylistic forms and to acquire the superior expertise of his models by borrowing from them.

The naive artist boldly attempts the most difficult of themes and precisely through the tension which arises from technical deficiencies and the truth of his inner vision, from the contrast of intellectual simplicity and visual imagery, he achieves that idiosyncrasy of creative expression that singles him out from other artists. Deformations and transformations of observed images are not a matter of stylistic intention but projections of his inner vision.

THE RECOGNITION OF NAIVE ART

From Paul Gauguin to Henri Rousseau

The revolutionary change in art that occurred in about the year 1890, largely due to Cézanne, Van Gogh and Gauguin, stood in contrast to an urban civilization that had become effete and superficial. Cézanne passed through and transcended the Impressionist's view of the world. In place of disintegration he sought stabilization and synthesis in composition. Matters of the mind took shape in the process of artistic creation and aspired to a new order in the world. Vincent van Gogh, a failure in the commercial art world, lay-preacher in the mining district of Belgium, discovered, in his search for the primeval brotherhood of mankind, a visual language of utterly instinctive authenticity which represented a cosmically intense response to objects in the world around him.

Paul Gauguin, bosun's mate, bank clerk and a "Sunday painter" in the initial stages of his career, detested the mechanized urban bustle of a Europe grown blasé and disillusioned. He turned his back on Paris and the middle-class way of life in order to find among primitive people the vital intensity of pristine forms and mythical imagery. He attempted to answer questions regarding the descent of man and his ultimate aim through the example of his life and work, by abandoning civilization and returning to the lost paradise of an archaic community. In the art of Europe and the world this turning back to the origins of man and society entailed a profound break with tradition. It was in this way that the rehabilitation of archaic and primitive cultures, the emancipation from the tyranny of Classical antiquity, began. The art of primitive peoples carried the ancient message, now revived, that the world was not what it seemed to the common gaze but what the artist knowingly felt about it. The abandonment of imitation, the surrender of devices designed to create illusion, implied the beginning of a new era. Just when the mode of representation of concrete objects seemed to have been discarded as outworn, *Henri Rousseau* stepped out of the soulless artificiality of the bourgeois world into the fabulous country of his pictures and transformed those things which had grown trite, and indeed well-nigh invisible, on account of their sheer conventionality into new entities, awakening them to new life and restoring them to mankind.

With Henri Rousseau, the customs official, the hitherto unknown creative activity of the naive artist emerged into the spotlight of publicity. The earliest of his pictures known to us date from 1880. After being introduced by Paul Signac and Maximilian Luce, Rousseau was represented in the exhibitions of the Salon des Indépendants from 1886 onwards. His pictures hung side by side with those of Signac, Seurat, Toulouse-Lautrec, Van Gogh, Bonnard, Matisse and Cézanne. In 1891, when Paul Gauguin made his journey to the South Seas and painted his "Women of Tahiti", Rousseau produced his first jungle picture. Like a sleepwalker, Rousseau followed a path of dreams made real, and a dream-like reality. In this he anticipated the modern notion of reality as a dialectical interplay of the visible and the feasible, of knowledge and vision. The real world is expanded to accommodate the possible world, Utopia is experienced at first hand; in response to his childlike magic touch, nature turns into a Promised Land.

An act of creation took place, a homecoming that breathed new life into things that had been reduced to mere items of commerce. Rousseau loved his fellow-men, but a fraternal feeling bound him also to the humble appliances of everyday life: a woman's hat, a sunshade, a paraffin lamp, a vase, a lantern — they all possess something, apart from their normal appearance, which is oddly individual. Rousseau conferred on these unpretentious objects a ceremonious and grotesquely poetic power of expression. From these simple mundane objects, seemingly paralysed and defunct, he constructed a magic world in which contact between men and things was re-established.

The specific nature of his hand is evident from the very outset — the clarity and hardness of the material from which man, animal, tree or leaf is carved. It is not only phenomena visible to the eye, but also those which are merely sensed, that go to make up the totality of his inspiration. Like the Byzantine icon-painters, Rousseau identified his compositions of form and colour with the objects which he was depicting. He already carried his image of the world firmly and securely within himself when he set out to give it visible form.

Painters of the Sacred Heart and their Successors

Almost fifty years ago, in the house of Wilhelm Uhde, friend and discoverer of Henri Rousseau, situated in the Faubourg St Germain, I gained my first deeper insight into the art of these painters. I gazed into the world of Vivin and Séraphine, Bombois and Bauchant. Why was I so affected by Séraphine's recondite flowers, plucked from the hereafter; those incandescent bouquets, embroidered with all the hues of ecstasy: harsh yellow, a disconcerting reptilian green, soothing autumnal wine-red and innocently devout turquoise? What is the origin of these floral expressions of yearning, which flourished in her imagination with almost elemental luxuriance? Perhaps the painter was inspired by the sentimental, glossy artificial flowers and floral tributes of wax and cellophane that one finds in provincial cemeteries and chapels? Perhaps *Séraphine* incorporated into her pictures the cosmic vision that is filtered through the windows of the church in Senlis? For although the pictures she painted may be manic repetitions of decoratively stylized floral patterns, they are also arabesques of an inner revelation, hieroglyphs fashioned from blossoms — intelligible in the final analysis only to the painter herself and to that God to whom she dedicated the sacred ecstasies of her letters.

The precincts of ecstasy were foreign to the postal inspector *Louis Vivin* (1861—1936). He communicated with the mysterious voices of the hereafter only in spiritualist séances. When he stood at his easel he painted the actual world as even more actual than it is. In the twilight of his old age when, as a pensioner, he was free to pursue his chosen vocation, he groped his way back into the past, to all the streets, squares and bridges he had trodden in the course of his existence. He entered into every minute detail with painful precision. He recorded not just the overall impression of the houses but every brick, not the bridge as a whole but every steel girder, not merely every tree but every leaf; the subdued brick-red of his walls, the bitter ashen grey of his skies, the bluish black of the war-memorial and the hopeless colour of the house-fronts are all in his paintings. And somewhere behind these terraced houses trembles the secret of existence.

Why are we fascinated by the churches and squares which Vivin conjures up on the ornamental surface of his paintings, dream-like scenes laboriously constructed, brick by brick, with all the patience of a craftsman? There is no depth of perspective in these paintings; everything is one-dimensional, bereft of background. People pass through the bluish atmosphere of the streets like dolls represented frontally, like the figures on Egyptian tombs. It is perhaps because we sense another landscape beyond Vivin's meticulous, graphic narrative. The ageing painter's childlike clairvoyance created this landscape where the laws of material and perspective do not hold. Behind the pedantically accurate *mise-*

Bauchant, André: Apollo Showing Himself to the Shepherds

en-scène the world is so true, naked and simple that we catch our breath as we recognize it.

What affects us in the case of *Camille Bombois* are the echoes of folk art, vulgarized and mixed with an unconscious dash of the surrealistic. Bombois imparts to every form that he creates something of the overflowing energy of his own vitality. Landscapes and objects have their own three-dimensional existence, and the space through which the painter leads us, the bridges we cross, the tree-lined avenues leading into the distance, all have, by reason of their brilliant illumination, long shadows and acute perspectives, a peculiar sense of depth. It is outlandish individuals in particular that claim his attention. Wrestlers, weight-lifters, clowns, sword-swallowers, fire-eaters, giant women, nude or in tights — the secrets of the human body in all its plasticity are put on show and loudly proclaimed. This is the glamour of fairground and circus, the display of abnormalities, the captivating glitter of circus equestriennes, the stirring sound of brass bands. The art of the folk-song, something of the folklore of the exotic and lurid peasant fantasy are endowed with the technical resources of the loud-speaker and the steam organ. Bombois paints the robust talk of athletes and

Vivin, Louis: The Cathedral at Rheims

sportsmen, of provincial prostitutes and betting-shops, the boastful words of scandalmongers and the melancholy longing for respectability and an illusory gentility.

André Bauchant, apart from Rousseau possibly the most important member of the group, was a gardener, as his father had been. He pursued this occupation throughout his life. Even when he painted he recreated the many-coloured floral abundance of the trees and fruits of his native Touraine. His mountains built of stones, men and animals all have something vegetative; they sprout organic growths. What prompted Diaghilev to commission stage-sets from Bauchant, who had no acquaintance either with the ballet or with Stravinsky's music? The combination of an elevated notion of Classical antiquity with mundane surroundings, the simultaneous divorce and combination of myth and irony which also preoccupied the artists of *Pittura Metafisica*, corresponded somehow to the spirit of the time. Without any deliberate attempt at irony or the grotesque, André Bauchant unwittingly expressed something of the same kind. He populated his grandiose historical paintings with Bauchants disguised as Greeks, Romans and ancient Germans. The historical compositions were followed by works of his late period: flowers and birds, peasant scenes and landscapes. The rural world is represented in flat, velvety pastel shades: metaphors of a mystic

Séraphine (Louis): The Tree

kind of dream reality. Bauchant the gardener, an Antaeus among painters, delights us with the floral masquerade of his dreams, dreams that are rooted in the fertile soil of his devout imagination.

These are the "Five" whom Wilhelm Uhde put on show for the first time in the Galerie des Quatre Chemins in Paris in 1928 under the name of "Painters of the Sacred Heart", and whose work he taught me to see and understand. However, he did not insist on this designation when we discussed the modern primitives on a later occasion. It now struck him as too emotive, and the critical assessment of naive painters no longer seemed to him to depend on their spiritual innocence; it should be governed also, and indeed principally, by the sheer aesthetic quality and the creative individuality of their works. Since those days

34

Bombois, Camille: Brothel at Two O'clock in the Night

many other primitive artists have made their appearance in France as well as in other countries and continents. In a sense the way was prepared for them by the "Five". In France, a country with an unbroken artistic tradition, where the modern primitives were discovered at an early stage, naive artists have their allotted place.

The typographer *Dominique Peyronnet* manifested a kind of poetic and supremely accomplished banality in representing the frozen landscape of his desires as seascapes, forest or river scenes. He drew his world with a needle-like precision.

René Rimbert is passionately devoted to an intensity of vision which relates to the insistent appeal of physical objects as they emerge into waking existence from the infinite silence and serenity of their physical substance. His streets, squares and house-fronts are shown in the light of their ephemerality. Human beings are submerged in them and scarcely ever visible. They are phantoms from the past, having only one foot in this street, in this world. We can see only half of Rousseau's face as he peers from a window. As in the Prague self-portrait, he is holding his palette in his hand, gazing out of the picture with an eye dilated by wonder and a sense of discovery. Rimbert calls this delightful little work "Douanier Rousseau's Window".

Pippin, Horace: The Bargain

North American Primitives
From Pioneer Times to the Present Day

Some three centuries ago there began to emerge in North America a kind of popular amateur art in response to the need felt by ordinary people to express themselves through the visual means available to the self-taught.

The less of artistic tradition the art of farmers, preachers, artisans and housewives incorporated, the nearer it was to the spirit of a young and developing nation. After the United States had broken away from the British colonial system the intellectual bridges which linked the country to the old continent also began to crumble. The newly awakened aspiration towards aesthetic expression now found an adequate form in the paintings of amateurs and naive professional painters. These works arose spontaneously from the need to communicate and to earn money.

In America the contrast between dilettantism and naive painting was not at first clearly marked. Many men and women painted in order to embellish their surroundings, to preserve the faces of their relatives for posterity or to record signal events from history or their own lives. Portraits, memorials, landscapes, still life pictures, genre paintings and allegories constitute the gallery of the popular painters. Parsons and teachers decorated marriage and birth certificates, ladies painted arrangements of fruit, flower-pieces and portraits of the deceased as keepsakes. So-called "folk art" arises from the combination of a graceful, and to some degree Romantic, idiom indulged in by amateurs with the practice of self-taught professionals who executed their works (accurate portraits, view of farms and so on) in accordance with the wishes of their patrons and in return for appropriate fees. The naive artists, generally coach-builders, cabinet-makers, house-painters or sign-painters, were craftsmen whose employment had made them familiar with the materials of painting. Their art was not a hobby but a source of income. There was as yet no firm dividing line between art and craft.

Most of the naive works that survive from the end of the 17th and the beginning of the 18th centuries are unsigned. The painters, called "limners", presumably from the practice of "illuminating" manuscripts and engravings, produced their works anonymously, like the painters of the Middle Ages. The itinerant limners roamed the wide-open spaces of America, decorating the farmhouses with stereotyped patterns, landscapes and frescoes and painting their "likenesses" of farmers and local worthies.

The limners' portraits simplify and typify their subjects. The instinctive search for summary simplification is underlined by the rigid immobility of the draughtsmanship and the harshness of the colouring. Portraiture remains dominant until the middle of the 18th century. Then followed landscapes and later genre pictures and historical scenes, which achieved a particular popularity in the middle of the 19th century. For two centuries the limners fulfilled the function of the camera, which had yet to be invented.

The best known of those popular painters who devised their own compositions is *Edward Hicks* (1780—1849). He travelled through many states, preaching

as a Quaker and painting pictures which celebrated peace among all men with a kind of old-fashioned dignity. His paintings of animals are particularly effective, whether he employs them allegorically, as in pictures of Noah's Ark, or selects them from everyday life, as in his pictures of farms.

Apart from historical and religious themes, scenes from everyday life and work and festivities are particularly popular. From Linton Park to Grandma Moses there is a tradition which binds the painter to the activities of the farmer and patriarchal village community.

The black painter, *Horace Pippin* (1888—1946), who might well be called a classic of American naive art, began to paint religious pictures at the age of ten. He left school at the age of fifteen and became a coal-heaver, then worked in a

Hicks, Edward: The Peaceable Kingdom

foundry and as a trader in second-hand goods. In the First World War he served in France and was severely wounded. Back in America he spent the remainder of his life in the production of numerous pictures: scenes from negro life, landscapes, memories of the war, religious themes and still-lifes.

The genuineness of his feelings gives his pictures an aura of melancholy and loneliness. At the same time there is a striving for communion and harmony. His interiors and group portraits from negro life manifest a harmonious relationship of form and colour.

John Kane, an important proletarian painter in the United States, was born in Scotland in 1860 and came to Pittsburgh at the age of nineteen. He worked as a miner, joiner, steel-worker and house-painter. With infinite patience and precision he painted portraits, interiors, festivities and the smoke-blackened factories in which he worked; a mass of detail is brought together by a strong sense of composition. His self-portrait is full of intense concentration. In an act of ruthless self-analysis, he represented his ageing nudity and the severe dignity of his self-awareness. In 1927 the Carnegie International Exhibition in Pittsburgh accepted his paintings. Kane was the first naive painter to achieve recognition in the United States.

One of the most remarkably individual phenomena among modern primitives or naive artists in the United States is *Morris Hirshfield* (1872—1946), who, at the age of sixty-five, began to paint fabulous animals and nude female figures gazing at themselves in the mirror of transparent erotic fantasies. When he retired from business in 1936 after a serious illness and devoted himself to painting, the patterns from his tailor's workshop found their way into the themes of his pictures: men and animals are tailored like ready-made garments and provided with childlike accessories. Behind these shapes, however, there vibrates something hectic, an element of the provocatively absurd. In 1939, works by him were exhibited at the Museum of Modern Art in New York in a show arranged by Sidney Janis, the collector and connoisseur of primitive art.

Field, Erastus Salisbury: The Historical Monument of the American Republic

When Hirshfield painted he first sketched in the outline of his subject. The application of pigments seemed to him like a sensual impulse within the framework of the creative act. But his febrile fantasies were brought under control, given an objective existence through the aesthetic process: every one of his figures is a representative symbol of his inner world, tokens of power, possessions, anxiety and seduction.

While Hirshfield drew his inspiration from the subterranean psychological sources represented by his instincts, *Anna Mary Robertson Moses*, known as *Grandma Moses* (1860—1961), turned unhesitatingly to visible reality. The little world of farming life was recorded by her from memory with a degree of idealization. Her art dwells contemplatively on these themes; it is a retrospective view and a final return to a life of fulfilment that had run its full course. What remain are the earth and the living things that spring from it. With the farsighted gaze of the elderly, she retrieved the events of her early youth of toil and celebration, sedate motherhood and the pilgrimage of a long life.

An inner serenity no doubt suffices to establish and express harmony and contentment in old age. But actual talent is necessary to extract from experience the joy of that affirmation of life and to transmit it to the world. Grandma Moses took the best passages from the diary of her memory in order to record them with a friendly smile and a happy ending, as is the custom of her country.

The Other America

Between the past and the present of the American continent lies a history of conquest, subjugation, enslavement and incipient upheaval.

The name Spanish-America points to the Spanish and Portuguese conquistadors; the term Indo-America refers to pre-Columbian cultures. But in the veins of America there circulates, together with Iberian and pre-Columbian blood, the blood of her involuntary inhabitants: the negroes "imported" from Africa.

The poets of Latin America hoped for a renaissance from the spirit of their Latin heritage. The signs of "Negritude" on the banners of militant liberation movements in America cannot be overlooked. But nowhere is the disparity in

Ycaza, Adela de: Poem by Ruben Darío

the development of the various races and peoples more evident than in the naive art of the two Americas. The limners of the 18th and 19th centuries were "proto-naive" artists; they had found a mode of expression which combined the sensibility of farmers and craftsmen in North America with reminiscences of European culture. In areas of Spanish-Latin culture the saints and demons of Catholicism combined with black and red deities to form a symbiosis that appealed to the popular imagination.

The colours and forms of the naive painter *Mario Urteaga*, from Cajamarca in Peru, remind us of the sumptuous vestments and draperies of the Inca empire, the fading glory of which was discovered on mummies. The Museum of Modern Art in New York acquired a picture painted by Urteaga in 1936, entitled "Funeral of a Man of Importance", in which he represents a social event of tragic significance in subdued colours with the artlessness of a folk-song. The drawing is conceived with serene clarity; the three-dimensional quality of the figures and gradations of colour evoke the clay gods and warriors on the pottery of the Mochica culture on the Northern coast of Peru.

In Mexico the colours and forms of Aztec culture lived on underground. The revolt against a feudal and academic order which set in after 1900, and from which monumental mural paintings emerged, also led to a new assessment of folk art. The anonymity of the folklore tradition was superseded by the individual creations of naive artists. Ezequiel Negrete paints ripening maize fields in a riot of radiant colour. The people's faces are sepia, since they are of Indian stock. Their work is hard, but it is a joy as well as a burden.

Felicindo Iglesias y Acevedo (born 1898), a grocer and wine-merchant living in Cuba, painted in 1939 a picture which shows with a naively emphatic explicitness the discovery of Cuba by Christopher Columbus. This infantile composition strikes us as being both visionary and uncannily stilted. In spite of the poverty

Negrete, Ezequil: Turkeys

of its artistic resources, it moves us by the intensity of the experience it expresses. It is as if Acevedo had perceived and awakened in his own heart the sublime and lethal adventure of that landing.

The professional embroideress, *Asilia Guillen* (1887—1964), lived in Managua, the capital of Nicaragua. Her native town of Granada had been burned down on some occasion, and this is the theme of "The Burning of Granada by American Troops".

Adela Vargas de Ycaza (born 1910) transposes the dark verbal music of the important Latin American poet, Ruben Dario, into the religious imagery of her naive visions. People, animals and plants are plunged into the aquarium blue of her psychic landscapes. Up above, the silver stars of hope shine down.

Julia Chevaria, a naive artist from Nicaragua, for her part, paints the terrestrial blue of the islands inhabited by the peasants and fishermen of Solentiname.

European Echoes

Whereas in the United States amateur painting grew up from the necessities of practical life, remote from schools and traditions, in England it was generally a genteel pursuit which went hand in hand with professional painting. These "Sunday painters" were aristocratic ladies, politicians, members of the middle-class, anything but outsiders, cultivated dilettantes who frequently painted landscapes and portraits full of atmosphere and characterized by refined taste and a sense of form.

The itinerant painters who once worked in pre-industrial times and were willing to paint homes, farms, the family and the domestic animals of the owner

Wilson, Scottie: The Village of Peace

in return for a modest fee, board and lodging, have largely been forgotten in the changes and upheavals which have taken place since then. It is only in our own age that individuals of humble social status have been able to indulge a childlike love of storytelling, to explore and describe the world with the eyes of the naive observer.

Alfred Wallis (1855—1942), a fisherman and shopkeeper from Devonport, was discovered by the painters Ben Nicholson and Christopher Wood. His work is characterized by a bold graphic line and subtle colours. His landscapes are rendered dramatic by disconcerting deformations.

Scottie Wilson (1888—1972), born into a Glasgow working-class family and incapable of writing more than his own name, began to express himself one day in a hitherto unknown language of pictures. His technique of hatching became his own personal handwriting, which conveyed his inner life to the light of day: plants, animals, places, faces were turned into calligraphic communications. The trees of life, populated by flamingo-coloured birds, are reminiscent of the strange, ecstatic bouquets of Séraphine of Senlis and Paul Klee's "Bird Garden". The naive painter *James Lloyd* (1905—1974), farmer, bus-driver, factory hand and lamp-lighter, was discovered by Herbert Read. He repeatedly tries to express in his pictures the affinity between man and animal, child and animal. Is it the case that the animals in his works are accorded that primeval idolatrous worship which preceded their domestication? Or is there growing up in the art of naive painters a renewed elementary sense of affinity with all creatures?

Anselme Bois-Vives, born in Spain, went to France as a young man and, though illiterate, succeeded in opening a grocery store. Wondering about the meaning of life, he began to paint. His compositions consist of people, animals and imaginary creatures resembling both the demons of primeval times and those demons of the atomic age.

Miguel Vivancos (born 1895), chauffeur, docker, bricklayer, soldier in the Spanish Civil War and the hero of Puigcerda, endured five years in a French concentration camp, where he brooded on the darkness of the shattered heavens. Then he began to communicate his dreams. He was painting on silk for the dress trade, but the stereotyped patterns bored him and he looked for something of his own to express. Perhaps he ought to be included among the French naive painters, as Juan Gris is associated with the School of Paris, although

Hatzimichali, Erse: At the Fair

Gris' painting was not merely executed in France but received its inspiration there. Vivancos' talent and his love of sumptuous and colourful display are an expression of the Spanish spirit and heritage.

The painting of *Valerico Moral Calvo* (born 1904) is neither decorative nor rhetorical, but rather grotesque and socially critical in its down-to-earth naive idiom. Calvo was employed as a dustman in Madrid and his themes revolve mainly round his work and the struggle for his daily bread. His colours are applied thickly, and his powerful brushwork seems to force its way into the material with elemental power, on occasion acquiring an intensity reminiscent of James Ensor.

Does Manuel Sanchez's abstract painting contain elements of stylistic refinement or of naive art? In the art of Islam contact with the living body is generally avoided and artists have had recourse to the symbolic power of ornament instead. The ornamental style derived from centuries of Arab rule in Spain is reflected in the art of the country's naive painters. Manuel Sanchez has a

Trillhaase, Adalbert: The Healing of the Mad

predilection for abstract structures, for the lines and colour combinations of a geometrical world. Archaic and modern elements are found side by side in his work as in many paintings by the Spaniards Picasso and Joan Miró.

The concept of the primitive in a literal sense is almost foreign to Italy. The grandiose idiom of antiquity, the harmony of Classicism and of the Renaissance, can only be reduced to a primitive level on occasions when they are relegated to the level of provincial life.

Among the artisans of an older Italy, particularly in smaller cities and towns, there were individuals who produced poetically idealized accounts of their lives which were no less powerful on account of the lack of formal training which they showed: portraits, family groups, landscapes, genre scenes, mythological glorifications of the struggle for national liberation. In the museums of small towns we find craftsmen's emblems, inn-signs and fairground pictures whose simple poetry and narrative strength bear witness to the talents of ordinary people. Sicily, Sardinia and Calabria are rich in amateur painting of both the sacred and profane kinds. The two-wheeled Sicilian cart is among the subjects carved and painted. Especially popular themes are episodes drawn from life, historical events, ballads and scenes from chivalrous romances. These were painted in the style of the 18th century, in a simple folk idiom with garish colours and strident rhetoric. Such works represent the beginnings of an incipient naive art.

The most important and individual of naive painters in Italy was *Orneore Metelli* (1872—1939), a shoemaker from Terni. He leads us through the fossilized architecture of his native city and sings its praises in a rhetorical narrative style. In his pictures, time and space seem as if petrified. The generous range of his palette and the subtlety of his forms were the outcome of an affirmative atti-

Dietrich, Adolf: Beagle

tude toward life: the revolutionary spirit of the shoemaker, an admirer of Garibaldi, is combined with a tender love for his art. His compositions are marked by the pride of the craftsman and an inner integrity: they now belong to the gallery of classical naive works.

In various parts of Italy during the last few years there has appeared a number of amateur and popular painters who show signs of being influenced by modern art movements: *Bruno Rovesti* (born 1907), *Nello Ponzi* (born 1897), *Pietro Ghizzardi* (born 1906), *Francesco Galeotti* (born 1920), *Enrico Benassi* (1902—1978), and others. *Bernardo Pasotti* (born 1910) paints his series of devotional pictures with fanciful intensity and all the care of a craftsman, but he is also influenced by trends in modern art.

Numerous cultures intersect on the island of Cyprus: influences from Egypt and Mesopotamia, from the Aegaean cultures and from the Mycenean art of Crete have all left their mark there. The compositions of the peasant cobbler *Michail Kkasialos* have a certain archaic severity and stringency. The deep ochre of his harvest studies reminds us of the gold ground we see in icons. Some of his pictures are naively devotional and the serenity of his works is apparent even in the paintings which depict the tragic events of his times; Kkasialos died in 1974 during the Turkish invasion of Cyprus.

In the case of the icon-like pictures of the Greek Aristodomos Papadakis, Byzantine liturgical forms are combined with peasant folk art. The pictures of the Athens housewife, *Effie Michelis* (1906—1984) have a childlike quality. She recreates the experiences of her intimate world with a delicate gradation of muted tones and simple directness. The capacity to view the towns and villages of Greece and its islands with an eye untroubled by convention and perspective gives her pictures all the magic of a child's drawing.

In Belgium and the Netherlands the term "primitives" was formerly used to refer to medieval Flemish painting, but it has changed its meaning. In the case of the neo-primitives, or naive painters, there is no trace of the fatalism or the introspection characteristic of the Gothic attitude to life. *Micheline Boyadjian* (born 1923) presents us with episodes, both grave and gay, culled from the vagaries and the joys of her childhood. She is the dainty little girl whom we see side by side with adults in her pictures — the prim, well-behaved little girl practising the piano, setting off for school, listening to the band in the park at some watering-place, painting at the artist's own easel. The theme which fascinates Micheline is the encounter with her own ego, the duplication, perhaps even the elimination, of her own personality.

Paps: Archers' Ceremony

Josephine Hermans (1895—1976) paints landscapes and compositions involving people and animals with cheerful humour and robust *joie de vivre*. In the works of the diamond-cutter, *Salomon Meijer* (1877—1965), the old houses of Amsterdam radiate a dull glitter; his landscapes and still-lifes, his genre and animal studies are based on observation of nature but at the same time transfigured by the poetry of artless innocence. The Amsterdam baker, Sipke Cornelis Houtman, also creates pictures of animal and street scenes with the vivid directness that comes from a childish sense of novelty. His interiors, artless projections of petty bourgeois existence, have the charm of detail — the kind of detail, however, that gives a clue to an entire mode of life.

Certain analogies with the workmanlike poetry of the North American limners can be found in the naive art of Swiss painters in the 18th and 19th centuries, who took their inspiration from folklore. The sturdy folk art of the mountain peasantry, which retains many of the technical features of the archaic art of herdsmen, degenerates in the course of time into souvenir painting of a falsely naive kind, a fate which has overtaken the declining folk art of a number of localities. It was not until the turn of the last century that interest in the simple originality of the naive was re-awakened — for example by the work of *Bartholomäus Lämmler* (1809—1865), *Johannes Müller* (1806—1897), and a number of others, including *Sibylle Neff* (born 1929) from Appenzell.

Adolf Dietrich (1877—1957), — woodman, railway worker and rope-maker — was a Swiss painter of considerable importance. His predilection for the minute and shapely object, his aspiration to articulate the harmony and the beauty of those unassuming details to be observed everywhere in nature — these qualities made him a pantheistic poet of the naive world. Gardens and fruit, birds, martens, mice and men are shaped with the rounded intensity of the

Meijer, Salomon: Surprise Contents

Quattrocentisti and the typical directness of the naive painter. His floral still-lifes, his aquarium, his animal studies and his portraits of himself and his father have the graphic precision of old masters and the delicate, prudently tempered palette of German Romanticism.

Among the most accomplished products of amateur painting in Germany

Balet, Jan: Beginning of Winter

Boyadjian, Micheline: Two Girls

49

Sauter, Aloys: A Likeable Unexpected Partner

must be numbered the pictures of the school-teacher, *Oluf Braren* (1787—1839), who was born on the North Sea island of Föhr. It is possible that the harsh, straightened circumstances of his life sharpened his innate powers of expression and directed all the intensity of his inner life towards his painting. He seems to have transferred to mankind the inspiration he draws from sea-shells, plants and reefs: he represents human faces as though they were flowers or rocks. The three-dimensional effect of the drawing and the crystalline luminosity of the colours emphasize the hermetic isolation of his figures. Taciturnity, astringency and insularity are all bound up together in a conception of the world that is both realistic and poetic. The solemn fervour that informs the mood of these pictures derives from a Romantic sensibility that is combined with a style based on classical models. In his lack of sophistication and his unselfconscious rigidity of expression Braren is to some degree a pioneer of naive art in Germany.

Adalbert Trillhaase (1859—1938) is the most individual of Germany's naive painters: a dreamer who tried in vain to force himself into a career after his

Wallis, Alfred: Ship in Front of the Bridge

commercial training. At the age of sixty he began to paint, mostly historical pictures or scenes from the Old and the New Testaments. The primitive and fantastic fairy-tale world of his paintings has absolutely nothing in common with the popular tradition of the village schoolmaster who dabbles in painting. Although these epic narratives deal with well-known themes, they have something uncannily inconsequential and oddly hallucinatory about them. These pictures are unwitting attempts to grasp dreams in visual terms and to interpret them in terms of line and colour.

The pictures painted by Friedrich Schröder-Sonnenstern have a certain affinity with those of Trillhaase, but there is no suggestion of childish innocence in the magic mirror of his vision. His eye is the eye of a voyeur; his pictures are totally uninhibited and seem like the feverishly erotic obsessive fantasies of an adolescent boy. And yet from this disordered psyche a naive imagination speaks of sin, existence and death. From primitive instinct and authentic artistic talent Schröder-Sonnenstern models his grotesquely fantastic world of forbidden dreams. His career was governed by the distorted imagery of his inner being: he was a postman, a spiritualist, a gardener, an itinerant preacher and a balladsinger, and had at times seen the inside of prisons and mental hospitals. It is

Metelli, Orneore: Self-portrait as a Musician

Spielbichler, Franz: The Hanging Garden of Semiramis

plain that certain features of his artistic idiom do not derive from the sphere of naive painting but from other frontier zones of the mind. But it is precisely these traits that are of interest in relation to the complex problems of primitive artists in the present century. Schröder-Sonnenstern's intensity of expression and the language of his instinct assure him a special place in the catalogue of naive painters.

Hagoort, Pieter: Horse-drawn Trolley Car

Peasant Naive Painters

In the Slav cultures naive painters can still draw from the dwindling resources of folk art. Most of them are peasant farmers whose imaginations are enriched by a store of memories relating to manners, customs and the forms of village life. Side by side with them are craftsmen and workmen engaged in painting and carving and already affected by the atmosphere of an urban culture.

In the case of artists in general, it is sufficient to absorb oneself in their work in order to comprehend it. In the case of peasant painters, however, life and work constitute an indissoluble unity, for naive artists have no inkling of the aesthetic view that is associated with advanced civilisation. Their true domain is life itself, or the dream of life. What they paint is a pictorial sequence of their labours and festivals, their christenings and burials, their commitment to the soil, their sullen revolt against excessive burdens — all this full of a rough vigour, peasant cunning and poetry.

Even as a boy herding his swine, *Ivan Generalić* (born 1914) used to carry a pencil and paper with him in order to note down in his leisure moments whatever he felt, saw or imagined. His early works have something of the unexpected rhythmical quality and the starkness of children's drawings. Sharp, clear lines pierce through the limits of logical perception; observation and invention merge with each other. Herdsman, dog, a herd of pigs in snow and sombre woodland; trees, man and animal: they stand side by side as creations of nature.

Many of Generalić's pictures are obverse paintings on glass. He has achieved the highest degree of mastery in this technique, which involves an ultimate and irreducible element of the fortuitous and the unforeseen. Colour becomes a miror of the heart: the deep green shimmer of the meadows, the pale yellow veins of phantom trees, the gently modulated white of the herdsmen's coats — there is delicate shading of tones, from golden brown to the brick-red of the foliage. In spite of the simplicity of their narrative themes, these paintings are governed by a feeling for space and proportion.

How are we to look at those trees which sprout like coral, the poetically naive tensions between reality and peasant myth invented by Generalić and now propagated in endless profusion by talented and untalented naive artists alike? Generalić could not be satisfied with an attempt to revert to the style of his early work. In the past the discrepancy between idea and reality was determined by technical factors. In time these factors were mastered. The perfection of his craft made the creative act both easier and more difficult. Ivan Generalić has retained his legendary vision, has retained his bond with his village, which for him signifies the world. At the point where innocence and experience meet he has abolished the boundary between naive art and the art of the professional.

There are not many naive artists who have reached those solitary regions in which categories cease to have any essential relevance. They have eaten of the fruit of knowledge but have not ceased to draw from that source which we call originality; they have entered into the timeless landscape of art.

I have dwelt on the creative crisis of this particular naive artist because the rare but feasible resolution of the dilemma contradicts our definition of the naive and must be regarded as an exception to the rule.

Amidst the rich diversity of contemporary art in Yugoslavia, besides Ivan Generalić and the school of Hlebine, Emerik Feješ, Ivan Rabuzin, Ilija Bosilj, and Matija Skurjeni perhaps deserve special mention.

The pictures composed by the old peasant *Ilija Bosilj* (1895—1972), with their hybrid creatures, half man and half animal, are occasionally reminiscent of cave paintings. Throughout the whole of his working life, Ilija had nursed a hostility to art as something sinful. Then, at the age of sixty, he quite suddenly began to paint, as though driven by an inner compulsion. He painted pictures on sheets, towels, bedsteads, cupboard doors and the walls of his roomy house. He filled these spaces with demons and deities of unknown origin, fabulous creatures, saints, kings, angels and imaginary animals. He painted in lurid, incandescent colours, sometimes on a green and gold background, sometimes on the deep blue background of the remote distance. Ilija's apocalyptic pictures grew out of a magically obsessive world. Saints with haloes in all the colours of the rainbow ride on two-headed birds, male figures with devoutly raised hands stride across the frame of the picture and animals leap out of it. Ilija's reality is different from that of our optical experience.

Up to this point we have been discussing those peasant painters who follow the plough and whose gaze dwells constantly within the sphere of nature. What of the craftsmen? We shall discuss them later in more detail, but they may be included at this point within the national framework where they belong.

Emerik Feješ (1904—1969) was a maker of buttons and combs. As is the case

Rabuzin, Ivan: Source of Life

with all urban painters, the dream of far-off places dwelt within his soul. With the help of picture postcards he undertook expeditions into worlds of half-real architecture constructed from the motley, dissonant mosaic of his simple mind.

It is not easy to decipher the individual mythology of *Matija Skurjeni* (born 1898), who has been a miner, a shepherd and a decorater in his time. All sorts of mysterious and apparently haphazard images are presented with a kind of objective sobriety. Apocalyptic visions, surrealistic reminiscences of his dreams, erotic desires provide him with his themes. The magic of his formal language lies in its cryptic nature: things do not coincide with their essential meaning. His proportions and his colour values are governed by a secret law of the imagination.

Among naive painters who project their pictorial themes into the realm of the decorative — not merely incidentally but as the fundamental form of their artistic idiom — the carpenter *Ivan Rabuzin* (born 1921) has achieved a kind of contemplative spirituality that verges on the abstract without leaving the domain of nature. Through a structural technique which sees the circle as the fundamental shape within nature, Rabuzin enters an ornamental Paradise. His landscape, composed of circles and curves, is reality transposed into terms of the naively poetic.

Šteberl, Ondrej: Poor Man and Rich Man

Kkassialos, Michail: Reapers Resting

The triennial exhibitions of naive art in Bratislava have demonstrated that in Czechoslovakia, Romania, Hungary, Poland and the Soviet Union peasant naive art derived from folk traditions is predominant.

In Czechoslovakia, the paintings of *Ondrej Šteberl* (1897—1977) describe his own introspective view of the world. Frequently he illustrates biblical tales or offers us his own subjective interpretation of a world that is simple and good-natured. His paintings are flat; their surface is rhythmically ordered without the aid of perspective and without concern for the laws of gravity. A childish and profoundly felt mythology is reflected in the one-dimensional patterns of his works, which combine men, animals, houses, copses, and cemeteries in harmonious simplicity and emblematic expressiveness.

Ludmila Procházková (born 1903) is emotionally tied to village modes of life. The ancient rhythm of communal rejoicing in her pictures constitutes an expression of an anonymous collective aspiration toward significant form. The circle of faces is impersonal; they are identical and seem mutually interchangeable.

Skurjeni, Matija: The Large Bird

Ilija (Bosilj): School of Apocalyptic Flying

Whereas Ludmila Procházková's colours, applied without blending or dilution in broad sweeps, bear a resemblance to the embroidery of folk art, the colours of *Juraj Lauko* (1894—1974) are spectral and evil: poisonous green, burning orange, bitter ash-grey and a painfully sweet shell-pink are placed side by side with diffuse strokes of the brush. The sky above the world of this sausage salesman is gloomy and overcast. The nightmares which are incorporated in his pictures are rooted in the soil of peasant superstition: a fortune-teller prophesying from cards, devils and witches, owls, skeletons, bats and magic number games — the hallucinatory memories of an introverted artist.

The symbolic language of *Natalie Schmidtová* (born 1895) is reduced to the simplest elements, cheerfully powerful in its expressive force. She paints a field traversed by a farmer with his plough; in the background are mountains below which a lake gazes up into the skies. In one of her pictures sits a woman spinning with a distaff in her hand and a hank of yarn round her neck. Slender, solemn female forms are gathered round a long table against a pale blue background. Alongside the folklore elements we can sense the civilized air of the town. Her hands may be clumsy, but the painter has learned to see things in a new light.

In Hungary, too, popular artists have abandoned the anonymous domain of

Generalić, Ivan: Crucified Rooster

a patriarchal society. In their childlike way the hands of these peasant artists are groping towards artistic self-consciousness.

Elek Györi (1905—1957) shows in his pictures the gradual disappearance of the division between town and country. He offers us spontaneously inspired and accurate accounts of weddings, fairs, the grape harvest and village dances; peasants, soldiers, musicians; a jaunt in an old-fashioned carriage. Everything is seen from the standpoint of someone who has returned home from the city.

András Süli (1896—1969), a peasant from Algyö, loved nature. He took it as his point of departure and occasionally painted whole series of related pictures on the same theme. But, in contrast to folk art, every single one of his variations is novel and expresses a different mood.

Holiday processions and the rhythms of everyday labour are represented with a picturesque kind of poetic force in the massed compositions of *János Gajdos* (1912—1950). The pictures of *Sándor Török* (born 1896) and *János Balázs* (1905—1977) manifest a popular narrative power.

The sombre piety of the Polish peasantry suffuses the naive art of that country with a devotional light. This is painting of an explicitly emotional and religious character, such as we find with Maria Lenczewska and Franciszek Janeczko. There are also reflections of inner tensions that verge on psychological derangement, like the obsessive mode of expression of *Edmund Monsiel* (1897—1962), who feels himself watched over by the thousand eyes of God, or the theosophical fantasies of *Teophil Ociepka* (1891—1978), with his saturnine primeval beasts and his nightmares, which may be an echo of the wars he experienced. And last, but not least, there is the most significant Polish naive artist, *Nikifor* (1895—1968), who gave shape to the concrete world round him and to the innermost hopes of his soul, using the most paltry material and the most banal of objects. Nikifor, a deaf mute, came from the mountain village of Krynicy. He soon forgot his own name and the beggar woman who was his mother and had recourse to the paint-brush as his sole means of communication with the world around him. The signs traced in his pictures are signals, bridges and roads, with saints in fur hats steering the chariot of eternal life.

Nikifor used to paint on the backs of cigarette packets, on chocolate wrappers and on the squared paper of school jotters, using the simplest of children's painting sets. It is here that we find recorded melancholy impressions of his pilgrimage through the villages of Poland, with the steeples and domes of little Orthodox churches set against the blue and sombre green background of his dreams.

Although more than a quarter of the earth's surface is still being farmed today and although half of mankind is engaged in agriculture, the agricultural population is faced with an economic and social revolution. The industrialization of agriculture and the influence of the mass media are beginning to replace the sense of family ancestry and the practice of fertility rites that formerly descended from father to son, and to initiate a transformation, indeed the elimination, of elemental forms of rural life. This is why everything that naive peasant artists retrieve from their store of experience is expressed as the echo and memory of earlier faiths, bygone patterns of life and work.

Although the process of change and disintegration that affects ancient peasant communities may last for some considerable time, it is inexorable. For this reason we must attach all the more importance to the art of naive peasant artists, who unconsciously reflect the dying radiance of an age and a landscape in which man, animal, plant and the whole totality of life constituted a single emotional complex within the realm of nature.

In some countries the coming together of the archaic and the modern is marked by the collision of social forces: the patriarchal tradition comes into contact with the planned society. It appears from the creative excitement in the work of many naive artists that they are both disconcerted and stimulated by finding themselves placed historically and socially between a fading communal tradition and the rise of a socialist collective. Where archaic cultures clash with technical civilization, however, there often arises a crisis in artistic creation.

Nikifor: Self-portrait

Popular Proletarian Painting in the Soviet Union

In the work of the Georgian painter, *Nikolai Pirosmanashvili* (1862—1918) the traditional imagery of custom and of a feudal society is combined with the real circumstances of his environment. Just as the rhapsodes of the ancient world recited the deeds of gods and heroes at the tables of princes, so Pirosmanashvili celebrated both the legendary and the actual life of his country in the hostelries of Tiflis and the neighbouring towns in return for his board and lodging: his mildly monumental, grandiosely artless pictures were created for wine-merchants, publicans, merchants and officials, for the diners and the drinkers in the local taverns.

Pirosmanashvili, Nikolai: Bego Greeting his Guests

In the course of years his mode of painting became more self-confident, his technique less constrained. But from the very beginning he manifested a spontaneous, directly experienced, optimistic vision of the world in epic terms. The chromatic range is not wide: against a background that is most often sombre, alabaster white, shell-pink, pale blue, rust-red and the variegated green of the vegetable kingdom shine out luminously. The ambitiously handled compositions occasionally bear the names of firms and restaurants, written in Cyrillic or Georgian script that produces a pictographic effect, as if the painter had deliberately used the letters for their calligraphic potential.

His paintings began to be collected only when interest in primitive and naive art started to grow, and works by him are in the State Museum of Tiflis. It may be that many people in Pirosmanashvili's homeland feel that the pictorially expressed humanity of his talent has captured more of Georgia's life and dreams than officially recognized art has done.

Pirosmanashvili died at a time when the Soviet Union was just coming into being. In the following decades a painting movement was encouraged as a form of self-taught folk art, a hobby which would offer relaxation and satisfy the need for creative expression. In this way a number of talented individuals emerged whose works belong to various trends of amateur painting. It is possible to detect two distinct lines of development. Many of these folk artists have taken the 19th century tradition of Russian realism as their starting-point. The artists working in this tradition, having achieved a degree of maturity through technical training, can handle the materials of academic painting with ease; their paintings are very much like those of professional artists.

We are interested more particularly in those artists whose technique is less accomplished, those who have not learned the laws of anatomy and perspective. Their imagination is more vividly pictorial and their mode of expression untrammelled by convention, because they have retained the instinctive vision and the sense of novelty characteristic of the child.

P. P. Leonov (born 1920), a plasterer from Kazakhstan, paints absurd

Amiryan, Gerasim: David Sasunski (detail)

nocturnal flights on carefully devised flying-machines, perilous circus turns, symbolic tests of human courage, daring deeds of naive artlessness.

The Russian farmhand and railway worker, *Ivan Mikhailoviċh Nikiforov* (1897—1971), puts together his mosaic-like group studies in a traditional style but with a modern palette of poetic subtlety: he shows us a roundabout with its rocking-horses in full flight, defying the laws of perspective, in front of a glassy, luminous sky, with a gaping crowd in the foreground.

Should we include *Gayane Khachaturian,* a woman painter from Armenia, among the naive artists? All her senses are focussed on the sheer beauty of things. In the case of her "Armenian Girl" she may have been inspired by Modigliani's long-necked women, with their melancholy, stylized eyes. She depicts four solemn seated female figures, with oval faces the colour of dates framed in black hair and with garments dark as a moonlit sky, beneath a canopy of expectant poppy-red — suggesting associations with Gauguin's "Women of Tahiti", although they are typical Armenian women. This is amateur painting with a naive note. Serge Diaghilev would perhaps have invited her to paint curtains for his ballet, as he once invited André Bauchant.

Africa between the Archaic and the Naive

Africa's strongly traditional tribal art is becoming extinct: contact with technology has undermined the power of the tribal gods and the artists who served them. Nevertheless, in Nigeria and in other African countries, naive art of a popular kind is still being produced. Powerfully expressive figurative pictures are being painted by painters from the lower middle class and from the growing proletariat. They paint commercial signs, murals in night-clubs, pictures for carnivals, political and historical episodes, landscapes and portraits. The influence of cinema posters, illustrated magazines and comics suggests certain affinities with the modern painting of the so-called New Figuration. A disintegrating tribal style coalesces with the Pop Art, plebeian style of the new generation, which has substituted machines and industrial production for the old gods.

The black "Manager" on the commercial logo of the Nigerian painter *Middle Art*, with his cool, commanding gaze and his hand slightly raised in greeting, is a variant form of the tribal chief or the Hollywood film hero. The bluish-grey figure on a sepia ground is the painter offering his services as a portraitist.

"The Lady in Blue", with her gleaming teeth and expressive eyes, her face turned slightly away from the observer, is the work of an unknown Nigerian painter; the coloured gentleman in a dinner-jacket has his arm round her neck, possibly in order to emphasize his rights of ownership.

"Family Trio" confronts us in static and conventional objectivity: three faces turned stiffly to one side, wide-eyed beneath black hair, a festive smile on their lips. The son, a miniature man, his mother with a lemon-yellow shawl and blouse, a pastel blue belt encircling the cheerful cinnamon of her skirt — these are the ice-cream hues of urban life, a dream of prosperous living, respectability and elegance.

The technical experience of these painters and their stock-in-trade are sometimes based on rapid courses or correspondence schools. A special branch of their art is obverse glass painting, which may well have begun in the form of

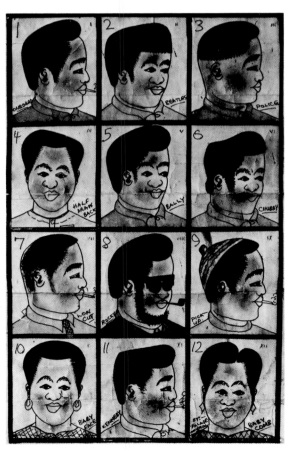

Imperial, Falade: Shop Sign   *Katarikawe, Jak: The Artist in Friend's Garden*

Middle Art: Story of Chukwumma and Rose

floral decoration on picture frames. It later became an independent genre and now, with its luminous colours and naively emblematic shapes, it forms an integral part of this popular art. This primitive, naive art, with its instinctive, bustling verve, may be just as important and embody just as much talent as the academic idiom which is taught alongside it in African art schools. During his travels in Africa Gerhart Schoenberner encountered this kind of popular and naive art and brought back examples of it. He was particularly interested in the Pop-art market and advertising motifs on shop-fronts and signboards.

The vast and rapid spread of urban civilization in our time has brought about a levelling of cultural standards. The more abrupt and seismic these convulsions are, the deeper the gulf between tradition and innovation. The massive movement towards the emancipation of nations and races entails the absorption into the sphere of modern technical civilization of millions of individuals hitherto bereft of a voice. The political subjugation of the African territories took place at a time when ethnography and the history of art were focussed exclusively on Europe, and there were no commentators who were in a position to appreciate the significance of primitive art. State schools and missions reinforced the African's feeling of inferiority. The most promising prospects for development and for a career seemed to lie in adaptation to the civilization introduced from Europe and a consequent denial of the indigenous past. Whereas European artists devoted themselves to the study of African idols and masks in order to revive imaginations enervated by intellect and the growth of technology, those peoples now awakening from the primeval slumbers of their forests were eager to free themselves both from the idols of their witch-doctors and the power of the white empires. A young Nigerian artist remarked to me, "We can no longer pray, because we no longer have a faith". Ancestral totems in the absence of the cult of the ancestors have become mere empty artefacts; the mask, without the dancers, has lost all its magic.

It is hardly possible to sustain the archaic mode of expression when its gods have died. It is probably equally impossible simply to adopt the artistic forms of a world which evolved in totally different social circumstances.

Black America

The inhabitants of Dahomey, Ife, Yorubaland and the Congo were transported to America as slaves centuries ago to provide cheap labour in place of the pre-Columbian peoples, who were becoming extinct.

In Haiti their descendants have revived the powers of their homeland, the spirit and the Gods of Africa, in the form of a naive art of intuitive intensity. The cult of Voodoo may be an eclectic synthesis of fading myths, demons and gods, but it provides the black people of Central America with a common sense of identity. It is in Haiti that this art has achieved its most integrated form.

Hyppolite, Hector: Queen Congua

The Africans imported into America bore with them their native traditions. In this way the saints and demons of Christianity came together with black gods and red gods to form a symbiosis in the popular imagination. In due course Haiti was rediscovered as an island with an artistic sensibility that found expression in a colourful narrative tradition. DeWitt Peters came to the island in 1943 on behalf of the United States Education Department in order to give English lessons. After six months he resigned from his post: he had discovered the powerful visual imagery of the Haitian naive painters and devoted himself henceforth to their artistic development.

Peters had made the acquaintance of the Voodoo priest, *Hector Hyppolite* (1894—1948), painter of mysterious rites and conjurations. Hyppolite was a specifically Voodoo painter, but he incorporated the Christian symbol of the

Cross in his ritual compositions. It was not long before other artists made their appearance in Haiti. *Philomé Obin* (1892—1977), in particular, tended to collect around him the more talented of the younger artists. He describes scenes from the present-day life of the island and from its history in a style which is naively realistic and literal. *André Pierre* (1914—1979), a lay practitioner of Voodoo, continued Hyppolite's work: most of his paintings are designed to illustrate the mythology of Voodoo.

Gérard Valcin (born 1923), both in his ritual paintings and his pictures of people at work, populated with a host of figures, reminds us of the communal symbolic language of African wood-carvers, with which he shares sets of rhythmically arranged parallel patterns and the manner of ornamentation.

Pierre, André: Sacrificing to Agoné and Sirene, Voodoo Goddesses of the Sea

Naive artists from all parts of the island find their way to Port-au-Prince, where their art centre and the galleries are situated. There is no other country where naive art has come to enjoy such wide support. There is some danger, however, that over-production is leading to the development of a popular cottage industry. Today the painters of Haiti stand between the ancient gods of Africa and the modern art-dealers.

The anachronistic spiritualistic faith of the Voodoo religion encouraged isolation from a hostile outside world and reinforced the sense of community among black people. From this sense of identity grew an art which was governed by a fundamental gift for expression through the visual language of colour and form. It was only members of the lower class who belonged to this secret association. The governing class, although themselves black, considered Voodoo and naive art as survivals of the primitive African past which should be discarded and repudiated.

In spite of an element of the banal engendered by the demands of tourism and the export business, the subject-matter of Haitian painting embodies a kind of veiled resistance: it evokes the ever-present panic-stricken memory of repression, the fight for liberty, wounds and wonders, martyrs and tormentors, masked deities and ecstatic piety, faith and superstition. Voodoo gods have their dwelling in Cuba, Brazil and El Salvador as well as in Haiti. A new Africa has established itself in America, and along with it an art which is not aggressive, like the Black Power movement, but which has something to say through its paintings in the confrontation of black and white on the American continent.

Japanese Naive Artists

It is generally the case that naive painters are recognized as such, and consequently appreciated, only in modern industrial societies. This is no doubt the reason why an advanced industrial state such as Japan is able to show a highly developed and characteristic tradition of naive art. It is true that very significant traditions of popular primitive art exist in India and in Bali, but creative personalities drawing on their own inner resources do not seem to have been able in these countries to free themselves from the constraints that bind them to an anonymous collective body. Japan is the only country in Asia where the evolution of a complex civilization poses a threat to traditional modes of life

Yamashita, Kiyoshi: Firework in Nagaoka

today and hence creates a climate favourable to the emergence of naive art.

Two Japanese naive painters, Kiyoshi Yamashita and Suma Maruki were artists of some importance. The life of *Kiyoshi Yamashita* (1922—1971) reminds us of the Polish artist, Nikifor: by transforming their feelings into pictures, both of them contrived to overcome their spiritual isolation and the contempt with which the world treated them as vagrants and beggars. Their works have enduring value in the canon of naive art. Although he was self-taught, the simplicity and the order we observe in Yamashita's pictures are bound up with the Japanese tradition: they are not merely simple-minded, but informed by a pure and authentic sense of rhythm and proportion, full of a fervent sense of discovery, such as we find in the art of children. In the oppressive loneliness of his existence, Yamashita looked for some countervailing force which would enable him to assert his personality, and he found it in the painstaking practice of the Japanese technique of collage known as *hari-e*. He made his first oil paintings by squeezing the paints directly from the tube. The result resembled the *hari-e* with their spots of colour, or perhaps the pointillist pictures of Van Gogh.

The name of *Suma Maruki* (1875—1956) is linked in my mind with the horrors of Hiroshima, for she lived through the destruction of that city. Suma Maruki was one of the numerous children of a peasant family. She never went to school and remained illiterate until the end of her life. She was already sixty years old when she began her first attempts at drawing. In the melancholy

Maruki, Suma: The Dog Named Ron

dream-garden of her pictures she has assembled the friends who accompanied her through life: snakes, cats, hens, ducks, many kinds of song-bird, and the miracles of trees, bushes and fruits.

Her palette has many varieties of green: through the dull jade-green of the foliage and the powerful green of ferns gleam pastel blue, old rose, alabaster white and the lilac of her luminous blossoms. These are not the ardent Lucifer bouquets of temptation such as were painted by Séraphine. There is no ecstasy in Suma Maruki's compositions; they are a creative expression of her childlike faith in life and in the future — in spite of Hiroshima and her hard life.

Peasant Painters in China

We are living in an age of social and artistic transformation. Wherever archaic cultures and primitive peoples come into contact with technological civilization, a crisis arises in the sphere of artistic creation. Contrasts between tradition and revolution, continuity and disintegration, manifest themselves.

The mass movement involving Chinese peasant painters during the past thirty years has no parallel in any other nation. It cannot be understood without some knowledge of local tradition and the social background: this is a culture which is thousands of years old, which is past and yet topical, in which everything changes, yet retains throughout its essential substance.

In China, as in other countries, popular peasant art was influenced by contemporary high art. At the same time it was strictly separated from painting and calligraphy, such as formed part of the education of all cultured individuals. Nowadays it is not the art of a privileged minority that is put on show but the paintings of workers and peasants.

Although peasant painting in contemporary China is descended from folk art and practised by amateurs, we are nevertheless justified in dealing with it within the framework of naive art. It is distinguished from the folk art of other cultures by the critical adoption of tradition and by a purposeful choice of themes.

The peasant painters set out to accomplish an educational and cultural mission by means of their pictures. They have no individual material interests. Large-scale pictures, sometimes painted on the white-washed walls of their villages, are worked on collectively by groups of artists. The improvement of the appearance of the village, the decoration of assembly halls and the edification of the observer are the aims of this activity, from which the participants derive creative pleasure and a sense of satisfaction.

The mural paintings are based on a tradition which can be traced back to the frescoes of Buddhist cave temples. Many works of these painters combine natural scenes, painted in bright, optimistic colours, with the collective labours of the workers. They are not so much scenes observed at first hand as a synthesis of fact and idea in an abstractly decorative form.

In Chinese, "writing" and "drawing" are represented by the same pictogram. Painting is a form of communication with the observer, a conversational exchange between individuals. The palette of these peasant painters utilizes powerful local pigments which correspond to the objects represented. As far as possible they manufacture their pigments themselves, in the manner of tempera colours. Commercial pigments are expensive and have to be employed sparingly.

Chinese engraving from the end of the 17th century

Zhu Xi: Granary Full of Golden Wheat

Chen Mujun: Roosters and Bamboos

The aesthetic traditions of a delicately modulated poetic form, of subtle suggestion and simplicity of line, are preserved in this kind of painting, but at the same time superseded. The individualism of high art is transformed into the collective aspiration of a new social structure. Plants are represented with a subtle delicacy of line, but the cultivation of those same plants in large quantities is represented as agricultural production and not as a form of decorative garden.

Many peasant painters have been trained on courses or by means of manuals; others have been instructed by art students or professional painters. Textbooks from the 17th and the beginning of the 18th centuries, the "Picturebook of the Hall of Ten Bamboos" and the "Manual of Painting of the Mustard-Seed Garden", offer the rudiments of classical Chinese painting; they are still in use and have popularized artistic styles of the past. Contemporary textbooks attempt to sustain continuity by adapting the old forms to new themes. Special pattern-books for the representation of human figures, machines, agricultural implements, animals and plants tempt the amateur painters to repeat or even to reproduce these models in a purely mechanical fashion.

The increase in technical skill, which enables the artist to operate more freely in the material of his art, can lead to deterioration in immediacy of expression and in the visual impact typical of naive work. The original element of childlike exploration and discovery often turns into the routine of the craftsman and purely formal decoration.

This painters' movement began in 1958 during the "Great Leap Forward" in the development of industry and agriculture. It originated in the county of Huxian, which is situated in Shansi province. Among the 430,000 inhabitants of this county there are today some 3,500 amateur artists, of whom 700 are women. The works which were produced during the Cultural Revolution were mostly in the form of posters and dealt with political and didactic themes. Figurative compositions in the idealized style of the European 19th century reached China via the Socialist Realism of the Soviet Union. The pictures which we find in exhibitions nowadays show artists to be freer in their themes and aesthetically more independent.

The conventionally traditional peasant folk art and its natural naivety are indications of a novel and unique movement in art. Nebojša Tomašević has grasped the significance of this movement and visited the peasant painters of Jinshan to acquaint himself with their landscape, their mode of life and their creative work, and to give an account of all this in the present encyclopaedia.

The Fifth Continent: Australia

It is barely a century and a half since Europeans first set foot in Australia. They found the aboriginal inhabitants living as nomads, with a mode of life and art forms characteristic of the Stone Age. They lived in separate tribal communities as fishermen and hunters and were still bound to the cycle of Nature. In the narrow, fertile belt surrounding this barren continent there may have been something like 300,000 dark-skinned inhabitants. In the course of a brief colonial history numerous tribes died out or were exterminated. Their surviving descendants were forced to adapt themselves to the conditions of a white civilization and now live a life cut off from their ethnic roots. It is estimated that about 50,000 members of this most ancient family of mankind still live in Australia.

One of them is *Dick Roughsey*, whom we might term a naive painter. It is possible that his picture of a man looking at a rock painting reflects the inner mood of the painter. In the shadow of a cliff sits the dark-skinned man, clad in white, gazing at a hunting scene engraved in the rock: a savage crocodile and a huntsman with a boomerang, and alongside them shadowy outlines of kangaroos and a snake. The painter seems to be seeking the path into the visual world of his ancestors. In terms of mythology, painting signifies an act of creation. The ritual pictures which would otherwise fade are renovated and redrawn each year by the elders of the tribe, so that their magic power will not vanish.

The other naive painters of Australia, who have made their appearance only in recent years, belong to the community of white immigrants. Remembered elements from their native lands and cultures may be detected in their pictures.

Douglas Stubbs, a painter born in Australia in 1927, studied for a time at the National Gallery School. The figures that he draws are bird-like creatures with long beaks and phantom faces. He has devised a mixture of primeval Australian and surrealistic modern myths. The boldly independent overall impression of his painting, the flowing brush-work, the emphatic polychromy of his palette — these features are based on the stylistic techniques of the professional painter, although they have their origins in the naive psyche of an eccentric individual.

Rafael Saldaña was born in Madrid and emigrated to Australia in about 1960. "Saint Francis and the Animals", which shows the holy man surrounded by tame creatures, is the theme of a triptych by him. It is reminiscent of pictures by the American painter, Edward Hicks, except that the latter brings peace to the world in the words of the Old Testament, whereas the Spaniard Saldaña embraces the animal kingdom within Christian legend.

Saldaña's landscape is harmonious, well-nigh paradisal. Do such landscapes really exist in Australia or is this a memory of Spain's Moorish gardens? The saint, who is giving the animals his blessing, has the face of Christ and is dressed in a star-spangled crimson garment. The glitter of the stars is repeated in the midst of the green meadows where the lamb lies down with tame lions and tigers.

NAIVE SCULPTURE

While the sheer originality, the poetic directness and the childlike charm of naive painting have obvious powers of attraction, naive sculpture has hitherto largely escaped the attention of art-lovers. This is all the more astonishing in that the imagination of professional artists, sated by the domination of the intellect and its technology, has been greatly inspired and rejuvenated by recourse to archaic and primitive sculpture and carvings.

In their search for wide-ranging cultural connections and affinities, the artists of the turn of the century looked not only to the early forms of primitive art but also to those latter-day manifestations of primitivism in the work of naive artists. We are concerned here with converging trends in which both painters and sculptors of modern times deliberately looked for analogies in elemental and unsophisticated works of art.

Africa's professionally skilled wood-carvers and workers in bronze, whose tribal communities are beginning to break up, find it difficult to assimilate to the larger political entities that are now emerging. In so far as they carry on producing work at all, it is in the form of bland airport souvenirs for the benefit of the tourist trade — replicas of a defunct craftsmanship. In these post-colonial times, however, many artists of humble origins, with little or no training, have emerged and are at work in many parts of Africa.

Among them is the wood-carver Yakobo, a member of the Makonde tribe, now settled in Tanzania; his group, "School", is a naively vivid and rhythmically pantomimic scene: four pupils are pushing their way towards the blackboard on which the teacher is writing mysterious ciphers — a scene from everyday life transformed into a deeply significant ritual. Joseph Ndandarika from Zimbabwe, who is self-taught, produces figures and objects in stone, wood and terracotta which relate to magic events.

The shepherd Samuel Wanjau learned to carve through making the wooden parts of home-made fire-arms during the struggle of his tribe for independence. He taught himself to give concrete form to his inner experience. His sculptures have a naively personal note, as though he were trying to impart a visible form to the souls of animals.

The Yoruba artist, blacksmith and metal-worker, *Asiru Olatunde*, hammers out myths and legends of his gods from aluminium sheet. In their artlessly imaginative way his works express a mixture of traditional tribal tales and biblical scenes. These densely populated compositions, which can be read as if they were hieroglyphics, remind us both of the sculptures of Ife and Benin and of the fabulous creatures that abound in naive paintings.

Although the European *avant-garde* turned to the inspiration of African sculpture in order to revitalize the effete art of civilized communities, the ritual sculptures of Haiti were almost totally disregarded.

Haiti is the home of many painters and few sculptors, and when we talk of Haitian art we generally think of painting. Little has been said hitherto of the forged or hammered artefacts of that country. The blacksmith and sculptor *Georges Liautaud* (born 1899) cut strange figures from sheet iron and copper: human beings, sirens, devils and Christ-figures. The mouths and eyes of his demons and gods are stamped out, their noses and breasts are hammered into

shape. Chains provide an element of movement. These figures suggest a synthesis of Christianity and the religion of Voodoo. The fetishist character of Liautaud's figures corresponds to the level of consciousness of the Haitian people and imbues them with magic powers.

Edgar Brièrre gave the name "Servants of Voodoo" to a scene with similar magic implications. In the middle of the group is the heart of the love-goddess Erzulie; to her right and left kneel two of the faithful, with faces carved on their knees. They are possessed by spirits, possibly the heavenly twins called Marassa, who represent the ancestors of mankind. A mighty hand rises above this group and points to the supernatural power emanating from the Loas.

Serge Jolimeau, creator of demons, masked heads and magical devices, has

74

Zagajewski, Stanislav: Altar

Schumann, Günter: The Shepherd Heinrich

shaped a symbolic wheel while representing *l'éternel retour*, the never-ending cycle of life. From four equal quadrants he has constructed the various elements of the world as he sees them: the natural and the supernatural, past and future. The centre is occupied by a crucified figure: Christ or a Voodoo spirit? Each of the quadrants is occupied by women, birds and an endless variety of animals.

In such elements of the unexpected and the incongruous, which are nevertheless formed into a unity, there is a certain latent affinity with Surrealism. At certain moments we may sense that the vulgar mannerism of such works emits a strange resonance somewhere between the mystic and the manic.

Naive sculpture in Europe lies generally on the borders of folk art. From a dying folklore arise original variations on themes that are linked to the past. Jedrzej Wawro, who worked as a stone-mason, lumberjack and rag-and-bone man, and Leon Kudla, former labourer, postman and small shop-keeper, produced highly original and deeply sincere variations on religious themes. The Last Supper carved in wood by an unskilled factory hand, Adam Zegadlo, continues popular tradition but also manifests features of individual expression.

In Romania it is Neculai Popa, an agricultural worker on the collective farm of Tirpesti-Neamt, who, through an imaginative use of formal expression, approximates the anonymous heritage of a folk tradition to the typical idiom of naive art.

The Slovak shepherd and small-holder Jozef Kemko invented men and animals that belong essentially to the imagery of popular tradition. Here we find Janošik, the legendary rebel epitomizing peasant resistance to feudal overlords, carved in natural wood without the benefit of colour, the patterns of his folk costume gouged out of the surface of the wood, his hat set straight on his round head. In spite of links with the past and affinities with folk art, Kemko has broken away from rigid traditional patterns and set his own personal mark on the collective memory of his people and class.

The architectonic solidity of Kemko's figures stands in direct contrast to the slender, plant-like wire figures of *Josef Kerák* (1891—1945). Their creator was a wire-worker and tinker who travelled from village to village repairing pots and pans. His witch from the world of Slav fable bears an owl, the creature of the night, on her hunched shoulder. Shadowy figures of men, women and animals, apparently shaped from blades of metallic grass, naive structures consisting of curves and three-dimensional modulations, give the impression of a kind of phantom substantiality reminiscent of the basket-work figures of Argentinian folk art, or perhaps of the figures in Oskar Schlemmer's "Triadic Ballet". In this way the primitive village artist's wire figures unwittingly come into contact with the sculptural idiom of modern art.

Naive wood-carvers in Hungary are linked via their themes with the countryside and the villages from which they come: sturdy peasant figures in folk costume, pious postures and narrative motifs. *István Orbán* shows a group at prayer with dull, devout expressions. A piece by *Antal Markovits-Horváth* (1851—1933), "Shepherds in Conversation", epitomizes an intense experience of nature. The figures are reduced to a set of simple rhythmic shapes which embody some latent meaning.

The sculptures of the Serbian peasant *Bogosav Živković* (born 1920) are not merely carved from wood: they are born from wood and have all the characteristics of that material. His human figures and imaginary animals have an outlandish and unexpected quality, and yet they seem familiar, as if we had encountered them in an ancient fairy-tale. He represents animal heads and human bodies, centaurs and mythical beasts that resemble the initials on old Serbian manuscripts. As in the case of Indian totem-poles on the north-west coast of America, where the heads of men and animals represent tribal ancestors and hence have more than a merely individual character, the heads of Bogosav's sculptures are their most expressive part.

The dynamic visions of *Milan Stanisavljević* (born 1944) force him to seek more complex possibilities. He tends to follow the structure of the tree-trunk less than Bogosav, the emphasis of his expressive idiom lying in the compositional grouping. His "Wedding Dirge" demonstrates the inexorable nature of human bondage. Rhythmically ordered groups seem to come together and then part again. On the rear of the pillar we witness a mysterious happening: a suffering figure, larger than life, with one hand on his breast, the other on his forehead. Tears have been carved on the face, as with Spanish Madonnas. The demonic and enigmatic implications of the work have been subjugated by a lucid and powerful sense of form.

The Dalmatian peasant and self-taught cartwright and wood-carver, *Petar Smajić* (born 1910), has created a work which he entitles "My Family". Two generations stand in orderly ranks, the family tree growing from the bottom upwards. The rigidly frontal pose of the group allows it no freedom, no mobility, no relationship between individuals. They stand there as though bound to each other, all strikingly alike, with small, childish hands and short arms, the men with flat Dalmatian caps on their heads, the women's faces strictly framed by their shawls, their feet firmly planted on the soil where they live and labour.

They have that grave demeanour, the simplicity and immobility that are inherent in the material, in the carver himself, in membership of the family and in the monotony of their whole existence.

The carved, and in some cases coloured figures of the Bosnian *Ðorđe Kreča* are evocations of childhood and death and of friendship with the trees, from whose material the life of the past and the life of the future takes its shape. His works have the ponderousness of idols and the fundamental solidity that springs from a sense of three-dimensional, concrete substantiality.

The symbolic shapes of archaic and exotic cultures, which find a latter-day echo in the carvings of these naive artists, can hardly be interpreted otherwise than as a resurrection of the collective unconscious that lies dormant in our

Bödeker, Erich: The Royal Family

Bogosav (Živković): My Life   *Stanisavljević, Milan: Wedding Dirge*

Bakos, Lajos: Doctor's House Call

souls. From the works of peasant sculptors we turn now to the domain of the craftsman. After decades of domination by abstraction, and precisely at the point where the human figure is beginning once more to make its appearance in art, the sculptures of the retired miner *Erich Bödeker* (1904—1971) tend to acquire an avant-garde function, without his being at all aware of this. His figures, shaped from wood and painted cement, offer a naive counterpart to Pop Art sculpture, the New Figuration, which tries to illustrate the desolation and depersonalization of the individual in an industrial society. In this connection his sculptures may be seen and assessed from a new aspect. Without parodistic intent, but guided by a lively, down-to-earth sense of humour, Bödeker has his own contribution to make to our view of our own age through the scenario of modern society which his sculptures offer.

When I went to visit *Hans Schmitt* (born 1912) in Walchstadt on the Wörthersee, I found him in his rain-soaked garden together with the brightly coloured lath figures that are reminiscent of Bödeker's squat sculptures. It may well be that the loss of his right hand in the war has obliged him to employ the surviving left hand with an instinctive spontaneity in pursuit of a direct simplicity. His fondness for angular and pointed shapes gives his compositions a humorously grotesque tension. Using the delicate probe of his premonitory instinct, he creates charming monsters, hybrid creatures of his elemental imagination, of a kind never seen on land or sea.

Neither Hans Schmitt, who has been a cow herd, farmer and hotel porter in his time, nor the former pitman, Erich Bödeker, are, properly speaking, industrial workers. They are marginal figures in the industrialized and technological world from which they take the materials of their sculptures.

Naive sculpture is not widely known and has been little studied hitherto. Although there have been a great many one-man shows and group exhibitions in galleries and museums since the first exhibition of naive painting in Knokke-Le-Zoute in 1958, there has so far been no equivalent comprehensive review of naive sculpture.

CLASSIFICATION AND PERSPECTIVES

In this introductory essay we have generally employed categories based on ethnic areas, continents and nationalities. This is not the only possible arrangement, but it provides the framework for the kind of summary needed in a reference work in which the items are in alphabetical order.

Whereas professional artists in the more advanced countries have broken away from their respective national traditions and now aspire to a kind of universality, the work of naive artists, which has its roots in peasant communities or in craft circles, still lives in a climate governed by a particular landscape or setting. There are, nevertheless, a number of other possible and useful ways of classifying their works, some of which we have already briefly mentioned.

Naive artists in farming communities tend not to see nature as a lost Paradise for which they yearn, but as a fact of their concrete existence, as the setting for their productive labours. What they are painting is something that belongs to them, the background to their everyday lives, the scene of bitter harvests and rural customs. These are not painters with a sentimental admiration for nature; they are thoroughly familiar with nature and it is from nature that they are obliged to wrest their daily bread by the sweat of their brow. The very real bond that the peasant artist has with his fellows and the countryside, his daily labour — this militates against any idealization of country life. The Romantic view is more characteristic of the reflective mode of thought we find in town-dwellers, among whom naive craftsmen painters are generally numbered.

Generalić, Josip: The Hlebine Jadwiga

Mejo, Oscar de: Violet-coloured Cake

In France, at the end of the last century and during the first decades of the present century, naive artists generally belonged to an ill-defined social group of craftsmen and middle-class people. The great master, Rousseau, combined the democratic awareness of the *citoyen* with the dignified respectability of the lower middle-class. The Douanier, the postal inspector Vivin, the gardener Bauchant and Bombois, who might be reckoned a member of the working class, were all brought up in a tradition of enlightened free thought.

In an age of scientific and technological revolution, of cybernetics and automation, members of the occupational group represented by craftsmen have either been absorbed into the industrial labour force or else have been obliged to transfer their activities from the production of goods to servicing and repair work. Living in this disintegrating peripheral zone of society, artisans often become outsiders, eccentrics and whimsical philosophers — something which can serve to inspire naive art.

It is to this guild of craftsmen that we would assign naive artists like the gardener André Bauchant from Touraine, the shoemaker Orneore Metelli from Terni, the painter and decorator Matija Skurjeni from Zaprešić, the watchmaker from Galilee, Shalom of Safed, the button-maker from Novi Sad, Emerik Feješ, and the trio of carpenters — Aloys Sauter, born in Stabrock, near Antwerp, Pal Homonai from Irig and Ivan Rabuzin from the village of Ključ.

Among the well-known naive painters are a number of women: Séraphine, the humble maiden and mystic gardener; Suma Maruki, who experienced Hiroshima and suffered there; Grandma Moses, who transformed the arduous years of her life on the farm into a celebration of life with the help of her brilliant palette; the Afro-American, Vivian Ellis, who paints the icons of her own black race; Micheline Boyadjian, who presents in the naive beauty of her paintings mirror images of her memories and her longing for a sister. We mention the names of these women without wishing to separate them from their male counterparts, to whom they are in no way inferior. A further social phenomenon in advanced countries is represented by those housewives who have taken up painting. In search of new ways to enjoy life they are often moved by a creative instinct which can in certain cases lead to the production of works of art.

Stefula, György: My Parents in Heaven

Not everything that is exhibited under the title, "naive art," has aesthetic value. It is true that many individuals who are searching for relief from the monotony of their professional occupations, or for a new interest in life, have been able to make a contribution towards a fresh view of the world through the directness of their narrative gift. Through the metaphor of childish observation they sometimes succeed in breaking through the closed circle of alienation and social isolation. However, as in every area of creative activity, the host of naive artists includes relatively few major talents.

RADIATIONS

The penetration of archaic and primitive elements into modern art was a significant event. It brought with it a kind of directness which ran counter to the prevailing technical virtuosity and the trend towards dissociative abstraction. Various ventures on the borders of spontaneous visual expression and self-conscious naivety may also be reckoned among the noteworthy and characteristic impulses in the art of our time. Many of my painter friends do not understand why I insist on calling them self-consciously naive. The word "self-conscious" seems to them — quite wrongly — to imply some sort of criticism. But why should it be held to the credit of Picasso or Modigliani that they were inspired by the primitive art of Africa and Oceania, whereas inspiration by the work of naive artists should be regarded as improper? The fact that educated and trained painters and draughtsmen should sense an affinity with a childishly direct mode of visual expression suggests that it is necessary in an excessively technical and artificial aesthetic climate to have recourse once more to those original sources which hold a promise of renewal.

The dividing lines between amateur art, naive art and professional art are often vague and indefinite: there are variants and transitional categories.

The continent which that Columbus of naive painting, Douanier Rousseau, discovered, the primeval paradise of fabulous fauna and mysterious flora, became the point of departure for Surrealism. Of Rousseau's "Sleeping Gipsy-Woman", Wilhelm Uhde said that this picture anticipated Cubism: "The later Picasso is splendidly adumbrated in this work." Did not Rousseau's "Footballers" also inspire Picasso's "Game with a Ball" and Delaunay's "Runners"? Edgar Tytgat's poetic artlessness and narrative gusto represent a sophisticated kind of naivety. Gifted Italian painters like Ottone Rossi have turned away from the bravura rhetoric of 20th-century painting to seek their inspiration in the realistic innocence of the Maîtres Populaires.

The desire for renewed contact with the figurative world and social realities in an age of alienation led Krsto Hegedušić, the moving spirit of the school of Hlebine, to combine the insights and techniques of modern art with the directness of a popular, naive view of the world. Many professionally trained artists regard the childlike sense of wonder of naive painters with admiration and envy. Among them are Dorothea and György Stefula, Jan Balet, the Italian American Oscar de Mejo, and the Spaniards Vallejo-Nagera and Isabel Villar. They are all good painters who have profited from creative contact with naive artists. Klaus-Jürgen Fischer wrote in his critical diary about certain qualities of naive painters which have inspired professional artists: "The naive painter submits totally to the fundamental human instinct for order, and he creates this order with the help of form and colour to the point of aesthetic mastery. The economical arrangement of space and surface is an aesthetic factor in which naive painters often prove superior to their professional colleagues. The latter have learned a good deal from the naive artists." Ever since the artists of the modern movement turned at the beginning of this century to the experience of the primitive, the artlessness of childish vision, the realism of peasant votive paintings as a source of inspiration, the influences of the naive vision on professional art have had to be taken into account.

Rimbert, René: *The Douanier Rousseau on the Road to Glory, Ascending to the Other World*

Ellis, Vivian: Iconostasis of Human Life

Lizzie Is Sick	*Funeral*	*Gifts for the Poor*
Lizzie Is Dead	*Hymn for Lizzie*	*Climbing Jacob's Ladder*
Wake	*Commemoration for Lizzie*	*Little David Making Music*

Any attempt to assimilate naive art to the historical principles governing the history of art, or to involve it in the ever-changing pattern of contemporary styles, would turn it into nothing more than a curious peripheral phenomenon, a fleeting "happening" marked by pure innocence.

It is not only professional art but also naive art that is going through a structural crisis in our scientific age. In spite of doubts and hesitations, however, it is becoming more and more certain that naive art, if it is genuinely naive and truly art, can and will survive, because it can help to overcome the growing estrangement of man from his own essential self.

Naive Artists
of the World
in
Alphabetical
Order

ABA, FERENC — Hungary
ABALJAEV, I. M. — USSR
ABBA (F. Abba Derbyshire) — Great Britain
ABELS, JEAN — West Germany
ACEVEDO, F. I. — Cuba
AGAPOV, M. M. — USSR
"AGUILERA" G. SILVA — Venezuela
AGUIRRE, JULIE — Nicaragua
ALADAŠVILI, A. — USSR
ALAMO, NEKE — Venezuela
ALBERINO, CARMELINA — Italy
ÁLDOZÓ, JÓZSEF — Hungary
ALEXANDRINE — Netherlands
ALLEGRETTI, F. — Italy
ALLEN, ELIZABETH — Great Britain
ALLIN, JOHN — Great Britain
ALVAREZ, A. A. — Venezuela
AMBARCUMJAN, O. — USSR
AMIRJAN, G. — USSR
ANDRADE, M. C. de — Brazil
ANDRADE, N. F. de — Brazil
ANDREEV, N. A. — USSR
ANDRUSZKIEWICS, M. — Italy

ANONYMOUS ARTISTS

from USA
from Canada
from Ethiopia
from Senegal
from Tunisia
from Romania
from USSR

APPENZELL PAINTING — Switzerland
ARAGÓN, J. R. — USA
ARANA, EDUARDO — Nicaragua
ARANA, JOSÉ — Nicaragua
ARCHER, JIMMY — Australia
ARELLANO, RODOLFO — Nicaragua
ARIMINI, I GUSTI A. — Indonesia, Bali
ARMAS, ARMANDO de — Cuba
ARNING, EDDIE — USA
"ARPILLERAS" — Chile
AUER, HILDEGARD — West Germany
AUXILIADORA, MARIA da S. — Brazil

Note

Names of artists from the USSR:

The conventional international spelling is given first, and they are alphabetised according to this. The specifically English transliteration is given afterwards.

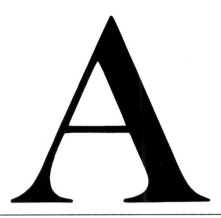

Aba, Ferenc: Villager

ABA, FERENC (1901) Hungary

Ferenc Aba, born in Vésztö, is a retired carpenter who has been carving small-size genre figures in wood since 1961. Ferenc draws his subject-matter from the everyday life of the people. Some of his works are marked by appealingly grotesque features. He has exhibited at many national and foreign exhibitions. *(See portrait of the artist, p. 110). M. I.*

ABALJAEV, IVAN MIHÁJLOVIČ (1901—1942) ABALYAYEV, IVAN MIKHAILOVICH

I. M. Abalyayev was born in the village of Butroma near Kimry, not far from Tver, now Kalinin, into the family of a poor peasant who did cobbling as a sideline. The town of Kimry and the surrounding villages were traditionally considered a "land of cobblers," from which place cobbler peasants travelled to Moscow in search of a livelihood. Peasants not only made boots but also carved out of local woods the necessary lasts as well as household utensils, window frames and cornices. Ivan Abalyayev learned the trade of a last-carver, but drudgery and want failed to kill his creative urges and sculptural gifts. Whenever he had a spare moment the boy would hide away from the prying eyes of parents and neighbours and carve wooden tops, building blocks and subsequently representations of birds and animals. He himself described his carving as an eccentricity. Unfortunately, he was killed in the war, having dedicated himself to what he called "wizardry in wood" for a mere thirteen years. In his multi-figure compositions, which deal with ordinary day-to-day life, he sought to convey his attitudes to both past and present. He imparted a class character and social affinity to the personages depicted, emphasising this by the choice of costume, hair-style and furnishings, and also through his titles, such as "A Holiday Feast in a Poor Man's House," "A Holiday Feast in a Rich Man's House," "In Search of a Livelihood," "Filching Leather from the Wife" and "The Family of a Shock Worker." With Abalyayev, his conventionalised representations of human beings are associated with the folk understanding of clan, rather than individual, features. Yet his figures are not that conventional; on the contrary they are detailed, even to the point of being a realistic copy of the original. This folk sculptor endeavoured to convey the character of the persons depicted, together with the relationships between them, discarding everything he considered superfluous. He regarded both image and medium as of equal importance, and though his figures are coloured in a somewhat restrained manner, the texture and mass of the wood can be sensed beneath the paint. One could say that the presentation of the wooden medium in its angularly plastic form and massiveness expresses the peasant's typical respect for wood, his love of this medium. Abalyayev's work was truly folksy in spirit: it was naive and consisted

Abalyayev, I. M.: A Holiday Feast in a Rich Man's House

of things done for his own pleasure and amusement. In 1935 he was represented at the First Exhibition of Amateur Collective-Farm Artists in Moscow. Today much of his work can be seen at what one may term "The Abalyayev Corner" in the Kimry Museum of Ethnography and Local Lore. *(See portrait of the artist, p. 110). N. Sh.*

ABBA   Great Britain
(FLORENCE ABBA DERBYSHIRE) (1920—1975)

Abba was born in 1920 in Chorley, Lancashire, where she lived until her death. She survived her husband by eleven years and it was during this period of her life that she turned to painting. Unable to afford brushes, she made her thick and complicated oil paintings with the tip of a needle. This technique in no way inhibited her. Indeed, all her pictures have a torrential zest not far removed from Expressionism at its wildest. Furthermore, possessed of a near maniacal religious fervour, she covered every surface upon which she painted with mystical imagery, reciting verses and singing prayers to them as she worked. Abba's pictures have rarely been exhibited outside Lancashire, but nine of them were included in "Northern Primitives" at the South London Art Gallery (Museum) in 1972. *(See portrait of the artist, p. 110). Sh. W.*

ABELS, JEAN (1895)   West Germany

Jean Abels was born in Angelsdorf and still lives there. His parents were farmers and all their eleven children were obliged to help on the farm from an early age. After leaving school he was trained as a carpet-weaver but from 1919 until his retirement in 1958 he worked on the rail-

way. Abels began painting two years after he retired.

He took up a number of themes — some of them on request — but, apart from scenes of the countryside and work on the farm, he had a preference for historical subjects, frequently choosing biblical tales and repeating many of them in different versions (they include the expulsion of Adam and Eve from the Garden of Eden, the marriage at Cana, Cain and Abel, Saul and David).

What a strange quirk of fate that this quiet, retiring, rather dreamy pensioner, with his delicate constitution, should one day have tried his

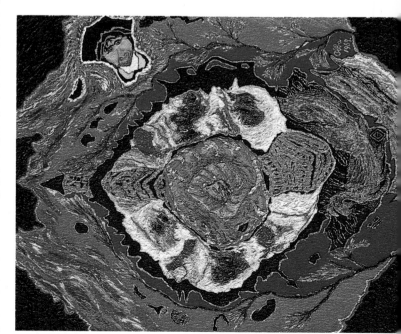

Abba (Florence Abba Derbyshire): Black Jack

hand at painting "from boredom." From then on he sat from morning till evening at his little work-table, where his small-scale studies took shape, painted with austere economy and focussed on the essential feature of each episode.

Abels's pictures are invariably slightly inept, painted with an awkwardness that is almost touching. Larger areas are firmly hatched in or else covered with dots. Sometimes he attempted to mould the pigments with a heavily charged, coarse brush, but it seems that the wooden panel absorbed the paint instantly, so that the outlines of the painted areas appear harsh rather than

ishly crude as these figures are from the point of view of the resources used, they nevertheless represent important pieces of a mosaic pictorial structure within an overall architectural concept which is astounding in the simplicity and grandeur of its shapes and colour combinations. In their harmonization of narrative, interpretation, colouring, technical reproduction, expression and form with all their anatomical, and particularly their perspective "errors," Abels's little pictorial panels are authentic evidence of an innocently intact and naturally naive interpretation of a world that is entirely free of blemish. *T. G.*

Abels, Jean: Holy Communion

fluid. It is noticeable that Abels employed a characteristic scheme of his own to represent faces. His palette is rich in contrasts, cool for the most part, with loud colours in small quantities only, and of a dry, cork-like consistency. He paints an almost greyish-blue bright sky, hilly pastures, often of a spring-like green, and reddish-grey or ochre-coloured mountains. Occasionally Abels employed a ruler: for example, to draw tiled surfaces with proper precision. Sometimes the pencil intrudes on the painting, outlines the shape of a table-leg, marks the edge of the table on the cloth that is draped over it. Space is experienced only as a plane surface; Abels rarely attempted to achieve three-dimensional effects by applying faint patches of colour. Figures could hardly be more economically rendered. Child-

ACEVEDO, FELICINDO IGLESIAS Y   Cuba
(1898)

Acevedo was born in Orense, Galicia, Spain. He went to school in France. In 1933 he emigrated to Cuba, where he became an importer of wine and spices. He took up painting in 1939, while continuing his profession. He was also a musician in a church in Havana, where he lives. His picture "Christopher Columbus Discovering Cuba" is a childlike composition which strikes the spectator as being both visionary and strangely stilted. In spite of the poverty of its artistic resources it is moving because of the intensity of the experience it expresses. It is as if Acevedo had perceived and awakened in his own heart the sublime adventure of that landing.

→

Acevedo, F. I.: Christopher Columbus Discovering Cuba

AGAPOV,   USSR
MIHAJLOVIČ (1903—1975)
AGAPOV, MIKHAIL MIKHAILOVICH

Agapov lived in Kungrad, a city in the autonomous republic of Kara Kalpak, Uzbekistan, and worked in a factory until his retirement in 1972, in which year he began to paint and was represented at a republic show of amateur art. He preferred genre scenes and also themes which expressed a civic spirit: for instance, in his panel "For Peace" ("Remember"), in which he depicted on the fringe of an intensely yellow field of wheat a woman holding a dead infant, with blood trickling from its mouth. A most memorable, truly anti-war, achievement, in which the artist, a man

Agapov, M.M.: Bread Cakes

of the people, gave rein to humanity's pain and shouted his "No!" to war. Several works are about the nearby Aral Sea, which is shown both calm and stormy. Or take his "Bread Cakes": a simple subject, merely an Uzbek woman baking the traditional national bread in the traditional national oven, the *tyndyr*, as her child plays on the brilliantly patterned carpet in the background. Familiar, common enough, yet conveyed with profound lyrical meaning, with emphasis on the vital feature. His compositions display a kind of circular movement that unobtrusively brings the viewer to the point the artist desires to make. (To express those aspects of life that stirred his mind, Agapov neutralised the spatial element, as it were, not only because circular movement is of universal significance, but also to pinpoint what is basic — a type of compositional arrangement that is extremely characteristic of the naive artist generally and is associated in some degree with binocular vision.) The circular composition is further enhanced by the use of bright colours, which imparts a certain dynamic stress. Agapov was represented at the USSR "Glory to Labour" exhibition of amateur art in Moscow in 1974. *N. Sh.*

"AGUILERA"   Venezuela
GERARDO SILVA (1920)

"Aguilera" (Gerardo Silva) was born in Barcelona, Venezuela. He was discovered by Luis Luksic in 1964 and went on to be chosen by Jacobo Borges for an exhibition in the Fine Arts Museum in 1966. As can be seen in the illustrations, he favours a picture on "two levels," selecting the most important part of his painting to be filled out on one panel (or what purports to be a panel), which is then stuck to the main picture area. Aguilera is an artist of prime importance to Venezuela, one who has been described as occupying a specially inspired corner of the naive art of his country. The only influences upon his personal imagery stem from the not always precise information he has been able to pick up from books and newspapers, emphasised in some part by a kind of untaught academicism, made even more bizarre because of a latent realisation of the purity to be found in the artistic products of madmen. *(See portrait of the artist, p. 111). Sh. W.*

AGUIRRE, JULIE (1953)   **Nicaragua**

Julie Aguirre married the painter Holner Madrigal. One day, drawn by the colours he had left on his palette, she also began to paint, encouraged by her husband. "I have painted a great many pictures and in them wanted to express the joy of life," she said on one occasion. In 1978 her husband was murdered by members of Somosa's National Guard. Filled with pain, she then began to portray the desire of her people for liberty. When the war ended and the country was liberated, her paintings took on a happier aspect. *(See portrait of the artist, p. 111). E. C.*

Aguirre, Julie: Village

ALADAŠVILI, ALEKSANDR (1909—1974) **USSR**
ALADASHVILI, ALEXANDER

Alexander Aladashvili was born in a peasant family in the Kakhetian village of Arbushiki in East Georgia. In the evening of his life he lived with his family in the Georgian capital of Tbilisi, where he had worked as a book-keeper before retirement. He first began to paint in about 1930, his works mostly dealing with the village life and farm work with which he was so familiar, such as wine-growing and harvesting. His unpretentious pictorial interpretation of the seemingly patriarchal mode of life and mores of the Georgian village recalls the naive world of Pirosmani. Yet, whereas Pirosmani sought to represent a combined rustic and urban environment, a borderline category which is almost always a fertile medium for naive art, the world that Aladashvili reproduced is of an epic, festive and truly popular nature. City life failed to modify the basis of the *Weltanschauung* of this colourful, gifted self-taught artist. A characteristic feature is his continual address to the seasons of the agricultural calendar. His colours are refreshingly direct and vibrant, reflecting as they do his frank perception and the picture he sought to present of the surrounding world. His works so greatly appealed to his fellow-villagers that in the 1930s they bore them aloft at demonstrations marking the national holidays — as the artist himself loved proudly to recall. This naive artist is of a type that can hardly be found among the self-taught artists of today, and in this sense he is probably more of a naive painter, more direct, than even Pirosmani was. The latter, who came from an urban milieu, was in his way a pioneer

"Aguilera" Gerardo Silva: Portrait of Raul Leon

naive artist in so far as he was the first in this country to be recognised as such. Aladashvili's subjects are more of today, unlike the subject-matter that Pirosmani handled. Aladashvili's characters are ordinary farmers, wine-growers, shepherds, vendors, especially those selling a kind of local yoghurt called matsoni. At all times he treated them with sincere and warm affection. He also adored reproducing, somewhat in the manner of a popular broadsheet, the personages and situations from the classical literature of his native Georgia. He was represented at USSR exhibitions of amateur art in Moscow. In 1970 he had a one-man show in the Georgian town of Telavi. Many of his works may be seen at the Museum of Popular Creative Art in Tbilisi. *(See portrait of the artist, p. 111). N. Sh.*

ALAMO, NEKE (1950) Venezuela

Neke Alamo is one of the Venezuelan naive artists associated with the "Pintores Populares de Caracas" who have been influenced by city life.

is random, underlining how the people are dwarfed by the majestic salon. *(See portrait of the artist, p. 111). Sh. W.*

ALBERINO, CARMELINA (1920) Italy

Carmelina Alberino is nicknamed Carmelina di Capri, not only because she was born on the isle of Capri into a poor fisherman's family, but also because she has lived there all her life, and because it is a recurring motif in her paintings.

She started painting by chance after buying a box of watercolours to entertain her sick son.

Aladashvili, Alexander: Bazaar

Certainly the subjects of her paintings have an urban ring about them which distances them from the village communes. "Coffee Time at Florencia's" is perhaps a little subdued. The colour range here is from pinks to greens and back again. A man, installed on a sofa, reads a book; a girl is painting on the patio, beyond which pink architecture — part castle, part ecclesiastical Romanesque — fronts a verdant and hilly landscape. The picture shown here, "La Hora de Café en el Taller de Pedro," makes happy distinction between the works of the four painters (two painting landscapes with figures, one a cat, and one with a blank canvas) and the sumptuous apartment, with its stage supporting three nudes (one black and two white). Again the perspective

Later she worked in oil on canvas. With the vigour typical of southerners who refuse to be defeated by want and poverty, she fills her canvases with all her instinctive vitality, the impetuosity of her people, a naive imagination pure and unadulterated. Originally, she painted what she saw around her, not so much in order to get down on paper a landscape or structure as to note their colours, which she places on canvas according to very personal and private rules. Later she no longer needed to be in direct contact with nature, having explored every corner of the island; in her small studio brilliant visions were born, showing the ever-changing appearance of her surroundings, the intensely blue sea and the bright sunlight.

Most of the scenes show lovely beaches, with fishing nets spread out over the sand; on the sea, with its changing colours, rock the rowing boats of fishermen occupied with their work, while the shore is lined with multi-coloured houses in gaudy hues from Pompeian red to blinding white and bright ochre ("The Small Marina"). The fact that the houses, squares, terraces, streets and beaches appear in constantly shifting relationships does not matter, because the artist's presentation is always suggestive and vital, full of charm and typically Mediterranean colours. All of these qualities have placed her among the most characteristic representatives of Italian naive painting, an artist of simple but authentic visual poetry and spontaneous naivety. *(See portrait of the artist, p. 110). D. M.*

ÁLDOZÓ, JÓZSEF (1892)   **Hungary**

József Áldozó was born in Himód. His talent was discovered at the end of the twenties. Most

Alberino, Carmelina: "The Grotta Verde" Restaurant

Alamo, Neke: Coffee Time in Pedro's Studio

of his watercolours show either people at work or a variety of domestic animals. An oil painting entitled "The Bishop Comes to Confirmation" evokes a solemn event of his youth. He exhibited at the "Original Talents" exhibition in 1937. Several of his works are in the Hungarian National Gallery in Budapest. *M. I.*   →

ALEXANDRINE (1903—1981)   **Netherlands**

Alexandrine (Alexandrine Kelder-Gortmans) was born in Djakarta, Indonesia. In her childhood she enjoyed the exotic nature of her birthplace. In 1916 she left for the Netherlands, where her Indonesian appearance aroused critical looks. The sudden change from one country to another caused her much suffering and Holland never inspired her. Nevertheless, she married a

Dutchman, the painter and sculptor Toon Kelder, by whom she had two children. In 1960 she spent a few months in Vence in southern France, where the Mediterranean environment reminded her of her youth. To express her joy, she began to paint.

Upon returning to the Netherlands, she continued painting, her memories remaining fresh. Anatole Jakovsky was one of the first to see her work and to arrange for it to be exhibited in Paris in the Bénézit Gallery (1964). But it was not until 1976 that she exhibited in the Netherlands (in the Frans Hals Museum in Haarlem, at

ALLEGRETTI, FERDINANDO (1908—1979) Italy

Ferdinando Allegretti, born in Fossombrone (Pesaro), moved to Terni, where he worked for a long time in the steel mills. Falling seriously ill, he was compelled to leave his job. This on the one hand cut him off from his social environment but on the other led him to take refuge in painting. Allegretti died in Terni in January 1979. His hard life left its mark and there is nothing gay or relaxed about his painting, no idyllic visions or dreamy overtones. Rather his works are a gallery of tormented human beings, some of them rejected as he had been and feeling the full brunt

Áldozó, József: The Bishop Comes to Confirmation

a group exhibition of Dutch naive art organised by Nico van der Endt). After the death of her husband (1973), she stopped painting.

It has unjustifiably been thought that Alexandrine was inspired by Henri Rousseau. At the beginning of her career, however, she had not even heard of him and drew her inspiration from her own experience. In a sense, her pictures are more "real" than the Douanier's, who never saw a jungle. The past and present are intermingled in her works, in which gorgeous blue-green nuances create an effect of melancholy. The gaiety of the past is stifled somewhat by the sadness of the present. Her themes are, for the most part, her youth in Indonesia, the landscapes of southern France and Paris. *(See portrait of the artist, p. 110). N. E.*

of life's cruelty. Even the landscapes, serving as a background for his scenes, are done in strong, decisive, frequently dark colours; the graphic work is instinctively primitive, making it seem that the painting has turned to stone and creating an unusually striking impression. These expressive features impel the spectator to delve for hidden psychological and other motives. *(See portrait of the artist, p. 110). D. M.*

ALLEN, ELIZABETH (1883—1967) Great Britain

Elizabeth Allen was born in Tottenham, London and died in Biggin Hill, Kent. She was one of seventeen children of a German father and an Irish mother. Elizabeth Allen had to use a crutch throughout her life because from birth she had two physical deformities — a twisted spine and a deformed leg.

From her father, who ran a tailor's shop, she learnt to become an adept seamstress. When she was twenty-five years old she left home to set up as a professional seamstress, first in Suffolk and subsequently in London, but it was not until years later, when she settled down in a cottage (built entirely of corrugated iron) in Biggin Hill, that she adapted her craft with the needle to the creation of outstanding pictures in patchwork, a brilliant series of which might have passed unnoticed had they not been discovered by a young art student called Bridget Poole, who showed them to the London art dealer Andras Kalman, after which they were exhibited. Elizabeth Allen was able to roam free in fancy or fact in the

ality. It was not until the mid-1960s that he returned to his easel, and this time he did not attempt to copy anyone. Since he was utterly without training and had no conception of any kind of technique, his first "original" paintings were basically naive, brash and lacking in style. He has continued in this manner ever since, except that he has become steadily more adept in painterly performance.

Paintings from the early years, when he still signed his pictures "Johny the Road," were already imbued with a simple attraction in combination with a freakish tendency to hit upon

Alexandrine: Out for a Walk

execution of her patchwork pictures. Their subjects were as diverse as "The Dream of Nebuchadnezzar" (rich not only in brilliant stuffs and colours but also in an inventive fantasy which seemed to know no bounds) and "Population Explosion," which shows a patient, uniformed nurse tending the needs of a tired mother in bed, while, set against the wall in what must have been a gigantic cradle, the heads of her septuplets can be seen. Every portion of cloth is stitched neatly into place, their colours as flamboyant and handsome as the brightly coloured children's sweets of long ago. *(See portrait of the artist, p. 111). Sh. W.*

ALLIN, JOHN (1942)　　　　**Great Britain**

John Allin was born in Hackney, East London. Originally employed as a heavy-lorry driver, he became interested in painting as a spare-time occupation. The first painting tasks he set himself (trying to copy reproductions of Rembrandt's pictures) proved wholly unsatisfactory and he totally abandoned what he had hoped would be an enjoyable expression of his person-

Allegretti, Ferdinando: Lady Violinist

Allen, Elizabeth: The Shrine

"ordinary" oddities (like his painting of a man who has climbed to a rooftop, clinging to the chimney as a personal demonstration — against or for what? who knows? — while a policeman from below tries, with professional patience, to dislodge him). "The policeman's uniform wasn't quite right," he remembers, "but I just felt I could not copy it from an official manual."

It is some while since Allin gave up driving heavy vehicles. Today all his time is devoted to painting, and he exhibits regularly at London's Portal Gallery, which has supported his work from the start.

ALVAREZ, ANDRES ANTONIO (1939) — Venezuela

A. A. Alvarez was born in Los Altos de Cumena. He lives and works in Caracas. Alvarez is by nature a farmer and was for a time employed on a coffee plantation. Later, in 1964, he settled in Barcelona, Venezuela, and worked as a policeman in Cotiza. It was here that he won a prize for a picture called "Police Day." Later he was appointed a police guard at the Museo de Bellas Artes, and in this way came to know many artists and was able to familiarise himself with important works of art. Alvarez's own painting

Allin, John: Petticoat Lane

Essentially an East Ender, he remembers that part of London before they began to pull it down: an area once famous for its industry, its small businesses, its mean streets and its Cockneys. And what he does not remember, he has learnt from members of his family and from friends. So it was natural that when the playwright Arnold Wesker wrote about the Cockneys and the Jews of the East End, he should have Allin as his illustrator — more than that, they produced a book together, Allin painting and Wesker writing in what has come to be regarded as a miracle of co-operation — the intellectual and the lorry driver both on the same job. Entitled "Say Goodbye, You May Never See Them Again," the book was published by Jonathan Cape and was an immediate success.

Since that time he has pursued his craft — sometimes steadily painting away for an ever-growing band of admirers, at others quixotically joining a circus, travelling with the troupe in their bus and even appearing himself under the big tent as a clown — all to find inspiration for a whole series of new paintings about the circus.

Although Allin has had many exhibitions, it was not until 1979 that he achieved world recognition; then he was awarded first prize for the Naive Picture of the Year from a six-man international jury in Morges, Switzerland. *(See portrait of the artist, p. 110). Sh. W.*

Allin, John: The Old Synagogue

falls into several stages. First, in the late 1960s, he concentrated on formal portraits; these are remotely akin to the work of the so-called "primitives" of 18th-century North America — artists who, with little or no training, sought to make exact likenesses of their contemporaries. Then, in the early 1970s, came his simple but colourful scenes of the world about him, crowded pictures which gradually became more and more careful in execution, still rich in colour but with their subject-matter organised in neat designs. *(See portrait of the artist, p. 111). Sh. W.*

Alvarez, A.A.: Portrait of Simon Bolivar

the Soviet border guards until his retirement. Having begun to draw and paint at the age of 65, in ten years he produced 225 oils and 100 drawings done from nature, memory and imagination. He mostly paints and draws old pre-revolutionary Armenia. He is undoubtedly a purely naive artist, as is illustrated by the two-dimensional representation (which seems pulled upward), the lack of sky, the narrative content and the *impasto*, which derives from a concrete sense of the paint. Ignorant of anatomy, he brings to his work a characteristically naive element of decorativeness. His disposition of volumes has a specific rhythm, the colour range is extremely attractive, and the still-lifes are concrete in a way that makes them akin with the compositional design of a signboard. He has had four one-man shows and has taken part in group exhibitions both in the Soviet Union and abroad. *(See portrait of the artist, p. 111). N. Sh.*

AMIRJAN, GERASIM (1914)   USSR
AMIRYAN, GERASIM

Gerasim Amiryan, born in Armenia, was formerly a building worker but is now an old-age pensioner. He was spotted by the interesting amateur artist Saak Saakyan (a methods expert

Ambartsumyan, Oganes: Meeting of the Revolutionary Committee

AMBARCUMJAN, OGANES (1905)   USSR
AMBARTSUMYAN, OGANES

Oganes Ambartsumyan was born in the village of Gudemnis in Armenia. His father and mother were peasants. He attended the ordinary ten-year secondary school, after which he entered a special military school. He served with

from Yerevan, working with amateur artists) and advised to work on his own. He likes to do portraits of friends and relatives and also thematic compositions. A sincere, artless chronicler with a childlike manner in his representation of crowded scenes, he believes it necessary to highlight details, considering every element important. His colour range is expressive and decorative and his imagery ornamental. He prefers to paint the old-time Armenian life and the mores of his own environment, with which he is familiar. Thus, his "Wedding" is a multi-figure composition in two dimensions which is splashed over the canvas in childlike fashion. Paintings are marked by localised pools of colour and reflect his philosophy as man and artist: the happiness of being alive and working. He has been represented in big group shows in 1974 and 1977, and at an exhibition of Transcaucasian amateur art in 1973. He has had a one-man show

ANDRADE, NEUTON FREITAS DE (1938) Brazil

Since the age of twenty-one Andrade has been living in São Paulo. He started painting in 1959 at the suggestion of his friend Americo Modanez. Some time later he was to take part in the X SPAM (1961) and this was followed with a one-man show at the Galeria Ambiente, São Paulo (also in 1961). He sold his pictures at the São Paulo Mini-Gallery and was also one of the young painters to take a stand at the Sunday Art Fair (the "Hippie-Fair" in the Praça de Republica, São Paulo). He became internationally known. In 1962 and 1963 he contributed to the Casa de

Amiryan, Gerasim: The Capture of the Yerevan Fortress

in Yerevan and has also been exhibited abroad. *(See portrait of the artist, p. 110). N. Sh.*

ANDRADE, MOACIR COUTO DE (1927)   Brazil

Moacir Couto de Andrade was born in Manaus, in Amazonas. He started painting seriously and working upon drawings in 1954, the year in which he joined the Madingada Club, where he came to be represented in a number of group exhibitions. This led to his participation in the Modern Art Salon of Manaus (1960), the 1st Salon of Plastic Arts at the University of Pará (1963) and many other exhibitions. In the meantime he held many solo exhibitions. Moacir de Andrade is particularly famous for his injection of the spirit of humanity into his folklore subjects. *Sh. W.*

Artista Plastico de São Paulo, and three years later he and his work were featured in an important article in the magazine Artes No. 6.

Neuton de Andrade is a painstaking naive artist. Intensely detailed, his pictures are illustrative almost to the point of being narratives. *(See portrait of the artist, p. 110). Sh. W.*

ANDREEV,   USSR
NIKOLAJ ALEKSEEVIČ (1940)
ANDREIEV, NIKOLAI ALEXEIEVICH

N. A. Andreiev was born in a village near Novgorod. Upon leaving secondary school, he entered an army college. After demobilisation in 1964, he was employed as a production technologist in a metal-working plant and subsequently as a designer-engineer at a factory making capacitors. He began to paint in 1961, in which year he enrolled in the visual arts department of ZNUI, the Extra-Mural People's University of

Art, in Moscow. After completing his studies there, he joined the staff, as a methods adviser, of the Novgorod Regional House of Popular Art of the Ministry of Culture of the Russian Federation.

He is fascinated by day-to-day living, mores, customs and the environment, as can be deduced from the titles of his pictures, such as "Marriage Money," "The Otvodin Wedding" and "Dancing by the Silver Poplars," to mention but three. He dreams of creating a stage-by-stage "history" of the old-time wedding ritual as reflected in the present-day ceremony.

contemporary surroundings — aspects of modern urban folklore can be discerned. In "Bride Money Wedding" (seen here), Andreiev introduces the motorcar and the guitar into the traditional scene. The formally arranged members of the families in their city clothes seem stiff and out of place in the romantic autumn landscape, with its graceful silver birch and rowan trees.

The laconic clarity of his means of artistic self-expression places him between village and town art. He has been represented at Russian Federation and USSR shows of amateur art. *(See portrait of the artist, p. 110). N. Sh.*

Andreiev, N. A.: Bride Money Wedding

Andrade, Neuton Freitas de: The Washerwomen

He paints not only from nature, but also from memory and on the basis of his own imagination. His works reveal naive features, but at the same time he seeks to attain a professional level of skill. In the episodes of the old-time marriage ritual — presented, however, in

ANDRUSZKIEWICS, MARIA (1891)   Italy

Maria Andruszkiewics was born in Lazise, Verona. Her life is one long tale of misfortunes, beginning when she was forced to leave elementary school in order to help her numerous family. Marriage to a Polish aristocrat permitted her to live a few years in relative ease. In the First World War, her husband was captured and interned in a POW camp in Austria. After the war, in spite of delicate health, Maria had to work to support her two daughters. In the Second World War her husband was arrested in Poland and sent to a concentration camp where he died. Maria was left alone to care for the family. She moved to Milan, where, in 1964, when she was already 73 years old, she saw the graphic work of an elderly lady and began to paint herself. Her work would probably have remained unnoticed if the writer, Dino Buzzati, had not discovered her one day.

Later Buzzati wrote of her: "She is an authentic naive artist who tells of life with the informal expressive force that certain bright peasants know how to use in writing of harvests, hail, fires in the hay loft."

Maria Andruszkiewics stands out for her exceptional sense of colour and unusual, severe synthesis of expression, particularly if her considerable age is taken into account. The chromatic timbre is achieved with bold strokes of the brush, producing a suggestive density and rough relief.

Her method is original, pure and instinctive, and could be called expressionistic. It is her colours especially that reflect the psychological reality of the painter's vision, supported and strengthened by an extraordinary sense of composition. In this connection, mention should be made of "Wedding in Cana," rich in delicate psychological implications: the figures are disposed in a typical iconography, as though turned to stone at the magical moment that precedes a miracle; the young couple, accom-

ANONYMOUS NAIVE ARTISTS

All prehistoric art is anonymous: the artists are unknown and unrecorded. The full significance of what we denote as art achieved its proper expression only with the development of individuality: it was the growing awareness of the individual personality that brought artists' marks, signatures and monograms into art.

Folk art, which had grown from an unbroken tradition, passed down from one generation to the next, allowed little scope for individual variations, and its practitioners, too, remain anonymous. With the demise of such folk art in our

Andruszkiewics, Maria: The Mushroom Pickers

panied by a procession of relatives, stop with awe in front of Christ, the central figure in the composition, while the Madonna timidly indicates that there is no wine. In the foreground, a servant has prepared pitchers full of water, soon to be transformed into wine. "The Mushroom Pickers," a suggestive and stylised depiction of a wood and a small village, breathes a sober realism, but the mood created is nevertheless an original and mysterious one.

Maria Andruszkiewics is without question an exceptional figure among the Italian naive painters, not only in terms of longevity, but above all for her unusual stylistic expression and wealth of symbols and specific colours.

It should be added that the artist writes simple, gentle and deeply inspired poems, testifying to a lyrical and spiritually profound soul. *(See portrait of the artist, p. 111). D. M.*

Andruszkiewics, Maria: Wedding in Cana

modern industrial society, subterranean creative forces began to seek a re-birth in individual form. In the transition from decline to rejuvenation, various marginal and transitional forms arose. The omission of the artist's name can on occasion signify deliberate concealment for religious or political reasons. Such cases are unlikely to occur in naive art and are not dealt with here. The artistic manner of a particular talented artist may be identified even without his signature, and this is true of naive art as of other forms of art.

We can offer here only a selection of illustrations of anonymous works of naive art.

unbelievable speed of about 20 miles per hour symbolises the transition of the material world into a state of motion.

The exciting "Boat with Prophet" from Senegal gives scope for various interpretations, political as well as religious. Is the black Prophet, aided by militant angels, about to consign a white colonial ruler and Arab slave-trader to the eager fish? This colourful scene from the tropics contrasts with the austere, sombre "Silver Black" set in a bleak Canadian landscape.

"The Slave Market in Tunis," with its clumsily spontaneous graphic line and uninhibited

Anonymous artist (USA): Touring Car

The Christian folk painting of Ethiopia, influenced by Syrian, Byzantine and Indian art of the Mogul period, combines fluent graphic stylisation with a decorative use of lively colours. The majority of Ethiopian artists remain anonymous: they frequently work to order and regard themselves as craftsmen. Their epic idiom, especially in the case of more modern secular themes, combines medieval serial episodes with sequences from films. In this way we get remarkable compositions such as "King Solomon Visiting the Queen of Sheba" and "Twenty-four Stages in the Life of the Olympic Marathon Runner Bekela Abebe."

"Touring Car" is a polychrome sculpture from the United States, made of wood and metal. It is a sincerely naive evocation of the incredible and miraculous experience represented by the dynamic mechanism of the early motorcar. The anonymous artist succeeded in conveying the astonished wonder of a past age, the car from the age of our grandparents. We can observe the pride of the owner as he grips the steering wheel firmly. Alongside him is his young son with a doll's face. And reclining on the upholstery of the rear seat is an elegant lady, her left hand raised prophetically, like a priestess of tourism. The

style of painting, bears a strong resemblance to the art of children — especially the figures lined up in the foreground, who may be intended to represent a slave-market. The composition of quadrilateral shapes and the skilful treatment of the rhythmically effective architectural background suggest the possibility that an experienced hand has deliberately adapted the style to suit the taste of the purchaser. Given the great demand for the products of naive artists, such deliberate adaptation is by no means inconceivable.

"Hunting Boar" by an anonymous artist from the Udeghe tribe is described by the art historian, Natalia Shkarovskaya, who has contributed the essay on naive art in the USSR. She demonstrates how a naive artist can be identified as a creative personality through exact analysis of his work. *O. B.-M.*

The anonymous folk master of the 1920s and 1930s, a student at the Leningrad Institute of the Peoples of the North, was a representative of the ethnic minority of the Udeghe, comprising only several thousand people, who live in the Amur River valley in the Far East. He evidently joined the Studio of Drawing before the Institute was

1　Anonymous artist: Silver Black (Canada)

2　Udeghe folk master: Hunting Boar (USSR)

4　Anonymous artist: Sir John A. Macdonald House (Canada)

5　Anonymous artist: King Solomon Visits the Queen of Sheba (Ethio

Anonymous artist: Boat with Prophet (Senegal)　8

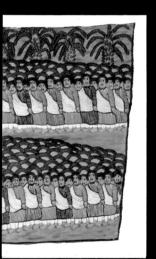

3   Anonymous artist: Twenty-four Stages in the Life of the
    Olympic Marathon Winner Bekela Abebe (Ethiopia)

6   Our Lady of Sorrows (Romania)   7   Adam and Eve with Serpent (Ethiopia)

9   The Slave Market in Tunis (Tunisia)

founded, when there was only a Northern Department and the Studio was supervised by the Leningrad artist Pyotr Sokolov. This may be inferred from his colourful decorativeness and the originality of his artistic mentality, which Sokolov always sought to encourage. His pictures are mostly live recollections of his recent life amidst the land of rivers and lakes, of hunting and fishing. The Udeghe Master uses the pure colouring, decorative in effect, which is characteristic of Northern naive artists generally, and of Udeghe applied art in particular. Pictures like "Hunting Boar" enable the viewer to comprehend the *Weltanschauung* of Northern ethnic minorities. *N. Sh.*

APPENZELL PAINTING   Switzerland

In Appenzell, Switzerland, at the end of the 18th and the beginning of the 19th century, a local style of naive painting developed in connection with the ornamentation of peasant utensils, cupboards and chests. In the 19th century, this type of painting was transformed into a pseudo-naive souvenir art.

As in many countries, the disappearance of folk art is not only the outcome of technical development, but also the ultimate consequence of a complex historical and social process. The anonymous forces that found expression in folk art continue to have an effect but covertly, in depth, and, since collectivity has been disrupted, impel toward a renaissance on an individual level. Folk art in decay is submerged in a lay art fusing the last rays of the collective and the primeval with the timeless desire for games and the eternal childlike wish to give form to whatever lives in man.

The painting of Swiss dairy farmers today still preserves aspects of this age-old shepherd art. In his study of peasant painting in the vicinity of Appenzell, Rudolf Hanhart notes that the "formal delineation of animals whose number probably once corresponded to the size of one's herd" is a conventional pictorial language, just like the one used quite early in the representation of animals in cave painting. Portraits of farmers and shepherds came later, together with pictures of shelters on high meadows, alpine landscapes and grazing herds.

Bartholomäus Lämmler was the most celebrated of this circle of lay painters. His narrative presentation of the farmers' lives shows a sense of rhythm, colour and form. Arranged in long strips of painting, as in Egyptian friezes, his black cows and white sheep dot the green carpet of a meadow.

Other painters of the Appenzell school are Johannes Müller (1806—1897), Johannes Zülle (1841—1938), Franz Anton Haim (1830—1890) and Johann Jakob Heuscher (1843—1901).

ARAGÓN, JOSÉ RAFAEL (d. 1862)   USA

José Rafael Aragón is one of the few early New Mexican *santeros* about whom there is some documentation, at least enough to provide an outline of his life. His birth date was not recorded, but his marriage in 1815 is registered in a Santa Fe census. In a later census he is listed as a sculptor, though he is known for having painted *retablos* (painted panels of saintly figures) and *reredos*, or altar screens, his first major one apparently being done for the Church of San Lorenzo at Picuris Pueblo, near Santa Fe.

Aragón, like other *santeros* of his time, was an itinerant artist and moved about the area until he settled in what is now Cordova, New Mexico. By this time he had developed a reputation as a master painter and was able to support himself fairly well with commissions from the churches in Santa Cruz and nearby villages. Aragón designed and made huge altar screens,

Aragón, José Rafael: The Soul of the Virgin

which consisted of enormous frames fitted with wood panels, then glazed with gesso and painted with tempera. He also supervised the decorations of the churches and chapels for which he created the *retablos*. Aragón did not always sign his work, hence a number of *retablos* that vary in style and carefulness of execution are attributed to him because of documentary reference or characterictics of composition. Christine Mather, curator at the Museum of International Folk Art in Santa Fe, suggests that the variations may be due to the fact that Aragón had a long career and so would have had time for his style to mature and change. Moreover, the fact that he signed himself "maestro" indicates that he was a director of a workshop. If so, many of the small *retablos* attributed to him may have been done by assistants in his shop. It is probable that some of the very large number of paintings attributed to Aragón were done by his sons (he had twelve children), who would have worked under his close supervision. *J. W.*

ARANA, EDUARDO　　　　　　　Nicaragua

Eduardo Arana was the first artist to begin painting in Solentiname, which later gained fame for its naive artists. Ernesto Cardenal, priest and poet, speaks of having found in Solentiname dried gourds used for water with carvings on them. They were the work of the peasant Eduardo Arana. Cardenal was struck by the thought that this peasant might also be a good painter and so supplied him with paper and coloured chalk. With these, Eduardo and his wife Rosita fashioned some lovely naive drawings. Later, the young painter from Managua, Roger Perez de la Rocha, gave Eduardo a brush and oils, with which he produced his first oil painting, also the first naive painting in Solentiname. Drawn by his example, other peasants began to paint. His wife also took up the brush, as did his son Alfonso, whose style recalls that of his father. *E. C.*

ARANA, JOSÉ (1948)　　　　　Nicaragua

José Arana was born in Solentiname, where he spent his childhood. Later he moved to an area bordering on Costa Rica and there became a

Arana, José: River and Village

Arana, Eduardo: Landscape

Arana, José: Entry of the Somosista Army into Solentiname

Archer, Jimmy: North Queensland

woodworker. In addition to carving lovely sculptures in wood, he also paints. A gift for fine detail is characteristic of his art (every board of the houses he paints in his pictures is done with precision). While fighting in the liberation war in Nicaragua, he was captured during an operation on the frontier and is now in prison in Costa Rica, where he has continued painting.

He has exhibited in Managua, Costa Rica, Peru, Venezuela and the USA. *E. C.*

ARCHER, JIMMY   Australia

Jimmy Archer is a full-blooded aboriginal, a member of the Lardil tribe, which lives on Mornington Island in the Gulf of Carpentaria.

He is married, with two children, and usually works as a game warden in an area known as "Quinkin Country" in the far north of Cape York Peninsula. Like all tribal natives, he feels compelled to go "walkabout" from time to time, and during these periods he is likely to return to Mornington Island for a period of months.

Jimmy Archer was encouraged to paint by Percy Trezise, himself an untrained but very successful painter. He also learned from his fellow-tribesman Dick Roughsey. Jimmy's tribal name is Junkinburri, and this is how he signs his paintings. He uses acrylics, usually on board, and draws his subjects from the landscapes of the North Queensland tablelands, the rain forests around Cairns, and the tribal legends of his area.

Arellano, Rodolfo: Country Cottage

His paintings have been shown in a number of mixed exhibitions and hang in many collections. They form an important link between the ethnic tribal paintings of the aboriginals and the naive pictorial records produced by white outback artists. *B. McC.*

ARELLANO, RODOLFO   Nicaragua

Rodolfo Arellano is a peasant living in Solentiname. Among naive painters, he stands out for his craftsmanship and wealth of themes. He has not given up tilling the soil because he feels that the rural atmosphere inspires him in his art.

He has exhibited in Peru, Costa Rica, Venezuela, the USA and in many naive art shows in Nicaragua. *E. C.*

ARIMINI, I GUSTI AYA (1964)　　　　　Indonesia, Bali

I Gusti Aya Arimini was born in Batuan. She started painting at the age of nine, initially under her brother, I Gusti Muriasa, who in turn was a pupil of the well-known Batuan artist I Made Djata. In her early years Arimini painted with oils or acrylic on canvas. However, when Radjin, the son of I Made Djata, reintroduced to Batuan the 1930s practice of painting with Chinese ink on paper, Arimini adopted this medium and has since continued to use it.

Armas, Armando de: The Luis Laza-Guana Valley

The inspiration for much of her present work is derived from remembered childhood tales of Balinese myth and legend, whose images Arimini recreates in a sensitive and meticulous manner.

Although it is unusual for a Balinese woman to paint (much less to prosper), Arimini has attained both success and recognition. Today, she is a respected member of the Wisma Pelukis (Balinese Artists Co-operative), and her work is to be found in many collections. *(See portrait of the artist, p. 111). J. F.*

ARMAS, ARMANDO DE (1904)　　　　　Cuba

Armando de Armas was born in Havana, Cuba, the son and grandson of veterans of the Cuban wars of independence. From 1917 to 1919 he studied dramatic art.

During the next fifty years he worked at various jobs, having been employed successively as a salesman, a public works employee, a post-office clerk, a businessman, and so on. Upon retirement in 1969, he began to paint, and soon after had his first exhibition. In the 1970s he participated in several group exhibitions in Cuba. In 1976 he was represented in a group exhibition, "Eleven Cuban Primitive Artists," at the Jamaica Institute (in Kingston, Jamaica) by landscapes, which reveal both competence in the realistic manner in which the scenes are represented, and a distinctive style, incorporating a good balance in design and use of colour, thus adding an element of integrity and a certain attractiveness to his work. *T. R.*

Arimini, I Gusti A.: Wedding Procession

ARNING, EDDIE (1898—1980)   USA

Eddie Arning was born near Kenney, Texas (near Austin), the son of German immigrants. For reasons never explained, he was put into a mental hospital when a young man and remained there for forty years until released in 1965 at the age of 67. An employee in the hospital, noting the way he embellished ordinary colouring books with the addition of original designs and unusual colour concepts, encouraged him to the point where he was doing his own drawings on blank paper. Using wax crayons at first, later pastel sticks impregnated with oil (Craypas), and

Arning, Eddie: The Breakfast

charm and saccharine are notably absent. Children, if they appear in these fabric pictures, introduce a note of drama, not of sweetness. "Home" is a battleground — not a homestead.

And the enduring wonder of it all is that this "distaff side" of art, which by its very nature (the gentleness of cloth quietly fixed in place by the patient needle) could so easily be no more than occupational therapy, in the hands of the *Arpilleras* becomes compulsively and magnetically attractive. Nameless these artists may be, but the messages they convey through their pictures are crystal-clear in meaning. *Sh. W.*

"Arpilleras": The Right to Return to One's Homeland

left without interference to choose his own subject-matter, he drew on his memories of his childhood on the farm — flowers, musical instruments, animals, pets, windmills, trees and ancient cars.

When his memories no longer seemed interesting to him as subjects, he found inspiration in magazine illustrations and advertisements. He chose his models according to some unexplained criteria, and while his source was recognisable, his drawing was never a copy but a stylised transformation or interpretation of what he saw. He said all he wanted to do was "make a nice picture," but he was proud of his work and of the recognition which he received. His patron, Alexander Sackton, a Texas art critic and historian, tells an anecdote wherein a friend offered Mr. Arning a Leger print to use as a model, but Mr. Arning rejected it, saying, "It's already a picture." *J. W.*

"ARPILLERAS"   Chile

The inspiration, the nature of the work and the anonymity of *Arpilleras* renders them a class apart, not only because they are individualism personified in Chile, but also because there is no similar grouping of naive artists anywhere else.

The other distinguishing characteristic about these artists in appliqué embroidery is that they are all women (if there are actually any male *Arpilleras*, they stay in the background). Maybe it is this sexual element that makes the works of the *Arpilleras* so vibrant.

Unlike so much folkloric art, in their work

AUER, HILDEGARD (1929)   West Germany

Hildegard Auer was born in Stuttgart and now lives in Maichingen in the south of Germany. She worked first as a stenographer and typist and was employed from 1951 onwards by the Eisenmann machine-tool factory in Böblingen. She began there as "maid of all work," became an administrator, then chief clerk, and finally managing director of the firm. At Eisenmann painting was cultivated and valued as a pastime, the firm organising annual exhibitions of amateur work. It was the results of these exhibitions that inspired in Hildegard Auer a desire "to try her hand." And so she began to paint at the beginning of the sixties. In her earlier oil paintings, which are of a totally private character, with themes derived from holidays in northern countries or from outings in the country, and expressive of her direct and naive relationship with animals and nature, Hildegard Auer reveals her power to comprehend and articulate the essential nature of certain animals, to get to the bottom of things, to eliminate everything that is merely incidental, to simplify everything — including colours.

Hildegard Auer, as a successful painter whose pictures are more frequently published and reproduced than those of the most eminent German naive artist, Trillhaase, has lost nothing of her intuition and her serious approach, but it is nevertheless apparent in her case how significantly natural originality may be impaired by the burden of intellect and a forced trend towards professionalism. With all due respect to the work of a highly talented self-taught artist, it is no longer possible to regard Auer's current paintings as authentic works of naive art. *(See portrait of the artist, p. 111). T. G.*

AUXILIADORA, MARIA DA SILVA (1935—1974)

Brazil

Maria da Silva Auxiliadora, born in Campo Belo in Minas Gerais, was a painter and draughtswoman whose early interest in art was inborn; first because she grew up in a family of naive artists (although none of them approached the eventual quality of her own work) and in the second place because from an early age she helped her mother with needlework, selecting the colours of the threads and pointing out where they should be included in the design of the fabric. By the age of 13 she began seriously to turn her attention to painting, but as an adult — coming from a poor and ill-educated family — she set aside her career in art and did not return to it until she had completed a course at primary school — which showed strong will-power, because to relinquish the pleasure of her painting was a great personal sacrifice.

Auxiliadora, Maria da Silva: Voodoo Ritual

Auer, Hildegard: Cows Near the Tanja River

After she settled in São Paulo in 1968, she became a member of the Embu Group, and was a regular and notably successful exhibitor at the Praça da Republica. Indeed, because of the impact her work made at the Praça, it was not long before she was able to branch out and arrange for her pictures to be exhibited abroad — in the USA, France, Yugoslavia and Germany. Maria Auxiliadora died of cancer in São Paulo.

The lingering memories of embroidery never quite lost their place in the paintings of Maria Auxiliadora. A lace-like quality intervenes to add its own decorative touches — almost, but not quite, in contrast with the bolder areas of colour. Rural scenes and customs persist in her subject-matter, but her pictures always emphasise primitive splendours at the expense of the hard epicentre of some of the worlds she has sought to evoke. *Sh. W.*

Aba, Ferenc

Abaljaev, I. M.

Abba (F. A. Derbyshire)

Alberino, Carmelina

Alexandrine

Allegretti, Ferdinando

Allin, John

Amirjan, Gerasim

Andrade, N. F. de

Andreev, N. A.

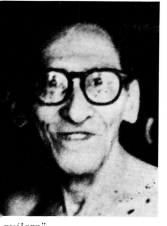
guilera"

Aguirre, Julie

Aladašvili, A.

Alamo, Neke

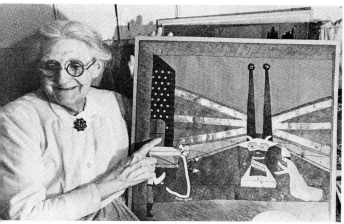
en, Elizabeth

Alvarez, A. A.

Ambarcumjan, Oganes

druszkiewics, Maria

Arimini, I. G. A.

Auer, Hildegard

BABEȚ, GHEORGHE — Romania
BACSKAI, ANDRÁSNÉ — Hungary
BAHUNEK, ANTUN — Yugoslavia
BAHUNEK, BRANKO — Yugoslavia
BAIRD, MARGARET — Great Britain
BAKOS, LAJOS — Hungary
BALAN, MARIJA — Yugoslavia
BALÁZS, JÁNOS — Hungary
BALET, JAN — West Germany
BAPTISTA, CARMEN — Bolivia
BARING, MARK — Great Britain
BARKER, NOËL — Great Britain
BASTIN, HENRY — Australia
BASTIN, MIREILLE — Belgium
BATARDY, MARIE-LOUISE — Belgium
BAUCHANT, ANDRÉ — France
BAZILE, CASTERA — Haiti
BDEJAN, ARTJUŠA — USSR
BECKER, HERMANN — West Germany
BECKLES, GILLIAN — Great Britain
BEER, ALOIS — Czechoslovakia
BEER, JUNE — Nicaragua
BELKOVIĆ, DRAGICA — Yugoslavia
BENASSI, ENRICO — Italy
BENEDEK, PÉTER — Hungary
BENEŠ, ALOIS — Czechoslovakia
BENOIT, JACQUELINE — France
BENOIT, RIGAUD — Haiti
BENSTED, JOHN — Great Britain
BÉRAL, JEAN — Switzerland
BERÁNEK, VÁCLAV — Czechoslovakia
BERECZKI GYÖRGY, ANDRÁS — Hungary
BEREZNEV, A. D. — USSR
BERMUDEZ, MARIO — Cuba
BIČJUNENE, MONIKA — USSR
BIGAUD, WILSON — Haiti
BINDER, JAKOB — Switzerland
BIREŠ, MIHALJ — Yugoslavia
BIRÓ, PAVEL — Romania
BLACK, CALVIN — USA
BLAIR, OSWALD — Australia
BLONDEL, EMILE — France
BLUMENFELD, TRISKA — New Zealand
BOCHERO, PETER — USA
BOCK, IDA — West Germany

BÖDE, FERENC — Hungary
BÖDEKER, ERICH — West Germany
BOGOSAV (ŽIVKOVIĆ) — Yugoslavia
BOIRON, ROSE — France
BOLLAR, GORKI — Netherlands
BOLOGNESI, FERRUCCIO — Italy
BOMBOIS, CAMILLE — France
BONNIN, MAURICE — France
BORDA BORTAGARAY, M. A. — Argentina
BORDONZOTTI, ALFRED — Switzerland
BORKOWSKI, MARY — USA
BOROSNÉ ENDRESZ, TERÉZ — Hungary
BOS, I — Belgium
BOTTEX, JEAN-BAPTISTE — Haiti
BOUQUET, ANDRÉ — France
BOURGEOIS, JEF — Belgium
BOYADJIAN, MICHELINE — Belgium
BRACHET, LISE — Belgium
BRADLEY, GEOFF — Great Britain
BRANDES, FRANZ — West Germany
BRAREN, OLUF — West Germany
BRAŠIĆ, JANKO — Yugoslavia
BREWSTER, JOHN — USA
BRICE, BRUCE — USA
BROWN, CLEVELAND — Great Britain
BROWN, CLINTON — Jamaica
BROWN, EVERALD — Jamaica
BUKTENICA, EUGEN — Yugoslavia
BUNJEVAČKI, DRAGIŠA — Yugoslavia
BURJAK, M. P. — USSR
BYRNE, SAM — Australia

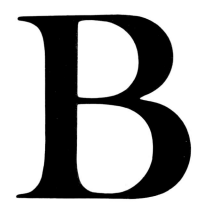

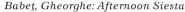

Babeț, Gheorghe: Afternoon Siesta

Bacskai, Andrásné: Ploughing

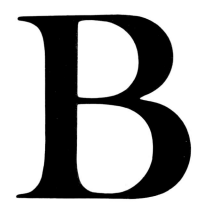

113

BABEȚ, GHEORGHE (1950)   Romania

Gheorghe Babeț was born in the commune of Brestovăț in the district of Timiș, and is employed as a locksmith in a machine-tool factory in Timișoara. He began painting in 1975, when he also started attending the People's Art School.

His paintings depict a world made up of recognisable forms, present in everyday life, the "small world" of the peasant and the man in the street. These the artist paints very carefully. Colours are boldly used, giving his canvases an atmosphere that defies definition.

Depicted statically, in the midst of a nature that is unrealistic in its luxuriance and exotic detail, his figures sometimes assume large dimensions and emit a message transcending their narrow framework and the ostensible motifs of the painter's narrative.

Babeț's paintings, done in oil on cardboard or canvas, and usually small in size, have won many national awards at collective exhibitions of Romanian naive art, and have been on display in a number of international naive art exhibitions in Austria, Sweden and other countries. *(See portrait of the artist, p. 162). M. Il.*

BACSKAI, ANDRÁSNÉ (1910)   Hungary

Andrásné Bacskai was born in Nagyhalász, where she still lives today. Of peasant origin, during her hard life she has always had to take care of her family and has only had time to paint since she retired. She paints on paper in a style reminiscent of children's drawings, her subject-matter consisting of ancient village customs, peasants at work, and the present appearance of her home town. Her compositions are highly successful and her work was shown at the exhibition of naive art in the Hungarian Agricultural Museum in Budapest, in 1980. The Museum of Naive Art in Kecskemét contains a number of her pictures. *M. I.*

BAHUNEK, ANTUN (1912)   Yugoslavia

Antun Bahunek was born in Varaždinske Toplice, Croatia, where he spent his childhood, and now lives in Zagreb.

When he was fourteen, he went "out into the world" to learn a trade. He became a house-painter but soon realised that it was far more profitable to paint angels and saints in the village churches. Sometimes the peasants asked him to paint something for them, and he would do a landscape or perhaps even a portrait. After completing his military service, he settled in Zagreb and got a job working for the railways, doing the lettering on railways carriages. Once retired, he devoted himself exclusively to painting. His favourite subjects are hilly landscapes with houses and churches, usually surrounded by greenery. The atmosphere he generates is always cheerful and optimistic, radiant and gay, bursting with life. Bahunek is fond of introducing into his landscapes galloping horses, birds, sometimes outsize, or deer and other animals. Once he laboriously drew some grains of wheat with the help of a disc. He found these shapes so pleasing that he started to produce entire paintings consisting of discs: the sky, trees and even horse's hide were portrayed by multi-coloured and different-sized discs.

While Bahunek's paintings have no sun or shade, he has succeeded in producing sunny, unreal landscapes — the creation of his rich imagination. By the interplay of circles and fantasy he has represented nature interwoven with unreal mythical beings.

The picture "Zagorje Landscape" shows softly rolling hills, the lines signifying order and harmony, with clumps of strange plants in colours

Bahunek, Antun: Zagorje Landscape

different from those found in nature. Against a pale blue sky, flecked with white, flies a spirited Pegasus. The whiteness of his outspread wings gives the painting a dimension of unreality, of the world of the imagination, while yet recalling Bahunek's native land of Croatian Zagorje.

Antun Bahunek has had one-man shows and participated in group exhibitions at home and abroad. *(See portrait of the artist, p. 162). N. T.*

BAHUNEK,   **Yugoslavia**
BRANKO (1945)

Branko Bahunek, born in Zagreb, Croatia, has been painting since 1960. The suburbs of Zagreb are his favourite theme. His father, Antun Bahunek, gave him his first lessons in painting, but while Bahunek Senior paints sunny, cheerful country landscapes, his son prefers scenes familiar to him since childhood — the outskirts of Zagreb.

Bahunek depicts the world of the poor who live on the fringes of big towns and have not yet forgotten their villages. They tend their tiny gardens and may have a yard in common with their neighbours, with a drinking fountain in the middle. There live the workers' families who often stand or sit in front of their gates. Among them are tradesmen, roving musicians, knife-grinders, flower sellers — in other words, a special kind of environment that is slowly disappearing. Most Yugoslav naive painters have turned to nature and village motifs. A smaller number, born in the

cities, seeks and finds inspiration inside town walls. Among the latter is Branko Bahunek, otherwise a house-painter, who lives and works in Zagreb.

In the painting "Acrobat" (1977), Bahunek portrays an acrobat displaying his talents on the pavement. A few spectators are ample reward for his efforts. And if a coin should come his way, his success is complete. For the people living on the outskirts of town, groups of street entertainers used to break the monotony of everyday life. The theme is one that is typical of all suburbs of big towns.

Bahunek, Branko: Acrobat

Baird, Margaret: Belle, Meg and Jake on a Horse

Branko Bahunek has had one-man shows and participated in group exhibitions at home and abroad. *(See portrait of the artist, p. 162). N. T.*

BAIRD, MARGARET (1891—1978) Great Britain

Margaret Baird was born in Chirnside, Berwickshire. She comes from farming stock, but at an early age adopted an independent line and took up dressmaking. During the First World War she joined a branch of the women's services (the WRAC), but it was not until 1966, shortly after the death of her husband, that — with no training whatsoever — she took up painting.

Her first picture (of a willow tree) was painted to amuse her grandchild (the son of her son-in-law, Jerzy Marek — the naive artist) when he had measles. So impressed was Marek with the

BALAN, MARIJA (1923) Yugoslavia

Marija Balan was born in the village of Uzdin, Vojvodina, most of whose inhabitants are Romanian. Like many girls of her time, she did not go to school. Besides doing housework and rearing children, she had to work in the fields side by side with her husband. On Sundays, dressed in the finery of the Romanian national costume, she would go to church with the other women, take a walk or watch young people dancing. Sunday was also a day for visiting relatives and friends, or attending engagement parties and weddings.

Balan, Marija: Death of a Daughter

Balázs, János: Imaginary Animals

result that he encouraged his mother-in-law to take her new-found activity seriously and regard painting as a full-time activity. Within four years she had been awarded the prize at the Madrid Sport-in-Art exhibition and competition.

As can be seen from the accompanying illustration, her style is direct and innocent of any sophistication.

She took part in many exhibitions in London and Manchester and in the "International Primitive Painters Exhibition" in Lugano. She died in Preston, Lancashire. *(See portrait of the artist, p. 163). Sh. W.*

BAKOS, LAJOS (1901—1975) Hungary

For twenty-eight years Lajos Bakos was a barber, and after that a worker on the railways. He began carving in 1967. His works were included in the 1972 exhibition entitled "Hungarian Naive Art in the 20th Century," in the National Gallery in Budapest. Most of them are group compositions reflecting a childlike view of the world and equally childlike in their method of presentation. In some of his works, he combines various materials (wood, leather, straw, and so on). Some of his compositions are exhibited in the Museum of Naive Art in Kecskemét. *(See picture, p. 78, and portrait of the artist, p. 163). M. I.*

In 1960 Marija Balan saw a picture exhibition in a neighbouring town and thought to herself: "Well, that would be a way of getting certain things off my mind."

So she began to paint the designs that she had woven on her Romanian national dress, showing both the costumes and the people who wore them. Then she went on to dances, engagement ceremonies, church-goings, funerals and everything that constituted an exceptional occurrence in the life of the Romanian peasant.

In the painting "Death of a Daughter" (1964), Marija Balan dressed the young deceased in a rich Romanian costume. The mourning women are in black, the contrast in colour stressing the irrevocable passing of youth and beauty. Lamenting the dead is women's work, for men must not show sorrow, even if they feel it, and so they pass the time playing cards.

Marija Balan has had one-woman shows and participated in group exhibitions at home and abroad. *(See portrait of the artist, p. 163). N. T.*

BALÁZS, JÁNOS (1905—1977) Hungary

János Balázs is an exceptionally talented naive painter of Romany origin. His life as a seasonal worker was a hard one and he began to paint only in 1968.

Balázs, János: Mecca and Mohammed

dreamed of far-off places, distant in time and space: his canvases show South Sea islands, strange fruit and idols from his imagination. His visions show the lifegiving but also destructive energies of creation and nature, and bizarre events. The compositions of János Balázs radiate a strange atmosphere and are characterised by suggestiveness, by crude, clumsy but lively drawing, and by monumentality. In his later works, figures prevail while the background is sketchy. His figures, one above the other, virtually fill up the canvas, although he introduces order into his overcrowded compositions. An autobiography, "Brush and Pencil," was published in 1977 in Hungarian and in English, together with a monograph by Ida Mihály. His paintings are in a number of Hungarian and Swiss museums. *(See portrait of the artist, p. 162).* M. I.

BALET, JAN (1913) **West Germany**

Painter and graphic artist, Jan Balet was born in Bremen and brought up in a climate of urban culture. He studied at schools of applied art in Munich and Berlin.

Then rejecting his academic background, but taking advantage of his talent for drawing and his ability to penetrate to the crux of things, he

As he led a lonely life, his imagination was not influenced by the torrents of visual information offered by others, nor by television. He

Balet, Jan: Bread

both consciously and instinctively found his way to a naive outlook.

In 1939 he left fascist Germany to work in the USA as a graphic artist, painter and illustrator of children's books. His fine draughtsmanship and childlike imagination evoke the life of our times, presented in the costumes of the *fin du siècle*. His tragic and grotesque scenes portray society's vanities in a vein of melancholy irony.

In "The Beginning of Winter" Balet shows what is probably the first snow of the season. A man wearing a heavy winter coat on his way to

BAPTISTA, CARMEN (1936)　　　Bolivia

Carmen Baptista was born in La Paz into a middle-class Bolivian family. Self-taught, she has never attended art school of any kind. She began painting in 1962 while living in Caracas, Venezuela. Since then, she has exhibited many times at group and one-woman shows. Married and with two children, she lives and paints in La Paz. In her artistic style, Carmen Baptista derives both from the Bolivian folk painters of saints of the 18th and 19th centuries and from modern sources. Pictures associated with Simon Bolivar and the winning of national independence dem-

Baptista, Carmen: Carnival in La Paz

the fields looks at a row of poplars, said to have been planted on Napoleon's orders, and sadly observes that winter has come again. He has grown old and holds his hands before his eyes to protect them from the brightness of the snow.

An especially characteristic painting is "Bread." In the background is a bakery or an apartment house. The scene is probably Paris: a bakery wagon, drawn by a horse, is surrounded by a crowd of people waiting to buy bread. Some are already holding loaves under their arms, while others are waiting for their baguette. All of them stand together, seemingly posing for a photographer. Mothers are there with small children. Who is the seller? Men wear scarves around their necks, as though it is cold, while the women, in their white aprons and blouses, are lightly dressed. A dog and a girl with a white ribbon in her hair are also watching from the crowd. This is Balet's style — something from the past and possibly something from present-day France as well. We have seen similar scenes in Holland where wagons with fruit and vegetables make the rounds obviating the necessity of leaving the house to go shopping. *(See portrait of the artist, p. 162). O. B.-M.*

onstrate a naive attitude toward history and historical personalities. Consequently, children and young people readily accept her works. She herself says that she tries to provide the spectator with a suitable visual means for experiencing history. In her view, it is necessary to develop a liking for the past "while ignoring the bronze and the marble."

She has exhibited in Caracas, Washington, New York and cities in Brazil. Her paintings are found in private collections in numerous countries of Europe and America. *(See portrait of the artist, p. 162). A. D.*

BARING, MARK (1915?)　　　Great Britain

Like every good ex-dancer and stage performer, Mark Baring is reticent about his date of birth or any hint that might lead to its discovery (he has even used the pseudonym "Mark Baring" throughout his life, to help maintain the inviolability of this secret). Suffice it to say that he is more than 67 years old (on evidence from 1983) and has led an adventurous, much-travelled life in ballet — all of which stemmed from the ballet scholarship he won from the Ballet Rambert's school in Drury Lane in 1938. Later he was to become the principal dancer with the International Ballet Company, and appeared in many productions. In 1956, when he found himself out of work in Paris, he turned to painting to occupy his time.

It was not until the 1970s, however, when he regretfully faced the fact that his career as a ballet-dancer was drawing to a close, that he exchanged the stage for the easel and took up painting as a career.

From this time, both in style and subject-matter his painting began to acquire its distinctive character.

Baring's subject-matter varies very little (it shows a concern with architectural elements within a precise composition), and his style is no-

Baring, Mark: The Place in the Park

BASTIN, HENRY (1896—1979)   Australia

Henry Bastin was born in Belgium and settled in Australia in 1920. Like many naives, he led a colourful and varied life before starting to paint. He worked on camel mail runs in the outback between Broken Hill in New South Wales and South Australia for some twenty years before going to Western Australia. It was after he moved to Queensland to work as an opal miner in 1956 that he started to paint. Since materials were not readily available he improvised by making brushes out of horses' tails. He was used to overcoming difficulties and being resourceful af-

Barker, Noël: The Butcher "Wainright & Daughter"

table for an exact and thin (anti-impasto!) application of paint.

Regular exhibitions of works by Mark Baring have taken place under the auspices of RONA (1977—81). *(See portrait of the artist, p. 162). Sh. W.*

BARKER, NOËL (1924)   Great Britain

Noël Barker was born in Leeds, Yorkshire. After a busy life working for the famous specialist in flower arrangement, Constance Spry, acting as a professional organiser of parties and social events, and raising a family, Noël Barker turned to painting in 1976. Then what had started as an instant enthusiasm became a full-time activity. Noël Barker, a self-taught naive, feels that she has learnt a great deal (from herself!) in her first five years as a painter. Her pictures, which initially verged on the primitive style, have become steadily more complex, and their humour, which originally had a simplistic flavour, has developed in both character and wit; the paintwork too has become increasingly precise. The painting shown here dates from the period when she was just beginning to find her bearings as an artist. She has been a constant exhibitor with RONA since 1977, and her pictures have been featured in many of the organization's exhibitions. They have also attracted a large number of collectors. Her first one-woman show took place in 1977 in a gallery in Fulham, London. *(See portrait of the artist, p. 163). Sh. W.*

ter so many years travelling through the remote regions of Australia.

In 1958 he had two exhibitions at the Melbourne Museum of Modern Art; after 1965 he painted full time and had a number of one-man shows in various cities. He lived in South Australia, where he died. *B. McC.*

BASTIN, MIREILLE (1943)   Belgium

Mireille Bastin, born "between two bombardments" in 1943, is the daughter of the painter Ginette Javaux but is nevertheless self-taught. Beginning to paint in 1974, she attracted the attention of critics at her first exhibition for the special quality of her naive art. The Belgian radio and television network devoted a broadcast to her and C. Monty included her in his book and film "The Other Belgium." The canvases of Mireille Bastin show a paradoxical preoccupation with malice, bitterness and even mischievous perversity, but this does not detract from the freshness of her inspiration. A rebellious naive artist, in order to challenge the authorities and the narrow boundaries of conformism she portrays girls who are anything but model, who stick out their tongues at nuns and others, raise their skirts, play tricks on their teachers, and provoke boys, but are restless and naughty rather than bad. Her portraits of officials are more an attack on the posts they hold than on them. At first glance, her landscapes are idyllic, but a closer look shows that in this artificial pastoral atmosphere there are those who devour and those who are devoured, depending on who the creature is: a tiny rosy piglet, a sheep with a ribbon around its neck or a big bad wolf.

The titles of her paintings, like the paintings themselves, reflect her rebellious spirit, alleviated by gentleness: "Isabel Has Twins," "Gudule Makes Balls," "Esther Washing with Ether." Her colours, actually half-tones, stress the drawing, which plays a primary role — a rarity in Belgium, where precedence is normally given to thick, pure colours. *J. C.*

BATARDY, MARIE-LOUISE (1943)   Belgium

Marie-Louise Christian-Batardy, born in Brussels, taught drawing for a year after attending a decorative arts school. Since 1974, she has devoted herself exclusively to painting.

In contrast to many naive painters in Belgium, within the framework of a rather severe construction she uses clear and often bright colours. A humorous and naughty irreverence is manifested in her works and their titles, as in the painting "Fritkot Royal," showing a shop selling fried potatoes and dedicated to the 150th anniver-

Bastin, Henry: Cockatoos

Bastin, Mireille: Abbess with Two Children

Batardy, Marie-Louise: "Fritkot Royal"

sary of the Belgian dynasty. Her work is appealing for its caustic but never malicious wit. Her works have been shown in many exhibitions in Belgium and abroad, especially in Latin America. *(See portrait of the artist, p. 163). J. C.*

BAUCHANT, ANDRÉ (1873—1958) France

André Bauchant was born at Chateaurenault and died at Montoire. His family was of modest means and lived in the working-class quarter of Chateaurenault, a small town in central France. School was obligatory and free, and the local school newly built. He attended until 1887, was a diligent pupil and gave proof of a highly inquisitive mind. He gorged himself on books but ended, nonetheless, following in his father's footsteps and undertook to become a gardener. In 1894, he began his military service but was discharged as the family breadwinner. Within a year, he was working in a nursery garden. Ambitious and imaginative, he went into the nursery business himself, starting on a small scale but expanding rapidly. He married in 1900. The war broke out on 2 August 1914, and on 2 September he was called up and forced to leave

Bauchant, André: The Apotheosis of Homer

Bauchant, André: The Gardener

his wife and plants. By now he was 41 years old. He embarked at Marseille for the front in Greece and the East. His shipboard duties left him enough time to watch the sea, unknown to him until then, and observe the light — so different from what he had known on the banks of the Loire — the mountains, and the coast edged by cliffs, with its shells, which he liked to colour. Though he returned in 1915, he was not discharged and did not get back home until 1919, when he was 46. His nurseries were ruined and

his wife had gone insane. He took her to Blutière, to the isolation of the woods there, and earned a living working in the fields of local farmers. Finally surrendering to an irresistible urge, he began to paint flowers and landscapes, the great moments in history, and famous legends. He painted, whether in small format or on huge canvases, both the real world and myths. He enjoyed a great success at the Salon d'Automne in 1927: Le Corbusier and Ozenfant came to see his work and Diaghilev ordered stage sets for his Ballet

Russe from him. He was one of the stars of the Maîtres Populaires de la Realité exhibition in 1937, and Maximilien Gauthier dedicated a work to him. He exhibited in Paris with growing frequency, while his canvases travelled to New York, London, Amsterdam and even Latin America. He also made designs for tapestries ordered by the state from the Beauvais and Gobelins factories: André Bauchant had become an established artist. His first wife died, and he remarried, taking his new wife to live in Montoire-sur-

le-Loire, where he died in August 1958. His death followed a long illness, but one which never forced him to set aside his brushes.

A great deal has been written about André Bauchant, and he had many exhibitions. It is not necessary, therefore, to reiterate here the leading place Bauchant holds among naive artists, the decisive role Wilhelm Uhde played in 1925 in making him known, or the recognition he won at the 1937 Paris exhibition and its reaffirmation with his retrospective at the Galerie Charpentier in 1941. In a letter of 1922 to Maurice Raynal, the artist himself best described the source of his art. During his travels, he wrote, he liked to see "the antiquities and curiosities of towns and cities," and a strong taste for beauty imprinted most of these on his memory. His first important allegorical canvases, among them "Pericles Justifying the Spending of Public Funds" or "Ulysses and the Sirens," date from 1921 and onwards. Legends, allegories, history, all provided material for his paintings. He could settle for a direct presentation ("Louis XI Planting Mulberry Bushes") or embark on allegorical transpositions, and work

trocento. It is true, as Maximilien Gauthier proclaimed, that the "Greeks and Romans of André Bauchant are no more convincing than those of Nicolas Poussin, Louis David or Thomas Couture. But they are no less so either." The smiling heroism of his paintings inspired by mythology or history is inseparable from the poetic dreaminess of his paintings of flowers. This is so much so that even half a century later "most of the works by Bauchant delight us for reasons which are above all of a strictly pictorial order" (M. Gauthier, 1937). André Bauchant began exhibiting in 1927. He participated in the following major exhibi-

Bauchant, André: Women Bathers

up different aspects of simple tales to produce actual cycles; the Ulysses cycle, for instance, is recalled by his "Shipwrecks" cycle. Little by little he abandoned history in favour of nature, which he painted in the aspects most familiar to him: flowers and the countryside. His is a huge opus, so that there are variations in quality. The spirit, however, is always the same, whether the subject is history or rural life, even when the hand sometimes varies. Muted colours, seemingly burned-out, are as frequent as bright and rich tones. His intelligent use of colour is in the classical tradition, although he had probably never heard of the rules involved. He was able to impart a rich glow and magnificence without sacrificing tenderness in compositions whose audacity evokes the *Quat-*

tions: Les Maîtres Populaires de la Realité, (1937 Paris, Zurich; 1938 New York, London); Palais des Beaux-Arts, Brussels (1949); Galerie Charpentier, Paris (1949, 1951, 1964); Knokke-le-Zoute (1958). He has been shown in galleries and museums in Paris, Tours, London, Tokyo, New York and Zagreb. *(See portrait of the artist, p. 163). Ch. Sch.*

BAZILE, CASTERA (1923—1965)   **Haiti**
    Castera Bazile was born in Jacmel and died in Port-au-Prince. When Bazile was helping De-Witt Peters (the American teacher who, in stumbling upon the hitherto undiscovered brilliance of Haitian naive art, became so engrossed with its beauty and its putative expansion — by encour-

aging more and more Haitian peasants to paint — that he totally changed his own life-style and devoted himself to his newly found enthusiasm by founding the Centre d'Art in Port-au-Prince) he found himself working for a man who quickly spotted him as a likely candidate to join the growing band of Haitian naive painters of quality.

Nor was DeWitt Peters to be proved wrong. Although until his meeting with the American, Castera Bazile had never touched a brush, fired by the enthusiasm and encouragement of this "Diaghilev" of Haitian naive art, he became trans-

naives, Bazile was amazing for the way in which he turned his genius as an artist to the task of fusing Christian and Voodoo themes. Together with some of his portraits, his paintings based on themes from Voodoo and from folklore constitute his finest work. Perhaps what specially sets Bazile apart from his famous contemporaries are the glowing colours that infuse all his paintings. Although other Haitian painters use bright, sometimes very bright, colours, few ever attain the astounding luminosity of Bazile's. The glow of the colours is heightened by Bazile's smooth techniques.

Bdeyan, Artyusha: Armenian Family

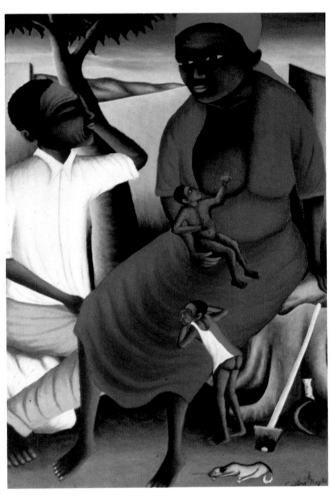

Bazile, Castera: Haitian Family

It was tragic that Castera Bazile died of tuberculosis in 1965, just too early to experience the full flood of world interest in Haitian naive art, and too poor to have been able to afford professional medical care and drugs.

The number of paintings which he left behind him was small, for he was a slow and fastidious artist. *(See portrait of the artist, p. 162). Sh. W.*

BDEJAN, ARTJUŠA (1926)　　　USSR
BDEYAN, ARTYUSHA

Artyusha Bdeyan was born in Tbilisi. His father and mother were office workers. He attended secondary school and is a photographer by profession, though he received no special education in art. He had always wanted to be an artist, but started painting only in the spring of 1979, when visiting one of his three brothers, the well-known Armenian ceramicist Amayak, in Yerevan. Spending the night at his brother's studio, he occupied himself by doing a painting which Amayak found of interest. As a result he moved to Yerevan and took up painting, which he does in oils on cardboard from memory or imagination. Using information from older relatives, he attempts to reproduce the life and mores of his ancestors in western Armenia. He also mirrors the life of old-time Tbilisi, remembered from childhood, and does remarkable still-lifes. He displays the characteristic traits of naive painters, such as frozen postures — perhaps this is due to his profession as a photographer — localised pools of colour and a static rendering of space. He has his own way of depicting the environ-

formed in the space of a few years from a houseboy into a fine artist. In fact, Bazile, although till then he had never taken such an ambition seriously, had always wanted to be a painter.

In 1951, like other Haitian painters discussed in this book, he found a wonderful professional opportunity in a commission to paint three enormous murals for Port-au-Prince's Holy Trinity Cathedral — a vast project which DeWitt Peters managed to negotiate with Bishop Voegeli. All the new murals and sculptures provided by Haitian naives were carried out while the Bishop was on holiday and he was transported with delight to discover his gleaming "new" cathedral on his return.

As in the case of many of the best Haitian

ment. The basic function of his works is discharged by composition; with the objects represented arranged now higher up, now lower down or along the horizon, should the composition require greater compactness. His figures are somewhat geometricised and graphic. The colour range is subordinated to overall mood, but seemingly without direct contact with imagery. He is naive in that he is fully dominated by his choice of means of expression, which are in themselves naive. In 1981 he had a one-man show at Yerevan's Museum of Modern Art. *(See portrait of the artist, p. 162). N. Sh.*

Becker, Hermann: The Joy of Leisure

BECKER, HERMANN (1884—1972)   West Germany

Hermann Becker was born in Breslau and died in Heiligenstedten, near Itzehoe. Becker was trained as a joiner, worked also as an aircraft mechanic and was employed as an agricultural labourer from 1920 until 1945. After retiring he devoted himself to bee-keeping but had to give up this pursuit because of ill-health. Out of sheer boredom he began to draw and then to paint at the age of 75. His favourite subjects are calm and peaceful landscapes with luminous clumps of cloud; a few isolated people or animals, suggesting a mood of sabbatical tranquillity, fit harmoniously into these landscapes. Becker was particularly adept in the use of oil crayons. He used them vigorously to cover the surfaces of the white card to which his subjects are austerely confined, so that the colour acquires a characteristic luminosity reminiscent of the transparent quality of paintings on the reverse surface of glass. With Becker it is particularly obvious that naive painters are not concerned with angles of lighting and the consequent formation of shadows. Characteristic of him is his capacity for omission and for reduction to a few major surfaces and colours that dominate the picture and give an impression of harmonious serenity and calm. *(See portrait of the artist, p. 162). T. G.*

BECKLES, GILLIAN (1918)   Great Britain

Gillian Beckles was born in Bournemouth. Her father was director of a publishing house. Having painted since early youth, she decided at the age of twenty-eight to join an art school in London. However, her training there was brief as she did not find that her favourite preoccupation of painting architectural subjects was understood. Caught up by her inspiration, she went out on the streets of London to paint. Thus originated her canvases portraying scenes of London squares, streets and churches. Later Gillian Beckles started painting the outskirts of London, as well as her impressions of the annual fairs held in small English towns, ships in harbour and English beaches. But houses remained her favourite theme.

Beckles, Gillian: Sunday Morning Prayers

For a time she worked in the Hanover Gallery in London and painted in her spare time. Although surrounded by the achievements of internationally known artists, she avoided falling under the influence of any of them. "Sunday Morning Prayers" shows a church interior filled with a muted morning light penetrating through the stained-glass windows, in an atmosphere of silence and holiness. *(See portrait of the artist, p. 163).*

BEER, ALOIS (1833—1897)   Czechoslovakia

Alois Beer was born in Dobruška. He was a very good and diligent pupil at school. Regardless of his obvious musical talent and aspirations, the boy had to become a turner. As a turner-journeyman he set out to gain some experience first at home and then abroad. He worked in Vienna, Ljubljana, Venice, Verona, and Milan. He kept a detailed diary he reworked at the end of his life, giving it then its final form — that of an authentic and topical chronicle. In 1862 he settled in his native Dobruška, where he made various artefacts from rare wood, amber, horn, and meerschaum. In 1886 he retired and began to devote himself to painting, which had been his dream and hobby since childhood. In 1892, at an Agricultural and Industrial Exhibition in Dobruška, a collection of Beer's drawings was exhibited, evoking general interest and admiration. Besides suffering poverty, he lost his two grown-up children in less than a year. He soon followed them in 1897.

Beer's literary and artistic creations — he was fifteen years senior to Douanier Rousseau — are rare for their balance and fine quality. He illustrated his travel notes, the pictures and texts together forming an inseparable entity. The former can be classified neither as autonomous

Beer, Alois: The Square

artefacts nor as illustrations in the real sense. To document reality had always been his modest aim. When he had no sketches of his own, he would make copies of picture postcards or of pictures and drawings in magazines. However, he retained the specific features of his own way of seeing and creating, so that even his copies of pictures from postcards and magazines are genuine, unique, and original.

Beer's discoverer, Karel Michl, participated in preparing the famous exhibition of Beer's works in Umelecká beseda in Prague in 1937 and in editing Beer's memoirs published in 1970. *(See portrait of artist, p. 163). S. T.*

BEER, JUNE (1933) Nicaragua

June Beer was born on the Atlantic coast of Nicaragua, where she spent most of her life. In that part of the country, the Nicaraguan Caribbean, the population is largely black and speaks English. June Beer is a mulatto. With great sensitivity, she paints life and landscapes in that beautiful region of Nicaragua. She now heads a workshop for naive painters set up by the Ministry of Culture. *(See portrait of the artist, p. 163). E. C.*

BELKOVIĆ, DRAGICA (1931) Yugoslavia

Dragica Belković was born in Hlebine near Koprivnica, in Croatia, where she attended school and where she still lives. She is a housewife who in her spare time carves in wood. Living in Hlebine, the home of one of the greatest names in Yugoslav and world naive art, Ivan

Generalić, and in a village where many peasants paint or sculpt, she had ample opportunity to see the results of their work. One day in 1967, she carved in soft willow wood a sculpture she called "Blind Woman Led by a Boy." Her carving of this work had been preceded by an eye affliction and fear that she was going blind. "I thought about this and felt that if I went blind, I could nevertheless carve." Also, she had plenty of wood in her yard, whereas glass or canvas had to be purchased in town.

This sculptor fashions figures of people and domestic animals from wood: not stiff or static

Beer, June: Fishing Boat

figures, but living, moving, acting, working, the facial expression always denoting a state of mind.

In the small carving "Peasant Women on Her Way to Market," Dragica Belković has with a few master strokes depicted a bent peasant woman whose face and figure reflect the long years of hard life that have worn her out. The basket she

Belković, Dragica: Peasant Woman on Her Way to Market

carries stresses the effort the old woman is making to go about her daily tasks. The figures she paints are usually of small size.

Dragica Belković has had one-woman shows and participated in group exhibitions at home and abroad. *(See portrait of the artist, p. 163).* *N. T.*

BENASSI, ENRICO (1902—1978)   **Italy**

Enrico Benassi, born in Casale di Mezzani, Parma into a peasant family, started playing music when he was sixteen. His musical talent en-

there are echoes in it of the Roman and pagan worlds. On the stereotyped and stylised scenes of a beginner are nevertheless grafted personal compositional structures, expressing an inborn sense of scenography and an instinctive use of rhythms perhaps traceable to Benassi's musical talent. "The Apostles," with its vibrant colours and solemn figures in rich tunics, recalls the brilliance of Byzantine mosaics.

Benassi's paintings were later enriched by other elements of composition, and by narrative cycles which intertwine to form what almost amounts to an illusionist vision. This is the

Benassi, Enrico: The Apostles

abled him to escape strenuous work in the fields from time to time. When he was twenty, he married and in the course of his married life had twelve children. He managed to feed his family by working at various occupations (feather salesman, hospital orderly, vendor) while at the same time continuing to play. When his children had grown and three of them had chosen to study music under his influence, he founded a family ensemble. To save money, he himself made and decorated the music stands and drums for his orchestra. Thus Benassi began to paint, although it was only in 1960 that he devoted himself to it on a regular basis. Benassi died in Parma.

With no training whatsoever, he worked in tempera on cardboard, which he chose as the means for transmitting his artistic ideas. Painting completely replaced music, so important in his life up to that point. His first paintings were reminiscences of stories he had heard during the long nights spent working as a hospital orderly. He called this his "Egyptian" period, although

Benedek, Péter: Family Gathering

period of his Cossack horseman against the background of oriental architectural structures, of troikas drawn by reindeer among castles and in the shadow of cupolas, churches and towers aflame like fireworks, with airy dancers pirouetting beside lakes on which float snow-white swans. An example of this kind of work is "Russian Fantasy," a clear condensation of Benassi's most characteristic themes.

The third and final period of Benassi's painting is notable for the close ordering of city buildings woven into a composition. Skilful strokes increase the decorative power of his works, taking

in the details of his still-lifes, there is always, in addition to the narrative element, the appeal of selected motifs and their inner beauty. He is a painter who regards the world cheerfully, with intense interest, while composing scenes which combine naive freshness, an analytic approach, and a radiant harmony. "Family Gathering" (1930) shows figures sitting motionless and as rigid as puppets around a table, but the expressions on their faces are wonderfully done. With thoughtful mien, they evoke memories of their dead father. Benedek also on occasion demonstrates a restrained humour and appealing gro-

Beneš, Alois: Adam and Eve in Paradise

them beyond ornamental hieroglyphics or the tracery of embroidery ("Madonna and Child," "Ancient Warriors"). All these are elements that have ranked him with the best-known and most expressive of Italian naive painters. *(See portrait of the artist, p. 162). D. M.*

BENEDEK, PÉTER (1889)   Hungary

Péter Benedek was born in Cegléd, where he lives today. In his youth he was a hired labourer. His talent was discovered during the First World War and he had his first exhibition in 1923 in Budapest. His gifts and the mental and emotional world of his painting — which does not fit into the framework of any romanticised view of the peasantry — attracted the attention of both public and experts. In his landscapes and interiors,

tesqueness. His art — irrespective of subject-matter — reflects characteristic Hungarian features. His works are to be found in the Hungarian National Gallery. *M. I.*

BENEŠ, ALOIS (1903)   Czechoslovakia

Alois Beneš was born in Otinoves, Drahansko. He attended elementary school only, became a trained miller, and worked at this job for many years in his native village. At the age of 52 he began to paint reminiscences of his youth. He is a master of reality, carefully noting the shape of things and doing his best to present his impressions as exactly as possible. Descriptive in his approach, he has always felt a penchant, though only in his heart of hearts, for romantic idyls, enabling him to express his joy in nature.

In 1963—1964 he displayed his works at the exhibition "Naive Art in Czechoslovakia" in Brno, Bratislava, Prague, and Ostrava. *S. T.*

BENOIT, JACQUELINE (1925)   France

Jacqueline Benoit, born in Paris, is an exception among naive artists because she has spent her life entirely dedicated to her art. Just before the Second World War, her parents moved with her to Orleans, where they opened a store. For several years she helped them out in their business but in 1954 began to paint. From then on she

![Benoit, Jacqueline: In the Gloaming]

Benoit, Jacqueline: In the Gloaming

has never stopped painting, remaining permanently in Orleans, where she has developed her art with acclaim and success.

Her work is above all a subtle reflection of transposed and reconstructed reality. Hers is an imaginary world of transparencies and halftones. Secrets barely uttered in audacious silences are the art of Jacqueline Benoit. Well-served by sound craftsmanship, she highlights meticulous drawing with a colour range of perfect harmony. With these, according to Raymond Nacenta, she "establishes a mysterious relationship between our senses and the wonders of nature."

She first exhibited in Paris in 1964 and her work has since been seen in many major exhibitions and the best-known galleries of naive art. *(See portrait of the artist, p. 162). Ch. Sch.*

BENOIT, RIGAUD (1911)   Haiti

Rigaud Benoit was born in Port-au-Prince. Before he started painting, he was a musician, but, with no other regular job, he went to work for DeWitt Peters as a chauffeur. At this time, for a hobby, he decorated home-made ceramics. He gradually turned to painting, and in this expansion of his creative energies he was, of course, encouraged by DeWitt Peters, who saw in him yet another likely Haitian naive painter of unusual talent.

Although Benoit has not been a prolific artist — in the sense of Préfète Duffaut or André

Pierre — his reputation today is firmly ensconced in the firmament of Haitian naive art. He is well thought of by visitors to the island republic, possibly because his figuration in paintings (unlike that of St. Brice or La Forest) is not difficult for ordinary people to appreciate, nor is it — as in the case of an artist like Gourgue — aggressively dark and oppressive. On the contrary, Benoit's "oddity" occurs in his selection of weird settings, as in his paintings "The Spoiled Wedding" (where a battle between brides for the groom is going on), "Adultery" (a rich interior where the act is about to take place, complete with accompanying

Benoit, Rigaud: Participants in Demonic Guise

guitarist), "Hell," and even "The Maiden's Dream of Marriage" (in which the "Maiden" features twice, once lying in bed dreaming and once with guests and future husband, she ready in bridal gown to take her wedding vows). These four pictures can be considered as a group. Broadly speaking, Benoit's favourite subjects are incidents drawn from daily life, folklore and Voodoo rituals.

At the start of his career as an artist, whenever possible he acted as manager of the "Artists' Cellar" in the Centre d'Art of which he was one of the earliest and most long-lasting associates.

Benoit is certainly an inspired illustrator, liking his pictures to tell stories rather than reflect reality.

He loves to paint pictures in which he is the dreamer of dreams, the creator of fantasies, a glorifier of women in an imaginative aristocratic scenario.

All these elements can perhaps be seen united in what has come to be his most famous painting, "Bioth," one of the best known murals in Holy Trinity Cathedral. For his first pictures he used a colourful palette, but this was to change. Step by step the sharp lines flowing from his brush became more important than the tints and hues that had once been so emphatic. This evolution in his style has made the illustrative side of

Bensted, John: The Rousseau Banquet

his work even more pronounced. *(See portrait of the artist, p. 162). Sh. W.*

BENSTED, JOHN (1920)   **Great Britain**

John Bensted was born in Dublin. A physician and pathologist, he now lives in Walton-on-the-Hill, Surrey.

This naive artist has twice shown with the Medical Art Society at their annual exhibition, but otherwise he has been presented to the public as a painter only through RONA exhibitions (1978—1980) — except for the "1st International Naive Art Exhibition in Britain" at Hamilton's, when his painting "The Rousseau Banquet" was the first picture to be sold (it is now in the Douanier Rousseau Museum, Laval, France).

Perhaps the best adjective with which to describe the special qualities of Bensted's work is "uninhibited." Maybe, having another profession, he feels that his painting career can proceed with an extra freedom that others, except those who are especially dedicated, can never quite achieve. At all events, his paintings seem to have an element of wry personal humor which can embrace a light-hearted street celebration of Queen Elizabeth II's Silver Jubilee. This is treated with exactly the same quirky gravity as his picture of the Garden of Eden, complete with an unclad dark-skinned pair, a white man — benign and fully clothed — and a tree with various letters and symbols cut into its trunk. *(See portrait of the artist, p. 162). Sh. W.*

BÉRAL, JEAN (1907)   **Switzerland**

Jean Béral (the name is a pseudonym) was born in Geneva and is a merchant. He has led quite an exciting life and travelled a great deal. Beginning in 1972, his development as an artist has a number of interesting features. His personal technique and great sensitivity to colour have increased the refinement of his painting, while his tones have become lighter and softer. Imaginary winter landscapes reflect an air of enchantment. His canvases present a world at once gay and nostalgic. In his "paradise lost," birds and animals have the right to be present, whereas man

Béral, Jean: The Lake

is always absent. In the springtime a grey heron seeks its mate, there is a flock of birds against the sky, butterflies are on the wing, time does not exist. Usually the artist places this paradise in the foothills of rockbound, snow-covered mountains, among sharp crags between which limpid rivers flow. Idyllic peace reigns in his pictures, and vegetation prevails in places where man has never set foot. His is a dream of the beauties of untouched nature. The style of this artist is like no one else's.

He has exhibited in Switzerland, New York, Quito and London, and received the "Prize of Switzerland for International Naive Painting" (Morges) in 1973. *(See portrait of the artist, p. 163). G. K.*

BERÁNEK, VÁCLAV (1915)   **Czechoslovakia**

Václav Beránek, youngest of the four children of a smallholder, was born in Bezdekov near Havlíckuv Brod. The games he used to play in the forests of his native Bohemian and Moravian hills are among Beránek's fondest memories. After leaving primary school he was trained as a carpenter and, following military service, completed a two-year course in the technical school at Hradec Králové, where he came into contact with Czech graphic art. He continued occasionally making drawings for family albums. In 1976, he went back to work in a railway workshop but found that this way of earning his living was little more than humiliating drudgery. At one time it looked almost as if he were trying to escape from the clutches of a senseless everyday life and seek refuge in a paradise. He continued to detest the realm of machinery and slavery that was manipulated by deceitful and malicious individuals, and bestowed his affections on his little orchard and the woods round Jihlava. This was his Eden, this was Nature, a fair, unsullied realm. He had a sense of well-being and liberty there, he was a human being who could talk to his bees and his flowers as he performed magical grafts on his fruit-trees. When he began to paint in oils

Lugano and participation in the Triennale in Bratislava.

"Even as a child I was touched by the beauty of nature and everything had the appearance of a fairy-tale. I used to watch how little plants sprang up out of nothing after the winter had passed, and how the grass turned green. I used to gaze at the great sun through dark fragments of broken bottles and arrived at the conclusion that the sun was at the back of all this magic," wrote Beránek.

Václav Beránek's pictures astonish us with their fabulous harmony of yearning and concrete

Beránek, Václav: Women in Landscape

in 1965, his first subjects were the flowers from his garden and his home. Beránek saw an amaryllis or a flowering cactus as solemn cult objects and formed their simple masses into generous arcs, so that Kandinsky would have spoken of them in terms of grandiose Realism. Later on come the pictures of the fabulous "Nymph Cycle" (1966—71) and with them Beránek's inspiration reaches its climax. Public recognition was linked with these pictures; important shows were held in Ústí and Rychnov in 1966, in Brno in 1968, and then at the International World Fair — Expo — in Montreal in 1967. In 1969 came an award in

detail, the coincidence, that is, of a wishful dream and reality experienced at first hand. We have the impression that the heavily painted structural surfaces are seething and exhaling their own aroma. It is hard to say whether Beránek wished to give his pan-erotic dream the highest degree of substantiality, so as to reconstruct in natural fashion the finer sphere of our world, or whether he idealised reality, so that it might manifest itself in the form of magic.

He is one of the great idyllic artists. His poetic — or childlike — power to perceive his surroundings only through a prism of the imagination, to set imagined symbols side by side on a surface, is massive and primal. The subsequent materialisation of these ideal signs, and, at the same time, their distortion or individualisation by means of preferred types of body and colour — all this evolves during the process of painting. That is to say, it is a secondary process.

Beránek's fairy-tale visions, however much they may be sustained by a lyrical nostalgia for nature, evoke a variety of joyful emotions, so that cheerfulness is coupled with mystery, and the sublime becomes a joking matter. Many seriously intended points and "encounters" in these pic-

BEREZNEV,   USSR
ALEKSANDR DMITRIEVIČ (1926)
BEREZNEV, ALEXANDER DMITRIEVICH

A. D. Bereznev was born in the village of Deryagintsy, near the city of Kirov (formerly Vyatka), west of the Ural Mountains. Losing both parents in infancy, he was brought up in an orphanage in Kazakhstan. After leaving school, he worked as vulcaniser and lorry driver. When the

Bereznev, A.D.: Seeing off Soldiers to the Fighting Front

Bereczki György, András: Peasant Wearing a Wide-brimmed Hat

tures have a pronounced comic effect. But it is this very factor which complements the range of values embodied in his authentic poetry. Beránek is numbered among the five most powerful naive painters of Czechoslovakia. *A. P.*

BERECZKI GYÖRGY,   Hungary
ANDRÁS (1872—?)

András Bereczki György was born in Vésztö; the year of his death is not known. His work attracted attention at the second exhibition of original talents in 1935. Initially, he fashioned his figures solely with the intention of presenting them as gifts. As he was a shepherd, he preferred making animal figures of clay: horses, cows, bulls, lambs, dogs. His animals wear a flustered and sometimes a thoughtful and serious look. Human figures, resembling stiff-legged puppets, wear wide-brimmed hats and are dressed in dolman-like robes decorated with large buttons of the kind worn at weddings. He also fashioned figures recollected from military service: hussars, officers, and infantry soldiers in authentic uniforms. Few of his works have been preserved because they were easily broken, having been made of unfired clay. His art was rediscovered in

Soviet Union was invaded by Germany in 1941, he was drafted into the army. He now lives in the small Ukrainian town of Kirovograd, where he supplements his war-invalid pension by working as a janitor. Though most of his subjects are imagined, he also likes to do still-lifes from nature. However, realising that his knowledge of the whys and wherefores of the visual arts was woefully inadequate, he enrolled in ZNUI, the Extra-Mural People's University of Art. Despite two or three years of postal tuition he is still very much the naive artist, with a childlike and, possibly, peasant mentality. The human figure is tentatively conveyed either in full face or profile, and though he adheres in some degree to the rules of perspective, this is merely to make things more expressive and present a bolder relief. His colour scheme is bright and festive.

He has been represented at local, republican and USSR exhibitions of amateur art. *(See portrait of the artist, p. 163). N. Sh.*

BERMUDEZ, MARIO (1923)   Cuba

Mario Bermudez was born in the city of Matanzas and received training at the Provincial School of Fine Arts there. His first one-man show was mounted in the art gallery of his hometown in 1968. He has also participated in several group exhibitions, including Salon 70, Primitive Painters in the Havana Gallery in 1971, in the exhibition "Primitive Cuban Artists in Socialist Countries" in 1972, and in 1976 in "Eleven Cuban Primitive Artists" at the Institute of Jamaica in Kingston, where he was represented by a selection of six paintings, characterised by an emphasis on figurative content and a boldness in design and in the use of colour, resulting in almost poster-like effects. Women, a neighbour, his

Bermudez, Mario: Portrait of a Woman

mother-in-law, or just a transformed palm tree, are recurring themes in his work. *T. R.*

BIČJUNENE, MONIKA (1910)   USSR
BICIUNIENE, MONICA

Monica Biciuniene was born in the village of Baubliai, near the small Lithuanian town of Rokishkis. As her parents were poor, they could allow her only one year of elementary schooling. "All I remember from childhood were pictures from the Bible," she recalls. "I didn't know what the visual arts were, let alone the theatre or the movies." She has had a chequered career, being by turn farm labourer, charwoman, messenger and night-duty nanny at a boarding school. Her husband, meanwhile, worked at the tailoring

trade. In 1960, her son Rimas (today a prestigious professional painter in his home republic), who was attending an art school for children in Vilnius, the capital, went home for his holidays to Pandelis, the small town where his mother, Monica, was then living. He showed her what he was doing at school and one day she decided to try her hand at painting. Secretively, when nobody was at home, she borrowed her son's paints and brushes and produced a picture that was much like a child's drawing. Shyly she showed Rimas the result and was amazed when he and his artist friends praised it. She began to paint in oils and

Biciuniene, Monica: My Family

gouache on canvas and a year later had her first one-woman exhibition in Vilnius, to which city she moved later after a granddaughter was born. Today Monica enjoys republic-wide fame as a naive painter. Her favourite subjects are genre scenes, domestic interiors, and landscapes of the village where she was born. Behind the childishly direct manner of presentation one discerns the roots of popular pictorial art; indeed, both children's drawing and pictorial folklore share a common preference for vibrant patches of colour, straightforward presentation and scattered composition, though this last is not that characteristic of Monica. Whatever she paints, be it "A Village Social," "The Festival of the Easter Eggs," "Calling on the Doctor with the Granddaughter," "Visiting the Farmyard," "The Wedding" or "My Lazdiyai District Is Twinned with German Erfurt," she always describes something close to her heart, something very real to her, something her very own. Her portraits are as metaphoric in their colour scheme and reflection of the sitter's features as would be the case in folk poetry. She also loves decorating furniture and various domestic articles. She also likes to travel and is especially fond of the countryside. Her observations are subsequently translated into pictorial form in such series as "The Seasons" cityscapes, or rustic scenes. Besides being represented at numerous exhibitions both in the USSR and abroad, she has had a dozen one-woman shows, one of which was a gala exhibition in Kaunas,

Bigaud promptly joined the Centre, and from that moment art filled his life. Meanwhile, his stature as an artist and his reputation were already growing; they reached a pinnacle with the completion of his fresco "The Marriage at Cana" for the Cathedral of the Holy Trinity.

Bigaud's career ran smoothly until in 1957 he fell victim to the first of what was to prove a series of nervous breakdowns. Although, on medical evidence, the last bad nervous crisis through which he passed took place in 1961, he remains to this day under a strict regime controlled by his family.

Biciuniene, Monica: P. Gudinas, Chairman of the Association of Folk Arts

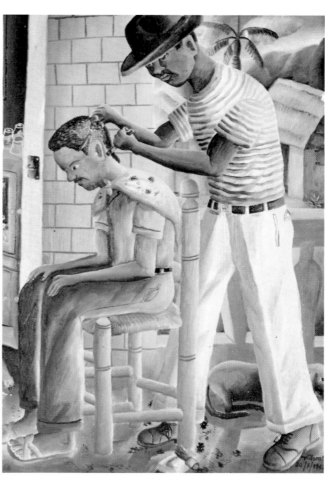

Bigaud, Wilson: The Barber

while another was held in 1982 in Moscow. She is a member of the Lithuanian Society of Folk Art. *(See portrait of the artist, p. 163). N. Sh.*

BIGAUD, WILSON (1931)   Haiti

Wilson Bigaud was born in Port-au-Prince. From the start he wanted to paint: after all, he had before him the example of his thriving neighbour, Héctor Hyppolite, by that time arousing considerable interest and already accepted by many as an inspired artist. But Bigaud could not have been more different, both in vision and with his naturally sophisticated painter's techniques.

When Bigaud decided that he had completed a picture of suitable standard he took it along to the Centre d'Art for inspection by DeWitt Peters. In the eyes of the American, here was yet another "natural," a man already betraying signs of an astonishing precocity, one who should immediately take up oil painting seriously.

Bigaud can be described as a case history of what happens when a Haitian is unable to conform and fails to accept the spiritual pattern of his homeland. Why did Bigaud go mad? With the laurels earned from "The Marriage at Cana" still fresh on his brow, he set to work on another painting: "The Last Judgement" (a title whose prophetic significance at the time escaped him).

With an access of Christian zeal he had applied himself to work on the fresco in the cathedral, while at the same time attending Voodoo ceremonies. The Christian ethic and belief did not disturb him, nor was he more than casually true to the Voodoo faith. However, the devils in the picture became steadily more real to him: it seemed that they were no longer attacking the angels but had turned all their vicious animosity upon him. It was when Bigaud completely associated them with the vengeful *loas* that he went out of his mind.

For long periods he ceased painting altogether. During the summer of 1969, when Sheldon Williams tried to make contact with him, no one knew his whereabouts.

Until 1957 he was the exponent of an almost Raphaelesque perfection. It seemed that, at the peak of his success, he could not go wrong: the smoothness of execution and the deftness of construction, combined with colours of great charm, all added up to a competence that was in no way impaired by sheer control.

Binder, Jakob: Winter

It would be outrageous to suggest that nothing the artist painted after 1957 had anything approaching a magic quality. It was simply that the old spellbinder had disappeared — or, if he still lived, was casting a different spell. *Sh. W.*

BINDER, JAKOB (1928) Switzerland

Jakob Binder was born in St. Johann, Austria and spent his youth in Kramsach in the Tyrol. An electrician by trade, since 1948 he has lived in various places in Switzerland and in 1963 married a Swiss woman. Influenced by the example of painters from Appenzell, in 1965 Binder began to devote himself to folk art. When a gallery in Zurich discovered him in 1972, painting became his principal occupation.

Binder is one of the most outstanding representatives of the younger generation of folk painters from Appenzell. Apart from traditional paintings portraying motifs from the Appenzell region and everyday scenes from the life of the livestock farmers (on which every detail has been worked out with precision), he also paints pictures in the naive-realistic genre for which he chooses other themes and colour values. The substance of these paintings reflects not so much the local and traditional achievements of the Appenzell painters as it does the spirit of folk art generally.

Apart from exhibitions in Appenzell, Zurich, Basel, and Winterthur, he has exhibited abroad: in 1975 in New York and later in London and

Innsbruck. In 1979 he won the international prize awarded by the public in Morges, Switzerland. *(See portrait of the artist, p. 164). G. K.*

BIREŠ, MIHALJ (1912—1980) Yugoslavia

Mihalj Bireš was born in Kovačica, Vojvodina. He had no schooling and was a farmer to the end of his days, painting in his leisure time.

In 1938, he became one of the founders of the group of peasant painters in Kovačica. Working on canvas, he did mostly portraits of peasants. Being poor, he spent the greater part of his life in

Biró, Pavel: Autumn

Bireš, Mihalj: Going to Market

employment as a hired hand or shepherd, until he managed to acquire a little land. His way of life left him little time for painting.

"I paint from memory the people I know in Kovačica, my friends and relations," he said. "Sitting through the long winter nights, I recall a dear friend and say to my wife that I am going to paint him. When that person later recognises himself in the painting, he is happy and so am I."

In the painting "Going to Market" (1972), Bireš painted his neighbours, a man and wife dressed in their best clothes for market day. As the woman was taller than the man, Bireš

of tiny wild animals and birds against a natural background changing with the seasons.

The paintings of Pavel Biró, occasionally melodramatically sentimental, have also been inspired by the writings of certain Romanian authors (Emil Gîrleanu, Al. Brătescu-Voineşti) who derived certain moral values from the lives of "mute beings."

The naive sincerity and gentleness of the artist's approach to events, the clear presentation of his themes and his rendering of the poetry of nature give Biró's paintings the charm of an independent artistic outlook.

Black, Calvin: Inside the Fantasy Doll Theatre

imagined that everything connected with the man should also be small — the broom he carried on his shoulder and the goat he led. In the woman's case, everything was the opposite, so her rooster looms bigger than his goat. Unwittingly, Bireš had made a psychological study of his neighbours.

Mihalj Bireš had several one-man shows and participated in group exhibitions at home and abroad. *(See portrait of the artist, p. 164). N. T.*

When the artist depicts an urban landscape ("Mureş in Arad") he selects wide spaces where nature fits into city life: a river, the sky, trees — all are allotted the same value as the works of human hands.

Small in size, done in oil on cardboard, the works of Pavel Biró have been shown at many exhibitions of naive art and have won national recognition. *(See portrait of the artist, p. 164). M. Il.*

BIRÓ, PAVEL (1885)   **Romania**

Pavel Biró, doyen of the naive artists of Romania and an agronomist by profession, discovered painting only after retirement.

In his works, this artist, obviously a storyteller given at times to didactic eloquence, endeavours to teach a lesson taken from life. He presents a world familiar to him: the struggle for life

BLACK, CALVIN (1903—1972)   **USA**

Calvin was born in rural Tennessee. Burdened at 13 with helping his widowed mother raise several brothers and sisters, in his spare time he taught himself how to read and write by studying mail-order catalogues. He also worked for a carnival, learning something of puppetry and ventriloquism from one of the women entertainers. His wife was to declare that he could talk and sing in nine different voices, and that he made his own musical instruments.

After his marriage in 1933, Black and his wife Ruby went to Northern California to pan for gold. The wet occupation and chilly climate aggravated his asthma, and so in 1953 they moved to the hot, arid desert in Southern California. He opened a rock shop, then began building a theatre and merry-go-round, and carving dolls. Now distributed among collectors and art dealers in California and New York City, Calvin Black's dolls were once the cast of his Possum Trot Tootum

Blair, Oswald: Tree with Birds

Doll Fantasy Theatre and the vocal riders on the wind-driven merry-go-round he erected outside his house. Possum Trot is a tiny community in the desert near Yermo, California. The dolls, dressed by Ruby Black, were jointed so that they could be animated, and fitted with cassette tapes so that they could talk or sing. Calvin wrote the songs they were ostensibly singing to his guitar accompaniment. Calvin also did a number of paintings, and built a magnificently humorous train engine, painted red.

Calvin died in March 1972. Ruby carried on with the rock shop but could not maintain the theatre and merry-go-round. The dolls inside survived more or less intact, but those on the merry-go-round, their clothes tattered by the searing wind, were transmogrified into eerie, fetish-like figures. Ruby died in February 1981. *J. W.*

BLAIR, OSWALD (1900)   Australia

Oswald Blair was born in Tenterfield, New South Wales. He is an artist who has tried his hand at many tasks besides painting.

His varied career began early. At the age of twelve he became a builder's mate and then a tailor's assistant. At sixteen he was apprenticed to a baker and worked in this trade for the next twenty years.

In the 1930s he became restless. The call of the Australian bush was strong and he set out to work as a station hand, kangaroo shooter, ring-barker of trees and scrub cutter. He travelled

Blondel, Emile: Notre-Dame de Paris

through the far north of New South Wales to Coopers Creek in South Australia and to Queensland before settling down in Sydney.

In Sydney Blair worked as a public servant until his retirement in 1967. It was after he had retired that he started to dabble with paint and brush and eventually found his own unique style.

His paintings have been hung in the Wynne Prize section of the Art Gallery of New South Wales at the annual showing of Archibald, Wynne and Sulman prize winners. They have also been shown in numerous other exhibitions. Some have been acquired by public and private collections and one hangs in the National Gallery of Victoria. *B. McC.*

BLONDEL, EMILE (1893—1970)   France

Emile Blondel was born at Le Havre and died at Pavillons-sous-Bois. He started as a cabin boy, worked as a longshoreman and farmhand, and ended in Paris as a bus driver, until he retired in about 1950. Highly disciplined in his ways, he had always been attracted to poetry and drawing. When he retired, he began to paint and within a few years had his first one-man show. Blondel is fond of well-composed landscapes firmly anchored on the surface of his canvases. Very often trees, river banks, or houses form a diagonal which imposes perspective. Groups of people, in unrelated little scenes, animate and impart rhythm to his pictures in a play of striking and contrasting highlights. He represents naive art drawn from the imagination, founded on references to the real world transposed with a great deal of poetry.

Blondel participated in the 1981 group show at the Galerie Mona Lisa in Paris, and had two one-man shows, in 1955 and 1964, at the Galerie Cambacérès in Paris. *(See portrait of the artist, p. 165). Sh. Sch.*

BLUMENFELD, TRISKA (1927)   New Zealand

Triska Blumenfeld (née Anderson) was born in Taunton, Somerset, in England, of New Zealand parents. She went to New Zealand with her parents and sister when she was three years old. At the age of fifteen, she left school and after the war went to live in Indonesia, took stenography and typing courses and got a job. Later she moved to Singapore. Sometimes she felt that she ought to take painting lessons to learn how to paint "properly," but actually never did so as she found great joy in painting the way she did. Until her departure for Rome (where she lived from 1970 to 1974), she had no idea that what she was doing was called "naive painting." Derna Querel, an Italian art critic, saw some of her works in Rome and had them included in a number of international naive art exhibitions. In 1974 she went to the South Pacific (to Fiji), continuing to paint even more intensively than before. *(See portrait of the artist, p. 165).*

BOCHERO, PETER ("PETER CHARLIE") (?—1962)   USA

Only the barest information exists about Peter Bochero. He is known to have emigrated

Blumenfeld, Triska: Village Taro Patch

from Armenia in about 1903, gone back to Europe briefly during the First World War, and returned to the United States to settle in Leechburg, Pennsylvania. He was evidently a friendly but retiring man, indeed, almost a hermit, who worked as a house painter, handyman and jack-of-all-trades. He worked and possibly even lived in a garage he rented behind a hardware store, and no one knew until after his death that he painted there in secret. He left 69 works, some on linoleum, some on cheap canvas-weight fabric, others on paper. The paintings, with their strange combinations of Western and Eastern

Bochero, Peter: Lady Liberty

religious symbology, exhortations against false promises by politicians and clergy, mystical events, space invaders and idolatry of Lincoln, suggest that underneath the quiet exterior was a personality in torment and despair. *J. W.*

BOCK, IDA (1909—1976)   West Germany

Ida Bock was born in Nadrejbie near Lublin and died in Maichingen near Stuttgart. At the end of an ill-fated life marked by persecution, expulsion and emigration to a town in Württemberg, she took up painting because she lacked the money to buy a picture. She had begun drawing as a child when obliged to spend many weeks in hospital, but real enjoyment came only when she was able to animate objects with the help of colour. This phase began in 1964. Ida Bock was brought up on a farm and had learned to take a firm grip of things and to see them in an elemental and uncomplicated fashion. Her pictures reflect this attitude: in spite of their bright and cheerful colours they never quite overcame a certain earthy density. She was always fond of painting women, flowers and domestic animals. Her interiors rarely have human figures but there are invariably flower arrangements or cats — playful, cosily curled up or affectionately fawning. With Ida Bock the act of painting was obviously the most zestful phase in the creation of a picture: the placing of the luminous pigments at exactly the right point, in correct relationship to other dominant highlights. To this was added the joy of rendering palpable the lustre and the transparency of successive layers of pigment and of effectively combining lucid blends of colour or decorative patterns painted on a common surface. The ornamental animation of the surface — patterns on walls, wallpaper, textiles, designs on vases, pots, plates and cups — was an unmistakable feature of Ida Bock's work. *(See portrait of the artist, p. 165). T. G.*

Böde, Ferenc: Gypsy Baron

BÖDE, FERENC (1925)   **Hungary**
Ferenc Böde was born in Vörösberény and is now retired as a disabled pensioner. He began

Bock, Ida: Adam and Eve

carving in 1970 to forget his illness, fashioning his figures from branches and roots of dry trees. With a few flourishes of his chisel, he changes the form of the wood. On occasion he carves bones or stones. He has had his works on display in group exhibitions at home and abroad. *M. I.*

BÖDEKER, ERICH (1904—1971) **West Germany**
Bödeker, who was born and died in Recklinghausen, worked as a miner for 41 years, 35 of

them underground. In 1959 he was forced to give up his job by the miner's disease, silicosis, and subsequently worked occasionally as a butcher. For his fifty-fifth birthday he was given a garden dwarf, but he did not care for it and, believing he could do better, he carved a dwarf of his own. Pleased with the result, which was much praised, Bödeker carried on carving. He later constructed figures from concrete and reckons to have produced about 1,000 sculptures altogether. Erich Bödeker is certainly one of the most prominent personalities among the naive sculptors of Europe, an unforgettable eccentric. He used to arrange week-end receptions in his backyard which were attended by people from all walks of life. He would receive his visitors amidst a motley crowd of newly-erected coloured cement figures of people and animals of all sizes. His sculpture is reckoned to be unique in the world of naive art. Bödeker had an impish sense of humour; he was a sturdy character, invariably optimistic in spite of his agonising affliction, given to cursing like a trooper, always eager for a chat or a joke with those he liked — and that included children. And just as Thegen, the celebrated naive painter from Schleswig-Holstein, always had his pattern-book with him, so Bödeker would take out of a cigar-box the snapshots of individuals and family groups that had been brought to him so that he could copy them in "building" his life-size sculptures. It is true that the public had to find its bearings. In the snapshot there might be a small baby waving its legs in the air. Where was he in the family group? Bödeker: "That's the lad with the blue jeans, there on the left! He's twelve years old now, but the only photograph his parents had was when

![Bödeker, Erich: Modern Society Considering the Quarrel between Adam and Eve]

Bödeker, Erich: Modern Society Considering the Quarrel between Adam and Eve

Bödeker, Erich: St. Christopher   *Bödeker, Erich: Madonna*

he was a baby. That was good enough. No problem, I just made him ten years older." In this natural and simple manner Bödeker solved all the problems that professional artists agonise over. He possessed an enviable kind of self-confidence without a trace of arrogance. Whenever he encountered anything novel he simply scratched his head under the leather cap and laughed with engaging boyishness: "O. K., I'll buy some cement and paint tomorrow." In the language of elementary shapes, abbreviations and fleeting hints Bödeker was in his element. Like all naive and unsophisticated artists, he had his own basic design for the human figure which recurs over and over again: lanky pillars with spherical heads perched on them, gawky arms and tubular legs. The face: beady eyes placed close together, prominent eyebrows just above them, a low brow, flattened skull, deep grooves running down from the nose, extended cheeks and chin, jug-handle ears, a thick line for the mouth.

The manner in which Bödeker contrived to bring out the facial features of his subjects, in spite of his very numeroùs commissions, has frequently been admired: he achieved this by minor additions or alterations to his prototype, often incorporating in his statue personal items belonging to his customer. What drew his vast circle of friends back to him again and again was the naivety with which he "built" his creatures, all of whom, animals as well as people, bore a striking resemblance to their creator. They were attracted not least by the ample sense of humour which was conveyed by all his creations. Bödeker was so attached to these creatures of his that he wished, when his time came, to die among his fairy-tale figures: the dogs, lions, giraffes, the cowboys, creel-carriers, St. Christo-

Bogosav (Živković): My Friends (detail from "Wall of Dreams")

phers, royal families and all the multifarious individuals and groups on which he had worked.

Bödeker's life-sized statues are displayed in museums and important private collections. Admirers of his art have founded a "Bödeker Association for Naive Art" to honour his memory. *(See portrait of the artist, p. 164). T. G.*

BOGOSAV (ŽIVKOVIĆ) (1920)   **Yugoslavia**

Bogosav Živković was born in 1920 in the village of Leskovac, near Stepojevac, Serbia, where he attended elementary school, and then helped his father, a poor peasant, on the farm. At the outbreak of war in 1941, he joined the struggle for national liberation; he was arrested and ill-treated. After the war, he learnt the furrier's craft, but poor health, particularly the wartime spinal injury suffered in prison, forced him to give up this work. He came to Belgrade and took a job as a doorman. He began carving in 1957, and first exhibited his works in 1960. He now lives in his native village, Leskovac, where he has created his "enchanted garden" — a place visited by peasants of the region and by art lovers from the city.

The chief material Živković uses in the realisation of his dreams are simple tree trunks, and these determine the vertical orientation of his sculpture. An essential quality of this sculptor's work is its absolute integrity with regard to its medium. The naive artist perceives the figures he carves as somehow contained within the wood. His task, his unquestioned calling, is to realise the suggestions of the wood — to release, and to preserve them.

His peasant's love of wood — the organic material provided by nature, which can be easily worked and moulded — may date from his childhood years. And from them may come his rootedness in nature, thanks to which he intuitively senses the human or animal figures lurking in the knots and branches and roots of tree trunks.

Živković's sculptures are not simply carved in wood: they are born of it, and still bear the essential character of the material. The men and fabulous creatures he creates are strange, surprising, and at the same time familiar, as though one had come across them while reading an old fairy tale. There are animal heads on human bodies, centaurs, miraculous beasts resembling the decorated initials of old Serbian manuscripts, and men and women not far removed from those on tombstones in country cemeteries and along the local roads. Flower stalks and tall columns composed of human figures, houses, exotic animals, and rank vegetation reveal the skill and imagination of this naive artist.

The more closely we examine Živković's work, the more we recognise how diverse and at the same time undifferentiated the faces of his figures are. Men have beards and grotesquely vine-like ears; women's faces are framed by the suggestion of a hair style and a headdress. Young girls wear long braids, and their arms appear to have fused together under their flowing gowns. Nuns have faces shrunken with resignation and self-denial, while the outlines of their bodies are concealed by their simple medieval robes. The creatures sprout intertwining limbs which metamorphose from man to animal and animal to plant; each figure braces itself on one below, or supports the next one in its climb toward the top of the column. In his nocturnal visions, menacing animals carry birds of death on their backs, while heads supporting houses portend still darker realms. Sometimes the faces display a faint attempt at a smile, but more often they are utterly passive in their meditation on their wooden existence.

Bogosav Živković is constantly concerned with an archetypal image, the sense of which is scarcely accessible to reason. This is pure, evolving form, feeding upon and reproducing itself, an indestructible chain of life in which things and creatures develop and decay, give birth to and prey upon one another. The artist is inspired by all metamorphoses; the world is a single whole, and all dead and living things are but ciphers of the manifold unity. Of course for Bogosav this is no conscious philosophy, nor even a rule of his life. He is not aware of the boundary between dream and reality; fantasy and factuality are one.

In his village of Leskovac, Bogosav, like the

Bogosav (Živković): Sun Goddess (detail)

French postman-artist Cheval, has created his "enchanted garden," full of vegetation of all kinds, with cottages and huts scattered here and there. The largest of these structures is his studio-gallery; inside there are peasant furniture and several of his carved pillars, while the walls are covered with his carved wooden reliefs. In the garden are stone tables, tree trunks from which plants sprout, water jugs, mill wheels. From the bushes peer the artist's mongrels and creatures from fairy tales, men's faces with drooping moustaches and women's heads with sharp, pursed lips. Some of these sculptures are carved in stone. On the bare branches of a tree, a wooden snake is entwined, the totem creature of the peasant-artist.

His carved wooden pillars have been displayed in many exhibitions all over the world and are found in many museums, including the National Museum of Modern Art in Paris. Some of his best known works are "Pillar of Dreams" (106 cm high), "Tall Nun" (114 cm), "Sun Goddess" (106 cm), "Carousel of the Century" (300 cm), "Rider on a Pig" (150 cm), "Monastery and Bird" (229 cm), "Eye to Eye" (200 cm). *(See portrait of the artist, p. 165).* O. B.-M.

b

142

Bogosav (Živković): My Mother with a Bird

Bogosav (Živković): Dreams and Thought

BOIRON, ROSE (1902) — France

Rose Boiron was born at Eygalières. Her love for the region of her birth is coupled with a lifetime attachment to her village. Her father was the local blacksmith and she attended the village primary school. Her first employment was as a seamstress in Avignon. A few years later she moved to Marseilles, where she became a city employee. After losing her husband, she returned and settled in Eygalières. In 1958, to entertain one of her children, she began to paint.

The art of Rose Boiron is forthright and a little frustrated, inspired by the landscapes of the Alpilles and the clear light of Haute Provence; it is a challenge to the incredulity of her own people. Her great power to dream with amusing and touching inventions is kept under control.

Her work has been shown in group exhibitions in France. *Ch. Sch.*

BOLLAR, GORKI (1944) — Netherlands

Gorki Bollar was born in Montevideo, Uruguay. He began painting in 1960 after seeing pictures by the Uruguayan constructivist, Joaquim Torres-Garcia, who had set up his own

Bollar, Gorki: The Miraculous Draught

Boiron, Rose: The Muse of Alpilles

workshop-school *(taller)* where artists worked together and gave lessons in an attempt to integrate the different branches of art. Bollar joined the workshop, where his teacher, José Gurvich, immediately discovered the naive artist latent in him and resolved to give him freedom to find his own way. Subsequently Bollar and three other artists founded their own *taller* to have greater freedom to work out their own ideas. Although one of the founders, Bollar felt himself an outsider and finally decided to distance himself from it. In 1966 the Taller de Montevideo, as it was known, received an invitation to visit the Netherlands from the Dutch Ministry of Culture. Bollar went on to England where he lived for some years and gained considerable recognition. In 1976 he went to work in Amsterdam at the invitation of the Municipal Museum, and rejoined the *taller. (See portrait of the artist, p. 164).* N. E.

BOLOGNESI, FERRUCCIO (1924)   Italy

Ferruccio Bolognesi, born in Mantua, was a bank clerk for years. He first began to paint in about 1957, but it was only in 1963 that he exhibited his work for the first time. In 1964, he met Mazzacurati who, in fact, "discovered" him. In 1967 he was awarded a prize *ex-aequo* at the First National Review in Luzzara. Since then he has progressed a long way, exhibiting both in

Bolognesi, Ferrucio: Piazza Virgiliana

Italy and abroad. A few years ago, after accumulating the minimum number of years needed to receive a pension, he stopped working in the bank to devote himself entirely to painting.

Bolognesi's painting stands out above all for his characteristic palette, and for his inclination toward special and suggestive chromatic rhythms deriving among other factors from the banal fact that Bolognesi is a Daltonist. But this circumstance does nothing to detract from the aesthetic impression made by his work. Furthermore, his very personal vision needs to be stressed: his is an imagination which is never an end in itself and which lends his work an original style. As De Grada puts it: "From the dark inertia of the subconscious there springs a graphic motif which is not inspired by geometry or purely decorative arabesques; rather it traces its source to something seen and then reworked by the imagination."

"Piazza Virgiliana," with its strong composition and exceptional colouristic counterpoint, provides an example of Bolognesi's stylistic originality: rectangles and squares, elements of a chromatic mosaic of floors, houses and streets, create a visual rhythm fitting in smoothly with the elegant and highly effective decorative components. Also worth mentioning is his delicate sarcasm, the mere suggestion of a satirical thrust in his various works and allegories that is not without a certain sense of theatre. It is not

therefore by chance that Bolognesi has of late devoted himself to designing scenery and costumes for the theatre. Another and no less important feature of his work is the virtually metaphysical aspect of his vision. For instance, in the painting "Cello Player," with an almost surrealistic virtuosity (but also with a naive surrealism not traceable to any cultural stereotypes) he creates with skimpy strokes a lyrical atmosphere pregnant with an intangible restiveness transmitted from the sky and round treetops to the musicians. *(See potrait of the artist, p. 164).* D. M.

BOMBOIS, CAMILLE (1883—1970)   France

Camille Bombois was born at Venarey-les-Laumes and died in Paris. His father was a boatman, and the family river-boat his childhood home. He grew up on the water until the age of 12, when he was sent to work on a farm. Later, he tried working as a road labourer and also as a wrestler with travelling circuses. Driven by an ambition to reach Paris, he went from town to town working, moving closer each time to the capital. At 24, in 1907, he finally found a job as a construction worker in Paris. For some time the idea of painting had been forming in his mind, and he practised drawing in his free time. He found work in a printing shop, struggling with the heavy rolls of paper at night, and took up painting during the day. This remained the pattern of his life until 1914 and the outbreak of the First World War. After his discharge from the army, he returned to his wife and home and immediately went back to painting. In the same spirit that had once impelled him to jump into the ring for his wrestling matches, he set up his easel one day in 1922 in the middle of the *foire aux croûtes* of Montmartre. In this setting of overwhelmingly bad paintings (*les croûtes*), a journalist noticed his work, and he was soon a centre of attention for all those in the Paris of that era who took a special interest in painters. Wilhem Uhde, Madame Grégory, Florent Fels, Maximilien Gauthier, among others, encouraged him to continue. Bombois was able at last to devote himself fully to his art. In 1937, he participated, along with Vivin, Bauchant, Jean Eve and Rousseau, at the Maîtres Populaires de la Realité exhibition, an event of great importance in the history of French naive art. After that he never stopped painting, covering the walls of his small house in Argenteuil with large nudes inspired by his wife and a proliferation of landscapes from his constantly resurging memories of the canals of Burgundy. He soon began exhibiting abroad, and his fame grew throughout Europe and the USA.

A forceful yet gentle idiom, a clear and forthright definition of his chosen subject, frankness and an abundance of well-combined colours summarily placed are all in the manner of Camille Bombois. "He paints as he lives, in great outbursts, but with everything clearly defined and specific, and not without that delicacy with which men of strength are so often endowed in their feelings. He likes clear-cut colours: the shiny black of an iron ball, the raw green of curtains against the rose thighs of dancers,

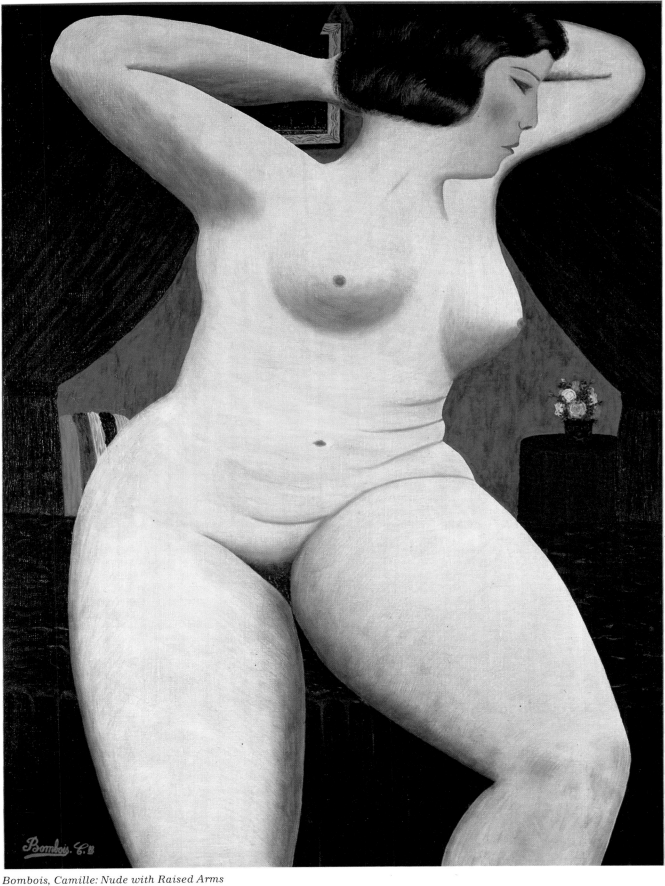

Bombois, Camille: Nude with Raised Arms

strong red velvets, aggressive yellows or the erotic violets of the circus or the drawing rooms of brothels," Oto Bihalji-Merin has written. Compositions are brought together around a form pruned to the initial truth of its volumes, with blocked-in backgrounds, and foregrounds used to simplify, to define a second approach to Bombois' nudes. Just as his nudes are composed starting from a full form, his landscapes are built around a central void: the luminous cavity of the arch in "The Bridge" (1923), the sun-bathed clearing in the forest of "The Bend in the Flowering River" (1928), the placing against the sun of the bushes in "The Chateau in the Green" (1928). The subject of the painting is heightened not by foreground treatment but rather by the other values brought into play, by sharp contrasts which enhance form. Bombois strove to give each element its due — leaves, pieces of wall, water surfaces — and this led him to neglect the sensuous forms of bodies in favour of more

Bombois, Camille: Self-portrait

tender descriptions of the fragments of nature he included. His work tells us the artist had a stance: he fused the Rabelaisian solidity of his women with the almost maternal intimacy of his vision of nature.

Camille Bombois exhibited in Paris and abroad. He was seen first in 1937 at the Maîtres Populaires de la Realité exhibition in Paris, Zurich, New York and London. Exhibitions followed in the best-known galleries and museums: the Museum am Ostwall in Dortmund, the Kunsthalle in Basel, at Knokke-le-Zoute (1958), and in New York, London and Zagreb. *(See portrait of the artist, p. 165). Ch. Sch.*

BONNIN, MAURICE (1911)   France

Maurice Bonnin was born in Naples. His mother was English. From secondary school he went directly to work, in 1928, for a major fashion house in Paris, where he remained until 1947 as a master furrier. Ten years later, he began to paint. Critical acclaim followed quickly on his first appearances before the public.

More recent works have shown a marked taste for the immobility of architecture. Maurice Bonnin draws with precision and elegance, adding colour by half-tones. The constant play of verticals brings rhythm into his pictures, and an

Bonnin, Maurice: "Le Lapin Agile" Cabaret

undefined light bathes most of the compositions.

He has exhibited in various Paris galleries. *(See portrait of the artist, p. 165). Ch. Sch.*

BORDA BORTAGARAY,   Argentina
MARIA ADELIA

M. A. Borda Bortagaray, a teacher, was born in Corrientes, an Argentine province encircled by two great rivers, the Paraná and the Uruguay. The climate is damp and warm, the vegetation lush and the people, a mixture of the indigenous Guarana Indians and European settlers, are gay and very fond of music. When she began illustrating the stories she composed for her pupils, this was the world Borda Bortagaray had in mind. Apart from these stories, she also wrote poems and plays for children. Her paintings show village streets with gauchos and their sweethearts on horseback; the great courtyards of the old colonial haciendas with their wells and their ivy; people resting under a huge tree native to the area, the "drunken tree," surrounded by multi-coloured flowers; Sunday dances to the sweet sound of national instruments, and, inevitably, the magnificent rivers of the area. These paintings, with their strange granular texture, abound in bright colours, confirming the artist's exceptional powers of observation, humour and vitality.

Borda Bortagaray, now living in Buenos Aires, is the doyenne of Argentine naive painters and the only one who has been painting without interruption for the last thirty years.

She has had many one-woman shows and participated in group exhibitions. In the second volume of the work "Argentine Art," her work has

real subject. Placing his easel in a street and surrounded by curious onlookers, he would start a painting that he later finished at home, in his modest flat.

His talent can perhaps be compared with that of Bauchant. He does not give his figures any veneer, and the impression they leave is one of physical strength. A man of likeable character, he did not work for the sake of money. Once he returned part of the payment he had received for a painting, stating that the price he had asked was too high. In fact, his prices were quite low. He loved colours, considering them a reflection of

Bordonzotti, Alfred: Landscape

Borda Bortagaray, M. A.: Morning in the Village

been described by the Argentine writer Manuel Mujica Lainez. *M. T. S.*

BORDONZOTTI, ALFRED (1906—1973)   Switzerland

Alfred Bordonzotti was born in Castelrotto, Ticino. A house-painter by occupation, he suffered an accident at work and after that began to paint pictures (1951). His work remained unknown until his first exhibition in the Pro Arte Kasper Gallery in Morges in 1973, the year he died.

Bordonzotti's talent was discovered late in his life. His pictures are not the product of his imagination; on the contrary, he needed to have a

joy and gladness through which he expressed his own joy in living. He exhibited in Switzerland, New York and London. *(See portrait of the artist, p. 164). G. K.*

BORKOWSKI, MARY (1916)   USA

Mary Borkowski was born on 28 March 1916 in Sulphur Springs, Ohio. Her ancestry is Appalachian and dates back to pioneer days. She went to a one-room school and enjoyed a childhood of rural outdoor pleasures. During the depression of the 1930s, however, the family moved to Dayton, where she still lives, and the hard times they endured later became the subject of some of Mary Borkowski's "thread paintings." Married and divorced at an early age, she worked as a manager of rental properties until her recent retirement.

Her fame as an artist has been won in two related but nonetheless different areas of needlework. Her grandmother and mother were skilled in traditional quilting, and Mary Borkowski carried what she learned from them into highly imaginative artistic realms, combining quilting with pictorial embroidery to portray patriotic themes centring on historical events.

She began creating thread paintings in 1965 after an intimate friend suddenly died. "I never made a painting, thread or otherwise, before in my life . . . suddenly the whole wasted pattern of living came crushing down upon me, and I wanted to put it down in some form to show why it happened." These works are intensely personal, their significance frequently rather tragic, "pieces of my life that shouldn't have been . . . the world of Mary Borkowski . . . expressions of awful truths and deep emotional experiences of self, of others, and God's creations." "The Crash," she said, was made out of a feeling "so deep about something so wrong I had to make it . . . the strange part is, after making it, all the original hostility I felt was gone."

Her thread paintings, she says, are "designs built in thread as with clay but in the same manner you would paint . . . there is no greater reward than looking at something you have created with your own hands." She is now trying her hand at painting with oils. *J. W.*

nating canvases on which he is fond of portraying figures in comic situations. Rich in tone, his work is modelled on the Flemish painting tradition and does not belong to any expressionistic or other school of art. Never having bowed to the ordinary conception of naive art, he has shown himself to be a profoundly original painter.

He has been exhibiting since 1979 and since 1980 has participated in group exhibitions in Brussels. *(See portrait of the artist, p. 165). J. C.*

BOSILJ, ILIJA see ILIJA (BOSILJ)

Borkowski, Mary: The Crash

BOROSNÉ ENDRESZ, TERÉZ (1919) Hungary

Teréz Endresz Borosné was born in Nagyesztergár, and now lives in Budapest as a retired worker. She creates her textured pictures from various materials: textiles, leather, plants, and so on. Her subject matter is largely inspired by folklore. She is distinctive for her knowledge of materials and her highly developed ability to combine them, as well as for her gift of using colour and her wealth of ideas. Her works were first exhibited in Budapest in 1975. Some of her paintings may be found in the Museum of Naive Art in Kecskémet. *M. I.*

BOS, I (1907) Belgium

Felix Alois Marie Van Bosstraeten, born in Wavre Notre-Dame, has had a bent for painting throughout his life. "The desire to paint," he once stated, "surprised me like the 'flu." He began by copying the masterpieces of the great artists, displaying a particular fondness for Renoir.

Since retiring, Bos has devoted himself to creative painting, inspired above all by Flemish sayings, scenes of everyday life and personal memories. "I paint them as I see them," he says, "and as I have never seen the inside of an academy, and have always worked without a teacher, it is understandable that my painting has nothing in common with classic painting. I have never met a naive artist who sees things the way I do."

A humorous element prevails in the fasci-

BOTTEX, JEAN-BAPTISTE Haiti

Jean-Baptiste Bottex and his brother Seymour E. Bottex (who is also well known as an artist in Haiti) share a number of similar themes in their pictures' subject-matter, yet each artist is wholly distinguishable. Both were born in Cap Haitien, but the two of them have long since moved south to Port-au-Prince.

J.-B. Bottex is deaf, a disadvantage which, however, enables him, once he is cut off in his beautiful studio in Pétionville with his wife, to divorce himself completely from the world outside and let his humour and fancies run riot in his painting.

He started his working life as a furniture-maker and for a while was employed as a teacher, before he turned to painting. He paints chiefly on masonite (the suggestion of DeWitt Peters, who realised that Haiti's humid atmosphere could too easily mean that a taut canvas in the West Indies would sag if it was taken to Europe or the United States). Bottex often allows a comic vein to creep into his paintings, as in "Susannah and the Elders" and in the picture of the encounter of Jesus with Mary Magdalene (shown here), which takes place in a completely Haitian setting, with the black, short-skirted Magdalene contrasted to the white, traditionally-robed Christ. But excerpts from the Christian story are not his only choice of subjects; he also depicts social scenes (often not without their humorous side) and has a number of beautiful pictures of animals to his credit.

In 1969 he was sent a number of crates full of high-fashion clothes designed by famous couturiers in Britain, with instructions to "make pictures" of each garment, and it is typical of Bottex that he chose to show off these examples of high-fashion design (for the 1969/70 season) among fantastic settings. *Sh. W.*

BOUQUET, ANDRÉ (1897)   France

André Bouquet was born at La Varenne-St-Hilaire. He worked first as a bronze setter and then as a cook and butcher's assistant, finally

tures in fresh and bright colours. His work is rooted in a simple and direct reality and enjoys great popularity among the general public.

His eye for minute detail and his precise rendering of architecture are well illustrated in "The Roofs of Gaillon" (shown here), which provides a clear, bird's eye view of the little town and surrounding countryside.

André Bouquet exhibited at Knokke-le-Zoute (1958), the Bratislava (1966) and the Zagreb Triennials (1970); his work has also been shown in galleries in Paris, Düsseldorf, Nantes and Munich. *(See portrait of the artist, p. 164). Ch. Sch.*

Bos, I: A Summer Night's Dream

Bottex, Jean-Baptiste: Mary Magdalene and Jesus

Borosné Endresz, Teréz: Return

Bouquet, André: The Roofs of Gaillon

finding employment as a foreman in a factory in the Paris region. This job allowed him more time for painting. He was drafted and sent to Indochina in 1919 and called up again in 1939. Since 1958 he has painted and exhibited constantly in France and throughout Europe. A great deal has been written about him.

André Bouquet is a perfect example of the naive artist who produces well-composed pic-

BOURGEOIS, JEF (1896)   Belgium

Jef Bourgeois, called the "prince of Marolles," was born in the poor district of Marolles, the Brussels folklore centre celebrated by a myriad writers and artists. He still lives there. It was in this area that he directed the Toone Puppet Theatre, for which he painted many backdrops. When the Toone Museum was opened, Jef Bourgeois became its custodian.

When he was seventeen, he joined the studio of the goldsmith-sculptor Wolfers, who encouraged him to study sculpture at the Saint-Josse Academy. He exhibited his first works in about 1926: sculptures retaining the hardness of their material, like the work of Rik Wouters. He was friendly with a number of painters, including Simonin, and this influenced him to take up painting himself.

Marolles is the centre of his inspiration, which derives almost exclusively from Brussels folklore. His paintings consist of "instinct and feelings and are full of sincerity and a great love

Bourgeois, Jef: The Actors of Toone Honouring the Manneken Pis

Belgian, and given birth to a child. She attended the Brussels Academy, where she had the good fortune to meet the painter, Leon Devos. He discovered that she had the qualities of a naive artist, and hoping that she would preserve them, allowed her to work without tutelage, thus endeavouring to protect her against all influences.

The presence of human beings, especially children, either explicitly or intimated, characterises her oils and gouaches. She places the human figure in a setting that, while bare, avoids coldness because of the magic of the ambience. A

Boyadjian, Micheline: The Easel

of colour" (Patesson). He works directly on canvas, without drawing first, and uses warm bright colours applied in thick layers. A lover of antiques, he inserts into his works some of the objects from his rich collection, especially examples of Brussels folk art which he patiently reconstructs from their ruined state resulting from bombings during the Second World War.

Recently, he has turned to the monotype, a genre he handles with virtuosity. He has exhibited mostly in Brussels. *(See portrait of the artist, p. 164). J. C.*

BOYADJIAN, MICHELINE (1923) Belgium
Micheline Boyadjian, born in Bruges is Belgian by birth, her maiden name being Evrard. Her talent was revealed after she had married a cardiologist, Noubar Boyadjian, a naturalised

highly refined scale of greys and other cool tones — browns, blues — surrounds and supports her forms, enlivened by accents of warm colours, all the more distinctive for being rare. The artist uses all possible chromatic means to make people and things weightless, thus giving them a dimension quite out of the ordinary and permitting their true identity to come to the fore.

Unlike Rousseau, she succeeds in imposing a third dimension while retaining the perspective of naive art. She often uses this perspective playfully, trying (as on the parquetry floor in "Waiting") to give a certain undulation to space expected to be static.

She exhibited for the first time in 1957, with a group, and won the prize of the city of Brussels. The following year, she received the Young Belgian Painter award, and the Koopall Prize.

She has had one-woman shows and participated in group exhibitions at home and abroad. Her paintings may be found in many museums. *(See portrait of the artist, p. 165). J. C.*

BRACHET, LISE — Belgium

Lise Brachet, daughter and granddaughter of university professors, wished to attend Ensaav de la Cambre but out of respect for her parents and the family tradition studied medicine and stomatology, in which fields she worked until recently.

Painting fascinated her and she devoted all

His problem is that he has a strong sense of outrage, and when he feels that he is being insulted or molested (and he is not inclined to reason why), he becomes violent, generally inflicting violence upon people in authority such as local councillors, with serious consequences for himself.

And yet he is a vibrant naive artist. If so many of his pictures are painted in gaol, they are nevertheless not lacking in brilliant colour, although in many cases the poignancy of their subject-matter and the way it is conveyed acts as a devastating contrast to the brightness of the

Brachet, Lise: The Path of Love

Bradley, Geoff: The Library

her spare time to it. A two-year stay in California, where her husband had an important position, freed her of obligations that would have prevented her devoting herself exclusively to painting.

"Perhaps my love of painting is all the greater for being hampered at the beginning," she says. Quite unjustifiably, the name of Chagall has been associated with her canvases and gouache, which are imbued with a genuine sense of magic. Attracted by the relationship between planes and colours, she does not feel that she has to introduce graphics into her works, in which colours are thickly applied. She makes her human beings and objects weightless and gives them a poetry totally free of the laws of gravitation. She has exhibited in Brussels galleries. *(See portrait of the artist, p. 165). J. C.*

BRADLEY, GEOFF (1946) — Great Britain

Geoff Bradley was born in Manchester. The background of this artist is one of sadness, punctuated by periods of personal tragedy. During his early adolescence he had difficult and disturbed times, mostly spent in "approved" schools (establishments to which the State sends awkward or criminally inclined children with a view to trying to reorganise their lives). Bradley is now serving his second term in prison (a nine-year sentence begun in 1981).

paint. One has only to recall "Lonely Christmas," a picture of his wife (who has now parted from him) gloomily sitting at a table surveying the yuletide banquet which he will not be sharing.

Often the subjects of his paintings (the children being bathed before the open fire at home, two friends absorbed in a chess game — in fact any aspect of life as he knows it in the world outside) are taken from ordinary experience, though he occasionally shows a vein of acid wit, as in "Safari," a painting of "pukkha sahibs" riding elephants at the Zoo.

His pictures (all of them small) have been seen in many exhibitions in northern England, and also in some RONA mixed exhibitions since 1979. He was included in the important "Northern Primitives" exhibition at the South London Art Gallery (the official show-place of the London Borough of Southwark) in 1972. *(See portrait of the artist, p. 165). Sh. W.*

BRANDES, FRANZ (1921) — West Germany

Franz Brandes was born in Dortmund, where he still lives. He is a miner who worked down the pit for 31 years, latterly at the coal face, but he had to give up his job because of silicosis and is now a pensioner. Brandes began to paint as the result of a bet. He started by copying, but soon observed that a copy was never "his own work" and went on to paint subjects chosen or invented by himself. He has frequently painted scenes in the mine-cage and in his place of work several hundred yards underground. On a number of occasions he was obliged to say to his workmates, who had little understanding of such sombre pictures: "Why shouldn't I paint what you and I do down there and let people see what it looks like down there?" Nevertheless, his memory tends to dwell nowadays on pleasant holidays, celebrations and ceremonies. He takes special delight in observing the expressions of his contemporaries, such as politicians, and incorporating these into humorous pictures. *T. G.*

deep within themselves and set apart by some magic spell from the event described by the painter.

In spite of their pictorial austerity and their strictly disciplined composition, these scenes from popular life captivate us with their lyrical sentiment and serene sense of poetry. Oluf Braren is considered to be the earliest amateur painter in Germany. "Oluf Braren had the faculty of wonder," remarked the art historian Franz Roh. "I recognise in this strange and tragic individual the very climax of amateur painting." An equally eminent connoisseur of naive painting,

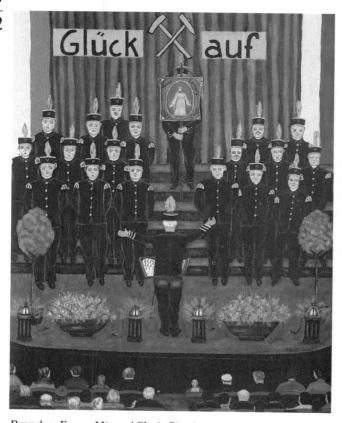

Brandes, Franz: Miners' Choir Singing

Brašić, Janko: Portrait of a Mother

BRAREN, OLUF (1787—1839) West Germany

Oluf Braren was born on the island of Föhr, where he also died. Braren was a village schoolmaster, first on the island of Sylt, then on Föhr. He used to collect sea-shells, bird's eggs and fossils, and also carried out studies of bird flight. In 1813 he published a book of his own paintings entitled "Pictures of Mammals. The First Hundred." He also devoted himself to portrait-painting. About thirty portraits of women and children in national costume and his two celebrated wedding pictures were probably commissioned. In 1822 he had to give up his post in consequence of a love-affair with one of his pupils; he lived from then on in great penury and died of consumption. The figures in Braren's portraits are invariably dressed in their Sunday best, their richly decorated costumes being represented in cool, unobtrusively luminous colours; they are caught in fixed postures or in solemn and restrained repose. All of Braren's people seem to be trapped in their own thoughts, sunk

Michailov, praises his pictures as "the finest achievements that we know in the whole field of amateur painting." *T. G.*

BRAŠIĆ, JANKO (1906) Yugoslavia

Janko Brašić was born in Oparić near Svetozarevo, Serbia, where he attended elementary school and still lives, farming and painting. Having started to paint in 1933, he is the founder of what is today known as the Oparić painters' group.

Most of his paintings are portraits of his fellow-peasants, done as records and to fix them in the memory. These portraits, the works for which he is most famous, comprise a fascinating gallery of psychological types, "the good and the bad, skinflints, liars, brave men and cowards." He is also fond of themes drawn from Serbia's history and the Serbs' battles with the Turks. In the warrior tradition, he celebrates in his paintings the praises of battles won by the Serbs.

Braren, Oluf: The Bride

The landscapes of the regions of Šumadija and Pomoravlje are simultaneously gentle and robust, rolling, hilly and restless. Janko Brašić, living there, has drunk deep of the traditions of his area and transmitted them to his extraordi-nary paintings. Portraying events and customs, he thinks of himself as an important chronicler of his region whose duty it is to record in paint-ing what the tellers of folk tales record in words.

In his fifty years of painting, Janko Brašić

Brašić, Janko: Panic

Brašić, Janko: A Fight in a Saloon

has devoted many canvases to Serbian customs. Some of his works have become a model for other painters in the Oparić area, where he is widely imitated.

He has included himself in some of his larger paintings, usually in national costume, but only if portraying an event in which he himself took part.

In the painting "Panic" (1967), people are running in all directions, pell-mell. About this painting, the artist says: "Many times during the last war, the people took to the woods when the German troops came to the village, for they knew

for the quality of his work, and second, for the fact that he was a deaf mute. He was born on 30 May 1766 in Hampton, Connecticut. His father was a doctor. By the time John was sixteen, he could read, write and converse well enough in signs to be understood, and according to his father's friend, the Reverend Cogswell, had a "genius for painting." He was also said to "have a good disposition." When twenty-two he took instruction for a while from the Reverend Joseph Steward, a successful self-taught painter. Brewster's first important paintings — and subjects — were his father and stepmother, done in about

Brewster, John: Portrait of Mr. James Eldridge, Jr.

Brewster, John: Portrait of Mrs. James Eldridge

from times of old that nothing good could come of the enemy. In the spacious courtyard of a monastery, an assembly was held. I remember it was in the autumn of 1943. In the midst of the festivities that followed, a peasant climbed up on a wagon, fired his pistol and yelled 'Hide, the Germans are coming.' In the twinkling of an eye, the monastery courtyard was empty, as though cleared by a storm. I stood to one side, watching, and then got on my horse and rode off into the cornfields."

Some of his best-known paintings are "Wedding in Dragačevo," "Cemetery," and "Portrait of a Mother."

Janko Brašić has had one-man shows and participated in group exhibitions at home and abroad. *(See portrait of the artist, p. 165). N. T.*

BREWSTER, JOHN (1766—1854)   USA

John Brewster stands out among early American itinerant limners for two reasons: first,

1795. He evidently painted a number of portraits in Hampton before moving, along with his newly married younger brother, to Buxton, Maine, which became his home, although he did go back and forth to Connecticut during his travels up and down the New England states painting portraits for prominent families.

Able as he was, he nonetheless must have felt some need to improve his ability to communicate, for in April 1817, at the age of 51, he enrolled in the Connecticut Asylum for the Education and Instruction of Deaf and Dumb Persons. He took three years of instruction, and the records list him as a self-supporting artist.

Brewster is not known to have painted any landscapes *per se*, but small outdoor scenes figure frequently as back-drops in many of his portraits. Other portraits contain details that suggest the furnishings and interiors in which many of his sitters live and are thus historical documents as well as fine paintings. *J. W.*

BRICE, BRUCE (1940) USA

Bruce Brice was born in the French quarter of New Orleans, Louisiana. He is young when compared to the majority of American naive or folk artists. Handsome, good-humoured and endowed with a healthy self-respect and pride in his work, Brice had made a name for himself as a prize-winning primitive artist by the time he was thirty.

His background was one of poverty, or certainly near-poverty. He was shining shoes by the time he was eight and "hamboning" it (rhythmically drumming on himself) for pennies in the

Brice, Bruce: "Shaft"

street. As a child he had wanted to be a puppeteer and entertained his playmates in Desire (a housing project) with marionettes and puppet shows. But painting was his obsession, he said, all through his school days, and as an adult, that's what he did in the time he had left over from working — as a city hall maintenance man, a bricklayer, house painter, tile setter, coffee grinder and picture framer, as well as selling toys in the local market. This experience is reflected in his scenes of urban life.

The success that followed his winning an award in a competition (the prize being a one-man exhibition plus the purchase of his work by the Delgado Museum) enabled Brice to devote himself entirely to painting. He uses oil, watercolours or acrylics, and sometimes works on two or more paintings at a time.

In a way, his subject-matter is autobiographical, for it is directly related to his experiences and the life of the black community. He might even be called an activist, for he raised enough money to produce two enormous murals that both commemorated and deplored the destruction of Treme, a black community, to make way for a parking lot for the new New Orleans Cultural Centre.

Brice's paintings are detailed, alive with colour and action, almost jazzy (he is a jazz fan), and as spirited as the people he so vividly portrays. *(See portrait of the artist, p. 164). J. W.*

BROWN, CLEVELAND (1943) Great Britain

Cleveland Brown was born in Jamaica. He is an expert contract carpenter who has been in Britain since 1959. He started painting — almost by chance — in 1974.

This new departure for him happened when he and his friend and co-worker, Cyril Houseley, were having a cup of tea in a shed on a building site and were wiling away the time flipping through the pages of some old illustrated magazines someone had left there. Conversation, at that point, was casual. However, in unison, they both decided that each of them could do as well — or better — painting "pictures" than the colour cameramen whose photos were in the magazines.

It was a genuine resolution. Brown and Houseley, when they had finished their work, went home to try their hand at painting. Cleveland Brown was very disappointed by what he painted. However, he did not fully give up the challenge he had set himself.

On a different tack, he paid a visit to London's Post Office Tower, bought a postcard of this modern monument and returned home to make his own picture of it. This proved to be the smallest painting he ever made, but it was the start of a career which (without interfering with his profession as a joiner) has earned him the acknowledged title of the greatest living naive artist in Britain.

At first, the only person who showed an interest in Brown's work (apart, perhaps, from his family and close friends) was Maggy Tolliday, the Arts Officer for the London Borough of Brent. But it was in vain that she sought to get the local council to share her admiration by including Cleveland in their borough exhibitions. Local interest in his works was virtually nil.

Indeed, it was not until Stanley B. Harries, the chief executive of RONA, was appointed to be in charge of the Greater London Jubilee Celebrations (Art) Committee in 1977, and visited every Greater London borough to find good naive artists (when, of course, he encountered Maggy Tolliday in Brent), that a real chance arose for Brown's pictures to go before the British public.

Brown, Cleveland: The Grunwick Strike

Harries immediately joined the Brent Art Officer in her enthusiasm for Cleveland Brown and in due course included his paintings in every one of the many exhibitions (starting with the Jubilee show in the Olympia stadium) which he mounted (and that includes every RONA exhibition from 1977 to the present day — in Britain, Greece, Japan and the United States).

"The Wedding of Princess Anne" was even taken to Morges, Switzerland, for the annual international naive art display at the Galerie Pro-Arte Kasper.

Brown only paints about four or five pictures

In the two pictures reproduced here the artist captures the tense atmosphere of the crowded streets, contrasting with the empty buildings. He wishes, it seems, to perform the function of a photographer, or the TV cameras, recording these dramatic events. He is also capable of wilder flights of fancy, as in "The Siege of the Iranian Embassy."

Not surprisingly, he has often been featured in the British national press and on television. His pictures are to be found in many important collections on both sides of the Atlantic. (See portrait of the artist, p. 164). Sh. W.

Brown, Cleveland: The Spaghetti House Siege

a year. The latest examples are very large. Although they tend to be expensive, it is rare that any of his big canvases is not pre-sold, either before completion or before it is first exhibited.

How can one best define the nature and style of Brown's work?

Born Jamaican, he has long since relinquished any formal connection with that island, claiming that he is British. He is indeed intensely pro-British and loves the Royal Family, who frequently feature in his pictures. A very different aspect of his choice of subject-matter appears in his bold depiction of sex. Other elements in his work are a sense of humour and a strong social conscience, beautifully underlined in his painting of the angry crowd confronting the police during the historic strike at Grunwick.

BROWN, CLINTON (1954)   **Jamaica**

Clinton Brown, son of Everald Brown, was born in Kingston, Jamaica. After his primary school education, he worked as an assistant to his father in the Ras Tafarian priesthood. He began painting in 1967 under the guidance of his father. He has exhibited in Jamaica (1969, 1972, 1977) and, through the Organization of American States, in Washington, D. C. (1972 and 1978). *J. G. S.*   →

BROWN, EVERALD (1917)   **Jamaica**

Everald Brown was born in St. Ann, Jamaica, and attended the Staceyville primary school in Clarendon. Brother Brown, as he is known to most, an unordained deacon in the

Brown, Clinton: A Son Is Born

Brown, Everald: Victory Dance

Ethiopian Orthodox Church, began painting and carving in the late sixties. His field of artistic endeavour is wide-ranging, and a most impressive spectrum of intuitive talent finds expression in dramatic productions of sacred pageants, complete with set and costume designs, musical arrangement and interpretation, with inspired performances in which the large family and the faithful brethren take part, to the accompaniment of unique stringed instruments, as if from another time and place, decorated with an iconography recalled assuredly from a past unknown but not forgotten, and ageless drums, all created by the artist, who humbly attributes his talent to divine inspiration.

He is, quite literally, a visionary whose works contain a strong spiritual influence and achieve, through the integration of elements of nature and the folklore of the island, a balance of cultural content uniquely Jamaican.

Brother Brown's paintings came to the public through the annual self-taught artists' exhibition at the Institute of Jamaica, the island's cultural centre. Internationally he was discovered by José Gomez-Sicre of the Museum of Modern Art of Latin America at the OAS in Washington, who visited Jamaica in 1972.

Brown has exhibited in Jamaica (1969, 1972, 1977), at the OAS, Washington (1972, 1974), and in El Salvador (1977).

The most recent development in Brown's work is his search in nature for objects which conform to his vision: that is, he simply recognises the artistry in a stone or a branch or a root and adds the finishing touches. *(See portrait of the artist, p. 164).* T. R.

BUKTENICA, EUGEN (1914) **Yugoslavia**

Eugen Buktenica was born in the village of Grohote on the island of Šolta, Croatia, where he went to elementary school and still lives. His occupations are farming, fishing and painting. Since 1964, he has been painting fishing motifs, for the most part on canvas. After a childhood disease, his hearing was impaired and he was excused military service. During the Second World War, he was arrested and interned in a concentration camp, where he contracted spotted typhus. Unmarried, he lives a lonely life, and when he wants company goes to a village dance

Buktenica, Eugen: Boat Watchman

Brown, Everald: Ethiopian Apple

where he observes the young people or may even dance himself. Rough in appearance, and barely articulate when he speaks, he is transformed when painting into a gentle artist of pastel colours and lyrical bent.

"When I started painting, I made my own brushes out of goat bristles and my colours from dust off the walls and woodcarver's glue. When the people in my village heard about this, they came to see my pictures. Some of them tried to persuade me to stop making a fool of myself and letting people laugh at me. But I kept on painting, mostly boats, fishing vessels. On one such

Buktenica, Eugen: To the Dance

boat, my late father took off for America."

In the painting "To the Dance" (1973), Buktenica shows the sea and boats sailing the peaceful waters and against this background a group of young men, dressed in their best, and wearing hats, riding donkeys two by two and obviously ready for some fun. A sharp and ironic observer of life and of his fellow villagers, he has portrayed the carefree young men of the island on their way to a gathering. Everything — the young men, the sea and the sky — are enveloped by Buktenica in the soft blue haze of a typical Mediterranean scene.

In the painting "Boat Watchman" (1972), a boy is shown sitting and watching a boat whose owners have gone to buy something in port. In the summer heat, the boy wiles away the time by eating a water-melon. In the background two boats are depicted, flattened between the coast and the rockbound island. One feels the heat of high noon in an Adriatic summer when all is still, both air and water. The island idyll is completed with two symbolic anchors and two names on the anchored boats: "Lucija" and "Nikola."

Eugen Buktenica has had one-man shows and participated in group exhibitions at home and abroad. *(See portrait of the artist, p. 164).* N. T.

BUNJEVAČKI,   **Yugoslavia**
DRAGIŠA (1925—1983)

Dragiša Bunjevački was born in Pančevo, Vojvodina. His childhood was spent travelling with his father in villages and small towns, where the latter entertained in bars. Dragiša's sister and mother also followed the father from place to place in the hope that he would someday settle down. The mother kept mentioning her small house in Novi Bečej to which, tired of wandering and hardship, she yearned to return. But the years passed. First the father died, then the mother, followed by the sister. Dragiša continued wandering out of habit and after many years arrived in Novi Bečej, where he settled and lived until his death. Thus was his mother's wish fulfilled.

Before coming to Novi Bečej, he spent seven years with a circus, grooming horses and helping

I have sold, but I'm happy when I sit up all night on a wooden packing case and meditate, while everyone else is sleeping comfortably."

In the picture called "Self-portrait," he placed himself in the foreground, making himself better-looking than in real life and wearing his best suit, which he never put on. His beard has been combed and he seems to be in a state of exhilaration. In the background there is a circus tent and in the middle, a bar and musicians with whom he spent long sleepless nights playing for drunken guests. On his left-hand side is a circus harlequin and on his right-hand side a circus

Bunjevački, Dragiša: Honouring Rousseau

Bunjevački, Dragiša: Self-portrait

the circus clowns. He travelled with the circus, carefree, happy to be part of a world he had become fond of while a boy, when taken to the circus by his parents. One evening, a high wind was blowing and his patron, an acrobat, fell from a trapeze and fractured his spine. "I then left the circus because life in it would never be the same."

After that, like his father before him, he played in bars. Tipsy customers wanted him to play without pause until dawn, plying him with liquor. He was unable to refuse because guests were known to beat up those who turned down such an offer.

When he first began doing paintings, he presented them as gifts to any acquaintance who happened to like them.

"I never had the intention of making a living from painting," he said. "For me it was enough that by painting I left the world I lived in and moved to another nicer and more interesting one. I could, for instance, buy a real bed to sleep in and pay for it with money earned from paintings

dancer. He was attracted to her while he worked in the circus but never had the courage to tell her. Besides Bunjevački, the picture holds a dog and a cat, faithful friends who lived with him in his solitary, overcrowded room.

Speaking of the painting "Hajduk Šandor," Bunjevački said: "This Šandor was a *hajduk* — an outlaw wanted by the authorities. He roamed about the countryside on a stallion and a baron's daughter fell in love with him. When her people learned she was seeing him in secret, they walled her up alive in the castle. Nowadays, at night, when you pass there, people say you can hear a voice calling, especially during storms. The *hajduk* disappeared long ago, killed in an ambush, but tamburitza players in bars sing about this legend. Unfortunately, a great tamburitza player, my friend Joško, died and I painted him in the clouds."

The artist had one-man shows and participated in group exhibitions at home and abroad. *(See portrait of the artist, p. 165). N. T.*

USSR

M. P. Buryak was born in the Ukrainian village of Kovalin, not far from Kiev. Her parents were collective farmers. At the age of thirteen, after five years at school, she lost the use of both legs due to a crippling nervous ailment and to this day is unable to fend for herself. To earn a living, she originally embroidered towels, blouses and shirts, but subsequently Liza Mironova, a peasant woman from a neighbouring village, aroused her interest in the painted paper panels

washed cottage. Gradually the more gifted of such peasant-woman painters began to make such paper panels for sale as an element of interior decoration. Some turned from traditional to individualised designs. Maria ventured into this new field in 1967, creating out of her own imagination compositions based on folk song and legend and also on historical events. In her efforts a palpable link with traditional folk painting and embroidery can be discerned. However, with her, the peasant mentality is re-interpreted in a naive manner. The prevalent features are a simplified form, fragmentary arrangement, and

b

161

Buryak, M. P.: Gardeners Having Dinner

Byrne, Sam: Block 10 Mine — Broken Hill

that she made. Painting of this order was traditional for the Ukrainian peasant woman, who each spring would thus decorate her newly white-

narrative element. Her means of artistic expression are wholly naive, though the roots lie in peasant art. She first exhibited in Kiev in 1972. In 1974 and again in 1977 she was represented at shows in Moscow. In 1979 the Kiev Film Studios made a documentary about her, entitled "Village Painters." *(See portrait of the artist, p. 165). N. Sh.*

BYRNE, SAM (1883—1978)   **Australia**

Sam Byrne was born in the Barossa Valley in South Australia. After moving to Broken Hill in New South Wales and working as a miner most of his life, he retired at the age of 73 and started painting full time. His early pictures showed mainly historical events relating to life in the mining town and aerial views of the growing city of Broken Hill. Later works recorded facets of his own working life and of the people around him. He worked in a shed at the back of his house, using ordinary house enamels. As his eyesight began to deteriorate, his paintings became more abstracted, but the strong, vibrant colours remained. *B. McC.*

Babeț, Gheorghe

Bahunek, Antun

Bahunek, Branko

Balász, János

Baptista, Carmen

Baring, Mark

Bazile, Castera

Balet, Jan

Bdejan, Artjuša

Becker, Hermann

Benassi, Enrico

Benoit, Jacqueline

Benoit, Rigaud

Bensted, John

...d, Margaret

Bakos, Lajos

Balan, Marija

...ker, Noël

Batardy, Marie-Louise

Bauchant, Andre

...kles, Gillian

Beer, Alois

Beer, June

Belković, Dragica

...al, Jean

Bereznev, A. D.

Bičjunene, Monika

Binder, Jakob

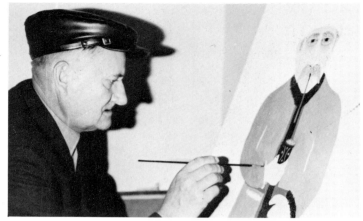

Bireš, Mihalj

Biró, Pavel

Bödeker, Erich

Bollar, Gorki

Bolognesi, Ferruccio

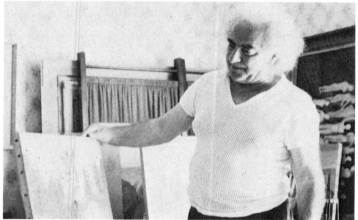

Bordonzotti, Alfred

Bouquet, André

Bourgeois, Jef

Brice, Bruce

Brown, Cleveland

Brown, Everald

Buktenica, Eugen

del, Emile

Blumenfeld, Triska

Bock, Ida

Bogosav (Živković)

bois, Camille

Bonnin, Maurice

Bos, I

Brachet, Lise

Brašić, Janko

adjian, Micheline

Bunjevački, Dragiša

Bradley, Geoff

Burjak, M. P.

CALLINS, CHARLES — Australia
CALVO, VALERICO MORAL — Spain
CAMERON, BARBARA — Australia
CAMPUAN, I NYOMAN — Indonesia, Bali
CAO JINYING — China
CAO XIUWEN — China
CARABASSA, TERESA — Argentina
CARTER, BERNARD — Great Britain
CASIMIR, LAURENT — Haiti
CASTAIN, AIMÉE — France
CECCARELLI, MARINO — Italy
CEDEÑO, JOSÉ ANTONIO — Cuba
ČERNJAHOVSKIJ, IVAN — USSR
ČERNOBROVA, SUZANNA — USSR
CHABAUTY, MALVINA — France
CHAVANNES, ETIENNE — Haiti
CHAVARRIA, JULIA — Nicaragua
CHECCHI, GIUSEPPE DE — Switzerland
CHEN MUJUN — China
CHERECHEŞ, ALEXANDRU — Romania
CHERY, JACQUES-RICHARD — Haiti
CHESHER, A. W. — Great Britain
CHICK, LORNA — Australia
CHURCH, HENRY — USA
CHVÁLA, JOSEF — Czechoslovakia
CLOES, NICOLAS — Belgium
COE, CLARK — USA
COELHO, J. I. M. — Portugal
COHEN, GABRIEL — Israel
COLAÇO, MADELEINE — Brazil
COLE, CHARLES FREDERIC — Australia
CONVEY, TONY — Australia
COOK, BERYL — Great Britain
COOPER, GLADYS — Great Britain
COULON, BERTHE — Belgium
COYLE, CARLOS CORTES — USA
CREPIN, BENOIT — France
CROCIANI, EMILE — France
CROIX, FRANÇOISE DE LA — Belgium
CROSSLEY, RALPH — Great Britain
CSAREJSNÉ HRABOVSZKI, I. — Hungary
CSIMIN, JÓZSEF — Hungary
CZENE, JÁNOSNÉ — Hungary

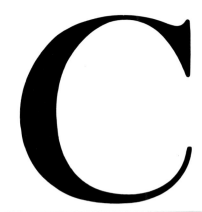

Callins, Charles: Honey Blossom Time

Calvo, Valerico Moral: Buen Retiro Park

CALLINS, CHARLES (1887—?)   Australia

Charles Callins, born in Queensland, worked for many years in printing offices. His retirement marked the beginning of his career as an artist: he did not paint seriously until 1947.

Callins spent a large part of his life sailing and fishing in waters around North Queensland. His paintings reflect this part of his life and are full of nautical memories.

He first exhibited with the Johnstone Gallery in Sydney in 1957. Gallery A in Sydney staged a large retrospective exhibition of Callins' work to celebrate his ninetieth birthday in 1977. *B. McC.*

CALVO, VALERICO MORAL (1904)   Spain

Everything that Calvo has experienced and suffered during his eventful itinerant career has been absorbed into the fanciful gallery of his pictures, his grotesque and lyrical tales. Calvo says: "The village where I was born in 1904 is called Aldezat, in the province of Burgos. I was carpenter in the Basque country, a road-worker and stone-mason in Valencia, a cook in the hotels and street cafés in Seville, a fighter for freedom in the Civil War and a prisoner following it. When I was released I drove a dustcart in the streets of Madrid. As I drove I used to look closely at the houses, the squares, the bridges — and also at the stone figures that the builders placed on the roofs of offices and palaces. I took very careful note of them, they became my silent friends."

Present and past — masters and servants — serfs and peasants at their communal tasks in the fields, Indians with feathered head-dresses such as Columbus and the Conquistadors used to bring back from America. Calvo explains to us what these figures from history or fiction signify and symbolise: "What I am thinking of is the equality of the races, the friendship of all living beings. At that time I had lost everything: freedom, sleep, hope — even fear. That was when the prison gates closed behind us. When the war was lost."

"Was it lost for good?"

Calvo gazes at us doubtfully. Then the rigid lines of his face soften.

"You have painted a picture of the King: Carlos and his family looking down from a palace window at the crowd applauding him on the Plaza Oriente."

"I would like to have a certain amount of fame and recognition."

"Not too much fame — see that you don't become too skilful, Calvo. If you gain everything, there are some things you can lose."

An inner power informs the soul of this painter as he applies his austere colours to the canvas with sensual passion: the expensively overloaded office buildings and banks, the romantic palaces of the Buen Retiro Park, with their mythological and historical figures, seem near enough to grasp, nearby and remote at one and the same time. So, too, the flesh pink of those male and female figures balancing on roofs and domes as they launch themselves with acrobatic daring into the azure infinity of the sky.

As Calvo, full of an inner unease, carries in his pictures, one after the other, my friend attempts to photograph them with all the agility of a tight-rope walker, as though he himself were one of those figures in the paintings. But we need more light. The sun-blinds are drawn up. The floral patterns of the wallpaper glow and mingle with the coloured highlights of Calvo's pictures.

As we depart the painter says to us: "I am self-taught, but not naive. I had no schooling and no teachers. I have learned from myself and from life. It's true my enemies say I'm a fool, in order to hurt me. But I am, and I remain, Valerico Moral Calvo and I paint my own truth." *(See portrait of the artist, p. 192). L. and O. B.-M.*

name of Toby Cameron, which were published in Sydney by Currawong. In 1960 she took up painting again, this time in oils, and studied for two years with Justin O'Brien.

Her painting "Outing on the Murray" with its turn-of-the-century steamboat and tiny animated figures is full of nostalgic charm.

Barbara Cameron is fanatically careful to achieve historical authenticity in her paintings. She has had numerous exhibitions since 1965 and her work may be found in public and private collections in Australia, Great Britain and the USA. *B. McC.*

Calvo, Valerico Moral: Recollection of History

CAMERON, BARBARA   Australia

Barbara Cameron was born in Sanderstead, Surrey, and arrived in Australia in 1934.

She was the youngest of six children and grew up in the midst of an artistic, musical, truly Edwardian family. Her older sisters and brothers and their entertainments — dancing, tennis, musical evenings, opera, the theatre — all these impressions coloured her vivid childhood memories. Both her parents were painters and Barbara showed talent and was encouraged to draw and paint in watercolour from a very early age. By the time she was eighteen she was illustrating professionally for the London press.

Marriage to a business executive, three children and travels in South Africa and Singapore put a halt to her professional career, although she continued to draw and paint to amuse her children. During the war she wrote and illustrated three children's books, under the pen-

CAMPUAN, I NYOMAN (1942)   Indonesia, Bali

I Nyoman Campuan was born in Campuhan-Ubud and started painting in 1970 with his friend and mentor, I Made Pugug. As a result of this association (which continues today) inspiration, enthusiasm and often even subject-matter are shared and a singularly beautiful interpretation of the local Young Artists style has been created.

Although in his work the influence of this involvement is conspicuous (scenes and themes often shared), Campuan has over the years developed his own style and distinctive use of colour. There is a great space and openness in his work, and although his use of colour, like Pugug's, is unusual and does not conform to nature, Campuan has developed a more sophisticated understanding of its use, and of the nuances that are possible.

Although he is considered a successful artist, and there is an almost constant demand for his paintings, Campuan still works daily in a nearby Government Health Clinic, content to reserve his artistic endeavours for his free moments, which are spent as a matter of course with his painting companion, Pugug. *(See portrait of the artist, p. 192). J. F.*

CAO JINYING (1931)   China

Cao Jinying was born in the province of Zhejiang. Her parents were killed during the Japanese occupation, and she was left, a seven-year-old child, to fend for herself. Wandering

Tongzhang, "I noticed some beautifully embroidered bed linen hanging in front of a house. The design, colours and style bore strong local features, but in many ways were different. There was a strong note of individuality, something the woman who did the embroidering had thought up herself. And so I made the acquaintance of Cao Jinying."

"The Whole Land Rejoices," done on a long piece of paper with a red background, shows a multitude of figures engaged in the Chinese game of *jayera*, with dragons and rocking rowing boats. In this painting, the art of embroidery has

C

169

Cameron, Barbara: Outing on the Murray

Campuan, I Nyoman: Ploughing the Rice Fields

Cao Jinying: The Whole Land Rejoices

about, she begged for food and so reached Jin Shan, where she found some relations. After the victory of the Chinese revolution, peasants were assigned to work brigades. Since 1950, when she was 19 years old, she has been tilling the land together with her husband. In her leisure time, she paints on paper, usually pictures of holidays she remembers from her childhood and also of the life of the village she belongs to now. Quite by chance she was discovered in 1977 by Wu Tongzhang, a painting instructor in Jin Shan. This man, an academic painter himself, has helped many peasants to take up the brush after having discovered in them a talent for painting.

"While passing through her village," says Wu

been transposed into the art of painting. The picture is full of life, gaiety and optimism.

"I remember," says Cao Jinying, "the gay holidays full of colour when the poor people were happy and carefree on that one day a year. From coloured paper they made dragons and lanterns." Her first painting was dedicated to the Fifth National Congress of the Party, which was being held at that time. Before she began to paint, she had never seen an artistic picture, except for the portrait of Mao Tse Tung. *(See portrait of the artist, p. 192). N. T.*

CAO XIUWEN (1955)　　　　　　　　　China

Cao Xiuwen hails from the Feng Wei commune. She graduated from secondary school in 1977 and became commander of a youth shock brigade as well as health officer in a peasant brigade. At school, she was fond of drawing and helped illustrate wall newspapers. On joining the brigade, she started painting and was soon a member of the Jin Shan painting group. Most of her subjects concern the life of women in contemporary Chinese society and are frequently autobiographical.

"When I began painting," says Cao Xiuwen,

Cao Xiuwen: Health Officer of the Brigade

"I was quite scared and rigid. I confided in a friend of mine, also a painter. She advised me to imagine I was embroidering and as soon as I did so, painting was easier. All the girls in our part of the country embroider beautifully and I also love it."

The painting "Health Officer of the Brigade" is obviously a self-portrait. Youthful fantasy and dreams of beauty could not be expressed better than they are in this picture. A healthy, cheerful girl, full of optimism, which is what Cao Xiuwen is in real life, stands in the foreground dressed in her best clothes. Usually she wears the green tunic of her brigade. In the background is a mosaic of flowers and a few butterflies. Other paintings by her show girls gathering medical herbs, ever an important occupation in China. Her technique and precision are features of traditional Chinese painters, in her area known for their lacquer painting. *(See portrait of the artist, p. 192). N. T.*

CARABASSA, TERESA　　　　　　Argentina

Teresa Carabassa, born in Buenos Aires, the youngest of nine children, took up ceramics in her youth. One rainy day in 1980, however, when she was in a depressed mood, a woman-painter friend advised her to paint a picture to dispel her gloom. She asked her friend how this was done, and then went right out, bought canvas and oils, and painted her first picture. Soon afterward, the future owners of a restaurant asked her to paint something to decorate their premises, where they were going to specialise in *parillada* (barbecued meat). This was the origin of her first

Carter, Bernard: Waterway

Casimir, Laurent: Cockfight

canvases, which she later developed into a series entitled "Details from the Life of a Cow." In the desire to merge various scenes from her life, she brings the animals of her childhood into the village houses where she lived at that time and thus creates absurd situations which she resolves in true painterly fashion. Her works are distinguished by imagination, wit and a fine sense of detail. *(See portrait of the artist, p. 193). M. T. S.*

CARTER, BERNARD (1920)　　　　Great Britain

Bernard Carter was born in London. Though he had the ability and the will to paint his own kind of "New Realist" pictures, Bernard Carter was for many years a schoolteacher. His most fulfilling career began when he was put in charge of the conservation of pictures at the National Maritime Museum, Greenwich, a post he held until 1977.

The work at Greenwich was specially attractive to him because quite naturally the emphasis in the museum's collection was on ships, the sea and waterways which formed the subject-matter of Carter's own art.

But whatever Greenwich gave him, he already had a profound knowledge of water and boats and was constantly increasing this understanding.

any satisfactory future. Searching for work in 1946, he came to Port-au-Prince, and in 1947, by good fortune, came upon the Centre d'Art, where he started to work as a painter. Three years later he became a member of the newly-formed Foyer des Arts Plastiques and thereafter the "scholarly" atmosphere of the Centre d'Art ceased to interest him. Although, by and large, freedom of expression existed at the Centre, parallel with this liberty there ran a sense of "duty" which in Casimir's case channelled an effervescent talent into hard work.

An all-out enthusiast, Casimir throws

Carabassa, Teresa: Unforgettable Moment

The illustration here shows the serenity of his water pictures: paintings on small wooden panels with a penchant for the subtleties of smooth sepias, cool greens and the blue of a generally unclouded sky. A frequent exhibitor at the Portal Gallery in London, he has also taken part in several RONA shows in the capital and outside Britain. *(See portrait of the artist, p. 193). Sh. W.*

CASIMIR, LAURENT (1928)   **Haiti**

Laurent Casimir was born at Anse-à-Veau and grew up in a peasant family with little hope of

himself heart-and-soul into any undertaking, especially when it is identified with the faceless majority. For him, personality is the character of the crowd and the crowd *is personality*. This is why his favourite subjects for painting are densely-peopled market scenes, carnivals, cockfights, and any location which by its nature acts as a magnet for the multitude. If his hand were not so deft, the brushwork in his paintings could be called crude and random. The best of his pictures are rich in strident streaks of red, orange, black and yellow, as in his "Cockfight," where the bright colours reflect the excited mood of the crowd of spectators. *Sh. W.*

CASTAIN, AIMÉE (1917)   France

Aimée Castain was born in Banon into a family of sharecroppers. Helped by her husband, she pursued as her life's work the only job she ever had the time to learn: shepherding the flocks entrusted to her care. Despite the hard life and, often, great difficulties imposed by her work, Aimée Castain has been able, since 1958, to reconcile her life as a shepherdess with painting. Apart from painting, she has published a collection of anecdotes and reminiscences.

Directly inspired by the Provence of her birth, she proclaims in her paintings her pleasure

CECCARELLI, MARINO (1909)   Italy

Marino Ceccarelli, son of a worker, was born in Spoleto. He started working as soon as he finished elementary school, going through a number of occupations: tailor, postman, barber, fireman and miner. It was as a miner that he met with an accident at work which compelled him to give up this occupation. Now 43 years old, he turned to doll-making for a living. Little by little his talent as a painter came to the fore, and he has never stopped painting since.

The basic features of his work are the simplicity of his vision of his native Umbria, detailed

Cedeño, José Antonio: Baracoa

in describing "her" landscapes: summers in brilliant sunlight, winters with snow enshrouding everything, villages perched in the shape of pyramids or small farmsteads hiding behind trees. Frontal views, pliant perspectives, docile lines, are characteristic of her style. Note must be made of the *Lavandes* (Lavender) series, small oils done most often in very diluted paint and evoking the blues of the fields of lavender around her. "I paint for things to be recognisable. My countryside is so beautiful, I see no reason to deform it," she willingly confides.

Some paintings by Aimée Castain are in the Laval Museum and in the Musée International d'art naif. *(See portrait of the artist, p. 193). Ch. Sch.*

composition and gentle poetic sentiment. Frequent themes are village festivities, processions, snow-covered fields and interiors.

In "Umbrian Landscape," one of the many works he has devoted to his native land, among the noteworthy features are the light illuminating hills and houses, the gaiety of the children at play and the endless perspective of rolling hills, calling forth a feeling of something mysterious and unknown.

After taking part in an exhibition in Rome in 1964 (Palazzo Barberini), Marino C. — as he always signs his name — also displayed his works in exhibitions in France, Sweden, Uruguay, Canada and the USA. *(See portrait of the artist, p. 193). D. M.*

CEDEÑO, JOSÉ ANTONIO (1939) Cuba

José Antonio Cedeño was born in Bayamo, Oriente, Cuba. He moved to Havana, where he studied at the Basic Secondary School, and at the same time received training as a mechanic.

Little or no information is available about his development as a painter.

The themes he chooses are usually figures in landscapes, where the figure is the dominant feature in the composition. Although the problem of perspective and proportion is resolved somewhat exaggeratedly in his work, the result is not unattractive, as he achieves a pleasing overall

Ceccarelli, Marino: Umbrian Landscape

balance through the use of a strong element of design and rich, rather impressionistic colour.

The vibrant colours of the Caribbean, intensified by the eerie light of an approaching storm at dusk, are seen in his painting of the harbour of Baracoa. The one solitary figure, running for shelter, emphasises the emptiness of the streets and water-front, the imminence of the downpour. This absence of human life is, in fact, uncommon in Cedeño's works.

He first participated in an exhibition in 1969, when he was represented in the Second Triennial Exhibition of Naive Painting in Bratislava, Czechoslovakia. Then in 1970 he took part in the group exhibition Salon 70, and again in another joint exhibition of primitive artists at the Havana Gallery in 1971. He was one of eleven Cuban primitive painters who exhibited in 1976 at the Institute of Jamaica in Kingston. *T. R.*

ČERNJAHOVSKIJ, IVAN USSR
CHERNYAKHOVSKY, IVAN

Ivan Chernyakhovsky was born in the late 19th century, and died between the 1960s and 70s somewhere in the Ukraine. Hardly anything is known about him. His works remained in the hands of a few collectors who "discovered" him in Kiev more than twenty years ago. In his youth he had been an *uhlan* in the tsarist army. Later in Kiev he had worked in a tramcar yard, where he painted cars and their numbers. Apparently his earliest paintings date from this time. His work is artless, totally unskilled, completely devoid of psychological probing or graphic representation.

Chernyakhovsky, Ivan: Chernyakhovsky, the Uhlan

Castain, Aimée: View of Brousses

His patches of colour are well demarcated, and all the figures depicted are as alike as two peas and well outlined. His self-portrait "Chernyakhovsky, the Uhlan" is reminiscent of the *lubok* broadsheet manner of late 19th-century urban folklore. Similar to some degree is his "Sorochinsky Fair," which reaffirms the link between his work and the urban folklore traditions of the late 19th century, survivals of which are still in evidence. This art, which found an outlet at fairs, markets, inns and sideshows, produced the greatest number of turn-of-the-century naive artists. *(See portrait of the artist, p. 192). N. Sh.*

Chernobrova, Susanna: House with Bush

ČERNOBROVA, SUZANNA (1945) USSR
CHERNOBROVA, SUSANNA

Susanna Chernobrova was born in Latvia. Her parents are office employees. She graduated in theoretical physics from Riga University in 1969. Her first attempts at painting date from 1968, but after enrolling in ZNUI, the Extra-Mural People's University of Art in Moscow, she took up painting seriously. She left ZNUI after two years of study to continue painting on her own. She draws largely on her imagination for subject-matter, preferring lyrical themes. Though she has some technical skill, she is really a naive artist in that her fantasies, though deriving partly from the objective environment, are more in the nature of a fairy-tale world, with falling snowflakes, flickering candles and floating toy balloons. Her very imagery belongs to a world of invention and fantasy. Her efforts seem to remind us of the sadness we feel at the changes and vicissitudes of life, its instability within the context of the canons that history has ordained. Her work thus recalls that of the noted Soviet illustrator Tyshler and even Chagall. She constrains her *Weltanschauung* to the form selected, which is again a palpable manifestation of her naive attitude, her penchant for a simplification of professional artifices, her desire to express what is her very own.

She has been represented at shows in Latvia and Moscow and has had two one-woman shows:

in 1977 at the editorial offices of the Moscow-based art magazine *Dekorativnoye Iskusstvo SSR*, and in 1978 in Riga. *(See portrait of the artist, p. 192). N. Sh.*

CHABAUTY, MALVINA (1901) France

Malvina Chabauty was born at Ferrière, a village near the coast in Vendée. She left her birth-place early to settle in the village where her husband worked as a bricklayer. For a long time she worked in watercolours, but was never quite satisfied with the results. She was eventually to

Chabauty, Malvina: Landscape

destroy everything from this period. In 1962 she met an artist who gave her all the equipment she needed for painting, and little by little she learned to use this. After 1965, she dedicated most of her time to her art, but since 1975, her work has slowed down because of ill health.

"I began to paint because of a need to express what I felt," Malvina Chabauty says. Her hand is inclined to the large and gesticulatory, and she constructs her canvases in an empirical fashion, eliminating unfilled space as far as possible. Her imagery flows, hurries, pushes about from canvas to canvas, but lyrically and with delicacy, in her effort to harmonise her colours, and she shows little concern for her drawing. She has exhibited in France. *(See portrait of the artist, p. 192). Ch. Sch.*

CHAVANNES, ETIENNE (1939) Haiti

Etienne Chavannes was born in Cap Haitien. As a young painter fresh from the patronage of Philomé Obin, Chavannes displayed an originality of style and equally an originality of subject-matter in his pictures. Experience in Cap Haitien and Philomé Obin's encouragement combined to instil in him a deep and serious awareness of mankind and of the way people applied themselves to hard work and a chosen style of life.

After he parted from Philomé Obin, he dedicated his art to recording life in his home town and its surroundings, peopled with ordinary folk each of whom still preserved hints of his or her individuality.

His manner of painting has the facility of a sketch, but a sketch amplified by colour and movement. He is not concerned to any great extent with depth and perspective, preferring to add character to his pictures with an underlying warmth and humour.

His cheerful market scene (shown here) is throbbing with life even though the individual figures, human and animal, seem stiff, almost frozen in their movements, as if caught by a camera.

Since 1971, Chavannes has been with the Centre d'Art. *Sh. W.*

Chavarria, Julia: Forest

Checchi, Giuseppe de: Jungle

CHAVARRIA, JULIA   Nicaragua

Julia Chavarria is a young peasant woman from Solentiname, where she was born, grew up and still lives. She has painted many canvases outstanding for their bright colours and radiant optimism.

In her painting "Forest" (shown here), the luxuriant, brilliantly coloured vegetation has a dynamic, flamelike quality, and seems to be closing in on the grazing deer. *E. C.*

CHECCHI, GIUSEPPE DE (1911)   Switzerland

Giuseppe de Checchi was born in Argentina, and is a florist by occupation. His painting is refined and quite bright in colour. For the most part he paints exotic flowers in a tropical forest setting. He is expressly a colourist and his beautiful flowers, with their imaginary backdrops are carefully executed. In this world of inaccessible forests he places red parrots, rosy and white birds, representing life in tropical regions as a jungle where there are no human beings. He won the Grand Prix at the Lugano Naive Art Biennial. *(See portrait of the artist, p. 192). G. K.*

Chavannes, Etienne: Market Day

CHEN MUJUN (1952)   China

Chen Mujun was born in the Xing Ta commune and has had five years of grade school. As a boy, he was fond of drawing. Later, in the brigade in which he worked, he was given an opportunity to paint. At that time in China it was thought that if every brigade had peasant painters, the level of mass culture would be raised in the process. A paper picture displayed by Chen Mujun took the fancy of his fellow peasants. The motif was one well known to all of them from days long gone by — a flock of ducks, such as may be seen in many Chinese villages, where they are a component part of the landscape. In this painting, which Chen has called simply "Ducks," a flock is caught in flight and portrayed in a rich scale of colours and in a harmonious composition. In the background is a building in deep perspective and against its façade is a row of bunches of red cherries. The atmosphere is that of a lush Chinese spring. Chen Mujun says: "I like doing pictures of ducks because, like every Chinese, I know well their lives, appearance, movements and colours. For us, ducks are a gift of nature, because without them the Chinese could not survive."

Chen Mujun had produced about 20 pictures by 1983. His spare time is spent in painting on paper, which is the only material he can obtain. He is a member of the Jin Shan painters' circle. *(See portrait of the artist, p. 193). N. T.*   →

CHERECHEȘ, ALEXANDRU (1944)   Romania

Alexandru Chere[s]hes, born in the village of Arunkuca, in the district of Cluj, has been painting since childhood. Later, after he had taken a job as a worker in an enterprise in Cluj-Napoca (to which he moved), he was attracted to painting on glass, a traditional art form in many towns in Transylvania, the home of the famous icons on glass. The town of Nikula is among the most famous of these and still enjoys its deserved reputation.

Living in Napoca, Alexandru Chereșeș first studied the compositional problems of icons on

Drawing his themes from the life of the village ("Welcoming the Bride") and from village traditions or events ("The Return of the Soldier"), the artist gives them increasingly free treatment. In his painting, Chereșeș recomposed and rediscovered artistic values already realised in traditional painting on glass and in doing so came to comprehend the scope of his artistic ability.

His "Rainmaker at Aruncuta" (shown here) recalls Orthodox icons, with its miniature scenes flanking the main picture and a framelike border above and below.

Preoccupations such as these were common

Chen Mujun: Ducks

glass, calling for a reconciliation of theme and substance through a lapidary but expressive synthesis of forms. While frequently retaining motifs already in widespread use, Chereșeș enriches them with new and personal artistic messages, introducing into his works original elements with the help of suggestive drawing, a rhythmical use of tones and colours over large areas, and a strict selection of details.

among the young naive painters of Cluj-Napoca. These young artists, together with Alexandru Chereșeș, became the members of a group of painters on glass (called the "Group of Six") who were soon rewarded with fame at home and abroad.

The "Group of Six," originally consisting of Mircea Corpodean, Petre Ghețu, Vasile Macavei, Ilie Roman and Alexandru and Mihai Chereșeș, later admitted another two members: Ilarion Mureșan, from Nicula, the venerable centre of iconographers, and Maria, sister of the Chereches brothers.

In spite of essential stylistic similarities, each of the painters of the Chereches family has constructed his or her own independent world. All of them show a mature handling of artistic elements, but each of them is attracted to different thematic aspects. They also demonstrate diversity in solving the problem of expression.

The group of artists from Cluj-Napoca is

small pictures of a child or children bearing enormous fruit or vegetables are a horrible example of this). However, his prestige is such that the double-sided cover of the catalogue of the big "Kunst aus Haiti" exhibition held in Berlin in 1979 bears a reproduction in colour of one of his works, as does the cover of Sheldon Williams's book "Voodoo and the Art of Haiti."

Chery, in fact, is one of those Haitian artists who often produces good work, but sometimes succumbs to the temptation to paint "pot-boîtes." (See "Naive Art in Haiti," later in this book, for an account of the art/finance syndrome in Haiti).

Chereches, Alexandru: A Rainmaker at Aruncuta

continuing a famous artistic craft — that of painting on glass — while enhancing it with some new definitions and modernising it as an artistic genre.

Other painters (Timotei Traian Tohăneanu, Vasile Frunzete, Traian Ciucurescu and others), while sustaining the tradition, interpret it in a new way and break new ground, sometimes with outstanding results.

(See portrait of the artist, p. 193). M. Il.

CHERY, JACQUES-RICHARD (1929)   Haiti

Jacques-Richard Chery was born in Cap Haitien. Since the early 1960s he has lived and worked in Port-au-Prince.

His best works are very good indeed but, like many of his countrymen, in his pursuit of the American dollar he sometimes enters an area of painting not far removed from "airport art" (the

After taking many jobs, including that of a barber, and later working as a watchman in the Arbonite Valley, because he was still a young man in 1951 he joined the Centre d'Art of Cap Haitien on Philomé Obin's recommendation, but stayed in it for only a year. He then left for Port-au-Prince, where he was taken into the working studio (more like an art factory) of Issa El Saieh, who paid him a regular wage in return for the regular production of a number of paintings a month.

Probably his most famous paintings all derive their subject-matter from his home near Cap Haitien, and he is particularly well known for the many versions he has painted of the Emperor Christophe's great fortress of "La Citadelle Forestière": its construction, inauguration and sinister presence. But the Citadelles are not the only subjects to be found in his best pictures — there are also beautiful Christmas and Carnival scenes in their local settings. And he did not confine his skill to crowded scenes. Careful and intimate portraits of people he once knew when he lived in the north showed another aspect of his talents.

All these paintings were rendered in a clear illustrative manner, with a sharp and brightly tinted palette (in strict contrast to his earliest work, which was all in watercolour). These glimpses of Haiti's historical past in the north and the sociological insight he exhibited in his depiction of friends and neighbours, however, all but vanished when he joined Issa in Port-au-Prince. *Sh. W.*

CHESHER, A. W. (1895—1972)   Great Britain

This artist spent all his life in Bedfordshire. Chesher was a man of the soil, his whole existence bound up with farming until his mid-forties, when he suffered two accidents in quick succession, first losing the use of one eye, and later getting his arm caught in a threshing machine.

In the face of these disasters, he needed something else to occupy his time and — quite by chance — he hit upon painting. Chesher was also fascinated with steam-powered machinery and its role in efficient agriculture. In his way, he was

Chesher, A. W.: Steam Traction Engine

Chery, Jacques-Richard: The Inauguration of La Citadelle

Chick, Lorna: South Wangaratta

an expert in this field, not only because of the accuracy that he could bring to painting complicated mechanisms, but also because of his memory of the old machines. In this manner he was able to make pictures of machines that had long gone out of service or even — except in his precise memory — been completely forgotten.

And so his pictures have not only artistic, but documentary value.

Chesher painted until a year before he died. The Portal Gallery, London, gave him many important special exhibitions, including a big retrospective after his death. *Sh. W.*

CHICK, LORNA (1922)   Australia

Lorna Chick was born at Wangandary near Wangaratta in North Eastern Victoria. She went to school in Wangaratta and since her marriage has lived on a farm at Wangandary.

Her painting began about 1964, when she was taking her two sons to evening classes in art at the Wangaratta Technical School. Her first success came with the 1967 Fairley Art Award, when her work was placed among the first five.

Her "South Wangaratta" (seen here) presents a bird's eye view of orchards and village, which resemble a carpet spread out in the midst of a vast landscape, an oasis of civilisation in the empty wilds.

Lorna Chick's work is included in the Shepparton Art Gallery collection, the Wangaratta Council collection, and in many private collections in Australia, New Zealand, America and London. Her most ambitious work is a ten by four foot canvas acquired by the National Gallery of Australia in Canberra in 1976. *(See portrait of the artist, p. 193). B. McC.*

CHURCH, HENRY (1836—1908)   USA

Henry Church's work might have languished unknown except for the chance discovery and research by the photographer, author and collector, Sam Rosenberg. Rosenberg had gone to Ohio to see an "Indian" sculpture that turned out to have been done by Henry Church, who had died in 1908. From Church's daughter, 70 years old when Rosenberg interviewed her many years ago, he learned the following:

Henry Church was born in 1836 in Chagrin Falls, Ohio, the son of a blacksmith who, along with his wife, was an abolitionist and a spiritualist. Too sickly to attend school, Henry was taught by his mother and allowed to wander in the wilderness at his pleasure. His father put him to work in the smithy when he was thirteen, and when young Henry tried to draw on the whitewashed walls with charcoal, his father gave him a beating. Because of his religious beliefs, he purchased a non-combatant status during the Civil War, which he commemorated by painting life-sized portraits of Lincoln and General Sherman.

After his father died in 1878, Church gave up the smithy to devote himself, until he died, to painting, sculpting and hunting, setting up a studio and art gallery above his shop. He did several carvings on nearby rocks, chiselled out his own tombstone — an angry lion with green glass eyes — and filled his front yard with a clutter of strange carvings.

His many skills and varied interests are symbolically represented in his "Self-Portrait with Five Muses." The oval shape is common in late 19th century portraits, but the picture is far from conventional. Church presents himself surrounded by his muses, male and female, hovering ethereally around his head amidst swirling mists. The feminine muse of Painting is adding the final touch to an eye, while the two muses of Music are charming his ear, playing instruments identical to the ones he himself

Church, Henry: Self-Portrait with Five Muses

made. The two male muses represent Sculpture and Smithing, the latter craft elevated to the level of an art by Church in acknowledgement of his debt to this profession in preparing him to become a sculptor.

The portrait itself is a fine study of a forceful personality, stern but lacking in humour. His impressive, partriarchal appearance is accentuated by the flowing beard and cap. The flowers and finely executed fruit in the foreground that fill out the composition are suggestive of well-being and prosperity.

Many of his paintings were destroyed by his daughter when she had to move into a house with limited storage space. Fearful that no one would care for them as she had, she destroyed them rather than let them be vandalised. Church married in 1895 and had two children.

Rosenberg's research indicated that many of Church's ideas for his paintings came from advertising posters and trade cards. *J. W.*

CHVÁLA, JOSEF (1906)   Czechoslovakia

Josef Chvála was born in Prachatice, the fifth child of nine in the family of a local night watchman. He wanted to be a confectioner, then a tailor, or locksmith, but started his occupational training as a bricklayer's apprentice. After working in a factory for some time, he took a chance and left for Belgium, where he checked tickets in a circus. After his return home he worked as a railway man and mason and later as a lumberman.

In 1936 Josef Chvála carved his first relief, representing St. Jacob's church in Prachatice.

of Karlstein with knights, of Svatá Hora, and even of St. Stephen's cathedral in Vienna. Religious themes, mainly his dreamy visions, represent another sphere of his interest. Most often he carved various likenesses of the Virgin Mary, while St. Florian and St. John Nepomuk were his favourite saints. Besides sculptures of saints he also carved Master John Hus.

Chvála's carvings, abounding in charm and poetry, were exhibited in 1966 in Prague, in 1968 in the House of Art in Brno, and in the South Moravian Museum in Znojmo. *(See portrait of the artist, p. 193).* S. T.

Chvála, Josef: St. Florian

Cloes, Nicolas: Vase with Flowers

However, he was able to devote himself fully to carving only when he was on the verge of old age. He has always been like a square peg in a round hole — as a child he was unable to cope with other children and as an adult never managed to make close contacts with people. Lonely, both in his life and thoughts, he found joy and happiness in wood carving, his only hobby and sole means of expression. His works were inspired by the history of South Bohemia, and his native Prachatice in particular. Over and over again he returns to the motif of Prachatice, representing the town as it was centuries ago, and on through the periods of its sieges and eras of prosperity. Apart from this, he has endeavoured to present various scenes in his reliefs — for instance, one based on a Bible story in which the Israelites delivered gold, precious vessels and silver rods to the Assyrians, with ancient Jerusalem in the background. He liked to carve motifs of the Old Town Square in Prague, and made reliefs of the castle

CLOES, NICOLAS (1889—1976)   Belgium

Nicolas Cloes was born in Othée and died in Liége. While still a schoolboy, he was fond of drawing. When his father died in 1897, Cloes, not yet ten, became the breadwinner of the family. After learning the trade of locksmith, he went to work first in the iron works in Liège and later on the Belgian railways, but was left without employment during the First World War. He became a singer and organist in the church in his home town, and subsequently in Stembert. In 1920 he married. After taking part in amateur singing and acting groups, he almost chose acting for his life's work. Under the influence of his brother-in-law, he began to paint in his spare time. But it was much later, in 1940, that, finding a great deal of free time on his hands as a result of the Second World War, he turned completely to painting. The painter Vetcour gave him the necessary technical instruction, while endeavouring not to influence his individual inspiration. Cloes attracted the attention of literary and artistic circles in Verviers, and this encouraged him, but he did not decide to exhibit until 1956.

After his early works he developed decisively: gradually he mastered his "trade," acquiring a sense of rhythm and widening the scale of his themes. Cloes is above all a colourist; he creates with colour on the basis of a rough sketch. His exciting but gentle landscapes are inhabited by anachronistic personalities. Beginning in 1940, he painted bouquets of flowers (originally with a monochromatic background) in detail, obviously inspired by real flowers. But he soon started producing strange, totally imaginary flora, which were particularly liked by the Surrealists, who paid him a great deal of attention.

"I work from my imagination," stated Cloes in an interview with Georges Schmits, who devoted an important monograph to him. "For instance, I have never been in the Congo, but sometimes a person is tempted to paint something he has never seen. The good Lord has made flowers, but I, too, can make some up out of my imagination."

Apart from his show in Verviers, he exhibited at a large exhibition of naive art in 1958 in Knokke-le-Zoute, and then in Brussels, Bratislava and Zagreb. *(See portrait of the artist, p. 192). J. C.*

COE, CLARK (1847—1919)　　　　　　**USA**
Considering that Clark Coe's "Killingworth Images" were, almost from their inception at the turn of the century, for many years a well-known tourist attraction in Connecticut, it is surprising that so little is known about their creator. However, he must certainly have been a compassionate man, endowed with that delightful if sardonic sense of humour typical of many a rural naive American artist.

There are differing versions of the *raison d'être* of the Killingworth figures, but according to a letter from a member of the Killingworth Historical Society, the facts are these. Clark Coe was born in Madison, Connecticut, married Miss Harriet Hull of Killingworth, and bought a farm there. "They had two children," the letter went on, "and their daughter Minnie died, so that the grandparents took care of her children. For their entertainment, Mr. Coe dammed the brook with staves and built the images."

The images were a group of "strange wooden figures," some almost life-size, others doll-size, made of barrel staves, tree stumps, driftwood, fence slats, and other oddments, and were dressed in cast-off clothing. Many of them had painted faces, and they were animated. As the water moved the water wheel, a bandmaster swung his baton at his busy wooden musicians, a mother endlessly rocked a baby in a cradle, a boy was spanked across his mother's knee. All day and all night, except during dry spells, a girl rode a pig, two children moved their swing, and twenty-two dolls rode in a Ferris wheel.

For many years, until he died on 26 October 1919, Mr. Coe left a box nearby for contributions to replace the clothes his figures wore. *J. W.*

COELHO,　　　　　　　　　　　**Portugal**
JOSÉ ISABELINO MARTINS
Childlike originality is not confined to those painters who come from the ranks of the people: there is some degree of it in the soul of every artist of any significance.

Coelho, one of the most imaginative naive painters of our time, was trained as an accountant and, as a principal officer in the accounts department of Porto University, is employed in a distinctly middle-class bureaucratic environment. It may well have been this that prompted him to break away and open up

Coe, Clark: Girl on a Pig

pathways of discovery in the realms of art. It was in 1966 that he began to compose the astonishing pictures that place him somewhere between Henry Rousseau's jungle paintings and the "Pleasure Garden" of Hieronymus Bosch. Coelho's world is one of *"Sueonos."* Dreams and nightmares, mysteriously terrifying or charming themes, fascinate the beholder. "The Consumers" shows a group of people on the verge of a flowery meadow; they are celebrating and enduring ecstatic scenes of temptation, pleasure and love between the walls of a narrow gorge. When they have tasted its delights some of those involved seek to escape from this paradise of pleasures. Half-clad or naked creatures, exhausted by the demonic passion of their dance, are trying in vain to scale rocky walls that divide them from the everyday world.

"Drugs" shows a meeting of addicts in the depths of a great shadowy forest. A man with long flowing hair and beard is showing his followers and disciples the fruits of the drug. All those sitting round him have long pipes resembling the *narghile*, the Oriental smoking-pipe. Four men and women clad in burgundy red and pale violet are clasped together in a narcotic stupor. On the right of the picture is a large shining white bed on which a naked couple are stretched out in a trance. A mysterious plant and a hypodermic needle on a small round table seem to suggest hashish or some other drug.

The left-hand side of the picture is dominated by the long, sinuous shape of the serpent of sin that has risen from the underworld. Round the snake a number of monkeys are busily filtering its venom into the world through a

the branches of the pine-trees. With their rainbow plumage they throng the grass, which is carpeted with the little flowers of Saint Francis of Assisi. This is the spirit of our time, the awakening realisation of man's need to conduct a loving dialogue with Nature and her creatures. The spirit of primitive Christianity as well as the bitter awareness of our atomic age have set their mark on this picture of the love we owe the creatures around us. Coelho finds the proper aesthetic form for each of his themes with instinctive sureness. His composition, the modelling of his figures, his feeling for space are

Coelho, J. I. M.: The Liberator of Birds

Bosch-like funnel. The terrestrial globe is transparent and we can just make out shell-pink human forms in erotic postures. The company assembled under the dense foliage of the forest is both seductive and ominous. The subdued earthy hues — dark brown, leaf-green, ochre with occasional touches of red — have an emotional significance and reflect a mood of fear and ecstasy. The picture is, in the last resort, enigmatic and permits a number of interpretations. The obsessive ideas of man's instinctive nature are set against man's poetic revolt against the bondage of all creatures.

In "The Liberator of Birds," a young man is kneeling beneath the dense tree-tops of a dreamlike forest, opening a tall bird-cage. He has already released a great many different kinds of birds that have taken refuge in the foliage and on

Coelho, J. I. M.: The Gluttons

independent of any academic tradition; they are full of naive poetic power. *O. B.-M.*

COHEN, GABRIEL (1933)   **Israel**

Gabriel Cohen was born in Paris to Sephardi-Jerusalemite parents. His father was a tailor, who also studied the Cabbala, and his mother was a seamstress. Having lived through the German occupation of Paris, the family moved to Israel in 1949. Gabriel, the sixth of eleven children, earned some money from odd jobs. He began to paint at the age of forty, while

Cohen, Gabriel: 92 Days around the World (part I)

working as a diamond-cutter and a night-watchman. At first he painted on cardboard, then turned to sack, sheets, plywood, canvas and lately to painting behind glass. He occasionally paints very large paintings: "92 Days around the

World" (1976) is made of three parts and measures 176 × 300 cm. A dedicated traveller, he paints panoramas of different countries and continents, mixing reality and dreams. Two landmarks always appear — the Eiffel Tower and the Dome of the Rock.

East and west, light and shade, playfulness and violence, historic grandeur and humorous detail alternate in his work. He covers an astounding range of subjects, including portraits, landscapes and fantastic scenes of religious or erotic significance. *(See portrait of the artist, p. 192). R. D.*

Cohen, Gabriel: Escape from Hell

COLAÇO, MADELEINE (1907)   **Brazil**

Madeleine Colaço was born in Tangiers, Morocco, and studied history at the Kasbah Palace School there. She then left for Portugal, where she first encountered and began to take an interest in tapestry, and where she married the famous Portuguese writer, Toma Tibeiro Colaço. Because they could not abide the Salazar regime, they emigrated to Brazil in 1940.

A keen naturalist, she is most at home when she is able to take trips to Manaus and Belém on her way to the Amazonian hinterland.

Her first experiments in tapestry, which led to her invention of a special technique now known as the "Brazilian stitch," took place in Rio de Janeiro, and here, at the Galeria Copacabana, she was awarded the first prize for her woven pictures in 1955. Her enthusiasm for this art form led to her founding not far from Rio a special village given over to the craft of weaving (Adela Artesana do Espriado).

Not surprisingly, in view of her strong interest in exotic flora and fauna, Madeleine Colaço has gained a reputation for tapestries filled with motifs based upon her research as a naturalist, but she is also well known for her renderings of Brazilian people from remote areas and for her colourful versions of the houses in which she lives.

A self-taught artist, she has become a supreme mistress of the various techniques and stitches used in tapestry, including her own *ponto Brasileiro* and the Portuguese *arraiolo* stitch. *(See portrait of the artist, p. 193). Sh. W.*   →

COLE, CHARLES FREDERIC (1875—1959)   Australia

Charles Frederic Cole was born of Kentish immigrant parents. He worked as a chief orchard inspector for the Victorian Department of Agriculture and the King Cole Apple was named after his family by him.

He wrote books on the propagation of fruit and garden trees, especially the walnut and hybridised camellias. He illustrated his own books and it is his experience in this field which accounts for his intricate and life-like flower paintings. It was his habit to measure each of his

CONVEY, TONY (1946)   Australia

Tony Convey was born in Melbourne, Victoria. He has worked as a musician, customs officer, diver, farm worker, cheese maker, on the railways and more recently as a prospector for a mineral company in the alps near Benambra. He began painting in Canberra in 1972 and published a book about mining folklore. He has won a number of art prizes, among them the 1974 Canberra Religious Art Award, the 1977 City of Wangaratta Art Award, and the 1978 St. James Award. His work may be found in numerous private collections throughout Australia. *B. McC.*

Colaço, Madeleine: Candomblé Bay

Cole, Charles Frederic: Winton Swamp

Cook, Beryl: Chips

flower subjects with a ruler in order to get a precise image.

As an artist he was untaught. His subjects were often imaginary and were inspired by the stories he heard from people while travelling around Victoria in his capacity of orchard inspector.

He was also a keen bird watcher, published articles in *Emu*, the magazine of the Royal Australian Ornithologists Union, and became well known for his discovery that the white and black backed magpie and its slightly different cousin were one and the same species.

In his paintings he frequently used metallic colours, which he obtained by grinding bronze and copper and mixing the fine metallic grains or dust with his normal painting medium. *B. McC.*

COOK, BERYL (1927)   Great Britain

Beryl Cook was born in Reading. A self-taught artist, she did not produce her first picture until she was 37 years of age — and even then it was a flash in the pan; after one picture she did not paint again until several years later.

At this stage, the Cooks were trying to live in Rhodesia with very little money. Then, to celebrate some special day (it is uncertain whether it was Christmas or Beryl Cook's birthday), her family got together and bought her a child's box of paints. With this incentive she produced a painting of an Indian lady, naked to the waist and distinguished by her large pendulous breasts. With a sense of humour which she shares, the family nicknamed this portrait "The Hangover." She did no more painting until her husband got a job in Britain and she and the family settled down in Plymouth. Then she became inspired to start again. The decision was entirely practical. The white walls of her new home, which she wanted to turn into a seaside boarding house, were bare, but decoration would be costly. To resolve this problem she started to

course that was to take her through exhibitions in the West Country (in Bristol and Plymouth), to the Portal Gallery, her exclusive agent in London, who now organise regular showings of her work.

Since 1977 she has become known to the public not only because of her exhibitions but also on television, in the press and through two books — "The Works" and "Private View" (Published by John Murray, London) — in both of which coloured reproductions of her paintings are accompanied by her own text. *(See portrait of the artist, p. 192). Sh. W.*

Convey, Tony: Tallandoon Tin Mine

paint pictures on wooden boards that she could nail up wherever she pleased. It was at this juncture that the strength of her innate talent for colour, composition and comedy began to make itself felt. Any doubts that guests might not like the "pictures" were quickly dispelled. Here was a natural artist, carefree to the point of shocking in her choice of subject, but at the same time equally plangent in her approach to bathos, bawdy or beauty.

Such earthy humour had not been seen in British art for at least a couple of centuries.

Today she no longer runs the guest house: her meteoric trail of success has brought with it a comfortable income. When, after filling the house with pictures, she ventured to let an antique shop show some in the window, this launched her on a

COOPER, GLADYS (1889—?) Great Britain

Gladys Cooper was born in Liverpool, and died in Preston, Lancashire. She is an artist who, in a subtle way, fills her paintings with an ambience of "mystery" (even in the example shown here — her naive version of "A Cricket Match" — there is an atmosphere of foreboding). She did not paint her first picture until she was 52 years old, and then only because she had attended a local lecture on the subject of "starting to paint."

When she approached the Wigan artist who had given the lecture he adjured her to get on with the business of picture-making but never to take lessons.

All Gladys Cooper's paintings have a doom-laden flavour, however innocent their style and subject. But this side of her nature did not extend into the other side of her life. She was well-known locally as a dispenser of homeopathic medicine and had a reputation for casting careful and often accurate horoscopes.

In the picture shown below, a violent wind seems to be bending the branches of the trees, but the children play on in the strangely deserted park.

She has taken part in many exhibitions in London, Lancaster, Manchester, several RO-NA exhibitions and many other exhibitions in northern England. *(See portrait of the artist, p. 193). Sh. W.*

Cooper, Gladys: A Cricket Match

COULON, BERTHE (1897—1979)   **Belgium**

Berthe Coulon was born in Brussels. After studying music and literature, she taught music and the history of art. It was only in her 70th year that she suddenly discovered in herself a desire to paint, which changed her life and occupied her entirely, while at the same time rejuvenating her.

A feeling for colour and movement, and a talent for doing crowd scenes, are characteristics of her art which has been highly praised by Anatole Jakovsky and Frederic Altman, who point out that she introduced something new into naive art. What message did Berthe Coulon have in mind when she said: "I have succeeded in drawing from within myself the elements of a real personality." The isolation of the human being at the end of this century is paradoxically expressed by her in motley crowds, successfully depicted in lively motion, where each person is only an anonymous number. Actually, a tragic feeling emerges from the ostensible gaiety which animates the closed ranks, and a careful look soon reveals that everyone is disputing the place held by another. The case of this teacher of art history is a unique one: her entire life was spent in studying the successive stages of contemporary art, but in the autumn of her life she decided to express herself in a manner which lay quite outside the boundaries of all those tendencies and styles — in a painter's tongue as simple as a child's soul.

Berthe Coulon was a keen spectator of foot-ball matches and bicycle races, where huge masses of people came together. In one of her works, her aim was to produce a portrait of the cycling champion Eddy Merckx. She exhibited a number of times in France, Knokke-Le-Zoute, Milan and Switzerland. *(See portrait of the artist, p. 193). J. C.*

COYLE, CARLOS CORTES (1871—1962)   **USA**

The striking works of Carlos Cortes Coyle are not well-known and indeed might have been forgotten altogether had he not sent some of

Coulon, Berthe: The Crowd

them to Berea College in Kentucky in 1942. Even then, according to a newspaper story, the crates containing them lay unopened for several years until a curious art professor, Thomas Fern, decided to investigate them. Fern found 47 paintings and a diary. The diary tells little of Coyle's life except that he was born in December 1871 in Bear Wallow (now Dreyfus) near Berea, and that as a young man he went west to Canada, Seattle, and San Francisco. He mentions a Hattie Mae Bracher, "mother of three children for me." However, most of the journal consists of a meticulous record of the size, cost, content and dates of commencement and completion of all his paintings, with comments on current events, history and life in general. He appears to have been an ardent lover of art, for in a letter to Fern he speaks of having seen Gainsborough's "Blue Boy" and "Italy's famous collection."

The paintings sent to Berea, done between the ages of 59 and 75, are on themes common in his writing: nostalgia for the past, Victorian idealisation of womanhood (especially mothers), interest in American history and worship of its heroes, and a love of nature. He seems not, however, to have had much faith in women as individuals. One of his most striking paintings (which may perhaps have had an autobiographical incentive) is a bitter allegory about Eve as the snake of divorce, ruining the man financially.

He lived and painted for twenty more years, but died impoverished and almost blind in Leesburg, Florida. He had been planning a 6 × 8 foot work on a biblical theme; after his death the large canvas was found in his room, empty. *J. W.*

Coyle, Carlos Cortes: Calling All Gods

CREPIN, BENOIT (1900)   France

Benoit Crepin was born in Hénin-Liétard, the descendant of an old northern family. He left school very young to go to work in the family furniture business. Later, he set up on his own as an interior decorator, while painting constantly for his own pleasure. At the age of sixteen, he was already making drawings of everyday life. He organised his first exhibition in 1942, and in 1943 founded the Art Society in his home town. His reputation as an artist grew and, since 1968, he has participated in most of the art shows in his region. He travelled to Martinique in 1977, returning home with an important group of canvases. Since that trip, poor health has forced him little by little to give up painting.

Sincerity and concern for authentic detail are the fundamentals of Benoit Crepin's art. He has produced canvases in many categories: landscapes, still-lifes, scenes from daily life — always with the same concern for true-to-life reconstructions. When it serves his purpose he does not hesitate to introduce techniques which are foreign to painting.

Benoit Crepin is a regular participant in the salons and exhibitions at Hénin-Liétard and Hénin Beaumont as well as in exhibitions elsewhere in France. *(See portrait of the artist, p. 192). Ch. Sch.*

CROCIANI, EMILE (1902—1979)   France

Emile Crociani was born in Santa Sofia, Italy. His parents were farmers, and he himself began to work in the fields at a very early age.

Crepin, Benoit: St. Joseph's Church, Martinique

He never attended school, but his mother undertook to teach him to read and write. His desire to become a portrait painter dates from this period. In 1924, he moved to France and two years later settled in Nice. He found work at the local gas works but never gave up his drawing. From 1950, painting assumed a growing importance in his life, due in large part to the encouragement of his son. He started exhibiting in 1956. He died in Antibes at the age of 77.

Rounded lines in constant quest, pearly colours and uphill perspectives are the main features of paintings by Emile Crociani. There is little variety in his range of colour; he is content to limit his palette to the few, essential colours necessary to evoke the sea, small villages and ports of the South of France.

Crociani had over ten one-man shows and participated in group exhibitions in the museums of Linz, Graz and Vienna. *(See portrait of the artist, p. 193). Ch. Sch.*   →

CROIX, FRANÇOISE DE LA (1931)   Belgium

Françoise de la Croix is the mother of four children. She lives in Laethem-Saint-Martin, until recently the centre of Flemish expressionists, although she is not one of them.

Her family on her mother's side was artistically inclined, so that her childhood and girlhood were spent in a dreamy atmosphere and in the adoration of beauty. Drawing attracted her early in life.

She studied decorative arts for four years in Antwerp but has been painting in oil as a self-

Croix, Françoise de la: Ghent Esplanade

taught artist since 1972. She has exhibited regularly, both in one-woman shows and with groups.

Victor Lecossois, whose work delighted her and with whom she maintained steady contact, (see page 384), drew the attention of Mimy de Néeff, Director of the Museum of Spontaneous and Naive Art, to her work and the latter agreed to exhibit it.

Françoise de la Croix paints in oils on glass or panel. Memories of childhood, family scenes, and local folk customs are the main sources of her pleasantly fresh inspiration. In interiors, she frames an object in the foreground, in a two-dimensional space, as is the case in folk painting. All of this has a common denominator — satisfaction in work: "I imagine the décor, whose point of departure is real, then, as in a puppet play, I give the décor life with my figures, with great love." She has exhibited mostly in Brussels. *(See portrait of the artist, p. 193). J. C.*

CROSSLEY, RALPH (1884—1966)   **Great Britain**

Ralph Crossley was born in Crigglestone, Yorkshire, settled in Grimsargle, near Preston, Lancashire, in 1910, and lived there until his death.

Crociani, Emile: Church in Vallauris

Crossley came from a large family of ten children. He himself was happily married until his wife's untimely death in 1936.

He was a successful bricklayer by trade, but the more than adequate wages his work secured him did not prevent him from pleading poverty and asking his neighbours to lend him money. This was only one aspect of a natural eccentricity which is also apparent in his pictures. These were not only supposed to tell a story; they were also expected to teach lessons. The "stories" were, more often than not, culled from press cuttings, and where possible he stuck the rele-

Rarely shown in exhibitions, his paintings have mainly been seen by individual collectors. They have, however, been displayed in several RONA exhibitions. *Sh. W.*

CSAREJSNÉ HRABOVSZKI, ILONA (1930)   **Hungary**

Ilona Hrabovszki Csarejsné was born in Cservas, which is where she still lives. Since 1974 she has been painting anecdotal reminiscences of her childhood, their substance revealed in their titles, such as "My Mother Grabbing My Father's

Crossley, Ralph: The Fight of the World for Civilisation Championship

vant cutting on the back of the painting, in case there might be some people who could not trace it in the painted image. Where newpapers did not come to his aid, the point he was making was clarified in the picture's title: for example, "My Sister 1948 — her soul has a fortnight's notice to find fresh tenancy."

Crossley's painting technique is careful and spare. All his pictures, however "literary," are fraught with a kind of compulsive atmosphere, created by his recording of a moment or occasion, be it ever so long ago.

Hat from His Head." Her works were displayed in the Museum of Naive Art in Kecskémet in 1979. Essay-length memoirs by her were published in Budapest in 1978 under the title "My Life Story." *M. I.*   →

CSIMIN, JÓZSEF (1920)   **Hungary**

József Csimin was born in Gola, Yugoslavia, the eleventh child of a poor village tradesman. Early in life he moved to Hungary, where he became a barber. He began to paint (on glass) in

1971; his works resemble somewhat those of the peasant-painters of Hlebine, Yugoslavia. His acute observation of the details of the village environment, and his faithful presentation of age-old cottage industries, make his works interesting to ethnographers, while the variety of his landscapes and the forms of plants and trees, combined with his winningly humorous portrayal of animals and their movements, give his paintings a special attraction.

His works have been shown in many exhibitions in Budapest, in Cuba, Japan, Belgium and East Germany. *M. I.*

CZENE, JÁNOSNÉ (1914)   **Hungary**

Czene Jánosné was born in Mako. During her working life, she has been a servant, agriculturalist, welder, and housewife. She began painting and drawing in 1969. Her painting, which sometimes shows a mixture of reality and imagination, is rich in ideas and symbols. Her written interpretations of her paintings are particularly interesting. Her pictures display a strong feeling for rhythm and colour.

Her works have been shown in group exhibitions in Budapest and Kecskemét and have also been shown abroad. *M. I.*

Csarejsné Hrabovszki, Ilona: Lunch at the "Red Dawn"

Csimin, József: Weaving and Spinning

Czene, Jánosné: I am not Selling the Colt

Calvo, Valerico Moral

Campuan, I Nyoman

Cao Jinying

Cao Xiuwen

Černobrova, Suzanna

Černjahovskij, Ivan

Chabauty, Malvina

Checci, Giuseppe de

Cloes, Nicolas

Cohen, Gabriel

Cook, Beryl

Crepin, Benoit

bassa, Teresa

Carter, Bernard

Castain, Aimée

Ceccarelli, Marino

Mujun

Cherecheş, Alexandru

Chick, Lorna

Chvála, Josef

ço, Madeleine

Cooper, Gladys

Coulon, Berthe

iani, Emile

Croix, Françoise de la

DAFTER, WILLIAM — Great Britain
DAŇKO, ŠTEFAN — Czechoslovakia
DAPRA, REGINA — Austria
DAVENPORT, NEIL — Great Britain
DAVIS, VESTIE — USA
DE KNIBBER, JAN — Belgium
DÉCHELETTE, LOUIS-AUGUSTE — France
DELAPORTE, ROGER — France
DELATTRE, LOUIS — Belgium
DELPLACE, RUPÉRT — Belgium
DEMONCHY, ANDRÉ — France
DEMPSEY, MICHAEL — Great Britain
DENDA, MARKO — Yugoslavia
DENNIS, MARGERY — Australia
DESNOS, FERDINAND — France
DEUS, WLADOMIRO SOUZA de — Brazil
DÉVÉNYI, ANTAL — Hungary
DIECKMANN, HENRY — West Germany
DIETRICH, ADOLF — Switzerland
DI GIROLAMO, GIOVANNI — Italy
DIKARSKAJA, ANNA PETROVNA — USSR
DINSMOOR, S. P. — USA
DIXON, JAMES — Ireland
DJANIRA, DA MOTA E SILVA — Brazil
DJELOŠEVIĆ, GORDANA — Yugoslavia
DJILATENDO, IBANEHE — Zaire
DOBRIĆ, DJORDJE — Yugoslavia
DOJA, GHEORGHE — Romania
DOKLEAN, SOFIJA — Yugoslavia
DOLAMA, ANUJKA — Yugoslavia
DONATI, VALENTINA — France
DOROTHY, SISTER — Australia
DRUNGILAS, ANTANAS — USSR
DUARTE, BENJAMIN — Cuba
DUFFAUT, PRÉFÈTE — Haiti
DUMITRESCU, GHEORGHE — Romania
DUNKLEY, JOHN — Jamaica
DŽALILOV, MADŽID — USSR

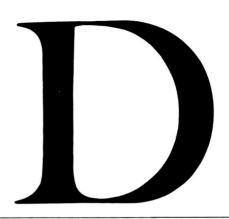

Dafter, William: Christmas

Daňko, Štefan: Constantine the Great and St. Helen

DAFTER, WILLIAM (1901)   **Great Britain**

William Dafter was born in London. A worker in a munitions factory, after the outbreak of the Second World War he was transferred to Blackburn, Lancashire. He did not start painting until after he had retired, and today he divides his time between making dresses for his wife, creating toys for his grandchildren, and painting.

Dafter's work often surprises the spectator. On the one hand, as in the illustration shown here, there is a clean-edged realism suggestive of the oleograph; life seems to have stopped and, no matter how full of action the subject may be, the air is still. On the other hand, quite another Dafter appears in paintings like "The Tears," a full close-up of a girl-child, hand over one eye, while huge teardrops well from the other. This is a painting pulsing with life, almost fierce in its directness. Dafter's pictures have mainly been shown in exhibitions in northern England, but he has also been on display in several RONA exhibitions. *(See portrait of the artist p. 216). Sh. W.*

DAŇKO, ŠTEFAN (1912)   **Czechoslovakia**

Štefan Daňko, the son of a Ukrainian smallholder, was born in Geraltov, Eastern Slovakia. After a few years at elementary school he lived first the life of a shepherd, later that of a farmhand. Those days, filled with singing and games, he remembers as the happiest of his life. At the age of twenty-four he set out on a new way of life — he entered a Greek-Catholic monastery in Mi-

chalovca, where he spent fifteen years. Later he worked as gardener, cook or janitor in various monasteries, ending up in Příbram, where he stayed until 1950. After an interval when he worked at laying floors he returned to Heiligenberg near Příbram as a cook. He was prompted to take up painting by the painters from Prague who were engaged in restoring the cloister frescoes between 1957 and 1959. But in Daňko's first attempts at painting we look in vain for any trace of the baroque illusionism of the Příbram frescoes. When he painted, and he did so at first with pigments thinned with flour and water, he somehow seemed to recall the icons and pictures in the monastery at Michalovca.

The rule of sublime verticality and the mystic central axis, the reduction of figures to types and the uniformity of detail are rooted, in Daňko's case, in popular as well as in "Byzantine" tradition. Daňko harked back deliberately to the latter, with its colour symbolism, its hieratic style and eternal impassivity. Byzantine painting was for him the only pure art. In fact, Daňko's paintings have more affinity with children's drawings than with Byzantine icons.

In 1962 he went to work as a miner and resigned himself to the fact that this meant the end of his painting. Gradually, however, he overcame the depression into which the ruined and desolate landscape in which he lived had plunged him, and now is once more able to recall, with his pastel paints to hand, the virgin beauty of the for-

![Dapra, Regina: Christmas Fair in Salzburg]

Dapra, Regina: Christmas Fair in Salzburg

ests, with their bee-hives, the huntsmen and the strawberry-seekers. He also paints variants of his older pictures with religious themes.

Since 1968 Daňko has been living once more as a servant in a Greek-Catholic presbytery in his native district. *(See portrait of the artist, p. 216). A. P.*

DAPRA, REGINA (1929)   Austria

Regina Dapra was born in Bad-Hofgastein. Between 1945 and 1951 she studied music at the Mozarteum in Salzburg and later at the conservatory in Vienna. After pursuing her musical career in Switzerland and West Germany, she married in 1960 and went to Salzburg. Since 1963 she has devoted herself exclusively to painting. The principal theme of almost all her paintings is Salzburg and its environs, shown totally submerged in greenery or on a wintry day (as in the illustration). In some of her paintings it is springtime and people are walking serenely or resting on benches — everywhere there is order and peace.

Regina Dapra has exhibited in many European countries and in the USA, and has won a number of awards. *(See portrait of the artist, p. 216).*

DAVENPORT, NEIL (1931)   Great Britain

Neil Davenport was born in Whitefield, Manchester. The first fifteen years of his working life were spent at a photographic studio, of which he became manager, but during all that period he was also painting pictures. How he came to be an accomplished self-taught painter is, in itself, a strange story. His father, after many years of successful professional life in the army, had become the bursar of Marlborough College, and so, quite naturally, when the time came for his son to start his serious education, it was to that school that he went. Like most children, Neil

Davenport, Neil: The Merry Widow

Davenport had a special hobby. In his case, it was his overwhelming enthusiasm — which he shared with a number of school-friends — for luxury cars of the 1920s. One day, he and his friends got together to answer an advertisement offering the inspection of a very splendid limousine, and, in due course, the dealer to whom they had written responded by sending the chauffeur-driven car to Marlborough College. He was not a little surprised to be met by school-boys, but he good-naturedly took them out in it for a spin.

Cars — vintage cars as they have become today — were the launching pad for Neil Davenport's artistic career. He painted these fabulous vehicles with a keen eye for exactitude, the result of fanatical study, and, for good measure, he let these car-portraits appear in the foreground of the luxurious settings in which they would normally be seen. Later, he concentrated on depicting either a world which was believable in hautmonde terms, or one which was Ruritanian in its atmosphere of Balkan plots, or one which was a dream interpretation of the hurly-burly of coups and revolutions in South America.

Davenport's style is neat and deft. The paint is thin, and the colours are bright, but never brash — they retain all the rich or gentle glamour of a vanished or disappearing world. His pictures are loved and cherished by collectors in many lands. He has had several one-man shows in the Portal Gallery, London, and mixed exhibitions abroad (in Hamburg, Zagreb, Basel, Geneva, Eck-en-Wiel and Paris). *(See portrait of the artist, p. 217). Sh. W.*

DAVIS, VESTIE (1902—1980) USA

Although Vestie Davis did not become a self-taught primitive artist (his own proud designation of himself) until he was forty-one, in the sometimes contradictory information he offered about himself he stated that when he was six, he was drawing on barn sides in Baltimore, Maryland, where he was born. There is no particular evidence that he persisted in this direction, though he once enrolled in a correspondence course in cartooning and took classes in photojournalism. None of this seems to have engaged his ambition, because in due course he was at gan doing New York City subjects. He would take several snapshots of a locality, paste them in a satisfying arrangement and do a sketch on tracing paper, carefully indicating on it the colours he planned to use. After the drawing was transferred to canvas, the painting was completed in two weeks.

In 1950 his wife persuaded him to display his work in the Washington Square Outdoor Art Show in Greenwich Village, where he was discovered by a local gallery owner. He then began painting almost exclusively on commission, doing only one painting at a time. At his death, only

Davis, Vestie: The Cyclone Roller Coaster

one time or another a circus barker, in the merchant marine, a news-stand manager, and finally, for many years, a funeral director and embalmer. He also played the organ in his local church in Brooklyn, where he moved with his wife Edna in 1947. He always maintained that such biographical details had no bearing on his life as an artist. He died of cancer of the lung.

His career as an artist began rather abruptly in 1947. A painting in a gallery window caught his eye, and he is quoted as saying, "I said to myself, I can paint that," adding that he promptly bought some artist's supplies and six prints to copy. He sold two of his copies (done, he said, in his own style) to his insurance agent. He then be-

an unfinished canvas and the tracing paper drawings he kept on file were left in his small apartment.

His early paintings showed unpeopled streets and meticulously detailed buildings — scenes similar to Vivin's. Later, he populated his scenes with hundreds of busy figures. He would, if asked, repeat a painting, but it was never an exact copy. As time altered him and the city, so did it, he said, change his view of the original work. *J. W.*

DE KNIBBER, JAN (1931) Belgium

Jan De Knibber, who was born in Geeraerdsbergen, Grammont, became a travelling salesman. Outside his work he surrendered completely to fantasy. One of his hobbies is electrical constructions. He enjoys making strange circuits, apparatuses for games, toys for children and adults, all of them reminiscent of Dadaistic machines. He is also an ardent collector of Asian art.

He began to paint in 1965. Like many Flemings, Jan De Knibber is a hard worker, literally sculpting his compositions in thick colours and often using a knife or finger, instead of a brush, thus gaining closer contact with the canvas. He is particularly attracted by pure colours and also uses pastels. Although his works are full of tiny

De Knibber, Jan: Spacemen

figures, particularly children, his canvases breathe, the coloured empty spaces giving them an airy effect. Like many naive artists, Jan De Knibber tells stories on his canvases, and is fond of hinting at local anecdotes which only the initiated can grasp. His mocking tales are based on a subtle and firm philosophy similar to Breughel's, but more gay than instructive. He has exhibited in Ostend, Brussels and Morges. *(See portrait of the artist, p. 217). J. C.*

DÉCHELETTE,   France
LOUIS-AUGUSTE (1894—1964)

Louis-Auguste Déchelette was born at Cours-la-Ville and died in Paris. He was brought up in the Lyon region by his grandfather and was apprenticed to a house painter. At sixteen, he did his *tour de France*, travelling as a member of the plasterers' guild. He first attracted critical notice in Paris after 1939 and the outbreak of the Second World War. His first one-man show was held in 1942. He eventually abandoned his trade completely to dedicate himself entirely to painting. He ended his life in solitude, forgotten by collectors and critics.

Paintings by Louis-Auguste Déchelette are few and command high prices. They circulate little, and, despite the continuing recognition his work enjoys, it has been some time since they have been exhibited. His work is very distinctive in the small world of naive artists. Each of his paintings is based on a play on words, a pun which serves as the title of the painting and is of-

ten untranslatable. He is an abrasive situation-comedy artist, whose work records the typical qualities of the French spirit. Déchelette most often painted in small format, with a restrained use of colour and an acute sense of harmony. Sobriety is his hallmark, but never at the expense of detail. This is especially true of his treatment of people, in which he has something in common with the miniaturist.

Déchelette's first one-man exhibition took place in 1942. From 1945, he participated in group exhibitions in the museums and galleries of Paris, Laval, Cologne, Milan and Brussels.

Déchelette, Louis-Auguste: Les Arts, Lese-Arts, Lezards

His work was also shown at Knokke-le-Zoute (1958). *(See portrait of the artist, p. 217). Ch. Sch.*

DELAPORTE, ROGER (1907—1969)   France

Roger Delaporte was born at Méru, near Paris. Few details are known about his life. He worked until 1950 as an ironsmith, making decorative pieces, but was forced after a serious illness to give up this work. He began little by little to paint in an effort, according to relatives, to overcome loneliness. From 1957, his work was seen regularly in Paris and he began to be known abroad. Several purchases of his work by the French government and the City of Paris shortly before his death firmly established his reputation.

Landscapes were most often the vehicle for artistic expression for Delaporte. His language is stern, and his idiom simple, but not to the exclusion of a highly refined technique. Clarity and exactness of colour, the use in each painting of local colour, and precision in drawing and perspective impart to each of his paintings a sensitive equilibrium.

His work has been exhibited in various Paris galleries. *(See portrait of the artist, p. 217). Ch. Sch.*

DELATTRE, LOUIS (1815—1897)   Belgium

Louis Delattre was born in Ghent and died there. He was one of the earliest known Belgian naive artists. Delattre was a fitter, a mechanic and a house painter; working as an *entrepreneur,*

pany. He lost both legs as the result of sabotage when he was with the occupation troops in Germany after 1918. It was only in 1938 that he decided to devote himself to painting.

In Brussels, the abstract painter Louis van Lint, a member of the "Young Belgian Painting Group," acquainted him with Robert Giron, director-general of the Brussels Palace of Art, after which Rupert Delplace exhibited pictures there for three years in succession.

He exhibited his masterly canvas "The Liberation of Paris" in 1946. At this time he began painting pictures of large dimensions. His dis-

Delaporte, Roger: St. Blaise Street and St. Germain Church

Delattre, Louis: The Visit of Queen Victoria to the Church of St. Elizabeth in Ghent in 1843

he went bankrupt and was sentenced to a term in prison, but was rehabilitated in 1869 by a decision of the Court of Appeals. By a strange coincidence, like Alois Sauter, he was the inventor of a device which he claimed to be a flying machine, despite the fact that it crashed during its first trial. This is the source of his nickname "The Flying Man."

For long, only two of his canvases were known, having been discovered by the painter Fritz Van Den Berghe: "The Market on Friday" and "The Rise of Prince Baudouin" in the collection of Frans Hellens. A recently discovered third canvas, reproduced here, "The Visit of Queen Victoria to the Church of St. Elizabeth in Ghent," was acquired by the Museum of Fine Arts in Ghent.

On the basis of these works alone, it is difficult to reconstruct the development of Delattre's art. After his death, his other canvases were put up for sale, bought and used again by local artists.

His works have been displayed in Knokke-le-Zoute, in other Belgian galleries and in exhibitions in Rotterdam and Paris. *(See portrait of the artist, p. 216). J. C.*

DELPLACE, RUPERT (1895—1951)   Belgium

Rupert Delplace, born in Herchies, Hainaut, was a geometer in the Belgian Railway Com-

covery of Ensor's work almost diverted him to academic painting, but he chose a naive style, using many symbols and religious themes, interpreted mystically. He continued to work until 1949, when old age compelled him to abandon painting. On the initiative of a Danish woman, Madame Hasselbach, the Director of the Gallery "Contemporaries," which monitors discoveries, organised a retrospective exhibition of his works (64 canvases), which attracted wide critical attention.

His clearly painted pictures, divided into planes on the model of the Sienese school and other painters of the past, were done directly on canvas, without any preliminary drawing. Light plays an important role. Lively, impressive in appearance, and a warm human being, Rupert Delplace enjoyed the support of his wife, a musician. He was modest and inclined to minimise the importance of his work, which was created sincerely and without any ambitions of achieving success. His work has been shown at many exhibitions in Belgium. *(See portrait of the artist, p. 216). J. C.* →

DEMONCHY, ANDRÉ (1914)   France

André Demonchy was born in Paris. He never went to school and, after the death of both parents, became a public ward at an early age. He went from farm to farm, working under very hard conditions until 1938, when he found a job with the railways. He was employed as an office worker in a post in Paris at his request. He claims to have always drawn, whenever he found the time. In 1944, he began to make gouaches and watercolours, selling them to help support his young family. In 1947, on the advice of Jacques de la Frégonnière, he did his first oils. He exhibited in New York in 1948 and in Paris the next year. Since then he has been a regular participant in all the major events of naive art. Critics have encouraged him, and the success he enjoys, in France and Belgium especially, is well founded.

Ever since childhood, he has loved painting. After leaving school, he at first tried all kinds of jobs before settling down for a while to plumbing, an occupation in which he had received some training. However, in the end, it was his painting which triumphed, leading to his being taken on by a publishing firm, initially as a junior but subsequently rising to the position of a director. At the start he was involved in the straightforward work of layout and design, but it was in the latter field that he was most at home. Today, a number of his paintings have been chosen for the cover design of paper-back books.

Delplace, Rupert: The Road to Paradise

Demonchy, André: Train Passing near Dormans

Dempsey, Michael: Couple in a Car

The initial inspiration for André Demonchy were the landscapes of Yonne, the region where he worked as a child. Throughout, he has always drawn on personal experience for the subjects of his paintings: the country fairs he visited, the world of railways, the cities he has loved. As he has moved ahead in his art, a growing grasp of perspective may be noted (in his scenes of Paris), and a real delight in putting as much detail as possible into famous buildings (in his cathedrals, for instance). Some canvases by Demonchy are undeniably reminiscent of Louis Vivin.

André Demonchy first exhibited at the Knoedler Gallery in New York. He has since exhibited at galleries in Paris, Nantes, Toulouse, Lyon and Zurich.

(See portrait of the artist, p. 216). Ch. Sch.

DEMPSEY, MICHAEL (1944)   Great Britain

Michael Dempsey was born in Dagenham, and now lives in Old Harlow, Essex.

Dempsey really started painting seriously after his move to Epping (still in his native Essex). He then added to his pictures of the local countryside by making trips up the East Anglian coast and recording what he saw. All his pictures have about them a sharp tidiness not often evident in the works of British naives, a kind of hard-edged decisiveness more often encountered on the Continental mainland (especially in the Lowlands of Belgium and Holland). *(See portrait of the artist, p. 216). Sh. W.*

DENDA, MARKO (1946)   Yugoslavia

Marko Denda, born in Vrbas, Bosnia, now lives in Igalo, Montenegro. He is a butcher who has been painting since 1966, and has also exhibited his pictures.

Most of his themes are associated with his occupation, which fascinates him. "A Shop Where Cuts are Sold" is the name of one of his pictures.

natural setting who, though naked, seem masked. On the yellow-green beach, a moment of summertime happiness has been immortalised: on a towel sits the reigning beauty of the beach in a bikini, listening to a song emanating from a tiny radio. The heads and limbs of all the people on the beach are made of cubes and pipes. The eyes of the men admiring the beauty stare from all sides.

All the other figures lie as though dead in the warm sand. None of them is looking at the silky green, shimmering sea, with its boats and swimmers.

Denda, Marko: The Beach at Igalo

Cuts of meat — heads, feet, legs — are distributed around the paintings as though on a chess board. In the foreground is the butcher and next to him a slaughtered body. The parts of the human body arouse fear and confusion.

"The Butcher Auctioning His Paintings" shows a group of prospective buyers standing motionless in a room where paintings are on show, the room presented in perspective. On a raised platform is a figure, perhaps talking about and selling the paintings. The room is small and threatening. The people in it look like dolls with movable limbs; they seem to be caught in the grip of some dark force.

Denda's paintings contain less humour and self-caricature than might be expected. His operating room, with its surgeons, assistants and nurses, is vaguely reminiscent of a butcher's shop.

"The Beach at Igalo" is the name given by Denda to a grotesque scene of nude people in a

The painting is arranged according to a scheme. The central part expresses dreams in reality, sometimes with gay cruelty. The colours, gently dissonant, increase the feeling of a cross between mockery and compassion. *O. B.-M.*

DENNIS, MARGERY (1922)   Australia

Margery Dennis was born in Sydney, New South Wales. She had no formal training in art until 1974, when she started to work under Marion Farley at the Lane Cove Art Society in Sydney. Almost immediately her warm, restful and beautifully picturesque paintings became a great success and her work was accepted for hanging in the prestigious Blake (1975, 1977), Wynne (1976, 1977) and Archibald (1977) Prize exhibitions.

People enjoy her vibrant landscapes and the pictures of flower stalls or ferneries where every detail is reproduced with loving care.

She has had a number of one-woman exhibitions, which were almost sold out, and has participated in various group shows.

Her works are in private collections in Australia and overseas. *(See portrait of the artist, p. 217). B. McC.*

DESNOS, FERDINAND (1901—1958)　France

Ferdinand Desnos was born at Pontelvoy and died in Paris. Poor health kept him changing jobs constantly. He tried working both in the provinces and in Paris, with his first stay in the

DEUS, WLADOMIRO SOUZA DE (1944)　Brazil

Wladomiro Souza de Deus was born in Boa Nova, Baia. At the age of fifteen he went to São Paulo where he started to work, first as a gardener and then later as a mason's apprentice, a waiter and subsequently in many different jobs. It was not until 1963 that he began painting pictures as a self-taught artist.

Wladomiro de Deus established his style early in his artistic career; his pictures are primitive in style and their subjects are mainly of a mystical or religious nature. These paintings are not

Deus, Wladomiro Souza de: Slaughter

Dennis, Margery: Fern Forest

Dieckmann, Henry: Public Urinal

capital in 1928. In 1931, he exhibited for the first time in the Salon des Indépendants. Nevertheless, he went back to live in the country and did not settle in Paris permanently until after the Second World War. He worked there as a concierge. His earliest canvas dates from 1923, and his first one-man show in Paris was held in 1943.

Ferdinand Desnos first recreated the world to which he belonged from the images accumulated during his childhood in the Tours region. Drawing was most important to him because it served the purpose of description. But he also liked to play with colour, using its possibilities to transcribe and carry his ideas into the realm of the imagination. He was deeply religious, and his faith provided him with an inspiration which was free of affectation, allowing him to enter an imaginary world of amazing invention.

Ferdinand Desnos exhibited mainly in Paris and Tours. *Ch. Sch.*

without a dash of humour, the comic element often being brash or ironic, as in "Our Lady of Aparecida in Mini-Skirt."

De Deus works in a clear-cut linear style, with all colour areas outlined in black or a dark hue. His work has been shown in many exhibitions, both group and personal. *Sh. W.*

DÉVÉNYI, ANTAL (1910) Hungary

Antal Dévényi was born in Budapest. A typographer, he has been in retirement since 1967, when he started to devote himself full time to painting and drawing. He is equally at home with pen, brush and chalk. Landscapes, idyllic scenes, pleasant old houses and streets are the themes he is most fond of. With wholehearted devotion, he endeavours to immortalise all the places where he has lived in his lifetime. Because of his childlike nature, he shows a greater predilection for portraying all the beauty he carries inside himself than for precise observation of the actual

DIETRICH, ADOLF (1877-1957) Switzerland

Adolf Dietrich was born in Berlingen, a hamlet on the shores of Lake Constance. Coming from a smallholding family, he took jobs as a day labourer, and worked on road crews and in factories. In spite of this heavy and exhausting work, he preserved a sensitivity which allowed him to reproduce the narrow world in which he lived with such microscopic precision and childish delight that it mirrors the world as a whole. Dietrich's biographer, Karl Hoenn, says that as a boy the artist "read in the book of nature, studied flowers and herbs, birds and caterpillars, and the

Desnos, Ferdinand: The Bridge of Arts or "The Last Supper on the Seine"

elements involved in his subject-matter. Since 1970, he has exhibited frequently in Budapest and the provinces. His pictures have been on display in group exhibitions of Hungarian naive art abroad. Daily newspapers and illustrated magazines often carry his paintings and drawings. *M. I.*

DIECKMANN, HENRY (1933) West Germany

Henry Dieckmann was born in Verden and now lives in Fischerhude, near Bremen. In 1948 Dieckmann began working with the German State Railways and is now an administrator in the locomotive repair works in Bremen. He was fond of drawing and painting even while he was at school. During the war he painted children's picture-books and exchanged them for foodstuffs. He showed his pictures for the first time in the Bremen flea-market in 1970. It is with pleasure that one recalls Henry Dieckmann's little pictures, executed with painstaking precision and patience: village life in Fischerhude and, even more vividly, the inexhaustible series of studies of lower middle-class life in Paris. Dieckmann developed his views of homely Parisian streets, their secluded corners, the bistros and urinals, with a wealth of invention and reflection allied with a highly developed taste for a discreetly refined range of colours. Then he was discovered by the advertising industry, and with success came routine, the pressure to produce to order; he was trapped, and the quality of naivety evaporated. *(See portrait of the artist, p. 217). T. G.*

Dévényi, Antal: Pilisi Lake

whole treasure-house of Mother Earth like a biologist, but drew them to his heart like an artist . . ." Gardens, fruit, stuffed birds, martens, mice, and men are formulated in his work with the plastic intensity of the *Quattrocento* and the immediacy of the primitives. He is an artist of untouched simplicity and at the same time a master of detail, a chiseller of forms. For him, the detail is an integral part of the whole. With staunch perseverance and a musing love of work he built up from his parts a perfect whole.

Dietrich worked with fine, thin brushes and a cautious application of colour. "He does it almost unconsciously," writes Karl Hoenn, "like one whose hand and brush are led by an inner voice, just as an inner vision enables him to paint from sketches made long before, since in the eye of his imagination the experience of the past is still a part of the living present."

His flower still-lifes, aquariums, animal pictures, self-portraits and renderings of children and young women have the precision in drawing of the old masters and the delicate feeling, the muted palette, of the German Romantics.

One can hardly point to stages of development in his work. Quite early he already had a sure sense for the delineation of surfaces and for living space. Still, there are successes and failures both in his early work and in that of his last years.

DI GIROLAMO, GIOVANNI (1932)   **Italy**

Giovanni Di Girolamo, born in Petrognano di Spoleto is of peasant origin. When he was twenty years old, he left his village and moved to the capital of the province, where he got a job as a watchman. He began to paint in about 1963, following a natural instinct to return in his thoughts to a world of dreams dissociated from the living conditions of the city.

His subject-matter is not, however, restricted to recollections of village life. On the contrary, he has done bright and buoyant urban "landscapes," suburbs crowded with houses and bold and orig-

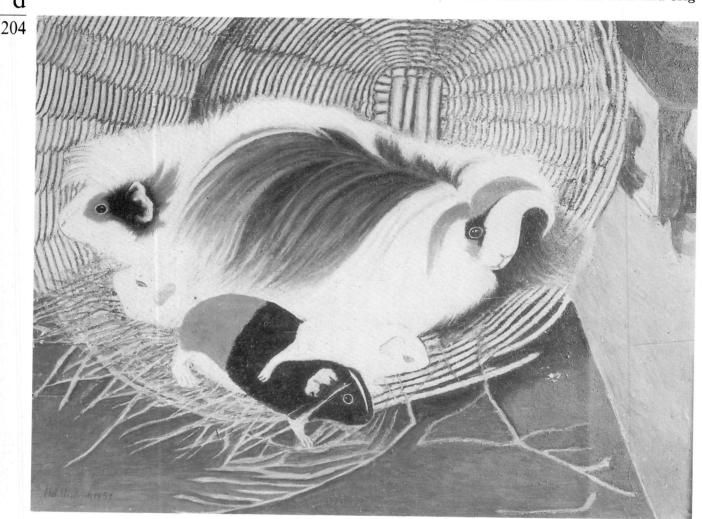

Dietrich, Adolf: Porpoise

Adolf Dietrich was a naive painter who painted with faith and instinct. He had perfected his craft through years of patient dedication; a solemn awe at the magical self-sufficiency of things, a preference for small things, bound him in brotherhood to Douanier Rousseau. His striving for the harmony and beauty which are in sympathy with the music of nature made him a pantheist poet of life. Adolf Dietrich was the first Swiss naive artist to win recognition internationally. His first known painting dates from 1905, and his first exhibition was held in 1909. He also took part in many important exhibitions in Switzerland and other countries. His works are in well-known museums throughout the world. *(See portrait of the artist, p. 217). O. B.-M.*

inal architecture. Also, there are his foreshortened forests and unusual feathery trees; his expansive, flowering meadows, where lovely young girls play, as if personifying the subconscious desire for a return to the happy time of innocent and untroubled childhood.

Di Girolamo's colours play an important part in his paintings, discharging a function, with their delicate nuances, on which the very composition of his pictures rests. The chromatic component is the most distinctive feature of his work. *(See portrait of the artist, p. 217). D. M.*   →

Dietrich, Adolf: In the Saloon

DIKARSKAJA, ANNA PETROVNA (1893—1982)
DIKARSKAYA, ANNA PETROVNA

USSR

A. P. Dikarskaya was born in a working-class family in the Volga city of Nizhni Novgorod, today Gorky. As a trained nurse she took part in the First World War and the Civil War. She began to paint by pure accident at the age of 67, totally untaught. In her works the accumulated wisdom of her years is revealed with frank emotion through a technique akin to that used in children's drawings. Her vision of the surrounding world is steeped in fantasy, yet is concrete, as is

Di Girolamo, Giovanni: Dancing in the Forest

more specifically manifest in her approach to historical subject-matter and events which she extracts from books. The very titles of her fantasised pictures, such as "The Execution of the Popular Hero Stepan Razin," "Ivan the Terrible and Malyuta Skuratov" or "Turks Attacking Armenians in 1731," to mention but three, reveal the diversity of her "historical" interests. She also produced numerous landscapes and still-lifes, characterised by resonant colour and individual rhythmical arrangement. However, the colouring is fragmented (the result of the spontaneity with which she created), and for this reason we may count her a naive artist. Unaware of perspective, she relied largely on colour, which blends, thanks to her ornamental skill, the result being a kind of "weaving" in colours that is typical of children's drawings and produces the effect of a carpet-like mosaic. This style derives both from the traditions of popular peasant art and from the immediacy with which she saw reality. She was represented at many group shows at regional, Republican and USSR level, and had two one-woman exhibitons. Some works are on view at the Museum of Popular and Amateur Art of the Russian Federation in Suzdal. *(See portrait of the artist, p. 216). N. Sh.*

DINSMOOR, S. P. (1843—1932)

USA

S. P. Dinsmoor was in many ways typical of many American naives in that his work is permeated with a wry humour and wit, while at the same time conveying a personal religio-political ideology. He is also an example of a fairly com-

mon American phenomenon, the environmentalist builder. Born in Coolville, Ohio, he was a Union soldier in the Civil War. After he was demobilised he taught in school in Illinois for a while, and also farmed. In the 1880s he moved to Kansas, then still pioneer country. He seems to have combined a strong *joie de vivre* with a passion for the Bible, from which he could quote long passages verbatim.

After he retired from farming in 1905, he moved to Lucas and built himself a "Cabin Home," which was constructed in log-cabin style out of limestone and concrete blocks. Equipped

Dikarskaya, Anna Petrovna: The Childhood of Ivan the Terrible in Moscow

Dinsmoor, S. P.: Garden of Eden (detail)

with its own electric generating plant, the house was finished inside with redwood, pine and oak. In 1907 Dinsmoor began working on his concrete "Garden of Eden." He wrote a little book about it, but never explained what prompted him to start it. Whatever it was, the project occupied him until his death in 1932.

The "Garden" consists of statuary that seems to be flying in the air about the cabin on tree-like supports. He portrayed Adam and Eve, effigies of the Devil, Capital, and Labour, an Indian Brave, and an angel, interspersed with animals and birds. He planted trees and shrubs to blend in

Cornwall is a part of England, an outcrop of the British mainland, and was approachable without too much difficulty even in times gone by. Ireland is still comparatively remote — especially Tory Island. This, to some extent, explains how Wallis — albeit after a long time — became an international figure in the world of naive art, whereas Dixon received far less recognition during the same period. Whether Dixon or Wallis is the more gifted artist is a point which could be debated endlessly, but one thing is certain: Dixon is without question the greatest self-taught painter to have come out of Ireland.

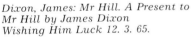

Dixon, James: Mr Hill. A Present to Mr Hill by James Dixon Wishing Him Luck 12. 3. 65.

Dixon, James: The Fairholm on the Rocks beside Alarin

with his concrete trees and built an ingenious lighting system to illuminate it all.

Near the cabin he built a mausoleum, where he lies in a glass-covered coffin with an axe by his side, so that, when the millennium arrives, he can quickly break out and join the angels. "This lid," he wrote, "will fly open and I will sail out like a locust . . . I have a cement angel outside to take me up."

At eighty he married a girl of twenty and fathered two children. Once famous, then neglected, the garden and cabin have been salvaged from decay and restored by Mr. and Mrs. Waybe Naegle and are a major tourist attraction in Lucas. *J. W.*

DIXON, JAMES (1887)   **Ireland**

A unique naive artist and an astonishing creature was James Dixon of Tory Island. Like the Cornishman Alfred Wallis (see page 605), he was a Celt — a race of people renowned for their poetry and vision, whether it takes the form of verse, drama, music or painting. But, again like Wallis, he was a simple man, capable of making pictures of primitive power and, like his Cornish counterpart, he was a man absorbed by the sea in all its aspects.

Born on the storm-tossed Irish island of Tory (which reputedly he never left), most of the time he lived and worked in undisturbed isolation, a local figure known to the other islanders as a fellow inhabitant whose eccentricity was to mess about with paint and produce crude pictures. Because of its inaccessibility and tempestuously bad weather, few visitors ever made their way to Tory.

Like Wallis, he was out of touch with anything connected with the world of culture. Like the Cornishman, he fashioned his pictures on old bits of cardboard or lining paper, working with stubs of pencil, chalk and paint.

The pigment he used was the colours scraped out from long abandoned cans of paint thrown away by their owners after the job of repainting a boat had been finished. Inevitably such a source of paint tended to limit the range of his palette.

The island's life was the life of Dixon. It was also the life of his pictures. The majority of these expressed the turbulence of sea and wind, but anything unusual on Tory was depicted by him. The unique and memorable occasion when the massive inflated German dirigible, the *Hindenburg*, floated across the sky over Tory was duly recorded in paint.

On the whole, the colours used in Dixon's pictures were dark and tenebrous, rarely straying outside the narrow compass of black, grey, grey-green and grey-blue, except for contrasting whites and off-whites, used where he deemed it necessary. Reds, browns and ochres also made their appearance sometimes, but these variations, apart from brown, were the exception rather than the rule.

To most of those who have been fortunate enough to come in contact with Dixon's paintings, the most outstanding feature of his amazing talent is the way in which he is able to turn

spent her early years in the little town of Porto União. In her day Djanira was reckoned the most important exponent of Brazilian naive art. As Flavio de Aquinto puts it, "She painted the simple domestic scene and peopled it with ordinary folk, humble or locally important, together with the creatures of the garden and countryside." This artist reduced these elements to their fundamental simplicity but, at the same time, introduced into her pictures telling details as well as an atmosphere reminiscent of her rural-based youth.

Returning to Avaré in 1930, she was able to blend local atmosphere with all the elements she

Djanira, da Mota e Silva: Football Teams

wind and weather into a palpable turmoil, angry and gripping in its intensity, rendering them with a fierce expressionism not generally to be found in the work of even the finest primitive artists. The painting illustrated here ("Mr Hill. A Present to Mr Hill by James Dixon Wishing Him Luck 12. 3. 65") is of a different kind. This portrait of Derek Hill, as well as being a painting of great quality, is more than just a memento. It was the artist Derek Hill who "discovered" James Dixon and, bit by bit, brought him to the attention of the world outside, an achievement comparable with that of the two artists Ben Nicholson and Christopher Wood when they stumbled upon Wallis.

Pictures by Dixon are now to be found in many parts of the world and a large number of them are in the important collection at Kettle's Yard, Cambridge. *(See portrait of the artist, p. 216). Sh. W.*

DJANIRA,   Brazil
DA MOTA E SILVA (1914)

Djanira was born in Avaré in the state of São Paulo. This self-taught painter and engraver

Djanira, da Mota e Silva: The Lonely Ones from Diamantina

had noted in the noisy café and market backgrounds of the urban ambiance of São Paulo (including the marine world of Brazilian ports and the coast), but it was not until she fell ill and was admitted to the hospital of São José de Campos that she was able to set aside the hustle of ordinary life to become a full-time painter.

Since her death some years ago, her pictures, which fetched substantial prices, have become much sought after. She took part in many exhibitions. *(See portrait of the artist, p. 216). Sh. W.*

DJELOŠEVIĆ, GORDANA (1935) Yugoslavia

Gordana Djelošević was born in Belgrade, where she still lives. She is a housewife who has been painting since 1960.

Many of her early works feature folkloric elements, but lately she has turned her attention to various parts of Belgrade and other towns she has visited, painting familiar streets, squares, buildings and other urban motifs. Although familiar, they are at the same time unrecognisable, because the artist has changed the architecture to correspond to some private scheme of her own. Sometimes she brings buildings closer together, narrows wide expanses or plants grass where only the dark grey asphalt lies. With precision and love she draws the façades of buildings, ornamenting them and producing a two-dimensional carpet without perspective but full of vibrant, strong and shining colours. Although no life is

Djilatendo, Ibanehe: Red Woman with Black Hat

Djelošević, Gordana: The Fountain on Terazije Square

noticeable behind the walls of her houses, the streets are not empty: people meet and talk on them, sometimes intermingled with a variety of animals. The vital yet restrained palette of Gordana Djelošević is an artless one; her perseverance, industry and talent promise further achievements. She has taken part in over fifty group exhibitions at home and abroad. *(See portrait of the artist, p. 216). N. T.*

DJILATENDO, IBANEHE (about 1885) Zaire

An early watercolour painter from Zaire, Djilatendo exhibited first in Geneva in 1930, together with his colleague, Lubaki. Further exhibitions followed in Brussels, Paris, Naples and Antwerp before and after the Second World War.

His works have been divided into three groups: coloured geometrical chess-board designs which bear a resemblance to tattoos or to the patterns on crockery and textiles in the painter's homeland; local scenes which resemble the graffiti on the mud walls of huts in Lulua villages; finally, black-outline drawings inspired by native fables or proverbs, their individual components frequently linked by curved lines.

His compositions, which bring plants, animals and men together in rhythmic designs on the surface of his pictures, possess a poetic delicacy and beauty. His palette is dominated by a delicate brick-red, shell-pink and a wide range of shades from grey to black.

An anthology of Congolese fables edited by Badibanga, with illustrations by Djilatendo, appeared in Brussels in 1931 under the title, *L'élé-phant qui marche sur des oeufs. (See portrait of the artist, p. 217). G. Sch.*

DOBRIĆ, DJORDJE (1931—1978) Yugoslavia

Djordje Dobrić was born in Veliko Selo near Bijeljina, Bosnia-Herzegovina, the youngest of

his father reconstruct their destroyed home. For a while he tended livestock but soon realised there was no future for him in the village. So, like many others in that post-war period, he left for the city to try his luck. As a person disabled in the war, at first he could only obtain a job in a bakery. Without resources, without a flat or any of the amenities of life, for about half a year he spent his nights sleeping on an office desk. Exhausted, he returned to his village, then back to the city, and again to the village. Finally, he was given the job of doorman in a bank in Skadarlija, the old bohemian part of Belgrade.

Dobrić, Djordje: Skadarlija — a Bohemian Quarter of Belgrade

five children in a poor peasant family. His father spared him from doing hard field work so that he could go to school, because it seemed that he had more aptitude for learning than the other children. But fate seems not to have looked kindly on Djordje Dobrić. His father's plans for him were interrupted by the war and his own family was caught up in the holocaust. With his brother and sister, he joined the Partisans in 1943 and in a battle against the Germans lost his right arm up to the shoulder. He was then only twelve years old. Hardly had he recovered from his wounds when word arrived that his brother and sister had been killed.

When the war ended he went back to his village. Weak and sickly, he tried, together with his one surviving brother, to work the land and help

Spending long hours at the bank entrance, he watched the young people strolling along Skadarlija, the pigeons fluttering overhead, and so on, and was taken by the desire to record these scenes. He had already learned to write his left hand and now started to paint. After a few tries, it seemed to him that he had succeeded and this encouraged him to continue.

Inclined to soft colours, he poured his lyrical nature out into his paintings, which he worked at slowly and punctiliously. He left approximately fifty pictures when he died.

In "The Pigeons of Skadarlija," a flock of pigeons seems to be engaged in a gentle conversation on a misty morning. Above them, a rosy-coloured pigeon, wings outspread, is ready to take off. Against the old Turkish cobblestoned street, where every stone is edged and shadowed, the pigeons seem unreal.

A similar effect is created by the painting "Skadarlija," showing people walking along the street. Three of them are turned toward the painter, as though frozen in their tracks, while others in the background move in both directions. With its pigeons and picturesque Skadarlija architecture, the painting is a mixture of dreams and reality.

Dobrić often compared himself with a pigeon, free to fly off wherever he wanted to, pecking away at bits of food and living from hand to

he moves, enriching them with elements from folk literature. On canvas he transforms them into veritable theatrical entertainments.

Doja's artistic solution for presenting his theme is in line with his own temperament; he preserves the melancholy tone of the poetry, while giving it a "happy ending."

Even on canvases for which he draws inspiration from his own daily life ("The Locomotive Repair Shop in Lugoz," "Winter"), the artist "orchestrates" everything in his own way and makes the scenes he loves so well, even livelier and more optimistic.

Doja, Gheorghe: The Dacians

Doklean, Sofija: All Souls' Day

In Doja's work the character of the composition is determined by the intense colours — especially in historical subjects (such as "The Dacians"); narrative elements have a rhetorical flavour and the expressiveness is decorative in nature.

Although painting since 1954, Gheorghe Doja began to exhibit only in 1965. Since then he has regularly participated in group exhibitions in Romania, where he has received many prizes, and in Switzerland, Yugoslavia, India, Sweden and other countries. *(See portrait of the artist, p. 217).* M. Il.

mouth, a gentle lover of life disappearing in the late night hours to the strains of music.

Djordje Dobrić had several one-man shows and participated in group exhibitions at home and abroad. *(See portrait of the artist, p. 217).* N. T.

DOJA, GHEORGHE (1928)   Romania

Gheorghe Doja, born in the commune of Tipari in the district of Timiș, is a metalworker in the railway workshop at Caransebeș.

Doja takes his themes from the love songs and poems popular in the environment in which

DOKLEAN, SOFIJA (1931)   Yugoslavia

Sofija Doklean was born in the village of Uzdin, Vojvodina, which was inhabited by Romanians. She went to elementary school in her village and is now a housewife who also works on the land. Since 1961, she has been painting in her free time.

Her beginnings as a painter resemble those of the other women painters of Uzdin. One day her daughter took a drawing to school. The teacher suspected that she had not done it all by herself and the girl admitted that her mother had helped her. As a result, the teacher visited Sofija

Doklean, bringing paper and colours, and persuaded her to paint.

Sofija Doklean says she likes to portray on her canvases all the various kinds of work done in the house: sewing, weaving and embroidering.

Sofija Doklean has had one-woman shows and participated in group exhibitions at home and abroad. *(See portrait of the artist, p. 216). N. T.*

DOLAMA, ANUJKA (1930)   Yugoslavia

Anujka Dolama was born in the village of Uzdin, Vojvodina, which was inhabited by Roma-

d
212

Dolama, Anujka: Dressing the Bride

nians, and went to elementary school there. She still lives in Uzdin. She is a housewife who also works in the fields and paints in her spare time the opulent Romanian national costumes and customs and life in the village. She began painting in the same way as the other women painters in Uzdin, whose works she once saw on display in the village school. Upon returning home, she decided to try her hand at painting, for while she had been at school, she had loved drawing and had been praised for her work.

In "Dressing the Bride" (1964), Anujka Dolama has used simple means to portray an important moment in village life — the dressing of the future bride before she leaves for her wedding. The dressing takes hours, for attention is paid to every detail. Necklaces of gold coins handed down from mother to daughter form part of the costume and of the dowry as well.

The bride in her finery, the embroidery on the bedspread and tablecloth, and the rug all stand out against the background of the decorated wall and red floor.

Anujka Dolama has had one-woman shows and participated in group exhibitions at home and abroad. *(See portrait of the artist, p. 216). N. T.*

DONATI, VALENTINA (1897)   France

Valentina Donati was born in Nikolaieff, Russia. Her parents were Italian and she spent her childhood in Italy. She lived in Florence for a long time, often travelling around the country. In 1928, she moved to France, where she settled permanently with her family. Her main concern

was bringing up her three children. In 1955, while travelling in Brittany, she began to paint, and two years later began to exhibit her work in Paris, other French cities and throughout Europe. She has received various awards and honours.

The paintings of Valentina Donati are above all opportunities for using colour. Everyday life and folk tales provide the principal sources of her inspiration. Her canvases are most often composed by aligning their elements in ranks from bottom to top, and her people are made to face front.

Donati, Valentina: Poultry Market in Lannion

Dorothy, Sister: Sorrento

Valentina Donati has had one-woman shows in Paris galleries and participated in numerous group shows in Amsterdam, Athens, Rome, Brussels, Milan, Florence and elsewhere. *(See portrait of the artist, p. 216). Ch. Sch.*

DOROTHY, SISTER (1920)   Australia

Sister Dorothy was born in Swan Hill in Victoria. She attended the local school until she was sixteen, when she went to continue her education at Genazzano Convent in the Melbourne suburb of Kew.

Although artistic, she decided against a career in art because she felt it was too bohemian and unrewarding.

While at Genazzano as a student, she decided to enter the convent and make teaching her life. She joined the Faithful Companions of Jesus and soon used her artistic talent to advantage by painting the "Spiritual Bouquets" given to the Superior on special occasions and feast days. These small, intricate cards were painstakingly painted in water-colours.

Sister Dorothy taught art, among other subjects, at Genazzano Convent for many years. In 1972 she was moved to the Stella Maris Convent at Frankston in Victoria, and there joined the Peninsula Art Group.

In 1968 he joined the Lithuanian Association of Folk Arts, which unites traditional folk craftsmen and amateur artists. He is now an old-age pensioner. He prefers historical themes, fairy tales and legends and adds inscriptions to his works, which reflect Lithuanian national art traditions and the mentality of his environment. He displays a versatile imagination, introducing into narrative paintings angels, devils, Death, *auto-da-fé* and other folkloric elements as well as patriarchal genre scenes from rustic life as in his "Ploughing," "An Old-Time Flax Harvest" or "Old-Time Harvesting." Space with him is virtu-

Drungilas, Antanas: An Old-Time Flax Harvest

Duarte, Benjamin: Symbols in the Landscape

Duarte, Benjamin: Mask

In 1975 she gained a Diploma of Fine Art (Painting) at Caulfield Institute of Technology and in 1976 was awarded the Mornington Art Prize.

Sister Dorothy's paintings are simply extensions of the lovingly composed votive cards which delighted her companions. *B. McC.*

ally tangible. He introduces a kind of tracery when arranging the narrative motives and also an expressiveness which indicates a certain involvement with the traditions of Western medieval art. He has been represented at exhibitions in his own republic and also at group USSR exhibitions in Moscow in 1974 and 1977. *(See portrait of the artist, p. 217). N. Sh.*

DRUNGILAS, ANTANAS (1914)   USSR
Antanas Drungilas was born into a working-class family in Salantai, a small town near Kretinga, Lithuania. A building worker by trade, he had only one year of elementary schooling. Because of bad health he worked as a night watchman between 1963 and 1967, when he began to draw with pencils and subsequently paint in oils.

DUARTE, BENJAMIN (1900—1974)   Cuba
Benjamin Duarte was born in Cienfuegos, Las Villas Province, Cuba, and died there. He sat for the entrance examination for the Teacher's Training College of Santa Clara, Las Villas, in 1924, and from 1931 to 1933 he dedicated himself to revolutionary activity against the dictator Gerardo Machado.

His style is informal and varied, depending on the theme, ranging from the Surrealistic in his figurative works, to Impressionism in his landscapes.

He exhibited at the Cienfuegos Gallery in 1951 and 1954, and again in 1956, on the occasion of the celebration of the 147th anniversary of the founding of that city; also in the Havana Gallery in 1967, and in the Salon '70 exhibition in 1970. He participated in the joint exhibition of Primitive Painters at the Havana Gallery in 1971, and was posthumously represented by four paintings in the exhibition "Eleven Cuban Primitive Paint-

Dumitrescu, Gheorghe: Holiday

Duffaut, Préfète: Boat below the Bridge

ers" at the Institute of Jamaica, Kingston, in 1976. *T. R.*

DUFFAUT, PRÉFÈTE (1923)   Haiti

Préfète Duffaut was born in Jacmel. It is hard to believe that his style and subjects were the product of a miserable childhood. With no affection from his stepmother, he more or less brought himself up, trying, whenever he could, to lose himself in a fantastic world of make-believe, the outward form of which appeared in drawings he made upon scraps of paper. At the age of twelve he started work, helping his father, who was a shipbuilder.

Duffaut's marriage proved to be a turning-point in his life. He and his wife settled in Jacmel, where they lived in a tiny house which he decorated with painted stars, decked with flags, and filled with vases brimming with flowers.

A second great turning-point occurred while Duffaut was on the lookout for work in Picmi (on the island of La Goave): the Virgin Mary appeared to him in a dream and commanded him to paint murals on the walls of the local church.

Duffaut obeyed the Virgin Mary's command. Where he was living, nothing like this had ever happened before. The murals proved to be fantastic in style, but their total effect was of a glorification of the Virgin Mary. Enthusiastic praise flowed in from parishioners. From this moment, the completion of the murals, Duffaut emerged as a naive painter — but one so different in manner and imagery from anything that Haiti had experienced before.

After he returned to his home (decorated by himself) in Jacmel, some American friends of De-Witt Peters took photographs of his pictures. These photographs secured Duffaut entry into the *Centre d'Art* in Port-au-Prince. The unique nature of the contortions of the landscape in so many of Préfète Duffaut's best known pictures are now widely familiar, but he has never forgotten the patronage of the Virgin and she is often the central figure in those paintings which he dedicates to her (notably in the two paintings he made for Bishop Voegel's Holy Trinity Cathedral in Port-au-Prince). It was Duffaut's gay, kite-flying youngsters and the brightly clad crowds thronging his extraordinary island landscapes, with their eccentric isthmuses and peninsulas, that brought Duffaut fame and success — but they are by no means the sole subjects he chooses for the wilder flights of his imagination. Voodoo and *le magic noir* also have their place in his pictorial fantasies and they evoke admiration even among the "unenlightened."

Generally Duffaut's colours are brilliant and cheerful (only occasionally do they suggest a less happy frame of mind), with the paint thinly applied; forms and outlines are almost calligraphic. *(See portrait of the artist, p. 217). Sh. W.*

DUMITRESCU, GHEORGHE (1913)   Romania

Gheorghe Dumitrescu, born in Tit, in the district of Dambovita, is a mechanic by trade who began painting in 1968. His canvases in which trees, grass and garden flowers bloom in a medley of colours, in effect show us scenes of everyday life transformed by the imagination of the painter.

In scenes of the interiors of houses or workshops, the artist introduces a little of the nature which surrounds him and exerts unending attraction for him. For even when he is painting (with minute precision) the details of the library, a china closet with vases, a table, following the principle of a "painting within a painting," he focuses on canvases on the walls, on which again are seen the colours of flowering meadows, lilacs in vases, gardens in spring.

Dumitrescu's works (oil paintings on cardboard and carvings in wood) have been shown in group exhibitions of naive art at home and abroad and have received many awards. *(See portrait of the artist, p. 217). M. Il.*

Dunkley, John: Banana Plantation

DUNKLEY, JOHN (1891—1947)   Jamaica

John Dunkley was born in Savanna-la-Mar, Jamaica. He left the island while still a lad of about fifteen, to join his father in Panama, and spent the next twelve years or so at first working and travelling in Central America and Cuba, and then as a sailor, including England, Scotland, and North and South America in his travels. For a while after, he lived and worked as a barber in Panama and began painting in his spare time.

Dunkley returned to Jamaica in the late 1920s, married, and continued barbering and painting. By the late 1930s his work had come to the notice of people who recognised his talent. He received further encouragement to continue painting and to exhibit in Jamaica and abroad. He first exhibited in 1938 at the St. George's Exhibition in Kingston, and was awarded a prize for sculpture. He was represented in the Exhibition of the Gallery of Science and Art (New York World's Fair, 1939) and at shows in Canada and England (1945 and 1946). In 1948, after his death, the Institute of Jamaica mounted a Memorial Exhibition. He was represented in the exhibitions in San Juan, Puerto Rico (1951), in the Institute of Jamaica (1960), in Atlanta (1969), in London (1971), in the National Gallery of Jamaica (1975, 1977, 1978, 1979), and in Caracas (1978).

Jalilov, Majid: Hodja Khizir

At the time of his death Dunkley had produced about fifty important works of painting and sculpture, revealing a highly individual style. Most of them were done in the last decade of his life. Totally self-taught and free from the influence of established movements, Dunkley is considered the master of the Jamaican naives and is also now widely accepted as Jamaica's greatest painter. *T. R.*

DŽALILOV, MADŽID (1909—1981)   USSR
JALILOV, MAJID

Majid Jalilov was born into the family of an Uzbek poet. Having qualified as a telegraph operator, in 1942 he completed in his spare time the full course of the Teacher-Training Institute in Samarkand. In 1970 he began to create painted sculptures of people and animals and also produce models of architectural structures. His major interest, however, was painting. His pictures are laconic from the standpoint of artistic expression and possess a static quality typical of naive art. He employed stereotyped motifs that are profoundly national in content. It is also quite likely that his liking for models prompted the representation on canvas of architectural design. His works display the decorative, carpetlike, mosaic quality characteristic of the applied arts of Central Asia, which undoubtedly influenced the artist. The colour scheme is saturated and profound, the product of contemplation. He was represented at all group exhibitions in his home republic and also at shows in Moscow since 1970. *(See portrait of the artist, p. 217). N. Sh.*

Dafter, William

Daňko, Štefan

Dapra, Regina

Delattre, Louis

Delplace, Rupert

Demonchy, André

Dempsey, Michael

Dikarskaja, Anna Petrovna

Dixon, James

Djanira, da Mota e Silva

Djelošević, Gordana

Doklean, Sofija

Dolama, Anujka

Donati, Valentina

enport, Neil

De Knibber, Jan

Déchelette, Lòuis-Auguste

Delaporte, Roger

nis, Margery

Dieckmann, Henry

Di Girolamo, Giovanni

atendo, Ibanehe

Dobrić, Djordje

Dietrich, Adolf

Doja, Gheorghe

ngilas, Antanas

Duffaut, Préfète

Dumitrescu, Gheorghe

Džalilov, Madžid

EBERT, ALBERT — East Germany
EDMONSON, WILLIAM — USA
EDZIEV, SOSLANBEK — USSR
EHM, ERNST — East Germany
ELENOK, TAT'JANA DMITRIEVNA — USSR
ELLIS, VIVIAN — West Germany
ELSA O. S. — Brazil
ENĂCHESCU, CONSTANTIN — Romania
ENNULAT, MINNA — West Germany
EPPLE, BRUNO — West Germany
ERKENS, SOFIA — West Germany
ERTUGANOV, ŠAMIL' — USSR
EVANS, MINNIE — USA
EVE, JEAN — France

Ebert, Albert: The Ebert Family

Edmonson, William: Angel

EBERT, ALBERT (1906—1976)   **East Germany**

Albert Ebert, born in Halle, was trained as a bricklayer. He began painting while in a military hospital. From 1946 onwards he was in a position to supplement his artistic education, with the help of the painter Carl Crodel, at the Academy for Industrial Design in Halle-Giebichenstein. He subsequently worked again as a bricklayer, and later as a stoker.

Although Albert Ebert aspired to a sophisticated style of painting, his early works, with their miniature-like poetic quality, in which he depicts people and events taken from his immediate surroundings, may nevertheless be included among the finest products of naive art.

His later works, as well as his drawings, retain no more than the expressive force that marks the picturesque naive idiom; otherwise they tend to belong, in the brilliance of their technique and the lithography, to the domain of professional art.

Ebert constantly sought to invest his existence with a poetic quality. This was perhaps the basic motive for his whole work. He tended to go beyond the confines of naive art in the manner in which he contrived, through his acute sense of reality, to attach deliberate statements to his inspired inventions. When he died, it was generally agreed that his art must be assessed on the basis of its consummate expressive technique, and that it is devoid of academic elements. *(See portrait of the artist, p. 228). K. C.*

EDMONSON, WILLIAM (1883?—1951)   **USA**

The son of former slaves, William Edmonson was born in Nashville, Tennessee. His birth is assumed to have occurred in 1883 but the Nashville directory for that year notes a labourer by that name, and, in subsequent years, an oil worker, railway worker, fireman, janitor for a hospital (1908—1931), and lastly, a stonecutter and monument carver (1933—1949). It would seem from this that he may have been much older than sixty-eight when he died in 1951.

Like so many southern blacks, Edmonson absorbed a simple but deep religiosity from his widowed mother and spoke of having visions of and conversations with God. In 1931 the hospital where he was working closed, and in that year or the next he began carving. He simply arose one

Yedziyev, Soslanbek: Tombstone in the Village Cemetery of Sindzikau

morning and told his sister he was going to cut some stone because God had spoken to him "like a natural man" and instructed him to do that. For the next fifteen years he produced numerous tombstones and carved a variety of stone preachers, women and angels (some of the last carrying bags!) as well as "critters" such as doves, turtles, horses, lambs and rabbits. He referred to his work as "mirkels" (miracles) which, he vowed, came from visions revealed to him in the sky.

As for his technique, totally untaught and living in a rural area, he had little chance to see works by other artists. He used flat chisels which he made himself and worked in limestone, which cost him nothing because he either salvaged it from demolished buildings or used discarded kerbstones.

Edmonson was "discovered" by a neighbour, Sidney Hirsch, who introduced him to the photographer Louise Dahl-Wolfe. She showed her photographs to Alfred Barr of the Museum of Modern Art, and thus Edmonson became the first black artist to be honoured there with a one-man show. He was then employed by the Works Pro-

jects Administration — Federal Art Projects — which he also regarded as the Lord's wish and doing. His work has since appeared in numerous exhibitions and galleries and can be seen in the Hirschhorn Museum in Washington, D. C. *J. W.*

EDZIEV, SOSLANBEK (1878—1953)   **USSR**
YEDZIYEV, SOSLANBEK

Soslanbek Yedziyev was born in the mountain hamlet of Khod. His father was a stone-mason who not only built houses but also made memorials for graveyards and roads; in fact the custom of many of the ethnic groups in the Caucasus of erecting roadside memorials, may be hundreds of years old. After learning at school how to write his Christian name and surname, Yedziyev moved, while in his teens, to the village of Sadon, where, like his father before him, he plied the trade of stone-mason and also worked as a house plasterer. Several years later he moved to the village of Sindzikau, where he lived to the end of his days.

His artistic talent was first revealed in the two-storey stone house that he built for himself in this village. Hewing the huge boulders which he had dragged out of the nearby mountain stream of Urodon, he carved out embellishments for his home; thus beneath the head of a young man symbolising eternal youth he adorned the front with an effigy of St. George transfixing the dragon with his lance, a girl playing a concertina, a sleeping woman and a highlander garbed in the national Cherkess tunic. Further, to make them more attractive and cause them to stand out from the natural hue of the rock, he painted them in plain colours, tinting the saint's horse white as the incarnation of the divine spirit and the dragon black as the embodiment of evil; the warrior saint is of a cerulean blue, as he lives in the heavens. These colours and also green and red are to be seen on all his sculptures.

Of greatest significance, though, in Yedziyev's work is the traditional type of memorial tombstone, in which genre he expressed his own aesthetic outlook. To this day one can encounter in Ossetia the traditional type of upright or horizontal tombstone, whose incised design indicates the trade or profession of the deceased. At the outset Yedziyev adhered to the traditional style, but later switched to a carved relief in place of the incised representation. Then he carved the figure in high relief, before finally turning to sculpture in the round. In the now overgrown village graveyards in the vicinity of Sindzikau there are thirty-odd tombstones on which Yedziyev depicted old people, children, young men and women, hunters, horsemen or musicians in bas-relief and high relief. Becoming interested in woodcarving, in the evening of his life, Yedziyev produced such objects as *ladzag* shepherd's staffs, goblets and chalices, which were exhibited at displays of popular applied art. Yedziyev's goblets and chalices are embellished with multi-figure narrative episodes centred on the national type of domestic utensil, a bowl for beer or for *koumyss* (a beverage made of fermented mare's milk) which is carved, as a rule, out of one chunk of wood. It is set amidst representations of bulls, horses or riders, which, like branches spreading from one tree-trunk, seem arrested in expectation of a gust of wind that will cause them to twirl as if on a merry-go-round. Yedziyev's work shows us how the traditional folk arts, by crossing into other systems of visual representation, may produce lasting works which widen our aesthetic vistas. Yedziyev was represented at several exhibitions in his home republic of Ossetia and also at USSR exhibitions held in Moscow. Some of his works have been acquired by the museum in Ordjonikidze, capital of the North Caucasian autonomous highland republic of Ossetia. *(See portrait of the artist, p. 228). N. Sh.*

ELENOK,   USSR
TAT'JANA DMITRIEVNA (1930)
YELENOK, TATYANA DMITRIYEVNA

T. D. Yelenok was born into a collective farmer's family in the hamlet of Maryansky near the South Russian city of Krasnodar. After four years of elementary schooling, she had seven years at a vocational school where she trained as a telephone operator. She has loved needlework, embroidery and knitting since childhood. After moving first to Krasnodar and subsequently to Moscow, where she works as a telephone and telegraph operator, she began to paint in oils.

Ehm, Ernst: Children's Portrait

Yelenok, T. D.: The Flying Proletarian

EHM, ERNST (1912)   **East Germany**

Ernst Ehm was trained as a tanner but was subsequently prevented from following his trade by a severe illness which led to paralysis of the right side of his body. He attended a school for the handicapped and was finally employed as a shoemaker in a large concern in Altenburg.

He finds the themes for his paintings in the immediate vicinity of Altenburg and in his own family circle. They are mostly portraits, frequently pictures of children, but there are also floral still-life studies and factory landscapes. Ehm's sense of composition and colour effect is exceptionally well-developed. His pictures are dominated by a brooding, solemn silence. The mode of reproduction is reminiscent of old photographs. The effect is involuntarily ironic, as if he were making fun of such photographs. The figurative pattern of the photograph, translated here into terms of painting, comes to life through the loving treatment of details. *(See portrait of the artist, p. 228). K. C.*

She had her first one-woman show in 1972 in Moscow during the World Student Games. She paints from memory and as imagination dictates, revealing a manifest connection with folklore, but of a present-day vintage. Her favourite subject, often repeated, is related in one way or another to the Soviet electrification scheme. She also borrows themes from fairy tales and from modern poetry. Also observable in her work are features characteristic of a child's vision of the world, as well as the reflection of ideals cherished by people of village stock who settled in the cities and assimilated urban aesthetic tastes through books, magazine illustrations, the cinema and the like.

Ambitious and eager for recognition, she has been represented at several group exhibitions and had works reproduced in periodicals; she also has works on view in the Suzdal Museum, where she painted a frieze.

(See portrait of the artist, p. 228). N. Sh.

ELLIS, VIVIAN (1933)　　　　　**West Germany**

Vivian Ellis, born in New Orleans, Louisiana, the daughter of a Baptist minister, has worked since 1961 as a nurse at the United States hospital in Munich. In New Orleans Vivian Ellis used to teach painting and handicrafts to the children who came to Sunday school and Bible classes, but she did not "really start painting" until she came to Munich. Although the world represented in the pictures of this intelligent and sensitive woman is frequently turbulent and hectic, it nevertheless retains a benignly serene atmosphere imbued with poetry. The religious back-

God's Creation. That's the only reason I turn to canvas and brush." This remark makes clear why a cheerful, optimistic and expansive atmosphere prevails in her pictures as well as in her personal life, which is totally occupied by service to her sick and helpless fellow-men and by devotion to her art. With incredible boldness Vivian Ellis embarked one day on a huge copper engraving, almost as large as a door, entitled "The Revelations of St. John on Patmos." She succeeded in capturing the bewildering flood of visionary revelations within a clearly ordered structure without forfeiting the excitement of the apocalyptic happenings.

Ellis, Vivian: Paradise

ground of the parental home, direct contact with the elemental forces of nature and the people of her homeland, but also a propensity for philosophical speculation have inclined Vivian Ellis to deal repeatedly in her paintings with the story of the Creation. With admirable courage and the recklessness that is characteristic of the truly naive artist she has recorded the history of the first human beings on her vast canvases — it is worth noting that they are always white-skinned in her pictures. She shows their carefree existence amidst animals that lie peacefully side by side surrounded by luxuriant flora and teeming fauna: "I would like to express my delight in

Much of her work is also concerned with memories of her childhood in far-off New Orleans.

It is the colours in particular which give her pictures their carefree freshness. They represent a broad range of very personal values. They are not elementary and are never applied *al prima* to the canvas. Every single shade is given its own specific value by means of careful blending: there are certain similarities to the palette of the "Nabis."

Apart from this, a profound delight in rhythm and in the fanciful use of ornament imparts movement and vitality to her genre pictures. The inventive alternation of oscillating and static shapes, of monochrome and patterned surfaces, is reminiscent of the work of Matisse. *(See portrait of the artist, p. 228).* T. G.

ELSA O. S.   Brazil
(ELSA DE OLIVEIRA SOUZA) (1928)

Elsa de Oliveira Souza was born in Recife, Pernambuco. Having taken the advice of Gerson da Silva (to whom she is now married) and Ivan Serpa in Rio de Janeiro in 1962, she became a painter, displaying a strong decorative streak and a natural surrealistic eccentricity.

Elsa de Oliveira Souza: The Wedding of Elsa O. S.

The women in her pictures (and many of the men) are notable for their large eyes and their solemn expressions. Interiors are carefully painted, with all details accented. Pictures of scenes outside houses are colourful and usually dense with action. Her painstaking methods, which in the work of others might appear laboured, escape such a criticism because they are to be absorbed by the atmosphere she is able to evoke. *Sh. W.*

ENĂCHESCU, CONSTANTIN (1905)   Romania

Constantin Enăchescu was born in the commune of Bujorul in the district of Galaţi. After serving as an apprentice he became a typographer and settled in the town of Bîrlad, where he still lives today in retirement. Having begun to paint in 1960, he had his first public showing in a group exhibition in Bîrlad in 1965.

Drawing for the substance of his paintings on romantic themes or events charged with tension, he has been largely inspired by the history of the wars fought by the Moldavian Romanians and instinctively chooses to paint in a monumen-

tal style. Using large surfaces and applying a strictly planned composition involving numerous figures, he invests their carefully studied movements with a certain romantic rhetoric, discernible in the proliferation of detail.

When portraying the cruelty of a military conflict ("August 1944 in Galaţi"), Enăchescu presents a gallery of types and psychological states of mind. The composition centres on one figure, who serves as a symbol; in a perfect crescendo, the foreground fits into the background, where the artist, like a stage designer, employs light to underline the cruelty of the scene.

Enăchescu, Constantin: Stephen the Great at Podul Inalt

Enăchescu paints in oil on canvas. Although he rarely exhibits, and when he does, only in group exhibitions, his paintings were on display with those of other Romanian naive artists at the International Meeting of Art and Culture in Lugano in 1973. *M. Il.*

ENNULAT, MINNA (1901)   West Germany

Minna Ennulat, a farmer's daughter, was born in Baltschdorf, East Prussia, and now lives in Hadamar. In 1945 she fled with her two sons across the frozen inshore waters of the Baltic. They finally arrived in Hadamar, where they found a new home. While they were furnishing their house, Minna Ennulat made a lamp-shade; because it looked dull she painted it. She was so pleased with the result that she began to paint pictures. There were years when Minna Ennulat, who had lost nothing of her effervescent temperament with advancing years, felt inclined to give up painting, mainly because she could not settle down on alien soil. Anyone who knows Minna Ennulat, whose works represent a major achievement in German naive art, is aware of how passionately she is attached to the landscapes and acquaintances of her youth, so it is hardly surprising that in her pictures she constantly recalls this unforgettable time. Here, firmly ensconced in the traditions of a village community, she is able to rediscover, even in an alien land, the inexhaustible repertoire of her pictures: the house where she was born, the church, the farm-house with its paddock and benches where one could sit and rest, elks, horses, and birds of every kind. All these tributes to village life are painted in bright, cheerful colours, for she has adopted an *al prima* technique of painting with primary enamels. She seems to view everything with the eyes of a carefree, happy child and interprets the world in this manner. Under her hand even the most banal and everyday objects and events undergo a kind of poetic transfiguration: the patterns of flower-beds spread out like coloured rugs on lush lawns, rows and clumps of trees and bushes, groups of people seated on benches and resting from the day's labour or strolling in a leisurely fashion through the beauties of nature, the shapes and the alignment of windows, gates and doorways, decorative painting, ornament in plaster and

overcome by an act of self-liberation achieved through the medium of painting. Pictures by Minna Ennulat are to be found in every important collection of naive art. In 1972 she was awarded a major prize endowed by the city of Hamburg. Recently, her advanced years and poor health have impaired her vitality and creative power. *(See portrait of the artist, p. 229). T. G.*

EPPLE, BRUNO (1931) West Germany

Bruno Epple, born in Rielasingen, and now resident in Wangen on Lake Constance, is a

Ennulat, Minna: Lorelei

wood, flocks of birds in the sky, swans, ducks, fish and water-lilies in and on the ponds and brightly coloured crowds of birds perched in the luxuriant foliage of the trees. From all these elements, and from many others added by her imagination, Minna Ennulat contrives to weave a bright and cheerful carpet of coloured images which is capable of astonishing us not simply because of the inventiveness of the artist, with her gift of rendering complicated things simply and reproducing the simple with a rich variety of inventive shapes, but also because her pictures bring home to us how the despair and hopelessness which threatened this vital woman can be

teacher of German and history at a grammar-school in Radolfzell. Epple was fond of drawing even when he was at school and in the intervening years painting has become his favourite sparetime occupation, although he tries not to neglect his other hobby — the writing of poetry and prose pieces.

Epple enjoys painting on days when he is not teaching and on Sundays (when he goes on painting late into the night), especially when he has a heavy load of professional work and is under stress. "That's when painting is like a kind of seduction. That's when I get the ideas for my best pictures. It's enjoyable to place one layer of pigment on another, building up and modelling things and discreetly emphasising them." The figures in Epple's paintings are as gentle in their treatment of each other as he is with his brush and pigments. Whether at work or in encounters with each other, their handshakes, embraces and other movements and gestures are tentative and shy. Strangely, almost mystically divorced from reality, they brood pensively in an atmosphere of serene contemplation. The colours that Epple chooses are correspondingly refined, never glaring, but possessing a discreet intensity. A broad range of whites, from pleasantly warm to frosty

noisseurs, and he has gained international recognition as well as a number of awards. *(See portrait of the artist, p. 228). T. G.*

ERKENS, SOFIA (1904)   West Germany

Sofia Erkens was born in Niederrhein, where she still lives today. At first, she worked in the office of a weaving workshop where her father was the technical manager. After marrying, she left her job and began painting to assuage the pain of the death of her daughter. Initially, she painted on glass but later she took up oils.

Epple, Bruno: Abandoned

Erkens, Sofia: Celebration of Hero's Day

and cold, dominates throughout, usually bordered by adjoining blue, black or brown.

Epple has nevertheless always been considered something of a controversial commuter in the various regions of German naive painting. This view has been more or less confirmed in his native country by the evolution of his work, which threatens to grow more and more inflexible and mannered. There is no doubt that Epple is capable of revealing psychic states with great delicacy by means of minimal modifications of facial expression and posture; he knows an astonishing amount about composition and colouring, is acquainted with the magic realism of the twenties and is a master of painting techniques. All this suggests that Epple's work no longer belongs in the category of naive art, but that behind these pictures there now stands an intellectually and professionally accomplished self-taught painter of considerable skill. Opinion is very much divided on this point. Anatol Jakowsky, for example, singles out Epple as "the best of contemporary German naive painters." Epple's precisely painted pictures are much in demand among con-

In the painting "Celebration of Hero's Day," an impressive monument stands against a blue sky. A heroic figure, probably the Unknown Soldier, wearing a blue uniform with bright red epaulettes, sits on a rock while an angel in light-coloured clothes touches his shoulder with one hand and points the other heavenwards: perhaps up there is the only hope for all those who lost their lives or disappeared in the war and will never go home again. Important personages in the social hierarchy, dressed in black and holding or wearing top hats, march around the monument. Full of piety, they are paying homage to the Unknown Soldier while the decorations on their chests show that survivors are, after all, better off.

In real life, celebrations such as these are far sadder, although sometimes the ceremonial is merely official. But this painting looks like a scene from a cabaret — despite the fact that a few faces reflect dismay at the recollection of war — especially since the hero on the monument seems to have come alive. Nature does not share in the solemn moment but lives its own life, the

green growing luxuriantly and tiny red flowers scattered gaily around the monument. *(See portrait of the artist, p. 229).*

ERTUGANOV, ŠAMIL' (1932)   USSR
ERTUGANOV, SHAMIL

A Tartar by nationality, Shamil Ertuganov was born in Moscow into a family of factory workers, who at about that time had moved from Penza to the capital. After leaving school he worked for a time as an electrician. Today he is a handyman in a shop. He has been drawing since

Ertuganov, Shamil: Moscow's Northern River Terminal

childhood. In 1973 he completed a course of instruction at ZNUI, the Extra-mural People's University of Art. He paints from nature and from memory, often reproducing what he may have seen on television. His art belongs to the category which we have conventionally designated as urban folklore, reflecting a combination of modern themes and the aesthetic tastes of the urban environment. To some degree his pictures are photographic, incorporating a tangible fixation of subject matter, especially in still-lifes. This evokes associations with the *Weltanschauung* of the signboard painters active at the turn of the 19th century. His colours are sharp and forceful, though the object or sitter is touchingly poeticised, displaying the integrity of an artisan approach to detail and accessories. The sitter is generalised, naive, a kind of cut-out isolated against the background — in much the same manner as that of the serf painters of the 19th century, who sought to imitate professional artists and what they considered the "grand style." Ertuganov has a keen eye for colour, which he uses sparsely, exclusively to single out the basic motif. In fact his main strength lies in his sense and feeling for colour. He is able to impart a piercing characterisation to a prosaic theme, even though it is wrongly handled. This is manifest in paintings on his favourite theme of Moscow sights, such as "The Pushkin Monument" and "The 'Leningrad' Picture Palace," to mention but two. He has been represented at numerous group exhibitions of amateur art, including several on a nation-wide scale. *(See portrait of the artist, p. 229). N. Sh.*

EVANS, MINNIE (1893)   USA

The works of Minnie Evans might be called visionary or mystic. She herself, however, is a jolly, open person, somewhat deaf and no longer the amply proportioned woman she was in 1935, when her strange dreams impelled her to put fantasy to paper.

Born in Long Creek, North Carolina (her mother was only 13!), she has, except for a trip to New York in 1966, lived all her life in the rural quiet of Wilmington, North Carolina. She never went beyond the sixth grade and until discovered by Nina Howell Starr in 1959 had little contact

Evans, Minnie: Untitled

with the world outside the Arlie Gardens in Wilmington, where she worked as gatekeeper and ticket-taker. After her husband died, she and her mother lived together until the infirmities of age made it necessary for them to move in with Minnie's son, his wife and children.

Her first drawings, two Klee-like line sketches in crayon on paper, were done on Good Friday in 1935. She had no explanation as to what impelled her except to say: "In a dream it was shown to me what I have to do . . . Something spoke to me like this, 'Why don't you draw or die?' Something had my hand." Her drawings amaze her as much as they do others. "When I get through with them, they are just as strange to me as they are to anybody else." Most of her work is in vivid primary colours, symmetrical in balance but not in the designs, which are full of eyes, heavenly figures, and lush, almost oriental phantasmagorias of leaves, birds, animals, flowers, devils and angels.

Though Minnie Evans has been written about in national magazines, has had several shows (one in the Whitney Museum), and is the subject of a short series of films on visionary artists, celebrity has not affected her work. She continues to create her strongly hued, inexplicable dream fantasies. *J. W.*

EVE, JEAN (1900—1968)   **France**

Jean Eve was born at Somain and died at Louveciennes. Coming from a family of railwaymen, he was sent to the trade school in Thiers to become a fitter. In 1917, he volunteered for the colonial cavalry in Algeria, which took him throughout North Africa and Syria. After his return to France in 1922, he tried a variety of jobs in the Paris region and in the north. He married in 1923 and, like his father, finally went to work for the French railways. The next years were of decisive importance in leading him to paint. A Courbet exhibition and another exhibition of

From the 1950s onwards, honours, medals and prizes made recognition official. After his trips across France, he always returned with a group of canvases which attested once again to his talent for landscape.

Jean Eve expressed himself principally through a classical vision of nature, his basic source of inspiration. Winter or spring landscapes, views of the villages of Burgundy or Provence — all are compositions firmly founded on the most severe rules of perspective and the distribution of coloured masses. Buildings are rendered with precision, vegetation is leafy, the

Eve, Jean: Landscape of the Ile de France

Flemish primitives were part of his discovery of painting, but it was his meetings with members of Art Vivant (George Charensol, Martin du Gard, Maximilien Gauthier) and with the painter Kisling which prompted him to paint. He first exhibited in 1930 in Paris, but it was the Maîtres Populaires de la Realité exhibition in 1937 which opened the doors to recognition for him. His success was confirmed with the Perls Gallery Exhibition of his work in New York in 1939. Within a few years, he gave up his job permanently — he was working as a toll-collector, as had Rousseau — and dedicated himself completely to painting.

lighting is soft and clearly directed. Each painting is above all a quest for harmony and pushes traditional definitions of naive art to their limits.

Jean Eve has been exhibiting since 1930. The exhibitions listed at which his work has been seen at present exceed 150. *(See portrait of the artist, p. 229). Ch. Sch.*

Edziev, Soslanbek

Ebert, Albert

Ehm, Ernst

Elenok, T. D.

Ellis, Vivian

Epple, Bruno

ulat, Minna

ens, Sofia

Ertuganov, Šamil'

, Jean

FAGUNDEZ CRUZ, AMADO — Venezuela
FARDOULYS, JAMES — Australia
FASANELLA, RALPH — USA
FAUCQ, JEAN — Belgium
FAUSTINO, JOSÉ — Nicaragua
FAVIER, CÉCILE — France
FAVRE, MARCEL — France
FEJEŠ, EMERIK — Yugoslavia
FELSKI, ALBINA — USA
FENNELL, VERA — Australia
FERDINAND, JEAN — Belgium
FEREOLI, ENRICO — Italy
FERNANDEZ, ANTONIO JOSÉ — Venezuela
FERNANDEZ, MARCELINA — Argentina
FERRARA, DANIEL — France
FERRARI, PIERINO — Italy
FIELD, ERASTUS SALISBURY — USA
FIELDING, DAVID — Australia
FILIPOVIĆ, FRANJO — Yugoslavia
FINSTER, HOWARD — USA
FIORIO, SERGE — France
FISHER, JONATHAN — USA
FLETES, IGNACIO — Nicaragua
FORTIN, EDMOND — France
FOUS, JEAN — France
FRACAROSSI, JOSEPH — USA
FRASSA, LUISE — West Germany
FREITAS, JOSÉ DE — Brazil
FRÍAS, GATO — Argentina
FRUNZETE, VASILE — Romania
FRYER, FLORA — USA
FUENTES, GLORIA — Argentina

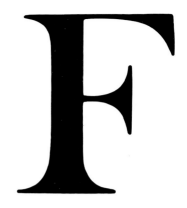

Fagundez Cruz, Amado: Reclining Nude   *Fardoulys, James: Migrations to Gympie*

FAGUNDEZ CRUZ, AMADO (1910)   **Venezuela**

Amado Cruz Fagundez was born in Petare. He now lives and works in Caracas. One of the titans of Venezuelan naive art, Fagundez is a man of natural efficiency. In his day he had had all manner of jobs (in a wine business, as chauffeur to the doctor Jesus Maria Pelaez, as a mechanic, then with the omnibuses, and finally as custodian of the art organisation "Germán V. Lira"), and all this was before he painted his first naive picture (1964).

"Doña Rosita," "Desnudo Reclinado" and "La Más Bella," show that he can be an artist of considerable strength, one who could even take his place alongside the finest of the German Expressionists. There is, however, another Fagundez who paints simple and more primitive naive scenes in which the figures (important nonetheless) are only a small part of the landscape or interior he has chosen to depict. Although these pictures might be considered less virile than those shown here, and certainly do not have the same impact, they are nevertheless extremely moving in their untutored style. *(See portrait of the artist, p. 248). Sh. W.*

FARDOULYS, JAMES (1900—1975)   **Australia**

James Fardoulys was born in Kythera in Greece. He came to Australia in 1914, and died in Brisbane.

In adulthood he travelled widely around Australia, painting water holes, gum trees, horses and cockatoos. In spite of his choice of typically Australian subject-matter, he approached his subjects always with the eye of a Greek.

After marrying a ventriloquist, James Fardoulys began to travel with show people, mostly in Queensland. Eventually he became a taxi-driver and retired when he was about sixty.

It was after his retirement that he began to paint seriously.

He had his first exhibition in Sydney at the Johnstone Gallery in 1966. He then regularly participated in group exhibitions and won a number of prizes, including the Warren Caltex Prize. *B. McC.*

FASANELLA, RALPH (1914)   **USA**

Ralph Fasanella, though he lives in a charming modern house with his wife (a schoolteacher) and two children in one of New York's nicest suburbs, always considers himself working class. He was born in New York City's Greenwich Village. Repeated rebellion against having to help his Italian immigrant father haul ice twelve hours a day led to three terms in a Catholic reform school (the subject of some of his paintings). During the Depression he joined the Workers' Alliance, fought in the Spanish Civil War in 1937, became a CIO (Congress of Industrial Organisations) organiser, and ran unsuccessfully for city councilman on the American Labour Party ticket. He never felt any ambition to become an artist until a girl friend who was a commercial artist persuaded him to do some drawing. This stirred him, and when he left his CIO job in 1945, he began to paint more purposefully. Unable to find a steady job because of his political background, he

Fasanella, Ralph: Family Dinner

worked in his brother's garage as a mechanic, and by 1947 was painting as much as ten hours a day, trying to portray the working-class heroism he had witnessed during his experiences as an organiser and factory employee.

Fasanella has over the years produced numerous large, heavily detailed, strongly coloured canvases on family life in the slums, the reform school, political campaigns, sweatshop life, and New York's crowded buildings and streets. He told a *New York Magazine* reporter: "There's no place like New York, and I want to get it all, hug it. I made a portrait of every window. Every face is a person I know. I painted in memory . . . my mother, my old man, working-class Italian families, Marcantonio (a liberal politician), injustice, Jews, Blacks, Puerto Ricans. I wanted the cars, the movement, the streets that pour people into sweatshops . . . the McCarthy era . . . the Rosenbergs . . ." *(See portrait of the artist, p. 248). J. W.*

FAUCQ, JEAN (1900—1978)   **Belgium**

Jean Faucq was born in Brussels, where he died. At one time, he kept a café in the Marolles quarter of the city. He painted only intermittently, selling his pictures in the Flea Market and in his café-bar. Most of his inspiration was drawn from places where the poorer sections of the population gathered, and also from Brussels folklore. A very prolific painter, he usually depicted street scenes. His canvases, on which pure tones lend dynamism to light grey and white areas, are filled with crowds that are never compact, always dispersed. This artist had no fear of empty

Faucq, Jean: Manneken Pis

spaces, unlike some naive painters, although he usually worked in a small format.

He is a lyricist by nature, more a serious painter than a humorist. The profound respect he feels for his craft is not at all at odds with his fantasy. Banal subjects are elevated by him and transposed to a poetic plane.

He exhibited a number of times in Brussels, Düsseldorf and Cologne. *J. C.*

FAUSTINO, JOSÉ   **Nicaragua**

In the south of the Nicaraguan archipelago of 38 islands Ernesto Cardinale founded a little community of fishermen and farmers devoted to painting. Strange pictures of paradise, inspired by naive faith, were produced here, in Solentiname.

José Faustino's beautiful landscape offers us a composition harmoniously constructed from three horizontal zones. The lowest of these is formed by the translucent clarity of the water, from which rise little islands with thickets of palm-like plants. A small boat pursues its course across the silky surface of the sea. The austere profiles of people and animals impart to the picture something of the hieratic quality we find in Egyptian reliefs. The second zone is formed by the dense olive-green forest, its bushes, grass and trees combining to create a bronze-coloured curtain. It is only when the spectator's eye has grown accustomed to the green patina that this curtain becomes transparent and reveals the secret life of people and animals in the forest. The third zone is that of the sparse upper levels of the forest, the pale yellow palm fronds and the gently stirring tree-tops that reach up into the azure

al wreaths, which she lovingly collected. Her first exhibition in Paris took place in 1959.

The work of Cécile Favier shows a strong discipline based on the rules of composition of academic art. Her paintings voice a concern to communicate the reality which inspires the artist by working with precise strokes and a feeling for detail pushed to the extreme. An atmosphere of calm deriving from a quest for harmonious colour combinations bathes each picture, even in some canvases which seem a little stiff.

Cécile Favier has exhibited in Paris. *(See portrait of the artist, p. 248). Ch. Sch.*

Faustino, José: *Village on the Sea*

Favier, Cécile: *Bouquet of Flowers*

blue of the sky. The blue above and the blue below combine to form the luminous unity of this landscape.

In the centre of the picture stands a house with a high-pitched shingle roof. On a bench by the door sits a man with a guitar, singing the heart-felt song of a devout life. A passer-by leading a white horse has stopped to listen; there is a woman with a basket of fruit on her head; a few tiny children. There they stand, spellbound by the music. The painter has contrived, in a moment of childlike enchantment, to capture the communion of man and primitive nature *O. B.-M.*

FAVIER, CÉCILE (1906)   **France**

Cécile Favier was born in Orcines, Puy-de-Dôme. Taken to South America by her parents as a child, she began painting landscapes there. On returning to France in 1918, she chose first to become a seamstress and later a florist. For her, handling flowers or textiles involved the same pleasure: the play of colours. She was inspired in both lines of work and by the aesthetics of funer-

FAVRE, MARCEL (1907—1972) France

Marcel Favre was born at Dingy-St-Clair and died in Paris. He finished elementary and secondary school in Annecy, served his term in the army and went to work for the government, rising to Chief Inspector of Taxes in his government career. In 1947, looking for a way to fill his free time, he bought brushes, canvases and paints. In 1949, while at Sable d'Olonne, he met Jules Lefranc, who encouraged him to paint and to exhibit. From that time onward he participated, in the Surintendants, the Salon Comparaison, and other group exhibitions. Marcel Favre was a

Favre, Marcel: Portrait of Jules Lefranc

painstaking perfectionist and painted only about a dozen pictures a year. These, however, were seen not only in France but also in London, Detroit, and Athens, winning him an international reputation.

Marcel Favre's art is one of meticulous description, of depicting the thousand reflections of water on carefully rendered leaves. He delighted to paint the port of Chaume in many different versions, applying touch by touch the colour accents which give vibrance to his canvases. We are also indebted to him for glimpses of the nooks and crannies of the towns and cities he knew.

Marcel Favre has had numerous one-man shows and participated in many group exhibitions. (See portrait of the artist, p. 249). Ch. Sch.

FEJEŠ, EMERIK (1904-1969) Yugoslavia

Emerik Feješ was born in Osijek, Croatia, one of fourteen children of a poor Hungarian family, and had to start earning a living early in life. From his father he learned how to make but-

tons and combs from animal bones, which could be had in quantity from the slaughterhouse, and continued in this trade until his death. He worked in Zagreb, Belgrade, Maribor, Novi Sad — wherever an interest was shown in his wares.

In the summer of 1969, he died at the age of sixty-five in a suburb of Novi Sad, in an environment differing greatly from those portrayed in his paintings. Buttonmaker, combmaker and daydreamer, a man who in his imagination travelled with his pictures, Emerik Feješ left behind, besides the buttons and combs, several hundred paintings showing imposing façades and squares

Feješ, Emerik: Parliament House in London

Felski, Albina: Logging Operation

from the world's metropolises. Coloured picture postcards, which he initially bought himself and later received from all over the world, were transformed by him with match-sticks and homemade colours into the fantastic architecture he dreamed about.

His second wife, Josephine, explained his technique: "Emerik painted at night, often until morning. Instead of a brush he used wooden match-sticks. He measured postcards with them

f

234

and transferred the subjects, enlarged, to paper. He kept his colours in the stoppers of beer bottles. He would put on two pairs of glasses to magnify the postcards, adding details as he saw fit. Colour gave him the most trouble. He used to get up at night to mix them if he recalled something. No one was entrusted with the secret of the way he made his colours, not even I. His colours cannot be erased from his pictures."

Emerik Feješ began to paint in 1949 and his passion for it never waned, in spite of his preoccupation with his main work. His first wife, dissatisfied with her husband for wasting precious

the postcard, it seemed to him that the square looked empty. He added tracks and a tram, like the ones in Novi Sad, and also a mother taking her child for a walk and a worker with a wheelbarrow who, dressed in his best, seems to be posing for a photograph taken by Feješ. He changed the colours of the façades and generally transformed the square in Basel, making it look the way he wished it to be.

Emerik Feješ has had one-man shows and participated in group exhibitions at home and abroad.

(See portrait of the artist, p. 249). N. T.

Feješ, Emerik: Basel

time on "stupidities" as though he were a child, burned up all his pictures one day. But even this did not distract him. Suffering from asthma and sciatica, he all of a sudden started travelling via his postcards and paintings to the most remote towns on earth. The more his sickness tied him to his bed, the more he painted the streets, squares, buildings, and monuments of world capitals. But he changed the colours and also left out everything on the postcards that did not appeal to him, while introducing numerous details of his own. The results were pictures entirely different from their models; the strangest thing is that he truly believed he was copying everything faithfully.

For instance, Feješ took a liking to the Swiss town of Basel, its architecture and its tower in the centre, and decided to paint it. As he copied

FELSKI, ALBINA   USA

Albina Felski's first award for painting was won when she was thirteen, but it was also her last for many years. She never explained why she did not continue this activity, though it was one of the pleasures of her school days. She comes from a working-class background and small-town life, having been born in Fernie, British Columbia, Canada, where her father was a coal miner. "That's where I had the great idea of painting a coal miner picture," she wrote. "I attended a Catholic school. My brothers would take me on fishing trips, and photograph pictures of grizzly bears, deer, mountain goats, wild sheep, moose. I would see all these lovely animals; that's where I get all my ideas on painting beautiful animals. I also travelled around all the National Glacial Parks . . . that's where I have ideas on painting lovely pine trees, spruce trees, lakes and rivers."

Mrs. Felski moved to the USA either during or shortly before the Second World War and worked in the shipyards as a riveter. She did not begin painting again until 1961, at which time she and her husband were living and working in Chicago.

She says her husband has always seen to it that her paintings were exhibited. "My paintings are all framed by him. I am very busy around the house and I work in a factory. I put a lot of details in my paintings because that is what I

FERDINAND, JEAN (1888—1972)   Belgium

Jean Ferdinand Hannoset was born in Brussels, where he died. His original intention was to study art but the First World War intervened and he found himself compelled to take up barbering. When he was in his fifties, he was again overcome by the desire to paint and by the love for the Belle Epoque that inspired all his works, which are poised on the very edge of a restless eroticism. His interiors also bear witness to that yearning: drawers full of underwear from 1900, a half-dressed mannequin for corsets — these were the models and the means of this artist.

Fennell, Vera: Stepping Out

remember. If I want to paint a picture of my experiences, I just close my eyes and remember the whole scene and draw it out on canvas, then I start from the top and paint down." *J. W.*

FENNELL, VERA (1939)   Australia

Vera Fennell was born in Czechoslovakia. Towards the end of the war, in 1944, her family moved to Vienna, and from there emigrated to Australia in 1958. In 1960 she joined the Tivoli Theatre in Melbourne, travelling to the Far East as a one-woman show between 1961 and 1967.

She finally settled in Australia on a permanent basis in about 1974, this country having always seemed to her the ideal place in which to live. She opened a beauty salon and started to learn drawing. At Christmas 1978, her husband presented her with a box of oil paints and some brushes. She became so inspired that she now paints at least five hours every day. Her pictures are strongly influenced by her European background: she often paints snow scenes, which are rare in the work of Australian naives. Her "Stepping Out" (shown here), with its atmosphere of old-world elegance and serenity, is redolent of a more leisurely age.

During 1980 she had a one-woman show at the Gallery Art Naive in Melbourne. *B. McC.*

Ferdinand, Jean: Buffalo Bill

He did not immediately achieve assurance in the painter's craft, and took time to acquire skill in keeping his colours uniform, and resourcefulness in transmitting to canvas pictures of the city of Epinal in which all the details were harmonised. Success came quickly to him, however, and his canvases were purchased even before they left his studio. Consequently, he had to be very careful to maintain his integrity as an artist. Collectors jealously guard his paintings, which hardly ever appear on the market.

He exhibited a number of times in Brussels. *(See portrait of the artist, p. 249). J. C.*

FEREOLI, ENRICO (1901) Italy

Enrico Fereoli, born in Sala Baganza, Parma, lives and works in Parma. Having been employed in a wide variety of occupations, such as carpenter, barber and locomotive engineer, he began to paint in 1955 but devoted himself to art only from 1958, after an illness compelled him to

FERNANDEZ, ANTONIO JOSÉ (1923) Venezuela

José Antonio Fernandez, born in Escuque, Trujillo province, Venezuela, now lives and works in Valera. At one time an auxiliary nurse in a hospital, Fernandez was discovered in 1958 by Carlos Contramaes. Ten years later he was able to hold an important exhibition of his works in Galeria 22, Caracas.

He is an artist who divides his time between sculpture (with which he began) and painting. His home and place of work have been described as seeming to be placed in a Garden of Eden. With

Fereoli, Enrico: Piazzale Serventi

Fernandez, Marcelina: Ploughman

Fernandez, Antonio José: Destruction of the Body

leave his job. All his artistic effort is concentrated on portraying the town in which he lives.

Fereoli's intention is to reproduce the attractions of Parma realistically and objectively, but the aesthetic effect he achieves far surpasses that of a simple photograph. His technique is exceptional and his canvases are imbued with a special atmosphere and a restrained serenity. In 1962, he had his first one-man show, and in 1964 took part in an exhibition in the Palazzo Barberini in Rome. *(See portrait of the artist, p. 249). D. M.*

something of the poetic imagination of a native, he seizes upon the dramatic moments that infuse his paintings. As can be seen, paint and figuration in these pictures are equally wild and fluid. Both these elements are evident also in his sculptures (which are modelled), but the ferocity to be found in the paintings cannot be matched in his other work. *(See portrait of the artist, p. 248). Sh. W.*

FERNANDEZ, MARCELINA (1898) Argentina

Marcelina Fernandez was born in Santa Fe. She is a housewife, and the only tenuous connection she had initially with art was her weaving and embroidery work. When she was seventy-two and widowed, she left for a distant province with many lakes, in the south of Argentina, and was delighted with the landscape, and with the variety and wealth of colour of the flowers growing there in such abundance. Upon returning to Buenos Aires, she began to weave wool into pictures, trying to depict the scenes she had loved so well. Encouraged by her son, she fashioned her pictures in a workshop set up in an old house full of birds and plants. These are the birds and plants seen in her works. Recently, painting on canvas, she has been evoking events from her childhood and fantastic tales from her imagination. "The gaiety of colours has helped me bear the sad fate of a widow," she says as she holds her brush, like a magic wand used to conjure up the past. *(See portrait of the artist, p. 248). M. T. S.*

FERRARA, DANIEL (1906) France

Daniel Ferrara was born at Mers-el-Kébir, Algeria, into a family of Italian descent and spent his entire childhood in North Africa. He went to work at the age of eleven and was variously employed as a cabin boy, electrician, sailor and, finally, longshoreman. He settled in Marseilles but had little time to spare for painting. In 1946, at the insistence of his wife, he produced his first canvas. With increasing frequency, his work began to appear at shows both in France and abroad. In recent years, he has painted much less.

Ferrara, Daniel: Longshoremen

Bright and changing tones and an almost excessively delicate treatment of his subject are the predominant features of much of the work of Daniel Ferrara. His canvases reproduce the longshoreman's life and the port at Marseilles. He has also painted a number of biblical scenes set against exquisite landscapes.

Ferrara has had one-man shows in Paris, Venice and Zurich. Over the years, he participated in the Salon Terres Latines, Salon Comparaisons and Salon d'Automne in Paris. His work was also seen at the first and second biennials in Bratislava, and he has exhibited in Japan, Switzerland and Denmark. *(See portrait of the artist, p. 248). Ch. Sch.*

FERRARI, PIERINO (1922) Italy

Pierino Ferrari was born in Parma, where he now lives in retirement. The diminutive of "Pierino" is at odds with his robust appearance, just as his earlier occupation of porter is at odds with the specific nature of his style as a painter — light touches with the tip of the brush. But such contrasts are not unusual among naive painters.

His powerful physique conceals a soul full of gentle sentiments, the source of a rich imagination and a freshness of approach. The subject-matter of his paintings differs from one canvas to the next. It may be reptiles whose scales glitter in rainbow colours, prehistoric monsters whose tails are decorated with miniatures in the form of musical notes; wild animals (bears, tigers, pan-

thers); village squares with a foreshortened perspective and surrounded by ornate houses; or, finally, religious scenes.

Whatever the subject, Ferrari uses fiery but controlled colour, rendering detail in the personal manner which is the most obvious feature of his elegant style. For instance, in "Death of St. Francis," the drama is transformed into an enchanted starry mosaic, with thousands upon thousands of flowers and white doves in flight seeming to accompany the ascension of the saint's soul to heaven.

(See portrait of the artist, p. 249). D. M.

Ferrari, Pierino: The Death of St. Francis.

FIELD, ERASTUS SALISBURY (1805—1900) USA

Erastus Salisbury Field was one of the outstanding early American itinerant limners. His bustling career as a portrait painter (but not his production as an artist) was brought to a slow halt in the middle of the 19th century by the invention and rapid spread of photography.

Field, fraternal twin to a sister, was born in Leverett, Massachusetts. As a child he showed so strong a talent and interest in sketching faces that his parents not only encouraged him by supplying him with paints but arranged for him to go to New York City to study with the artist Samuel F. Morse. According to his biographer, Mary Black of the New York Historical Society, Morse found the 19-year old Field to be a "tractable and useful" student. The lessons, however, came to an abrupt halt when Morse's young wife suddenly died and Morse went off to Europe. Several years later Field documented his short but happy life as an art student by painting his memories of Morse's studio.

Field returned to Leverett shortly after Morse's departure and embarked upon what was to become a lucrative profession as an itinerant portrait painter. He travelled extensively throughout Massachusetts, into Connecticut and as far north as Vermont. In 1831 he married Phoebe Gilmur, who bore him one child, a daughter, Henriette. Though the country was heading toward the financial crisis of 1837, Field himself seems not to have had any money problems. His relatives and friends not only kept him busy and paid him well, but recommended his talents to other friends and their relatives elsewhere. Ac-

fairs held by the American Institute of the City of New York. In 1848, according to his daughter, he returned to Massachusetts to manage his father's farm.

Here began the decline of Field's career. Samuel Morse had just returned to the States with the daguerrotype. Field learned to use the camera and followed Morse's precept of "accumulating models" by making photographs of his sitters to be enlarged later on canvas. Even so, orders for his work and hence his income fell off, and Field began more and more to paint large, imposing landscapes, evidently as much for his

Field, Erastus Salisbury: The Garden of Eden

cording to Mary Black, many family and social connections in Massachusetts and Connecticut can be followed through Field's portraits.

In about 1841, for reasons so far undiscovered, Field and his wife and daughter moved to New York City, and judging from the directories of the period, seem to have moved from one address to another in Greenwich Village. By this time his style had matured, its direct hard-edged delineation giving way to a softer feeling and his draughtsmanship much improved. That his success was still at its peak was shown by in the fact that several of his paintings were exhibited in

own pleasure as for sale. When his wife died, he and his daughter moved to Plumtrees, Massachusetts, where he built himself a two-room studio and began to paint large fantasy landscapes, many with religious or historical themes.

Field must have been a genial old man, for fond stories have been recorded by people who knew him when they were schoolchildren, telling of how they would visit his studio at recess time to sit and listen as if mesmerised to his exciting descriptive stories about the massive allegorical paintings lining the walls of his studio from top to bottom and end to end.

He died on 28 June 1900, the oldest voter in his county, the last remaining and one of the most striking representatives of a very special period in the history of American art. *(See portrait of the artist, p. 249). J. W.*

FIELDING, DAVID (1944)   Australia

David Fielding was born in Wales but lived in London until he was six. His parents then moved to the south island of New Zealand and later to Tasmania, where he went to school and, for a short spell, to university. Eventually he and his

Fielding, David: Boys Playing Football

family settled in Adelaide. He attended the South Australian School of Art for two months but was urged to leave because he could not conform to the teaching there. He did some theatre designs, also greeting cards. In 1969 he illustrated a book for Angus and Robertson and in the same year returned to England. Since then he has divided his time between the United Kingdom and Australia, but all his inspiration comes directly from his early impressions of colonial architecture and the unique colours produced by the harsh Australian light.

In 1976 he began to paint full-time, drawing his subjects mostly from the suburban life around him. He likes man-made parks and gardens and architectural subjects which serve to capture the tension between the natural and the so-called civilised worlds. His buildings are often "ugly" — a mixture of styles spanning the various historical periods. He satirises suburbia, municipal bad taste and people's idiosyncrasies, and finds inspiration in the ridiculous. The paintings often carry long and involved titles.

David Fielding works painstakingly on small canvases, using a pointillistic technique with a highly glazed finish which emphasises the detail and the vibrant colouring.

In 1978 he received a study grant from the South Australian Council for the Arts which enabled him to travel to England once again.

His work is represented in private collections in Australia and the United Kingdom as

well as in the permanent collection of naive art at the Swan Hill Regional Gallery. A greetings card was produced from one of his paintings to raise funds for the Melbourne Blind Institute. *(See portrait of the artist, p. 249). B. McC.*

FILIPOVIĆ, FRANJO (1930)   Yugoslavia

Franjo Filipović was born in Hlebine, Croatia. A poor boy, after completing four grades of elementary school, he began to till the soil. In his spare time, he watched his senior fellow-villager, Ivan Generalić, painting, and under his influence

Filipović, Franjo: The Harvest

began to paint on glass the life of the people of this Podravina region. Hlebine, a village comprising a few streets and a hundred or so houses, has remained a permanent source of inspiration for Franjo Filipović. He still lives there, farming, and, in his free time, painting.

"I have no need to think up themes because there are plenty of them in our village and every peasant here knows what they are. If you were to ask any peasant to name the various kinds of work you have to do on the farm, he would certainly tell you two hundred kinds right off. So I have enough themes to last me my whole life."

In "Harvest" (1975), Franjo Filipović portrays summer in Hlebine: work in the fields tying up sheaves of ripe wheat. The farmer and his wife cultivate their land themselves and both of them are dedicated to their work. Behind the wheat-sheaves extends an idyllic landscape of gently rolling hills, green grass and yellow-reddish wheat, still unharvested. In the background, among the trees in bloom, village houses are seen. The sky is a pleasant blue and on it white clouds sail. There is nothing to upset the peace and quiet of the scene except the industrious hands of the peasant couple hurrying with their work, a scene that has repeated itself every summer for centuries.

Franjo Filipović has had one-man shows and participated in group exhibitions at home and abroad. *(See portrait of the artist, p. 248). N. T.*

FINSTER, HOWARD (1916)   USA

The Reverend Howard Finster is both a painter and what is termed an environmentalist — that is, a builder of a personal universe. Genial, almost obsessively talkative in interviews, he is a Baptist minister, who was born in Valley Head, Alabama, and now lives in Summerville, Georgia, where he has turned his two-acre backyard into his "paradise garden." Now retired from preaching, Finster said he had preached for forty years and then asked the Lord, "Is there anything else you want me to do besides pastoring? Well, just show me. So it came to me to build

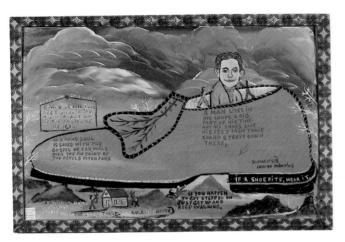

Finster, Howard: A Man Lives in His Shoes

gradually made it his main activity, with encouragement from various writers and art critics. The work of Giono especially has been an important source of inspiration for him.

Fair stalls, merry-go-rounds, Provençal landscapes, knotted grapevines, are all a part of Fiorio's iconography, all rendered in a style of drawing reminiscent of the Italian primitives. From canvas to canvas he maintains a recognisable palette of bright but restrained colour, from which derives a subtle and delicate atmosphere, a "strange poetry of the immobility of air," to quote Fleming's description of Fiorio's work.

f

241

Fiorio, Serge: The Herd

a paradise and decorate it with the Bible. I wanted to put every verse in the Bible in this park."

His "garden" is a complex, grotto-like structure of white painted concrete into which he has inserted hubcaps, broken mirrors, bottles, photographs, television screens on which he has done paintings in car lacquer, wood panels with burned-in designs, and assorted memorabilia.

This all began in 1976, when he was 60. He dipped his finger into a can of paint and saw a face inscribed on it and realised God intended him to paint "Sacred Heart," the first of over 2,000 paintings and constructions he has since done. His paintings, except for his portraits of his favourite presidents and of famous figures, are usually as densely detailed as a Bosch panorama, with small figures in violent action in a variety of settings, the whole interspersed with written admonitions of the dangers of evil, the pleasures of Paradise, thoughts on political issues, women's liberation, energy conservation or current events. *J. W.*

FIORIO, SERGE (1911)   France

Serge Fiorio was born at Vallorbe, Switzerland. After trying various occupations, among them miner, ditch-digger and photographer, he settled in 1947 at Montjustin in the Basses-Alpes. He bought a farm there and helped to bring new life to the small hamlet of Montjustin, where he still lives today. After painting for some time, he

The work of Serge Fiorio has appeared since 1956 in numerous galleries in France, Belgium and England. *(See portrait of the artist, p. 248). Ch. Sch.*

FISHER, JONATHAN (1768—1847)   USA

Alice Winchester wrote that Jonathan Fisher was "a clergyman, not a painter . . . by temperament an artist, a poet, and a naturalist; and by necessity a craftsman, teacher, architect, surveyor, inventor, and more besides." Indeed, judging from his personal journal, he must have been a man of incredible energy, talent, persistence and organisational ability to have done all that he did. He was born in New Braintree, Massachusetts. His father died when he was nine and the boy went to live with his uncle, a minister, who taught him Latin, Greek and theology. Fisher worked his way through Harvard, spent three years as a divinity student, became the first minister at Blue Hill, Maine, married, and with his wife brought nine children in a house he planned himself, decorated with his own paintings, and furnished with furniture and a woodwork clock of his own making. He farmed, raised livestock, made his own farm implements, surveyed his land with homemade instruments, and earned money making and selling buttons, sleighs, pumps and other useful equipment. "He believed in the virtue of labour and the value of learning," writes Mrs. Winchester. He learned Hebrew and

French and acquired an understanding of the Penobscot Indian language. Further, he was an eclectic reader with an aptitude for mathematics and "a passion for natural history." He also found time to get involved in the social and moral issues of his time, such as the abolition of slavery and the rights of Indians, teaching and founding schools, and attending to the various offices of his calling as a minister. He retired in 1837.

This amazing man found time throughout his life to embellish his notebooks with watercolour sketches and drawings, copy engravings of animals and birds to bind in a leather-covered al-

and was able to take time off from his business and visit museums. Eventually he bought artist's equipment and painted his first canvases. The outbreak of war in 1914 put a temporary end to these initial excursions into art. By 1930, he owned several grocery stores in Paris, but in 1940 he sold up, left his wife and withdrew to Nièvre with a new companion. This is when he began to paint in earnest. Most of his works date from this period (1940—1945). In 1946, the couple returned to the Paris area, to Le Bourget, and set up a small grocery shop where Fortin hung his best paintings amidst the vegetable stands and

Fisher, Jonathan: A Morning View of Blue Hill Village

bum, draw from life and from nature, and produce paintings in oil on canvas or board (paintings ranging from portraits and scenic views to still-lifes and nature studies, and occasionally a biblical, allegorical or literary subject inspired by prints), and to illustrate a primer with his woodcuts. His most important oil is his striking self-portrait and a view of Blue Hill. He painted for pleasure and rarely sold his work. *J. W.*

FLETES, IGNACIO   **Nicaragua**

Ignacio Fletes, born in the town of Leon, moved to Solentiname when he was sixteen years old. There he later married a peasant woman. Although a townsman, he became integrated into the life of the village of Solentiname, where he learned to paint and became a naive artist. *E. C.*

FORTIN, EDMOND (1881—1955)   **France**

Edmond Fortin was born at Argy, in Indre, and died at Le Bourget. An orphan from the age of six, he was brilliant at school, a frequent truant, and enraptured by drawing. At thirteen, he was given a job as a farmhand and later entrusted to an uncle in Paris, who gave him a start in the grocery business. He married well in 1906

shelves of canned goods. He refused to sell to his customers or any of the others who besieged his store seeking to buy. His paintings were dispersed, however, after his death.

Edmond Fortin made subtle use of repetition. He drew impeccably and had a preference for melting tones of singing greys. His starting point was a meticulous view of nature and an exact appraisal of each object which he included in a composition, with each placed as an independent element which contributed nonetheless to the overall effect; the line-up of trees, piles of stones, groupings of houses, ranging of greenery, formations of birds in flight challenge and balance one another as vibrant parts of a living whole.

Edmond Fortin's first exhibition was in 1905 at the Galerie Herbinet in Paris and the last in 1970 at the Laval Museum. *Ch. Sch.*

FOUS, JEAN (1901—1970)   **France**

Jean Fous was born in Paris and died there. Because his father was a picture framer, he came into contact with the world of painting very early. He travelled a great deal as a young man, returning finally to Paris to become a dealer at the Marché aux Puces in Paris. His first paintings, inspired by the atmosphere of the "junk" market, date from the war. He began selling his own paintings in 1944, and soon established a reputation.

Lively scenes, market stalls, vignettes of the unusual or amusing in the life of the market or moments of celebration are the subjects Jean Fous paints. Strollers, lined-up wares or buildings are drawn so as to stand out clearly, enhanced by frank, sustained colours. His treatment bears witness to an amused and tender eye for a Paris investigated in all its aspects. Jean Fous usually painted in small format.

Jean Fous' work has been shown in Paris and London galleries and he participated in the

Knokke-le-Zoute show (1958). *(See portrait of the artist, p. 248). Ch. Sch.*

FRACAROSSI, JOSEPH (1886—1970)   **USA**

Like many another American naive artists, Joseph Fracarossi felt no particular desire to paint until he was well advanced in years, seventy-one to be exact. In a biographical note he said he visited the Open Art Show in Greenwich Village and "thought I could do something, too, to show, so I started to paint." He participated in other Washington Square shows, an exhibition

Fletes, Ignacio: Bathers   *Fortin, Edmond: Prairie and March Birds*

Fous, Jean: The Flea Market

sponsored by the Union Square Bank, an exhibition at the Mystic Show in Connecticut (1966), in which he won second place.

He said he was born in 1886 in Trieste (then Austrian) and left school after the seventh grade. "I made a try at many different trades and finished working steady as a baker." He spent two years in the Austrian army, and in 1914, while working as a ship's baker, found himself aboard a vessel that had to remain anchored off Brooklyn for three days to avoid capture. Fracarossi chose to stay in the USA, and after an accident blinded him in one eye, gave up baking and

Frassa, Luise: The Factual State — And No One Noticed What Was Happening

painter and they gave her brushes, paints and canvas as a present on her fiftieth birthday. She arranged a tiny attic as a studio and sat there painting — preferably late at night. She was never at a loss for subjects: childhood memories, incidents from her travels, impressions of the world around her. She attempts to catch in her pictures the whole diversity of life, with its light and dark sides.

She is at best when depicting metropolitan types and their attitudes in the city streets or in social gatherings, as in the work illustrated below. *T. G.*

Fracarossi, Joseph: United Nations Building

"made a try on embroidery . . . women's dresses. I liked it and went on for fifty years."

He loved painting, and though he sometimes worked from photographs and illustrations, he more often studied at first hand the scenes he wanted to paint by climbing rooftops, crossing bridges, and walking along waterfronts.

His dealer, Morris Weisenthal, said that Fracarossi lived alone in a "small, clean, workmanlike flat. I recall a bulletin board with notes and papers attached, a quotation from Camus, the name and address of a neighbourhood funeral parlour." Poor health forced Fracarossi to leave New York and live with his son. Small-town life bored him and he wrote, "I feel to be alive in a grave." He continued to paint, however. Of his work, he remarked that his detailed style required "lots of time to do and then who will be interested? Oh I know it is the pleasure of painting to keep in mind, I could always give away the paintings . . . but I figure people really appreciate only when they part with their money to get it." He died in Coventry, Rhode Island. *J. W.*

FRASSA, LUISE (1921)   **West Germany**

Luise Frassa was born in Kassel, and now lives in Cuxhaven. Her early wish to become a painter was not realised: she took up a commercial career in a publishing house, married and had three children. She sometimes used to tell her children about her childhood ambition to be a

FREITAS, JOSÉ DE (1935)   **Brazil**

José de Freitas was born in Vitória de Santo Antão, Pernambuco. A painter and draughtsman, he first began work as a self-taught artist after he had set up residence in Rio de Janeiro.

One of the most distinguished Brazilian art critics, Walmir Ayala, has described him as "masterful in his handling of a primitive technique out of which he has been able to fashion his own interpretation of biblical themes" expressed with irony and humour in composite pictures. These often divide into as many as twelve different sections, each telling its own chapter of the story he presents, in much the same manner as that employed of old, when artists crowded the entire narrative into the picture area of one panel, with the main characters reappearing at appropriate moments in chronological order. This system is in no way upset when Freitas tackles subjects like the seaborne attack on the city of Troy. *Sh. W.*

FRÍAS, GATO   Argentina
(SUSANA DIAZ DE VIVAR)

Gato is the artist's nickname: it means "cat." Gato Frías was born in Madrid, her father being

Frias, Gato: The Convent of Los Naramos (detail)

Freitas, José de: Oedipus Rex

an Argentine diplomat, her mother Spanish. She spent her childhood in Andalusia, came to Argentina when she was fourteen years old, and went to a boarding school. She felt lonely, and dreaming, together with painting, were her favourite pastimes. She has painted since she was a child, but, as is usual among naives, she never thought her work possessed any worth apart from the pleasure she got from it, and consequently never showed it to strangers. Married very young, she went to live in the country. In 1974 she and her ex-husband opened a restaurant and instead of spending money on posters decided to hang some of her paintings. There she was spotted by two industrial designers who, dazzled by her talent, called in a specialist on naive art. Gato thought it was all a big joke. "Then I was told I was a naive

artist and not the clumsy painter I thought I was."

Her first exhibition, in one of Buenos Aires' best art galleries, was a notable event. All her paintings were sold on the opening night, and from then on she became Argentina's most famous naive artist.

She paints with exquisite detail and colour, like a master of the Middle Ages illuminating some Book of Hours or a Persian miniaturist. She is a true poet, her eyes perceiving an untouched world where everything is fulfilled: white winged horses mingle with angels and saints and naked couples kiss blissfully under the flowers, while serene monks gather oranges in the orchard to the tune of songs and prayers. She is deeply religious, with a very individual point of view: whenever she wants to symbolise chastity she paints a couple holding a child in their arms! Lately she has been painting historical works. Some of them represent battles Argentina fought in the 19th century to win independence from Spain. Constructing her pictures with craftsmanlike care, she follows the tradition of Candido Lopez (whose paintings she had never seen) not only in terms of historical accuracy but in her scrupulous and refined treatment of multifarious detail. These pictures are remarkable achievements of colour and movement; consequently, close concentration is required from the spectator. Her work expresses the happiness of her warm, humble and loving heart. *(See portrait of the artist, p. 249). M. T. S.* →

FRUNZETE, VASILE (1942)   Romania

Vasile Frunzete vas born in Răşinari, where he settled down to work as a hydrologist after completing his studies. Though he began painting in 1959, it was not until ten years later that he crystallised his vision of the world in his own personal forms.

Frunzete's compositions, done in oil on glass or wood, show the influence of his predecessors (folk artists who painted icons) in the synthetic draughtsmanship, achieved with a simple, even and expressive line. Some critics compare it with the *cloisonné* technique used in stained glass windows. Unremittingly firm, the drawing is precise in its enclosure of forms, whereas the colours, equal in intensity, spread out in large patches, dominated by pure red, blue and yellow.

The artist takes his subject-matter from folk customs, from the ostensibly banal preoccupations of everyday life ("Cutting Wood around the House," "At the Well"), from colourful personalities (Laie Kjorul) or from events in Romanian history, such as "The Rebirth of My Nation" (shown here), which achieves a skilful synthesis of diverse elements and a dynamic rhythm expressive of the country's eventful past. He sometimes introduces written signs, though, in contrast with other naive painters, he gives them a plastic significance.

In addition to twelve one-man shows, Vasile Frunzete has taken part in many group exhibitions of naive art and has received a number of awards. *(See portrait of the artist, p. 249). M. Il.*

f
246

Frias, Gato: The Battle at San Lorenzo

FRYER, FLORA (1892—1977)   USA

Flora Fryer was born in St. Paul, Minnesota. She chose nursing as a career. After her graduation from nursing school in 1917, she joined the armed forces as a nurse and served in Europe. After the war was over she seems to have travelled widely (to judge from the subject-matter of her paintings), spending much time in France. She moved to the Seattle, Washington area in 1943 to work in the rural Public Health Nursing Service, from which she retired in 1960. She began to paint in 1962, and wrote, "I am convinced my paintings are related to the environment of

Frunzete, Vasile: The Rebirth of My Nation

Fuentes, Gloria: The Red Chair

my early childhood. Painting is a pleasure; it is also fulfilling the desire of early childhood, and the need to be busy." She never married, and apparently had no near relatives, for she chose to leave those of her paintings that remained unsold (she had had several exhibitions in Seattle) to a friend and colleague, Donna Ferguson. Flora Fryer died in Seattle. *J. W.*

FUENTES, GLORIA   Argentina

Gloria Fuentes was born in Hendaye, her father being an Argentinian and her mother Filippino. Living first in France, she later moved to Chile and after her marriage settled in Buenos Aires. She has always been noted for her vivid imagination and innate craftsmanship as seen in her embroidered rugs, enamelware, and the charming drawings which cover the walls of the rooms of her three children. In 1978, she showed some of her ink drawings to an art critic, who encouraged her and advised her to improve her technical skill, but at all costs to preserve the

Fryer, Flora: The Maxi

richness and originality of her painterly vision. Although it would be possible to claim that Gloria Fuentes sometimes approaches Surrealism, those houses, wonderfully painted in colours applied like a whisper revealing dreams, certainly depict the territory of her childhood. What is expressed here, however, is not the conventional paradise lost, but something much more awful: the abandonment and desertion of the only place that was truly ours. *(See portrait of the artist, p. 249).* M. T. S.

Fagundez Cruz, Amado

Fasanella, Ralph

Favier, Cécile

Fernandez, Antonio José

Fernandez, Marcelina

Ferrara, Daniel

Filipović, Franjo

Fiorio, Serge

Fous, Jean

, Emerik

Favre, Marcel

Ferdinand, Jean

Fereoli, Enrico

ari, Pierino

Field, Erastus Salisbury

Fielding, David

, Gato

Frunzete, Vasile

Fuentes, Gloria

GAGLIANO, GIUSEPPE — Italy
GAGUA, IRINA — USSR
GAJDOS, JÁNOS — Hungary
GALEOTTI, FRANCESCO — Italy
GARCIA, CARLOS — Nicaragua
GARCIA, MANUEL — Nicaragua
GARDE, SILVIA — West Germany
GATTO, VICTOR JOSEPH — USA
GAWŁOWA, KATARZYNA — Poland
GAZIVODA, PREDRAG — Yugoslavia
GAŽI, DRAGAN — Yugoslavia
GENDRON, ERNEST — Canada
GENERALIĆ, IVAN — Yugoslavia
GENERALIĆ, JOSIP — Yugoslavia
GENERALIĆ, MATO — Yugoslavia
GENK, WILLEM VAN — Netherlands
GENTILI, ALDO — Italy
GERARD, FRANÇOISE — Belgium
GERLACH, FRIEDRICH — West Germany
GERLACH, LUDWIG — West Germany
GERLIKENE, PJATRONELE — USSR
GEYER, RUDOLF — Austria
GHEȚU, PETRE — Romania
GHIZZARDI, PIETRO — Italy
GIBBONS, CHARLES W. — Palau
"GILVAN," PAULO — Brazil
GLUHOVSKAJA, G. G. — USSR
GOLDING, WILLIAM — USA
GÓMEZ, CRISANTO — Venezuela
GOOSSENS, CORNELIUS — West Germany
GOULDING, ARTHUR — Great Britain
GOURGUE, JACQUES-ENGUERRAND — Haiti
GRAHAM, ANNE — Australia
GRAHAM, M. E. de — Nicaragua
GRAMS, ERICH — West Germany
GRAND-MÈRE PARIS — France
GRANDMA MOSES — USA
GREFFE, LÉON — Belgium
GREGOIRE, ALEXANDRE — Haiti
GRGEC, PETAR — Yugoslavia
GRIGORESCU, GREORGHE ION — Romania
GRIGORJANC, KARAPET — USSR
"GRIM," MAURICE GRIMALDI — France
GRIMMEISEN, FRANZ JOSEF — West Germany
GROSSIN, FERNANDE ("MEMÉE") — France

GUBÁNYI, IMRÉNÉ — Hungary
GÜDEL, HELEN — Switzerland
GUEVARA, ALEJANDRO — Nicaragua
GUEVARA, GLORIA — Nicaragua
GUEVARA, LUIS HARRERA — Chile
GUEVARA, MARITA — Nicaragua
GUEVARA, MIRIAM — Nicaragua
GUILLEMINOT, RENÉ — France
GUILLEN, ASILIA — Nicaragua
GUIRAUD, JEAN-BAPTISTE — France
GUTTMANN, ROBERT — Czechoslovakia
GYOVAI, ESZTER — Hungary
GYÖRGY-SZALMÁS, BÉLA — Hungary
GYÖRI, ELEK — Hungary

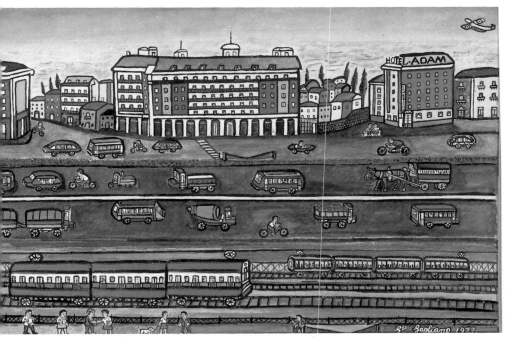

Gagliano, Guiseppe: Palmanova Street in Milan

Gagua, Irina: Little Girl Keke

GAGLIANO, GIUSEPPE (1897)   Italy

Giuseppe Gagliano was born in Centuripe, Enna, a large Sicilian village situated on a plateau, where he still lives today. Up to the age of seventy, he worked as a shoemaker and then, like so many other naive artists, in his old age felt a powerful need to express himself in painting for his own personal satisfaction. Never did it occur to him to exhibit or to let his secret be known. That he gained fame is due to the efforts of his son and a few admirers from his home town who saw to it that his works were displayed.

Gagliano's favourite themes are the landscapes of Centuripe, the houses clustered on the hill-tops or scattered in fan-shaped formations over the slopes, and the fields where various kinds of farm work are in progress. These scenes, issuing from intense emotional recollection, are presented in typically bright Mediterranean colours: from the golden yellow of wheat to the vivid red of fiery sunsets and the vibrant green of the fields, and in between a wide scale of nuances. In "Harvest," there is a broad gamut of pure colours, strong and contrasting; in the centre is the farmer's home, on the right a group of

hired labourers is arriving, and in the foreground the farmer is paying workers to harvest the wheat fields discernible on the horizon.

Gagliano also paints towns, but less frequently. Such, for instance, is the painting portraying the chaotic traffic of Milan, where Gagliano's son lives, a work rich in earthy colours, details and realistic elements perfectly harmonised.

But the predominant themes are nevertheless those associated with Gagliano's Sicily, with his native land. It must be stressed that his vision is purely his own and is not rooted in Sicilian folk tradition, with its dolls and waggons. His work is not folkloric decoration but recollection full of love, a "remembrance of things past," a valuable eye-witness account of an ancient land. *(See portrait of the artist, p. 288). D. M.*

GAGUA, IRINA (1937)   USSR

Irina Gagua was born in Tbilisi. A musician and choirmaster by profession, who graduated from Tbilisi Conservatoire in 1966, she teaches at a school of music. She began to paint in 1970, working from memory and now and again from time-yellowed photographs. She both paints and draws with pencil: mostly portraits (usually of children or family groups), landscapes, and a doll's house world. Her dolls are garbed in stylised period costume. The theatricalised, naive make-believe of her world (with its colourfully dressed women) is generally characteristic of the modern primitivist. Some of the oils reflect a more manifestly national tradition, expressed in their style of ornamental, carpet-like mosaic. Like many other primitivists, Gagua prefers to depict the obsolescent. She has had three one-woman shows: in Tbilisi, in Riga and in the

acquaintance of the peasant painter Alek Györi in 1931 and, following in his footsteps, devoted himself to painting. He exhibited for the first time in 1937 at the "Original Talents" Exhibition in the Jenö Bálint Gallery. In 1938, his paintings were shown in the Netherlands. By now he had attracted the attention of critics, some of whom praised his imaginative power, while others stressed his artistic sensitivity.

At some stage in his career he had begun visiting picture galleries and reading the biographies of great artists in fictional form. He was also inspired by experiences from his childhood. In

Gajdos, János: The Fair

physicist township of Dubna outside Moscow. *(See portrait of the artist, p. 288). N. Sh.*

GAJDOS, JÁNOS (1912—1950)   **Hungary**

János Gajdos abandoned his trade of shoemaker in order to pursue his dreams. He came to Budapest in the thirties, during the time of the Depression, and then went all over Austria and Germany as a hired labourer. He made the

his daydreams he returned to the world of bazaars and amusement parks, of church weddings and happy Christmas ceremonies. The places where these events occur are often imaginary landscapes, with strange buildings. Gajdos was a nature lover and portrayed lumberjacks working in forests of giant trees, whose branches bore the nests of birds with coloured plumage. Even in barren areas along the banks of rivers, flocks of birds are seen. Nature and man working in nature appear in his pictures in an intimate relationship. His early paintings are as multi-coloured as a kaleidoscope, with long processions of figures; later he also chose more sombre themes, portraying the life of the city's poor.

Living in want, he became seriously ill. In 1949 he was given an opportunity to further his education but was too ill by then to profit from it and died the following year.

Since his works began to be rediscovered in the sixties they have been exhibited at home and in Czechoslovakia, Germany, Cuba, Belgium and Greece. *(See portrait of the artist, p. 288). M. I.*

tures and rich with suggested magic; more rarely, young girls appear as symbols of the spring of life and eternal joy.

In some works, such as "The Market-Place," Galeotti has achieved an exceptional harmony and originality: the painting is framed by a wreath of flowers and fruit; before our eyes spreads a market-place under the open sky, crowded with peasants and white Tuscan cattle. Along the top is ranged a series of gentle hills and among them nestle deep blue lakes, village houses, medieval towers (Galeotti lived in such a tower for years). This painting illustrates the art-

Galeotti, Francesco: Market-Place   *Garcia, Carlos: Bullfight*

GALEOTTI, FRANCESCO (1920)   **Italy**

Francesco Galeotti, born in S. Adriano di Marradi, Florence, of peasant parents, is a farmer. A prisoner of war in Egypt during the war, he came back to Italy after his release and continued his strenuous life as a tiller of the soil. His closeness to nature fired his imagination and he began to draw, demonstrating from the very beginning a gift for clear and authentic style of expression.

The most notable element of his subject-matter was established at the very beginning and is often repeated: intertwining and twisted bushes, recalling tropical lianas, which have remained in his memory from his prisoner-of-war days and are sometimes transformed by him into vine leaves. This floral backdrop is the framework for his compositions and also for that typical barnyard fowl — the turkey — that appears so frequently in his works, as in "Family of Turkeys."

Other canvases have as a background a village, done in his habitual ripe colours, with turkeys scattered around a sunflower, as if taking part in a ritual, while the usual liana frames the entire composition ("Sunflower Holiday").

In other pictures, the figures of peasants move about in a milieu abounding in rustic fea-

ist's fresh inspiration, the rare and genuine purity of his work, and the elegance of his lines.

Galeotti, who still lives and works in S. Adriano di Marradi, has remained faithful to his original inspiration, rarely leaving his hills and the peace he finds in his beloved sunflowers and his ubiquitous turkeys, with the secretive stillness which surrounds it all.

At the beginning of the sixties, thanks to the critic C. L. Ragghianti, Galeotti received public recognition at an exhibition of drawings in Florence, and his work has been in many exhibitions since.

(See portrait of the artist, p. 289). D. M.

GARCIA, CARLOS (?1955)   **Nicaragua**

Together with Marina Ortega, Carlos Garcia is one of the most gifted naive painters of Nicaragua. He was born in Solentiname and still lives there. Before he began to paint, he lost an eye in an accident in the fields.

The subjects of his paintings vary and his style is a singular one, though notable for well-organised composition.

He has exhibited in Managua, Cuba, Poland and West Berlin. *E. C.*

GARCIA, MANUEL (1939)   Nicaragua

Manuel Garcia was born in Masaya, in the native quarter of Monimbo. After living in various parts of Nicaragua he finally settled down in Managua, where he resides today. Under the supervision of the Nicaraguan painter Rodrigo Penalba, he began to paint in 1964. He has worked as an illustrator in the weekly newspaper *Extra*, published in Managua, and is now employed as a designer in the Department of Crafts of the Ministry of Culture.

Most of his paintings portray the folk festivals of Nicaragua.

Garcia, Manuel: The Monimba Native Quarter

He has taken part in group exhibitions in Germany, France, Brazil, Guatemala and Salvador, as well as in many in Nicaragua. *(See portrait of the artist, p. 289).* E. C.

GARDE, SILVIA (1943)   West Germany

Silvia Garde, born in Bad Godesberg, now lives in Lohmar. Together with her husband she owns a stud-farm where they breed thoroughbreds. Because her husband is a painter, and because his materials and implements were "always lying around so temptingly," she tried to paint a picture of her own one day. That was in 1965, and she has been painting ever since. Silvia Garde finds her subjects in her own stables: horses, dogs, cats. She made her début with little pictures that possessed a kind of poetic serenity and were characterised by candour and judicious observation, while being devoid of any element of routine. What fascinated the observer was the fact that reality and imagination were harmoniously combined in all her pictures. People and

animals — however three-dimensionally solid the horses may be — always remain at a magic distance from the spectator, seeming to float effortlessly free of the force of gravity. *(See portrait of the artist, p. 289).* T. G.

GATTO, VICTOR JOSEPH (1890—1965)   USA

Victor Joseph Gatto was born to impoverished Italian immigrants in New York City's Greenwich Village. When he was seven, Theodore Roosevelt visited his school and praised his blackboard drawing; and from then on, Gatto

Garde, Silvia: Three Girls Jumping Rope

Gatto, Victor Joseph: The Peaceable Kingdom

said, he wanted to become a painter. Poverty, however, prevented him from pursuing that career and he was forty-five before he gave in to the urge. In the interim he became a featherweight boxer (at twenty) but left that profession ("too rough") to work at odd jobs to help support his mother, with whom he lived. He also worked as a steam-fitter and plumber.

In 1937, no longer able to repress his childhood ambition, he bought cheap paintbrushes and some pigments which he mixed with oil. He applied his colours with an impasto-like technique so that his work is marked by a combination of texture and bright colour. In the beginning he painted wild animals — lions, tigers, leopards, elephants — in the jungles, relying only on his memories of visits to the zoo. The source for their jungle settings was primarily his imagination, for he never travelled widely nor outside of the USA. In about 1945, hoping to sell his work, he displayed it at the Washington Square Outdoor Art Show. The first person to buy one of his paintings (for five dollars) showed it to a collector, Ivan Black, who not only hastened to buy more Gatto paintings but gave him a 25-dollar weekly retainer, so that he could devote more time to his art.

Wherever she lived, she painted the walls and ceramic stoves with flowers and other ornaments. At first, she worked very hard for some relations, living in a tiny unheated room without a proper floor. Though tired to the point of exhaustion, she painted on the walls pictures of the Madonna, angels, birds and flowers. A Cracow collector, making the rounds of the villages, noticed her work and persuaded her to paint pictures by bringing her plywood and colours. Painting gave her great pleasure and was one of the few experiences in life which she enjoyed. She paints in tempera on a hard surface: largely

Gawłowa, Katarzyna: Supper

Gawłova, Katarzyna: Holy Communion

Black persuaded the Barzansky Galleries to mount a one-man show for Gatto, which proved sufficiently successful to enable Gatto to devote himself entirely to painting. He worked as if driven, sometimes as much as thirty-six hours at a stretch, and extended his subject-matter to include biblical scenes, recollections of his boxing days, and events which he witnessed during the visits to Miami, which he now could afford to pay.

He used his kitchen as a studio, with a slab of glass for his palette, and, as his primary light source, an overhead 40-watt light bulb. After his mother died, he moved to Miami and continued to paint with the same fervour. When his eyesight began to fail, he persisted, even against doctor's orders, using a magnifying glass to help him paint details. He died in Miami. *(See portrait of the artist, p. 288). J. W.*

scenes with saints, for she is profoundly religious. (Once, after the Devil had led her into temptation, she drew a picture of him on cardboard and pinned it to a chest of drawers.) Her first exhibition, with an unusually festive vernissage, was held in the Ethnographic Museum of Cracow in 1977. On that occasion, she remarked: "I paint because I have grown to love painting, but I am afraid that if God gives me everything in this world, perhaps I will not fare so well in the next one."

Gawłowa's paintings are in museum collections in Cracow, Warsaw and Toruń, and in the collections of L. Zimmerer and J. Lodzinski — the connoisseur who discovered her and concerned himself with her welfare. Her works have been displayed in many exhibitions in Poland and abroad. *(See portrait of the artist, p. 288). A. J.*

GAWŁOWA, KATARZYNA (1896)　　Poland

Katarzyna Gawłowa was born in the village of Zielonka near Cracow, where she still lives. While still a child, she started working on her parents' farm, and learned to read and write by herself. Although she carried milk to Cracow every day, contact with the city did not change her, and she seems to have lived out of her time. When she was thirty-six years old, she married, but was left a widow after only a few years.

GAZIVODA, PREDRAG (1952)　　Yugoslavia

Predrag Gazivoda was born in Cetinje, the former capital of Montenegro. A lithographer by occupation, he has asserted himself as an authentic naive artist with paintings portraying pure and innocent fantasies, dominated by the beauty of Lake Skadar (Scutari) and the arduous life of the inhabitants of this area. Gazivoda's characters, old and wrinkled but proud, are nameless heroes placed in a beautiful landscape and portrayed at their daily work or leisure, their struggles and their prayers. Where there are no figures, the paintings are dominated by rose-hips or pomegranates, by fish and gulls, by rowing boats and the solemn peace of a Sunday dawn seen from a house of stone. He achieves his vision by refined colour and a specific kind of mastery of his material, also by an inborn talent for characterisation, pure even in its distortions and clumsiness. This is also the case in his ink drawings, which, despite the absence of colour, show a richness of nuance and a subtle interplay of tones.

Gazivoda, Predrag: Fishing on Skadar Lake

ly in front of the church, and at other times working in the fields; he has also portrayed patients in their sick beds, pale and bored, sitting near an open window through which the fresh country breeze blows. These pictures recalled his brother Branko, a talented sculptor, who lay paralysed for over twenty years, cared for by Dragan.

Gaži seemed to wish to record everything he saw in the village and around himself, especially the nature he loved so well, for he felt that urbanisation and industry would soon destroy all the beauty of the countryside. He therefore strove to immortalise whatever had not yet been trans-

Gendron, Ernest: Mao Tse-tung

Predrag Gazivoda had a one-man show in Cetinje in 1980. He has also taken part in a number of representative exhibitions at home and abroad. *M. L.*

GAŽI, DRAGAN (1930—1983) Yugoslavia

Dragan Gaži was born in Hlebine, Croatia, in the immediate vicinity of Ivan Generalić's home. He rarely left his village. While he was in elementary school, his gift for drawing was noticed. After receiving his first lessons in painting from Generalić, in 1946 he began to put down on canvas whatever caught his eye in his surroundings. In due course Gaži developed into one of the Hlebine circle of painters, in which he ranks at the top with Generalić, Kovačić and Večenaj.

During the winters, when there was no work in the fields, he walked about for hours with drawing pad and pencil, taking down details that intrigued him: clouds scudding across the sky, birds on the wing, fences, trees and flowers. As he never stopped tilling the soil, it was natural for him to take his subject-matter from the fields where he spent so much time. His neighbours and other peasants are always present in his pictures, but he also painted the endless landscapes of his native Podravina region. Loving horses, he depicted many of them and was sad to see them disappearing from the countryside so quickly. His palette consists largely of pastel colours. His figures are shown sometimes at festivities, usual-

formed by the dreadnought of relentless modernisation.

On one occasion he invited friends and neighbours to an exhibition of his and was delighted when they recognised themselves, their houses and gardens.

The painting "Building a House" (1973) shows everything realistically. In the autumn, when work in the fields is finished, the roofs of houses are examined and repaired in preparation for winter. Then neighbours come to help, for many hands do the job more quickly. In the background, Gaži abandoned realism, and it is this combination of reality and a child's view of the world that is so characteristic of his work.

In "Friends in the Vineyards" (1976), two slightly tipsy friends, their arms around each other, are drinking the new wine after the harvest. With their powerful chests and strong hands, they are typical of the farm labourers of the Podravina region. Against the background of the wide open spaces of the Podravina plains, merging with the horizon, they invest the painting with a strong and convincing effect.

Gaži has had one-man shows and participated in group exhibitions at home and abroad. *(See portrait of the artist, p. 288). N. T.*

GENDRON, ERNEST (1912) Canada

Ernest Gendron was born in the Quebec village of Saint-Marc-des-Carrières. His parènts were poor, and as soon as he was able, Gendron moved to Montreal as a way of escaping the same fate. He enlisted as a commando in the Canadian Army during the Second World War but saw no action. Nevertheless, his training provided him with a skill that he could use and he turned to boxing in a run-down Montreal gymnasium. As a way of supplementing the fifty cents a bout he received for fighting, Gendron became, by turns, an acrobat, singer, and comedian. In 1950 he began to paint. His works are extremely painstaking, with layer upon layer of enamel paint, built up with the use of wooden match sticks

GENERALIĆ, IVAN (1914)   Yugoslavia

The village of Hlebine, not far from the Hungarian border, lost most of the year in the mists of the Podravina lowlands, has won worldwide renown through the fame of one of its inhabitants: the former cowherd and peasant, Ivan Generalić. In this little place, with its dozen or so narrow winding streets, hundred-odd houses, and church in the middle, Ivan Generalić has spent most of his life. His painting has been inspired by the traditions of his region, the wisdom of his countrymen and the plain, stretching as far as the eye can see.

Gaži, Dragan: Building a House

instead of a brush. Gendron has never liked brushes and his first experiments were conducted with the aid of a blade of grass to carry the paint. This meticulous and obsessive method is a compliment to Gendron's feeling for his work. Most of his paintings deal with heroes and their fates. The assassination of John Kennedy is a recurring theme. He has also produced icon-like portraits of his other personal heroes: De Gaulle, Charlie Chaplin, Norman Bethune, and Quebec popular and political figures. Gendron still owns almost all of his works and shrewdly calculates that their worth is in direct proportion to the fame of the individual portrayed. *Th. L.*

Generalić was born to a poor peasant couple, Mate and Terezija Generalić. When he was small, he loved climbing trees and gazing at the horizon, peeping over high fences and into neighbours' barnyards, observing the animals or trying to guess, at a distance, who was walking along the road to and from the fields.

He attended elementary school in his village. While still a boy, but already working in the fields, he started drawing on a pad of crumpled paper kept hidden under his patched shirt. He sketched everything he saw around him: the peasants in different circumstances, and the village in various seasons. He first caught the attention of intellectual circles in Zagreb when he exhibited in 1931 with a well-known progressive group of Croatian painters calling themselves "Earth." With his fellow-peasants, Mirko Virius and Franjo Mraz, he painted scenes of rebellion provoked by the social injustice felt by the peasants of his district.

Ivan Generalić still lives in Hlebine in the immediate vicinity of the house where he was born and spent his childhood. Although he has become famous and well-known galleries throughout the world vie for his paintings, he himself has remained the same in many ways. He still spends considerable time at village gatherings, in the homes of his fellow-citizens when they celebrate some event or other, at the local football club, of which he is honorary president, in conversation with children who visit him and with the painters of Hlebine, for whom he has set an example.

His outlook on life reflects the wisdom of the Podravina peasants, acquired through generations of struggle and hard life. When he is with them, he seems at first glance no different from them, either in his dress or in his sturdy appearance, with his large hands and hawk-like nose, typical of the men of Podravina.

What is it that this peasant, this former cowherd, offers the world as a painter, a world full of educated and talented artists?

The torch lit at the close of the last century in a poor Paris suburb by the naive dreamer Henri Rousseau was taken up far from Paris by the young farmer, Ivan Generalić, who had never heard of Rousseau. Both of them, one painting in the city and the other in the country, enriched world painting in theme and form, and perhaps most by offering something for the soul and the dreams of alienated man. Rousseau escaped from his urban environment by turning inward to a fantasy world; Generalić, on the other hand, invites us into his world, where the values of a life associated with nature were proved long ago.

During Generalić's exhibition in Paris in 1953, the well-known French critic, Marcel Arland, wrote: "Generalić has not come to Paris as a conqueror, but he disarms and wins us because the small world he brings with him is truly his world and he needs no other guides. The earth gave birth to him and he possesses its grace, wisdom and charm. In his paintings one feels a gentle conversation in progress between people and animals."

Whatever Generalić does traces its roots to peasant common-sense and healthy farm life. He takes life at its source, like water, and transfers it to his pictures. When he paints a field, the spectator feels the invisible processes unfolding in the plant and animal world: the power of the old bull and the blood flowing in his swollen veins; the message of the rooster which sometimes heralds misfortune; the seed in the fields germinating and growing; the crops ripening. The people in his paintings always seem to radiate a message, to be feeling some emotion, to be in movement, working. He paints eternal themes always close to man: weddings, funerals, religious processions, fairs, farm work, peasant customs and beliefs, landscapes in every season of the year. What he paints is not a faithful reproduction because he takes what he sees — hills,

Generalić, Ivan: Deer Courting

houses, people — and with his creative power rearranges these according to his own taste and need. When he was in Paris, he took pleasure in the Eiffel Tower. He had no desire to stay in Paris but he did want to immortalise in some way the edifice that had attracted him so strongly. And what could be more natural for him than to transpose it to his native Podravina, to paint it surrounded with Bosnian sheep and Hlebine cows and to hang the painting in his studio in Hlebine, where he could look at it the livelong day?

Ivan Generalić's first exhibitions, held before the Second World War, were applauded by progressive students and workers and attacked by the authorities and official critics because his paintings, both in theme and in conviction, carried a message of dissatisfaction with, and of a refusal to compromise with, the social situation.

This is obvious in canvases such as "Requisition" (1934), "For Taxes" (1934) and "The Djelekovec Revolt" (1936).

During the war, his friend, the naive painter Mirko Virius, was executed by the invaders. After the war Generalić dedicated to his memory the painting "Virius's Death" (1959). Although Virius is known to have died in a concentration camp in Zemun, Generalić laid him out on the green grass of Podravina, where he had walked so many times in his life, and placed around him a row of lighted candles. The heavy labourer's hands are crossed and peaceful, while his bare feet feel no more cold. A rooster approaches him as though recognising him and communicating something, perhaps thanking him for having fed and cared for him. The bright red colour of the rooster finds a counterpart in the red roof of a house and of a group of people in the distance.

After the war, one exhibit followed another, as did the highest recognition and awards. Gradually Generalić's fame spread beyond the borders of his own country. Working tirelessly, he created his finest paintings: "Deer Courting" and "Woodcutters" (1959), "The Horned Horse" (1961), "Scarecrow" (1964), "Hlebine Mona Liza" (1972), "Old Bull" (1972), "Cold Winter" (1973) and others.

Generalić has stimulated young peasants living near him to paint. Under his influence, talented individuals took up the brush and began to work on glass, as he does. Soon a large circle of painters formed, some of them creating a style of their own and even winning fame.

Ivan Generalić has done a great deal to popularise naive painting. His paintings and thousands of reproductions of his works are seen and easily recognised all over the world.

In "Woodcutters" (1959), three apparently identical woodcutters in red caps are cutting wood. In front of the woods Generalić has painted a peacock on the right, in the left-hand corner a cow and cart, and in the centre two women. The figures are not, in fact, repetitive: each one differs from the others. Above the woods fly birds of a kind found nowhere in nature. In the foreground are light-coloured bushes, the tones gradually darkening to suggest the depth of the woods. But the artist has fashioned nature himself rather than copying what he saw around him.

The painting "Underneath a Tree" (1943) gives the spectator a feeling of autumn in the air, with a gamut of rich colours, from white to yellowish-brown and brick red. A couple stands serenely, untroubled by the coming winter, against a background of vine-covered hills. Autumn has brought a good harvest; nearby pigs are feeding and one feels how the freshness of autumn is slowly taking hold. The day is drawing to a close; and Generalić has done a masterly job of lighting the painting with the last rays of the warm autumn sun. "Deer Courting" (1959) is anything but monotonous or tedious, although

Generalić, Ivan: The Fire (detail)

Generalić, Ivan: Gipsy Wedding

the artist has used only four colours; he has achieved an exceptional harmony by using a wide range of delicate greenish tones. By painting the same stag four times, head raised and calling to his mate, he has created a symbolism, the call of the wild, the quality of life in nature.

Generalić for the first time took part in the "Earth" exhibition 1931 in Zagreb's Art Pavilion. He has participated in group exhibitions in Paris (1953), São Paulo (1955), Knokke-le-Zoute (1958) and has had one-man shows in forty countries, including the major cities of Germany (Frankfurt, Cologne, Munich in 1961), in London (1961), Zurich (1964), New York (1966 and 1977), Venice (1970), Florence and Geneva (1971), Rome (1974), Milan and Amsterdam (1975). He has won the major naive art awards throughout the world. *(See portrait of the artist, p. 289). N. T.*

Generalić, Ivan: Underneath a Tree

GENERALIĆ, JOSIP (1936)   Yugoslavia

Ivan Generalić was already seriously dedicated to naive painting when his son, Josip, was born in 1936. The parents wanted their son to become a teacher, an occupation that enjoys great prestige in rural districts. But Josip, growing up beside his father, and spending most of his time in his favourite place for play, his father's studio, absorbed the colours and motifs of the Podravina area. When Ivan went to the fields to work or to observe nature, he took with him his son, who, while playing, entered more and more into the world of painting and began to

father and son had entirely different memories, because Ivan had spent his childhood in poverty, surrounded by the poor, whereas Josip's youth was a happy one, spent in an aura of abundance.

Josip Generalić feels that he had a harder time persuading people to accept him, that they were more disinclined to recognise his talent and worth as a painter, and even the authenticity of his creative efforts, than was the case with other naive artists. But it was precisely this doubting of his talent that made him persevere and moved him to prove that his painting had value not because he was named Generalić but because he

Generalić, Josip: Guyana '78

draw people and landscapes in the way his childish eye saw them.

Nothing came of his parents' wish for him to become a teacher, as Josip was more interested in painting. He felt it on the one hand as an inner need and on the other as a challenge to his famous father. Fortunately, Josip realised that it would not do to follow the path trodden by his father, as many other painters were doing, and that he should find his own way of expressing himself and his own style. Like his father, he chose for his subject-matter the life and scenes of Podravina and memories of his youth. But

was gifted and had something fresh to communicate to the world through his pictures.

His themes are quite new: he paints spacemen barefooted on the moon with a Hlebine cow; sometimes he portrays actresses of world-wide fame, or a city baby in a carriage with a nipple in his mouth, coming to the village for a visit and looking at the animals in as much wonder as they look at him! A Hlebine Yadwigha boldly lies nude on a sofa, observed with curiosity by cows and cowherd, while in the background stands the Podravina village, peaceful and submerged in green. The women in Josip

Generalić's paintings, frequently holding a symbolic fish in their hands, are no longer peasant women either in appearance or behaviour and stand out in contrast to the landscape in which he places them. They are endowed with big, strange eyes, and their naked bodies show that they have been sunbathing in bikinis, but not on the river banks where the painter has now put them.

Josip Generalić has a fresh vision of Hlebine, achieving a symbiosis of the old and the new by painting modern figures in the old landscape. In "Hlebine Yadwigha" (1973), referred to above, a

number of pigs and I used to take them to pasture," says Mato Generalić."While the pigs rooted for acorns in the woods, I would make figures of animals out of mud. Once my brother Ivan Generalić came into my yard and saw the mud figures. Looking at them, he said: 'Listen, brother, don't go on working in mud, work in wood. Wood is worth more and lasts longer.' "

The Generalićs had a vineyard and Mato took part in all the activities surrounding wine-growing. He portrayed all this in his sculptures. Other subjects were brides and grooms, relations and friends. He thus created a gallery of peasant

Generalić, Josip: Tears for a Dead Bird

Generalić, Mato: Woman Churning Butter

nude woman on a sofa has sailed into the Hlebine landscape, with all its Podravina attributes, her appearance recalling the Douanier's painting "Dream." Here, she is not only a nude shepherd girl of the kind imagined by young men, and by Josip in his youth, but the personification of the concept of woman as the beginning of everything, as in the Bible. Thus his paintings on themes from his childhood also express his philosophy of life.

Josip Generalić has had one-man shows and participated in group exhibitions at home and abroad. *(See portrait of the artist, p. 289). N. T.*

GENERALIĆ, MATO (1920)   Yugoslavia

Mato Generalić, brother of Ivan Generalić, was born in Hlebine, Croatia, where he lives. A farmer with four grades of elementary school, in his spare time he carves in wood, having begun in 1950. Thus he has worked as an artist during a period which has witnessed the growth of international interest in Yugoslav naive art. Ivan Generalić has encouraged him. "We had quite a

portraits and a picture of the whole of village life. His figures are mosaic-like, with the strongly accented hands of labourers, large feet heavy from work, and faces revealing a particular state of mind, giving his figures the character of psychological portraits.

Mato Generalić has had one-man shows and participated in group exhibitions at home and abroad. *N. T.*

GENK, WILLEM VAN (1927)   Netherlands

Willem van Genk, born in Voorburg, was left motherless when he was five years old. In school, he would do nothing but draw. His father spanked him regularly and finally sent him to a poorhouse because he refused to do his lessons. Considered mentally backward, he was assigned to jobs for the unfit. He now lives alone in The Hague, where he receives social welfare assistance.

The world he paints is a terrible one. Having grown up without love, in loneliness, he could only escape in dreams of far-off places. He developed a singular drawing style on the basis of which he was superficially ranked with the naive painters. Van Genk's forms are frequently spontaneous and immediate, but his subject-matter differs radically from that of the average naive painter. Actually, he belongs more with the practitioners of *art brut* (artists who are in many cases disturbed) with the "loners," who create an art of irrational fears. But Van Genk's fear is explicitly rational. He presents a picture of reality that we can recognise. He seems to be calling our attention to facts that can destroy our happiness at any moment, insofar as that happi-

bling an octopus, hovers over the world of Japan. Danger lurks everywhere, according to this artist, although it does seem that while warning us he is also having a good laugh at us behind our backs, fascinated by the power that constitutes the essence of our world — the power of self-preservation. *(See portrait of the artist, p. 289).* N. E.

GENTILI, ALDO (1906)   Italy

Aldo Gentili, born in Genoa, moved from there to Pisa, where he got a job as a street-

Genk, Willem van: Madrid

ness exists. He observes the world around him with a sharp eye, but an eye glazed with fear. It is fear of a world governed by unknown, magical forces, endangering us ordinary mortals. Wherever we may be, Van Genk points out to us the dangers surrounding us. He sees tanks as steel monsters that will some day smash men of flesh and blood, as though they were insects spattered against a windshield. His trains rumble in the dark; his locomotives draw to a stop, their whistles blowing and their brakes screeching like mad forces checked in their advance for a moment. Straight as an arrow, a rocket is ready to take off into space. A volcanic hulk, resem-

cleaner. He began to paint in 1952 to compensate for the monotony and boredom of his lowly occupation. Roaming the length and breadth of the town he had adopted as his own, one day he decided to note down some of the things that had caught his eye. And so Gentili the painter was born. In spite of the materials he worked with (plywood, cardboard, remnants of canvas) and the unusual colours he used (plain enamel from tin cans) in order to save money, he has achieved interesting results. Whatever he paints (fresh scenes of fields full of flowers and greenery, or the seashore with its counterpoint of bright blue, or, even more frequently, his characteristic urban landscapes), his fast, decisive and instinctive strokes always impress the eye. Through a bold contrasting of dense tones and colours, the use of distinct and very functional lines, his paintings gain in attraction.

Representative examples of his work are "Cathedral in Arezzo" and "Pisa" (or "Cathedral in Siena"), in which the wealth of form is enhanced by white clouds and by the rhythmic play of perspective in the windows, some of which are enlivened by snow-white fabrics carried by the wind. *(See portrait of the artist, p. 288). D. M.*

GERARD, FRANÇOISE (1951)   **Belgium**

Françoise Gerard, born in Brussels, comes from a cosmopolitan family: Italian, Belgian and French. Drawing attracted her while she was still a child. In her ninth year, exploration of her grandmother's attic, with its clothing and other objects dating from 1900, confirmed her in her desire to be an artist, which she became during her difficult youth, finding that her art helped her to overcome many problems. She married the writer Luc Canon. The desire for release led her to the art of the fairy-tale, of poetry and childlike freshness. She attracted the attention of

Gerard, Françoise: The Gate Keeper's House

Gentili, Aldo: Pisa

the painter Désiré Haine (who painted her portrait) and of writers such as Guy des Cars, Marcel Jouhandeau, Désiré Denuit, Louis Scutenaire, some of whom entrusted her with the illustration of their works.

At her very first exhibitions in Belgium, Françoise Gerard enjoyed an extraordinary success, later confirmed abroad, especially in the USA, where she stayed on several occasions and frequently exhibits.

She recently abandoned naive painting and is working in a very personal style, related to the movement known as the New Subjectivity.

Works dating from her naive period are mostly in private European and American collections, and rarely appear on the market. *(See portrait of the artist, p. 288). J. C.*

GERLACH, FRIEDRICH (1903—1972)

West Germany

Friedrich Gerlach was born in Herten, and died there. He became a miner at the age of fourteen, beginning as a stable-lad, then becoming a coal-face worker. He had no love of his work, which left him with poor eyesight and a bad heart when he retired after forty-six years of service. For this reason he immersed himself in his leisure time in all sorts of pursuits: he took up astronomy and philosophy, and was particularly keen on nature study. He wrote about his observations and started painting, his studio being a

lessly long flights of steps leading to luminous heights or into the dark void. If we look more closely we can often make out the artist himself in these scenes.

Throughout his life Gerlach was inspired by light and the manner in which it can be soundlessly dramatised. He makes it creep down staircases, he pours it over the pinnacles of precipices or the pillars of distant castellated temples; gruesomely cold and harsh, it falls fleetingly on rocky cliffs, engulfs a cratered landscape with its magic vibrations, moulds the massive stone blocks of walls, boulders, colonnades and dying trees.

Gerlach, Friedrich: The Holy Bomb

Gerlach, Friedrich: Illusions

tiny kitchen which he shared with his wife. His painting surface was set up on the narrow kitchen table, with tubes of paint ranged meticulously in front of it. It was here that his unique book "The Tale of the Stone Inability" took shape, handwritten page by page and illustrated with numerous coloured vignettes. In this work, cast in the form of a fairy-tale, Gerlach's critical and generally pessimistic views of the world and of humanity are reflected. The accompanying miniature illustrations anticipate almost all the visions and nightmares that are typical of the work that was later to make him famous.

Insidious fear rears up in Gerlach's pictures: nightmares crouch mutely between the façades of houses; terrified fugitives are duped and harried by ponderous shadows, spectres and phantoms; a solitary figure flits past, helpless and defenceless in endless deserted rooms, with empty railway tracks or coldly whitewashed walls. The scenes often signify war, suggesting the powerlessness of the masses who have a foreboding of the fate that awaits them, and the despotism of their rulers. In vast laboratories dedicated to destruction, in stone strongholds, in camps full of nameless prisoners, the menace of anonymous powers is manifested. Then there are pictures which offer a glimpse of unattainable goals: end-

It is possible to detect the difficulty which the technical manipulation of his material presents, the stubborn determination with which he overcame the problems offered by pigmentation, light, shade and perspective. Perspective was almost an obsession. It was his favourite means of suggesting remote goals but also a method of conveying a presentiment of infinity and fear of unseen things, of something apparently ineluctable hanging "in the air."

Gerlach insisted that everything he ever dreamed must be recorded in this manner. The way in which he contrived to compose his pictures is all the more astonishing because the aggressiveness of the thousands of blobs of colour set side by side, and his obstinate concern with minute detail, might well have tended to obscure the simple overall structure of the composition.

Although the content of his pictures (in which lamentation, accusation, and philosophical introspection combine with the everyday scene to form a new world of images) was always of supreme importance to the painter and the motive which impelled him to take up brush and palette, technical mastery nevertheless remained for him a prime concern — one to be pursued with fanatical zeal. He never became a routine artist. Friedrich Gerlach is without doubt the most important painter to have emerged from the mining community of the Ruhr. His pictures are now few and far between and fetch high prices in the art market. Most of his works are to be found in national galleries and in private ownership. They have repeatedly been shown in international exhibitions. *(See portrait of the artist, p. 288). T. G.*

GERLACH, LUDWIG (1900—1972)   **West Germany**

Ludwig Gerlach was born in Herten, where he died. He began work as a miner on his fif-

Gerlach, Ludwig: Return from Sertao

talent. Before retiring on an old-age pension in 1972, she lived in the Lithuanian village of Mazrimai, where she worked on a collective farm. Subsequently she moved to Vilnius to live with her artist son. Fond of needlework and embroidery, she created her own compositions on curtains and rugs, with the tree as the central motif, surrounded by people and occasionally by animals — a stereotype of symmetrical composition observable in the popular art of several nations. In 1976 she began to paint in oils, her subjects being drawn solely from her own imagination. The genre of embroidered rug influenced her paint-

Gerlikiene, Petronele: Noah's Ark

teenth birthday and worked his way up from stable-lad to foreman on the coal-face, completing thirty years in the pit. In 1922 he was seized by the urge to see the world and set off for South America, where he worked on a ranch until 1927. His first oils were painted in the fifties, but most were done after he retired in 1960.

In his relatively modest output Ludwig Gerlach was fond of reminiscing about his adventures in South America as a young runaway who had absconded from his job in the mines. These are pictures done from memory, dominated by a lush green which suggests a cheerful mood.

When viewed from a distance, the pictures give the impression of a grandiose general plan of composition; looked at more closely, they reveal an extraordinary amount of meticulous detail. Every inch is painted in with minute care in a pattern of constantly varied and delicately articulated shapes and lines. These are pictures painted with utter commitment, with patient persistence and loving involvement — but with interludes of sheer despair when the anatomy, the spatial proportions or the precise choice of shades "simply wouldn't come out right." *T. G.*

GERLIKENE, PJATRONELE (1905—1979)   **USSR**
GERLIKIENE, PETRONELE

Petronele Gerlikiene was born in Chicago. In 1908 her parents returned to Lithuania. Though uneducated and illiterate, she possessed great

ing, as can be seen from the draughtsmanship. Her approach was intuitive; however, her feeling for colour also related to the creative process, which resulted in what might be termed an unfinished state. She first exhibited at a group show of Lithuanian amateur artists in 1976 in Vilnius, where she subsequently had two exhibitions devoted exclusively to her work. *(See portrait of the artist, p. 289). N. Sh.*

GEYER, RUDOLF (1897)   **Austria**

Rudolf Geyer was born in Hossenreith, near Oberplan (then in Austria, but now in Czechoslovakia). Geyer's parents came from Steyer, in Austria. Trained as a mechanic and fitter, he worked as a coppersmith in various factories in Germany and Czechoslovakia between 1920 and 1945. He married in 1934. After the family were obliged to emigrate in 1945, they settled first in Aigen, Mühlviertel, and then in Linz, where Geyer found work in the Voest iron and steel plant in 1946. He retired in 1960, and settled down in Kremsdorf, near Linz, where, together with his daughter and son-in-law, he built a house in 1964. Geyer had been fascinated by painting from his earliest youth. His teacher at the Viennese Mechanics' Institute continuation school, Professor Linzbauer, wished to send him to art school, but conscription into the army put an end to any hopes of a professional training. An exhibition arranged by amateur painters in his firm encouraged him to take up painting. His subjects can be divided into three groups: religious themes; architectural pictures; experiences and events from his youth, sometimes reconstructed from stories told him by his parents.

The theatrical producer, Harald Benesch, commissioned him to design the sets of his production of Smetana's opera, "The Bartered Bride," for the State Theatre in Bonn in 1971. This turned out to be a great success for Geyer, and constituted a milestone in the artist's career and reputation. His work is marked by an unselfconscious deftness of touch, luminous and remarkably refined colours, and an authentically

forms, sometimes even symmetrically distributed in a scene ("The Council of Shepherds"). The addition of decorative elements to the principal figures does not disturb the general effect, while the broad strokes of pure colour and the modulated lines create a serene harmony ("The Harvest").

In other works (such as "Vase with Flowers"), the artist concentrates on details and at the same time introduces certain technical innovations.

Petre Gheţu has shown his oil paintings on glass in exhibitions of work by the Group of Six,

Geyer, Rudolf: The Main Square in Linz

Gheţu, Petre: The Harvest

naive originality. Innate formative skill enables him to construct pictures that are lucidly and convincingly organised. His gift for graphic narrative, combined with a powerful sense of communion with nature and a heart-warming sincerity, give his pictures an inimitable directness, originality and freshness of appeal.

He has exhibited mainly in Austria, West Germany and Switzerland. *(See portrait of the artist, p. 289). F. N.*

GHEŢU, PETRE (1953) Romania

Petre Gheţu is a member of the Group of Six — young painters who work on glass and live in the Cluj area. He was born in the commune of Sag, in the district of Timiş. He is closer than the other members of the group to the traditions and artistic language of the painters of icons on glass because, while working as an instructor at the National Art School in Turda, he tried to find the explanation for the continuity of the icon painters' art, and also studied contemporary ways of interpreting its specific features.

In his compositions, Petre Gheţu approaches space through a proportionate relationship of

most of which he has participated in, and has received considerable recognition at home and abroad. *(See portrait of the artist, p. 289). M. Il.*

GHIZZARDI, PIETRO (1906) Italy

Pietro Ghizzardi was born in Viadana, Mantua, into a peasant family, and is himself a tiller of the soil. In about 1940, he began to draw on paper the faces of people around him, mostly his family and friends. Later, in 1950, he took up painting. Lacking money for the necessities of art, canvas and colours, he decided on a "do-ityourself" approach. For material he took rough corrugated cardboard, used for packing nails manufactured by a factory in the vicinity, and for colours a product that he made himself.

Together with the rest of his family, Ghizzardi moved to Boretto, Reggio Emilia, and, in spite of their lack of understanding (they once burned all his works), persisted in his art, kneeling at night in his darkened room on the floor, where he first drew on and then coloured his cardboard, always in the same format — 50 × 70 cm. The years passed and one by one the members of the family died. Ghizzardi remained alone with his old mother. Quiet, reticent, and under his mother's influence, he never married. He made his living by doing the most ordinary kinds of work, such as street-cleaning.

Early in the sixties, he started to paint more intensively; this was the peak period of his productivity. Short of cardboard, he began to use both sides of what supplies he had, probably a unique case in the history of naive painting.

Ghizzardi later began to paint less and showed signs of fatigue; at the same time his inspiration seemed to weaken. He also changed his technique, using smooth cardboard. In 1976 he

subconscious links with the mother who had had so strong an influence on the painter's psychological development. Ghizzardi also painted very gentle figures (as in "Giuliana") and a wonderful gallery of personalities, from Verdi to Sophia Loren, and from Columbus to Garibaldi.

Ghizzardi also painted animals. In one painting a very human-looking dog with gentle eyes stands in the midst of the marshy vegetation of the River Po, while a water bird flits about, completing an effective composition. The purity of this painter and his naive dimension are best expressed in certain landscapes, such as "View of

Ghizzardi, Pietro: Dog

Ghizzardi, Pietro: Woman of Mantova

aroused curiosity anew and gained publicity with the publication of a book of his memoirs *Mi richordo anchora* (the spelling mistakes in the title are his).

Ghizzardi's portraits are among his most characteristic works. One of the most remarkable of these is "Dina" (1963). On cardboard with a sepia background "Dina" is painted in rich rosy forms and with exceptional sculptural power. Ghizzardi's models posed dressed. He usually painted two versions: one modest and strait-laced, which he presented to the model, and the other a free version transformed into a nude which the model frequently knew nothing about. The stress on the breasts is typical (see also the painting "Mantovana"), although less as an erotic symbol than as a feature of the archetype of the woman-mother — the protoparent — and of the

Boretto." In this picture, the artist, working on cardboard, drew two rows of houses at right angles, separated by a street which, in this kind of perspective, looks as though it runs along the rooftops, while the people walking along the street appear to be lying on it.

Ghizzardi is one of the outstanding naive artists of Italy and of our time. His "cardboards" radiate a strong and profound suggestiveness of the mystery of life and man, although they appear to be the products of instinct and the subconscious.

Athos Campanini, from Reggio Emilia, became Ghizzardi's agent and patron, organising his first exhibition in 1965 in Guastalla and the second one in 1967 in Boretto. In the latter year Dino Menozzi made a documentary film about him (16 mm). Subsequently Ghizzardi exhibited more and more frequently, both in Italian cities and abroad. In 1975, an important monograph by L. Orlich was published, in which the author carefully analyses the characteristics of Ghizzardi's personality and art. *(See portrait of the artist, p. 289).* D. M.

GIBBONS, CHARLES W. (1894) — Palau, Caroline Archipelago

Charles Gibbons was born in Ngaraard village, Palau. His grandfather, James Gibbons, was a West Indian of English ancestry who

Gibbons, Charles W.: Village Feast

"Gilvan", Paulo: The Baptism of Bandits

jumped ship in Palau in the 1800s and later became an adviser to the highest Palauan chief. Charles's father, William Gibbons, became a man of means and a leader of the community, and in 1901 was appointed Governor of Palau by the then German administration.

Following family tradition, Charles's own life has been eventful and varied. As a youth he attended various missionary schools both in Koror, the capital of Palau, and on Yap, another island in the Caroline group. On Yap he learned blacksmithing and also worked in a telegraphic cable station. He then spent a year on Saipan, where he studied German, before returning to Yap. At this stage in his life Gibbons was introduced to watercolours, although many years and adventures would pass before he took them up seriously as an artist. In 1910, Gibbons took employment with the Governor of Yap and accompanied him to Ponape, where he assisted in the suppression of the Ponapean Sokehs' rebellion. Gibbons remained on Ponape as an administrative assistant to the Governor until 1917, when, with the defeat of the Germans at the end of the First World War, the Japanese took over the administration of these islands and Gibbons was ordered back home to Palau. Here he first served in the Japanese constabulary and later worked as a farmer until the end of the Second World War. With the cessation of hostilities and the occupation of the islands by American military forces, Gibbons' knowledge of languages (Palauan, Ponapean, Yapese, Japanese and English) earned him an ap-

pointment with the new American government. In due course he was appointed District Judge and served in this capacity for eleven years before finally leaving government service to join the staff of the Palau Museum in 1959.

It was at the museum that Gibbons really began to paint. Visual material was often needed to illustrate the various exhibits and Gibbons tried his hand at creating the scenes required. Delighted with his own efforts, he continued to paint, now as much for his own enjoyment as for the benefit of the museum, concentrating more and more upon depicting traditional Palauan life and the customs that are too quickly disappearing. Inspired by the old legends recounted by the village elders and by his own and his father's recollections, Gibbons' paintings are a unique chronicle of a bygone era.

The former director of the Palau Museum, Hera Ware Owen, took a strong and early interest in his paintings and her enthusiasm and encouragement were a great inspiration to Gibbons' work. Owen successfully organised an exhibition of his paintings at the University of Washington in 1971 and at the University of Guam in 1973.

Gibbons now lives in the same small blue-painted corrugated iron shack in which he was born. Frail and aging, until only recently he could be seen each day riding his bicycle the two miles to the museum, where he would sit and paint. Today, unfortunately, his strength is not often equal to a bicycle ride, and he prefers to sit in his small house and dream of times passed. Most of Gibbons' paintings have found their way into private collections all over the world, but fortunately the Palau Museum has retained a sufficient number to do justice to the honour not only of a great naive painter but of a fine man who so clearly recalled and chronicled the past for everyone to enjoy. Undoubtedly Gibbons will always be remembered as the most important painter that Palau has known. *(See portrait of the artist, p. 289).* J. F.

"GILVAN," PAULO (1930)   **Brazil**

Paulo "Gilvan" was born in Recife, Pernambuco. Originally he achieved fame as a founder of a vocal group called the Trio Trikitan — which became popular not only in Brazil but in many countries of the world.

Today he has built up a new reputation as a naive painter. Although in no way pretentious, he has in the main injected into his works a strong moral timbre which appears either in his versions of stories from the Bible (both Old and New Testaments), in pictorialised incidents from the lives of Limpiao and Maia Bonita (the almost

Glukhovskaya, G. G.: The Young and the Old

legendary bandit of the wild lands in the Brazilian north-east and his wife) or, in some cases, a synthesis of both. On occasion, he also paints pictures of rural fiestas. But despite this plenitude of subject-matter, his people tend to be standardised (although never quite repetitive) because, as he once explained to a critic, they are all "alike". His colours are recognisably distinctive; he uses acrylic enamels and plastic paints on the smooth side of cardboard. *Sh. W.*

GLUHOVSKAJA,   **USSR**
GALINA GRIGOR'EVNA (1908—1981)
GLUKHOVSKAYA,
GALINA GRIGORYEVNA

G. G. Glukhovskaya was born in the South Russian steppe-land city of Rostov-on-Don, the

Gómez, Crisanto: Village Girls

daughter of office employees. She worked as a cartographer and stenographer, and began to paint only in 1969, after retirement. She painted from nature, but preferred portraits. The influence of her occupation of cartographer can be seen in her pictures, with their clear silhouettes and smooth lines. She had a deep feeling for nature and was able to express moods through colour and texture.

Her *Weltanschauung* was rooted in an urban environment. She was regularly represented at exhibitions after 1970 and also at group shows of amateur artists on a USSR level and in Czecho-

Golding, William: Bodie Island

slovakia, East Germany, West Germany and Poland.

(See portrait of the artist, p. 289). N. Sh.

GOLDING,   **USA**
WILLIAM (1875—1943)

What little is known of William Golding comes from the records of the Marine Hospital in Savannah, Georgia, and two surviving letters of several he wrote to a Miss Stiles. Golding was born in Savannah, where he was hospitalised four times between 1925 and 1935. A fellow-patient recalled him as quiet, dignified, self-educated and deeply religious. Miss Stiles, who apparently acted as his agent, must have asked him about his life, for he wrote to her to say that on 15 July 1882 (when he was seven or eight) he and a friend went to the wharves to watch the ships. The captain of a ship invited the small black boy aboard and entertained him in their cabin. "When I wanted to go ashore, I could not, for I was at sea, about fifty miles off shore . . . and that is how I left home. I never saw home again until 25 March 1894. All that time since I left I have been all over the world . . . from England to China, Japan, India, South America, around Cape Horn twenty-three times. Am old now, fifty-nine, so I have to give up going to sea. Now I only goes in my sleep."

Golding evidently started drawing in 1932, possibly during one of his periods in hospital, but if he ever indicated why or how, that story is lost in those letters to Miss Stiles, which were destroyed in a fire. But whatever moved him, the numerous drawings now in the hands of collectors and dealers are a charming diary of the many ports he visited and the several ships he sailed on. All of them, done with pencil and crayon, are small, usually 9 × 12 in, and all are graced with the presence of a sun, which, pale in the first sketches, became brighter and more glorious as his work grew stronger. *J. W.*

GÓMEZ, CRISANTO
Venezuela

Crisanto Gómez was born in Santa Cruz de Aragua; for the last forty years Gómez has been

g
272

Goossens, Cornelius: Lion

living and working in Bella Vista near the Villa de Cura of that city.

By occupation a farmer, he loves the poetic themes which he has discovered in his animals, but he is also closely concerned with the semi-urban life which he depicts in his other pictures. All of his paintings are executed in a thick impasto, applied with a palette knife. They are in the true, uncomplicated naive manner. Houses are more or less square. Cars are just containers for drivers and passengers. Trees are a little more complex. But all his subjects are rendered in heavy pigments broken into a myriad colours, of which the principal one is a sunlit pink. In this way, wholly unconsciously, he has been able to introduce a flavour of Impressionism as subtle as it is raw in its mode of application. *(See portrait of the artist, p. 290). Sh. W.*

←

GOOSSENS, CORNELIUS (1894—1976)
West Germany

Cornelius Goossens was born in Wolsdrecht, Holland, and died in Erkrath-Hochdahl. It was here that he spent his life and began "knocking together" animal sculptures intended for his garden when he retired. Goossens trained first as a bricklayer and then worked as a diamond polisher in Amsterdam and Idar-Oberstein. Together with Erich Bödeker, Goossens made figures for the "Fairy Forest" at Glüdern near Solingen. Goossens's garden, where, to the delight of his admirers, he set up a whole menagerie of brightly painted cement animals, is reminiscent of the atmosphere in Bödeker's garden, with its host of animal statues and figures, but

the uniquely astounding naivety of Bödeker's cement creatures is not so generally evident in Goossens's work. *(See portrait of the artist, p. 290). T. G.*

GOULDING, ARTHUR (1921)
Great Britain

Arthur Goulding, born at Bradford, went to live in Kirkham, near Preston, and is now in Blackpool.

Originally Goulding was a member of a musical group made up from his family. Much

Goulding, Arthur: Encounter

Gourgue, Jacques-Enguerrand: Voodoo Objects

respected, they toured the music halls, including London's famous Windmill Theatre. But since 1965, when he painted his first picture, he has divided his life in half — sometimes carrying on as a professional musician, sometimes devoting himself to his painting. He is a trained musician, but as a painter, completely self-taught. Usually he paints with a careful neatness. He favours romantic subjects with a touch of mystery. In a painting like "The Family," he plays tricks with mirrors, so that not only do the main figures appear but the rest of the members of the family are picked up in mirror images.

"Encounter," shown here, is a more traditional subject. A girl encounters a lone swan; the possible reference to Lohengrin suggests that Goulding is an incurable traditional romantic.

He has taken part in many mixed exhibitions in London, Lancaster, Paris and Lugano. *(See portrait of the artist, p. 290). Sh. W.*

It may seem fair to compare him with Wilson Bigaud, but it is true to say that both men possessed an extraordinary gift (although, as we have seen, Bigaud was to lose his in terrible circumstances) — the gift of being able, without academic knowledge or training, to use artistic technique with an effortless expertise that a professional artist would envy. On the other hand, Gourgue has painted pictures of great simplicity and innocence. Gourgue paints many subjects: daily life, folklore, Voodoo (he has a strong understanding of its many forms and complications), the mountains, the forests, peas-

Graham, Anne: Boy with Monkey Bali

GOURGUE, JACQUES-ENGUERRAND (1930)

Haiti

Jacques-Enguerrand Gourgue was born in Port-au-Prince, the son of a French psychiatrist who married a Haitian (later to become a Voodoo Mambo priestess).

He does not care to speak much about his parents, whose union was to prove unsatisfactory — a bad marriage which contributed to his unhappy childhood.

His life changed when he went to school. Once he was there, painting became his overriding passion. By the time he had reached the age of 17, he joined the Centre d'Art, letting eleven artistically fruitful years pass by before he painted his "Magic Table," which is now in the permanent collection of the Museum of Modern Art, New York.

ants in their homes and also about their business. Sometimes he leaves behind the world he knows and paints pure fantasy — in styles ranging from the near-primitive to the ultra-sophisticated. At ease with direct realism, he is also capable — if the mood takes him — of injecting beguiling elements of Surrealism into some of his pictures (even though Surrealism, as a movement, is unknown to him).

The forms and figures in Gourgue's paintings are easy enough for anyone to understand; the spirit, the meanings — often semi-symbolic — that underlie outward appearances are another matter; even for Haitians their interpretation is not always straightforward. Gourgue can often be a purveyor of visual mysteries.

Nowadays, Gourgue lives in Spain with his Spanish wife and their daughter, but once every year he always returns to Haiti, the homeland and sole source of his inspiration. *(See portrait of the artist, p. 290). Sh. W.*

GRAHAM, ANNE (1925)   Australia

Anne Graham was born in Vienna, where she studied under Professor Cizek. In 1939 she emigrated to Australia, where she continued to study at various art schools. Later, in Italy, she worked under Emilio Greco and in Salzburg under Oscar Kokoschka. She was lecturing for a time at Melbourne University and is a founding

Graham, Mercedes Estrada de: Night

member of two groups called the "Essentialists" and "Figuratives Now."

She is represented in the state and regional galleries of Victoria, Western Australia, Queensland and New Zealand as well as private collections all over the world.

Anne Graham has worked on relief murals, fountains, book illustrations and art films. She portrays mankind in a kindly and humorous way, superimposed on magical surroundings. Often she uses "cut-ins," free-shaped or oval canvases to emphasise the interplay of subject-matter. Satire sometimes appears in her work, revealing that side of her which is the sophisticated intellectual. Her colours and shapes, however, remain as direct and vibrant as those used in the peasant paintings of her native Austria.

In 1979 UNICEF selected her painting "Children Playing" for a greeting card to mark the International Year of the Child. *(See portrait of the artist, p. 291). B. McC.*

←

GRAHAM,   Nicaragua
MERCEDES ESTRADA DE (1941)

Mercedes Estrada de Graham was born in Managua, capital of Nicaragua, where she spent her childhood. Married in 1961, she later moved with her husband to Panama. Her first paintings, done on stones, were made to resemble fantastic animal forms. When she came to use canvas, her paintings were lively in colour and extremely precise in execution. She says she first felt the desire to paint when she saw the works produced

by the painters' school in Solentiname. Lately, her paintings have been on the theme of the Spanish conquest of Panama of which they are (in romantic terms) a condemnation; they depict the tropical forests of Panama and in them Indians and Spanish conquistadors.

She has exhibited in Nicaragua and Panama. *(See portrait of the artist, p. 291). E. C.*

GRAMS, ERICH (1924)   West Germany

Erich Grams, born in Altenfelde, East Prussia, now lives in Neuerburg, Eifel. Grams's

Grams, Erich: Trees in Bloom

Grand-Mère Paris: Seven Large Peaches

family came to Westphalia in 1928. Grams became a miner and worked underground until 1948. During that time he was involved in two serious accidents and on medical advice he moved to the densely forested region of the

Southern Eifel in 1966, taking with him his large family — he had no less than ten children. Here Grams renovated a disused smithy and painted it all over with synthetic paints, even covering the roof with flowers and animals. This was not done for artistic expression but for a purely practical purpose: the plastic component in the paint was designed to insulate the building against damp. But painting the walls and the roof in a monotonous conventional pattern struck our miner as too prosaic. Grams continued his technique of total coverage in the interior of the house. In its new guise the former smithy quickly became a

certainly a good deal of observed detail, culled from woods and fields, but we tend to be captivated rather by the poetic force and sure grasp of form with which Grams has created a world of images full of temperament and exuberant fantasy. These scenes, and also the chairs, tables, cupboards, vases and platters that are totally covered with painted flowers and beasts, manifest the same *horror vacui* as in the painting of the building. In accounts of naive art, Grams is treated as a unique case. No wonder that museums and collectors have purchased many of his paintings and decorated items. *T. G.*

Grams, Erich: The Pond Near the Castle

popular attraction, and its occupant, the invalid miner, still racked with pain, came to be highly respected. When the building had to be evacuated, Grams went on to paint his new home in the same way. By now Grams was producing paintings, which are done on both sides — and on the frame, into the bargain. In his expressive brush-work — spontaneous, fluent and overflowing with narrative gusto — Grams conjures up brightly-coloured meadows, covered with luxuriantly-blossoming trees and flowers and crammed to bursting-point with all sorts of beasts — man usually being excluded. His creatures fly and crawl, hop and leap, swim and chatter, play and wrestle with each other, doze or lurk in wait, so that the spectator, fascinated by this exuberant display of animal spirits and the many-coloured cascades of lush vegetation, wonders in mild irritation whether he is watching paradisal frolics in the Garden of Eden, or whether there is something deadly earnest behind these scuffles. In such pictures there is

GRAND-MÈRE PARIS   France
(ELISE NONCLERCQ) (1906—1982)

Elise Nonclercq, known as Grand-Mère Paris, was born in Quarouble and died in Paris. After attending elementary school in the little village of her birth in the north, she became a storekeeper in Lesquin and in Paris, where she sold antiques. She married and was widowed early. In 1963 she was shattered by the death of a granddaughter. This tragedy pushed her to seek an outlet for her pain. In addition to the poetry she had been writing for some time, she turned to expressing herself on canvas. "The Death of Françoise" was her first major painting. In 1965, her work, exhibited at a gallery of the Palais Royal caught the attention of newsmen waiting for the results of the presidential elections. De Gaulle was re-elected, defeating Mitterrand, and Grand-Mère Paris, the name she used from then on, soared to national and international fame. She exhibited in Paris, Hamburg, Lille and Brussels, but without giving up her antique shop. In

December 1982, just before she died, she was planning an exhibition of her paintings in the village of her birth.

Grand-Mère Paris disrupts conventional space in her pictures with a highly personal audacity. Inverted perspectives, subjects aligned on major diagonals, people strung across the face of a painting — these are features suggestive of the broad line of compositions which sometimes end up speaking the language of tapestry.

Grand-Mère Paris had a large number of shows in France after 1955 and participated in many group shows in France and abroad: in the

GRANDMA MOSES (1860—1961) USA
(ANNA MARY ROBERTSON MOSES)

Anna Mary Robertson Moses, familiarly known as Grandma Moses, is by now almost a legend in the annals of untaught American artists. Others may be more striking, but none have been so widely publicised. She was born in Washington County, upstate New York, in 1860, married in 1877, and lived with her husband on a farm in the Shenandoah Valley in Virginia for twenty years before moving back to New York State. Her husband died in 1927 and she remained on the New York farm with her youngest son.

Grandma Moses: A Beautiful World

United States, Canada, Belgium, Italy, Germany, Yugoslavia, Switzerland, Czechoslovakia and Austria. Her work has also been shown at the Salon d'Automne, Salon des Artistes Français, Salon des Comparaisons and elsewhere. *(See portrait of the artist, p. 291). Ch. Sch.*

As a child, Mrs. Moses liked to draw and was encouraged by her father, who gave her white new sheets to work on. "It was a pennie a sheet and lasted longer than candy. I had to have pictures, the gayer the better," she wrote. She coloured her drawings with berry juice, "anything that was red and pretty. I dabbled in oil painting . . . then the long years went by," she wrote to Sidney Janis. She was seventy before she began to paint again, in between her routine daily tasks of canning, baking, cooking, gardening and making jellies. Her first pictures were done in yarn, but arthritis in her fingers made that too painful. Finding a piece of canvas left from a threshing-machine cover, she tried painting a scene with housepaints. It pleased her, so she ordered some artists' supplies by mail, and thus began the many memory paintings of rural farm and country life for which she became famous.

She first displayed her paintings along with her jams and jellies at local fairs, and when they

number of paintings. Unable to do so because of his health, he sought to drown his sorrows in alcohol.

His art is characterised by minute graphics and a singular perspective. Among his best-known works are a still-life and "The Wedding Procession." But the most important ones are those depicting the old Paris, by reason of which he is often classified with the French naive artists, although he kept his Belgian citizenship.

He exhibited in Paris, Knokke-le-Zoute, Brussels and elsewhere in Belgium. *(See portrait of the artist, p. 290). J. C.*

Greffe, Léon: Wedding Procession

Gregoire, Alexandre: Holiday

did not sell there, undaunted, she had them shown in a drugstore window. This was in 1938. A collector of Americana saw them, bought four, showed them to a dealer who, charmed, arranged an exhibition of her works in New York City. Her first paintings were priced at three dollars each at the fairs. Today some sell for about 50,000 dollars, and many have been reproduced in magazines, as Christmas cards, and on so-called "collector's plates." Mrs. Moses died in 1961. *(See portrait of the artist, p. 291). J. W.*

GREFFE, LÉON (1881—1949)   **Belgium**

Léon Greffe was born in Charleroi and died in Paris. He was the youngest of six children in a miner's family. Himself a miner, he married Sidonie Goffin and lived alternately in the district of Charleroi, Brussels and Liège. In 1926 he moved to Paris.

Most probably he did no painting before his arrival in Paris. He and his wife obtained employment there as the *concierges* of a building on the Quai de la Mégisserie, across the way from the Palace of Justice. Greffe painted in a maid's room in the attic, which explains the origin of his paintings, with their bird's eye view of the old quarter in the centre.

He was discovered by Anatole Jakovsky, who regularly visited the couple. Jakovsky organised Greffe's participation in an exhibition of "Sunday Painters," where he was discovered by the director of the "Le Dragon" gallery, who proposed that they sign a contract for Greffe regularly to produce for the gallery a certain

GREGOIRE, ALEXANDRE (1922)   **Haiti**

Alexandre Gregoire was born in Port-au-Prince. For ten years he was a private in the army and went on to be a musician in the Palace band. In 1968 he was brought to the Centre d'Art by Gérard Valcin, who taught him the rudiments of art and encouraged him to take up painting. Using bright colours and a bold linear technique, he seems to be at ease with any subject, whether it be large decorated bowls of fruit (with a woman standing on one side and a man on the other) or his own version of the statue of *l'esclave marron*, which dominates the central square of Port-au-Prince. Using Voodoo as a source, he is happy to find inspiration in an underwater painting of "Maîtresse, La Sirène" at play with the fishes. Back in the less spiritual purlieus of the country's capital he discovers a brothel, whose less salubrious features he sanitises.

It has been suggested that people — men and women alike — all bear the same features in Gregoire's pictures, and may well all be self-portraits. *Sh. W.*

GRGEC, PETAR (1933)   **Yugoslavia**

Petar Grgec was born in Kloštar Podravski of poor parents who soon moved away in search of work. After completing his military service he left for Karlovac, took a job as a technical assistant in construction work, and married. In his spare time, he painted subjects from his native Podravina region.

He set up his first exhibition of about forty works — drawings and watercolours — in his backyard when he was eleven years old, nailing the "paintings" to the fence for the public (consisting of his companions, neighbours and relatives) to see. He drew everything he found attractive: from the marshes beginning at his house, to farm animals from his barnyard and the willow groves at the end of the village. To his great chagrin, after only one hour his "exhibition" was closed — by rain.

His principal preoccupations are willows and horses. In his childhood, in the marshy landscapes of his native district, he had ample opportunity to see willows and from his grandfather

GRIGORESCU, GHEORGHE ION (1904)   Romania

One of the most famous Romanian naive painters, Gheorghe Ion Grigorescu, was born in Glîmbocel, a remote village in the Arge district. After graduating from college, he worked as a dentist in various towns, finally settling in Cîmpulung Muscel.

Thanks to the painter M. H. Catargi and others who drew attention to amateur painters in Cîmpulung Muscel, Grigorescu emerged from obscurity in 1965 and since 1966 has been steadily exhibiting at home and abroad.

Grgec, Petar: My Horse

Grigorescu, Gheorghe Ion: The Yellow Armchair

heard tales of the houses once upon a time built on willows by the inhabitants of the area. There thus took shape in his imagination an unreal, fantasy landscape which he constantly paints in different variations and with new distributions of colours. For the painter, the willow is a symbol of indestructibility, for the more you cut it the more it grows. Grgec grew to love horses while still a child, but his great dream of owning a horse has never come true. Perhaps that is why he always shows them riderless, galloping, full of power, grace and beauty.

In the painting "My Horse" (1969), Grgec has portrayed an untamed black stallion, rearing powerfully. Set against a blue-red sky and the hazy Podravina plains, the horse is a symbol of childhood desires and fantasies, and of man's longing for beauty and the unattainable.

The painting "Pumpkins" (1972) shows large, ripe pumpkins in a heap in the foreground. Also in the picture are three trimmed willow trees, with young shoots already sprouting from the old trunk. Just as nature renews itself every year, so do the old willow trees. In the background, against a ruddy sky, are haystacks and the broad expanses of Podravina. The painting is a simple composition, reminiscent of home and childhood.

Petar Grgec has had one-man shows and participated in group exhibitions at home and abroad. *(See portrait of the artist, p. 290). N. T.*

Although he is acquainted with Romanian and European academic painting, especially with the Impressionists and post-Impressionists, Grigorescu's works do not in general reflect their influence, apart from some hints in theme and composition. Despite this, Grigorescu, self-taught, succeeded in discovering for himself the true functions of colour, the expressive values of line, the inherent power of monumental composition.

Grigorescu's vision of life is optimistic, albeit with nostalgic overtones, as in "The Yellow Armchair" and "The Linden Tree."

Grigorescu paints in oil on cardboard, and most of his works are of modest dimensions. He has exhibited his work, mainly in group shows of Romanian naive art, both at home (where he has received many awards) and abroad. *M. Il.*

GRIGORJANC, KARAPET (1870s—1930s)   USSR
GRIGORYANTZ, KARAPET

Karapet Grigoryantz belonged to that category of guild-type craftsmen active in Tiflis, now Tbilisi, between the late 19th century and the 1950s. Though it had been assumed that none of his work had survived, the Tbilisi art historian Irina Dzutzova discovered some of his paintings in Georgian museums and, digging him out of obscurity, managed to piece together some particulars about his life. It was established that he had been born into an impoverished Armenian family towards the close of the 19th century in the village of Kulaiya, in what is now the Soviet

Republic of Azerbaijan. Subsequently, when his brother moved to the highland town of Telavi in Georgia, he took the young Karapet along with him to assist him in the shop he opened there. However, noticing his gifts for painting and poetry, Karapet's brother put him to school with a local priest, who taught the boy Old Georgian and instilled in him a love of reading.

At the end of the 1880s, already well into his teens, Karapet went to Tiflis to study the rudiments of painting under the German artist Helfong. In 1895 the local authorities gave him permission to start a painting establishment,

Russian poet, Sergei Yessenin, when on a visit in Tbilisi to see his famous colleague, Vladimir Mayakovsky. Taking Yessenin along to see the restaurant's "portrait gallery," depicting among the many notables such great men as Pushkin, Shakespeare, Christopher Columbus and Shota Rustaveli, Mayakovsky spoke of the many local painters of humble origins, such as Pirosmani, Vano Hodjabegov and Grigoryantz, and deplored the fact that their talent achieved only posthumous recognition. Grigoryantz also carried out the decor for several popular wine cellars and for the Russian Bank in Tiflis itself, executed

Grigoryantz, Karapet: Girl with Flower

Grigoryantz, Karapet: Fisherman

where Grigoryantz painted billboards for the local railway, guild gonfalons and street signs. Later he produced numerous signboards for wine bars, cellars, shops and barber's establishments in the city; these are, in effect, easel paintings. Examples of still-lifes of this period by Grigoryantz, surviving in Tbilisi today, are greatly reminiscent of Pirosmani's style in the choice of subject-matter, the spatial arrangement, the use of localised splashes of colour and the generalised and materialised character of the subjects depicted. Over the many years that his painting establishment functioned, Grigorynatz discharged several memorable commissions, as, for instance, the decor for the Simpatia Public Restaurant, which attracted the eye of the

commissions for the landed nobility, and painted the gonfalon for the carpenters' guild in the small town of Akhalkalaki, on whose field he depicted Mount Ararat, with Noah's Ark. On the field of another gonfalon (for the hansom-cab drivers' guild in Telavi) he depicted local urban architecture. One can deduce from extant reproductions that the men's faces had been given an Oriental cast. Despite the distinctively national features and types, the figures depicted seem unreal and unattributable to any definite time or place. Grigoryantz's work is typical of urban folklore, the handiwork of a talented journeyman artist, as is illustrated by the presentation and imagery (which appear to have been culled from the popular street broadsheet), the flatness, the frontal postures, the static, frozen faces and the abundant use of localised patches of colour. Grigoryantz often painted from photographs and reproductions.

Grigoryantz also essayed his hand at poetry and produced a play, "The Fratricide," which was staged in 1904. He is also known to have illustrated volumes of verse by Georgian folk bards. Though a record of his biography was taken down in 1938, all trace of him was subsequently lost. Summing up, one could say of him that he was the last of that constellation of urban folk painters who depicted so well the bohemian

Grimaldi, Maurice: Landscape with Shepherd

vivacity of colourful old-time Tiflis. *(See portrait of the artist, p. 290). N. Sh.*

"GRIM,"   France
(MAURICE GRIMALDI) (1890—1968)

Maurice Grimaldi, known as Grim, was born at Raon l'Etape and died in Paris. Grim's interest in drawing and painting seems to have dated from his early childhood. He went to work, however, for the Nancy Post Office, and was drafted into the army to serve in the First World War. After the war, he returned to the Post Office, working as a travelling postal employee on the Paris—Strasbourg line. Louis Vivin was his supervisor. Little by little, he began to paint and attracted special note at an annual PTT Exhibition. But he waited to retire, in 1957, to dedicate himself fully to his art.

To tell a story was not Grim's major concern when he painted. Nature was his most frequent inspiration, and he brought it to life in his work, putting together grandiose compositions of trees or banks of greenery in successive planes to define his perspectives. His work is notable for its immense variety of greens, including various nuances of leaves.

Grim exhibited in many galleries in Paris and Munich and in several Italian galleries. *Ch. Sch.*

GRIMMEISEN,   West Germany
FRANZ JOSEF (1921)

Franz Josef Grimmeisen, born in Cologne, now lives in Essen, a dentist by profession. Per-

iodically he takes time off for expeditions into remote areas of the Sahara, where he shares the life of the nomads and recuperates from city life and the stress of his profession. He started to paint more or less by accident. The generally cheerless backyards of the Ruhr suburbs, with their industrial enclaves, are the "happy hunting-ground" of this medical man who is now obsessed with painting.

It is here that he prowls about, once his consulting hours are over, occasionally molested as he tries to record in his sketch-book odd details of buildings or an unusual juxtaposition

Grimmeisen, Franz Josef: Backyard

of colours. The evening is then devoted to evaluating the spoils of his expedition as he proceeds through the backyards of the Ruhr, a pursuit that often lasts long into the night.

The longer Grimmeisen immerses himself in his picture, the more he tends to give free rein to his imagination and his fondness for idyllic scenes. This is why these little pictures never turn out in the end to be representations of social evils laid bare with a critical probe, but turn into restrained, poetically and aesthetically appealing views of suburban streets and courtyards, in which an artist enamoured of detail and pictorial narrative can find full scope for his feelings.

Grimmeisen has participated in numerous exhibitions and one-man shows at home and abroad. His work can be found in museums and private collections of naive art. *(See portrait of the artist, p. 291). T. G.*

GROSSIN, FERNANDE ("MEMÉE") (1886—1975)　　France

Fernande Grossin, known as "Memée" Grossin, was born in Bordeaux and died in Biarritz. Growing up at the turn of the century, she chose to become a dressmaker. The handling of colours, feathers and silks was for her the attraction of this profession. At twenty, after marrying, she went to live on the island of Réunion. She

gusto undertake to recreate the neighbourhood and its life. Memée Grossin was more spontaneous in her approach than many of her generation and would more often capture a given moment than work towards a more general statement.

From 1964, her work was seen in galleries and shows in Paris and Cannes. She participated in the Bratislava Triennial and in the "World of Naives Exhibition" in Spoleto, later exhibiting in Lugano, Milan and Turin. Her work has also been shown in the Netherlands and Belgium. *(See portrait of the artist, p. 291). Ch. Sch.*

Gubányi, Imréné: Thatching the Roof

Grossin, Fernande: Cyclone in St. Leu

Güdel, Helen: Winter

GUBÁNYI, IMRÉNÉ (1920)　　Hungary

Gubányi Imréné was born in Homokmégy, the child of a landless labourer. While still at school, she painted in watercolours and up to the time of her marriage occasionally painted pictures on the walls of peasant houses. She was also fond of drawing designs for embroidery work. Later, with folk motifs as her model, she decorated plates and pitchers. She began painting on canvas only in 1977. Village life is portrayed in decorative interiors and attractive paintings of streets. She paints her pictures from memory, the result resembling stage scenery. On her canvases she uses colours popular in her native district for embroidery and wall paintings: bright red, pink and light blue. Her work has been shown in the Museum of Modern Art in Kecskemét (1978), and in a number of exhibitions abroad. *M. I.*

explored it from end to end, recording images and colour with her camera. Her photographs from these years have much in common with her later paintings. Soon after her return to France in 1936, her husband died. By the outbreak of the Second World War her three children had grown up and she withdrew into the country in the Vienne region. To keep herself busy, she began to paint. She would later claim to friends that she had been waiting for this moment for forty-five years. After the war, she returned to Paris and began to paint the streets of the capital.

Memée Grossin retained from her stay on Réunion a fascination with pure colours and a preference for lively scenes. In Paris, she would set up her easel on a pavement and with great

GÜDEL, HELEN (1936)　　Switzerland

Helen Güdel was born in Zurich. The first influence on her was that of her father, an interior decorator, followed by that of her uncle, a painter whose success in his chosen field was subject to a series of ups and downs. Her mother was quiet and determined, a typical woman of the Appenzell area, who went to a great deal of trouble to bring her up in the traditional bourgeois way.

After her father's early death, and her failure to pass entrance examinations for different art schools, Helen Güdel was persuaded by her mother to follow a more ordinary course in life. She graduated from a school of commerce and then did secretarial work in Zurich, Paris and San Francisco. In 1962, she married in Bern a man who was a teacher and economist, and thus continued to follow the beaten path. But soon she returned to the ideals of her youth. In spite of (or perhaps because of) the obligations imposed on her by her growing family (she had three sons), she turned with increasing frequency to paper and pencils. Initially, she was inspired by her children, her husband and motifs from their apartment. However, spending more and more time in the summer cottage of her uncle in the Appenzell area, she came to replace her pencil and drawing block with brush and oils, and produced her first naive paintings. Later she also

He has exhibited in Peru, Costa Rica, Cuba and the USA, and participated in group shows in Managua. In Paris his works were on display in an exhibition organised by Bernard Dreyfus. *(See portrait of the artist, p. 291).* E. C.

GUEVARA, GLORIA (1954)　　　　**Nicaragua**

Gloria Guevara was born in 1954 in Solentiname, where she spent her childhood. She was a participant in the attack on San Carlos in 1977. At present she works in social organisations. The poster made of her painting of Christ on

Guevara, Gloria: Paintings, Sculptures and Handicrafts of Solentiname

took for subjects parts of the towns of Bern and Zurich as well as the valley of Emmental, where she spent weekends and holidays. She has exhibited in towns in Switzerland, in London and in Paris. *(See portrait of the artist, p. 291).* G. K.

GUEVARA, ALEJANDRO (1949)　　**Nicaragua**

Until the age of seventeen, Alejandro Guevara worked the soil on an island in Solentiname, where he was born. Then he joined the Comunidad de Ernesto Cardenal settlement. In 1977, he left to fight as a guerrilla on the side of the Sandinista National Liberation Front against the Somoza dictatorship.

His canvases frequently portray scenes of the war. He is now a captain in the Sandinista People's Army.

Guevara, Alejandro: Fortress (San Juan River)

the Cross, his clothing and face those of a Nicaraguan peasant, was widely distributed in Western Europe. The artist now lives in Rio San Juan, in the south of Nicaragua.

She has exhibited in Cuba, Costa Rica, and the USA, and in a number of group shows in Managua. *E. C.*

GUEVARA, LUIS HARRERA (1891—1945)   Chile

Luis Harrera Guevara was born in Santiago, Chile. After studying law, Guevara qualified as a

Guevara, Luis Harrera: The Beach

Guevara, Marita: Somozista Guards' Fortified Encampment in San Carlos

practising solicitor. Very much later, he abandoned his legal practice and started to dedicate all his time to painting. At the beginning he experienced great difficulty in persuading his fellow Chilenos to accept the nature of his artistic vision. His works were shown in several mixed exhibitions and in some one-man shows. As can be seen in the painting illustrated below — typical of Guevara at his strongest — he favours as subjects urban complexes and the intricate architectural planning of Chilean towns. In Chile, naives, except for the *Arpilleras*, have been placed in two categories: instinctive (ingenuous) and magical. Guevara has been dubbed "the ingenuous painter of cities." His dark linear detail and rich and luminously tenebrous colours yield the sort of veracity to be found in the descriptive line enveloping the structure of buildings in the pictures by the late Nikifor, except that in Guevara's

Guevara, Miriam: "Los Chiles" Dock in Costa Rica

case the dream-like unreality of the Polish artist's combination of imagination with reportage is missing; or rather, it is replaced by a crowded urban bustle and suntanned tints — so far from the Baltic, even in its northern summertime. *Sh. W.*

GUEVARA, MARITA (1955)   Nicaragua

Marita Guevara was born in Solentiname, where she lived until her marriage. She then moved to the port town of San Carlos, where she resides today.

She began painting in 1968 for her own amusement, but also in the hope of giving pleasure to others. At present, she is the head of a small workshop of naive painters in San Carlos and is also active in social organisations.

She has shown her work in Venezuela, Costa Rica, Peru and the USA, as well as in exhibitions in Managua. *E. C.*

GUEVARA, MIRIAM   Nicaragua

Miriam Guevara was born in Solentiname, where she lived until the Sandinista Front of National Liberation captured San Carlos in 1977; she took part in the attack. From then onwards she lived in Costa Rica.

She began to paint when she was thirteen, following in the footsteps of her brothers and sisters. In many of her paintings, she has used a dark palette. In Costa Rica, she continued painting her recollections of landscapes associated with her childhood. Eventually she returned to her homeland and she enrolled in college.

She has exhibited in Peru, Costa Rica, Cuba, the USA, and in a number of group shows in Managua. *(See portrait of the artist, p. 290).* E. C.

GUILLEMINOT, RENÉ (1900) France

René Guilleminot was born in Bagneux. At the age of twenty-four, he began to paint in his free time. He earned his living teaching sports: boxing, wrestling, weight-lifting. He was the all-in wrestling champion, first of France, and later of Europe. After retiring, he turned to painting full time and very quickly, following a major ex-

Guilleminot, René: Bowlers

Guillen, Asilia: Geyser in Guatemala

hibition in Sweden, became known and began to sell widely. He died in the Midi, where he had been living for many years.

The world of sport is the main subject of René Guilleminot's paintings, some of which convey the atmosphere of the human encounter at boxing matches. Guilleminot also left a number of landscapes and scenes from the life of villagers in the Midi. These have the same clear tone and economy of line of his sports pictures and confirm his gift for sharp observation.

René Guilleminot exhibited in France and Stockholm. *(See portrait of the artist, p. 290).* Ch. Sch.

GUILLEN, ASILIA (1887—1964) Nicaragua

Asilia Guillen is the most famous naive painter of Nicaragua. Born in Granada, Nicaragua, she made her living by doing very fine and precise embroidery work. The writer Enrique Fernandez Morales persuaded her to try her hand at painting. He took her to the Fine Arts School in Managua and introduced her to the Director, the painter Rodrigo Penalba, who welcomed her by giving her a brush and paints.

"Never in my life did I feel so shy as I did that afternoon when, in my sixty-third year, I sat on a bench in the School of Fine Arts to paint my first picture in front of the mocking eyes and laughter of the youngsters there," she said later. She completed that first picture at home and never went back to the school.

Guttmann, Robert: Hanukkah (Festival of Light)

After her death in 1964, her paintings grew in value. Few are now still in Nicaragua.

She exhibited with great success in Brazil, the USA, the World's Fair in Belgium, a Biennial in Mexico, and in the exhibition "Naive Art of the New World" in the Museum in Baden-Baden and other towns in Germany. *(See portrait of the artist, p. 291). E. C.*

GUIRAUD, JEAN-BAPTISTE France

Jean-Baptiste Guiraud was born at Saint-Chinian, in Hérault. Almost nothing is known about his life. His birthplace is known because of an inscription on one of his paintings, signed and dated 1896. This date confirms that Guiraud was still actively painting in that year.

GUTTMANN, ROBERT (1880—1942) Czechoslovakia

Robert Guttmann was born in Sušice and died in Auschwitz. He spent his youth in Planá on the Luschnitz, where he attended the Czech school, although he came from a German-speaking commercial family. After moving to Prague in 1895, he read Herzl's books and became a convinced Zionist. From 1897 he took part in Zionist congresses in Western Europe, travelling to them on foot. Guttmann longed to serve great ideals and hence to gain something of their reflected glory. In about 1900 he had attended a course run

Guiraud, Jean-Baptiste: View of Parliament

The few works by Guiraud which have been identified share a highly developed elegance of line, more restrained than that of Louis Vivin, richer in detail and more muted in colour. In most of his paintings, there is a repetition of the date and signature at different points in the composition. Persuasive in his message and excellent in the execution of his work, Guiraud ranks as a first-class artist. We can only regret that so few of his paintings survive. *Ch. Sch.*

by the Academician L. Kirnig. His yearning and his restlessness found vent in a somewhat hysterical manner and in his painting.

During the 1920s, magazines followed the escapades and the *bons mots* of this eccentric, who was celebrated for his long journeys on foot.

In 1928 his first exhibition was opened in the Monopol publishing house in Prague. At that time Prague Zionists were already turning away from Robert Guttmann. They were no longer prepared to tolerate his outlandish manner, and disapproved of his long hair, his lavish bow-ties and his blue velvet jacket. He was exhorted to give up this mode of dress, but never did.

Guttmann's pictures were as original as his ideas and aphorisms, full of contrasting images and innovations, characteristic of his egocentric attitude, that verged on megalomania. His Jewish genre studies are filled with a strange and mysterious atmosphere. Some describe the miracle of an alchemist who succeeded in extracting a grain of glittering metal from a slimy mixture of elements; they are full of gleams of hope in an atmosphere of racial nostalgia. Others are as garish as the paintings of a ten-year-old child. Against a blue background he arranges picturesquely contrasting tints, his instinctive sence of

specific atmosphere. Her drawings were used to illustrate a collection of archaic texts of Zsuzsa Erdélyi entitled "I Tramped the Hill, I Walked the Earth," published in 1974. Eszter Gyovai began exhibiting in 1971. Her works are in the Museum of Naive Art in Kecskemét. *M. I.*

GYÖRGY-SZALMÁS, BÉLA (1908—1961)   Hungary

Béla György-Szalmás had a harsh childhood and adolescence, and a manhood marked by war and want. He died fairly young, in Budapest.

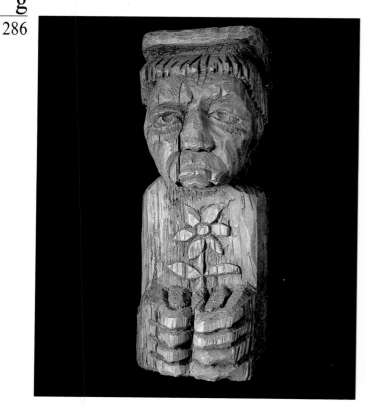

Gyovai, Eszter: Lipi with Flower

György-Szalmás, Béla: The Poor

ritual symmetry and rigidity investing them with the mystical regularity of barbaric ornament.

Guttmann said that he was "an uncompromising disciple of the modern style, but with a touch of realism, indeed of accuracy." But most of the objects in his pictures are merely approximations, as if they stemmed from ancient memories, and instead of details there is the radiance of magic substances.

His first biographer, the psychiatrist A. Heller, wrote about his painting: "In spite of all these technical and artistic limitations, it is not difficult to detect something childlike and original that is, in turn, reminiscent of something sacred." *(See portrait of the artist, p. 290). A. P.*

GYOVAI, ESZTER (1924—1977)   Hungary

Eszter Gyovai had eight years of schooling. She began carving her reliefs and small figures after occupational disablement. Folk ballads and the archaic texts of folk prayers captured her imagination. The work of this artist is marked by a strong feeling for style and the creation of a

During his lifetime, he worked as a wage-labourer, seasonal labourer, and for a brief period in the thirties as a painter of scenery for the theatre, but he was discharged from this job for political reasons. While working as a wage-labourer, he attended evening school for technical drawing courses in 1942. During this period, he produced temperas and coloured pencil drawings, naive in their stylisation and possessed of a feeling for the decorative. Through a form of assistance extended to artists from 1950 onwards, he was able to be independent. It was then that the subject-matter of his paintings and his style changed. He continued his studies, producing excellent drawings with a sure hand and a perceptive treatment of his theme. His works have been shown at home and abroad. *M. I.*

GYÖRI, ELEK (1905—1957)   Hungary

The male members of the Györi family were respected masters of the blacksmith's trade for a number of generations. Elek Györi learned that trade, too. His native village of Tiszaladány is in the neighbourhood of the wine-growing Tokay hills. He produced his first pictures in 1932 and won recognition in 1934 after the "Original Talents" Exhibition, in which his works were on display. His peasant genre paintings are imbued with a strong and vital feeling and good humour. He loved village festivities, and particularly autumn and winter, with their wealth of occasions for holiday-making. The village of his childhood has been perpetuated in his paintings: costumes and customs that have since disappeared; the motions made by peasants when working and handed down from one generation to another.

Györi admired the vivid processions of winter weddings. The wedding party comes for the bride in a sleigh drawn by four horses. Pistol shots and shouts echo in the snowy silence. The painter used vivid colours with natural ease and set them off with white, black and murky tones. Scenes with many figures are placed for the most part in landscapes with a high horizon. The source of his inspiration always remained village life. Also worthy of mention, apart from his paintings, is his autobiography of more than three hundred pages, as a document of the fate and aspirations of a gifted peasant. In 1940, he enrolled at the

Györi, Elek: Wedding Procession

Györi, Elek: Tokay District

Academy of Art, with the desire to become a schooled painter. But the years spent in the Academy, one might venture to say, hindered rather than helped him, since his inborn skill at expressing himself seemed to be stunted there. In the last decade of his life, however, he found himself again.

From 1934 onwards, he exhibited almost every year in Budapest. His works have been shown at home and abroad in the Netherlands, Czechoslovakia, Switzerland, Germany, Belgium, Greece and Cuba. *(See portrait of the artist, p. 291). M. I.*

Gagliano, Giuseppe

Gagua, Irina

Gajdos, János

Gatto, Victor Joseph

Gaži, Dragan

Gentili, Aldo

Gerard, Françoise

Gawłowa, Katarzyna

Gerlach, Friedrich

otti, Francesco

Garcia, Manuel

Garde, Silvia

ralić, Ivan

Generalić, Josip

Genk, Willem van

kene, Pjatronele

Geyer, Rudolf

Ghețu, Petre

Ghizzardi, Pietro

ons, Charles W.

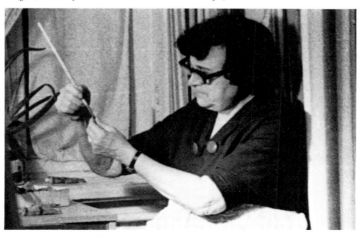

Gluhovskaja, G. G.

Gómez, Crisanto

Goulding, Arthur

Gourgue, Jacques-Enguerra

Greffe, Léon

Goossens, Cornelius

Grgec, Petar

Grigorjanc, Karapet

Guevara, Miriam

Guilleminot, René

Guttmann, Robert

ham, Anne

Graham, M. E. de

Grand-Mère Paris

Grandma Moses

mmeisen, Franz Josef

Grossin, Fernande

Güdel, Helen

Guevara, Alejandro

illen, Asilia

Györi, Elek

HABETH, MARIA — West Germany
HAČATURJAN, GAJANE — USSR
HAGOORT, PIETER — Netherlands
HAIM, FRANZ ANTON — Switzerland
HALÁK, PETR — Czechoslovakia
HALSBAND, GERTRUDE — Great Britain
HALUPOVA, SUZANA — Yugoslavia
HAMBLETT, THEORA — USA
HAMPTON, JAMES — USA
HÄNDEL, HELENE — East Germany
HARADA, TAIDJI — Japan
HATHAWAY, RUFUS — USA
HEBER, NATAN — Israel
HEGEDUŠIĆ, MARTIN — Yugoslavia
HEIL, ELI MALVINA — Brazil
HELIMIŠI, HASAN — USSR
HENC, KATARINA — Yugoslavia
HENNIN, GASTON — France
HERMANS, JOSEPHINE — Netherlands
HERNÁNDEZ, CAMILA — Mexico
HERNÁNDEZ, ROLANDO — Nicaragua
"HERÓDEK" (KAROL WÓJCIAK) — Poland
HERTMANN, KARL — West Germany
HESSING, PERLE — Great Britain
HEUSCHER, JOHANN JAKOB — Switzerland
HICKS, EDWARD — USA
HIGGINS, ROMA — Australia
HIRSCH, EMMA — Australia
HIRSHFIELD, MORRIS — USA
HLINOMAZ, JOSEF — Czechoslovakia
HOLMAN, BETTY — Great Britain
HOLZER, MEIELI — Switzerland
HOLZHANDLER, DORA — Great Britain
HOMA, JÁNOS — Hungary
HOMONAJ, PAL — Yugoslavia
HORNYÁK, LAJOS — Hungary
HOSTETTLER, ELISABETH — Switzerland
HRUŠKA, JAN — Czechoslovakia
HURM, KARL — West Germany
HUSARIK, JAN — Yugoslavia
HYPPOLITE, HECTOR — Haiti

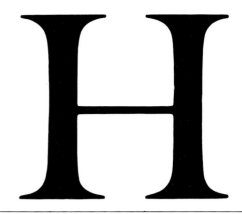

Khachaturian, Gayane: Playing Chess

Habeth, Maria: Harvest (detail)

HABETH, MARIA (1908)   **West Germany**

Maria Habeth, born in Duisburg, lives in Ersdorf, near Bonn. Her days used to be spent working in the household, the garden or the fields. She took up embroidery because Sundays were so dull in the little village where she grew up. With needle and thread she embroidered linen clothes with freely invented patterns, flowers and landscape themes, all in rather subdued colours. In her old age, when Maria Habeth had the painful experience of seeing the old half-timbered houses she loved vanishing one after the other, it occurred to her that she could perpetuate this vanishing world of old houses, lush meadows and cornfields in embroidered scenes. No wonder that these gracious pictures, created with needle and thread in defiance of all the traditional rules of embroidery, have found eager admirers and are frequently exhibited. *T. G.*

HAČATURJAN, GAJANE (1942)   **USSR**
KHACHATURIAN, GAYANE

Gayane Khachaturian was born into an Armenian family in Tbilisi, capital of the Soviet republic of Georgia. Her mother was a Zog, member of an ethnic group, which legend associates with Jewish tribes, but which in Armenia are regarded as Armenians and are much respected there. In her teens she attended an art school for children, but after a grave illness, which apparently affected her psychologically, she ventured to work on her own — even though she has to be in the proper mood to create, needs to feel the resisting texture of the painter's medium and works to a musical accompaniment. Hers is an agonising search for her own manner, for a means of expression, for symbols with which to depict her own characters, the trees, the moon, a horse, or a lion. Her fantasies derive from an inner emotional impulse, while her subject-matter is highly metaphoric, enhanced by a wide gamut of tonal values. All the many phases she has gone through tend towards theatrical make-believe. Her technical skill derives more from an acquaintance with professional painting than from professional training, while her *Weltanschauung* stems from the typically Caucasian scenery, with its mountains, vividly coloured fruits and verdant green, and the peculiar Eastern way of life and mores of the Caucasians, with their national and social attitudes and their eroticism. The world of her painting is flat with no drama, no social upheavals, no personalised or historical reminiscences, no psychological probing; the characters that populate it are not real flesh-and-blood people or beasts, but symbols, as static as the elements of a stage set. Rather this is a reflection of a dreamland world devoid of movement and of genre detail. Over the past few years, her works have become more complicated, with an increased emphasis on detail and an abstract play of colour. Is she really a naive artist? And is she herself naive? Certainly she is not naive in her manner of thought. Yet the knowledge she draws upon to reflect that world

Khachaturian, Gayane: Dreaming Wind

in forms and shapes corresponding to her own intuition has not prevailed over her artless sincerity. Her work stems, in effect, from the human heart, and her amazement at the eternal riddles that nature and life propound, coupled with the opportunity offered to her of expressing these riddles in paint in accordance with her own inner observations, are, in substance, naive.

Gayane Khachaturian's work is in private collections and in the Museum of Modern Art, Yerevan (capital of the Armenian Republic). She has had several one-woman shows in Yerevan, and has been represented in exhibitions in Tbilisi and elsewhere in Georgia. Articles and essays have been devoted to her and her paintings and a television documentary was made about her in Armenia. Meanwhile her tiny studio has become a tourist attraction. In 1982 she was accepted as a member of the Union of Soviet Artists. *(See portrait of the artist, p. 316). N. Sh.*

HAGOORT, PIETER (1887—1975) Netherlands

Pieter Hagoort was born in Strijen, near Rotterdam. At the age of sixteen he started to work as a stable boy for the Rotterdam streetcar line, then drawn by horses, and two years later became a coachman. After three years he was transferred to the Hoorn-Enkhuizen line, where he became head of the streetcar service. When horse-drawn streetcars were abolished in 1918, he went to work as a postman in the villages of Grootebroek and Bovenkarspel, north Holland, where he remained until retirement. Once retired, he felt the urge to tell stories about the

Hagoort, Pieter: Street with Canal and Horse-drawn Streetcar

horse-drawn streetcars, but as he could not do so in words, he did it with pictures. It thus happened that in 1957, when he was seventy, he started painting in watercolours, gouache and oil. He depicted only his recollections, not because he felt that the past had been better than the present, but because he thought of himself as an historian rather than as a painter.

Of all naive painting, Hagoort's work is most typically Dutch: gay, fresh colours, compositions in straight lines, clear portrayals and idealised memories of youthful days. Although some development did take place in his work, it remained childlike and spontaneous. He did not have a very high opinion of his paintings, and even called them "messes," in comparison with works by academically trained artists. Hagoort lived in the conviction that he had never had enough talent to attend the Academy. He was satisfied with what he knew and surprised that anyone took an interest in him. Dr Lus Gans discovered him in 1960 and gave him the incentive to persevere with his painting. Hagoort won his first prize in 1970 in Zagreb "Naive '70" and had a one-man show in 1973. He died in Grootebroek. The Westfries Museum in Horn displays his works regularly. *(See portrait of the artist, p. 316). N. E.*

HAIM, FRANZ ANTON (1830—1890) **Switzerland**

Franz Anton Haim, a member of the group of painters from Appenzell (see page 104) was born in Unter-Reute, and died in Fendrig, Leimensteig. He was a farmer, whose painting brought in some additional income. He even painted the walls of his rooms. Two small details have been preserved — a cow and a horse — from the façade of his house.

As with other Appenzell artists, Haim's open-heartedness and lack of sophistication are his principal features. To some extent he looked to his predecessor, Bartholomäus Lämmler,

Haim, Franz Anton: Three Herders Playing Cards

although the way he depicted cows in the wide open spaces of the Swiss hills and valleys is more reminiscent of the work of Johannes Müller. While themes are often repeated in his works, his creative originality permeates them all.

Haim usually has a sunny setting for his scenes of livestock going to summer mountain pasture in the Appenzell area. His works, however, include some subjects quite rare among the Appenzell painters: a picture showing only one cow with herdsman and dog, or hunters after game, or even a portrait of a herdsman puffing a pipe. Also unusual is the theme of the painting "Three Herders Playing Cards," in which, despite the clumsy perspective, the cardplayers' concentration on their game is expressed. Even the dog near the table seems interested in the outcome.

HALÁK, PETR (1948)   **Czechoslovakia**

Petr Halák, born in Teplice, comes from a working class family and is a skilled mechanic specialising in measuring apparatus. He was formerly a stoker and at present works as an electrician in a water-supply station in Prague. He painted his first pictures and self-portrait in 1968, but started painting in his own particular style after his return from the army in 1970. He has had no special artistic training. Halák is a man with an enquiring intelligence, and an interest in poetry, photography and music. Halák wants to create an unrenewable world of his own. His artistic world is rooted in an original realm of myths, naive poetics and self-expression. He does not describe reality, but contemplates the world and himself and seeks for the meaning of life. The stories he presents with a touch of balladry always have some deeper connotation. Halák places his own type of tall figures (mainly nudes

Halák, Petr: So Join Us

with expressive eyes) on ample canvases, painting them in nuances of the basic colours, without any great contrasts. His colours are subdued in accordance with the gravity of the content.

Halák exhibited his works for the first time at the Third Triennial of Insitic (Naive) Art in Bratislava in 1972, where he was awarded the Grand Prix of Rousseau le Douanier by the International Jury. (See portrait of the artist, p. 316). S. T.

HALSBAND, GERTRUDE (1917)   Great Britain

Gertrude Halsband was born in Mosseley, near Ashton-under-Lyne. It was her childhood dream to become an artist. In fact, while still in her teens, when her mother asked her what she would like for a birthday present, she promptly replied, "A canvas, brushes and paints." It was not what her father, who ran a local fish-and-chip shop, had expected.

After completing her first picture, she went on to paint another much larger one (not on canvas): a nude for which she had to be her own model. The big nude was actually bought for a meagre sum by the local RAF station (war with Germany had either just begun or was in the offing) and was hung in the mess.

When Gertrude Halsband left school she had to go out in the world and make a living. She turned to designing and making dresses and millinery and, because she worked for such long hours, had virtually no time left in which to paint. She did not stay long in the north but eventually made her way to London, where she met her tailor husband and subsequently went to live with him in a small flat above the Fire Station in Knightsbridge, where she lives to this day.

Sometime in the late sixties, the couple found that they were at last earning enough money to make ends meet and it was at this juncture that Gertrude was able to put aside her needle in favour of the brush.

This important decision led to an exhibition of her works at the Portal Gallery, London, and the inclusion of many of her pictures in the gallery's mixed exhibitions for several years thereafter. Her original Portal exhibition had been in the late 1970s, but from 1977 onwards she was well represented in RONA exhibitions in London, Manchester, Rome, San Francisco, Tokyo and Athens, as well as taking her place in the 1st Exhibition of International Naive Art in Britain (Hamilton's, London, 1979) and among the four British naive artists exhibited at Harrods in Knightsbridge the same year.

Nearly all of Gertrude Halsband's paintings — always excepting her portraits of cats — are of scenes she remembers from her childhood up north, and so the buildings, roads and streets are shown as they were long ago. So too are the people, with their period haircuts and style of clothes directly associated with what country folk expected to wear in the 1920s and the early 1930s. She has even painted (1980) a picture of her father's fish-and-chip shop, thronged with long-forgotten customers.

An assiduous neatness and care invests all her pictures, but it should also be emphasised that she deserves credit, not only for the craft she exhibits in her actual painting, but also for her personal delight in weaving people and places (often crowded and complex) into dense and sometimes convoluted compositions. *(See portrait of the artist, p. 317).* Sh. W.

HALUPOVA, SUZANA (1925)   Yugoslavia

Suzana Halupova was born in the village of Kovačica, Vojvodina, inhabited by Slovaks, where she went to elementary school. She does housework, cultivates her farm, and has been

painting since 1964. Under the influence of her neighbour, Jan Sokol, an older naive painter, she began to paint themes from the life of the Slovaks in Kovačica. As time passed, she restricted herself to painting children and their pastimes.

Halupova was for long the only woman painter in Kovačica, in contrast to a neighbouring village, Uzdin, where only women paint. The children in her paintings are all dressed in Slovak national costume, once the rule and now the exception in her village. In depicting children, Halupova has created a number of

Halsband, Gertrude: Our Street

Halupova, Suzana: The Death of the Husband

types. One is a naughty, aggressive child, another is placid. But all the children have round pink cheeks and are bursting with health. Her painting is therefore essentially different in theme and approach from that of the other painters of Kovačica, of whom there are about thirty. Halupova occasionally departs from her favourite theme of children and paints something from her own life, such as "The Death of the Husband" (1968). In a Slovak room, simply furnished, with the obligatory clock on the wall, her dead husband lies on the bed. As custom demands, the dead must be dressed in their best clothes before the relatives arrive. On a table are left-over medicines and a lighted candle. A red vessel with water in it harmonises with the flowers in a red flowerpot on the sill.

Suzana Halupova has had one-woman shows and participated in group exhibitions at home and abroad. *(See portrait of the artist, p. 317).* N. T.

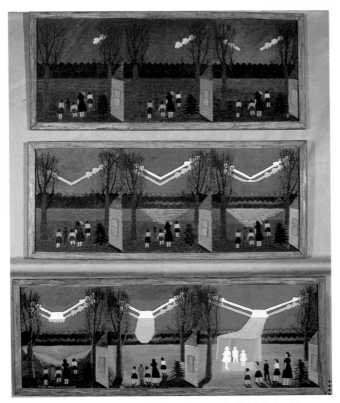

Hamblett, Theora: Heaven's Descent to Earth (triptych)

HAMBLETT, THEORA (1895—1977)   USA

Theora Hamblett painted her dreams recalled from years back, events and games from her childhood, "spiritual visions," and her memories of other people's memories. The mundane facts of her life are scattered piecemeal throughout the explanations she wrote for each painting reproduced in her privately printed books, "I Remember" and "Dreams and Visions." (The explanations, too, are fascinating vignettes of early 20th-century life in small town America.) She was born on a farm near Paris, Mississippi, the youngest child of her father's second marriage. Her childhood and youth were occupied with farm chores, games and school in Paris. On graduating from high school, she taught for a while, then attended Mississippi Southern University in Hattiesburg, after which she taught school in Paris, and in Oxford, Mississippi, where she remained.

It is not clear whether or not she had retired before she started painting in 1950. She wrote that an art department had been added to the

university nearby, giving her the opportunity, now that she could at long last afford it, to take lessons. However, "Abstract art was the favourite subject taught; that did not embrace my wishes for painting." She went her own way, sharing her activity with two like-minded friends, one of whom persuaded her to try painting "in colour" the dreams she so vividly remembered. Her first "dream painting," "The Vision," was donated to the Museum of Modern Art in New York by its purchaser. Another, "The Golden Gates," depicting two visions she had of "my Savior" just prior to and during an operation to repair a

Hampton, James: The Throne of the Third Heaven of the Nation's Millenium General Assembly (detail)

broken hip, was bought by Betty Parsons, the gallery owner in New York City. At her death, Theora Hamblett left behind quite an extensive body of work. *J. W.*

HAMPTON, JAMES (1909—1964)   USA

Grandiose in concept but fragile in structure, James Hampton's shiny "Throne of the Third Heaven of the Nation's Millennium General Assembly" was found in a garage in Washington, D. C. and is now ensconced in the Museum of American Art there. Hampton, born in Elloree, South Carolina, was the son of an itinerant black gospel singer and preacher who abandoned his family to follow his "calling." When he was nineteen, young Hampton moved to Washington, D. C., where he worked as a short-order cook and then as a labourer until called up by the army in 1942. Described as thin, timid and bespectacled, he was in a non-combatant unit which took him to Texas, Seattle, Hawaii, Saipan and Guam. Discharged in 1945, he took a job as a janitor with the General Services Administration in Washington.

Outwardly Hampton lived a quiet, solitary life, but in his mind a lively one, for, when he was twenty-two, he reported in one of his "writings" that God, his angels, and later other biblical figures, including "the great Moses appeared in Washington, D. C. April 11, 1931." It was these visions which inspired Hampton to put together his complex assemblage. He rented an unheated garage for fifty dollars a month and spent all his evenings and week-ends assembling his big work. It is made entirely of discarded materials, such as old furniture, light bulbs, cardboard boxes, desk blotters, kraft paper, plastic sheets, electric wiring and other objects commonly found in rubbish baskets. These were ingeniously arranged and covered with gold, silver and aluminium foil taken from cigarette packages, wine bottles, gift wrappings and such like. Hampton was known to carry a sack to collect these materials.

On the back of various parts of this throne, Hampton affixed diary-like labels documenting

Händel, Helene: Altenburg Castle Park

the dates of his revelations, such as: "This is true that on October 2, 194—, the Great Virgin Mary and the Star of Bethlehem appeared on the Nation's Capital." A bulletin board announced: "Where there is NO vision, the People Perish." Hampton declared he would finish his throne before he died, but after his death by cancer in 1964 unfinished pieces were still scattered around, as if waiting for his decision as to where to put them. That the throne survived destruction was due to an effort of the garage owner. *J. W.*

HÄNDEL, HELENE (1899—1979) **East Germany**
Helene Händel was born in Altenburg and died in nearby Plottendorf. As in the case of the West German naive painter Minna Ennulat, her painting ranges over a wide area. She took her artistic inspiration from the collections in the Lindenau Museum at Altenburg. What is recorded in her clearly ordered pictures is governed by the closely observed world of the little provincial capital where she lived out her life. Like many naive painters, Helene Händel believed that she could overcome or obscure the primitive nature of her work by sheer application and extreme precision and thus gradually attain a higher level of artistic expression. The linear structure of her meticulously designed pictures has a compelling effect. She developed her own particular approach to colours and shapes independently of other naive painters working in Altenburg at the time. Her paintings on canvas are reminiscent of ancient folk embroidery. *(See portrait of the artist, p. 317). K. C.*

HARADA, TAIDJI (1940) **Japan**
Taidji Harada, born in the province of Nagano, is a graduate of the Misashino Art Academy. Although he is art-aducated, in contrast to Yamashita, his style is more naive.

When he was one year old, he contracted infantile paralysis, leaving him lame in both legs. But he was born with a cheerful disposition and lived in a warm, pleasant climate in his native Shinshu, surrounded by a happy family.

After beginning his creative work, he came into contact with and was most impressed by the Yugoslav peasant painter Ivan Rabuzin and the

Harada, Taidji: Lullaby in the Village

French painter Henri Rousseau, although he went on to discover his own artistic world.

Today, the biggest Japanese newspaper, *Asahi Shimbun*, publishes his pictures once a week under the heading "The World of Taidji Harada," in which, presenting landscapes from all over Japan, he creates the atmosphere of each region with a rich poetic spirit. His fresh youthful pictures have spread throughout Japan, gaining growing popularity among readers. *(See portrait of the artist, p. 317). S. K.*

HATHAWAY, RUFUS (1770—1822) **USA**
Rufus Hathaway, a direct descendant of one of the earliest English settlers in America, was born in Freetown, Massachusetts. The details of his personal life are scanty, but it is known that he was both an artist and a physician. His first known portrait was signed and dated 1790, when he was twenty. In 1795 he became an itinerant painter and moved to Duxbury, Massachusetts,

and there married Judith Winsor, the daughter of a prominent merchant who persuaded young Hathaway to take up medicine as a more secure and lucrative profession than limning. He did, but he also continued to paint and to carve.

Rufus not only painted his in-laws, but also did a charming rendition of his father-in-law's house. While a number of the surviving portraits Rufus painted are in private hands or museums, most of the miniatures he is also known to have painted have disappeared: only four survive. Hathaway's portraits are delightful records of women's and men's fashions of his day. *J. W.*

HEBER, NATAN (1902—1975)   **Israel**

Natan Heber was born in Poland and came to Palestine with his wife and children in 1936. He made his living as a ritual slaughterer *(Schochet)* on Mount Carmel in Haifa, where he lived. He began to paint when he was sixty, having had to give up his poultry shop for health reasons. His impulse to paint came from his need to commemorate members of his family killed during the Holocaust. His first painting remained at the entrance to his home, serving as a memorial. Other paintings followed, describing the Chassidic *stetl* of his childhood in a severe,

Hegedušić, Martin: The Hired Hand

Heber, Natan: Sabbath Eve

Hathaway, Rufus: Lady with Her Pets

graphic, style. He often painted the Jewish holidays as celebrated in the Diaspora, but unwittingly added details of celebrations that are customary only in Israel. Heber's is a man's world, and the dominating colours are the black and grey of the Jewish men's clothes. But women are also present in the background. *(See portrait of the artist, p. 316). R. D.*

HEGEDUŠIĆ, MARTIN (1923)   **Yugoslavia**

Martin Hegedušić was born in the village of Hlebine, where he has always lived. A farmer, he sculpts in the evenings, especially in the wintertime when he can devote himself to his passion for carving his fellow-peasants in wood and depicting the hard life they lead. He works in the wood of the linden tree, soft and easy to handle, and prefers to make figures of small format.

His sculpture "The Prisoner" represents, according to the artist, his recollection of the concentration camp inmates he saw during the war. Bound and helpless, man surrenders to his fate. His head bowed and his eyes fixed on the expectation of the worst to come, his prisoner is eloquent testimony to the destiny of many people during the war. *(See portrait of the artist, p. 316). N. T.*

HEIL, ELI MALVINA (1929)   Brazil

Eli Malvina Heil was born in Palhoça. Before dedicating her life to painting and drawing Eli Heil worked as a teacher of physical education. As a naive self-taught artist she is easily distinguishable among the large number of artists painting in the same vein in Brazil by her fierce, almost aggressive style. One could almost say that her pigment swirls like a mighty flood, were it not for the deftly defined areas allotted to each colour. The images may be in tumult, but the colours manage to escape anything suggesting confusion. *Sh. W.*

Heil, Eli Malvina: Village in Morro

HELIMIŠI, HASAN (1907—1976)   USSR
HELIMISHI, HASSAN

Hassan Helimishi was born in the small Turkish town of Hopa. His father was a cobbler of the Kartvelian Laz ethnic group. Having received an elementary schooling, he worked as a cobbler and subsequently as a photographer, now and again doing painted copies of photographs for customers. In his teens he composed lyrics which he sang to guitar accompaniment. Involvement in the underground Communist movement led to him being sentenced to prison for life, but he managed to escape and swim across to the Soviet Georgian village of Sarpi in Adzharia. He then moved to Batumi, where he worked at a footwear factory. In 1932 he was sent to Leningrad to study at the Institute for the National Minorities of the East, but, having been crippled in an accident he was unable to complete the course. In 1936 he returned to Batumi, married and moved to Sukhumi. One period of his life was spent in subarctic Vasyugan, where he built himself a house. He returned in the 1960s to Tbilisi where he conducted Turkish conversation classes at the local university. After retiring on a pension in the mid-1970s, he hoped to get back to the seaside and show his pictures to the villagers of Sarpi. He did not live long enough to do so, but after his death his body was taken there by friends and buried on a cliff overlooking the sea. Mostly

painted from memory and imagination, and mostly in gouache on cardboard, they are scenes from the day-to-day life of the Laz, one of the oldest Kartvelian tribes of seamen and fishermen, of whom he was a member. His colour scheme is restrained and gentle, but based on contrasts. In part, his rendering is reminiscent of the Persian miniature, while, as regards the relationship between figures and their spatial disposition or the presentation of perspective in his flat, two-dimensional compositions, these elements are associated more with traditional Persian oils. Artistically, he is akin to the pioneer

Helimishi, Hassan: Laz Cormorant Hunters

Henc, Katarina: The Old Man

naives in their primitive understanding of the objective world and their devotion to the ideals and mentality of their environment, which they sought to convey by characteristic means. Yet he is profoundly national as regards form, colour scheme and other basic elements. In 1979, a posthumous one-man show of his work was mounted at the Georgian State Museum of Art. *(See portrait of the artist, p. 316). N. Sh.*

HENC, KATARINA (1948)   Yugoslavia

Katarina Henc was born in the village of Sigetec, near Koprivnica, Croatia. She went to elementary school in her village, then to high school in Zagreb, where she also studied Yugoslav literature and philosophy at the university. Although she wanted to enroll in the fine arts academy, she desisted from fear of the entrance examination and returned to Sigetec, where she still lives. Since Sigetec is only a few kilometres from legendary Hlebine, it was natural for her to acquire Hlebine mannerisms when she first started to paint. Later, she evolved her own style

Hennin, Gaston: Street of the Vagrants

of expression. She introduced a dark scale of colours and a dramatic note into the painting of the Podravina area. Her pictures are concerned with the problem of loneliness, mostly of elderly people in the village, who seem to be apathetically living out their last days on earth. They no longer talk to each other, as they have nothing more to say; they vegetate until their meaningless, inexorable death.

In "The Old Man" (1973) she depicts a man awakened by noise, rising from his bed in a dark room and holding a candle in his hand. Near his feet is a bowl tipped over by a cat and spilt milk. Her sense of detail is illustrated by the hardly visible old clock on the wall, its mother-of-pearl face constituting the only light point in the background of the painting and in the darkness of the room. Katarina Henc seems to want to express in her paintings her feeling of compassion for the lonely people of the village.

Katarina Henc has had one-woman shows and participated in group exhibitions at home and abroad. *(See portrait of the artist, p. 317).* N. T.

HENNIN, GASTON (1907)   France

Gaston Hennin was born in Lyons. He moved to Paris in 1936 and set himself up as an upholsterer and decorator. This line of work brought him jobs for shows staged in Paris theatres. He had married in 1932. So far the idea of painting had not occurred to him. In recalling his

Hermans, Josephine: Paradise

past, Gaston Hennin mentions many names of music-hall fame: Vincent Scotto, Kiki de Montparnasse, Fernandel, Andrex. There was also Maurice Utrillo, whose portrait he painted after he had passed fifty. This was Hennin's first painting. Soon afterwards he stopped working, toured Europe visiting museums, and then started to paint in earnest. He exhibited first in local shows, before appearing in Paris, and was eventually seen abroad.

A frequent subject for Gaston Hennin are towns and cities he has seen in his travels. But, he concentrates chiefly on the streets of Paris, producing a lively inventory of its neighbourhoods, some of which have disappeared or been radically changed. Picturesque architectural features, presented in detail, are characteristic of his work which is based on careful sketches, which he then transfers to canvas. The canvas itself is often of his own making.

Gaston Hennin has been exhibited in France since 1957. *(See portrait of the artist, p. 317).* Ch. Sch.

HERMANS, JOSEPHINE (1895—1976)   Netherlands

Josephine Hermans was born in Arnhem, the daughter of a Flemish family. An unmarried mother, excommunicated by the Roman Catholic Church, she was able to bring up her child only through a great deal of effort, working as a cleaning woman in an Amsterdam hospital and also sewing in her spare time. After retiring, she began to paint — "something I had always thought about," as she herself said. In the fifties she was discovered by Willem Sandberg, Director of Amsterdam's Municipal Museum, who bought four of her works for the Museum. In the meantime, her pictures were also purchased by the Boymans-van Beuningen Museum in Rotterdam and the Frans Hals Museum in Haarlem. At the end of the fifties she left for Zurich to join her daughter. In 1961 she exhibited in the Gewerbe-Museum in Basel. A one-woman show was held in 1978 in the Hamer Gallery in Amsterdam.

Hernández, Camila: Maternity

The world she portrayed in oil or water colours, a world full of fantasy and movement, had lived inside her head for a long time. She painted the "Singing Fountain in Prague" and "Field of Roses in Bulgaria," which she had probably never seen except on postcards. Her paintings show white birds seemingly cutting the air in their flight; flowering fields, with hills in the background; a procession with tall red trees like palms. Her work is like a long poem full of life's joy as her rich imagination sees it and as her free choice of colours presents it. Josephine Hermans is a perfect example of how serious and profoundly exciting poetry can be when created with simple, almost childlike means. *(See portrait of the artist, p. 317). N. E.*

HERNÁNDEZ, CAMILA   Mexico

Camila Hernández lives in San Pablito, a village on the slopes of the Witch's Mountain, a peak of the Sierra Madre in the State of Puebla.

She comes from the Otomi Indian tribe, which lives in Mexico. There is evidence that, like some other members of her tribe, she is a *curandera*, or medicine woman. Like members of most Mexican Indian societies since pre-Hispanic times, the Otomi use the bark of the amate tree to produce a rich-textured paper that is used for magical as well as utilitarian purposes. In the former case, images are cut

from the paper and endowed with powers of good and evil, depending on the spell cast by the medicine woman.

There is a limited range of colour in the bark, from pale honey to dark brown. Images cut from dark paper symbolise evil, the lighter paper being reserved for the forces of good.

Unhampered by preconceptions of any sort, Camila Hernández produces compositions on bark of exquisite simplicity. They are reminiscent of early cave drawings, exhibiting a fine selection of detail and a strong awareness of space. *J. G. S.*

Hernández, Rolando: Bombardment in Esteli

HERNÁNDEZ, ROLANDO (1957)   Nicaragua

Rolando Hernández was born in Somoto and spent his entire childhood there. He moved to Managua and worked there as a mason. A few years ago, he succeeded in achieving his life's ambition — to paint the lovely valleys and villages of his birthplace. This he has done in a series of memorable pictures distinctive for their warmth and for the artist's abundant use of red and ochre.

He has exhibited in group shows in his home town of Somoto and in Managua. *(See portrait of the artist, p. 316). E. C.*

"HERÓDEK"   Poland
(KAROL WÓJCIAK) (1892—1971)

Karol Wójciak "Heródek" was born in the village of Lipnica Wielka, where he lived all his life. Different from other people, he was the village buffoon, made fun of by the others. But still, he was popular, especially with children, to whom he told tales of the saints, although a speech defect made him hard to understand. A shepherd from early childhood, he learned to read and write. When he was eight years old, he was given his first suit. Wanting to enhance it, he cut holes in the cloth and stuck flowers in them. Shocked, his father banished him from home. He lived his whole life in his places of work, usually barns. While still a child, he carved birds, and later, under the influence of his neighbour, a sculptor, he turned to religious subjects: Jesus, the Madonna, saints and angels. Deeply religious, he was convinced that his sculptures would make people live a more holy life in accordance with the tenets of the Roman Catholic religion, and that he would thus escape punishment in Hell. Often he kept his sculptures with him in the meadows. He painted them, staining Christ's red clothing not with paint but with his own blood. Wójciak considered his figures altogether realistic and could not understand why the priest did not want them in the church. Living in a mountain village, far from other centres of population, he played for dances and weddings on a primitive fiddle which he had

"Heródek" (Karol Wójciak): Madonna and Child

made himself from a board and two wires. When he was about forty, he was taken seriously ill, his sickness being diagnosed as atrophy of the thyroid gland.

In 1959 officials of the Museum in Zakopane took an interest in "Heródek," but it was only in 1966 that the first articles about him appeared in the press. Soon he was famous. Exhibitions of his sculptures were organised in Zakopane and Cracow, and his work aroused the interest of art critics, psychologists, musicologists and experts on folk music and dancing. His works are contained in collections of the ethnographic museums in Zakopane, Rabka, Cracow and Warsaw. *(See portrait of the artist, p. 316). A. J.*

HERTMANN, KARL (1918)   West Germany

Karl Hertmann was born in Recklinghausen, where he still lives. He worked as a miner until 1966, being engaged latterly in building and securing roadways underground. Chronic bronchitis obliged him to retire on a disability pension. He has three hobbies which occupy his spare time: his flower and herb garden, his bees, and his painting, which he mostly pursues in the winter. The subjects he chooses are taken from his domestic surroundings: his family, disabled miners on benches in the park, the humble but beautifully tended paradise of the allotments, and the

Hertmann, Karl: Miners' Orchestra

people whom Hertmann observes carefully and long, and slowly but surely works into his compositions. He knows his subjects well, for they belong to his own circle and walk of life. There are few echoes here of his former employment, except for pictures of a miners' band.

Hertmann's approach to everything is cautious, and this is true of the evolution of his work. It is possible to detect in his pictures the determination with which he has toiled away at his painting, the persistence with which he has experimented with one brush technique after another. He sums it up as follows: "Painting is my tonic, a form of relaxation. I don't often fail to get what I want. I'm not showing off, I can make a go of anything I put my mind to. I've got luck."

Hertmann's pictures are to be found in important collections and exhibitions of naive art. *(See portrait of the artist, p. 316). T. G.*

HESSING, PERLE (1908)   Great Britain

Perle Hessing was born in Zaleszczyki, at that time a province of Austria. In Chernovtsy, where she spent her childhood, her thoughts and the philosophies which developed from them were strongly influenced by her father, a man of great erudition, by profession a bookbinder and printer specialising in writings dealing with ancient Jewish teaching and lore. It is necessary to speak of the nature of his knowledge and expertise because these were passed on to his daughter in the form of stories which he narrated to her in the evenings after his work was done. This is why, allowing for inevitable interventions from the world outside her imagination, Perle Hessing's pictures are imbued with an informed and specialised flavour of the history of Israel and her people, starting from beyond the beginnings of recorded history.

Both she and her husband Siegfried fell victims to the Nazis during the Second World War, but when peace was declared, they were able to emigrate to Australia. It was in that country that, after a short visit to Europe (including some time

Hessing, Perle: The Golem

spent in London), she suddenly decided to become a painter. For the next eight years she spent her time going to all the major cities of Australia and devoting herself to her painting, before making the decision to live in London.

Hers is the art of story-telling — simple, direct, sad or melancholy, richly coloured or sombre. The story dictates the form and emotion to be found in the painting. As an artist, Perle Hessing made her name in Australia and that country was a source of much inspiration to her.

The list of exhibitions in which she has participated is long: from 1963 until 1980 she has had seven one-woman shows and has taken part in over twenty mixed exhibitions. *(See portrait of the artist, p. 317). Sh. W.*

HEUSCHER, JOHANN JAKOB (1843—1901)   Switzerland

Johann Jakob Heuscher, who belonged to the Appenzell group of painters (see page 104),

was born in Herisau and died in St. Gallen. His work (producing designs for embroidery and textiles) influenced his painting, as did his acquaintance with peasant painters from Appenzell.

Heuscher was chiefly interested in painting peasant houses. A feature typical of his works are the small black birds always flying across the sky, a hallmark giving evidence that a work is his, even if unsigned. In portraying individual houses, he is punctilious in elaborating every detail, almost always showing the owners and the members of their families, together with cows, dogs, cats and chickens, deployed statically.

Heuscher, Johann Jakob: View of Estate in the Thaa Valley

Heuscher displayed unusual sensitivity in his rhythmical distribution of forms over the entire surface of a painting, placing people and trees around buildings or depicting a garden.

HICKS, EDWARD (1780—1849)   USA

Edward Hicks is undoubtedly one of the most famous of the early American untaught artists, noted even in his own time for the many variations he painted of the "Peaceable Kingdom." One of his biographers, Eleanore Price Mather, comments that Hicks was "a supreme folk artist, but not a typical one," because while other folk artists of the time were either anonymous or known only within a limited area, Hicks, through his preaching, published writings, and his paintings, was familiar to thousands.

Hicks was born in Bucks County, Pennsylvania. Eighteen months later his mother died and his impoverished father placed him in the comfortable home of Elizabeth Twining, a Quaker woman who cared for young Hicks as one of her own. When he turned thirteen, the age when boys of his era began vocational training, he became a coachmaker's apprentice, alternating hard work with tavern sprees in Philadelphia. At twenty, after a prolonged bout of illness which he was convinced was cured solely by divine help, he was overcome with remorse for his profligate life, gave up dancing and singing, and in 1803 formally joined the Quaker Society of Friends. He married Sarah Worstall and became a Quaker minister.

As a Quaker preacher, Hicks received no pay, and so continued his labours as a coach painter. At the same time, he found it necessary to augment that income by painting household furniture, fire buckets and trade and tavern signs. In doing the last, he learned how to draw figures and cope with space as well as develop the conventions of decorative borders, lettered banners and stylised heraldry animals that would appear in his later work.

In 1803 Hicks and his growing family moved to Newton, in Bucks County, where they remained. However, Hicks's ministerial duties required that when he "felt the call," he must not only speak at Friends' meetings in his home town

Richard Westall, an English academic painter who in this work illustrated the famous biblical prophesy of Isaiah (11:6) that at the coming of the Messiah, the lion would lie down with the lamb, the leopard with the kid, the calf and the fatling, and "a young child shall lead them."

Hicks arranged and rearranged this composition in each of the approximately sixty "Peaceable Kingdoms" he painted at various intervals. Similar in theme though these paintings appeared to be, each was different, not only in composition but in symbolism. Some of the paintings subtly recorded a bitter conflict within the Socie-

Hicks, Edward: Noah's Ark

but "carry the message" of the Holy Spirit to others. Consequently, though afflicted with tuberculosis, when the "spirit" moved him he undertook long journeys to speak in other Quaker communities. One of his stops was at Niagara Falls, and it inspired a famous landscape now owned by the Metropolitan Museum of Art in New York. Though based on an 1822 map by Henry S. Tanner, Hicks put in alterations and touches that make the painting uniquely his.

His first "Peaceable Kingdom" was painted in 1820. It was derived from an engraving which was itself in turn a rendition of a painting by

ty of Friends (one which found Hicks and a cousin actively at odds with each other), others dealt with American history, such as Penn signing a peace treaty with the Indians, and still others were direct allegories of conquering the savage within oneself — a matter that troubled Hicks. By then his "Peaceable Kingdom" paintings did indeed reflect a coming to terms with, if not life, then impending death.

Hicks did not limit himself just to "Peaceable Kingdom" paintings. He did others of equal merit on seemingly more prosaic subjects, such as the hauntingly beautiful "Noah's Ark," now at the

Philadelphia Museum of Art, "The David Twining Residence," and "Cornell Farm" at the National Gallery of American Art in Washington, D. C. *(See portrait of the artist, p. 317). J. W.*

HIGGINS, ROMA (1909—1979)　　　**Australia**

Roma Higgins was born in England and arrived in Australia in 1914, just before the outbreak of the First World War.

She lived with her family on a farm at Bungalow, near Byron Bay in northern New South Wales. It was a simple life, full of simple pleas-

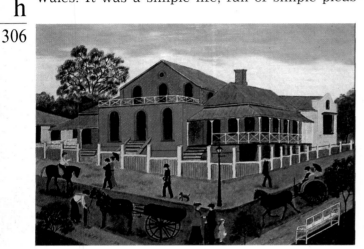

Higgins, Roma: The Old Courthouse

ures — musical evenings, church, fêtes, picnics and weddings in the garden. She has captured the atmosphere of those early years in her detailed, cheerful paintings, which have become collectors' items since her sudden death.

Although she had a few lessons in art, Roma Higgins remained virtually untrained. In 1972 she sold her first painting at a Queensland Cultural Centre Exhibition. From then on she started to paint seriously, holding a number of one-woman shows in various Australian capitals. Her work has twice been reproduced on covers of records for the Australian Broadcasting Commission. In 1978 she became one of a very small number of overseas naives to exhibit at the Portal Gallery in London. *B. McC.*

HIRSCH, EMMA (1932)　　　**Australia**

Emma Hirsch was born in Frankfurt, West Germany; she came to Australia as a child and lived for a time in Brisbane and Melbourne. She married an Australian but prefers to paint under her European name.

Completely untrained, she started painting as a hobby after her children were grown up and she had spare time on her hands. She now travels widely, but always considers Australia as her home and uses Australian landscapes as background for her many figure compositions. Her subjects are often urban ones — city beaches, terrace houses, back gardens and domestic scenes.

Emma Hirsch has been included in a number of group shows in Victoria, Queensland and

Western Australia and she had a one-woman show at the Gallery Art Naive in Melbourne in 1979. In that year also, one of her works was acquired for the permanent collection of Australian Naive Art at the Swan Hill Regional Gallery, where she had a solo exhibition in 1980.

Her work hangs in many Australian and overseas collections. *B. McC.*

HIRSHFIELD, MORRIS (1872—1946)　　　**USA**

Morris Hirshfield, perhaps one of the most unusual and distinctive of the 20th-century

Hirsch, Emma: The Gardener

American naives, was "discovered" in 1939 by the New York gallery owner Sidney Janis. At the time Janis was searching for works for a show of "Contemporary Unknown American Painters" to be held at the Museum of Modern Art and was invited by another dealer, Hudson Walker, to have a look at some new paintings he thought would be appropriate. It was here that Janis saw and was pleasurably "shocked" by Hirshfield's first paintings. He then and there took away the canvases with him. Janis later arranged for Hirshfield to have a one-man show at the Museum of Modern Art. Recognition by so prestigious an institution in no way affected Hirshfield's work, for, secure in his pride in his work, Hirshfield continued to paint sensuously mysterious, often subtly erotic works, one after another, until his sudden death in 1946.

Hirshfield was born in a tiny Russian-Polish village near the German border. He told Janis that as a youngster he had "exhibited artistic tendencies — not in painting but in sculpture," and, at fourteen, had carved a six-foot tall prayer stand for his synagogue. However, when he left Europe at the age of eighteen to come to New York, for practical reasons he went into the garment industry and later became a slipper manufacturer. Nonetheless, he reported that he never quite stifled the desire to "produce artistically, to paint or carve." When illness forced him to retire in 1937, he finally had time to satisfy that early longing and began working in tandem on two paintings, one of a cat, the other of a young girl

Hirshfield, Morris: Inseparable Friends

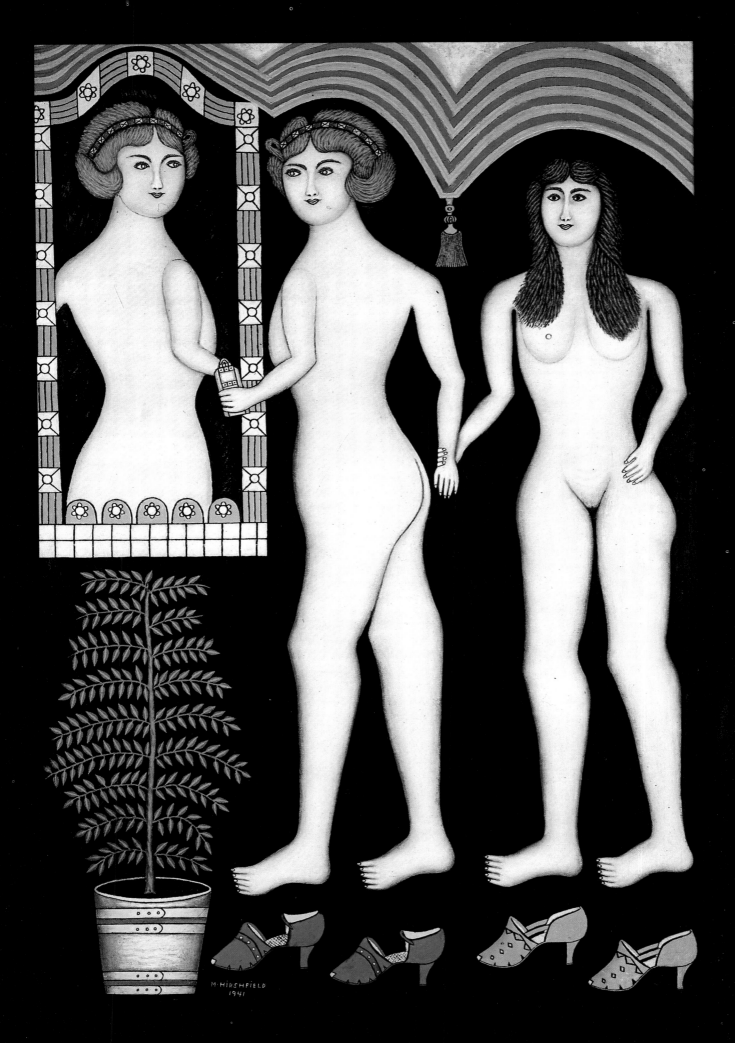

on the beach. The paintings took him two years to complete because, he said, "... my mind knew well what I wanted to portray but my hands were unable to produce what my mind demanded." When the paintings finally satisfied him, he took them to the Brooklyn Museum to be photographed. The then director, John I. H. Baur, encouraged his efforts by recommending that he show his paintings to Hudson Walker.

Janis has analysed the elements that contribute to the uniquely effective qualities of Hirshfield's work. His occupational background accounts for the meticulous textural detailing, so reminiscent of fabrics, as well as for his tendency toward bisymmetry, which echoes the bisymmetrical balance of the clothing and slipper patterns which he used to make. Less obvious, but nonetheless present in his religion are the design elements such as tassels, draperies and six-pointed stars, and his lions have their ancestry in the curtains that protect the ark holding the Torah scrolls and in the Lion of Judah. And finally, but by no means the least important, are the psychological components in Hirshfield's work: the unconscious but discreetly modest sexuality evidenced particularly in his paintings of nudes. These seemed to embarrass his wife, who, together with his then grown children, gave Hirshfield little or no encouragement. Like the families of many other naives, they were unappreciative of his talents until his paintings turned out to have a respectable market value. His own belief in himself, however, was so strong that he frequently worked on his paintings for eight and ten hours a day. In the brief nine years of his career as an artist, Hirshfield produced 77 paintings in all.

Hirshfield made preliminary drawings, but, according to Janis, they were commonplace and gave no hint of the vividness he achieved with paint and brush. It is interesting to note that, like other naives, Hirshfield, possibly aware of contouring by means of shadowing tones but unable to achieve it, often resorted to heavily building details, such as a nose or buttocks, with paint to give the illusion of three-dimensional depth. *(See portrait of the artist, p. 317). J. W.*

HLINOMAZ, JOSEF (1914—1978) Czechoslovakia

Josef Hlinomaz was born in Příbam and died in Prague. He attended the secondary modern school in Příbam, achieved good marks in drawing and thought of taking up a career as a painter. However, instead he went to study at the Academy of Dramatic Art in Prague and graduated in 1939. He began painting in 1942. After 1945 he embarked on a successful career as an actor with the satirical theatre. Hlinomaz was one of the most popular Czech comedians and a brilliant writer of satirical essays. His pictures also belong to the satirical and grotesque genre, only their mode of expression and their affiliations stem from the naive tradition. He deliberately chose the primitive idiom and cultivated it as his own natural form of expression. Hlinomaz felt that strict method and technical discipline were bound to be the death of the original inspiration and imaginative power that are the glory of

painting. The unfettered imagination remains, despite its owner's technical ignorance, the source of inventive vision. All this applies to Hlinomaz's work, which is also marked by its wilful thematic independence.

Hlinomaz's pictures are, above all, a fantastic drama. It is as if we had been wakened at midnight in the midst of a masked ball. We no longer know what is real and what is merely a dream: what we see is half reality, half exaggeration, and the greater the verisimilitude, the crazier reality seems. It is a fantastic vision. We do not know in which direction to look, for fear of miss-

Hlinomaz, Josef: The Congress of Dogmatics (detail)

ing something. Entire panoramas, more reminiscent of the film than of the theatre, are frozen at the critical moment, as in the final scene of Gogol's "Government Inspector."

"He is a latter-day Bosch," states a journalist's slogan, referring to the overburdening of the pictures with phantasmagorias, the assimilation of human facial expressions to those of animals, and the proliferation of emblematic allegory. In tiny grotesques and in broad panoramas we are confronted with the grinning face of Nonsense.

In the seventies Hlinomaz himself defined the trend of his art as "Surneonaivism," and even composed his own manifesto. Seen from the angle of his imagination, everything had the appearance of a grotesque gargoyle. *(See portrait of the artist, p. 316). A. P.*

HOLMAN, BETTY (1911)   Great Britain

Betty Holman was born in Camborne, the daughter of an engineering family. She now lives in St. Ives, Cornwall. Betty Holman did not start painting until she was forty-nine years of age, and then only because she found a canvas her sister had left behind her on the Spanish island of Ibiza (where she resided from 1958 until 1967). Thereupon she managed to borrow some brushes and paints from an artist and five years after that she had an exhibition in Ibiza, which proved a triumph. Since that time her pictures have been seen in Britain, Holland and New York.

Holman, Betty: The Church

Her work tends to have haphazard perspective and carefully prepared flat passages. The subject is generally the life and landscape of Cornwall.

She has had one-woman exhibitions in London, Ibiza and Amsterdam, and a number of mixed exhibitions since 1978. *(See portrait of the artist, p. 316). Sh. W.*

HOLZER, MEIELI (1925)   Switzerland

Meieli Holzer was born in the village of Sutz-Lattringen, on the shores of Biel Lake, where her parents were teachers. Her mother had artistic talent. From early childhood, Meieli too demonstrated an artistic bent. Upon completing her education, she went to art school in the town of Biel, where she studied ceramics.

In 1945 she married a young engineer. After travelling widely, she and her husband arrived in Rio de Janeiro with their two children and spent six years there. During her travels, Meieli took advantage of every opportunity to paint.

After returning to Switzerland in 1959, enriched by many memories, she persevered in her painting, although it was only in 1975 that she finally decided to display her work at a group exhibition of naive art in Zurich and at an Art Fair in Basel. She had her first one-woman show in Bern in 1978. Since then, Meieli Holzer has been invited to exhibit in many towns in Switzerland. Some of her pictures are in Germany, France, Benelux and Spain.

Her painting is not romantic. On the contrary, she is interested in real life and not in nostalgia for the past. She makes no effort to

Holzer, Meieli: Winter Evening

convey a message; her vision is simple and her only aim is to find beauty wherever it happens to be.

In 1981, she received a "Special Recognition" award at the International Exhibition of Naive Painting in Morges, in the Pro Arte Kasper Gallery, and in 1982 became a member of the "Henri Rousseau" Group whose members are the best naive painters of today. *(See portrait of the artist, p. 316). G. K.*

HOLZHANDLER, DORA (1928)   Great Britain

Dora Holzhandler was born in Paris, and is now based with her husband George in London. She escaped the Nazi occupation of France, having joined her father in England at the age of six. As soon as the war was over, she returned for a while to France, where she stayed with relatives. Jewish/Slav in origin (her family had fled Poland to avoid a pogrom), as can be seen in her work, she has been able to establish a "bridge" between Occident and Orient — an unusual feature in art of any kind — and this has been given a particular eloquence because of her embracing of Buddhism. It is, she claims, her Buddhist faith — present in every aspect of her life — that gives her pictures their air of simple serenity.

In France she had studied French literature and, to a certain degree, French philosophy. This background, together with her knowledge of the Jewish religion and her Jewish upbringing, followed by years of study of Buddhism, have culminated in a rich understanding of human nature and endeavour which she has been able to express in painting.

Dora Holzhandler has three daughters, and babies, motherhood and children (especially little girls) all find their place in many of her canvases. The maternal instinct is a powerful element in her art. Like few painters, she has completed a number of self-portraits which show her in a state of easily discernible pregnancy, even at the point where the birth of the new baby is imminent. There is an understanding innocence in all these mother/child celebrations in paint.

only one or two pictures — the prince Buddha himself with perhaps a single attendant.

Sometimes exact and careful, sometimes rough and turbulent, her paint is laid on canvas or board with a sweeping personal technique, all of her own making. Bright or tenebrous, her colours are always rich. Often the decorative elements in her pictures (walls, floors and upholstery, the fine fabrics of dresses, table tops and carpets) are built up to form a mosaic of black and white tiles, Islamic in their dominance. Women wear finery, often Tibetan in character, as do the children. Cars and buses shrink in size

Holzhandler, Dora: Lovers

Homa, János: Father Handing Over His Job to His Son

Next in importance for Dora Holzhandler, after motherhood, babies and children, comes the home. Her theme of domesticity is equally personally handled. The lady at the dressing table is Dora, the woman shopping is Dora, the lady in the garden is Dora (these may not necessarily be self-portraits, but they all represent Dora Holzhandler, just the same). Love and a kind of natural leisure abound. The couple entwined upon a bed or couch never quarrel.

The third of these recognisable categories in her painting is Buddhism: religious festivals and ceremonies, priests with the faithful sitting at table, scenes of personal meditation and — in compared with humans. The message throughout all this amiable medley is of Peace, coupled with the assurance that "Flower Power" never dies.

The list of the exhibitions in which Dora Holzhandler has participated is long. Her work has also been acquired by collectors all over the world.

(See portrait of the artist, p. 316). Sh. W.

HOMA, JÁNOS (1900—1951) **Hungary**

János Homa was a farm worker, fond of telling fairy tales and playing on the zither made

craftsman's house. It was his task to paint caskets, which he did in a room which was empty except for himself and the caskets and entered by no one during the whole day. When the paint on the caskets was dry he would carry them to the homes of the dead. He was often requested to nail down the coffin lid and on these occasions he could not avoid seeing the face of the deceased. At night he dreamed of funerals and woke up frightened. This went on for four years and during this time, he learned nothing of his craft.

But he did learn it when he started working on his own. Fond of wood, he became famous for

Homonaj, Pal: Petrovaradin Fortress

Homonaj, Pal: Family from Srem

by himself. He began carving when he was thirty-one years of age. All his themes, chosen from folk legends, show an archaic view of the world. In "The Word on the Hill," a terraced slope serves as the background for groups of figures in different positions and facing each other, but all of them concentrating their attention on a suggestive chief figure sitting in the centre of the composition "Father Handing Over His Job to His Son" consists of two figures, an old and feeble father surrendering to his tall, strong son the symbol of his occupation — the shepherd's staff. János Homa is the outstanding representative of Hungarian naive sculptors. His works are in the Hungarian National Gallery in Budapest, the Museum of J. Damjanich in Szolnok, and the Museum of Naive Art in Kecskemét. *M. I.*

HOMONAJ, PAL (1922) **Yugoslavia**

Pal Homonaj was born in Irig, Vojvodina, where he attended elementary school. As he liked making his own toys, his father, a hired labourer, sent him to learn the cabinetmaker's trade. During his apprenticeship he began working at four in the morning and finished at nine in the evening, also sleeping at the master

his carving. When he began to paint he was already over forty, and felt an irresistible desire to leave some trace of his childhood recollections, his village and the hills surrounding it. Today he lives in Novi Sad and devotes himself exclusively to painting.

His paintings are distinguished by the lyrical tones of his soft pastel colours. As though on a wall covered with unusual wallpaper, valleys alternate with humpy wooded hills. Lines divide the plateaux from the valleys, the separation stressed by the use of another colour. His villages, half-concealed, peep from behind hills; harvesters reap grain along the slopes or rest in the shade, while the livestock is peacefully at pasture and shepherds play games.

In the painting "Petrovaradin," Homonaj shows the famous fortress of the same name, resting on a cliff overhanging the Danube, with its military barracks and old clocktower. The Yugoslav flag is being raised, while sailors on a warship stand impeccably to attention. The motif is a rare one for Homonaj, but the painting's vertical composition is highly effective. In "Family from Srem" Homonaj shows the gentle hills of his district, covered in pine. The slopes are furrowed and the whole resembles a tapestry.

In the middle of the painting a family group has unyoked the oxen to give them a breathing spell. The painting shows a lyrical experience from an idealised childhood.

Pal Homonaj has had one-man shows and participated in group exhibitions at home and abroad. *(See portrait of the artist, p. 317).* N. T.

HORNYÁK, LAJOS (1918) Hungary

Lajos Hornyák, born in Pestujhely, is now a disabled pensioner. In his childhood and youth he was very good at drawing but began to paint

Hornyák, Lajos: Forest Area from Bakonje

only in 1965. Inspiration for his work is drawn from several sources. As a young agronomist he spent considerable time in the provinces, making the rounds of estates, farms and forests. Memories of this are transferred to his paintings, along with various festivities, dancing during harvest time and gay May Day celebrations. He also has a deep admiration for the paintings of others and is inspired by them, although he has his own expressive forms and a singular sense of colour. Hornyák paints the streets of old towns, rococo palaces, coaches and four, and town-dwellers.

While the dimensions of his works vary, he is fond of elongated paintings. In 1978, he had an exhibit in the Hungarian National Gallery. He also exhibited at the Naive Painters Exhibition in Zagreb in 1977. M. I.

HOSTETTLER, ELISABETH (1921) Switzerland

Elisabeth Hostettler was born in Zofingen. She attended applied arts courses in Basel and Zurich, and later in Leicester, England where she spent three years. She is married and has five children. Originally, she designed posters and then, given an incentive by competitions and prizes from the French magazine "Elle," she began to paint. Her favourite themes are the people of small towns and villages going about their daily work or celebrating a holiday. Actually, she wants to portray whatever is worthy of being saved from destruction in this fast-changing world.

She has exhibited in Switzerland, Germany, Belgium, Italy and England. *(See portrait of the artist, p. 317).* G. K.

HRUŠKA, JAN (1918) Czechoslovakia

Jan Hruška was born in Leštice, near Brno, and attended the elementary school there. He was later employed as a pharmacist in Brno. In 1967, at the age of almost fifty, he began to paint. Bouquets of flowers — heather, tulips, forget-me-nots and mysterious clusters of blossoms, sometimes passionately fluttering in the breeze, sometimes artlessly slumbering — such were the subjects of Hruška's first pictures. They attracted attention from the very outset on account of their unique technique. They present the appearance of little pictorial mats, seeming to be embroid-

Hruška, Jan: A Small Square Surrounded by Houses

Hurm, Karl: Coloured Ceramic Stove

ered or knotted, but, surprisingly, the "threads" consist of oil pigments. These threads were delicately applied over a period of weeks or months, allowed to dry slowly and then raised layer by layer. The artist's industry and devotion were much admired, but spectators were also charmed by the splendidly coloured texture that gleamed and sparkled like enamel. Every single fibre offers the splendid colour of its own particular material, and together they form magnificent structures, comparable to medieval gems and the miniatures in illuminated manuscripts. The painter's favourite subjects are gardens and, in

HURM, KARL (1930)   West Germany

Karl Hurm, born in Württemberg, now lives in Weildorf. After an apprenticeship as a painter and decorator Hurm took over his father's fruit and vegetable business, which he built up into a fruit wholesaler's. He had to abandon his work in 1970 because of poor health. His wife goes to work and he does the cooking and housework, but he still has time for his hobby, painting. He prefers landscapes or interiors with people and animals; reality and imagination — sometimes sheer fantasy — come together to form a synthesis. It is remarkable how someone so

Hostettler, Elisabeth: The Main Square

particular, city market-places. It is here that Hruška liked best to stroll at random. It seems that the market has just finished; the hucksters and craftsmen who filled the open space a moment ago with the sound of their voices have departed. Now there is only empty space. But between the old house-fronts that look like elaborately flounced costumes the echo of memories still hangs in the air. It looks as if these grand mansions were about to join in a round dance under the leadership of the splendid Town Hall. These market-squares retain a strict symmetry and a serene, harmonious dignity; they suggest heraldic shields in which a flat regularity of structure is replaced by spatial depth. Their space is scenic, not that of a town view. The charm of a ritual happening is constantly preserved, even in works so seemingly objective. *A. P.*

much given to the cheerful company of a circle of friends can lapse into a profoundly reflective mood as he sits in front of his canvas in the quiet of his room, plunging into a world in which all the salient contrasts of life, the diversity of human temperament, the many-coloured glow of his paints, can begin to fade and merge. Hurm contemplates the attitudes of his fellow-men from a proper distance — from above, in strictly spatial terms. We see them sitting or standing about in over-large rooms, silent, evasive, as if waiting for something. All his figures are squat and burly. This is the characteristic scheme of Hurm's paintings. Characteristic, too, is his fondness for a sublimated style that is reflected in his palette, the colours of which are mainly delicate and subdued. *(See portrait of the artist, p. 317).* *T. G.*

HUSARIK, JAN (1942) Yugoslavia

Jan Husarik was born in the village of Padina, Vojvodina, mainly inhabited by Slovaks, where he went to elementary school and where he still lives. He is a farmer who has been painting since 1958, mostly on the subject of thirst.

Padina is situated on the edge of the Deliblatska Peščara, a sandy area, and Husarik remembers that in his childhood the Padina peasants' greatest problem was the shortage of water. The village had a well from which water was drawn by a horse going around and around. Now there is a water main supply, but the childhood

Husarik, Jan: White Horse

memory of the problem presented by the water shortage has been recalled in his paintings.

In "White Horse" (1976), Husarik has placed a woman, tired out by work, going to fetch water at the end of the day. A thirsty horse is rearing, while his owner tries to calm him. A peasant cart loaded with barrels is ready to move. In the background is the village of Padina and red clouds that promise no rain.

Husarik has had one-man shows and participated in group exhibitions at home and abroad. *(See portrait of the artist, p. 317). N. T.*

HYPPOLITE, HECTOR (1894—1948) Haiti

Hector Hyppolite was born in St. Marc and died probably in Port-au-Prince. This naive artist remains — and justly so — the most renowned of all the naive painters of Haiti.

To a large extent this is due to the flood of unstinted praise which the late André Breton, the self-appointed doyen of the Surrealists, lavished upon him when he visited Haiti in 1945.

And not only could Breton speak and write about Hyppolite in this manner; he also organised a series of Hyppolite exhibitions (1947) in Prague, Paris, Basel and Berlin which blazoned the artist's name across Europe. In its own way this step which Breton took in bringing Hyppolite's name before a world public achieved as much for one artist as he was able to accomplish for the entire Surrealist movement. What amazed Breton, in those early days, was the utter purity (the Frenchman knew nothing about its motivation), the innocence, the idiosyncratic

vision, and the sheer magic that Hyppolite could evoke with a brush (frequently, at the outset of his three-year artistic career, fashioned from chicken feathers) loaded with ordinary house paints and spread across the coarsest of materials (with the image sometimes emphasised in pencil or, if he thought fit, with pigment manipulated by his finger).

Breton, a man of considerable artistic flair, was absolutely correct in his very positive assessment of Hyppolite. But who and how was the origin of his natural genius? A small thin man with shoulder-length hair, he was the son of an

Hyppolite, Hector: The Nude Queen

houngan priest and his grandfather had been an houngan as well. His sense of African heritage was so strong that he even planned a 5-year pilgrimage of that continent where he would seek for his roots — the world and tradition of his forefathers before they had been taken as slaves first to Brazil and thence to Haiti. It follows that, since childhood, he had been deeply imbued with Voodoo lore and practice, all in preparation for the day when he too would become an houngan.

Starting with decoration of the doors and walls of his Voodoo houmphor temple — signs, symbols and vévérs (the magic notations which could act as a welcome and simultaneously an evocation of the loa spirits), he also allowed himself, as a house painter-cum-cobbler might, to ornament in paint any other building or shack which offered this opportunity, and so it was that DeWitt Peters, on one of his rambles through the countryside, came upon a little bar at Mont Rouis (close to St. Marc) which Hyppolite had chosen to embellish in this way and over whose entrance the artist had painted a sign: Ici la Renaissance.

Primitive, with wild colours, aggressive yet heart-warming, the decoration of this bar showed a vibrant talent which DeWitt Peters immediately recognised as important and which led to his meeting with the artist and shortly after that to the coming of Hyppolite to the Centre d'Art in Port-au-Prince. It was here that Breton made contact with his arresting works. By this time Hyppolite had been persuaded to paint actual pictures, rather that what stopped short at decoration; indeed, towards the end of his life he complained that painting was taking up too much of his time and was interfering with his Voodoo

foregrounds and backgrounds (whose true meaning is the world of once-upon-a-time). Thus various loas (the absolute expression of magic) are brought together in company with the birds who act as their messengers (there are no birds left in Haiti today).

The collective impression given by Hyppolite's paintings is one of hypnotic power; the compulsive effect on the spectator is created by a sustained series of flashes of insight proceeding through the painter's works — a peering into the secret world confirmed through the snake-eyes of Damballah. In his work, the artist speaks from a

Hyppolite, Hector: *General Bauron Sacrificing to the Divinity Bobo*

duties. During his three years as an active painter he produced (it is impossible to discover the exact figure) between 250 and 600 finished paintings, of which 80 are known to have survived.

Naturally, most of this artist's works owe their inspiration to religious (or, rather, to spiritual) experience, but this could also be applied to historical heroes reincarnated through the power of the loas as men. Apart from their instant visual beauty, his paintings need to be read: subjects which in the technical sense could be classed as profane rather than spiritual are found, on closer examination, to be rich in religious symbols — flowers (signifying everlasting life), flags (which are really wings) and empty

complete understanding of the loas: how they should be served, what are their special requirements (different in each case), and the key to nature itself (a macrocosmic analysis only known to the finest houngans). It is typical of this remarkable man that he is one of those (and, in their day, there have been many) who has entered into a state of matrimony with la Maîtresse Sirène (the loa of the seas and waters, and of many other physical and psychological attributes besides), a mystical union he greatly prized because it helped him to investigate the double-sided nature of the spirit of the female loas, adding another dimension to his knowledge of the world of Voodoo. *Sh. W.*

Hačaturjan, Gajane

Hagoort, Pieter

Halák, Petr

Heber, Natan

Hegedušić, Martin

Helimiši, Hasan

Hernández, Rolando

"Heródek" (Karol Wójciak)

Hertmann, Karl

Hlinomaz, Josef

Holman, Betty

Holzer, Meieli

Holzhandler, Dora

band, Gertrude

Händel, Helene

Harada, Taidji

c, Katarina

Halupova, Suzana

Hennin, Gaston

Hermans, Josephine

sing, Perle

Hicks, Edward

Hirshfield, Morris

nonaj, Pal

Hostettler, Elisabeth

Hurm, Karl

Husarik, Jan

Ikonomou, Stathis

Ilija (Bosilj)

Invrea, Irene

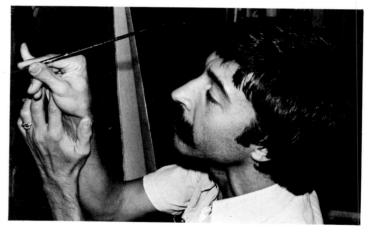

"Ivonaldo" (Veloso de Melo)

Iaponi, Araujo Soares de: Victory of Cavalry in the Battle with Golden Lion

IAPONI,   Brazil
ARAUJO SOARES DE (1942)

Araujo Soares de Iaponi was born in Sao Vicente, Rio Grande do Norte. In the main the paintings of this naive artist, gifted with an innate sense of composition and decoration, have either been based on traditional themes of peasant lore and legend or draw their inspiration from the Bible and the stories of the Christian saints. But there is another side to Iaponi, who also includes among his finest paintings subjects dealing with aspects of Candomblé (an ancient belief with African origins), with pride of place given to the Orixa spirits and the control they exert over a wide span of Brazilian society. This latter category of his work is particularly influenced by local beliefs and folklore, so that it is not surprising to find among his chosen subjects themes like "Henri, King Conongo and his Retinue," "The Children of Cearamirem," "The Coronation of the Kings of Congo" and the "Festival of the City of Caico."

Of all the multitudinous throng of naive and primitive artists of Brazil, Iaponi can be counted as one of the ten most popular, exercising an appeal which seems to attract a very wide public. *Sh. W.*

IKONOMOU, STATHIS (1928)   Greece

Stathis Ikonomou was born in Katachori, into a family of poor peasants. Until the age of twenty-two, he worked as a hired hand. In fact, his entire childhood and youth were spent in

Ikonomou, Stathis: Easter

Ikonomou, Stathis: A Theodorakis Concert

Ilija (Bosilj): The Elm Tree →

hard labour, want, war and occupation. Arriving in Athens in 1953, he took up various jobs but found true joy only in the painting he devoted himself to in his leisure time. In 1964 he opened a small boutique in Athens selling Greek handicrafts and also exhibiting his first works, as well as his objects made of copper.

Ikonomou is self-taught. His subject-matter is closely associated with his life, springing partly from memories of childhood and youth and partly from his current existence. He has succeeded in achieving an individual style in naive art and certainly differs, and distances himself, from those who turn out in quantity pseudo-naive products which are erroneously presented as naive art. He has shown his work at group exhibitions first in Greece, and then in France, the Federal Republic of Germany and Switzerland. His paintings have been purchased by museums of naive art and are also found in many private collections. *(See portrait of the artist, p. 318). O. B.-M.*

ILIJA (BOSILJ), (1895—1972)   Yugoslavia

Ilija Bosilj, usually known as Ilija, was born in Šid, Vojvodina, the ninth child in his family. He had four years of elementary school in Šid and subsequently spent his whole life there, tilling the soil. Late in life, he fell seriously ill with paralysis and was bed-ridden; he died in Šid. He began to paint in 1957, in the sixty-third

year of his hard-working life. As he neared the end, having lived through wars, met many people and participated in many events, he began to ask himself what life was all about? Although he was a good storyteller, he was not literate enough to formulate in words his philosophy of life, so all of a sudden, without any experience or preparation, he began with an unskilled hand to draw on paper unusual depictions of the world that do not fit into any known categories of work by naive peasant painters.

The first picture he tried to paint was supposed to portray his guardian saints, Cosmas

toward colour. He always painted straight out of the tube, without using a palette. He did not mix colours, except sometimes right on the painting itself. He had an odd way of choosing colours. Sometimes when I was at home, he would ask me to hand him his colours. 'Which one?' I would ask. 'Anyone,' my father would answer. He even allowed children to hand him colours at their own discretion. Normally, a drawing would take shape in ten minutes. He could finish a metre of painting in a few hours. He worked at intervals. At the height of work in the fields, he did not paint. He would start slowly, waiting for his hard-

Ilija (Bosilj): The Tower of Babel

and Damian. But the two main figures flowed together and one figure with two faces was the result. When he stepped back from his finished work, the farmer was shocked by what he had done. The painting seemed to cast a spell over him, for he felt that with this two-faced figure he had represented the double aspect of life in general — day and night, good and evil. From then on, these Janus-headed figures of men and demons constantly recurred among his themes. While most peasant painters remain tied to visible reality, in Ilija's pictures we discover icons from a religion of his own making.

His son, Dr. Bašičević, has written about his father: "... My father had a strange attitude

ened hands to loosen up. He often worked until dawn, not differentiating between daylight and artificial light. My father is not a narrative painter. His most interesting opus, which he christened "The Iliad," after his own name, represents an imaginary world according to Ilija. The relations prevalent in that world are also singular."

Various themes are dealt with in Ilija's painting, which can be divided into three phases: white, gold, and multi-coloured. The Apocalypse, themes from the Bible, folk songs and history predominate; however, he also paints strange birds and animals, especially serpents, and has also painted completely modern motifs, like spacemen.

Ilija Bosilj, the elderly painter, said: "It is hard to know what is good and what evil. It seems to me that a man is like a handkerchief with two faces. Even animals are not without hypocrisy. So in my pictures men and animals often have two faces. It is easy to paint, but it is hard to get to know life."

Sickness and paralysis made it impossible for Ilija to continue the creative work which he began so late in life. The pagan and biblical world he carried inside himself, erupting from within him, disappeared as suddenly as it had appeared. And so one of the most unusual of naive painters

cannot see ahead of you for the tall corn, but only above you, skyward?

In his painting "Noah's Ark" (1963), Ilija gives his version of the famous biblical vessel. It is a raft on which the animals are assembled under the direct threat of the coming flood; snakes, crocodiles, pigs, snails, and some indistinct but clearly fabulous creatures with heads at either end. Noah stands silhouetted in his boat, a bird perched on his shoulder, his hands clasped, like a bright flower. A rabbit peeps up over the railing.

Noah's weightless silhouette and the insubstantial animals resemble scissor-pictures as

Ilija (Bosilj): Noah's Ark

stopped creating — a man whose pagan and saintly figures represent the play of man's imagination throughout all periods down to the present day.

In "Elm Tree," the link between generations is most apparent. Is it the tree of life, the tree of good or evil, simply a genealogy, or all of them at the same time? Perhaps from this multitude of forms, animals and birds, man emerged. In this painting many of the figures are two-headed, with opposing forces pulling each head in their own direction. Is the world created by Ilija based on tales, on man's experience, or on the products of the rich imagination of a peasant from the spacious Vojvodina plains, where in summer you

they stand in conversation; they seem more appropriate to a ship of fools than to a lifeboat in the midst of a great catastrophe. It is as though the Bible story had been used only as an excuse for some comments on the strange and burlesque adventures of a crew of men and animals.

"The Tower of Babel" (1961), signed prominently by the artist, like many of his works, again shows a highly individual approach, combining elements of several biblical episodes — the serpent from the Garden of Eden, animals from Noah's Ark — with certain Byzantine features (the peacock, the saint with a halo). The men resembling bank clerks perched on the outside of each storey represent the various future races and language-speakers whose over-ambitious building activity prompted the Lord to disperse mankind over the face of the earth.

Ilija has had one-man shows and has been represented at group exhibitions at home and abroad. *(See portrait of the artist, p. 318). N. T.*

IMPERIAL, FALADE — Ghana

Pseudonym of a sign-painter from Ghana who lived for some time in Bobo-Dioulassou, Upper Volta, and apparently returned later to his homeland. No further details about him or his whereabouts are available. Whereas all his colleagues paint with oils on wood or work in sheet metal, Falade Imperial produces hair-dresser's advertisements done with Indian ink on paper and touched up with watercolours. *(See the picture on p. 62). G. Sch.*

INIGUEZ, SILVIO (1907) — Cuba

Silvio Iniguez was born in Havana.

The themes of Iniguez's paintings are landscapes with figures, usually realistically rendered, and yet sometimes quite fantastic, as is

Invrea, Irene: Panther Walking on Daisies

Invrea, Irene: A Rhinoceros Loner

Iniguez, Silvio: The Dream

the case of "The Dream," which portrays a chocolate-coloured nude reclining on a white towel in an idyllic setting.

In 1964 Iniguez had an exhibition in the National Salon of Painting and Sculpture, and in 1969 he participated in the Second Triennial Exhibition of Naive Art in Bratislava, Czechoslovakia. In 1970 he exhibited in Salon '70 and in 1971 took part in the joint exhibition of Primitive Painters in the Havana Gallery. In 1976 he was included in the exhibition "Eleven Cuban Primitive Artists" at the Institute of Jamaica in Kingston. *T. R.*

animal, nimble and agile, stepping silently, and apparently with a troubled air, along a sea of daisies on a hill whose curve is bordered by distant and ominous white glaciers, giving the entire composition a strange feeling of infinity.

Irene Invrea was able to transform her own desire for happiness, peace and forgetfulness into a space and time without limit, with the help of her patiently worked painter's stories, delicate in their graphics and thin and elegant in their lines. The serenity of the lines, despite their geometric repetition, coincides with the modulations of magical colour, giving her pictures an

"Ivonaldo", Veloso de Melo: The Rowboat

"Ivonaldo", Veloso de Melo: Bulls

INVREA, IRENE (1920)   Italy

Irene Invrea, born in Diano D'Alba, Cuneo, now lives and works in Turin. The loss of her husband in 1962 was a painful turning-point in her peaceful and pleasant existence, but, with her buoyant and optimistic temperament, she found the strength to react positively to a tragedy that seemed to threaten her very life.

Although unsure of herself at the beginning, Irene Invrea soon found the elements of her own personal painter's language: she depicts unpolluted nature, where space opens and spreads vertiginously; where vegetation, airy palm trees and a multitude of luxuriant flowers fill the eyes with joy. And then there are the blue rhinoceroses, symbols of strength, which have, however, become harmless ("The Rhinoceros Loner") and all the other animals living in her earthly garden. "The Panther and the Daisies" shows this

intense poetry and profound suggestiveness. *(See portrait of the artist, p. 318). D. M.*

"IVONALDO"   Brazil
(VELOSO DE MELO) (1943)

Veloso de Melo — "Ivonaldo" — was born in Curuaro, Pernambuco. In 1966 he started painting and came to live in São Paulo. This successful naive artist might well be described as a *macho* painter, because he emphasises in his bright, bold flat colours the dominance of the male element, a focus which is clearly evident whether his pictures contain people or not. A good example of this characteristic is to be found in his famous series, "Bulls." Ivonaldo's imagery is uncomplicated. What sophistication appears in his painting has been introduced largely *sotto voce. (See portrait of the artist, p. 318). Sh. W.*

JANKŮ, MARIE — Czechoslovakia
JAURISOVÁ, HELENA — Czechoslovakia
JEAN-JEAN, LÉOPOLD — France
JEAN-GILLES, JOSEPH — Haiti
JESUS, ISABEL de — Brazil
JEUKEN, JOHAN — Netherlands
JEVTOVIĆ, DUŠAN — Yugoslavia
JIANG GUOHONG — China
JIMENEZ, ELBA — Nicaragua
JOHNSON, TAPLOE — Great Britain
JONAŠ, MARTIN — Yugoslavia
JONES, DEE — Australia
JONES, FRANCES — Australia
JONES, FRANK — USA
JORDÁN, ARMANDO — Bolivia
JOSEPH, JASMIN — Haiti
JOVANOVIĆ, MILOSAV — Yugoslavia
JÓZSA, ENDRE — Hungary
"JUCA" (OVÍDIO MELO) — Brazil
JURAK, DRAGUTIN — Yugoslavia
JUROVATÝ, LADISLAV — Czechoslovakia
JUŠČUVENE, MAGDALENA — USSR

Janků, Marie: The Bridegroom's Yearning

Jaurisová, Helena: Outdoor Mass at Bardejov's

JANKŮ, MARIE (1891) Czechoslovakia

Marie Janků, born in Vitejeves, has always worked on a farm. Leading a hard life and disappointed by her fate, she dissociated herself from ordinary people and their truths. Her complete break with the outside world drove her to imagine a new, blissful life, and in her paintings she escaped into a better world. She began in 1960 by painting on the walls of her house. Her first subjects were bunches of flowers, then houses were added. Her life was completely changed by painting. "I used to be inhuman, bad, before. Everything is different now. I have never experienced such joy of life as I do now." Marie Janků is a visionary who transforms the essence of everything in her imagination. The gates of paradise opened to her and she saw flowers and flame-shaped trees there, and was captivated by the energy and will of love, eternal spring and youth. There are hidden passion, unfulfilled dreams, unreciprocated tenderness and anger in her pictures of clouds, water, rocks, blossoming trees, birds and human figures. Marie Janků found her redemption in them. The first exhibition of her pictures was held at the Prague Na Zábradlí theatre in 1962. Since then she has taken part in many exhibitions both at home and abroad. *(See portrait of the artist, p. 342). S. T.*

JAURISOVÁ, HELENA (1904) Czechoslovakia

Helena Jaurisová, daughter of a small peasant farmer, was born in Krušovice, near Rakovnik, where she attended the elementary school. She married at the age of twenty-two and spent thirteen years in Eastern Slovakia and the Carpathians of the Ukraine with her husband (a head gamekeeper) and her two children. After the dismemberment of the Czechoslovakian Republic she was obliged to move back to Bohemia. Since 1950 she has lived in Jilemnice in the foothills of the Riesengebirge, where she took up employment, first as a shop assistant and then as a quality-control supervisor. In 1966 she decided to take up painting. Since 1969 she has been exhibiting her paintings of village life ("Naive Painters in Bohemia"). The reality represented in her simple, cheerful scenes is light-hearted — this is what Jaurisová understands by "beautiful." Her mode of painting is also astonishingly simple: from memory she projects flat outlines of people and objects onto the background. These direct pictograms have a certain amount in common with those of L. Procházková, but Helena Jaurisová's figures are sometimes piled up by way of contrast and thus suggest a teeming crowd of pilgrims or the rejoicing and rhythm of a wedding.

Alongside her recollections of the Ukrainian Carpathians, Jaurisová describes the daily life of her neighbours and the annual village festivities: the spring festival in the foothills of the Riesengebirge, followed by the first sheep grazing; after the Corpus Christi processions come weddings and hop harvests; in the autumn we see the recruits taking leave of their families, or the gamekeepers at the Duke's shoot; and with the first snow firewood is dragged from the forest and the pigs are slaughtered. The cycle of the calendar is concluded with the long winter evenings spent telling stories as feathers are stripped from the poultry. *A. P.*

JEAN-JEAN, LÉOPOLD (1877—1948) France

Léopold Jean-Jean was born at Matha and died at La Roche-sur-Yon. Abandoned as an infant, he was brought up as a ward of the state. Sources who knew him in his later years confirm that he led a life of travel and adventure, during which resourcefulness most often had to substitute for good fortune. He often recounted the

d'Art in Port-au-Prince, the first institution that brought Haiti's artists together.

Although Jean-Gilles adheres to many elements that characterise naive painting — two-dimensional rendering, brilliant colour, the selection of his country's people and landscapes for subject-matter, and a certain innocence of vision — he has reached a more advanced stage. This is most evident in the luminosity that pervades his paintings and in the astonishing precision with which the various elements are interwoven, particularly in the still-lifes and works in which crowds appear. Even his colour

Jaurisová, Helena: Street in Jelemnice

story of his stay in Indochina, in anecdotes richly mixing fact and fiction.

The rare works — a few dozen at the most — left by Jean-Jean cannot be described only as paintings. He worked into his pictures shells, cordage, wood cut-outs and so on, in addition to actual painting, enhancing the visual impact with these reliefs. He framed his own works, executing the frames with as great care, often, as the actual pictures. His most frequent subject is the sea, although landscapes by him are also known, displaying the same straightforwardness and bright colours as his seascapes. In most cases he painted on panelling. *Ch. Sch.*

JEAN-GILLES, JOSEPH (1943) Haiti

Joseph Jean-Gilles was born in Hinche, Haiti. He attended the workshop of the *Centre*

Jean-Jean, Léopold: Seascape

seems to have added intensity, in spite of the fact that he has been living in New York for several years, far removed from the tropics.

Since 1965, Jean-Gilles has participated in numerous group shows in the United States and had his first one-man exhibition in 1971 organised by the Organization of American States, Washington, D. C. *J. G. S.*

JESUS, ISABEL DE (1938)   Brazil

Isabel de Jesus was born in Cabo Verde, in the state of Minas Gerais, where she lived for seven years until her father, who was an explorer, moved to Paraná. For three years she was a novice before going into service as a nurse. A few years later she went to São Paulo to work as a domestic before dedicating all her time to her work as a self-taught artist.

Her own special style, which verges on the fantastic (images appear in the form of unrecognisable birds, beasts and fish tangled up in complicated bizarre vegetation) is dependent on bright coloration, much of which is linear in character. Her pictures tend to be small in format. *Sh. W.*

Jean-Gilles, Joseph: Haitian Landscape

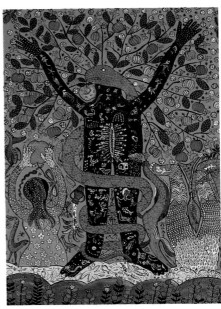

Jesus, Isabel de: Adam and Eve

Jean-Gilles, Joseph: Procession of Women

JEUKEN, JOHAN (1909—1982)   Netherlands

Johan Jeuken was born in Venray and died in Amsterdam. At the age of nineteen, he took up the tailor's craft and later, with his wife's help, opened his own shop in his home town. With his family he moved to Amsterdam in 1947 and there his two sons enrolled in the Academy of Art. For reasons of health, he had to stop working in 1963. After a few gloomy years, in 1967, at the request of his wife, he made a sketch of their new garden, which he could easily do because, as a tailor, he had had to draw so many patterns. Now drawing was such a pleasure that he began to use his grandchildren's oils. In the meantime, his sons, who had become academic painters, advised him to attend a short amateur painters' course where he would have full freedom of expression. He tried to paint like a "real" artist, but his sons persuaded him to remain what he was and to evoke the past in his paintings. But as he, like Sal Meijer, considered himself a craftsman, he wanted to perfect his technique. Also, it became his aim to present the historical truth realistically. He resembled Hagoort in the sense of wanting to record events.

He left a total of some hundred paintings about life in old Venray. His motifs are processions, laundering, the livestock market, gymnastics, carnival time, peasant funerals, student excursions, and so on. All events portrayed by him have a sunny cheerfulness, thanks to his exceptional feeling for light. In recent years, he also painted scenes of Amsterdam. He had a number of one-man shows in Amsterdam and one in the Noord-Brabants Museum (1973). He also participated in the "Naives '77" exhibition in Zagreb. *(See portrait of the artist, p. 342). N. E.*

JEVTOVIĆ, DUŠAN (1925)   Yugoslavia

Dušan Jevtović was born in Gornja Trnava, Serbia, where he spent his childhood and went to

a militiaman, serving in villages and small towns throughout Serbia.

"Many of the scenes in my paintings were taken directly from my life in the militia. I saw many human dramas and even had to take part in some of them. If two men start a fight, in Serbia another fifty will immediately join in on one side or the other, and before you know it you have a full-scale riot."

The painting "Winter Wedding" shows a milling crowd. Trumpet players are blowing their instruments; everything is in motion; people are arriving from all sides, bumping into each other,

Jeuken, Johan: Procession

elementary school. When he was twelve, his father sent him to the village blacksmith to learn the craft.

The master craftsman, his family and his apprentices all slept together in one room. Work went on far into the night. While the apprentices made preparations for the next day's work, the women wove and spun in the fitful light of an oil lamp. While they worked, they talked about village events and told superstitious tales of spirits and spooks. Dušan drank it all in and it remained engraved in his memory. After learning his craft, he opened a blacksmith's shop, where he shod horses. Soon after, the war began. Like many of the young men of his district, Dušan joined the Partisans and remained with them to the end of the war. He then took a job as

yelling, gay. Against the white snow the largely red figures (red is his favourite colour) strike a contrast in which the nightmarish side of village festivities is underlined.

"When I begin a picture I cannot imagine what it will turn out like. Memories well up and figures appear. Where I had thought of doing ten figures, I do so many that I can no longer count them," says Jevtović.

Dušan Jevtović has had one-man shows and participated in group exhibitions at home and abroad. *(See portrait of the artist, p. 342). N. T.*

JIANG GUOHONG (1961)   China

Jiang Guohong is from the Hang commune and works in the Tuan Jie agricultural brigade.

Jevtović, Dušan: Winter Wedding

Jiang Guohong: Bamboo Forest

Having begun to paint in 1978, she is a member of the Jin Shan circle of painters.

"When I finish my work in the fields and come home, it is my greatest joy to paint. In our village, I saw some pictures painted by young brigadiers. I decided to try and now I think I could never give it up. I love nature and beautiful colours. We are surrounded by bamboo from which peasants make their homes and many articles for household use. The bamboo grows tall, its stalk is strong and flexible and when the wind blows it only bends over." In "Bamboo Forest," Jiang Guohong portrays a scene in which the tied bamboo stalks create the effect of trees. She has used soft, pastel colours, darkish green, green and blue, while in the middle of the picture, for contrast, stands a cherry tree in blossom. In the foreground a group of Chinese peasants, unconventionally clothed, is moving with baskets swung on shoulder poles. Against this scene, with no sky, yellow birds flutter in the air.

Jiang Guohong has turned for her inspiration mostly to nature — to the Chinese landscape which in her part of the country is distinctive for its bamboo. *(See portrait of the artist, p. 342).* N. T.

JIMENEZ, ELBA (1940) **Nicaragua**

Elba Jimenez was born in Solentiname and has continued living there, bringing up her many children. In her free time she paints scenes of the peaceful, picturesque life surrounding her: fishing, feeding the chickens, slaughtering pigs.

She has exhibited in Managua, in Costa Rica and in Peru. *E. C.*

JOHNSON, TAPLOE (1955) **Great Britain**

Taploe Johnson was born in Britain of Gambian descent. A leather cutter by trade, he lives in London's East End, but it is his ambition to return one day (although he has never been there) to Africa, the land of his forefathers. This tall, dark-skinned man, with a mat of natural red hair, is a peaceable fellow with exquisite manners, so it is a sad irony of fate that he has two major defects — an inability to stay in a job (there always seem to be misunderstandings with his employers) and a facility for falling foul of the law (not for heinous crimes, but for relatively minor offences). It follows that Johnson is not a rich man. As a person who too frequently had time on his hands, he turned to painting, at

Johnson, Taploe: Almost Home

Jimenez, Elba: Pirate River

first merely to while away his leisure, but soon from a newly kindled enthusiasm. However, since Johnson is liable at a moment's notice to abandon his latent talent, it is difficult to assess him properly as even a part-time painter.

When he paints, he makes pictures of a crude yet absolute honesty, treating subjects deep in social significance. His first public success, in a fashion typical of his eccentric pattern of life, came with the exhibition of a very large painting called "The Ink Spots" at the official Summer Exhibition of the Royal Academy in 1976.

"The Ink Spots" contained large "portraits" of black youths, obviously out of work, leaning and sprawling against an urban background in a poor district; an empty and long since abandoned gin bottle was among the debris on the pavement. Taploe and the Ink Spots all appeared in a moving television programme about the artist in the same year.

Whenever possible — but all too infrequently — his pictures have been shown in RONA exhibitions. *(See portrait of the artist, p. 343). Sh. W.*

JONAŠ, MARTIN (1924)   **Yugoslavia**

Martin Jonaš was born in the village of Kovačica, inhabited by Slovaks, not far from Belgrade, where he still lives. In elementary school, drawing was his best subject. In summer his parents tilled the fields and in winter practised the leatherworking craft. He accompanied his parents to the fields, watered the horses in the intervals between ploughings, and chased birds. When winter came, his favourite pastime was listening to stories told by the adults until far into the night. When peasants came to their house to buy leather jackets, Martin would slip under the big round table, his favourite hiding place, and listen to grown-up talk. In his imagination, he experienced the events described as

Jonaš, Martin: Village Saloon

Jonaš, Martin: Departure for the Fields

though they were taking place right there before his very eyes. But equally impressed on his memory were the large, calloused hands of the peasants, resting on their knees under the table, and the muddy boots on the farmers' feet.

During the war he was taken away to do forced labour, but fled and joined the Partisans. After the war, he went back to his village, only to find his parents ill, his brother an invalid with only one leg, and their house badly damaged. Jonaš rolled up his sleeves and went to work, repairing the house and cultivating the fields. Returning exhausted at night, he recalled the one-time visitors and the tales he had heard as a small boy sitting underneath the table. He began painting those recollections. The first exhibition in which he participated was held in 1952 in the village during the celebration of the 150th anniversary of the founding of Kovačica.

Initially, he used a great deal of blue, a favourite colour in Kovačica (many houses are painted blue), but then moved on to the colour of sunflowers and pumpkins. Later his palette expanded.

In the painting "Café" (1961), a group of peasants sit talking after a hard day spent in the fields. The figures of the peasants, whom he knows so well, are dressed in the leather jackets made by his father and himself. Powerful hands and feet signify the strenuous work they do on the land. In the background is a wall painted blue — the colour of the Slovaks — and a large

Jones, Dee: Autumn Fire

earthenware stove like those found in every Slovak homestead and without which a winter could hardly be endured in these plains buffeted by bitter winds.

Martin Jonaš has had one-man shows and participated in group exhibitions at home and abroad. *(See portrait of the artist, p. 343). N. T.*

JONES, DEE (1933)   **Australia**

Dee Jones was born in South Australia. She had no formal training in art but began painting in 1966 and first entered a work in a mixed exhibition in 1968. In the same year she had her first one-woman exhibition in Adelaide, South Australia, and has continued to show widely in both solo and group exhibitions.

The following is quoted from Audio Pack ("The Artists Talking" series): "Dee Jones is best known for her descriptions of life and places in the McLaren Vale area of South Australia. The seasons, work cycles and patterns of vineyards, orchards and farmland are constant subjects. Human figures always appear, some observed and some remembered from childhood. Other subjects include interior scenes and descriptions of Greek life based on travel memories. Most paintings are characterised by painstaking attention to detail, decorative areas of bright colour and a dominant sense of all-over pattern. Dee Jones has been described as a 'sophisticated primitive' or as painting with 'sophisticated naivety.' Whilst she is not entirely happy with these categories, she admits that they go part of the way toward describing the contradictions in her style. Themes recur throughout her work: the

timeless pattern of growing and gathering food, survival and isolation. Her descriptions of the land and its people never remain as topographical description. They emphasise the dignity of rural labour and express a delight in the colours, textures and patterns of a bountiful nature." *(See portrait of the artist, p. 343). B. McC.*

JONES, FRANCES (1923)   **Australia**

Frances Jones was born in Sydney, New South Wales. From 1940 to 1945 she eagerly studied painting and drawing at the Julian

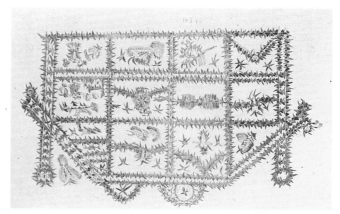

Jones, Frank: "Hoorin" Devil House

Ashton Art School and the East Sydney Technical School.

For a time she worked as a textile designer and ceramic decorator. Later she had two extended trips to London and Europe, one in 1956 and the second in 1972. This gave her a chance to study Florentine and Venetian masters in Italy.

Although Frances Jones has had extensive training in art, her attitude towards her subjects and her interpretation have remained essentially naive. Her paintings, especially her still-life subjects, have an utterly timeless, serene quality which emphasises her love for all manner of life.

Frances Jones has been included in many group shows from 1964 onwards and has had many solo exhibitions. Her paintings are to be found in public and private collections, including the College of Advanced Education, Canberra A. C. T. *(See portrait of the artist, p. 343). B. McC.*

JONES, FRANK (1901—1969)   **USA**

Frank Jones was born in Clarksville, Texas, the son of a part-Indian, part-black mother who abandoned him in infancy. When he died in prison, he had achieved enough fame by his intriguing "devil house" drawings for his death to be reported in the newspapers and mourned in the prison publication. As a young man given to daydreaming, Jones was something of a town character and the butt of practical jokers. He himself, however, was not a mischief-maker and worked at odd jobs to support himself, his mistress and her two troublesome sons. In 1949, accused of involvement in a murder committed by one of the sons, he was sentenced to life imprisonment. A small, rather frail man, he was given portering chores in the recreation department.

Around 1955, as he swept up the litter, he began salvaging stubs of red and blue pencils and scraps of wrapping paper to draw on. A custodial officer noticed his drawings and decided to enter one in the prison art show. It won first prize and brought him the patronage of a Dallas gallery, which then supplied Jones with sheets of paper and colouring pencils. Jones' subsequent works won a number of awards and were featured, as well as collected, all over the country.

Jones' drawings to some extent resemble each other. They are basically "houses" divided into "rooms" and are peopled with a variety of devils — twin devils, winged ones, king and queen devils, fish and women devils. He was quoted as saying: "I think about the Devil quite a bit. I'm trying to keep him away from me." He gave his houses names, such as "Black Devil in China House," "Philippine House," "Jap Devil House." Asked to explain his work, he simply said, "I draw what I feel." *(See portrait of the artist, p. 342). J. W.*

Jordán, Armando: A Windy Day

JORDÁN, ARMANDO (1893—1982)   **Bolivia**

Armando Jordán was born in Irapan, in a *yunga* area (with deep valleys in the Bolivian Andes), but while still very young left for Santa Cruz, where he later taught drawing. Eventually, he became director of the college where he taught, and still later an official in the Ministry of Education. During a retrospective exhibition in the National Art Museum in La Paz in 1973, the public was pleasantly surprised to see his great skill in depicting typical scenes from the life of eastern Bolivia. At the bottom of his pictures Armando was in the habit of writing "reproduction forbidden," while on the back he

Jones, Frances: Apples in a Bowl

noted down details about them: the names of the people in the painting, the names of villages, streets and so on. Many of the citizens of Santa Cruz could recognise themselves in his pictures, set in a typical Bolivian environment. Towards the end of his life, Jordán started to paint political themes, particularly those concerned with Bolivar, his country's favourite son.

For almost half a century Armando Jordán was the sole representative of naive painting in Bolivia.

Armando Jordán is the chronicler of the town of Santa Cruz. Convincingly and eloquently,

bring any of those ambitions to fruition. Instead he became a builder.

It was only in 1948, when the American sculptor, Jason Seeley, came upon him in the furnace of the brickworks where he had found a job that Joseph found his first artistic opportunity. Seeley had brought his sculpture students and some of their works to be fired in the furnace, some thirty pieces, including some of his own. This prompted Joseph to make copies of some of the sculptures and, when he showed them to Seeley, the American immediately steered him to the *Centre d'Art*.

Jordán, Armando: Procession of Our Lady of Cotoco

he has portrayed various scenes from the everyday life of this city and its environs, and people from various classes. "I know the folklore of this country, the people and their customs, because I have spent my whole life here. And that is what I like painting most," said Jordán on one occasion. In his paintings, he liked to tell the story of an event, or to point out a human virtue or failing. Although he did not exhibit often, his name and his paintings are known throughout Bolivia. *(See portrait of the artist, p. 342). A. D.*

JOSEPH, JASMIN (1924)   Haiti

Jasmin Joseph was born in the town of La Grande Rivière du Nord. A man who has passed through many crises, both physical and spiritual, Joseph grew up as the child of a very poor peasant family who could not afford to educate him. Even in his early days he was alive with artistic intention, allowing himself to pass through many creative phases, but unable to

Today Joseph is famous for the way in which he developed this talent. It was he who was selected by Selden Rodman as the principal sculptor for the Stations of the Cross and the choir stalls when the Cathedral of the Holy Trinity was decorated and refurnished by Haitian naives.

Joseph left the brickworks in 1950 in order to paint pictures. He was in poor health, having been poisoned by the furnace fumes emitted during the curing of the bricks. It was about the same time that he gave up Voodoo for Protestantism, a conversion that was immediately reflected in his work, which, so far as painting was concerned, had been centred upon Voodoo until that time. He now turned to Christian themes, abjuring his love for animals in favour of painting subjects which point to a moral.

His style and methods as a painter have been as varied as the stages of his life's development. Sometimes he works in thick oil paint overlarded with subtle glosses, another time he will completely change his palette to play with rich and glowing colour ensembles and tonal variations which are almost *sotto voce*.

From the start, any money Joseph made from art he put straight into his education, so that he could read and write in order to be a lay preacher. *(See portrait of the artist, p. 343).* Sh. W.

JOVANOVIĆ, MILOSAV (1935)   Yugoslavia

Milosav Jovanović was born in the village of Oparić, Serbia, where he lived until 1970, when

Asked to describe the painting "Flowers of the Night," Jovanović said: "It is very difficult to describe a painting because it is the outcome of an experience that one carries inside oneself for a long time. I am not a painter who paints what he sees or whatever inspires him at the moment. So this picture, too, contains all the phases of my life: rural and urban. In the village there are flowers, light, nature and animals. When I look back from this city gloom to my life in the village, I see an idealised picture of it. But once you leave the village and move to town, you cannot go back anymore. The city tires you, poisons you with

Jovanović, Milosav: Flowers of the Night

Joseph, Jasmin: The Seduction of Education

he moved to Belgrade. He has been painting since 1955 and exhibiting since 1960. His themes are of village life as seen through his own lively imagination. While he still lived in the country, he came into contact with the doyen of Serbian naive painting, Janko Brašić, who influenced many painters around him and, initially, also Jovanović. Talented and dissatisfied with himself, he soon started investigating in his paintings various aspects of his own life in a village environment that did not understand him.

Since he was attracted by many innovative devices appearing in the rural districts, especially the radio, the new medium of communication, he trained to be a radio repairman and worked at his trade in the village.

Jovanović is distinguished by a special method of painting. He applies pure colour to canvas in the form of dots, creating compositions that merge on the surface and achieve a specific quality. Every painting is the product of long and careful work.

smoke and you live like a prisoner. And there are many temptations in town." In the foreground of the painting is one such temptation — a nude — and in the right-hand corner a man with his eyes open wide, excited by the challenge.

In another painting, "Women," the artist has created a gentle colour contrast with his pointillist technique. Everything seems to consist of molecules and atoms, like a dandelion easily puffed away by the least breeze. The cohesive link is the theme of women in the village and in the city, with everything their life comprises, and also the differences between the village woman, her head and body covered, and the city woman, her long hair undone, her body nude and voluptuous. The clothing of the former represents the limitations imposed on the village woman by the men of her environment, while the nudity of the city woman reflects her much greater freedom in many respects. Next to each woman, the painter has placed a white lamb as the symbol of maternity.

Milosav Jovanović has had one-man shows and participated in group exhibitions at home and abroad. *(See portrait of the artist, p. 343).* N. T.

JÓZSA, ENDRE (1906)   **Hungary**

Endre Józsa, born in Sümegcsehi, is a retired worker. His works, bearing the hallmarks of an archaic mode of expression, are composed face-front and there is a lack of proportion between the heads and the stiff, motionless limbs. They were presented for the first time in 1980 at an

In the first place his favourite subjects were drawn from the scenes and activities of his native village, Pirai, from what he had seen and experienced as a youth. It did not matter how many years had elapsed since his last visit; confrontation with the simple life and what it had meant to him were to be the raw material of nearly all the pictures that flowed from his brush. He was able to bring the same innocence even to those rare paintings which were of places and situations outside Pirai, pictures like the sad memorial he painted to record Brazil's defeat by the Netherlands in the World Football Cup Final.

"Juca" (Ovídio Melo): School Parade

Józsa, Endre: Woman Feeding Chickens

"Juca" (Ovídio Melo): French Lesson

exhibition in Kecskemét, followed by an exhibition entitled "Agriculture in Naive Art" in 1980 in Budapest. *M. I.*

"JUCA" (OVÍDIO MELO)   **Brazil**

For those who are not Brazilians, the name "Juca" requires some explanation. A *Juca* is a man who never gives up; he will plague somebody — probably a stranger — with a request. He never takes "No" for an answer; he will nag and nag until the hapless victim gives up.

In his painting Ovídio Melo believes that he has the same dogged determination. From the moment he started work on his first paintings he has persisted with single-minded determination to persuade everybody that he must be recognised as a good and genuine artist. This is why he chose the pseudonym "Juca."

Jovanovič, Milosav: Women

It is only recently that he has looked about him, instead of into the past, to find fresh subjects to conquer.

In a way, Ovídio Melo and Juca are different persons. Juca is the painter, a vigorous naive artist. Ovídio Melo is a denizen of another world, a public arena where he pursues a diplomatic career which took him to London as First Consul and then later to Bangkok as Brazilian Ambassador to the Court of Thailand. In one guise he is the talented painter with his peasant background, in the other the official representative of his country, a man who has a job to do on the other side of the world. *Sh. W.*

JURAK, DRAGUTIN (1911)   **Yugoslavia**

Dragutin Jurak was born in Pušica in the Hrvatsko Zagorje district of Croatia. A retired carpenter's assistant, he lives in Zagreb, where he used to work making scenery for the Croatian National Theatre. He began painting his fantastic constructions in 1960, using ink and flowmaster on silk. Simple and modest, having had no schooling, he probably discerned in the backdrops for theatrical productions the contours of his future phantasmagoric buildings and towns.

Asked what his pictures represent, Jurak replies: "They are old towns where modern people could live today. There are towers linked by iron, decorated with carving and built on a hill

JUROVATÝ, LADISLAV (1923)   Czechoslovakia

Ladislav Jurovatý was born in Lúky pod Makytou, where his father was a local smith. He himself trained as a locksmith and worked in the building industry. In his time off, faithful to family tradition, he devoted himself to working with iron and wires in an endeavour to revive interest in craft objects made from true materials. Bending iron and wire into artistic forms, he became thoroughly acquainted with the nature of iron, learning that it was not passive and could be more expressive than stone and more malleable than wood: when heated it yielded easily to

Jurak, Dragutin: Castle of Joy

from which a majestic view may be had. Then come the streets, squares, football fields. I would like to build into such a town everything our seamen have seen as they wandered the earth and stopped at the big ports of the world, things they told me about. My favourite pastime is listening to the stories of our seamen when they talk about where they have been and what they have experienced. I know that no country could build such a city, it would be too expensive, but if countries would get together, then it would be possible."

Dragutin Jurak has had one-man shows and participated in group exhibitions at home and abroad.

(See portrait of the artist, p. 343). N. T.

hammer beats. He had to master a whole range of strokes to find out which were the proper ones, to hit the right places for obtaining the effect he wanted. He had to calculate their number, to discover the place on the anvil he should hit in order to achieve the desired result. His hammer beats changed intensity and rhythm as he strove to find the right "tune" to express his mental state. Thus Jurovatý created a new sculptor's principle, stemming from his aims and artistic feelings. His works are introverted, created from an inner urge. They embrace space and shape it. Concave or protruding, they are almost ascetic in their simplicity. His wire sculptures are also extremely lively, directly reflecting his experience. Ladislav Jurovatý exhibits both at home and abroad and has gained many commendations for his works, some of which are found in the collections of the Slovak National Gallery and the Slovak National Museum. He lives in Bratislava. *(See portrait of the artist, p. 343). S. T.*

JUŠČUVENE, MAGDALENA (1914)   USSR
JUSCIUVIENE, MAGDALENA

Magdalena Jusciuviene was born in Lithuania. Her father was from an intellectual family, and her mother of peasant stock. After several years at school she began work and has been postmistress and collective farmer. Today she is retired on an old-age pension. She has been painting from girlhood, but always from imagination, mostly with recollections, songs and stories as her subject-matter. However, she prefers to reproduce reminiscences of wars lived through and past events. Her wide ranging artistic outlook embraces the dramatic, the tragic and the radiant, and her imagery is often symbolic. She has been represented at exhibitions in the Lithuanian cities of Kaunas, Kapsukas and Vilnius, and also in Moscow and Leningrad. *(See portrait of the artist, p. 343). N. Sh.*

Jusciuviene, Magdalena: Matchmaking

Jurovatý, Ladislav: Head

Janků, Marie

Jeuken, Johan

Jevtović, Dušan

Jiang Guohong

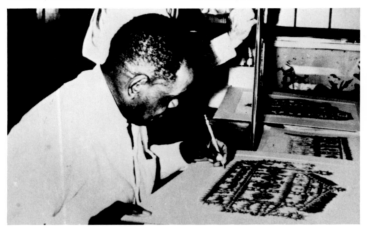

Jones, Frank

Jordán, Armando

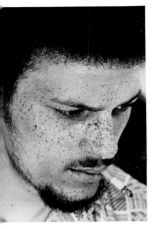

ason, Taploe

Jonaš, Martin

Jones, Dee

Jones, Frances

Jovanović, Milosav

eph, Jasmin

Jurak Dragutin

ovatý, Ladislav

Juščuvene, Magdalena

KADA, ISTVÁN — Hungary
KADARKUTI, RICHÁRD — Hungary
KALUME-DIKOTE — Zaire
KANE, JOHN — USA
KANGARAS, CHRISTOS — Greece
KÁPLÁR, MIKLÓS — Hungary
"KAPO" (MALLIÇA REYNOLDS) — Jamaica
KARWAN, I KETUT — Indonesia, Bali
KASLING, CHARLES — USA
KATARIKAWE, JAK — Uganda
KATONA, JÓZSEF — Hungary
KAZMIERCZAK, K. E. — West Germany
KAZ'MINA, M. G. — USSR
KEMBENG, IDA BAGUS — Indonesia, Bali
KENE (LJUBIŠA JOVANOVIĆ) — Yugoslavia
KER HOVE — Belgium
KERÁK, JOZEF — Czechoslovakia
KIABELUA, ALPHONSE — Zaire
KIŠ, ELENA — USSR
KKASSIALOS, MICHAIL — Cyprus
KLEKAWKA, FRANZ — West Germany
KLINGER, EMIL — West Germany
KLOPOTAN, FRANJO — Yugoslavia
KLOSS, MARIA — West Germany
KLUCSIK, ISTVÁN — Hungary
KLUMPP, GUSTAV — USA
KNJAZOVIC, JAN — Yugoslavia
KNJUKŠTAJTE, ELENA — USSR
KOCHOL, ĹUDOVÍT — Czechoslovakia
KOEHN, HANS — West Germany
KONDAS, PAUL — USSR
KONRÁÔSSON, ÍSLEIFUR — Iceland
KOPRIČANEC, MARTIN — YUGOSLAVIA
KORN, HALINA — Great Britain
KOROVKIN, A. N. — USSR
KORSAK, MARIA — Poland
KOSTOPOULOS, DIMITRIS — Greece
KOŠUT, TIVADAR — Yugoslavia
KOVAČIĆ, MIJO — Yugoslavia
KOYONGONDA, LOUIS — Zaire
KRANS, OLOF — USA
KRATOCHWIL, SIEGFRIED — Austria
KRAUSS, GERLINDE — West Germany
KRAWCZUK, BRONISŁAW — Poland
KREČA, DJORDJE — Yugoslavia

KREITMEIR LISA — West Germany
KUNERT, MAJA — West Germany

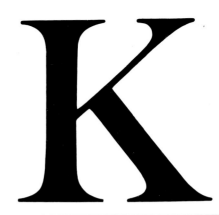

345

Kada, István: Brother's Farm

KADA, ISTVÁN (1904)   **Hungary**

István Kada, born in Törökszentmiklos, was first a blacksmith, and later a mechanic. He produced his first oil painting in 1941, but has been painting regularly only since the seventies. His subject-matter is drawn from village life, though his angle of observation differs from that of other peasant painters. He pays great attention to detail and does a thorough job of solving problems of composition. He has exhibited a number of times in Budapest and in the provinces. His paintings are in the Museum of Naive Art in Kecskemét. *M. I.*

KADARKUTI, RICHÁRD (1926)   **Hungary**

Richárd Kadarkuti was born in Erszébetfalva, today part of greater Budapest. A locksmith

Kadarkuti, Richárd: Outskirts of Town in the Rain

by trade, he went on to study economics with the help of a scholarship. He has been painting since 1967, his subject-matter being largely the environment of his childhood: workers' districts in the suburbs, with their single-storey houses, streets full of potholes, dilapidated trolleycars. His memories radiate the special appeal of the atmosphere of cinemas on the outskirts of town, of saloons heated by iron stoves, of children playing in the circles of light thrown by street lamps, of exciting Sunday games and fun. He has also painted the members of his family and his friends. In these paintings, for which his models

Kalume-Dikote: The Flogging

posed, the background tells a great deal about the person portrayed. Since 1973 his paintings have been regularly displayed in Budapest. In 1977, he exhibited at the "International Naive Art Exhibition" in Zagreb, and in 1979 in Paris. *M. I.*

KALUME-DIKOTE (1930) Zaire

Kalume-Dikote, born in Lusambo, Kivo, usually signs his pictures as "Kalume." No personal details are known. He finds his subjects in scenes of traditional village life and in contemporary urban settings. His pictures show huntsmen returning from the hunt or peasants returning from their work in the fields, or else markets and dance-halls.

In "La Chicotte" (The Flogging) he follows the example of many of his predecessors in choosing a historical theme from the era of colonialism, a theme that plays a central part in the popular painting of Zaire. Although the scene has been represented innumerable times, his version achieves a peculiar power of suggestion, as though he had succeeded for the first time in investing this traumatic experience with its authentic iconographic expression. *G. Sch.*

KANE, JOHN (1860—1934) USA

Because he so superbly and in such provocatively imaginative detail portrayed the American industrial scene on canvas, John Kane has been referred to as one of the most significant American painters of the 20th century, naive or otherwise. Born of Irish parents living near Edinburgh, and the son of a miner, he was himself working in the coal mines at the age of fifteen. At nineteen, together with his stepfather and an older brother, he emigrated to Braddock, Pennsylvania, and from then on laboured at a number of different jobs, never, until his paintings began to sell late in his life, earning much above the poverty level. At one time or another he worked as a "gandy dancer" (laying rock roadbeds for the railways), worked in the steel mills, mined coal in Alabama, Kentucky and Tennessee, and moved back to Braddock, where he worked first as a miner and then as a street paver. But he considered Pittsburgh, Pennsylvania, as his home. It was that city to which he always returned and which was his favourite subject. "The city is my own," he told his biographer, Marie McSwigan. "I have worked on all parts of it, building the blast furnaces... the mills... paving the tracks... The filtration plant, the bridges that span the river, all these are my own... I see it both the way God made it and as man changed it."

Kane was described as kindly, tall, lean and muscular, fond of boxing. In 1891 he was struck by a train and lost a leg, but was so agile with his artificial limb that few knew that he was disabled. He married Maggie Halloran in 1897 and took a job painting railway coaches. He later said this was how he learned to mix colours. During his lunch hour he would draw on the sides of the box cars, fill the drawings in with colour, then, when lunch was over, cover them with paint. When that job came to an end, he got one colouring enlarged photographs, and after that became a house painter. He did not mind being poor or miss his leg, but in 1904, when a much-longed-for son died a day after birth, Kane was intensely grieved. He began to drink so heavily that his wife took their two daughters and left him, and Kane became a wanderer, earning a living where and when he could as a house painter and carpenter's apprentice. He also painted whenever he could, trying three times to enrol in art classes but never having enough money for tuition. He obviously had faith in his basic abilities anyway, for he said, "...I was not put out... when all three... attempts failed, for I believe generally God finds a way to help those inclined to art. And so it was in my case."

His sturdy determination paid off: he twice submitted work to the Carnegie International and was rejected, but in 1927 he tried again and was accepted. Kane was then sixty-seven years old. He became a celebrity and as a consequence was permanently reunited with his wife. Kane's future work was included in all Carnegie Internationals thereafter and was sought by museums and collectors elsewhere as well. Kane died of tuberculosis. *J. W.*

KANGARAS, CHRISTOS Greece

Christos Kangaras was born in Granitsa, Evrytania, Central Greece. He was first a shepherd boy and later a farmer. In order to earn a living he worked in many parts of Greece, including Mount Athos, and finally settled down in the town of Lamia, Central Greece, where he brought

Kane, John: Self-portrait

up a large family. His remarkable talent for painting became apparent when he was a child. His repertory includes wild flowers, landscapes, expressive portraits of local characters, farming and pastoral scenes, and festivities of the mountainous region of Rumelia, done with a genuinely naive poetic and lyrical vision. He also paints religious themes and icons. Some of the paintings in the series "The Christ of Rumelia," represented by the figure of a young shepherd holding a sheep, are particularly impressive. This series, and a number of landscapes as well, recall Byzantine hagiography and the stylisation of By-

Kangaras, Christos: The Threshing

zantine painting. His work is marked by a variety of colours and a sensitivity in rendering the light and shade of foliage according to the season of the year and the time of day.

Kangaras organised his first one-man show in Athens in 1968; this was followed by a number of others, and participation in group exhibitions. In 1978 paintings of his were included in the exhibition of Greek naive painters organised by the National Gallery (Athens) in Dortmund, Germany. Works by the artist are in the collections of the Municipal Gallery of Thessalonike, the Agricultural Bank of Greece, the Waggon Gallery, and in many private collections in Athens, London, Paris, New York and Italy. *A. T.*

KÁPLÁR, MIKLÓS (1886—1935)   Hungary

Miklós Káplár was a shepherd, an assistant cowherd, a butcher, a porter, a waiter, a hired labourer during harvest time, and a student at the art academy. One day in 1910, when he was unemployed, he entered the Museum of Fine Arts in Budapest by chance, simply to get warm. What he saw there inspired him to dedicate himself to painting. He accepted a night job in order to be

able to paint during the daytime. Many years later, he enrolled in the Academy of Fine Arts. In the last six years of his life he found his principal motif — the Great Plain — where he had spent his childhood. Dogged by want, he painted the plain in the winter and in the summer, at dawn and at noon: the shimmering of mirages, the murk of a coming storm, the shepherds tending their herds at the crack of dawn, faces sculpted by the wind and sun and the typical look on such faces. His best works are kept in the Deri Museum in Debrecen and in the memorial house at Hajduböszörmény, which bears his name. In the

Káplár, Miklós: The Village in Winter

"Kapo" (Malliça Reynolds): Orange Paradise

thirties his paintings were displayed in the "Original Talents" exhibition and in the National Salon. He frequently exhibited at home and abroad. *M. I.*

"KAPO" (MALLIÇA REYNOLDS) (1911)   Jamaica

Malliça Reynolds, or "Kapo" as he is better known, is perhaps the best known Jamaican naive artist internationally, having exhibited in New York (1952, 1969), Los Angeles (1964, 1968), Cuba (1976), Venezuela (1978) and in 1978 at the Museum of Modern Art of Latin America in Washington, which acquired a painting for its permanent collection, as did the Stedelijk Museum in Amsterdam. He was invited to exhibit in London at the Hamilton "International Exhibition of Naive Arts." His exhibitions in Jamaica have been numerous, and among his awards are several silver and gold medals.

His best known paintings are idyllic landscapes in which rural life in Jamaica is portrayed in an extraordinary combination of colour and design. However, it is generally felt that Kapo's inventive genius can best be experienced through his carvings and figurative paintings.

Besides being an artist, Kapo is the spiritual leader of a small congregation of Lion revivalists, the St. Michael's Revival Apostolic Tabernacle, of which he was ordained Patriarch Bishop in 1976.

mastering techniques and materials and developing his own style and visions. Today, painting either with watercolours, oils or Chinese ink on paper, Karwan has emerged as one of Bali's most talented artists.

Karwan's favourite themes of festivities and ceremonies are rendered awe-inspiring by the mass and perfection of detail, his meticulous use of rich, almost luminescent colour, and by sheer size as well. Karwan's paintings are exceptional even in Bali, where perfection and detail are almost a way of life. He works slowly but constantly on his paintings, taking in some instances as

Karwan, I Ketut: Cremation

Here are parts of his own account of his life: "I was born 1911 the 10th day of February in Bynloss, St. Catherine ... I ... went to school when I was nine years old ... At the age of 16 I left school. Looking back on myself, I can remember as far back as my creeping days, and forty years ago when I started as a self-taught artist, scraping on a stone with home-made tools, never having seen before a piece of sculpture in any medium. Happily for me, Guiding Lights appeared in my life — a number of prominent men who took interest in my work and encouraged me." *(See portrait of the artist, p. 374). T. R.*

KARWAN, I KETUT (1942)　　Indonesia, Bali

I Ketut Karwan was born in Batuan. Like so many Balinese artists, he began painting seriously in 1953, when at the age of eleven he received his first lessons from his father, the painter I Nyoman Reneh. Upon his father's death some years later, Karwan continued on his own,

long as four years to complete a canvas to his satisfaction. He has participated in many exhibitions, both in Bali and overseas. Karwan's work was prominently featured in "Art of Indonesia," an important show at the Pacific Asia Museum in Pasadena, California. He has also exhibited in the show "Bali, Morning of the World" at the Muckenthaler Cultural Center in California. *(See portrait of the artist, p. 374). J. F.*

KASLING, CHARLES (1901)　　USA

Charles Kasling is an example of what is almost a *sui generis* type of American eccentric: the kind who chooses to build an individualistic, not to say peculiar, environment for himself in the middle of nowhere. Kasling, who must have earned his nickname "Driftwood Charlie" because of his extensive travels, has not disclosed where he was born. He told a California journalist, Peter Odens (who found him through the present writer) that he had travelled the seven seas with the US Navy, but when or for how long he did not reveal. He did say: "I've seen a lot of the world. When I retired (which may have been around 1965) I cut off my beard — didn't want to compete with the hippies. I spent eight years in Death Valley — Zabriski Point. I got to dislike some of the people, so I came here." "Here" is a not easily discovered spot in the desert outside Yuma, Arizona, near the border of southern California. Finding idleness a bore, he gave some thought as to how to occupy himself and decided. "Well, I'd been a part-time engraver. [He did not identify in what circumstances.] So I became a

Kasling, Charles: World of Lost Art

part-time engraver here, engraving rocks." He told Jacqueline Airamee, his first discoverer, that the figures he made for his "Charlie's World of Lost Art" came "out of my head" and were based on what he'd seen abroad. "I never do Americans. These are Orientals, Buddhists, Columbian, Peruvian, Chiefs, Indians." His tools were "a spoon for cement, a kitchen knife for pumice, files for harder stones." However, some of his sculptures were made of less permanent materials, such as mud, and these have crumbled of their own weight or been eroded by wind. Moreover, while publicity brought visitors, it also brought vandals. *J. W.*

KATARIKAWE, JAK (1940)　　　　　**Uganda**
Born in the Kabole area, Kigazi, until 1965 Jak Katarikawe never had any education and consequently was illiterate. It had never been his intention to be an artist. As with so many intuitive naives, he began his painting almost by accident. "Doodles" that he made for his own amusement suddenly seemed to him to have a genuine potential as actual pictures. It was for this reason that he turned to the traditional medium of oil colours. Up to this time he had earned his living by driving a taxicab and by supplying the greengrocer trade with home-grown vegetables. It is

difficult to define any true influences in the works by this artist. Certainly it would be wrong to ascribe the origin and motivation of the images he has created to any painter, teacher, training centre or school. Nevertheless, the inescapable conclusion must also be that these paintings are in no debt to any local tradition either, since they do not suggest ethnic Africanism of any kind. His pictures appear more in harmony with European and American art than with that of the African continent.

Katarikawe plainly shows sound ability in his methods of work, but no signs of derivation.

Katona, József: On a Small Bench

Kazmina, Maria Georgiyevna: Holiday Feast

He paints in luminous colours, often soft-edged, and, except for eccentricities of perspective and angle, his work is recognisably figurative. Despite the remoteness of his homeland from Europe and America, he has successfully exhibited his paintings in Switzerland and the USA (as well as in East Africa). *(See the picture on p. 62). Sh. W.*

KATONA, JÓZSEF (1912)   Hungary

József Katona, born in Kunszentmárton, was disabled during the Second World War. Since 1975, he has been producing compositions containing numerous figures and he also makes mobiles. His works have been on display at several exhibitions in his country. He also had an independent exhibition in Kecskemét in 1978. *M. I.*

dubbed him, had a hard life; in his later years he suffered from a terrible eye disease, while his wife, with whom he had toured the Rhineland on a tandem bicycle in their carefree youth, spent her last years as a helpless invalid.

"The Sunday Painter," a self-portrait, captures better than any words can the milieu in which he was at home, the atmosphere in which he felt at ease, his cheerful dreaminess. This work is entirely representative in its sensitive style, impressionistically *dégagé*, rich in nuances of colour, full of atmosphere, never blatant or ostentatious.

Kazmierczak, Karl Eduard: The Sunday Painter

KAZMIERCZAK,   West Germany
KARL EDUARD (1894—1969)

Karl Eduard Kazmierczak was born in Helbra and died in Duisburg. Trained as a fitter, he was employed for more than forty years with the August Thyssen steel works in Duisburg, finishing up as a pump maintenance fitter in the filter plant. Following occasional earlier attempts, Kazmierczak began to paint and model on a large scale after his retirement.

The feature that most obviously marked Kazmierczak as a man and a painter was his irrepressible sense of humour. A highly versatile individual, he approached everything in the same carefree manner, an optimist to the end of his days, given to philosophising in a wryly teasing tone. In spite of this, "Uncle Karl," as his friends

Kazmierczak possessed an instinctive sense of composition, a feeling for balance and tension in terms of colour and shape. In common with some other naive artists, he was in the habit of committing to paper the heartfelt thoughts and experiences he could not express with his brush. *(See portrait of the artist, p. 374). T. G.*

KAZ'MINA,   USSR
MARIJA GEORGIEVNA (1904—1980)
KAZMINA, MARIA GEORGIYEVNA

M. G. Kazmina was born to a peasant family in the village of Studinenskoye, near Archangel in North Russia. After four years of schooling, she had to work to assist her family. On her marriage she moved to her husband's relatives in a village near Kaluga in Central Russia and worked as a seamstress. During the Second World War, when her husband and elder son were at the fighting front, she was evacuated with her other children to the Soviet hinterland. In 1946 she moved with her family to Klaipeda, a Lithuanian port. She started painting unexpectedly at sixty-three, after one of her sons, then a student of the Extra-mural People's University of Art (ZNUI), asked her to paint something and provided her with canvas, paints and brushes. At first embarrassed, Kazmina then painted a street scene depicting two gossiping old ladies, which

Kembeng, Ida Bagus: A Story from the Book of "Tantra"

caught her relatives' fancy. She took up painting systematically at home and gained popularity after several exhibitions, thanks to her colourful, sincerely motivated works. These have much in common with children's drawings, being devoid of linear perspective, proper composition and planes. Indeed, she seems to ignore all that, transferring everything seen directly to the surface of the canvas without any spatial arrangement. Her figures are conventional and two-dimensional, with merely a few attributes to identify them as human beings. As a rule she paints familiar rustic life, with its characters, mostly womenfolk spinning, mushrooming, dancing, or trading at the market-place. She had her first one-person show in 1970 in Palanga, a Baltic seaside resort near Klaipeda. She has been represented at many group shows both in her home republic and on a national scale in Moscow. *(See portrait of the artist, p. 375). N. Sh.*

KEMBENG,   **Indonesia, Bali**
IDA BAGUS (1897—1952)
Ida Bagus Kembeng was born in Tebasaja, Ubud. As a young man, Kembeng trained as a classical *Wayang Kulit Dalang* (puppet master) and also became known as an accomplished painter in the traditional Wayang style. By the late 1920s, influenced by Ida Bagus Mokoh and other members of the priestly family of Tampaksiring, with whom he had close ties, Kembeng began

painting, with Chinese ink on paper, the images of Balinese village life that would soon make him famous. Kembeng in turn inspired other artists of the eastern Balinese villages and before long this new secular style of painting was sweeping the island. In 1929 Kembeng received a commission from Rudolf Bonnet to paint a large mural on the wall of his Ubud house. Bonnet sent one of Kembeng's paintings to the 1937 "Exposition Internationale des Arts et des Techniques" in Paris, where it won a silver medal.

Married quite young, Kembeng had three sons, Ida Bagus Wiri, Ida Bagus Made and Ida Bagus Belawa, all of whom became painters. Ida Bagus Made became quite famous in his own right.

Shortly after the end of the Second World War, Kembeng suffered a severe heart attack which made it impossible for him to paint, and cast a gloom over the life of this warm and kindhearted man.

Kembeng's paintings can now be found in several museums, including the Colonial Museum, Amsterdam, the Puri Lukisan, Ubud, and in many prestigious private collections. J. F.

KENE   **Yugoslavia**
(LJUBIŠA JOVANOVIĆ) (1956)
Ljubiša Jovanović, nicknamed Kene, was born in the village of Vranovac — near Svetozarevo, Serbia, into a family of small farmers. Since completing eight grades of elementary school he has continued living in his native village, where he fashions a puzzling and naive world of dreams. His story is neither pleasant nor sentimental. In his father's house, the light was dim, and his parents had no love for each other. Only twelve when they parted, Ljubiša felt he would have to make and paint his own life.

He began painting while still young and had certainly seen the works of Breughel and Bosch, also, to a far greater extent, old Orthodox icons in churches. His paintings resemble a new kind of icon on which the saints and demons could be figures from his village. The intensity of his colours and his individual draughtsmanship reflect a pictorial vision drawn from the soul.

The hollow tree trunks in his landscapes are transformed into dangerous field guns, while a newly green meadow can take on the contours of a phallus. Kene believes in the things he paints, in the good and bad demons man harbours within himself, and fears their goggling, bulging eyes. His is the fear and the gentleness of a true naive painter.

In "The Dream," who is the pale, square-faced man lying on the olive green carpet of the earth and arousing the curiosity of the people gathered around him? Is he the drowned, the sick or the prodigal son returned? Larger than all the other figures, he has taken off his clothes and lain down to sleep. With large, worried, clairvoyant eyes, his mother bends over him. A white bird resembling a heron chirps in his ear. To his left and right squat his uncle, aunt, grandmother and a child extending his hand to the sleeper.

The artist has had a number of one-man shows and participated in group exhibitions in Yugoslavia. *O. B.-M.*

Kene (Ljubiša Jovanović): The Dream

KER HOVE (1921)

Belgium

Behind this pseudonym is concealed a member of the Belgian nobility who has found in naive art relief from the stiffness of his environ-ment, and freedom in the expression of satire. Born in Ghent, Ker Hove is a Doctor of Law. In artistic terms, he is altogether self-taught and has been drawing since childhood. Although he started by modelling in clay, he finally chose painting in 1960, the year he left Kortrijk for Brussels, as this medium permitted him greater freedom in conveying his critical message.

Ker Hove paints vigorously, with "full" colours in the Flemish way. His technique is rough and direct. Sometimes he gives his figures animal-like qualities, when he places them in the context of a stiff social order and of the conformism which he rejects. His inspiration is equally direct: disrespect for taboos, a rebellious eroticism, the mocking of the self-satisfied, making fun of stupidities — all of this in an atmosphere of

his emotions and ideas, an effort to treat his ideas aesthetically by means of a delicate balance of material, forms and colours. The form is elementary, simple, suggestive and lively. Kerák achieved his effects by a specific technique — combinations of twisted wire. He thus created his transparent figures in an exactly defined volume, manifesting the great boldness and self-confidence typical of his approach. He captivates us with his highly personal expression, his natural naivety with its specific charm, difficult to define and endowed with rare poignancy. Kerák's wire sculptures are the property of the Povážske Mu-

Ker Hove: The Last Temptation

Kerák, Jozef: The Tinsmith (detail)

pleasant freshness and good-natured humour which is far from aggressive sarcasm (such as imbues the work, for instance, of an Ensor), which would, if present, remove his work from the category of naive art.

Ker Hove long refused to exhibit, wishing to keep for his own personal satisfaction the works he had created: "Each one of my paintings leaves me a little emptier; when I sell a canvas, I seem to be losing a part of myself."

He has exhibited in many galleries and exhibitions. *(See portrait of the artist, p. 375). J. C.*

KERÁK, JOZEF (1891—1945)　　**Czechoslovakia**
Jozef Kerák was born in Velké Rovné. As a tinker he walked with his bag over almost all of Central Europe. By virtue of his individual imagination, his inventiveness, and rare artistic potential, he exceeded the boundaries of a tinker's work and, without any knowledge of the basics of sculpture, tried to give expression to his poetical fantasies in works which have no practical application. In his wire sculptures he dealt most often with fairy-tale motifs (princesses, witches and so on), as well as with themes reflecting his own deepest views. His work "The Tinker and his Son," marked by the subdued nature of the figures, sincere humanity and convincing treatment, is a unique transposition of an idea which he had long cherished in his mind and finally expressed in life-size sculptural form. It is a direct, sincere and not at all pathetic interpretation of reality, an attempt to seize and express

seum in Žilina. They were exhibited for the first time in Prague in 1962 at the exhibition of Amateur Artists of Czechoslovakia. They were also shown at the 1st Triennial of Naive Art, in Bratislava (1966) and at several exhibitions both at home and abroad.

Kerák died on 25 June, 1945. *S. T.*

KIABELUA, ALPHONSE　　**Zaire**
This self-taught portrait and landscape painter, born in Basilongo, lived in Léopoldville, Kinshasa, where he worked as a house-boy for European settlers. At the end of the forties he joined the circle round the Belgian painter, Laurent Moonens, who had formed a group of self-taught painters which soon became known as the

"School of Stanley Pool" (Pool Malebo). When Moonens was commissioned to establish an academy of fine arts in Lubumbashi in 1951, Maurice Alhadeff, an American philanthropist, took on the responsibility of supporting the painters and selling their work in Europe and the United States.

Kiabelua, known to his colleagues as "Douanier Rousseau," achieved fame with his austere portraits, which, in a strange manner, all bore a stronger resemblance to ancient masks than to the sitter. His later landscapes and townscapes, rhythmic compositions with strongly decorative

birch trees on the bank of a stream, in the midst of which floats a boat surrounded by white swans, with people garbed as characters from icons seated in it. Another picture depicts a woman amidst rushes and in front of her a swan and a rowing boat with a man at the oars; above her are symmetrically arranged birds; in the left-hand portion is a moonlit landscape. Though different, all these planes are organically interconnected. The ornamental frame is composed of stylised, brightly coloured two-dimensional flowers. Also in evidence are survivals of aspects of peasant folk-art genres such as painting on

Kish, Yelena: Lions

Kiabelua, Alphonse: Portrait of a Woman

features, such as he still paints, are no less typically African in their own way, but they have not had the success which marked the work of his early years. *G. Sch.*

KIŠ, ELENA   USSR
KISH, YELENA

The works of Yelena Kish were discovered by the Minsk artist V. Basalyga in the 1970s near Slutsk, a town not far from the Byelorussian capital of Minsk. Executed in oil on canvas in the 1930s and early 1940s, they were shown as rugs. The painting, decorative and naive, served as embellishment. The centrally positioned narrative picture is enclosed in an ornamental frame. The people and swans depicted attract by virtue of their artless representation, static immobility and folkloric metaphor. Like most naive artists, Kish sought to tell a story and display a familiar or fantasised world. Thus lions ramble beneath

chests and on glass; they are coupled with expressions of semi-cultured urban aesthetic tastes, with preferences for pictures of moonlit landscapes, ponds with swans and the like. These characteristic features of old-time urban folklore bring to mind the itinerant painters who offered their naive pictures and "rugs" at fairs and market-places. All that we know about Kish are a few particulars provided by elderly people to the effect that in the late 1930s and early 1940s she was about fifty and often visited villages to paint on commission. She has not been represented at a single exhibition. *N. Sh.*

KKASSIALOS, MICHAIL (1885—1974)   Cyprus

Michail Kkassialos, born in Asha, Cyprus, used to work as a smallholder and shoemaker, and later ran an antique shop, so becoming acquainted with sculptures, ceramics and the work of goldsmiths and coppersmiths. It was in 1960 that he began to paint. He is indebted to a tradition of popular art and the ancient and variegated cultural landscape of the island has cast reflections on his pictures — Byzantine hieratic shapes, a wealth of colours from the East and the Mediterranean can be detected here, there and everywhere. His compositions have a certain archaic austerity and the stringency of Orthodox icons. The dark ochre background to his pictures of harvest and work in the fields is reminiscent of the gold ground in ecclesiastical pictures of the saints. They are naive cult pictures in which knowledge and feeling are fused.

In spite of the vivacity of these pictures of people at work, they nevertheless radiate an intense serenity. Kkassialos lost his life during the Turkish invasion of Cyprus in 1974. *O. B.-M.*

KLEKAWKA, FRANZ (1925)   West Germany

Franz Klekawka, born in Dortmund, where he still lives, is a trained steel erector and is still employed in a gigantic steelworks. When did his

theless, he turned out in the end to be the painstaking and critical chronicler of the industrial world of the Ruhr.

What Klekawka tries to do is to show as realistically as possible the Ruhr and its people, their work in the pits, the steelworks and the factories, the crowds of people in shopping centres and busy streets, but also the more contemplative aspect of the industrial cities and their inhabitants "after working-hours." In the last few years Klekawka has begun painting his place of work on a much larger scale than previously, recording the machine-shops, the steel rolling-mills, the

Kkassialos, Michail: A Village Carnival Custom

painting begin? "When I wanted to buy a picture for my first home, I found that all those I liked were too dear; I couldn't afford them. So I began to paint one myself in oils. That was in 1957. My first original picture was an industrial scene. I would never have put anything like that on show, but then we got more leisure time because of the 45-hour week, and the newspapers were all saying, 'The working man will only go boozing in his spare time.' I was so furious I put this picture in for a 'hobby show' at Hoesch's. I actually got a book prize for it."

From then on many people began to take an interest in this cheerful, boyish, working man and to admire his obvious talent for realistic illustration. Klekawka was initially reluctant to return to his workaday world "after working hours," and it is to this natural reluctance that we owe a series of vivid, idyllic "free-time pictures" and scenes from country life, for example, "Corpus Christi Procession in the Sauerland." Never-

wage offices and works canteens, meetings of workers and management, and the election of workers' representatives on the board of management.

It obviously pleases him to "fire" powerful patches of colour into a subdued background of buildings or landscape, thus achieving startling contrasts: brightly coloured trade-union banners, individual house-fronts, placards, striking clothes, dresses or pullovers. Orange, lemon yellow, acid green, lilac, ultramarine, suddenly dart out from groups of figures that are predominantly clad in grey, brown and black, imparting a sudden shock to the eye. In this way Klekawka is able to animate with his bright shades the dreary monotony of the endless assembly sheds, sooty roofs, belching chimneys, stark steel winding-gear and blast-furnaces and shabby streets, so that we can bear to look again and to discern some colour in a "Pit Land" shrouded in smoke and soot.

Klekawka, Franz: Procession

Klekawka, Franz: In Memory of Erich Bödeker

The painter, who has been much lauded and rewarded with prizes, shows and lucrative sales, has remained a plain, sociable person. When he has finished his shift in the factory he sits down almost every day in his cosy flat, which is adorned with pictures and statues exchanged with his artist friends. He crouches on a footstool in front of an armchair covered with a cloth which serves as an easel and paints the colourful pictures that are so much loved. *T. G.*

KLINGER, EMIL (1893—1974) East Germany

Emil Klinger, born in Bavaria, moved to Altenburg with his family at an early age, and worked underground for forty years in the Kriebitsch mine near Altenburg. When he was pensioned off in 1958 he started to paint and continued to record impressions from his surroundings until his death.

In his best works Klinger took as his starting-point observations and experiences from the world around him. Whatever he committed to canvas was in no way overlaid by any kind of artistic refinement. His former place of work, the

poor but happy childhood — poor because the father was a labourer with five mouths to feed. Franjo had always wanted to paint and actually started to do so while he was an orderly in a Zagreb hospital. His motifs are a combination of the landscapes of his native district and outsized butterflies and birds, which cover most of the sky. When a boy, he made a small "hospital" in his backyard and there treated birds with broken wings or legs, the victims of hunters or children. On his canvases, the big birds represent freedom and recall for him the moment when he set his little patients free and they flew away after being

k

358

Klinger, Emil: Festive Procession

pit, a view of an Altenburg farm or a park — all were created with a natural feeling for colours, their values and their effects. The spontaneous freshness of conception and reproduction derived from a kind of vitality and *joie de vivre* that was deeply rooted in the artist's personality.

He was fascinated, above all, by gatherings of people on festive occasions or in public places. The individual figures are frequently rather uniform in appearance and form dense groups, represented in a childishly naive manner. Details, drawn with loving care, suggest a kind of dreamy serenity. The background is generally formed by Altenburg house-fronts — the Pohlhof, the Strassemzeile, where the painter lived, the Lindenau Museum, the Castle Pond. Side by side with such observed scenes there are often fictional elements, illusions derived from books or films. Flowers play a special part in his pictures, and here his sense of pictorial values is effectively deployed. *(See portrait of the artist, p. 375). K. C.*

KLOPOTAN, FRANJO (1938) Yugoslavia

Franjo Klopotan was born in Presečanj, near Varaždin, Croatia, where he still lives. He has been painting since 1959. Once a photographer and also a hospital orderly, he has devoted himself exclusively to painting for a number of years now. Klopotan went to elementary school in his village and high school in Varaždin. He had a

Klopotan, Franjo: The Large Butterfly

healed by him. Against the laws of perspective, the higher they fly, the bigger they are.

"In many of my paintings, the landscape is imaginary and everything I paint is more the product of my imagination than of reality. My paintings have been called fantastic although that is not my goal. I simply take a canvas, imagine a landscape where I would like to be at that moment, and let the birds fly heavenward. Some of them may be men turned into birds, representing their desire to fly away, to travel in their thoughts," says the painter. In "The Large Butterfly," Klopotan has painted one such imaginary landscape. In the foreground is a vase of blue flowers. A closer view shows the vase transformed into a human skull.

Franjo Klopotan has had one-man shows and participated in group exhibitions at home and abroad. *(See portrait of the artist, p. 375).* N. T.

KLUCSIK, ISTVÁN (1946)   Hungary

István Klucsik is a smeltery worker. Though deliberately experimental in his artistic outlook, he is a naive painter whose inner world, its discovery and portrayal, is of overwhelming importance. He was left alone early in life, which explains why many of his experiences are rooted in loneliness. While still a child, he was awakened to the magical beauty of nature. For a long time he was inclined to fall into a state of ecstasy at the sound of music, which he listened to partly as an escape from his problems. Music likewise inspired him to paint, and he translated the sound

Kloss, Maria: The Stations of the Cross

Klucsik, István: Autumn Landscape

KLOSS, MARIA (1940)   West Germany

Maria Kloss, born in Ronsperg, Czechoslovakia, now lives in Schnellhöfle, near Lorch. She was a factory hand until her marriage in 1963. Her husband is a painter and graphic designer, and this is what prompted her to begin painting in 1964.

Her early pictures of animals, particularly cats, soon found admirers, because she did not paint the cuddly, playful kittens so beloved of the ordinary run of bogus naive painters. Here the creature is shown in keeping with its predatory antecedents and its animal instincts — motionless, tensely poised to spring. Kloss's cats all have their gaze rivetted on an imaginary spectator, but between them and this spectator there is erected the same transparent but impenetrable partition that is also potentially present in the artist's representations of encounters between human beings: cryptic psychological studies that should not blind us to the very capable handling of composition.

Her early pictures, dating from about 1970, were more straightforward, more laboured and painted with more devoted persistence than her later work. They are more subtle and affectionate than the later paintings, which are frequently too "pop," with their bright colours and their blatant poster appeal — very much the work of a well-versed professional. T. G.

effects of Gershwin's "Rhapsody in Blue" into painting by the use of nuances of colour. His welding machine gave him the idea of perpetuating the wonderful colours of light, fire and flame. In his landscapes, he always seeks the beautiful side of nature. A valley is lit by the autumn sun, whose rays of light fall on it in geometric forms, illuminating the strange vegetation of multi-coloured meadows and slopes, and the yellowish-red bushes resembling new mushrooms or huge flowers. In several of his pictures, the blanket of flowers, tropically luxuriant, recalls the organic growth of nature. His first exhibition was organised in 1977 in the Hungarian National Gallery. In 1979, his paintings were also exhibited in Paris. M. I.

KLUMPP, GUSTAV (1902—1977)   USA

There is in the child-like painting of Gustav Klumpp a certain innocent sexuality and eroticism, even a touch of the voyeur. He wrote: "My philosophy of painting is expressed in the visualisation of painting beautiful girls in the nude or semi-nude and fictitious surroundings... of dream-like nature. This is one reason I love to paint and I was trying to accomplish something particular at the Golden Age [a club for retired people] and as an inspiration to other Senior Citizens, to beautify the place where it is displayed."

Klumpp's father was a photographer in the Black Forest area of Germany. Gustav was apprenticed as a printing compositor, then emigrated to the USA in 1923, spent two years in a lithographic factory in Rocher, New York, and became a linotype operator in New York City. He retired in 1964 and moved to a housing project in Brooklyn. When he visited the Red Hook Senior Citizen Center there, the director suggested Klumpp try painting. "I said I have never painted in my life, but I'll try. I don't want to be told anything, I want to make it different from the others." As a test, he painted a reproduction of Lincoln, a few

KNJAZOVIC, JAN (1925) Yugoslavia

Jan Knjazovic was born in the village of Kovačica, Vojvodina inhabited by Slovaks, where he went to elementary school. Except for his stint in the army and brief trips to exhibitions, he has spent his whole life in Kovačica and is thoroughly acquainted with Slovak customs and traditions. In his paintings, he has recorded their national costumes, work in the fields, housework and, in particular, festivities. To make it easier to depict the multifarious theme of village life, with the peasant's talent for simplification and systematisation he has divided his subject-matter

Klumpp, Gustav: Art Gallery Saluting a Painting of a Nude

landscapes, and then, "I decided to paint fantasies, like the 'Wedding of the Mermaid.' This was a thrilling experience."

After his paintings were displayed at the Brooklyn Museum, he began selling them and would use the money to go to burlesque shows on 42nd Street. These inspired several paintings.

Klumpp never married, though he did have a girl friend for sixteen years, a relationship he ended because she lived too long a subway ride from his new home. A few years before he died he seemed to anticipate his death in some of his paintings, particularly one in which he shows a man reaching for a distant heaven. *J. W.*

into two categories: day and night. Everything the peasant does is divided into these two opposites. For night Knjazovic uses ultramarine; for daytime, acid green, bright red and pale blue.

Asked how he avoids repeating himself in his paintings, Knjazovic replies: "Life in the country is much richer and more varied than it is in the city, although the opposite appears to be true at first glance. For instance, the farmer's return from the fields can be represented in a hundred ways. I can show peasants against the background of the Kovačica houses in whose windows lights are aglow. Or I can paint a late bird flying in solitude across the sky. I can paint in a tired horse moving slowly, placing one foot before the other, so exhausted the whip no longer helps. Or, painting the trek back from the fields at night, I can show a woman hurrying her oxen along, and so on."

Thus has Kovačica and its life remained the favourite subject-matter of this painter, loving the people who rejoice in their work. Slowly, men and animals and nature withdraw from the green colour of day and melt into the ultramarine of night.

Knjazovic has a standard array of figures, whom he distributes about the canvas according to need or as the fancy takes him, and in doing so succeeds in depicting all aspects of the folklore and rich life of the Slovaks of Kovačica. How-

blacksmith, her mother a seamstress. After leaving school she worked in Vilnius, the Lithuanian capital, as a photographer. Between 1972 and 1976 she attended an amateur art studio at the trade-union palace in Vilnius, but showed her teacher, R. Biciunas, only finished work. In 1974 she took up painting as a profession, doing oils on cardboard exclusively from memory, imagination and photographs. She lives today in the small Lithuanian town of Rumsiskes, where she works as art designer at the local museum of folk mores. When photography first emerged (and even today), the poses of the people portrayed

Knjazovic, Jan: The Dance

ever, this very standardisation of figures detracts somewhat from the power and spontaneity he showed during the earlier part of his career.

The painting "Dance" (1954) graphically portrays the atmosphere of a village dance, where the peasants give free rein to their cheerful mood to the sound of music. In the background, leaning against a blue ceramic stove, a boy and girl watch the dancing and lend the picture a naive freshness.

Jan Knjazovic has had one-man shows and participated in group exhibitions at home and abroad. *(See portrait of the artist, p. 374). N. T.*

KNJUKŠTAJTE, ELENA (1950)   USSR
KNIUKSTAITE, YELENA

Yelena Kniukstaite was born in a Lithuanian village in the region of Zemaitii, her father a

Kniukstaite, Yelena: My Family

were akin to those of old-time portraits, indicating the desire to attract the eye of the viewer. All this is in evidence in Kniukstaite's pictures — for instance, in "My Family," painted from a photograph. She is of the opinion that anything the camera catches is affected by subjective notions. Her touching representations of animals are evidently borrowed from 19th-century illustrations — or perhaps from sculptured piggy banks, though they are two-dimensional. She has been represented at republican and USSR group shows of amateur art. *(See portrait of the artist, p. 374). N. Sh.*

its build-up of architectural space. Attention is drawn to his application of what he observed in paintings by the old masters and to a manner of classic representation manifested mainly in the emphasis he laid on beauty and the delight he took in the environment. His landscapes, too, are endowed with a soulful tenderness. In his most typical picture "The Shepherd," painted with a moral in mind, he managed to depict his specific experience of reality with especial power. The life of a shepherd, closely bound to the magnificent rhythm of nature, represents his idea of a man living in harmony with all the forces of the

Kochol, Ľudovít: The Shepherd

KOCHOL, ĽUDOVÍT (1896—1974)
Czechoslovakia

Ľudovít Kochol was born in Jamník, one of four children of a local mason. After completing primary schooling, he followed the family tradition and became a skilled mason too. From early childhood he worked hard as a bricklayer and mason, his occupation shaping his character. He became a man of clear-cut opinions and steely logic. Calm observation, certainty and originality manifest themselves in his painting, to which he began to devote himself in 1929.

Kochol had always been concerned with the essentials of life. Visits to his native village and its surroundings evoked deep feelings and memories of childhood. He was deeply attached to his mother in particular. When painting her portrait, he tried to grasp her character and endow the picture with all her features, which he loved dearly. The portrait has a profound, inner meaning, is impressive in composition and logical in

universe. The content of the work is enhanced by the clear and sincere means of expression.

In spite of his strenuous calling, Kochol remained sensitive, and this enabled him to present reality with the fresh approach of a child. Tenderness, clarity, and naivety are the most characteristic features of his pictures. However, his emotional, naive presentation is always coupled with his rational striving for objectivity. His pictures are almost plastic, as if two dimensions did not suffice for him and he was trying to make the surface three-dimensional, partly as the result of his use of photographs, picture postcards and pictures from calendars. Kochol had always linked his own experience with perfectly realistic interpretations, so that objects in his carefully balanced pictures retain their natural forms. The formal unity of his paintings gives them a kind of pictorial lyricism. The heart-felt, poetical presentation of his feelings and the beauty of form in his works raise them to the sphere of poetry.

Kochol exhibited his pictures from 1950. He participated in several international exhibitions, including the Triennial of Insitic (Naive) Art in Bratislava. *S. T.*

KOEHN, HANS (1897—1964) West Germany

Hans Koehn was born in Treptow, and died in Dortmund. He was employed for twenty-five years as a fitter in the mines until heart disease obliged him to give up work at sixty. One day his grandchildren asked him to paint a picture of a castle. He got himself oil paints and a hardboard

Koehn, Hans: Woman Rider

panel and in 1958 he painted his first picture — a fine, brightly coloured "Castle." From then on Hans Koehn found subjects and happenings around him which he recorded with a steady and leisurely hand on the snow-white base of his painting surface.

There is invariably just a whiff of poetry about his pictures, whether the subject be the castle for his grandchildren, a pond with water-lilies, or scenes from the race-course that he saw when he looked out of his sitting-room. His declared aim was to bring people, animals and nature into a harmonious relationship with each other. *(See portrait of the artist, p. 374). T. G.*

KONDAS, PAUL (1900) USSR

Paul Kondas was born in Pauastvere, a village near Piltsmaa in Estonia, then part of the tsarist Russian Empire. As a boy he helped his father, a farm labourer, not only in field work but

also when ferrying loads to the local railway depot. After attending the local parish school, he entered high school in 1921, and then spent two years in the law department of Tartu University. However, he was forced to leave due to pecuniary circumstances. He taught in and was headmaster of a secondary school and a school for young factory workers in Viljandi, where he now lives in retirement.

He began to paint while still in high school. He developed a passion for art, believing it capable of doing good and of changing people's lives. This accounts for his lifelong enthusiasm for painting,

Kondas, Paul: Eating Wild Strawberries

music, literature and sculpture. First he did watercolours and used gouache and crayons. At sixteen he turned to oils, and also did decorative work, mostly for local schools, using egg distemper, pastels, charcoal and powder paints. When young, he painted from nature not only people, animals, birds and forests but also clouds, lakes and waves. Subsequently he painted from memory and imagination, his highly diversified subject-matter revealing a proclivity for fantasy. Many pictures are associated with ancient national pagan notions and customs, such as "Devils' Treasure on Mid-Summer Night's Eve." He fills his paintings with nymphs, the spirits of his forefathers and other supernatural figures. He also paints genre scenes. The horned characters of Estonian folklore emphasise not only the erotic but also the pagan, their obligation as mummers being to entertain, for which they are rewarded with sausage, stew, wine and jellied meats. These creatures are in their way akin to the Slav carollers, lifted out of pagan rites into Christmas festivities. Kondas is somewhere on the borders of the naive. His mature efforts produce the impression of having been cut out and pasted onto the canvas, while the objects depicted display a certain rhythm. He has been represented at two exhibitions in his own town, had a one-man show in the Estonian capital of Tallinn in the summer of 1980, and in the winter of that year took part in a group exhibition of Estonian naive artists in Tartu. His works have been incorporated in the short film "Sunday Painters," made at the Tallinnfilm Studio. *(See portrait of the artist, p. 375). N. Sh.*

KONRÁÐSSON, ÍSLEIFUR (1889—1972) Iceland

Ísleifur Konráðsson was born to unmarried parents. When a year old, he was adopted by a good-hearted spinster, but she died when he was only in his teens. His adolescence was passed on the bay of Húnaflói, a part of the big Steingrims-fiord peninsula in North-West Iceland, one of the wildest, hardest parts of the country and notorious as a hide-out for criminals. Its isolated people, cut off from the mainstream of Icelandic life, were more attuned to a culture a century older than that which existed elsewhere in the country; they included a few craftsmen who could

Ísleifur's career as a painter cannot be charted in terms of stages of development, for his first picture was as rich in quality as his last.

Each picture "began" at the left-hand bottom corner, whence his finely-tipped brush travelled upwards, branching out where composition or design dictated. Every picture was conjured up from memory, occasionally aided by, but not copied from, snapshots which he had once taken.

After finishing his first picture at the age of seventy-two, he painted every day, holding his first show in 1962. By the time of his death in 1972, at the age of eighty-three, he could look

k

364

Konráðsson, Ísleifur: Farms under the Glacier in the Skatafell National Park

Konráðsson, Ísleifur: Seabirds Perching on Coastal Rocks along the Northwest Shore

carve from designs dating back to before the Middle Ages.

Against this harsh yet fascinating background (belief in witchcraft persisted there for long after it had vanished elsewhere), Ísleifur soon absorbed the prevailing atmosphere of the supernatural.

Later he spent five years in Copenhagen as a heavy-duty porter at the railway station; when he could stand the smoke and steam no longer, he signed on as a seaman, even crossing the Atlantic to New York. But the skyscrapers daunted him and he never went ashore. Although he wanted to go back to Copenhagen, he never saw that city again, passing the rest of his working life employed on the docks of Reykjavik.

His life was depressing: he had hardly any money, no family, no wife and children, nothing he could call his own. Yet there was one vital compensation. Every summer, without fail, with his box camera, he walked over Steingrimsfiord's mountainous ranges, or through the lands that lay on its southern side; he also travelled to equally remote areas, entering secret caves and visiting forgotten spots renowned in folklore. During these annual excursions, if any place or detail caught his eye, he photographed it.

Ísleifur Konráðsson retired at 70. No explanation for what happened next has ever been given. Suddenly he entered an artist-craftsman's store and bought paints, canvases and brushes. Then he asked his Reykjavik landlady to cover the sofa in his room with plastic. From then on this was to serve as his easel.

back on eight exhibitions, most of them held in Reykjavik's Home for Retired Seamen.

Konráðsson did not begin to paint until he had reached an advanced age, but those last ten years, when he created his pictures, proved him to be a natural artist, imbued with special powers drawn from a stockpile of experience, sensibility, and a profound knowledge of Icelandic folklore at its most esoteric. This man of the people developed something akin to second sight when confronted by a homeland that still preserved ancient beliefs and echoes of history forgotten by those who were living in the mainstream of the 20th century. (See portrait of the artist, p. 375). Sh. W.

KOPRIČANEC, MARTIN (1943) Yugoslavia

Martin Kopričanec was born in Molve near Koprivnica, Croatia. His father died when he was three years old, leaving his mother to bring up him and his sister by cultivating the small plot of land they possessed. At school, he drew very well and often, for holidays, the teacher would ask him to decorate the schoolhouse with drawings of the village and nature. His love of painting never deserted him. He still lives in his village (Molve) and paints, mostly on glass, the way of life of the peasant which he knows so well at first-hand. At times he portrays weddings, when the whole village joins in the festivities and the rough faces of the peasants radiate a cheerfulness expressed in the paintings. Or he may depict a christening or simply the village itself, the thatched houses sleeping peacefully under a thick blanket of snow. He particularly favoured subjects associated with his mother. He often places a portrait of his mother in the middle of the village scene as a tribute to all widowed mothers who have brought up their children patiently and devotedly, sacrificing their own personal lives to do so.

In "Mother" (1975) Kopričanec has painted himself as a child being cared for by his mother, who resembles a brood hen guarding her chicks from a surprise attack by a hawk. In the background is his native village flooded by the sudden thawing of the snow.

Kopričanec, Martin: Mother

Martin Kopričanec has had one-man shows and participated in group exhibitions at home and abroad. *(See portrait of the artist, p. 375).* N. T.

KORN, HALINA (1902—1978)   Great Britain
(HALINA JULIA KORNGOLD)

Halina Korn was born in Warsaw and died in Roehampton. Brought up in the family of a Polish businessman, Julian Korngold, and his wife Anne, who had had a French upbringing, Halina Korn (the name she chose when she became a painter) was a fluent linguist, speaking not only her mother-tongue, Polish, but also French, German, Russian and English. Her parents, three brothers, sister and nieces and nephews were all killed by the Germans during the occupation of Poland in the Second World War.

Halina Korn, on holiday in France at the time, escaped, and when the Germans entered Paris she was already working on the staff of General Sikorski's Polish Government-in-Exile at Angers in the Loire Valley. It was from there that she made her way to England, where in 1948 she

married the Polish artist Marek Zuławski, with whom she lived in London for the rest of her life. Her marriage gave her British citizenship, but although London had now become her home, she also found time to travel extensively to France, Italy, Spain, Poland and the United States.

Victor Musgrave, an authority on unusual art, sees her, with Scottie Wilson, as one of the two outstanding painters, both impossible to categorise, to have emerged in Britain in modern times. To make acquaintance with her pictures is truly a sensational experience — not the sensation of shock, but rather one of awe and mystifi-

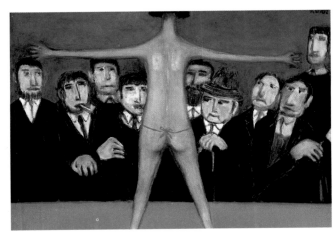

Korn, Halina: Striptease

cation. On the one hand there is often the simplicity of the imagery, while on the other is that nagging realisation that you are in the presence of something "different," something deep and vibrant upon whose essential nature you cannot put your finger. Her techniques and methods as an artist are so easy, gentle, and innocent. The clue to all this "otherness" lies in the artist herself. She was the victim of an incurable cycle of manic-depression — and as if this were not a heavy enough burden for one who loved the social whirl and the intense activity of artistic creation, she was also a serious cardiac case, so that for the last twelve years of her life she was rendered a permanent invalid, unable even to paint. And yet even that is not a total truth. At the Priory Nursing Home, where she died, she did produce her last painting — an anonymous frontal portrait of a doctor in his white coat, aggressively etched against a black background.

Halina Korn's pictures are in a number of museums, several of them in Poland, and have been shown in many exhibitions. *(See portrait of the artist, p. 374).* Sh. W.

KOROVKIN,   USSR
AL'BERT NIKOLAEVIČ (1935)
KOROVKIN, ALBERT NIKOLAYEVICH

A. N. Korovkin's mother was a factory worker. Having always wanted to paint, between 1963 and 1976 he attended the art studio of the railwaymen's club in the Urals city of Sverdlovsk, where he lives and works as a highly skilled glass-blower. Having gone through the phase of naive storyteller in his painting, he is now intuitively searching for increased complexity by attaining more sophisticated means of expression. His pictures, decorative and with clearly demarcated local pools of colour, reveal a certain amount of make-believe and also sarcasm. In the means of expression employed, Korovkin is more draughtsman than painter, possibly because his mentality is that of the applied artist, as he has demonstrated in a series of glass objects. He has been represented at various city and republican exhibitions and also at two USSR shows in Moscow (in 1974 and 1977). *(See portrait of the artist, p. 374). N. Sh.*

he felt the need to express his childhood memories in pictures painted in his own spontaneous manner. He portrays his village's traditional occupations, religious ceremonies, farming scenes, manners and customs, and all kinds of everyday events, reconstructing details with the help of his imagination, in a rather primitive but highly personal technique, notably influenced by Byzantine art. His slender figures, with their somewhat severe but very expressive faces, are particularly interesting. His preference for rather dark, earthy primary colours, his thick canvases and his often violent brushstrokes are also distinc-

Korovkin, Albert Nikolayevich: *Amateur Artist Korovkin Flying off to a Moscow Show*

Korsak, Maria: *Crater Lake*

KORSAK, MARIA (1908)   Poland

Maria Korsak was born near the town of Nowogródek (now in the USSR). In her youth, she lived on her parents' farm, painting throw-rugs and also weaving. The war years were very hard for her. In 1958 she returned to Poland as a repatriate and settled in Warsaw. While on her way to her native land, she had decided she wanted to paint. That was a condition she laid down to her husband, whom she had not seen since 1939. She has painted hundreds of pictures, most of them bought by foreign tourists. A fine selection of her paintings is kept in the State Ethnographic Museum in Warsaw and in the collection of L. Zimmerer also in Warsaw. Her work has been displayed at many one-woman shows in Poland and abroad, and in all group exhibitions of Polish naive art. *(See portrait of the artist, p. 374). A. J.*

KOSTOPOULOS, DIMITRIS (1939)   Greece

Dimitris Kostopoulos was born in Pyrgos, Ilias, in the Peloponese. He is a self-taught artist who started to paint when he was a child. Later,

tive. In addition to his secular paintings, the artist has given evidence of his talent for hagiography, developing a personal type of folk hagiography derived from Byzantine style and technique.

His painting "Making Noodles," illustrated here, shows the traditional preparation of food for the winter. The Byzantine influence is clear in the style of the figures and the trees, and also in the gold foil decorated with flowers forming the upper and lower parts of the frame of the picture. In addition to his painting the artist also works in wood; he has made wooden decorative reliefs for fire-places and wooden sculptures representing ships and Gorgons.

Kostopoulos' work has been shown in numerous one-man shows in Athens and in group exhibitions in Greece, Florence, Munich and Paris. Works by the artist are in the collections of the Ministry of Culture and Sciences and of the Bank of Greece, in the Ion Vorres collection, Paiania, Attica, and in many private collections in Athens, Germany, Italy, Spain and the USA. *A. T.*

KOŠUT, TIVADAR (1947) Yugoslavia

In the town of Novi Bečej, situated on the low-lying plains of Vojvodina, a group of self-taught artists — farmers, craftsmen and workers — came together to form an association for the pursuit of naive art under the name of "Selo" ("The Village").

They gathered round a good-natured workman, popular philosopher and self-taught painter by the name of Dragiša Bunjevački. This group, which pursued common aims and a common mode of development, included Jovan Sijačić, Janoš Mesaroš, Georgije Popov, Dušanka Vujačić-

Our illustration shows his picture "The Last Supper," with its pale gold ground of cosmic light: Christ and his disciples are grouped round a circular table, their hands raised in ecstatic consternation. Certain of his pictures display a symmetrical balance of structure from top to bottom and left to right. Even if they are turned upside down, his figures still convey a sense of spatial symmetry.

Along with the childishly naive quality of his expression, Košut possesses a decorative sense of rhythm and a feeling for the musicality of colours. *O. B.-M.*

Kostopoulos, Dimitris: Making Noodles

Košut, Tivadar: The Last Supper

Kiselički, Svetozar Kiselički, Tivadar Košut and his wife, Katarina.

Košut works in a factory producing building materials, as well as in a pottery workshop, but he is noted above all for his highly imaginative, childlike pictures, totally devoid of perspective. He is inclined to choose circular or elliptical shapes, possibly from a conscious desire for the harmony of enclosed forms. In his "Bull-fight" the arena forms the enclosure where dangerously cavorting bulls and the bullfighters offer a scene that hovers between death and play.

KOVAČIĆ, MIJO (1935) Yugoslavia

Mijo Kovačić was born in the village of Gornja Šuma, Croatia, a hamlet of a dozen or so scattered houses which takes its name from an ancient forest dividing Yugoslavia from Hungary. He went to elementary school in the neighbouring village of Molve as there was none in his own village. Every day the boy walked ten kilometres to school and back, a feat both strenuous and dangerous in the wintertime and bad weather. The first strong impressions of his childhood, associated with the forest he had to pass through every day to and from school, have been a source of inspiration for his painting. Surrounded by woods and marshlands, cut off from the world, especially in the wintertime, when the snow is piled high, this was an isolated life. Mijo Kovačić remembers the stories he heard his elders telling around the hearth when he was a boy. These tales, some of them true and others made up, concerned events that had taken place in the nearby forests, where every tree acquired strange forms, as in fairy tales, in the eyes of the lost and frightened passer-by.

Mijo Kovačić still lives in the same village, where he has built a house and married, but he has less and less time to work the land that he now cultivates more out of habit than need.

Inspired by the work of the famous peasant painter, Ivan Generalić, Kovačić began to paint in 1953 and soon stood out from the other peasant painters by his talent for large-scale compositions and his brilliant technique, especially in portraits of peasants, who in his paintings assume the appearance of biblical figures. He is fond of painting tragic events when people are under strain: elemental disasters, fires, floods, and so on. His peasants are constantly in motion, especially when they give way to panic caused by events they cannot explain, such as northern lights, solar eclipses, earthquakes. He remembers that when he was a child people formed processions to pray for rain during the great droughts that alternate with floods in his district. All these subjects are found in his pictures, where people are almost always placed in a wide landscape, with Podravina's houses in the distance, giving the painting great depth and awakening a feeling of the immensity of nature, with its eternally repeated cycles, so familiar to the painter and many generations of his ancestors.

from early morning until late at night. "From a big composition," says Kovačić, "I sometimes take one person whom I find attractive and then give him or her special treatment, going into a great deal of detail. I like to paint people who interest me because of their appearance or behaviour, who remind me of the old stories from my childhood, when I loved most listening to tales about wars and the destinies of people who, wandering lost in our forests, were never heard of again."

In "When the Rivers Swell," Kovačić has portrayed spring in his village. The snow has thawed

Kovačić, Mijo: Winter Landscape

A distinctive feature of his paintings are the trees, which seem to rear in threat to the lowering skies and bluish-purple clouds. And when nature is calm, a state Kovačić also records from time to time, with rivers flowing peacefully and fruit trees in bloom, a bright blue sky lends richness to all the other colours in nature.

In "Grandfather's Tales," the wrinkled face and bony hands of the old man bear witness to the hard life of the Podravina peasant, who, whipped by wind and rain, works in the fields

but the woods are not yet in leaf; the houses are surrounded by water and menaced by the spring floods; some people in an overloaded rowing boat are returning home; a group of peasants stand around a bare tree taking bird's eggs from a nest to stay their hunger. This message about want in a flooded village is accented by Kovačić in the forms of the hungry dog and the birds gathered about the skull of a drowned animal. The entire scene is rendered more dramatic by the ruddy glow on the roofs of the houses, the people and the water, and particularly by the restless branches seemingly lit by lightning.

At first glance, "Winter Landscape" is an idyllic portrayal of a cold winter morning in a Podravina village. The steep roofs of the houses are piled high with snow and everything is calm and quiet. But looking more closely at the painting, one sees the peasants in the cold grey dawn, dressed in their heavy winter boots and clothing, sleepy and chilled, going to their work. Winter is releasing its grip, it seems; snow is thawing on the trees and in the background flows a river of glacier-like green. The atmosphere of nature

artist. Born Olof Olson in Silja, Västmandland, Sweden, he emigrated with his parents in 1850 to join a colony, in Bishop Hill, Illinois, of reformist dissidents from the Established Church of Sweden. The colonists were encouraged to develop whatever skills they seemed best suited to and twelve-year old Olof, being skilful with his hands, was sent to train in a blacksmith's shop and then a paint shop. It was the latter that prepared him for the vocation he was to take up after a stint as a soldier during the Civil War. He worked for a time for a portable photographic gallery, an experience that figured in his paintings, then in 1865

Kovačić, Mijo: Grandfather's Tales

Koyongonda, Louis: Portrait of a Man

awakening and people in the early winter dawn is unusually suggestive in a work worthy of a painter of the Dutch school.

Mijo Kovačić has had many one-man shows and participated in group exhibitions at home and abroad. (See portrait of the artist, p. 375). N. T.

KOYONGONDA, LOUIS (1918)   Zaire

Louis Koyongonda, born in Kisangani, Basoko, is married with six children and lives in Kinshasa. In the course of his travels he came to know various countries in Africa and the Near East. He has been painting since 1935. He makes his living by decorating tablecloths and tablenapkins. The few oil paintings he has done, mainly portraits, manifest a sure sense of colour and a remarkable concentration of expressive power. G. Sch.

KRANS, OLOF (1838—1916)   USA

Olof Krans, according to all accounts, was as delightful a personality as he was a remarkable

moved and set himself up as a house painter and decorator. Apparently at that time he met, for the first time, a professional artist and became interested in adding art work to his already long list of skills. By 1880 he was advertising himself as a "highly skilled portrait and landscape painter." In the meantime, however, he also painted houses, barns, signs, and fireplugs, did wallpapering, painted theatre backdrops and even restored old paintings. When asked, he would compose a poem for the signs he painted or write a speech for a community dinner. Though he had been painting portraits for some time, the first truly public display of his art took place in 1894: a stage curtain done for the new community centre — for sixty-five dollars! — called a "View of Bishop Hill in 1885." After that he painted several pictures of the colony, and also quite a few *Efterbilde*, pictures based on photographs or illustrations. His own self-portrait, done in 1908, is an *Efterbilde*, as is a most remarkable portrait of his elderly mother, done in 1900. Two years before his death in Alton, Illinois, in 1916, Krans donated his historical paintings to the Bishop Hill Old Settlers Association. J. W.   →

Krans, Olof: Self-portrait

KRATOCHWIL, SIEGFRIED (1916) Austria

Siegfried Kratochwil was born in Karlstift, a foresters' settlement, in Lower Austria. His parents lived and worked in Vienna, his mother as a chambermaid, his father as a baker's assistant. He spent his childhood, however, with his grandparents in Karlstift, and his school days in Vienna. His school holidays were spent in Karlstift, where he developed a love of nature and of freedom. From 1930 to 1933 he trained as a fitter and tool-maker, but was unemployed for a time after his apprenticeship, and was prepared to accept any work that was offered him. He was employed as fitter in a repair shop, as an electrician, cloakroom attendant and factory hand, among other jobs. He married in 1939, but then fell seriously ill. Since he was unfit for military service, he worked during the war in an armaments factory.

His daughter Erika was born in 1941. He finally managed to find employment in his proper profession in a goldsmith's workshop.

While his daughter was at school he used to help her with her homework, and in this way started to draw and paint. He soon felt an urgent need to carry on with his painting. In the hospital and during his convalescence he tried to fill an inner void "by painting." He has painted "rather more regularly" since 1959.

His pictures are full of minute and precise detail, painted with pigments which he carefully prepares himself. Many of his paintings are

Kratochwil, Siegfried: Rowing

Krauss, Gerlinde: Procession

crammed with events, action and people — things are happening all over the place. Subsidiary episodes — often observed with a great sense of humour — fill out the picture to the brim. He repudiates any sort of training in drawing or painting, because he "would have to do the same thing over again, but do it in accordance with the wishes of others." His literary leanings are manifested in the poems, written on the back of his pictures, in which he describes the events in the pictures themselves. Inspired by his work in the goldsmith's workshop, which involves engraving and etching, he has also taken up cold-point engraving.

He has exhibited mainly in Austria (Vienna), but also in West Germany. In 1978 he exhibited in Zagreb, Yugoslavia. *(See portrait of the artist, p. 375). F. N.*

KRAUSS, GERLINDE (1941)   West Germany

Gerlinde Krauss, born in Kolbermoor, now lives in Rosenheim. A qualified nursery-school teacher, who has worked from time to time in children's groups, youth clubs and holiday homes, she seems to be generally a cheerful person, a "hippy," who lives a carefree life from day to day. She has profound religious faith, however, and a sense of social commitment, despite her anarchic mode of life. She has taken a vow of poverty, devoted herself to serving her fellowmen and regards her painting in a missionary light, as a task allotted her by the Lord. "I want

Krawczuk, Bronisław: Gliwice in Winter

to paint joy. I know very well that the world is nothing like as perfect as I paint it. I don't paint the world as it is but as it might be. It could be happy and joyful, if only we had love." *(See portrait of the artist, p. 375). T. G.*

KRAWCZUK, BRONISŁAW (1933)   Poland

Bronisław Krawczuk was born in Panasówca, where his father worked on a large landed estate. When he was a boy, Bronislaw contracted a serious disease which left him with a partial muscular paralysis that prevented him from studying and working as he wished (he had hoped to be a locomotive engineer). After the war, when eastern districts belonging to Poland before the war were incorporated in the USSR, he did light work in a kolkhoz. On one occasion, greatly impressed by a stained glass window which he saw in a church, he started collecting bits of glass and painting on them. His little pictures found buyers and he also earned money by painting slogans and "obligations assumed" on kolkhoz agricultural equipment during the harvest time and various state anniversaries. He returned to Poland as a repatriate in 1957, settling in the town of Gliwice, Silesia, together with his wife and children. While working at odd jobs — night watchman, porter, stoker in a boiler room — he yearned for the fields of his native village, comparing it with smoke-blackened Silesia, which was somehow alien to him. He painted what he could remember but after a few years started doing Silesian landscapes as well. He visited exhibitions of "real" painters and read art books. But Van Gogh was the only artist who made an impression on him. People began to take an interest in his paintings and he received first prize at several amateur competitions and exhibitions. Different from other painters, he created a world of his own. Soon his fifteen-year-old son Eugeniusz began to paint in a different but interesting style, followed by his daughter Zofia. Krawczuk's works are in many Polish museums and collections (among

KREČA, DJORDJE (1936)   Yugoslavia

Djordje Kreča was born in the village of Budimlić Japra, near Banja Luka in Bosnia-Herzegovina. His father was killed in the war, leaving him an orphan. He wandered from one place to another with the fleeing refugees until liberation came and he was taken into a home for war orphans. He attended elementary and secondary school in Bihać and forestry school in Split. During this period of his schooling, he also wrote poetry and acted in an amateur theatre. After leaving school, he worked as a forest warden in a number of places. In 1964, he tried his hand at

Kreča, Djordje: Partisan Shield

others, in museums in Zabrze, Bytom, Wrocław, Cracow, Warsaw, and in the collection of L. Zimmerer). He has had many one-man shows in Poland and abroad (West Germany and Switzerland) and has taken part in all important group exhibitions of Polish naive art. *(See portrait of the artist, p. 375). A. J.*

painting but a year later was already carving in wood. Speaking of the themes he likes best, Kreča says: "I would like to leave behind, for the generations to come, a portrayal of the wartime suffering and struggle of our people for freedom. Therefore, my carvings depict heroes from folk songs, historical personalities and brave men from the last war."

Kreča works in wood and, less frequently, stone. Some of his wood carvings are as much as eleven metres high. From time to time he does reliefs telling the story of certain events. Kreča's sculptures are original in form, for he dresses his firmly carved bodies in clothes answering the personality of the wearer. Euphemia, a princess who figures in Serbian medieval history, is depicted in the nude. The sign of her aristocratic origin is her headgear and an opulent cape falling full-length to the floor. Only the closed eyes and the wrinkles around the taut mouth reveal the controlled sorrow of the unfortunate woman, who entered a convent after her husband was killed in battle.

Djordje Kreča is a sculptor whose works portray the turbulent history of his people, every generation of which has been caught up in the turmoils of war.

Kreča has had one-man shows and participated in group exhibitions at home and abroad. *(See portrait of the artist, p. 375). N. T.*

KREITMEIR, LISA   West Germany

Lisa Kreitmeir was born on a farm in Oberammergau and has spent her life there. Prior to her marriage she was a seamstress in the costume department of a theatre, and she has remained loyal to the theatre as a member of an amateur dramatic society. Lisa Kreitmeir's husband is a wood-carver, and when he and some friends mounted a private exhibition in the Kreitmeir home, those members of the family (including Lisa) who were not artists also took part by way of a joke. Since then she has devoted every spare moment to painting.

Lisa Kreitmeir's palette has a predominantly cheerful complexion: bright hues reminiscent of the coloured façades of Bavarian houses banish every trace of sadness even from pictures with problematic themes. But there are few such pictures in Lisa Kreitmeir's work, in which many other events are depicted. There is a drunken farmer actually standing on the kitchen table swinging the bell that has been newly cast for the village chapel. In another picture we see a meeting of the folk costume group, and in others a performance by the farmers' dramatic group or a sentimental ballad. Lisa Kreitmeir observes all this with the joyous eye of someone who knows and loves her native region and is indefatigable in drawing — but with a brush — all the joyful or comic tales she can recall. Although her figures are not contrasted with each other in physique, movement or facial expression, with the result that they seem to be members of one great clan, she contrives to avoid schematic simplification and stereotyped monotony. Their gestures and the reactions registered on their faces are never in danger, however, of relapsing into extravagant sentimentality. Although the events are often highly dramatic and very hectic, there is nothing unduly emphatic or obtrusive. A discreet but vibrant tension can be felt in many of her pictures, both in the association and contrast of scenic elements and in the constructive assembly of colours, bodies and shapes. Her pictures are among those most sought after for exhibitions of authentic naive art. *T. G.*

KUNERT, MAJA (1924)   West Germany

Maja Kunert, born in Riga, now lives in Flensburg. Once an actress and then a travel journalist, she is an intellectual, sensitive and open to impressions. She had a very productive period when she used to paint secretly and in reticent solitude, free from deadlines and the perils of publicity. When she later began to produce little pictures on a commercial basis, she found herself at odds with her own individual mode of creation. Maja Kunert is fond of telling stories in her pictures, but she has a sense of proportion and never overloads them. She uses a magnify-

Kreitmeir, Lisa: *Village Theatre*

Kunert, Maja: *In the Realm of Friendly Diver-Parrots*

ing-glass to apply her very delicate brushstrokes, placing stroke by stroke with patient persistence to form a lush meadow covered with flowers, to impart vibrant life to a thatched roof or to represent the wintry magic of snow-crowned trees by the application of hundreds of dots. *T. G.*

Karwan, I Ketut

Kazmierczak, Karl Eduard

"Kapo" (Malliça Reynolds)

Knjazovic, Jan

Knjukštajte, Elena

Koehn, Hans

Korn, Halina

Korovkin, A. N.

Korsak, Maria

nina, M. G.

Ker Hove

Klinger, Emil

Klopotan, Franjo

as, Paul

Konráðsson, Ísleifur

Kopričanec, Martin

čić, Mijo

Kratochwil, Siegfried

Krauss, Gerlinde

vczuk, Bronisław

Kreča, Djordje

LACKOVIĆ, IVAN — Yugoslavia
LADA, JAN — Poland
LA FOREST, WESNER — Haiti
LAGRU, DOMINIQUE — France
LÄMMLER, BARTHOLOMÄUS — Switzerland
LAUKO, JURAJ — Czechoslovakia
LAURENT, PETERSON — Haiti
LAVRIČ, BORIS — Yugoslavia
LAZAROU, STAMATIS — Greece
LEBDUSKA, LAWRENCE — USA
LECAROS, JUANA IZQUIERDO — Chile
LECOSSOIS, VICTOR — Belgium
LEDESMA, VALERIO — Argentina
LEFEVRE, PIERRE — Belgium
LEFRANC, JULES — France
LEMAN, MARTIN — Great Britain
LEMBERGER, SHIMSHON — Israel
LEONOV, PAVEL PETROVIČ — USSR
LEWIS, VICTOR — Panama
LIAUTAUD, GEORGES — Haiti
LIČKOVÁ, ANNA — Czechoslovakia
LIEBERMAN, HARRY — USA
LIGABUE, ANTONIO — Italy
LISTER, MATHILDA — Australia
LLOYD, JAMES — Great Britain
LÖBEL-BOCK, DOROTHEA — West Germany
LOHSE, FREDERICO — Chile
LOLIŠVILI, TENGIZ — USSR
LONČARIĆ, DRAGICA — Yugoslavia
LOPEZ, CÁNDIDO — Argentina
LORETJAN, AGAVARD — USSR
LOVAK, BRANKO — Yugoslavia
LUBAKI, ALBERT — Zaire
LÜTHI, HANNY — Switzerland
LYSENKO, IVAN IVANOVIČ — USSR

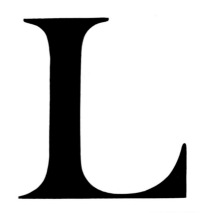

Lacković, Ivan: Winter

LACKOVIĆ, IVAN (1932)　　　**Yugoslavia**

Ivan Lacković was born in the village of Batinsko, Croatia. Before devoting himself completely to painting, he was a hired labourer and the village postman. Moving to the city, he came to belong to the class of naive painters who, living in town, idealise the country. His explanation is typical: "We were four brothers and our father died when I was thirteen. I somehow succeeded in finishing four grades of elementary school, although the schoolhouse was six kilometres away from where I lived and I had to walk twelve kilometres a day. That was not hard when the weather was nice, but when the winds and rain began and mud formed, I barely made it to school and back. At the same time, I helped till the land, the little we had. Then I began to work as a hired hand in a forest greenhouse, and also as a postman. After I married, my wife and I decided to go to Zagreb and look for work. Then, as now, everyone living in the country talked about moving to town and getting a job in a factory."

In Zagreb, Lacković became a postman, taking letters to the surrounding villages and countryside. In his postman's bag, he carried a tablet and drew whatever struck his eye. In the evenings, he would work the sketches up into paintings, using ink or colours. Much earlier, while he and his wife still lived in Kloštar Podravski, to brighten up his wife's old house he had painted

Lacković, Ivan: White Flowers

on the white façade his ideal world: flowers and angels in heaven. The drawing teacher from a neighbouring village saw his work and in 1957 took him for his first visit to the Gallery of Primitive Art in Zagreb.

Lacković usually paints winter scenes; however, his winters are not harsh but gentle and lyrical, with their characteristic blue sky, bare branches delineated in immense detail, and people dressed in their Sunday best. There is no pessimism in his depiction of the country. His paintings radiate a kind of optimism, a village idyll, giving the country precedence over the city. This

Lacković, Ivan: Along the Way

is actually the result of his own romanticism, which he passes on to the viewer. His world is clean, lovely, clear in colour; inside his houses something is going on, there is a warm hearth. Everything is seen through misty windows, through which lamps shimmer while above smoke spreads across the roofs.

In "White Flowers" (1968), Lacković shows a bouquet of white flowers in a pot with a broken handle standing on a small mound against a dense young forest and hazy sky; a combination of realistically portrayed flowers and naive background, the picture has a convincing and sculptural quality.

In "Along the Way" (1967), two peasant women are returning to their village at night. One is carrying a lantern to light the way and the other a cane for defence against wild animals or dogs. The darkened surface of snow shaded by branches against a reddish-blue sky recalls a biblical picture of pilgrimage. "Procession" (1969) shows a winter morning and the faithful marching in a procession. The long skirts with aprons in a different colour, worn by the peasant women in this area when they go to church, and the pro-

cession coming from two directions against the white houses and church in the background, suggest a holiday mood. It is an idyllic picture of a village that respects tradition.

Lacković has had many one-man shows and participated in group exhibitions at home and abroad. *(See portrait of the artist, p. 402). N. T.*

LADA, JAN (1911)   Poland

Jan Lada, born in Czarnocin, has lived in Warsaw since 1951. His father was a blacksmith and he himself worked as a mechanic and lock-

Lada, Jan: Sibyl Prophesying before Kings and Pagan Rulers

smith from his fifteenth year onward. Since early youth he has been interested in art and painted pictures, either religious scenes or landscapes. He is also absorbed by history, mythology, legends and mysterious tales. Having learned the technique of linocuts, he invented his own way of producing colour tones. Lada, who does not sell his work, retired in 1976 and finally has enough time for painting. His linocuts are in Warsaw in the National Museum, in the State Ethnographic Museum, and the collection of L. Zimmerer. *(See portrait of the artist, p. 402). A. J.*

LA FOREST, WESNER (1927—1965)   Haiti

Wesner La Forest is said to have lived in the countryside where he decorated masks and various ritual instruments required for Voodoo rites. No paintings by La Forest would remain were it not that at some time during the 1960s he had deposited a number of pictures in the cellar of the Centre d'Art in Port-au-Prince. Less is known about the man than about his pictures; no one recalls having met him except casually and infrequently. He died from an epileptic fit.

But the scanty evidence provided by the paintings from the cellar show him to have been an artist of mysterious talent. These few pictures are redolent with atmosphere; most show a single figure, but there are also several portrait heads. Backgrounds and foregrounds are notable for absence of detail, amounting sometimes to emptiness. La Forest's colours are grey or near-greys and earth tints, all rubbed into sheets of card or similar fragments of material. None of the pictures are large. Close in feeling to the decoration of houmphor temples, they sometimes include signs and symbols which indicate an expert familiarity with all aspects of Voodoo.

It was only after his death that paintings by Wesner La Forest reached the art market and were exhibited in Port-au-Prince. Their impact on the public was electric. Discriminating collectors realised that here was an artist, albeit dead and unknown, who possessed a truly independent identity, and the few pictures which had come to light were quickly bought. *Sh. W.*

edges of his canvas. The hallmarks of his work are his methodical approach and a thoughtful refinement and restraint in the handling of colour and detail. He draws clearly and without hesitation, achieving a subtlety of line in his later work which is reminiscent of the "Japanese" school. His reading fed his thoughts with images whose sources were very close to those Henri Trouillard would also choose a few years later: the history of man and the sources of creation, the Garden of Eden and the mythology of the original paradise. Dreamland vegetation and creatures of fantasy help to enrich the philosophical premises of this

Lagru, Dominique: La Côte Sauvage

La Forest Wesner: Figure on Horseback

LAGRU, DOMINIQUE (1873—1960) France

Dominique Lagru was born at Perrecy-les-Forges. He died in Paris. His childhood was spent in the region of his birth. An orphan, he started tending livestock at the age of twelve and later held a great variety of jobs, including those of miner and building worker. In 1902 he settled in Paris and was to suffer successively the deaths of his wife and three children. A long period of unemployment followed, during which he tried working as a copyist. He then became a highly active trade-unionist and began to read intensively. An inter-trade-union library became a major focus of interest. He found much to learn and understand in the historical and philosophical works he devoured. The history and origins of man were his particular interest. In 1948, he tried to render on canvas the images born of his reading. His first efforts gave him great satisfaction, and he continued to paint without stopping until his death. He lived an isolated life and refused to visit museums as a safeguard against outside influences on his painting.

Dominique Lagru painted flat. He would start at one end of his canvas and develop gradually his overall composition, working towards the

La Forest, Wesner: Man, Animal and Large Hand

gifted artist. From 1951, Lagru exhibited in several Paris galleries. He took part in the world exhibition of naive art at Knokke-le-Zoute (1958). His work was shown in Switzerland and Austria. *(See portrait of the artist, p. 402). Ch. Sch.*

LÄMMLER, BARTHOLOMÄUS (1809—1865) Switzerland

Bartholomäus Lämmler was born in Herisau and died in Unterach. His principal occupation was painting, although it is said that toward the end of his life he worked as a farmhand. He is also said to have succumbed finally to alcoholism.

Lämmler was one of the first and most important painters of the Appenzell school of peasant artists (see p. 104). Herds and summer mountain pastures were, however, not the only subjects painted by him, for initially he decorated furniture (cupboards and chests) with great success.

moving along the very edge of the boulders. Although they are small, it is obvious that they are city people on an outing. The picture is divided horizontally into two unequal parts by a road leading from the valley to the mountain. Also proceeding along this path are people who are disproportionately small in comparison with the animals around them. Against a lowering sky birds seem to be fleeing from portents of a storm. The meadow is dark green, as there is no sunlight.

Lämmler's paintings abound in details not found in works by the other peasant painters of Appenzell. His radiate freshness, immediacy and

Lämmler, Bartholomäus: Pasture Lands under the Peaks of Kamor, High Kasten and Staubern

The themes he painted on these articles of furniture vary greatly: hunting, herding, newly-weds in their gala clothes (usually those who commissioned the work), horsemen, and so on. Also of interest are the pictures he painted on the bottom of milk pails, usually one or two cows with a herdsman and a dog. On one of these, a herdsman full of the joy of life is portrayed with a cow. Both hands are raised and he has stopped his ear with one finger, the better to execute a "yodel." A dog gambols about him and the cow.

The painting of a pasture under a cliff, shown here, is one of his best works in this genre. Equal-sized cows and goats are shown in the valley vertically, one above the other. The animals are in movement, each in its own way. Lämmler makes his figures of a size to accord with the importance he assigns them. A gay note is struck by the small goats and people in profile,

naivety, in addition to an exceptional painterly talent. He was the first of the great and well-known peasant painters of Appenzell to serve as a model for later artists in that area.

LAUKO, JURAJ (1894—1974) Czechoslovakia

Juraj Lauko was born in Szarvas, Hungary, where his parents emigrated from Slovakia. The youngest of nine children, he was supposed to become a potter but eventually received training as a butcher and was very successful at his job. After the Second World War Lauko left his native village for Bratislava, where he worked for nine years as a butcher. However, serious heart disease compelled him to retire, after which he devoted himself to creative activities. To be exact, his beginnings as an artist date from the twenties. He himself commented on them in the following way: "I made first-class hard dripping, which remains white and does not melt even in summer, in one vessel, and ordinary dripping, the kind every butcher has, in another. I made a sculpture of a fat pig of the hard dripping as an advertisement and put it in my shop window. Soft dripping ran like a waterfall from its back. It was a great sensation. Then I realised for the first time something I'd felt since early childhood, that I could mould and shape things, that I could create something." Then Lauko started to sculpt. In 1928 he painted his first picture — a self-portrait and a portrait of his wife. When he retired,

ing of individual episodes. Though, unlike most other naive artists, Lauko makes preliminary sketches and arrangements of the elements of his pictures, yet the improvised contours of figures literally grow before our eyes. Out of proportion and in that sense deformed, they are rather clumsy in their movements. However, he always saw them in their relationship to the whole work, as a part of it. The impressive colour scale of his compositions — intense, warm and fiery hues — also underlines the fresh and direct character of his paintings. Lauko usually used clear and bright colours only. Juraj Lauko began showing

Lauko, Juraj: Christmas Eve

creative activities became an inseparable part of his life.

Spontaneity and the elementary nature of his approach to the act of creating determine the specific character of his expression. He captivates people first of all by his freshness and sincerity. His works are notable for their naivety, rhapsodic features, immediacy and artistic clarity. Attracted by the simplicity and sincerity of village life, he made that his principal theme. He created an almost film-like cycle of pictures, a whole story called "A Year in a Village," consist-

his works in 1962 at the "All-Slovakian Exhibition" in Prague. He also had a number of one-man exhibitions and participated in international exhibitions of naive art. He died in Bratislava. *(See portrait of the artist, p. 403). S. T.*

LAURENT, PETERSON (? —1958)   **Haiti**

Active as a smith for the railway of St. Marc, the area in which he lived and died, Laurent did not begin painting until 1940, just four years before the foundation of the Centre d'Art.

At first he was noted for his forceful still-life compositions, but later he expanded his subjects to include all manner of images: Haitian country life, American warships, animals, fish and Voodoo.

In the middle of the eighteen years that were to span his entire artistic career Laurent made it clear that nearly all his pictures were acts of homage to the loas, whether they showed vases of flowers for the altars, fish for Agoué (loa of the deep) or animals for sacrifice.

Always capable of extracting sharp character from a pencil-point, he would then often go on

Laurent, Peterson: Conversation

to build up a thick texture on his paintings and to flood them with warm, earthy tones. *Sh. W.*

LAVRIČ, BORIS (1933)   **Yugoslavia**

Boris Lavrič was born in the village of Naklo, near Kranj in Slovenia. A telephone mechanic in the Iskra Factory in Kranj, where he lives, he has been painting since 1969, mostly on glass, subjects suggested by his imagination.

"In my pictures, I want to portray a non-terrestrial world, as I see it. The telephone and radio already reach other planets, so why not man, especially in his thoughts?" says Lavrič.

In his paintings, people are travelling somewhere in strange devices, or on roosters, horses, flowers, unreal beings. Some of them are panic-stricken human beings or souls torn between earth and space, between eternity and nothingness, holding on to their flying vehicle by a thin wire, the way in which a drowning man would grasp at a straw. In the painting "Fiery Horses" (1979), spirited horses prance like storm clouds in a flaming red sky above the sharply pointed peaks of unknown planets.

Boris Lavrič has had one-man shows and participated in group exhibitions at home and abroad. *(See portrait of the artist, p. 403). N. T.*

LAZAROU, STAMATIS (1917)   **Greece**

Although Lazarou's artistic inclinations were noted while he was still a schoolboy, he became an ironmonger. Since 1964 he has devoted himself exclusively to his many-faceted artistic activity. His astonishingly rich subject-matter includes mythological figures and scenes; various historical scenes (particularly from the Greek revolution against the Turks in 1821, and from the time of the Second World War and the German occupation), mermaids, Gorgons and sphinxes, figures of Alexander the Great; birds and fish. In his paintings the life of the Greek farmers, shep-

Lavrič, Boris: Fiery Horses

Lazarou, Stamatis: Threshing in Skyros

herds and fishermen, the beauty of the Greek landscape and his experiences in the ironmonger's shop have been his main sources of inspiration. An artist of many talents, he carves wood and stone, paints, and makes woodcuts, ceramics and pyrographs on gourds with equal mastery. A rich imagination, an incredible inventiveness and a strong emotional content give his work some of its distinctive qualities; its genuinely poetic atmosphere recalls that of a fairy tale.

Lazarou has had a number of one-man shows in Athens and Piraeus, and took part in

his spare time. His first sale was in the late 1920s, to Louis Kaufman, the violinist, and his pianist wife. Through the Kaufmans, young Lebduska met the dealer Stephen Burgeois, who offered him a show. The show never materialised; Lebduska either drank up or was robbed of the money given to him for paint and canvases. However, he persisted in his efforts to become an artist and did have a number of successful exhibitions. Lebduska was fond of painting portraits of friends. He also liked painting animals, and a number of them were intended to be four-footed personifications of favourite friends. At one time,

Lebduska, Lawrence: The Collector. Portrait of Louis Kaufman

Lecaros, Juana Izquierdo: Dressed in Mourning

many group exhibitions in Athens, Piraeus and other parts of Greece. In 1978, some drawings, wood engravings and a painting by the artist were included in the exhibition organised by the National Gallery in Dortmund, Germany. *A. T.*

LEBDUSKA, LAWRENCE (1894—1962)   USA

Lawrence Lebduska's career as an artist and the calibre of his work fluctuated according to the state of his health and his ability to control his alcoholism. He was born in Baltimore, Maryland, while his parents were temporarily living there. His father, a Bohemian who made stained-glass, took the family back to Europe when Lawrence was five, and Lawrence, too, studied his father's craft, as well as decorating, in Leipzig. In 1912 he returned to the USA and soon found work as a wall decorator for the interior designer, Elsie de Wolfe. After three years, he set up his own business and began easel painting in

possibly to pay for his drinks, Lebduska painted murals on three floors of a speak-easy known as Nino's, covering the walls with country scenes remembered from his childhood and youth in Bohemia. He also enjoyed painting foreign landscapes, getting his fantastic ideas for them from travel books given him by the Kaufmans. Lebduska "disappeared" for twenty years, between 1940 and 1960, was "rediscovered," but died just a few years later. *J. W.*

LECAROS,   Chile
JUANA IZQUIERDO (1920)

J. I. Lecaros, born in Santiago, hovers between the two naive styles recognised in Chile — the instinctive (ingenuous) and the magical. She never quite remains in one corner or its opposite. Perhaps it is her colours, often squarely at odds with reality, that bring her near to the world of the brain's non-dominant (eccentric and spiritual) zone — as in the picture here of "Dressed in Mourning." And yet she can create a cool still-life: a table spread for coffee, the two cups, saucers and spoons as regular as the single round fruit carefully placed off-centre, with only a full vase of flowers (subduedly gay in colour) to half-join with, half-withdraw from, such correctitude.

It is true that she spent some time at the Faculty of Fine Arts in Santiago, but to the people of Chile she belongs to the untaught. Her unquiet sensitivity, the informal and unacademic way in which her pictures develop and the attraction she has found, like so many other Chilean autodi-

A gay blade in his youth, Lecossois knew all the bars and colourful dance halls in his area. Loving women, he felt that their beauty should be underlined by fancy dress. These feelings: nostalgia for youth and for the *Belle époque*, love for the women's fashions at the turn of the century, the holiday atmosphere he adored ("It's always Sunday in my pictures," he used to say) determined his themes and his inspiration. The focus is on gaiety, women and dancing. Fairs reflected his outlook on life, with their folklore, processions, merry-go-rounds and tent shows — and of course the dancing in the cafés, former barns

Lecossois, Victor: Hotel at the Golden Leaf

Ledesma, Valerio: Palermo

dacts, in religious subjects (again with a hint of the magical) make her for them an undiluted naive; for the people who share her vision, no relic of the Santiago art school remains.

Lecaros has had numerous exhibitions both in Chile and in countries overseas. *Sh. W.*

LECOSSOIS, VICTOR (1897—1976)   Belgium

Victor Lecossois was born in Hal and died in Assche. He started working in 1912 as a messenger boy carrying telegrams for the Belgian Railways, and continued later as a toolmaker in the workshops of the same enterprise. An accident compelled him to retire, but he could not make ends meet on an invalid's pension. He therefore tried his hand at making radios, which did not sell well, and also at embroidering bedcovers. He began painting after his wife asked him for a still-life to embellish her dining room.

His interest whetted, Lecossois continued painting. Through reproductions, he discovered the Impressionists, whose use of colour delighted him as a good Fleming, which he was in spite of his French name (he was the descendant of a grenadier of Napoleon's army who married and settled down in Flanders). It is interesting to note how this entirely self-taught painter applied with virtuosity the technique of the short stroke and the mutual emphasising of complementary colours by bringing them into close contact with one another.

transformed into dance floors. Another theme is the village pub, where a peasant, leaning on his elbows, slowly downs his beer, surrounded by pottery and bright copper objects, enjoying the warmth of a Louvain stove. Also, not far from Lecossois' home horse races were regularly held: a chance to portray elegant society.

When Lecossois died at a ripe old age, it was truly the death of an artist: when he painted, he would shut himself up in a small room, and finally the fumes from the paint and other art materials proved fatal.

Lecossois always sought to portray the personalities and social roles of the people presented in these country settings, even when he only intimates these by drawing in silhouette.

He exhibited at the Triennial at Bratislava, at the exhibition of naive artists in 1970 in Zagreb, and in galleries in Brussels. *(See portrait of the artist, p. 403). J. C.*

LEDESMA, VALERIO (1896)   Argentina

Valerio Ledesma, born in Cuba del Vini, Spain, was thirty-four years old when he went to Argentina to join his brother, and took employment as a janitor. In 1965 the owners of the El Taller Gallery learned that an old man living in very modest circumstances was doing some fine painting. When they visited him, they found his room completely decorated: he had painted the walls and furniture and also hung his pictures. At that time, he was working as a travelling sales-man selling lace and other kinds of handwork. With a huge bag around his neck he would make the rounds of the fairs in Buenos Aires, always ready to turn tail and run when he spied the po-lice, as he had no sales license. He made life more pleasant by painting, sometimes without in-terruption for days on end. The owners of the El Taller Gallery invited him to exhibit on their pre-mises, and the result was his first and only one-man show. A few years later he announced that he no longer wished to paint because painting provoked in him a "black nausea." What he

Biting but not sarcastic, sharp but not cruel, ironical but never malicious, Pierre Lefèvre, a si-lent man, is obviously a case of a person who communicates exclusively through his painting. Certain figures are placed in comic situations, and reduced on occasion to animal types, whom they resemble either in physical appearance or in psychological state. But the question arises of whether Pierre Lefèvre does not also work in the opposite direction, in which case one may ask: does he animalise people or humanise animals? Or does he link them up in a dichotomy which he has maliciously devised?

Ledesma, Valerio: Adam and Eve

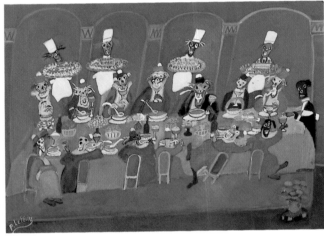

Lefèvre, Pierre: Supper of the Dead

meant by that was never established, and it is not known why he stopped working as he did. Never again did he take a palette in his hands.

His pictures show scenes from the Bible ("Adam and Eve" was reproduced in the cata-logue of the Third Biennial of Naive Art in Bra-tislava in 1972) and also certain sections of Bue-nos Aires. His most characteristic works are landscapes, as seen in photographs or in dreams, and totally unreal. In these paintings there are usually trees with lacy leaves in the foreground, distant mountains and figures of people, shown from the back and facing a long road stretching out in front of them. *M. T. S.*

LEFÈVRE, PIERRE (1926)   **Belgium**

Pierre Lefèvre, born in Etterbeek did not quite finish elementary school and worked at various trades before becoming a janitor in a ministry.

While a young man, he tried drawing events he had witnessed. He therefore developed early in life a gift for observing men and objects — the gift of a born psychologist. Hoping to train him-self for the profession of painter, he enrolled in evening courses in the Academy at Etterbeek. His teachers were taken aback by the strange way in which he imbibed their teaching and soon learned that it was useless to try and make a tra-ditional painter out of their exceptional pupil. Nevertheless, he was awarded the Gold Medal for composition, which is not in the least surpris-ing, bearing in mind the innate virtuosity he dis-plays in filling space with dense, lively crowds.

In everyday life, Pierre Lefèvre resembles his work. He goes around Brussels, seemingly calm ("I am an ordinary person," he says) but "breathing in people," as it was aptly put by Mad-ame de Néeff, who discovered him. His watchful eye misses nothing, and in a naive but unusually sensitive manner, by the most ordinary means, he presents the results of those keen powers of observation that perhaps only an authentic naive artist can develop.

He has exhibited frequently in Brussels and other places in Belgium, in Paris and in Nice. *(See portrait of the artist, p. 402). J. C.*

LEFRANC, JULES (1887—1972)   **France**

Jules Lefranc was born in Laval and died in Paris. His career as a painter must certainly have had its origins in his meeting in 1901 with Claude Monet, to whom he was introduced by Monet's niece Anne Bergmann. The son of an ironmonger, he entered the trade himself in 1901, and a few years later was able to buy his own shop in Paris. After returning from the First World War and having settled once again in civil-ian life, he met Louis Aragon (in 1920). He mar-ried in 1924 and four years later completely aban-doned his trade to dedicate himself exclusively to painting. He exhibited that same year in the Sal-on des Indépendants and established a lasting friendship with René Rimbert. In subsequent years, Jules Lefranc participated in all the major Paris exhibitions. In 1937, he moved to Les Sables d'Olonne, and had his first one-man show in Paris the next year, at which he was presented by Jean Cassou. In 1940 he exhibited in New York and in 1947 in Lyons (the catalogue contained an introduction by Aragon). A retrospective exhibition of his work was organised before his death by the Museum of Les Sables d'Olonne.

The ability to be concise and to synthesise, and a quick intuition for colour transpositions, are among the features of the art of Jules Lefranc. His work ranges far and wide, extending from landscapes to port structures, from the old streets of Laval to the quays along the Seine, from the country cottages of picture postcards to freighters on the high seas. He often made use of

pavements, greenery. Undeniably less striking, these more laborious works lack the immediate impact of his best work and do not have that "Cartesian light" singled out by Aragon. The real Jules Lefranc is somewhere between these two extremes. Jean Cassou described him as a re-creator of images "at the height of their colour." His *oeuvre* runs to 800 catalogued works.

Between 1928 and 1960, Jules Lefranc appeared in many group shows in Paris, London and New York. In 1964 and 1966 there were several one-man shows. *(See portrait of the artist, p. 402).* Ch. Sch.

Lefranc, Jules: The Launching of the Normandie

Leman, Martin: What Shall I Wear Tonight?

illustrations, sketching carefully conceived compositions by tracing, with the colours he planned duly noted — the practice of René Rimbert among others. Lefranc transferred this careful preliminary sketch to canvas, weeding out all unnecessary detail in the process. What remained brought into focus the essential, retaining only the original volume of his subject. The almost photographic vision characteristic of Jules Lefranc is indeed reminiscent of Moholy-Nagy. At the same time, Lefranc painted several canvases in minute detail, including his châteaux series, and his picture of Mont St. Michel. In these, his concern for detail led him to elaborate on the actual elements of the composition: walls, roofs,

LEMAN, MARTIN (1934) Great Britain

Martin Leman was born in London. His life as a boy, as a youth, and even as a young man, was not a happy one and he rarely alludes to it. His father was a fruit merchant in Covent Garden Market, but such a way of life was not the example Martin sought. After serving two years in the army, he worked and trained as a typographer, a means of livelihood for which he also had no liking. Virtually his only pleasurable escape from what he considered to be occupational drudgery lay in playing chess. Then, in 1960, he turned to painting. Even if today his pictures of cats have become his most famous attribute (and one which has kept him increasingly busy, first in painting cat "portraits" but subsequently as an illustrator whose cat paintings have been reproduced in many books — to such an extent that he has come to be known as the acknowledged cat-painter of Britain), there is another side to his art which many collectors regard as more valuable. This is his cynical, humorous and deft portrayal of young women whose bedrooms and "salons" (they are usually to be found "indoors") convey a centrally-heated atmosphere, as in the case of the painting "What Shall I Wear Tonight?"

Martin Leman paints with extreme delicacy, with a fastidious brush that leaves no hint of a stroke on canvas or panel. The result is as smooth as silk-velvet: and Martin handles his paintings like fresh eggs, and expects others to do likewise.

Apart from numerous exhibitions at various galleries in London, since 1977 he has appeared in all RONA exhibitions taking place in England and abroad. His work is also in the hands of

Lemberger, Shimshon: Two Holding the Talit

many collectors in Europe, the USA and Japan. *(See portrait of the artist, p. 402). Sh. W.*

LEMBERGER, SHIMSHON (1910)   Israel

Shimshon Lemberger was born in Poland and came to Palestine in 1933. He first lived on a *kibbutz* and later worked as a builder. He began to paint at sixty, having had to give up work for health reasons. His first works were plaster reliefs that he coloured. Later he turned to canvas. A painter of stories of the Bible, Chassidic folktales, scenes from the life of the Zionist pioneers, love scenes and family lore, he works in a very meticulous manner. His Bible paintings show him to be very knowledgeable in traditional Jewish learning and exegesis. Like Shalom of Safed and Natan Heber, he subconsciously blends stories of Israel's past with those of modern Israel. In a painting of Adam and Eve, he paints Eve placing flowers on Abel's grave, a scene that could only have been inspired by ceremonies at Israeli war cemeteries. Lemberger occasionally divides his canvas into parts that make it possible for him to tell a story consecutively, from beginning to end. Intrigued by the precision of kinetic art, Lemberger once tried to make a three-dimensional work in plaster, *à la* Agam. *(See portrait of the artist, p. 403). R. D.*

LEONOV, PAVEL PETROVIČ (1920)   USSR
LEONOV, PAVEL PETROVICH

After secondary school, Leonov became a house plasterer and worked at numerous building sites. Between 1962 and 1968 he studied at ZNUI (the Extra-mural People's University of Arts), but since he often moved from place to place, it was always hard to trace him. He is now believed to be living somewhere in Central Asia. He attracted notice while a ZNUI student and was represented in several exhibitions. Some of his paintings are of a panoramic nature, such as his "Window-Circus" or "Window-Rehearsal."

Leonov, Pavel Petrovich: Window-Rehearsal

They are composed in such a fashion as to present a view from a window or a view of a stage. The association is further enhanced by the surroundings in which these scenes are set, especially the stage sets that throw into relief, as it were, ladies in historical costume, exotic flowers, or a group of animals. His subject-matter has in many cases evidently been suggested by the topical, contemporary issues of industrialisation and environmental protection, which are emphasised by wedding fantasised urban architecture to wild, exuberant nature. There is an ever-present tinge of exoticism, the artist's reaction to the complexity of today's issues as seen through the prism of his own *Weltanschauung*. He regards himself as a "truth-seeker," as a "promoter of new ideas," and often dares to criticise, which may in part explain his many changes of job. His ideal is to achieve complete harmony between technology and nature in the world of today. This explains his approach to a problem that is usually a painful one for any self-taught or amateur artist — how to preserve one's own individuality, one's own unprejudiced attitude. His colour schemes are highly expressive. His "Russian Rescuing Travellers from Wolves in Africa" could be seen as an interpretation of the author's internationalist feelings. These features attract the eye at the many exhibitions at which he has been represented, including, among others, the 1970 ZNUI Jubilee Display. *(See portrait of the artist, p. 403). N. Sh.*

LEWIS, VICTOR (1918)   **Panama**

Born in Colón, Victor Lewis is self-taught. He paints between assignments at the local cinema,

ment buildings in Panama and in private collections in Panama, Ecuador, and Costa Rica. *J. G. S.*

LIAUTAUD, GEORGES (1899)   **Haiti**

Georges Liautaud was born in the town of Croix de Bouguets, Haiti, where he received his primary education and studied mechanics. Later he took up the blacksmith's craft and, over the years, he hammered out at his forge agricultural implements, branding irons, and crosses for the cemetery of his native village. In his hands, the

Leonov, Pavel Petrovich: Russians Rescuing Travellers from Wolves in Africa

where he does the lettering and design of the signs for the façade.

All of Lewis's paintings focus on his native Colón, which lies at one extreme of the Panama Canal. He creates his own world when he tries to depict the world around him. What he sees he renders with absolute veracity. His forms are solid and well-defined and the interplay of luminous colours is based upon reality, but it is a reality heightened by the intensity of the burning light of the tropics.

He has participated in many national exhibitions in Panama and Cuba, and in 1977 received first prize at the annual Xerox Salon in Panama City. His paintings hang in numerous govern-

crosses became genuine works of art, combining, in a curious example of religious syncretism, the Christian symbol with motifs characteristic of Voodoo rites. In 1953 one of these crosses came to the attention of DeWitt Peters, the founder and director of the *Centre d'Art* in Port-au-Prince, who invited Liautaud to create works of purely artistic significance. In his compositions Liautaud makes use of iron (generally from empty petrol drums) and, occasionally, tin sheets. He cuts, grates, or perforates the pieces, combining them to form flat, two-dimensional creatures of fancy — strange beasts, mermaids, and the like.

Georges Liautaud participated in an exhibition outside his native Haiti for the first time in

1955; he has taken part in significant exhibitions of naive art in Europe, Brazil and the USA. *J. G. S.*

LIČKOVÁ, ANNA (1895—1975) Czechoslovakia

Anna Ličková, born in Děčín, attended only five classes at primary school and spent almost her entire girlhood in Čadca, nursing in local well-to-do families. At the age of nineteen, she married a slaughterhouse watchman. After her two sons were born, they found it difficult to make ends meet and worked hard for a living.

composition. She usually started with details and worked up to the whole, simply covering empty spaces as she came upon them. Only in the end did she paint on larger surfaces. To make a point, she frequently presented several absolutely equivalent scenes in her pictures. Such an accumulation of motifs often lacked the orientation of figures, which seem independent of the rest of the picture. However, they always fulfilled their artistic function, constituting a sort of frame for her stories, characterised as they are by the differentiated and fantastic character of her settings. Her non-intellectual, emotional approach

Lewis, Victor: Walking with a Blue Parasol

Liautaud, Georges: Crucifixion

Ličková began to paint in 1953. She seems to have retained the enchanting qualities of her youth even in her sixties and they are reflected in her works. Many of the motifs of her pictures show that Ličková, with her child's vision, was richly endowed with creative power and inventiveness. Her paintings are the expression of her unlimited ability to humanise all things, living and inorganic; to monumentalise human life; to give an emotional charge to each single thing she decides to paint, however unimportant. Ličková drew on her own memories of past events for her works, which are evocations of states of mind and moods deeply rooted in her self. With persistence and charm she retraced memories of childhood that, transformed by her imagination, take us back to the childhood of humanity. Ličková's creative abilities were so exuberant that she not only painted on canvas and paper but felt the urge to cover all the empty spaces in her flat with her paintings. She painted on the glass of her cupboard, on the chair seats and on the floors. That the concept of a whole is not dominant in the composition of her pictures reveals her inability to understand the continuity of things. She clung to particulars to the detriment of coherence. She did not make her pictures a synthesis but rather a combination of parts, composing them in sections unlinked by the principles of

Ličková, Anna: The Song of the Millers's Lovely Wife

to the treatment of composition is almost instinctively direct. Ličková employed basic colours: by using them directly from the tube rather than mixing them, she achieved a clear, intense harmony.

Her works have been shown at many important exhibitions in Slovakia, Bohemia and abroad. *(See portrait of the artist, p. 403). S. T.*

LIEBERMAN, HARRY (1876—?)　　**USA**
Harry Lieberman, born in Poland, studied to become a Hasidic rabbi but in 1906 forsook that

and when Rivers assured him that his style was unique, one no trained artist could improve or emulate, Lieberman promptly bought a full line of art supplies and began a prodigious outpouring of ideas in brilliant colour, spending as much as fourteen hours a day at his easel. Within two years he had the first of several one-man shows on both the West and East coasts of the USA.

Except for his floral pieces, Lieberman's bright, spirited paintings, done in acrylics, are on themes from the Hebrew and Yiddish literatures, the Talmud, the Cabala, the Old Testament, his Hasidic origins and current events. Each

Ličková, Anna: Village

career and emigrated to the USA. He went into the garment industry in New York but left it after a year or two to become a successful wholesale confectionery manufacturer. In 1950, then seventy-five, he retired to live in Great Neck, New York, and to "return to the enjoyments of the mind," to read and study as he had done when young. He also joined the Golden Age Club, where, in 1956, pure chance led him into painting. His chess partner fell ill and it was suggested he try the art class. He was both amused and challenged by the notion, never in his life having so much as dipped brush into paint. His first tries won such praise that he joined an adult art class under Larry Rivers. Piqued when Rivers seemed to be ignoring his work, Lieberman asked why,

painting has a little explanatory essay fixed to the back. "I believe a painting should have a reason," he said, "and the people should know what is the reason. I try that my paintings show the idea — but I still put on the back what it is."

Lieberman has said that his art is the most important work he has ever done and is the medicine that keeps him alive. "I don't believe there is a life upstairs. I believe the life I got here is paradise, because I do believe if I'll die tomorrow a hundred years later my paintings will be here and people will enjoy them." *J. W.*

LIGABUE, ANTONIO (1899—1965) **Italy**

Antonio Ligabue was born in Zurich. His mother, Elisabetta Costa, an Italian emigrant, never revealed to him the identity of his father. When he was only nine months old, Antonio was entrusted to the care of a Swiss-German family with whom he remained until 1919. In 1901 his mother married Bonfiglio Laccabue, who later adopted Antonio and gave him his name, Laccabue, subsequently changed by Antonio to Ligabue. Little Antonio went to elementary school in St. Gall, where the teacher claimed that he "did not learn easily." He was by nature unpleasant,

Arriving in Gualtieri, he began to lead a strange and unstable life, going hungry, living in a deserted forest hut on the banks of the Po. From time to time he found work as a farmhand, which he did not enjoy because his co-workers made fun of and insulted him for speaking the language poorly. In the meantime, he did some sign-painting and also decorated the tents of travelling circuses. He continued wandering in the forests and drawing further and further away from people. In 1929/1930, he made the acquaintance of Mazzacurati, a painter and sculptor living in Gualtieri. After days of carefully trying to ap-

Lieberman, Harry: Before and After

aggressive and explosive, with sudden emotional outbursts, fierce and uncontrolled reactions. As a result, he was committed to an institution for disturbed adolescents where he underwent treatment. His teachers there noted that he calmed down during crises by drawing animals. He was committed in 1917 to a psychiatric clinic in Pfefers, where he remained for several months. His drawing skill was duly noted there, although he was also assessed as "mentally weak." After that came a long period of wandering. To make a living, he worked as a farmhand, preferring to live in close communion with nature and animals. In May 1919 he was expelled from Switzerland for "threatening public security and for vagrancy."

proach him, Mazzacurati succeeded in overcoming Ligabue's mistrust. Ligabue visited the painter's studio where he was given canvas and paints, and thus was his artistic talent discovered. After a while, Mazzacurati left for Rome and Ligabue was placed in Gualtieri's home for the needy, where he painted like mad in the conviction that painting represented for him the whole meaning of life.

His earlier experiences, want and vagrant life aggravated his excesses, manias, phobias and restiveness. He was committed three times to the neuro-psychiatric clinic in Reggio Emilia, from which he was definitely discharged in 1948. In 1949, he exhibited his works in Reggio Emilia for the first time, but had his first one-man show only in 1955 in Gonzaga, Mantua, where not a single one of his pictures was sold. His first big exhibition, in the Galleria Barcaccia in Rome, was opened by G. Vigorelli.

He received official recognition during the first Anthological Exhibition in Reggio Emilia (May-June 1965), where his work was presented by L. Orlich. But the same year, Ligabue died in the Home for the Aged in Gualtieri, where he had lain half-paralysed for three years.

After his death, his works began to be studied and evaluated. On the tenth anniversary of

ancy of the composition. The subject matter becomes broader. There are many self-portraits, also cockfights, village landscapes, and coaches hurtling along a natural background constituting a synthesis of the Po Valley and Switzerland.

The third period (1952 to 1962, when the artist stopped painting because of his paralysis) is a time of discontinuity. Apart from a few excellent works, a general decline in quality is unmistakeable.

Despite the poorer quality of some of his work, Antonio Ligabue remains the most important Italian naive artist, thanks to the diversity of

Ligabue, Antonio: Dogs Attacking a Boar

the painter's death in 1975, the commune of Gualtieri organised another big exhibition of his collected works, while a third was set up in Milan in 1980. A very fine monograph on him was published by Ricci of Parma (1967), with a text by Zavattini and introduction by Mazzacurati. Three documentary films in colour have been devoted to him: two by R. Andreassi and one by Dino Merozzi.

Ligabue's exceptional production is usually divided into three periods. The first (from 1930 to 1938/39) features muted, pastel colours, among which brown, grey, soft pale green and delicate blue prevail, as, for instance, in "A Lion Attacking a Gazelle."

Characteristic of the second period (1939—1952) are warmer and more vibrant colours, achieving density and relief in the buoy-

his themes, the variety of his techniques (drawings, graphics, paintings, sculptures) and his exceptionally rich expressiveness. Instinctive primitivism and unerring intuition, gentle poesy and harsh ferocity alternate and interweave in an unrepeatable and unique entity. *(See portrait of the artist, p. 403). D. M.*

LISTER, MATHILDA (1889—1965)   Australia

Mathilda Lister was a neighbour of the painter Donald Friend when they both lived at Hill End in New South Wales.

Mr Friend encouraged her to develop her obvious talent, which eventually won her the Darcy Morris Memorial Prize and got her accepted for the Blake Prize for Religious Art competition in Sydney in 1959.

Mathilda Lister's paintings were inspired by early pioneering history and feature bushrangers, goldminers and horsemen as well as biblical subjects. *B. McC.*

LLOYD, JAMES (1905—1974) **Great Britain**

James Lloyd was born in Alsager, Cheshire, and died in Skirpenbeck, near York. In his day Lloyd was regarded as not only unique but also as probably the best naive artist living in Britain at that time. He passed through a whole variety of jobs, starting as a schoolboy in Cheshire, following a day at his desk by getting his father's livestock settled for the night, and only then amusing himself with his early attempts to paint.

At first he just made drawings in black-and-white (in Indian ink on sturdy paper or white card). The switch from one kind of a job to another which coloured his working career rendered life hard for a non-professional who had to keep his wife and a rapidly expanding family. Painting time was in the evenings. Gradually the urge grew upon him to cut loose from his black-and-white compositions and take to colour.

Even as a rural worker he had somehow discovered, albeit at second-hand through reproductions, the masterpieces of Constable and Turner. For them his admiration knew no bounds, especially for the expertise of the former in his pictures of stretches of water. But how to emulate them?

Poring over the coloured illustrations in books, he came to realise that these pictures were being reproduced by a complicated system of minute coloured dots (screens). This was, of course, in the days before the printing revolution represented by offset-lithography. Why should he not imitate the work of the process-block engraver? It would mean adapting a technological method to handicraft, it would take a very long time and it would be extremely tiring for the eyes, but it would be worth it. So began the artistic career of the man whom the television director Ken Russell described as "dotty Lloyd" (Russell — after making two films with and about Lloyd, in one of which this non-actor played the part of the Douanier Rousseau to perfection! — became a close friend of the great naive artist).

Lister, Mathilda: Finding the Holduman Nugget

Ligabue, Antonio: Self-portrait

Virtually every section of each of Lloyd's paintings was built up out of tiny dots applied with an extra-fine brush. All his pictures were created in watercolour and gouache, but in a way in which these sensitive media had never been employed before. And all the paintings were limited in size so that they would fit the surface of the kitchen table upon which he worked.

The paintings were uniquely beautiful and extraordinary in execution, but of little interest to anyone in the area around York where he and his family now lived. Without some kind of promotion, the world might never learn of his remarkable talents. His wife Nancy tried to sell parcels of his pictures through a local farmer and this operation brought in a few shillings. Then she took the plunge, getting in touch with the eminent art critic, the late Sir Herbert Read, who, together with the well-known communist art critic John Berger, paid Lloyd a visit.

What they saw convinced them that they had encountered an artist of considerable quality. They bought an armful of Lloyd's paintings for one hundred pounds and took them to London. James himself could never remember how many pictures they got for that sum — even in those days, so little money.

How important contact with Read and Berger was to prove was soon evident in an approach made to Lloyd by Arthur Jeffress, who owned a gallery in London. The pictures reached the Arthur Jeffress Gallery in time for exhibition, but not long after Jeffress committed suicide.

What followed was to become a central influence upon James Lloyd's life and career as a naive artist. Admittedly for very little money (a regular stipend paid in instalments and, a little later, increased to a slightly larger sum, but of no great magnitude), James Lloyd was taken up by Eric Lister and Lionel Levy of the Portal Gallery, London, and exhibited there as a star of the stable. This meant that he was able to acquire a reputation as an artist outside York, and see his pictures travel to Holland, Yugoslavia (Zagreb) and other parts of the world. Pictures by Lloyd could now be found in many important collections in Europe and the USA.

Quite apart from natural ability — a gift for beautiful composition, a love of farm animals that he could transmit in paint, an astonishing

suck from the breast of a naked witch standing at his shoulder, or even in the big picture "St. George and the Dragon" — a much favoured subject with so many artists in days gone by, but in Lloyd's case imbued with an indefinable quality that could only proceed from so complex a personality. *(See portrait of the artist, p. 402). Sh. W.*

LÖBEL-BOCK,   West Germany
DOROTHEA (1921)

Dorothea Löbel-Bock was born in Berlin, where she still lives. She is employed making

Lloyd, James: Lamb

understanding of the countryside and its magic, a quaint talent for injecting special personality into portraits (including his strange painting methods) — what else singled out James Lloyd from his contemporaries? Possibly it was the mystery of his nature.

On the outside, Lloyd seemed an easy-going man — fond of a gamble, with an enduring love of liquor, and a spry sense of humour not always easy to follow. But this is only a skin-deep assessment of his character.

The man most famous for pictures like "Cat & Mouse" in the Tate Gallery, but who also painted his own version of the "Beatles" and portraits of well-known personalities, had a less familiar characteristic which, when it appeared in his works, was both gripping and intriguing. This side of Lloyd might be seen in the triple portrait he made of a French girl (an amazing psychological study), or in the picture of a stallion taking

ladies' underwear, but she is also a trained photographer. Persuaded by a painter friend to act as a model, she was reluctant at first, but then sat as a model at the Berlin Academy until 1965. In 1959 she went to Yugoslavia with her husband, who was then an art student. Since he spent all his time drawing she soon grew bored, until one day he said, "Right, now you paint something, too!" Dorothea did, and ever since then she has been in the grip of "painting fever."

This lively, optimistic Berliner has both feet planted firmly on the ground and finds it easy to make contact with other people. She paints in oils and chooses as subjects the quiet, idyllic corners of her home town. These include the spaces between the blocks of flats, almost totally enclosed courtyards which children choose as their playgrounds.

These romantic corners of Berlin are most attractive to paint when the winter snow casts its spell over the townscape. And in Berlin as it used to be — there she can give free rein to her imagination. "A theme I feel I have to paint over and over again is the gipsies — perhaps because I have a drop of gipsy blood myself?" Dorothea Löbel-Bock paints without inhibitions or undue respect for the pitfalls of technique: "I can't allow myself to think; you have to do it like this or like that, because otherwise I might take fright at what I've set out to do. I daren't lose my spontaneous approach or I couldn't go on painting."

Every one of Löbel-Bock's paintings consists basically of its sum total of coloured surfaces and

the execution of the pictures has a matching speed of performance.

For Lohse, there are only two themes from which to choose when he is about to start on a fresh picture — the simple life of Los Vilos, or scenes from the Bible. The painting shown here belongs to the first category, but it is worth bearing in mind that besides "The Five Wounds of Christ," "Armageddon, the Ultimate Battle," "Eve" and "The World's First Crime" (all of them with a flavour of magic or the Apocalypse), another element in this artist's work can come rushing to the fore. For Lohse has a rich vein of ex-

Lloyd, James: Feeding Time

Löbel-Bock, Dorothea: Iceskaters on the Lake

structures. Everything is approached from a painterly standpoint, the works sometimes having all the lustre of the Impressionists. Her paintings are invariably cheerful and conciliatory in tone, but what the figures in them might be thinking or saying it is impossible to guess: she merely describes their doings and their setting, which time and again has the appearance of an Arcadia. *(See portrait of the artist, p. 402). T. G.*

LOHSE, FREDERICO (1913)   Chile

Frederico Lohse lives and works in the spa of Los Vilos in Northern Chile, some 250 kilometres to the north of Santiago, where he is able to carry out his painting in peace and quiet. For him the village, with its gentle vistas of the wharfs and the silent and sure craft of the fisherfolk, provides an ideal background for the contrasting turbulence of his painting.

Lohse did not start painting until he was fifty-five years old, and when he did at first he was satisfied with rapid sketches. It was not until he came in contact with the sculptress Rosa Vicuna that his work took a more serious turn. Señora Vicuna liked the sketches he had done in oils and she encouraged him to continue. Now he entered a stage of intense concentration, and his new works began to show evidence of high quality. This artist is incapable of painting pictures slowly. He works with complete spontaneity and

pressionism in his artistic make-up. The raging floods in "Naufragio" would be a credit to many artists working within the compass of Der Blaue Reiter or Die Brücke. *Sh. W.*   →

LOLIŠVILI, TENGIZ (1929)   USSR
LOLISHVILI, TENGHIZ

Tenghiz Lolishvili was born in Tbilisi, the son of an office clerk. When his father was drafted in 1941 after war broke out, he had to enter a trade school to assist the family. At the age of fourteen he worked as barber in an army hospital. He attended a school for young workers at the same time and completed eight years of schooling. A barber by trade, he has had no artistic education. He first attempted drawing in 1970 when sick with the 'flu, to pass the time and entertain his little boy. He paints from imagination and only when on holiday, away from his job as a hair stylist at the Intourist Hotel in Tbilisi. A highly talented naive, he prefers to depict national rites and customs and the old-time Tbilisi of his boyhood, when he himself participated in various festivities that have now virtually died out. His conventional approach — a laconic, somewhat stereotyped style of presentation — reveals a similarity with children's drawing. He has been represented at a republican exhibition in Tbilisi, at the Transcaucasian Exhibition of Amateur Artists, and at a USSR exhibition in Moscow in 1977. Earlier, in 1973, he had a one-man show in Tbilisi.

(See portrait of the artist, p 402). N. Sh.

LONČARIĆ, DRAGICA (1956)   **Yugoslavia**

Dragica Lončarić was born in Hlebine, Croatia, where she went to elementary school and still lives. As a girl, she was fond of drawing, which she started to do in 1968. She remembers

Lohse, Frederico: Manna from Heaven

the visits paid to her elementary school by Ivan Generalić, the celebrated painter, who taught the children how to draw. Growing up in Hlebine, cradle of naive painters, she had the opportunity to visit many exhibitions of the work of peasant painters: the village has a gallery, built with the assistance of Ivan Generalić, where the peasants display their paintings and sculptures. Dragica Lončarić could easily have fallen into a mannered type of art in imitation of the Hlebine way of painting on glass prevalent among many of the artists from the village and surrounding area. Aware of this danger, she tried to be different and, while using the same village themes, succeeded in presenting them differently and in creating not only her own types of people and houses, but also her personal palette. In "Raftsmen," she portrays the Drava River that flows through the plains where she lives, a frequent subject of the naive artists in the Podravina region. In the past, its course unregulated, it did the peasants as much harm as good. In the foreground, peasants are waiting for a raft, fastened to a wire to prevent it from being borne away by the swollen spring waters and steered by an old raftsman. In the background are houses lit by the sun, penetrating through rain-bearing clouds. The dark yellow colour accentuates the action, making for a dynamic rather than a static effect.

Dragica Lončarić has had one-woman shows and participated in group exhibitions at home and abroad. *(See portrait of the artist, p. 403). N. T.*

LOPEZ, CÁNDIDO (1840—1902)   **Argentina**

Cándido Lopez was born in Buenos Aires, at a time when the first local painters were being taught in the studios of artists who had come from Europe. In a cultural environment dominated by academism, he arrived at a phase, after the usual beginning, where the features of his paintings brought him close to the naives. When war was declared against Paraguay, Lopez volunteered. In large notebooks (still preserved) he made careful sketches of all the battles. His right hand was torn off by a shell and this event was decisive in his career as an artist. He learned to

Lolishvili, Tenghiz: Feasting

Lončarić, Dragica: Raftsmen

paint with his left hand, but this completely changed his vision of things and the way he expressed himself. Forgetting the period he had spent in the studio of his Italian teacher, and ridding himself of all academic conventions, he painted in the fresh and meticulous manner of a

Lopez, Cándido: Self-portrait

true naive artist. At a time when a very meagre palette was in fashion (it should be remembered that Impressionism reached Argentina only in 1902), Lopez painted sub-tropical vegetation as it was. "People who had never seen these areas criticised me for misusing colour," Lopez once complained.

His works were not intrusively heroic, as demanded by contemporary norms; they had no central figures commanding the attention of the beholder, nor did his figures strike lofty poses. Cándido Lopez told tales that moved him deeply, as he himself explained, but in his paintings the

Lopez, Cándido: Disembarkation

woods and rivers are just as much the heroes of his tales as are the men and animals. Even the size of his pictures is unconventional (1×1.50 metres) and testifies to his intention of painting "a piece of history." As he was very concerned to portray the historical truth of battles, he showed his sketches to General Mitre, future President of the Republic. After receiving praise from the general, he began his great undertaking, devoting his entire life as a painter to depicting his unforgettable experiences in the war against Paraguay. Relying on his sketches, "done without artistic pretensions," as he later told friends, he was to paint fifty-two pictures in a period of twenty years.

Although he was motivated by the conscious desire to bear witness to events, and ostensibly less to express himself as a painter, his painterly qualities could not help coming through spontaneously in his work. When he died in 1902, he was quickly forgotten. It is to the credit of contemporary criticism that his work is again seeing the light of day. (See portrait of the artist, p. 403). M. T. S.

LORETJAN, AGAVARD (1902)   USSR
LORETIAN, AGAVARD

Agavard Loretian, born in Turkey, is a retired farm-worker now living in Armenia. After a serious illness between 1960 and 1972, he began to draw and make collages, manifesting a graphic ability and a link with folklore traditions that hark back to early Christian art (as will be remembered, Armenia was the first country in this part of the world to adopt Christianity). This is an approach to the traditional aspects of medieval

Armenian art as reflected through the Weltanschauung of the naive artist, an approach which is, incidentally, something of a paradox, in that the means the medieval artisan employed to convey his feelings are identical with the conventional means of expression that the modern naive artist Loretian uses. However, for him this is easier, since he has before him, as models, the actual buildings of medieval Armenian architects; hence all that remains is to reproduce them to the best of his ability by means of pencil, watercolour or other medium. His attitude derives from his outlook as a devout Christian who

Loretian, Agavard: An Armenian Church

brings his pictures as votive offerings to Armenian churches, which is where they can be seen. He has not been represented at any exhibitions. (See portrait of the artist, p. 403). N. Sh.

LOVAK, BRANKO (1944—1983)   Yugoslavia

Branko Lovak was born in Hlebine, Croatia, where he spent his childhood and went to elementary school. On his way to school, he used to pass by the house of his famous neighbour, the peasant painter Ivan Generalić, and stop to watch him painting in his backyard. He was thus stimulated to try painting himself, and was lucky enough to be given some initial instruction by Generalić. Lovak soon left the land and Hlebine and moved to Zagreb, where he lived until his untimely death in 1983. For a time, he worked as a window dresser while also painting pictures of village life: field work — reaping the harvest, resting in the shade, tending herds of cattle. In fact, cows are his most frequent subject.

In "Milking Cows" (1971) Lovak dealt with a well-known Hlebine theme. The cows are in red and yellow fantasy colours, while the rooster, cat and woman are painted realistically. After he moved to Zagreb, his landscapes and village motifs were no longer the product of direct observation and experience. He began to produce a more

LUBAKI, ALBERT (working 1926—1936) **Zaire**

This artist, the date of whose birth is not known, is regarded as the first modern painter of what is now Zaire. An ivory carver by profession, he began to paint in 1926, when he was about thirty, encouraged by a French colonial official. His wife Antoinette, who signs pictures of her own, used to copy his pictures. In 1929 his paintings were exhibited in Brussels for the first time. Further shows followed — in Geneva, Paris, Naples, Antwerp, and then, again, in Brussels.

His wash drawings, remarkable for their directness and graphic simplification, display a

Lovak, Branko: Milking Cows

decorative variant of the Hlebine heritage: pleasant pictures, but lacking the earlier depth and conviction.

Branko Lovak had several one-man shows and participated in group exhibitions at home and abroad. *(See portrait of the artist, p. 402).* N. T.

shrewd power of observation and a childlike delight in discovery, somehow combining instinctive and rational perception. The everyday rural life of men and animals, the cruel fight for survival in natural surroundings, the clash between traditional modes of life and the technical civilisation imported by the colonial rulers — these are three of the themes which he illustrates in an abridged form, with drastic directness, deadly accuracy and great power of expression.

When we look at his work, we must still feel a powerful sense of regret that it was not possible for this master of draughtsmanship to create his own cartoon films, as the Nigerian film-maker, Moustapha Allassane, has done. The sad truth is that Lubaki, in spite of having the opportunity — rare at that time — of exhibiting in Europe, continued to live in dire poverty and had to stop his creative work prematurely in 1936, when he was only forty, simply because he did not have the means to buy paper and watercolour paints. His pictures, like those of his colleague Djilatendo, are among the most precious documents of African art in this century. *(See portrait of the artist, p. 403). G. Sch.*

LÜTHI, HANNY (1919—1982)　　**Switzerland**
Hanny Lüthi was born in Meiringen, where she spent her entire childhood in a large family. Long winter nights were passed in reading, playing music and painting. After completing her studies she worked for two years in the Curie Foundation in Paris. She was married to a doctor, and had two children, a son and a daughter. Her spare time was taken up with painting,

Lüthi, Hanny: The Big Square in Winter

Lubaki, Albert: Leopard Devouring an Antelope

Lubaki, Albert: Women Feeding Chickens

which was, for her, a pleasure and refuge that she could not forfeit. Of her painting, she said: "I also like to put on canvas things that do not exist, or to revive something that lived for a mere moment." She exhibited in Switzerland and abroad. *(See portrait of the artist, p. 403). G. K.*

LYSENKO, IVAN IVANOVIČ (1921)　　**USSR**
LYSENKO, IVAN IVANOVICH

I. I. Lysenko was born into a peasant family in the village of Zolotonozhka, Drabovsky district, in the Cherkassy region of the Ukraine. In 1952 he graduated from the Kiev college which trained workers in the field of cultural enlightenment. He was by turns a village librarian and an art designer, and is today head of a club. He has also founded a picture gallery, in addition to the local museum of ethnography and local lore that he started. His favourite subject-matter relates to the life, mores and day-to-day work of the villager. His work reflects the outlook of a villager who has come into contact with urban culture. Lysenko has been represented at several group exhibitions at republican and USSR level. *(See portrait of the artist, p. 403). N. Sh.*

Lysenko, Ivan Ivanovich: Winter Festival in the Village of Drabovo

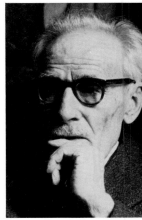

Lacković, Ivan

Lada, Jan

Lagru, Dominique

Lefevre, Pierre

Lefranc, Jules

Leman, Martin

Lloyd, James

Löbel-Bock, Dorothea

Lolišvili, Tengiz

Lovak, Branko

o, Juraj

Lavrič, Boris

Lecossois, Victor

berger, Shimshon

Leonov, Pavel Petrovič

Ličková, Anna

Ligabue, Antonio

arić, Dragica

Lopez, Cándido

Loretjan, Agavard

ki, Albert

Lüthi, Hanny

Lysenko, I. I.

MACZÓ, MIHÁLYNÉ — Hungary
MAEDER, KARL — West Germany
MAGYAR, VIKTOR — Yugoslavia
MAIRENA, OSCAR — Nicaragua
MA JALI — China
MALDONADO, ALEX — USA
MALONEY, ELLEN — Australia
MANDEVILLE, ANNE — France
MANDIĆ, PETAR — Yugoslavia
MANOUSSAKI, ATHENA — Greece
MANSO, CARLOS — Argentina
MARADIŠVILI, ŠALVA — USSR
MARAN, ANUJKA — Yugoslavia
MAREK, JERZY — Great Britain
MARENCO, CARLOS — Nicaragua
MARIN, MARIO — Nicaragua
MARINGER, LUCIEN — Belgium
MARKAKIS, ANTONIS — Greece
MARKOVÁ, CECILIE — Czechoslovakia
MARKOVITS-HORVÁTH, A. — Hungary
MARKȘ, RAE — Australia
MARUKI, SUMA — Japan
MARX, SOPHIA — West Germany
MASON, GWEN — Australia
MASTAJTENE, MARITE — USSR
MATAMOROS, RUPERTO JAY — Cuba
MAVEC-TOMLJENOVIĆ, M. — Yugoslavia
MAXIME (VOYET) — France
MAYERL, WILLIBALD — East Germany
MAYORGA, PABLO — Nicaragua
MAZIN, IGNATIJ ANDREEVIČ — USSR
MAZUR, FRANK — USA
McCARTHY, JUSTIN — USA
McCLAREN, SYDNEY — Jamaica
MEHKEK, MARTIN — Yugoslavia
MEIJER, SAL — Netherlands
MEJIA GODOY, ARMADO — Nicaragua
MEJO, OSCAR de — USA
MELIAŠVILI, IVAN — USSR
MENTRUP, ANNA — West Germany
MESSINGER, MENACHEM — Israel
METELLI, ORNEORE — Italy
MICHAŁOWSKA, MARTA — Poland
MICHELIS, EFFIE — Greece
"MIDDLE ART" (AUGUSTIN OKOYE) — Nigeria

MIHUȚ, PETRU — Romania
MILLÁN, CARMEN — Venezuela
MILLÁN, VICTOR — Venezuela
MILLER, ANTHONY — Great Britain
MILLER, LOUISA — USA
MILOJEVIĆ, DOBROSAV — Yugoslavia
MIL'TS, EL'FRIDA MARTSOVNA — USSR
MIRONOVA, E. F. — USSR
MITRĂCHIȚĂ, GHIȚĂ — Romania
MITRAKAS, YANNIS — Greece
MOKE ART P. — Zaire
MOKRY-MÉSZÁROS, DEZSÖ — Hungary
MONSIEL, EDMUND — Poland
MOORE, ROSS — Australia
MORAÏTIS, ZAPHEIRIS — Greece
MORALES, ELSA — Venezuela
MORENO, RAFAEL — Cuba
MORGAN, GERTRUDE — USA
MOSES, KIVETORUK — USA
MOTOROŽESKU, MARIORA — Yugoslavia
MRAZ, FRANJO — Yugoslavia
MUCHA, SZCZEPAN — Poland
MÜLLER, JOHANNES — Switzerland
MURAEV, M. V. — USSR
MURRAY, ANDREW — Great Britain
MUSCH, JEAN-LOUIS — Belgium
MUSUSA, PUNGU — Zaire

Maczó, Mihályné: Threshing

Maeder, Karl: The National Park of Jungfernheide with Water Tower

MACZÓ, MIHÁLYNÉ (1908) Hungary

Mihályné Maczó, born in Hajdudorog, has been a farm labourer, a worker in a tobacco factory, and a housemaid. Since 1967, she has been painting pictures made of the seeds of various plants in a technique resembling mosaic. Her decorative scenes reflect the suffering of the peasants at the beginning of this century. Carefully worked out to the last detail in grains of wheat, these pictures show archaic scenes set on a plain. Her compositions are harmonious, both in colour and in form. She is the author of a two-hundred-page autobiography, an interesting document about the way of life, the harsh fate and love of life of the village poor, the girls and women of her native district. She has received prizes for her paintings and for her writing as well. Her works are housed in the Museum of Naive Art in Kecskemét and in the Ethnographic Museum in Budapest. *M. I.*

MAEDER, KARL (1891—1968) West Germany

Karl Maeder was born in Bromberg and died in Berlin. After serving his apprenticeship as a fitter, he was employed from 1922 onwards in the Siemens-Schuckert works in Berlin.

When he was about forty-eight years old he had to carry out some repairs in an artist's studio. There was a half-finished painting on the easel and the painter was discussing with a friend the problems of finishing it when Maeder intervened in the conversation with some "well-meant advice." The painter said he should finish the painting himself, if he knew so much about it, and Maeder actually began to paint and finished the picture in a couple of hours. Back home, he bought himself the necessary materials and from then on spent his free time painting.

Karl Maeder was something of an eccentric, with a naive outlook on life and a way of expressing himself that was not always intelligible to others. Years ago, long before naive painting was fashionable, he used to appear from time to time at the Rosen Gallery in Berlin, or, later on, at Springer's, and unpack his pictures of parks and woodlands. Maeder's passion was his trees, those he had actually seen as well as those he invented. He also had a fondness for cloud formations which lie menacingly or drift distractedly, lashed by the wind over broad, serene landscapes, reminiscent in their cold blue or leaden grey folds of El Greco's painting of drapery. Most of his pictures have a sluggish, earthy heaviness; even in the case of subjects as familiar to the Berliner as the water-tower in Jungfernheide Park, Maeder's pictures have a suggestion of something impenetrable, magic, familiar but not cosy. These are the sort of landscapes we might come across in bad dreams.

Maeder's pictures are not numerous but they have been included in many representative exhibitions and are much sought after by museums and private collectors. *T. G.*

MAGYAR, VIKTOR (1934—1980)   Yugoslavia

Viktor Magyar was born in Metlika, Slovenia, where his father was a worker. After completing elementary schooling in Metlika, he went to Kamnik to continue his education. Then, desirous of becoming a teacher, he went to school in Ljubljana, from where he graduated. After eight years of teaching in the mountain locality of Čatež, he moved to Grosuplje, where he died.

"I paint the fresco of life as I see and understand it," he said. "To me, the world seems egg-shaped, the mountains, trees and people. When I was a young and inexperienced teacher, I

greenish white ground, three participants in a carnival are ringing bells to announce the end of the long cold winter and with it all that winter brings — sickness and dark forces. Looking at his painting, the spectator can imagine the moment when the mummers withdraw and people rush pell-mell from their houses, slide like children downhill, and liven up the atmosphere again.

In "Winter" (1974), Viktor Magyar has covered his hills and housetops with snow. The branches are there, as if to halt the movement of the hills and provide colour contrast. Dark red

Mairena, Oscar: Rural Festivity in Solentiname

Magyar, Viktor: Carnival

wandered around the hills, meeting people along the way, in the fields or in the backyards of their houses. I watched them working on the steep slopes, saw them rejoicing, getting tipsy, playing Slovene songs on the accordion."

His first pictures were done in the green colour of the meadow and vineyards, and later ones in the red of an Indian summer or the blue of the winter sky. All of them radiate a feeling of unreality, with their figures rigid, the way children would draw them. Nature has been transformed into a fantastic version of itself, as though the hills and houses had been cut out of cardboard and pasted on a wooden board. The houses have no foundations or chimneys, and do not seem meant to be lived in. The fences of dead branches have the appearance of a backdrop placed there for a small, temporary village stage. But all these elements in the paintings of Viktor Magyar are interlinked, leaving a strong impression of a world which only he has seen, or which no one else has perceived in the same way.

In "Carnival" (1975), Magyar portrayed men wearing masks at the end of Lent. The hills are edged with branches, with white houses on the peaks, placed as though on stacks of hay. On the

figures represent masked men with the attributes of birds. Magyar often identifies people with flocks of birds or herds of animals, and human behaviour is compared with life in nature.

Viktor Magyar had one-man shows and participated in group exhibitions at home and abroad. *N. T.*

MAIRENA, OSCAR (1948)   Nicaragua

Oscar Mairena was born in Leon but in early childhood moved with his parents to Solentiname, where he now lives. During the civil war, he was persecuted for his paintings, as were other painters from Solentiname. He is skilful at moulding cement shapes and at carving animal figures in wood, which he then colours.

He has exhibited in Managua, in Venezuela, the USA, Germany and other countries. *E. C.*

MA JALI (1955)   China

Born in the village of Po You in Hu county, Ma Jali did not go to school. Like the other girls in her village, she began working in a farm brigade raising wheat and cotton. In summer she helped gather the harvest in this agriculturally rich part of the country. Her work included taking the wheat to the road passing through the village, and then spreading it on the asphalt so that the oncoming traffic would partly thresh it. Then the grain would be taken to a nearby field specially flattened with rollers for the final threshing. When this was over, work would commence in the cotton fields. At the age of seventeen she painted her first picture, which she named "Drying the Cotton," showing members of her brigade spreading cotton to dry on racks. Horse-drawn carts wait to take it to the communal storehouse. Ma Jali felt shy about showing her first painting, but her talent was quickly noted and she was encouraged by her brigade members and later by the local teacher. She joined the village painters' group and painting became her favourite pastime. Every evening, after work on the land and in the house, she spent what little free time was left depicting in watercolours the many activities of her brigade in which she took part. She has painted about fifty works, some of which hang in the local gallery built to display the best examples of peasant painting in the region.

(See portrait of the artist, p. 446). N. T.

MALDONADO, ALEX (1901)   USA

Born in Mazatlán, Sinaloa, Mexico, Alex Maldonado emigrated to California with his

Ma Jali: Drying Cotton

Maldonado, Alex: A Return of Christ in This Atomic Age

family in 1911. His father died in 1914, and little Alex sold newspapers, took care of the milkman's horse, and did other odd jobs to earn money. The family lived in North Beach, a "tough" neighbourhood in San Francisco, and Alex learned boxing for self-protection. By 1917 he was "moonlighting" as a professional boxer, while at the same time working in the shipyards, first as a riveter and then for several years as a clerk. When he retired in 1971 he had been a shipping clerk in a canning factory. During all this time he was living with his mother and his sister Carmen, who says she "programmed him into having a hobby, painting." He had never taken any drawing lessons and, she said, "draws and paints only what comes from his mind."

He started drawing with pencil, then went on to watercolours, and finally to oil, which he prefers. Maldonado's paintings contain fantasy overlaying actuality, and have the "otherness" of space travel in their evocation of unreal vistas that sometimes go outward onto the very frames of the painting. "I used to start with a house, but like no house you ever saw. I read the encyclopedia, about petrified bones, astronomy, the galaxy, nebula. Only part of the picture is on the canvas. There are always more buildings underneath or more sky beyond the top."

In 1973 one of Maldonado's paintings won the KQUED TV Station annual auction award in San Francisco, and his works are now in collections in New York, Chicago, California and Japan. *J. W.*

remained in the Retz region throughout her life, except during the Second World War, when she worked as a *résidente sociale*. On her return home, she took up painting and, after several encounters with Yugoslav naive artists, adopted the technique of painting on the back of glass. She recently published her autobiography.

The work of Anne Mandeville has shown, as it has developed, an increasingly sound craftsmanship. Whether she is employing traditional techniques or painting on the back of glass, her subject is always richly elaborated, and she reveals the world in all its great diversity,

Maloney, Ellen: Rengeville — Toowoomba

Mandeville, Anne: Tree with Eggs

MALONEY, ELLEN (1900—1976)   **Australia**

Born at Toowoomba in Queensland, Ellen Maloney was always interested in drawing and painting. When she was a child her family often found it difficult to supply her with art materials and it was not until the mid-1950s that she began to paint seriously. She completed an art diploma by correspondence course and held her first one-woman exhibition at the Darling Downs Institute of Advanced Education in 1975.

Ellen Maloney took prizes in many local exhibitions and her largest painting, "Noah's Ark," was acquired by the Toowoomba City Gallery. Her subjects were taken from the surrounding countryside and depicted the life of the people who lived around her.

Each of Ellen Maloney's paintings had its own history and for this reason she rarely parted with any of her works, preferring to remain surrounded by these milestones of a long life. *B. McC.*

MANDEVILLE, ANNE (1915)   **France**

Anne Mandeville was born at Frossay. She felt an affinity for art at an early age and attended the School of Fine Arts in Nantes. She

depicting landscapes, stories, legends, and so on. Among her finest paintings is the recent series of variations on the theme of whatever sends out roots.

Anne Mandeville has been exhibiting since 1961. Her work has been seen at the Henri Rousseau Museum in Laval. She participated in 1969 at the Second Biennial of Naive Art in Bratislava and has also exhibited in Rome, London, Lugano and Zagreb. *Ch. Sch.*

MANDIĆ, PETAR (1938)   **Yugoslavia**

Petar Mandić was born in Zdenac, near Sanski Most, Bosnia-Herzegovina, where he went to elementary school. A metalworker by trade, he is employed in a foundry. Since 1958 he has been painting motifs from the Bosanska Krajina (Bosnian March) area: men who work in the factory, casting iron, and others who live in the village, tending herds or cultivating the land. Most of his pictures are autobiographical and tell of his transformation from a peasant into a metalworker.

In "Self-portrait" (1973), Mandić places himself in the foreground with the bicycle he rides to work and back. In the centre are factories from whose smoke-stacks red smoke rises to a horizon made ruddy by it. Red often dominates.

"Circumcision" is another painting where the artist has used red to create atmosphere. Male relatives have gathered to assist the "expert," while the child, blindfolded, must endure the painful masculine ritual. *(See portrait of the artist, p. 446). N. T.*

MANOUSSAKI, ATHENA (1928) **Greece**

Athena Manoussaki-Ebers was born in Heraklion, Crete, and moved to Athens just before the war. Starting painting in 1957, she never attended art school and had no thought of becoming an artist, since this privilege seemed to belong to other members of her family. She married an American painter, Bob Ebers, and in 1964 moved to New York.

Athena's works are a sincere expression of a deep love of life and of the emotions caused by simple, everyday things. Past and present, reality and imagination, coexist happily in her work. Some of her themes are scenes from Greek life: island interiors, market-places, squares, harbours, coffee-houses and taverns by the sea,

Mandić, Petar: Self-portrait

Mandić, Petar: Circumcision

Manoussaki, Athena: A Tavern on a Greek Island

interiors of churches, and so on. Her colours are generally much brighter than in reality; this is true even in a country like Greece, with its dazzling sun and its villagers' preference for striking colours, noticeable in every aspect of their folk art. Her sophisticated personality helps her make the most of a remarkable sense of the ornamental, expressed through her simple displacement of objects without perspective. Although she has the ability to visualise ingenious scenes that never existed, her travels and her life in New York have undoubtedly enriched her subject-matter. She has gradually started to use new materials in combination with oil.

Athena has had successful exhibitions in Stockholm, Athens, Chios, Boston, New York, St. Louis, Stamford, and London. *A. T.*

MANSO, CARLOS (1928) **Argentina**

Carlos Manso, born in Buenos Aires, studied piano and composition, completing his schooling in Brazil, the USA, Spain and Portugal. He was a scholarship student and teacher of music in New Delhi and at the Music Academy in Bahia (Brazil), where he first drew closer to painting. As a well-known pianist returning from a guest appearance, he once stayed over in Bahia. He himself says of this occasion: "I wanted to buy one of the lovely paintings by the naive artists of Bahia showing a colonial church, and a 17th-century wooden figure of the Madonna. I did not have enough money for both so I decided to buy the figure and do the painting myself." Returning to Buenos Aires, he hung his work over his piano but said nothing about the identity of the artist. When his pupils and friends pressed him to reveal it, he admitted that he had painted it. And thus the musician became a painter. Nostalgic in the big city, he paints the fields and villages where he spent his childhood. His lines and colours are soft: sown flax, like a green coverlet, and endless rows of sunflowers represent man's inexhaustible dialogue with nature. *M. T. S.*

sion. His somewhat archaic statuary is akin to the works of ancient sculptors who adorned the walls of Georgian shrines. His painting is as sincere and artless as his sculpture, but more derivative. He has been represented at many exhibitions since 1937. Most of his work is at the Gori Museum and at the Museum of Georgian Folk Art in Tbilisi. *N. Sh.*

MARAN, ANUJKA (1918—1983) Yugoslavia
Anujka Maran was born in the village of Uzdin, Vojvodina, which is inhabited by ethnic

Manso, Carlos: Wedding

Maradishvili, Shalva: A Georgian

MARADIŠVILI, ŠALVA (1899—1973) USSR
MARADISHVILI, SHALVA

Shalva Maradishvili, a sculptor and painter, was born into a peasant family in the Georgian village of Uriatubani, and, like Pirosmani, hails from the fertile Kakhetian Valley in Eastern Georgia. He had no schooling, and all his life grew fruit and grapes. He was a "sacred heart" — sincere, unselfish, well-intentioned, kind, loved by neighbours and children. He began to draw and mould in soap in boyhood but made his first sculpture at the age of twenty-five. His special field was the embellishing of house and village wells and springs with sculptures and reliefs. His debut was arranged by the celebrated Georgian artist Lado Gudiashvili (who also knew Pirosmani) in 1937, for celebrations of the 800th anniversary of the Georgian national poet, Shota Rustaveli. Also in 1937 he exhibited at the Moscow show commemorating the 20th anniversary of the October Revolution and at the Paris World Fair.

He produced over a hundred sculptural pieces in basalt, marble and local stone. On friezes and bas-reliefs, and in figures in-the-round, he depicted Georgian peasants wearing the traditional national felt cap, shepherds with water gourds, celebrities and Georgian national heroes. His concept of artistic form is in harmony with the traditional, national styles of expres-

Romanians, and died after a life spent doing house and field work. From 1956, she began to paint in her spare time. She was the first one in her village to do so, but her example was soon followed by another fifteen women. Having had no education, she knew nothing about painting and had not even seen any paintings, with the exception of the iconostasis in the Uzdin church, the work of the well-known Vojvodina painter Konstantin Danilo. Dressed in her best Romanian national costume, on Sundays she would regard the richly worked iconostasis from which ascetic-looking saints glared fixedly at the faithful. She also gazed at her fellow-peasants in church, wearing their best clothes, and thought how pleasant it would be if she could paint herself, the members of her household, her relations and friends.

"I took some colours, not real ones, and began to work on cloth that I did not know how to stretch when I started. So I did my first pictures which I dared not show anyone lest they laugh at me. The village teacher heard about them, came to see, and told me to continue." Her favourite subjects are Romanian national costumes, and the life and customs of her village.

In "Red Horse" (1963), she painted a meeting between a young boy and girl engaged in the village custom of sizing each other up. The girl is wearing a rich Romanian costume, and is at the right age for marriage; she seems to be posing for a photographer. He is passing by on a fancy horse and has stopped for a moment, as though struck by her beauty. The well-fed horse reveals the boy to be from a prosperous household. The young man will ride past the girl several times to call attention to himself. And so acquaintance begins wordlessly. When the time comes, his parents will visit her parents to ask for her hand.

Anujka Maran has had one-woman shows and has participated in group exhibitions at home and abroad. *(See portrait of the artist, p. 446). N. T.*

MAREK, JERZY (1925) **Great Britain**

Jerzy Marek was born in Poland. His early interest in painting and wood-carving came to an abrupt end with the outbreak of the Second World War, and it was many years before this enthusiasm for art came back into his life. Since the war, he has lived in Preston, Lancashire.

Jerzy Marek is a versatile man. He is an accomplished designer of modern bridges, an inspired promoter of naive and primitive painters and sculptors from England and Poland.

As can be seen, his style is careful and fluent. His early pictures are of runners, boxers

Maran, Anujka: Red Horse

Maran, Anujka: Procession

Marek, Jerzy: Outing

and other participants in sport. His recent paintings include some on romantic themes, while others are compositions built round one or more cats.

He has taken part in many mixed exhibitions in England and abroad. *(See portrait of the artist, p. 446). Sh. W.*

MARENCO, CARLOS (1958)   Nicaragua

Carlos Marenco was born in the native quarter of Monimbo in Masaya and has lived there ever since. Active in demonstrations

Marenco, Carlos: *Little Devils' Dance in Masaya*

Marin, Mario: *Procession of the Eucharist*

against the Somoza dictatorship, he was persecuted for his part in them.

He began to paint when he was twelve, using left-over colours. Very devout, he paints religious pictures which show in detail the customs and folk traditions of the people. "For me," says Marenco, "painting is something magnificent. By painting pictures, we Nicaraguans can show others who we are and what we are like. I paint especially for the peasants and schoolchildren, so that they can become acquainted with painting."

He has exhibited in Masaya and Managua, also in Costa Rica and other countries. *E. C.*

MARIN, MARIO (1954)   Nicaragua

Mario Marin works only on cardboard, using tempera covered with a dense layer of shiny shellac which gives his pictures a distinctive appearance. Mostly he paints scenes from the life of his native town of Boaca: processions honouring saints, the market-place, Sunday afternoon in the park. "I love painting and have managed to establish good contact with people," he says. And his works reflect this, being full of life and light.

By occupation he is a cabinetmaker. Excellent at working in wood, he sculpts in this medium, although he is principally a painter.

He has exhibited in Boaca and Managua. *E. C.*

MARINGER, LUCIEN (1903—1981)   Belgium

Lucien Maringer died in his native Ardennes, which he hardly ever left. He was called the painter of the Ardennes by Joseph Delmelle.

He grew up on his father's farm, drawing "good men" in his spare time from agricultural work, which he had to start doing early in life. He dreamed of becoming a postman, attracted by the prestige of the uniform. Finally he did come to wear a uniform, but it was that of a railwayman. In 1927, when he was twenty-four years old, he had a serious accident at work and was then given the job of cloak-room attendant at the station of Libramont. The painter Marie Howet discovered his talent and gave him painting lessons when he was already thirty.

Maringer used thick colour applied straight onto the canvas, without a preliminary drawing. He was inspired particularly by the life of the Ardennes — not by the work, but by the celebrations and holidays. "Village Comedy" is a product of his narrative imagination and can easily evoke the novel "Clochemerle," transposed to the Ardennes. He also loved landscapes, still-lifes, and especially floral pieces. Religious themes are likewise characteristic of his work. His "Signs of the Cross" (in the church in Gouvy) is portrayed as everyday life, with the addition, along Christ's road or underneath the cross, of a number of "sinners" — actually local types, loutish soldiers depicted as German troops of the occupying forces during the Second World War.

Enthusiasts for naive art have objected to the fact that Maringer received some artistic training. But this training was brief, and Marie Howet, aware of how special a case her pupil was, limited herself to teaching him only how to observe and how to use colour. *J. C.*

MARKAKIS, ANTONIS (1922)   Greece

Antonis Markakis, born in Crete, works as a guard at the archaeological site of Hagia Triada.

His painting surprises the viewer with its spontaneous wisdom and technical peculiarities. His works show remarkable qualities in the disposition of volume and form, and in the distribution of motifs. The beautiful plain of the Messara, where Markakis lives and works, is an endless source of inspiration for his painting. His vision embraces details that would go unnoticed by the ordinary visitor, and he records them in a highly individual way. Unusual blue olive trees are a dominant element of many compositions. A few indirect Byzantine influences may be detected only in the rendering of schematic rocks and of

Maringer, Lucien: Confiscation

the outlines of houses. The artist became acquainted with the techniques of Byzantine hagiography on Mount Athos and has also produced a few icons. The "saddle" of Mount Psiloriti — which he incorporates in several landscapes, regardless of their exact location — adds another genuine Cretan touch to his work. The artist's themes are taken from his immediate surroundings; the plain of the Messara, the Psiloriti mountain range, flowers, trees, birds, antiquities and scenes from Cretan agricultural and pastoral life are transformed through the remarkable quality of his colour and his notable technical skill. The views of the Minoan palace of Phaistos are particularly impressive. In these the antiquities are an integral part of the landscape; the artist does not give them a predominant place because of their archaeological importance.

Markakis took part in group exhibitions in Athens and on Crete, and in the Bratislava Triennial of Naive Art; he has also had one-man shows in Athens, Heraklion, Crete, and England.

A. T.

MARKOVÁ, CECILIE (1911)   Czechoslovakia

After leaving intermediate school, Cecilie Marková trained as a milliner and later became chief saleswoman in a milliner's shop in Kyjov, Moravia. Her first drawings are reminiscent of the patterns drawn by spiritualist mediums. On 18 October 1938, at ten o'clock in the morning, Marková experienced a definite, almost physical compulsion to draw. From that time onwards she set aside certain days on which she drew and painted. It was at this period that she lost her beloved husband and she put all her love into the symbols that she drew.

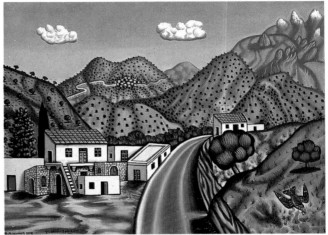

Markakis, Antonis: View of the Messara Plain

Marková pursues her art in a firm belief in irrational spheres and powers. She believes in the existence of "another" world with other laws, a world that is linked with the world of our planet. She is convinced that her astral blossoms, the soul-faces and the orphic landscapes are actually messages from distant worlds and hence a means of understanding the cosmic psyche. The art of Séraphine or Zemánková proceeded from similar premises. Her statement about the instantaneous generation of the symbols is important: "I firmly believe that there exists a definite power which guides me. A spirit living on another planet who manifests himself in this manner... I am alone and yet I am not alone." She speaks as follows of her imaginative insight when she paints: "I paint without any model, without any idea, I never know beforehand what it will be and how it will turn out." Such connections with the ideas of occultism place Marková's work outside the uninhibited simplicity of naive painting. But her ecstatic utterances differ from the stereotypes of those spiritualists who express themselves in drawings. Marková absorbs elements of popular ornament from her native Moravian Slovakia and incorporates in them mystic elements and figures. *(See portrait of the artist, p. 447). A. P.* →

MARKOVITS-HORVÁTH,   Hungary
ANTAL (1851—1933)

Antal Markovits-Horváth, a carpenter by trade, was disabled by a fall from a roof. He then began to carve, first drawing his figures with a carpenter's pencil and then fashioning them with a pocket knife and razor blade. His compositions on biblical themes, might show, for instance, a group gathered around the manger in Bethlehem. But he was also adept at portraying the heroes of folk tales and typical figures from his immediate surroundings. Private collectors began showing an interest only after his death. The Museum housed in the Rakos Palace in Budapest contains many examples of his work. His works were on display in the exhibitions of "Original Talents," which began in 1934, and were shown again in 1972 in Budapest and in six museums in other parts of the country, as well as in several European countries and Cuba. *M. I.*

MARKS, RAE (1945) **Australia**

After completing her secondary education, Rae Marks decided to take up art studies. She prepared for a Diploma of Art at Swinburne College of Technology in Melbourne, Victoria. She is married and now lives with her husband and family at Eltham in Victoria. Rae Marks paints the everyday things around her. Her

Marks, Rae: Late Night Reading

Marková, Cecilie: Christ's Head

pictures show people, old houses with verandas, gardens and animals. They are a lovingly constructed record of a simple life style. *B. McC.*

MARUKI, SUMA (1875—1956) **Japan**

Suma Maruki, born a farmer's daughter in Hiroshima, married a farmer, brought up a family and tilled the land, leading an ordinary life until her husband was killed when the atom bomb was dropped on Hiroshima and she herself sustained injuries (she was seventy at the time).

Nonetheless, she remained lively and cheerful, finding consolation and meaning in work. To have something to occupy herself with in her old age and overcome a feeling of loneliness, she started painting when seventy-four at the urging of her son and daughter-in-law, who were painters.

Some of the pictures she painted are: "The Cow," "The Mother Cat," "Late Autumn," "Birds," "Friend of the Earth," "In Front of the Garden," "Animals." As these titles show, her themes are taken from life in the village. In her last eight years (the years during which she painted), she produced several hundred works.

Markovits-Horváth, Antal: King Matthew in Disguise

Maruki, Suma: The Cattle Dealer Comes to the Village

Maruki, Suma: Animal Kingdom

Her paintings have been shown in numerous exhibitions and many of them were awarded prizes. *(See portrait of the artist, p. 447).* S. L.

MARX, SOPHIA (1896)   **West Germany**

Sophia Marx, born in Frauenberg, now lives in Cologne. She would like to have become a painter, but as she was "only a girl" she had to learn housekeeping. After her marriage she ran a boarding-house. She began to paint in 1950, when she had given up this occupation and her children were grown up.

Marx, Sophia: Ball in Gürzenich

The range of subjects chosen by this jolly Rhinelander is varied, but she shows a preference for country scenes: "I would never take visions of nuclear war and such horrors as subjects. The world that I paint is intended to help the spectator relax and to cheer him up."

Her numerous pictures of scenes from Cologne, especially the area round the Cathedral, are inspired by this purpose and are far removed from the hurly-burly of city life. They are brightly animated scenes, picturesque and imbued with an idyllic cosiness. Sophia Marx quite naturally seizes on the rousing celebrations that are customary in the Rhineland. She has absolutely no misgivings about how to cope, for example, with the countless dancing couples and the bewildering array of tables and decorations. Sophia Marx attempts to achieve all these effects from the pigments alone, which she applies with a flat brush, working one wet colour into another, so that the individual objects in her pictures flow softly into each other.

Her pictures have become popular over the years because of her brisk and colourful style, and also because of their edifying subjects, taken directly from life. Unfortunately she has produced an increasing number of rather meretricious "pretty-pretty" pictures. *(See portrait of the artist, p. 447).* T. G.

MASON, GWEN (1922)   **Australia**

Gwen Mason was born in Melbourne, Victoria. She went to school in Bendigo, Victoria, where she received some basic art training.

Mason, Gwen: The Intruder

Although she remained very interested in the visual arts, she had no formal education in drawing and painting.

Her early activities included showcard and ticket writing and she was, for a time, a tracer at the Ordnance Factory in Bendigo. Later she designed copper repoussé objects and illustrated children's books.

In 1976, in the despair of deep grief caused by the successive deaths of several members of her family, Gwen Mason started to paint. A new world opened for her as she translated her earlier embroidery pictures into oils. The influence of this craft is still evident in her joyously detailed paintings. Her imagination received much stimulus from frequent travels around Australia and abroad. In 1978 she journeyed as far as China.

Gwen Mason's work is to be found in many private and institutional collections, and in the permanent collection of Australian Naive Art at the Swan Hill Regional Gallery. She had a one-woman show at the Australian Galleries, Melbourne, in 1980 and has participated in a number of group exhibitions. *(See portrait of the artist, p. 447).* B. McC.

MASTAJTENE, MARITE (1919) **USSR**
MASTAITIENE, MARITE

Marite Mastaitiene was born in the Lithuanian village of Deviaikiskiai, near Kedainyai. She has had only four years of elementary schooling. Before retiring in 1978, she did work in Kazakhstan and subsequently at the May Day Collective Farm near her native village, where she lives today. Like other village girls, she loved needlework and embroidery and was fond of painting congratulation cards and stage sets for amateur art shows. She was forty-odd when she began to do decorative hangings, on either linen

Mastaitiene, Marite: The Shepherd

or black cloth. Having learned to prime canvas, she began to paint pictures, among them a series based on recollections of the farm work, customs and holiday-making of her native village. She is naive in artistic expression; even though the colour is not folkloric, yet it is not drawn directly from nature. In this respect, she is like a child, who, while seeing how things are really coloured, subconsciously translates the colouring into the realm of fantasy. With her the subject-matter is all-important, as can be gauged from her works "The Festival of the Shepherds," "Village Dances," "The Festival of the Mummers," "The Christmas Table," "Hunters in Winter," or "Driving the Cattle out to Pasture." Integrated into their author's own concepts of space and colour, they are profoundly patriarchal in their philosophy. One cannot say that her pictures are identical with children's drawings but rather they are a personalised, imaginative, lyrical interpretation. She was first represented at a 1973 group show mounted in the club of the Eighth of March Collective Farm, and subsequently at two group shows in 1980 in Kedainyai and Vilnius. She is a member of the Lithuanian Association of Folk Arts. (*See portrait of the artist, p. 446*). *N. Sh.*

MATAMOROS, RUPERTO JAY **Cuba**

Ruperto Jay Matamoros is considered one of the most important Cuban naive painters. Born in San Luis, Oriente Province, he moved to Havana and in 1937 he entered the Free Studies

of Prado Street, where many other artists trained. Already in 1939 he had exhibited in the Prado Gallery. Mainly figurative and realistic in style, his work covers varying aspects of life in Cuba, including current events of national importance.

In 1963 he exhibited in the Gallery of the Union of Cuban Writers and Artists in Matanzas and later participated in various exhibitions in Cuba and abroad. In 1969 he received an award at the Second Triennial Exhibition of Naive Art in Bratislava, Czechoslovakia. He took part in the Salon '70 (1970) and in the joint exhibition of

Matamoros, Ruperto Jay: Bathing in the River

Primitive Painters (1971). In 1976 he was included in the exhibition "Eleven Cuban Primitive Artists" at the Institute of Jamaica in Kingston. His work is in the collection of the National Museum in Havana. *T. R.*

MAVEC-TOMLJENOVIĆ, **Yugoslavia**
MARICA (1920)

Marica Mavec-Tomljenović was born in Radeče, Slovenia, but has lived in Zagreb since 1921. She has had a secondary school education, looks after her home and raises flowers, and has been painting since 1969. Her subjects are nudes, interiors, the Upper Town — the old part of Zagreb — portraits of family and friends, scenes of everyday life and family celebrations, usually held in light, spacious rooms such as this artist would like to have in real life.

Since she was already fifty when she began to paint, it was natural that she should turn to family themes. As though composing an album, she produces pictures of events in the daily life of the household, or those seen in the street through a window. The painting "Iris and Her Pet" shows a segment of life that could have been caught by a camera: a girl with her pet in the foreground, a doll on the couch and a painting of a nude on the wall. Soft pastel colours reflect a serene and happy family atmosphere.

She has had one-woman shows and participated in group exhibitions at home and abroad. *N. T.*

Mavec-Tomljenović, Marica: Iris and Her Pet

MAXIME (VOYET) (1896) France

Maxime Voyet, known simply as Maxime, was born in Jondonnière. He became a bricklayer, but after the First World War went to work for the railways and became a stoker on steam locomotives. He had little free time, and was able to dedicate himself to his art only after he retired.

The main source of inspiration for Maxime is the railways: stations, trains moving across open country, and so on. He places the well-known elements — the locomotive, signals, typical stations — in an idealised setting, organising the whole composition with ease. Large numbers of people are grouped in virtually independent scenes, animating these gaily coloured paintings, with their sharp and pure lines. In Maxime's view, the coal and smoke of locomotives never dirty the atmosphere.

Since 1958, Maxime has exhibited at numerous galleries and shows in Paris, Nantes and Tours, as well as at the Museum of Modern Art in Paris and the Laval Museum. *Ch. Sch.*

MAYERL, WILLIBALD (1896—1977) East Germany

Willibald Mayerl was the son of a coalminer. At the age of 16 he also went down the pit and worked underground at the coal-face and in various other functions. After qualifying at the mining academy in Freiberg he became, in

Maxime (Voyet): Train Running Through the Countryside

Mayorga, Pablo: Rural Homestead

succession, a deputy and senior deputy in the coalmining industry. He retired in 1954.

Willibald Mayerl started painting in his spare time in 1930. He first exhibited his pictures — scenes of the miner's life — in the *Kunsthütte* in Chemnitz and subsequently in the City Museum of Zwickau. In his early period he painted with a consistent precision of detail associated with "Magic Realism." The social criticism contained in his pictures of miners made them suspect to the Nazi regime, and for that reason he was not permitted to exhibit again until 1945. With the change of the social system that followed 1945, Mayerl's painting underwent a transformation in style. The depressive mood and the sombre symbolism of his pictures gave way to a more positive manner of representation. The meticulous veracity of detail was abandoned in favour of more generously sweeping brushwork, without varnish. Mayerl's painting can easily be linked historically with the socially critical realism of progressive proletarian art in the twenties and thirties. *G. C.*

these gifted folk artists, since he fused the traditional canons of folk painting with his own individual style. The artist was born in the small provincial Volga town of Gorodets. His father, a dyer who ran his own establishment, coloured wooden domestic utensils much in the traditional style of folk painting. After gaining a notion of the "three R's" at the local parish school, the boy was despatched to his uncle, also a dyer with his own workshop, in the village of Kurtsevo, where many gifted artisans lived. Fascinated by paints, chapbooks and popular broadsheets, the boy began to contrive his own pictures, learning the

Mazin, Ignatii Andreievich: Nursery

Mazin, Ignatii Andreievich: Working in the Old Days

MAYORGA, PABLO (1955)   Nicaragua

Pablo Mayorga, a farmer born in Solentiname, began drawing as a child. Many of his stylised animal drawings decorate the walls of the church in his home town. Later in life he took up painting. Of all the artists in Solentiname, he has the most distinctive personal style. Mayorga also carves in wood, which he paints once the work is finished. He has exhibited in the USA, Costa Rica, Germany and several times in Nicaragua. *E. C.*

MAZIN,   USSR
IGNATIJ ANDREEVIČ (1876—1941)
MAZIN, IGNATII ANDREIEVICH

Mazin, like many other Russian peasant painters of the Volga region, was discovered in the mid-1920s, conspicuous even then among

craft and designs from Varvara Konovalova, one of his uncle's employees and daughter of the well-known master of ornamental design, Sidor Konovalov. In those days a common article which local craftsmen loved to adorn before taking to market was the distaff. Besides serving a practical purpose, it also had a ritual meaning in that it was usually chosen as a present from father to daughter upon her wedding or as a gift from groom to bride, and seen as symbolising wishes of good fortune and prosperity. Mazin also engaged in the embellishment of distaffs, manifesting, however, a distinct preference for non-traditional festive scenes of bustling wharves, river paddle-steamers, wedding feasts, gipsy choirs, fairs and carnivals and bear-tamers with their muzzled beasts. His characters are always fashionably garbed and coiffeured, dandyish and flirtatious, attracted to the urban *dolce vita*. In his pictures Mazin tells a story, dividing the design — as in a broadsheet or in a comic, for that matter — into a series of episodes, accompanied by such explanatory remarks as "Mazin having his first party," "Mazin listening to the priest at school," or "Mazin with his wife." Figures are flat, disposed exclusively in the foreground, and always look out at the viewer with kind intent. Depicting, in his early period, sailors, nannies with their small charges, grannies, fashion-plates and members of the Old Believers' breakaway sect, and, in more recent times, farm team leaders, Red cavalrymen, toy-makers,

Mazin, Ignatii Andreievich: Children Playing with Dolls in Olden Times

nursery-school tutors and children wearing the red Young Pioneer tie, he invariably selected the more beautiful and impressive aspects. These pictures conclusively demonstrate how the imagery, conventionality and immediacy of the colour characteristics of the old peasant art, no longer associated with a specific domestic article such as the distaff, were affected by *fin-de-siècle* urban aesthetic tastes, with their penchant for what was thought attractive and pretty. Like his fellow Volga folk painters, Mazin also turned to the picture and panel proper. Whenever he depicted contemporary subjects, the characteristic features of naive realism and an immediacy of vision are especially manifest in a manner untypical of peasant art. In 1927 Mazin was invited to Nizhni Novgorod (now Gorki), whose museum commissioned him to adorn distaff brakes with pictures of the Russian national wedding ritual. These pieces were subsequently exhibited at a show at the Institute of the History of the Arts in Leningrad. In his declining years Mazin painted a series of panels for museums in Moscow and in Zagorsk, a monastery town sixty kilometres from the Soviet capital, and also for the station of the children's railway in Gorki. Thus, in 1933 he executed a series of panels for the Zagorsk Museum of Toys.

Only in the 1930s was Mazin first noticed and described as representative of the folk arts and crafts. However, today one can scarcely regard Mazin's output as fully in the folk tradition.

Mazin's works have been displayed time and again at various exhibitions of peasant folk arts and crafts and have been reproduced in art books. *(See portrait of the artist, p. 446). N. Sh.*

MAZUR, FRANK (1910)   USA

Frank Mazur, born in Lozowa in the Ukraine, never anticipated when he emigrated to the USA in 1921 that he would become an artist. He worked for most of his life as a taxi driver, living alone in Brooklyn. Suddenly, deeply moved by the 1967 Six Days War in Israel, he felt a need to "do something" and began to study Hebrew, in the hope of visiting Israel some day. He also enrolled in a painting class in the Brooklyn Museum Art School. "As to what made me interested in the fine arts, that is a mystery, unexplainable, because I do not know myself." Not

Mazur, Frank: The Wailing Wall

satisfied with the painting class, Mazur joined a sculpture class under Toshio Odate, who recognised immediately the primitive strength latent in Mazur's work and let him create freely.

Mazur's work is qualitatively different from that of other naives who concentrate on religious themes because it derives from such a personal identification with the history of his people, while that of other artists is often, in a sense, a "memory copy" of established iconography. Mazur was at first extremely emotional and shy about his work, but after two one-man shows and twelve group shows, he is both proud and modest. However, he continues to work with the same fervour and his pieces have become larger and more powerful. He works primarily in wood and stone, though he has done some terra cotta pieces. *(See portrait of the artist, p. 446). J. W.*

McCarthy, Justin: Ava Gardner

failing to pass the bar examination, never practised. He began to paint in 1920, thus releasing an urge harboured from his visit to the Louvre. In the meantime, he earned his living in diverse ways, and during the last thirty years of his life raised and sold vegetables. He never married.

When he was seventy he began to supplement his income through the sale of his paintings. In 1960 he displayed some of his work at an outdoor art show in Stroudsburg, Pennsylvania, and through a felicitous coincidence was found by Dorothy and Sterling Strauser, themselves artists and devotees of naive and folk art. The Strausers, who are also dealers, persuaded McCarthy to "go professional," and since then his work has won prizes, has been included in museum shows, and is now in a number of collections.

McCarthy's paintings have something of a stylistic resemblance to German Expressionists, and in addition to his Paris memories, were inspired by films, television, illustrations from magazines and newspaper stories. He called himself a "painter of the human form," and claimed, "I paint for money, period. I paint what I can sell. I have no message." Even so, he manifested a highly personal, unconsciously ironical vision of life and its theatrical events, expressing it with bright colours, thickly applied to canvases crowded with figures. *J. W.*

McCarthy, Justin: George Washington Crossing the Delaware

McCARTHY, JUSTIN (1892—1981)   USA

Justin McCarthy was born in Weatherly, Pennsylvania. He was the son of a well-to-do newspaper executive, from whom he inherited the stone mansion on a 17-acre estate where he was brought up and lived until his death. After a trip to Paris when still in his teens, he entered the University of Pennsylvania to study law, but,

McCLAREN, SYDNEY (1895—1979)   Jamaica

Sydney McClaren died on 11 October 1979, at the age of 84, in Morant Bay, Jamaica, near where he was born, only days before he was to receive the national award of Officer of the Order of Distinction. At the time, he was represented by eleven works, paintings and sculptures, in a major exhibition, "The Intuitive Eye," mounted by the National Gallery of Jamaica and devoted mainly to Jamaican naive artists, among whom McClaren had earned a very special place. His artistic career spanned a period of over twenty years, but his rise to national prominence came only in the last decade of his life. Among the other exhibitions in which he participated were those devoted to self-taught artists at the Institute of Jamaica between 1970 and 1977, the exhibition of West Indian Art at the OAS in Washington in 1972, "Eight Jamaican Primitives" in Havana, in 1976, and the Annual National Exhibitions at the Gallery of Jamaica in 1977 and 1978.

McClaren, Sydney: Creative Imagination

His paintings, nearly all of which are delightful depictions of well-known or easily recognisable street scenes in Kingston and other Jamaican towns, are a joy to behold: full of action, with great attention to detail and with a purity of vision one might expect from a child. Besides being aesthetically pleasing and fairly precise records of the way things were, they leave the viewer little doubt about how McClaren felt about his country and his fellow-men.

The following passages are excerpts from his autobiography, written in 1978: "I, Sydney McClaren, born at Spring Garden, St. Thomas, on the 18th March 1895, in the Year of Our Lord, reached 6th Grade in Primary School. After leaving school, I went to learn the Coach Building Trade. After finishing, motor cars started to come into the island. The owners of carriages put them away, and got motor cars in their place. The trade that I learned did not have any use to me, so I started to do some farming on my father's little plot of land.

"In the yard in which I was living, one day I took a bit of cardboard and pencil and started to draw the house, trees, fencing, etc. After showing it around, people praised it, so I was more interested and discovered that my mental faculties started to work by my concentrating on Art.

"Then my motives drove me to action, and without a teacher I found myself doing the 'Fine Arts' Drawings and Paintings." *T. R.*

MEHKEK, MARTIN (1936)   Yugoslavia

Martin Mehkek was born in the village of Novačka, Croatia, where he went to elementary school. When he was eight, his father died and

Mehkek had to do a man's work, as is the custom in the farming areas.

Marrying in 1955, he moved to his wife's village of Gola, where he still lives. At present he divides his time between tilling the soil and painting, for which he was given incentive by Ivan Večenaj, the well-known naive painter from Gola.

His first works manifest a primordial power. In these early paintings, rigid and rough, he portrayed woodcutters and troughmakers. Both man and the wood he cuts down or works are strong and sinewy. Particularly impressive are

Mehkek, Martin: The Servant

his later works, such as "Woman with Candle" and "Man with Cat." Lovingly, but unsentimentally, he has immortalised the poor and insignificant men and women who inhabit the world unnoticed.

Later, Mehkek concentrated on two subjects graved in his memory from his childhood: village servants and gipsies.

Village servants are usually placed in a winter setting, when their life is more miserable than in other seasons. Their suffering and prematurely wrinkled faces are seen against open spaces, often at sunset, when bare branches, snow-covered houses and birds borne by the wind stand out against the ruddy sky. As a boy, Mehkek had spent much time with gipsies in their tents and twig huts, and was especially fond of watching the gipsy women smoking clay pipes and exhaling large smoke circles. The scene was all the more fascinating for the boy because village women of that time never even dreamed of smoking, for doing so would have put them on a par with the gipsy women.

In his earlier paintings, Mehkek fashioned a gallery of profound psychological portraits. His later ones are less poetic and some of them even seem like masks from which no inner life radiates. Since he had limited himself to two themes, stylisation and repetition set in as time passed, undercutting his originality.

He has had one-man shows and participated in group exhibitions at home and abroad. *N. T.*

MEIJER, SAL (1877—1965)   Netherlands

Sal Meijer may rightfully be called the father of Netherlands naive art, the counterpart of Henri Rousseau in France. It is not only that both, each in his own country, head a long column of artistic descendants, but that both were also professional painters who discovered their own road. Formally speaking, too, there are points of contact between them: Sal Meijer's flowers resemble Rousseau's, and "Easter Park" (probably dating from between 1914 and 1930), showing a warm, sun-drenched Sunday afternoon in a park full of greenery, is very similar to

diamond cutting from his uncle. In the evenings, he attended drawing school and in 1904 received a diploma and a certificate licensing him to give drawing lessons in grade school. This he never did, however (in contrast to Rousseau), but continued cutting diamonds, and from 1914 onwards supported himself as an independent artist. In the meantime, he learned engraving — for a good cutter that was probably not difficult — and was adept at selling his small engravings, mostly of Amsterdam. He also mastered many other techniques: lithography, pastels, watercolours, graphite and pencil (especially for portraits

Meijer, Sal: Toren Dyke in Amsterdam

Rousseau's treatment of the same subject, both in form and substance. It is possible, but not certain, that Meijer saw Rousseau's pictures hanging in the Municipal Museum in Amsterdam during the twenties.

Sal (Salomon) Meijer, born in Amsterdam, was fond of drawing in elementary school and did it well. When he was thirteen, he learned

of women). Although Amsterdam dominates his work, he also portrayed other towns and regions (Delft, Amersfoort, Zandvoort, Brugge, Frankfurt, Switzerland). When he moved to Blaricum in 1930, pictures began to appear of Gooia (a flat area between Hilversum and Amsterdam): villages, farms, pastures and fields. He won fame particularly for his paintings of felines, works that were presumably commissioned. Like no one else, he was able to achieve a remarkable expression in his cats.

His technique is based on drawing in layers, with a long period for drying, and on mixing oils with colourless varnish to give his paintings a slightly shiny effect. He painted in dots and lines — a technique which lends his works a quality of soft fullness.

In spite of the professional factor, Sal Meijer remained irrefutably a naive painter, unconcerned with the artistic conceptions of his own time or the past and retaining his own poetic

Mejia Godoy, Armado: Cockfight

vision, transmitted to his works with great virtuosity. But his point of departure was always the visible world. He had an eye for the details of everyday life, although he invested the reality he saw with the magical force of visual enchantment. Sal Meijer died in Blaricum. *(See portrait of the artist, p. 447). N. E.*

MEJIA GODOY, ARMADO (1946)   Nicaragua
Armado Mejia Godoy was born in Somoto, a small town in the north of Nicaragua. As an agronomist, he has been in regular contact with villages and peasants. He has also participated in work on archeological excavations. After making the acquaintance of the naive painter Manuel Garcia in 1972, he also began to paint. In Somoto, Armado founded a painters' workshop, attended by peasants and craftsman from the surrounding area. He himself paints small towns, the backwardness of inaccessible areas, woodcutting in the forests and so on. Armado took part in the underground struggle of the Sandinista Front and as a result had to flee to Costa Rica. There his painting became invested with an even more candidly political substance. Since the liberation, he has been painting battles once waged in his area, the entry of the guerrillas into the villages and similar scenes. *(See portrait of the artist, p. 446). E. C.*

MEJO, OSCAR DE (1911)   USA
Oscar de Mejo, a musician and painter born in Trieste and now living in New York, hovers on

the border between spontaneous pictorial expression and a self-conscious naivety. He began to draw when he was sixteen; since 1949 he has been painting professionally and exhibiting his work.

The figures in his paintings are reminiscent of woodcuts: "Farewell to Elba" (1970), "Mazzini in Prison" and "Women's Lib" (painted in 1979 and reproduced here) show a sense of emotional involvement and a talent for the articulation of tragic and tragi-comic situations.

In his grotesque inversion of the radical demands of the women's movement, the painter

Mejo, Oscar de: Women's Lib

shows the male as disarmed and vanquished. The domineering lady, with her huge violet-feathered hat and a violet and white frilled costume in the style of the *fin de siècle*, stands in a victorious posture, straddling her former lord and master. The man in the top-hat and tail-coat, typical of the middle class, lies spread-eagled beneath her feet. What the scene offers is a dubious interpretation of history. However, the rigid poses and the mask-like expression of the faces suggest to the spectator that he should not take too seriously the popularly humorous implications of the scene. *O. B.-M.*

MELIAŠVILI, IVAN (1896) USSR
MELIASHVILI, IVAN

Ivan Meliashvili was born in the Georgian village of Tianeti and orphaned at the age of fourteen, when an epidemic struck down the entire village, including his parents, who were poor peasants. He made his way to Tbilisi and had four years of schooling. When the First World War broke out he was called up. In his younger years he travelled extensively, hiking throughout Georgia and seeing much of Tbilisi and its environs. He married late in life, at the age of sixty-nine, as he had not had the time or the

MENTRUP, ANNA (1913) West Germany

Anna Mentrup, born in Wanne-Eickel, now lives in Herne. She had a hard time in her youth, first on a farm and then as the mother in a miner's family. Now a grandmother, she has forgotten her tribulations and likes to return in memory to the rustic idyll of her youth or to Germany's "Black Country" in the closing years of the last century. Her pictures are always serene, although the social conditions in which miners lived then were anything but rosy. But from the combination of reality and creative imagination there emerge works of art which

Meliashvili, Ivan: The Poet Vazha Pshavela with Family

Mentrup, Anna: Windmill on a Pond

resources before. For sixty years he was nightwatchman at a Tbilisi kindergarten, where he saw the children drawing and felt impelled to do the same. Though old and living on a pension, he continues to work. Completely deaf, he could not explain when he first began to paint. However, his manner shows that he began long ago. He paints in oil on canvas or draws with crayons on paper, taking his subjects from nature, from photographs and his imagination.

Meliashvili's formative environment was similar to that of Pirosmani, and, like the latter, he addresses himself to national art; he is obviously familiar with ancient Georgian mosaics and their technique, as for instance, in his "Queen Tamar" and "Vazha Pshavela with Family." His Paliashvili opera pictures likewise indicate a knowledge of the Georgian miniature. He reveals features of children's art in the patches of colour and in the almost complete integration of the composition with the surface of the canvas, yet his imagery is characteristic of an adult mind. He invests his characters with an air of patriarchal mores. However, his art is in a different category — rather an outpouring of naive talent betraying an affinity with other modern naives, such as Lolishvili.

Meliashvili was represented at a group republican show in Tbilisi in 1974. Some works are on view at that city's museum of Georgian Folk Arts; recently the State Museum of Arts of Georgia acquired several of his paintings. *(See portrait of the artist, p. 447). N. Sh.*

obey the special laws devised by Anna Mentrup. A fondness for symmetry, a leaning toward systematic order and a reduction of flowers and trees to elementary forms: these are obvious features. All of them are imbued with her predilection for strict accuracy, achieved with constantly resharpened crayons. With these she patiently covers the surface of her pictures, line by line. *T. G.*

MESSINGER, MENACHEM (1898) Israel

Menachem Messinger was born in Poland, the son of the beadle of the local synagogue. At eleven he was carving walking sticks in order to help his mother make a living. In his youth he played the violin and the mandolin, wrote poetry and participated in his *stetl's* Yiddish theatre. He came with his family to Palestine in 1932, and worked at odd jobs until he finally set up a sauna in Haifa in 1963. He began to paint when he was nearly seventy, using gouache on paper. He has also produced silk-screens, and recently tapestries were made of his work. His subject-matter ranges from stories of the Bible to Jewish history, geography, current events, and religious and national symbols. He combines flat areas with others drawn in perspective, and uses brilliant colours. His brushstrokes are bold and expressionistic in character. His paintings possess a traditional, ornamental quality, reminiscent of synagogue decorations in Eastern Europe. *(See portrait of the artist, p. 447). R. D.*

→

METELLI, ORNEORE (1872—1939)   **Italy**

Orneore Metelli was born in Terni. After learning the craft of shoemaker from his father, he began to help him run his shop. Industrious and possessed of an innate sense of beauty, the young man soon became an excellent shoe designer, taking part in many Italian and international exhibitions, receiving prizes, diplomas and gold medals.

At the international exhibition in Paris in 1911, his designs were so good that they were withdrawn from the competition and he was appointed a member of the jury. But Orneore

Messinger, Menachem: Birds (detail)

Metelli, Orneore: The Venus of Terni

Metelli, Orneore: Procession in Collescipoli

was not satisfied with being a shoe designer and nothing more. Always a lover of music, he played first trombone with the municipal orchestra for many years.

In 1922, when he was fifty, an age when the paths of a man's life are already ordained and he continues along them out of habit, Metelli felt the need to satisfy his love of beauty by trying his hand at painting, without any object except to amuse himself. Little by little, he became a faithful interpreter of the peaceful life of the small town where he lived, of its atmosphere and interesting customs.

Usually, as one of his biographers states, he painted in the evenings, after a day spent working at the shoemaker's craft. The fact that he worked by the light of a powerful lamp explains the special quality of his colours, which tend to cool tones, giving his compositions a rarified and almost metaphysical atmosphere.

In composition, too, his paintings are precise and not without their carefully reconstructed details, although his main endeavour is directed to getting to the crux of the matter — to the basic features of, say, a cityscape, albeit naive in vision. As was cleverly noted by L. Bigiaretti in a short essay in 1957, Metelli conceived a rather unusual theory that "permits the shadows of objects to fall only where they do not upset the composition."

Metelli remained insensitive to all classical influences although, as Bigiaretti says, he sometimes tried his hand at copies, to which he always added something of his own — some impulse, some bold innovation — as, for instance, when he made Giorgione's "Storm" even stormier by copying it from a postcard.

"How Quiet!" and "My Self-portrait" may be considered typical examples of his work as a

In "My Self-portrait," Metelli presents himself in an oval characteristic of the 19th century; he is dressed in the uniform of a bandsman with decorative buttons on his jacket, in keeping with a position the artist proudly flaunts.

The "provincial" Metelli was as proud of his skilful designing of elegant shoes as he was of his trombone playing; often on his canvases next to his signature, a small pair of boots can be seen — sometimes a man's, at other times a woman's. He died without completing his last painting, symbolically entitled "Departure from the Theatre." *(See portrait of the artist, p. 446). D. M.*

Metelli, Orneore: Blessing Animals

painter and of his simple psychology. The former captures the feeling of pregnant silence associated with action: seminary students in pairs are out walking and must, even then, strictly respect the law of silence; in a pale and subdued light the monastery closes the horizon and only a donkey, accompanied by a peasant, injects a different note into the serene atmosphere.

MICHAŁOWSKA, MARTA (1900—1971)   Poland

Marta Michałowska was born in Romanów, the daughter of a landowning family. She worked as a sister of mercy in a hospital during the First World War and there met a wounded Russian prisoner-of-war with whom she fell in love. As he was a painter, she started painting alongside him. But her parents soon broke up their idyll

Michałowska, Marta: Portrait of Mother

Michelis, Effie: Square in Heraklion

'Middle Art': The Manager in Charge

and married her against her will to a Polish officer. With her husband, she moved from one garrison to another. After the Second World War, left alone with her daughters when her husband remained in England, she went to live in Lublin, eastern Poland. After she had brought up her children and had more time for herself, she went back to painting (in 1959). Usually she painted at night — dream landscapes, imaginary worlds. She had her first one-woman show in Gdańsk in 1961. Her paintings have been on display in many exhibitions of Polish naive art in Poland and abroad and are contained in the collections of the State Ethnographic Museum in Warsaw and particularly in the collection of L. Zimmerer in Warsaw. *(See portrait of the artist, p. 446). A. J.*

MICHELIS, EFFIE (1906—1984)   **Greece**

Effie Michelis was born in Athens. She studied art by visiting many museums and art galleries in Europe and the USA and also attended courses and lectures on various aspects of art and aesthetics. Traditional Greek architecture, represented by beautifully drawn and sensitively coloured houses or churches, plays an essential role in the majority of her pictures; these are never merely postcard-like views of tourist sites, but have the specific features of an individual style marked by simplicity and clarity. An illuminating account of her approach was given by the artist herself: "In my paintings I do not set things down as I actually see them, but as I know them to be. I avoid shadows, I enlarge what seems to me more important, and reduce what I feel to be secondary. All this of course occurs unconsciously, for when I paint I never think."

"MIDDLE ART" (AUGUSTIN OKOYE)   Nigeria

Born in Nri, Middle Art is now living and working in Onitsha, Nigeria. His true name is Augustin Okoye; Middle Art is the name he has chosen for himself. Although with no art training, Middle Art found that he could earn his living as a designer of posters, an occupation he was pursuing even before the Biafran War, after the termination of which he returned home to find that his property had been sequestered.

Something of his poster design techniques can be seen in "Suffering Stages of Life" (a kind of strip cartoon which takes his existence from

"Middle Art": Suffering Stages of Life

Michelis has had one-woman shows in Greece and elsewhere and taken part in many exhibitions abroad. Since 1952 she has participated in all Panhellenic exhibitions and in other group exhibitions in Athens and other parts of Greece. In 1975 she showed her works in the large exhibition of naive painting entitled "Die Kunst der Naiver" in Munich, and in the World Salon of Naive Painting in Paris.

Works by the artist are in the collections of the National Gallery, Athens, the Municipal Gallery of Athens, the Municipal Galleries of Thessalonike, Argos, Kalamata, Rhodes, Ioannina, the Ministry of Education, the Ministry of Culture and Sciences, the Bank of Greece, the Henri Rousseau Museum of Naive Art, Laval, France, and other collections. Her paintings have been awarded medals and prizes in Athens, Paris, Madrid, Istanbul, among other centres.

(See portrait of the artist, p. 446). A. T.

the time of the war until the present day). This is not an uncommon method of picture-making in Africa. One has only to recall the story-telling works of Ethiopia (past and present), which, in their own way, relate in infinite detail and frequently with many "pictures within a picture" an even more complex series of events than those encompassed in the life of Middle Art. Such artists as he are in fact continuing an ancient tradition of multi-situational picture-making which was certainly well established in Europe during the period of the great illuminated manuscripts.

But Middle Art is not a naive in the true sense. After the Biafran War he fell in with the European Ulli Beier at whose Institute of African Studies in Ife he was encouraged to broaden his poster art activities to the point where he was making pictures instead of posters. *(See portrait of the artist, p. 446). Sh. W.*

MIHUŢ, PETRU (1927) **Romania**

Petru Mihuţ was born in the village of Brusturi, in the commune of Hălmagiu in the district of Arad, where he worked as a miner.

Mihuţ began painting after meeting Ion Nita Nicodim, who exerted an obvious influence on many of the painters in that area. The ties between Nicodim and Mihuţ became even closer after the marriage of their children (Rodica Mihuţ-Nicodim has also been painting since 1973). Mihuţ has succeeded in finding his own individual style, accepting only certain features typical of the painters of the village of Brusturi.

Mihuţ, Petru: Making Jam

Petru Mihuţ registers every ostensibly banal moment of life as though it were a holiday, transforming ordinary events into real folk festivals, with the participation of people, animals, birds — in fact, of all nature ("With the Livestock at Pasture," "Making Jam").

Typical of his work is a refined feeling for composition and decoration, a happy intermeshing of balanced forms and an explosive abundance of colours, permitting him to reach exceptional artistic heights, especially in his later works.

Many paintings (oil on canvas) with a historical theme ("The Surrender of the Turkish Banner") or a moralising content ("Heaven and Hell"), have been shown with increasing frequency in exhibitions of naive art in Romania. They exemplify the achievement of this artist, who is the winner of a number of national awards and is also well-known abroad; he has taken part in group exhibitions of naive art in India, Canada, Egypt, France and other countries. *(See portrait of the artist, p. 447). M. Il.*

MILLÁN, CARMEN (1915?) **Venezuela**

Carmen Millán was born in Clarines, Anzóategui, between 1915 and 1920. She began painting seriously in about 1950 under the tutelage of her husband, a well-known naive painter, Victor Millán.

Carmen Millán works with her husband — a rarity in naive painting — and shares with him a great sense of creativity and imagination, although their paintings differ radically. Victor uses vivid colours and generally defines his figures against an intricate background, while Carmen shows a preference for neutral colours and massive figures interwoven in a tight composition. *J. G. S.*

MILLÁN, VICTOR (1919) **Venezuela**

Victor Millán was born in Punta de Araya in the province of Sucre. With Feliciano Carvallo, Millán founded an art centre for "marginal" art in Mare Abajo (1959). He has been described as a "true man of the coast," very outgoing and always prepared to promote the interests of naive art,

Millán, Carmen: Women

not only for himself but for all Venezuelan artists in this field.

Millán's works are immensely popular (in both senses), perhaps because of their clear imagery. There is an element of showmanship in his art, as seen in the painting of "Adam and Eve" illustrated here. *Sh. W.*

MILLER, ANTHONY (1914) **Great Britain**

Anthony Miller, born in Stockport has been confined to hospital since the age of six. A natural artist, he has sight in only one eye. His experience of the world about him has been limited to three areas — everything below the level of the television set on the hospital wall, what he sees in television programmes, and what he sees on his few expeditions outside the hospital walls. Miller can neither read nor write, but these failings are amply compensated for by

Millán, Victor: The Jungle

Miller, Anthony: Bedroom

Millán, Victor: Adam and Eve

his inspired draughtsmanship (which, however different, can remind one of the drawing of the Pole Nikifor). Using, like Wallis and Dixon, whatever comes to hand, he makes his pictures on scraps of hardboard or pieces of cardboard from old shoe-boxes.

Generally, Miller lets his images take form from a mass of light pencil lines filled in with soft watercolour tinting — again in a manner reminiscent of Nikifor. With this technique he is able to achieve remarkable — even dramatic — effects of light. "Going to the Lights," a scene of urban sprawl and congested traffic lanes, is a good example of this remarkable facility. But sometimes he also uses deep and luminous colours, as in the wholly imaginary "Bedroom," painted from a rich, warm palette.

Miller's pictures have been shown in a number of mixed exhibitions, as well as in five RONA exhibitions. *Sh. W.*

MILLER, LOUISA (1906) USA
Louisa Miller was born in Glenbeulah, Wisconsin. In 1972 she gave the bulk of her paintings, which were done between 1944 and 1968, to Viterbo College, a Catholic institution in La Crosse, Wisconsin. She did so (she explained during a telephone interview in 1973) not only to help the college but because she was worried

Miller, Louisa: Boy in Blue   Milts, Elfrida Martsovna: Bird Market in Trubnaya Place in Moscow

about the possibility the pictures might be hijacked ("There's an awful lot of that!") and smuggled out ("That's illegal!"). She donated the works with the proviso that the school should not sell them one by one but only as "one piece," for to do otherwise would "spoil the whole meaning of folk art"; they were "there for the children who never see real painting." She remarked, "There's thirty years work there," and said she no longer painted.

Mrs. Miller, who lives in a rural area near Augusta, Wisconsin, did not explain what motivated her to begin to paint at the age of thirty-eight, nor why she suddenly decided to stop, except that she had her garden and her cats to take care of. Her paintings seem to be primarily either biographical in content or else vehicles for memories of her childhood and youth. *J. W.*

MILOJEVIĆ, DOBROSAV (1948) Yugoslavia
Dobrosav Milojević was born in Donje Štiplje, near Svetozarevo, Serbia. After finishing his elementary schooling, he remained on the family farm. In 1971, he began painting, his

incentive being the example of the painter Milan Rašić, whose style he initially imitated. He later moved to Svetozarevo, where he now lives and devotes himself exclusively to painting. His themes are taken from nature and Serbian village life. Milojević approaches his subject-matter optimistically, painting the village in gay colours and showing the peasants dancing or courting. A humorous note frequently informs his work. Asked how he selects his colours, he says: "I used to tend sheep, and if there were fifty in the flock not all of them were white. Some were black or spotted. If real sheep can differ in colour, those in my paintings can differ too. I also paint other things in colours that seem suitable. Sometimes I simply use the colours I have at hand. The main thing is for the painting to come out looking nice." In "The Goats" (1973), Milojević placed a monastery in the foreground and his village in the background. In fact, there is no monastery, but he has put one there to make the village more beautiful. Dobrosav Milojević has had one-man shows and participated in group exhibitions at home and abroad. *(See portrait of the artist, p. 447). N. T.*

MIL'TS, USSR
EL'FRIDA MARTSOVNA (1903—1974)
MILTS, ELFRIDA MARTSOVNA
E. M. Milts, a Lett, moved to Moscow with her parents in her childhood and lived there all her life. After high school she worked as an accountant. During the Second World War she cut timber and did other war work. Her personal life was closely interwoven with that of the city she had loved since childhood. In her girlhood she had spent some time at an art studio,

learning the fundamentals of painting and drawing, but in the evening of her life she adhered to a style of her own, even though she attended ZNUI, the Extra-mural People's University of Art. Her example is in its way an answer to that question which has always exercised the minds of art critics: whether underivative artists should be given instruction or not. At any rate her teacher, B. N. Otarov, always gave her every encouragement in her effort to express everything she remembered or that excited her. Thanks to his tactful attitude and understanding of her artistic gifts, she was able to preserve her

Milojević, Dobrosav: Goats Around the Monastery

underivative individuality of manner. Her work is extremely sincere and artless. She preferred to depict the Moscow of the past as she remembered it from childhood or as it is seen on popular broadsheets — more specifically, old-time Moscow mores and urban scenes, and also architecture, as, for instance, "The Bolshoi," "The Rumyantsev Library" (now the Lenin Library), "Kozlov Lane," and "Trubnaya Bird Market." She tried to convey on cardboard, paper or canvas events she had experienced, heard or read about, or seen in picture-books. The result was a naive, almost childlike style, blended with the wisdom of experience. Her compositions are intricately ornamented decorations on a flat plane with carefully delineated detail. Her colour range creates a definite rhythm not infrequently in harmony with classical Russian architecture. Her practice was first to make a pencil drawing and then paint it, treating every element as of identical importance. The architecture she depicted is lace-like, expressing her fondness for embroidery and delicate needlework. Many of her works bear inscriptions — which is typical of folkloric artists — such as "In our yard we had a

janitor named Maxim. Today his son Ivan Maximovich is a factory manager who has been decorated with an order," or "The house in which I live is most handsome." In 1973 she had a solo exhibition at ZNUI, the Extra-mural People's University of Arts. *N. Sh.*

MIRONOVA, USSR
ELIZAVETA FEDOROVNA (1929)
MIRONOVA, YELIZAVETA FYODOROVNA

Y. F. Mironova was born in the Ukrainian village of Soshniki, south of Kiev. She lost her

Mironova, Yelizaveta Fyodorovna: The Cossack Mamai

peasant father at an early age. Like every Ukrainian country girl she learned to embroider and to decorate cottage walls for holidays. However, after she moved to Kiev, her approach changed. She now paints mostly in gouache on paper or cardboard. Though she is no longer a peasant artist who both farms and paints from necessity (today she is a member of the USSR Union of Artists), some critics relegate her work to the category of peasant popular art, while others class it with amateur art. Despite the folklore mentality which it expresses, her work, like that of many similar artists, is distinct from traditional popular art since it contains an element of urban culture. As she started with decorative compositions rooted in Ukrainian cottage wall-painting, she displays a characteristic *penchant* for filling the entire surface of the sheet of paper or cardboard with ornament. Her flowers (flat and with few petals) are reminiscent of the well-known Ukrainian wild flower — the mallow. She often introduces figures of human beings, birds and beasts. She also depicts old legends and customs in paintings peopled by dignified characters shown full-face. Her compositional arrangements are often symmetrical, with horses or birds ranged along the sides of a tree, reminiscent of old icon composition of canonical embroidery. Not infrequently she adds inscriptions associated with Ukrainian folklore and ballads. The artist has also been commissioned to illustrate children's books. She has had many one-woman shows. Since 1963 she has been represented at all republican and USSR exhibitions of both popular and professional art. Her paintings have been exhibited abroad on many occasions. *(See portrait of the artist, p. 447).* N. Sh.

MITRĂCHIŢĂ, GHIŢĂ (1904) Romania

A peasant and former member of a farming cooperative, now retired, Ghiţă Mitrăchiţă was born in the commune of Bîrca, district of Dolj. Before the war he tried to find employment in various trades in Bucharest and Craiova. In 1965 he began painting.

When working on a historical subject, Mitrăchiţă resembles the tellers of folk tales who, in recounting a legend, take from it only certain details from which the other parts naturally follow and become clear. For instance, in the painting "Mihail the Bold and the Turks", the artist is not concerned with the verisimilitude of the Ottoman soldiers' clothing, but he does not forget that the Romanian commander was left-handed and depicts him holding his weapon in his left hand.

Done in oil on cardboard, the works of Ghiţă Mitrăchiţă have been on display in international

Mitrăchiţă, Ghiţă: Peasant Wedding in Oltenia

His paintings depict, on one and the same canvas, scenes from two worlds: the Romanian village as it was before the Second World War and the modern village. Obviously the painter is endeavouring, by this comparison, to point out the basic differences between the two ways of life.

Even when this method of contrast is not used in the painting itself, it is present in the verse composed by the painter and inscribed in a space on the composition, thus becoming one of its component parts.

Perhaps more than other Romanian naive artists, Mitrăchiţă reflects the direct influence of folk art: the use of patterns, of decorative chromatic rhythms; the total organisation of space; the narrative and sometimes even declamatory unfolding of action.

group exhibitions (in Italy, Switzerland, Argentina, Mexico, India and Sweden) and in one-man shows in Romania. *M. Il.*

MITRAKAS, YANNIS (1936) Greece

Yannis Mitrakas was born in Provatona, Soufli, Thrace; he now lives in Aliveri on Evvoia, one of Greece's major islands. He made his first pictorial investigations in historical and genre painting with a symbolic content; he has subsequently proceeded to the creation of the austere, monumental figures that are the distinguishing feature of his work. These are today's "Saints"— the supporters and at the same time the victims of contemporary society. Typical examples of these are the ascetic coalminers of Aliveri, their expressive faces reflecting their psychology and their helmets sometimes transformed into haloes; the sea-captain's wife patiently awaiting her beloved; the sailors and the immigrants, and also the farmers toiling in the fields.

Mitrakas is well acquainted with the secrets of Byzantine hagiography; at the same time he is able to give a very personal expression to his reflections and social criticism. His style is a mixture of neo-Byzantine and folk elements. His egg-temperas are marked by clear and somewhat hard outlines; these, together with the dark and rather limited scale of colours, emphasise the seriousness of the themes, focusing attention on

their deeper meaning and not on their decorative qualities. The purpose of his painting is not to entertain but to express a deeply personal concern with the sorrows and problems of society he lives in. The inscriptions in Byzantine script which are often added to the pictures summarise their meaning with a militant and critical intent. His latest work consists of highly expressive portraits and pictures of wild flowers grouped with simple everyday objects. The faces of his figures are harassed by everyday problems, but they never lose hope; on the other hand, the flowers become symbols of relaxation.

Mitrakas, Yannis: The Saints of the Underground

Mitrakas, Yannis: Lost Fatherland

Moke Art P.: Bandundu

Mitrakas has organised a number of one-man shows in Athens and in various Greek towns; in 1982 he was awarded a Ministry of Culture and Sciences prize for the painting "Lost Fatherland," illustrated here, and exhibited at the Municipal Library in Chalkis. *A. T.*

MOKE ART P. (1950)   Zaire
Born in Ibe, Bandunda, Moke follows a familiar pattern for naives who come either from countries which the so-called sophisticated world dubs "new" or from older nations still caught in the toils of a backward and not very prosperous economy. A brief glance at his first encounter with "art" makes this abundantly clear. On a visit to Kinshasa in 1963, when he was only thirteen, he came upon a market in the Place du 27 Octobre which was doing a roaring picture trade with tourists. This direct trading fascinated him, and at the same time he was able to lay hands on some discarded paint tins which were virtually empty but contained just enough pigment to catch the fancy of a boy who now decided that he wanted to paint. With a palette conjured up from these finds he painted his first pictures on old bits of cardboard.

From these early beginnings he eventually went on to become a full-time artist. Untutored in every sense and with an unsophisticated background, at the start he made pictures of village life and of sunsets, but after a while he tired of these subjects and turned to something more adventurous. His next group of paintings, mainly mythological in character, proved particularly successful with Europeans. It was the money from the sales of these pictures to foreigners that enabled him to purchase canvases and proper artist's oil colours. The example of his work shown here — "Bandundu" — offers a fair sample of his competence. It shows President Mobutu with his bodyguard of leopards (indicating that the President dare not enter

Hungarian fairy tales. He was loath to part with his pictures and so, in the forties, took a job painting ceramic objects, which enabled him to earn his livelihood and to remain free.

At the exhibition "Naive Art in the 20th Century" in Budapest in 1972, Mokry-Mészáros' artistic achievements, reflecting his unusual view of the world, caught the attention of the public. Commemorative exhibitions were organised in 1978 in Miskolc and in the Museum of Naive Art in Kecskemét. His works are in the Budapest National Gallery, in the Herman Otto Museum in Miskolc and in Kecskemét. *M. I.*

Mokry-Mészáros, Dezsö: Life on an Alien Planet

Mokry-Mészáros, Dezsö: A Place to Stay

Bandundu without this kind of protection). Perhaps because of the traditional style of his painting and because of his "realism," Moke has had wide success as an untutored artist. *Sh. W.*

MOKRY-MÉSZÁROS,   Hungary
DEZSÖ (1881—1970)

Dezsö Mokry-Mészáros, a graduate of an agricultural college, travelled throughout Europe, Asia and Africa during his adventurous life. On the Isle of Capri he frequently met Maxim Gorky. In the primeval forests of India he collected insects for a European scientific institution. In his autobiography he mentions that in 1913, through the good offices of a Swiss zoologist, he took part in a scientific expedition to North Africa.

He began painting early in life. His inclination for the exotic was a determining factor in his choice of subject-matter. In 1905, some cells observed under a microscope served as the inspiration for a series of pictures entitled "Life on an Alien Planet." He was attracted to nature in its pristine state and to primitive peoples, and it is to this interest that one can attribute his pictures on themes from primeval times and art. In the twenties, he began making ceramic statuettes: sturdy, singular figurines with the features of oriental idols. In the thirties he painted domestic landscapes, motifs redolent of the atmosphere of

MONSIEL,   Poland
EDMUND (1897—1962)

Edmund Monsiel was born in the town of Wożuczyn, where he died. He completed four grades of elementary school and three years of teacher training school, and developed an interest in photography. At home, he acquired a healthy respect for craftsmanship, as his father was a capable itinerant cabinetmaker and his brother the same. In 1923, he opened a haberdashery shop which the Germans confiscated in 1942. Fearful of being arrested, he hid in his brother's attic in a small room, to which no daylight penetrated, and remained there until the liberation in 1944.

It was there in that attic room that he first began to paint by candlelight on small pieces of paper. First he did faces, then representations of God, and later scenes filled with hundreds of eyes.

After the war he lived all alone in a state of total self-denial, working at the weighing machine in a sugar factory. He was deeply religious and sensitive to all evil, especially immorality. In his drawings, he endeavoured to pit himself against evil and to warn mankind against it. Frequently on the back of his drawings he would write words of caution and appeal, written with pathos and in imitation of the Bible. When he died, his family did not attach any significance to the drawings he left behind. Many were destroyed, but about five hundred were preserved. A posthumous exhibition in 1963 caused a veritable artistic sensation in Cracow, and later in Warsaw. His works have been displayed on a number of occasions in Poland and abroad, and have also been reproduced. Drawings by him are in collections of the National Museum and Ethnographic Museum in Warsaw, in the Ethnographic Museum in Cracow, in the collection of L. Zimmerer, Warsaw, and in the collection of *L'art brut* in Lausanne.

(See portrait of the artist, p. 447). A. J.

cately coloured desert landscape which later inspired many of his paintings. He had a normal education and attended the University in Melbourne, where he still lives today. He began to paint in 1974, without formal training, but it was not until he had completed three years of an English honours course in 1977 that he took up full-time painting and writing. In 1979 he was awarded a Young Writers' Fellowship by the Literature Board of the Australia Council, which enabled him to work on a novel about the complexities of family life in the Melbourne suburbs.

Moore, Ross: Desert Lake

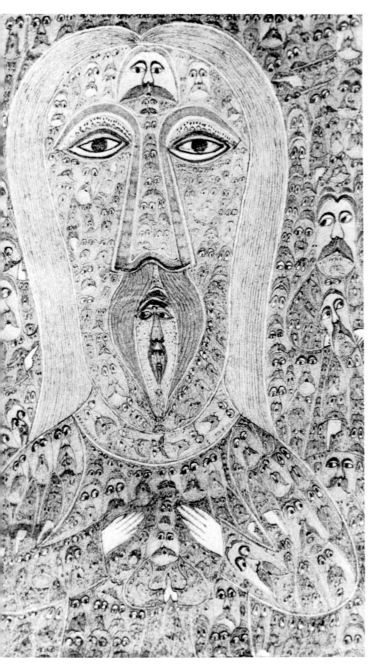

Monsiel, Edmund: God the Father

MOORE, ROSS (1954)   Australia

Ross Moore was born in Broken Hill, New South Wales, and spent his childhood there, surrounded by the strangely delicate and intri-

Moore's method of painting is to envisage a complete image in outline, draw it out and then fill in textures and colours. Because he does not work directly from reality and disregards traditional perspectives and colour relationships, his work has qualities of fantasy even when everyday objects are the subject.

His drawings and sculptures complement the paintings. He often works on three areas side by side in order to portray the same idea from different viewpoints.

In 1979 Ross Moore had an exhibition of three years' work at the Realities Gallery, Melbourne, and later he was engaged on a series of large bird paintings. He is represented in numerous private collections and in the Swan Hill Regional Gallery, Victoria. *(See portrait of the artist, p. 446). B. McC.*

MORAÏTIS, ZAPHEIRIS (1900—1979)   Greece

Zapheiris Moraïtis was born in Asia Minor and started to paint and to carve wood and stone while still a child. Together with other refugees, he went to Sarti, a village in eastern Chalcidice, Macedonia, to escape the results of the catastrophe in Asia Minor in 1922. Completely illiterate, he spent some time working in a quarry in Lavrio near Sounio, and was considered peculiar or even a little mad by his compatriots. His sculptures incorporate his own vision of the Greek national ideals and accomplishments.

His favourite heroes originate from Homer, from ancient Greek history and mythology, and from the history of the Greek Revolution against the Turks in 1821. To these stories he adds imaginary details and suitable verses. His figures are taken from illustrated primers but from these he proceeds to highly original reconstructions of compositions and of details. Some of his sculptures are granite reliefs; others have the shape of the classical Greek *heroum* (a shrine or chapel dedicated to a deified or semi-deified dead person), with figures and scenes painted in casein on their fronts, and with sculptures dec-

MORALES, ELSA (1924)   Venezuela

Elsa Morales was born in Rio Chico, where she lived for forty-five years until the first big exhibition of her paintings in the "Industrial" Art Gallery at the end of 1969. Today she lives in Caracas.

Elsa Morales, as can be seen in the accompanying illustration, is one of those Venezuelan naives dedicated to giving full play to rich, deep colour.

Where her colours do not define any outline, she fills in the missing edge in a deeper hue. (See portrait of the artist, p. 446). Sh. W.

Moraïtis, Zapheiris: Untitled

Morales, Elsa: Waiting for a Happy Day

orating their tops and sometimes their sides as well.

His figures recall western primitivism, while his monsters, with their wide-open mouths, have an accidental similarity to the gargoyles of Gothic cathedrals, and are unrelated to the medieval Greek world.

Moraïtis was virtually unknown until 1970, when he was discovered by chance by two students of archaeology. His works are to be found in the Faculty of Philosophy of the University of Thessalonike, in the archaeological museum of Thessalonike, and in private collections in Athens, Thessalonike and Paris. *A. T.*

MORENO, RAFAEL (1887)   Cuba

Rafael Moreno was born in Huelva, Spain and moved to Cuba in 1919. Before turning to painting as a means of livelihood, he followed a truly amazing variety of trades. At various times he was employed as a bricklayer, a farm labourer, and an apprentice to a bullfighter. In his colourful career he has also been in turn the proprietor of a grocer's shop, of a fruit store and even of a shooting gallery.

In 1930 Moreno went to La Playa, a small district on the outskirts of Havana which abounds in cabarets and bars noted for their typically creole atmosphere. He soon obtained employment there and, although he had no experience whatsoever in painting, he was given the job of creating murals in the various bars of the locality.

His work happened to come to the notice of Mme. Kate Perls and M. Pierre Loeb, both well-known in French art circles. Loeb decided to make Moreno his *protégé* and at once supplied him with all the necessary materials for the production of oil panels. Encouraged and stimulated by the interest taken in him, Moreno began to paint with tremendous enthusiasm and sincerity. His work "The Garden of Eden" is a masterpiece of its kind, indicating the potentialities of "popular" Cuban painting. *J. G. S.*

several newspaper stories, she had become a bride of "Our Father and Christ" when, at a call from Heaven, she took up gospel singing and street preaching many years before. "I was having a good time, going to the picture shows and I like to dance, but by and by He called me and the red light come on and I heard the voice of Jesus saying, 'Come be with me'..." She was energetic and good-humored, and her gravelly voice and original songs made her well known.

Several years ago, while not giving up her music, she did give up her street preaching when "God told me to leave the streets and find a new

Morgan, Gertrude: *Christ Is the Head of This House*

Moreno, Rafael: *Backyard in Marianao*

way to speak the Gospel..." Her "new way" was to draw and paint, depicting her sermons and thoughts on whatever material she could find at hand, including toilet paper rolls. She used the least expensive ball point pens, pencils, crayons and watercolours available, and began turning out a stream of works which corresponded to her preaching. Not content that the message should come through illustrations alone, she wrote her exhortations and biblical quotations profusely around the figures as a calligraphic background. She sold her brightly coloured, childishly primitive drawings to help maintain her one-room "mission," which was painted all white. These drawings were, almost from the very beginning, avidly collected and have been shown in several exhibitions, while Sister Gertrude has twice been the subject of documentary films on naive artists. *(See portrait of the artist, p. 446). J. W.*

MORGAN, GERTRUDE (1900—1981)   USA

Born in New Orleans, Louisiana, Gertrude Morgan, known as Sister Gertrude, was always dressed entirely in white to indicate her permanent celebration of the fact that, as she said in

MOSES, KIVETORUK (1908)   USA

Eskimo art traditions have always been centred more on bone and walrus ivory carvings than on drawings. Hence, Kivetoruk (James) Moses is an interesting deviation from tradition.

Born near Cape Espenberg, Alaska, he lived or worked in several other Alaskan communities before settling in Nome. He left school at the end of the third grade to learn the traditional Eskimo pursuits of reindeer hunting, fishing and trapping. Injured in an aeroplane accident in 1954, he began to paint — though what motivated him is not recorded. Generally, he works in pencil and Indian ink on cardboard, which he then tints with coloured pencils or watercolours and, on occasion, photograph colouring pencils. His subject-matter is almost always some historical event or his own interpretation of Eskimo folk

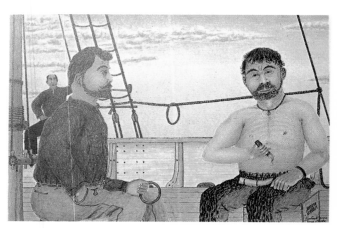

Moses, Kivetoruk: The Medicine Man and the "Cutter Bear"

tales and folklore. He is married, and his wife Bessie has acted as his secretary and assistant since his work began to sell. *J. W.*

MOTOROŽESKU, MARIORA (1928) **Yugoslavia**

Mariora Motorožesku was born in the village of Uzdin, Vojvodina, which is inhabited by ethnic Romanians. With no schooling, she does housework and farms, painting in her spare time. Her themes are the rich national costumes, life and customs of the Romanian peasant. As she began painting in 1962, she belongs to the earliest group of Romanian women peasant painters.

"I love going to exhibitions by the women of Uzdin occasionally organised in the schoolhouse," she says. "I like to see what the other women are painting, not to copy them but to enjoy their work. I have not been to any other kind of exhibitions."

Mariora Motorožesku stands out among the Uzdin painters for her composition and colours. Although all their themes are similar, her figures are, by comparison, less static, livelier and shown in movement; one feels the link between them, their communication with each other. In "Carnival Time" (1966), using a narrower palette of toned-down colours, she shows people in masks, evoking contrast and drama, the atmosphere of winter, the mystery hidden behind the masks.

Mariora Motorožesku has had one-woman shows and has participated in group exhibitions at home and abroad. *(See portrait of the artist, p. 446). N. T.*

MRAZ, FRANJO (1910—1981) **Yugoslavia**

Franjo Mraz was born in Hlebine. After his elementary schooling, he farmed until the Second World War, while at the same time heading a group of naive artists, the precursors of naive painting in Yugoslavia today. With him in the group were the now celebrated Ivan Generalić and Mirko Virius, who was killed during the war.

When twelve years old, he received a gift of watercolours; this event marked the beginning of his work as a painter, in which he persevered tirelessly until his death. "My mother once sent

Motorožesku, Mariora: Carnival Time

me to town to pay a tax. I passed by a shop window with paints and paper and bought them, as I could no longer live without them. Of course, I did not pay the tax. When my mother found out, she complained to her neighbours, who paid their taxes regularly, and they said that I would be a wanderer, never a real man. They were right about the first, and I sometimes wonder if it wouldn't have been better for me to have remained a peasant. When I went out into the field, I always carried a tablet and drew while the cows slowly pulled the cart. Sometimes it took me two hours to get to the field. During that time, I used to look around, and while the cart creaked along, I sat in it drawing, without a care in the world."

In 1931, Mraz and Generalić were guests at the exhibition of the "Earth" group in Zagreb. Five years later, Mraz founded a group of peasant painters, the first of its kind in the country, which included Generalić, Virius and later Ćaće. There followed a series of exhibitions of pictures on social themes which were frowned on by the authorities. Then came the war and painting was interrupted. Mraz was arrested but managed to jump off the train which was taking him to a concentration camp. The train stopped and enemy soldiers opened fire, while Mraz fled through corn fields. Then he joined the Partisans, with whom he remained until the end of the war. Moving to Zagreb, he took a job for a while but then went back to painting, although he never returned to his birthplace of Hlebine. (The younger Generalić did remain in Hlebine, and it was his influence that became decisive among the peasant-painters there.)

Mraz, Franjo: At the Well

Mraz, Franjo: Springtime

Mraz later moved to Belgrade, where, in a tiny room in a building set aside for academic painters, he worked for over twenty years. A few years before his death he left Belgrade and despite his advanced age (he was seventy by then) went alone and discontented to live in Dalmatia. When he died only Generalić was left of the original three famous Hlebine painters.

In his post-war work, Franjo Mraz first drew away from naive art and then went back to it again. But his eyes were forever trained on the village, on the life of the peasants whom he did not regard as strangers but as people whose feel-

deserved rest awaits them. An old woman is watering the horse. A village barnyard, an oasis of peace, is often seen in his paintings.

Franjo Mraz has had one-man shows and has participated in group exhibitions at home and abroad. *N. T.*

MUCHA, SZCZEPAN (1908)   Poland

Szczepan Mucha was born in the village of Szale, where he still lives. One of a large family that could barely eke out a living on their farm, after three years at school he began, as a young

Mucha, Szczepan: Demons

ings he shared and of whose tasks he had first-hand experience. In his paintings, the peasants seem to be talking while their faces show gladness or sorrow. As a man, he stood somewhere midway between the village and the town, and the same may be said of his painting. He could not go back to the village but could not be happy in town.

In "At the Well," as in many other paintings, Franjo Mraz expressed his nostalgia for the village. The painting is done with naive realism. With its last rays the setting sun illuminates a corner of his birth-place, Hlebine. He has arrived from the fields in a cart with his two children. Children are always welcome when farm work is in progress in the fields, because they can fetch and carry and help in many ways. A well-

boy, to work in the woods. For a number of years he was a woodcutter, then he became a sawyer and later a forester. Involved by accident in a poaching scandal in 1958, he was sentenced to six months in prison. He felt this to be an injustice, the result of an error on the part of the court. Unable to return to his forester's job, he rented a small plot of land and began raising bees. Isolated from people, he started to suffer from a feeling of fear. Around his house he built a high fence and carved human heads at the top of some of the slats. In front of his house he placed sculptures of the devil, spooks, witches, and figures of various kinds with names on them such as "spy," "scoundrel," "Herod." They were placed there because he wanted to be left in peace and also to conceal his not strictly legal practice of collecting wood and boards. He carved in wood a great deal, but everything he did, he did for himself and was astonished when officials of the museum in Sieradz showed an interest in his work. Soon he became famous and his sculptures were purchased by the museums in Sieradz, Warsaw, Łódź, Toruń and Cracow. Many of them are in the collection of L. Zimmerer, Warsaw. Tourists visit him, a film has been made about his work, and he has won prizes at competitions. His carvings have been displayed at many exhibitions in Poland (one-man shows in the State Ethnographic Museum in Warsaw in 1980, in Sieradz in

valleys and hills, trees, animals and people. He worked out details minutely and endeavoured to attain perspective by reducing the size of objects and figures receding into the background.

The painting illustrated here contains an innovation in the sense that a herd of cows is moving along a wide curve in the shape of the letter S; in the distance hills are followed by high mountains. The line of clouds coincides rhythmically with the contours of the hills. In the foreground left and right, trees are depicted faithfully and vigorously. Skill is shown in portraying the herd moving slowly toward the mountains.

Müller, Johannes: Taking the Livestock to Highland Pastures

1957 and 1958, in the town of Rawa Mazowiecka) and abroad. *(See portrait of the artist, p. 447).* A. J.

MÜLLER, JOHANNES (1806—1897) Switzerland

Apart from painting, Müller also made toys and repaired clocks. He also decorated furniture (his work in this field was fashionable in his day) and executed paintings on the bottoms of milk pails. Sometimes, when painting a large number of these, he repeated himself and sacrificed freshness of approach, but he always remained a fine craftsman. Apparently, he started painting larger pictures only after the death of Lämmler, when scenes from the life of herdsmen (taking their herds to summer mountain pastures) became popular with the inhabitants of Appenzell.

Müller's paintings are noted for the broad spaces and depth of the landscape portrayed, achieved by depicting extensive areas containing

Müller, an Appenzell painter (see p. 104), was admired by many later painters in Appenzell — in fact, by the whole new generation that appeared in the second half of the 19th century.

MURAEV, MIHAIL VLADIMIROVIČ (1903—1960) USSR
MURAYEV, MIKHAIL VLADIMIROVICH

M. V. Murayev was born in the village of Prichizh in Komarichi district, previously part of the Ukraine, and now within the Bryansk region of Soviet Russia, the largest of the Soviet Republics. Of peasant stock, he had a rather desultory schooling. Till 1935 he lived in various townships around Voronezh and before the Second World War taught drawing and draughtsmanship in a school for young factory workers. He began to draw and fashion figures in early boyhood, though his family opposed this. He mostly used plywood, wood and canvas as his basic media and always painted his sculptures. Partly blind toward the end of his life, Murayev moved to Radogoshch, where he lived with his daughter until his death. In the regional seat of Bryansk the Local Folk Arts and Crafts House displays several of Murayev's wooden sculptures, notably those of Pushkin, Leo Tolstoy, Lenin and Karl Marx, and also some of his paintings. His work is at variance with the traditional canons of peasant art, especially in his sculptures. He demonstrated great potential and intellectual sophistication in his painting. Besides landscapes, mostly portraying his native village, he painted genre scenes showing, for instance, his parents drinking tea. In this picture, the colour scheme of primary blues, yellows and reds is harmonious and the spatial composition is well arranged. Murayev was represented at regional and republican exhibitions even before the war. *(See portrait of the artist, p. 447). N. Sh.*

MURRAY, ANDREW (1917) Great Britain

Andrew Murray was born in Tientsin. As is the case with so many self-taught artists, Andrew Murray's original ambition was far removed from painting.

He was the son of two missionaries, and his early years were intimately bound up with religious activities in foreign lands; indeed, it was as a religious journalist in Cape Town in 1956 that, almost by chance, he stumbled upon the art of painting, which was to become his eventual *raison-d'être*.

Murray, Andrew: Daniel in the Lion's Den

Murayev, Mikhail Vladimirovich: My Parents Drinking Tea

He is the grandson of Sir James Murray, the first man to edit the "Oxford English Dictionary" and perhaps something of his grandfather's tenacious determination and drive accounts for the way in which this outwardly mild-mannered and gentle man set about making a success of his new calling. Although he became an artist by chance when a friend gave him a box of paints, brushes and canvases, no other element of his painter's career was left to chance.

The murky colours of the first pictures — quite exceptional in their quirky tenderness — gradually gave way to brighter tints. The biblical

studied it, I only looked and felt. My themes? Exceptional moments of banality."

A patient perfectionist, Musch loves the hard and slow technique of painting on glass because of the play of perspective.

His work might be defined as a dialogue between persons and scenery inspired by the *Belle époque*, and as the transmission of elements of reality to the world of the theatre at the moment that the actors "take the stage."

He has had one-man shows and has participated in group exhibitions in Brussels and Paris. *(See portrait of the artist, p. 447). J. C.*

Musch, Jean Louis: Never Again

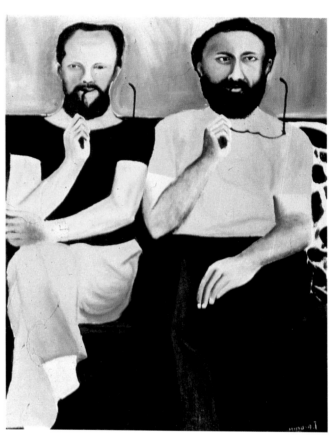

Mususa, Pungu: Portraits of Ch. Hénault and J. M. Lahoye

pictures (often charged with quiet humour) were interrupted for a while when he settled in London and set out upon a series of views and vistas of the British capital. Soon he was painting all the famous tourist spots. Possibly it was through this group of paintings that he achieved his widest fame, because very many were turned into postcards and greetings cards, thus reaching people who in the ordinary course of events would never have come in contact with his work.

Murray is a regular exhibitor at the Portal Gallery, London. His pictures have been shown in a number of mixed exhibitions abroad. *(See portrait of the artist, p. 447). Sh. W.*

MUSCH, JEAN LOUIS (1935)   **Belgium**

Jean Louis Musch (Musch is a pseudonym) was born in Ixelles. Having received a diploma in Romance languages, he taught French at the Brussels Academy.

He has enjoyed drawing since childhood. His love of traditional art led him to painting and then to designing costumes for amateur theatricals. A long bout of immobility, caused by an operation on his larynx in 1976, gave him considerable free time, which he used to try painting on glass. "Why painting?" he asks. "Because I never

MUSUSA, PUNGU (1931)   **Zaire**

Pungu Mususa was born in Sheki, a village of the Kabinda region. He was educated at elementary and technical schools and worked at various jobs, being at one time a government clerk. He spent a number of years in Nairobi, Kenya, returning to Zaire in 1970. He now lives with his wife and six children in Kisangani. When he lost his job in 1972 he began to paint. His representations of traditional village life are marked by a sure sense of composition and a broad, sweeping style which grasps the essence of a situation without becoming too deeply involved in detail. His originality emerges in his portraits, which combine technical ability with an essentially naive conception of pictorial art. *G. Sch.*

Ma Jali

Mandić, Petar

Maran, Anujka

Marek, Jerzy

Mastajtene, Marite

Mazin, Ignatij Andreevič

Mazur, Frank

Mejia Godoy, Armado

Metelli, Orneore

Michałowska, Marta

Michelis, Effie

"Middle Art"

Moore, Ross

Morales, Elsa

Morgan, Gertrude

Motorožesku, Mariora

ková, Cecilie

Maruki, Suma

Marx, Sophia

Mason, Gwen

jer, Sal

Meliašvili, Ivan

Messinger, Menachem

huţ, Petru

Milojević, Dobrosav

Mironova, E. F.

Monsiel, Edmund

cha, Szczepan

Muraev, M. V.

Murray, Andrew

Musch, Jean Louis

Nadera, Ida Bagus Made

Nalivajkene-Jonelite, J.

Naumovski, Vangel

Neervoort, Leo

Nikifor

Nikiforov, I. M.

Noot, Gré

NADERA, I. B. M. — Indonesia, Bali
NALIVAJKENE-JONELITE, J. — USSR
NASI, RINA — Italy
NAUMOVSKI, VANGEL — Yugoslavia
NEERVOORT, LEO — Netherlands
NEFF, SIBYLLE — Switzerland
NICODIM, ION NIŢĂ — Romania
NICOLAOU, KAITI — Greece
NIKČEVIĆ, MILAN, — Yugoslavia
NIKIFOR — Poland
NIKIFOROV, I. M. — USSR
NOOT, GRÉ — Netherlands
NUEZ, GILBERTO DE LA — Cuba

Nadera, Ida Bagus Made: Village Scene

Nalivaikiene-Jonelyte, Jadviga: Odessa Port in 1918

NADERA,   Indonesia, Bali
IDA BAGUS MADE (1915)

Ida Bagus Made Nadera was born in Tegalinggah Gianyar. In 1932 he moved to Ubud, where he became a painter in the classical *Wayang* style. However, Nadera soon came under the influence of radical Ubud and Batuan painters and by late 1933 was already painting in the new secular *Desa* (village) style. Nadera remained in Ubud for approximately six years and during this period studied for a time with both Walter Spies and Rudolph Bonnet. In the summer of 1935 he painted in the new secular style the doors, walls and window frames of the Hotel Campuan (Walter Spies' home) and later the same year joined the prestigious Pita-Maha (Balinese painters' association). Later in the following year he was asked by the Rajah of Gianyar to paint a picture for the royal palace. Both paintings are in Chinese ink on paper and reveal not only his mastery of this medium but also the wholly Balinese character and intent of his work.

With the coming of the Second World War he ceased painting, resuming his art at the end of hostilities in 1945. His style now changed immeasurably. Although Nadera's themes are still rooted in the life of Bali and in the Hindu religion, over the years he has changed to a more sophisticated European technique. *(See portrait of the artist, p. 448).* J. F.

NALIVAJKENE-JONELITE,   USSR
JADVIGA (1897—1969)
NALIVAIKIENE-JONELYTE, JADVIGA

J. Nalivaikiene-Jonelyte was born in a Lithuanian village. After marriage, she moved with her husband to his native Ukraine. She first began to draw in the 1940s, after seeing herself painting in a dream. Though her husband was angry and her neighbours ridiculed her, she persisted, subsequently developing into one of Lithuania's best-known naive artists. The themes she depicted were girlhood reminiscences, harking back to the times of the Civil War in the Ukraine, together with those social upheavals which she accepted as part of her own life story and which in her pictures she combined with folk legend, fantasy and a dreamland world. Though of peasant stock, she is a typical representative of what can be termed urban folklore, with an attitude to form and line that is characteristic of the outlook of the lower middle classes in the city. Though her works to some extent recall children's drawings, they are far more complex. In fact, they are symbols in which a religious morality has been wedded to a modern outlook, as in "Peace Will Overcome War," "The Chapayev Machine-Gun Carriage" (Vassily Chapayev was a famous Civil War hero) or "Odessa Port in 1918." The colours are bright, well demarcated, and to some degree folkloric. A highly individual naive artist, she is of that small group who work folk tradition into modernity, stylistically as well as thematically. She has been represented in numerous exhibitions, and has works in Lithuanian galleries and private collections. Some of her pictures have been reproduced on postcards and in magazines, catalogues and books. *(See portrait of the artist, p. 448). N. Sh.*

NASI, RINA (1915—1976)   **Italy**

Rina Nasi was born in Curtatone, Mantua, and moved to Guastalla, Reggio Emilia, when she married. A housewife, she did not begin to paint until 1971. She took up painting to fill in the

Nasi, Rina: The Four Seasons

emptiness of her life, to make up for the lack of social contacts in the isolated place where she lived — among the sandbars of the Po, which often flooded them. In other words, she painted for herself, modestly and in secret. Rina Nasi, a plain, unspoiled peasant woman, produced spare, "primitive" graphics, basic line drawings, enriched chromatically by extremely bright colours and strong contrasts: vivid red, brilliant green and blue tones merge in a strange way with black and intense yellow-orange, all the colours being obtained from ordinary shellacs. *D. M.*

NAUMOVSKI, VANGEL (1924)   **Yugoslavia**

Vangel Naumovski was born in Ohrid, Macedonia, where he has lived ever since. He wanted to become an academically trained painter, but the work of the talented youngster was not what the art academy in Skopje expected of its students and in consequence he was compelled to leave. In the first phase of his work, figures were strongly accented and themes were taken from the Macedonian region and its past. In time, his painting shed its figurative character and became largely abstract, with touches of reality. Naumovski does not paint life as he sees it around him, but his emotional experience of that life — its substance, what life actually means.

"I see life as twofold," says Naumovski. "Public life and personal life. The latter is the essence

of my creative work. There is reality and there are wishes. The hope that our wishes will be fulfilled keeps us alive and enables physical existence to be maintained. I am inside all these wishes and my painting reveals this. This means that whatever I wish for is accessible to me in my paintings."

He uses colour freely, bypassing or even going counter to academic rules. In his pictures, meadows and lakes are in the sky, the sun rises from the earth, trees grow everywhere. But his paintings are firmly composed, and give an impression of optimistic Surrealism.

Naumovski, Vangel: Girls of Ohrid

"Girls of Ohrid" is the best example of the spectrum of colours Naumovski applies to his canvas: three female figures, symbols of birth, trigger an explosion in outer space. The painting seems to signify the origin of all things. Here are a symbolism and eroticism rarely found in naive painting.

The artist has had one-man shows and has participated in group exhibitions at home and abroad. *(See portrait of the artist, p. 448). N. T.*

NEERVOORT, LEO (1908—1981)   **Netherlands**

Leo Neervoort was born in The Hague and died there. His whole life was spent in the city, where his father had a shop in which Leo had to help even as a small child. On finishing his schooling, he worked there day and night. After five years, he took a job on the railways, with which he remained for nine years, doing various kinds of work. Later, he made his living in different ways. After the war, he obtained employment in a hotel, then worked in a warehouse and later was a shop foreman in a china factory. In 1956, he became a messenger for the State Printing Enterprise, where he remained until his early retirement in 1964.

Neervoort began painting in 1957. Previously, he had spent his leisure time collecting stamps. When his colleagues discovered that he painted, he was persuaded to join the Association of Amateur Painters. To his great surprise, the president praised him, saying that he had no need to study as he already knew how to paint. Witty and always ready with an anecdote in the dialect of The Hague, he spent his last years at

soldiers in parade dress, bands of musicians in different coloured uniforms, the roofs of houses — all of these had such an attractive rhythm that he subconsciously gave them an abstract quality. By the originality of his expression, Neervoort won a notable place in the history of naive art. Normally he used gouache, although he also painted in oil. Some works by him can be classified as amateur art because of the extremely conventional conception of nature and of towns. He won first prize in Zagreb in 1973 and had a one-man show in 1977. *(See portrait of the artist, p. 448). N. E.*

Neervoort, Leo: A Suburb in the Netherlands

Neff, Sibylle: Cleaning Up

home as an invalid. The sight of the gay crowds on the Queen's birthday gave him a great deal of pleasure and he always depicted it in an unusual composition. Rows of people jostling each other,

NEFF, SIBYLLE (1929) **Switzerland**

Sibylle Neff, born in Appenzell, comes from a family of tradesmen. She continues the tradition of the "alpine painters" of Appenzell. With delicate, childlike feeling she paints her experiences and memories: an outing of the village school, the celebration of a holiday, the transfer of the herd to high pastures. There are a pleasant sense of movement and a painterly vision in the sincere and patient work of this gifted, emotional naive painter. *O. B.-M.*

NICODIM, ION NIŢĂ (1909—1980) **Romania**

Ion Niţă Nicodim was born in the commune of Hălmagiu in the district of Arad, and spent his whole life in his native village.

It was only in 1963 that he devoted himself to painting, although his talents were well-known to the villagers before that and he had frequently been invited to paint pictures on the walls of new houses.

As a self-taught painter (who also made his own equipment), Nicodim gradually created his own world under the influence of tradition and the natural beauty surrounding him. Although his themes and source of inspiration were always similar, the artist, perfecting his painting technique and gaining in experience, gave an increasingly nuanced portrayal of a poetic conception of reality. His themes derive from ostensibly banal customs and everyday village life, but are presented with a singular and independent vision: the seasons with their wealth of colour ("Spring"), men and women on festive days ("The

theni, Kavalla, and the threading of tobacco leaves in the courtyard of their traditional Macedonian house (illustrated here), are among them.

Her egg temperas are marked by simplicity, fresh, spontaneous expression, nostalgic feeling and a love of nature. Her scale of colours shows a certain preference for shades of brown and green; the primitive character of her human figures is more pronounced than that of her landscapes.

Nicolaou's little-known work maintains all the purity of an artistic personality which is still in the process of development. *A. T.*

Nicodim, Ion Niţă: Tree Planting

Nicolaou, Kaiti: Threading and Drying Tobacco Leaves

Wedding"), or historical subjects interpreted in an altogether modern fashion, stressing the indivisible tie between man and nature.

The canvases dating from the last period of his life are precise in composition and carefully worked out in their details. Naive painting in Romania was influenced by his work and he even took the initiative in founding a group of naive painters in his native village, outstanding among whom are Rodica Nicodim, Petru Mihuţ and Petru Roman.

The works of Nicodim, painted in oil on cardboard or canvas, have been displayed at many national and international exhibitions and have been awarded prestigious prizes, among them the award of the city of Lugano in 1973. *M. Il.*

NICOLAOU, KAITI   Greece

Kaiti Nicolaou was born in Serrai, northern Greece, but moved to Athens, where she is employed by the National Organisation of Handicrafts. As a child she showed a certain talent for painting, but, like a number of other naive painters, started to devote time to it in maturity, when her family no longer demanded so much from her. Her subject-matter consists of memories of her birthplace and impressions from trips to different parts of Greece: weddings, christenings, funerals, landscapes and the ruins of Serrai and its surroundings. Nicolaou is probably at her best when painting things that particularly impressed her as a child: the gathering of tobacco in the family tobacco field in the village of Mous-

NIKČEVIĆ, MILAN (1942)   Yugoslavia

Milan Nikčević was born in Straševina, near Nikšić, Montenegro. After completing his secondary schooling he studied at a school of advanced catering. At present he is a truck driver in the picturesque coastal town of Budva. Nikčević has

Nikčević, Milan: The Serf

travelled along an unusual road, from the making of jugs and the fashioning of figurines in wood to the production of monumental naive sculptural compositions. His inspiration is drawn from the people around him (his mother, children and so on), personalities and scenes from the near and distant past, and men and women who have had a hard life (prisoners, beggars). Of late, he has turned increasingly to the folklore of Montenegro ("Montenegrin Man and Woman," "The Gusle Player" and the like). Skilful in stylising forms and perceptive in his use of characteristic details, Nikčević also creates sugges-

to be a painter. On the back of his pictures, Nikifor stamped a round seal bearing the name of Nikifor-Matejko: he had taken the name of the renowned Polish painter Matejko as the sign of his profession. When he could not make a living by selling his works, he begged. A speech defect obstructed communication with other people — hence the legend that he was a deaf-mute. Deeply and naively religious, he formed his conception of God, Heaven and Hell more from the paintings seen in Orthodox and Catholic churches than from the preaching of clergymen. Illiterate, he tried to conceal the fact and also to

Nikifor: Nikifor on the Road

Nikifor: A Byzantine-style Church

tive compositions from everyday life ("Mother and Child," "Girl with Doves") or sculptures based on literature and folk tales ("Bloody Tale," "Tower of Skulls"). He had his first one-man show in Belgrade in 1977 and has taken part in a number of exhibitions of naive art at home and abroad. *M. L.*

NIKIFOR (1895—1968)   **Poland**

Nikifor was born in the vicinity of Krynicy, where he died. He was by descent a Łemko (a Ukrainian tribe); his mother was a washerwoman and he did not know his father. After her death, the boy wandered about the countryside begging. He began to paint very early in life; some pictures have been preserved dating from his thirteenth year. Even at that age, he wanted

increase the importance of his paintings by drawing in certain expressions, frequently having no connection with the subject-matter and also wrongly spelled. To sell his paintings, he went from village to village and travelled to towns such as Tarnow, Nowy Sacz, Lvov, Cracow and Warsaw. He made pencil drawings of the buildings he saw, especially town houses, railway stations and churches, and collected illustrations of Secession architecture. He imitated it while transforming it in his own fantastic way. Some themes he kept coming back to, such as the "Painters' Feast," for he believed that in the other world painters would sit down at the table of the Lord because they were better than other people in the sense that they could not only copy the world but shape it to fit their own will and imaginations. Convinced that he would find in the other world the justice that eluded him in this one, he frequently portrayed himself as a Bishop-Wise Man, a Bishop-Judge (condemning to damnation those who had done him injustice), as a musician and as a painter with a large easel. He worked from morning till night, never repeating himself. When painting a series of pictures on one theme he did each one as a successive phase in movement, like the frames of an animated cartoon. His later works show development in comparison with the earlier ones — colour sensitivity is greater, the creation of atmosphere is intensified and composition has

many international exhibitions. Two books and several hundred articles have been written about Nikifor and he has been the subject of three documentary films. *(See portrait of the artist, p. 448). A. J.*

NIKIFOROV, USSR
IVAN MIHAJLOVIČ (1897—1971)
NIKIFOROV, IVAN MIKHAILOVICH
I. M. Nikiforov was born to poor peasants in the village of Monakovo, near Vereya, not far from Moscow. After the boy had had two years at

Nikiforov, Ivan Mikhailovich: Wedding

improved. In the last years of his life, he was assigned a guardian and obtained an apartment containing many of the things he had dreamed of possessing all his life (several radios, a dozen watches) and a car in which he was driven around. He even got an identification card and official surname — Krynicki. However, he was already very ill, sad and tired of life. The people who came to watch him work fatigued him and so did painting itself. He worked as though it were an obligation, and it became ever harder for him to do, while the results grew worse.

Nikifor painted at least ten thousand pictures — on sheets of paper, on the pages of notebooks, on cigarette cartons, and even on scraps of paper glued together. His works are in many museums and private collections in Poland and abroad. He has had about ten one-man shows and his works have been on display in

the local parish school, his father, recently back from the Russo-Japanese war in 1906 and working as a coachman in Vereya, apprenticed him to a Moscow artisan — the lot of many children of poor families in tsarist Russia. During the First World War he fought in the tsarist army as a private. After the October 1917 Revolution he joined the Red Army and fought the Whites. In the 1930s he served as chairman of the collective farm set up in his native village. Later his wife persuaded him to move to the township of Pushkino, not far from Moscow, where he worked at the railway station as a porter. In 1942 he was badly injured when unloading a waggon. After a long period of convalescence, he worked as a railway guard before eventually retiring on a pension. In 1960 he began to write short stories and an autobiographical novel, "My Life," which he illustrated with pictures, having borrowed watercolour paints, Indian ink, paper and brush from a granddaughter. Shortly before his death he was accepted as a member of the USSR Union of Artists.

After his work had been noted at exhibitions, he had been encouraged by professional painters and had several articles written about him.

In its decorative style, Nikiforov's work recalls the patterns of folk art. He did not seek to convey any deep inner meaning, simply reproducing nature, people and animals as such, which makes his work akin to children's drawings. His compositions consist of a decorative surface upon

duties as a wife and mother, she found the time to go to night school. In any event, she wanted to engage in some outside activities. As her husband had no consideration for her ambitions, the couple divorced in 1961. She remarried in 1964. For a time, she was head of the service section in a large hotel. Upon leaving that job, she received a box of painting equipment from the manager. A guest in the hotel, a teacher in an art academy, had noticed some flowers beautifully arranged by her and said they showed artistic talent. Gré Noot had never thought of painting. But her daughter, a sculptress, suggested that she take a

Noot, Gré: Foekepotterij

Nuez, Gilberto de la: The Forties

which people, houses, trees and individual details are superimposed. The colour scheme, with splashes of yellow, blue, red and purple scattered over the white ground of the paper, produces the impression of a mosaic-like village rug or patchwork blanket. The artist sought to break out of the confines of inner restraint and convey his own naive understanding of the beauty around him. Though he was totally ignorant of perspective and human anatomy, his handling is confident and detailed, while the "wrong" technique imparts the immediacy of a story told with lively warmth in a free and easy manner. Besides autobiographical, rustic or urban scenes, which served as an inexhaustible source of subject-matter, he also liked drawing narrative pictures, setting out the contents of books, songs and ballads. His naive pictures — folkloric, integrated and consistent — mirror the popular mentality of the village and town that he chronicled pictorially. He was represented at numerous exhibitions, including some on a republican and USSR level. Some water-colours were exhibited at a show of railwaymen amateur artists in France. His work may be seen at the Museum of Folk and Amateur Art of Soviet Russia in Suzdal. *(See portrait of the artist, p. 448). N. Sh.*

NOOT, GRÉ (1914)   **Netherlands**

Gré Noot was born in Enschede. When she was twenty-one, she married a warehouse worker by whom she had five children. Despite her

few art lessons. In 1970, she already had an independent exhibition of water-colours, gouaches, and oils at Zwolle.

Gré Noot paints her youth, "the happiest time of my life." It is her wish to transmit that happiness to others, to the rest of the world, so unhappy and threatened by urbanisation, pollution and nuclear weapons. She herself is always happy when strolling through the woods, listening to birds chirping. Her work is distinguished by emotion, expressed through strong colours. Local folk customs are a frequent theme. In one painting, she shows children making the rounds of houses and begging for sweets. The children and a lush nature transform life into a gay holiday. *(See portrait of the artist, p. 448). N. E.*

NUEZ, GILBERTO DE LA (1913)   **Cuba**

Gilberto de la Nuez was born in Havana. The outstanding aspect of his work is the themes chosen — usually strong socio-political commentaries on current and historical events. His style, bordering on a hybrid of magazine illustration and caricature, is of lesser importance and is subordinated to the message. Gilberto de la Nuez took part in the exhibition of "Primitive Cuban Painters in Socialist Countries" in 1972, and in 1973 mounted a solo exhibition in the Amelia Pelaez Gallery in Havana. He was represented at the exhibition "Eleven Cuban Primitive Artists" at the Institute of Jamaica, Kingston, in 1976. *T. R.*

Oad, Jan

Obin, Philomé

Obin, Sénèque

O'Brien, Patricia

Ociepka, Teofil

Ol'šaneckaja, L. V.

Ončú, Ana

Orbán, István

OAD, JAN — Canada
OBIN, ANTOINE — Haiti
OBIN, PHILOMÉ — Haiti
OBIN, SÉNÈQUE — Haiti
OBIN, TÉLÉMAQUE — Haiti
O'BRIEN, PATRICIA — Ireland
OCIEPKA, TEOFIL — Poland
ODDIE, HARRY — Great Britain
ODENTHAL, EDUARD — West Germany

O'KELLY, MATTIE LOU — USA
OLATUNDE, ASIRU — Nigeria
OL'ŠANECKAJA, L. V. — USSR
ONČU, ANA — Yugoslavia
ORBÁN, ISTVÁN — Hungary
ORDAVO, ALDO — Italy
ORISEKNÉ FARSANG, E. — Hungary
ORTEGA, MARINA — Nicaragua
ORTIZ, BENITO — Cuba

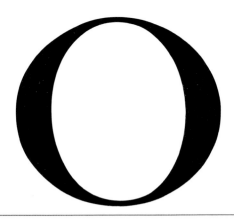

Oad, Jan: Witch Trial in Mara

Obin, Antoine: Wild Bull

OAD, JAN (1889)   Canada

Jan Oad was born on the island of Kihnu, near the Estonian coast, the son of a carpenter and joiner. At school, which he attended for four years, his teacher would sometimes allow those pupils who were making progress to stay behind after hours to draw. Later, already at work as assistant cook aboard a steamer plying a local route, Oad spent part of his pay on a box of water-colours and oil paints, especially to paint the sailing boats he knew so well. He had married rather early in life and had to work hard. He went out on fishing boats, worked as a mail carrier, carted rocks and bricks to Riga, helped to build sailing vessels, did locksmithing, and signed on as seaman on both Estonian and foreign ships. Wherever voyages took him, he always showed a keen interest in pictures seen in portside taverns, shipping offices and homes. He often painted pictures for his mates, who wanted to have a reproduction of a ship or of a picture from a magazine as a souvenir. During the Second World War, Oad landed in Canada, where for many years now he has been living in Toronto, today retired on a pension. He was discovered by M. Soosaar, a cameraman of the Tallinn Film Studios, who in the winter of 1980 mounted in Tallinn, the Estonian capital, an exhibition of pictures by self-taught seamen artists, among whom were H. Widrik, M. Sutt, M. Mikhel, N. Sulev and P. Roosaid. The exhibition included several transparencies of Oad's work (though not of pictures of ships), sent from Canada. Overwhelmed by nostalgia, Oad decided to produce a pictorial account of the 220-year-old history of his birthplace, the island of Kihnu. He shows us scenes of the Baltic Sea near the coast, the island's lighthouse, a wedding, a village barber blood-letting, a shipbuilder, the forging of a ship's anchor, a launching, harvesting, hay being mown, women crossing the gulf with piglets on their way to a fair, the importation of salt from Sweden, and the wrecking of the good ship "Rock City" off Danish shores, together with its legendary Kihnu skipper, Jann. In 1963-4, already well past the prime of life, Oad attended evening art classes at Danforth Technical College, painting landscapes and portraits. Of the 150 pictures he has today at home, some one hundred relate the history of his native island. It would be distressing if these pictures of a talented, self-taught Estonian seaman-artist should be lost. *(See portrait of the artist, p. 456).* N. Sh.

OBIN, ANTOINE (1929)   Haiti

Antoine Obin was born in Cap Haitien, the youngest son of Philomé Obin. His father's pupil, Antoine Obin has achieved sufficient individuality in his paintings (although he is well-established in the "Obin" tradition) to claim a place as an independent artist. He has almost as great a sense of precision as his father and, like him, favours warm, sombre colours, seeks to achieve a sense of space in his pictures and tries to monumentalise the main characters in them. *Sh. W.*

OBIN, PHILOMÉ (1892—1977)   **Haiti**

Philomé Obin was born in Bas Limbé. He is associated with Cap Haitien, where he has lived and worked throughout a long life. Essentially, Philomé Obin is regarded as the "Patriarch" of Haitian art, although some would say that such a title refers to northern Haiti rather than to the whole republic, because there is unquestionably a dividing line between art of the north (domi-

as monuments to the suffering and death — Haitians call it the Crucifixion — of the patriot Charlemagne Péralte, killed in an ambush during the American Occupation (the Cacos War of 1918—1922), when Péralte's body was tied to a door and brought back to the American Marines' headquarters, to confirm beyond doubt that he had been killed, thus quashing any rumours that he was still active on the anti-American front. Obin's picture of the colossal funeral (painted in 1946) is among his most complex works. Even more moving is his version of Péralte's death, showing Péralte (naked except for a loincloth)

Obin, Philomé: Jean-Jacques Dessaline on the Road to General Headquarters in Crete-à-Pierrot

nated by Obin) and that of the south (dominated by Hippolyte), which has influenced many widely divergent talents.

The turning-point in Obin's career occurred in 1944, when the Centre d'Art was opening and Obin met DeWitt Peters; when he submitted his works for inspection, the American immediately recognised the artist's gifts.

Philomé Obin is famous among collectors of his paintings for the neat and precise records he has made of scenes and personalities from Haitian history. Perhaps among the most arresting of these are the paintings he produced

strapped to the door, propped up in the sand and clutching the standard of Haiti, whose yellow banner-pole is topped with a cross. His black-robed, weeping mother, standing close by, symbolises the Virgin Mary. Both these pictures, in their own ways, are among the most poignant to have come out of Haiti.

The style of this artist is totally figurative, every detail being sharply edged and faultlessly delineated. The paint is thinly applied, but telling in its frail precision. Obin was also one of the famous contributors to the murals of the Cathedral of St. Trinité in Port-au-Prince.

Obin lived and worked in Cap Haitien, ancient black capital of Haiti, where he had established a school of painting from which have come not only his relatives — sons Antoine and Télémaque — but many of Haiti's finest artists. *(See portrait of the artist, p. 456). Sh. W.*

OBIN, SÉNÈQUE (1893—1977) Haiti

Sénèque Obin was born in Cap Haitien, where he died. He began as a coffee merchant, but in the early 1940s, encouraged by his elder brother, painted his first pictures. He presented

Obin, Sénèque: National Holiday

Obin, Télémaque: Hunting Guinea Fowl

himself at Port-au-Prince's Centre d'Art in 1948. The younger brother of Philomé Obin by one year, he is inevitably associated with him in people's minds. It should be pointed out, however, that though the two brothers have much in common as artists, and both favour scenes from Haitian history, Sénèque did on occasion seek subjects from a wider range of subject-matter. But what distinguishes Sénèque's work from Philomé's is his enthusiasm for black

pigment, which he uses in more than a few of his works. *(See portrait of the artist, p. 456). Sh. W.*

OBIN, TÉLÉMAQUE (1913) Haiti

Télémaque Obin was born in Cap Haitien, the son of Philomé Obin. He was a watchmaker until, at 35, he surrendered to the attractions of the life of a painter. Strongly influenced by the work of his father, he favours historical scenes from Haiti's past, but, in contrast to Philomé, he has a strong lyrical strain, which is most pronounced in paintings devoted to the beauties

O'Brien, Patricia: Girl Before a Mirror

of nature. It is not surprising that his favourite colour is green. *Sh. W.*

O'BRIEN, PATRICIA Ireland

Patricia O'Brien, a painter of Anglo-Irish stock, spent time in London and the Channel Islands before taking up permanent residence in St. François, near Grasse, in Provence.

Her ambition to become a painter stems from her father, who, although an accomplished musician like his wife, was also an artist.

As can be seen in the accompanying illustration, without formal art training she has found her own way to becoming a competent artist, even if she betrays her love for the great Italians. Nevertheless, her choice of scene and subject-matter is undeniably original, with its emphasis upon the lonely, independent status of women.

She has taken part in several group exhibitions in England and abroad and has had some one-woman shows in London and Dublin. *(See portrait of the artist, p. 456). Sh. W.*

OCIEPKA, TEOFIL (1891—1978) Poland

Teofil Ociepka was born in the town of Janów Slaski, and died in Bydgoszcz. Coming from a miner's family, he had only an elementary school education. After his fourteenth year, to support his family following his father's death in a mine disaster, he worked, though sickly, as an assistant administrative clerk on the railways, and as a locomotive engineer in the mines. As a boy he mixed little with other lads of his age, preferring to read, especially books about hypnosis and the occult. His interest in these matters later developed even further under the influence of a friend who was a theosophist. When he was fifty-six years old, he began to paint, in order to express and hand down to others the truth about the world, to deliver them from evil and to introduce them to a state of mystical beauty. He painted mysterious flowers, jungles, unknown worlds and creatures, the spirit of the mines, symbolic scenes of religious inspiration and later

his subject. Indeed, it is always the horse which is the key to his pictures, but not the horse of "now"; it is always the horse of "then."

He has taken part in several RONA exhibitions. *Sh. W.*

ODENTHAL, EDUARD (1929) **West Germany**

Eduard Odenthal was born in Cologne, where he still lives. He completed an apprenticeship as a fitter, but after the Second World War tried his luck as a boxer and as an itinerant craftsman. He also worked as a carpet salesman

Ociepka, Teofil: Lion from Saturn

Oddie, Harry: Cumberland Forge

— when he was chided for withdrawing from life — cycles with such titles as "Life on Saturn" and "Life on the Moon," in keeping with the texts of theosophist books sent him by his mentor and friend. He was "discovered" in 1948 and after exhibitions in Cracow and Warsaw became famous; about 200 articles were written about him, as were two books, and a film was made. He had many exhibitions in Poland and abroad (among others, one-man shows in Vienna and São Paulo). Fame, the rising prices of his paintings, marriage in 1959 with an enterprising widow some ten years younger — these were all instrumental in his beginning to repeat himself and in his losing the inner need to transmit his ideas to others. Several of his works are in the possession of the Polish State Ethnographic Museum in Warsaw. *(See portrait of the artist, p. 456). A. J.*

ODDIE, HARRY (1896) **Great Britain**

Harry Oddie was born in Darwen, Lancashire, and now lives in Preston. For thirty years he worked first as a fitter and then as a foreman-tester at Leyland Motors. But before that he had served in the army with the Royal Horse Artillery, whose horses he clipped and groomed. This was like a hangover from a lost era and it had a lasting effect upon Harry Oddie. From it he gained intimate knowledge of horses, their work and their way of life, so that when he came to start painting (at the age of seventy-two!) it was natural that he should turn to horses for

and had his own business at one time. In 1965, while Odenthal was trying to help his young daughter with her drawing, a spark was kindled in him which drove him to paint in every free minute turning him into a passionate painter with a totally distinctive palette and great intensity of expression. Townscapes, and views of streets and squares, are the subjects which his inquisitive painter's eye seizes on greedily. The confident and matter-of-fact manner in which Odenthal assembles buildings, trees and people to form a colourful, rhythmically organised and harmonious whole suggests that the task is little more than child's play to him.

A sensitive and rather touchy person, Odenthal is fond of observing the people he meets. He has succeeded in creating highly personal interpretations of various social *milieux*: droll, lanky figures with spidery legs, generally in an intellectual environment. He is often so fascinated by an event that he bases an entire series of pictures on it. On occasion he uses his art to criticise or even to pillory people or institutions and is equally ready to do the same thing in verse or prose.

Odenthal, who has an international reputation, is represented in the most important collections of naive art. *T. G.*

O'KELLY, MATTIE LOU (1908) **USA**

Mattie Lou O'Kelly, one of eight children, was born on a farm near Maysville, Georgia, where she lived until she was in her thirties. She was thirty-five before she worked outside her

Odenthal, Eduard: Aachen

Odenthal, Eduard: Family L.

O'Kelly, Mattie Lou: Cotton Picking on the Hills of Georgia

home. Her first job was in a local sewing plant, and from there she went from one kind of work to another, seldom if ever happy in any occupation. She worked in a mill, then in a school lunchroom, became a store clerk and tried being a housekeeper. She said that reading was her most enduring pleasure, and that her interest in painting was first stirred when a sister "came home from Atlanta with paints. She liked to copy pictures, but I wanted to do my own."

Her father died when she was young, and she stayed with her mother. When her mother died — Miss O'Kelly was in her fifties — to keep herself busy with a hobby she began to paint, ordering her materials through Sears & Roebuck catalogues. She offered her "hobby work" for sale at local festivals at prices ranging from one to ten dollars. Noticing an announcement in an Atlanta newspaper about an exhibition to be held at the High Museum, she asked if she could show her work there, but was not accepted. However, she was told that she could offer her paintings for sale in the museum shop, and it was there that

promises, they separated and each went his own way. Mortified, the woman went back to her father and then again returned to live in the forest, taking with her a large water vessel which she carried on her head. Passing by a big tree, she slipped and fell; the pitcher broke, the water spilled and thus was born the River Otin in which she disappeared.

Her father, King Oba, went to look for her but instead found the River Otin and the broken pitcher.

This legend speaks of two irreconcilable contradictions in the Africa of long ago — the

Olatunde, Asiru: Festive Procession

Dr. Robert Bishop, then with the Henry Ford Museum in Dearborn, saw her work and became her agent in 1975. She has been in several shows at the Jay Johnson American Folk Heritage Gallery since.

Miss O'Kelly's paintings are based both on her memories of rural life and on contemporary scenes that appeal to her. Those who are familiar with Czech and Yugoslav naives will notice that her work has some stylistic and compositional similarities to theirs. *J. W.*

OLATUNDE, ASIRU   Nigeria

In times long gone by there ruled in Otan Aiyegbay a king called Oba, whose wife gave birth to a daughter with four breasts. The child, named Otin, was a source of shame to her father. When she grew up, she became self-conscious and shy. One day, she told her father, King Oba, that she wished to go away and live in the wilds, far from people, which she did. In the forest she met a hunter and told him her story. Taking pity on her, he decided to marry her but on one condition: that she would never make him a meal from a certain kind of forbidden leaf. For his part, the hunter promised that he would never reproach his wife for her defect.

At first, they both kept their promises and were happy and satisfied in their marriage. But one day the wife, despite her promise, made her husband a meal from the forbidden leaf. Angry, the husband started to upbraid her for her physical shortcoming. As both had broken their

love and pain of a father for his abnormal child and his relief at the loss of that child who was unacceptable in a world of harsh natural selection. Here, too, is the good she does by sacrificing herself for that implacable environment in presenting it with a river, so necessary in the heat of Africa.

This fairy tale from the Yoruba tribe, and many other similar ones passed down by word of mouth, is the subject dealt with by Nigeria's most famous contemporary artist, Asiru Olatunde, from Oshogbo, a town over one hundred kilometres from Lagos, capital of the federal state of Nigeria.

The mystical and imaginative Olatunde draws inspiration from the wealth of folklore in his country. Thanks to his unquestionably great talent, he has succeeded in arriving at an individual expression, departing essentially from the traditional style of creativity of his region. Taking pagan and biblical stories, he transforms them into artistic compositions in which everything is possible, as in pagan magic.

In Oshogbo, the muezzins call to the faithful from their low-lying, one-storey mosques, while bells perform the same service from the Catholic and Protestant churches. All three religions vie with one another for the souls of the still-illiterate Africans, most of whom are bound to animist beliefs, with all their rituals and superstition.

In this atmosphere of spiritual intermingling, Olatunde has for twenty years been creating in beaten aluminum a wondrous mythical and biblical world, which has sprung from his fertile imagination. Judged on the basis of what and how he creates, Asiru Olatunde is a rare and highly individual personality.

He began life as a blacksmith, a craft he inherited from his father, but illness prevented him from working at it for long. He then became a drummer, a calling much esteemed in Oshogbo. Twenty years after stopping work as a blacksmith, Olatunde began to produce the works of art that were to bring him fame at home and abroad.

Initially he made small ornaments of copper, but later turned to aluminum, which he could

fragile, in contrast to the roughly ornamented background, symbolising the harshness of the world, in which the figures are often helpless and alone.

Asiru Olatunde would probably not be what he is today had he not made the acquaintance of Suzanna Wenger, an Austrian sculptress living in Oshogbo; she was the first person who realised his abilites and helped him with advice and encouragement.

Olatunde frequently exhibits in Nigeria, and also in Germany, the USA and other countries. *N. T.*

Olshanetskaya, Lidia Vladimirovna: My Granddaughter's Wedding

procure in greater quantities, thus enabling him to fashion works of larger dimensions. Carefully beating the surface of the aluminum, he creates compositions consisting of several rows along which the story unfolds. The scenes are solemn and even somewhat mournful, while the size of the figures depends on the role assigned to them in the story. The forms of the figures are both the product of his imagination and his personal vision and of the story itself, which begins as a rule in the lower right-hand corner and then climbs in two, three or more rows toward the upper edge.

There is no drama in Olatunde's compositions; the mood is contemplative, with strong lyrical and poetic accents. Human figures are

Ončhu, Ana: The Christening

OL'ŠANECKAJA,   USSR
LIDIJA VLADIMIROVNA (1899—1975)
OLSHANETSKAYA, LIDIA VLADIMIROVNA

Olshanetskaya's father was an impoverished aristocrat from the Russified German Berg family and in his younger years was an actor. Her mother came from the Circassian family of Aga-Gamza, whose descendants adopted the Orthodox faith. After graduating from school she married, and after the Revolution worked as an office clerk in the Ministry of the Merchant Marine. She first began to paint, using tempera, after her seventeenth birthday. Her subjects were drawn from nature and imagination. In her interiors (her favourite genre), as a rule she disposed the figures and lightly tinted furnishings in a somewhat childish manner, as, for instance, in "My Granddaughter's Wedding." As her compositional arrangement is imprecise, the colouring is fragmented, yet nevertheless attractively vivid and somewhat folkloric. Her choice of theme indicates a link with the art of urban folklore. Yet because of the fragmented colouring, it is rather a borderline case between urban folklore and typical children's drawing. Thus one painting is entitled "The Nursery," a theme often encountered in turn-of-the-century poetry, song and painting. Olshanetskaya's many paintings are today in the possession of her son and daughter and grandchildren. They were exhibited for the first time in 1980 at a group show of Moscow amateur artists timed specially to coincide with the 1980 Olympic Games. *(See portrait of the artist, p. 456). N. Sh.*

ONČU, ANA (1931) Yugoslavia

Ana Onču was born in the village of Lokve, Vojvodina, but after marrying moved to Uzdin, another village inhabited by ethnic Romanians. With no schooling, she is a housewife who paints in her leisure time. Starting somewhat later than most of the other women-painters in her village, Ana Onču has presented her vision of Uzdin and the life and customs of the Romanian community. Her colours are softer than those of her colleagues, and not so opulent or gay, so that the action she portrays is more sculptural in effect. Her works include no landscapes, which,

O
464

Orbán, István: Believers (Pious Old Women)

strangely enough, the women peasant-painters of Uzdin do not take as a theme. Her preoccupation is with concrete events that have been repeated in a prescribed manner for centuries.

In "The Christening" (1972), Ana Onču portrays this joyous moment in the life of every family. The parents and relations, dressed in their best, move toward church in a column headed by the proud mother. The red fence around the churchyard, contrasting with the black and white church, endows this painting with the solemn and spiritual atmosphere associated with the act of christening.

Ana Onču has had one-woman shows and participated in group exhibitions at home and abroad. *(See portrait of the artist, p. 456). N. T.*
←

ORBÁN, ISTVÁN Hungary

István Orbán comes from a peasant family. After the First World War, he spent several years in France as a political emigrant. His views on society are apparent in his works. Most of the figures he fashions are lonely old men, patiently enduring their fate. Figures of shepherds, farmers and pious old women, whom he knew in his youth, as well as those of the unemployed and of strikers, are carved from bent branches or the trunks of fruit trees with coloured bark. Adaptation to the features of his material has led him to a stylisation of sorts. He has also done polychromatic statues. Since 1967 he has exhibited in Budapest and in other parts of the country. *(See portrait of the artist, p. 456). M. I.*

ORDAVO, ALDO (1913) Italy

Aldo Ordavo was born in Viareggio, where he lives today, a retired teacher. He began painting in 1960, doing peaceful scenes with spare, basic lines, especially the landscape of Viareggio and the sea, with its limitless horizons and sudden dangers. Later Ordavo enriched his repertory with lifelike figures of frightened birds, strutting roosters and extraordinary purple elephants, also seasonal landscapes containing human and animal figures in bold colours.

A cosmic joy, radiating from his paintings as a result of his enviable purity of invention,

Ordavo, Aldo: Venice in the Snow

Orisekné Farsang, Erzsébet: Husking Corn

reflects the artist's cheerful spirits nurtured by the fresh intuition typical of the pure in heart.

In this sense, there is something characteristic about the work "Two Roosters," in which the fowls are drawn in arabesques of vivid colours, like emblems, standing against a snowy, fairy-tale background. A publisher commissioned Ordavo to illustrate Phaedrus' tales and for this work he won much praise. *D. M.*

ORISEKNÉ FARSANG, Hungary
ERZSÉBET (1929)

Erzsébet Orisekné Farsang was born in Pazmand, where she still lives today. Her pictures portray landscapes of her native district, and are also a cheerful chronicle of work in the fields and domestic chores. Since 1962, many of her paintings have travelled to exhibitions at home and abroad. Her works may be found both in private collections and in the Museum of Naive Art in Kecskemét. *M. I.*

ORTEGA, MARINA (1955)   **Nicaragua**

Marina Ortega was born in Solentiname, and it was there that she developed as a painter. Her painting dates back to childhood, when her talent was already apparent. She is now one of the most famous artists in Nicaragua, her works standing out for their extraordinary colours and precision. This *penchant* for minute detail is obvious even on the large canvases she sometimes paints. The artist now lives in Masaya and has devoted herself exclusively to her painting.

She has exhibited in Managua, also in Venezuela, the USA, Germany and other countries. *E. C.*

ORTIZ, BENITO (1896)   **Cuba**

Benito Ortiz was born in Trinidad, in Las Villas Province in Cuba. He left school after

Ortega, Marina: A Church in Solentiname

Ortiz, Benito: Castle in the Forest

reaching the fifth grade and has worked at a number of jobs, including shoemaking and as a sugar-cane worker; he retired from the latter occupation only recently.

Both his subjects and his style are simple and unsophisticated, being reminiscent of a genre of decorative illustration, produced by a myriad Latin-American artisans, which is generally grouped under the heading of folklore or popular art; but for its intricacy of design, as in "Castle in the Forest," his work could easily be mistaken as belonging to the former category.

Ortiz took part in the Salon '70 exhibition and the exhibition of Primitive Painters in 1971. In 1976 he participated in the exhibition "Eleven Cuban Primitive Artists" at the Institute of Jamaica, in Kingston, and in 1978 in the International Exhibition of Naive Painting in Caracas. His work is in the collection of the National Museum in Havana. *T. R.*

PACHTA, JOSEF — Austria
PAGANO, LUISA — Italy
PAGE, DEROLD — Great Britain
PALADIN, BRUNO — Yugoslavia
PALLADINO, ANGELA — USA
PALLETA, KARL BORRO — West Germany
PALUŠKA, MARTIN — Yugoslavia
PANKOV, K. A. — USSR
PAPS (W. RUSCHE) — West Germany
PARADE, MADELEINE — France
PAŘÍK, ANTONÍN — Czechoslovakia
PASOTTI, BERNARDO — Italy
PĂTRAȘ, ION STAN — Romania
PAVELESCU, EMIL — Romania
PEARCE, BRYAN — Great Britain
PEČNIK, GRETA — Yugoslavia
PEPERSACK, LOUISE — Belgium
PETELINŠEK, FRANCISKA — Yugoslavia
PETER, ALFRED ERNEST — Switzerland
PETERNELJ, JOŽE — Yugoslavia
PETERNELJ, KONRAD — Jugoslavia
PETRANOVIĆ, TOMISLAV — Yugoslavia
PETRESCU, SIMONA — Romania
PEYRONNET, DOMINIQUE — France
PHILIPPE-AUGUSTE, SALNAVE — Haiti
PIC (TEARLACH S. HIGGINS) — Great Britain
PICKET, SARAH — Canada
PICKETT, JOSEPH — USA
PIERCE, ELIJAH — USA
PIERRE, ANDRÉ — Haiti
PILI-PILI — Zaire
PINDER, GEORGE — Great Britain
PINTARIĆ, JOSIP — Yugoslavia
PINTO, JOSÉ — Brazil
PIPPIN, HORACE — USA
PIROSMANAŠVILI, NIKOLAJ — USSR
PLASMEIJER, JOOP — Netherlands
PLASTININ, VASILIJ VASIL'EVIČ — USSR
PONZI, NELLO — Italy
POP, MARIA — Greece
POSZ, MARIA DE — Austria
POVOLNI, MIHALJ — Yugoslavia
PRESSLEY, DANIEL — USA
PRIJMAČENKO, M. A. — USSR
PROCHÁZKOVÁ, LUDMILA — Czechoslovakia
PUGUG, I MADE — Bali

PUJA, FLORIKA — Yugoslavia
PURYGIN, LEONID ANATOL'EVIČ — USSR
PUŠKARIĆ-PETRAS, MARA — Yugoslavia

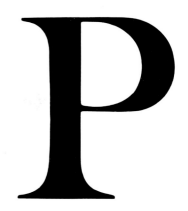

Pachta, Josef: Outdoor Pool

Pagano, Luisa: Village Landscape

PACHTA, JOSEF (1902)   Austria

Josef Pachta was born in Vienna. He trained as a compositor. In 1939 he changed jobs and moved to the Post Office. During the war he was taken prisoner by the French and began to paint from pure boredom. He had considerable success with his pictures, which he exchanged for bread with fellow-prisoners and French officers. After his release Pachta thought no more about painting until he retired. Now that he had enough time — as he had when he was a prisoner — he started painting again. He now lives in Vienna.

His pictures contain hints of social and moral criticism, as well as a certain irony. Although they might seem rather too simple, he manages to achieve in them an amusing mixture of actual and fictional events. He loves detail and devotes to it all his skill, blending humour and an original power of observation in his densely populated scenes. He belongs to the best tradition of Viennese popular humour. Pachta exhibits in Austria and in the Federal Republic of Germany. *(See portrait of the artist, p. 494). F. N.*

PAGANO, LUISA (1895)   Italy

Luisa Pagano was born in Voghera. In due course she moved to Milan, where she studied music. After completing her studies, she became a highly esteemed opera singer. In her forties, an affliction of the vocal chords prevented her from continuing her career.

Evacuated to Ormala in 1944, she began to paint from a subconscious need to continue working in art of some kind. Thus, in her fifties Luisa Pagano the painter was born and returned to her birthplace of Voghera. Although totally uninitiated in painting techniques and with no specific knowledge of art, Luisa Pagano soon found her own way of expressing herself, leaving much to instinct, to immediacy, to the poetic gift.

Her works fall into two categories. In one, she depicts the ordinary forms of everyday life, a microcosm of real-life episodes and customs. In the other she turns inward to the desires born in dreams, to the vision of a perfect and idealised world. These two levels of expression, often intertwining, are justified and harmonised by the simplicity of the pictorial structure. Some of the scenes of provincial life, at times so concrete and detailed, by their composition and chromatic scheme succeed in transcending mere descriptiveness.

The most outstanding feature of Luisa Pagano's painting is the "visual musicality" of her works. See, for instance, the "Village Landscape," featuring wide spaces, slow rhythms and a sensitive colour-scale enlivened by the white of the houses.

Luisa Pagano has exhibited in Paris (1950), Munich (1953), and Rome (1957). She also took part in the big Rome exhibition in the Palazzo Barberini in 1964. *(See portrait of the artist, p. 494). D. M.*

PAGE, DEROLD — Great Britain

Derold Page was born in Johannesburg, South Africa. After the Soweto riots he came to live and work in England.

As a child Derold Page spent his holidays on a farm and so came to have a special affection for animals. After leaving school he went to work in the city at a design shop, of which he shortly afterwards became the manager. Without any training, he specialised in the design of high-fashion dresses, which he decorated either in appliqué or with fabric paints — sometimes with the addition of shells and porcupine-quill beads.

Paladin, Bruno: The Ship "Good Hope"

The dresses, with designs of animals and landscapes, came to be worn by women of the theatre and film world and by frequenters of art galleries.

Then he retired to a mountain village to concentrate upon painting, a new step in his creative development. When Page came to settle in England, in a 14th-century Somerset cottage, he spent two years transforming a room into a "Jungle" ambience that was to serve as background for a television documentary film featuring him as the "eccentric couturier" of South Africa.

Clothes he had found to be too impermanent a medium for art work, even though many of those who had dressed in what had come to be known as his "wearable art" subsequently framed his garments to hang in permanent splendour, just like pictures. Since those days he has limited his range to painting pictures and furniture, though recently he has begun to experiment with the carving of his own frames.

He has participated in several RONA exhibitions. *(See portrait of the artist, p. 494). Sh. W.*

PALADIN, BRUNO (1951) — Yugoslavia

Bruno Paladin was born in Rijeka, Croatia, where he now lives. This young man, formerly a car mechanic and a sailor on ocean-going ships and now a draughtsman and graphic artist, has brought new artistic form to the already considerable wealth of Yugoslav naive art.

Back in Rijeka after his period as a sailor, he took a job and in his spare time began to

Page, Derold: A Basket of Somerset

Palladino, Angela: The Nude on the Grass

paint the landscapes of Istria, the sea, coastal life and folk customs. Having started to paint in 1973, he exhibited his first picture three years later.

The rockbound coast of the Adriatic, small settlements, shipyards and ships are the favourite themes of this artist. The painting "Red Way" shows two islands linked by a red line in the blue expanse of the Adriatic and, along the edge, the Dinaric mountain massif. Small plots of land, enclosed by grey stones to prevent the rain from washing away the soil, have been sown by the artist with various crops whose colour scheme creates a firm composition, completed by

classics. In 1959 she emigrated and married an American, Tony Palladino, a graphic designer and creative director.

After her children were born, Mrs. Palladino found herself restless. During a brief illness she began idly sketching and, at her husband's urging, started to paint. His attitude to her work was diametrically the opposite of her old art teacher's (though he has given her no direct assistance), and from then on she began to work more seriously. Recently Mrs. Palladino has experimented with ceramics, resulting in masks that are totally different from her paintings. *J. W.*

Palleta, Karl Borro: Columbus-Cocktail-Titbits

a village church and belfry. His technique sets him apart from the Hlebine manner and other techniques typical of various groups of painters in Yugoslavia.

Paladin has had one-man shows and has participated in group exhibitions at home and abroad. *(See portrait of the artist, p. 494). N. T.*

PALLADINO, ANGELA (1929) USA

Angela Palladino was born in Trapani, Sicily. Her father, Italian by birth but brought up in the USA, had gone to Italy on a visit and married there. Political events interfered with his plan to return to the USA, and so he remained in Italy. Angela Palladino is another of those naives who never thought she would become an artist. Indeed, she tells with amusement how her lack of artistic abilities and ineptness with pencil or paint irritated her art teacher in the Italian elementary school she attended in Trapani. Her ambitions were in the direction of literature and she went to Rome to study the

PALLETA, West Germany
KARL BORRO (1898—1972)

Karl Borro Palleta was born in Mariaschein, Ore Mountains, and died in Berlin. He was a trained chef, but also served apprenticeships as a pastry-cook and as a butcher. He was employed as head chef in famous international hotels. In 1949 he opened a hotel of his own, but had to give up work a year later on account of ill health. Palleta used to paint whenever he had the leisure, but took up the pursuit in a big way only after he retired. He had the air of a well-bred man of the world and was something of a character. He was very proud of his inventions in the way of tasty canapes. These tit-bits devised by the ingenious chef Palleta, became a source of inspiration for the painter Palleta. In his pictures he reviewed once more all the culinary works of art with which he had once gained prizes and awards. His "truffle sketches," for example, were as delicate as cut-outs and turned a ham into a poem. "I'm a precision worker," he used to say. Every pistachio that he used for garnishing, every globule of caviare that he applied to an egg to represent a mouth or a nose, every truffle that he sliced up, provided the outlines of a scene which was featured in his oil paintings. These pictures are provided with highly detailed recipes, sometimes pasted on the back of the pictures. They reveal, as does a brief glance at his style of painting, that he is a precise and meticulous snapper-up of unconsidered trifles, who submerges himself with infinite love and patience in every minute detail. His "Self-portrait from Memory," done with special care, is his masterpiece.

![Paluška, Martin: The Trough]

Paluška, Martin: The Trough

Palleta remained until the end an alert and inquisitive individual who sought his inspiration in magazine reports, films and television, reproducing them courageously on his canvases. Palleta's "Tit-bits" pictures are unique in subject-matter and style, and consequently much sought after by galleries. They have been shown in numerous international exhibitions. *(See portrait of the artist, p. 495). T. G.*

PALUŠKA, MARTIN (1913)   **Yugoslavia**

Martin Paluška was born in the village of Kovačica, Vojvodina, the home of ethnic Slovaks, where he attended elementary school. For part of the time he tilled the land and the other part he spent working in the village mill as a miller. One of the founders of the Kovačica group, he has had considerable influence on the other naive painters in his village. His themes are the life and customs of the Slovaks in Kovačica: weddings, dances, visits, and also portraits.

"When I finished my apprenticeship as a miller, I came back home to Kovačica and people heard that I had learned to paint. They asked me to paint tombstones for them, to decorate their verandas and spinning wheels, which I did with pleasure. The village storekeepers asked me to paint their signs for them and, on wooden panels, pictures of the goods they sold: sugar, coffee, bottles, glasses, halters, and so on. I thus improved my technique before I started painting our life and customs."

In "The Trough" (1967), Paluška has painted a scene repeated in the Vojvodina villages for ages: peasants leading their cattle to drink in the early evening. We also see excited dogs getting in the way of the livestock.

Martin Paluška has had one-man shows and has participated in group exhibitions at home and abroad. *(See portrait of the artist, p. 495).* N. T.

PANKOV,   USSR
KONSTANTIN ALEKSEEVIČ (1910—1942)
PANKOV, KONSTANTIN ALEKSEYEVICH

K. A. Pankov was born in the village of Saranpaul, near Berezovo in the northern Urals. His father was a Nenets, his mother a Mansi. In the late 1920s he went to Moscow to attend a two-

Pankov, K. A.: Blue Lake

Pankov, K. A.: A Fishing Collective Farm in the 1930s

year course for training government and party functionaries to work in the national areas. As a star student he was invited to enrol at the Leningrad Institute of the Peoples of the North, and completed this course also with honours. He then took part in the postgraduate courses there, having won repute as an artist. The Institute operated an art studio, where the professional painter, A. Uspensky, instructed Pankov and his comrades (such as Izhimbin Natuskin, Kilya-Pyachka, Terentyeva and other gifted representatives of the northern ethnic minorities) in the use of oils, watercolours, crayons and gouache — which media were totally new to them. Pankov's works reflect the mentality of a taiga trapper, child-like and naive, transferred to paper and canvas by techniques he had been taught.

His outlook was that of the semi-primitive hunter. For him, as for many other students at the Institute, not only the artist's materials, but even the alphabet, houses, railway, trams and electricity were all absolutely novel.

For Pankov, space has rhythm and dynamism. He painted rivers, mountains, racing reindeer and birds in flight. He saw the tundra as a living map of images, on which he could chart past, present and future. He also indicated signs of the new times, the changes that Soviet power had wrought in the tundra. In their student years Pankov and his fellow-students participated in

PAPS
(WALDEMAR RUSCHE)
West Germany

(1882—1965)

Waldemar Rusche was born in Naumburg and died in Lilienthal, near Bremen. An internationally famous ophthalmologist and chief consultant of the ophthalmological department of a Bremen hospital, when he retired from this demanding career at the age of seventy he was concerned to find a hobby with which he could occupy his newly discovered leisure hours.

In his youth Paps had travelled about the world as a ship's doctor, and now he had time to

Paps (Waldemar Rusche): The Market-Day

an exhibition at the Russian State Museum in Leningrad in 1929. In 1937, for work exhibited at the Paris World Fair they won a Grand Prix. Two years later, they produced panels for the Pavilion of the North at the USSR Exhibition of Economic Achievement in Moscow, and also for the foyer of their Institute.

Pankov's works are in the Russian State Museum and Museum of the Arctic and Antarctic, both of which are in Leningrad, and also in private collections. Besides books, two documentary films have been devoted to him; one was made in Leningrad after a script by D. Moldavsky, the other in Sverdlovsk after a script by G. Gor in collaboration with the Mansi poet Yuvan Shestalov. *(See portrait of the artist, p. 495). N. Sh.*

look round his North German home town. He was fond of painting cottages and large farmhouses, with their brickwork and half-timbering — especially in winter, because the whiteness of the snow gives the colours a special luminous quality. At other times he painted bunches of flowers, compact clusters and rampant sprays of blossom, bursting with life and vigour, surging out of pot-bellied vases with irrepressible energy. He was fascinated by small sea-ports. He felt an irresistible urge to discipline in his paintings all that he saw there, and to combine it harmoniously with the picturesque sea of houses: the jumble of closely moored fishing-boats, with their tangle of masts, sails and rigging, the throng of fishermen, tradesmen, shoppers and idle spectators.

Paps was virtually intoxicated by this delight in the organisation and orchestration of his material; the supreme examples of it are two little masterpieces painted with incredible boldness: two variations on a rifle-club festival in an idyllic small town.

In order to turn the innumerable figures into real people, he put on his old magnifying spectacles. Thus, every face, however minute, has eyes, mouth and nose and an expression all its own.

Pictures by Paps are now rare and much sought after. *(See portrait of the artist, p. 495).* T. G.

enjoyed painting, particularly landscapes copied from postcards and calendars. When he retired in 1960 he settled in Nová Ves, near Mladá Boleslav, with his wife, a gifted embroidress. Parting from city life and from his friends was a painful experience. To escape the oppressive solitude and boredom Pařík tried his hand at carving and trimming dolls. At the suggestion of his son he enlarged the scale of his figures. Gradually there came into being Babinský, with his robber band, who kept the sculptor company as he drank his beer. In 1963-64 Pařík's painted statues were included in the exhibition "Naive Art" in Czechoslo-

Parade, Madeleine: Barnyard

Pařík, Antonín: The Robber

PARADE, MADELEINE   France
(MARIE PAULAINE SEIGNEURIE) (1904)

Marie Paulaine Seigneurie, known as Madeleine Parade, was born in Paris. She grew up in a family of musicians and showed considerable musical talent as a child. At the age of four she began playing the piano and eventually became a music teacher. She lived with an artist and in 1962 discovered for herself the joys of painting. She exhibited her work for the first time the next year and ever since has been a regular contributor to exhibitions of naive art both in France and abroad.

Madeleine Parade chooses fresh and delicate colours with which to express the bright notes created by the large masses of greenery or houses which she depicts on her canvases. A classical approach to composition underlies the elements highlighted in her pictures by constant colour contrasts. The work of Madeleine Parade has enjoyed growing popularity over the years.

She has participated in several group shows, both at galleries and in salons, and has had one-woman shows. *Ch. Sch.*

PAŘÍK, ANTONÍN (1904—1976)   Czechoslovakia

Antonín Pařík was trained as a mechanic and from 1927 worked in the Prague textile mill where he ultimately became a foreman. During the 1930s he carved toys for his children. He later

vakia. In 1965 he held his first one-man show, which was followed by sixty others at home and abroad.

Pařík spent most of his life in Prague, but his statues are hardly typical of urban naive art. His robbers and gamekeepers are formed from roughly-carved birch logs, with details added by means of bark and switches. The lurid colouring with enamel paints adds to the powerfully primitive effect. In this respect these works are akin to the pilgrims of the Slovak wire-worker Kerák or of the Polish carver Żegadło, which stem from traditional folk craftsmanship. Pařík's carved figures have in fact more direct ancestors in the mountain spirit Rübezahl, the millers and fiendish figures that are fixed to water-mills beside the waterfalls in the Riesengebirge, so that they "work" alongside the mill. They may also be related to the figurative bee-hives of Wallachia. From time immemorial folk wood-carvers have contrived their idols from the substance of the forests — roots, forked branches, moss or tree-stumps — which they see as the dwelling of good or evil spirits. Pařík's race of wooden figures also includes Romantic heroes and hence symbols of a faith in miraculous changes of fortune. At his fifty-fifth exhibition in 1971 he placed on show a group of bandits alongside historical figures like Wallenstein and the grotesque head of a water-sprite (made from a coffee-mill). The robber-band, consisting of about forty figures and covering an area of ten square metres, moved from city to city and did much to increase the artist's extraordinary popularity. *(See portrait of the artist, p. 494).* A. P.

PASOTTI, BERNARDO (1910)   Italy

Bernardo Pasotti, son of an industrialist, was born in Milan. Encouraged by his parents, he enrolled in the Academy of Fine Arts in Milan (Brera). Having graduated, he exhibited a number of times between 1935 and 1938. However, between 1938 and 1947 he experienced several crises. His

demonstrated an interest in him: R. Carrieri, O. Vergani, L. Borgese, De Grada, D. Buzzati. In 1958 he took part in the exhibition in Knokke-le-Zoute, where he represented Italy together with Metelli. In 1964 he exhibited in Rome.

He was also among those represented in the Great Review in Milan in 1974; in 1977 R. Degni and W. Carlino included him in the Italian section of the exhibition of naive art in Zagreb. Finally, in 1981, there appeared an excellent monograph on him and his work prepared by Degni and Carlino. *(See portrait of the artist, p. 494).* D. M.

Pasotti, Bernardo: Zeppelin

Pasotti, Bernardo: Baroque Church in Monza

work became more and more uneven and profound changes set in. Little by little, he drew away from what he had learned at school, finding his own original, bold solutions, confusing the public and critics.

His exhibition in Milan in 1948 marks his first appearance as a naive artist. He is a rare case, if not the only one, of a naive artist with an Academy diploma.

The predominantly vivid tones in his paintings are boldly distributed, sometimes making for gaudy contrasts which are nonetheless harmonious in their effect.

His painting "Corso Roma" is an example of the author's poetic world; the "classical" architecture of the palace, the empty paved street, with the diagonal trolley lines leading us dynamically outside the painting — all this could suggest a rarified metaphysical atmosphere, were it not for the serene faces of the mother and daughter in front of a shop, the vegetable vendor, the elegant elderly couple and the cyclist, who mitigate the tense rhythmical silence and make it more human, peaceful and ordered.

The work "Cathedral in Cremona" is highly symbolic. The architecture of the church stands out in its light tones in relation to the ruddy background of the belfry and roofs and the blue sky. Human figures are lacking but the statues on the façade and the angels on the flanking columns are a dynamic equivalent to them.

Between 1950 and 1958, many critics and other persons active in the field of culture

Pătraş, Ion Stan: Decoration on a Cross in the "Cheerful Cemetery" of Sapînţa

PĂTRAŞ, ION STAN (1908—1977)   Romania

Ion Stan Pătraş was born in the commune of Săpînţa in Maramureş, where from his early youth he worked as a woodcutter, a traditional occupation in the area. In time, he gained renown for the wooden crosses he fashioned for village cemeteries.

Taking as his point of departure the carving of ornamental motifs in wood, widespread in Romania, Pătraş, in discharging the commissions he received from peasants, introduced personal accents, largely geometrical designs interwoven with figural elements. Later he enriched his repertory by colouring the carved wood, finally adding short verses complementing the picture.

In the collection of crosses by Pătraş in Săpînţa called "The Cheerful Cemetery," intended for the tourist trade, there is in fact nothing gay. What the artist has tried to do is strike a balance between the tragic events of daily life and man's inevitable fate.

From 1961 on, Pătraş displayed his works in group exhibitions in Romania and abroad and received many national awards, as well as the

Pearce, Bryan: Newlyn Harbour

Pavelescu, Emil: Entry into Bucharest of Tudor Vladimirescu

award of the International Triennial of Naive Art in Bratislava in 1972. *M. Il.*

PAVELESCU, EMIL (1949)   Romania

Born in Chernovtsy and now living in Bucharest, Emil Pavelescu is a driver by profession who now chauffeurs an ambulance. Although frequently a witness of dramatic and even tragic events, in his painting, which he took up in 1973, Pavelescu has preserved the qualities of freshness and humour. The latter attribute sometimes takes the form of parody or comedy, even in compositions inspired by history ("The Battle at Posada," "Vlad Tepes").

In addition to painting, Pavelescu also produces sculpture ("Old Man with a Pipe"); his figures border on the grotesque, a characteristic of his work in general.

Many of Pavelescu's paintings are inspired by the urban scene. Sometimes when he depicts a joyful or festive occasion ("The Entry into Bucharest of Tudor Vladimirescu"), Pavelescu transfers to his canvas scenes or figures that have nothing to do with his principal theme. In the midst of the ceremonious welcome given to Tudor Vladimirescu, a number of boyars in long-sleeved tunics and a few Turks in turbans (obviously all opponents of Tudor) are seen fleeing or falling into the river. On a roof, a cat, made restive by these events, seeks a better refuge.

Pavelescu paints in oil on canvas. Since 1974 he has participated in national and international

Pečnik, Greta: Earth

Pepersack, Louise: Departure

exhibitions; and was the winner of the Golden Plaque awarded in Trebnje, Yugoslavia, in 1978. *M. Il.*

PEARCE, BRYAN (1929) Great Britain

Bryan Pearce was born in St. Ives, Cornwall, the physically handicapped son of a butcher. Because of his affliction it seemed at first as if Bryan Pearce could claim no more than the care and attention lavished upon a chronic invalid by his mother. Then, in 1954, he began attending art classes with Leonard Fuller. Admittedly, he showed both natural flair and enthusiasm, but initially this use of his time had a primarily therapeutic purpose. It was not foreseen that his work would capture attention at exhibitions, first in his native St. Ives, and subsequently in Monte Carlo and Sportono (1959—1962). This man, who seemed to live in a private world which, except through his paintings, no one but he could enter, began what was to be a series of paintings and drawings mainly depicting St. Ives and its environs but sometimes ranging in subject as far as Porthleven on the other side of Cornwall.

Pearce paints exactly what he knows. Sometimes hills and buildings are rendered in a straightforward frontal manner. In other works, particularly those which he describes, often in the title, as "all round," the perspective seems to have gone berserk, so that houses and other buildings fan out from the centre of the picture, those at the top being painted without eccentricity (upwards, from front door to roof) while those to the left and right spread out sideways, and those at the painting's base are completely upside down.

Today, Pearce is recognised as one of Britain's finest naive artists. It is largely because of his mother that his exceptional talent has been exported from local Cornwall to ensure his work a place in important collections, museums, and leading galleries. *(See portrait of the artist, p. 494). Sh. W.*

PEČNIK, GRETA (1924) Yugoslavia

Greta Pečnik, born in Oplotnica near Maribor, Slovenia, now lives in Piran, in Istria. When there has been time to spare from looking after her husband and two children, she has withdrawn into a favourite corner to draw and paint themes suggested by her imagination, many of them with erotic overtones. Bright in colour, her figures are symbols of fidelity and passion.

"I am particularly fond of red," says Greta Pečnik, "and often wear red dresses. I had an elementary school education. My childhood was hard as my father drank."

The painting "Earth" shows our planet as an anxious elderly mother hovering over her children. The sky is red hot. On her hair and shoulders, resembling a mountain massif, white snow glitters. Surrounded by trees, people are exploring the earth, discovering its charms and the endless treasurehouse of food and everything else provided for the human race. Lit candles are symbols of discovery.

It is characteristic of Greta Pečnik's work that she does not dress her figures, as other art-

ists do, in the type of clothing worn in her area; she does not link them up with any specific area, for she believes her themes are eternal and close to all people, no matter where they may be on this earth.

Greta Pečnik has had one-woman shows and participated in group exhibitions at home and abroad. *N. T.*

PEPERSACK, LOUISE (1890) Belgium

Louise Pepersack, although a Belgian, has often been classified as a French naive artist.

Petelinšek, F.: Brother   *Petelinšek, F.: Old Mara*

She claimed to have been "born at the age of fifty," that is, in 1940, during the Second World War, when she decided to attend the Brussels Academy. Attracted by her art, the painter Jean-Jacques Gaillard visited her regularly to give her technical advice.

Louise Pepersack left for Vence in 1946. Extremely sociable, she went to the openings of all the art shows and moved in artistic circles. Having a sense of the ridiculous, she often mocked critics who tried to discover in her work "phases," the last of which was qualified as "oriental," which she considered very funny. Stories from the Bible (the Tower of Babel), the Iliad and the Odyssey are all related in her canvases and gouaches, in which a linear treatment prevails. Above all a poet, she depicted strange cities, and farces resembling those of Ghelderode. A black line, often thick, outlines the contours of planes and figures, set in a dream-like décor. Oddly enough, nothing has been published on this artist, and exhibitions of her works have been only intermittent, since she sold pictures whenever the fancy took her. *(See portrait of the artist, p. 494). J. C.*

PETELINŠEK, FRANCISKA (1905) Yugoslavia

Franciska Petelinšek was born in the village of Sveti Pongrac, near the Slovenian town of

Celje; she moved to Duga Resa in Croatia after completing her primary schooling, and spent her entire working life in a textile factory in this pretty small town. Only after her retirement in 1962 did she begin carving wooden figures. Her subjects are often unusual people she has met, frozen in energetic action. Their expressions are reminiscent of the faces of martyrs depicted in Croatian and Slovenian village churches, which are themselves the work of self-taught artists in many cases. Besides carving individual figures, often following the shape of a branch, she also covers the surfaces of birch or poplar branches

Peter, Alfred Ernest: Cathedral

with several interrelated figures. She has been represented in many group exhibitions in Yugoslavia and abroad. *N. T.*

PETER, ALFRED ERNEST (1890—1980)   Switzerland

A. E. Peter was born in Aubonne, Vaud, the son of a banker. He attended high school in Lausanne and then went on to study music. In 1911, he moved to Paris. After the death of his wife in 1955, he began to paint in order to forget his sorrow. Initially, he made small drawings during his travels and later these grew into his first pictures. He has been called the "Utrillo of naive art." His paintings of Montmartre, which he loved, resemble the works of the great Utrillo, but, presented in the naive manner, they possess complete authenticity in their genre. Peter is ranked among the outstanding naive artists of Switzerland.

One of his first exhibitions was held in Paris in 1964. He exhibited in Lugano (1969), in the Pro Arte Kasper Gallery in Morges (1972 and 1975), and in various exhibitions of the Henri Rousseau Group. *G. K.*

PETERNELJ, JOŽE (1927)   Yugoslavia

Jože Peternelj was born in Jarčja Dolina, Slovenia, where he went to elementary school and then cultivated the land until he was twenty-

four years old. He then moved to Žiri, where he got a job in a shoe factory.

Since he retired in 1981, Peternelj has devoted himself exclusively to his painting. The picture "Every Peasant Has His Pleasure" shows a Slovene peasant pouring water over his wife who is having a bath in a barrel. Of course, there is a curious neighbour, hidden, who is watching this somewhat erotic scene.

In "Poor Man's Funeral" (1962), Peternelj painted the kind of funeral usual in Slovenian villages. First the "standard-bearer" followed by the priest and two assistants, the cart bearing the

Peternelj, Jože: *Every Peasant Has His Pleasure*

Peternelj, Jože: *Poor Man's Funeral*

Petranović, Tomislav: *Women Bathing*

deceased, and then the relatives. Against a realistic background the painter has shown the poverty of the deceased and his family by substituting a donkey for a horse. The status of the dead man has been shown symbolically by the absence of a coffin. The dark scenery comprising a pine forest, naked trees, snow-covered roofs and lowering clouds, all rendered in a firmly drawn composition, dramatise man's last moments on earth.

Jože Peternelj has had one-man shows and participated in group exhibitions at home and abroad. *(See portrait of the artist, p. 495). N. T.*

In his painting, Konrad Peternelj portrays both aspects of life. The painting "Work Break" falls into the first category: the family has stopped work to have lunch, the housewife has brought food and the tired members of the household are seated, ready to have a bite to eat. The gloomy autumn sky and the ravens are harbingers of winter. Only the boy, also working with his parents, somehow found the energy to climb a tree.

Konrad Peternelj has had one-man shows and participated in group exhibitions at home and abroad. *N. T.*

Peternelj, Konrad: Work Break

PETERNELJ, KONRAD (1936)   Yugoslavia

Konrad Peternelj, born in Stara Vas, near Žiri, Slovenia, is employed in the local footwear factory as a shoemaker. Since 1958 he has been painting, mostly on glass, themes from the life of forest workers. In his workshop he spends eight hours a day making shoes. After he finishes work, he enters, through his paintings, another world: the magnificent mountain scenery and pine forests which surround him. Life in his district seems to be divided into two parts: the working part (preparing wood, putting preserves in jars, repairing the roof and doing everything necessary to make the country home cosy and comfortable in the winter); and the other, more enjoyable part (family gatherings around the big ceramic stove, telling tales far into the night, weddings and christenings, enjoying feasts).

PETRANOVIĆ, TOMISLAV (1934)   Yugoslavia

Tomislav Petranović was born in the village of Prvča, near Nova Gradiška, Croatia. A drawing teacher, he taught his subject in the elementary school in Nova Gradiška. A few years ago he started devoting himself exclusively to painting, taking inspiration from his childhood, from ancient tales full of strange happenings conceived by the imagination of unlettered peasants. Some of his paintings are on the theme of war and violence. For this he has an explanation. "Just as the war was about to begin, my father, a railwayman, got a job as a guard. Once a transport arrived carrying Jewish people. It stood near our house almost two whole days. The Partisans had wrecked the track so the train had to wait. Without food and water, the prisoners cried out for help. On the sly, mother and I carried water to them all day long, but sadly we had no food to give them."

This painter also strives to portray his vision of Slav mythology: fairies and divinities, surrounded by imaginary flowers. These mythological tales are inspired by the Slavonian plains. From the flood waters of the Sava River mirroring willows and other plants, or from the clear waters of streams, water-sprites rise as in the tales heard in childhood. Such creatures are related to the old Slav goddess of Spring, Vesna.

In "Women Bathing" (1973) — inspired by spring, when underground waters swell, the

materials, thus carrying on an old tradition of Romanian folk art.

In addition to one-woman shows in Constanta, the artist has participated in many group exhibitions and has won various awards. *(See portrait of the artist, p. 495).* M. Il.

PEYRONNET, France
DOMINIQUE (1872—1943)

Dominique Peyronnet was born at Talence and died in Paris. He completed a *tour de France*, associated with his occupation, before going to

Petrescu, Simona: Milking Goats   Philippe-Auguste, Salnave: Carnival

marshes grow green and only the chirping of birds breaks the deep silence — the two sprites dressed in white resemble village girls. In a conscious desire to differ from the other Podravina painters, Petranović makes his figures slightly grotesque (with unnaturally large hands, symbolic of physical labour), although they are not caricatures.

Tomislav Petranović has had one-man shows and has participated in group exhibitions at home and abroad. *(See portrait of the artist, p. 495).* N. T.

PETRESCU, SIMONA (1952) Romania

Simona Petrescu uses painting rather than reality as a medium for experience, for illness ties her down to her wheelchair. She has, however, kept up direct contact with folk art and with peasant painting on glass. In spite of the difficulty of moving around, she has visited the big museums and even regions in Romania famous among ethnographers for their folk art.

Although certain influences are apparent in her work, she has evolved her own style, characterised by a soft and sensitive line, stressing the poetry of her subject-matter, and a lyrical pathos. Her paintings are also notable for their gentle humour and joyous chromatic relationships.

Active in applied arts as well, Simona Petrescu fashions "masks" by combining diverse

work in a printing shop in Paris in 1902. He specialised in lithography, and his growing knowledge of colour led him to try painting. His first works date from 1920. In 1932 he exhibited in the Salon des Indépendants. As with many of the artists of his generation, he was actually discovered by the public at the 1937 Maîtres Populaires de la Réalité exhibition. He continued to work in his printing shop until he reached retirement age.

Louis Aragon, in a preface written in 1947, referred to certain new trends at the end of the 19th century as a "kind of new pre-Raphaelism" — a term which might be applied to the works of Dominique Peyronnet. His paintings are few, but each was received at the Salon des Indépendants of its day as a major event: "The Castle of the White Queen" in 1934; "Crossing the Moselle," (which won the Paul Guillaume Prize) in 1936. Each of these canvases shows an absolute mastery of technique as well as genuine inspiration. Purity of expression, refinement of execution and in the use of colour, perfect balance of its composition — all these qualities are present, whether the painting be large in scale ("Town Crier from the Garde-Champêtre") or intimate in feeling ("The Model," "The Reclining Woman").

Dominique Peyronnet had one-man shows in 1964 in Salzburg, Rotterdam and Paris. He participated in the 1932 Salon des Indépendants and the Salon de l'Ecole Française and also in the group shows at the Kunsthalle in Bern (1958), in Knokke-le-Zoute (1958) and in the Maison de la Pensée Française, Paris (1960). *(See portrait of the artist, p. 495).* Ch. Sch.

PHILIPPE-AUGUSTE, SALNAVE (1908)   **Haiti**

Salnave Philippe-Auguste was born in St. Marc. Starting life as a solicitor with a poetic streak, Philippe-Auguste, comfortably married in Port-au-Prince with eight children, did not take up painting until he was 55 years old. He first visited the Centre d'Art in 1960, at a time when carnival. Lately he has moved from such well-trodden ground and has introduced a touch of the grotesque into his work. *Sh. W.*

PIC (1893—1980)   **Great Britain**
(TEARLACH S. HIGGINS)

Pic was born of Scottish parents in Belgrano, Buenos Aires, and died in London. Following an uncomfortable period at Malvern College (1910 onwards), he attended London University and obtained a degree in engineering. In 1930, Pic (the name he always used as a painter) married

Peyronnet, Dominique: Town Crier from the Garde-Champêtre

he was chiefly engaged in writing articles and poems for the press and painting only in spare moments. Finally, for economic reasons (he had to support his family) he chose to devote himself to painting.

The results were outstanding. Today his jungle pictures are amongst the most prized works in Haitian painting — a remarkable achievement for a man who had to shoulder the responsibilities of a Magistrat de la Paix at three periods in his life.

Everything that Philippe-Auguste paints is first carefully drawn on transparent paper and then transferred to hardboard. With a strong *penchant* for green (sometimes with black in the background), he creates precise, yet romantically lyrical, pictures which evoke the world of

the artist Kate Elizabeth Oliver. They went to live at Barra, in the Outer Hebrides, where both of them could paint in peace. In the same year that they settled in Barra he held his first one-man show (at the Wertheim Gallery in London). Further one-man shows followed and his pictures were also exhibited in Paris and Rome. He joined forces with Jan Wieliczko of the Centaur Gallery in London, who organised special exhibitions of his works, the latest of which was held posthumously in 1981. His works have also been shown in mixed exhibitions.

Pic could paint pictures of mysterious creatures in dream landscapes, romantically conceived figures accompanied by horses, or exact depictions of wild animals (as in "Tiger"). *(See portrait of the artist, p. 494). Sh. W.* →

PICKET, SARAH   Canada

Little is known of the life of Sarah Picket, except that she was a schoolgirl in Kingston, New Brunswick, where, in 1848, she painted the watercolour of the steamship "Sarah." It was not unusual for girls of this period to be taught watercolour painting and stencil work as part of the training of a "finished" young lady. Sarah Picket, while obviously very "finished," broke the constraints of formalised and sterile popular conventions with her own disciplined but freely imaginative work. The only known examples of her work are contained in the school exercise

related to the area. However, in his biographical notes on Pickett, Sidney Janis remarks that Pickett had a fine disregard for facts. For instance, he put George Washington in a lush green landscape during a time of the year that normally would have been cold and snowy. Further, he showed the first president facing a house that was built long after he was in New Hope (then known as Coryell's Ferry). Pickett, like many another naive, was inclined to paint what he knew rather than what he saw.

Pickett's friends recalled that he worked on his paintings for years, changing the composi-

Pic (Tearlach S. Higgins): Man and Friend

Picket, Sarah: The Steamship "Sarah"

book from which the painting of the "Sarah" is taken. Interspersed with her mathematical homework is a series of carefully executed geometrical fantasies. Shapes within shapes are rendered with the same fine line and brilliance that marks the drawing of the "Sarah." In view of the disciplined exuberance of this other work, it is no wonder that young Sarah self-confidently named this beautiful and sturdy vessel after herself. *Th. L.*

PICKETT, JOSEPH (1848—1918)   USA

Though only four of his works are known to survive, Joseph Pickett, according to those who knew him, painted many more. He was born and died in New Hope, Pennsylvania. Until he married, his summers were largely spent roaming around the area as a carnival concessionaire of shooting galleries, cane racks and knife boards; he would return to New Hope for the winter.

At the age of forty-five he married and opened a small grocery and general store in New Hope. He promptly decorated the store window with a landscape filled with maple trees. He evidently started painting seriously in the late 1890s — possibly, according to friends, to do something as a substitute for the adventurous life he had once lived. At first he used house paints, then he turned to artists' materials. If his surviving paintings are a clue to his interests, he seems to have preferred historical subjects

tion, adding more and more colour until he achieved relief-like textures that were sometimes half an inch high. In addition, he would use sand, broken shells or other extraneous materials to achieve certain textures or colours.

After Pickett died, his wife put the store and its contents up for auction. When only one dollar was offered for each painting, Mrs. Pickett bought them back herself and gave one to the New Hope High School. Lloyd Ney, a New Hope artist, saw two others on sale in the old store building, bought them for fifteen dollars, and then traded them with a local art dealer for frames. The paintings later found their way into the home of a Mr. and Mrs. Price, who lent them to the Newark Museum in New Jersey for an exhibition, "American Primitives." From there they went on to appear at the Museum of Modern Art in New York in 1932 in an exhibition entitled "American Folk Art, The Art of the Common Man in America," organised by Holger Cahill. Pickett's paintings are now owned by the Museum of Modern Art and the Whitney Museum in New York City and the Newark Museum in New Jersey. *J. W.*

PIERCE, ELIJAH (1892—1984)   USA

Elijah Pierce was a black man and, like many another American black naive or folk artist, something of a religious visionary who looked upon his art as a form of sermonising or missionary work. Pierce told Boris Gruenwald, a young artist who discovered him in Columbus, Ohio, in 1972: "Every piece of work is a message. All my carvings are preaching one important message — love one another."

Tall, gaunt, quiet in speech and manner, Pierce was born on a rural southern farm close to Baldwin, Mississippi. Piety became a permanent force in Pierce's art and life because of an odd incident in his youth. As he told it, "I was laid out for dead once for not doing what the Good Lord told me to do... I went into the house one evening.... Sears & Roebuck [a mail-order

he promised her a whole zoo and began carving every animal he could think of. This led him into creating his now noted story carvings. The profiled figures in these plaques were first done as separate pieces, mounted on a board backing, and then painted. Later he began carving his action-filled scenes, in bas-relief to begin with. Most of Pierce's pieces were painted with gloss colours and heavily varnished to intensify their sheen, which is occasionally heightened with sprinklings of glitter. Pierce has always been an avid fan of the "funnies" (cartoon strips), and they seem to have influenced not only the composi-

Pickett, Joseph: Manchester Valley

merchandising company] had sent a catalogue that day and I reached over my Bible to look at the catalogue ... and He laid His Hands on my head and I fell outta the chair.... My mother and sister ... laid me out on the bed ... and I heard the Voice say, 'I told you to read the Bible and you disobeyed Me, so I'm just showing you My Power....' They were screaming when I came back ... and I said, 'Hush, Mother, I know what's the matter' ..."

All this may have kept Pierce on the straight and narrow path of sanctitude but it did not curb a restlessness that grew in urgency as he grew in height.

Pierce's first carving — done, as all his work is, with a pocket knife — was an elephant, made for his wife's birthday. She was so fond of it that

tion but also the colouring of his work. During the thirties, Pierce and his wife would spend their summer vacations driving from state to state in the South, selling his art work at country fairs and markets. At the same time he would give a sermon or preach to explain the moral purpose, implication or meaning of his carvings. Frequently Pierce would give a "picture" to an admirer or friend. Today Pierce's work is exhibited in museums and commands quite high prices, but he did not regret having given away any of it. "I get a kick out of giving as they do in receiving."

In 1982 Pierce, 90 years old and devotedly attended by his third wife, worked in his barber shop and carved till his last days. *J. W.* →

PIERRE, ANDRÉ (1914—1979)   Haiti

André Pierre was born in Port-au-Prince and died in Croix-des-Missions. Like Hyppolite, he might never have become an artist had it not been for a chance encounter, not with DeWitt Peters, but with Mme Odette Rigaud, the wife of a Haitian doctor and an expert in the mysteries of Voodoo.

Mme Rigaud bought govi jars (for the preservation of the physical and sacred elements of the dead, in order to protect them against malevolent spirits) decorated by Pierre. As a strong believer in Voodoo, soon to become a la-place (the man managed to persuade him to paint pictures (on flat rectangles) which included not only the loas, but also complex backgrounds — a step which Pierre took with reluctance, because he declared that he had received as yet no precise commands from the loas to paint pictures in this manner. Throughout his life, he was unwilling to paint unless the loas told him to do so; their instructions were not only direct commands to paint, but also included exact descriptions of the subject of the picture itself.

Later on, in spite of valuable commissions for his pictures, there were to be long periods

Pierce, Elijah: Story of Job

Pierre, André: Mistress Siren

who prepares a houmphor temple for special occasions), and eventually to replace M. Isnard (the local houngan priest) when the old man died, Pierre was already an expert in all matters relating to this complex faith.

Pierre's decoration of the houmphor temple, and of the jars, caused Mme Rigaud to encourage him to paint on the interiors of gourd shells (curved surfaces which allowed him to depict individual pictures of different loas, albeit against a plain grey background); she further

Pierre, André: The Voodoo Divinities Damballah, La Flembeau and Jean Danton

of artistic inactivity because the loas were silent.

Pierre did not merely record the Voodoo rites and ceremonies, but — more essentially — the life and habits of the loas themselves. People, if they appear in his pictures, are always shown paying their respects to the loas, whose presence in the same picture is so natural that only their attributes and costume distinguish them from the humans.

Pierre always remained poor. Despite a growing clientèle for his pictures, completed or yet to be painted, he probably spent most of the

picture he repudiated everything he had learned and began again from the beginning. He reverted — or, rather, advanced — to utterly elemental forms of expression, in order to give adequate expression to the myths of his people ("Mammy Wata," 1976). *(See portrait of the artist, p. 494).* G. Sch.

PINDER, GEORGE (1895)   Great Britain

George Pinder, born in Manchester, did not start painting until he reached retirement in 1962. Entirely self-taught, he reserves the early

Pili-Pili: Mammy Wata

Pinder, George: While London Sleeps

money he earned upon the houmphor temple, especially after he became the established houngan. Toward the end of Pierre's life, Kurt Bachmann, a great patron of his work, showed the aging André Breton colour slides of his paintings, but the great Surrealist poet and philosopher, who only had a few months to live, never saw the paintings themselves. Nevertheless, Breton (who had said that if Hyppolite could have come to Europe he would have changed the face of modern painting) did declare that in his opinion André Pierre reflected the soul of Haiti.

Alas, even before his death in 1979 Pierre was suffering from failing eyesight — a physical handicap that brought his artistic career to a premature end. *Sh. W.*

PILI-PILI   Zaire

Discovered by Pierre Romain-Defossés (1878—1954), for whom he worked as a servant, Pili-Pili is a self-consciously naive artist. Of all those artists in Zaire who passed through his master's school and later exhibited in Europe and the USA, Pili-Pili is probably the most remarkable.

He learned the painter's craft so consummately that he was able to transform traditional animal motifs and create a number of compositions of supreme ornamental subtlety and superb technical expertise ("Snake Attacking a Bird's Nest", 1960). Fifteen years after painting this

hours of the morning for his painting, and generally spends the rest of the day in his garden or carrying out household chores. His style has an attractive luminous quality and at times — as in his seashore pictures — approaches Impressionism. Perspective in his works is arbitrary, but never irksome, and figures, too, lose nothing in stature, however distant from the front of the picture.

As well as being included in a number of exhibitions in northern England, George Pinder's work has been on display at several RONA exhibitions. *(See portrait of the artist, p. 494). Sh. W.*

PINTARIĆ, JOSIP (1927)   Yugoslavia

Josip Pintarić, born in the village of Mala, not far from Nova Gradiška, Croatia, took up carpentry after completing elementary school, married, and went to work as a woodcarver. Josip plays the violin well and even now frequently performs at weddings, together with his brothers. He began to paint in 1960 and was soon noticed by the then director of the Croatian Museum in Zagreb, who organised Pintarić's first exhibition in Vukovar. In 1972, he gave up woodcarving to devote himself exclusively to painting. His first pictures were commissioned by brides-to-be in the village. At the same time, he began to paint for himself, usually pictures of nature. In depicting trees, he meticulously paints every leaf, every branch, the whole forming a mass of luxuriant vegetation, rising skyward from the fertile earth on which every plant prospers. The sky is rarely seen in his paintings. Usually only a yellow light from the sun filters through, radiating in all directions. When he portrays men or women, they are sturdy, firm of step, with large labourer's hands that are always busy and reflect vitality and strength.

"People and nature in my paintings are bound up with the marshes surrounding me," says Pintarić. "Strange tales have it that mysterious animals live in the marshes. Sometimes, in the summer, peasants cautiously enter the marshes with their livestock and bathe all together. When I was a child, my father told terrible stories of people disappearing in the marshes. They used to say that in the wintertime when the wind whistles, if you listen hard you can hear their voices calling for help. I feel the need to paint all these stories I heard in my childhood."

In the painting "The Unknown" (1972), in front of an ethereal, imaginary wood stands the frightening figure of an unknown man. Next to him is a mythical bird that is trying to fly away but, being tied, cannot. The largely concealed

Pintarić, Josip: The Unknown

Pinto, José: Jaguars

face of the unknown person represents everything that can take you by surprise in the marsh — and that everything can only be evil.

Josip Pintarić has had one-man shows and has participated in group exhibitions at home and abroad. *(See portrait of the artist, p. 494).* N. T.

PINTO, JOSÉ (1932)   **Brazil**

José Pinto was born in Ilhéus, Baía. He became a painter in 1948, when living in Salvador. Five years later he left for Rio de Janeiro.

Pictures by Pinto are usually concerned with biblical subjects and have a simple and ingenuous attraction.

His first exhibition was also a solo one (Galeria Nuestra Senhora de Paz, Guanabara, 1969). He has been featured in many group exhibitions. *Sh. W.*

PIPPIN, HORACE (1888—1946)   USA

Horace Pippin ranks among the best of the American artists, let alone naive painters, of the first half of the 20th century. A black man, he was born in West Chester, Pennsylvania. After his mother died, Pippin moved to Paterson, New Jersey, in 1911. He worked for a while as a fruit powerful work is his triptych on the hanging of John Brown, the anti-slavery activist of the American Civil War era.

Sidney Janis once asked Pippin for his life story, and Pippin wrote that, when he was a youngster, he picked up a magazine that had a sketch of a funny face in it, and an offering of a prize to the person who could "make me." Pippin entered the contest and won a box of coloured pencils. He then found some muslin, cut it into squares and drew biblical scenes on each square. These were sold to an elderly woman, who returned them to young Pippin with the

Pippin, Horace: Domino Players
(The Phillips Collection, Washington)

packer and then found work at the American Brakeshoe Company. In 1917 he enlisted in the army at Fort Dix, New Jersey, and the end of the year found him in Brest, France. He was wounded so severely in battle that his right arm was paralysed.

Pippin kept both a written and a pictorial diary of his experiences during the First World War. The written one, according to one biographer, Selden Rodman, documents Pippin's patriotism in "clichés and traditional patriotism." The sketches, however, and Pippin's later paintings, say something else — that Pippin found war horrible and horrifying.

After his discharge from the army, Pippin went back to West Chester, married a widow with a son, and augmented his disability pay by doing light work. He told an earlier biographer, Sidney Janis, that he had enjoyed drawing since early childhood, and the urge to continue was so strong that he refused to let his injury stop him. For a time he drew by supporting his right arm with his left hand. Then he developed some exercises to strengthen the crippled arm, and in 1929 began to use paints. His most famous and possibly most

remark, "You sure make bum things." She had washed his doilies and naturally washed out his art work.

Pippin also told Janis that his work was first seen by Dr. Christian Brinton, an orientalist who had it exhibited in the West Chester Community Center. This led to Pippin's paintings being included in the "Masters of Popular Painting" show at the Museum of Modern Art in 1938 and in several subsequent exhibitions as well.

Asked how he painted, Pippin indicated that he gave considerable thought to the picture he wanted to paint. ". . . If it is a worthwhile picture, I paint it. I go over the picture in my mind several times and when I am ready to paint it I have all the details that I need. I take my time, and examine each coat of paint carefully to be sure that the exact colour I have in mind is satisfactory to me . . . my idea is that [a man] paints from his heart and mind. To me it seems impossible for another to teach one of Art."

While working on the fourth version of another painting, "Holy Mountain," Pippin suffered a stroke and died in 1949. *J. W.*

Pirosmanashvili, Nikolai: Kathetian Epic

PIROSMANAŠVILI, NIKOLAJ (1862—1918)
PIROSMANASHVILI, NIKOLAI

USSR

The Georgian artist better known by the brief appellation of Niko Pirosmani is the best known primitive artist of the USSR both inside and outside the country. There are, of course, other artists like him, but only he was to acquire such universal fame, the epithet of genius, and only he has a memorial museum in his birthplace, and has had hundreds of articles and monographs written about him, international exhibitions mounted specially to show his works and documentary and feature films made about him. His role as pioneer is obvious. He was discovered at the start of this century by Russian avant-garde artists. These were three friends: the Zdanevich brothers, artist Kirill (1892—1969) and poet Ilya (1894—1975), who subsequently emigrated to Paris where he was known as Ilyzad, and Mikhail Le-Dantu (late 19th century — 1917).

Not only the Futurists were interested, but also some Georgian artists who regarded Pirosmani as a vehicle of the distinctive national character. Pirosmani's biographers do not see eye to eye on his life story. To this day art students and historians argue as to when he was born in the East Georgian village of Mirzaani, what he did throughout his life, when he died, and also where he is buried. At the age of twelve he went to Tiflis (today Tbilisi), capital of Georgia, to live with the Kalantarovs, a family of rich merchants and his father's former masters. Treated with kindness in this home, where he lived up to the age of twenty-eight, he drew and read avidly, especially the national poet Vazha Pshavela (Luka Razikashvili), and learned much about the national movement of the Georgians and their great people. Young Niko's drawings caught the eye of the professional painter, Gevorg Bashindjagyan, who, noting his original talent, gave him advice. After nearly sixteen years at the Kalantarovs, Niko, a most romantic soul, wrote a love letter asking one of the daughters, Elisabed Hankalamova, a wealthy widow ten years his senior, for her hand in marriage. She treated the proposal as absurd and Niko had to leave. He attempted to start a business of his own, opening a signboard

Pirosmanashvili, Nikolai: Donkey's Bridge

painters' workshop with a friend, also an amateur, G. Zaziashvili. However, they went bankrupt and in 1890 he took the job of brakeman on local goods trains operated by the Trans-Caucasian Railway Office.

In 1894, at first by himself, and subsequently with one Dimitr Alugishvili, Pirosmani opened a dairy shop. After losing this job, he became a tramp, earning a precarious livelihood painting pictures and signboards for wine cellars and wineshops, greengrocers', butchers' and dairy shops. Thus he became a wine cellar artist. It was above the entrance to one of the taverns, the "Varangian" on Tiflis' Railway Square, that the Zdanevich brothers and their friend Le-Dantu spotted in 1912 a signboard which Pirosmani had painted of a sea battle involving the celebrated Russian cruiser "The Varyag" ("Varangian") sunk in the Russo-Japanese war, after which the tavern was named. Entering, the three young men were enchanted when they saw among the pictures on the walls a portrait of the owner and "The Young Bear" and "Queen Tamara." The tavern-owners fed him, gave him a place where to sleep, and provided him with some money for

paints and the black oilcloth on which he painted without preliminary preparation.

Though the signboard themes were often suggested by the customer, Pirosmani painted what imagination dictated, and in this respect adhered to a definite style. In short, the analogous outlook of the painter and his customer found expression in the representation of a solid, understandable, objective world. Pirosmani's still-lifes are, in their way, signboards, while his signboards are, in turn, still-lifes. To a certain extent Pirosmani has chronicled history, depicting men and women of diverse trades and professions and social status as well as the customs and mores of the past. Apart from signboards, the basic genres to which he addressed himself were single and group portraits, the representation of animals, scenes of feasting, and the "epics," the epithet somebody bestowed upon his pastoral panoramas of his beloved Georgia, which are indeed presented in an epic vein. Some pictures deal with village life. His range of subject-matter and types and his style are fairly stable, while his portrayal of the overall environment and story is, despite the expressive nature of some details, exceedingly static and objectivised, as if isolated from the time of day or night, the atmospheric or climatic condition, the action, or the place. Meanwhile his rather restrained colour scheme quite accorded with the palette characteristic of Georgian folk art. His portraits, though named, do not depict real personages but are rather symbols, since they do not present particular features but the popular conception of the Georgian, of the Eastern person, a trait found in 18th-century Persian painting and in Georgian painting of the 18th or 19th centuries. He is thought to have produced some 2,000 pieces, but only about 200 are extant, most in the State Museum of the Arts of Georgia in Tbilisi, and some in private hands. Pirosmani loved depicting various animals such as the deer, hart, lamb, lion and bear. With him they are symbols of man's kind helpers, figures seemingly borrowed from folk tales.

The girls of Ortochala, the "red-light district" of old-time Tiflis — the Ortochala Venuses as they were once dubbed — over whom men would fight with knife in hand, are always depicted in white. Pirosmani pitied these prostitutes and pictured them in white as if to grant them indulgence for their sins. All his feasts and picnics, generous abundance in pictures produced by a penniless tramp, are seen as if they are occurring in a fairy tale — poetic dreams of a blissful life of peace and harmony. The professionals who invited Pirosmani to a session of their Association of Georgian Artists in 1916, and even provided him with some pecuniary assistance, failed to understand him and could not accept his work. Evidently the time had not yet arrived to comprehend a different system of visual representation, that of urban folklore, which is akin to the broadsheet, signboard and icon. His own milieu could not understand him either. In all eyes he was an eccentric drunkard, a crank. The latest research indicates that interest in this genius remains undimmed. Unfortunately Piros-

Pirosmanashvili, Nikolai: The Actress Margarita

mani's fame, and the understanding of his art, were posthumous. In the spring of 1918 this great painter, who did more by his art to convey the mood of Georgia and its people than his now forgotten opponents, died a sick beggar: where — nobody knows. *(See portrait of the artist, p. 495). N. Sh.*

gives his paintings a rather tense and moody aspect.

He had an important one-man show in 1978 in the European Academy in Berlin, with a catalogue in colour and a foreword by Hans Hesse. *(See portrait of the artist, p. 495). N. E.*

PLASMEIJER, JOOP (1942)   **Netherlands**

Joop Plasmeijer was born in Amsterdam, where he lived for ten years. After elementary school, he went to secondary school for a few

Plasmeijer, Joop: Interior

PLASTININ,   **USSR**
VASILIJ VASIL'EVIČ (1907—1983)
PLASTININ, VASILI VASILYEVICH

V. V. Plastinin was born in a working-class family in the old Central Russian town of Vladi-

Plastinin, Vasili Vasilyevich: Prince Alexander Nevsky Massing Troops in the 13th Century to Defeat the Enemy

years, and from his fifteenth year on worked in a factory as a metalsmith. Having made the acquaintance of a painter and seen his works, he said in jest that he would be able to paint just as well. When he tried it, to his great surprise he found it gave him much satisfaction. In 1969, he won the Talens Prize, a significant incentive for him, for, as a naive figurative painter, he had feared that he would achieve nothing in a world where only abstract art was held in esteem. In the meantime, he decided that he did not want to work in a factory for his whole life and at the beginning of the seventies resolved to devote himself exclusively to painting, despite not having had any education in art. He now lives in Hengel with his wife and two children.

His first paintings were mostly of fantasy cities, but later on real life took precedence. His best works are portrayals of Dutch middle-class homes where symmetry, humour and a somewhat subconscious symbolism play an important part. The orderliness of the middle classes is to him a source of entertainment, although he is not a moraliser. Also characteristic of him is his use of strong colour. Deep blue, restlessly applied,

mir. For forty-five years between 1926 and 1971, he worked on the railways, beginning to paint only after retirement. Plastinin reveals folkloric features, even though he gravitates to more complex manifestations, as indicated by his choice of subject.

Like most elderly people, he has a predilection for depicting reminiscences and past experiences, as well as the history of his native city and his country generally. In his historical "epics" he reveals traits characteristic of the *lubok* broadsheets, even of the icon. He presents the actual architecture of the city, such as the celebrated Cathedral of St. Demetrius and the Golden Gates and also that gem of Russian architecture, the Cathedral of the Intercession of the Holy Virgin that stands on the banks of the Nerl River. These historical pieces are not only in a *lubok* manner; they also produce the impression of a motley-coloured carpet. However, the actual episode depicted is secondary to the impressive grandeur of the architectural relics. Thus, if we take "The Killing of Prince Andrey Bogolyubsky," the actual murder is presented merely as a secondary episode within the overall architectural composition. Elsewhere the figures of Russian soldiers are depicted in a most conventional way, which prompts one to assign Plastinin to the ranks of folkloric naive artists. He has been represented at group shows in Vladimir and also at a republican level. Some pieces are exhibited in the Museum of Folk and Amateur Art of Soviet Russia, in Suzdal. *(See portrait of the artist, p. 495). N. Sh.*

PONZI, NELLO (1897) Italy

Nello Ponzi, born in S. Maria del Piano, Parma, kept a small village store selling odds and ends. Then, after working as a puppeteer, and writing a number of works, he began his "career" as a painter and sculptor in 1945.

In his small town in the foothills, he lived a quiet life, completely taken up with his two activities: as shopkeeper and as painter-sculptor. He evaded the influence of contemporary culture and remained strongly tied to his peaceful and patriarchal view of life. Both in his sculpting

Ponzi, Nello: Lumberjacks

(modelling and adapting stones taken from a nearby stream) and in his painting, his themes are taken from fantastic tales, ancient legends and biblical episodes. The world of his sculptures has primitive and archaic aspects and therefore, by chance, points of contact with the Bogumil gravestones in Bosnia-Herzegovina, but also with the spare and primitive Romanesque bas-reliefs by Viligelmo. In his painting, which he worked at for almost thirty years in the strictest secrecy, he shows distinctive characteristics, with regard both to technique (he dissolves coloured powders in vegetable oils, often olive, in the way village housepainters used to do several decades ago, and applies the result to pressed wood) and to subject-matter (a specially suggestive iconography, typified by squat figures with astonished looks on their faces).

In "The Foresters" his primitive world is symbolically represented. The woodsmen are descending a slope in single file with pack donkeys. The landscape is one of old castles (abundant in his area), rolling hills and foaming brooks. The light blue sky and white paths are sometimes stained with yellow ochre spots — the result of oxidised olive oil.

The special features of his painting, purity and pathos, are apparent in "Flight from Egypt," with its archaic medieval atmosphere and spare simplicity, and in "Dream," where the author portrays the death of his wife in an allegory in which he himself appears, with a winged dragon — the symbol of death — and angels. *(See portrait of the artist, p. 495). D. M.*

POP, MARIA Greece

Maria Pop was born in Phaleron, near Athens, studied music and acting, and began to paint in 1952. She has travelled to many European countries, where she has visited museums and exhibitions. Her favourite subjects are old houses, with their warm, mellow colours; courtyards; little shops where the human presence has left its imprint; gatherings, processions, festivities, and all the simple little things that man cherishes. She works with traditional materials, such as tempera, egg-tempera, and oil. Her pictures are marked by a distinctive quality of

Pop, Maria: Procession

composition, warm colours and a pure tenderness and sensitivity. All are rendered with remarkable vivacity and sincerity. She endeavours to render even the slightest details as accurately as possible. The human presence animates her scenes without ever becoming the predominant element. Following a folk custom, she adds explanatory inscriptions to her paintings.

Maria Pop, who lives in Athens, has had several one-woman shows in the capital, Thessalonike, and Volos, and has taken part in group exhibitions in Athens, other parts of Greece, and abroad. She has been represented in several Pan-hellenic exhibitions, in the Alexandria Biennial (1974), and in the exhibition of naive painters organised by the National Gallery in Dortmund, Germany (1978). *A. T.*

POSZ, MARIA DE (1929)   Austria

Maria de Posz was born in Budapest. Venezuela was the homeland of her choice, but since 1962 she has lived in Salzburg.

Starting to paint in 1964, she showed a predilection for landscapes, gardens, multitudes of people, recollections of the tropics of Venezuela, and finally the life of Salzburg. She also paints scenes of the folk customs of her new homeland, Austria, of which she has grown very fond.

Her paintings have been reproduced on picture postcards (UNICEF 1973) and record jackets. She has exhibited in Austria, Germany,

Posz, Maria de: Downpour in Salzburg

Pressley, Daniel: A Summer Day Chore

POVOLNI, MIHALJ (1935)   Yugoslavia

Mihalj Povolni was born in the village of Padina, Vojvodina, inhabited by ethnic Slovaks. He is a farmer, without schooling, who occasionally paints in his free time subjects from the life of the Slovaks in Padina. He thinks of himself as a chronicler of the life and work of his village and tries to paint so that "coming generations will know how life was lived in Padina. Everything is changing quickly now, and our nice customs are disappearing," says Povolni.

In "Pig Slaughter" (1973), Povolni seems to have done a portrait of his wife and himself, as

Povolni, Mihalj: Pig Slaughter

Switzerland, and the USA, and has been awarded prizes. She is a member of the Henri Rousseau Group. *(See portrait of the artist, p. 494).*

he has painted his own yard. When winter comes to the plains where the painter lives, with snow and freezing winds blowing through Hungary and Romania from the Russian steppes, the peasants slaughter their fattened pigs for food during the cold season. Such a scene is shown in the painting. On the chair is a bottle of brandy, from which a swig is taken every once in a while to get warm. Everything is bathed in a rosy light against the trodden snow.

Mihalj Povolni has had one-man shows and participated in group exhibitions at home and abroad. *(See portrait of the artist, p. 494). N. T.*

PRESSLEY, DANIEL (1918—1971)   USA

Gregarious and something of a man-about-town, Daniel Pressley was so dedicated to his art that he spent long hours at it, yet still found time to keep a journal which was a combination of diary, autobiography, statement of personal philosophy and sketchbook. In it he wrote: "With only a limited Grama [i.e., grammar] school learning, I Daniel Pressley, born at Wasamasaw, South Carolina, when asked my age my answer is that an artist doesn't really have an age — because it's an artist creation that counts; if his creations are youthful then the artist is young no matter how old in age his age time." Actually, Pressley was born in 1918 and died in 1971. He moved to Ohio, married, had two daughters, was divorced, and left for New York in about 1943 to work for a plumbing supply firm. He was housebound by a prolonged illness and, though he recovered, never worked again but devoted himself entirely to painting and wood-sculpture. He participated regularly in the Greenwich Village Outdoor Art shows, where a fellow artist, Marcia Wilson, bought his work and was asked by him to photograph portions of his journal

T. Floru, who was amazed by the riotous imagination and decorative sense this talented peasant woman demonstrated. In that same year of 1935 she was invited to work at the experimental workshop of the Kiev Museum of Ukrainian Art, in its way a studio of folk art, where there were several outstanding peasant painters, among them I. Gonchar and P. Vlasenko. After Maria Priimachenko was taken to see a performance of the Ukrainian opera "The Zaporozhye Cossack Beyond the Danube", she produced an intricate composition that subconsciously adhered to the popular type of painting, presenting the stage

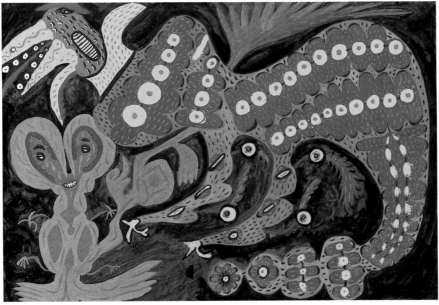

Priimachenko, M. A.: Green Beast

Priimachenko, M. A.: Glory to the Unknown Soldier

shortly before his death. He recorded that he "began to Draw and Carve when at actual age of 6 years. I hated farmwork because there was year in and year out, Dig up, Dig and Destroy. I wanted to do something that could live forever, something I could look at for years without destroying. I youster [used to] go down to the swamp and study the bright moon and wonder if the same moon shown down on other people in other parts of the world."

Sections of this journal were entitled "A footnote of the artist life and thoughts are filed here" and "Footnotes by Daniel Pressley oil painter and sculptor folk art." *J. W.*

PRIJMAČENKO,   **USSR**
MARIJA AVKSENT'EVNA (1908)
PRIIMACHENKO, MARIA AVKSENTYEVNA

M. A. Priimachenko was born in the village of Bolotnya near the Ukrainian capital of Kiev, from which place she has never moved. As a little girl she began to draw figures in sand, sought for what she called "blue peat," (which apparently was swampland clay), embroidered, did needlework, and moulded figures and animals of dough to embellish pies and cakes, which is quite in keeping with a time-hallowed tradition. She was discovered in 1935 by the Kiev lady painter

action as a flat, two-dimensional scene, with stripes, and adding a band of village musicians. The bond with traditional popular imagery is revealed in Priimachenko's allegorical and personified works, the flowers and animals stemming, as they do in folklore, from associative concepts. Thus, we have the modish sea serpent, the bureaucratic toad, and so on. She also loves to personify the plant and animal world. Priimachenko was rediscovered by art historians and painters in the 1950s. She turned to complex thematic compositions centering on either the struggle between good and evil or on satire. Priimachenko has also shown great talent as an illustrator of books for children published in the Ukraine. Widely known in the Soviet Union, she holds the distinguished title, Merited Master of Folk Art of the Ukraine, and is a member of the USSR Union of Artists. Besides being represented in all the important group shows at different levels, she has had several exhibitions devoted exclusively to her work, which has also been reproduced on picture postcards, in booklets and in the many monographs and articles written about her. After seeing an exhibition of her work Pablo Picasso exclaimed: "I kneel before this marvel, the art of this Ukrainian woman of genius." *(See portrait of the artist, p. 494). N. Sh.*

PROCHÁZKOVÁ, LUDMILA (1903)   Czechoslovakia

Ludmila Procházková, born in Heršpice, is a housewife and lives in Slavkov. She started painting in Damborice in 1941 where, in the hard times of the Second World War and the German occupation of Bohemia, she wanted to participate actively in the ethnographic movement and thus to revive the roots of her national culture. Hoping to help restore the noble character of old folk culture, she followed traditional folk art in her paintings, presenting the old ideas and collective memory in a cycle showing the customs of a

Procházková, Ludmila: In the Yard

patriarchal village. Her sense of reconstruction is amazing. Procházková's links with folk art are found in her interpretation of old ceremonies, customs, dances and figures in national costumes in paintings on glass and on canvas. They represent the whole cycle of man's life in moments of Sunday contemplation. Procházková's scenes of Haná, the country of her childhood, are bright, transparent, festive and genuinely poetic. She has participated in several exhibitions on both national and international levels since 1956. *(See portrait of the artist, p. 494).* S. T.

PUGUG, I MADE (1940)   Indonesia, Bali

I Made Pugug was born in Penestanan Kaja. A little over a generation ago the Young Artists movement was born in Pugug's home village of Penestanan. Today, the artists of this movement are numbered in hundreds, most, unfortunately, having but mediocre ability, though a few, such as Pugug, possess exceptional talent. Pugug comes from an agricultural family, and in his youth worked first as a contract farmer and later as a gardener at the Ratna Warta Museum in Ubud. In 1959 he took the position of cook to the Dutch artist Arie Smit. Smit had earlier been instrumental in the development of the Young Artists movement, but although Pugug stayed with Smit until 1961 he apparently had no interest in painting at that time. It was not until some years later that he began his career as a painter. In the spring of 1969 he returned to study under Arie Smit and the Penestanan artist, I Made Sekar. Pugug soon showed himself to be an imaginative but controlled painter. His interpretation and development of the Young Artists style possess the innocence and naturalism that one would expect, but transcend what has

become a standard formula and breathe freshness into what has become a hackneyed approach. Pugug's exotic scenes of village and agrarian life are painted in bizarre and extraordinary colours. Abundant vegetation seems to crowd in from all sides, but still does not disturb the stillness and peace of the central theme.

His paintings reveal his obvious joy in the world around him. He has been exhibited at the Ratna Warta Museum, at the Arts Centre of Denpasar, Bali, and in many private galleries in Jakarta, London, New York and Los Angeles. *(See portrait of the artist, p. 495). J. F.*

Pugug, I Made: Cockfight

Puja, Florika: The Wooing

PUJA, FLORIKA (1920)   Yugoslavia

Florika Puja, born in the village of Uzdin Vojvodina, inhabited by ethnic Romanians, has been painting Romanian national costumes and customs since 1962. After marrying, for a number of years she worked with her husband in the fields in addition to doing the housework. When she took up the brush, other women in her village, Anujka Maran and Marija Balan for instance, were already transferring to canvas the Romanian designs they had previously embroidered.

Florika Puja's subjects are village events and customs. Whomever she paints is carefully dressed in the Romanian national costume, which she herself wears. In "The Wooing" (1974), well-to-do farmers mounted on red horses are escorting a sleigh drawn by two gaudily turned-out steeds. Also in the painting is a village dog barking at the red horses and a wide muddy street with a row of houses painted like Easter eggs. "I paint my horses, cows, and dogs in colours that suit me," says the artist. "Why should I look to see what colour a horse is?"

Florika Puja has had one-woman shows and has participated in group exhibitions at home and abroad. *(See portrait of the artist, p. 495). N. T.*

manifestation of childhood dreams and ambitions. His carved and painted folding triptychs are naive in spirit; power of characterisation is somewhat limited by the fragmented manner of depiction, evidently caused by the artist's desire to give emotional expression rein. Almost everything is symmetrical, with, as a rule, a centrally positioned blossoming tree or self-portrait, or the representation of some other person. Purygin's frequently symmetrically paired animals, flowers or people suggest a certain analogy with the biblical legend of Noah's Ark and the animals that "went in two by two."

Puškarić-Petras, Mara: Christmas

Purygin, Leonid Anatolievich: In Defence of Animals

Purygin has been represented at two exhibitions and is now a member of the youth section of the Moscow chapter of the USSR Union of Artists. *(See portrait of the artist, p. 495). N. Sh.*

PUŠKARIĆ-PETRAS, MARA (1903) Yugoslavia

Mara Puškarić-Petras was born in Novigrad Podravski, Croatia, where she still lives. Left a widow in 1923, while still a young woman she was compelled to bring up her child herself. She was sixty when she began to paint by chance, while helping her granddaughter do her homework. She works mostly on lesonite and occasionally on canvas.

Speaking about the themes of her pictures, she says: "I like to paint my village, especially the tower in front of which all sorts of things happen: weddings, funerals, births, entertainments. I like painting everything the way it was in my youth."

But what is most interesting in the world of this old woman, hardened by labour and time, is her lyrical, emotionally refined, poetic feeling for and vision of everything that happened in her youth. Never sentimental, she is simply and exceptionally poetic. Her concentration on singing the praises of the past reveals a sensitive and gentle woman's soul. At exhibitions throughout the world she is often called the Grandma Moses of Podravina.

She has had one-woman shows and has participated in group exhibitions at home and abroad. *N. T.*

PURYGIN, LEONID ANATOL'EVIČ (1951) USSR
PURYGIN, LEONID ANATOLIEVICH

L. A. Purygin was born into an office-clerk's family in the town of Naro Fominsk, not far from Moscow. After eight years of general schooling he attended evening art classes at the Surikov Art College in Moscow, but was forced to give them up after a year as the frequent journeying to the capital took up too much time. He entered employment as a joiner at a local toy factory, but nevertheless did not abandon painting. Currently he lives in Moscow. He is a true urban naive, displaying what might be considered certain mental aberrations as expressed in a marked religious fervour combined with a certain eroticism, the whole expressed in a theatricalised

Pachta, Josef

Pagano, Luisa

Page, Derold

Paladin, Bruno

Pařík, Antonin

Pasotti, Bernardo

Pearce, Bryan

Pepersack, Louise

Pic (Tearlach S. Higgins)

Pili-Pili

Pinder, George

Pintarić, Josip

Posz, Maria de

Povolni, Mihalj

Prijmačenko, M. A.

Procházková, Ludmila

eta. Karl Borro

Paluška, Martin

Pankov, K. A.

Paps

rnelj, Jože

Petranović, Tomislav

Petrescu, Simona

Peyronnet, Dominique

smanašvili, Nikolaj

Plasmeijer, Joop

Plastinin, V. V.

Ponzi, Nello

ug, I Made

Puja, Florika

Purygin, L. A.

RABUZIN, IVAN — Yugoslavia
RADKE, ZENON — Poland
RAFFLER, MAX — West Germany
"RAINBOW ARTS" (ENUGU) — Nigeria
RAMHOLZ, FELIX (MUCHE) — West Germany
RAMIREZ, MARTIN — USA
RAŠIĆ, MILAN — Yugoslavia
RASMANÉ, NITIEMA — Upper Volta
ŘEHA, VIKTOR — Czechoslovakia
ŘEHÁK, ANTONÍN — Czechoslovakia
REPNIK, ANTON — Yugoslavia
RIEC, RAYMOND — France
RIGAS, YORGOS — Greece
RIMBERT, RENÉ — France
RISTIĆ, PETAR — Yugoslavia
RJAUBA, STASIS — USSR
RODA, I NYOMAN — Indonesia, Bali
RODRÍGUEZ, JOSÉ A. — Cuba
RODRÍGUEZ, MANASES — Venezuela
ROEDER, JOHN — USA
ROGGERI, TONI — Italy
ROUGHSEY, DICK — Australia
ROUSSEAU, HENRI — France
ROVESTI, BRUNO — Italy
ROY, LOUIS — France
RUAN ZHANGJUN — China
RUBAŠKIN, S. J. — USSR
RUGGERI, ALFREDO — Italy
RUSEWICZ, MICHAŁ — Poland
RYBKOWSKI, WŁADYSŁAW — Poland
RŽEVSKIJ, N. A. — USSR

Rabuzin, Ivan: The Rooster

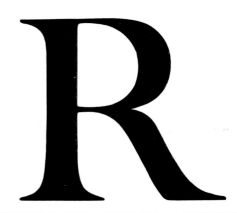

Rabuzin, Ivan: Vineyards

RABUZIN, IVAN (1921)   Yugoslavia

Born in Ključ, Ivan Rabuzin returned to his birthplace after long years of absence and wandering, during which he also served an apprenticeship and worked in a factory in town.

In his village, surrounded by a countryside that has changed but little since his childhood, Rabuzin today paints out-of-the-ordinary landscapes, illuminated by a bright light seemingly radiating from the hills and clouds.

"The cheerfulness and beauty of my childhood were always dampened when there was no sun, when rain or snow fell, but joy returned with the clear skies and the disappearance of the clouds," says Rabuzin.

Optimism is the hallmark of his paintings, for he depicts a world better than the real one. The world of his paintings breathes harmony; in it there are no shadows, no struggle, no hatred.

Most of his landscapes have no people in them, and if they are inhabited, it is usually by only one person. This is the case of the painting "Greeting to the World," where a young nude woman emerges from behind forested hills, encircled by large flowers in soft colours. In each hand she holds a big blossom pointing skyward, where feathery, elongated, identical rosy-white clouds sail. In the foreground a large sun at the bottom of the picture has lit the enchanted landscape and dispensed a benevolent warmth, enabling everything to germinate, turn green and grow. Thus in the painting, sun, warmth and woman are transformed into symbols of fertility and growth. The world is vast, fertile and variegated, and everyone is welcome in it. In fact, the landscape bears a message, a philosophy of life and a view of the world that Rabuzin, a lyrical painter, transmits to the viewer through his creativity.

Radke, Zenon: Lady with Dog

"The motifs of my paintings are landscapes," says Rabuzin. "In my pictures, I beautify nature. In other words, in nature I create an order that suits me, I create a world that pleases me and that appears the way I want it to."

In the painting "My World," against a Zagorje landscape a boy is holding a picture of his village. The houses are in perfect order, the fields have been ploughed and these, together with the woods, constitute the world Rabuzin lives in. The village is only a fragment of the landscape; it could be a microcosm of the universe. The boy, his eyes wide open, stands firmly in that sunlit world, not worried in the least by the small round clouds resembling a necklace of pearls. Similar is his "Landscape" (1965) with its meadows nodding with wild flowers, its wooded hillocks, its identical treetops in sunlight, its blossom-covered branches and the sun, a symbol of warmth and life.

Ivan Rabuzin has had many one-man shows and has participated in group exhibitions at home and abroad. *(See portrait of the artist, p. 516). N. T.*

RADKE, ZENON (1921)   Poland

Zenon Radke, born in the town of Łapy, now lives in Gdańsk. In his early childhood, his parents moved to Daugavpils, in Latvia, where he lived until 1943, working as a mechanic. After returning to Poland, he settled in Gdańsk, where he is employed as a mechanic. Art has held an attraction for him since early youth. After visiting museums and exhibitions, he himself tried his hand at painting for the first time in 1964. A year later, on the basis of his works, he was admitted to membership of the Association of Polish Artists. His paintings are in state collec-

"Rainbow Arts": Untitled

tions and in the collection of L. Zimmerer, Warsaw. He has had one-man shows in Gdańsk and Stockholm and has participated in group exhibitions in Neuchâtel, Stuttgart, Hamburg, London, Bratislava and other cities. *(See portrait of the artist, p. 516). A. J.*

RAFFLER, MAX (1902)   West Germany

Max Raffler was born in Greifenberg, where he still lives. His father was a farmer, and Max followed in his footsteps. Raffler is generally reckoned to be the most distinguished of the peasant painters in Germany.

What is so astounding in Raffler's pictures is the matter-of-fact, indeed instinctive assurance with which he integrates people and objects into space and into the landscape. There is never the slightest trace of intellectual calculation in the construction of the pictorial scenery or in the juxtaposition of coloured areas or events. With almost somnambulistic instinct and without the slightest misgivings concerning the handling of crowds, herds, masses of trees and agricultural implements, he crams his canvases to the point of overflowing, if necessary, with hundreds of objects. Line by line, he assigns every object to its place, calms down movement, places areas of stillness between masses of bodies, discreet shades alongside bolder chromatic combinations and creates order and rhythm effortlessly.

In the course of his life Raffler has painted his way patiently right through the Holy Scriptures, from the story of the Creation to Christ's death on the Cross. The supreme achievement among his religious pictures is the Stations of the Cross, which he provided for the Maria am Wege church in Windach and which has brought renown to this tiny village. If we immerse ourselves visually in these pictures, our eye is captivated at once by their structure — the piling up of horizontally ordered elements, such as rows of people. "Wedding Breakfast" is a typical example because, among other things, it reveals

Friends say he likes to describe his works as examples of "contemporary experience."

Although the picture shown here officially bears no title, it is known as "Market Day after the End of the War" and is reckoned a typical painting by this artist. It carries a strong propaganda message because the cyclist is transporting yam — a staple food in Nigeria and one that had been in acutely short supply during the Second World War. So, in its way, "Untitled" is a symbol of great public joy. It is Market Day, the War is over, and again ordinary citizens are able to buy yams, whose harvest is back to normal.

Raffler, Max: Wedding Breakfast

Raffler's ability to impart rhythmic movement to the pictorial surface by means of an interplay of colour and shapes that is rich in variation and full of inner tensions.

There is scarcely another naive painter who has been exhibited so often or whose works are so frequently found in galleries or private collections. Raffler himself, however, seems unaffected by his success. *T. G.*

"RAINBOW ARTS" (ENUGU)   Nigeria

The Nigerian naive "Rainbow Arts," whose real name is Enugu, now lives and works at his studio in Enugu in the Province of Anambra in eastern Nigeria. In Nigeria itself his paintings of the Ibo people are well known. In Europe and the USA he would be regarded as a full-time popular painter whose appeal to all kinds of people helps to earn him a good living from his pictures.

It is in this sort of way, by reflecting the strong feelings of the populace at precisely the time when such reactions are at their strongest, that Rainbow Arts has earned his popularity as a Nigerian naive painter.

The subjects he paints may be "obvious," but for those who see his work they are nonetheless trenchant. *Sh. W.*

RAMHOLZ,   West Germany
FELIX (MUCHE) (1868—1947)

Felix Ramholz was born in Querfurt and died in Ramholz, Rhön where he had been an estate manager since 1901. He was actually called Muche, and was the father of the Bauhaus architect Georg Muche, but his pseudonym as a painter was taken from the place where he lived. At the age of forty-eight Ramholz began collecting paintings — by no mean artists, at that: Chagall, Feininger, Klee, Marc. At sixty he was seized by a desire to paint himself. Very few of his pictures became known to the public, but what showpieces they are: humorous studies of mankind with all its follies! Ramholz was something of a joker, and Georg Muche has many amusing tales to tell about him. As for his painting, his palette was imbued with Biedermeier sentiment, his colour values were bold and generous. The splendid alternation of structured and plain coloured surfaces should also be mentioned. There is self-confident manipulation of the objects portrayed, delicately matched in their colour values. Ramholz also handles delight-

fully anecdotal themes, where he himself occupies a central position. The comedy of the moment never degenerates into mere caricature and always retains something of gentle humour. *(See portrait of the artist, p. 516). T. G.*

RAMIREZ, MARTIN (about 1885—1960) USA

The extraordinary, strongly patterned and carefully organised drawings by Martin Ramirez were done in the California state mental hospital, where he was put in the mid-1930s and where he

Ramholz, Felix: The Husband

Ramirez, Martin: Untitled

Rasmané, Nitiema: Portrait of a Man in a Blue Jacket

Rasmané, Nitiema: Tailor Here

died. Facts about him are sparse. He was born in Mexico (in about 1885, it is assumed) and emigrated to California possibly in about 1915, the year in which he seems to have become mute. In about 1935, deemed incapable of caring for himself and labeled as paranoid and schizophrenic, he was placed in the mental hospital. Ramirez was not deaf but was so withdrawn that no one was able to discover why he would not or could not talk. After he had been in the hospital for ten years, a doctor discovered that Ramirez was saving pieces of discarded wrapping paper, scraps, old menus, and other trash, which he pasted together with glue made by chewing bread to make large sheets, and was drawing on the paper with crayon and pencil stubs. Ramirez produced almost two hundred drawings between 1945 and 1960 which the doctor stored in his garage, where they were found by Jim Nutt, a California artist who shared his discovery with his dealer, Phyllis Kind.

Like the work of most mentally or emotionally disturbed people, Ramirez's drawings are in all likelihood pictorialisations of troubling phantasmagoria, but they do at the same time suggest his Mexican upbringing, and the frequency of wild animals indicates a possible rural environment. *J. W.*

RAŠIĆ, MILAN (1931)   Yugoslavia

Milan Rašić was born in Donje Štiplje, near Svetozarevo, Serbia where he had four years of elementary schooling. He helped his father farm until 1970, when he left the village and moved to Svetozarevo to devote himself exclusively to painting, at which he had been working on and off since 1960. His very individual style, ideal-

is disintegrating, how the young men and women are leaving it, while only the weak old men stay behind. They depart, as I did, leaving the fertile land, living crowded into small city flats and walking on asphalt all day long."

In "The Funeral" (1967) Rašić shows the road to a cemetery. Behind the ox-drawn cart, bearing the coffin of the deceased, the family is weeping. Instead of music, birds chirp in the trees.

In "Church Festivity" (1968), a village church, in form and dimension resembling a monastery, stands in the middle of the painting. In the courtyard in front of the church, peasants dressed

Rašić, Milan: Church Festivity

Rašić, Milan: The Funeral

ising country life, immediately appealed to the young men in his village, who tried imitating him.

His paintings show, as from a bird's-eye view, peasants going about their daily tasks. Because the spectator is looking down at the village below he does not see the sky but only the barnyards enclosed by fences. Circling like a falcon over the village (where the church holds the central place, as a symbol of rural peace and tradition) he can note every detail. All around are seen tiny peasants tilling the soil, feeding their livestock or taking part in some festivity. The livestock comes home from pasture; women are drawing water from a well; a boy and girl are embracing on the grass. All these scenes are set in farmyards, underneath trees and among flowers. In his paintings, Rašić endeavours to safeguard the idyllic life of the village from change.

Asked why his village is so sunny, so harmonious and gay in colour, so full of flowers, although villages in Serbia are not so neat and orderly, Rašić replied: "I see how fast the village

in national costumes of rainbow colours are dancing and enjoying themselves. Rašić is fond of portraying church festivities accompanied by music.

Milan Rašić has had one-man shows and has participated in group exhibitions at home and abroad. *(See portrait of the artist, p. 517). N. T.*

RASMANÉ,   Upper Volta
NITIEMA (1946)

Born in the village of Damzoussi, Upper Volta, the son of a peasant, Rasmané grew up in his native village. He was brought up in the Roman Catholic faith, and his Christian name is Emanuel. At the age of ten he moved to the capital, because the family could no longer make a living on the land.

Rasmané never went to school. He did various odd jobs, learned to repair radios and one day began to draw.

"Whenever I see someone, I have an urge to paint him," he said, and "God has shown me how I have to paint." He makes a living for himself and his three children on his modest income from sign-painting for hairdressers and other people, and from occasional portraits, which he copies from photographs.

He lives in a little mud hut, without water or electric light, situated in a suburb of Ouagadougou, where there are neither regular streets nor house-numbers.

His advertising placards are to be found in every part of the capital: he is the most popular, celebrated and sought-after sign-painter in Upper Volta.

(See portrait of the artist, p. 516). G. Sch.

Řeha, Viktor: The General Yermenko Mine

Repnik, Anton: People from the Poorhouse

Riec, Raymond: Endymion's Slumber

ŘEHA, VIKTOR (1898)   Czechoslovakia

Viktor Řeha, born in Hrabová, was already working on a farm when he was seven years old. From the age of fourteen to sixty-two he worked as a miner and then as a voluntary national health service worker. He started painting in an amateur artists' club in 1950. As he felt the urge to bear testimony to the events that had excited him most, he treated farmers' and miners' themes, by which he wanted to convey something significant. His actions take place on several stages. His time planes exist almost side by side, presented with cartographic care. The poetic content of his pictures is rounded out by verbal commentaries.

Řeha has participated in several exhibitions. *S. T.*

ŘEHÁK, ANTONÍN (1902—1970) Czechoslovakia

Antonín Řehák, was the son of a joiner and the eldest of nine children. He attended elementary school in Sveti Kopeček, near Olomouc, for eight years. His father was called up during the First World War and Antonín had to help his mother look after his younger brothers. After the war he was employed in no less than nine different trades: as stone-breaker, soldier, labourer in a sand-pit, concrete worker, locksmith and cabinetmaker, followed by work in the

chemical industry and in a workshop for making toys. From 1928 onward he tended the gardens of the shrine at Sveti Kopeček. As years went by he laid out beautiful gardens on the "Sacred Hill" (Sv. Kopeček), became well-known in the area, and was much sought after as a gardener and as a man well versed in the ways of nature. He had a secret bond with nature, it was said, and knew how to master her. When he began to paint systematically in 1960, his pictures of green parks were so laid out that they almost suggested the designs of a landscape gardener. Řehák always liked drawing with pencil and crayons. In pictures drawn from memory and in the paintings "from nature" he showed himself to be a sharp observer with a well-nigh photographic memory.

As a rule his oil paintings are preceded by a clear sketch. Along the main axes of a dry linear concept Řehák arranged little pictures and flowers, bushes and cottages and then filled these with detail, as though he were transplanting flowers from a hot-house to the flower-beds. When he fills in the outlines it is as if he were embroidering an old-fashioned decoration and trimming it with tiny pearls taking the design from his memory or devising it in response to his feelings. In this way, by allowing his fancy free rein, distorting and dislocating the image, he achieves a lyrical tension which adds a new dimension to the actual scene. The bright image shimmers and shines with the solemn stillness of morning.

The oil painting of Karlovy Vary ("View from the Pension Aleš") is one of his principal works, painted from his memories of a stay in the famous spa on the Ohře.

A second series of Řehák's pictures is ranged round the "Sacred Hill," with its baroque Pilgrims' Church. The splendour of Sunday Mass is extended to the framework of nature. But beyond the awe-inspiring pomp lies the cosiness of Řehák's "Sacred Hill" — the little village grave-

REPNIK, ANTON (1935)　　Yugoslavia

Anton Repnik was born in Sveti Vid, near Vuzenica, but now lives in Gornja Muta near Dravograd, Slovenia. For a time he was employed in a factory as a foundry worker, but then he fell sick and was left an invalid. He has been painting since 1959, largely chosing social themes. The son of a poor family of many children, he himself has seven. Burdened by life's problems and his own illness, he has found relief in painting.

Repnik paints the people of his district: women working in the fields, reapers, plough-

Řehák, Antonín: Karlsbad (View from the Pension Aleš)

yard on the bank of the green pond, with its weeping willows and its ducks. There stands his summerhouse — his studio, nowadays a sleepy hollow. He used to keep poultry there, breed pigeons and fish and keep bees; he had a pony to help him bring his drinking water from afar. *A. P.*

men, workers from the factory where he was employed. Weighed down by problems, they labour hard for their living, because life in that area is not easy. In his first phase, he used dark and gloomy colours, reflecting his spiritual and material state. When his health improved, the colours grew lighter, warmer and more cheerful, but his paintings forfeited some of their power and his figures became slightly stylised.

In "People from the Poorhouse," Repnik shows elderly persons in an enclosure, like sheep. In this narrow space, a crowd of the homeless stagger as though gasping for air, like a net full of fish drawn out of the sea.

Anton Repnik has had one-man shows and has participated in group exhibitions at home and abroad. *(See portrait of the artist, p. 517). N. T.*

RIEC, RAYMOND (1905)   France

Raymond Riec, born in Landerneau, started to draw in his earliest childhood and has recounted how he used to draw on the sacks of grain sold by his grandmother. He attended

Rigas, Yorgos: Threshing

school up through his *baccalaureat*, but to earn a living worked at a variety of small jobs: streetcar conductor, driver, night porter, and so on. For a time he was a hawker at fairs. His discovery of the Mediterranean and later of the Red Sea led him to painting. He exhibited for the first time in Paris in 1960.

From canvas to canvas, Raymond Riec invents new flowers, suggesting unheard-of perfumes. He brings into being a nature of sumptuous colours, an inseparable mass, to all appearances. Careful examination will always reveal, however, a space between two leaves or two vines inviting the eye to glide, in complicity with the painter, to the heart of the painting. Riec's manner is opulent: he likes sharp colour contrasts. He builds the successive planes of his compositions through a game of reciprocal lights and darks.

Raymond Riec has exhibited since 1957 at a number of Paris galleries. *(See portrait of the artist, p. 517). Ch. Sch.*
←

RIGAS, YORGOS (1921)   Greece

Yorgos Rigas was born in Zoriano, a mountain village in Doris, Central Greece, and lives in Athens, where he works as a tricycle transporter. But the memories and experiences of his life in his village were kept alive in his mind until 1976, when he started painting. Traditional farming and cattle-breeding tasks, almost forgotten customs; people walking in the country or along the coast, and sometimes relaxing in coffee-houses and taverns: these are all part of his repertory. The milking of cows; the building of houses; organ-grinders and old-time photogra-

phers; marriage festivities; women fetching water, feeding hens or working in the fields, and above all, views of his little mountain village and of its surroundings are all represented in his painting. He says that the aim of his work is to bring beauty and joy to people's homes. Anxieties, conflicts and problems have no place in his timeless and still world.

The simple symmetrical arrangement of trees, houses, tables and benches; the stiff and somewhat clumsy figures and the calm chromatic contrasts offer the viewer a pleasant surprise.

Ristić, Petar: The Pipe Player

Rigas has taken part in group exhibitions and has had two one-man shows in Athens. *A. T.*

RIMBERT, RENÉ (1896)   France

René Rimbert was born in Paris. His father was a picture framer, so that his contact with the world of painters and modern art started at an early age. He made friends with the Cubists and from 1920 received encouragement from Marcel Gromair. In the same year, he exhibited for the first time at the Salon des Indépendants. Like Vivin and Grim, he worked for the Post Office, remaining in its employ until 1956. The turning-point in his career came in 1923, with a trip to Germany and Belgium. His discovery of the Dutch 17th-century masters, notably Vermeer, impressed him deeply. During this same period, he met Max Jacob, also Picasso and André Breton. The "Peintres de la Réalité" exhibition in 1937 was a major event, confirming his talent, as it was in general for second-generation naive artists such as Jean Eve or Jules Lefranc. In 1964, he received the Critics Prize of the "Primitifs d'Aujourd'hui" exhibition at the Galerie Charpentier.

Each painting by Rimbert is the result of a painstaking technique, and the outcome of diligent preparatory sketches and tracings, with each colour carefully chosen. Flemish influence is present throughout, both in the treatment of light and in the exceptional quality achieved by transparencies and subtle nuances. A total mastery of drawing allows Rimbert to impart a distinctive vitality to each of his pictures. His preference for an almost photographic approach to his subject enables him to play with perspectives and space.

René Rimbert has had four one-man shows in Paris and has participated in many major group exhibitions, from the "Les Peintres de Coeur-Sacré" show in 1928 to the Triennial of

In the painting "The Pipe Player," Ristić has caught his father at rest after working strenuously in the woods. Reclining on some ferns, he is keeping his worries at bay by playing on an instrument he himself has carved from wood. The area around him is bare, with the exception of two flowers in the foreground, which seem to symbolise the rare moments of leisure. His wife is calling him home, where his family is waiting for him.

"My father was barefoot and his clothes were ragged," says Ristić, "and he had to do everything himself. He felled trees, sold the wood and with

Riauba, Stasis: Master Craftsman

Roda, I Nyoman: Barong Landung

Naive Art in Zagreb in 1973. *(See the reproduction, p. 83 and the portrait of the artist, p. 516). Ch. Sch.*

RISTIĆ, PETAR (1927) Yugoslavia

Petar Ristić was born in the village of Rujkovac, near Leskovac in Serbia. His father was a poor peasant who sent his son to a trade school to learn a craft. But before he could finish his apprenticeship, the war broke out and Ristić, though not yet of age, nevertheless engaged in the fighting. He remained in the army, and after a number of promotions retired with the rank of lieutenant-colonel. He now lives in Koper, Slovenia.

In 1954, he began painting, on glass, motifs from his birth-place and associated with the childhood interrupted by the war. His village is situated near a river on a plain; on somewhat higher ground are the homes of a few landless peasants, and it was in one of these that Petar Ristić was born.

"The difference in standard and status was tremendous between the people who lived near the river and those of us who lived on the rocky slope," says Ristić.

the money brought home flour, sugar, and other necessities. In painting my childhood, I am paying a debt to him for the hard life he led to bring up his children." *(See portrait of the artist, p. 517). N. T.*

RJAUBA, STASIS (1904—1982) USSR
RIAUBA, STASIS

Stasis Riauba was born into a Lithuanian peasant family, and in his teens worked as a farm labourer. After the First World War he continued agricultural work. Riauba's work falls into several tentatively defined categories, paramount among which are sculptures, which, though suggested by folklore, have been metamorphosed by the artist's imagination. The peasant mentality always spots the farcical in the day-to-day; this is illustrated by his "The Count from Plataiai," "The Robber" and "The Miller and the Devil." Another category may be called by one of his titles, "The Anthropoid," and includes "The Monkey Concertina Player" and "Grappling with the Dragon." A third category consists of such fairy-tale personages as "The She-Devil" and "The Witch" and also incorporates the popular Lithuanian Saint George, known in Lithuania as

St. Jurgis. A fourth category comprises portraits of representatives of the bourgeois world, such as "The Gentry," "The American," "The Kulak" and "The Policeman." Most deserving of note is the first category of characters, carved mostly of wood and also decorated with fur, leather and fabric. They are not infrequently painted, as many sculptural pieces of the 19th and early 20th centuries were. He was also among the Lithuanian folk sculptors who collaborated in executing memorial posts or pillars to mark the centenary of the birth of the noted Lithuanian composer-artist Ciurlionis; these were set up along the

one of cock-fights, drunkenness, arguments, surreptitious erotic interludes and other occurrences among his fellow Balinese villagers — reveals an aspect of Balinese life otherwise virtually unknown to outsiders. Roda's robust, earthy visions seem to be derived from an inner urgency to create and compose with a directness and passion that link him with the best of the European naives.

Roda is also a musician; he makes, plays and teaches the flute as well as illustrates little booklets of fingering charts and notation for Balinese music and dance. His paintings enjoy consider-

Rodríguez, José A.: The Kiss

wayside from Varena to Druskininkai, popularly termed the "Ciurlionis Way." From 1960 Riauba was represented at all republican and USSR exhibitions. His works have been acquired by several Lithuanian museums and have also been reproduced in art books. *(See portrait of the artist, p. 516). N. Sh.*

RODA, I NYOMAN (1928)   Indonesia, Bali

I Nyoman Roda, born in Ubud, stands apart from other Balinese painters in both the style and the content of his work. Although he was trained in the classical *Wayang* style, in the mid-seventies Roda veered away from these methods and themes.

Roda's approach differs radically from that of his peers primarily in his uninhibited use of materials. He paints directly onto his canvases, departing from the usual Balinese practice of first conceptualising an entire composition in pencil outlines. The world which he depicts —

able popularity and can be found in many major collections overseas as well as in Indonesia. *(See portrait of the artist, p. 516). J. F.*
←

RODRÍGUEZ, JOSÉ A. (1930)   Cuba

José A. Rodríguez (El Monje), born in Sancti Spiritus, began working at the age of fourteen on the Central Adelaida Sugar Estates. Then he worked at various jobs — shoe-shine boy, mason, clerk, and so on. In 1965 he took classes at the Vocational Centre of Plastic Arts at Sancti Spiritus, and in 1966 exhibited paintings in the UNEAC (Union of Cuban Writers and Artists) Gallery. In 1970 he participated in Salon '70 and in 1971 in the joint exhibition "Primitive Painters," in the Havana Gallery. In the same year he mounted a one-man show at the Cuban Spanish Society in Havana, and in 1976 took part in the exhibition "Eleven Cuban Primitive Artists" at the Institute of Jamaica in Kingston. Some of his work involves elements of pre-Columbian Maya

Rodríguez, Manases: The Mad Woman

Roggeri, Toni: St. Francis

Roeder, John: Bay with Islands

Indian mythology in theme and design; its remarkable graphic and chromatic qualities make it difficult to confuse with the work of any of his colleagues. *T. R.*

RODRÍGUEZ, MANASES   Venezuela

Manases Rodríguez of Caracas is the odd-man-out so far as Venezuelan naive artists are concerned. Perhaps the closest to him in style is Julio Cesar Perez, but Perez's work does not have the same acrid flavour that marks Rodríguez's paintings. As in the picture shown here, his

Roughsey, Dick: Willy Long at Mushroom Gallery

favourite colour range consists of blue, black and white (in reproduction his pictures may seem like drawings, which they are not). *(See portrait of the artist, p. 517). Sh. W.*

ROEDER, JOHN (1877—?)   USA

In December 1961, the Richmond California Art Center held a retrospective exhibit of the work of John Roeder, then eighty-three. Dean Wallace, a "San Francisco Chronicle" reporter, described him as "far more than a primitive. He is a visionary, a sage, a poet, a magician and a clown." James Eakle, an art historian and teacher in the area, said Roeder's work "represents a unique religious and philosophical approach to art."

Roeder was indeed a fascinating artist. The son of a stonecutter, he was born in Bollendorferbruck, Luxembourg, in 1877. In 1901 he emigrated with his wife and two children to the USA, where he worked for a time as a pipe fitter for Standard Oil near Richmond. He bought a small ranch, but sold it after ten years to become a gardener at the Richmond Union High School. It was at this point that he began to build a small village in his back garden and to construct life-size sculptures out of cement which he painted. He was a Roman Catholic and built a small chapel decorated with paintings (some on glass), sculptures and many of his own poems. According to Vincent Porcaro, who knew him and collected his work, his chapel was converted from a chicken coop and resembled a Voodoo or fetish shrine.

Roeder retired in 1947 and devoted himself to painting, but in 1952, suffering periods of blindness, he began once again to construct assemblages, of baskets and canes. Then in 1958 he resumed painting, signing his work, "John Roeder, Blind Man." *(See portrait of the artist, p. 517). J. W.*

ROGGERI, TONI (1927) — Italy

Toni Roggeri was born in Pieve Modolena, Reggio Emilia, and still lives there, working as a blacksmith. Roggeri's youth was a combination of poverty and hard physical labour. It was natural, therefore, that when he started painting in 1969, simple, ordinary people inspired him such as old men with bodies bent and misshapen by hard physical labour. In his first paintings, people are only discreetly present: small figures submerged in a natural setting of living colour. With time, their presence becomes more apparent, stressed, resolute, and finally fills up almost all the available space. His sharing of man's suffering and poverty becomes ever more intensive.

Even the drama of the painting "St. Francis," where the saint receives the signs of God's will, expresses the concealed human tragedy of every man. Only the skeleton of a tree in the background, a few birds and two sunflowers (symbols often found in Roggeri's iconography) are mute witnesses to the event, depicted in flaming, tremulous tones of bright red and orange. Works which are at first glance thematically less significant, such as the "Balloon Seller," likewise convey a feeling of melancholy over man's fate, the mutability of things and life on earth. Only the dancing balloons and ubiquitous sunflowers lend a note of cheer to the severe composition.

Roggeri also does woodcarving and sculpting. *(See portrait of the artist, p. 517). D. M.*

ROUGHSEY, DICK — Australia

Dick Roughsey is not quite sure how old he is but he was born shortly after Europeans first landed on his home island, Langu-Narnji, in the Gulf of Carpentaria (Mornington Island). He is a full-blood aboriginal whose tribal name of Goobalathaldin means "turbulent seas." Hence his other name: Rough-sey. He lived a tribal life until he was about eight years old and was then educated to the fifth grade standard by the Presbyterian Mission. He returned to his tribe until the outbreak of the Second World War when he started working on northern Australian cattle stations, on a supply ship in the Gulf of Carpentaria and at an Ansett Airways Lodge on the Norman River. There he met an Ansett pilot, Percy Trezise, who encouraged him to paint and later explored and rediscovered many of the cave paintings of Cape York Peninsula together with him.

Dick Roughsey is a man of many talents. As an artist he has had numerous exhibitions in all the states of Australia. His paintings may be found in public and private collections in Australia and overseas.

As a writer he has a number of successful books to his credit. "Moon and Rainbow" is the story of his tribe and "Giant Devil Dingo" is a mythical story from his aboriginal heritage.

Dick Roughsey is a former chairman of the Aboriginal Art Board and a member of the Institute of Aboriginal Studies. *(See portrait of the artist, p. 516). B. McC.*

ROUSSEAU, HENRI "LE DOUANIER" (1844—1910) — France

Henri Rousseau, called Le Douanier, was born in the small town of Laval, which is situated in the northwest of France. He was the son of a plumber.

In his own mind Rousseau was a small-time artisan with feelings of inferiority, who looked up to the pinnacles of official art and respected the academically educated. He linked the idea of fame and social status with the name of the painter Bouguereau, although he did not simply copy the latter's work. Having become a painter by virtue of talent as well as instinct, he provided a new stimulus for a world grown weary of civilisation. He became a symbolic figure at a turning-point in the evolution of art, because his painting was imbued with those qualities which, in the early years of the 20th century, produced such movements as Fauvism, Cubism and Surrealism.

Naive painting, which had always existed but had only now been discovered, officially began with Rousseau. An essential part of modern art, it has survived the manifold comings and goings of artistic styles in our time.

Henri Rousseau was surrounded by the masterpieces of French art, so that his view of art could not possibly coincide with the pictorial concepts of primitive races. The synthesis of man and landscape, which he considered to be his own invention, depicts man in his environment. "I Myself — Portrait-Landscape," painted in 1890, tells us of this symbiosis of man and nature. It seems as if the painter is hovering in mid-air, rather than standing, like the angel in a medieval Annunciation, soaring up into icy mountains of cloud, flanked by earthly and cosmic balloons and by the sun, at his back, a Seine bridge and a ship with the ensigns of all nations that has just docked after a voyage from the remotest regions of Time. Rousseau, pathetic and sublime at one and the same time: this is how he saw himself and how we remember him: a lonely individual rising in hope from the wretchedness of poverty to create the work that paved the way for the most remarkable artistic adventure of our time.

Rousseau's intimate association with a strange and often emphatically exotic landscape has been linked with the war in Mexico, where he is alleged to have served as a member of a regimental band. He did nothing of the kind: this hypothetical expedition into the jungle is simply one of a series of legends that have grown up around the figure of the Douanier.

In order to understand Rousseau's yearning for far away places, for unknown landscapes, we have to visualise the middle-class narrowness, the conventional and arid nature of the world in which he lived. Rousseau's exotic landscapes, inspired by popular magazines, catalogues, herbariums and botanical gardens, formed the archetypal vegetation of his imagination and the dream-like ramblings of his yearnings: a lost paradise regained through art, miraculous and terrifying.

Without being aware of it, Rousseau constituted the profound contrast to that process of dissolution so authentically represented by Expressionistic painting.

Some twenty years before Picasso's Negro period began, Rousseau had unwittingly set the seal on the richness and the power inherent in the original vision of primitive peoples, for naive artists are the "primitives" in the art of civilised nations.

turn brought him into contact with the circle of friends who constituted the youngest and most radical generation of artists. One of his most faithful friends turned out to be Robert Delaunay, who defended his artistic methods and supported him by buying his pictures. In his studio Rousseau organised those sentimental *soirées familiales et artistiques*, concert evenings and receptions attended by pupils and their parents as well as by the artistic avant-garde: Apollinaire, Delaunay, Picasso, Max Jacob, Georges Braque, Maurice Vlaminck, Georges Duhamel, Jules Romains, Brancusi, Marie Lau-

Rousseau, Henri: The Sleeping Gipsy

It was no accident that Rousseau found his way into the avant-garde. From what had originally been a slightly ironic partiality for the comic side of the primitive style ridiculed in the press, there eventually grew an understanding and admiration for Rousseau and his aspirations. Of particular significance was his encounter at an early stage with Alfred Jarry, who, like Rousseau, came from Laval.

Jarry, the tragic clown and creator of Ubu Roi, was the first to detect in his friend Henri Rousseau that turning away from literary refinement and intellectual mannerism toward unaffected naturalness and a poetically grotesque vision that somehow marked the whole age. Through him Rousseau came to know Paul Gauguin, who, like Toulouse-Lautrec and Pissarro, admired the Douanier's idiosyncratic colour-schemes. In Gauguin's studio he met Mallarmé and Degas. In 1907 there followed the meeting with Guillaume Apollinaire, which in

rencin, Felix Fénéon and Philippe Soupault, who wrote a fine and affectionate account of Rousseau.

Many art critics speak of a development in Rousseau's work. In Rousseau's later works there are indeed technical refinements, greater confidence, more freedom in the style of painting. But there is no suggestion of a creative force grounded in experience which was not there from the very beginning.

The continent which Rousseau, the Columbus of naive painting, discovered, this paradise of the primeval, of legendary creatures and mystic plants, was, at one and the same time, an anticipation of and the lyrical prelude to Surrealism. In Rousseau's "Sleeping Gipsy," painted in 1897, the woman lies dreaming under an ancient green sky in the solitude of the desert. The picture is dominated by the silence of sleep and by a profound and dreamy sense of security, while, at the same time, terror in the shape of the lion leans over the slumbering woman. The dark-skinned gipsy reclines like an island in her inner monologue between the desert of the sky and the desert of the earth. A jug and a mandolin stand beside the sleeping figure. Henceforth these objects would inhabit the dreams of the Surrealists and the space of the Cubists.

In 1907 Rousseau painted his picture of the "Snake-charmer." The black figure of the woman playing the flute stands with her back to the luminous green sky and the shining river-bed. She is taming the dangerous snakes with her melody. From the darkness of the jungle vegeta-

embedded in the sombre tissue composed of lianas, ferns and the luxuriantly fantastic trees of the jungle. She is listening to the notes of a magic flute. A dark figure is playing the tune, while tigers, elephants and birds look on from the undergrowth. The magic of this picture somehow lends credibility to the Surrealistic furnishings of the primeval forest. Rousseau believes in his own vision, as if he had actually experienced this world of legend and fable. In this way an alien time and an unprecedented space become the local habitation of a substantial waking dream.

Rousseau, Henri: Portrait of a Woman

Rousseau, Henri: Child with Puppet

tion the powerful bodies of the serpents stretch out to join in the dance. Their eyes gleam mysteriously from the gloom; weird leaves like clumps of lances, feathery shoots from a primeval age, rear up as though cut out of some hard, unyielding material. The whole world of plants, the waters, the moon and the pink flamingoes listen enchanted to the song of the snake-charmer.

In that same year Picasso painted "Les Demoiselles d'Avignon," a key picture of the avant-garde. The elemental proportions of African ju-ju masks were assimilated into the experiment of early Cubism. This was a premonitory change of direction which linked Picasso with Rousseau.

Henri Rousseau's last work, "The Dream of Yadwigha," was painted in 1910. She is lying naked on the red velvet sofa in the Rue Perrel,

Apart from his painting, Rousseau also tried his hand at music and writing. On the door of his little house in the Rue Perrel was a sign: "Cours de diction, musique, peinture et solfège." He wrote short dramatic pieces, of which "The Vengeance of a Russian Orphan" was the best-known. Music, poetry and drama, however, lie on the fringe of his artistic activity: painting remains the profoundest expression of his being.

Rousseau's most celebrated works now hang in the great museums of the world: "The Snake-charmer," "The War" and the portrait of the artist's first wife belong to the Louvre; "The Walk in the Forest" and the "Portrait of Pierre Loti" are in the Kunsthaus, Zurich. "Jungle Landscape at Sunset" and the first version of "The Muse inspiring the Poet" is in the Kunstmuseum, Basel, while the later version is to be found in the Pushkin Museum, Moscow, which also owns

"The Bridge at Sèvres," "The Fortifications" and "Horse Attacked by a Jaguar." "I Myself — Portrait-Landscape" is in the National Gallery of Prague, "The Ballplayers" in the Guggenheim Museum, New York, and "The Dream of Yadwigha" and "Sleeping Gipsy" — which the mayor of Laval refused to purchase — are numbered among the most admired works in the Museum of Modern Art, New York.

In Laval, Rousseau's birth-place, is the Douanier's fine but unassuming painting, "La Moisson au Château," discovered some time ago by Henri Certigny. In the Laval Museum we also

After military service, he was employed as a farm hand. In 1937, he says, he was called up again and thus began a series of misadventures. He fought on a number of fronts, from Spain, where he was wounded, through Greece and North Africa, to Albania, where his lungs were affected. Sent away to recuperate, he deserted and thereby ended his career as a soldier. In 1947, in the hospital of Castelnovo Monti, Reggio Emilia, he began to paint in watercolours and tempera, to while away the time. Mazzacurati took note of his talent and thus started the artistic adventure of "village painter CE" (CE

Rousseau, Henri: The Dream of Yadwigha

find the pictures of those classic French naive artists who followed in Rousseau's footsteps: Camille Bombois, André Bauchant, Séraphine, Louis from Senlis. Jules Lefranc, the naive painter who also came from Laval, provided the funds for this Henri Rousseau Museum.

Rousseau died a lonely death in the Hôpital Necker on 2 September 1910. The funeral took place at the public expense in the cemetery of Bagneux. There were seven mourners present, including the painter, Paul Signac. His mortal remains were removed to the Parc de la Perrine in Laval in 1947. (*See portrait of the artist, p. 516*). O. B.-M.

ROVESTI, BRUNO (1907)   Italy

Bruno Rovesti was born in Gualtieri, Reggio Emilia. While still a child, he helped his family do the hard work in the fields and tend livestock.

standing for *celebre* — famous) as he called himself and as he signs most of his pictures.

Rovesti's technique is extremely simple: at first he prepares the canvas and then, without forethought or corrections, produces his extraordinary compositions, which trace their roots to the inexhaustible wealth of folk legend. He also depicts everyday life, work in the fields, peasants and woodmen — everything that he himself has seen and experienced. The woods and plains of the Po Valley are the protagonists of his poetic art. Sometimes there also appears a human face, which he paints with a characteristic look, half-way between naivety and a strong, penetrating expression (as in the painting "The Mason").

Rovesti sometimes paints luxurious gardens, non-existent in reality although situated in specific locations, with flowering bushes, rendered in vibrant, harmonious colours, largely red and various tones of green, with very elegant shadings. There are paintings of squares, villages and landscapes, done in strong and resolute colours bordering on harshness but, nevertheless, mitigated and softened by the unusual harmony of the composition.

Rovesti's vision consists of atmosphere and meaning — here extremely odd, there lyrical — with fantastic, almost dreamy intonations, and at times with a wealth of symbols, the whole imbued with extraordinary purity and innate simplicity.

(See portrait of the artist, p. 516). D. M.

Rovesti, Bruno: Hillside Village

ROY, LOUIS (1891—1979)   France

Louis Roy was born at Niort and died at Le Gué d'Alleré. Born into a very poor home, he began his apprenticeship as a cooper at the age of eight. He never went to school and began painting at about the age of fifty.

The artistry of Louis Roy lies largely in his drawing. His paintings testify to a hard conquest of a means of expression by an artist who above all wanted his work to be easily understood. Colour serves most often to pull a composition together. Frequently distorted perspectives, details nullified by their overstatement and by the complexity of simultaneously occurring events, are the most notable features of Louis Roy's paintings.

Louis Roy had one-man shows in 1965 and 1966 and also participated in many group exhibitions. *(See portrait of the artist, p. 517). Ch. Sch.*

RUAN ZHANGJUN (1960)   China

Ruan Zhangjun was born in the tiny town of Ting Ling, in the Jin Shan region. After completing secondary school, he was assigned to work in the Jin Shan Cultural Centre. South of the Yangtze River flow many streams and rivulets. The land is divided into small plots and surrounded by water. On the surface of the water grows a plant which the Chinese call "water bells," used for feeding pigs. In the summertime, this plant is covered with red and white flowers.

"In their rowing boats, the brigadiers set out to gather these flowers. I have often gathered them myself," says Ruan Zhangjun. "This scene inspired my first picture, which I called 'Water Bells.' The gathering, typical of the summer in our part of the country, has been going on for centuries." Ruan Zhangjun has so far based most of his paintings on this motif. The picture "Water Bells" has been on display in Canada, together with the works of other painters of the Jin Shan area. It attracted attention for its naively realistic portrayal of the harvesting of these water flowers. *(See portrait of the artist, p. 517). N. T.*

Roy, Louis: Clocktower in Rochelle

Rubashkin, Samuil Yakovlevich: Succoth

RUBAŠKIN,   USSR
SAMUIL JAKOVLEVIČ (1906—1975)
RUBASHKIN, SAMUIL YAKOVLEVICH

S. Y. Rubashkin was born in the Byelorussian town of Vitebsk, famous as the birth-place of Marc Chagall. He completed his higher education in 1928 at the USSR State Institute of Cinematography in Moscow, where he was trained as cameraman; he subsequently worked in this capacity at the Soviet Union's largest feature film studios. He always liked to draw, and started to paint regularly by pure chance when in 1959 a woman artist friend from Leningrad provided him with paint and brushes. After that he could not tear himself away from painting. He worked not only in oils but also with crayons and felt-tipped pens, producing landscapes, still-lifes and genre scenes, mostly done from memory. Once, when ill in bed in a darkened room, he related childhood memories to friends, and, after recovering, reproduced them in a series

RUGGERI, ALFREDO (1912—1977)   **Italy**

Alfredo Ruggeri, born in S. Savino al Trasimeno, Ascoli Piceno, moved to Rome, where he worked as an office employee and began to paint in 1952. His compositions — with their remarkable colours, in which reddish-brown tones prevail — issued from a medieval tower in the centre of Rome, where Ruggeri, withdrawn and reserved by nature, retreated from everyday life, from the chaotic rhythms of the metropolis. There for years he sheltered and nurtured his imagination, while satisfying his profound desire to transmit to canvas pictures of his native

Ruan Zhangjun: Water Bells

reflecting typically Jewish customs and mores which Rubashkin had observed in the *shtetl.* His "Wedding," "Barmitzvah," "Sukkoth," "Passover" and other such pieces, which comprise the high-water mark of his work, are primitive in the means of expression used, two-dimensional, bright and artless. Indeed, wherever he attempted to invent, the immediacy was lost, yielding to dilettantism. He was represented at several exhibitions and in 1975 had a one-man show at the film club in Leningrad. Some of his works are in the possession of his widow in Moscow; others are in private collections. *(See portrait of the artist, p. 517).* N. Sh.

Umbria, simultaneously lush and harsh, seemingly enchanted, a serene and dream-like heaven on earth, with an abundance of crops. Nature was profoundly transformed by Ruggeri, who presented his version of it, radiating a secretive feeling of the poet's dream-like vision, full of solemn silences. This atmosphere is found in the work "Small Town," in which, against the dark backdrop of the trees, there stands, like an unexpected apparition, a tiny town, its soft whiteness making the melancholy foliage of his district seem even darker. Ruggeri died in Rome. *(See portrait of the artist, p. 516).* D. M.   →

RUSEWICZ, MICHAŁ (1912)   **Poland**

Michał Rusewicz, born in the archduchy of Wilno (now in the USSR), at present lives in the small spa of Jerzmanice Zdroj, Poland. After seven grades of school, he followed his father into the forest to work and eventually became a forest ranger. In 1943 he was sent to forced labour in Germany. After the liberation, he went back to Poland and worked in the forests around the town of Znin, and after 1953 in Jerzmanice Zdroj. He has been painting since his retirement in 1973, having previously also done some art work between 1936 and 1939. His paintings are in the collections of ethnographic museums in Wrocław and Warsaw. *(See portrait of the artist, p. 517). A. J.*

worker, he graduated from a German school (Poland was divided at that time). After the death of his parents, the fourteen-year-old boy had to earn his own living and take care of his younger sister. Moving to Westphalia, he took employment as a worker in the Krupp factories. When war broke out, he was called up and, during fighting at the Somme, crossed over to the Allied side, joined the Foreign Legion and lived in Algeria for several years (a period which suggested the themes of many of his pictures). He returned to Poland in 1922 and worked for eight years in a warehouse as well as doing other

r

514

Ruggeri, Alfredo: Small Town

Rusewicz, Michał: A Couple in Highland Clothes

Rzhevsky, Nikolai Alekseyevich: View of Courtyard and Lane

RYBKOWSKI, WŁADYSŁAW (1894)　　　**Poland**

Władysław Rybkowski, born in Swadzyń, now lives in Poznań. The son of a railway

odd jobs. During the Depression, he was unemployed, although he did some whitewashing from time to time. He also painted merry-go-rounds and shooting galleries. After the Second World War, he worked as a manual labourer. Following the death of his wife in 1954, he moved to Warsaw to live with his son. Seriously ill, he took a job as a night watchman, spending entire days and nights in a small wooden watchman's hut, keeping guard over a construction site for the opera. Having nothing else to do, he painted the inside walls of the hut as well as all the equipment and objects inside it (including even boxes, ashtrays, a pen-holder and a cane). Then he began painting pictures, together with their frames on canvas (frequently using both sides),

cottages, small yards, gardens and orchards and is apparently a nature-lover. In his artless works he strikes a lyrical note. Realising that his knowledge of painting was inadequate, between 1974 and 1978 he applied for advice to instructors at ZNUI, the Extra-mural People's University of Art. As a result his works are a combination of the naive and the professional. His compositions are static and devoid of psychological insight. Pools of colour are well demarcated, even though there is a certain amount of brushwork. He was represented at a USSR group show in Moscow in 1974. *N. Sh.*

Rybkowski, Władysław: Kingdom in the Jungle

or on cardboard, boards or metal sheeting. In his paintings, he went back to the world of the Grimm fairy tales he had loved in his youth, linking up that world of tales and fantasy with elements of reality. After being discovered in 1965, he devoted himself exclusively to painting. His works are in many Polish museums (Warsaw, Cracow, Poznań), in the collection of L. Zimmerer, Warsaw, and in foreign collections. He has had one-man shows in Warsaw and Poznań, and his works have been on display in all foreign exhibitions of Polish naive art, among other in Zagreb ("Naivi '73"). *(See portrait of the artist, p. 517). A. J.*

RŽEVSKIJ,   **USSR**
NIKOLAJ ALEKSEEVIČ (1903)
RZHEVSKY, NIKOLAI ALEKSEYEVICH
     N. A. Rzhevsky had a university education. He used to live near Moscow but his present whereabouts are unknown. Rzhevsky started to paint while in his teens, but took up painting seriously only upon retirement. He likes to depict

Rabuzin, Ivan

Radke, Zenon

Ramholz, Felix

Rasmané, Nitiema

Rimbert, René

Rjauba, Stasis

Roda, I Nyoman

Roughsey, Dick

Rousseau, Henri

Rovesti, Bruno

Ruggeri, Alfredo

ić, Milan

Repnik, Anton

Riec, Raymond

Ristić, Petar

ríguez, Manases

Roggeri, Toni

Roeder, John

, Louis

Ruan Zhangjun

Rubaškin, S. J.

ewicz, Michał

Rybkowski, Władysław

SALDAÑA, RAFAEL — Australia
SAMBA, WA NBIMBA NIZINGA — Zaire
SAUTER, ALOIS — Belgium
SAVAKIS, YORGOS — Greece
SAVIĆ, KRSTO — Yugoslavia
SAVINOV, VASILIJ TIMOFEEVIČ — USSR
SAVITSKY, JACK — USA
SAVU, ALEXANDRU — Romania
SCARBOROUGH, JOE — Great Britain
SCHAAR, MONIQUE — Belgium
SCHEPIS, A. A. C. — Brazil
SCHILLING, HEINRICH — West Germany
SCHMIDTOVÁ, NATALIE — Czechoslovakia
SCHMIT, ILONA — Netherlands
SCHMITT, HANS — West Germany
SCHULZ, ELFRIDE-MARIA — West Germany
SCHUMANN, GÜNTER — East Germany
SCHWARTZENBERG, SIMON — France
SEEMANN, FRITZ — West Germany
SEIFERT, MAX — West Germany
SELIVANOV, IVAN EGOROVIĆ — USSR
SERAFINI, GIUSEPPE — Italy
SÉRAPHINE (SÉRAPHINE LOUIS) — France
SERGEEV, GRIGORIJ SERGEEVIČ — USSR
SGRO, MERCURIO — Argentina
SHALOM OF SAFED — Israel
SHEN DEXIAN — China
ŠIJAKOVIĆ, DJORDJE — Yugoslavia
ŠILHÁN, VÁCLAV — Czechoslovakia
SILVA, FRANCISCO DOMINGOS DA — Brazil
SILVA, MARINA — Nicaragua
SIRKOVIĆ, STEPA — Yugoslavia
SIVÁŇ, ŠTEFAN — Czechoslovakia
SKOULAS, ALKIVIADIS — Greece
SKURJENI, MATIJA — Yugoslavia
SLEEP, JOSEPH — Canada
SLOOT, JENTJE VAN DER — Netherlands
SMAJIĆ, PETAR — Yugoslavia
SMIRNOV, VLADIMIR BORISOVIČ — USSR
SOBOTA, JÓZEF — Poland
SODANG, IDA BAGUS — Indonesia, Bali
SÖHL, MANFRED — West Germany
SOKOL, ANA — Argentina
SOKOL, JAN — Yugoslavia
SOOMER, JEANNE DE — Belgium

SÓWKA, ERWIN — Poland
SOY, ANCENT — Kenya
SPASIĆ, ČEDA — Yugoslavia
SPATHARIS, E. — Greece
SPENCER, SAM — Canada
SPIELBICHLER, FRANZ — Austria
STANIČIĆ, MATIJA — Yugoslavia
STANISAVLJEVIĆ, DRAGIŠA — Yugoslavia
STANISAVLJEVIĆ, MILAN — Yugoslavia
STAPEL, RUDOLF — West Germany
ST. BRICE, ROBERT — Haiti
ŠTEBERL, ONDREJ — Czechoslovakia
STEFULA, GY. and D. — West Germany
STEINMANN, HEINZ — Australia
STEPANOV, SERGEJ GEORGIEVIČ — USSR
STÉPHANE, MICIUS — Haiti
STERN, EMMA — West Germany
STEVANOVIĆ, DOBRIVOJE — Yugoslavia
STEWART, ERIC — Australia
STUBBS, DOUGLAS — Australia
STURZA, GHEORGHE — Romania
SU JUNLIANG — China
SÜLI, ANDRÁS, — Hungary
SULLIVAN, PATRICK J. — USA
SUND, MEIKE — Netherlands
SUTOR, EDWARD — Poland
SVOBODA, JAKUB — Czechoslovakia
SZABÓ, ANIKO — Argentina
SZAKÁCS, JÁNOSNÉ — Hungary
SZCZYPAWKA-PTASZYNSKA, H. — Poland
SZEKERES, MIHÁLYNÉ — Hungary
SZELECKI, MIHÁLY — Hungary

Saldaña, Rafael: St. Francis (part of a triptych)

Samba, Wa Nbimba Nizinga: "Les Dessinateur Samba & la Sirène"

animals reflect the love which this artist seems to feel toward the world around him.

He has had shows in Tasmania and at the Gallery Art Naive in Melbourne and his works are to be found in many private collections. *(See portrait of the artist, p. 560). B. McC.*

SALDAÑA, RAFAEL   Australia

Rafael Saldaña was born into a large family in Madrid. His career in art began when — as a very young child — he was given a box of coloured pencils and a sketch pad for Christmas. These were the most treasured gifts he ever remembers. When he was six years old his family moved into the country and he discovered the joys of rural life: animals, plants and the daily round of chores which also involved the children. Years later he entered the Spanish Navy and travelled to France and England, where he learned English.

In about 1960 Rafael Saldaña emigrated to Australia, living first in the eastern states, before settling in Tasmania, where he now paints. He has had no formal training in art, yet his paintings explode with vitality and colour. His landscapes are mysteriously dramatic; his birds and

SAMBA,   Zaire
WA NBIMBA NIZINGA (1955)

Born at Madimba, while still a child Samba came in contact with the art of painting, when doing odd jobs at a workshop near his parents' home. As a further inducement to enter this new world he made the acquaintance of the Zaire artist Masunda, who, while he did not actually teach him anything, helped to make the possibility of being an artist real to him. As with Middle Art of Nigeria, but in a totally different fashion, he likes to let his pictures tell stories, a talent for which he receives recognition through the caricatures and strip cartoons he makes for the bi-monthly "Bilenge."

Samba is an entirely self-taught artist. When he is not painting and drawing he is employed as a stamp-cutter. More often than not written texts are incorporated into his pictures. This "aspect" of his art occurs in all the "Sirène" pictures, an example of which, "Le Dessinateur Samba et la

Sirène," is shown here. The "Sirène" paintings help to emphasise the transatlantic links which persist in the works of Voodoo art (Haiti) and Candomblé/Macumba art (Brazil), both of which are the products of those who were once African slaves in Central and South America. *Sh. W.*

SAUTER, ALOIS (1875—1952) Belgium

Alois Sauter was born in Stabroeck and died in Chaumes-en-Brie, not far from Argentière, in France. Although he lived in France for much of his life, he retained his Belgian citizenship. Nevertheless, he is sometimes erroneously classified with French painters.

The son of a cartwright, and a cartwright himself, as was his brother Cornelius, he was obsessed by the idea of inventing. At the age of fourteen, he constructed the model of a tricycle, followed by a pedal-driven rowing-boat, an armoured tank, a *perpetuum mobile* and "an apparatus with sails which also flies by flapping its wings" which he named "Sauteral." He poured all his savings into this machine, which flew no longer than the one constructed by another Belgian naive painter, Louis Delattre.

He made his home successively in Kapellen, Anvers, Jumet, and Charleroi. In 1904, he married Alphonsine Detrait, whom he soon divorced, leaving with his brother for France. As a seller of antiques in Neuilly-sur-Seine, he lived with Marie Gatelier, who called herself the muse of Neuilly and wrote strange poems. It was she who persuaded Sauter to start painting. She died in 1931 and he then decorated his pictures with his late wife's poetry. Sauter married again and moved to Chaumes-en-Brie. An Italian grocer discovered twelve of his pictures and sold them to an antique dealer. Only eight of these works have been found, including the famous "Buffet" from the collection of Félix Labisse. "A Likeable Unexpected Partner" shows the face of Marie Gatelier and, like "Buffet," is typical of his endeavour to fill the entire canvas, which is bathed in gloom and redolent of the atmosphere of works by Clovis Trouille, but without the latter's erotic touch. Domestic animals, in addition to people and objects, fill up the darkened space. Other works are strongly inspired by a petty bourgeois ambience. His purely pictorial qualities are the delight of painters such as Albert Dasnoy, who considers his canvases "condensed and extremely unusual." The manner in which he presents his themes resembles a photographer's and is rightly described by Anatole Jakovsky as "fleeting."

He exhibited in Knokke-le-Zoute (1958) and also in Paris, Rotterdam and Brussels. *(See reproduction, p. 49). J. C.*

SAVAKIS, YORGOS (1924) Greece

Yorgos Savakis was born in the Plaka, the heart of old Athens, and has lived in this area all his life. His subjects are centred on the life of old Athens: scenes in the central market and the fish market, celebrations and carnival customs, Christmas carols and religious festivities, old trams, cinemas, churches, taverns and coffee-houses, old curio shops, the flea market, an so on.

But these joyful and nostalgic images of the past are not Savakis' exclusive source of inspiration; references to the Second World War, the German occupation, and the excitement of the liberation are found in his canvases as well. His brush-strokes are nervous and hurried but never fail to render all the details of his themes; his colours are usually much too bright, and reflect his preference for red, blue and green, sometimes producing bold contrasts.

Savakis has had several one-man shows in Athens and in various cities of Europe, Australia and the USA. Paintings by the artist are to be

Savakis, Yorgos: Carnival at the Monument of Lyssicrates

Savić, Krsto: The Swineherd

found in the Museum of Folk Art, Athens, in the Vorres Museum, Paiania, Attica, and in private collections in Athens, Europe and the USA. *A. T.*

SAVIĆ, KRSTO (1931) Yugoslavia

Krsto Savić was born in Maradik near Novi Sad, Vojvodina, and since 1956 has been painting motifs of village life. After finishing elementary school in his village, he farmed for a while and then began house painting, mostly whitewashing the exteriors of houses.

"I was too weak for farm work and had to find something easier to do. Painting houses, I learned something about colours and also occasionally added designs and various kinds of ornaments to the walls. At home I drew on paper and painted on canvas, the way I had seen one of the teachers in school do," he says.

In "The Swineherd" (1960), Savić painted an old occupation which has practically disappeared from the Vojvodina countryside. At the sound of the bees would stream out. Savinov was active when progressive Russian intellectuals were enthusiastic about folk art, especially sculpture, which they purchased and collected even to the point of setting up museums; examples are Tretyakov, the founder of the Moscow Art Gallery named after him, and the merchant Shchukin. The Yegorevsk merchant Bardygin bought many works from Savinov, and housed them in a museum which he built specially for the purpose, giving free access to the public at large. (The building now houses the local ethnographic museum.) The artist carved a seated, rather

Savinov, Vasili Timofeyevich: Moujik (Bee-hive)

Savitsky, Jack: The Miner's Week

static figure of Bardygin, showing him with an intense look, as if posing for the camera; indeed, it is quite likely that the carver did it from a photograph.

Savinov's works have been shown at more than one exhibition of popular applied art, and examples are in the museums of Zagorsk and Yegorevsk outside Moscow and in the History Museum in Moscow itself. *N. Sh.*

a trumpet, the doors of pigsties would be opened and the pigs inside would rush out to join the herd being taken by the swineherd to pasture outside the village. In the background are the neatly painted façades of village houses, all in lovely pastel colours, perhaps the very ones painted by Savić.

Krsto Savić has had one-man shows and has participated in group exhibitions at home and abroad.

(See portrait of the artist, p. 560). N. T.

SAVINOV, VASILIJ TIMOFEEVIČ   USSR
(mid-19th — early 20th centuries)
SAVINOV, VASILI TIMOFEYEVICH

Vasili Timofeyevich Savinov was born into a peasant family in the village Timerevo near Yegorevsk in the Moscow region. After finishing at the local school with honours, he did some farming, going to Moscow now and again to earn more, a common practice with the local peasantry. He took up woodcarving as a hobby. He later stayed all the time in the village, and built himself a cottage and workshop. Working in a popular tradition, he gave full rein to his imagination by carving bee-hives in the shape of peasants, farm women and bears, from whose eyes

SAVITSKY, JACK (1910)   USA

Jack Savitsky, the son of a Russian farmer who emigrated to the USA and became a miner in Pennsylvania, was born and brought up in Silver Creek, Pennsylvania, the first of five children. He says that as a child he much preferred drawing to learning to write. He left school after the sixth grade, and though he ultimately became a miner, like his father, he tried his hand at a few other trades, among them taxidermy, which he learned through mail-order instruction books. He also did some sign-painting for the local used-car company, and painted fantastic birds and animals on the mirrors of the local speakeasy.

By the time the mine he worked for shut down in 1959 he was in any case unable to work as a miner any more, having by that time become victim of miner's asthma, or "black lung" disease, as it is more commonly known. His son then suggested that since he could not do heavy work any more, he should take up his old pastime of painting. It was a lucky suggestion, for shortly after he began painting, he entered some of his work in a local exhibition, where it was discovered by Sterling Strausser, a painter and enthusiastic supporter of and dealer in works by contemporary American folk artists. Savitsky's works have since found their way into numerous collections and several museums.

Savitsky is very prolific, and the walls in every room in his house, including the kitchen and bathroom, are covered from floor to ceiling, and from end to end, with his paintings. His work can to some extent be categorised as memory painting. However, even though his style has almost a comic-strip, cartoon-like quality, neither that nor the bright colours which he uses entirely disguise the bitterness of some of his recollections of the hard life of the coal miner. *J. W.*

Savu, Alexandru: On the Sabar River

SAVU, ALEXANDRU (1932)   Romania

Alexandru Savu was born in the village of Poenari-Ulmi, near Bucharest, and began earning his livelihood as a house painter. Later he joined some groups working on the restoration of frescoes in Romanian churches.

Returning home and painting pictures in his free time, Alexandru Savu was discovered in 1972, when he had his first one-man show.

Although in constant contact with traditional Romanian wall painting, Alexandru Savu has retained his personal signature as an artist; independent in his conceptions, he deftly unifies various visual details taken from his own recollections, or from newspapers, books or famous works of art. Notable elements in his work are a refreshing sense of humour (frequently found in Romanian naive art) and the influence of well-known love songs and melodies.

Even when the artist's subject-matter is taken from history or legend, his chromatic range is fresh, optimistic and cheerful, reflecting his own joyful attitude toward life, apparent even when the events dealt with are tinged with melancholy.

First brought to public notice at the international naive art meeting in Lugano in 1973, the works of Alexandru Savu, painted in oil on canvas or cardboard, have since been shown at group exhibitions in Argentina, Mexico, the Federal Republic of Germany, Yugoslavia, Sweden, and other countries. *(See portrait of the artist, p. 560). M. Il.*

SCARBOROUGH, JOE (1938)   Great Britain

Joe Scarborough was born in Pitsmoor, Sheffield. Although he had not shown any talent as an artist while he was still at school, he now set about "copying" illustrations out of books in the public library, particularly pictures by the artist Montague Dawson and masterpieces by the Impressionists. The latter certainly invaded his mind to such an extent that his subsequent personal style — with its thick impasto and its bright, often primary, colours — must owe these godfathers of modern art a most enduring debt. But it was while he was still a coal miner at

Scarborough, Joe: Two Tram-cars

the Thorpe Hesley Colliery that the absolute transformation from "someone who just wanted to paint" into an artist took place. One day he came up from the pit-face into the glare of radiant summer sunlight and made the fundamental decision to give up the good money he was making from coal and paint pictures instead.

It was a big sacrifice. Now, to support his wife and family, he relied on small sums of money earned from the sale of bric-a-brac off a barrow, from doing the occasional temporary menial tasks, and from the rare sale of a picture at a rock-bottom price — all so that he could have time to paint.

The only "public" places in which he could show his pictures were pubs and working men's clubs — and the financial return from these was either nil or very small. Then, by a stroke of luck, into one of these indifferent "shows" strayed the Secretary of the Crucible Theatre, Sheffield, who arranged an exhibition of his works at his theatre. It proved an instant success; the paintings were offered and all of them were bought by visitors to the theatre on the first day.

Scarborough was then approached by a businessman, who was also a collector and art dealer, called Cyril "Sheppy" Caplan, who made a deal with him to arrange the exhibitions and sales of his pictures. Scarborough became so successful that for many people he was "Mr Sheffield." He held many exhibitions, particularly in Sheffield,

tries, she is also inspired by objects brought back from her travels. The theme of the sea coast is freely interpreted by her in a symbolic sense: on a canvas of hers, men who are taking various kinds of shells from the sea are counterbalanced by a siren who at the same time draws from the sea debris thrown into it by human beings.

Monique Schaar is always prepared to eliminate elements which are not necessary for her theme, and to leave empty spaces.

She has had many one-woman shows and has participated in group exhibitions at home and abroad. *(See portrait of the artist, p. 561). J. C.*

Schaar, Monique: Memory of a Journey

and took his pictures to the USA. Eventually the pace proved too fast for him: warnings of deteriorating health forced him to part from "Sheppy" Caplan, who released him from their contract without rancour.

Scarborough has had an important exhibition at the Portal Gallery, London, and under the auspices of RONA has had his pictures on show in Athens, Tokyo, San Francisco, Rome, Sheffield, Manchester and other provincial British centres, as well as on several occasions in London. He can also boast of being represented in a number of public collections as well as in the homes of art-lovers all over the world. *(See portrait of the artist, p. 560). Sh. W.*

SCHAAR, MONIQUE (1939)   **Belgium**

Monique Schaar, born in Brussels, did not permit three years of art studies to spoil her authentically naive inspiration. She is the wife of a lawyer, and her favourite theme (touched with a restless humour) is the world in which justice is dispensed. She often uses symbols: for instance, the tortoise is the incarnation of the slowness of justice. As a collector of the folk arts of all coun-

SCHEPIS,   **Brazil**
ANGELO ARMANDO CASSAVIA (1928)

Angelo Armando Cassavia Schepis was born in Rio Claro, but now lives in Rio de Janeiro. He specialises in assembling slivers of acrylic plastic or glass and creating mosaics out of these unlikely materials; the results are pictures which have a natural sparkle quite unlike the productions of any other self-taught artist in Brazil. All these mosaics are figurative, and Schepis is not afraid to be downright sentimental in some of them. Like so many self-taught Brazilian artists, he favours religious subjects — the creation of scenic drama out of Christian observance. *Sh. W.*

→

SCHILLING,   **West Germany**
HEINRICH (1898)

Heinrich Schilling was born in Essen, where he still lives. He worked as a miner until 1927 and was subsequently employed as a panel-beater and sheet metal worker until he retired in 1963. Schilling had always sketched and painted in his leisure time — except during the Nazi period, when he "just couldn't." Since his retirement this quiet, reserved former miner has found a new lease of life in the production of woodcuts and linocuts.

In his woodcuts Schilling succeeds in capturing the miniature idyll of gardens and backyards that forms an oasis in the midst of the industrial landscape, with its dirt, smoke and noise; he employs an absolute minimum of lines and surfaces.

There are very few oils by him, but the finest of them "The Harbour," is a small canvas in which Schilling succeeds in reproducing with astonishing simplicity the atmosphere of the Ruhr "after working-hours." *T. G.*

expressed in colourful decoration. Humour and musical rhythms, joy and fragrance coalesce to form a single sensation.

Specialists wondered how an untutored woman was able to design entire compositions with such deftness and decorative sense and how she was able to reduce people and things to such lapidary proportions.

Schmidtová's ideograms correspond to tribal ideas which have not been overlaid by the "leaves" of later experiences nor affected by psychic changes associated with puberty. The sum of those primal experiences which she

Schepis, Angelo Armando Cassavia: The Ball

Schilling, Heinrich: The Harbour

SCHMIDTOVÁ, NATALIE (1895) Czechoslovakia

Natalie Schmidtová was born in Dobrinka, which was situated in the Russian administrative district of Tambov. She never went to school. Her father, Lavrentij Maslikov, emigrated with his family to Prikanovka, in Siberia, where free land was on offer. Natalie Maslikova passed her happiest years between 1911 and 1915 in Novorossisk and on the Black Sea coast as a parlourmaid and nanny. From 1915 to 1919 she lived in Prokurovka, near Voronezh, where she became acquainted with an Austrian prisoner of war, Rudolf Schmidt, a mechanic by trade, whom she later accompanied to Moravia. From 1919 to 1940 the Schmidts lived with their two daughters in the vicinity of Bystřice. During the Second World War she began to paint at the instigation of her daughter, Milada. A new phase in the history of naive painting in Czechoslovakia began with her first exhibition in Prague in 1946. The exhibition was subsequently transferred to Paris by Dorra Maar. In its importance Schmidtová's work offers a parallel to that of Nikifor.

Schmidtová's gouaches and tempera paintings may be divided into two separate thematic groups: traditional village life and "exotica." When, after the Second World War, she was unable to persuade her husband to emigrate to the South Seas, she tried to realise her desire for exotic lands in another way. She began to undertake painting excursions.

Schmidtová attempted to cast a spell over her future fate by painting the plucking of flowers, festive gatherings and visions of the South Seas. This wish-fulfillment on paper is rendered more intense by a special mood

Schmit, Ilona: Church at Kloeting

garnered in the life-cycle of a Russian village has remained the sustaining structure of her being. By means of this process, later visual experiences (for example, films or reproductions of works of art which she has seen) have also been absorbed and transformed according to an elementary childish code. *(See portrait of the artist, p. 561). A. P.*

SCHMIT, ILONA (1943)   Netherlands

Ilona Schmit was born in a concentration camp in Goslar, Germany. Her father, a Dutchman, had been interned for opposing fascism. Her mother, a German, became a naturalised citizen of the Netherlands after the war.

her pictures, she presents men and animals with wit, while also giving them a new role, idealising and romanticising their peaceful togetherness.

Ilona Schmit exhibited in 1977 in Zagreb at the "Naivi '77" exhibition. *(See portrait of the artist, p. 561). N. E.*

SCHMITT, HANS (1912)   West Germany

Hans Schmitt was twelve when he moved with his parents from Frankfurt to the country. Starting out by tending herds of cows, he later became a baker's helper, a servant in a hotel, and

Schmidtová, Natalie: Dreams of the South Seas

After graduating from secondary school in Haarlem, she obtained employment as a secretary. Dissatisfied with her job, she took private lessons in pottery and textile printing. She married and had three daughters. Apart from her household duties, she found time for pottery and tapestry weaving and even exhibited her work on one occasion. After divorcing her husband, she moved to south-west Holland, to the sea- and wind-swept area of Zeeland. Feeling the need to do something new, she decided to paint. Her early works show an uncanny resemblance to the paintings of Pieter Hagoort: the same straight lines, the same fresh nuances. But the young Ilona Schmit studied to master a technique and after three years her mode of expression matured in both form and substance. Her orientation to man and nature is characteristic of her. In the well-regulated countryside which we see in

a coal carrier. He lost his right hand in the war. In 1977, after he had retired, he started carving from bits of wood and other odds and ends a series of bizarre polychrome figures — naive, vital and immediate. Using saws, hammers, nails, screws and paint, he created figures from the Bavarian Alps. Gnomes, wood sprites, pairs of lovers, shepherds, blackamoors, masked figures and comic animals from fables people the world of his fantasy. He is distinctive for his singular forms and for his method of creating wooden collages by stacking tone on tone. He was discovered by the Munich collector, Hans Schaffner. The well-known art historian and connoisseur of naive art, Oto Bihalji-Merin, initiator of the exhibition "Naive Artists of the World 1974," considers Hans Schmitt a specially talented naive sculptor. The works of this artist, made of bits and pieces, undoubtedly fall within the category designated as "poor art." Perhaps the necessity of working with his left hand alone forced simplicity on him, but it is the kind of simplicity that tells of a sure instinct and spontaneity. His predilection for angular and pointed forms gives his compositions a humorous, grotesque note. *T. G.*

SCHULZ, ELFRIDE-MARIA West Germany

Elfride-Maria Schulz, born in Berlin, now lives in Hanover. She was trained as a nursery-school teacher but practised her profession only

The setting of her biblical narratives is therefore the present day. E. M. Schulz's pictures are almost exclusively painted in light shades: luminous yellow, fresh green, blossoming white, cheerful red, a buoyant sky-blue.

She produces fewer pictures than she would like, perhaps half a dozen a year. As a mother with a numerous family who also provides free care and accommodation for a number of house guests, she has only the early morning for her painting.

Elfride-Maria Schulz has painted a bedroom scene which shows her talent in a more amusing

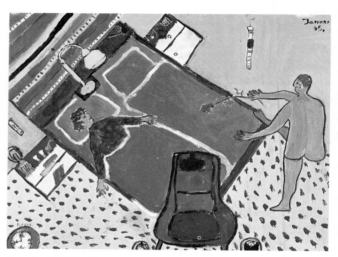

Schulz, Elfride-Maria: In the Bedroom

Schmitt, Hans: Human Being and Sunflower

Schumann, Günter: The Chemie Leipzig Football Team

with her own five children. When she was obliged to lie motionless for a long time because of a cracked vertebra, her husband built her a frame that hung at an angle over her bed. He bought her a box of watercolours, and she began to paint. She found that she was making progress and has gone on painting ever since then. "I never go looking for subjects or deliberately pick them. They just come. Because I live with the New Testament particularly, that is, with Jesus, I would like to tell other people through my pictures that Jesus is here today, in our time and in everything round us."

light; the unintentional comedy of the representation conveys the intimate family episode splendidly, and the bird's-eye view, an angle which is difficult even for professional painters, is effectively used. The picture is dominated by the manner in which the romantic lover, holding a seductive red rose, leaps into the bed, and by the languidly reclining young woman. The charm of the picture lies in its combination of a recklessly bold handling of space and childishly naive draughtsmanship, as in the displaced back panel on the bed and the ledges on the wardrobe. *(See portrait of the artist, p. 560). T. G.*

Schumann, Günter: Giraffe Named "Long-legged Emma"

SCHUMANN, GÜNTER (1941)   East Germany

Günter Schumann, born in Neuwernsdorf, has worked as mock-up maker, truck driver and turner. After attending teachers' college in Leipzig, he went on for specialised training in Schneeberg. Since 1969, he has been working as a free-lance artist in Zwenkau near Leipzig.

Günter Schumann's wooden sculptures are full of feelings of friendship, laced with gentle humour, for the creatures of this world. Regardless of what they represent (giraffes, hippopotami, deer, grandfathers and grandmothers, children or football players), they are always the

composition is perhaps reminiscent of Bödeker's ironic representations of people. *O. B.-M.*

←

SCHWARTZENBERG, SIMON (1895)   France

Simon Schwartzenberg was born in Paris. An artist of great sensitivity, he had a deep love for music. He began to paint at the age of fifty-seven in the time he could spare from the small haberdashery business which he ran. His work began to be known in the 1960s.

Distinctive in style, Simon Schwartzenberg's pictures are well drawn, but with inverted

Schwartzenberg, Simon: Paris, Place de la République

Seemann, Fritz: The Yellow Villa

product of a spontaneous imagination or of a sense of reality brightened by sincere human warmth.

The love of folk tales is so strong in Schumann that one could imagine a whole children's town peopled with these figures. He is a gifted sculptor for whom wood is not dead matter to be worked, say, like cement. Wherever possible, he tries to delve into the inner being of the wood and subordinate his carving knife to the grain of the wood and the anatomy of its growth. Thus, the figures of animals and human beings seem to have sprung from the wood, as though an unseen force of nature had helped the carver.

His sculptures show a tendency toward the lyrically grotesque. "Grandmother and Grandfather" seem like figures from an ancient ancestor cult. The members of a football team (in more than life size, eleven figures in all) are framed by the poles of the victor's goal after the game has been won. Almost comic in their dignified pride and self-satisfaction, these sportsmen, idols of the masses, stand all in a row. The

proportions and perspectives in constant upheaval. A pleasure in painting and the audacity of his brush combine to achieve a balance, buttressed by opulent colour in each work.

Simon Schwartzenberg has appeared in Paris galleries since 1962 and has also participated in group shows: at the First and Second Triennials of Naive Art in Bratislava (1966 and 1969) and at the Museum of Naive Art in Zagreb (1968 and 1970). *(See portrait of the artist, p. 560). Ch. Sch.*

SEEMANN, FRITZ (1908)   West Germany

Fritz Seemann was born in Löwenberg, Silesia, and now lives in Itzehoe. He studied geography and mathematics and then trained as a teacher of sport. Not being "acceptable" to the National Socialists as a teacher, he worked as a bookseller and then in a travel bureau until the war broke out. When he retired in 1970 he was a secondary school teacher. Whenever Seemann could spare an hour he was to be found working away thoughtfully and carefully at his painting.

The content of his pictures is a mixture of memories, travel experiences, fantasies and dreams. What he most likes painting is the forest with its animals, huntsmen, poachers, smugglers, lumberjacks and old women gathering berries. *(See portrait of the artist, p. 560). T. G.*

SEIFERT, MAX (1914)   West Germany

Max Seifert, born in Eppendorf, Saxony, now lives in Düsseldorf. A retired police inspector

Seifert, Max: Threshing with Flails

with a neatly trimmed moustache, he looks like a smart Englishman of the old school. Even when he was on duty he was a welcome guest in those pubs in the old centre of Düsseldorf where artists congregate.

Max Seifert projects into his pictures an individual manner of looking at things — sober, objective, always seeking a balanced view. It is hardly surprising that he escapes as often as possible from the atmosphere of the big city in order to "recharge his batteries" and to seek subjects for his paintings in the country; but he is just as keen on popular themes of the day, such as pollution, space travel, the problems that arise between different generations — themes that are more universal than current political events. In the case of such pictures the intellectual content sometimes clashes with the carefree naive style of the painting. *(See portrait of the artist, p. 561). T. G.*

SELIVANOV, IVAN EGOROVIČ (1907)   USSR
SELIVANOV, IVAN YEGOROVICH

I. Y. Selivanov was born near Archangel, in northern Russia. His parents were poor peasants and Ivan and his siblings had to beg to keep alive. At the age of thirty he moved to Prokopevsk, a town near Kemerovo in Siberia, where he worked as a stove-maker until retiring on a pension. He began to paint in 1953 after seeing a picture displayed in a shop window. Lacking skill, he learned about the Extra-mural People's University of Art (ZNUI), where he studied under the instructor Yuri Aksyonov, with whom he established a long-standing friendship by corre-

spondence, even to the point of doing his portrait. He starts with an initial drawing, done from life. Special talent lies in his ability to faithfully reproduce the object or sitter at once, with almost the skill of a professional artist. However, he is individual in his approach. When limning his wife, a herd of cows, a little girl with hens or his self-portrait, he uses restrained tonal values, accenting the outline with pencil, which thus imparts a sense of relief. His figures are static, frontal. He is one of that category of folk artists who come to understand by themselves the laws of art, be this drawing or painting. He has been

Selivanov, Ivan Yegorovich: Self-portrait

represented at many ZNUI, republican and USSR exhibitions. His works have been reproduced in periodicals. Some are exhibited at the Museum of Popular and Amateur Art in Suzdal. *(See portrait of the artist, p. 561). N. Sh.*

SERAFINI,   Italy
GIUSEPPE (BEPPE) (1915)

Giuseppe Serafini, born in Montelupo Fiorentino, Florence, worked for a long time in a local factory, decorating pottery (plates, pitchers, souvenirs), while secretly indulging his passion for drawing and painting. Those were years of want, humiliation and even cruel intolerance on the part of some of his acquaintances, who mocked him and his work. Serafini reacted by withdrawing into his shell, into dignified isolation. Later, his talent was discovered and he achieved success, putting an end to his poverty.

Serafini works according to a precise ritual. He first makes a drawing on thick cardboard, with unusual ease and rapidity. Then with ordinary ballpoint pens he presses the basic lines of the drawing into the cardboard, and these form the backbone, the underlying structure, of the work. Sometimes a few days go by before he continues, the next stage being to apply colours, consisting of printer's ink, with broad strokes of a brush, or, more frequently, a spatula. Finally, after the colour has dried, comes the last phase: covering the picture with a secret mixture based on thinning fluid, making it possible to tone down and even out the strongest colours and giving the picture the special illumination and

Serafini, Giuseppe: The Peasant

dark nuances characteristic of this painter's work.

Serafini's themes at first glance seem to harbour an accusation, a protest, an ideological commitment, but a second glance will show that such preoccupations are alien to his work. His implicit message, his artistic commitment, consists only in his telling the story of that silent, suffering, weak and unprotected part of mankind to which he himself belonged and which, in spite of his success, he did not reject psychologically. That this is so is patently clear from many of his works, such as, for instance, "The Peasant": the subject's worried glance speaks not of demands but of suffering in silent resignation.

The painting "Figures with Sunflowers," a very effective composition, contains female figures who reveal that they belong to the people, that their lives are hard and strenuous. Nevertheless, they are powerfully rendered in all their human dignity.

Serafini's works show a clear identification of theme and form, articulated in strong, clear and decisive lines and in lively, glowing combinations of colours. *(See portrait of the artist, p. 560). D. M.*

SÉRAPHINE   France
(SÉRAPHINE LOUIS) (1864—1942)

Séraphine Louis, known simply as Séraphine, was born at Arsy, Oise, and died in Clermont de l'Oise. Her birthplace was a small Oise village where her father was a watchmaker. The elder of two daughters, she was orphaned very young and had to leave school, despite her record

as a hard-working and well-behaved child. She went to tend livestock, as was expected of any young girl of her circumstances. But already at her young age, she spent the free time allowed by her occupation in drawing. At fourteen she became a housemaid in Compiègne, and four years later was in a convent, helping the sisters with their housekeeping. She remained there for the next twenty years, until her desire for independence led her to leave the familiarity and security of the convent to find employment as a housemaid once again. A series of employers led her eventually, in 1904, to Senlis. In 1906, she

Séraphine Louis: Tree of Paradise

took rooms of her own and decided to earn her living as a day maid. She was forty-two by then and began to give colour to her own world. She painted her furniture and dishes, on cardboard and wood. Many of these works she traded with local merchants in exchange for her daily needs. She remained in Senlis in 1914 despite the German invasion. She painted flowers and fruit arrangements. By 1927, she had become something of a local character in Senlis and was invited to hang three of her paintings at an exhibition organised by a local charitable organisation at the Hôtel de Ville. Wilhelm Uhde saw them and was greatly impressed. He bought all three works and offered Séraphine a guaranteed income, to ensure her a living and allow her to give herself entirely to her art. Her devotion was total from 1927 to 1930, reaching an almost mystic intensity. She took to painting at night, became increasingly unstable and tense, and finally paranoiac. She was admitted in 1932 to the mental hospital at Clermont de l'Oise in a

SERGEEV, GRIGORIJ SERGEEVIČ (1913) USSR
SERGEYEV, GRIGORI SERGEYEVICH

G. S. Sergeyev was born into a working class family in the Ukrainian town of Zaporozhe. In the following year the family moved to another Ukrainian town, Kherson, where Sergeyev lives today. After four years of secondary schooling, Sergeyev was apprenticed to a locksmith at the age of fourteen and has been a factory worker ever since. He was interested in drawing in childhood, but because of family circumstances he could not acquire any special training in that field. Only in 1970 did he start to paint properly.

Sergeyev, Grigori Sergeyevich: River Crossing in 1919

Sgro, Mercurio: Going Downtown

state of complete breakdown, and remained there until her death in 1942.

"With incredible concentration, a strong intelligence has fixed on this canvas until all the problems of balance, harmony and the distribution of space have been resolved." This is the appraisal of Wilhelm Uhde of the works he discovered at that 1927 exhibition. Accepting, not without difficulty, the imperatives of the canvas' surface, Séraphine imposed an internal vision both opulent and monumental. She far exceeded the limits which are conventionally believed to apply to naive painters. Hers is an accumulation of forms emerging from an abstract background; a symbolic fabric going well beyond the simple presentation of still-lifes; a feeling for space which drove her to paint on bigger and bigger canvases; a secret chemistry of colour the principle of which disappeared with her; a cosmic vision owing nothing of its dimensions to the constricted life of Senlis.

After her works were shown in Senlis in 1927, Séraphine participated in international shows in Paris, New York, Bratislava, São Paulo, Geneva, Bern, London and Rome. *Ch. Sch.*

He mostly paints from memory and imagination and also does woodcarving, which he likes to inlay with mother of pearl. Like most elderly naive artists, he prefers to take past events as subject-matter. With him this is mostly various chapters in the story of this seaside city. His means of expression are laconic and artless, but each plane is worked out in scrupulous detail. He has been represented at several group shows. Some of his works are on view at the Kiev Museum of Folk Arts and Crafts. *(See portrait of the artist, p. 560). N. Sh.*

SGRO, MERCURIO (1910)   Argentina

Mercurio Sgro was born in Calabria, Italy, but when he was three months old his parents decided to move to Argentina. He worked first as a mason and later in the iron and steel industry. In 1974, already retired, he suffered a serious accident in which he broke his leg. After surgery, he was forced to rest for several months. As inactivity depressed him, to entertain him his brother-in-law offered him oils and a brush. And Mercurio, who had never painted a stroke in his life, joyfully started at the age of sixty-three to cover his pasteboard paper with pictures. Mercurio, a city dweller who has never been out in the country, paints his parents' recollections of their little town in the south of Italy. Recently, quite sure of himself, he started to paint with acrylic, mixing areas of pure colours (gay roofs, vivid clothing) with delicately hued renderings of trees and meadows. *M. T. S.*

SHALOM OF SAFED (1882—1980)   **Israel**

Shalom of Safed was born in Safed as Shalom Moskowitz. He was a watchmaker when the painter Yosl Bergner discovered his talents — hence his nickname Zeigermacher (watchmaker, in Yiddish). He began to paint stories

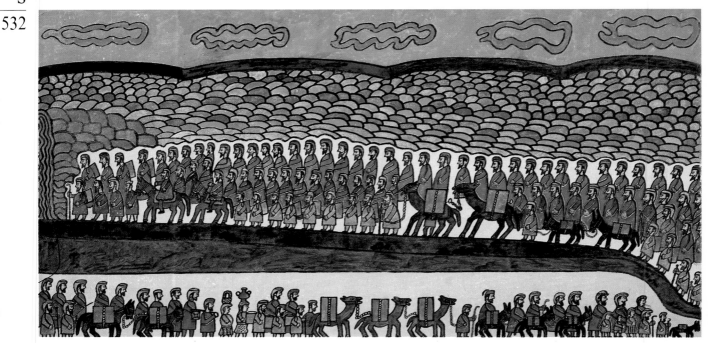

Shalom of Safed: Exodus

from the Bible when he was about seventy years old. These remained his main subjects. He mostly used watercolour and gouache, later acrylics, and painted on paper rather than on canvas. Also lithographs were made from his works.

A horizontal division of the paper and a technique of relating the story in strips are typical features of his work. Sometimes whole phrases from the Bible are copied by Shalom into his painting, to explain the theme. Occasionally explanations in Yiddish also appear. Shalom's paintings draw a parallel — subconsciously, no doubt — between life in biblical times and life in Israel today. Houses very often resemble the standard Israeli habitats, and biblical heroes wear modern coats and hats, like those worn by the old of Safed today. The wicked often have the face of Hitler. Shalom's fascination with clouds is worth noting: there is no end to the variations on their form in his work. *(See portrait of the artist, p. 560). R. D.*

SHEN DEXIAN (1929)   **China**

Shen Dexian is from the Xing Nong commune. Before he joined the Jin Shan group of

peasants in 1974, he spent his leisure time painting flowers and birds above the brick stoves which Chinese peasants usually decorate with ornamental designs. Because of the scarcity of wood and other fuels, the stoves are rarely lit. When they are lit, the entire Chinese peasant family considers it a holiday. Since 1974, Shen Dexian has used all his spare time to produce watercolours of scenes from contemporary Chinese life.

"When I come in from the fields," says this painter, "I begin to paint and that is the greatest joy in life for me. In the brigade, I do one kind of

Shen Dexian: The Artificial Pearls

work, whereas in my paintings my life becomes different, many-sided. I live with all the people whose lives I paint. For the most part, we peasants stay in our village. But once in 1976 I went to Shanghai on business. Along the way I came upon scenes that differed completely from my own life. I saw peasants floating in barrels. They were planting shells in the water in order to obtain cultivated pearls. I was enchanted by the scene and painted it the minute I reached home. I called the painting 'The Artificial Pearls.' The boat in the middle of the picture is the product of my imagination as there was none there. I needed it to break the monotony of the identical barrels." The painting has been exhibited with the works of other painters belonging to the Jin Shan group. *(See portrait of the artist, p. 561). N. T.*

ŠIJAKOVIĆ, DJORDJE (1901—1980) Yugoslavia

Djordje Šijaković was born in Cetinje, Montenegro, and died in Skopje. In early childhood, he went with his parents and elder brother

In his brief career as a painter, Šijaković enriched naive art with his individual approach to painting, his largely green, grassy backgrounds and his figures of people with large heads and soulful eyes.

Šijaković had one-man shows and participated in group exhibitions at home and abroad. *(See portrait of the artist, p. 561). N. T.*

ŠILHÁN, VÁCLAV (1906) Czechoslovakia

Václav Šilhán, born in Jirkov, comes from a glass-blower's family of seven children. Initially,

Šijaković, Djordje: Searching for Happiness

Šilhán, Václav: Maya

to the USA, where he attended grade school and high school. The family lived in a number of American cities as the father moved around looking for better jobs. When Šijaković was fourteen he came back home and worked as a clerk for the British at the Trepča Mines until 1941. During the war he was interned in a prisoner-of-war camp. After the war, he changed jobs several times, always accepting with fortitude employment in many backward parts of Macedonia.

After a life of travel and work, Šijaković impatiently looked forward to his pension. Fortunately, one day, already retired, having nothing better to do, he watched his son mixing colours and painting. Previously, he had no interest in painting, as other things had appealed to him. Now he felt a desire to paint and soon this became the overruling passion of his life. His subjects are shepherds, elderly people gnarled from the wind and the rain, gipsies always on the move or others who have grown tired of eternal motion and settled around Skopje and other towns in Macedonia.

In "Searching for Happiness" (1973), gipsy wagons are going off in all directions. Full of gay men and women, they are being drawn by gipsy horses to fairs and carnivals, to weddings and other festivities where gipsies are always welcome. Since music is in their blood, they and their instruments are always found wherever they can help keep sorrow at bay and make life more cheerful, if only for a while.

he worked as a glass-blower at home, then he moved to Jablonec, where he was manager of a small glass works. After being in charge of various aspects of production in the Jablonec glass works in Lučany, he retired in 1966. His main hobbies were bee-keeping and chess. After retiring, Šilhán gave up the chess he had been so fond of in favour of bees and painting, pursuing the latter in winter, while in summer he devotes all his attention to his bees. "My bees are my kingdom. I would not touch my brush for all the money in the world if my bees are out." As an artist, he started by painting a landscape at the beginning of winter in 1966.

At present Šilhán paints mostly nudes. They are his dream, his idea of beauty. He takes inspiration from other works or photographs. But his variants on these are so specific that to speak of mere copying is simply out of the question in his case. His nudes are actually variations on a theme that comply with the rules of his clear vision. He can stylise shapes and form them in harmonious combinations of clear colours; he also knows how to arrange the space of a picture decoratively. His manner of painting is pure and genuine and his naivety is refined. Simple compositions have the impact of lapidary forms, while the more complicated ones generate interest by the addition of details.

Pink, white, blue, and light violet are used on dark violet, green and other backgrounds. Šilhán occupies a highly individual position in naive art. *S. T.*

SILVA, FRANCISCO DOMINGOS DA (about 1910) — Brazil

SILVA,   **Brazil**
FRANCISCO DOMINGOS DA (about 1910)

Born in Alto Tejo, Silva left home to take up residence in various areas, settling finally in Fortaleza. During this time he was employed in all manner of jobs, passing through a number of vicissitudes until in 1935 he turned his attention to finding out if he could become an artist. For anyone with such eccentric and fantastic vision — let alone one who was self-taught — it was some time before art enthusiasts started to take notice of him. Although he started exhibiting his pictures in 1943, it was not until 1965 that he

Silva, Francisco Domingos da: Intruder

disabled. First with pencil and paper and later with canvas and oils, from his bed he created an imaginary and idyllic village world with himself always in the foreground. In fact, his paintings were stories on paper or canvas about various events that would have taken place in his life if he had had a normal youth like other country boys. In 1962 he began exhibiting soft pastel-coloured paintings, together with Janko Brašić and other Serbian naive artists. Probably Stepa Sirković is the only painter in Serbia who has never attended an exhibition of his works. Because of his disablement, he never leaves the

Silva, Marina: The Cove

received what was to all intents and purposes an accolade — a commission to create a whole series of pictures. Since that time Francisco da Silva has been both accepted and recognised.

He is surely the most fantastic of all Brazil's self-taught artists, having a visual language all his own. The figures in his pictures are all loosely related to animals, birds, fish, reptiles and insects, but there the recognisable element in his work ends, because along with cheerful and uncharted coloration, all these "figures" have a kind of roulette-wheel chance distortion. His technique as a painter is extremely linear and even colour blocks are often made up from a linear base. *Sh. W.*

SILVA, MARINA — Nicaragua

SILVA, MARINA   **Nicaragua**

This young artist, from the archipelago of Solentiname on the Lake of Nicaragua, has painted a large number of pictures and taken part in many exhibitions at home and abroad. Among the members of the Solentiname school, she stands out for the precision with which she paints details, especially leaves, grass and flowers. Her favourite subject is the landscape of these tropical islands. *(See portrait of the artist, p. 561). E. C.*

SIRKOVIĆ, STEPA (1932) — Yugoslavia

SIRKOVIĆ, STEPA (1932)   **Yugoslavia**

Stepa Sirković was born in Drlupe, near Mt. Kosmaj, Serbia, and still resides in the village of his birth. As a child, he contracted infantile paralysis and was left seriously

house. His subject-matter is joyful: engagements, get-togethers, men waiting for their sweethearts, first love, an autumn wedding.

In the painting "The Wedding," a gay procession, consisting of the groom's men dressed in their holiday clothes, horses, and the bride and groom, is passing through the village to the great satisfaction of the peasants. They are all in a good mood, dancing, while among them are the eternal itinerants: gipsy musicians, violinists with the strings of their violins in disarray, and so on. The wedding party is arriving at the home of the groom. A boy has climbed up on the roof to watch, as boys will. Later all of this will be repeated. A grown-up, good-looking young man will climb down from the roof and take his place alongside the bride. This painting, like many others, is the product of the artist's imagination and recollections of childhood, when Stepa Sirković was still able to clamber up trees and on roofs, before his illness took hold of him and condemned him to his bed forever.

Stepa Sirković has had one-man shows and participated in group exhibitions at home and abroad. *(See portrait of the artist, p. 561). N. T.*

SIVÁŇ, ŠTEFAN (1906) — Czechoslovakia

SIVÁŇ, ŠTEFAN (1906)   **Czechoslovakia**

Štefan Siváň was born in Babín, where he still lives. He has worked as a farmer and a cartwright. Love of wood made him turn to carving both as a job and as a hobby. Wood was a godsend for Siváň, and he learned all about its qualities. While still a boy, besides working on the farm, he carved kitchen and shepherd's tools and utensils in his spare time, as well as carts, sledges, ladders and many other things. He gradually extended the scope of his themes from various tools and useful objects to sculpture. He carved figures for Nativity scenes which he carried around the village, singing Christmas carols. In the sixties he began to carve larger sculptures (even larger than life), and made them his specific medium of artistic expression. Though Siváň's works are part of folk art and culture, they exceed these boundaries. A rare phenomenon among Slovak carvers, Siváň is unique by virtue of the spiritual richness of his

Gallery, the Slovak National Museum in Bratislava and Martin, the Orava Gallery in Dolný Kubín and many other museums and galleries in Czechoslovakia and abroad. *(See portrait of the artist, p. 560). S. T.*

SKOULAS, ALKIVIADIS (1902)   Greece

Alkiviadis Skoulas was born in Anayia, Crete. He only became aware of his remarkable talent at the age of seventy. With the simplicity of his pure heart and the certainty of his true artistic instinct Skoulas gives life to tree-trunks

Sirković, Stepa: Wedding

Siváň, Štefan: Flight into Egypt

Skoulas, Alkiviadis: Village Scene

and roots that he transforms into figures. Isolated male and female figures, often identifiable as figures from both ancient and more recent history, group scenes, religious compositions, animals and snakes, trees, birds, an eagle trampling on a snake are all part of his repertory. In addition to his work in wood he has also made some figures of stone.

In his paintings he tells us stories with the help of sensitive and usually light colours. Scenes from his village's traditional life and occupations (mountains, shepherds, sheep, milking, ploughing, spinning and hunting) are some of his most typical subjects. The arrangement of houses in rows placed one on top of the other is a kind of naive representation of his village's position on a mountain slope. The houses have simple roofs and clearly recall children's drawings. His family portraits are also noteworthy; in these the strict and somewhat inept frontality, the charmingly disproportionate rendering, the limited scale of colours (with a certain emphasis on black) contribute to a highly expressive effect.

Undoubtedly the most authentic representative of his village's living tradition, Skoulas is a remarkable figure among the naive artists of Greece. His work has been shown in two one-man shows (one in Athens and one in Anayia) and in a few group exhibitions in Crete. *A. T.*

expression. All this stems from his abilities and disposition and from the rich mosaic of his everyday life, revealing both his inspiration and his style. Siváň fashions shepherds, Orava bagpipers, women milking cows, cows with calves, horseback riders, Jánošík (the Slovak Robin Hood), bee-hives in the shape of human figures and other themes. He is able to transform the poetry of simple common people into the structure of wood. Skilled in producing variations, he uses the same motif in different ways, all of them marked by his personal style. His figures seem to be symbols of life-giving force.

Štefan Siváň has had one-man exhibitions in the Orava Gallery in Dolný Kubín and in the Tatra Gallery in Horný Smokovec in 1974. He has also shown his work in several international exhibitions. His works are in the Slovak National

SKURJENI, MATIJA (1898)   Yugoslavia

Matija Skurjeni, born in Vaternica, near Zlatar, Croatia, had no schooling. His father, a woodcutter, was killed when crushed by a falling tree-trunk while Matija was still a boy. The mother then had to feed her eight small children alone, so Matija left home when he was only twelve to seek work. He was taken in as an apprentice by a house painter for whom he also did all the housework in return for room and board. In the First World War, as a soldier in the Austrian Army, he found himself, not yet eighteen, at the Russian front, where he was for all parts of the world, bearing not only passengers but also their dreams, visions and desires. Although Skurjeni worked for the railways many years, he did very little travelling. Waiting for the trains to come in or pull out, he voyaged in his mind to faraway places, following the trains and their passengers to their destinations. What he wished for during the day turned into dreams during the night.

In the lower part of the painting "Passing Trains," a series of black trains are making their way through a tunnel. As in an aquarium, the transparent blue-green of the vegetation merges

Skurjeni, Matija: Passing Trains

wounded. Upon returning to his village, he took a job in the mines, where he remained twelve years. He then moved to Zagreb and worked for the railways for thirty years, until his retirement in 1956. He now lives in Zaprešić, a small town near Zagreb.

Matija Skurjeni differs from most naive painters in that he draws the inspiration for his paintings from dreams. He frequently wakes up during the night in the middle of a dream and, while it is still fresh in his mind, notes it down, describes it and makes a sketch of it. Sometimes, if he is really wide awake, he even begins to paint. Many of his canvases show trains leaving

with the cosmic blue of the sky. Small churches and houses seem to be floating in a two-toned world.

Where is the boundary line between reality and dreams? Perhaps it is in their intermingling that the source of the artist's inspiration lies — the merging of dreams and reality that gives his pictures their special charm of a mixture of the real and unreal.

In "Crossing the Sava," Skurjeni has painted himself and his friend, also an artist. He dreamed that he was on the banks of a swollen river during a storm. The wind was so strong that trees bent under its force. Shelter had to be found. He looked across the river and there on the other side everything was calm. An orchard in bloom seemed like an ideal refuge. But how to get there? And as might happen in a dream, the painter raised his hands skyward and the wave-tossed Sava split in two. Along the edge of the blue sky, two large white clouds sail toward each other, resembling two mythical spectres. As in the biblical story of Moses, a miracle brought salvation. The painter portrayed the separation of the storm-tossed river and in contrast to man's misfortunes showed a peaceful, pastoral landscape in the background.

They lead a settled family life, whereas in the case of the other couple, life together seems to be just beginning. The charm of the picture lies in the unreal vision of the painter, stressed by characteristic clouds of unusual form and bare trees against a full moon, creating a specially romantic atmosphere.

In addition to subjects from dreams and the gipsy cycle, the painter has produced a considerable number of pictures that are fantasies, as he himself calls them. "I have always fantasised and never could regard things realistically. I had my own way of looking at every thing and every

Skurjeni, Matija: Animal Kingdom

One cannot help noticing that by using blue tones, interrupted only by the white of the waves, the flowering orchard and the clouds, the painter has achieved a contrast between two utterly different situations without resorting to colour contrasts.

In "Gipsy Love," a subject this artist has dealt with several times, a man and woman in the moonlight, the latter visible only from the reflection in the fenced-in pool and the somewhat darker tones in the foreground, are portrayed in the throes of a conflict between desire and morality. The man has taken a long step in the direction of an empty tent, while the woman seems to be hesitating before doing the same. Behind them is a gipsy nag, without which life for the family is unimaginable. Always on the move, sometimes covering long distances, the gipsies are dependent on their horses. In contrast to this drama, in the background stands a row of huts and gipsy families gathered about a fire.

person, changing them to suit my mood," says the painter.

With the tip of his brush, as though guided by a magic power, Skurjeni uncodes almost subconsciously the tension between dreams and reality. He paints hallucinatory figures, fantastic animals, heavenly landscapes full of melancholy, and from his own innermost visions brings forth bouquets of flowers and strange creatures. Over the years, his motifs have changed, but his pictures remain within the sphere of inner experience, mysterious in form and colour but convincing nevertheless. In his feeling for theme, colour and composition, Skurjeni belongs among the very best Yugoslav naive artists, while set apart from other naives by his individuality.

Skurjeni works in oil on canvas; his paintings are usually small in size. He has frequently exhibited and has won recognition at home and abroad.

(See portrait of the artist, p. 560). N. T.

SLEEP, JOSEPH (1914—1978)　　　　Canada

A concise account of Sleep's life is given in his autobiography: "My mother and father were from England. I was born on the boat coming at sea. The Government have me born in three different years: 1914, 1916, 1918. Education: East St. John School, New Brunswick. I was a devil. I never wanted to go to school: went as far as grade 2. Various jobs: fisherman, jack-of-all-trades. 1973 while at the Halifax Infirmary they gave me posters to colour and I started drawing my own and I aint stopped since. Done about 500 pictures this year [1977-78]."

538

Sleep, Joseph: Untitled

Sleep started to paint in 1973. In that year, while recovering from a bout of chronic alcoholism, he was given large colouring sheets printed with intricate borders and large flower arrangements. This experience not only launched him as an amateur painter, but provided him with a method which he continued to employ in all his work. Borders and the use of over one hundred different tracing patterns became a feature of Sleep's painting. From these patterns he assembled a fantastic universe of carnivals, murals with every living creature he could imagine either on land or in the sea, and still-lifes of birds, animals, and flowers. *Th. L.*

SLOOT,　　　　Netherlands
JENTJE VAN DER (1881—1963)

Jentje van der Sloot, born in Schalsum, Friesland, had to leave school when he was nine to help his parents in the fields. Undecided in choosing a calling, he tried many occupations. He was coffee-house owner, salesman, book-keeper, street photographer — always on the move. Finally, he reached Amsterdam. When his daughter fell ill, he returned to Friesland.

When his wife died, Jentje withdrew even further into himself. Once retired, he began to paint. Initially, he reproduced postcards but his brother, who had attended a fine arts academy, advised him to look around for himself and paint nature. Only after the death of his brother did Jentje succeed in finding his own style. Already old in 1958, he packed up eight of his paintings

and went to The Hague to show them to the director of the Academy. His work was met with great enthusiasm at the Free Academy. This recognition was a turning-point. He was to live only four years more, but from the artistic point of view they were the most significant years of his life. He exhibited in a one-man show at the Free Academy and in the Van Hulsen Gallery in Leeuwarden, as well as in a group show in Basel.

When he died in 1963, he left about sixty pictures behind him. These works are among the most outstanding in Dutch naive art. He had a strong feeling for composition and his paintings

Sloot, Jentje van der: Hotel in Friesland

possess dramatic force, bringing them close to Expressionism.

His subject-matter is his native land: defiant and harsh, whipped by storms and wind, but full of unearthly poetic gentleness. In spite of the gloomy green of his palette, the overall effect of his work is anything but gloomy. One would rather describe it as an exceptionally complete image, both sweet and rough, of a naive reality. *(See portrait of the artist, p. 560). N. E.*

SMAJIĆ, PETAR (1910)　　　　Yugoslavia

Petar Smajić, born in Donje Dolce, near Split, Croatia, began to work in wood at the age of seventeen while still a shepherd. His first sculptures, carved in wood while he tended sheep, portrayed historical personalities, fearless riders on horses, dressed in festive array, and so on, after which he started doing ordinary people: peasants from the rock-strewn Dalmatian Karst — tall, straight, bony, and whiskered, with Dalmatian caps on their heads. Smajić had his first exhibition in 1934 in the Galić Salon in Split. At that time, the person who helped him most was Dr. Vidović, who, finding Smajić's naive sculptures exceptionally attractive, bought up all the figures he produced for the next four years and also offered him suggestions about expanding his subject-matter.

"Dr. Vidović asked me to do a man and woman together, which I did for the first time as I had never attempted that before. When I was twenty-four years old, an illiterate workman and shepherd, I had the first exhibition of my works, a great recognition for me. Our countryman, the celebrated sculptor Ivan Meštrović, was a member of the jury of the Galić Salon. I had forty-two sculptures on display. Meštrović liked all of them and was satisfied with my output."

It was thus that Smajić paved the way for naive sculpture in Yugoslavia with the assistance of Ivan Meštrović, just as in another part of Croatia, a year earlier, Ivan Generalić had launched naive painting with the help of the academic painter, Krsto Hegedušić.

For his sculptures, which are, as a rule, small in size (about 30 cm on the average, the largest being 5 metres), Smajić used maple, easy to come by in the unproductive Dalmatian Karst.

One of Smajić's best works is biographical. He thought it altogether natural to do a carving of his family of ten. In this sculpture of 50 cm he

Smajić, Petar: My Family

ranged all the members of his family by size. He and his wife are in the first row and the smallest children are above, at the top. The sculptor thinks that such a hierarchy should also exist in the family: first come those who are older and then the youngest. This patriarchal approach to the family is present in all his works: portrayals of a traditional way of life, forms which have disappeared or are disappearing, conceptions that are changing. Smajić's work differs from that of other sculptors in the sense that his carvings are of people who live in the Dalmatian highlands, leading a hard life. He also carves animals but as

Smirnov, Vladimir Borisovich: Square

a rule only tame ones, those who live with or serve man. For twenty years now, Smajić has been living in Ernestinovo, near Osijek.

Petar Smajić has had one-man shows and has participated in group exhibitions at home and abroad. *(See portrait of the artist, p. 561).* N. T.

SMIRNOV,   USSR
VLADIMIR BORISOVIČ (1953)
SMIRNOV, VLADIMIR BORISOVICH

V. B. Smirnov was born in Byelorechensk, in the Kuban, south Russia, the son of a railwayman. He took up drawing in childhood, and also tried to compile city plans from match-box labels and razor-blade wrappings. Subsequently he seriously studied architecture. After a term of national service (in the armed forces he drew posters, did wall newspapers, and so on), he took a job at the Moscow Likhachev Autoworks. He began to exhibit at amateur art shows and attended a night school. His main love is architecture, however, as man's handiwork. Initially he was interested in West European architecture, more specifically Gothic churches, palaces, castles and panoramic views of London, Paris and Venice. The paintings which result are highly expressive urban fantasies which combine a good visual memory and an element of imagination. His works seem ephemeral, like fairy-tale visions, and in some manner are reminiscent even of the 17th-century French artist Jacques Callot, with whom he is totally unfamiliar. Smirnov himself believes his "architectural fantasies combine with fantasies in technique." He is no copyist and is not interested in landscapes and panoramic views as such; rather he seeks to link city with city, or building with land

and the like. Thus, he combines Mexican ziggurats with Indian shrines, and Egyptian pyramids with Grecian temples. He is fascinated by Atlantis and the Seven Wonders of the World, scenes which he fills with many ancient and sophisticated machines of his own imagination. In his views of Russian cities he takes for his points of departure some stereotyped panoramic engravings produced by Western artists working in Russia since the time of Peter the Great. Smirnov favours pencil and watercolour, but often uses grisaille and sometimes combines techniques. He has had two shows of his own,

Sobota, Józef: Home Altars

and has been represented at exhibitions of amateur art (in 1977) and in group shows of the Moscow Association of Graphic Artists, of which he is a member. *(See portrait of the artist, p. 561).* N. Sh.

SOBOTA, JÓZEF (1894—1980)   Poland

Józef Sobota was born in the town of Regut, where he lived until he died. He was illiterate and, living in the vicinity of Warsaw, did not know folk art, or the sculptures of the wayside chapels. With only a small farm, he had to work also in a sawmill in order to make a living. There, in 1940, he suffered an accident, which left him an invalid, unable to walk. There was no money for treatment. In 1972, an angel appeared to him in a dream and advised him to put leeches on his legs. After a few months he felt the blood coursing in his veins and started walking. In another dream an angel appeared also, telling him that in gratitude to God the Father he should place along the roads ten little wayside altars. As he could not buy either figures or lithographs, he had to carve them himself in wood. Soon his work was noticed by ethnographers passing by his village. Sobota was given medical help and orders started coming in for sculptures for state collections (the museums in Warsaw, Cracow and Toruń), and for private ones, especially that of L. Zimmerer, Warsaw. This he considered repayment of the debt owed him by God for his prayers. *(See portrait of the artist, p. 562). A. J.*

Sodang, Ida Bagus: Women Bathing

SODANG, IDA BAGUS (?—1937)
Indonesia, Bali

Ida Bagus Sodang was born at about the turn of the century in the coastal village of Sanur, in the south of Bali. Little is known of his early life other than that he received a classical Balinese education in story-telling, music and puppet theatre, all of which were instrumental in preparing him for his later career as a painter.

Although the secular painting movement was conceived and nurtured in the inland towns of Batuan and Ubud it was not long before its influence spread to other centres, the most notable being the village of Sanur. As this new type of painting made its presence felt, Sodang emerged almost immediately as one of Sanur's leading painters and most powerful exponents of the new genre.

Whereas the painters of Ubud and Batuan painted the lush vegetation and animals that surrounded them, the painters of Sanur chose to depict the sea and its mysterious life. The sea is regarded by the Balinese as a low and evil place, with monsters lurking in its depths. The early secular artists of Sanur recreated these fears in their paintings, but none better or with more potent insight than Sodang. Few of his disturbing but brilliantly executed images of aquatic malfeasance survive. *J. F.*

SÖHL, MANFRED (1942)
West Germany

Manfred Söhl, born in Melno, West Prussia, now lives in Hamburg. He has been a policeman since 1960, but spends every free moment painting with obsessive enthusiasm.

At the end of the sixties, connoisseurs of naive art looked forward eagerly to every new picture by Manfred Söhl, who was at that time doing duty on patrol in the Hamburg red light district, St. Pauli. Much sought after were (and still are) those small-scale oils in which Söhl, with his unmistakably painstaking and subtle style and palette, guides us into the daily life that swarms in and around the brothels. The pictures are unspectacular, anything but depraved, detached, imbued with a poetic atmosphere; they promise suggestive glimpses of St. Pauli life but they are cosily intimate rather than wickedly

Söhl, Manfred: Two Sailors in St. Pauli

provocative. The style is neutral, the gestures and poses of the girls are restrained, their gazes are pensive and the whole scene is quiet and peaceful.

At that time Söhl served as model and inspiration for another spare-time painter, Peter Behr, who was also based at the St. David police station. Söhl's earlier pictures should also be noted: straightforward, disciplined North German landscapes (with their dykes and low-lying islands) or the landscapes painted in Yugoslavia, in which a serene joy radiates from the brilliant blue sky, the ebullient white clouds and the lush green meadows.

Connoisseurs began to take notice of these delightful little pictures in international exhibitions. It is regrettable that the originality and spontaneity which is characteristic of some authentic naive painters like Manfred Söhl is, in some cases, eventually lost. His earlier pictures deserve to be remembered, for in them an elemental freshness and instinctive assurance have not yet given way to the deliberate calculation, sterile routine, and smooth, mannered virtuosity which mar his later productions. *(See portrait of the artist, p. 562). T. G.*

SOKOL, ANA (1902)   Argentina

Ana Sokol was born in the Ukraine and came to Argentina as a child. After she divorced her husband, she opened a beauty parlour for men, women and children in the port district, where her main clients were sailors. The owners of the Art Gallery of El Taller spotted her colourful embroideries and offered her canvases and colours, encouraging her to paint. She discovered that there were stories she wanted to tell, and excerpts from the Bible she wanted to depict for others. Her colouring is vivid and her awkwardness is full of grace. The baroque expla-

Sokol, Ana: Adam and Eve

nations of her paintings which she offers turn a visit to her into a joyful occasion. *(See portrait of the artist, p. 562). M. T. S.*

SOKOL, JAN (1909—1982)   Yugoslavia

Jan Sokol was born in the village of Kovačica, Vojvodina, the home of ethnic Slovaks, where he went to elementary school. He was a farmer who began to paint in his free time in 1937. The group of naive painters in Kovačica was founded by him and a few associates.

His subject-matter is the life of the Slovaks: work in the fields, family and church festivities, funerals.

"I am frequently preoccupied with the end of life," he said. "I see how quickly life passes. On the one hand, the sun rises and flowers are everywhere, but soon a man is old and stands before his grave. That is why in my paintings I use white and black. White is for youth and happiness, and black for the end and sorrow."

In "The Funeral" (1966), Jan Sokol portrayed just such an end. On the coffin is the name of the deceased. In the background stands the mourning family. To the right are the men and to the left the women and these two worlds, the male and the female, are separated by the clergyman. The painter has used a simple method to detach the women's black kerchiefs and the dark hair of the men from the dark background of the sky: painting the roofs of the houses white. But he also knew how to break up the whiteness — by painting one of the relatives bald. In both technique and subjects Jan Sokol changed little over the years.

Jan Sokol had one-man shows and participated in group exhibitions at home and abroad. *(See portrait of the artist, p. 562). N. T.*

SOOMER, JEANNE DE (1925)   Belgium

Jeanne de Soomer, born in Brussels of Flemish parents, is self-taught in a number of fields, which has enabled her to work at various professions.

She has alternately been interested in several kinds of art: music, sculpture, modelling. Painting became her chosen means of expression

Sokol, Jan: The Funeral

in 1975, for she discovered that the language of painting came most naturally to her: "For me," she says, "painting soon became a drug. To feel firm on my feet, I have to paint every day."

Gifted with humour of a mischievous rather than harsh character, Jeanne de Soomer is influenced by folklore and Belgian history as a source of inspiration. Her approach to her themes is a happy one and she makes the effort to invest her anecdotes with an atmosphere of freshness and good will. To tell a tale she divides her canvas into sections, as the painters of votive pictures and altars did once upon a time. She has an inborn sense of composition and frequently fills up the entire space at her disposal with compact masses. The main features of her work are lyricism, poetry, dreaminess and a sense of mischief.

Jeanne de Soomer has participated in most of the group exhibitions of naive artists in Brussels. She won an award in Zagreb and also received recognition for Belgium at the International Competition in Morges. *(See portrait of the artist, p. 563). J. C.*

SÓWKA, ERWIN (1936)   Poland

Erwin Sówka was born in Katowice, where he still lives. From a miner's family, he himself worked as a miner for seventeen years. When he was fifteen, he painted his first picture, moved by his admiration of nature. Serious and contemplative, he regards his painting as a means of self-expression, and brings to it his theosophical experience and thinking about the religions of the ancient East. He is fascinated by the secrets of Sumer, Egypt, Mesopotamia, and by magic and unknown worlds. "In creating, I study myself and thus come to know my own character," says Sówka. He uses oil because he considers it more permanent than other media, and he is reluctant to part with his pictures. The scenes he depicts are fantastic representations of man and his destiny to which he assigns the significance of moral warnings. His works are in the collections

His pictures are designed to counteract commercialised tourist art by means of a language and style of their own. His favourite motif seems to be the streets of Nairobi, with their dense motor traffic and swarming crowds of people. This is the vision of a world which is thoroughly untypical of Africa. It is represented in flat surfaces, with simple lines, powerful brush-strokes and a wide range of colours — striking but lacking the full richness of life.

More original is his portrait of the country's patriarchal President, Kenyatta, whom Soy depicts in a pose of mask-like and rigid dignity.

Soomer, Jeanne de: Football Game

Sówka, Erwin: The Queen of Sheba

Soy, Ancent: Kenyatta

of the State Ethnographic Museum in Warsaw, in museums in Bytom and Zabrze, and in the collection of L. Zimmerer in Warsaw. He has exhibited in Poland and abroad. *(See portrait of the artist, p. 563). A. J.*

SOY, ANCENT (about 1940)   Kenya

Ancent Soy was born as a member of the Kamba tribe, and now lives in Nairobi. Even as a child he began making clay figures. After leaving missionary school, he became a salesman in a souvenir shop. He learned painting from a friend.

His poster design for the Olympic Games in Munich (1972) shows a different style again. Along with works by Bill, Grieshaber, Hundertwasser, Kokoschka and Vasarely, it was singled out for an award, and made Soy world-famous overnight. His picture of slim, graceful young sprinters training for the championships to come is a rhythmically structured composition, in which the painter shows himself, unexpectedly, to be a master of commercial art. *G. Sch.*

SPASIĆ, ČEDA (1922—1979)   Yugoslavia

Čeda Spasić was born in the village of Barinac, near Leskovac, Serbia. He died in Belgrade, where he had been living since 1948, employed variously as a construction worker, watchman and doorman. In his leisure time, he drew, but tore up his drawings. When he reached the age of forty, he started painting with oils on canvas. Hemp-workers were a frequent subject, since every homestead in his native village was engaged in working with hemp. He also painted other subjects associated with village customs and wartime events, working slowly, as he was far from strong.

Of the painting "Gipsy Wedding," Čeda Spasić said: "Once, when I went to visit my village, I heard the sound of the *zurle* [a type of clarinet]. Gipsies were singing, dancing and

Moreover, a large number of his pictures have a rather theatrical character; this is particularly true of the highly decorative buildings, shown in some of them, which derive directly from his colourful stage designs. His repertory is astonishingly rich and varied; he favours a scale of rather discreet colours, with some emphasis on yellow, blue, beige, white, brown and touches of red. He also painted historical scenes — battles with Turks and the like. A painting illustrated here shows a man captured by the Turks — Athanassios Diakos, the favourite of the Greek folk poets. Spatharis organised one-man shows and

Spasić, Čeda: Gipsy Wedding

Spatharis, E.: The Hero Athanassios Diakos

having a good time. The colours, and the ritual being followed there in the field under the open sky, caught my fancy."

In another painting, "Harvest," the painter treated the theme of work in the fields. The harvesters are working in a row. Some go faster, others slower. The women are dressed in ornate skirts, making them look like poppies. The wheat crop is a good one and the colour of the ripe sheaves against the small houses on the hill is like a cheerful concert, glorifying fertility. *(See portrait of the artist, p. 563). N. T.*

SPATHARIS, EVGHENIOS (1924)　　　Greece

Evghenios Spatharis, born in Athens, is the son of the well-known player of the shadow theatre *(Karaghiozis)* Sotiris Spatharis and has followed his father's profession since 1942. In this capacity he has performed in nearly every part of Greece and with his troupe also took part in folk theatre festivals in Paris, Brussels and Rome.

The influence of the shadow theatre is clear both in the subject-matter and in the details of Spatharis' paintings. In some cases he paints *Karaghiozis* or other figures of this theatre; in others the subject is taken from one of its plays.

took part in group exhibitions in Athens and in other parts of Greece; in addition, his paintings have been shown in Paris. *A. T.*

SPENCER, SAM (1898)　　　Canada

Sam Spencer became a trapper at the age of fourteen and later worked as an itinerant carpenter in Chicago, Florida and Mexico. In 1924 he returned to Canada and settled down to farm near Punnichy, Saskatchewan. His grandmother's decision to throw out a calendar picture that she had been saving, because she had no frame for it, prompted Spencer to begin his carving career in 1927. He began by carving frames but soon moved to carving the whole picture. Picture and frame became one, and all of Spencer's later work was done in what he described as "solid block carving." Spencer's work continued to depend heavily on commercial art sources, such as calendars and postcards. From these sources he extracted the dominant figure and set it in bold relief. The entire carving was then painted in an enormously complex series of dots, which give the surface depth and a rich texture. Each carving was completed with a layer of varnish which was renewed yearly until the piece began to recede behind the veil of this cracking and rough, fissured finish. Spencer works slowly and has completed about one work a year since he began. He has now ceased to carve; his works have been purchased by Canada's National Museum. *Th. L.*

SPIELBICHLER, FRANZ (1899—1975)   Austria

Franz Spielbichler was born in Trübenbach, Austria. He was the illegitimate son of a painter and never met his father. He grew up in very poor circumstances, never went to school and

Spencer, Sam: Charlie Conachor

had to work even as a child, in order to help support the family. His childhood amid the romantic mountain landscape at the foot of Mount Oetcher bred in him a strong sense of communion with nature and left him with impressions which subsequently reappear in his pictures. He was employed as a workman, and later as a conscript, in armaments factories, and in 1917 he was posted to the Isonzo front. During convalescence from a severe illness, he was sent to an island in the Black Sea. After the war he worked as a miner, a building labourer and a construction worker building mine galleries underground. For a considerable time he was unemployed, but a contract with the Russian Trade Mission in Vienna took him and his family to a magnesite works in the Urals, to major building sites in Siberia, to the Caucasus and finally to Moscow.

In 1936 he returned to his Austrian homeland and once more found himself unemployed.

In 1938 he found work in a file factory, but was called up into the army again in 1939. He was taken prisoner in Russia and not released until 1946. His circumstances improved to the point where he was able at least to buy the equipment necessary for his painting. He painted, so he said, as a form of relaxation from heavy and monotonous labour.

It was during his convalescence on an island in the Black Sea that Spielbichler was encouraged to follow the example of a sergeant who painted watercolours, but it was not until he had reached an advanced age that he was able to

Spielbichler, Franz: The Ice-skating Rink

devote himself consistently to his painting. "Partly I copy, and partly I try to paint from nature in the open air, otherwise I simply use my imagination." This is how he himself described the range of his work. In fact, it is precisely the "false" perspective and the imaginative richness of his cosmic visions that constitutes the charm of his works. He died in Lilienfeld, Lower Austria. He exhibited in Bratislava (at the First Triennial in 1966), then in Austria, West Germany and Switzerland. *F. N.*

STANIČIĆ, MATIJA (1925)   Yugoslavia

Matija Staničić was born in Dalmatia, near the town of Baška Voda. For a while she worked as a housekeeper for the Bihalji family, but after that all trace of her was lost.

She drew and painted strange, simple and fascinating pictures, but only when there was no one in the vicinity. Once, when the Bihaljis were out of town, she covered their house — the walls, closets and shutters — with her paintings and drawings. She painted on burlap or old bedsheets, on cardboard or paper. She seemed to paint on the spur of the moment, in the way small children do who, while playing, try with signs to capture the picture they have of life and the world.

The picture reproduced here is in a way her self-portrait. A magic power emanates from the slender figure in a black dress, like a priestess of some unknown deity from primeval times. The face, in profile, is as white as flour and the lips are thin and taut. The outsize yellow eye, framed in emerald green, is unmoving, hypnotic, staring into the distance under the black arch of the eyebrow. From a hair net black curls fall onto her shoulders, painted *en face*. In her right hand is a bunch of white and red flowers. The left hand, wearing a black glove, is raised as though in greeting. A black bag hangs from her arm. The dress reaches to her feet, peeping out parallel to each other like the claws of a bird. The broad, simple strokes recall Minoan wall paintings. The flowers running down the right side soften the picture. Matija Staničić works, so to say, secretly, for her own pleasure and has never exhibited her works. *O. B.-M.*

STANISAVLJEVIĆ, DRAGIŠA (1921) **Yugoslavia**

Dragiša Stanisavljević was born in the village of Jabučje, in Kolubara district, Serbia. He still lives in that same village, where he also went to elementary school, working the land and sculpting since 1956. For his sculptures, he uses wood which he drags out of the river, some of it hundreds of years old. In the water the wood is impregnated, turns black, and becomes very hard and difficult to carve. Why did Dragiša Stanisavljević decide to work in precisely this kind of wood when there are forests full of other kinds in his vicinity? It is not difficult to guess. The wood

Staničić, Matija: Woman with Flowers

Stanisavljević, Dragiša: Jesus Crucified

from the river is monolithic, monumental, challenging for a sculptor, in addition to which it has an enduring quality highly appreciated by a peasant.

The sculptor says about the themes he chooses: "I work in my spare time, mostly in the winter. During the long nights, I carved spacemen. I put the moon at the top of a tree, two rockets underneath it, one Russian and one American, and beneath them two pilots. Then I made a parachute and at the base of the sculpture some people looking at what is happening in the sky. I did the sculpture in 1967 when our peasants were very much interested in these rockets."

Stanisavljević approaches his themes with the realism he sees in certain actions, occupations or names. Symbols representing good or evil, and betrayal, are present in his work. A pregnant unmarried woman is still called a sinner in the village. To designate her as such, the sculptor will assuredly put in her portrait elements that symbolise sin and temptation: a serpent and the like. The sculpture "Jesus Crucified" differs from the work of other naive sculptors in Yugoslavia in the way Jesus is presented, for his powerful figure resembles that of the labourers of the Kolubara district. In the background are carved figures like those on the stone portal of a medieval church. At the bottom are Adam and Eve and above them is the serene figure of a mature woman; across from them is a young pregnant woman, nude. The fact that she has no clothing on serves to reveal her pregnancy but also her curves, skin and voluptuousness. On one side of the head of the crucified Christ are two calm nuns and on the other an old woman with her grandchild.

The artist has had one-man shows and has participated in group exhibitions at home and abroad. *(See portrait of the artist, p. 563). N. T.*

STANISAVLJEVIĆ, MILAN (1944)   Yugoslavia

Milan Stanisavljević was born in Jabučje, in Kolubara district, Serbia. He went to elementary school in his village, worked with his father Dragiša on their farm, and carved in his spare time. Soon sculpture became his principal occupation. He won international recognition and requests for him to exhibit his work came in from all over the world. Because of the difficulty of communicating with the world from his idyllic but remote village, and of transporting his sculptures in wood (which are as heavy as lead), Stanisavljević moved to Belgrade. Portraying life and people through his own eyes and feelings, he differs from other sculptors in a number of ways, including his working method. Stanisavljević does not sculpt life the way it is on the outside, realistically, but depicts his internal world. Following in his father's footsteps, he uses oak which topples over from age into the Kolubara River or is uprooted by the Kolubara when that river changes course. He hauls it out of the muddy river bottom, where the oak may have lain for hundreds of years. In the water, the oak is slowly impregnated and transformed into a black, hard wood which presents a great challenge to this robust sculptor. The work of Milan Stanisavljević is too individual to be classed with that of the other sculptors of Yugoslavia, no matter how great, or with that of any of the groups or schools in existence in that country. His sculptures are original works of art, evolving from the authentic world of the village and from a philosophy with a strong streak of the mythical. Patriarchal morals and religion form the roots which feed the powerful personality of this artist.

Stanisavljević, Dragiša: Spacemen

Stanisavljević, Milan: The Wedding Dirge

"In the sculpture 'Birth' I depict a mother as a large embryo, a large grain of the fruit that gives birth to a child," says the sculptor. "Instead of her eye, I imagined the head of the child, and from her mouth emerge his legs. That is the nucleus that remains, that is the seed that grows. The mother dies and disappears, while the child continues to look at the world through her eyes."

Since Milan Stanisavljević does not deal in his work with external effects but with the essence of things, his ability to present variety is in proportion to the wealth of his spiritual world and talent. Love, the prime mover and elixir of

Stanisavljević, Milan: Self-creation

life, is shown by him in various ways, depending on what is involved: love for a mother, a sweetheart, a friend. Love for a girl: three eyes and two noses; on one side a man and on the other a girl; they are bound together not only physically, in the marriage register, but spiritually as well. Stanisavljević has shown love for a friend in an unusual way in the sculpture "Measuring": since conversation is a kind of unlocking, instead of an ear there is a lock; the man speaking is shown in profile — instead of a nose, he has a scale with a heart on it; two legs stand on the two pans of the scale. Love for a mother has already been

Stapel, Rudolf: Winter in Westphalia

described in the sculpture "Birth." Each state of the spirit is shown in its own way, revealing Stanisavljević as a varied and impassioned sculptor. The critic O. Bihalji-Merin wrote the following after a visit to the house and "studio" of Milan Stanisavljević while the latter was still living in the village:

"Hens and chickens peck about the barnyard; near the fence is an old bee-hive made of reeds held together by dried mud. Here again we come across his important sculpture 'Wedding Dirge.' Rhythmic groups, members of a fantastic wedding party, move toward each other and away from each other. A horse-drawn cart seems to fly. Men with farm implements, animals, musicians playing the bass and accordion, people singing and dancing. A floating nude. At the bottom, as heavy as caryatids, is a pair of parents. On the other side of the column the space is dominated by the great figure of the Redeemer, one fist on his chest, the other at his forehead and tears flowing down his face, Christ as escort, the peasant as sufferer."

Milan Stanisavljević has had one-man shows and has participated in group exhibitions at home and abroad. *(See portrait of the artist, p. 562). N. T.*

STAPEL, RUDOLF (1925) West Germany

Rudolf Stapel was born in Hamburg, where he still lives. Trained as a motor mechanic, he was a lorry-driver for many years and is now laboratory assistant in a Hamburg school. He began to paint while he was temporarily unemployed and at a loss for something to do: it turned out to be an inspired idea which has given Stapel a rich and happy life.

He invariably tries to look for his subjects outside the city (his favourite sources are villages and small towns in Schleswig-Holstein and Lower Saxony) and he tends to discover those subjects which, in his view, other people pass by unheedingly. Stapel does not allow himself to be hurried when he is painting, and he can summon up the stamina to pursue a picture down to the very last detail. He tends to see his own nature in

St. Brice, Robert: Queen Erzulle

the manner of his painting: sober and objective, but slightly dreamy. His colour schemes are correspondingly firm and cool: certain objects look as if they were petrified; the waves appear to be frozen.

Stapel speaks of 120 to 150 hours as being necessary on the average for the completion of a picture. If we note how precisely objects are located in the landscape, observe the patience with which he represents brick houses and stone walls, placing stone by stone with painful accuracy and in imaginative variety, painting each with the most delicate of brushes, then it is indeed all the more remarkable that Stapel never loses sight of the overall structure of his pictures, which is simply and liberally conceived and full of a restrained rhythmic tension. *T. G.*

ST. BRICE, ROBERT (1893—1973) Haiti

Robert St. Brice was born in Pétionville and died in Port-au-Prince. The son of a very poor family, St. Brice had to try his hand at many jobs; this situation lasted for years until, quite by chance, the American artist Alex John came to stay at his home as a paying guest.

The Haitian was greatly intrigued by the way in which Alex John could paint pictures and he decided to follow his example. He came to the Centre d'Art in Port-au-Prince at a time when he was already deeply involved with Voodoo and had become a houngan (priest).

To gain a true insight into St. Brice's art it is necessary not only to comprehend the integrity lurking in his "rough and primitive" style, but also to realise that the impetus and inspiration

ing in 1963 when he was immobilised for several months following an injury. He started exhibiting works in tempera and oils in 1966.

In Šteberl's work we recognise one of the most remarkable phenomena to have appeared in the firmament of naive art during the last twenty years. Šteberl's dream reality has a certain resemblance to medieval imagery. His devotional pictures suggest an affinity with stained-glass windows, especially with those flat figures ornamentally linked by the ramifications of lead. The reality of the senses in both cases is barely represented by graphic indications — the whole

Šteberl, Ondrej: Šteberl Arrives in Heaven

Šteberl, Ondrej: The Couple

for his art was spiritual and mystical. For this artist, the most important element in painting was the dictates of the "inner eye" (he had no interest in ordinary reality); he saw the creation of a picture as a holy act in close harmony with the magic of Voodoo. He was not a descriptive painter of Voodoo "life and activities," nor was his manner that of the richly imaginative André Pierre (who was also deeply immersed in Voodoo lore and mysteries). No, in his unique way, St. Brice was like a transatlantic Expressionist, but an Expressionist outside physical life and one who turned emotionalism into the "realism" of his inner eye. The outcome of his preoccupation was a loose and hectic painterly style. *Sh. W.*

ŠTEBERL, ONDREJ (1897—1977)   Czechoslovakia

Ondrej Šteberl, son of a vintner, was born in Pezinok. Even in his youth, which was passed in poverty, his introverted nature was manifest. The wretched conclusion of the First World War found him suffering from malaria on the Albanian front. After working as a craftsman he became a postman in 1928. Šteberl began paint-

work is open to spiritual influences and is sustained by faith in a profounder truth apprehended by the inner eye.

Šteberl's large body of work can be divided thematically into three groups. Alongside biblical and symbolic scenes ("The Good Samaritan," "Crucifixion," "Christ Knocking at the Door") we find innumerable themes from the country life of earlier times (huntsmen and shepherds, woodsmen, girls in peasant costume, mowing, dances, the grape-harvest) and also splendidly idyllic urban scenes ("In the Boat," "Bathing," "In the Garden," "A Walk"). The folk who make their appearance in these pictures are unmistakable.

Šteberl's emblematic images must be nourished by very distant memories; the "concepts" abstracted from them may be passed through a psychic lens. This lens focuses them, reduces them to a scheme, and then proceeds to transform and re-arrange them. Šteberl used to build up his compositions from the lower edge of the picture, like a façade. He arranged his flat areas, with their cellular concepts, side by side, rather like an Egyptian scribe or a Coptic carpet weaver. The artist's work has won him several awards. *(See portrait of the artist, p. 562). A. P.*

STEFULA,   West Germany
GYÖRGY AND DOROTHEA

György and Dorothea Stefula were born in Hamburg. The year of birth is known only for György — 1913. Both belong to the category of consciously naive artists who have preserved so much of their childlike imagination that their craftsmanlike skill only adds another dimension to their wondrous discoveries. György comes closer than Dorothea to the painterly expression of the true naive artist. A house painter, he was working one day, painting the fence of an airport, when he was caught up in the desire to become

The Stefulas have been displaying their paintings both together and separately at exhibitions since the end of the forties. *(See the reproduction, p. 81 and the portrait of the artist, p. 562).* O. B.-M.

STEINMANN, HEINZ (1943) Australia

Heinz Steinmann was born in Switzerland and arrived in Australia in 1958. Without formal art training he has evolved a distinct style using mixed media, including inks — to achieve an effect of vibrant, lush tropical vegetation. His sub-

Steinmann, Heinz: Cape York Fantasy

an artist. In this he was helped by the professional artistic experience of Dorothea.

Among the most impressive works by György Stefula is his painting "Parents in Heaven." With great mastery of his craft and a primitive inspiration, he painted a fine-looking couple representing his mother and father from the distant past. Floating on clouds, full of youthful strength, the elegant jockey hailing from Hungary, dressed in a blue-green and orange costume, wears a melancholy expression on his face and stands next to a lovely girl in white — the artist's mother, a gracious Frenchwoman attired in a wedding gown and holding a branch of myrtle in her hand. The figures of the young couple are framed with flowering branches and national flags.

jects are mostly inspired by the unspoilt wilderness areas of Northern Queensland and in particular the Cape York Peninsula, where he lives with his sister in Port Douglas. He is passionately involved with all issues relating to wilderness preservation, with the delicate balance of flora and fauna and the urgency of recognising their needs in the face of encroaching civilisation.

Heinz Steinmann's pencil portraits show amazing skill and sensitivity, and he is able to draw with both hands simultaneously.

He has had one-man shows at a number of commercial galleries in various states and has participated in numerous group exhibitions.

His work is represented in the Queensland Art Gallery and many private collections. *(See portrait of the artist, p. 563). B. McC.*

STEPANOV, SERGEJ GEORGIEVIČ (1923)
STEPANOV, SERGEY GEORGIYEVICH

USSR

S. G. Stepanov was born in Orsk, a town near Orenburg. After seven years of schooling he went to work. He fought in the Second World War and was invalided. Since 1959 he has been state farm time-keeper and locksmith. He began to draw when a child. He entered ZNUI — the Extra-mural People's University of Art — in 1966 and studied under A. Aizenman. His colour scheme is bright; now and again a sense of texture is conveyed. His ZNUI studies have not af-

Stepanov, Sergey Georgiyevich: State Farm Woman Worker Ozhogin with Cucumber

fected his concepts. The obvious charm of his work derives from the artist's fondness for the objects and people pictured. Planes are conveyed through conventional lines designating one or another level; horizons are usually high, even though the artist is aware of the rules of perspective; most of what is portrayed appears directly in the flat plane of the canvas. He has been represented at many exhibitions, including ZNUI shows in 1970 in Moscow, a 1972 show in Orenburg devoted to the 50th anniversary of the creation of the USSR, the "Glory to Labour" Exhibition in Moscow (1974), the "Amateur Artists to Their Motherland" Exhibition (1970), and a 1982 exhibition, both in Moscow. *N. Sh.*

STÉPHANE, MICIUS (1912)

Haiti

Micius Stéphane was born in Bainet. A cobbler, he used to make little sculptures out of chalk in his spare time. When he saw these small carvings, DeWitt Peters was not impressed and persuaded Stéphane to take up painting instead. In 1948 Stéphane joined the Centre d'Art, making his way to Port-au-Prince some eight years later. Since his wife is blind, he has lived a quiet life, staying mostly indoors. Unlike so many other Haitian artists discussed in this book, Stéphane, although a religious man, is not a believer in Voodoo.

Stéphane, Micius: Scaring off Birds

When he began painting, Stéphane chose as subjects childlike descriptions of the coastal life he had grown up with in his home village of Bainet. As a painter, he is poised on a knife-edge between primitive and naive; in an extraordinary way he comes close to the *folklorique* imagery and expression of the best peasant art in Europe. He elevates the most ordinary circumstance into a work of art.

After urban exposure (of himself and his pictures) in Port-au-Prince, he settled down to city-life.

With practice and increasing expertise, Stéphane has refined some of the rougher techniques which he originally employed, but without sacrificing the primitive character of his work. His colours tend to be dry and earthy; muted oranges and terracottas vie with pale acid greens and blues, and even the paint itself looks as if it has been through a refiner's fire. *Sh. W.*

STERN, EMMA (1878—1969)

West Germany

Emma Stern was born in St. Wendel, Saarland, and died in Paris. Together with her husband she ran a textile business in Lebach and continued to manage it single-handedly after his death in 1920. Emma Stern had known better days, filled with satisfaction in her work and ambitious plans for the future, before she was forced to flee from the Nazis and seek refuge in Paris, where she began a new life. The terrors of the occupation and the cruel death of a son who was gassed robbed her of all her appetite for life. After the liberation of the land where she had found refuge, however, she tried to start all over again. She was seventy when she began to tinker with crayons and watercolours, more or less accidentally, from weariness and boredom.

What strikes one in all her pictures is the sheer painterly quality of her work, which reaches a level and an intensity that is rare among naive painters. The draughtsmanship of her pictorial narratives manifests all the characteristics of the unspoiled naive vision — flat structures, absence of perspective, groups of figures on the same level, viewed horizontally or

Stern, Emma: Return from Work

Stern, Emma: Family Supper

from above, in rows or in rising ranks, figures and faces either full-face or in profile. In her handling of colours, however, Emma Stern reaches out beyond the manner and the potential of naive painting and shows a cultivation of painting technique which prompts astonishment and admiration. She must have loved the Impressionists and their picturesque world. The colours glow in her flowerbeds and clusters of blossoms, as they did with the Impressionists. The lustre of her favourite colours, red, yellow, violet, embedded in lush green, is utterly and unmistakably characteristic of her palette. At times, however, these colours are obscured and overcast. Such pictures have an oppressive heaviness and they break in like bitter memories.

In the wealth of this gifted woman's posthumous work there can be found almost all the narrative situations that arise in life. But certain favourite themes which clearly had a deep appeal for her constantly recur in a variety of guises: for example, scenes from the everyday life of industrial workers, park scenes, trees in blossom and flowerbeds, still-life studies and those particularly charming accounts of family life and family celebrations.

It is hardly surprising that Emma Stern's pictures are nowadays among the most sought after treasures of naive art. Those who knew of

Stevanović, Dobrivoje: Fire in the Village

her in Montparnasse realised it even when she was alive. *T. G.*

STEVANOVIĆ, DOBRIVOJE (1948)   Yugoslavia

Dobrivoje Stevanović was born in the village of Bošnjane, Serbia, but moved to Varvarin, where he is employed as a metal worker. He has been painting in his spare time since 1969. His themes centre on the life of the peasants living in the valley of the Western Morava River: harvest time, fires, fairs, gipsy dancing, millers, Christmas. Although he exchanged the fertile fields of the Morava Valley for factory smokestacks, as many peasants did (more because it was fashionable to do than out of necessity), Stevanović finds inspiration for his pictures in the landscapes of his childhood, with the winding rows of houses of blood-red brick, enclosed by wooden fences, where life progresses according to a set pattern.

In the painting "Fire in the Village," Stevanović portrays the drama of a fire: a house is in flames and the blaze has already swallowed up most of the roof; the members of the household are saving their animals and furniture and together with their neighbours are helping to put out the fire. Their efforts are hardly synchronised, as everyone is doing whatever happens to have come to mind at the moment; they are all carrying vessels filled with water and moving in various directions, while from a scaffold a few peasants pour water on the fire. In this painting the people seem aware that their endeavours will not be of much help.

Dobrivoje Stevanović has had one-man shows and has participated in group exhibitions at home and abroad. *(See portrait of the artist, p. 563). N. T.*

STEWART, ERIC (1903—1970) Australia

Eric Stewart's paintings were not discovered until after his death in 1970. The artist Clifton Pugh came upon the first of them in a second-hand dealer's shop and subsequently located others in various parts of Victoria.

Stewart, Eric: Legend of Everlasting Water

Sturza, Gheorghe: Wedding in the Country

Eric Stewart, a nightwatchman with the Post-Master-General's Department, learnt a little about painting when he was in hospital recovering from tuberculosis. He tried to conform to traditional techniques until about 1967, when he became terminally ill.

From that time, Eric Stewart's style of painting changed, a change which produced his powerful pictures of aboriginal legends. He was inspired by Roland Robinson's book, "Aboriginal Myths and Legends," which he seemed to understand instinctively and translated into painted epics. *B. McC.*

STUBBS, DOUGLAS (1927) Australia

Douglas Stubbs was born in Leongatha, Victoria, and studied for a while at the Melbourne National Gallery School.

His colourful paintings of fantastic birds and landscapes, mythical beasts and other-worldly people first attracted attention at the "Melbourne Herald" Outdoor Exhibition, an annual event in which hundreds of amateur and as yet unknown artists have a chance to show their work in a large open-air display sponsored by Melbourne's evening paper.

Stubbs' pictures are mostly large-sized and intricately worked in a mosaic-like style. His combination of technique and fantasy creates uniquely fascinating pictures. In 1963 Douglas Stubbs had his first one-man show with the East Side Gallery, Melbourne, and in subsequent years held very successful exhibitions at the Australian Galleries and Toorak Galleries, Melbourne.

(See portrait of the artist, p. 563). B. McC.

STURZA, GHEORGHE (1904) Romania

Born in Botosani, northern Moldavia, Sturza remained in his home town to work as an electrician, and began to paint (in oil on cardboard) only after retiring in 1969.

The artist sent his first work to Bucharest in support of a project for the planning of rural settlements in Romania. "The Village of the Future," which came by indirect ways to the attention of the jury of the National Exhibition of 1969, won first prize, to Sturza's astonishment.

In his early works, Sturza obtained topographical views of the scenes that interested him, collecting documentation, taking measurements and making sketches and notes. On the basis of this information, he then built up his pictures, often using a ruler and compass. With an inborn feeling for composition and an exceptional ability to achieve a plastic synthesis, he succeeded in producing, through the medium of colour, a refreshing pictorial effect.

Although he is fondest of painting landscapes (on which he impresses his own personal vision), many of his works are inspired by the urban scene: a meeting on the street, a coffee break in a factory courtyard, waiting at a bus stop.

Painted vertically as a rule, and sometimes even without a horizon, the works of this artist which the peasants recognised themselves. In his picture "Drying Hot Peppers," Su Junliang presents a vivid scene, with all the figures in motion, hurrying to complete this task, which has to be done while the good weather lasts. The dynamism is enhanced by the lavish use of red and its masterly distribution. Su Junliang's work has been exhibited in the local gallery, specially built to house peasant paintings. An army delegation which came to the village looking for talent liked his work and persuaded him that he would have greater scope to develop his hobby in the army. He now continues painting as a soldier. *N. T.*

Su Junliang: Drying Hot Peppers

are imbued with the accents of a moving lyricism, which is apparent in the soft, fresh colours ("Eminescu's Park").

Sturza's works have won many prizes, and have been on display in group exhibitions abroad and in one-man shows in various Romanian towns.

(See portrait of the artist, p. 562). M. Il.

SU JUNLIANG (1952)   China
Su Junliang was born in the village of Wunan in Hu county, a place about 45 kilometres from China's old capital of Xian, from which eleven dynasties ruled.

Being of peasant stock, he joined the village farming brigade, working in the fields and often serving as a watchman against birds and other potential thieves. He took up painting in 1974 and soon became popular among his fellow-villagers thanks to his colourful scenes of village life, in

SÜLI, ANDRÁS (1896—1969)   Hungary
The pictures of András Süli are childlike observations in colour of the world around him. He never learned to draw, with the exception of lessons in elementary school. As a youth, he did farm work. When he was eighteen, he went to war and was taken prisoner. After returning to his homeland, he learned the basket-weaver's trade, in which he distinguished himself for his skill. The period during which he painted was a brief one — the six years between 1933 and 1939. His works were on display in the "Original Talents" Exhibition of 1934 in Budapest, and were also exhibited in the Netherlands. All his canvases are based on reality, on his immediate world. Fowl and four-legged domestic animals in the barnyard, the figures of a farmer and his wife looking after their livestock, a family enjoying a festive luncheon at a large table set in the guest room, decorated furniture, the pious atmosphere of church interiors — all these are of equal signifi-

cance for this painter. In his minutely and carefully painted landscapes, multi-coloured flowers glitter in the fresh green grass; along the rivers sail large ships, smaller boats and rafts. His paintings — in the dense, shining colours used by painters of miniatures — are well-conceived in terms of their composition. Today, only some thirty or so paintings by Süli are known to us, most of them in museums. He threw many of his paintings into the fire at the end of the thirties in a moment of profound bitterness. After that he never again took up a brush. He received belated satisfaction from a retrospective exhibition of his

Virginia. Here he became a playground manager, then a house painter, which so rearoused his interest in "fine art," that he began to paint — on wrapping paper, old window blinds, cardboard.

In 1916 he enlisted in the army, and when he was discharged in 1919 had become a sergeant. He went back to Wheeling, married in 1920, and once more became a house painter. Apparently that trade was neither very lucrative nor time-consuming toward the end of that decade and the early part of the next, because he said that during the Depression he "had much time to paint." Unable to afford lessons, he tried copying, and

Süli, András: Family at Lunch

Sutor, Edward: Figure

works in 1969 in Bratislava, at the International Triennial of Naive Art, and from the prize awarded him. He passed away the same year. Since 1969 his works have been displayed at many European exhibitions and in Cuba. *(See portrait of the artist, p. 562). M. I.*

SULLIVAN, PATRICK J. (1894—1966)   USA

The work of Patrick J. Sullivan is not often seen in exhibitions or often reproduced in books on American folk or naive art. Nonetheless, he is a striking and important artist. Where other naives might paint memories, or scenes from their lives, Sullivan was moved by history and current events, which he conceptualised in very personal interpretative imagery.

Sullivan was born in Braddock, Pennsylvania, the youngest of twelve children. His father was Irish, his mother English. When he was two, his father died, and his mother, quite ill at the time, placed him in an orphanage, where he remained until he was fifteen. The training he received in its print shop gave him, he said, "the idea of dabbling in painting, but I never gave much thought to it." He went with his mother to McKeesport, Pennsylvania, and worked in a sheet-iron mill before moving to Wheeling, West

Sullivan, Patrick J.: Haunts in Totalitarian Woods

once copied a Hoffman painting of Christ, but altered it to make it more "masculine." Then in 1937 he produced his first "all original canvas": "Man's Procrastinating Pastime," a pictorial essay on the need for man to overcome his evil self and "courageously... perform good deeds..." He entered the painting in the Society of Independent Artists' annual show, and it was discovered there by Sidney Janis, who promptly got in touch with Sullivan and subsequently put three of Sullivan's works into the Museum of

Modern Art's exhibition, "Masters of Popular Painting," in 1938.

Sullivan's studio was a corner of the bedroom, his easel a kitchen chair. He worked slowly and carefully, building up his pigments to achieve a relief quality. He used dime-store brushes and mixed his own colours, using pigments ground in oil and "pure linseed oil fresh daily." At the age of forty-seven (in 1931) he gave up house painting because, as a seasonal trade, it did not earn him a good living. Jobless for some time, he finally found work in a steel mill, but it was so exhausting that he was unable to paint.

of wild flowers. On trips to France, she found new scenes for her paintings.

Some of her pictures (for example, the large canvas "Gorkum outside the Port" (1962), belonging to the Municipal Museum in The Hague) are among the most poetic in Dutch naive painting. *(See portrait of the artist, p. 562). N. E.*

SUTOR, EDWARD (1917)   Poland

Edward Sutor was born in Nowy Targ, where he still lives. From a large and poor worker's family, he has had seven years of grade school

Sund, Meike: People of Gorinchen

Svoboda, Jakub: An Old Gipsy Settlement

He wrote to Janis: "Sometimes I am too tired to eat or sleep. I haven't touched a canvas in months — my head is full of good pictures and I want to paint very much." *J. W.*

SUND,   Netherlands
MEIKE (1923)

Meike Sund, born in The Hague, has pleasant recollections of drawing lessons in school and visits to exhibitions and museums with her class. When she left school, she decided to become a photographer. At work she made the acquaintance of the painter, Thijs Overmans, whom she married in 1950. At that time, she still had no intention of trying her hand at painting. A trip to France and the beautiful surroundings of the Cévennes mountains awakened memories of her childhood. A skinny city child, she had twice been sent to the country to gain strength. She says: "I think I began painting out of nostalgia for paradise lost. My first pictures are recollections of youth and my stay in the Cévennes. I called them 'Spring,' 'Summer,' 'Autumn,' and 'Winter.' With these four paintings I made my debut at a group show in 1958 in the Panorama Mesdagu in The Hague. Interest was shown in my work and since then I have been painting as an occupation. I started searching for motifs in my own environment." Her devotion to nature grew even stronger when the family moved in 1960 to a small, picturesque place on the banks of the Maas. There she found everything she needed: a cemetery, nuns, a forest of chestnut trees in all seasons, old men, strollers, nosegays

and has worked as a hairdresser. During the occupation, he was sent to forced labour in Germany and after an abortive attempt to escape was interned in a prison camp, where he was tortured. He returned home with serious damage to his skull and intermittent loss of memory. Occasional treatment in a specialist hospital only helped to alleviate his symptoms. In 1958, he began sculpting in wood and stone — always the human figure. The stone he used was transported by him in his cart, sometimes many kilometres, and he would wander the forests for hours searching for the right kind of waste wood. His figures are sometimes painted or given a patina. Their size ranges from small to large, at times reaching a metre and a half. With different configurations of sculptures (some of them representing his family) he has composed a theatre of sorts where he is the author and the sole spectator. At times, he goes back to the terrible concentration camp experiences, burns his sculptures in crematoria, buries them in the ground and then exhumes them. He creates exclusively for himself, from an inner need, and is indifferent to reactions to his art, favourable or otherwise. In 1970, his works were exhibited in Nowy Targ, Zakopane, Cracow, and Warsaw. His sculptures are in the Tatra Museum in Zakopane and in the collection of L. Zimmerer, Warsaw. *(See portrait of the artist, p. 563). A. J.*

SVOBODA, JAKUB (1875—1943) Czechoslovakia

Jakub Svoboda was born in Ivančice. He tried several jobs after being trained as a confectioner: he gave zither lessons and concerts, painted gables and plates, drew pictures to illustrate events which had taken place both in his own day and in the past in Bohemia and in other countries, illustrated the songs he himself composed, but most often painted and decorated houses. He lived as a free-lance jack-of-all-trades. His pictures are marked by his natural, inborn feeling for the poetical aspects of everyday life and his sense of the permanent values of human existence. Absorbing impressions and the essence of his experiences, he made an effort to present them faithfully in his pictures. He was so

loved to sit peacefully on the balcony of her house and sketch the surrounding buildings. That same love of buildings induced her, a few years ago, to study architecture. In 1973 she started drawing Christmas cards with city landscapes of Buenos Aires on coloured paper. These were reprinted with great success. A new series, in 1975, of town scenes in larger sizes has been even more successful: magazines and newspapers reproduce them. Even if the pictures closely depict the actual buildings, the imaginary colouring and the capricious perspective render these familiar yet unfamiliar. It is the city we all know but no

Szczypawka-Ptaszynska, Helena: Sculpture

precise in his depictions that his anxious observation of the principles of realism frequently resulted in naturalism. In spite of Svoboda's emphasis on detail, his pictures possess a genuine, heart-felt atmosphere and the charm of tender lyricism. *S. T.*

meanness has ever touched it; houses and streets exist in serene beauty, with a new-born happiness. It is a city where people can live in harmony. *(See portrait of the artist, p. 563).* *M. T. S.*

SZABÓ, ANIKO   Argentina

Argentine by choice, Aniko Szabó was born in Germany of Hungarian parents and arrived in Argentina when she was three years old. Her father, a well-known portrait painter, taught her to draw very early in life. She started with carbon pencil and after a time experimented with watercolours, crayon, pastels and other techniques, except oil ("Oil scared me to death"). She

SZAKÁCS, JÁNOSNÉ (1924)   Hungary

Jánosné Szakács was born in Tiszaeszlár into a peasant family with many children. After completing elementary schooling, she became a house painter. When her health deteriorated, she turned to working as a cleaning woman. Although she has been drawing since childhood, she began painting only in 1976 and exhibiting in 1979. Painting helps her overcome occasional periods of bad health. *M. I.*

SZCZYPAWKA-PTASZYNSKA, HELENA (1897—1978) — Poland

Helena Szczypawka-Ptaszynska was born in the village of Mościska and died in the village of Maluszyn. An exceptionally small child at birth, she was seriously afflicted with rickets and had difficulty in walking. Her parents, who were not well-off, were swineherds. Deeply religious, sensitive and good, she was convinced that she had to be considerate toward both human beings and animals. Her kindness to geese and cows, and especially to pigs (whom she loved above all) was far from the village norm. The concept of the

was pleased when someone bought a figure from her, or even accepted one. She used a knife, chisel and borer and above all an axe. Her creative work, ignored by those around her, was highly thought of by artists, collectors and art-lovers.

Her sculptures are in the museum in the town of Sierpc, in the State Ethnographic Museum in Warsaw, the Ethnographic Museums in Cracow and Toruń, and in private collections, including that of L. Zimmerer in Warsaw. She exhibited in Sierpc, Cracow and Warsaw. *(See portrait of the artist, p. 563). A. J.*

Szabó, Aniko: Landscape of Buenos Aires

Szekeres, Mihályné: Shoeing Horses

Szelecki, Mihály: Construction of Mountain Railway

Szakács, Jánosné: The Crèche Carriers

"beautiful" was associated in her mind with that of the good and useful. Two values towered above all others for her — honour and respect. She had four husbands, who died one after the other. When she was twelve years old, she began to sculpt, especially horses and horsemen (cavalrymen, Cossacks), an evocation of the playthings no one had ever bought her. She knew how to make carts and even wheels, also barrels. Constantly carving, she looked upon this work as the highest possible source of satisfaction and

SZEKERES, MIHÁLYNÉ (1924) — Hungary

Mihályné Szekeres, born in Makó, was discovered by professional artists. For a brief period, she took part in the work of an amateur painting circle in her home town. Animals are her favourite subject. Her paintings have been shown at various exhibitions in Hungary. *M. I.*

SZELECKI, MIHÁLY (1911) — Hungary

Mihály Szelecki was born in Bugac. He has been a shepherd and shopkeeper, and has been painting since 1968, mostly watercolours. Done on paper from a drawing tablet, his pictures show the beauties of the barren landscape in the area where he was born, events from the life of shepherds and cowherds, and the hard life of road labourers. Acquainted with traditional musical instruments, he himself also plays. His works are in the Museum of Naive Art in Kecskemét. *M. I.*

Saldaña, Rafael

Savić, Krsto

Savu, Alexandru

Scarborough, Joe

Schulz, Elfride-Maria

Schwartzenberg, Simon

Seemann, Fritz

Serafini, Giuseppe

Sergeev, G. S.

Shalom of Safed

Siváň, Štefan

Skurjeni, Matija

Sloot, Jentje van der

...aar, Monique

Schmidtová, Natalie

Schmit, Ilona

...ert, Max

Selivanov, I. E.

...n Dexian

Šijaković, Djordje

Silva, Marina

Sirković, Stepa

...ajić, Petar

Smirnov, V. B.

Sobota, Józef

Söhl, Manfred

Sokol, Ana

Sokol, Jan

Stanisavljević, Milan

Šteberl, Ondrej

Stefula, György

Sturza, Gheorghe

Süli, András

Sund, Meike

ner, Jeanne de   Sówka, Erwin   Spasić, Čeda   Stanisavljević, Dragiša

nmann, Heinz   Stevanović, Dobrivoje   Stubbs, Douglas

or, Edward   Szabó, Aniko   Szczypawka-Ptaszynska, Helena

564 TACHATAKI, EIRENE — Greece
TANIUCHI, ROKURŌ — Japan
TELES, LADARIO RIBEIRO — Brazil
TERENT'EVA, M. — USSR
THEGEN, C. CH. — West Germany
THEOPHILOS — Greece
TINGATINGA, EDUARDO SAIDI — Tanzania
TISNIKAR, JOŽE — Yugoslavia
TOGOG, IDA BAGUS MADE — Indonesia, Bali
TOHĂNEANU, TIMOTEI TRAIAN — Romania
TÖKE, IMRE — Hungary
TOLSON, EDGAR — USA
TONIATO, UDO — Italy
TOPLJAK, PERO — Yugoslavia
TÖRÖK, SÁNDOR — Hungary
TORREZAPICO, JOSÉ — Argentina
TOWERS, WILLIAM — Great Britain
TREBLA — Belgium
TRET'JAKOV, K. I. — USSR
TRILLHAASE, ADALBERT — West Germany
TROUILLARD, HENRI — France
TROVIC, JACQUES — France
TSCHISTJAKOW, A. N. — West Germany
TSIRONIS, THEMIS — Greece
TU JIANRONG — China
TVERDOHVALOV, A. M. — USSR
TWINS SEVEN SEVEN — Nigeria

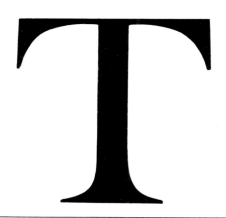

Tachataki, Eirene: An Old-time Couple

Taniuchi, Rokurō: Some Freight Trains in the Small Town of Joko

TACHATAKI, EIRENE   **Greece**

Eirene Tachataki was born in Archanes, Crete, where she still lives and works. She is a self-taught painter and, at the same time, a school-teacher and folklorist; she also makes embroideries with Byzantine and Cretan motifs that she does not copy but draws herself. Her naive style is marked by Byzantine and post-Byzantine influences and specifically by those of the Cretan school and the school of the Ionian Islands. She sometimes frames her works with motifs, such as peacocks and flowers, which are taken from embroideries; these motifs alone constitute the theme of some of her paintings. Her subject-matter largely consists of scenes from the traditional life and culture of Crete: illustrations of figures in typically Cretan costumes, Cretan interiors and exteriors, lyre-players and celebrations, Cretan manners and customs, the island's agricultural occupations, folk songs and so on. Her representations of couples dressed in old Cretan urban costumes recall old photographs. The figures are natural-istic, carefully drawn, sensitively coloured and highly expressive.

Tachataki has presented her work in two one-woman shows and in group exhibitions in Athens and Crete. *A. T.*

TANIUCHI, ROKURŌ (1921—1981)   **Japan**

Rokurō Taniuchi was born in the suburb of Ebisu in Tokyo. Upon completing the primary school of Komazawa Jinjō, he worked as an apprentice and waiter, at the same time publishing cartoons and sketches in newspapers and magazines.

In 1955, he won first prize for cartoons in the magazine *Bungei Shunjū* for the work "A Child Who Went Away." The following year he edited the magazine *Shūkan Shinchō* (issued by the publishing house of Shinchōsha), and at the same time was in charge of the cover page for the same magazine. He depicted a world of childlike imagination and poetic feelings of nostalgia for his home country, and developed an original style that won him numerous admirers. Later on, during the twenty-five years before his death, he produced more than 1,300 cover pages of magazines and book covers.

A sufferer from poor health since childhood, he worked passionately for child welfare and engaged in social work; he gave his time to the Institution for Mentally Retarded Children

half-Indian, this man from the Baiano backwoods bases his art more on the description of true events in the "Cordel" literature of his Indian people than on primitive African styles, which so often influence the naive art of so many of his fellow-countrymen.

In his case, all the "true stories" that characterise his pictures emanate from the Baiano countryside. However grotesque his figures, they are based on persons known to the artist.

Because of his "interpretation" of real events, coupled with the use he makes of uncomplicated colouration, other self-taught artists who

Teles, Ladario Ribeiro: Ladies of the Night

Taniuchi, Rokurō: Blue Melody

Terentyeva, M.: Reindeer Drive

(Nemu no Kigakuen) free of charge, teaching the children painting.

He left numerous works: "Travel Picture-book," "Song of a Naive Child's Heart," "Picture-book of Distant Days," and others in which, with his original paintings and writing, he developed a world rich in lyrical feeling. *(See portrait of the artist, p. 580). S. K.*

show their pictures in the Praça da Republica on Sundays have given him the title of "the most primitive painter of the Praça". *Sh. W.*

TELES,   Brazil
LADARIO RIBEIRO (1924)

Ladario Ribeiro Teles was born in Afranio Peixoto, Lençois, Baía. He came to live in São Paulo in 1960, but only for a while. Today he resides in Osasco. Teles took up painting because he was encouraged by another naive artist, Americo Modanez. Of mixed blood, half-white,

TERENT'EVA, M.   USSR
TERENTYEVA, M.

In the 1930s, together with K. Pankov, Izhimbyn, Natuskin and others, M. Terentyeva was a student at the Leningrad Institute of the Peoples of the North, and attended the artist A. Uspensky's *atelier*, where she painted most of her pictures, some of which are now exhibited at the Leningrad Museum of the Arctic and

Antarctic. In these works, which mainly present the nomadic world of reindeer and tents familiar from her childhood, space seems curved. Like Pankov, she tends to the highly decorative, which is why both preferred the large format and monumentality, combined with highly expressive colouring that imparted the feeling of tri-dimensionality to the flat plane.

One of the first women of Arctic minorities to take up painting, Terentyeva was represented at group shows of Institute students in 1929, 1936 and 1939 and won a Grand Prix at the 1937 Paris World Fair. *N. Sh.*

perfect union of content and style. Both are approached with disarming naivety and simple directness. The childish spontaneity of his approach is clearly manifested in the draughtsmanship of his figures, animal or human, who are shown either in profile or full face, although he had observed them from all angles during his life and knew their contours by heart. It is also striking that his herds, waggon-trains and Sioux Indians are invariably travelling from the right-hand side of the picture towards the left. Yellow — a cold yellow — is rarely absent from his paintings, and so is blue, both the warm and the

Thegen, Carl Christian: Salome's Dance

THEGEN, CARL CHRISTIAN (1883—1955)   West Germany

C. Ch. Thegen was born in Oldesloe, near Lübeck. "Krischan" Thegen, an internationally famous classic of German naive painting, had an unsettled, materially under-privileged life. He was in turn a farm-labourer and a zoo attendant, operated a fairground roundabout, and worked as a clown, an amateur vet, a shepherd, a butcher and a gardener in the Holstein town of Oldesloe. He lived the life of a tramp until the last, dying in 1955 as a result of falling from a hayloft where he had spent the night. The unique standing of Thegen's pictures in the history of naive art in Germany is not derived, however, from the anecdotes that have accumulated around this eccentric figure. It is true that his themes are generally of a highly popular kind: herds of animals, stables and byres, farms, circus scenes and, above all, those romantic notions of life in different lands which he concocted from Wild West films and children's comic-books. The fascinating feature of his pictures, however, is the

cold shades. Reddish brown, green, orange and black: these he handles in a masterly fashion, conjuring up for us with the simplest of means a radiantly cheerful world that comes into being as effortlessly and joyously as fanciful dreams compounded of his knowledge of the actual world and of a yearning for far-off places.

Geist described the appearance of this genius, who was at the same time an eccentric, a tramp and an adventurer: "He was like a piece of human flotsam, bent forward as he walked, shuffling along, thrusting himself on with a stick that was not too thin to be used to ward off the dogs that sniffed round him or to urge on a recalcitrant horse that had caught a whiff of the knacker's yard. His small, squat body was clothed in a jacket that buttoned up to the neck and in grey, crumpled trousers of coarse cloth. His heavy shoes were designed for third-class roads. In the summer he used to wear a peaked cap jauntily set to shield his little watery blue eyes from the sun; in the winter it was an old felt hat." *(See portrait of the artist, p. 580). T. G.*

THEOPHILOS (CHATZIMICHAIL) (1873—1934) — Greece

Theophilos is undoubtedly Greece's most famous naive painter. A picturesque and peculiar figure, endowed with a naive wisdom and a genuine artistic talent, he may have seemed like a village fool to those who did not understand his vision.

Theophilos was born in Varia, Lesbos. His maternal grandfather was a hagiographer, and his own gift for painting became apparent in his schooldays. Having lived elsewhere, in 1927 he returned to his native island and remained there

Theophilos: A Newly Married Couple from the Pelion Area

until his death. In 1929 he met his compatriot Stratis Eleftheriadis (Tériade), who later became a famous art critic in Paris, and this brought him the joy of some recognition. Two years after his death, the first major exhibition of his work was held in Paris (1936), on the initiative of Tériade, who was also the moving spirit behind the foundation of a museum to house the artist's work in his birthplace (opened in 1965). It is unfortunate that many of his works were wall-paintings and have been destroyed.

Theophilos' visual impressions came from Byzantine and post-Byzantine art and from popular architecture. He painted on the walls of houses, grocery stores, coffee-houses and mills, and also on tin, wood, canvas, trays, carts, pillows and naval bags. His themes are scenes from ancient, Byzantine and modern Greek history, portraits of mythological and historical heroes and various local characters, and scenes from the Old Testament and the 17th-century Cretan romance "Erocritos." *A. T.*

TINGATINGA, EDUARDO SAIDI (1937—1972) — Tanzania

This artist was the founder of the Tingatinga school, whose members were also known as the "square painters from Dar es Salaam." He was born in the village Mindu, in Tinduru district.

For ten years he walked 10 kilometres a day to a missionary school. After ritual initiation into the ranks of adult males, he followed tradition and left his village, obtaining employment in the north of his country as a gatherer of sisal. Turning eighteen, he found a job in Dar es Salaam as assistant to a gardener working for a

Tingatinga, Eduardo Saidi: Four Birds

Tingatinga, Eduardo Saidi: Antelope with Birds

colonial official. Later on, after returning from work, he began using remnants of paint to work on masonite boards left over from the renovation of his house.

In 1961, his country won independence and black servants found themselves unemployed. In 1968, Tingatinga lost his job. Recalling his attempts to paint, he decided to try his luck. He procured masonite boards and bicycle shellac in all colours. Soon he sold a few pictures.

Not long afterwards, he found employment as a cleaning man in a large hospital, but continued painting in the afternoons. His wife displayed his pictures at the market-place and he started doing well. A relative, January Linda, who cut and prepared the masonite boards, and his half-brother, S. G. Mpata, also began painting.

for his paintings, which he first started producing in 1952, from the work he does. He has spent almost thirty years in the hospital.

Tisnikar's biography is a moving story of the fall and rise of a man, of the uncertain beginnings as a painter, of the nerve-wracked alcoholic Tisnikar was for many years. After nervous breakdowns, treatment for alcoholism and several attempts at suicide, his powerful and original talent helped him triumph over himself and, as the dedicated chronicler of man's last moments on earth, he has created a moving world of the resurrected dead. His paintings are

Tisnikar, Jože: Encounter with the Truth

Through the good offices of Scandinavian lovers of naive art, in 1971 Tingatinga and Linda had their first exhibition abroad, and it was a great success. Soon afterwards, the painters parted ways. A distant cousin, an unemployed street cleaner by the name of Adeuzi Mmatambwa, became Tingatinga's assistant. After Tingatinga's death in 1972, his pupils and collaborators continued working. *G. Sch.*

TISNIKAR, JOŽE (1928)   Yugoslavia

Jože Tisnikar, born in the village of Mislinje, near Slovenj Gradec, Slovenia, now lives in Slovenj Gradec. He is employed in the pathology department of a hospital and takes his themes

dark green and blue, the colours of the dissecting room and of formaldehyde.

In the painting "Loneliness" (1973), Tisnikar has portrayed a sick and lonely man in the last stage of life.

"I've seen people like that. If their illness lasts a long time their friends and relations, and those closest to them, slowly abandon them. My picture shows a man like that. He stands alone in front of the void seen in the background. Leaning against the wall, he tries to keep on his feet with what little strength he has left."

Jože Tisnikar has had one-man shows and has participated in group exhibitions at home and abroad. *(See portrait of the artist, p. 580). N. T.*

TOGOG, IDA BAGUS MADE (1913)   Indonesia, Bali

Ida Bagus Made Togog was born in Batuan. An early member of Pita Maha, Togog has always been, as he is today, one of Bali's most productive and imaginative painters. His lively, humorous works, which have changed little in style since the 1930s, are a revealing source of every aspect of Balinese life and legend. He has had a long and distinguished painting career and today ranks among the most celebrated of Balinese artists. Togog's works can be seen in all Balinese museums, have been shown in many

In works such as "Avram Janku" or "Mihal the Bold," the artist, in addition to group scenes, introduces elements of landscape with the intention of unifying the composition in terms of plasticity and stressing the monumental proportions of the principal figure. Other works are inspired by events from village life ("The Peasant Household") and the desire of the artist to portray the appeal of the countryside.

Tohăneanu has participated in many group exhibitions and has exhibited independently at home and in Belgium, Switzerland and the USA. *(See portrait of the artist, p. 581).* M. Il.

Togog, Ida Bagus Made: Cremation

Töke, Imre: A Shepherd with His Bride

international exhibitions and have been reproduced in many publications. *(See portrait of the artist, p. 580).* J. F.

TOHĂNEANU, TIMOTEI TRAIAN (1915)   Romania

Timotei Traian Tohăneanu was born in Intorsura Buzăului, in the district of Covasna, and after a hard life took vows as a monk in the monastery of Simbata de Sus.

He began painting in 1953 and in this respect took after his forebears, painters on glass, whose works could be found in many places in the Făgăraş region. Tohăneanu's intention was to produce a series of paintings to embellish the monastery church. From the simple process of copying without taking account of style, he evolved toward an understanding of the real artistic values of the folk icons on glass, the painters of which were also the founders of schools, like Sava Moga and Matei Timforea. These icons he collected and sometimes even interpreted in his own works. Tohăneanu founded in the monastery a modest painters' workshop which, thanks to its impressive collection of icons, attracted lovers of painting from different walks of life.

TÖKE, IMRE (1927)   Hungary

Imre Töke was born in Alsóujlak. Since childhood he has made his living working as a shepherd. Töke has been carving for several decades, at first producing objects of everyday use, following the traditions of folk art. Today he largely sculpts figures in beautifully ornamented capes, shepherds, and peasants at work. A special feature of his somewhat grotesque faces are the almond-shaped eyes, unusually shaped lips and timid look. His works have been on display in many exhibitions in various parts of the country and in Budapest. He has also exhibited in Austria. M. I.

TOLSON, EDGAR (1905)   USA

Edgar Tolson's sculptures stem from a tradition of wood whittling, although he has for many years — at least, since his sculptures caught the interest of serious folk art collectors — called himself "the woodcarver." Described as a "hard drinking, tobacco-chewing, storytelling native philosopher of Campton," Kentucky, Tolson was born in Lee in that state. He was partially disabled by a stroke in 1945 but continued to carve. A descendant of 17th-century English pioneers who settled in the Appalachian Mountains, Tolson has been a preacher, farmer and itinerant worker. Married twice, he claims to have fathered eighteen legitimate children, to have participated in mountain feuds, and, while on a week-end orgy, to have burned down two of his houses and blown up his own church during Sunday prayers.

His carvings (some of which he has painted, others of which he has left in the natural wood, particularly those of the past few years) cover a variety of subjects. Many of them are based on biblical themes.

Tohăneanu, Timotei Traian: Peasant Household

Toniato, Udo: Carpenters

Tolson has said of his work: "A person makes those things; if you could open his skull and look inside you would see the piece there, perfect as it's made. You don't make it with your hands, you make it with your mind and you form it with your hands." (*See portrait of the artist, p. 581*). J. W.

TONIATO, UDO (1930)　　　　　Italy

Udo Toniato was born in Borgoforte, Mantua, into a poor family that later moved to Guastalla, Reggio Emilia. The penultimate of fifteen children, he lived a life of self-denial and poverty which he bore manfully, preserving his vitality, good humour and sharp wit. In 1967, he took up painting by chance after a series of diverse occupations: mason, factory worker, varnisher, footballer, and even a worker in the rice fields.

His inspiration derives from the experiences of his life, evoked with a dash of nostalgia and a

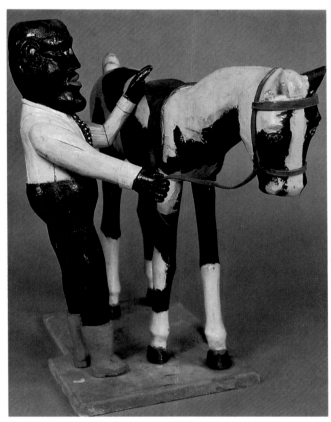

Tolson, Edgar: Man with Pony

subtle, malicious humour. Toniato thus became a bard of the land in the Po River Valley, a folk story-teller and at the same time a troubadour, his vibrant and poetic imagination merging with his suggestive recollections. His simple and direct poetry gently touches and transforms banal everyday reality and lends intimacy to his work as a painter. He thus avoids the trap of a mannered approach.

His paintings depict specific persons whose expressions brook no misinterpretation, so unequivocal are they. Failings and virtues are shown with considerable irony, though the feeling of sympathy is stronger than the desire to criticise. His themes, sometimes unjustly thought of as "minor," are supported by a simple philosophy, a vital sense of life, and instinctive common sense. The work "Woodcutter" may be taken as an example, with its chromatic brilliance and assured handling of figures and masses. (*See portrait of the artist, p. 581*). D. M.

TOPLJAK, PERO (1948) Yugoslavia

Pero Topljak was born in Djurdjevac, near Koprivnica, Croatia, where he attended elementary school. He is a farmer who, having received an incentive from the art of Ivan Generalić, has been painting since 1965. His subjects are village life and the landscapes of the Podravina area.

"There is no shortage of subject-matter. The Podravina area is spacious, the horizons are wide," he says.

In "The Autumn in the Village" (1975), Topljak follows the style of the famous Podravina painters, especially Kovačić, and shows a multi-

Topljak, Pero: Autumn in the Village

tude of people doing various tasks. They are going to the fields, repairing their houses, resting under a big oak tree, harnessing oxen. All the kinds of work that a peasant does in one day, at various places, have been put in the foreground of Topljak's picture.

Pero Topljak has had one-man shows and has participated in group exhibitions at home and abroad. *(See portrait of the artist, p. 581).* N. T.

TÖRÖK, SÁNDOR (1896) Hungary

Török Sándor, born in Bocsár, is a retired office worker. Impelled by some inner compulsion, he began to paint on his seventieth birthday. For a whole year previous to that, he had dreamed of painting the walls of his room in lavish colours. He paints the things he dreams of, and attaches mysterious captions to his surrealistic visions. For instance "Venus and Adonis on the Planet of Venus with Their Animals." In some of his works he treats the social problems of our times: examples are "The First Family Tree of Blacks," "The Dreams of Poverty." Since 1970, his paintings have been displayed at many exhibitions in Budapest, in the interior of the country and abroad. *(See portrait of the artist, p. 580).* M. I.

TORREZAPICO, JOSÉ (1896) Argentina

Torrezapico was born in Sama de Longreo, Oviedo, Spain. He started studying medicine but stopped at the age of twenty-six when he decided to come to Argentina. Once there he worked in a shoemaker's shop and for several years served as a waiter at the racetrack restaurant of Palermo, in Buenos Aires. When he was sixty-five years old he retired, but as his pension was meagre he decided to live in the lovely public gardens of Buenos Aires, "Plaza Francia," exactly at the spot where they bordered on the old People's Home. He stayed there, sleeping on wooden benches.

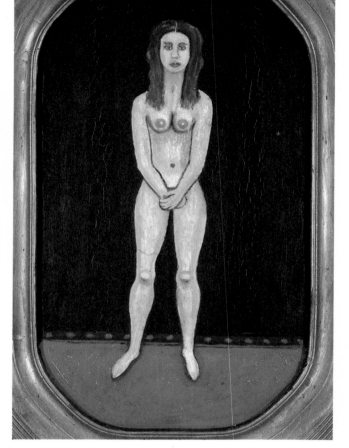

Torrezapico, José: Nude

After finding some books by Khrishnamurti at the bottom of a rubbish bin, he became a follower and has practiced meditation ever since. He started to paint on a sudden impulse, a sort of *satori*. He was sitting under a tree when he saw the large bare wall of the Home flashing white under the sun, and an uncontrollable urge possessed him to do something with it. He then picked up a nail from the ground and started to draw on the wall. Some passers-by, students of the nearby School of Fine Arts, obtained brushes and paint for him. The result was a very beautiful mural painting. People started coming to see him. Among them was a well-known journalist who interviewed him for the local radio and obtained for him a free location in a hotel. A short time later, the Mayor of Buenos Aires, un-

Towers, William: Men's Singles

Török, Sándor: Venus and Adonis on the Planet of Venus with Their Animals

der the pretext that people who came to see the mural were trampling the grass and destroying the flowers, had the painting whitewashed.

Approached by the owners of El Taller (the first gallery in Buenos Aires to be devoted to naive art), Nina Rivero, Nini Gomez and Leonor Vassena, Torrezapico presented his paintings in two one-man shows in 1964 and 1965. He also participated in several group shows in Buenos Aires. In 1967 he was represented in "Contemporary Primitives of America" in Madrid, and in 1972 in the 3rd Triennial of Insitic Art in Bratislava, Czechoslovakia. All of a sudden he became popular. Newspapers offered him full pages and art collectors sought him. In the middle of this unexpected glory, the El Taller Gallery moved to larger premises. Torrezapico, angered with his lady-friends from El Taller because paintings other than naive had been shown at the opening, left Buenos Aires and headed for the pampas. Though every effort was made to locate him, he was never heard of again. *(See portrait of the artist, p. 580). M. T. S.*

TOWERS, WILLIAM (1935)   Great Britain

This entirely self-taught painter from Lancashire specialises in the making of appliqué pictures (he also paints, but by far his finest works are the outcome of cloth, cotton and needle). These are based on long experience as a professional knitter, rugmaker and in the design and execution of hand-made patchwork quilts.

Possibly partly because of his professional expertise, but mainly because of his unique naive feeling and vision, Towers, through his best works, exerts a subtle fascination. His colours are muted, never strident. Few who come in contact with his appliqué pictures for the first time will not scan them, if only cursorily initially, and then be drawn back for a closer inspection.

Towers was included in some mixed exhibitions in and outside Britain. *(See portrait of the artist, p. 581). Sh. W.*

TREBLA (1913—1983)   Belgium

To understand this pseudonym, one need only read it backwards, when it emerges as Albert. This inversion symbolises the artist's method of painting: his works can be regarded from four sides and one gains the impression that the right place for them would be the ceiling. In Belgium, all television viewers know the painter Trebla, for he was the Director of the "Floating Museum" which participates in all the Intervilles broadcasts.

He spent his childhood in Furnes, which in the First World War was right in the middle of the battle at the Yser. The enemy occupied his home town. Soldiers' graffiti on the walls impressed the boy. One of them, of large dimensions, has remained for posterity: it was signed Jean Cocteau, who was then in the French marines.

In a talk, Trebla stated in his picturesque language: "My monolines reveal a spiritist graphology with the creative power in the grip of the occult sciences." Light colours in the Ensor manner help him to paint a world which we might be tempted to place on the "special plane" which the occultists call astral. He is likewise inspired by ballet, opera and dances. The question arises of whether Trebla's unusual work should be classified as naive art or *art brut*.

He has exhibited in Belgium, France, Germany and New York, and has taken part in more than forty television shows. He has also received international and national awards. *(See portrait of the artist, p. 581). J. C.*

TRET'JAKOV, KONSTANTIN IVANOVIČ (1896—1982)
TRETYAKOV, KONSTANTIN IVANOVICH

K. I. Tretyakov was born in a village near Archangel. His peasant father often went to St. Petersburg, then the Russian capital, to earn a livelihood as a roofer. After five years at the village school, Tretyakov was apprenticed to the art workshop of the merchant Batukhin, in St. Petersburg, which produced sundry church-ware. After some time as a messenger boy, he was despatched to the art workshop of the Solo-vetsky Monastery in Northern Russia. Even here, however, the monk icon-painters did not allow him to paint until he had spent some eighteen months doing various chores and grinding paints. Subsequently Tretyakov lived in Archangel itself, where he hired himself out to merchants and painted signboards, landscapes and other pictures.

After the October Revolution, the Economic Council of the town of Shenkursk, which is not far from Archangel, appointed him as head of an art workshop producing portraits of Lenin, posters and slogans for the revolutionary holidays, and signboards. Three years later the local Communist Party committee assigned him to serve in the militia, where he stayed for fifteen years. Afterwards he was appointed curator of a local museum and then head of a local club.

He has produced several hundred pictures, mostly landscapes of northern Russia, genre scenes and reflections of events in which he was involved or which he witnessed. He held his first exhibition in 1920, in the village of Blagovesh-chensk, near Archangel. His next exhibition was held in 1925 in Shenkursk. Later he had shows in various nearby villages. His work mirrors the mentality of the urban fringe with its low cultural level and he may be ranked among the typical Russian urban folklore artists. But he has also produced works which have associations with the mid-19th-century Venetsianov school, most of whose representatives were of the urban Third Estate. Over the years the artist's outlook modified, and this was reflected both in his choice of motifs and his skill: some works reveal a dilettantism, a striving to acquire professional knacks, and lack the specific features of the urban primitive artist.

He has been represented at group exhibitions at various levels and has had several one-man shows. Many of his works may be found in museums in the town of Velsk near Archangel and in Archangel itself. *(See portrait of the artist, p. 581). N. Sh.*

TRILLHAASE, ADALBERT (1859—1938) West Germany

Adalbert Trillhaase was born in Erfurt, and died in Königswinter. The son of a businessman, he became a businessman himself, married an industrial heiress, and inherited a considerable fortune. In 1919 he moved to Düsseldorf.

Trillhaase has been described as being "driven by a kind of inner restlessness." He was said to be suspicious, quarrelsome, apprehensive and introverted almost to the point of suffering from a persecution complex. Cut off from the outside world, he is said to have sought security

Trebla: A Giant Step

Tretyakov, Konstantin Ivanovich: The Village of Voskresenskoye near Arkhangelsk in 1923

within his family, which he ruled in patriarchal fashion.

When Trillhaase started painting at the age of sixty, he seems to have been impelled to choose subjects haunted by fear, distrust, duplicity, terror, injustice and ineluctable demonic forces. It is reported that he read a great deal: especially books on travel and history, and, above all, the Bible. He had a preference for Old Testament tales, and he is said to have spent many a night brooding over these.

Bible stories are a prominent, even the central, theme in Trillhaase's pictures. What strikes us straight away in this eccentric genius' paintings and drawings is his incredibly consistent intuitive sense of the total integration

Trillhaase, Adalbert: The Witch of Endor

of narrative within pictorial space, his trance-like assurance in the balanced placing of centres of gravity in terms of shapes, planes and colours, in the seductive choreography of masses, and in the alternation of active and passive elements. He had a fine sense of priorities in the organisation of the scenic action in his pictures and for the precise application of coloured segments to subtly differentiated backgrounds — superlative effects that bear witness to the fascination that Trillhaase's work radiates. The effect is enhanced by the fact that the spectator is confronted directly by the happenings in the

classic artist marks the very peak of naive painting in Germany.

Only rarely, however, was Trillhaase able to free himself from the spell of biblical history and apply his vivid imagination to mythological themes or everyday episodes.

Trillhaase was received with open arms by the artists associated with "Mother Ey," who then represented the avant-garde of the so-called "Young Rhineland"; he would sit silent and unapproachable in their midst. Later together with them he was to be branded by the Nazis as "degenerate." *T. G.*

Trouillard, Henri: Old Laval

Trillhaase, Adalbert: Twelve-year-old Jesus in the Temple

pictures, as if he were involved in and drawn into them. At the same time his works are devoid of importunate emotion or any trace of sentimentality, although they are crammed with action: turbulent movement, outbursts of feeling, exhortation and gesticulation, admonition, dispute, and rapt attention. With the objective fidelity of the historical chronicler that is totally in keeping with his characteristically restrained and lapidary style, Trillhaase was capable of representing the orgiastic "Dance round the Golden Calf" with the same compelling force as Jacob's fairy-tale dream of angels climbing the heavenly ladder.

Trillhaase never located any of his Bible pictures in an ecclesiastical setting, but a museum fortunate enough to possess one of his rare grandiose works may well construct an "altar" on which to display it. The work of this

TROUILLARD, HENRI (1892—1972) France

Henri Trouillard was born and died at Laval. A few lines hardly suffice to summarise the vicissitudes, disappointments and adventures which pursued him throughout his long life. He was a carpenter by the time he turned fifteen and then worked his way in several stages through the traditional guildman's *tour de France*. He was very unsettled during this period, passing from shop to shop until the outbreak of World War I. Captured by the enemy in 1916, he escaped, travelled to North Africa, married and then came home to Laval, where he opened his own carpentry shop. He also began to sell antiques and to arrange a studio in which to paint; this was his period of the "Tunisian Oasis" series. He was sent to prison several times, was an avid reader and was deeply interested in the theory of evolution and the future of man: his canvases reveal these different aspects of his thought. He died in poverty, rejected little by little by his environment, but leaving behind a controversial and widely studied opus.

Henri Trouillard had no equal when it came to colour and drawing, and in some of his major compositions gave proof of his abilities as a realistic painter, capable of emotion, precision and enjoyment. He considered some of his canvases to be preliminary studies for more important works — try-outs, in a sense, of his ideas. He would say: "There are no more beautiful colours than there are beautiful notes on a violin — only their correct appreciation can add up to harmony." And in practice, there is a constant pursuit of harmony in his work and an effort always to create a special atmosphere for each painting as he tried to develop a philosophy which often carried him far from the beaten paths of naive art. His rendering of the major periods in the theory of evolution (*"Autrefois* No. 1 and 2"), of the absurdity of war, of prehistoric periods, and of the atomic threat, mark the highlights of a line of philosophical meditations to which his works bear vigorous witness.

Henri Trouillard began exhibiting in 1957; his last exhibition was in 1981 at the Maison de la

Trovic, Jacques: Botanists Studying Orchids

Culture in Rennes. *(See portrait of the artist, p. 581). Ch. Sch.*

TROVIC, JACQUES (1948)　　　　France

Jacques Trovic was born at Anzin. He became a student of the Academie d'Arts Plastiques at St-Amand-les-Eaux, where he began making mosaics, paintings and above all tapestries. He exhibited locally at first, then later throughout France; also he has shown his work abroad. He still lives with his mother and sister in a small miner's house in the working-class suburb of Valenciennes.

Most important in the work of Jacques Trovic are his tapestries, usually done in "patchwork." Above all his vision is monumental, and this is also reflected in his mosaics. Forceful volumes and a decorative choice of materials and colours are the special features of the large-size works he seems to like best. Great precision in working with the wools he applies to his textile base allows him to add details to each work with constant inventiveness.

Jacques Trovic has been exhibiting since 1978. *(See portrait of the artist, p. 580). Ch. Sch.*

TSCHISTJAKOW,　　　　West Germany
ALEKSEJ NIKOLAEWITSCH (1904)

A. N. Tschistjakow, born in Sukhum, Russia, now lives the life of a solitary recluse in the spartan surroundings of his room in a Bethel home in Bielefeld. It is to Deacon Werner Pöschel, himself a distinguished artist, who works in a Bethel mental hospital, that we owe the discovery of this truly unique individual.

If only Tschistjakow would exchange his pen more often for a paint-brush! But even his six known pictures represent a major contribution to naive art. "Before the Murder," conceived in his

Tschistjakow, Aleksej Nikolaewitsch: Before the Murder

imagination, he claims, is the fourth of his works. With an unrelenting precision in his miniaturist style and a lucidity that penetrates to every corner of his pictures, Tschistjakow describes mournful events or catastrophes which are nevertheless devoid of anything in the way of emphatic gesture or melodrama. The composition of his pictures is so clear and so imaginatively diversified that the scene can be taken in at a glance, but what we see in his pictures is not so transparently obvious as it might seem: they involve a kind of personal mythology which presents the detached spectator with a series of puzzles. A striking peculiarity of Tschistjakow's work is his habit of setting his small, discreetly coloured pictures in broad frames which he constructs of paper and cardboard and then colours. Onto these frames he then pastes ornaments, elements of figures — which bear a symbolic relationship to the subject of the picture. The effect is of a peep-show, in which the spectator feels he is looking at a scene from a drama. *(See portrait of the artist, p. 581). T. G.*

TSIRONIS, THEMIS (1942)　　　　Greece

Themis Tsironis was born at Pyrgos and now lives in Athens in an area largely inhabited by students. Restless and unconventional in his youth, he emigrated to Canada, but then returned to Greece, where he took up painting and photography.

Tsironis selects elements from different sources — ancient legends, popular mythology,

Byzantine and folk art, old photographs, post-cards and lithographs — then adapts these to his own original and imaginative personal pictorial idiom. Their meaning is emphasised by the addition of epigrammatic and sometimes rather humorous inscriptions on characteristic ribbons, the colours of which create contrasts with those of the letters. In the painting illustrated here, the winged boy is identified as Icarus fallen into the sea.

Personifications are another typical element of Tsironis' painting. The month of May is shown as a bearded, dark-haired youth, wearing a

TU JIANRONG (1948)   China

Born in the village of Datun in Hu county, Tu Jianrong joined the village farming brigade, working in the wheat and cotton fields. Lotus plants are also cultivated in the local ponds. Tu Jianrong began painting in 1974. As he was that year engaged in washing lotus roots, his work inspired him to depict this activity in his first painting, "Washing Lotus Roots." This picture drew attention to the young man's talent, and he was then encouraged further by the local teacher and by the admiration of his fellow villagers. He has since produced many paintings of village life,

Tu Jianrong: Washing Lotus Roots

flower wreath on his head and flanked by birds and a butterfly. Winds are shown as winged youths.

In his recent works Tsironis shows a renewed interest in Byzantine history and in the Greek War of Independence of 1821. This has resulted in the creation of expressive portraits of the most famous heroes, enriched with new elements, and of original scenes with a large number of figures.

Tsironis' painting has only been given one individual exhibition in Athens, together with his photographs of wild flowers. The artist has his own ideas and ideals about the function of art, and does not rush to prepare works in order to show them in a gallery. He does not seem to believe in the unique character of a work of art, and transfers his most attractive compositions to posters, postcards and prints. *A. T.*

and has exhibited in the local gallery, purposely built to exhibit the works of more than 200 regional painters. He has also exhibited successfully elsewhere in China. *N. T.*

TVERDOHVALOV,   USSR
ALEKSANDR MIHAJLOVIČ (1906—1977)
TVERDOKHVALOV,
ALEXANDR MIKHAILOVICH

A. M. Tverdokhvalov, born in the Kuban town of Slavyansk near Krasnoyarsk in southern Russia, was a trained civil engineer. After retiring on an old-age pension in 1967 he took up painting as a hobby, though he had never learned drawing. He produced landscapes, copied reproductions of Italian masters from a ten-volume edition in his possession, and also drew from nature. His paintings for the most part are in the vein of modern urban folklore, with vibrant colours, minute detail and well conveyed perspective. The means of expression reflect his inability to achieve the professional skill he sought, and also — as is the case with virtually every naive artist — his desire to preserve his outlook, the mentality of his milieu. Though he depicted contemporary subject-matter, there was a definite liking for past events which is revealed in a peculiar associative recollection.

At the USSR "Glory to Labour" show in Moscow in 1974, his picture "Winter" evoked such keen interest that it was reproduced as a New

for ten years, worked for a short time as a driver and salesman, formed a "Young Boys' Orchestra," lived for a while as an itinerant musician and demonstration dancer for a patent medicine salesman, became a member of Duro Lapido's theatrical company, then formed another band and, finally, a theatrical company of his own.

In 1964 he enrolled in Georgina Beier's school for experimental art and began drawing. It seemed that cold-point etching was the ideal medium for him, that which he used in illustrating the texts of Yoruba story-teller, Amos Tutuola.

Tverdokhvalov, Alexandr Mikhailovich: Pyatigorsk, a National Health Resort

Tsironis, Themis: Icarus

Twins Seven Seven: Flying above New York City. To Gunter Péus

Year card in millions of copies, and was also featured in various periodicals. Tverdokhvalov has been represented at several group shows. *(See portrait of the artist, p. 581). N. Sh.*

TWINS SEVEN SEVEN (1947)   Nigeria

Taie Salau or Taiwo Olanayi, to give Twins Seven Seven his real name, is a musician, dancer, singer, song-writer and graphic artist. He was born in Ibadan, the son of a dyer and cloth-merchant. He was educated at the mission school

The ghosts and demons in these drawings with their wealth of fantasy inhabit a world which he has invented, but which is as natural to him as the real world. His outline compositions, encrusted with bright colours, are engraved on wax plates, shaped with patient precision and an untrammelled delight in story-telling. After a visit to the United States, where his work was shown, he began to use new motifs.

The income from the sale of his works shown in large-scale exhibitions in Europe has helped to finance his theatrical activities. He has worked much more, in recent years, for the recording industry. *(See portrait of the artist, p. 581). G. Sch.*

Taniuchi, Rokurō

Thegen, Carl Christian

Togog, Ida Bagus Made

Török, Sándor

Tisnikar, Jože

Torrezapico, José

Trovic, Jacques

ăneanu, Timotei Traian

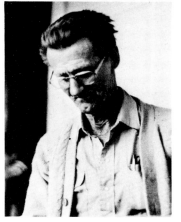
Tolson, Edgar

Toniato, Udo

Topljak, Pero

vers, William

Trebla

Tret'jakov, K. I.

Trouillard, Henri

uistjakow, A. N.

Tverdohvalov, A. M.

Twins Seven Seven

Ubau, Yelba: La Palometa (an isle at Solentiname)

UBAU, YELBA — Nicaragua
UTKIN, M. D. — USSR

UBAU, YELBA (1955)   Nicaragua

Before the liberation war (1977), Yelba Ubau taught in a little village schoolhouse in Rio Papaturru, located in an area bordering Costa Rica. Her interest in painting dates from her first meeting with the artists of Solentiname. Since then, she has been painting steadily, making fast progress. Her themes are the jungle and village, the surroundings she is used to. Her colours are vivid, sometimes accented with bits of white, and in the pictures something is always happening.

She has exhibited in the USA, Costa Rica, Germany and several times in Nicaragua. *E. C.*

Utkin, M. D.: The Dubrovsky Collective Farm

UTKIN, M. D. (active 1920s—1930s) **USSR**

This self-taught artist was active in the 1920s and 1930s, but relatively little is known about him. Evidently he was one of the young artists who started out in the first years after the Revolution. ZNUI (Extra-mural People's University) has in its possession his "The Dubrovsky Collective Farm," painted in 1931. Utkin's picture is reminiscent of the traditional decorativeness that was characteristic of amateur painting of the time. He sought not the illusion of space but a rhythmic pattern. Time is frozen; the icon-like figures of the collective farmers are static and appear suspended. The result is reminiscent of the decoration on Russian distaffs and old chests and coffers. The socially active motivation co-exists with an outlook grounded in a patriarchal upbringing and the acceptance of national art tradition. Amateur artists like Utkin regarded a picture as something that must be meticulously made. For them this was not a game of creation and intuition, but hard and devoted work — which explains the naive gravity and sincerity of his expression. The painting "The Dubrovsky Collective Farm" has been reproduced in periodicals in recent years. *N. Sh.*

VALCIN, GÉRARD — Haiti
VALDES, SIMÓN — Cuba
VALERIUS, MAX — West Germany
VALERO, SALVADOR — Venezuela
VALLA, SERAFINO — Italy
VAN DER STEEN, GERMAIN — France
VANKÓNÉ-DUDÁS, JULI — Hungary
VARFOLOMEEVA, E. I. — USSR
VASILESCU, CONSTANTIN — Romania
VEČENAJ, IVAN — Yugoslavia
VELÁSQUEZ, JOSÉ ANTONIO — Honduras
VIDOVIĆ, BRANKO — Yugoslavia
VIDRIK, GEORG — USSR
VIEILLARD, LUCIEN — France
VILLAZON VEGA, CARMEN — Bolivia
VINTILĂ, PETRU — Romania
VIRAGHOVÁ, ZUZANA — Czechoslovakia
VIRIUS, MIRKO — Yugoslavia
VIŠNIK, A. D. — USSR
VIVA, ROSINA — Italy
VIVANCOS, MIGUEL GARCIA — Spain
VIVIN, LOUIS — France
VLADIMIR (BEDENIKOVIĆ) — Austria
VOGL, HILDA — Nicaragua
VOIGT, FRIEDERIKE — West Germany
VOLKOVA, E. A. — USSR

Valcin, Gérard: Voodoo Ceremony around a Holy Tree

VALCIN, GÉRARD (1923)   Haiti

This happy man who only betrays a hint of anxiety when he talks about Voodoo and the *loas* was born in Port-au-Prince. Because his family had very little money, he stayed in school for only three years before taking up work as a tile setter. Valcin wanted to be a painter, yet he held the work of those artists he knew in scant esteem and did not consider any of his own work worth showing until he took an example of his painting to the Centre d'Art in 1959. DeWitt Peters thought highly of his style and offered to buy the picture.

What was it that DeWitt Peters discerned in the work of this young man who, until then, had been wholly unknown to him? Perhaps it was because of the extraordinary way in which he can infuse his pictures with "the rhythm of the drums" (the magic bush-telegraph of Voodoo) which seem to permeate every part of his paintings with their pulsing insistence. Or perhaps it was the sheer perfection of his pattern-making figuration woven into fantastic harmony

(another strong hint of the absolute "togetherness" created by a Voodoo congregation as it gathers towards a spiritual climax). Or again it may have been the faultless technique he employs to achieve the smooth uninterrupted execution of images and their surroundings in his works, a satin finish which yields to no man.

Valcin has won enthusiastic respect from a wide selection of viewers and collectors (he won the international prize for Naive Painting in Yugoslavia), but even fame can have its drawbacks. Rumour, no doubt unfounded, has it that not all of his paintings are his own, that he finds others to carry out his instructions, or even that he was perhaps never, and at no time, a painter at all! The absurdity in all this gossip is reflected in the question that if Valcin is not the author of his works, who is? A painter capable of capturing only a portion of his magic would long ago have declared himself and made his own name.

For us, the public, what is important is that the paintings exist. *Sh. W.*

VALDES, SIMÓN (1891)   Cuba

Simón Valdes was born in Santiago de las Vegas, Havana. He attended public school in 1897, and began working in a tobacco factory in 1904. As a young man he travelled to the United States and lived in Tampa and Key West in Florida, but returned to Cuba by 1917, and switched from being a tobacco-worker to a clerical job. In 1924, he sat for the civil service exams successfully, but decided not to take the job. Eventually he became a cashier and operator.

In 1927 he published a selection of stories entitled *Motivos del Sorozón y de la Farsa*. He

Valdes, Simón: "Cane Juice"

published poems in 1954 and in 1963, under the titles *Tornasol* and *Trece Romances*, respectively.

In 1970, he took part in the Salon '70 exhibition and had the honour of having the National Museum acquire all of his exhibited paintings. In 1971, he participated in the exhibition of Primitive Painters in the Havana Gallery, and in 1976 in the exhibition "Eleven Cuban Primitive Artists" at the Institute of Jamaica, in Kingston. All his works charmingly combine elements of erotic fantasy in an uninhibited and imaginative manner, the result of which is amusing and enjoyable not only to the viewer but, one imagines, the artist as well. *T. R.*

VALERIUS, MAX (1908—1978)   West Germany

Max Valerius was born in Bollingen, Lorraine, but lived and died in Dortmund. He worked as a miner, from the age of thirteen, suffered severe illness towards the end of his life and finally died of that agonising miner's disease, silicosis. He was never downhearted, however. "I have learned from necessity to work for a better future and to paint that future."

A painter needs good eyesight and Valerius' eyes were not of the best. Bad sight and failing hearing sometimes drove him almost to distraction, but he had a clear idea of his mission: "I'm a miner, body and soul, and an active trade unionist and also someone who has committed himself to art and to this industrial country of ours on the Ruhr; someone who can see social issues clearly. And that's what gives my pictures their special character." Valerius was referring to the themes of his pictures, and two of these in particular, "The Last of the Miners" and "The Miner's Problems," are the kind of titles he had

Valerius, Max: Miner's Problems

in mind. The latter, painted during the coal-mining crisis, is a cry of distress on the part of someone who sympathises with the fate of the miners and sees the mining industry perishing and along with it the miners' livelihood.

Of course, there are also pictures by Valerius which celebrate the lighter side of life and of nature. As an enthusiastic tourist and a member of a nature-lovers' association, he came to know the whole of his home countryside in the course of walking tours and later painted bright and cheerful pictures from his memories.

In his technique Valerius alternates between oils and tempera. His brush drives energetically through the heavily applied mass of pigment and shapes movements and trends in the form of flames, clouds and bushes; even the ponderous masses of industrial plant, sheds and scaffolding are swept up into the vigorous assault of this brushwork. But in all scenes from the coal-face the dominating colour is black, which penetrates the others, overlays them, permeates them and injects into them an oppressive heaviness like that actually experienced by miners in their daily work. *(See portrait of the artist, p. 602). T. G.*

VALERO, SALVADOR (1915)   Venezuela

Born in El Colorado, Escuque, province of Trujillo, Valero still lives and works in the *barrio* of his native village.

After a busy life as photographer, ambulance attendant and typographer, he began work as a naive painter in 1956 and exhibited at the Salon of the Ateneo de Valera where he was recognised and admired by writers of the Sardio Group.

In the wide variety of Venezuelan naive artists, Valero can claim to be one of the best, if not the best, of the "pictorial" naives in his country. Everything in his paintings is figurative, but figurative with just that naturalness that stamps him out as an unadulterated autodidact. True, he paints in an exact manner, but this is an aid to visual clarity and does not stray far into the realms of trained or academic efficiency where perspective is concerned.

VALLA, SERAFINO (1919)   Italy

Serafino Valla, born in Luzzara, Reggio Emilia, now lives in Reggiola, where he is a shop-keeper. In 1964 he began to paint motifs from everyday life, ordinary and anonymous: life and work in the fields and in suburbs where trades-men live. This is the subject-matter of many naive artists but in Valla's case it acquires a new and convincing significance because of his stylistic features.

Valla achieves an enchanting visual effect, sensitive and expressive, with what is in fact a simple composition where essential elements are

Valero, Salvador: Anatomy Lesson

Valero, Salvador: Girl from the Andes

Valla, Serafino: The Harvest

Generally his colours are clean, bright and distinctive, and a dark or black line surrounds all the principle elements of all his works. *(See portrait of the artist, p. 602). Sh. W.*

clearly and precisely stressed, with a palette containing only a small number of primary colours and no tonal nuances, and with a balanced utilisation of large canvases. Central to his compositions is always man, homely and symbolic representation of a reality spiritualised. *(See portrait of the artist, p. 602). D. M.*

VAN DER STEEN,   France
GERMAIN (1897)

Germain Van der Steen was born at Ver-sailles. Notwithstanding his Flemish-sounding name, he is authentically Parisian, a member of a family which has lived in the capital for genera-tions. Sent abroad to England when very young, he returned in due course with an Oxford University degree. He was called up during World War I, gassed in the trenches and returned to civilian life to open a paint and home-mainten-ance store. Afflicted by insomnia, he took to painting the dreams he was denied by his sleep-lessness. He painted the birds and cats of a phan-tasmic animal kingdom at night and, during the day, continued behind the counter in his store near the Etoile. Over eighty and retired, he still works with his pastels and oils.

The canvases of Van der Steen are striking in their pictorial force and well-conceived colour. Particular mention must be made of the variety of the cats he depicts, a variety he adds to with each new canvas: poetic or jocular cats, wise or sassy felines, fictitious animals with more reality than the real. Violence of colour and dynamism of line have often led Van der Steen off the course travelled by more conventional naive artists.

Germain Van der Steen has had fourteen one-man shows since 1946 and has participated in group shows in France, Belgium, Switzerland, Holland, Italy, Austria, Germany, Yugoslavia, the United States, Brazil and Israel. *(See portrait of the artist, p. 603). Ch. Sch.*

The painter has produced many variants of the festivities associated with the slaughtering of pigs in winter, with weddings, Christmas, Easter, the decoration of the Maypole, and even funerals. There is variety in her compositions and her colours are cheerful and decorative. Her book, "My Village Galgamács," which she illustrated with 170 drawings, was published recently. Since 1966, her paintings have won acclaim at numerous exhibitions in Hungary, Czechoslovakia, Italy, Switzerland, West Germany, Belgium, Greece, Japan and the USA. *(See portrait of the artist, p. 603). M. I.*

Van der Steen, Germain: The Cat

Vankóné Dudás, Juli: Field Work in the Summer

VANKÓNÉ DUDÁS, JULI (1919)   Hungary

Juli Vankóné Dudás, painter and winner of the "Master of Folk Art" award, was born in Galgamács. Her father was a shepherd who liked to tell her fairy tales, and also spoke to her of superstitions and ancient customs. Later, Juli Dudás gathered around herself the young people of her village and organised a drama group which put on performances showing holiday and working customs. Subsequently she drew these scenes, and the drawings are now the property of the Ethnographic Museum in Budapest. After marriage, she was unable to practice her favourite pastime for many years. It was only in the 1960s that she began to paint on canvas in oils. Her pictures are cheerful scenes of young and old at work in her village. Her works portray the life and traditions of an ethnic group. Weaving is in progress inside the village houses, while in the fields peasants are ploughing, sowing and reaping. Harvesting is done collectively and in a festive mood; young men and women are bent over their work. In the winters, the young people are shown at spinning bees, the girls working and the young men entertaining them.

VARFOLOMEEVA, EFIMIJA (NINA) IVANOVNA (1919) VARFOLOMEYEVA, YEFIMIYA (NINA) IVANOVNA   USSR

Y. I. Varfolomeyeva was born of peasant stock. She worked as plasterer and house painter, before retiring on an old-age pension in the Urals town of Azbest, where she now lives. She first began to paint, without any training, in 1973, preferring themes with a civic ring, such as the Soviet people's heroic work in the hinterland during the past war. Her basic means of expression consists of the simple depiction of the subject, with lack of spatial depth and clearly demarcated patches of colour. These pictures are deeply sincere, artless, and are marked by what one could term stereotypes or eternal axiomatic truths, as illustrated by such pictures as "The Yard of the House I Lived in When a Child," "Winter in the Village," or "Harvesting in the 1930s." In the last-named, she has elevated the harvesting scene into a symbol of the work that has fed man over the centuries. Besides being represented at republic-level group shows, she has had two exhibitions devoted exclusively to her work. *(See portrait of the artist, p. 603). N. Sh.*

VASILESCU, CONSTANTIN (1901)

The sculptor Constantin Vasilescu was born in Bucharest. After finishing technical school, he became a metalworker in Ploeşti. Retiring in 1964, he began to sculpt.

Through diligence and hard work, he created a world modelled in wood with specific typological characteristics. It is a world inspired on one hand by his own experience of life, and on the other by his encounter with the works of Ion Creangă, a writer whom Vasilescu resembles in his interpretation of life and events.

In his woodcarvings, he attaches equal significance to secondary elements in the composition, adding details characteristic of various individuals — for instance the stethoscope in "The Medical Check-up."

Even when a composition comprises a large number of elements, and the artist has been inspired by something he read ("Uncle Kirpek the Bootmaker") or a painting once dear to him ("The Stagecoach"), it retains expressiveness regardless of ostensible simplicity in the treatment of volume. While he has not had many one-man shows, Vasilescu's works are regularly

Varfolomeyeva, Yefimiya Ivanovna: Winter

Vasilescu, Constantin: The Medical Check-up

Večenaj, Ivan: Night in Bethlehem

included in collective exhibitions in Romania, where he has received many awards. He has also participated in exhibitions of Romanian naive art in Japan, Italy, East Germany, Sweden and other countries. *(See portrait of the artist, p. 603). M. Il.*

VEČENAJ, IVAN (1920)   Yugoslavia

Ivan Večenaj was born in the village of Gola on the left bank of the Drava River in Croatia, the son of poor peasants. His birthplace lies on the border with Hungary and until recently the only way to reach town was by a dusty path running in the direction of Koprivnica. The oldest of six children, Ivan completed elementary schooling and then as a very young boy had to go to work as a hired hand to help his father feed the large family.

He became fond of painting in his youth and was the best in school at drawing. However, it was only after he married and reached his thirty-third birthday that he emerged as a painter. Although originally under the influence of the painters in Hlebine, which is just across the river from Gola, he slowly drew away, not so much in terms of technique as in subject-matter, introducing biblical figures into his Podravina landscapes.

"I paint local subjects: diggers, funerals, weddings, cowherds and swineherds, but I raise

Like Creangă, Vasilescu has a subtle sense of storytelling and from his small sculptures creates scenes representing an entire epoch. Although small in size (rarely larger than 20 cm), his sculptured compositions appear almost monumental from his synthetic treatment of volume and suggestive stylisation.

Večenaj, Ivan: Jesus in Podravina

these to the level of a general theme. All these things have been going on for centuries. It seems to me that by the introduction of biblical motifs, the subjects of my paintings become eternal, timeless."

Although Ivan Večenaj paints his district and its people, their life and their customs, he invests his paintings with something of a mystical quality. Sometimes the theme is purely biblical as in the paintings "The Last Supper" and "Moses and the Red Sea." Speaking of his painting "Jesus in Podravina," he says: "I put Jesus on the Cross because that is the way it is in the Bible, but I placed him in the Podravina region."

"In the painting of Moses," explains Večenaj, "there are no stone tablets, and instead of the Ten Commandments I have painted birds around Moses. By its colour, each bird represents a commandment. The white birds are associated with God and parents. The rooster represents the commandment: Thou shalt not covet thy neighbour's wife. Behind Moses is Mt. Sinai. The dawn is a sign of a better life waiting in the Promised Land which Moses never reached."

In addition to his more realistic paintings based on his Podravina landscape, Večenaj has done some where mystical and fantastic elements drawn from his inexhaustible imagination are more pronounced.

Ivan Večenaj has had many one-man shows and has participated in group exhibitions at home and abroad. *(See portrait of the artist, p. 602). N. T.*

VELÁSQUEZ, JOSÉ ANTONIO (1906)   Honduras

José Antonio Velásquez was born in Caridad, Honduras. He has followed a number of occupations, including telegraph operator, barber, teacher and finally mayor of the small municipality of San Antonio de Oriente. This town,

His art appears there in altar decorations, processional banners and simple commercial lettering.

In his painting, he has taken an honest and direct approach, analysing all the elements in the landscape — almost counting the cobblestones in the road. He endeavours to show all details realistically and precisely. He uses the smallest of brush strokes to obtain nuances, shades and a bizarre richness of green.

The artist has presented his work in the capital of Honduras, Tegucigalpa. He exhibited in the USA for the first time in 1949 and in the

Velásquez, José Antonio: Morazan Square in Tegucigalpa

where silver was once mined, is the central theme in the paintings of this artist.

Velásquez began to practice his art at an early age, producing drawings on paper. It was not until 1933 that he started to work in oil. With a minute detailing of reality, he depicts the people and environment of San Antonio de Oriente. In this small town, located in the pine hills of Honduras, Velásquez, his wife and six children lived for over twenty years (until 1954).

first Hispano-American Biennial in Madrid in 1951. He has exhibited in all the larger cities of Latin America and Europe and his works are found in museums and private collections throughout the world. *J. G. S.*

VIDOVIĆ, BRANKO (1947)   Yugoslavia

Branko Vidović was born in Sisak, Croatia, the same year his father, a baker, moved to

Karlovac, where Branko learned the trade of house painter. In Germany, where he had gone to work, he had a serious road accident, leaving him unable to practice his trade. Returning to Karlovac, he started painting in 1973, first on the model of the painters of Hlebine but later, drawing on the strength of his talent, finding his own mode of expression.

City life provides him with the subjects of his pictures: vagabonds, porters, cafés, dancing.

In the painting "Late-Night Guests," Vidović presents a café atmosphere and in his own original way depicts the last customers warding

Vidrik loved the sea, which, along with three-masters and other boats under sail, he painted in every weather. As he himself often built sailing vessels, he was familiar with tackle and rigging. On the other hand, the depicted seamen and fishermen are flat, disproportionate, conventionally awkward. Ever uppermost in his mind was the sea, which, like his fellow Baltic seafarers he revered as a mysterious semi-divine element upon which prosperity and life itself depended. No wonder the sea with him is now turbulent now quiescent, now light, now dark, but never romanticised. This attitude to the sea, shared by

Vidrik, George: The Rescuers

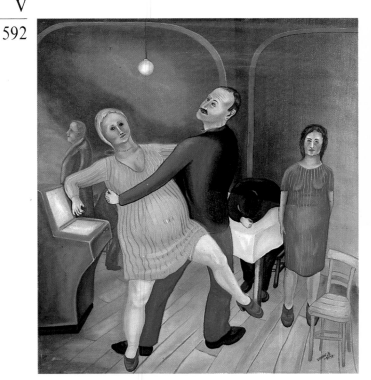

Vidović, Branko: Late-Night Guests

off fatigue to have a bit more fun. Behind a couple executing some steps to the tune of a juke box, a requisite of cafés on the outskirts of town, stands another couple, obviously tired, with rigid limbs and dull expressions, and apparently in the midst of a quarrel. *(See portrait of the artist, p. 602). N. T.*

all Kihnu Island mariners, may be compared to the pagan's deification of nature in antiquity, his veneration of trees, rocks and water. However the ships that Vidrik and his painter colleagues depicted are toilers of the sea, catchers of fish and carriers of cargoes, not the Flying Dutchman of legend. In their works there is nothing of that romantic uplift which one finds in the pictures of Dutch and English marine painters. Rather the ships of Vidrik and the other Kihnu naive painters call to mind the clippers and whalers that 19th-century American self-taught artists loved to paint to adorn the walls of homes, shipping offices, or dockside taverns. Like these American naives, Vidrik always presented his ships sideways amidst heavily stylised waves, but with tackle and rigging shown in the minutest detail. There is no perspective or foreshortening, the pools of colour are sharply demarcated, and now and again some legend or other is inscribed within the painting itself. *N. Sh.*

VIDRIK, GEORG (1904—1942)   USSR
VIDRIK, GEORGE

George Vidrik was born on the Island of Kihnu (now part of the Estonian Soviet Republic) which lies in the Gulf of Riga, an arm of the Baltic Sea. A sailor and fisherman, he died in Nazi-beleaguered Leningrad after arriving there aboard the "Rhine," with military equipment from Tallinn. His works were discovered by Mark Soosaar, a Tallinnfilm Studio cameraman, who, having assembled and restored the naive paintings of Kihnu Island seamen, mounted an exhibition in the Estonian capital of Tallinn in January 1980, and then made a film about them, entitled "The Kihnu Island Primitivists." Vidrik was clearly the most striking among them.

VIEILLARD,   France
LUCIEN (1923)

Lucien Vieillard was born in Toulouse. From early childhood he showed a marked inclination for the arts and a special talent for drawing. After secondary school, he studied law and became a court employee. Up until 1966, he focussed entirely on this career. In that decisive year, he rediscovered paints and brushes during a family holiday and within a few days had produced seven canvases. Anatole Jakovsky, whom he met in 1968, encouraged him to persevere with his painting. From then on painting was his only profession and his career evolved towards worldwide recognition for the excellence of his work.

Lucien Vieillard's art is one of immobility and silence. People have no part in the majority of his compositions. His paintings are dominated by a quest for atmosphere, while encompassing a full range of pure colours. The predominant importance of line intensifies the pervading presence of structures. The severity of his perspectives reflects his pursuit of firmly enclosed planes. Most of his scenes are built around a main diagonal — a road, a street corner or a rail-

Santa Cruz. *(See portrait of the artist, p. 603). A. D.*

VINTILĂ, PETRU (1922)   Romania

Petru Vintilă, born in Orşova, has won fame as a writer, poet, dramatist and journalist. He began writing in 1945 and is a member of the League of Writers of Romania and winner of the League's Award for 1961. Restless and productive, Petru Vintilă organised his first independent exhibition in 1973 (although he once admitted that he had been painting on and off

Vieillard, Lucien: The Old Bayard Crossroads

Villazon Vega, Carmen: Festival

road track — which creates space and gives depth. Immobile but not frozen, each canvas is a moment of expectation, a prelude to wisdom.

Lucien Vieillard has had seven one-man shows to date in as many galleries and has participated also in a number of group exhibitions. *(See portrait of the artist, p. 602). Ch. Sch.*

VILLAZON VEGA, CARMEN (1952)   Bolivia

Carmen Villazon Vega was born in Vallegrande in the Santa Cruz district of Bolivia. Her parents, who were teachers, moved to Santa Cruz when she was thirteen. No longer did she see the mountains so typical of Vallegrande for in her new surroundings there was only lush vegetation. Nor was there, anymore, peaceful village life. After graduating from college, she did various kinds of work in the advertising sections of newspaper houses and printing companies. Later she took up painting. Scenes from early youth alternate with city themes on her canvases, most of which are dominated by groups of people in a gay mood, listening to music and song or, conversely, in a sad mood, for instance attending a funeral. The colours seem to be adapted to these different moods — sometimes rich multi-coloured vegetation and people dressed in bright-coloured clothes, and elsewhere gloomy clouds with people dressed in black.

She has participated in exhibitions in Bolivia and received first prize at the "Humberto Vasquez Machicado" Biennial of Fine Arts in

Vintilă, Petru: Venice

since 1935) on the premises of the League of Writers.

This artist, while well-acquainted with modern European painting, has developed his own painterly language, perfectly articulated in the severe compositions in which draughtsmanship, impressively accurate, is the basic artistic element.

In his more recent works, the artist elaborates upon familiar themes from literature, embellishing them from the richness of his imagination.

Although draughtsmanship is paramount in Vintilă's painting, and although he achieves purity of form with the help of sharp lines, it is colour that in most of his pictures creates a dense atmosphere full of optimism. Bright, clear, full of white or warm colours (from yellow to red), his chromatic scale sometimes reveals an "academic" influence.

Petru Vintilă has had some striking one-man shows at home and abroad (New York 1978) and in recent years has regularly participated also in collective exhibitions of Romanian naive art. *(See portrait of the artist, p. 603). M. Il.*

Vintilă, Petru: The Butcher

VIRAGHOVÁ, ZUZANA (1885—1979)   Czechoslovakia

Zuzana Viraghová attended only primary school, was never employed and spent all her life as a housewife. After her husband died and she remained alone, art became part of her life.

Her works, filled with balladic poetry and the charm of quiet reminiscences, present a simple view of the characteristic countryside of South Slovakia, although there is an emotional charge in her themes. Her artistic means of expression reveal the beauty of the apparently drab countryside and add more profound meaning to the subject, showing a human relationship to the countryside and through it her feelings and philosophy, limited by her lack of any wider experience. She painted her self-portrait among red roses in a poetical and lyrical manner, revealing her vivid sense of her own characteristics. Her drawings, like her paintings, are suggestive and spontaneous.

Viraghová uses means and forms of expression in her works which are not codified by traditions or customs, but are typical only of her own artistic manner. The synthetic character of the author's vision, rare conciseness and simplicity, pure means of expression, delicate palette, immaterial nature, softness, the non-structural character of the trees employed as a background and intimate details of nature are the most characteristic features of her works.

Zuzana Viraghová began showing her works in 1960 and participated in international exhibitions. *(See portrait of the artist, p. 603). S. T.*

VIRIUS, MIRKO (1889—1943)   Yugoslavia

Mirko Virius was born in Djelekovac near Hlebine, Croatia. He had four years of elementary school and then started to work the land and tend livestock. He married, and when World War I broke out, was sent to the Russian Front as a soldier in the Austrian Army. Soon captured, he spent the next few years in Russia as a prisoner-of-war. Far from home, after a hard day's work he would sit of an evening with an oil lamp by his side and dream about home, his village and his family, all of which he committed to the paper he so assiduously collected in camp. After returning

Viraghová, Zuzana: Self-portrait

from captivity, he continued drawing but it was only in 1936, after teaming up with Mraz and Generalić, that he began to paint seriously.

With his calloused peasant hand, Virius recorded scenes of the kind of life he knew well. As that life was nothing if not hard and meager, he opted for social themes in his painting: the peasant in debt, overburdened by taxes.

In the middle of 1943, Mirko Virius was killed in a fascist camp in Zemun. Thus did the holocaust of war take the life of one of the famous Hlebine trio of peasant painters: Franjo Mraz, Ivan Generalić and Mirko Virius. In the decade preceding the war, these men, as the "Hlebine Trio", exhibited their works in the towns of Yugoslavia, works inspired by the village, the hard country life, the social injustice of the regime of that time. New in many of its aspects, and thematically unpalatable to official circles, their painting had a decisive effect on other peasant painters and marked the beginning of the so-called "Yugoslav miracle" in naive art.

Mirko Virius left behind some paintings and drawings most of which were purchased after the war by the Gallery of Primitive Art in Zagreb, where they reside as testimony to the talent of this peasant who painted in his spare time.

"There was no financial incentive for our painting," says his colleague and friend Ivan

anything else, stronger even than the fear that we might be arrested as communists because of the themes of our paintings."

The painting "Quarrel during Ploughing" shows how hunger for land at a time when many peasants were landless caused frequent quarrels in the fields. A farmer has harnessed his oxen and ploughed up his neighbour's field, which was enough to set off an argument in which hoes came into play and men grabbed at each other's throats. A woman is running with a hammer to help her husband. The picture seems to be divided in two by the line running across the

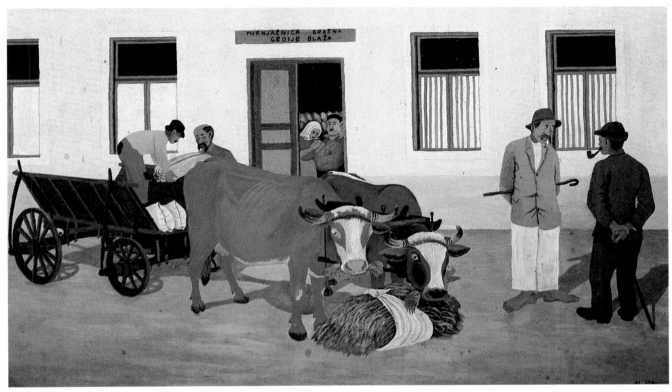

Virius, Mirko: Unloading

Virius, Mirko: Quarrel during Ploughing

middle. In the foreground, by simple means, the place of the action is designated dramatically, while the peaceful pastoral background gives the impression of a backdrop for a drama of life that is constantly repeated.

In another picture, "Unloading," this eternal act, repeated virtually every day, was plastically represented by Virius in the manner typical of him. A long one-storey cottage, with blinds half-drawn and a sign above the entrance, is the backdrop for an event in village life. A couple is watching while two peasants unload sacks.

Mirko Virius' work has been displayed in one-man shows and in group exhibitions at home and abroad. *(See portrait of the artist, p. 602).* N. T.

Generalić. "We painted and spent the little money we had on brushes and paints. Many of our neighbours thought our painting a waste of time. But we had to paint just as we had to eat or sleep. The desire to paint was stronger than

VIŠNIK,   **USSR**
ALEKSANDR DMITRIEVIČ (1872—1964/5?)
VISHNIK, ALEXANDR DIMITRIYEVICH

A. D. Vishnik was born into a peasant family in the village of Ostapya, near the Central Ukrainian city of Poltava. He worked as roofer. A journeyman artist familiar with the naively realistic art current in the Ukraine in the 19th and 20th centuries, he may even be considered its heir. To some degree Vishnik imitated this artistic manner. 19th-century Ukrainian art borrowed heavily from the classical ideals of professional painting and in this respect copied what might be termed the "grand manner." The origins of the static immobility and hieratic postures in Vishnik's painting should thus be sought in those traditions of Ukrainian art that are associated with the typical stiff portraiture. The spatial arrangement is fairly complex and

if by magic scenes from Naples, Amalfi and Sorrento, interiors with wide open windows overlooking the sunny bay of Naples and Mediterranean gardens with flowers of all colours.

After 1946 she went back to Naples, where she still lives and works. The warm but gentle palette of Rosina Viva, her harmonious compositions of flowers are the product of an innate naivety, a happy innocence. The picture "Living Room" is important, with its solid constructional basis and piles of painted objects in an unusual mutual balance. On the table in the foreground is a large ceramic vase with interesting decorations

Vishnik, Alexandr Dimitriyevich: Self-portrait with Family

Viva, Rosina: Living Room

the colour scheme, partly derived from the natural environment, is intense, near-realistic. His known works include "Self-Portrait with Family" and "Taras Bulba and His Sons" after Gogol's famous novel. In 1972 he was represented at an exhibition of Poltava amateur art arranged by Kim Skalatsky, curator of the Poltava Art Gallery. *N. Sh.*

VIVA, ROSINA (1920)   Italy

Rosina Viva, born in Anacapri, was married while still very young to a Swiss who became a rich industrialist in Naples. During the Second World War, she left with her husband for Switzerland where they both remained until 1946. During this period, she felt nostalgic for home and the Naples sunshine and could not reconcile herself to the peaceful life she led in that secure country. It was then that she took up painting and on her canvases there suddenly appeared as

and a beautiful bouquet of blue and yellow flowers, while the patterns on the curtain, on the china in the closet and on the jewellery box provide a harmonious counterpoint. *(See portrait of the artist, p. 602). D. M.*

VIVANCOS, MIGUEL GARCIA (1895)   Spain

Miguel Garcia Vivancos was born in Mazarrón, in Murcia. He worked in Barcelona as a docker, lorry-driver, house painter and glazier. During the Spanish Civil War he led the defence of Puigcerda and was forced to take refuge in France in 1938. During the German occupation he was imprisoned in a concentration camp. He made his way to Paris in 1944, where he was employed in painting patterns on silk for the wholesale clothing trade. He did his best to free himself from the purely mechanical nature of this work and to represent his own feelings and

Vivancos, Miguel Garcia: Notre Dame de Marais

experiences. He painted scenes from the every-day life of ordinary people, still-life pictures in brilliantly luminous colours, and, above all, the streets and squares of small French towns. In "Notre Dame de Marais" (1964), the Gothic church stands under a pastel blue sky, the centre and the pride of the town. On the left is the inn with its red and blue striped awning; beyond it, on the left and right, are little doll's houses. It is near mid-day: the light falls straight down on the inn-keeper standing in front of his door as he waits for his customers. A family group, husband, wife and child, are moving in the direction of the church. Vivancos depicts the paving-stones and the bricks of which the church is built. It is a narrative work, as brightly coloured as a postcard but imbued with a naive poetic power. *(See portrait of the artist, p. 602). O. B.-M.*

VIVIN, LOUIS (1861—1936)   France

Louis Vivin was born in the Vosges and died in Paris. His father was a school teacher and his mother kept a grocery store. After elementary school, he entered the industrial trade school at Epinal where he got his start in industrial drawing and painting. While still a child he was painting the landscapes of his native Vosges on walls and on doors at home and on canvas. In 1878, he went to work for the Post Office (PTT) as a travelling postman on the *Lignes de l'Est* railroad. Throughout, he continued to paint as a hobby. In 1892 he moved to Paris, though remaining a postal employee on the railroad. He moved quickly up the ladder despite a certain excess of imagination for which he was criticised by his employers. In 1904, his only daughter died in childbirth and Vivin assumed the care of the surviving child, transferring all his affection to this grandson. He began to exhibit at the Salon of the PTT Art Society. The First World War greatly complicated his job, but when it ended he returned to his painting. His inspiration, however, had changed: his smiling landscapes had become scenes of bloodshed and death. Less understanding bosses at the Post Office refused to give him a well-earned promotion and he applied to retire. He left the Post Office in 1922. From this point on, he painted continually despite the initial lack of interest in his work. With the help of Wilhelm Uhde, he exhibited in 1925, and the show enjoyed a great success. His canvases sold and his reputation began to grow. He was particularly fond of Parisian landscapes. In 1934, he suffered a stroke from which he never fully recovered. Two years later he died from another stroke.

A few paintings by Louis Vivin from 1880—1890 are known, but his work began in earnest in 1922 when he retired and began to paint regularly. The main subjects of his paintings come from the places he knew best — Paris, the quays of the Seine — or things he saw in the course of his career, such as Reims Cathedral or

Vivin, Louis: Hunting Boar

the Belfort Lion. However, he did not ignore still-life and subjects drawn entirely from his imagination — hunting scenes, for instance. There was an evolution in his work from an almost obsessive concern with precise and excessive detail in realistic reconstructions to, gradually, a simplification of his compositions, a restriction of his palette to only a few colours, and a rejection, a total absence in fact, of the rules of composition. "A Bus in Front of Ste-Eustache Church," "L'Hotel de Sens," in the Béziers Museum, or "Notre Dame de Paris" at the Museum of Modern Art are good examples of this synthesis in vision in which each brick, each flagstone, each detail of a building are part of a rhythm induced by the accumulation of increasingly abstract surfaces. At the same time, they are constant reminders of reality, but the reality recalled is reduced to its essentials, transposed and simplified, rid, one might say, of the fatigue or dust of daily existence. Louis Vivin focussed his attention on something specific, a monument or a church, and avoided, always, a more encompassing view. He placed his subject on a diagonal, suppressed all perspective by a generalised flattening of space and allowed nothing to survive, except for the vibrations of colour.

Louis Vivin was among the artists whose work was seen at the celebrated *Les Maîtres Populaires de la Realité* exhibition in 1937. His paintings have been seen since in Amsterdam, Berne, Basel, New York, Knokke-le-Zoute, Baden-Baden, Salzburg and in the major cities of Yugoslavia (1970). *(See portrait of the artist, p. 602). Ch. Sch.*

VLADIMIR (BEDENIKOVIĆ) (1944)   Austria

Vladimir Bedeniković, who signs his works "Vladimir," was born in Zagreb, Yugoslavia, but has lived in Salzburg since his nineteenth year. Although a trained machinist, he worked as a caterer in Austria. After spending some time in

Vivin, Louis: Portrait of My Father

France and England, he took a job as a steward on ocean-going ships.

Inspired by Maria de Posz, the naive painter from Salzburg, he began painting in 1974. That same year he was awarded a scholarship to art school. Wide open spaces, meadows and animals are his main themes. His favourite colours are yellow, blue and green. Paintings by him show extraordinary attention to detail, with every blade of grass, every wave on the water, minutely executed.

He has exhibited in Austria and other countries and is the recipient of a number of awards.

Vladimir (Bedeniković): First Flight

He is a member of the Henri Rousseau Group. *(See portrait of the artist, p. 603).*

VOGL, HILDA (1930)   Nicaragua

Hilda Vogl spent her childhood and youth on an estate in Nicaragua, but when the Somoza dictatorship took power she was compelled to leave the country. As a refugee, she started putting on canvas her recollections of her homeland, mostly scenes of poor settlements, huts of straw and palm leaf, naked children, the poverty of the peasants in the midst of the luxuriant beauty of tropical vegetation. Poverty is not portrayed picturesquely but as something deserving social condemnation. When she returned to her homeland after the revolution, she chose different themes, such as work in the villages, life in the cooperatives, and courses for illiterate peasants. *(See portrait of the artist, p. 603).* E. C.

VOIGT, FRIEDERIKE (1882—1968)   West Germany

Friederike Voigt was born in Willingen, County of Waldeck, and died in Kassel. The daughter of a farmer, she learned the usual housekeeping skills, married and moved from city to city with her husband, who was a railway employee, finally ending up in Kassel. Like countless other women, Friederike Voigt spent her entire life working and caring for her husband and children — she had ten. After her husband's death, and when her children had grown up, she used to make "Grandma Voigt" dolls for her grandchildren and embroider wall-hangings with patterns devised by herself. Her work was so fanciful that all her daughters and her relatives wanted to have tapestries, each of which was more splendid than the last.

One of her admirers was shrewd enough to put brushes and pigments in her way. She began to paint quite naturally, choosing especially bunches of flowers and rustic still-life studies. She would make incessant excursions into her own youth, into her beloved rural home, thus

Vogl, Hilda: Yard Full of Cotton

Voigt, Friederike: Wedding Procession

bringing into her city flat the homestead of her childhood, the village people with their work, their customs and festivals. It was not these pictures, however, but the flower pictures — Grandma Voigt's favourite subjects — that brought her fame and admiration. There is nothing in German naive painting to compare with their simple, unassuming beauty and their flawlessly pure and inimitable style.

The flowers and fruit in her pictures can blossom only in peasant gardens, they can flourish only in free nature, in lush meadows and by the roadside. They are not as delicate as the artificially propagated hybrids to be found in hothouses. When we look at them we have the same sensation as when we listen to folk songs sung in a natural, heartfelt and artless manner. With Grandma Voigt all these flowers show themselves in their finest aspect and in luxuriant abundance. It is easy to see right through them and to understand them — and this is the way they are painted: down to earth, with no fancy

Voigt, Friederike: Basket with Flowers

tricks or ideas. Voigt's painting is comparable to painting done on the reverse side of glass or to the ornamentation of peasant furniture. But unlike many of these examples of traditional folk art, Voigt's flower pictures do not give the impression of being schematic, prosaic, routine craftsmanship. All her pictures radiate a unique freshness, a spontaneity of inspiration, a directness of approach; they have an aura of matchlessness. In her most impressive pictures she might well be compared with another artist who proclaims the grand simplicity of nature in all its flawless serenity — Paula Modersohn-Becker. The manner of composition is also reminiscent of her, a certain earthy heaviness in the colouring, the consistently one-dimensional style of representation.

As Friederike Voigt stated repeatedly, painting was not a strenuous pastime. It was entertaining and the most appealing work in the world. She was out to enjoy it, and to give others enjoyment. The good-humoured visitors to galleries whom we see absorbed in her pictures, and

the fortunate owners of one of her flower studies will bear witness to that. *T. G.*

VOLKOVA, ELENA ANDREEVNA (1915)   USSR
VOLKOVA, YELENA ANDREIEVNA

Y. A. Volkova was born into a Ukrainian working-class family in Chuguyev, a town near Kharkov. She was fond in girlhood of moulding pitchers, cups and saucers of clay, and of embroidery. She was a nurse during the war, and it was not until her fifties that she essayed painting in oils on canvas and cardboard. She paints,

Volkova, Yelena Andreievna: Gala Festivities on the Banks of the Irtysh River

without any preliminary draughtsmanship, from memory or imagination. Feeling that her knowledge of the basics of art were inadequate, she enrolled as a student in ZNUI, the Extra-mural People's University of Art in Moscow, where, incidentally, she now lives as an old-age pensioner together with her artist son. Her favourite themes are still-lifes and scenes of popular festivities, which appear from a distance like colourful mosaics. Her ZNUI classes scarcely modified her artistic concepts and aesthetic attitudes, which derive from her small-town upbringing and are largely influenced by peasant morals and mores. In her works nature lives, which is why her still-lifes are not really inanimate; the objects depicted are tangible and the manner of their presentation on canvas or cardboard is as down-to-earth as the objective set to reproduce the surrounding environment. The colours employed are bright, gay, and well-demarcated, and the objects depicted are modelled with loving detail. Volkova has been represented at Soviet Russia and USSR exhibitions and has also had a show exclusively of her own work. *(See portrait of the artist, p. 603). N. Sh.*

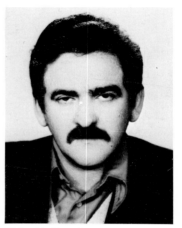

Valerius, Max

Valero, Salvador

Valla, Serafino

Večenaj, Ivan

Vidović, Branko

Vieillard, Lucien

Virius, Mirko

Viva, Rosina

Vivancos M. G.

Vivin, Louis

 Der Steen, Germain

 Vankóné Dudás, Juli

 Varfolomeeva, E. I.

 Vasilescu, Constantin

 lazon Vega, Carmen

 Vintilă, Petru

 Viraghová, Zuzana

 adimir (Bedeniković)

 Vogl, Hilda

 Volkova, Elena Andreevna

604 WALLIS, ALFRED — Great Britain
WALTHER-VISINO T. — East Germany
WANG JINXI — China
WARCZYGŁOWA, ZYGMUNT — Poland
WARE, CHRIS — Great Britain
WARREN, SELBY — Australia
WATTERS, MAX — Australia
WATTYNE, JACQUES VAN DE — Belgium
WEBER, RUDOLF FELIX — East Germany
WEERT, JAN VAN — West Germany
WEN ZHIJIANG — China
WESTBROEK, WILLEM — Netherlands
WIDJA, IDA BAGUS — Indonesia, Bali
WIĘCEK, LUDWIK — Poland
WILLIAMSON, CLARA McDONALD — USA
WILLSON, MARY ANN — USA
WILSON, SCOTTIE — Great Britain
WIMMER, ALFONS — West Germany
WITTLICH, JOSEF — West Germany
WNĘK, MARIA, — Poland
WÓJTOWICZ, MARIA — Poland
WU SCHENGGIN — China
WYERS, JAN — Canada

Wallis, Alfred: Cornish Coast

WALLIS, ALFRED (1855—1942)   Great Britain

Alfred Wallis was born in Devonport and died in St. Ives. Today he is renowned as Britain's greatest primitive artist. At the beginning and for most of his life, when he did not paint at all, this Cornishman was a withdrawn character who at first joined up with the St. Ives fishing fleet, a livelihood which meant working aboard coastal vessels, although he sometimes ventured into the North Sea.

Born the son of a master paver who married a woman from the Scilly Isles, he knew little of the creature comforts of a cosy home. Life was bleak, pleasures few. A natural recluse, Wallis did get married — but his wife was twenty years older than he. It was in 1922, three years after her death, that he started to paint, at the age of sixty-seven; even then he kept this occupation a secret from all but his closest friends. As a painter, his reputation was purely local. Only a few were allowed to see his pictures, and not many more knew about them.

Intensely religious, almost to the point of being a God-fearing fanatic, he made it a rule to drape his paintings in black on Sundays so that they would not offend the Lord.

When he left the sea, he had tried to scrape together a living selling secondhand odds and ends, things which people had thrown out when they had no further use for them. Little money came from this, and by the time his wife died he had already abandoned even this activity.

Still in the early 1920s, it was into this lugubrious and sombre world that the two artists Ben Nicholson and Cristopher Wood came. Almost by chance, they learnt of Wallis, the "anchorite" artist, and went to see him in the lonely cottage where he lived. At first, as with all strangers, they were unwelcome; but possibly because they too were "artists" and because of their immediate and spontaneous enthusiasm for his pictures, hostility and coldness were gradually overcome. Through these two artists he acquired many admirers.

Yet, after his wife's death he still felt there was little left for him. His painting perhaps, and of course the Bible. But things were slowly changing and in 1962 — admittedly twenty years after his death — a Wallis exhibition was mounted in the Piccadilly Gallery, London, the first of many.

It is now hard to believe how rapidly his reputation has grown. Good paintings by him are

Walther-Visino, Therese: Arrival at Midnight Mass

to be seen in museums like London's Tate Gallery and New York's Museum of Modern Art.

Like James Dixon, or even Bryan Pearce (like Rousseau too with his dreams of Mexico — only in Wallis's case it was Newfoundland), this bad-tempered hermit lost every shred of artistic sophistication — however mild — when he settled down to paint. With an eccentric rejection of any kind of perspective, he painted things straight-on. Like Dixon, he made what use he could of scrapings from the bottoms of discarded cans of paint and made his pictures on bits of wood or old carton, often very irregular in shape. Like both James Dixon and Bryan Pearce, his indifference to traditional perspective would sometimes take him aloft and, especially when his subjects were drawn from the coastline or the landscape, he would paint them as if he was seeing them from above. This also applied to views of the shipyard at St. Ives — although not to the portraits of the ships themselves. *(See portrait of the artist, p. 618). Sh. W.*

WALTHER-VISINO, THERESE (1898—1981) — East Germany

Like the American farmer's wife, Mary Robertson-Moses, who found her way into art history as Grandma Moses, Therese Walther-Visino painted episodes from her life in the naive manner that reflected her simple beliefs. In these drawings of actual or fictional happenings she invited the spectator of her work to share her personal joy, her merriment or her fervour in relation to all the curious things she remembered. Therese Walther-Visino was born in Leipzig-Gohlis. From 1917 until 1924 she studied

Wang Jinxi: The Iron Bridge

music in Dresden and subsequently worked as a teacher of music; she was also conductor of a school orchestra. After the death of her husband in 1964 she took up painting and drawing. She limited herself at first to drawing, but gradually ventured on to painting. In 1971 she was discovered by the publisher, Verlag der Kunst, in Dresden, who organised her first show.

Even while she was still alive a large part of her vast production found its way into the Dresden Museum of Folk Art ("Museum für Volkskunst").

Together with numerous "rural" studies which manifest a lyrical and romantic conception of landscape, she painted cheerful still-life studies. In her narrative pictures certain figures often appear to be drawn on a larger scale, in keeping with their significance for the painter. *(See portrait of the artist, p. 618). G. C.*

WANG JINXI (1955) — China

Wang Jinxi is from the Feng Wei commune where, having completed secondary school, he works as an agriculturist in the Chang An brigade. While still a boy at school he loved to draw and his artistic talent won him the position of editor and principal illustrator of the school wall newspaper. After school, he returned to his brigade, joined the Jim Shan circle of painters and began to paint subjects associated with the history of the village. A brigade exhibition of his pictures aroused a great deal of interest among the local peasants and he was encouraged to continue painting. His most notable work is "Iron Bridge" recording the ceremony of the opening of a new bridge in his village. He has imagined a procession of boats in two queues with young people in colourful tunics contrasting with the uniforms he and his comrades wear. The bridges now are iron, replacing the semicircular wood-carved bridges Chinese peasants had built for centuries to span their canals. There is much motion in the picture and a festive air is achieved with numerous waving flags. The boats course through the water, trailing a wake behind them. *(See portrait of the artist, p. 619).* N. T.

WARE, CHRIS (1904) Great Britain

Chris Ware was born in Aldershot, Hampshire. After education at the Silesian College in South Farnborough, Hampshire, during the Second World War he worked as a photographer with the Royal Navy, frequently working alongside Lord Mountbatten. He is an accepted master photographer.

It was not until the 1960s that he started to paint, and as he fell in love with France, he is busy immortalising in his paintings what he regards as the real character of that country as exemplified for centuries by ordinary people.

Warczygłowa, Zygmunt: The City

Ware, Chris: Le Touquet Restaurant

WARCZYGŁOWA, ZYGMUNT (1922) Poland

Zygmunt Warczygłowa was born in Poznań, where he still lives. He is from a worker's family (his father is a precision mechanic) and had seven years of elementary schooling. During the war, he was sent to forced labour in Germany. Returning to Poland after the war, he worked as a fisherman, later as a labourer and from 1952 to 1964 as a streetcar conductor in Poznań. Illness obliged him to take a disablement pension in 1964. During the war, he began to paint "in order to forget." He prefers small formats and uses ink, chalk and gouache. Since 1966 he has had about ten one-man shows in Poland and has participated in Polish exhibitions of naive art abroad. His works are in the collections of the Ethnographic Museums in Warsaw, Cracow, and Poznań. *(See portrait of the artist, p. 619).* A. J.

This artist's admirers are not only attracted by his translation into paint of the traditional France, they are also amazed at his swirling control of paint — for architecture and landscape — and his often witty realisation of the character of the French people, especially in the countryside. This two-sided expertise with paint-and-brush and psychology singles him out as an artist of the highest quality.

Paintings by Chris Ware — he hates to sell them because for him every time it is like the loss of a child — have frequently been seen on view in and around Richmond, Surrey, where he lives. He has been well represented by Gallery 359, Nottingham and the White House Gallery, Over Hadden (he was for instance a star of the show "The Last Man on Earth" in Nottingham). He has been included in RONA exhibitions (1978-80), and was in a special show of British

Naive Artists at Harrods, London. *(See portrait of the artist, p. 618). Sh. W.*

WARREN, SELBY (1887)　　　　Australia

Selby Warren was born in Bathurst in New South Wales. He worked at various occupations in the country, becoming adept in the skills of the shearer, rabbiter, miner and cutter of railway sleepers. It was this last occupation that gave him the inspiration for his most famous work, "The Sleeper Cutters," which hangs in the Australian National Gallery in Canberra. Selby

Warren, Selby: Coach

Warren is now regarded as one of the grand old men of Australian naive art. *B. McC.*

WATTERS, MAX (1936)　　　　Australia

Max Watters, born in Muswellbrook in New South Wales, is a self-taught artist who began painting seriously in 1956. Whereas his first pictures were mainly figures and portraits, he now concentrates on landscape work. His landscape subjects are usually taken from the area he knows best — the Upper Hunter Valley in New South Wales.

It is his usual practice to make sketches on the spot, using pastel crayons and pencil, then develop these into full paintings in his studio. Watters uses a colour range to suit his particularly bold interpretations and employs a certain amount of artistic licence with regard to colour. It is this boldness of approach which has set him apart from other naive artists.

He is represented in the National Collection in Canberra, in many galleries and private collections in Australia, the USA, Great Britain, Germany and Singapore. *B. McC.*

WATTYNE, JACQUES VAN DE　　　Belgium

Jacques van de Wattyne, a teacher, devoted himself to reviving folklore in areas bordering on Hennuy and Belgian and French Flanders whose centres are Ronse and Ellezelles. While engaged in these activities, including festivals, popular

celebrations, reconstructions of historic events, collection of folk objects, and the like, he has produced paintings which he calls "folk art."

In cases where his pictures, drawings or engravings deal with local folkways, their principal theme is magic and other supernatural phenomena. Apart from other things, he has done a series of frescoes depicting the twelve phases of the initiation of witches which were printed in a calender.

He asserts that "folk art," as he conceives it, does not confine itself only to painting but also encompasses the theatre, poetry, folk music. He

Watters, Max: Isolated House

Wattyne, Jacques van de: Entry of the Devil into Ellezelles

hopes that his work will give impulse to the renaissance of all those forms of art that can be considered as instruments of dialogue, as the reintegration of traditional values into contemporary life. Van de Wattyne considers himself belonging to "an art that is witness to a return to sources."

He has exhibited in Brussels and in France. *(See portrait of the artist, p. 618). J. C.*

WEBER, RUDOLF FELIX (1900—1973)

Rudolf Felix Weber was born in the village of Mittelherwigedorf, near Zittau. His father was a weaver, his ancestors had been masons, weavers and carpenters. He lost his mother at the age of two, and his father when he was ten. In 1911 his grandparents took him to Zittau. He was apprenticed to a baker in Dresden, called up into the army in 1918, then worked as a journeyman baker in Zittau from 1919 to 1922. There followed a period of unemployment, then further training as a commercial clerk. For some time he worked

Weber, Rudolf Felix: The Mountain Village of Oberlausitz

in the Olbersdorf electricity works near Zittau. From 1939 until 1948 he was either in the army or a prisoner of war. Later he worked in the Olbersdorf creosoting plant.

Weber's father used to paint murals and he encouraged his son's artistic leanings, including his fondness for the violin. For a short time the boy took drawing lessons with A. Schorich in Zittau; otherwise he simply taught himself. Throughout his life Weber painted pictures for village weddings and birthdays, utilising the walls of sheds and huts as well as albums and display cases. In every situation in which he found himself during his life, he sought to overcome the blows dealt him by fate by means of his painting.

From 1950 until his death, hardly a week-end passed without Weber taking part as a fiddler in concerts arranged for holiday visitors and without a spell of painting. These two passions, the violin and the paint-brush, dominated his daily life.

His pictures record experiences and impressions of his native district. His style of painting favours stark contrasts of heavily applied layers of pigment. *(See portrait of the artist, p. 619).* G. C.

WEERT, JAN VAN (1871—1955)   West Germany

Jan van Weert was born in the Netherlands and died in Düsseldorf. He led an unsettled nomadic existence before settling down in Düsseldorf in 1922. He was a much-travelled man of the world who had ridden his own horses

Weert, Jan van: Winter Landscape with View of the Town and the Mailcoach

in show-jumping competitions in Paris and Budapest, for he was a bloodstock breeder among other things. It is hardly surprising that Van Weert should have relived the palmy days of his youth and recalled his horses when he turned to painting as his hobby in old age. Those were the good old days, and when he set about recalling them they were bound to be bathed in a romantic glow. His favourite subjects, which recur in numerous variations, were horse-drawn sleighs and mail coaches.

Van Weert had a particular fondness for colours. "Everything must match, down to the finest shades, otherwise the entire picture is a dead loss; sometimes you nearly give up in despair before you find exactly the right shade for a little roof or a fence." It was not just the colours, however, that he went on trying out until he managed to combine all the contrasting values of his paintings into a harmony that is both lively and elevated. Just as important to him was the exact placement within the picture of the horse sleigh, the four-in-hand mail coach, the windmill, the castle and the trees, the direction to be taken by the trotting horses, the manner in which he might involve buildings and rows of trees and relate them to these movements, so that all the elements of the picture might be joined in perfect harmony, in spite of their various shapes and shades, the contrasts of rest and motion, of the fleeting and the cumbersome. The figures that feature in this board game with the same unchanging accessories might have been taken from a collection of tin soldiers and set down in the snow-covered scene.

Van Weert's pictures rapidly found their way into the art world and are much in demand with galleries and private collectors. *T. G.*

WEN ZHIJIANG (1945)   **China**

Born in the village of Jiangcun in Hu country, about 45 km. from Xian, the capital of old China, Wen Zhijiang comes from a farming background. In 1961 he was among the first peasants to take up painting. They were encouraged

Wen Zhijiang: Picking Persimmon

by the authorities, provided that they portrayed the various working activities of the brigade, while all other subjects, whether depicting landscapes or scenes of enjoyment, were frowned upon. This attitude on the part of the authorities throughout the period known as the Cultural Revolution prevented artists from showing the full scope of their imagination and talent.

His 1965 painting "Picking Persimmon" shows a dense grove of persimmon trees, whose fruit is much sought after in China as a delicacy. The colours are rich, suggesting that the harvest was bountiful, and the painting conveys a feeling of rejoicing and contentment. Wen Zhijiang, who now works in the village veterinary station, treating sick animals, has become a well-known painter who has exhibited his work in the local gallery and other places in China. *N. T.*

WESTBROEK, WILLEM (1918)   **Netherlands**

Willem Westbroek, born in Rotterdam, learned house painting after finishing elementary school while also, from the age of fourteen, taking drawing lessons from the painter H. Bieling. As house painting had taught him how to use colour, he thought of becoming an artist. However, unemployment was widespread when he was a youth and, in order to survive, he had to do various jobs, among them working as a confectioner, dock worker, locksmith and a copper engraver. In 1942, he enrolled in the Academy of Fine Arts in Rotterdam. Contacts

Westbroek, Willem: The Hitch-Hiker

with the world of art led him at first to paint in the classical manner, i.e., in the style of the "Hague School" of Dutch Impressionism. Since academic painting did not satisfy him, he began to search for his own personal expression. In the fifties, he painted a green landscape much admired by his friends from the Academy. It was they who told him that he was, in effect, a naive painter.

At the end of the 1950s, Westbroek finally found his genre and painted only dark-green, highly stylised landscapes resembling parks. These serve as a worthy backdrop for his symbolic, human situations. With much wit and a gentle irony, he portrayed the relationship between a man and a woman, with symbolism playing an important role, as in a fairy tale: a royal egg that must be hatched in a palace; a dignified-looking carriage, bearing nude princesses, on its way to the royal summer home. Everything is precisely portrayed, as though experienced in a dream. He has a refined technique and his intense green colour shades easily from dark to light, giving a suggestion of space.

He has had only one solo show ("De Doelen," 1969, Rotterdam), but in Amsterdam he has frequently displayed his works at exhibitions, and also exhibited in Zagreb in 1973 and 1977 ("Naivi"). *(See portrait of the artist, p. 619). N. E.*

WIDJA, IDA BAGUS (1912)   Indonesia, Bali

Ida Bagus Widja is one of the second generation classical Batuan artists who started painting relatively late in the 1930s and is now one of Bali's foremost painters.

Widja's success and recognition has apparently meant little change in the circumstances of his life. A quiet, unassuming man, he fasts to cleanse himself spiritually before painting.

Like so many Batuan artists, Widja was in his younger days influenced by the early radical examples of the painters I Ngendon, Tombelos and I Patera. However, since the 1950s he has

and singular in its portrayal of Balinese life. Widja's crowded, overflowing canvases reflect the restless, seething scenes typical of active Balinese village life. Celebrations, festivities, rites of passage and simple day-to-day activities are all handled with droll, impish humour. Widja works slowly and carefully, delighting in infinite detail and perception, building into his canvases every facet and item, however minute, of the scene around him. Disregarding perspective completely, he works in a flat plane, as to be found in the traditional paintings of the *Wayang* style. The lack of perspective does not, however,

Widja, Ida Bagus: Barong Dance

Więcek, Ludwik: On Genezaret Lake

developed a style that, while retaining much of the 1930s influence, is still highly individualistic

detract but enhances the vibrant, primitive quality of his colourful work.

Widja's paintings are to be found in the Denpasar Art Centre, the Australian Museum, the Amsterdam Museum and the Puri Lukisan in Ubud. He is also represented in private collections on several continents and is published in numerous books and magazines. *(See portrait of the artist, p. 619). J. F.*

WIĘCEK, LUDWIK (1930)   Poland

Ludwik Więcek was born in the vicinity of Nowy Sacz and now lives in the village of Wilczyska. Lame and illiterate, he is employed as a farm labourer. As trusting as a child, he is cordial in his relations with people. All his paintings are in oil on a hard surface, either board or panel: religious scenes or scenes from real life, copied from cards or reproductions. These he treats as themes which have to be elaborated. His works are in the collection of the Ethnographic Museum in Cracow and in the collection of L. Zimmerer in Warsaw. *(See portrait of the artist, p. 618). A. J.*

WILLIAMSON, CLARA McDONALD (1875—1976) USA

Clara McDonald Williamson was born shortly after her pioneer parents arrived by covered wagon to settle in Iredell, a Texas frontier town. Clara's recollections of her pioneer youth are in her paintings, for she said, "Of course, that was my world . . . all I knew . . . and all I had to remember and put on canvas. I think a painter ought to paint what she knows." As the eldest child, she had to help with the children and household chores, so her school was catch-as-catch-can, three days one week, two the next,

pleasure in learning new things, and a delight in life itself. Widowed at sixty-eight, with nothing special to do and used to being busy, she enrolled in an evening painting class at the Dallas Museum, where she was discovered by Donald Vogel, who later became her dealer. *J. W.*

WILLSON, MARY ANN USA

It is a pity that more is not known about Mary Ann Willson, for in the annals of American folk art she is indeed unusual. Only twenty of her works are known, and along with Eunice Pinney

Williamson, Clara McDonald: The Day the Bosque Froze Over

if she was lucky. But her avidness to learn was phenomenal, and she managed somehow to keep up with her classmates.

At age twenty, considered a spinster, she was invited by an uncle to come and work for him in Waxahachie. This ushered in a period of freedom for her as an emancipated woman (which she was not to experience again until after her husband died when she was in her late sixties) and she thoroughly enjoyed being responsible to and for no one except herself. Marriage to a widower with two children helped her achieve her desire to have her own home.

In 1920 they moved to Dallas, where Clara not only aided her husband in his business but ran a boarding house as well. Still, she managed as always to cling to her sense of humour, her

she shares the distinction of being among the earliest (and the more primitive of the two) water-colourists found so far. The little information available on this pioneer artist is contained in a letter written around 1850 by "An Admirer of Art" and enclosed in a portfolio of her works found in 1943 by the Harry Stone Gallery of New York City. The Admirer letter says, "The artist, Miss Willson and her friend, Miss Brundage, came from one of the Eastern States," and remarks that they bought a few acres and built or "formed" a house of logs in Greenville County, New York. "One was a farmer and cultivated the land . . . while the other made pictures which she sold to the farmers and others as rare and unique 'works of art.' Their paints, or colours, were made of . . . berries, bricks and occasional 'store paint'

Willson, Mary Ann: The Prodigal Son Reclaimed

[which] made up their wants [needs] for these elegant designs. The two maids left their home in the East with a romantic attachment for each other and which continued until the death of the 'farmer maid.' The artist was inconsolable . . . and removed to parts unknown."

The writer of the letter (possibly Thomas Cole, who owned some of the paintings) often visited the ladies, he said, and commented on how they "boasted how greatly they were in demand [the paintings]. Why, they go to Canada and clear to Mobile! [Alabama]."

Miss Willson's paintings were boldly decorative and many seemed directly inspired by academic prints. Her interpretations, however, and colours were decidedly original, and in the opinion of Jean Lipman, "as primitive as those of ancient Egypt, as modern as those of Matisse." *J. W.*

WILSON, SCOTTIE (1888—1972)   **Great Britain**

Scottie Wilson was born in Glasgow, of immigrant Russian Jewish parents. The patterns of childhood — dogs, fishes, fountains, paper doilies, net curtains, animals at the zoo, everything he saw and felt — must have impressed a latent poetic sensibility, for they were all ultimately to be transmuted on paper into an enchanted world. His pictures were haunted by the atavistic echoes of many civilisations, the curvilinear forms of ancient Celtic designs, the triangular incisions of African carving, the irreg-

on the back of glass, pictures on ceramic, pictures devoid of hatched lines, pure abstractions, and so on.

His works represent an exploration of the psyche, forever obliquely transgressing erotic and other taboos. He never tried to copy from life — he abstracted from life to form his own iconography, which remains totally and uncompromisingly original. Thus his claims to greatness rest on utter originality; creation of his own cosmogony; creation of his own superlative techniques; and a poetic vision, to which we may add that Scottie, like many outstanding masters, was

Wilson, Scottie: Untitled

Wimmer, Alfons: Portrait

ular rhythms of South Sea sculpture. Yet one can only guess at the sources of his magical cities, vases, totems, phantoms, gargoyles and ghosts — racial memories or the ability of a visionary poet, for that is what he was, to bring together exterior and interior worlds to create an entire cosmogony of his own.

How did it come about that a barely literate Glasgow ex-newspaper boy and market trader should have suddenly started drawing around the age of thirty-eight and become one of the great figures of modern art, sought not only by the museums and private collectors but by artists like Picasso and critics such as André Breton?

In the construction of this immense *oeuvre* it is possible to distinguish a large number of quite different phases or periods, in which technique as well as imagery undergo marked transformations. Much research remains to be done in order to identify them. One can suggest some by subject-matter — ice castles, "crusader" cities, vases, fountains, totems, metaphysical pictures, mandalas and other conceptions — and some by technique, or a merger of imagery and technique — black and white pictures, pictures painted

also a prophet, constantly foreseeing in his pictures events to come.

Scottie fought for beauty and the recognition of beauty by those to whom he tried to show it, but it was never a banal conception. He cast his work upon the world like a benediction, actually giving it away in the early days; he valued it highly in terms of aesthetics and not in terms of money. Those lucky enough to possess one of his works return to it again and again as a source of optimism, of a kind of innocent purity shining forth in what Scottie often called, rather slyly, "this wicked world." Even in the years before his death, at eighty-four, Scottie's work continued to radiate the joy and aspirations of youth.

Scottie Wilson is often included as a highly personal and individual contributor in exhibitions of mainstream as well as naive art. His position is therefore virtually without precedent, since he participated in the historic Surrealist exhibition at the Hayward Gallery in 1978 and was selected by Victor Musgrave to fill a prominent position in his international survey of Art Brut at the same gallery in 1979, sponsored by the Arts Council of Great Britain. He is also represented in numerous public collections, notably the Tate Gallery in London, the Musée de l'Art Moderne in Paris and the Museum of Modern Art in New York.

A theory as to how Scottie began to create and became an artist has been proposed by Victor Musgrave in his monograph, *Scottie Wilson*, published by the "Collection de l'Art Brut" in Lausanne.

The innocence and absolute authority of his work is likely to outlast many of his contemporaries.

(See portrait of the artist, p. 618). V. M.

works during the Second World War. As the result of an accident he suffered a severe injury to his hand which forced him to give up his hobby for a number of years, but he began to paint once more in 1957. Josef Wittlich is one of the few naive artists whose work is spoken of in superlatives; he is accepted without reservation, exhibited and bought up by museums and galleries.

Wittlich was a shy man, small, uncommunicative, a bachelor, shut up in the voluntary seclusion of a dormitory belonging to his factory.

By an irony of fate Wittlich was discovered precisely at the time when the Pop-Art wave

Wittlich, Josef: One of the Stations of the Cross

Wittlich, Josef: Soldiers on the Move

WIMMER, ALFONS (1922) — West Germany

Alfons Wimmer was born in Weller, a small village in Bavaria where today, together with his siblings, he runs the farm inherited from their father; they are engaged in intensive stockbreeding. Wimmer likes to play his concertina, but in the late autumn and winter months he also finds time to carve wooden figures. These are on a small scale but they have the same originality and rudimentary formal idiom as Bödeker's sculptures. He is fascinated above all by nude figures, and that is just as well, for it would be difficult to find anywhere else naked female figures of such astonishingly primitive expressiveness. They point back to the earliest manifestations of creative activity, with contours similar to rock paintings; they are reminiscent of the archaic idols and the ritual carved figures produced by primitive peoples. Wimmer's figures do not turn out to be copies from nature. Wimmer achieves unity of form with a minimal range of shapes and a reductive stylisation conveyed by a technique of notching. *T. G.*

WITTLICH, JOSEF (1903—1982) — West Germany

Josef Wittlich was born in Glattbach, near Neuwied, and lived in Höhr-Grenzhausen, where he worked in a pottery factory. Wittlich was fond of painting even in his youth, but he lost all his

arrived in Germany. With some consternation critics realised that Wittlich's pictures, which were first shown in Stuttgart and Hanover in 1967, bore a remarkably close resemblance to Pop-Art. In both cases there were themes taken from the catalogue of our consumer society and represented with an ironical undertone, bold "pop" colours, banal photographs as models, alienated pictures of pictures. Wittlich had been painting in this fashion for years before he was discovered!

A designer had discovered him while he was on a conducted tour of the pottery factory where Wittlich worked as a labourer. He came across huge, crudely coloured pictures painted on paper, nailed to beams and girders, or else pasted on the walls of the lofty sheds, often scrawled or adorned with pin-up photos. "Our Joe paints that stuff," explained the smiling workmen. On these vast surfaces which have the visual impact of the brilliantly coloured cartoons that serve as the designs for stained glass windows, a war is being waged — there is no other word for it. A surging, riotous turmoil covers the whole surface from side to side, and above it all there is a dense forest of brightly coloured fluttering banners. Was it Wittlich's intention to trivialise, or even to glorify such a detestable thing as warfare? God forbid! What fascinated him was the brightness of the uniforms and the luminous patches of the banners, the massing together of groups of individuals, action and reaction, the sequence of rest and motion, the confrontation of contrasting figures and clashing colours — this was what interested, stimulated and excited him. He believed he could represent all this best in his imaginary battle scenes. Whether the uniforms were historically accurate, whether it was possible to identify the nationality of the banners in his pictures — all this was a matter of indifference as far as he was concerned. He located his colours and other attributes wherever they best fitted into his picture, made changes without

must have possessed to be able to construct such well-balanced compositions, in spite of this handicap and in spite of the complex movements and colour schemes in his pictures! It was a search for such harmonious effects that constituted the adventure of painting for him. He reckoned that the draughtsmanship was the most difficult part. The base was white cartridge paper in large rolls. He began by marking out a frame which was divided into different colours and surrounded the area of the painting. The paper was soon enmeshed in a network of delicate lines marking out the contours. Wittlich noted in each surface

Wnęk, Maria: Portrait of Lenin in May Day Parade

Wójtowicz, Maria: Flowers

hesitation or made additions on the spur of the moment if only he could enhance the idea of his picture.

Wittlich selected his figures from history books and yellowing illustrated magazines with accounts of wars in the last century or the First World War. He said he needed these models because it was the best way to learn about facial expressions and bodily movements. It was incredible to see the tiny table on which these pictures were painted on a scale to which no other naive painter in Germany has dared to aspire. Wittlich could never see the whole of his picture at once because there was room on the table-top only for a section of the paper — the remainder of the sheet hanging down over the edges. What a phenomenal power of imagination and what a sure sense of proportion Wittlich

area which colour was to be used. He later applied the colours, using dense tempera pigments of spectral purity. Bold and luminous areas of colour in challenging juxtaposition border on or jut into other zones with more subtly differentiated shades. Wherever empty spaces showed up in the vortex of action, he instantly devised patterns which constituted the superficial structure of the picture as a whole. Finally, Wittlich took a fine brush and outlined in a kind of absent-minded fashion all the figures and surface areas of his picture. And so another battle scene was completed. *T. G.*

WNĘK, MARIA (1921)   Poland

Maria Wnęk was born in Olszanca near Nowy Sacz where she now lives. She learned to read and write, and worked for many years as a cleaning woman. She is very religious and considers her painting, especially in recent years, as a mission, an opportunity to point to a moral. Her imagination is the source of her subject-matter and in her paintings she frequently gives expression to feelings of fear and jeopardy. In some, she portrays imaginary disasters. Her paintings are done on cardboard to which she often adds, on the back, words of explanation, prayers, or warnings. Her works are in the collections of museums in Cracow, Warsaw and Nowy Sacz. She has had a number of one-woman shows

WU SHENGGIN (1945)   China

A farmer working in the village farming brigade, Wu Shenggin, born in Yincun, a village in Hu county, took up painting in 1973, after seeing the work done by other village painters. Before long, however, he developed a distinctive style in depicting the familiar subjects of farming life, emphasising the rhythmic repetition of geometrical shapes. In his picture "Silkworms" (1973), peasants are shown placing silkworms ready to hatch into baskets, in the same manner as has been done in China for thousands of years. The mulberry leaves make a delightful colour

Wu Shenggin: Silkworms

Wyers, Jan: Those Good Old Threshing Days

and participated in group exhibitions in Poland and abroad. *(See portrait of the artist, p. 619).* *A. J.*

contrast. Wu Shenggin continues to work on the land and paints in his free time. *N. T.*

WÓJTOWICZ, MARIA   Poland

Maria Wójtowicz was born and lives in Cracow. She grew up against a background of traditional folk culture. Her father was a locomotive engineer and her mother had a farm. During art lessons in school, her teacher objected to her using all the colours available to her. She met her husband, a graphic artist and painter, when she was sixteen years old. Whereas her ideal was a quiet life, he loved company and adventures, worrying her when he did not appear at home for days on end. She claims that her anxiety over him made her begin to paint, in order to soothe her nerves and prevent her from thinking that something awful might have happened to her husband. This was at the end of 1968. Soon after she had a public showing of her works in Cracow and was popularised by the television, numerous articles, and a documentary film (1974). She has had a number of one-woman shows in Cracow, Milan, Rome, Cologne, and so on, and her works have been displayed at all important exhibitions of Polish naive art in Poland and abroad. Her pictures are in the collections of Polish museums (among others, the National Museum in Cracow, the State Ethnographic Museum in Warsaw) and in many private collections in the country and abroad. *(See portrait of the artist, p. 619). A. J.*

WYERS, JAN (1888—1973)   Canada

Jan Wyers was born in Steenderen, the Netherlands, and died in Regina, Saskatchewan. He moved to Canada to take up wheat farming in 1916 after having spent three years in the United States. Wyers originally turned to sketching as a way to combat boredom while recovering from an illness. It wasn't until he began to work as a guard at a prisoner-of-war camp during the Second World War that this hobby became a serious pursuit. One of the German prisoners provided Wyers with a few books and some rudimentary lessons in painting. The end of the war brought Wyers back to his farm, but he continued to paint during the idle winter months. Wyers sold his farm in 1960 and retired to a one-room shack in Windhorst, Saskatchewan, to paint and invent the odd bit of machinery. While he occasionally returned to memories of his birthplace for inspiration, most of the paintings are records of the Saskatchewan prairies. His style is vivid and full of heavy-bodied men and animals engaged in work or resting after the exertion of ploughing or hauling. Wyers did turn to commercial sources for some of his work, however. Calendars and colouring books provided images of the King and Queen of England, and animal studies. Such paintings show less immediacy than the farm paintings or portraits. *Th. L.*

Wallis, Alfred

Walther-Visino, Therese

Ware, Chris

Wattyne, Jacques van de

Wieçek, Ludwik

Wilson, Scottie

ng Jinxi

Warczygłowa, Zygmunt

ber, Rudolf Felix

Westbroek, Willem

Widja, Ida Bagus

nęk, Maria

Wójtowicz, Maria

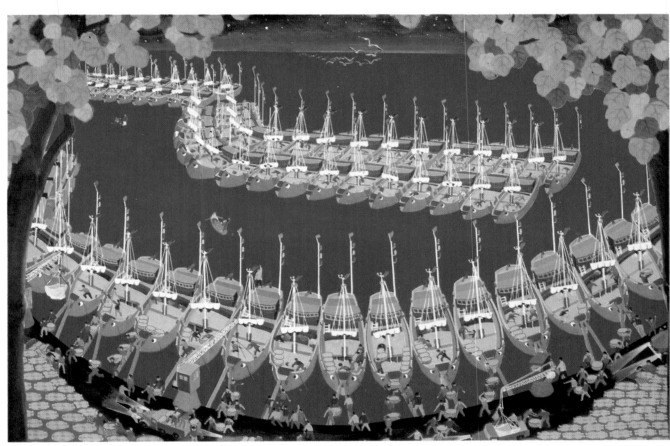

Xia Zengqiang: A Busy Fishing Port

XIA ZENGQIANG (1955)   **China**

Xia Zengqiang was born in the town of Zhangyan, Jinshan county. He attended senior high school and began painting in 1975. "A Busy Fishing Port" is a typical work, displaying a brilliant sense of composition, fine handling of colour and great precision of detail. Boats play an important part in the life of this region, with its many rivers, canals and sea coast. The neatly ranged, identical vessels, however, make this an idealised rather than realistic scene.

They seem identical, but upon closer examination, one can see that on each vessel the arrangement of sacks and human figures is different. It is really a busy fishing port with all people in dynamic movement.

Xia Zengqiang is now a handicraft worker in Qianxu commune, Jinshan county. *N. T.*

Xue Deliang: Reclamation of Land from the Sea

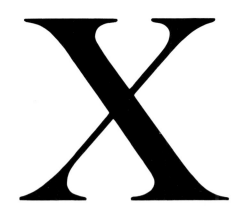
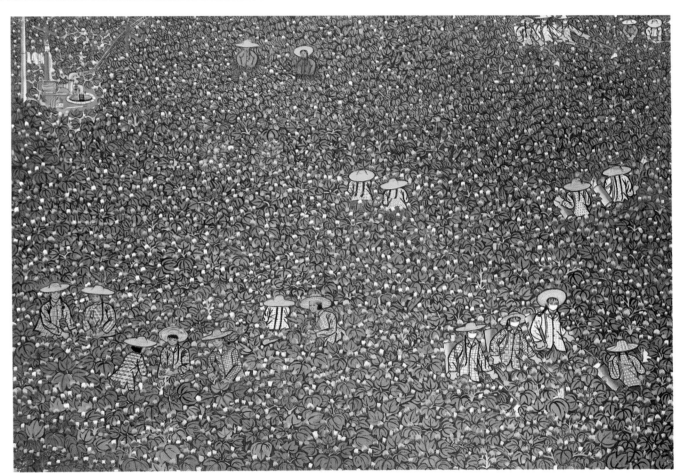

Xu Hengke: Spraying Cotton

XU HENGKE (1927—1975)   China

Xu Hengke is a native of the village of Yekou in Hu county, near Xian, the ancient capital of China. He was born in 1927 and spent his life working on the land, becoming a member of the local farming brigade. In his region the farmer's life is a particularly busy one since there are two harvests annually: one of wheat and one of cotton, both commodities of vital importance for the Chinese economy.

The peasant-painter's awareness of this is one reason why they figure so prominently in his work.

Xu Hengke started painting in 1970. His work "Spraying Cotton" dating from 1974, is akin to pointillism with the dots of white cotton. By the distribution of figures, this talented painter achieved the right perspective.

Xu Hengke continued working in the fields by day and painting in the evenings until his death. *N. T.*

XUE DELIANG (1957)   China

Xue Deliang was born in Jianquo village in Tingxin commune, Jinshan county. He went to junior high school and began painting in 1975. Of peasant stock, he works on the land in the local commune. A good example of his work is "Reclamation of Land from the Sea," illustrating the immense labour invested in increasing the area of much needed arable land. This scene of night work, illuminated by tractor beams, has a somewhat surrealistic feeling. Xue Deliang has skilfully achieved a sense of depth and of the scope of the work involved. *N. T.*

Yamashita, Kiyoshi: The Island of Sacura

YAMASHITA, KIYOSHI — Japan
YAXLEY, W. E. (BILL) — Australia
YCAZA, ADELA VARGAS DE — Nicaragua
YOAKUM, JOSEPH — USA

Yamashita, Kiyoshi

Yoakum, Joseph

Yamashita, Kiyoshi: Toshigu Shrine in Ueno

YAMASHITA, KIYOSHI (1922—1971)   Japan

Kiyoshi Yamashita, son of poor farmers, was one and a half years old when his family's house burned down during a great earthquake in Kanto. At the age of ten, he lost his father. His childhood was spent in poverty. At the age of three, he contracted a serious illness and, probably as a result, began to stutter. In elementary school, he was a backward pupil, mocked by the other children and given to rough behaviour. When he was twelve years old, he was admitted to an institute for mentally-retarded children, where he learned to make collages and from these seemed to find some spiritual stability.

In 1937 a small exhibition was held of works by the children of the institute. His own travelled to all parts of Japan and were exceptionally well-received, winning praise from top painters and writers. However, even the stability he had attained did not satisfy him and he suddenly fled from the institute to become a vagabond. After returning just as suddenly as he had left, he spent his days making collages and writing a diary.

In 1953 the press gave him considerable publicity and the "Exhibition of Kiyoshi Yamashita," held soon after, become exceedingly popular.

In 1961, while travelling in Europe, he worked constantly on sketches, collages, oil paintings, paintings on porcelain and batik. (See portrait of the artist, p. 622). S. K.

YAXLEY, W. E. (BILL) (1943)   Australia

Bill Yaxley was born in Melbourne and spent his childhood in Shepparton in northern Victoria.

He began to paint about 1960. During this time he supported himself as a gold prospector, a driller and a factory hand, travelling around Australia and later going overseas to Canada and the United Kingdom. He also worked for a time

YCAZA, ADELA VARGAS DE (1910)   Nicaragua

Adela Vargas de Ycaza was born in 1910 in Granada (Nicaragua). She worked in a flower shop and after her marriage to Luis Ycaza Reyes moved to León. The former flower seller began to paint in 1967, at the age of 57, at the urging of her son Alberto.

Adela de Ycaza paints scenes from history, the Bible and popular legend. The poems of Felix Rubén Dario, friend of Mallarmé and Verlaine, also stirred her fantasy. Dario's symbolic poesy about Spanish-Indian ancestors fused the traditional and modern movements. Adela de Ycaza

Ycaza, Adela Vargas de: Sonatina

in New Zealand, fruit picking, scrub cutting and prawning in various districts.

With his family Billy Yaxley has now settled down on a fruit farm in Queensland, dividing his time between his trees and animals and his compulsion to record on canvas the country life around him.

He was encouraged in his art by John Maynard, Director of the Auckland Museum Gallery. B. McC.

translates his humanistic dreams into naive visual images.

The religious themes in the paintings of Ycaza often blend with the themes of great literature. Christian saints occasionally merge with figures from the myths of Africa and of the Indians. The religious and legendary world of Ycaza's images does not resemble the pious vision of medieval mystics: her genuine gift gives her artificial scenery a festive radiance.

The champion of naive art in Central and South America, José Gomez-Sicre, became aware of her and arranged to have her works shown. She has exhibited in major shows of naive artists in South and Latin America as well as in the United States. *O. B.-M.*

YOAKUM, JOSEPH (1888—1972) USA

The more Joseph Yoakum's fascinating, strangely patterned drawings were exhibited, the more varied became the reports of the chronology of his life. Said to be half back, half Indian, he was born on the Navajo Reservation at Window Rock, Arizona. He told one biographer

from grocery bags and were fantasy or "spiritural" *(sic)* interpretations of real scenes recalled from his travels. He displayed his works in the window of his home, offering them for sale at a quarter of a dollar each, and was thus discovered by John Hapgood, a college instructor. Hapgood arranged to exhibit the work (at better prices) in a local coffee house, and Yoakum's work ultimately reached the Phyllis Kind Gallery in Chicago and was given a small one-man show at the Whitney Museum in New York. Yoakum died on Christmas day, 1972. *(See portrait of the artist, p. 622). J. W.*

Yamashita, Kiyoshi: Self-portrait

Yaxley, W. E.: On the Way to Andy's Place

that he drove a delivery wagon in Walnut Grove, Missouri, was a railroad porter, worked in a roundhouse; another summary of his life says that in 1901 he ran away to join a circus, went to China with Buffalo Bill, joined the Ringling Brothers Circus as personal valet to John Ringling, and subsequently went around the world as a stowaway and hobo, travelling through Europe, Russia, Palestine, China, Siberia, Australia and Canada. He said he saw service in France during the First World War, and continued his travels, this time through South and Central America and Mexico. During his *wanderlust* years he managed to marry twice, and father five children. He finally settled in Chicago's South Side, spending his time reading and studying the Bible.

Yoakum began to draw in 1962, impelled, he said, by a dream in which "the Lord gave me instructions." His structurally similar yet individualistically patterned drawings were first done with pencil or ballpoint pens on brown paper

Yoakum, Joseph: Imperial Valley, California Bay

Zagajewski, Stanisław

Zakarjan, Gajk

Zarapišvili, Emma

Zaznobin, Vladimir Nikolaev

Zelenka, Horymír

Zhu Xi

Žil'cov, Fedor Aleksandrovič

ZAGAJEWSKI, STANISŁAW — Poland
ŽÁK, VÁCLAV — Czechoslovakia
ZAKARJAN, GAJK — USSR
ZANGOUDAKIS, DEMETRIOS — Greece
ZARAPIŠVILI, EMMA — USSR
ZAZNOBIN, VLADIMIR NIKOLAEVIČ — USSR
ZELDIS, MALCAH — USA
ZELENKA, HORYMÍR — Czechoslovakia
ZHANG FENYING — China
ZHONG DEXIANG — China
ZHU XI — China
ŽIL'COV, FEDOR ALEKSANDROVIČ — USSR
ZISSIS, SOTTIRIS — Greece

ŽIVANOVIĆ, SLOBODAN — Yugoslavia
ZOGRAPHOS, PANAYOTIS — Greece
ZOGRAPHOS, TASSOS — Greece
ZOMER, ANNA — Netherlands
"ZU CAMPOS", JESUINO — Brazil

Žák, Václav: Red City

ZAGAJEWSKI, STANISŁAW (1927)   Poland

Stanisław Zagajewski, born in Warsaw, now lives in Włocławek. When he was barely two years old, his mother abandoned him on the doorstep of a church. He spent his childhood and early manhood in church educational institutions, doing various kinds of work: gardener, shepherd, cook, bookbinder, tailor, mason, porter, watchman and so on. In 1962, he began modelling in clay, devoting all his spare time to his hobby. For years he lived in Warsaw in a small hut without any heating. There he modelled his visions in clay: birds, strange animals, religious scenes, conceived expressively and unconventionally. In 1972 he moved to Włocławek and found employment in a ceramics factory, which gave him the opportunity to fire his sculptures. He is extremely religious and each year makes the pilgrimage to Czestochowa. Half of what he earns is donated to the Church and with the other half he lives a modest life. Despite his small means, he helps poor students. "Jesus Christ has not given me talent so that I should use it for commerce," he says. He had his first exhibition in Warsaw in 1963. Since then he has had many one-man shows in Poland and abroad, and his works have been on display in group exhibitions in the USA, France and West Germany. The Museum in Włocławek possesses about a hundred of his works; a smaller collection is in the State Ethnographic Museum in Warsaw and some are in the collection of L. Zimmerer. *(See the picture, p. 74 and the portrait of the artist, p. 626). A. J.*

ŽÁK, VÁCLAV (1906) Czechoslovakia

Václav Žák was born in Velké Kyšice, near Kladno. At the age of four the right side of his body became paralysed as a consequence of convulsions and this condemned him to the life of an outsider, as far as practical activity was concerned. In 1927 he began buying and collecting animal skins. In 1952, after a visit to Mariánské Lázně, he began painting. After modest beginnings, an absolute deluge of imaginative power was unleashed. No surface was safe from Žák's mania for painting. Apart from glass panes he painted doors and staircases, walls and

Zakarian, Gaik: In a Cobbler's Workshop

Zarapishvili, Emma: Dance

rabbit-hutches. He decorated his house-front with Jan Kozina and Kuneš of Bělovic, heroes from Bohemian history, three metres tall. This house in the bleak district called "America," near Unhošt, along with its artistic tenant, have become a legend in Prague intellectual circles since 1960. Not unnaturally, from 1962 there ensued not only one-man shows and television programmes but a literary account by Bohumil Hrabál, from which a film was subsequently made. Žák's wildly expressive fairy-tale pictures have become familiar to visitors to many international exhibitions. The cripple has shown the philistines his worth.

The popular storytellers' archetypes are reproduced in a very generalised form in Žák's ideal world, which has remained fixed on the level of a child. Unknown riders, unknown cities, towers, monuments and sights, unknown rivers and birds emerge from the subconscious in a surge of brilliant colours. *A. P.*

←

Zangoudakis, Demetrios: Ploughing Scene

ZAKARJAN, GAJK (1925) USSR
ZAKARIAN, GAIK

Gaik Zakarian was born to an Armenian family in Athens. After residing in Lebanon from the age of three, he was repatriated in 1946 at the age of twenty-one to Soviet Armenia. He has been electrician and cobbler. He began to paint in 1963 when, moving into a new flat, he wished to decorate it. He has only a general elementary schooling. The favourite subjects of his oils (on cardboard or canvas) are the human being and his life, and still-lifes. He prefers genre scenes from a familiar environment, especially dealing with work, such as "Carpet Weaving,"

"Baker," "Basturma" (a national dish) or "Cobblers," in which last picture he lovingly depicts the tools of the trade, the lamp and other accessories, as he does in the carpet-weaving picture. Actually these accessories, which are now dispensed with in modern work processes, are partly responsible for the singular charm of these pictures; they provide the background for the life of the people he depicts, who are clearly out of proportion. The author made his debut at a group showing in Yerevan in 1965, while in 1982 he had a one-man show at the Yerevan Museum of Modern Art, where some of his pictures are on view. *(See portrait of the artist, p. 626). N. Sh.*

ZANGOUDAKIS, DEMETRIOS (1940) Greece

Demetrios Zangoudakis was born in Peristeri, a working-class district of Athens, and still lives in the same area, where he works as an ironmonger. The artist has installed an elementary sculpture workshop in primitive premises where he also keeps hens. Zangoudakis' subject-matter is a reflection of the crossing of different influences and stimuli: some of his sculptures may be interpreted as his instinctive response to his surroundings and contemporary Greek reality, while others are the more typical creations of a naive artist of his particular background. He uses an individual technique of fitting together small fragments of sheet iron in order to make figures of men and women and sometimes other things as well. Such works are hollow inside and the artist has deliberately left joinings uncovered in order to produce a more decorative

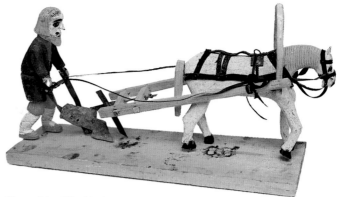

Zaznobin, Vladimir Nikolayevich: Ploughman

ZAZNOBIN, VLADIMIR NIKOLAEVIČ (1900—1981)   USSR
ZAZNOBIN, VLADIMIR NIKOLAYEVICH

V. N. Zaznobin was born of peasant stock. He fought in the Russian Civil War in 1919 and in the Second World War. A carpenter by trade, he lived in the village of Gorky near Yaroslavl, a hundred or so kilometres from Moscow. In his garden he kept amusing mobile wooden figures of a bear and a blacksmith alternately hammering at a forge or sawyers working in turn, or an old woman weaving at a loom. Along with Zhiltsov, he was one of the inventors of popular carved wooden "statues." These wind-driven scarecrows are capable of acting out "performances" reminiscent of the mummers of old. Zaznobin made them of aspen, painted them and provided them with clockwork arrangements not only to make them move but also to act and produce noises. He also contrived multi-figure compositions on rustic themes such as "Threshing" and "Flax Scutching." He combined creative fantasy with living reality. Though these wooden figures follow the rules of peasant art, they are largely reminiscent of ancient Russian pagan idols wherein the subject-matter determined the approach to shape. They are highly conventional, frontal and symmetrical. He also carved simple, static, rather crude, wooden statues. He was represented at all-Russian exhibitions in 1973 and 1977 and at a USSR exhibition in 1974. In 1981 he had a one-man show at the History and Art Museum of Pereslavl-Zalessky near Yaroslavl, where many of his works are preserved. He has works in Suzdal, Yaroslavl, Moscow and Leningrad Museums. *(See portrait of the artist, p. 626). N. Sh.*

Zeldis, Malcah: Lincoln in Front of His Tent

effect. His small sculptures, up to half a metre high, are differentiated by both their technique and their subject-matter. They usually show everyday scenes and occupations such as ploughing, the work of the ironmonger and the woodcutter, a girl watering flowers, a fish, a spider, or flowers. These are made of small iron tubes and other iron fragments.

This artist's work is virtually unknown to the wider public and has only been shown in one or two group exhibitions in Athens. *A. T.*

ZARAPIŠVILI, EMMA (1940)   USSR
ZARAPISHVILI, EMMA

Of Tartar nationality, Emma Zarapishvili was born in the city of Yangiul in Uzbekistan. In 1957 she moved to Tbilisi, having married a Georgian graphic artist. Her style is gifted, emotional, temperamental. Every aspect of her work derives from fantasy, from her resurrection of the past. Emma Zarapishvili's works are highly expressive, revealing a fullness of vision, while the somewhat deliberately deformed image betrays a link with professional art. The colourfulness and specific approach impart a full-blooded, even sensual, note. Though the subject is somewhat abstract, the artist seeks to generalise, arriving at this aim through a unity of drawing and colour. She has been represented at republican and USSR group exhibitions of popular and amateur art and in 1969 had a one-woman show in Tbilisi. *(See portrait of the artist, p. 626). N. Sh.*

ZELDIS, MALCAH (1931)   USA

Malcah Zeldis was born in New York but grew up in Detroit, Michigan. Her mother had been a dancer, and her father, who ran a window-washing business, a competent "Sunday painter." When Malcah, at sixteen, ventured into painting, they suggested she would do better to direct her sights toward marriage. She did marry, at nineteen, and moved to Israel, where she tried to paint again. Though encouraged by a prominent Israeli artist, the birth of two children and work on a collective farm temporarily stifled her ambition.

Zeldis's work is a very personal perception of her own life, her experiences, her feelings. Thus, though there are memories of childhood and family, street scenes where she lives and the like, her emotional reactions to larger events such as Hiroshima and My Lai, or her readings about Lincoln, have produced paintings that are as personal as any of her family scenes; she is essentially doing a biography of herself through her work — not a biography of external events, necessarily, but of her internal life. She has said that "as an artist you are creating yourself in your art, you are wrestling with yourself. You create yourself through your work." She and her family, or people she has met are somewhere in almost all her paintings. The moods of her paintings change as does the tenor of her life. *J. W.*

The titles of this self-taught painter's pictures sound symptomatic in themselves: "Red Flowers," "Childhood Is Done," "Red Scarf," "Autumn," "Factory," "Black Cloud." The last is a heavily painted picture, which consists of decoratively interlocked symbolic areas, and possesses unusual expressive power. *(See portrait of the artist, p. 626). A. P.*

ZHANG FENYING (1931)   China

Zhang Fenying was born in Feng county. She attended elementary school and is now a

Zelenka, Horymír: I Dreamed of a Young Girl

Zhang Fenying: Dressing Table

ZELENKA, HORYMÍR (1931)   Czechoslovakia

Horymír Zelenka spent his childhood in Pozorka, where he attended elementary and intermediate schools. He always liked drawing and intended to become a potter. However, his parents apprenticed him to a confectioner. Later, he went on to study food science at the Technical Academy in Prague. Even then he used to draw and write poems. He was subsequently employed as a confectionery expert with a state firm. When naive talent was being searched for in 1962—1963, a correspondent in the cultural field wrote: "There are any number of amateur painters here, but only one of them has true individuality — Zelenka." The tempera studies that were submitted confirmed that their author was no intruder in the landscape of naive art. Poems, literature and history also helped to inspire Zelenka's vision. His powerful expressiveness is based on the contrasts offered by thickly painted, leaf-shaped structures, in which yellow and gold are designed to enunciate something exquisite and supernatural.

member of the seed farm of Caojing commune, Jin Shan county. Since starting painting in 1978, she has shown a talent for depicting rural customs, traditional folk tales and domestic scenes. Typical works include "Dressing Table" and "Making Rice Dumplings on January 15 of the Lunar Calendar." "Dressing Table" illustrates the artist's idea of prosperity, with treasured objects which are probably more wishful thinking than reality for most peasant households. *N. T.*

ZHONG DEXIANG (1955)   China

Zhong Dexiang was born in Xinnon village in Fengwei commune, Jin Shan county. He attended junior high school and began painting in 1976. More than most of his fellow-painters he is inclined to lyrical, romantic subjects rather than farming activities. Characteristic works are "Duck Cages" and "Nightfall." In the latter, the static, formalised bushes contrast with the movement of the innumerable birds gathering at dusk. *N. T.*

ZHU XI (1952)   China

Zhu Xi is from Quian Yian Yu commune. He is a graduate of a secondary brigadiers' school, where he was first introduced to traditional Chinese painting. He loved drawing and copied the pictures, especially those of flowers and birds. After finishing school, he worked in an agricultural brigade and joined the Jin Shan circle of painters.

"I love autumn best, not only because of the fruits of nature but also the gorgeous golden colours. The work of farm labourers is then crowned by nature and the rich harvest that

ŽIL'COV,   USSR
FEDOR ALEKSANDROVIČ (1894)
ZHILTSOV, FYODOR ALEXANDROVICH

F. A. Zhiltsov resides in the village of Vertlovo near Yaroslavl. He used to carve wind-driven scarecrows of aspen or alder, and now makes wooden figures of soldiers jointed by wire, in memory of the past war in which he fought. He likes to place these figures on a fence. As a result, long-distance truck drivers going through Zhiltsov's village often stop to look and sometimes buy these figures with their pipes, concertinas, military insignia and charcoal-drawn

Zhong Dexiang: Nightfall

Zhu Xi: Girls Making a Net

rewards their efforts." The first picture painted by Zhu Xi, "Granary Full of Golden Wheat," portrays the riches of autumn. In the foreground, Zhu Xi has painted the making of thatch roofs. In the background a silo is being filled by conveyer belt, with the same belt repeated five times in a row to accentuate the richness of the harvest. In the middle ground, people in the fields are gathering crops and a multitude of peasants are carrying wheat in sacks. Everyone seems to be in a hurry. To show all the work done during harvest time, the young artist has placed the wheat field between the silo and conveyer belt. The painting is given cohesion by the colour of old gold. *(See portrait of the artist, p. 626). N. T.*

moustaches. The figures are chunks of wood enlivened by human features imparted by means of a knife. The arms are nailed on. Painted red and blue, the figures wear medals, sashes and stars made of paper, foil or tin. The carver displays features in line with traditional folk art, even though he was the first in the neighbourhood to carve such figures. Earlier generations carved domestic utensils, bee-hives and birdhouses, but Zhiltsov, out of a creative urge, struck out into the woods across the stream and started carving figures which, though archaic in form, are traditional in that they proceed from a mentality associated with the patriarchal mode of life and a genetically-inherited understanding of the canons of collective peasant art. However, as he seeks self-expression he is a true naive amateur artist. Among his soldier figures are representations of his wife, whose efforts to bring up their children during the war he equates with martial heroism. In a gust of wind his wooden soldiers twirl, dance and wave their arms. He was represented at all-Russian group shows in 1973 and 1977, and at USSR shows in 1974 and again in 1977. His works are in museums and private collections. *(See portrait of the artist, p. 626). N. Sh.* →

ZISSIS, SOTTIRIS (1902)   Greece

Sottiris Zissis was born in the village of Halastra (Pyrgos) near Thessalonika and has been living in this city ever since 1937. He worked as a zincographer, and started to paint systematically after he retired. His subjects are scenes from the Balkan Wars of 1912—1913 and from the German occupation of Thessalonika in the Second World War, picturesque old customs, farming occupations and other aspects of village life: the heroes of the Balkan Wars, the cobbled narrow streets of the old city of Thessalonika, its horse-drawn trams, its street-cleaners, the

ŽIVANOVIĆ, SLOBODAN (1943)   Yugoslavia

Born in the village of Gornji Račnik near Svetozarevo, Serbia, Živanović is an agricultural technician by profession, who now lives in Svetozarevo. In 1968, he started painting in oil on canvas, using a filigree-like technique, which gives his pictures the beauty of intricate lacework, as is well illustrated in the reproduction of his "Basket Weavers" (1970). He has been represented in many group exhibitions in Yugoslavia and abroad, and has had one-man shows in Svetozarevo and Belgrade. *N. T.*

Zhiltsov, Fyodor Alexandrovich: A Soldier and His Wife

Zissis, Sottiris: Village Wedding at Roumlouki

Živanović, Slobodan: Basket Weavers

outskirts of town and the town walls, its street butchers, its lemon and yoghurt vendors, its old houses and the difficult times of its German occupation form one cycle of his repertory. Other paintings illustrate his memories of everyday life in the village: Macedonian dances, night work in the village, the beautiful tales told by his grandmother, different festivities, threshing, the celebration of May Day, the crossing of the River Vardar before bridges were built, winter in Macedonia, the village oven, or the sieve-makers. In the typical manner of folk painters he adds explanatory inscriptions to his compositions, in his case characteristic excerpts from different writers, in order to help the viewer understand their content.

Zissis' work is not very widely known. It was presented in two one-man shows in Thessalonika and in a group exhibition in Piraeus. *A. T.*

ŽIVKOVIĆ, BOGOSAV see **BOGOSAV (ŽIVKOVIĆ)**

ZOGRAPHOS, PANAYOTIS   Greece

Born in Vordonia, a village in Laconia in the Peloponnesus, Panayotis Zographos worked as a hagiographer until 1836, when he was hired by General Ioannis Makriyannis, a leading figure of the Greek Revolution of 1821, who wanted illustrated records of its main battles. Zographos was helped in this by his two sons (one named Dimitris and another whose name is unknown), though it is uncertain whether they all worked first series for himself and giving away the other four: one to the king of Greece, and the other three to the ambassadors of Britain, France and Russia. These series differ considerably from one another. His aim was to circulate them in various parts of Europe to tell people the real story of the Greek Revolution. The originals of these were discovered in 1909 in Rome by Ioannis Gennadios, and are now in the Gennadion Library in Athens. The eight surviving oil paintings of the first series are in the Historical Museum, Athens. The series given to the British ambassador is in Windsor Castle, but the fates of the series given

Zographos, Panayotis: The First Battle of the Greeks against the Turks on the Alemana Bridge

simultaneously or the sons took over after their father's death. The work, started in 1836 and completed in 1839, consisted of five series of twenty-five pictures each, the first comprising oil paintings on wood and the other four watercolours. It seems certain that Panayotis Zographos was responsible for the first series, and also for the mosaic decorating the general's courtyard. The wealth of colours, rhythmic movement and ability to combine events from different times and places reveal him to have been a genuine folk artist trained in the tradition of post-Byzantine ecclesiastical painting. In contrast, the work of his sons is somewhat academic in style, displaying a knowledge of perspective and skilful drawing.

On the completion of the commission, Makriyannis announced his intention of keeping the to the French and Russian ambassadors are unknown. With the exception of three pictures, the others show famous battles and events of the Greek Revolution. The scenes are in miniature, producing a tapestry-like effect; the schematic rendering of the costumes and horses recalls Persian miniatures. The modelling of the figures and lack of interest in naturalistic representation of landscape attest to the influence of Byzantine art. Certain features also remind us of the general's cartographic studies; these, together with a love of polychromy, sometimes lead to excessive stylisation and emphasis on the purely decorative. However, the final product is always genuine and charming, full of life and emotional warmth. *A. T.*

ZOGRAPHOS, TASSOS   Greece

Tassos Zographos was born in Livadia, a town at the foot of Mount Parnassos, and never set eyes on the sea until the age of eleven. With the outbreak of the war he moved with his family to Athens, where he experienced famine and extreme hardship. His first works, done during the occupation, were linocuts and lettering for resistance leaflets. After the war he started working for the theatre mostly as a stage-designer, distinguishing himself in this field. He also worked for the cinema, for many films made in the period 1955—1975.

standing on deserted shores with some reminiscences of the past, Mediterranean gardens, the Greek flag, old-fashioned chairs and cameras, are some of his favourite motifs. The *gorgones* invariably resemble his wife Effie; long-haired and broad-hipped, imposing and irresistibly attractive, they seem like a personification of ideal femininity. In addition, his typical figure of a hero of the Greek War of Independence of 1821 sometimes shares the features of his heroic father, who greatly influenced his ideas and beliefs.

Zographos believes in the existence of two basic colours, white and black, and says that the

Zographos, Tassos: Karavi-Karavaki

Zographos draws his inspiration from the folk tradition. Showing a healthy respect for it, he has made a skilful attempt to extend and revive it. Painting with his heart rather than his mind, he concentrates on the subjects he loves and enjoys, and this may be the secret of the fascination exerted by his pictures. In reality he uses a rather limited number of elements in infinite ingenious and attractive combinations. In addition to the sky, the sea and the earth, the winged youths that may stand for Eros or for personifications of winds, or even for *bouzouki* players, neoclassical houses, mermaids *(gorgones)*, ships, orange and cypress trees, pebbles, cobbled courts, flowers and flower-pots, ships departing and leaving smoke behind, garlands, white gateways, elaborate iron doors or half-open doors with a nude female emerging from them, famous couples with attributes characteristic of the period in which they lived, or unknown couples

others simply complement them. He makes the most of space, which is not treated like something conventional, but plays the same role as in the theatre — a background for the theme.

Zographos has held two one-man shows in Athens and one in Yannina, and has taken part in group exhibitions in Athens and Piraeus. *A. T.*

ZOMER,   Netherlands
ANNA (1899—1970)

Anna Zomer was born in Houten, and died in Bunnik, both villages in the immediate vicinity of Utrecht. A peasant her whole life, she began to paint in 1954 after seeing, by chance, the pictures of a woman painter in her neighbourhood. She sought her subjects in her surroundings: peasant homes and picturesque places like Amelisweerd. Just because she was a peasant, she directly experienced the seasons of the year and one of her most famous works is an allegorical painting of all twelve months. After retiring, she lived in a house on her family's land, devoting herself entirely to painting. A very religious person, she participated in the processions in Lourdes, France, and in Kevelaer, Germany, which provided the material for several of her paintings. Also well-known is her interior "Gentleman Reading in Ijselmuide," a touching painting of an elderly man sitting near the window of a Dutch middle-class drawing room. Opposite him is an empty chair. A widow had painted a widower. *N. E.*

"ZU CAMPOS", JESUINO (1939)　　Brazil

Jesuino Campos — "Zu" — was born in Vitória de Conquista, Baía. He first started painting when he became employed as a guide and nightwatchman for the Sacred Art Museum, Baía.

Zu Campos favours religious representations, usually carried out in glossy house paints. His pictures are not always on routine flat surfaces; they also appear as decoration on children's pushcarts and similar toy vehicles. His images are generally rendered against black or dark backgrounds. *Sh. W.*

Zographos, Tassos: Gate by the Sea

Zomer, Anna. A Gentleman Reading

"Zu Campos", Jesuino: Dance

Historical Surveys
of Naive Art
in Individual Countries

AFRICA
ARGENTINA
AUSTRALIA
BELGIUM
BRAZIL
CANADA
CHINA
CZECHOSLOVAKIA
FRANCE
EAST GERMANY
WEST GERMANY
GREAT BRITAIN AND EIRE
GREECE
HAITI
HUNGARY
INDONESIA (BALI)
ISRAEL
ITALY
JAPAN
MEXICO
NETHERLANDS
NICARAGUA
POLAND
ROMANIA
SWITZERLAND
USA
USSR
VENEZUELA
YUGOSLAVIA

Gerhard Schoenberner

AFRICA

During the last two decades, technical communication between the industrial nations and the African continent has developed rapidly. Whether our knowledge and mutual understanding has been advanced correspondingly is open to doubt. On both sides there is frequently nothing more than a superficial recognition of certain features and phenomena with no understanding of their origins or significance.

Although few places now remain where no European has ever set foot, our information is inevitably still patchy and imperfect. This is true, amongst other things, of African art. For this reason a topical survey of naive art based on the author's own observation as well as accounts by others cannot be complete. Nevertheless, certain characteristic features and lines of development may be identified which can be observed in a number of places in Africa.

The General Situation. The African continent is involved in rapid technological, economic, social and cultural change. Colonialism introduced new economic structures, languages and political systems which have continued to have their effects even after the achievement of independence. Although they affect only part of the population, technology, coupled with the market forces of the capitalist consumer society and its ideology as epitomised in the cheap imported products of the entertainment industry, change the actual circumstances of life as well as the consciousness of individuals living in this environment.

The urban African despises evidence of cultural achievement in his own past, regarding it merely as the expression of a primitive and backward society, whereas the photographic naturalism of American cinema posters appeals to him as true art. Mass-produced consumer goods made of plastic and synthetics, with their labour-saving potential, seem to him a vast improvement on the hand-carved bowl and hand-woven, home-dyed cloth.

The descendants of the wood-carvers and bronze-founders have discovered new customers in the tourist market, whom they supply with series-produced, highly polished copies that retain nothing of the inner tensions and the expressive power of the originals. Production is determined by whatever finds favour, that is, by whatever can most easily be sold, so that the bad taste of the new class of purchasers gradually distorts the product beyond recognition. The art of the craftsman becomes a mere traffic in art, tribal art degenerates into "airport art" (Frank McEwen), which offers the last remnants of a great tradition in a banal and marketable form.

The standardised souvenir pictures offered for sale to travellers at African airports are of similar quality: hunting scenes with wild animals, women grinding millet against a background of mud huts, canoes on a moonlit river bank crowned with palm trees. We must, therefore, devote all the more care and attention to singling out those original talents and artistic experiments that fortunately also exist in abundance, although are more difficult to find.

Early Beginnings. The first discovery of a black African naive artist dates back more than half a century. It was in 1929 that works by the Congolese artist *Lubaki* were first exhibited at the Palais des Beaux Arts in Brussels, at the instigation of Gaston-Denis Périer.

This first exhibition was followed in the next few years by a number of others in Geneva, Brussels, Paris and Naples, which brought to public notice three younger artists besides Lubaki — *Djilatendo, Ngoma* and *Masalai*. All four were ivory carvers who had begun to produce drawings and watercolours that incorporated traditional designs, motifs and scenes from African life with a technique entirely new to Africa.

A combination of extreme simplicity and finesse, poetry and a secure sense of form constitutes the high aesthetic appeal of these pieces. Lubaki and Djilatendo in particular are still unrivalled in this respect. In their works, the decorative animal motifs adopted from rock drawings and the reliefs that once adorned the carved double doors of mud huts are combined with figurative elements to form narrative pictures of great beauty. Their works are amongst the finest products of African art in this century. Both these painters made the transition to professional status and stand apart from the general line of development. They achieved a standing in art which accorded them a place in the black continent comparable to that occupied by Frenchman Henri Rousseau among the naive artists of Europe.

Sign Painters. The first thing that strikes the foreign visitor nowadays, even before he comes to discover individual artists, are the various forms of applied art that form part of the general impression of African towns and cities. Everywhere in West Africa, in the states of the Sahel zone, as well as in Central Africa and Zaire, in streets and market places, on mud huts and corrugated-iron shanties are crude sign-boards, on which small craftsmen proclaim their skill and shopkeepers advertise their wares. Modes of production and the products, the craftsman and his customer are depicted in a simple pictorial language. These advertisements are aimed at visitors from the surrounding rural districts unfamiliar with the town and often illiterate. Nevertheless, there is frequently a caption in French or English, the language of the former colonial power, indicating the trade, less frequently the name of the proprietor: "Ici bon coiffeur," for example, or "Couture, hommes et femmes." The lettering is partly done by hand but stencils are also used. A tailor sits at his sewing-machine in conversation with a customer; a number of dresses and pairs of trousers in the upper part of the picture illustrate his wares — above that stands the legend, "Ici tailleur." A mechanic, a spanner in his hands, tinkers with a motor-bike: the lettering recommends him as "Bon spécialiste pour toutes marques," although his clientele probably also travel by bicycle.

The most common of these signs belong to hairdressers. They mostly display a range of hair-styles with fanciful names, from Cock's Comb and Ape's Cap to Policeman, Afro, Beatles and Kennedy Cut. Usually the signs are fastened to the outside wall of the "Salon de luxe" that they advertise. Sometimes life-size figures are also painted on the inner surfaces of the door-shutters through which the shop is entered.

The classical colours of advertisement predominate: blue and yellow or red and green. The pictures are done in oil-paints or motor-car enamels on cardboard, plywood or hardboard and secured with nails or wire attached to the upper edge, or else by holes bored at the corners.

What we have here is plebeian street painting with elements of pop-art, inspired, it is true, by cinema posters, magazines and commercial advertising, but nevertheless possessing a distinctive style of its own. Often the sign painters decorate lorries and adorn discotheques with murals. Some of them also supply large-scale portraits painted from photographs in which they exhibit the full range of their talents. Whereas the rows of full-face pictures on the hairdressers' signs seem stiff, as though cut out of cardboard, the artist strives in these portraits to achieve plasticity and individual expression. These painters are, for the most part, little more than working-class individuals without formal training who earn a fairly precarious living in this fashion. They tend not to regard themselves as artists, but sign their paintings all the same for purposes of advertisement. In the larger towns and commercial centres where more is commissioned, the successful among them have established stalls which also serve as their studios. These are often garnished with portraits of domestic or foreign politicians or pop-stars which are meant to attract the attention of passers-by and to serve as examples of the artist's talent.

In their spare time, one or two of these commission painters also work on landscapes, self-portraits or narratives in a comic-strip style on themes taken from cheap novelettes, a form of market literature particularly popular in Nigeria.

In recent years the printed advertising placards of large foreign companies which now feature on shops selling gramophone records or bicycles have ousted the cheerful and fanciful sign paintings in many places. Their originality has declined along with their number, since the remaining customers, hairdressers and small craftsmen, tend to take the new images as their model. Even in Upper Volta, where the most original signboards are still to be found thanks to the absence of mass production, it is necessary to make one's way to the streets and markets in the suburbs in order to find good examples of such work.

Truck Art. Another feature of applied art in everyday life is the painting of commercial vehicles, known as "truck art." In Ghana, the popular *mammy lorries*, which serve as mini-buses, are adorned with pictures of flowers and pious legends reminding the passenger that he is in fact placing himself in God's hands the moment he boards the vehicle.

In Nigeria, truck art has developed into a popular genre which can be called naive only in exceptional cases, but which should at least be mentioned in passing. Here, too, we find floral motifs and aphorisms, not always of a devout kind, often proclaiming the robust slogans of the drivers. Not only the rear of the driver's cab and the sides of the vehicle, but even the doors and the mud-guard are covered with small-scale drawings. The main designs are situated, however, on the tailboard of the truck. Here it is the manly heroes of urban youth that rule — James Bond and Superman, Django, Bruce Lee and Kung Fu, extricating themselves by brute force or by dint of superhuman powers from the most perilous of situations, eliminating their adversaries with revolver or karate blows, and thus commanding the respect of all around them. All this is painted with some skill and technical accomplishment, with brisk and energetic brushwork of a rough and banal kind; the scenes are clearly copied from the still photographs of cinema advertisements but are modified and simplified to give even more the effect of garish placards.

Jack Prichett and the photographer Lawrence Manning spent a number of months interviewing the lorry drivers with the aim of registering the frequency of particular motifs and the locality of their origin. It would appear from their survey that the images copied from the cinema are generally to be found in commercial cities in the industrial north of the country.

Side by side with scenes of brutal combat, there are occasionally pictures of hunting, in which traditional and modern elements are mingled: the huntsman who has just brought down a lion with his bow and arrow is clad in blue jeans and high-heeled cowboy boots. Amongst the animal themes which occur throughout Africa, the most common are birds of prey and lions, both of them symbols of power. Another popular subject that also occasionally turns up as a painting over the front door of houses is the mosque, denoting that the occupier has been on a pilgrimage to Mecca — an indication of the influence of Islam, another form of cultural assimilation.

Individual Talents. Amongst the *protégés* of European art teachers and patrons who have established workshops and art schools in many parts of Africa with varying success and encouraged or guided numerous talented individuals in this way, there are also a number of naive artists. Some of them have acquired international reputations. Although their works may be found today in private collections and museums on both sides of the Atlantic, they lived — and still live — for the most part in poverty. They have had no share in the economic boom which brought prosperity to quite a number of naives in Europe — although often at the cost of commercialisation and consequent loss of their naive creative power.

The first place among the numerous artists of Zaire is occupied by *Alphonse Kiabelua*, who belonged to the circle associated with the Belgian painter Laurent Moonens in Kinshasa. His portraits, which resemble old masks in the purity of their form and deliberate stylisation, are quite near to the traditional spirit of his great predecessors Lubaki and Djilatendo.

In a group of painters originating from the school of Pierre Romain Desfossés (1878—1954) in what was then the Belgian Congo — among them some of Desfossés's houseboys — who put their work on show in Europe and the United States after the war, the most noteworthy is possibly *Pili-Pili*. A consciously naive painter, he pursued a line of development toward the perfection of the craft, only to return to his origins, touching the extremes in both directions.

In Nigeria, which, along with present-day Zaire, can boast the largest number of artists known by name, Ulli Beier, in collaboration with Susanne Wenger and Georgina Betts, discovered a whole series of talents in the sixties, of whom three may be regarded as naive.

The musician and dancer, *Twins Seven Seven*, who sings songs written and set to music by himself, uses a dry-point engraving technique to conjure up the submerged world of Africa's ghosts and demons in drawings of fanciful complexity. The coppersmith *Asiru Olatunde* also utilises new materials and new techniques to revive myths and legends from the past: his large-scale compositions hammered on aluminium sheet are reminiscent of the old reliefs carved on wooden doors.

It was not tradition but the modern pop world of advertising which inspired *Middle Art*, possibly the most original sign-painter and portraitist in Africa. At Beier's suggestion, he created original works alongside his commissioned pieces; in these he departed from the mere professional competence of the craftsman and discovered his own personal mode of expression.

The number of part-time painters, among whom are several significant naive artists, is growing in Africa as elsewhere. Many of them remain undiscovered simply because they live in the provinces. Others achieve world-wide renown, like *Ancent Soy* from Nairobi in Kenya, who won first prize in the competition among the African states for the best design of a poster for the twentieth Olympic Games in Munich.

"Square" Painters. Finally, we must mention the so-called "square" painters of Dar-es-Salaam in Tanzania, a group of self-taught artists who have become internationally known. *Tingatinga*, the son of a farmer, who found himself unemployed after working for many years as house-boy in European families and was obliged to seek his living elsewhere, began painting in 1968. He used sheets of Masonite which he cut into square sections, and unmixed enamels, of the type employed in painting bicycles and cars. He rapidly gained success with his pictures of animals and people from the rural life of his childhood. Four of his relatives, *January Linda*, *Simon G. Mpata*, *Adeusi Mmatambwe* and *Kasper Henrik Tedo*, who worked for a time as his assistants, soon became his pupils and eventually his rivals. *Tingatinga* died in 1971, but his school continued. A whole cluster of painters working in his style has since grown up in Dar-es-Salaam and two other places, but frequently they do not have his originality and talent. The best of them is certainly *Hashim B. Mruta*, a cousin of the founder, who combines imagination with a highly discriminating sense of colour values.

Generally speaking, this is popular painting governed by market demand and directed exclusively at foreign customers. A limited number of well-tried motifs — pictures of birds, tortoises and other creatures, as well as scenes from village life — are constantly repeated in a stereotyped fashion with little variation. The pictures are on a large scale and in a homogeneous style, deftly painted in garish colours with a sense of effect but a lack of the depth of inner experience. They have the cheerful simplicity of children tempered by a knowledge of what is likely to please.

Mammy Wata and La Chicotte. In many places in Africa there already exists a naive popular painting that is bought by the local inhabitants. Various pictorial motifs dominate according to region and religion. In those districts of West Africa which have a wealth of rivers, as well as in south-east Nigeria and in Zaire, people still believe in water-spirits, envisaged in various forms and of both sexes. Some are supposed to live in the depths of the water. In popular painting and sculpture, the water-spirit is often represented as a kind of mermaid, who sits like the Lorelei on a rock, combing her long hair, except that here she tends to surround herself with serpents. The most usual name for the *Ndem mmo* (Spirit of the Water) is *Mammy Wata*.

Bill Salmons believes that the imagination of the native population may have been nourished by the sight of the sea-cow, a mammal that frequents the Niger delta, and by their impression of the figure-heads of European schooners that had sailed round these coasts and put in at local harbours ever since the 16th century.

In Zaire the "femme poisson" is also called *mambu muntu* (Crocodile Woman) on account of her shape. The drowned and the demented are regarded as her victims. But it is also considered that she brings good fortune and wealth to anyone who succeeds in gaining her favour. For this reason the miners in the province of Shaba adorn their quarters with her picture.

As Francine Ndiaye rightly points out, the popularity of the miraculous "femme sirène" demonstrates all too clearly "the sense of impotence of the copper miners in Shaba, who constitute a crassly exploited proletariat, for whom wealth can be achieved only through the agency of magic." In this respect there is a manifest link with European folk-tales, which came into being in the age of feudalism and mass poverty. The Mammy Wata pictures represent a popular type of art which is not always naive but often appears to be sweetish and appealing.

Another motif of popular painting in Zaire is equally widespread and reminds us of Belgian colonial rule. It shows a prison yard with a black prisoner being beaten under the supervision of a white warder. This scene, recurring over and over again in various versions, is also purchased by an exclusively working-class clientele, who see in this historical representation a symbol of the continued suppression of the dispossessed.

Paintings on Glass. Paintings on the back of glass panels constitute a particularly attractive variation of naive art found from Benin to Tunisia. It has equal appeal for tourists and for local inhabitants. It is a technique said to have been imported from the Arab world by pilgrims visiting Mecca. In Nigeria it was originally restricted to decorative borders featuring flowers, ornaments and popular sayings. Photographs were placed in the blank space left in the centre of the glass. Later on, lions and elephants, kings, women and motor-cars were painted in the same fashion and the pictures sold for conventional hanging.

The frequency of particular themes varies according to region. In Senegal the paintings on glass generally illustrate devotional tales. They show scenes from the Koran, angels, saints and the prophets of Islam in brilliant colours. Nowadays, however, there are also profane subjects, historical themes like the banishment of Amadou Bamba, the founder of the Murid sect, by the French colonial power, or portraits of an African beauty, decoratively painted in a dazzling variety of colours with a confident simplicity worthy of a black Matisse. The paintings, craftsmanlike in execution but totally naive in theme, are sold by the painters on street stands.

In the bazaars of Tunisia one can also find glass paintings, often small in size, that show either calligraphic representations of verses from the Koran or repetitions of particular motifs from its legends: Adam and Eve with the serpent, Abraham on the point of sacrificing his son, scenes at the court of the Pharaoh. The most frequent items are episodes from the life of the holy Saidna Ali, the fourth Caliph worshipped by the Shiites, who was married to the Prophet's daughter; his sons Hassan and Hussein also occur frequently. Mohammed's horse, Al Bourak, who sometimes assumes the form of a female centaur, is always represented with huge wings.

Occasionally we find paintings on glass by Berbers which have their own individual themes and style. They, too, repeat certain conventional images, but in contrast to the religious paintings of Islam, they are mostly not copied from models but are original works, as naive as children's drawings, but painted with a subtle sense of colour in pastel shades that correspond to the desert landscape. Their favourite theme is the slave market.

Otherwise, the Islamic prohibition of figurative images in the Maghreb states and the whole of Arab North Africa seems to have impeded the development of naive or popular art and restricted the pursuit of drawing and painting to a small stratum of middle-class intellectuals. Some time ago a book appeared in Tunis which introduced six self-taught painters to the public, but the attention devoted to them should be regarded mainly as an echo of the current boom in naive painting. Some early and very original works by anonymous Tunisian artists displayed at the second Triennial of Naive Art in Bratislava in 1969 suggest, however, that in North Africa as well there must be powerful and original talents which have remained undiscovered, possibly owing to religious tradition and the absence of public interest.

Ethiopian Popular Painting. Ethiopia represents a special case within the continent of Africa. It is a country of great ethnic and linguistic diversity that feels affinities with the world of Christianity and Judaism rather than with the Arab world. Large sections of the population embraced Christianity as early as the 4th century. Few works of art have been preserved from the period before the 14th century although murals and decorated ceilings in the numerous churches, icons, portable screens and illuminated books from more than half a millennium which we can still admire today, constitute evidence of a great tradition of religious painting. Rustic and popular in tone, it served, like the *biblia pauperum* of the European Middle Ages, to educate and edify the mass of the population. Although experts have identified Nubian, Byzantine, Italian and Indian influences operating at various times and affecting motifs and style, it is nevertheless obvious that the basic repertoire of stylistic techniques and pictorial forms of expression has survived almost unchanged through the centuries.

Among the characteristic features of this style are the firm delineation of all figures and objects, which gives the pictures the appearance of coloured drawings, the predominance of tempera and the use of unmixed natural colours, where red, green, blue and yellow prevail. As in Byzantine paintings, the pictures are two-dimensional; spatial illusion of perspective and shadow are unknown. Ethiopians are shown full-face, foreigners usually in profile, identified in more recent works by the additional attributes of spectacles, cigarette and camera. Unmistakable are the almond-shaped eyes, from the corners of which the pupils gaze expressively; they appear in animals as well as men in all the pictures.

The themes of the popular painting which also thrived outside the Church were for the most part the life of Christ and legends of the Virgin Mary and the saints. Even nowadays, pictures of St George, Ethiopia's national saint, slaying the dragon remain highly popular. An equally frequent topic is the visit of King Solomon to the Queen of Sheba; another is the fabulous Emperor Menelik I, the child born of their love.

At the end of the last century, this popular painting turned more and more towards secular themes, no doubt due in part to purchasers from abroad. Like the ecclesiastical painters, those who succeeded them regarded themselves as artisans and have therefore remained nameless ever since.

While the eastern part of the country acknowledges Islam, the Coptic faith is predominant in Upper Ethiopia. In popular paintings, the history of these two regions, which were locked in fierce combat in previous centuries, is represented exclusively from the Christian point of view. The battle at Lake Tana in the 16th century, the victorious battle against the Italians at Adua (1896) won by the Emperor Ras Makonnen, father of the Negus Haile Selassie, who was deposed in 1977, and the struggle against the Italian occupation from 1936 to 1941 are all repeatedly painted. Equally favoured are the highly detailed pictures of village life. These have great ethnological value because they record costumes, tools and methods of work as well as traditional customs.

In keeping with ecclesiastical models, anything from twelve to seventy-two individual scenes are accommodated in one picture, ranged in rows, one above the other, each row being in turn sub-divided. Formerly, the sufferings of a saint or the life of a ruler were depicted in this manner. Now everyday themes are treated in the same way. For example, "Life and Work in the Country," or "Twenty-four Scenes from the Life of the Olympic Marathon Winner, Bekela Abebe." A comparison with the historical models, however, reveals an undeniable coarsening of artistic technique.

Along with the stiff, stencil-like, small-scale pictures done on parchment, the supreme craftsmanship of which gives them the appearance of prints, we also find large paintings on canvas, in which themes and style, suggested by traditional models, achieve remarkable vitality through their naive originality and humorous charm.

Sculpture. While there are numerous recognisable varieties of popular and naive painting, the situation with sculpture is much more complex. The decline of tribal art, once of great importance, led to a situation in which typical samples of work in wood and bronze can be admired almost only in European museums, whereas Africa itself is flooded by mass-production pieces designed for the tourist market. Nowadays considerable efforts are necessary to unearth even authentic copies of original masks and figurines, which are often "pickled" to make them look old, since the true originals have become rare and impossibly expensive.

Among the wood-carvers of the Makonde in Kenya and Tanzania, whose highly developed craft is also increasingly threatened by commercialisation, there can still be found individuals who have assimilated their ancient heritage and are capable of developing it in true creative vein.

In this respect the so-called "Colon" sculptures, only lately discovered by the international art market, are remarkable: these are representations of European officials and policemen with their black servants, which bring to life scenes and figures from the colonial era when they were created. Here, the traditional art of woodcarving discovered a novel set of themes that only disappeared with the independence of African States in the sixties of our century.

An attempt to absorb elements of ancient folk art is also shown in the work of a number of artists who co-operated, under the guidance of Susanne Wenger, in decorating the Sacred Grove of the Yoruba tribe in Oshogbo; this is particularly true of the severe, sacred wooden figures by *Kasali* and the carved tree trunks of *Buraimoh Gbadamosi*, reminiscent of totem poles. The cement reliefs and sculptures produced by the former brick-layers, *Ojewale*, *Lani* and *Adebisi Akanji* are also worthy of mention; they have revived a craft previously practised in their trade to decorate the walls and archways of rich people's houses with animal figures done in cement relief.

How far sculptures that hark back to a historical tradition can genuinely be regarded as naive remains a matter of theoretical dispute. The issue is more straightforward in the case of the larger-than-life painted cement figures that the Ibibio set up as monuments to their dead.

Naive spontaneity also marks the perishable coloured clay sculptures of the Igbo, to which again Ulli Beier first drew our attention. Although designed for holy places, they remind us in their themes and style of the painted cement figures done by the German miner, Erich Bödeker. In both cases the artist shapes a human reality in an unsophisticated and grotesque manner and with great satirical precision; it is not the individual but the social type, the attitude, that is fixed in the form of typical stance or gesture: the petit bourgeois in the borrowed finery of a colonial official's uniform, as well as the Ruhr miner in the bourgeois disguise of his Sunday suit.

Conclusion. There is no naive art as such in Africa. All contemporary African art is naive. These two statements are contradictory, and yet they have something in common: good arguments can be advanced for both — and both are untrue.

What *is* true is the fact that it is more difficult here than anywhere to define the naive, because the boundaries are even vaguer than elsewhere. (To the present-day observer, all archaic, pre-classical art seems in a certain sense naive, even when, as with black African art, it has strictly codified rules and achieves a high degree of expression and abstraction).

Among the painters and sculptors of Africa, fully trained professionals and intellectuals are to be found as well as large numbers of self-taught artists. And just as there are among academic painters both original artists and others who are merely skilful imitators of the European modern idiom, so it is equally true that the clumsiness of the amateur is not necessarily naive, while the skill of a craftsman and artistic sensibility may well go hand in hand with a childlike soul and an element of poetic originality.

Present-day African art did not emanate from the ancient cultural tradition because its supreme achievements were burned by missionaries as evil idols, stolen by the colonisers, concealed in ethnological museums. Traditional African art was only discovered at the beginning of this century and understood by European artists who drew their inspiration from African art.

After five centuries of European domination, the art of African naive painters and sculptors, like the art of their professional brethren, reflects the general crisis of consciousness, a distorted relationship to tradition, the ambiguous influence of Western industrial society and the groping search for a new genuine cultural identity.

Maria Teresa Solá de Dandolo
NAIVE ART IN ARGENTINA

The first painters in Argentine territory were the Sonavirones Indians, called "The Indian Painters" by the Spanish conquistadors. In precisely wrought mural chronicles, they portrayed themselves as hunters, herdsmen and warriors. They stalked the deer, the wild cat and the puma; as herdsmen, they raised guanacos, ruminants resembling the llama, and also vicuñas, the Peruvian llama. As warriors, they bravely defended their freedom from other Indian groups, like the Inca, who tried to subject them. While other Indians in the Cordoba area were gradually subdued, the Sonavirones were the sole ones to keep their independence. In their painted chronicles, there all of a sudden appeared a strange creature, half man, half animal, against whom the Sonavirones battled. Thus was the arrival of the Spaniards and their horses in South America depicted on the walls of caves. Much time was to pass before the appearance of other autochthonous painters.

In contrast to literature, painting got off to a late start in Argentina. For the most part, paintings came to the country from upper Peru, where many indigenous artists had imbibed Spanish influence and thus given rise to colonial painting, with its fresh and naive depictions of the saints.

Toward the close of the 18th century, Argentina was visited by itinerant painters, traders and persons who simply wished to see exotic countries. Versed in the arts, they carefully recorded the life and customs of inhabitants of Buenos Aires and the surrounding pampas.

The first original Argentine painter, *Cándido Lopez*, was born in 1840 in Buenos Aires. Although he was a graduate of the Academy of Fine Arts, it was only after a tragic accident that he began with authentic immediacy to portray the world around him. In his works is found the vision of the original primitives and of their descendants — the naive artists.

Argentine painting after that partially reflected trends in modern art. In saying this, it should be kept in mind that Buenos Aires held a special position as the capital of Argentina with eight million inhabitants, the centre of a country of 2,800,000 square kilometres and a total of 28 million people. Its drawing power has always been great in terms of cultural tendencies.

On the other hand, Buenos Aires itself has always had its eyes trained on Europe (particularly Paris, and more recently New York), where it sought its models. In contrast, the interior of the country nurtured artistic forms tracing their roots to the Indo-Spanish tradition, but without the special intensity achieved in other Latin American countries. It should be mentioned that the local indigenous cultures, while interesting, never succeeded in acquiring the power of Inca, Maya or Aztec cultures. Hence the need to seek cultural models abroad. Once assimilated, these models breathed life into Argentine painting, whose strength and quality awakened the admiration of critics such as André Malraux. But this fact does not in itself alter the circumstance that Argentine art has no deep autochthonous roots. Perhaps this explains why naive art spontaneously developed from folk art, as an isolated phenomenon in Argentina until quite recently, especially if compared with the situation in Peru, Mexico, Haiti and Brazil (a strong current of African origin being characteristic of the latter two countries).

There is no doubt that the indifference of dealers and collectors to any art not faithfully reflecting trends in Europe generated an unfavourable climate if not for the emergence of naive painting, then certainly for its discovery.

While modern art was developing with all its "isms," naive painters also existed, for naive art is not the product of an ideological stance or the result of an evolution of successive artistic premises. In contrast to various movements, naive art lives in a kind of eternal "time present" of its own. But the marginal character alone of this type of expression, which only recently came to rank as "serious painting," led to a situation where true naive painters rarely called themselves that. Usually, a naive artist does not have technical knowledge (although the rapid progress of individual painters is typical of these autodidacts) and when comparing his work with accepted art he may feel uncertainty. Consequently, a naive artist discovers himself only after someone has qualified him as such. It is also worth mentioning that naive painting is infectious — when one such artist succeeds, others immediately ask: why not I? However, if naive painting is to develop, it needs to be recognised; individuals and institutions must take an interest in it.

In Argentina, a veritable boom in naive painting was unleashed in 1963 by three sensitive, intelligent and well-informed women. Knowledgeable about world trends, and loving the spontaneity and purity of naive art, Matilde Rivero, Leonor Vassena, and Nini Gomez were resolved to popularise it. From the very moment the El Taller (Workshop) Gallery opened, a multitude of authentic and fake naive artists came to the fore in Argentina. Those were the years when many appeared or were discovered: *Torrezapico*, *Valerio Ledesma*, *Borda Bortagaray*, *Ana Sokol* — all spontaneous naive artists without any academic education. The relative simplicity of their paintings does not diminish the imaginative vitality of their themes and use of colour.

Twenty years later, there is a large number of new painters and new buyers of naive art, a variety of international exhibitions and a place assigned for this painting against the will of, but with growing alacrity, by specialised criticism. This bears testimony to the fruitful results of the El Taller Gallery. It is also interesting to observe that the new naive painting offered a more perfect picture and greater visual refinement the more new sections of society were incorporated in the practice of this genre. There was *Gato Frías*, with her highly complex visions, *Carlos Manso* with his urban scenes, *Marcelina Fernandez* with her recollections of childhood, the urban landscapes of *Aniko Szabó*, the innocent world of nature and the cartoons of *Mercurio Sgro*, the humour of *Teresa Carabassa*, falling between the ironical and the gentle, and the mysterious solitude of the houses of *Gloria Fuentes*.

One hears, for instance, of a village schoolteacher who began ten years ago to teach painting to children in a remote area in Quebrada de Humacuaca, on the slopes of the Andes. In Chucalezna, the boys and girls who tend the goats and llamas and help out their families by painting, demonstrate that a wealth of expression is waiting to be manifested and recognised.

An exciting task awaits: to sift out from the abundance of new urban painters the ones who are authentically naive and to find ways of discovering and supporting those in the cities, villages or mountains who paint in the silence of their enchanted world where time stands still.

Bianca McCullough

NAIVE ART IN AUSTRALIA

Australia, with its ancient aboriginal population and unique flora and fauna, is a very new land, historically speaking. In the late 18th century, when the first white men stepped onto its virgin shores, there was no welcoming prettiness to make their pioneering efforts easier. Among the motley crew alighting from battered sailing ships were very few who were trained in the luxuries of artistic pursuits. They were mostly adventurers, convicts and remittance men who were paid a yearly pension in return for their undertaking not to embarrass their wealthy English families with their presence again. Their talents and inclinations leaned heavily towards sculduggery, excesses of all manner, philandering and avarice. The officers and men who sailed their ships to this new continent, as well as the men who came out to govern the place had little time for peaceful, leisurely pursuits such as painting or music-making. Their time was spent exploring, establishing communities, contending with lack of supplies, convicts, natives and the very nature of this unpredictable land, where floods and droughts, extremes of heat and cold, and the immensity of distance took a continuous toll.

Yet, by and by, from such a crowd emerged a group of people with definite artistic talents and a mind to employ them. Some had skills which originally had got them into trouble with the law. For instance, forgery, although broadly speaking within the sphere of artistic endeavour, was neither appreciated nor rewarded with anything better than gaol and deportation. Yet the talent could be, and was, turned into some of the earliest pictorial records of the Australian landscape and the lives of the settlers. Generally such paintings are now classified as "Colonial School" and the label of "naive" is reserved for later, wholly untrained artists.

The former included such outstanding artists as Joseph Lycett, Thomas Wainewright, Thomas Watling and William Gould.

The earliest professional artists were employed as cartographers, botanical and zoological illustrators and topographical artists aboard the expedition ships. People like Conrad Martens and John Glover have left us with a wealth of unique paintings, in that they portrayed the strangeness and size of the coastal regions interpreted through the medium of 19th-century romanticism and a classical palette.

Later, during the gold-rush years, a great number of "colonial" paintings were produced by the amateur miners and prospectors who came from diverse countries and many differing social backgrounds. Within the last half century, these quaint and often beautifully executed records of Australia's development have been rediscovered and appreciated by galleries and private collectors.

As settlement spread from Victoria in the south to the wilderness areas of Cape York and Arnhem Land in the north, and from Sydney on the east coast to Perth on the Indian Ocean, a new breed of Australian emerged. He was immensely self-reliant, adept at anything from farming to sheep shearing, droving and prospecting, and he had established a respectfully cordial relationship with the inherent dangers of an inhospitable land.

He and his families often lived in complete isolation, on landholdings which were measured in thousands of square miles and covered areas larger than many European principalities.

The stage was set for the truly naive painter. Uninfluenced by artistic conventions, often without proper education or the necessary artistic tools, the impulsive "Innocent Observer" set out to record in his spare time or after retirement from a physically arduous job, what he had absorbed through close contact with nature and animals. If the paints available were house enamels and the brushes had to be improvised from horsehair or frayed twigs, this did not deter the painter. Since there was no market for his works and no recognition from outsiders, the subjects and execution stayed completely personal — truly innocent, unselfconscious and spontaneous.

What did emerge were the clear outlines of our unique animals — kangaroos, wombats, snakes and lizards and the flight patterns and shapes of cockatoos, eagles and waterfowl. Similarly, the shapes of giant eucalyptus trees and ancient ferns became integrated into the backdrop to bush shanties, wells, and the stark shapes of mining equipment against spinifex patterns of the arid inland.

During the 20th century, and especially since 1933, a new wave of immigrants has drastically changed Australian living patterns, what we eat, drink, wear and expect culturally. Melbourne is now a city with the second largest Greek population anywhere in the world, including Greece. Italians, Yugoslavs, Turks, Lebanese, Christians, Jews and Moslems, to mention just a few, contribute to the kaleidoscope of racial origins and cultures. It is only natural that this would reflect also in the work of those artists who are closest to the roots of such a community. Although they might have lived most of their lives in Australia, they have carried over into their work a style reminiscent of their background. In *Fardoulys'* work we often find Greek undertones; *David Fielding's* little houses relate to his English architectural family background; *Rafael Saldaña* brings to his paintings of birds and tropical landscapes the subdued intensity of his Spanish origin.

Aboriginal primitives, like *Dick Roughsey*, have successfully bridged the gap between traditional tribal art with its rock or bark surfaces and pigment colours, and the white man's tools, to create typical landscapes and tribal scenes. Aboriginal paintings of the wilderness areas and the northern-most island settlements are historically and culturally significant.

Certainly, spontaneous local art must reflect certain regional peculiarities whether they be the colouring of a landscape, the dress and implements of the people in it, or the recording of ritualistic events.

Just as we see in the paintings of Italian *Naifs* a recurrence of clerical figures in cassocks and wide black hats, so we find tent-riggers, gold-diggers, bushrangers and miners in Australian pictures. These people form the matrix of our society, which has drawn strength and inspiration from their way of life and their legends. The legends live on in the heart of the outback people, who furnish us with most of the naive artists.

Animals figure largely in naive pictures, probably because a love of nature includes a love of both wild and domestic creatures. In Australian paintings we find typically Australian animals — dingoes, emis, kangaroos and rabbits. If we look closely at them, their expressions are almost human and there is no portrayal of danger or dislike. *Sam Byrne's* "Rabbit Plague" paintings are those of an amused observer, not a hunter.

In recent years, naive painting has become a respectable and recognised art form in this country and through exhibitions in various city galleries, many urban naives have been encouraged to show their work in public. They have added another fascinating aspect to the mainly rural pictures we have come to love.

A small artistic miracle took place in Broken Hill, a mining town in the semi-desert inland of Australia, hundreds of miles from the capital cities. In 1973 five men, each with a completely different background, formed a group called the "Brushmen of the Bush." They are now well known in London, Los Angeles and Rome, and their uniquely Australian paintings hang in major collections all over the world.

The members include an accountant, the regional manager for the Australian Broadcasting Commission for that area, an ex-miner, a professional kangaroo-shooter (boxing champion), an explorer, and one of Australia's best known local landscape artists. Following their first overseas exhibition in 1975, they returned to London in 1976 where the Duchess of Kent opened their show. In 1977 Prince Charles also opened a show of theirs, this time in Canberra.

Paintings of the Brushmen of the Bush have opened the way toward international appreciation of Australian indigenous paintings, which in time will become fitting ambassadors for a country which is still largely *terra incognita*.

Jacques Collard

NAIVE ART IN BELGIUM

Naive art in Belgium does not have a specific or structured history. Since it is typical of naive art to grow in any kind of soil and in full freedom, like a wild flower, how is it possible to postulate for naive art foundations which, in art history generally, represent tendencies and movements? This is all the more applicable to Belgium where there are no "villages of painters" or schools as there are in some countries, notably the Slav. We may therefore say that in Wallonia, in Brussels, in Flanders, there are naive painters, but not groups of naive painters.

Also, is it possible to claim that there are in Belgium regional sources of privileged inspiration where the naive artist, sensitive to his surroundings, is tempted to reproduce or to tell stories? Properly speaking, no. Whereas in industrialised Hainaut, certain painters, like *Joseph Caupin*, are inspired by the world of work, there are many more Caroloregian, Borain or Brussels naive artists who are motivated by flight from the monotony of everyday life.

Folklore is something else again as it is in itself an escape, a flight. In this respect, the attachment of the naive artist to his native area is just as noticeable in Brussels, with its rich history and tradition, as it is in other centres, likewise steeped in the past.

Whom to Include? Can a complete listing of our naive artists be made? Certainly not. How can there be an enumeration of all those who practice this art as a hobby which many of them consider a private affair, not very likely to interest their contemporaries, and who therefore do not seek recognition by the usual means of exhibitions in galleries? This was very well understood by Christian Bussy and other collectors as they rummaged through attics and made the rounds of fairs in the hope of discovering the past as well as the present, and frequently happened upon the remains of works once undoubtedly fuller and richer, upon artists whose names are unknown or whose signatures may be illegible. From this derives the need constantly to revise nomenclatures. But on what grounds? The criterion of quality? Of course, but it must be handled prudently in a promenade down the pathways of naive art.

Where does naive art end and academic art begin? There is a typically Belgian reply to this question. In this land of painting, where there reigns, in this domain as in others, a veritable cult of craftsmanship, of a "job well done," even the majority of naive artists feels the need to learn the rudiments of art either at an academy or an art studio. One might even venture to say that a Belgian would feel guilty about practising a craft he had not studied, and the craft of painting, as a kind of national activity, is no exception. Such preliminary training, which does not at all detract from the authenticity of Belgian naive artists, is manifested to varying degrees, depending on the individual.

Edgard Tytgat presents the most striking example of an accomplished artist who remained a perfectly naive painter, although the history of our national art persists in classifying him among the Brabant Expressionists.

But what about Ensor, a case that helps us to detect the link between the gift of childhood and a susceptibility to phantasmagoria, which is also, in an adult, a symptom of escapism, albeit a different one. I know someone will say that the shop selling masks and other curios, where Ensor spent his childhood, left its mark on the adult man, and that he made very skilful use of this burden from his youth. But sarcasm in Ensor's case killed off the unrealised power of the naive artist...

At another pole, *Micheline Boyadjian* shows that a perceptive academy professor (in this case Leon Devos) can discover in time a pupil's gift for naive artistic expression and strive to preserve it while leaving full freedom of interpretation.

Chosen Fields? Georges Schmits asks: are there regions in Belgium where naive art flourishes? His answer is instructive in the sense of what has already been said: yes, there are regions where naive art "buffs" have discovered "different" artists. Near La Louvière, Marcel G. Lefrancq, member of the Surrealist Group of Hainaut, found a few whom he presented to the public during his studies, in prefaces to catalogues and at exhibitions, with the help of Robert Rousseau, art critic and Director of the Hall of Fine Arts in Charleroi. Similarly, in the region of Verviers, the Surrealist André Blavier is dedicated to finding and promoting them. This does not mean, Georges Schmits recognises, that other regions of Belgium which do not yet have their Wilhelm Uhde are not just as rich. Mimy de Néeff, founder of the Museum of Spontaneous and Naive Arts, has devoted recent years to discovering them. The results of her work account for many of the pages of this encyclopaedia in the parts dealing with Belgian naive art.

There are many in Brussels. In the Flemish provinces there are outstanding individuals, but only systematic investigation will reveal the extent to which Flemish naive artists demonstrate the inborn sense of colour typical of their land.

Pioneers and Veterans. Georges Schmits — we mention him frequently because of the importance of his book "Naive Art in Wallonia and Brussels" — has formulated a theory which coincides quite well with the facts of the near and distant past and holds true for Belgium as for other countries. In his view, naive art in the form we know it, appeared after 1840 and grew gradually in popularity thanks to the technical, economic and social phenomena characterising the second half of the 19th century. The harsh life of the working class and the lack of leisure among workers before they won certain social gains prevented the flowering of popular forms of art, among which naive art has top priority.

The predecessors of the present naive artists actually appeared in Belgium between 1840 and 1860. Given the insufficient data about them, difficulties regarding illustration and considerations of space, they cannot be included in this encyclopaedia. Only the most important among them will be mentioned, those whose names are known to us. For the rest, we refer the reader to the works of Georges Schmits and Albert Dasnoy, as well as to various catalogues from exhibitions, a list of which is provided in the bibliography of this encyclopaedia.

François Funcken from Verviers (1848—1916) worked in many crafts before arriving at naive art by way of decorative painting and jobs done for fairs. His life of a wanderer was not followed by his son, *Armand Funcken* (1875—1940). A born musician, he nonetheless adopted his father's craft, but rose from the level of decorative work for fairs to the painting of theatrical backdrops, developing an anecdotal art, pithy in its burlesque features, which he placed on view in his drug store.

Two self-taught sculptors appeared in the early decades of the century. Born in 1887, *Adolphe Baivier* of Ligne, using in a new way the tools of his parents who made clogs, created a series of historical bas-reliefs illustrating the beauties of the town of Mons. He died in 1962. The Brussels Museum of Art and History has twelve of his panels in its folklore department. The other, *Edmond Delebois* (1897—1959), carved religious reliefs with his shoemaker's tools.

The compositions of cellist *Incolle Maximin* (died in 1953) enchanted the writer Thomas Owen, who went under the name of Stéphane Rey when writing criticism. Owen gave himself to discovering this artist's works but never came to know him personally. The mine worker *Théophile Damien*, a Protestant, found in the Bible themes for the paintings done in his few hours of leisure. *Guillaume Thurion* (1898) from Verviers sought inspiration in photographs and newspaper printing plates; manysided in his talent, he left behind crayon drawings and birds fashioned of various materials. *Céleste Pedoux* of Liège (born in Hollogne in 1901; died in Embourg in 1960) was a white-collar worker, a well-educated man who portrayed seascapes and flowers on his canvases.

Should mention be made among naive painters of the work of the writer *Maurice des Ombiaux* (1868—1943), a self-taught painter? Obviously, naive painters like to tell stories, but is every spontaneous storyteller *ipso facto* a naive artist?

Graphic Artists or Colourists? The range of Belgian naive artists in this encyclopaedia demonstrates the endless variety of their artistic expression. As stated above, it is practically impossible to detect currents or tendencies among them. While recent group exhibitions, primarily those organised by Mimy de Néeff in the Museum of Spontaneous and Naive Arts, made more lasting meetings and contacts possible, there was no reciprocal action as a result. The history of our naive art (and this must be repeated time and again) has been and remains a history of individual roads.

Mireille Bastin irreverently portrays a distorted world of young girls far from demure in their behaviour. *Marie-Louise Batardy* also reveals a world of childhood but with greater naivety and less sharpness; she proves that one can remain an authentic naive artist in spite of an art education and drawing lessons. *Lise Brachet*, a dentist, renouncing preliminary drawing, succeeds in creating an enchanted atmosphere, in certain aspects akin to that of Chagall, by working only in colour. Other naive artists also display the colour sense inborn in Belgians, which some say — though it is open to discussion — is more frequently found in Flanders than Wallonia. It is found in *Jan De Knibber, Bos I. (Alois van Bosstraeten), Ker Hove*, admittedly in the country's north, but *Nicolas Cloes, Pierre Lefèvre, Nadine Frison, Jef Bourgeois, Jacques Van Der Wattyne*, also confirm that this sense is found in the south, which may also be said of *Lucien Maringer*, a poet of Belgian Luxembourg, where he was born and lived. Flemish in inspiration, *Victor Lecossois*, in contact with the Impressionists whom he admired, acquired an expressly French palette of luminous nuances: is this atavism on the part of a descendant of Napoleon's soldiers who settled in Flemish Brabant? In contrast to this, linear strokes are used by *Françoise de la Croix* from Ghent, *Micheline Boyadjian* from Brussels but of Bruges origin, *Jean-Louis Musch, Jean Faucq, Jean Ferdinand*, all from Brussels. Two outsiders are also graphic artists: *Pepersack*, a Belgian living in Paris, and *Carolus Paepen*, a Fleming from Mol, who turned to painting thanks to his compatriot *Jacob Smits*, a colourist whom he admired although he was not subject to his influence; his work is on the borderline between the naive and the fantastic, though he owes nothing to Bosch or Ensor.

Many Women? It is often said that the number of women naive artists in Belgium almost equals that of men. How can this be explained? By saying that women have more free time than men and strive to fill it by painting? Probably partly for this reason. But this does not explain why many women naive painters also have other occupations and are in some cases, like the dentist Lise Brachet, even professionals. I do not think there is a single explanation for this, particularly as, in Belgium, women are also numerous in other artistic trends. We may therefore say that this is just one more illustration of the innate devotion of Belgians to painting and, within the frameworks of the general advancement of women that is a feature of our epoch, of the desire of women to assert themselves in the art field as well.

Hopes, Promise. Finally, it would be a mistake not to cite various contemporary naive painters, not widely known because they are modest and therefore not incorporable in the nomenclature containing biographical data. *Leopold Haro*, an office worker on the railways; *François de Metsenaere*, an entrepreneur from Mons; the baker *Leon Bellin*, from Ghislenghien; the mason *Ruelle; Alfred Noel*, miner; the gardener *Lucien Plancq*; Madame *Maxy*, another discovery of Thomas Owen; *Jean-Baptiste Mergeay*, farmer and cabinet-maker, born in 1877, who died when he was ninety; and *Gabriel Bohet* (1909—1977) who became a painter while in a POW camp in Germany. We might end with the names of some young painters who have been attracting attention lately and hold out much promise.

Jeanne Cremers (born 1922) produces paintings with a childlike air. *Reine Thumerel* (born 1922), painter and poet, has had his creative activity handicapped by an illness contracted in Buchenwald. *Michel Provost* (Mikke), (born 1946 at Ellezelles) is marked by anxiety, a rare but not ostracising feature in a naive artist. *Luc van Hacter* uses stones in his landscapes. *Jean-Pierre Hostier*, a Brussels lawyer, known for a decade already, was born in 1940. Finally, should *Machri* (born 1949) be denied the attribute of naive simply because she studied art? Her career began much earlier as she has been painting since childhood, her works distinctive for a "gift" that is mysterious because it escapes definition "in scholastic terms" as Mallarmé would say.

Conclusion. We must salute the unknown naive artist, symbol of all those who have been omitted here because they have not won fame . . .

But can we approve of their keeping their works to themselves, works that are for them, above all, a release, an escape, the creation of the Secret Garden without which this grey and colourless world would be stifling?

But fame, the Belgian naive artists would reply, means that you have to accept the merchandising of art and all of its sometimes sordid imperatives. All who search for authentic naive artists will say I am right in claiming that the worst adversaries of authenticity are the dealers and their hangers-on. Because naive art has its paradox: the dealers and merchandisers have only one word on their lips, "authentic." However, when they are brought a real discovery which, precisely because it is real, does not fit into any "naive" standards (of which there are many), they cry: "This is not saleable!"

Why? Because they serve a public which, more and more disillusioned by those who "caught the last train," throw themselves on the "naive artists" as though they were the "last refuge of value." They created this stereotyped, and therefore false, image of naive art. Thus they are the ones who were the first to encourage the proliferation of counterfeit naive artists.

Two more questions arise at the end: are all naive artists — artists? The answer depends on the substance attributed to this word. The attribute of naive cannot be denied everyone who has had an art education if his works show him to be imbued with the naive spirit. But this also means that in choosing we are guided by certain formal criteria, manipulated with a degree of flexibility, for instance: to the extent that naive inspiration is sincere so that the work, in its manner of execution, remains legible.

The final question: can a naive artist develop in the direction of other forms of expression besides the naive? A naive painter in her youth, *Françoise Gérard* in time developed toward academic art, despite the success she achieved as a naive artist, especially on the other side of the Atlantic.

Should we then deny the significance of the naive period of these artists who have evolved? Or, because of the spirit of the system, of geometry, as Pascal would say, should its authenticity be disputed?

We thank Madame de Néeff, Director of the Museum of Spontaneous and Naive Arts, Mr Eeckhout, Chief Curator of the Museum of Naive Art in Ghent, and art critics Mr Georges Schmits, Jean Dypreau and Tilmany, for the valuable assistance rendered us.

Sheldon Williams

NAIVE ART IN BRAZIL

As large as Europe without the Soviet Union, Brazil has been a refuge for emigrés from many different lands, especially those of Europe, who have intermingled with the two dominant elements of the population: the Portuguese and descendants of slaves from various parts of Africa. Something of this complicated pattern of mixed humanity is reflected in the rich and explosive variety of the arts of Brazil, a multitude of styles and a bewildering range of content.

But, as with Haiti, it is the impingement of the spirit world of the ex-slaves (and also often of their beguiled masters) upon painting and sculpture that has ensured a special fertility and inspiration amongst the country's numerous and brilliant naive artists. This is no freakish chance since the slave ships went first to Brazil and it was only after this landfall that part of the human cargo was trans-shipped to Haiti.

Not without difficulty, substitute the many forms of Candomblé (or Umbanda, or Quimbanda, or Macumba and other off-shoots from the main branch) for the Voodoos of Haiti (not as many, but equally independent), and the parallel is complete. For, like the current acceptance of Voodoo in Haiti, Candomblé has now achieved nationwide compliance (and sometimes, this attitude amounts to a great deal more) with its urgent primitivism, garish finery and mysterious rituals. The transmuted tribal beliefs of the descendants of the slaves, however adulterated by centuries and distance from Africa, are vivid, compulsive and powerful. Their influences are now stretching out to entwine the intellectuals and the educated, a large number of whom have tried Candomblé and found it to their liking.

This interest among Europeans in Candomblé, and to some extent agreement with its diverse aims and objects, dates back to the early years of the Portuguese conquest. A fair proportion of those who had left home to find fortune overseas were persons of little consequence; in fact, Portugal was glad to get rid of them. Relatively quickly, though unofficially (this side of their lives, real though it was, remained on the whole covert, at least to start with), they fell into the thrall of their buxom black housekeepers (sometimes elevated to the position of full-time "mistresses") who introduced them to Candomblé practices and respect for the Orixas (spirits) and Exus (personal spirits — part benevolent, part devilish).

A few hundred years later, this infiltration of African tribal beliefs and mysticism into the minds and manners of the Portuguese settlers has paid off; it is not only they but also later arrivals from other parts of the world who to a greater or lesser extent have become prone to the attractions of Candomblé.

Because these beliefs exert a powerful influence over so many artists (especially naives and primitives), Brazilian naive art's imagery is naturally and immediately understandable to a large sector of the public insofar as subject-matter is concerned and, at the same time, excites a healthy appetite among buyers. Such persons fully understand the *dramatis personae* and symbolism which are part and parcel of Brazilian naive art. For them, such art is so genuine that it must be "the real thing," the essential Brazil. These people encourage it, and often become enthusiastic collectors of what they consider to be prime examples of this side of their country's culture.

The works of artists like the late *Djanira*, whose primitive paintings of family life — especially those she made during the days of her greatness — were never short of buyers, in their way set the pattern for the popularity of Brazilian naive art. Djanira was able to inculcate a South American Indian flavour into her pictures, alongside the legacy from Africa, so that they were in their own way near to the heart and spirit of a still older Brazil.

Silvia de Leon Chalreo makes Rio de Janeiro a place of peace and simplicity (very different from an extension of the "International Beach" which is all that many tourists discover), peopled with crowds of near-matchstick individuals. Unlike Djanira, she is a lady who, in spite of her personal simplicity of style, sees art-and-culture as a single entity. She is famous for lending a helping hand to young artists whose paintings may be entirely at variance with her own. She follows her own course, but is full of interest in the work of others and concern for their welfare.

Mary Lino comes from the wide and far-away Mato Grosso. Though she has been in London, and is now in Paris, everywhere she goes she takes with her a fairy-tale imagery of her own part of Brazil with its synchretisation of the folklore of Candomblé and Christianity desperately intermingled: bright colours, cleancut forms, brought together with a peasant's sophistication that defies explanation.

Djanira, Silvia, Lino — they are fine artists wielding an innocent brush. *Zu Campos* transports one into a world as jet-black as his skin, but everywhere lit with figures and fancies of stained-glass brilliance. He paints on wood, sometimes carved in low relief, and his works can take all sorts of shapes, from the routine rectangle to a child's go-cart. Campos, like Mary Lino, has managed to muddle up the figures in his paintings, so that sometimes they go by their Christian names, sometimes by the names of the Orixas — the same system of synchretisation to be found in the Voodoo art of Haiti.

Araújo Japoni is a naive who revels in his own "sophisticated" techniques, although his vision is that of an innocent, full of invention that embraces the entire span of Brazilian life from Christ to Oxalá. *Ligia Milton*, a housewife of Salvador in Bahia, protests: "How can you class me as an innocent autodidact?" but paints simplistic architecture that, even allowing for the bright colours (a natural phenomenon of Brazilian naive art), has a purity that only the best naives attain.

Four women artists have been mentioned. Like it or not, the emphasis in so much of this painting is of an aggressive femininity. Not only from the hands of women, but endemic in the output of many of the male artists. There is good reason for this. Unlike Voodoo, in Candomblé the predominating operatives and final arbiters of liturgical practice (and any of its "new" reforms) are women.

So, in Brazilian naive painting, it scarcely matters what the intentions or subjects chosen by the artists are. In the majority of cases an emphasis on the female (or feminine) is in command. Though in manner or appearance a work may be masculine, the background tenor of such painting has the authority of a matriarchy or the spell of woman's power. In many instances it has a soft near-decorative finish or, at the other end of the scale, insists upon a contradictory fierce, even vitriolic, shrewishness. Of course, there are exceptions, but even so, such heresy, whether casual or deliberate, only tends to italicise the central female role in the art of creation.

Sometimes, as in the work of *Sante Scaldaferri*, the imagery is direct and, if you are familiar with the cast-list of your Candomblé, there is no problem in recognising the figures in his pictures, and grasping their symbolic meanings. Despite his Romance origin, his works are homage to the Orixas — a clear proof case of how powerful a hold this Candomblé way of life can acquire upon even the most unlikely of subjects.

The late Genaro was not a naive. Yet this gifted and highly decorative painter and weaver of tapestries, successful and well-known, left behind him his widow *Nair de Carvalho*, who unquestionably is. Perhaps because of his reputation, her talents did not come to the fore until after his early and tragic death. Nair de Carvalho paints sumptuous scenes and luxurious pleasures; clearly she was not unaware of the richness and luxury that pervaded her late husband's paintings.

Antonio Maia is a wholly different case. Apart from the late Djanira, he is probably the best known of the Brazilian naives abroad. Although he was thirty-one years of age before he held his first exhibition, the utter simplicity of tightly drawn forms and primal colours (often strangely at variance with their subjects) made an instant impact on the public. The stark side of the influence of Candomblé and all other kinds of spiritual experience is given a visual emphasis that few works have equalled, except perhaps the wonderful totemistic symbols of the non-representational *Rubem Valentim*, whose devotion to the Orixas has found its way to a huge public in flat and carefully painted immense signs and symbols that fill his paintings. *Maia*, whose imagery, however simplified, is immediately recognisable, is the only artist (and he a naive) who can match the arresting splendour, and mystery, of the magic configurations of Rubem Valentim.

Remote from this hard-edged precision stands *Ovídio Melo*, the career diplomat (currently Ambassador to the court of Thailand) who signs his pictures "Juca", a special name which he believes sums up his artistic struggle. In Brazil, this is what people are called when they perpetually nag and demand to have something of another which their unfortunate victim plainly does not want to give them. A Juca never gives up. He continues his persecution, sometimes over years, until he finally gets his way.

To Ovídio Melo, this is the pattern of his painting. As a stern self-critic he is always trying to win something which he deems to be only just within his grasp: a difficult task.

To start with, most of his pictures, in fact all the early ones, were based on memories of his native village, Barra do Piraí. They were essentially a reportage-of-yesteryear, redolent with "local" colour, simple in the sense that every detail told a story. Later, as his horizons widened, he took the same unsophisticated style to catalogue important events like the terrible defeat of Brazil by Holland in the World Football Cup game of 1974, or the innocent account of a diplomatic moment, "After Presenting Credentials" of 1979.

Juca paints like his name, doggedly, with little or no attention to finesse. His duty as a painter is to record what he knows. It is all the more surprising then to find that he has a good natural sense of composition which, however honest and untutored the paintwork, ensures that every element of the picture falls into place.

The great romantic among these painters is *Floriano Teixeira*, a story-teller, most of whose canvases are packed with incident. The nude lies with her arms entwined above her head, her body loose and at ease on the extended length of the white table-cloth trailing on the floor. An old man and his son are seated for dinner, a big tureen, two bottles of wine and a couple of decanters before them. But this is only part of a large and complicated picture. There are windows, other characters, a hut, even a towering Venetian-red cliff topped with houses and bigger buildings, with a bullock somewhere at the base of the escarpment. Not unexpectedly, he has been commissioned to paint several large murals.

Teixeira paints thinly. His tints are subtle, and all his paintings are complex, but not in a way that bewilders the beholder.

There seems to be no avenue that the autodidacts of Brazil have not explored. Teixeira is perhaps the most carefully refined of those mentioned here, but like so many of them, he is individualistic. *Valdomiro de Deus* and *Eli Heil* come close to falling into the category of primitive, but in every other way they could not be more different. De Deus paints firmly and with descriptive line whenever he wants to leave no lingering doubts in the viewer. His composition is straightforward and uncomplicated. Eli Heil, on the other hand, is full of *Sturm-und-Drang*; fiercely painted areas curl and twist into enormous patterns in whose interstices are slotted figures, animals, flowers and houses. In de Deus' paintings, people are drawn large and occupy vital parts of the picture; in Heil's works they are crowded, along with everything else, into what space they can find.

Naturally, Brazil has its naive traditionalists, men like *Paulo Pedro Leal* and *Gerson de Souza*. Each is closer in spirit to the European naives, but both share a definable Brazilian accent. Leal's "Battle of Ypres," crowded with corpses, troops, ruins and aircraft, although set in Europe, could just as easily be taking place in Brazil. His portraits have the same international rapport. Gerson comes nearer in feeling to Maia, except that in his case his sharp-edged variation of figuration is closer to European tradition than that of the ultra-Brazilian Maia. Nor are his figures or faces as geometrically simple.

Then there are the off-beats. *Angelo Schepis* is a good example. He works diligently (after careful drawings and preparation) at elaborate mosaics made up from thousands of fragments of plastic. The colours tend to be rich. The subjects — when they are not out-and-out Candomblé — are homesteads and other glimpses of peasant life.

Elza O. S. (Oliveira Souza) has discovered a way of painting wide-eyed black-eyed maidens (long the bane of the European art market where they have become monstrous in reproduction in shops which sell "art" prints). This seems an unfair way in which to introduce Elza O. S., but it is worthwhile, if only to demonstrate what, consciously or unconsciously, she has had to overcome. Even if there are some who will be quick to point out where they believe her challenge to this down-market ugly visual fiction has failed, it is true to say that she has a large enough body of good work behind her to make the occasional gaffe allowable.

A close friend of hers and of other artists (Isabel de Jesus, for example) is *Crisaldo Morais*, a prolific naive artist who specialises in fleshy and rubicund portraits of the Orixas. His canvases, generally on the large side, are brightly coloured and show the spirits to have a dark complexion and heavy features.

There remain the fantasists.

Isabel de Jesus mentioned above, like Eli Heil, crams her pictures with swirling detail, but there the resemblance stops. The paintings by de Jesus are in the main peopled with creatures out of imagination. Fishes, yes — but what fishes! A whole insect kingdom still awaiting its catalogue by some unorthodox lepidopterist.

More fantastic is *Francisco da Silva*. When he calls one of his pictures "Iguana Wrestling with a Monster of the Mountains," that is definitely what he means. You may not be able to recognise the iguana, but the monster is unmistakable. Da Silva knows exactly what he is painting. For him, these are real creatures. Many esteemed collectors, both in Brazil and overseas, share his fantasist understanding of the "other world."

The nineteen Brazilian naive artists so far mentioned give only a scattered impression of what the country has to offer in this art form. A roll-call including all the naive artists, most of them of high quality, would run into hundreds of names. The examples chosen here have been picked out to convey not only differences in style, but also varying intention, love of simplicity and innocence, craftsmanlike determination to rinse unvarnished truths from absolute complication, subtle romantic messages or emotional primitive statements — all these and many more aspects.

In doing this, much play has been made of the basic feminine control or inspiration that underlies so much of Brazil's creativity — particularly in the realms of naive art. Although this is very much a man's country, because of woman's dominating role in most of Candomblé the distaff side has a large slice of national character in its thrall.

One blatant exception to this female imprint upon Brazilian culture is the naive artist *Ivonaldo Veloso de Melo*. Quite apart from a careful strategy of social comment which sometimes seeps into the carefully painted but deftly simple forms which occupy his pictures, Ivonaldo is an unqualified *machismo* painter. Men are in the ascendant. The bulls in his pictures carry wide sweeping horns on their heads and are clearly equipped for mastery. But they are controlled by men. It is men who are at the forefront at the cattle market. The bull which haunts the Iberian peninsula — through Ivonaldo — has the same symbolic powers in Brazil.

Thomas Lackey

NAIVE ART IN CANADA

A very prosaic problem attends any discussion of naive art in Canada: the study of such art is still in its infancy. We have been long enough in recognising the contribution of folk art to our culture; naive art, a much less common contribution, has yet to receive the attention that it deserves. The artists are practically unknown and this makes it very difficult to comment with any assurance on what has influenced individual artists or even how large a body of work they have produced. Not only the artists but also the sympathetic observers are scattered and isolated.

Canadian artists are struggling to grasp a culture which is neither quite folk nor purely North American in origin. Our European roots are recent and confused. The disparate immigrant groups that make up what is smugly referred to as the "Canadian mosaic" are both geographically and politically isolated. Memory is their only link to the roots of their culture, and it fades and is altered by lack of contact. American mass culture intrudes and renders much of what was once a genuine expression of folk culture as tourist *kitsch*. Unlike our American neighbours, we have no common thread of myth to bind our national consciousness, none of the simple verities of Grandma Moses. The house and barn paintings from Galt Ontario are not joyous or feverishly populated but isolated and stark; they speak to no one else and barely speak to each other across the ambiguous ground on which they stand.

Because of the cultural confusion of a country that has retained ethnic identities instead of submerging them in an American "melting pot," the general tradition of decorative folk painting remains strong. The 1745 *Ex Voto* from Quebec is evidence of both the religious foundation of that province's settlement and the continuity of a folk painting tradition in the New World. It is irrelevant that this work is almost indistinguishable from its European contemporaries; it is part of the root of a tree that continues to flower in this country. Successive waves of immigrants have brought a fresh eye and a renewed desire to describe and depict their new environment. Their images vary widely from frenzied to awestruck or nostalgic. Most of these works are naive only in the sense that they cannot reconcile their new circumstances. But through the confusion and the mass of folk expression that is solely concerned with transmitting the symbols of a culture in the throes of accommodating itself to a new world, come some works of vision and expression of what this new land might offer. Young *Sarah Picket's* drawing of a steamship, as a piece of ebullient capitalistic optimism, contrasts beautifully with *Richard Coates'* serene "Quaker Madonna," who cradles two infants and supports the banner of "Peace." These two works may perfectly express the poles of the North American promise: material gain, and freedom from religious persecution. One of the realities confronting 19th-century immigrants to Canada was the overwhelming vastness of the land itself. The theme of isolation and man dwarfed by nature recurs repeatedly in Canadian popular painting. The carving of the schooner "Porto Weir" floats breathlessly on a grey-green ocean as an agonisingly lonesome symbol of men who work on this life-sustaining but unforgiving sea. "Porto Weir," inscribed in the paint of the background, so minimally as almost to defy reproduction, hovers like an epitaph over this ghost ship.

Despite their dimly recognised contribution, contemporary Canadian naive artists represent a vital continuity with the work of their historical predecessors. The modern work is not an aberration but an affirmation that the spirit of an art that extends itself into a larger world is still alive. In looking at the contemporary work, it is important to avoid the easy solution of choosing paintings of charm and simplicity and offering them up to the world under the generous umbrella of the term "naive." Charm and simplicity are not substitutes for a clarity and force of vision which carries itself effortlessly across cultures and time. Any other use of "naive" in an art context calls up the worst sin that can be charged against that word: it is patronising. The selection of 20th-century works is advisedly limited. We do not yet know the extent of the contribution that naive art has made to Canada. Appreciation and its search for gratification are only beginning.

The five contemporary artists are chosen because they represent the best range of influences: folk, work, mass culture, and a sense of space. *Ernest Gendron*, from Quebec, has combined folk symbolism — stars, hearts, birds and floral motifs — with an obsessive and vibrant patterning to frame his nostalgic and cynical relief paintings of media heroes. The price of an individual painting is based on Gendron's appreciation of the international fame of the subject: up to $300,000 for a portrait of Charlie Chaplin. *Sam Spencer* also draws from popular culture images, but with a completely different intent. Spencer has carved an icon, a homage to a hockey hero whose image has come to him from the pages of a sports calendar. It shares with the anonymous painting of the fox from Prince Edward Island a powerful sense of the survivor: one a latter-day knight errant conquering with grace and strength, the other keeping the world at bay with guile and a mythic aura. "These Good Old Threshing Days," by *Jan Wyers*, is a celebration of the time when the vast loneliness of the prairies is reduced to a human scale with the communal effort of harvesting. It is a joyous affirmation of man's labour. *Joe Sleep's* joy is that of a man discovering the whole world at once. All living things are his delight. He

absorbed the whimsy and colours of the carnivals he worked for and combined them with elements of children's book illustrations and patterns given him by a hospital nurse to create an ingenuous peaceful kingdom.

Nebojša-Bato Tomašević

NAIVE ART IN CHINA

In the fertile plains extending further than the eye can see north of Hanchow Bay lies the small town of Jin Shan, a county seat. This entire part of China is famed far and wide for its rice fields and rivers teeming with fish. It is crisscrossed by many streams and tributaries of the Great Canal, the longest man-made waterway on earth, dug by Chinese peasants two thousand years ago so that these rich prairies could supply the imperial city of Beijing with food. Add to this the multitude of lakes, the meandering rivers, the streams and ponds, and the resulting picture is a huge mosaic comprising the land with its settlements as large green stones and the spreading blue-green waters as separation lines.

Travelling from Shanghai one day in January 1980, I arrived in this region, where life unfolds much as it did in bygone times, searching for naive peasant painters, known in that country as the "Jin Shan painters" from the name of the county seat near which they live.

Sailing in a small boat patched together from different materials and powered by a diesel motor belching forth a vast amount of pungent smoke, our group, made up of a dozen or so escorting Chinese and myself, moved slowly along the canals and tributaries of this wondrous land. For over two hours, we made our way, turning and twisting, in the direction of the villages we were to visit and the painters we sought. On either side, peasant work brigades, organised on military lines, were working in the fields. Thousands upon thousands of peasants, men and women wearing the same grey jackets and trousers, patiently stood in long lines ending at the waterways we were negotiating. Some of them were scooping up water in wooden vessels and, using the same system employed for the building of the Great Wall, the canals and the many ancient buildings dotting China, the vessels were then passed from hand to hand over distances of up to a kilometre, where each plant was watered separately. On all sides the canals could be crossed by arched bridges in familiar "Willow-pattern" style and decorated with Chinese symbols. Ahead of us on our canal, as on others running parallel with ours or at right-angles, swam such huge numbers of ducks that from time to time our boat had to stop. Near each flock was a peasant standing guard and holding a long bamboo pole. In the evenings, it was his job to return them to his village, since they were collective property.

The huts of the villages we passed were made of mud, their windows without glass and only here and there covered with paper, yet they were impeccably neat and reminiscent of scenes familiar to us from traditional Chinese paintings.

Finally, we arrived at a tiny village, altogether about a dozen houses, the abode of the woman-painter *Cao Jinying*, whom her fellow-peasants call "the clever girl." This fifty-year-old peasant woman, numbered among the best painters in this region, welcomed us at the threshhold of her commodious, freshly swept home.

In the kitchen stood a wooden table with carved legs and in the corner an earthenware stove. In the next room, reached from the kitchen through a doorway without a door, was a broad wooden bed with a canopy. A vertical wooden plaque on the headboard was carefully carved with birds in flight. The white pillows and bed sheets were covered with dark-blue printed patterns. Being the only piece of furniture in the room, the bed obviously served several functions; the family sat and chatted on it, making it a sort of family corner. On the wall hung several coloured drawings and over them a photo of Mao Zedong of the kind found in houses and offices throughout China.

Wu Tongzhang, employed in the cultural centre in Jin Shan, deserves much of the credit for the development of painting in this region. He told us how once, when walking through the village, he had noticed the interesting bed linen drying on a clothes line, as well as embroidered articles — cushion covers, mosquito netting, children's coats and caps. Their design, style and colours were typical of this area before the revolution. When asked where she had acquired all these articles, Cao Jinying, whose home it was, explained that they were part of her trousseau and that she had done the embroidery herself. Before the revolution, her mother had been one of those Chinese peasant women who capitalised on their embroidery skills to feed the impoverished family. Until late into the night, she had embroidered clothing for the trousseaux of girls from wealthier families. Cao Jinying learned embroidery from her mother, but she sometimes did her own designs rather than working in the accepted tradition. After a fashion, her work resembled painting, although she had never in her life seen a picture, with the exception of photographs of Mao Zedong after the revolution. When she showed the rest of her embroidery to Wu Tongzhang, he was astonished and delighted. Every piece was a different picture, vivid and rich in colour, the figures arranged firmly in a composition, bearing some similarity to the embroidery that once upon a time was created by women south of the great Yangtse River.

Her artistic talent having been discovered, Cao Jinying joined the painting circle in the cultural centre and produced her first work, called "The Whole Country Rejoices." Done on a long piece of paper, this depicted many figures performing the dances of the lanterns, the dragon and the rocking boat against a red background. In this picture, for the first time, the art of embroidery was translated into the art of painting. The work is vivid, gay in atmosphere, breathing optimism. Another picture of hers, "Our Fish Pond," a favourite theme with Chinese painters, is done in the traditional colours of indigo and white.

Her neighbour, *Shen Dexian*, born in 1931, initially painted scenes of village life on walls and above the earthenware stoves for his neighbours. Fires are rarely lit, for there is not enough fuel, and when they are, this is a special occasion for the whole family. The stove is highly valued, and it is a widespread custom to decorate the space above it: "After work," says this painter, "I spent the little leisure time I had drawing scenes of our life and some of my childhood. In 1974 I joined a group of painters. One day I sat watching peasants afloat in barrels planting oysters in the hope that these would one day breed pearls. The scene recalled tales told by my grandmother about pearl fishers. These tales always ended with a large pearl being found by chance by a young girl to whom it brought wealth, lovely clothes and a life of ease. And so I did my first painting on this subject. Later came others, mostly about our village and life."

After 1972, when two young peasants from Feng Wei commune first painted a number of watercolours associated with the history of their village, about three hundred talented peasant-painters began depicting folk tales, customs, everyday life and, to an even greater extent, the life they would like to lead. The approximately two thousand paintings they produced in ten years ranked the Jin Shan artists among the leading naive painters of China. Something of this success is certainly due to the rich tradition in this area in embroidery and in the fashioning of painted lanterns. The scenes of everyday life depicted on these not infrequently depart from the traditional to present an individual experience and vision of familiar scenes on the part of the lantern-makers. Mention should also be made of the tradition of paper cut-outs and story-telling with the help of these; the carving of wooden bowls, furniture and window-frames; the making of paper flowers to decorate the window-sills of houses; and the lacquer-work, mostly ornamental wooden boxes.

For centuries, all of this belonged to the domain of peasant folk art, and was the only kind always accessible to the indigent peasantry.

In seeking out painters and selecting works, the Jin Shan Centre, and the afore-mentioned pedagogue Wu Tongzhang are guided by the same principles and criteria that apply in Europe.

"There are ten times more peasants painting than those we have mentioned," Wu Tongzhang told us. "Most of the peasant painters do amateurish work, copying others or working in the traditional Chinese style. These do not interest us. We concentrate on individualistic styles. This type of art must differ from other familiar forms in China. We insist on a creative form of painting, with each painter possessing his own mode of expression and outlook. This does not preclude the exchange of experience among painters. They can learn from one another, but not imitate each other. The most important feature is originality, for without this, a work has no value. We have many naive painters in China in various provinces and regions, but our painting differs from theirs. We stress our specific features and wish to express our rural characteristics. We do not teach the painters drawing, or perspective, or copying or anything else resembling rules, which would kill their spontaneity. The greatest enemy of our painters is the rich one-thousand-year painting tradition surrounding them. Except for the truly talented, it is hard to escape its influence."

In other provinces throughout China, there are painters' groups and talented individuals whose work, although not altogether free of classical influence, can in many of its features be considered naive painting in the sense that we understand it.

For instance, in the Husyen district of Shansi province, a group of painters, appearing in 1958, grew quickly to number several thousand artists distributed among about five hundred peasant brigades, which again belong to twenty-one communes in the district. Of these painters, many are ordinary amateurs imitating traditional forms or turning out posters glorifying the labour victories of the prevailing system. However, among them are many painters who invest with their own individual vision even works that are commissioned, and whose subject-matter is specified.

More than any others, these painters had to bend their creative efforts to the service of everyday tasks. Work, work and only work for the benefit of the revolution had to be depicted in one form or another on the majority of paintings. At that time, the period of the cultural revolution, there was no latitude for romanticising. But even in these cases the human spirit succeeded in informing daily labour with the strength of its talent and imagination and in creating a fantasy world, a lovelier world painters have to portray if they are to survive intact as personalities.

The painter *Chen Mujun* from this province, in his painting "The Banks of the River Laoho," shows a number of activities going on at the same time, but does so in idealised fashion, giving gloss to the hard truth of the working day with his pastel colours. Brigade members pick cotton in a field resembling a field of flowers; prancing horses drawing carts pass along the way; on the river bank flowers are in bloom; in the upper part of the painting is a tree heavy with fruit being picked. Everything is shown as being in perfect order, as part of nature in which the painter has placed man, whom he observes from a bird's eye view. In the upper right-hand corner, almost unnoticed, is a tractor serving as contrast and as the herald of the new order, technical progress and industrialisation.

Another painter, *Wu Shenggin*, in his painting "The Raising of Silkworms," having chosen a theme almost as old as China, could not help imbuing his work with the warmth and fondness the Chinese feel for this type of activity. Baskets with silkworms look like baskets of flowers, while only the figures of people, somewhat stiff, reflect stylised Chinese painting.

The peasant-painter movement was particularly intensive in the Husyen district in the province of Shansi during the Chinese cultural revolution, but it bore all the hallmarks of commissioned and "guided" art. In other districts and provinces of China, like the Jin Shan district described above, naive painting emerged later and was thus spared some of the strictures placed upon that of an earlier period. With each passing year in China, new groups of peasant-painters are emerging, and among the many, some genuine naive talents. It is safe to say that naive painting exists in greater or lesser measure in each of the twenty-one provinces of China.

The flourishing of peasant painting (and in that framework the segment that represents naive painting) can partially be explained as the result of efforts being invested by cultural centres in the districts and provinces to discover talented self-taught painters. However, it is quite certain that this growth would not be so vital were it not for a significant fact: the desire of these peasant-painters to relieve the grey monotony of life, imposed by the organisation of peasant brigades, where the peasant is part of a vast political movement, of standards fixed by plan, of competition for greater production; where individuality is lost in a welter of daily political activity and bureaucratic machinery.

Painting, mostly done on paper for there is no canvas to be had, and with colours made by the artist because oils are expensive and therefore inaccessible, is an escape from everyday existence into a world of fantasy where the peasant lives his other, imaginary life. It offers him the possibility of "doing his own thing," of expressing himself in forms and colours representing his own personal view of life, in contrast to the life that suddenly wrenched him from tradition, a life mapped out in the Party laboratory and offering prescriptions outside the cultural heritage of the Chinese peasant.

If all the people in a brigade wear the same shoes and clothing, live the same lives year in and year out, as repetitive as a production line, what could be more natural than for the sensitive Chinese peasant, perhaps more civilised than any other peasant on earth, to conjure up in his paintings another world in which he would like to live. This he does the day he begins to paint. In painting, he seems to divest himself of his grey uniform and don luxurious clothing, to participate in rich weddings, to dance and to enjoy an abundance of things that are scarce in real life.

It needs to be stressed once again that what has been said above relates to the minority of peasant-painters who, talented and sensitive, do not reconcile themselves easily to reality. Clashing with it and with everything that stifles their personalities, they leave this world behind and in their paintings travel to another where man is not simply a cipher in a mass of humanity, only one of a billion citizens, but the centre of a world revolving around him.

But in order to understand to some extent the new that is emerging in the artistic creativity of the Chinese man, the spontaneity that differentiates it from the traditional painting of this great country, it should be remembered that self-taught painters are found in the cities, too, predominantly among industrial workers. Their art has not been duly investigated and is probably less authentic and original than that created by the peasant-painter for the simple reason that the revolution changed the life of workers in the cities less than that of the peasants in the villages. There are, however, certain purely Chinese features.

With a population of one billion, the longest-lasting civilisation in the world, no great migrations of peoples such as were experienced by other countries, and with a long and relatively peaceful tradition in everything including creative effort, China is also specific in what is known as naive painting.

For centuries there had been passed down from one generation to the next a precise, minutely drawn kind of painting, usually on silk, depicting in a strictly prescribed way, and for a relatively small circle of the privileged, the beauties of the Chinese landscape and nature, ancient buildings, temples and palaces, and everyday life, particularly that of the upper classes. Painters had no need or incentive to move beyond the accepted and decreed mode of expression of Chinese art.

The victorious revolution of 1949 brought tremendous social changes, almost unimaginable to the European mind. Largely a peasant country with over eighty percent of the population living in the countryside, it was changed overnight, in what may safely be called the greatest revolutionary undertaking in world history, when all land was expropriated and collectivised. Every peasant together with the members of his family found himself a member of a peasant production brigade where he was assigned the kind of work the brigade commander thought suited him best. Mao Zedong's great leaps in industry and agriculture, which later acquired all-embracing proportions in the cultural revolution, further emphasised the collective spirit, life and work in common, while suppressing whatever bore the hallmarks of individuality in every field of human endeavour.

Everything was made to serve the revolution, to fulfill its goals at a high cost in human suffering and self-denial, to the tune of endless slogans and marching songs. Paradoxical though it may seem, it was precisely during the cultural revolution, when Chinese tradition and the cultural heritage of the former ruling class were anathematised, that Chinese peasant painting was given a free rein, with talented individuals paving the way for this type of creative endeavour. Folk and peasant culture, including painting, were looked upon with favour in contrast to the culture of the small and privileged ruling class.

What are the most popular subjects by Chinese naive peasant painters?

Apart from scenes glorifying work, the victory of the revolution and success in building up the country which predominate (though much of this work might be excluded from the category of naive painting on the grounds that it is not spontaneous individual expression), the main subjects of Chinese naive art are the nostalgic depiction of life based on the tales told by older family members of various customs and celebrations, legends, fantasies about the kind of life the painter would like to lead in contrast to his present existence. If life is grey, hard, collective, daydreams are not.

Finally, it needs to be said that Chinese naive painters, in contrast to naive painters in other parts of the world, have no material incentive for their work. There are no buyers, because society lives on the edge of subsistence. If a foreigner should happen to come along, as I did (although this rarely occurs), the money for the painting is accepted not by the painter but by the central district administration. In such a case, the administration fixes a price close to the price for such paintings in the rest of the world, while the peasant painter gives up his work consoled by the knowledge that his picture will give satisfaction to its new owner, just as it did to him while he was creating it. Something belonging to his inner self, something springing spontaneously from him and experienced by him, in other words, a part of him, goes out into the unknown world which he can reach only in his thoughts.

Arsen Pohribny

NAIVE ART IN CZECHOSLOVAKIA

The origins and development of naive art in Czechoslovakia are still a matter of some obscurity. Although certain decades still have to be investigated and a whole series of details and relationships have yet to be studied, some points of principle have already been established. It is on these that we shall base our division into periods as well as our evaluation.

Problems of origin and evolution require a methodical approach not only from the point of view of artistic creation and the ideas of naive artists, but also from the aspect of the growing public interest in naive art (in the first place, an élite which made its appearance mainly in Bohemia), an interest manifested particularly in the quantity of publications. The latter put an end to anonymity, while, at the same time, fostering social awareness and appreciation of naive pictures. It is not surprising that a process of professional specialisation should ensue, involving art collectors, critics and theorists, so that the dynamic interaction of the two aspects mentioned produces structures so complex as to amount to a distinct cultural phenomenon. This progressive evolution by no means follows an even course. During the years 1965—1972 a boom in "fresh talents" was unfortunately accompanied by a "frenzy of discovery"; anything that was not obviously professional and was somewhat clumsily drawn was hailed as "naive" and accorded corresponding publicity.

If we pursue both the methodical aspects already mentioned and keep in view the affinities between naive art and modern art, relatively good criteria for a division into periods emerge. It was post-Impressionist art and sensibility that opened people's eyes to the values of the primitive in art. The interest thus aroused was soon to be elevated to the level of a creed; the cult object of primitive peoples or the pictures of Douanier Rousseau may be cited as examples of new tradition. If we consider the celebrated banquet given in honour of the Douanier in 1908 as marking a turning-point, then we have established a significant point of departure which is valid for the Czechoslovak scene among others.

This was preceded by a phase of what might be called proto-naive art — popular pictures and objects created by small-town artisans and the efforts of dilettantes. The years 1908—1919 and 1919—1945 mark two phases of the initial stage, during which cultural interest in primitive modes of expression and in other paraphrases of naive style came into being. The ambivalent aspect of the intermediate period (1945—1957) must be regarded as a time of misguided popular academic style, but also as years of preparation for authentic naive artists. The most decisive and vital phase of the development (1957—1972) took place under much more favourable political and cultural circumstances. The last few years (since 1973) have been marked by a certain disillusionment and slackening of interest and have the characteristics of decline in other respects as well.

In the proto-naive works produced before 1908, three groups may be distinguished. In the first we include paintings on mangers and pottery and not obverse glass paintings which had tended, in the interests of illustrative narrative, to loosen the self-contained system of folk art by means of the artist's own ideas and observations of nature (*A. Salzmann*, born 1870, and a series of anonymous artists).

We find the representatives of the second group among small-town artisans who manufactured to the orders of their fellow-citizens all kinds of imposing signs, guild banners and, particularly noteworthy, targets for marksmen; carved and trimmed emblems and plaques for houses, invariably with that same popular hieratic matter-of-factness that we might mistake for magic realism. They engraved as required, or as the spirit moved them, the events featured in sentimental legends, visions or the deeds of patriotic heroes; or drew lithographs of playing-cards and illustrations for calendars.

The majority of the third group, amateur artists, were also bound to such patterns and visions of the all-pervading reality of their small towns. From illustrations to chronicles or diaries it was only a short step to the historical devotional pictures of *B. Kasparides*, the panoramic views of towns by *F. Michálek*, or the enchanting water-colours of *Jakub Svoboda* from Ivančice (1875—1943). The documentary drawings and sentimental scenes of the most celebrated of this group, *Alois Beer*, a wood-turner from Dobruška (1833—1897), were always highly esteemed, and selections of them have been repeatedly reissued.

A fundamental change of direction took place at the beginning of the early phase (1908—1918). Various Symbolists, Expressionists and Cubists declared their allegiance to the tradition of so-called Primitivism. In Prague, the painter E. Filla and leading critics reflected on the general cultural relationships with the primitive artists of all ages. The first reproduction of a painting by Rousseau appeared in *Umelecký měsičnik* (Art Monthly). These are features, then, which parallel the avant-garde scene in Paris or Munich.

Shortly before the First World War, the painter Josef Čapek developed an intense interest in local, anonymous folk-painting and described in wonderful essays the naive representation of everyday as well as festive occasions. Those contained in the cultural supplement *The People's Painters* are particularly evocative (first published in *Kmen* in 1918). Even today these essays are among the most perceptive ever written on the mentality and the creative work of naive artists.

With the advent of a new generation after the war (1918), we may detect a yearning to see the world quite differently, "with the eyes of a new-born child." The naive experienced a boom, above all as a source of inspiration, but also as the focus or the formal principle of various trends. The young Czech artists of the "social tendency" (the painters P. Kotik, M. Holý, K. Holan, Piskač, the sculptors O. Gutfreund, B. Štefan, J. Kubiček and others) and the Romantic Poetists (A. Hoffmeister, J. Wachsmann, O. Mrkvička and especially the brilliant F. Muzika and J. Procházka), all revered the Douanier Rousseau and admired the gentle austerity of his archaic style. Some of these artists were also moved by the dreamy magic visions of *Jan Zrzavý*.

While Wilhelm Uhde was launching his "Painters of the Sacred Heart" and the Americans were taking note of the "limners," other countries were offering only meagre contributions to the community of naive painters. Thus there appeared in Bohemia in 1932 (following a one-man show) a monograph on the well-known roving eccentric *Robert Guttmann* (1880—1942). Not long afterwards, some articles appeared on *A. Beer*, whose "Notebooks" were exhibited in "Umělecká beseda" in 1937 with a catalogue preface by J. Čapek and K. Michl.

Above all it was Jan Zrzavý, the Russian Grigorij Musatov in Bohemia, and M. Galanda and L. Fulla in Slovakia — professional painters — who established continuity in primitive art. The essential issue was the existence of a general cultural principle and of a method. During the initial period, the works of naive artists served the intellectuals as a path to emancipation, but also as a stylistic and intellectual confirmation. This came about, if only for a short period, by way of a deliberate identification in terms of imagery but also by way of theoretical contributions (V. Nebeský, V. Kramář, F. Kovarná, K. Teige and others).

The phase between 1945 and 1957 is marked by promising new departures at the outset and by a subsequent idiosyncratic deviation in development. *Natalie Schmidtová's* exhibition in Prague (1946), which stimulated a good deal of comment, was reckoned to be the first swallow in a new summer. Unfortunately, as far as naive art is concerned, we had to wait sixteen years for the summer thus heralded.

The hiatus which succeeded the upheaval of 1948 resembles a one-way street in which traffic was regulated by a cultural policy dictated by Socialist Realism. Other views, including Magic Realism and Primitivism, were banned as hostile. This constraint was also reflected in the amateur art movement (LUT) which was organised on a broad basis by the state. Innumerable courses in graphic art inculcated the same depersonalised quasi-realistic stereotypes in a great diversity of talents. In the amateur art shows of the fifties, many highly expressive deviations, such as those of naive artists, were almost always eliminated as being aberrant. This happened at the same time as dozens of naive artists were beginning their careers in France and popular talents in Haiti and Yugoslavia were enjoying their first world-wide acclaim.

But naive art, like modern art, for that matter, had its secret history outside the great exhibitions during the fifties. People ignored the official criteria and went on dreaming and painting; a new departure was in the making. As early as the forties, alongside *Schmidtová* (1895—1981), the milliner *Cecilie Marková* (1911) was already drawing her astral world of flowers, the actor *Josef Hlinomaz* (1914—1978), the gardener *Antonin Řehak* (1902—1970), *Ludmila Procházková* (1903), *Viktor Řehak* (1898) were painting only intermittently, while in Slovakia the folk artists *J. Kerák* (1891—1975), *J. Kemko* (1887—1960) and the Realist *Ludovit Kochol* (1896) were busily at work. In the fifties a number of artists began to try their hand at painting — *Anna Ličková* (1895), *V. Matoušek, Marie Janků* (1891—1975), *Václav Žák* (1906), *Alois Beneš* (1903), *Štefan Daňko* (1911), *Zuzana Virághová* (1885), *L. Pokorná* (1904—1979), *Karel Chaba* and others. In this way a great deal of material accumulated in readiness for the soaring success of the following phase.

With the weakening of the dogmatic attitude after 1956, a variety of creative styles and criteria was gradually established. Alongside the main trends with their affinities to the "great abstract" artists, works conceived in the spirit of the "great realists" played a certain part in the process of renewal. Rousseau, Zrzavý and Galanda once more began to influence the work of the younger generation as represented by the pictures of *V. Kómarek, J. John, J. Kolinská, W. Chlupač, Z. Sekal, Vl. Beneš, A. Karásek, K. Černá* or by the illustration in many children's books. This regeneration of the values embodied in magic realism (1957—1960), represented in the work of professional artists, stimulated an understanding for the experiments of actual naive artists and hence paved the way for the next phase. Further impulses came from abroad, e.g., from major shows in Brussels, Knokke, Baden-Baden, but also more directly from the travelling exhibition "Primitive Folk Artists of Yugoslavia" (Prague 1959), which can probably be regarded as the model for certain combinations of styles in Czechoslovakia.

As early as 1960, authentic naive artists were already significantly represented, at the instigation of Štefan Tkáč, in the "Review of Amateur Art in Slovakia" (a selection of works was brought to Prague in 1962). Arsén Pohribny rapidly organised a Czech version which confirmed this shift toward an authentic local idiom: "32 Folk Artists and Self-Taught Painters from Bohemia and Moravia." This was the period that laid the foundations for the heyday of naive art — the period of most "discoveries." This was the impression created by the very first one-man shows (Chaba, Janků, Žák in Prague; Hubaček, Ličková, Lauko in Bratislava).

By the summer of 1963 things had progressed so far that the director of the Art Museum in Brno, Adolf Kroupa, was in a position to plan the first national retrospective exhibition of naive art. The unexpected interest shown by over 100,000 visitors and the active participation of the media reached new heights when the exhibition was repeated in Bratislava, in Ostrava, and in the National Gallery in Prague (1964). In the National Gallery the exhibits were rearranged in line with critical criteria and supplemented by examples of proto-naive works and a roomful of professional paraphrases. In this way the ground was laid for the theories contained in the publication "Naive Art in Czechoslovakia." The two authors, Pohribny and Tkáč, submitted their texts in 1967, and continued to act as the main initiators of the propagation of naive art.

In the following period (1965—1969), the number of events increased threefold. A small, self-contained realm of naive art came into being in Czechoslovakia with its own distinctive characteristics. Regional exhibitions educated the public on a wider basis; the overall scene was enlarged by important discoveries; international activities found a favourable response. None of this would have been possible without the part played by institutions and without increasing specialisation.

In the years 1964—1966, a series of Czechoslovak collective shows took place for the first time abroad. These seemed very important at the time, but they pale into insignificance compared with the First Triennial in Bratislava (1966), the prestige of which was much enhanced by the theoretical contribution of Oto Bihalji-Merin. The four shows comprising the Triennial offered such a wealth of material and new impulses that they warranted a special article. As the venue of a theoretical symposium, the Triennial made possible a lively exchange of ideas and the establishment of various criteria. The Slovak public were able to convince themselves that the works of indigenous naive artists were worthy to stand alongside a selection of works from abroad, and were able to observe the qualities and the individual character of the native works. The continuing series of Triennial exhibitions in Bratislava (1969, 1972, 1975) proved increasingly valuable while other major exhibitions in Lugano (from 1969), and in Zagreb (from 1970) pursued other paths toward a clarification of the international situation.

At the Triennial, at Expo '67 in Montreal, but above all at various regional exhibitions (e.g., "Pictures of the Simple-hearted" in Aussig, 1966) it became clear that sustained public interest prompted naive artists to more intense and more mature activity. This kind of climate facilitated the discovery of new talents, amongst others such outstanding painters as *Ondrej Šteberl* (1897—1977), *Václav Beránek* (1915), *Anna Zemánková* (1907), and the sculptors *A. Pařík* (1904—1976), *A. Kudera* (1895), and *J. Chwala* (1906), whose unusual works crowned the galaxy of Czech naive talents. This phase of consolidation and soaring success reached its climax in a sense in the opulent exhibitions "The Nymph Arising from the Pool" (Brno, June 1968) and was mirrored in the Czechoslovak collections presented in 1969 in Lugano, Bratislava, Reggio Emilia and Amsterdam. Ever since this breakthrough, Czechoslovak naive artists have been welcome guests at innumerable foreign exhibitions.

The autonomy of naive art and the high value set upon it was confirmed by its institutionalisation. Even prior to 1964, the Slovak National Gallery had set up a special section which, in addition to its important organisational function, collected naive works. In Bohemia its counterpart is in the regional gallery in Leitmeritz, not to mention the numerous public collections as, for instance, that of the Ethnographic Department of the National Museum.

The major period concluded with the decline (1970—1972) of this profuse florescence of art. Czechoslovak naive painters gained international success and even awards. Beránek, Šteberl and Halák enjoyed particular success in Italy ("Incontro con i primitivi," Prato 1971, Padua 1973) and in Germany (repeated exhibitions in the Galerie Gurlitt, Galerie Zimmer, the Clemens Sels Museum in Neuss, 1972). The Third Triennial with the retrospective show and a collection of prize exhibits by the great naive artists brings this felicitous period to a close.

A relatively large number of shows by individuals and tiny groups, often outside the cultural institutions, may be regarded as the main characteristic of the latest phase of development (1973—1983). The galaxy of names was impoverished by the death of A. Řehák, A. Ličkova, M. Janků, O. Šteberl, H. Jaurisová, J. Hlinomaz, A. Pařík and others. The overall picture was redeemed, however, by newly-discovered artists — *V. Šilhan*, *M. Šitalova*, *E. Valčikova*, *M. Polanska* and others, and *J. Bezák*, *P. Halák*, *J. Šafránek*, *M. Matoušova* among the younger painters. Although there can be no question of a boom in naive art in Czechoslovakia, it is nevertheless under threat even in a country which lacks the seductive temptations of an art market. The rarity of larger collective exhibitions must be attributed to a "co-ordinated" cultural policy. The sad fate of the Fourth Triennial in Bratislava is symptomatic of this policy: this fourth and last exhibition was denied a catalogue and was closed prematurely.

This final phase is partly reminiscent of the period between 1948 and 1956. Now, too, numerous authentic works are being created which are far removed from official art and its exhibitions, but which will have to bide their time before they are published. The heirs of J. Hlinomaz and the poet Egon Bondy enjoy relatively widespread but only half-public popularity. A whole series of young painters (*E. Švankma-*

jerová, J. Šafránek, P. Bílek, A. Vadurová, E. Srncová, etc.) and illustrators accentuate the humorous tendency of the naive style to the point of absurdity. Behind the stolid, down-to-earth pose, a point of social criticism is often concealed.

It is not this temporary relapse but the peak of achievement in Czech and Slovak art which is of importance, and which represents an enduring standard of excellence. That was demonstrated, in fact, by the major exhibition "The Art of the Naive" (Munich 1974, Zurich 1975), by lesser shows and also by a number of monographs of naive art. As a brilliant example of one case where the collection of Czech naive artists served as a crystallisation point, we may quote the outstanding Novotny Collection in Offenbach, which has also been publicised in a monograph.

Charles Schaettel

NAIVE ART IN FRANCE

It was in 1885 at the Salon organised in Paris by the Independents that Henri Rousseau first presented his world to the public. In the following years he continued to exhibit a variety of canvases, which were received with scorn and derision by public and critics alike. Henri Certigny, in his work "La Verité sur le Douanier Rousseau" (The Truth about the Douanier Rousseau), recorded in 1887 some contemporary comments: "Our ears are still ringing with the gales of laughter provoked by Rousseau's canvases." Three years later, another critic remarked on the: "imbecile subjects, treated foolishly with sterile pretensions to great art, things grotesque, suitable only for mantlepieces and fairground tents, such as a certain *Portrait-Paysage*." The reference is to none other than the famous picture in Prague Museum entitled: "I Myself — Portrait-Landscape" — a new genre of which Rousseau proudly declared himself to be the inventor.

These judgements illustrate the total incomprehension whose consequences Henri Rousseau was to suffer as long as he lived. It mattered little that he was noticed by Signac as soon as he began to exhibit, that he was invited by Seurat to join the Independents, along with Odilon Redon, or even that he was presented to Camille Pissaro: the great majority of critics and the public at large, accustomed to the products of contemporary artists and receptive only to paintings strictly subordinated to academic rules, reacted to Rousseau's work with outbursts of indignation and rejection. He asserted, however, that his greatest desire was to follow his elders on the path of "great art." He liked to cite Gérôme or Bouguereau as the models of classical painting he wished to emulate, so as to become a historical painter like them. But in his paintings he used a completely different language to express an imagination too personal for him to have any chance of being admitted to the company of recognised and respected artists.

Historical perspective allows us to see that the work of Rousseau was resented for being in total contrast to the culture of the intellectuals. Part of his imagination indeed came from popular culture, disregarded up to that time; with his free and ingenuous treatment, Rousseau rejected the painting conventions of his age. Many years had to pass before it became clear that the artistic means used by Rousseau signified not a lack of skill but a freedom of expression and approach previously unknown, and inconceivable in the artistic climate of the time, despite the efforts — likewise much disputed — by the Impressionists.

It is enough to say that the Douanier's work appeared at a particularly sensitive moment in the history of French painting, when divergent currents of academicism, coupled with the appearance of new movements (such as Cubism in the early years of the 20th century) were preparing the public for a new vision of art. In this respect, the 1920s were a turning-point in the evolution of the aesthetic mentality, under the influence of a new generation of musicians (Satie, Poulenc, Honegger), writers (Tzara, Cocteau, Breton) and painters (Picabia, Juan Gris, Braque, etc.). In this context, Rousseau's works in the eyes of *avant-garde* intellectuals were naturally charged with a challenging power, inducing Apollinaire, Alfred Jarry and Picasso to stage the famous banquet in 1908, whereby Rousseau — an artist who transformed profane inspiration into the world of dreams and imagination, though paradoxically trying to identify himself with officially-accepted painters — was honoured by artists who were still unknown to the public.

But already in the early years of the century, artists who corresponded to the very criteria of naivety for which Rousseau was reproached were painting regularly and even exhibited in the Salon of Independents. George Schmits, in an article published in 1971, pointed out that as early as 1901 a critic of the magazine "Revue Blanche" referred to "naive artists among whom Rousseau is numbered," while in 1912 (the year in which Wilhelm Uhde discovered Séraphine Louis), the poet Guillaume Apollinaire explained to his readers in the paper "L'Intransigeant": "There is the Dufy-Friesz trend, the Valloton trend, the trend of the Douanier Rousseau and the Matisse trend." Few people were aware that there were other artists under the Douanier's banner, but some critics realised that a new generation of artists was following in the footsteps of Henri Rousseau, finally accepted as an artist of some standing. The intellectual *avant-garde*, eager for novelty, discovered and confirmed the place that had been gradually gained by naive artists. This is why Georges Schmits underlines the importance which should be ascribed to the "enthusiastic commitment," although tardy, with which Guillaume Apollinaire in 1913 announced the Berlin exhibition of a score of Rousseau's works. Also deserving mention is the exhibition in 1923 in Paris which a group of artists, among them Albert Marquat and Jean Cocteau, dedicated to *Paul-Emile Pajot*, sailor and painter of the Vendée, who created from 1893 onwards. Nor should we forget the farsightedness and intuition of Wilhelm Uhde who presented, in the Painters of the Sacred Heart exhibition of 1928, naive artists who were later to receive undivided acclaim: *Camille Bombois, Louis Vivin* and *André Bauchant*.

The public at large discovered that these artists belonged, in many respects, to the common people: Louis Vivin, born in 1861, was a postman; André Bauchant, who came from Tours, was a gardener; Séraphine Louis was Wilhelm Uhde's house-keeper at Senlis.

The 1930s confirmed the importance of these artists. The unflagging activity of a dedicated élite (Maximilien Gauthier, René Huyghes, Raymond Nacenta in the domain of criticism and galleries, Andry-Farcy in that of museums, etc.) contributed, by the growing number of exhibitions and critical writings, to a more profound analysis of this phenomenon.

But as far as France was concerned, it was necessary to wait until the sixties, when naive art began to enjoy greater favour with cultural institutions and more interest was shown in rehabilitating important artists, painters and sculptors, whose work had previously been little appreciated. This state of affairs was due, in part, to the fact that these artists had worked in isolation, each in his own region, even long before the Douanier became the main yardstick of naive art. There were, for instance, *Jean Désir* in Tulle, who painted his "Investigation for the Arrest of Marshal Ney" around 1815; the painter *Houdry* and his gouache relating to a battle of a *franc-tireur* from the 1st Company of Indre-et-Loire; the sculptor *Jean Molette* who carved a large Calvary in the Alps (1848) and a statue of Napoleon I (1852); the sculptor in marble, *Fournier*, from the Ile-de-Ré, who was working between 1855 and 1889.

The need to classify naive art often led to these works being grouped together with sign-painters, weathervane-painters, and the producers of votive paintings. What they share is the same evocative power, the same formal naivety and knowledge of the poetry of nature. But the symbolism of an *ex-voto* or the social function of a sign over a craftsman's shop — having found their own place — can no longer be confused with artistic painting. And so, in various ways, the public became aware of the world of *Jules Lefranc*, an ironmonger by profession, the sailor and farmer *Emile Blondel*, the cook *Narcisse Belle*, who was encouraged by the critic André Salmon.

Naive art no longer appeared an aberration of "official" art, a kind of deformation of naturalism. It came to be accepted as possessing a certain autonomy and originality which assured it a rightful place in the artistic creativity of its epoch.

But the terminology remained very imprecise, despite numerous attempts to define the essence of naive art. Through exhibitions such as "One Century of Naive Art" (1933), "Popular Masters of Reality" (1937), or "Primitives of the 20th Century" (1942), efforts could be perceived to find a "middle" term which would express at the same time the subordination of naive art to realistic modes of expression, its kinship with the so-called popular (folk) art, and the completely personal poetic contribution of each individual artist. Wilhelm Uhde, as we know, chose the expression "painters of the sacred heart," René Huyghes spoke of "painters of instinct." None of the terms proposed was satisfactory; nor are the more recent efforts (Anatole Jakovsky: "Those painters who treat every day as Sunday," or Patrice Walberg: "Immediate art").

It is therefore under the term "naive art" that we will finally classify the works of these artists that the French public is now discovering. The interwar period brought to light such different painters as *Dominique Peyronnet*, who drew attention at the 1937 exhibition, *René Rimbert*, whose first works aroused the interest of Gromaire and Max Jacob, or *Jean Eve*, to whom Maximilien Gauthier dedicated several of his works, and who immortalised Gauthier in a celebrated portrait. After the Liberation came the discovery of a whole galaxy of talented painters who were to shape the course of naive art in France: *Maurice Loirand* of Nantes, a painter of small harbours on the Atlantic coast; *Maurice Grimaldi*,

known as Grim, with his luxuriant landscapes; the story-teller *Jean Fous*, a real chronicler of the Flea Market. Some of them, such as *Marcel Favre* or *Dominique Lagru*, head groups of naives at Paris exhibitions. Mention should also be made of those, such as *Ferdinand Boilauges* and *Ernest Bray*, who are known by only a very small number of works. It should be added that intellectuals — painters of a different kind, writers — have also contributed to the discovery and acceptance of some of these artists. Picasso and Jacques Prévert discovered *Emilienne Delacroix*; Louis Aragon wrote an important preface to the catalogue for an exhibition of the already mentioned Jules Lefranc; *Elie Lascaux*, whose works, on the artist's own admission, border on the naive, corresponded with Raymond Quenaud and Michel Leiris. Some of these left for a while the strict domain of painting for book illustration: *André Demonchy*, a Paris chimney-sweep, and *Auguste Déchelette*, a plasterer's mate, to illustrate the works of Marcel Aymé, and *Serge Fiorio*, those of Giono.

Naive art has gained the right of citizenship in the realm of French culture. Museums and galleries display constant interest in these artists. The number of publications and reviews about them is steadily increasing, while fresh exhibitions further rouse public interest. The appearance of more and more new artists and discovery of new works testify to the vitality of naive art, and constitute a general phenomenon not confined to France. In less than a century an art which was usually regarded with disdain in France, as the expression of a small group of fringe artists, has greatly expanded and has gained a wide following among the public and the critics as a whole.

Successive waves of artists, mostly painters, have enriched and confirmed the value of the production of previous generations. After the immediate postwar wave, already mentioned, an interesting generation of artists and visionaries appeared, many of whom have helped to change the traditional concept of naive painting: *Ferdinand Desnos, Henri Trouillard* or *Dominique Lagru* brought to their work a strong poetic feeling or, better to say, allegorical quality; *Baglione Antigore, Jacqueline Benoit, Emile Crociani* give colour autonomy and a dominant role in creating atmosphere in the picture. *Lucien Vieillard* and *Maxime Voyet* favour line over colour, their drawing giving their works precision and realism. In this output we again find the main subjects treated by naives: tranquil landscapes (*Cécile Favier, Malvina Chabauty*), anecdotes (*Fernande Grossin, Edmond Fortin*), nature and flowers (*Marie Pincour, Georges Freset*), etc. At the present time the main theme preoccupying these artists is the conventional representation of the reality that surrounds them (*Geneviève Peyrade, Simone Le Moigne*), through colourful or poetic notes (*Robert Masdurand, Benoît Crépin*) or through explosions of colour which transpose forms and volumes (*René Guilleminot*). Some are more concerned with reproducing the reality of the village or countryside they know (*Gaston Hennin, Marcel Sénéchal, Jean Schubnel*); others prefer compositions in which their imagination has free rein (*Rose Boiron, Germain Van der Steen*). All of them, with an infinite richness of means, transfer to canvas the images they carry in themselves or create in a variety of personal styles. This allows young artists of a very wide range (*Gérard Laplau, Sylviane Gratio*) to coexist, shoulder to shoulder, with those who have been practising their art for a long time and whose work conforms to a more restrained tradition (*Grand-Mère Paris, Henri Guisol*).

The naive artists, more and more numerous, find themselves today in the situation in which their incredible commercial success has led to a growing number of stereotyped and insignificant works. The general public, however, welcomes a new generation of artists who are willing to paint to order. The banalisation of subjects and codification of artistic means lead, through the establishment of clichés, to the spread of a kind of "naive academicism" and commercialisation, degrading the cultural values of naive art.

But, confronted by the firmly established positions of some artists, and despite the danger that a not inconsiderable part of current naive production may for this reason confine itself to mere exploitation of skill, deprived of all meaning, we must bear in mind the presence in many French museums of regional or local artists of great worth. Their works, collected and preserved in their time, testify, today more than ever before, to the indisputable existence of confirmed talents, such as the ones mentioned above. It should, finally, be stressed that there is a constant renewal of inspiration in the work of these artists, as seen from one exhibition to the next, and the maintenance of quality.

From the standpoint imposed by art criticism, there has been talk about some sort of principle of evolution of naive art through various epochs. As an expression of an individual sensibility, not claiming relationship with any theory, naive art could not be interpreted in any such light. Changes in aesthetic conceptions led French cultural workers to turn to different modes of approach and presentation. The highly individualistic artists, whose activity necessitated a clear differentiation from the naives, have been grouped separately. Because of their quite idiosyncratic artistic conceptions they could not be assimilated with the naives, particularly on the level of form *(Bojnev, Camille Vidal)*. For this reason, artists such as *Raymond Isidore, Gaston Chaissac, Aristide Caillaud, Joseph Crépin*, who previously appeared in publications devoted to the naives, can no longer be included in them, being rightly regrouped, under various headings, in the sphere of "singular artists," where the naive artists do not have their place.

As for the latter, they have managed to overcome the obstacles that novelty, suspicion and various attempts at renewal have placed in the path of their expansion and recognition. Naive art, freed of the ambiguities that repressed it, now constitutes a unique testimony to the permanence of the attitude of the artists themselves. Regardless of epoch or fashion, their language remains consistent. The critical writing that has accompanied them in recent decades has not changed the judgement passed on them back in 1947 by Tristan Tzara. Indeed it remains truer than ever. He declared: "The naive confirm that surprises are reserved for those who, regardless of all their troubles, find, like Rousseau, their profound justification in a freedom based on the hope which is left to them, at least on the spiritual plane, and in spite of the unstable and wretched situations in which they find themselves in the present-day world — the hope of an ample and fraternal harmony whose purity the many Douaniers are always prepared, as far as possible, to defend."

Gert Claussnitzer

NAIVE ART IN EAST GERMANY

Naive artists working in the territory of the German Democratic Republic are no longer in a position, as in other countries like Poland or Hungary, to draw on the "subterranean streams of an ancient and dwindling folk-art." What passes for folk art is largely mass-produced and bears only a superficial resemblance to the original designs. The growing influence of industrialisation and its demands have disrupted formal principles and impaired original powers of observation. In certain areas commercial interests have also intervened on a considerable scale and have tended to silence the natural creative abilities of popular artists. In certain districts, like the Erzgebirge, the Vogtland and the Thuringian Forest, where until a few decades ago there was still a thriving cottage industry, evidences of artistic work in wood and glass based on the traditional designs of folk art may still be observed. But these products can be considered folk art only in a limited sense, since their manufacture is no longer based on a distinct social and aesthetic consensus. In some cases, the process of alienation has advanced so far that there is serious concern about the continuation of the tradition in future generations and about the further spread of mechanisation. What is true of these regions could be equally easily demonstrated by reference to other areas, like Lusatia (Lausitz). It follows that there is nowhere in the country a set of deeply rooted patterns or models which might have nourished naive painting. The various naive artists and sculptors who may be listed here are of urban antecedents and actually have little in common with folklore traditions; one or two of them, in fact, have certain links with the style of contemporary professional art.

The painter *Albert Ebert*, a resident of Halle, was long regarded as the sole naive painter in the German Democratic Republic. Although he received his training from the professional painter, Carl Crodel, and subsequently practised a highly sophisticated style of painting, his poetic miniature-like representation of everyday scenes are generally reckoned to be among the choicest products of naive painting. Apart from a whole series of recognised painters and graphic artists, Albert Ebert has also encouraged many amateurs, such as his fellow citizen, *Peter Michael Glöckner*, a practitioner of *verre églomisé* painting.

Ewald Schönberg from Dresden, a carpenter by trade, made his mark in the 1930s with a number of naive pictures. He founded an academy of painting and graphic art in Dresden, where talented workmen could acquire the rudiments of artistic training. A number of his pupils contrived to retain their naive and original powers of observation, for example, *Marie Domschke*, who settled in Lauenstein. Others became professional artists and pursued careers which conformed to the general trends of painting in Dresden.

The development of a broadly based organisation of amateurs in the form of a "Popular Art Movement" has nothing whatsoever to do with folk-painting and forms of primitive art. The painting and drawing clubs organised in factories and community centres are generally supervised by professional artists and very rarely offer naive painters scope for the creative development of their original talents, so that naive art in the German Democratic Republic remains basically a peripheral feature of the artistic scene. Nevertheless, there are one or two places where appropriate notice is taken of the idiosyncratic products of naive amateur artists, e.g., the Lindenau Museum in Altenburg, where naive paintings are collected and support and encouragement given to naive artists within the amateur art movement. This activity is based on a long tradition associated with this museum. It is in Altenburg that we find preserved the work of one of the very first naive painters of the region that now forms the German Democratic Republic, the drawings and water-colours of the master coachbuilder, *Christian Friedrich Schadewitz* (1779—1847). To this very day, naive painters in Altenburg relate instinctively to the unpretentious but frank pictures by Schadewitz. We might mention in this connection *Emil Klinger*, who began painting when he retired and recorded the tranquil aspects of the town in a manner that was frequently somewhat enigmatic. Then there is *Ernst Ehm*, who was obliged to change his calling after a severe illness and found fulfilment in painting. His works, which are full of a sense of composition and colour, deal with themes taken from the family circle and his place of work. Naive painting in Altenburg was brought into prominence in the person of *Helene Händel*, an artist who has created, as an adjunct to the craft of embroidery, a whole picturesque universe that stems from her fondness for decorative shapes. *Willibald Mayerl*, a miner from the Erzgebirge, belonged to the school of social realists as early as the 1930s. By reason of his revolutionary themes he was one of the few artists who were more widely esteemed beyond the limited circle of the amateur art movement. *Therese Walther-Visino* also found a place of honour in a public gallery during her lifetime. She depicted the story of her own life in a set of splendidly terse shapes and figures and in a manner reminiscent of Grandma Moses. *Johanna Kaiser* in Pirna and *Rudolf Felix Weber* in Lusatia (Lausitz) are included among those who composed their pictures from a deeply felt urge to communicate their ideas and emotions. The creative originality of their work manifests an ardent uninhibited longing to express themselves. This general feature of naive art may be found sporadically in a number of regional centres in the Democratic Republic of Germany today.

Thomas Grochowiak

NAIVE ART IN WEST GERMANY

The existence of amateur painters and sculptors whose pictures and sculptures we nowadays consider as naive art can be traced in Germany right back into the 18th century. Their history, on the other hand, did not begin until that point in time when progressive artists and collectors, as well as open-minded art-historians, critics and art dealers, discovered and encouraged these eccentric individuals who had hitherto been ignored or derided, thus rescuing them from anonymity. A summary of the discoveries currently being made more or less by chance among the holdings of regional museums of local or popular art would undoubtedly extend our historical knowledge by the addition of any number of outstanding "village geniuses." It is by no means uncommon, for example, to be confronted in

south German village churches by *ex voto* pictures in which the local amateur painter was required to represent an event for which he had no pictorial model. Consequently he was obliged to seek an original and purely personal interpretation of his commission. Similar cases may be found in northern ports among the portraits of skippers and ship's figureheads and in many other places in the form of marksmen's targets, trinket boxes, and souvenir albums. Elsewhere we come across portraits and ceremonial pictures — often painted by schoolmasters — which reveal the hand of a naive painter in technique and idiom. Such evidence of naive art remains the exception, however, a departure from the rule by which the popular artists of earlier ages were bound in terms of tradition, theme and manner.

The Friesian village schoolmaster *Oluf Braren*, who lived on the island of Föhr at the turn of the 19th century, is regarded as the earliest amateur painter in Germany: "Oluf Braren possessed the faculty of wonder" is how the art historian Franz Roh summed it up: "In this strange and tragic figure I see the supreme achievement of amateur painting in Germany." An equally eminent connoisseur of naive art, Nicola Michailow, extols his pictures as "the most magnificent achievements known to us in the whole field of amateur art."

A sympathetic view of these "outsiders" developed later in Germany than in France, where naive art had been recognised and acknowledged as a special genre and a new form of expression ever since 1908 when the banquet in honour of Rousseau had been given at the "Bateau Lavoir" — although to begin with this appreciation was evident only in artistic circles and linked primarily to the work of the Douanier. It was Wilhelm Uhde's legendary exhibition of the "Peintres du Coeur Sacré" in 1928 that marked the unobtrusive but long overdue entry of naive artists into official art circles — but whom would he have discovered in his German homeland had he cared to look round? One single name, that of *Adalbert Trillhaase*, bears witness to the existence of naive art in Germany during the twenties — but it is a name of impressive significance. Trillhaase was the discovery of those artists of the "Young Rhineland" group who used to hold their meetings at "Mother Ey's" in Düsseldorf. He was their "Rousseau" and enjoyed considerable prestige. For the authorities of the Nazi regime, Trillhaase was a "decadent," a pathological idiot whose pictures could not be tolerated. To this day the work of this classic artist marks the climax of naive painting in Germany.

There is evidence from the catalogue of an exhibition at the Berlin Academy of Art as far back as the year 1786 that even then there were certain unorthodox artists untrammelled by tradition who had a perceptive eye for the characteristic idiom of the amateur painter: "There would be many more such, did not a laudable modesty and a certain fear of censure restrain many estimable lovers of art."

As far as I have been able to establish, it was the National Gallery in Berlin that first began to purchase naive art in 1930. It was then that Ludwig Justi acquired three oil paintings by *Adolf Dietrich* for the collection — an isolated but far-sighted experiment in its time. A single reference to Nicola Michailow's analytical article in the "Zeitschrift für Kunstgeschichte" for 1935, "Toward a Definition of Amateur Painting," represents the sum total of critical or scholarly comment on naive art in Germany during these years. A depressing result, when all is said and done: the list of works branded as "decadent" by the Nazis and removed from the galleries of Berlin, Frankfurt and Kassel included among others pictures by Bombois, Vivin and Dietrich.

After 1945 it was Hans-Friedrich Geist who exhibited amateur works in Lübeck as early as 1947 and by his articles in cultural magazines such as "Das Kunstwerk" and "Werk" encouraged other establishments to seek out, collect and display the work of naive artists. It was thanks to articles by him that *Carl Thegen* was discovered and brought to the notice of the art world. The people of Hamburg were able to see amateur work in their gallery as early as 1948, and Thegen was featured along with others. In 1955 the Landesmuseum of Schleswig-Holstein followed this lead, as did the Altona Museum in Hamburg in 1966. The Kunstverein of Oldenburg also mounted a show of naive painting.

In a first, rather elementary attempt at a study of the "Sunday painters," published in 1956, August Ehlers surprised his readers with a discovery from about 1930 when he reproduced the work of *Felix Ramholz*, estate manager and the father of the Bauhaus designer Muche. Ramholz had been seized with the desire to paint at the age of sixty. He painted delightfully anecdotal genre pictures of "straw widowers" and husbands kicked out by their wives, in which the comic instant never descends to the level of mere caricature and the fine harmony of gay colours invariably holds its own.

In the Ruhr district Leonio Reighers revived the memory of the classical "painters of the simple heart" in 1952 with an exhibition in the Dortmund Museum am Ostwall. But the most effective stimulus to the study of naive artists and their peculiar fascination was provided at this time by Jongher W. Sandberg, who inspired West German artists and art-lovers. In the Stedelijk Museum of Amsterdam, which under his outstanding direction became a meeting-place for all those in the modern art world, there was always a collection of naive art side by side with the topical productions of the international art scene. This was no doubt one reason why pictures by a small handful of such "outsiders," admired for their naive vision and straightforward, elementary representation of the world, gained the acknowledgement and sympathy of many artists and a small élite of the aesthetically aware — in particular, abstract and non-figurative painters and gallery directors like Vömel in Düsseldorf, who discovered *van Weert*, or Springer in Berlin, who introduced *Maeden* to the public. This situation changed perceptibly with the continued increase in leisure time, when a considerable number of large industrial concerns, especially in the Ruhr, offered their employees opportunities for the creative use of that leisure, together with the chance to exhibit work publicly. This was done in Württemberg, for instance, by the Böblingen firm of Eisenmann. It not only organises annual exhibitions on its own premises, in which outside contributors are also invited to show their work, it also maintains an impressive permanent collection of naive works and issues lavish publications. In 1953 the German Trade Union Congress — DGB — made the exhibition "Work and Leisure" the focus of the Recklinghausen Festival which it organised for its members. Side by side with leading "classics" of naive art were to be found pictures and sculptures by miners, furnace-men and workers from factories and commercial firms. In those years, when new perspectives were opening up, Recklinghausen became the centre for naive artists in all of the Ruhr. A few years later the Trade Union Congress extended its campaign and its exhibitions of creative leisure activities to embrace the whole of the Federal Republic. These events often attracted more visitors than did the great museums. They reached a climax in 1971 with the exhibition, "Works and Workshops of Naive Art," which made a significant popular impact and turned out to be a meeting-place for many of the most important amateur and professional artists from all over Europe. It was in wide-ranging factory and trade-union shows of this kind that these few authentic painters and sculptors were discovered who have since come to be known as the "painting pitmen of the Ruhr" far beyond the boundaries of their homeland: *Bödeker, Brandes,* the two *Gerlach* brothers, *Grams, Hertmann, Kamierczak, Klekawka, Koehn, Schilling, Thewissen and Valerius.* The wood and cement sculptures of Bödeker, who later won the sculpture prize at the Triennial in Bratislava, and the pictures of Friedrich Gerlach with their obsessive nightmare visions have gained international esteem, while Klekawka's lively and brightly coloured studies were awarded the international prize for painting at the exhibition of naive art in Zagreb in 1970.

One thing is worthy of note: while it is rare to find naive artists in other parts of Germany who tackle the seamy side of life in their work or seek to offer solutions to social problems, those artists who make their living as miners or steelworkers in the Ruhr are by no means inclined to evade such subjects.

It is much more difficult and much rarer to track down naive artists in the country than it is in the large firms and factories of the cities. Since they pursue their hobby in the intimacy of their homes or farms, their activity seldom goes beyond the family circle and remains unknown to the general public. It happens only occasionally by sheer accident that one or the other of these artists is rescued from obscurity because a professional artist, the director of a museum, the owner of a gallery, a writer, a collector or an enthusiast for modern art has stumbled across him. This is unfortunately not always to the advantage of the artist concerned, if this particular branch of the art trade sets out to capitalise on him. In this case only very stable and determined individuals succeed in carrying on as before, at their own pace, determined to allow themselves time to finish their pictures as they think fit, ignoring the distraction of lucrative offers and commissions. The rural world with which these peasant painters live in daily harmonious contact provides an inexhaustible source of themes and subjects. In most cases their roots in their farms or their villages go back for generations; they feel at home and at ease there and in their daily work, the rhythm of which shapes their lives within the rise and fall of the seasons. This is amply evident in the richness of *Raffler's* work. As a rule they have no occasion to seek refuge in some substitute world, to free themselves from subjugation to wretched and monotonous drudgery by means of wishful fancies.

If occasionally, as in the case of Raffler or *Ennulat,* their subjects range beyond the horizon of their customary rural landscape, we should not interpret this as a flight from the narrowness of their everyday lives or a yearning for distant places — unless it is the home-sickness we detect in the work of *Minna Ennulat*. These are either excursions into cities or landscapes overrun by tourists, prompted by an understandable need for a change of theme, or — as is often the case — a response to friends or "customers" who have brought or sent postcards with the request that the artist should copy them.

By way of introduction to those naive artists who live in cities and frequently have intellectual jobs, we might make the following points. It is not possible to lump together everything that goes by the name of naive art, for even among authentic naive artists there are, roughly speaking, two distinct groups with different points of departure. There are what might be called elemental naive artists and those who come from the intellectual professions or have an intellectual background. The distinction between these groups is not always hard and fast. But there are also cases of professional painters who deliberately adopt a naive manner, such as the academically trained *Jan Balet* or *György Stefula* and his wife *Dorothea* — quite apart from imitators catering for a commercial market. How is it possible to draw distinctions?

The situation is relatively simple and unambiguous with such elemental painters as *Abels, Ennulat, Grams, Hertmann, Raffler* and *Thegen*, or the sculptor *Erich Bödeker*, to name but a few typical figures, who lived, or are still living, in a state of grace reminiscent of St Francis of Assissi, with a kind of imperturbable self-assurance, and who paint in the same manner, displaying an enviable natural simplicity, undismayed by intellectual influences and immune to any kind of distraction. Doubts and misgivings, various experiences calculated to inhibit creative activity, such as the *avant-garde* of our artistic community is exposed to nowadays in its search for new attitudes and concepts or in coming to terms with new aesthetic possibilities and tendencies while taking account of the astounding increase of scientific knowledge, changes in society and in outlook — none of this constitutes any kind of bewildering impediment for these naive artists in the creation of their own pictorial world. Naive artists of this fundamental kind care little or nothing for what is permissible in the field of art, for what must or should be done, for in their case knowledge will never gain the ascendancy over inner ideas and modes of representation that are guided primarily by instinct. In their view everything has its own integral and self-contained identity: outlook on life, consciousness and attitude, interpretation and mode of expression, above all, that technically uncomplicated, reductive manner of representation that might indeed be called primitive in comparison with the work of academically trained painters. It is here that we come face to face with the primeval and unspoiled paradise of the naive painters.

One would be inclined to think that one particular group of naive artists would be constantly exposed to the danger of losing their innocence and the fundamentally naive mode of expression, namely those whose disposition or profession requires intellectual awareness and strict scientific logic together with the need to size up the real world critically and analytically, or, indeed, to inculcate those qualities in others. Can anyone who knows and understands so much really be

"naive"? And are not such individuals putting on a pretence of innocence when they paint in this manner? Such "individuals" — e.g., *Paps* (the pseudonym of Dr Waldemar Rusche) an ophthalmologist of international reputation, *Fritz Seemann*, who used to teach mathematics, *Vivian Ellis*, etc. — every one of them untrained in the arts of painting and sculpture, but generally highly qualified experts in their own subject, are involved in a world of norms and rationality that makes all kinds of complicated scientific and technical demands. No wonder that someone who knows so much, and is obliged to know so much, sometimes wants to switch off and forget that knowledge, to surrender for once to his yearning to be simple and uncomplicated; and should he be seized with the desire to articulate his feelings in pictorial form then he is naturally inclined to see the world with an innocent eye and to paint it without constraints of intellect, theory and schooling, spontaneously, just as it comes into his head, devoid of rules and training. The end-product may be totally trivial, but if, by some lucky chance, this innocent creative act reveals an original and intuitive visionary power of a highly individual kind — that might some day be discovered by the experts — then we are face to face with a truly naive artist.

Anyone who is acquainted with the personalities already mentioned and who has watched them paint is bound to confirm that intellect and innocence are not mutually exclusive in their mode of life.

This kind of balancing act, poised between naive innocence and intellectual awareness may, however, represent a danger for a naive artist if he is assailed by doubts arising from certain aesthetic issues which have assumed prominence in his mind. The same is true if he becomes involved in the intellectual and productive process of modern art through association with professional artists and tries to combine this contemporary art with his own naive painting. If we look at it in this light, then it must be admitted that the pictures of some of these amateur painters — *Auer, Dieckmann, Epple, Garde, Kloss*, for instance — in spite of all their qualities would have to be assigned to the peripheral area of naive art, if we are concerned to devise strict categories. It is here that one of the critical issues regarding the assessment of the naive emerges; it affects even the judgement of experts and gives rise to a difference of opinion.

It should have become obvious by now that innocence and originality cannot be learned or taught!

It would be foolish to accept the view that "to be of a naive mind" is something like a guarantee of quality, as far as pictures are concerned. Even in the case of naive art there are valid standards, as for all art, and the brief moments of glory are just as rare here as anywhere else.

What matters as far as quality and value goes is the greater or lesser degree of originality, creative imagination, poetic intensity and power of expression, the fascination of a new vision embodied in pictorial form, the unique quality of the impromptu, the unmistakable mark of an individual's "handwriting" (however awkwardly it may be formed and however crassly at odds with standards of technical perfection and academic doctrine), an individual idiom and set of forms as well as an original range of colours; last, but not least, there is that perfect union and harmony of all these structural values, which, as always, constitutes the value and the quality of a work of art. In the 1960s, which were particularly productive years in the history of naive art, discussion of its nature flared up passionately. German museums were opening their doors more and more to the pictures and sculptures of contemporary naive artists, who in turn were increasingly represented in the international art fairs of Cologne and Düsseldorf. At this time the art trade was dominated by naive galleries that had sprung up everywhere offering their dubious products for sale. Publications by H. Geist and Juliane and Franz Roh offered interesting matter for discussion, but it was Bihalji-Merin's book, "Das naive Bild der Welt," published by DuMont in 1959, that turned out to be the much praised and widely discussed "gospel." In 1961 Dietrich Mahlow organised a major exhibition in Baden-Baden (subsequently in Frankfurt and Hanover) under the title "Das naive Bild der Welt," in the catalogue of which international experts recorded their views. Georg Schmidt's objective and illuminating study, "Was ist ein peintre naif" seemed especially helpful to many people. It ought to be mentioned that the Basel exhibitions "Laienmaler" in the same year and the Rotterdam exhibition of 1964, "De Lusthof der Naieven" gave an added stimulus to the naive art scene in the Federal Republic of Germany. Naive art had long since transcended the intimate circle of enthusiasts, but it undoubtedly owed the further increase of its popularity to a Grandma Moses exhibition of 1962/1963, shown in Bremen, Düsseldorf and Mannheim, as well as to the first fascinating shows of naive art from Yugoslavia and Poland which were put on by West German museums and private galleries.

There is no doubt that Germany's participation in the Bratislava Triennial exhibitions of 1966, 1969 and 1972 provided a further impulse for the promotion of naive art in the Federal Republic, particularly in view of the success enjoyed by German painters. The same is true of the "Naivi" exhibitions held in Zagreb in 1970 and 1973. The symposia in Bratislava, Recklinghausen and Zagreb, in the course of which artists, scholars, critics, collectors and informed laymen hotly debated the concept and definition of naive art, did a great deal to dissipate the sceptical reservations of German curators and critics and to gain new supporters for naive art. Dieter Honisch's essay, "Three Naive Artists," which appeared in 1969 in the catalogue of the Folkwang Museum, Essen, also served the same purpose, as did lectures by experts from abroad, such as Ludwig Gans (Amsterdam), A. Jackowski (Warsaw), Boris Kelemen (Zagreb) and Arsen Pohribny.

An unprecedented boom in naive art extended the frontiers of the German art scene until the late 1970s. Museums in Dortmund (1952, Dr Reyghers), Recklinghausen (1954, Prof. Grochowiak) and Neuss (1969, Dr Feldhaus) established collections of naive art. Neuss acquired the Dorne collection in addition. Berlin and Hamburg (Altona Museum) supplemented their collections considerably by the acquisition of works by contemporary naive artists. It is impossible to give a comprehensive list of the numerous newly-begun private collections, among which the most prominent in range and quality are those established by Messrs Eisenmann (Böblingen), Fritz Novotny (Frankfurt), Charlotte-Lotte Zander (Munich), Holzinger

(Munich) and Dallmeier (Hanover). Rolf Italiaander opened to the public his comprehensive, if somewhat uneven, collection in the Rhade Museum. Reference should also be made to the unique collection of Polish naive popular painting founded by the journalist, Ludwig Zimmerer, in Warsaw and enlarged in recent years by the addition of German naive works donated by the Ludwig Zimmerer Foundation. The fact that the Federal Republic of Germany has since 1974 possessed its own excellent collection of naive works, maintained by the Institute for Foreign Relations and permanently on tour throughout the world, may give some idea of the esteem which German naive painters now enjoy.

There has been an uninterrupted series of first-class exhibitions organised by museums and artistic associations, often accompanied by lectures and discussions; there have been a number of new publications, among them some controversial contributions by authors such as Bihalji-Merin, M. T. Engels, Fritz Novotny and Thomas Grochowiak. During the 1970s two events in particular aroused interest throughout the Federal Republic and produced strong reactions both among the supporters of naive art and those who took a sceptical view of it: in 1972 the announcement of a painting competition by a Hamburg illustrated magazine attracted no less than 12,000 amateur painters, led to the discovery of a number of hitherto unknown naive artists and produced very mixed public reactions. In 1975 Bihalji-Merin was able to mount a fascinating major international exhibition in Munich, "The Art of the Naive," which gave occasion for further discussion of naive art. There was reason enough for such discussion: numerous galleries were concerned to foster and to exhibit authentic naive art — Franke, Holzinger, Charlotte in Munich, Vömel and Zimmerer in Düsseldorf, Abels and Buchholz in Cologne, Springer in Berlin, Mensch in Hamburg, to name only a few of the galleries that were active in this field in the 1960s and the early 1970s. Alongside these galleries, however, many "dealers in naive art" shot up, riding high on a wave of nostalgia and swamping the market with bogus naive works designed to meet public taste. Trained painters were employed in the mass production of deliberately inept pictures of a secure and cosy world. Such counterfeit naive works could be bought in department stores and were advertised on television as valuable investments. Courses and schools for naive art were founded. In no time at all derogatory references to painting housewives and grannies were going the rounds. In view of this fashionable craze, it is no wonder that many museums have now reverted to their previous reserved attitude towards naive art. In the meantime the naive boom has already passed its peak, so that the work of genuine naive artists can once more be seen in its true perspective and given its due. Following the disarray of this period the Kunsthalle in Bielefeld assumed the task in 1981 of "explaining and clarifying by way of demonstration and example what can properly and rightly be regarded as naive art." This rewarding exhibition, "Naive Art — Past and Present," was also shown in the Altona Museum, Hamburg. It aroused admiration, speculation and controversy. An Erich Bödeker Association, founded in Düsseldorf in 1983 with headquarters in Hanover, intends not only to preserve and catalogue the work of the man who was probably the most important German naive sculptor, but also to encourage authentic naive artists by means of symposia, exhibitions and publications and to establish criteria which will lead to a better understanding of the whole phenomenon of "naive art."

Sheldon Williams

NAIVE ART IN GREAT BRITAIN AND EIRE

The great gap that separates the naive and primitive art of these islands from a rich past is the sociological change that overcame them at the time of the Industrial Revolution. In cultural terms it was a long and seemingly empty period. As will be shown, Irish and British naive art appeared to vanish for a hundred years until a slow process of resuscitation began in the early 1920s.

When the peasant population disappeared, leaving the land for the factories, every kind of untutored painting which had previously flourished, became rare, "unusual," sometimes even eccentric. Worse, it also turned into something essentially private, known only to the artist's immediate family and perhaps a circle of close friends.

Before analysing the full effect of this disastrous and dramatic change of life-style among Britain's erstwhile peasants, something needs to be said of the lost world and origins of Irish and British autodidacts.

Before the Industrial Revolution. As far back as the Roman occupation, the British were recognised as natural sculptors. The Imperial Romans residing in the British territories admired their skills and strangeness. At one time there was even a small export trade of British carvings to Rome herself. The few examples of this sculpture that remain display the true flavour of naive craftsmen, being utterly independent but at the same time betraying a "family" likeness.

But when the legions withdrew from Britain, there followed uncharted centuries of social chaos. Some monasteries held out against this general collapse, albeit briefly, although in relatively peaceful Ireland splendid illuminated manuscripts were made. In the broader sense it was not until the Middle Ages that the artists and craftsmen once more found regular employment decorating churches and monasteries (not always with great respect, as those examples of their work set high in niches or in the uppermost recesses of sacred buildings, out of sight or almost invisible to the human eye, testify to this day). It was a period when there were no accepted, professionally-trained artists. The most ancient of British shrines with their painted and carved embellishment owe their individual and personalised freshness to the concept and imagery of these early and genuine naive craftsmen.

Even when some sort of social stability was at last restored, this naive tradition was maintained. True, the sophistication of tutored art was gradually building up a contrary trend, but its challenge to naive art took hundreds of years to reach large-scale development, culminating in the founding of the Royal Academy in 1768. It was at this point that the clear distinction between the trained élite (official) and the untaught artists was drawn.

The Last Flowering of Naive Art Before the Industrial Revolution. For the rich, paintings could be commissioned at a high price from an artist of the Royal Academy. For those who had some money but not nearly enough, there remained the itinerant artists, men who, although untrained, had the requisite amount of artistic ability to make pictures. Often for bed-and-board and very little pay, they could produce paintings that their hosts could afford. The clientele for such artists were usually made up of prosperous farmers. They wanted painted records of their prize cattle or favourite dogs.

Human portraits were different. If the farmer himself wished to appear in the picture perhaps holding his horse's bridle, this meant that a special kind of itinerant painter was needed. Among these roving artists there existed such a category. Those who could paint portraits were known as "face-painters" and could demand a higher fee. There was, needless to say, a wide range of quality among these artists, from the most primitive (the cheapest) to the most skilled — within whose ranks were the amazing *Sartorius* family, emanating from the Low Countries, who over three generations were able to string together a faithful band of buyers and supporters.

After the Industrial Revolution. There may well have been naive artists working away in industrial obscurity, but hardly anything is known of them and their names are lost. It was not until the 1920s that Ben Nicholson and Christopher Wood — both of them modern artists of taste and distinction — stumbled upon the recluse, *Alfred Wallis* (1855—1942).

Wallis was an ill-humoured misogynist who only started to paint at all after his wife died (she was twenty years his senior). He was also a religious fanatic, and very poor.

Nicholson and Wood immediately recognised the primitive genius of the old man. They were totally undeterred by the odd shapes of many of his paintings, frequently on rough scraps of cardboard or fragments of wood coloured with the crude industrial paint left over from the painting of boats, the dregs of pigment at the bottom of discarded cans.

Getting to know Wallis was a slow process, and when that had been achieved, it took even longer to bring him to the attention of art lovers, aesthetes and art critics. So it was many years before his works became the cherished prizes of intelligent collectors, first in Britain and subsequently all over the world.

Like Rousseau, Wallis proved to be a man of unsubstantiated memories. As an ex-seaman, he liked to recall, in some of his pictures, journeys that he perhaps never took but which became the subjects of some of his finest paintings.

On Sundays, all his pictures at his home in St Ives, Cornwall, were draped in black cloth so that the sight of them would not give offence to the Lord on His holy day.

Although Wallis did not die until 1942, his emergence as a painter of great value — albeit a primitive — marked the slow revival of the affection of the British for naive art (until then, artists like Rousseau and Séraphine had been regarded with genuine respect, but realisation of the virtues of naive artists had not been extended to those at home).

Thereafter, the art enthusiasts of Britain were prepared to treat naives seriously instead of regarding them as artistic freaks. Slowly at first, these painters came out of their secret places and felt encouraged to show the world what they could do. Of course, there are still artists who shrink from the glare of publicity, and, for diverse reasons, wish to stay in the shadows. A Ben Nicholson or a Christopher Wood might tempt them to change their minds, but the chance of such an encounter is unlikely.

There were a few notable but isolated enthusiasts who early spotted the promise of naive and primitive artists in Britain and Ireland. Chief among these were the late art critic Herbert Read and the aesthete H. S. Ede; but until the mid-thirties this sort of painting had no real promoters in the commercial sense.

It was not until the late Arthur Jeffress opened his gallery in London's Davies Street that any regular showplace could be found for the works of these painters. After his tragic death, it was left to Eric Lister and Lionel Levy, who were just beginning at the Portal Gallery, to pick up the pieces. (The Portal Gallery at that early stage of its development was experimenting with many different kinds of contemporary art, but it was after its directors visited the Arthur Jeffress Gallery that they most probably acquired a strong taste for naive art, which was to become the mainspring of their exhibitions.) Apart from the discovery of works by *James Lloyd* at the Arthur Jeffress Gallery, Eric Lister in particular became aware of the strange element of poetry that haunted the pictures of so many of the British naive artists that he subsequently came to admire.

On the fringe of such activity was Andras Kalman, the main business of whose Crane Gallery in Manchester was transferred to the Crane Kalman Gallery in London. Kalman had already started showing naives in the north and he continued to display them at his new gallery, but he was also interested in a wide selection of modern art. As well as international and British naives, he occasionally put on view the best British naive art of the 18th and 19th centuries.

A man of similar tastes is Christopher Bibby of the Rutland Gallery, but he too only exhibits the same kind of occasional concern for naives.

What this meant was that at that time (1930s—1960s) naive art in Britain and Eire appeared in very few galleries, and all of them were in fashionable London, attracting only a small coterie of dedicated supporters and collectors. Only on rare occasions did British naive art come in contact with a broad public.

The big breakthrough in Britain came — curiously enough — as a part of the Jubilee Celebrations of Queen Elizabeth II. Stanley Harries was asked by the Celebrations Committee to organise an exhibition to be shown in each of the Greater London Boroughs (1977). It was when he took the decision (warmly received) to exhibit "London's Naive Painters" that the ice broke. The first showing at County Hall was shortly followed by a display at the Art and Antiques Fair, the stand for which was donated by the organisation of the Olympia Stadium.

Other exhibitions took place at the National Theatre, London University, the Guildhall, even aboard a floating gallery off the Victoria Embankment. These were the first of many such venues.

At last the British got the full flavour of their naives — first, London's naive painters, later naives from all over Britain, and eventually contemporary naive art from overseas as well.

Within a year, the bringing together of naive artists from every quarter by Harries led to the formation of RONA (the Register of Naive Artists), an international organisation which, from its permanent headquarters at St Katherine's Dock, acted as a catalyst for many varied artists of this sort.

Dimitrios Papastamos

NAIVE ART IN GREECE

While the naive art of many European countries may be interpreted as a conscious reversal to a childlike way of seeing the world in the middle of the technological era, this is not at all the case with its equivalent in Greece. With the exception of ecclesiastical art, Greek folk and naive art was the unique medium of artistic expression for the people of that country, who were completely isolated under the Turkish occupation, and could not have a regular intellectual and artistic development for a period of about four hundred years.

Greek naive art is a spontaneous artistic manifestation in painting, sculpture wood-carving, embroidery, the goldsmith's and the silversmith's crafts, and weaving. which has flourished in many areas of Greece, e.g., in the north-eastern Aegean Islands, the mountainous regions of northern Macedonia, the villages of the Pilion and of Epirus, etc. This indigenous art, distinguished by its simple and humane character, developed independently of any external influence, and without being directly inspired by foreign exotic civilisations. Thus it retains the essential features of a rich artistic tradition of many centuries, and often recalls the splendour of ancient Greek sculpture, or the stately religious character of Byzantine art.

The main themes in the repertoire of Greek naive artists are taken from everyday life and occupations, or from mythological, heroic and historical events, which are treated as something familiar to all Greeks. This is the reason why Greek folk and naive art never resorts to compositions dominated by fear, nightmares, secret desires, imaginary landscapes and psychedelic fantasies. Apocalyptic visions, dreamlike memories, erotic desires, have no place in the naive art of the Greek people, whose Mediterranean character will not tolerate psychological tensions, and who manage to overcome all difficulties, helped perhaps by Dionysius' wine and by the openness of their conversation.

Everything in Greek naive art is full of the nostalgia for the simple pleasures of the past and pure landscapes and villages unspoilt by modern civilisation. Such compositions are totally deprived of dreamlike exoticism, because the Greek naive artist is able to see the merry side of life, in a way which reduces the pressure of heavy manual work, and transforms the daily struggle into a pleasant game.

Panagiotis Zographos, the first representative naive artist of the recent past, painted his own version of the history of the Greek Revolution against the Turkish occupation in 1821, following the directions of General Makriyiannis, a leading figure in those events. However, his work is not as widely known as that of *Theophilos Hatzimichail* (1867—1934) from the island of Lesbos, a pioneer in the field of naive painting with a recognisably Greek flavour. His work served as a source of insipiration to many subsequent folk and naive painters.

Theophilos was one of the itinerant painters who travelled from village to village in order to fulfil the requirements of a certain commission. He is reported to have worked in Smyrna, and later on in the villages of Pilion in Thessaly, where he decorated coffee houses, little shops, drawing-rooms, wealthy homes and mansions. His subjects range from Greek mythology, treated as a series of true and lively stories, to the Greek Revolution of 1821, or to the simple life of shepherds and peasants engaged in the olive harvest, the kneading of bread and the work of the greengrocer.

The thousand-year-long Byzantine history does not seem to be unknown to him, because he often depicts Constantine Palaeologus fighting against the Turks on the walls of Constantinople. Theophilos' historical paintings show a juxtaposition and mixture of elements and people from different periods, typical of the rich imagination of the naive artist, which does not obey the rules imposed by precise knowledge. He also favours street scenes (e.g., the dancing bear, the barber cutting the hair of his client in the middle of the street) as well as portraits of well-known village characters, heroes of the Greek struggle for independence, views of cities and simple decorations with flowers. His figures are life-size, and always in the middle of a clearly Greek landscape. The proportions of the limbs and those of the different objects vary according to the degree of importance attached to them. The outlines and the use of the effects of light and shadow prove that Theophilos adheres to the tradition of religious painting which grew out of Byzantine art during the time of the Turkish occupation. At the same time, the painter presages something completely new and revolutionary, which determined the character of the subsequent developments of this art.

Greek naive sculpture made its first appearance in the island of Tinos, which had a rich native tradition in the carving of marble reliefs with religious and every-day scenes, and exclusively decorative motifs related to the Byzantine tradition. The work was in low relief, the facial expression of the figures simple, and their limbs disproportionate. The scenes represented took place in a calm and simple atmosphere, attesting to the joy of life and the moderation of the island's inhabitants.

The sea serves as another source of inspiration to Greek naive painters, because of their country's intense seafaring activity. Various types of ships with masts, which travelled across the Aegean Sea for centuries, different maritime adventures and the rough faces of the sailors appeal to the imagination of naive painters. *Nicolaos Christopoulos* (1880—1967), a painter from the area of Pilion, specialised in lively pictures of proud ships, as well as in others showing the hard labour involved in the constant struggle against the dangers of the sea. The type of naive art which made its first appearance during the 19th century finds a lively expression today in the work of contemporary painters, whose naive style is either instinctive or conscious. *Stamatis Lazarou* (1916) is a self-taught artist, whose work includes wood-carvings, paintings on canvas and shells, and stone and clay sculptures. His subjects are mythological and historical scenes, with some emphasis on

the incidents of the Greek Revolution of 1821, Gorgons and tritons, religious figures, the occupations of peasants and fishermen, and colourful landscapes. His wood-carvings, which often depict fishermen, workmen and peasants, are imbued with a humorous and carefree disposition. He often compresses his figures, together with the characteristic tools of their profession, in a small area, and this obliges him to show them one on top of the other.

Yannis Theophilis (1926), *Spyros Paliouras* (1875—1957), and *Christos Kagaras* (1920) draw their inspiration from village life which still remains untouched in many areas of Greece.

Various events like weddings, religious festivals and processions, dances in village squares, etc., which have now lost their import-ance and are mechanically repeated in the cities, continue to be represented with all necessary detail and appropriate significance. Such scenes are not merely pictures created by the artist's naive imagination. They retain their close connection with the life of the Greek people. Some consciously naive painters, like *Maria Pop, Effi Michelis* (1906—1984), *Takis Sideris* (1929), *Nicolaos Nakis (Kartsonakis)* (1899—1977) are firmly rooted in tradition, and have spent their whole life trying to discover untouched popular painting and the ways of the village people.

Vassilaros, Fotios Rammos, Christos Psarianos, Kostas Karampalis, Eugene Spatharis (1924) and *Mollas*, the great reformer of the Greek shadow-theatre called "Karagiozis," which flourishes in Greece today, paint scenes and figures related to the texts of this type of theatre.

Karagiozis, this very old shadow-theatre which combines simplicity with the hard realities of life, has some influence on the paintings of Nakis as well. Pop and Sideris are well acquainted with island life, and paint old houses, religious processions and characteristic small shops that are continuously under the threat of the destruction caused by technological progress and modern civilisation.

The freshness and simplicity of naive art continuously appeal to many modern artists, who incorporate a variety of elements taken from folk and Byzantine art into the art of today.

Sheldon Williams

NAIVE ART IN HAITI

The history of naive art in Haiti stretches back to a century ago, but it did not become fully-fledged until DeWitt Peters, an American school-teacher, stumbled upon the paintings of *Hector Hyppolite*, first in the form of household decoration (painted with feathers dipped in housepaint) and then used as an adjunct to his work as Voodoo priest. Voodoo is the key syndrome of Haitian naive painting and sculpture.

The existence of this "spiritual way of life" (and death) did not come from indigenous people of Haiti, the now extinct Arawaks, but from the Haitians, the descendants of the black slaves who, although mainly imported from Brazil, came originally from Africa, or to be more precise, the Yoruba, Nago, Ibo, Congo and other tribes. It is amazing that nothing on the African continent in the way of naive art can compare with its sudden efflorescence on this island in the Caribbean.

It was DeWitt Peters who laid the foundations of what was to become the Centre d'Art in Port-au-Prince (inaugurated in 1945), and it was as a result of his enthusiasm for his new-found artists that he was able to persuade Bishop Voegeli to commission so many works from them for the decoration of the new Episcopalian Cathedral in that city.

Haitian naive art draws its inspiration, character and development from the overwhelming influence that Voodoo has had not only on its subject-matter but also on its very existence. There is a wry saying in Haiti that ninety percent of the population are Roman Catholic, but one hundred percent are Voodoo.

This is so true that those who go to Mass in the morning will probably be found at a Voodoo ceremony in the afternoon. The very hierarchy of the Roman Catholic saints is matched and paralleled by the Voodoo *loas* in such a way that when the cult was officially prohibited it was easy to switch from Voodoo nomenclature to Christian without in any way interfering with the proceedings.

Voodoo is absolute. So it is not surprising to find clear evidence of it in the artists' work and inspiration. Many of them might never have painted any pictures at all had it not been for the "command of the *loas*." In fact, they frequently depict either the *loas* themselves or the ceremonies that take place when they are worshipped.

The artists themselves fall into three categories, temporal, not stylistic (in the main, although they all have a Haitian accent, the independence of their paintings makes them stand out as individuals): those who are pre-DeWitt Peters (few in number and frequently anonymous); those who were discovered or encouraged by him (the artists who came to the forefront after his death); and those who have since made a "career" for themselves in naive art.

In all three groups there are degrees of quality and, not unnaturally, account must be taken of the increase in the number of artists as a natural outcome of the sudden world interest in naive art (a visit from André Breton helped) in the island where Christopher Columbus first dropped anchor in his attempt to find a western route to the East Indies. This upsurge of excitement abroad led not only to the discovery of a wealth of fine artists, but also to the emergence of an excessive number who at best might be described as second-rate (in view of this situation, there has been a growing tendency to distrust all "newcomers" and show a marked preference for the works of the older generation).

Furthermore, this attitude has become steadily substantiated because of the rising tide of *faux-naifs* or those who are simply trying to cash-in on a tourist influx of US dollars or other hard currency.

As far as the relationship between art and money in Haiti is concerned, a number of the island's artists fall broadly into one of two groups: those whose work can be "good" but which frequently falls into the category of "potboilers"; and those who never rise above the level of ethnic kitsch. They can either be the victims of desperate endeavours to earn as much as possible (and the Devil take standards!), or, as is also too often the case, they can fall into the hands of ruthless promoters of their works who, while being efficient businessmen, seek profit first and quality second, and then only if it is quickly marketable. It is natural that money

making should have a crucial and oppressive role in a country where the majority of the population is so poor.

In a country notorious for its devastating unemployment and extremes of poverty, it can hardly come as a shock that some of the poor with only a vestige of talent as artists have sought to take advantage of the unwary with a terrible cultural confidence trick. This ploy is certainly not unknown in other parts of the world, but it is perhaps at its most prevalent in Haiti.

Of the great names existing in the time of DeWitt Peters, who remains? *Philomé Obin* and his family are still productive, and it is worth pointing out that the Obins, unlike so many of their contemporaries, do not rely upon Voodoo as the lynchpin of their works. Philomé (he was hard at work as a painter in Cap Haitien long before the arrival of DeWitt Peters), in particular, prefers to dwell upon Haiti's past, so that most of his pictures are of dreams or scenes of elegance costumed in an ambience unknown today.

Jean Enguerrand Gourgue is altogether different. With his capably handled sophisticated brush (albeit, untrained), he is a recognised devotee of Voodoo and very often evokes its sinister side (the Left Hand) in his paintings. True, his pictures betray marked gradations in quality, but the best of them are magnificent, even if in many cases they exude an inescapable eeriness.

Then there is the sad story of *Wilson Bigaud*. Discovered by Hector Hyppolite when he was only fourteen years of age, at one time he was hailed as the "Raphael" of Haitian paintings — his pictures were so limpid and beautifully constructed, a truly miraculous autodidact. But he took the fatal step of defying the *loas* of Voodoo. (Maybe, in western terms, his "crime" was one more of omission than commission?) At all events, it was to have serious consequences.

The mistake came about — long after he had completed his paintings for the Episcopalian Cathedral — when he was undertaking a huge canvas of "The Last Judgement." The picture, relating the terrible division between those destined for Heaven and those cast into the outer darkness of Hell, was naturally filled with figures, not only human ones but also the Angels (for the saved) and the Devils to take the condemned below.

This important painting was well in hand when he received his first warning. In dreams, the ultimatum was put to him: either you stop glorifying Christianity and show your loyalty to Voodoo, or you take the other course and will be punished accordingly. Bigaud's reply was that he had no special wish to paint "Christian" pictures, and the whole matter was, as far as he was concerned, trivial. (He put it badly. He inferred that, with no strong disposition for Voodoo, what could it matter?)

The initial proof for Wilson Bigaud that the *loas*' threat was serious came when the Devils in his picture came alive and started to plague him (he was never to complete this painting). Thereafter, Bigaud's standard of painting declined, and he became the victim of persistent attacks of mental instability. Occasionally he would produce a painting of relatively high quality, though not in the same class as his early works, but in general his work degenerated.

After years of recurring mental illness, he eventually became the puppet of a Mambo (Voodoo priestess). She kept him in the backwoods, churning out worse and worse paintings which she would subsequently sell for a few dollars on her trips to Port-au-Prince.

Even in the sunny "honeymoon" period of DeWitt Peters, Haitian artists were poor (the good times, financially, were for them a long way off). *Castera Bazile*, a wonderful painter who died early, in need of medical attention he could not afford, was a houseboy at the "Centre d'Art," while his contemporary *Sisson Blanchard*, although he was able to sell a few paintings, had to augment his income working as a yard boy; *Rigaud Benoit* even acted as DeWitt Peters' chauffeur.

One of the last great talents of the Haitian Renaissance was *André Pierre*. In his bright colours and crude representation, Pierre painted *loas* in total actuality. He painted them engaged in their extraordinary activities and in the centre of their lavish ceremonies. This exceptional artist only painted when he received direct orders from the spirits to do so. As a "la place," the position held by Voodoo servants with duties to prepare the *houmphor* (Voodoo temple) for meetings and ceremonies, before they are elevated to become *houngans* (priests), he was close to the sources of his inspiration. Because his work called on him to carry out the entire fabric of active Voodoo expertly and with extreme care, he was exceptionally well-informed about all the details relating to the *loas* and this complex "spiritual way of life."

Alas, André Pierre is no more. Almost as a sardonic twist of fate, his eyes, which had seen so much more than the ordinary man is vouchsafed, failed him at the end. But not before he had set out on canvas many secrets of the *loas* and their complicated existences.

The great Haitian artists were plentiful — *Gérard Valcin* (who won the international first prize for naive painting at Zagreb), *Robert St Brice* (perhaps the most "primitive" of all the Haitian painters), the amazingly inventive *Préfète Duffaut*, the mysterious "missing man" *Le Forest* (no one ever saw him and only his equally mysterious paintings remain as testimony of his skill), the supreme peasant artist *Micius Stéphane*; their sheer individuality and natural genius made an unprepared world gasp.

Some survive. Others have moved forward to help write another chapter in the history of Haitian naive art. There are some good artists among them; *St Louis Blaise*, *Etienne Chavannes*, *Yves Lafontant* and *Murat St Vil* (sophisticated in his paintings of magic islands half lost in a greedy sea), but they have not somehow achieved the artistic charisma of those who preceded them. They have character, ability, sound talent, but they lack the 'x' element of the Bottex brothers: *J. B. Bottex's* painting of Mary Magdalene on a balcony spotting Jesus in the crowd below is enormously powerful both in its philosophic content and in its humour — Mary Magdalene, black of course, is so obviously a member of the oldest profession (we only see her from the back, her nubile frame propped against the balustrade); or, at his best, *J. R. Chéry* with his picture of the inauguration of "La Citadelle" by the Emperor Christophe; or the humanity that is summoned up by *Salnave Philippe-Auguste* in his "Youth and a Girl," which defeats all arguments against miscegenation.

We live today (1984) in a period of marking time. While some of the old men still make their fine paintings (Alexandre Grégoire is not what he was and some of the fire has gone out of him; Chéry paints too many cute children carrying giant gourds and melons), the new artists, so rich in ability, have still not discovered the touchstone that could raise the quality of their pictures to the level of those of their illustrious forebears.

As well as the favourites of the past, some of them still painting, there are bright lights on the horizon. *Audes Saul* is young, but he may yet live to deserve the crown of laurels.

Ida F. Mihály

NAIVE ART IN HUNGARY

Any investigation of the precursors of naive art in Hungary must take into consideration talented men of the people who stood out in village communities for the mastery of their painting, carving and, in general, decoration of churches. If one goes back to around 1830, this category would include the first significant generation of shepherd carvers. On wood or bone, using relief as their technique, they gave a succinct accounting of the life lived by shepherds. The figures depicted by them, dressed in richly ornamented and motley shepherds' capes, tend their flocks, drink wine, carouse, dance to the tune of the fiddle, the bagpipe and flute, or receive favours from their sweethearts. Carved wooden drinking vessels, decorative figures on shepherd's staffs, human faces or animal heads, bear witness to the singular imagination, expressiveness and extraordinary sculptural sensibility of these artists.

In certain parts of Hungary, among the decorative figures on carved furniture and on the painted backs of benches we find shepherds, hunters, gendarmes, revellers, Hussars or scenes from everyday life.

In the 1860s it was the custom in vine-growing villages along the north shore of Lake Balaton for newly married couples to place votive statues of their patron saint before their houses or along the road. In graveyards, stone-carved monuments rise to heights of three or four metres. These were the origins of a rustic late religious art not commonly found elsewhere. Amateur wood-carvings of the so-called Kiskun Madonna were shown in growing numbers at Alföld.

In the first decade of our century, it was the custom in certain villages beyond the Danube for pupils taking exams to present each other with drawings, some of which are found in the graphics collection of the Ethnographic Museum in Budapest. The pictures show young girls in the festive Sárköz costume going about their chores, watering flowers or playing ball. These drawings cannot be classified as anonymous folk art because they bear the stamp of individuality.

Interest in naive art in the present sense of the words appeared with discovery of the works of the peasant painter *Péter Benedek*. During the First World War, the art critic Jenö Bálint was the first to call the attention of the public to his drawings, having perceived that Benedek was a more sincere, fresher and richer interpreter of the life of his peasant world than were professional painters. In his pictures are found passionate love or grotesque motifs portrayed with winning humour. His first exhibition in 1923, a later one in Budapest in 1928, and another in Vienna in 1929, aroused the interest of critics and the public at large in his art and personality. Newspapers carried reports on him and his paintings found purchasers. His success set an example for many previously unknown and neglected painters of talent in the countryside.

The thirties brought a flowering of a singular type of art, faithfully reflecting the life of the Hungarian peasantry. Thanks to trail-blazing by Bartók and Kodály in the field of research in folk music, *literati*, too, showed a growing interest in folk culture. A segment of the intelligentsia, considering the peasants the most original and authentic part of the population, set itself the task of collecting and saving from oblivion the achievements of folk art that were beginning to be forgotten. Encouraged by earlier results, Jenö Bálint organised in Budapest's National Salon in 1934 a large group exhibition of works by newly-discovered "original talents." The newspaper "Reggel" published articles on talented individual artists, thus popularising them among the public.

In the years that followed, these popular artists became widely known through exhibitions and the press. Bálint rented, on a permanent basis, a gallery in Budapest for showing and selling their works. Later, in 1935, he founded an association and a newspaper named "Original Hungarian Talent." The fame of these creative peasants spread beyond the boundaries of their own country. Many foreign papers began to write about them, they were invited to exhibit abroad, and their work was covered by mass communications media.

During the Second World War and immediately afterwards, interest in the art of these creative peasants waned. But since the sixties exhibitions of the work of peasant naive painters have become more frequent, and repercussions of Hungarian naive art have reached foreign experts.

To supplement the works already in its possession, the Hungarian National Gallery purchased Patai's private collection consisting of approximately one hundred naive paintings of the thirties. Together with the Ethnographic Institute, the Gallery organized an exhibition under the heading of "Hungarian Naive Art in the 20th Century," shown also in numerous museums in the country's interior, and then in Regensburg, in Cuba, in Belgium and in Greece.

Hungarian peasant painters show equal interest in everyday life and festive occasions in their community. Some of the themes dealt with are the villages, ploughed fields, wastelands, groves along the banks of rivers, the rare woods of the Alföld, vineyards on hillsides, vegetable gardens, flower gardens, barnyards and guest rooms. In most cases, the pictures are crammed with human figures. Scenes of intimacy are rare — only here and there do we find a betrothed or married couple, a mother nursing her baby, such as may be seen, for instance, in some of the watercolours and pastels of Péter Benedek.

András Süli's works are childlike observations of the world around him, wonderful in their simplicity, for his way of looking at things radiates the purest naivety. The interiors of peasant homes, small objects, barnyards and village gardens with lawns and flowers, the banks of rivers, country railroad stations, car drivers and passengers on the roads, are portrayed in dense colours on his paintings, whose decorative composition is well-conceived. The paintings of *Péter Benedek*, master of delicate drawing and refined colours, depict the painter's surroundings, including the intimate atmosphere of the inside of peasant homes with individual objects shown in detail in the manner of still lifes. The uninhibited interplay of details in these pictures is combined with sweep in execution.

Holy days, harvest festivities, revelry during grape-picking time, groups of youths in their holiday finery going to call on the prospective bride of one of them, a peasant cart loaded with the dowry, pillows and boxes of a young woman just married, crowds jamming coloured tents, are themes that have been dealt with by virtually all peasant painters. This is true also of the women of Galgamács. *Elek Györi* portrays several versions of gay wedding parties in horse-drawn sleighs. His paintings radiate a pithy vitality, dynamism and humour. On the canvases showing village feasts, many figures are found — men and women sitting with dignity and eating at large tables. The paintings of dancers in couples or doing a reel are painted with gusto, freshness and wit.

The works of women painters from Galgamács depict the gaiety and high colour of groups of young women sitting by the light of oil lamps and spinning or flirting with young men. Whereas the "original talents" painted almost all the kinds of work done in the villages during the various seasons of the year, in the paintings of *János Gajdos* we find the figures of the urban poor and seasonal workers. On his huge canvases, the lame and the blind, as well as beggars, are dispersed among the crowds hurrying to church service. His winter scenes show skaters on frozen rivers or city rinks. He has also painted scenes from the soldier's life: recruitment, the send-off given young men on their way to the army, units on the march, Hussars. Naive painters frequently depict floods, children and elders fleeing from danger, families saving what little they have in the way of property and livestock, and events from their own lives. The thought of death is expressed in the paintings of peasant artists, obviously preoccupied with the spectacular aspect of rituals by portrayals of funerals or the dead lying in state.

The life of Hungarian peasant painters is portrayed on all these pictures with elementary realism or gentle lyricism. Their observation of the world around them is imbued with childlike purity; with brush and paint they have recorded popular customs from the first half of this century and village life in different parts of Hungary.

Since the sixties, a growing number of retired persons have turned to art and spend their leisure time painting and carving. In various towns and villages throughout the country amateur art clubs have been founded where young and old work side by side with the help of a painter or sculptor. Among them are creative talents whose view of the world is typical of the naive artist. On closer examination, it is apparent that their subject-matter and styles vary considerably. Among the naive painters in the villages, traditional subjects are still popular. The artistic world of naive painters in the cities is different and their experiences are more individualised. Most of them deal with real-life themes but there are some among them who prefer to paint places and figures outside their immediate environment, events from the past, or projections into the future. The influence of education is obvious in their imaginative paintings. For *János Balázs*, a painter of Romany descent, an obsession with the fantastic is characteristic. An inclination to meditate on the puzzle of life has taken his brush to regions far removed in space and time. On his canvases are found South Sea islands with their luxuriant vegetation, strange idols, myths about the beginning of the world and cataclysms. The sun, the life-giving or destructive energy of water, the mystery of death — these are the basic themes of his paintings. *Lajos Hornyák* is attracted by the great masters whose works he sees in museums. While using them as his model, he nevertheless gives his forms and compositions individual treatment, investing them with his own feeling for gay and decorative colour. Idyllic regions as well as city scenes, drawn by pen, with thin brush-strokes or in pastels, are the favourite of *Antal Dévényi*. *István Klucsik* in his paintings seems carried away by a nature resembling paradise.

The paintings of the naive artists predominantly show groups in a landscape. Their pictures are frequently symmetrical and animals and buildings face forward. In most cases, human figures are composed of several linked forms. On his paintings on glass, *József Csimin* depicts a number of events going on at the same time, regardless of whether he is painting men at work or a motif from a fairy-tale. In the plastic oil paintings of *Dezsö Mokry-Mészáros*, the movements of the figures parallel the background of the picture, of the lines of the landscape, recalling backdrops. In the work of *János Balázs* the basic elements are placed beside or above each other, so that space is rendered in what is virtually an oriental fashion.

Naive painters usually work in oil but also use tempera, watercolours, pastels and ink. Two special techniques are also found: *Mihályné Maczó* works with coloured mosaic-like wheat grains, while *Teréz Borosné Endresz* achieves a plastic effect in compositions worked in cloth, leather and other natural materials. Sculptures and wood-carvings portray the figures of animals and human beings in various situations and are characterised by an exceptional power of observation.

Most of the artists who carve in wood live in the villages: the descendants of shepherds, they include carpenters and barrel-makers, but also factory workers. Few of them carve life-size figures or figures from legends and history. The most original works among them are the figures of revellers by *Joachim Asztalos*. The sedately composed groups of statues by *Janos Homa* feature an archaic conception of form. Social and political criticism is the hallmark of work by *István Orban*. *Károly Nagy*, an intellectual from Budapest, may be considered a master wood-carver. His figures of sinners in grotesque situations bear witness to a highly unusual power of insight.

In summing up opinions about Hungarian naive art, it is safe to say that the psychological profile of the artists differs and that the themes they deal with and ways of expressing themselves likewise vary. Their works reflect specific national features and a dedication to local customs, since most of them are closely associated with the village and the peasant way of life.

Many of their works are found in public collections: the naive art collection of the Hungarian National Gallery in Budapest contains no less than seven hundred paintings, sculptures and graphics. The recently founded Museum of Naive Art in Kecskemét has possibilities of expanding its collection and exhibiting the works it has collected.

John Fowler and Karen Mills

NAIVE ART IN INDONESIA (BALI)

About mid-way in the southern chain of the Indonesian archipelago lies the 2,300 square-mile volcanic island of Bali. Since the arrival of the first settlers from the mainland of Asia thousands of years ago, Indians, Chinese, proto-Polynesians, Arabs, Javanese, Dutch and others have passed this way, each leaving their mark upon the face and culture of the people. Today the island is home to over 2,500,000 Balinese, the majority living in their ancestral family villages, surrounded on all sides by the life-sustaining rice fields.

Bali's religious life is markedly complex. The venerated old Balinese deities are merged into the beliefs and deities of the old Javanese-Hindu-Buddhist pantheon to form a uniquely Balinese religion.

Although contact with the western world had extended over several hundred years, Bali remained virtually unmolested until the middle of the 19th century, when Dutch expeditions were sent to the island. By 1906, after fierce resistence by many of Bali's independent kingdoms, the entire island was finally brought under Dutch colonial rule. This western intrusion resulted in the shattering of traditional continuity in a society dominated by caste feudalism, religion and cosmic magical influences. Dutch democratisation sharply reduced the power and wealth of the ruling classes, greatly curtailing royal and priestly patronage of the arts, which at that time were almost totally of a religious nature.

Traditional Painting. The original and traditional style of painting, introduced into Bali by the 9th century, was in the style known as "Wayang". This style was, and still is, strict in form, execution, subject-matter and medium, lending a formalised and stiff appearance with little of the freedom, richness and colour now usually associated with the art of Bali. Almost all faces are presented in three-quarter view if they are human beings, gods or demons, and in profile if they are mortal animals or fish. The subject-matter of the paintings was almost invariably scenes from the Hindu epics of Ramayana and Mahabhrata and the indigenous Balinese or Javanese legends, known as *Malat*.

These paintings were used for the festive decoration and embellishment of temples, pavilions and palaces, and for family and village ceremonies, or to illustrate the combination calendar-almanac-horoscopes that guide the Balinese in determining the most auspicious day to plant, sow, make certain offerings, look to financial matters, or engage in any of the countless activities of uncertain outcome.

The classic Wayang style reached its zenith during the 15th century when, after the fall of the Madjapahit Empire, most of the Hindu-Javanese court fled to Bali. Some of the finest extant examples of Wayang painting can be found adorning the ceilings and walls of two most impressive buildings: the "Kerta Gosa" (ancient Court of

Justice), and the "Bale Kambang", Floating Pavilion, both located in the city of Kelungkung.

Although Wayang painting suffered a slight decline in the early 20th century owing to the Dutch invasion and resulting social upheaval, it has continued to this day and has, in fact, enjoyed a recent rejuvenation under the leadership of a young painter named *Nyoman Mandra* of Kamasan. Although the traditional Wayang style can hardly be considered "naive", the foundation of all Balinese painting is nevertheless firmly rooted in this old religious art. Almost all contemporary Balinese painters still first draw and then colour-in the image, still portray vegetation in the stylised Wayang manner and most faces in three-quarter view and, in a hundred other small but significant ways, remain influenced by the Wayang traditions.

Secular Painting. In the 20th century, as communications opened between Bali, Indonesia and the rest of the world, and the first trickle of tourists with their unfamiliar customs and cultures appeared, the style and subjects of Balinese painting began to change. In the late 1920s and early 1930s, painting and music flourished. Balinese artists in the villages of Ubud, Batuan and Sanur, as well as individual artists from other villages, began for the first time to draw subject-matter from their imaginations and environment, creating small, almost miniature masterpieces reflecting scenes from village life and Balinese legends and myths. Although they no longer followed the strict traditions and purity of style associated with the classic Wayang, these new secular painters of the thirties continued to work with the same care and love of detail that had been previously devoted to the religious classics.

Batuan. Of the three major painting villages, it was the inland village of Batuan in the southeast that produced the leading and most powerful exponents of what is known as the "thirties style." Alive with tensions and power and filled with sumptuous and fantastic detail, these images present, with almost photographic clarity, dramatic scenes of village and ceremonial life. Devoid of almost all perspective, depth or light effect, the paintings of the thirties have an originality and naiveté that is truly magical.

Almost all works during this era were done on paper with Chinese inks and locally made water-based colours. The artists did not sign their works in those days. No pride of authorship could attach to such a gift from the gods. Today, in the museums of Bali and collections throughout the world, there are hundreds of exquisite paintings whose authors are now unknown. Surely some are still alive, working once again in their village rice fields, their passing enthusiasm and talent long ago spent on only a few masterpieces. Yet others, such as *Ida Bagus Togog, I Made Djata* and *Ida Bagus Made Widja*, have continued to paint and develop their talent, keeping them in the forefront of Balinese art to this day. Togog and Widja continued in a style varying little from their original one of the thirties, and each has trained a son to perpetuate his tradition. These two families are the proponents of what is now known in Batuan as their "old" style. Djata, on the other hand, soon developed a more realistic style of painting, more acute and precise in detail, often displaying an almost sophisticated sense of perspective and proportion. Over the years Djata has had many pupils and followers in his "new" Batuan style,

unquestionably the most talented and successful of whom is his son, *Wayan Radjin*, an innovator in his own right.

Ubud. Approximately ten miles inland from Batuan lie the villages of Peliatan and Ubud and several surrounding communities such as Tebesaya and Padangtegal. Elevated, cool, and surrounded by a myriad of rushing rivers and streams, Ubud was the chosen home of European painters Walter Spies and Rudolf Bonnet and of many of the founding and pre-eminent members of the Pita Maha Association of Balinese artists. *Ida Bagus Kembeng, Anak Agung Gede Soberat, Ida Bagus Made Nadera* and *I Gusti Nyoman Lempad* were all fine artists of the thirties who lived and worked in this area and whose contributions to the artistic renaissance of Bali was profound and far reaching. Here there was a much greater diversity of styles and individual interpretation than was to be found in Batuan and other more homogeneous painting villages. The images created by many artists bore a strong affinity to those of Batuan, although the relatively realistic definition of the human anatomy and the sophisticated use of light and dark colours would indicate that the Ubud artists had assimilated some of the techniques of the Europeans. Other Ubud artists such as Lempad and, to a lesser degree, Soberat, were never part of this mainstream village movement and developed their own unique images and styles.

Local artists were instrumental in the creation of the "Puri Lukisan" (Painting Museum) in Ubud, with an extremely fine collection of paintings not only from Ubud, but representing almost all the fine known Balinese artists of the thirties and since. Today, Ubud is still regarded as a major art centre although, since the death of Lempad in 1978, most of the art produced there can only be described as commercial or "tourist" art.

Sanur. On the south coast of the island lies Sanur, a large village that boasted several very fine artists of the 1930s. Here *Ida Bagus Nyoman Rai, I Gusti Made Rundu, Ida Bagus Sodang* and others created their own distinctive parochial style. Although the sea is regarded by the Balinese as low, evil and the home of feared monsters, the painters of Sanur chose it as their favourite theme. Perhaps for the painters of coastal Sanur these scenes of marine life took the place of the luxurious vegetation images of the inland villages. Painting in a style that was perfectly flat and totally without perspective or depth, they created a somewhat Escher-like co-mingling of marine creatures, intertwined schools of fish or flocks or marine fowl, reptilian monsters and other human-faced apparitions from the unknown deep and beyond.

Today Sanur is a leading centre of hotels and services for tourists. As a result, little of what was traditionally Balinese naivety is seen in the art created in Sanur today. Nonetheless, the works of some of the early Sanur painters of the thirties are considered among the finest of Balinese "primitives." Probably the largest collection of these is held in the Gedung Kertia Library in Singaradja, North Bali.

Pita Maha. In 1935 an island-wide painters' association was formed with the guidance of Spies and Bonnet. This society, known as "Pita Maha," was created firstly to assist and instruct Balinese artists; secondly to counteract the tourist demand for Balinese art of commercial or common appeal, and thirdly to further assist in the promotion and development of fine local arts and in their exhibition abroad. A committee comprised of Spies, Bonnet and two leading Balinese artists selected paintings of Balinese artists that, in their opinion, were of the highest quality. These paintings were sent for exhibition to the Netherlands, the USA, Britain, France, Jakarta and other parts of Indonesia. In these creative and fertile years, Pita Maha had as many as a hundred and twenty-five active members.

With the outbreak of the Second World War and the occupation of the country by the Japanese, the Pita Maha organisation foundered and subsequently disbanded. In 1945, the Japanese surrendered but the cessation of hostilities was immediately followed by the struggle for Indonesian independence from the Dutch, finally recognised in 1949. The newly acquired independence brought a measure of somewhat turbulent normality. However, by this time Bali was becoming a tourist mecca, creating a demand for mass-produced art. During the intervening years, many of the old masters had either died or retired, and much of the earlier momentum had been lost. It is only today that the spirit that created the Pita Maha is reawakening and the serious artists are beginning to communicate and organise to overcome the deterioration of quality threatened by continually growing tourist demand.

Contemporary Painting. Something of a hiatus existed until the early 1960s when Arie Smit, then resident in Bali, assisted in developing what later became known as the "Young Artist" school of painting. The support and enthusiasm of Smit and the introduction of canvas and bright oil paints resulted in the birth and proliferation of this new and vibrant style. The Young Artist school was, and still is, largely comprised of boys and young men, most of whom come from the Sudra-class farming families in Ubud and the complex of small villages, primarily Campuhan and Penestanan, that surround it. These young artists paint idyllic villages, agrarian and some ceremonial scenes in an innocent, naive style and with a festive, carefree air. The lush vegetation of their environment is painted with a multi-coloured extravagance that surrounds and envelops the central theme of the painting.

Unfortunately, much of the original spontaneity of this style has been lost, since the majority of the young artists who paint in this style today have little time for reflection or development but are caught on a treadmill fulfilling the demands of "art shops" that sell to the endless stream of tourists and even wholesale to large shops in Italy, Germany and Brazil. There are, however, still a few painters of this school, such as *I Made Pugug* and *I Nyoman Campuan*, who are imaginative and take both pride and care in what they create. It is doubtful whether the Young Artists school, perhaps the most strictly "naive" of today's Balinese painting, will achieve its full potential or receive the critical recognition awarded to other areas of Bali's art.

As always, however, Ubud breeds innovative artists, and new styles are still emerging. One such innovator is *I Nyoman Roda*, perhaps the only primitive on Bali who applies his images immediately and directly onto his canvas rather than first drawing the outlines and then filling in the colours, the method employed by practically every other Balinese naive.

The growing commercialism that the Batuan artists saw destroying the art of their own and other villages induced them to group together, with the assistance of the curator of the *Puri Lukisan*, Anak Agung Gede Muning, and withdraw to the farthest corner of Batuan, forming the *Wisma Pelukis*. This organization, comprised of Batuan's leading serious painters including Widja, Djata, Radjin, *Ketut Karwan* and even seventeen-year-old *Gusti Ayu Natih Arimini*, Bali's first recognised woman painter, has, in the spirit of Pita Maha, been instrumental in preserving the integrity of the art of Batuan, elevating it to a position that should be envied and emulated by the sincere artist of every other painting village on the island.

Pengoseken. Hidden in the rice fields between Ubud and Peliatan is the village of Pengoseken, home of *I Gusti Ketut Kobot*, an early member of Pita Maha. As a noted artist of the 1930s, Kobot was fascinated with the stories of Hindu and Balinese mythology. His personal interpretations of these stories were notable for the great wealth of detail in which the vegetation and figures were painted. His work in the intervening years has culminated in the perfection of an almost surrealistic style and the emergence of a new and original interpretation of the classic stories. In association with his brothers, *Kaler* and *Baret*, Kobot founded what might be termed the "Pengoseken school of fanciful Hindu-Balinese mythological art." While the style of this school cannot be thought of as naive, it reflects an honest dedication to skill and craftsmanship.

The pressure to fulfil the demands of a guaranteed but relatively unsophisticated market has bypassed Bali's finest artists. While many works of Widja, Togog, Djata, Radjin, Lempad, Kobot and others are to be found not only in Bali's museums but in museums and private collections throughout the world, these artists have not as yet been universally recognised, sought after, or even understood. Thus, painting in relative obscurity and within the traditional structure of family and village communities, Bali's unsung masters are able to devote sufficient time, be it one year or three, to the creation of a single canvas. Behind the walled enclosures of the Balinese village and family compounds, time has but little meaning, and satisfaction comes from pride in one's work and tranquility of the soul.

Ruth Debel

NAIVE ART IN ISRAEL

Every study of modern art in Israel will mention the role played indirectly in it, by the work of Henri Rousseau. Eager to find a new artistic language through which their unique experience could be expressed, young artists from the Bezalel School in Jerusalem (founded in 1906) rebelled against their academic teachers and went to Paris in the 1920s. Rousseau's "innocence" matched their need to return to basics, because they felt they "began anew," exiles returning to their ancient land, rediscovering its landscape and remodelling its culture. These artists, among them Reuven Rubin, assimilated Rousseau's influence and when they returned to Jerusalem created what has since been recognised as the beginning of modern painting in Israel — "The Eretz-Israel School."

Even before the creation of the State of Israel popular or naive artists must have lived in the Holy Land, whether Jewish, Christian or Moslem, but there is very little record of their existence. In an exhibition called "Arts and Crafts in 19th-Century Eretz-Israel," held at the Israel Museum in 1979, three Jewish folk artists were represented: *Moshe Mizrahi* and *Shlomo Janiwer*, originally from Jerusalem, and *Joseph Zvi Geiger* of Safed. It is now commonly accepted that *Shalom of Safed*, the best known contemporary Israeli naive, has in his own way, continued their tradition.

Israeli museums, especially the Haifa Museum, have collected and shown works by local naive painters through the years, but the first attempt at presenting an overall picture of naive art was made in 1966 by the Israel Museum. Since there is no catalogue of that show, it is hard to discover how many artists were represented in it. The Tel Aviv Museum followed in 1970, this time with a catalogue listing eighteen participants. Occasionally, but not often, curators include works by naive painters in theme-exhibitions: "From Landscape to Abstraction, from Abstraction to Nature," at the Israel Museum, 1972, included *Shalom of Safed* and *Moshe Elnatan*. "Artist and Society," at the Tel Aviv Museum, 1979, included Elnatan and *Gabriel Cohen*.

Naive artists do not enjoy great popularity in Israel, and find it much easier to sell their works abroad than at home. They have made their mark at international exhibitions, such as those in Munich and Zurich in 1974. Anatole Jakovsky included five Israeli naive artists in his Lexicon, while West German television made a documentary about them in the series "Naives of the World."

The following are included in this encyclopaedia as the most important. *Shalom of Safed* (died 1980), *Natan Heber* (died 1975), *Gabriel Cohen* (born 1940), *Shimshon Lemberger* (born 1910) and *Menahem Messinger* (born 1900). There are women among naive painters in Israel, but none of them has yet produced an important *oeuvre*.

The above-mentioned artists only rarely knew of each other. Raised in traditional Jewish families, they still reflect different cultural sources through their work: Shalom of Safed was a typical Jewish-Palestinian artist, continuing a tradition known from the 19th century, but probably as old as the Jewish post-biblical settlement of the Holy Land. Moshe Elnatan and Gabriel Cohen are Jews from the East, who imbibed the Moslem culture which surrounded their ancestors in Iraq, Persia and Turkey. Natan Heber, Shimshon Lemberger and Menahem Messinger came from Poland and their work stems from the culture of the East-European *stetl*.

Dino Menozzi

NAIVE ART IN ITALY

It is not a simple task to speak of the beginnings of naive art in Italy or chronologically to determine its commencement and emergence. In the first place, only a small number of critical and historical studies have been written on the genesis of this phenomenon and, secondly, the very concept of naive art emerged fairly recently, parallel with the appearance and development of the naive artists themselves.

It would appear that critical thinking about naive artists in Italy was heralded by the interest aroused among the *avant-garde* and critics by the "Rousseau case." In this connection valuable testimony is provided by something written by A. Soffici in 1910 in the magazine "La Voce": "... if there is a painter who, by means of minor deceptions, invocations, or even ordinary technical mastery, does not know how to burnish and pictorialise his meagre and impoverished vision of reality, if there is a painter who — in a word — does not know how to paint in the way that painting is understood by the academic school and also by a large section of the critics and the public, cultivated or uninitiated, then that painter is assuredly Rousseau."

For quite some time, however, thinking on these matters was confined to a small élite, despite the fact that the first signs of a new criticism began to appear during the showing of a number of specialised exhibitions abroad.

On the other hand, in Italy there is not any widespread critical consciousness about the phenomenon of naive artists, as naive art is still too isolated a presence. In order to be conscientious as chroniclers, we must mention O. Metelli, who began to paint in 1922 but became known to the wider public at a big posthumous exhibition in 1946; L. De Angelis, who made his start in 1920 but exhibited for the first time in 1926; Di Terlizzi, beginning to work in 1928; Astarita, who won fame in 1931; to say nothing of the secret phase of painting by A. Ligabue, who though he commenced painting in 1930, waited until 1955 to exhibit in public; and the first feelers in painting by P. Ghizzardi in 1940. The lack of a logical link, and of any consistent critical link, between these isolated artistic events, means that we are still far from a systematic and adequate theoretical survey.

It would therefore be quite safe to assert that the origins of naive art in Italy emerged virtually unnoticed somewhere in the middle twenties and numbered extremely few practitioners. For at least two decades, naive art lingered in the shadows, practised, one might venture to say, almost in private. It was only at the beginning of the fifties that people began to sit up and take notice, to publish reviews, short essays and critical studies about one or the other naive painter. Between 1941 and 1952, L. Bartolini wrote a number of perceptive studies on Ligabue's painting, helpful in later critical revaluation of his work. M. Valsecchi, his interest aroused by R. Viva, admitted in 1952 that: "this will not even be an opportunity to talk about an alleged rebellion against culture; in the final analysis it will make a contribution of sorts to the spiritual history of its time, a handful of modest and fragrant violets among the exotic and refined garden paths of contemporary aesthetics." C. Belli, who was among the first to notice Di Terlizzi, spoke in a work dedicated to A. Grande in 1958 about the phenomenon of naive art, generally, although in a sense dissociating himself from it.

The repercussions of an important exhibition of naive art in Knokke-le-Zoute, during the World Fair in Brussels in 1958, were too faint by the time they arrived in Italy to have any visible influence on criticism. The first critical picture of the whole movement was presented in 1960 when the Saggiatore Publishing House of Milan issued the book "Contemporary Naive Painters" by Oto Bihalji-Merin, after which acceptable critical standards could be applied, fitting into the international panorama and permitting analysis of Italian conditions, even if only briefly.

An appreciable number of distinguished persons in Italian cultural and critical circles are, however, interested in individuals of undoubted talent. To recall a few: R. Vigorelli, who presented *Ligabue* in Rome in 1961; C. L. Ragghianti, who demonstrated an interest in *Galeotti* in 1960; S. Quasimodo and R. Carrieri, who wrote on *Ceccareli*; O. Vergani and L. Borgese, who presented *Rovesti*; A. Mezio, who discovered and launched *Pagano*. But in spite of these authoritative voices, the problems of naive art have still not been placed in their proper perspective nor widely felt; no need has as yet arisen for deeper investigation to reveal whether the phenomenon of naive art exists at a national level; much prejudice, doubt and mistrust still prevail.

Certain important happenings may be taken for an easier determination of the stages of development of Italian naive art: the naive exhibition in the Barberini Palace in Rome (1964), the anthological premiere of Ligabue in Reggio Emilia in 1965, the founding of the Naive Art Award in Luzzara (province of Reggio Emilia) in 1967, and the launching of the journal "L'arte naive" in Reggio Emilia (1973).

The exhibition in Rome of "Italian and French Naive Painters" (1964) marked the first phase of development consisting of the discovery of fresh personalities in the world of naive painting and in the creation of critical consciousness among individuals and the public at large, thus leading to the first, albeit incomplete, codification of naive art in Italy.

For purposes of possible historical-critical comparisons, note should certainly be taken of the presence of Italian naive painters who, in addition to Metelli, took part in this exhibition, and stress laid on the fact that these were still isolated cases impossible to arrange into homogeneous groups: *Allegretti*, whose graphics possess an inborn naiveté; *Benedettucci*, *Cappuccio*, *Carmelina di Capri* with a fascinating pictorial expression rich in warm Mediterranean hues; *Ceccarelli* with his poetic vision of his native Umbria; *L. De Angelis*, *Di Terlizzi*, *Fereoli* with his "metaphysical" urban paintings of Parma; the Romans *Grande* and *Imbrogno*; *Ligabue*, impressive for his rare creative power; *Lissia*, whose images breathe a boundless but serene imagination; *Mozzali* with his earthy, witty folk implications; *Pagano* with his characteristic visual musicality; *Pasotti*, a boundary case of a painter, who after finishing his studies, returned to an exceptionally lyrical vision of things; *Pera*, a gentle painter of the rough world of the villages around Chieti; *Rovesti*, the disorderly but suggestive countryman of Ligabue; *Ruggeri* with his secretive poesy full of solemn, visionary silences; *Viva* with his fascinating chromatic compositions, laden with nostalgia and memories.

Some outstanding articles on the exhibition were written by V. Guzzi, J. Recupero and L. Trucchi. Guzzi defined the naive painter as: "a self-taught painter who does not start from precise positions regarding culture but nonetheless succeeds in creating some of its forms."

J. Recupero delves extensively into the critical problem of the naive painters, pointing up the difference between naive and folk art. L. Trucchi firmly asserts that the naive artists, "a large and complex family of irregulars, have now already entered with full rights into the history of modern art." M. Ventureli, describing the exhibition, notes that the naive artists belong to no artistic group, school or movement. As may be concluded from these few quotations, naive art is drawing considerable attention from the public, which is becoming more curious, its interest aroused by new and important discoveries of individual "cases", among whom the most recent is *Ligabue*, familiar only to a select circle of critics: namely, in 1964 M. de Micheli introduced him in Milan with lively and intense sympathy. With the appearance of Ligabue, the second stage of development was embarked upon, distinctive for the definitive affirmation of naive art.

In 1965 in Reggio Emilia the first important anthological exhibition was held of Ligabue's work, marking him as a painter of excellence. We selected the paintings for that exhibition after careful work on research, cataloguing and photographic documentation. By one of those inexplicable twists of destiny, the artist died a few days after the opening of the exhibition in Reggio. The press, illustrated magazines and television began to take an interest in his hard life, his works and the exhibition then in progress; official criticism, no longer in a position to ignore him, was compelled to deal with his works. Thus began a rush for his paintings, scornfully rejected during his lifetime by so many "experts."

Motivated by the desire to reap profit from the exceptional artistic success of Ligabue, several painters in the Po Valley who had previously worked in complete privacy came out into the open and revealed themselves to be important naive artists; others, taking their cue from the unexpected upsurge of Ligabue's esteemed and naive painting, launched the lamentable phenomenon of imitation, of "mannered" naive art, of the mushrooming of a multitude of improvised discoveries and dealers.

The numerous impulses and suggestiveness flowing from Ligabue's work led us to embark on a study of the phenomenon of naive art, which spread with extreme rapidity, especially in the Po River Valley. Others also took note of the thriving new phenomenon, among them O. Zavattini who, supported by the municipal authorities of Luzzara, established in December 1967 the National Award for Naive Art; thus began the third stage of development, the phase of institutionalisation. Taking advantage also of the facilities of museums, a structure was created, in the wish to collect and systematically study everything connected with naive artists, to justify the rosiest expectations regarding extensive critical systematisation of this phenomenon. Artistic personalities arousing lively interest appeared for the first time. We also draw attention to the robust paintings of *M. Andruszkiewics*, the surrealist visions of *F. Bolognesi*, the gentle and naive works of *M. Colombo*, the dreamy and poetic paintings of *Di Girolamo*, the village themes enriched by the new and original style of *F. Galeotti*, the disturbing female figures of *P. Ghizzardi*, the idyllic, dreamy, refined and elegant visions of *I. Invrea*, the fragrant and tasteful poetic world associated with the childhood of *A. Ordavo*, the impressive and unconscious realism of *Pasqualini*.

The initiative from Luzzara was applauded as an event that could explain in national frameworks many theoretical issues and questions concerning the affiliations of naive art, although the definition of naive art contained in the Award stipulations, instead of clarifying concept, actually caused even more confusion. From the fourth year of bestowal of the National Award (December 1970), references were abolished to the specific features of naive art, so that the theoretical problem of the affiliation of this art was in fact abandoned. However, for a number of reasons, including insufficient vigilance on the part of official academic criticism, the phenomenon spread like wildfire and began to encompass pseudo-naive artists and dilettantes.

The exhibition in Lugano (1969), the Second Triennial in Bratislava (1969), Naive Art '70 in Zagreb and Meeting with Naive Artists in Prato (1971), passed almost unnoticed by the members of the jury of the National Award in Luzzara. With the public at large unable to find its bearings, in 1971 one of our publications came off the press, "La grafica naive nella bassa padana" (Age, Reggio Emilia), constituting the first attempt in Italy to collect and document the most acceptable critical articles and methodology for classifying naive artists. Thus work began on studying, cataloguing, discovering and calling attention to the best and most influential naive paintings. In 1973, following the exhibition "Contemporary Italian Naive Painters" in the Gallery of Naive Art in Zagreb (1972) and Italian participation with *Ghizzardi* in the exhibition Naive Art 1973, this work led to the founding of the magazine "L'arte naive." This magazine, endeavouring to make a selection and to stave off excessive publicity, represents the sound evolution of naive art and proposes a consistent critical revision of this phenomenon.

Those who succeeded, in the plethora of exhibitions, in finding their bearings among the numerous initiatives in various parts of Italy and who kept abreast of the appraisals offered by "L'arte naive" and the few well-organised exhibitions (mention must be made here of "La grande domenica" — Rotonda, Besana, Milan [1974]) and the IV International Biennial "I Naifs — I Candidi" organised by the Fair Council in Milan in 1980) could not help noticing how varied and characteristic, how charming and suggestive authentic Italian naive art is, and how, if we look closely, it is possible to identify painters whose style and subject-matter can be grouped together and through this the artists classified into specific homogeneous groups. What links them together may be their environment or ethnic relatedness or perhaps simply temperament. Instead of classifying them by generation, an unsuitable method, it would be better, given the limitations of space, to provide a concise but inclusive survey showing how the broad spectrum of Italian naive painters could be divided up today.

We indicated as far back as 1971 that it might be necessary to refer to one group as the "Po River Group", comparable to the Hlebine school in Yugoslavia. In this group, apart from *Ligabue, Rovesti, Fereoli* (participants in the Rome Exhibition of 1964) and *Colombo, Ghizzardi, Macca, Pasqualini* (present at Luzzara from 1967), whom we have already mentioned, new personalities have been appearing in later years, some of them extremely significant, like *Benassi*, with his instinctive and scenographic rhythm of composition; *Nasi*, with his effective primitive stereotypes; *Ponzi* and *Roggeri*, who

portray the existential themes of man with emotion and original techniques; *Toniato*, who sings the praises of the Po region and whose works are a merger of flights of feverish and poetic fancy with earthy anecdotes of everyday life; and other less familiar but still stylistically differentiated painters such as *Colibri, Ferrari, Pecchini, Savazzi, Valla,* and *Verzelloni.* All of them, together with others on a lesser plane, bear witness to the wealth of inspiration and vitality of the Po region — erroneously called a school by some — which certainly must be considered the most important in Italy.

The Umbrian group, whose founder is *Metelli*, with his highly elaborated and ambiguous atmospheres, includes *Allegretti, Benedettucci, Ceccarelli* and *Di Girolamo.* The number of prestigious members of this group has not grown significantly with the passage of time. On the other hand, the Roman region, including *Grande, Imbrogno, Lissia, Ruggeri, Pardo,* has been enriched by new representatives such as *Ciancaleoni,* and *Rotunno* with his original figures structured in bilateral symmetry, and the emigrant *Dallos,* a naturalised Roman.

The southern region, with *Carmelina, L. De Angelis, Di Terlizzi, Viva* (all of whom were in Rome in 1964), has been endowed with the suggestive morphological variations of *Gagliano, Pomili* and *Ezechiele,* particularly noted for the brilliance of their chromatic expression, thoroughly in keeping with the expansive Mediterranean temperament of the population there and the warmth of the sunny south.

No less interesting and worthy of attention is the Lombardy group, represented by such distinctive artistic personalities as *Pasotti, Pagado* and *Andruszkiewics,* to whom may now be added new names such as *Bini, Melis, Caffi.*

The Torino group, in which *Invrea* stands out, comprises *Prato, F. De Angelis, Maiolo, Berganton.* This group is distinguished for its particularly elegant and refined characteristics, almost as if the proximity of relatives on the other side of the Alps has somehow influenced the formation and development of their art, investing it with precision and delicate, poetic lines.

In Sardinia, too, there is a rather large "colony" of naive artists, unified by a thousand-year-old tradition, their painting drawing inspiration from their ancestors. Outstanding among them is *F. C. Pau*, the dry and down-to-earth interpreter of the Sardinian soul filled with myths and rituals lost in the mists of time; and *Pillitu* and *Cadoni*, who are also successful sculptors.

Finally, the "isolated" ones should not be forgotten, those who appeared in places where naive painting has not flourished to any appreciable extent: *Bortolami* (from Valdagno) with his sombre, intimate paintings; *Bragato* (of Padua) with his lyrical and delicately airy works; *Gentili* (of Pisa) with his powerful and instinctive expressionism reproducing the urban landscapes of his city; *Sartori* (from Trento) who is fondest of themes from everyday life; *Serafini* (from Montelupo Fiorentino) with his extraordinary forms and resourceful poetic vision focused on the pain and resignation of mankind.

In the hope that this historical survey provides sufficient elements for a wide insight into Italian naive painting, we should like to stress in conclusion the significance of the role which, practically against their will, the naive painters play: they reveal authentic cultural values, instinctively portraying this world from unsullied sources, drawing their themes from the genuine and indestructible inspiration of their creative impulses.

Sumio Kuwabara

NAIVE ART IN JAPAN

It is very difficult to explain the phenomenon of Japanese naive painting. Although there has been a great deal of research into naive painting in Europe and America, there has been almost none in Japan, so that it is not entirely clear whether naive painting existed there at all.

There are two reasons for this. The first is that Western and Japanese art are based on entirely different traditions. As the concept of naive painting has grown from the tradition of Western art, it is difficult to conceive of the birth of Japanese naive painting based on a tradition different from that of Western art. The second reason is linked with this question, too. In studies on Japanese art, no one has ever concentrated on research in naive painting. Hence it may be said that researchers on Japanese art have never analysed Japanese naive painting from a specific viewpoint. Folk art in Japan can hardly be included in the field of naive art; as a kind of refined artisan's work, perfectly professional in technique, it does not fit into this category. These are only some of the considerations posing difficulties in any discussion of naive art in Japan.

For naive painting to be born, there must be an art based on realism, as in Western Europe. In other words, naive painting cannot appear without the tradition of realism, the purpose of which is a reproduction of real objects. Without the background of an academic aestheticism of art and the techniques of realistic representation, both of which have developed since the Renaissance, naive painting, at the opposite pole from academicism, would never have been born. Naive painting, therefore, may be considered as a "child" of Western realism who does not resemble his "mother". Consequently, in Japan, where the tradition of Western realism was lacking, conditions for the birth of naive painting were very unfavourable.

Here one might say, to the surprise of many people, that the Japanese genre painting of "Ukiyoe" was the naive painting of Japan. However, if considered from a somewhat different viewpoint, Ukiyoe painting is seen to have, to a certain extent, the same characteristics as naive painting. These are paintings without light or shade, without nuances of colours. The technique of Ukiyoe painting, which reduces objects to thin black lines and flat colours, is far from the Western aesthetics of realism. To the eyes of French Impressionists, prints of Ukiyoe painting probably looked like primitive paintings from a small island in the Far East. The beauty of naivety was discovered by Western traditional aesthetics, so it might be said that the prints of Ukiyoe painting are a kind of naive art which Western aesthetics noticed by chance. If we accept such a viewpoint, then the prints of Ukiyoe painting may be considered the origin of naive painting in Japan.

However, we should turn our attention to the appearance in the middle of the 18th century of a kind of painting similar in style to the naive painting of Europe and America. First of all came the relief paintings of "Ukie." The term Ukie denotes a kind of illustration of a street or the inside of a house, based on perspective representation imported from Europe. The name is derived from the fact that buildings and figures seem to be shown in relief. Many Ukie pictures have survived — by Okyo Maruyama, a painter from Kyoto (1733—1795), by Masanobu Okumura, an Ukiyoe painter (1686—1764), etc. Ukie, which appear to be seen through a *vue d'optique* device, are said to have been very popular in those days. Although the painters were professional makers of specialised prints, they had no knowledge of Western realism, so that their works remained immature.

Next there appeared a series of pictures belonging to the early phase of painting under Western influence. At that time, the only "window" through which Japan could look at Europe was Holland, because Japan had trade relations only with that country. Many Japanese painters who came to know Western realism via Holland experienced a kind of shock. They were surprised to find that objects in the paintings looked quite realistic and resembled actual objects. These Western pictures, with light and shade and colour nuances, seemed to be done in three dimensions and to represent real objects. While French Impressionists discovered the Japanese painting of Ukiyoe, which is quite the opposite of realism, Western realism impressed Japanese painters, who now endeavoured in some way to paint in a realistic style, *Kōkan Shiba* (1738—1818), *Shozan Satake* (1748—1785), *Naotake Onoda* (1748—1780), *Denzen Aodo* (1748—1822) and others are considered typical painters of this trend. Unfortunately, their paintings could not approach the level of Western painting, remaining unsophisticated and immature since Japanese painters had not learned in practice the aesthetics and techniques of Western realism. Their works are very close in style to the naive painting of Europe and America. If we call them naive painters, then we may say that naive painting came into being in Japan in the second half of the 18th century. However, if we do not take into account the fact that these painters belonged to the Kano school, we may arrive at a wrong conclusion. (For example, Kōkan was at the same time an outstanding painter of Ukiyoe prints.) That these painters began to produce naive paintings soon after they came into contact with Western realism is an important factor. In the history of Japanese art their paintings are called "paintings from the early phase of influence of the West European style." They differ from paintings in real Western style from the second half of the 19th century, but they have never been considered from the viewpoint of naive painting.

After that, European realism was gradually absorbed by the Kano school and the *Bunjinga* (literary painting). On the other hand, by the middle of the 19th century there appeared on the scene a new movement of artists who were keen on introducing Western painting into Japan. A representative painter of this group of artists was *Yuichi Takahashi* (1828—1894). In Yokohama he learned the technique of oil painting from Charles Wigrman of the "London Illustrated News," and then studied under Antonio Fontanesi, an Italian artist who visited Japan at the invitation of the Japanese Government, and produced numerous oil paintings. However, as Takahashi did not entirely master the aesthetics and techniques of realism, many of his pictures resemble naive painting in style. In the second half of the 19th century besides Takahashi, artists like *Horyu Goseida* (1826—1892), *Seiji Tokonami* (1824—1897), *Shozaburo Yokohama* (1834—1884), sometimes produced portraits and landscape paintings in oil in the same crude style. As there was no tradition of oil painting in Japan when European realism began to influence Japanese painting, Japanese artists were faced with great difficulties, as may be gathered from the crude style, naivety and simplicity of their works.

At the end of the 19th century and the beginning of the 20th century, many Japanese painters who had studied in Europe became active in the art world. In the Tokyo Art Academy, the Department of Western painting was set up in 1896, and started offering an art education based on Western realism. From this point, under the influence of Western art, academicism began to develop in Japanese painting, although in fact, while the absorption of Western realism was in progress, some deviation occurred and Japanese realism took shape. Since a long time elapsed before Japanese academicism was established, certain conditions were therefore lacking for the birth of naive painting in the real sense of the word. At that time Japanese art had reached a stage close to the phase of development of naive art in the West, although conditions were still not ripe for the birth of genuine Japanese naive painting.

Real interest in naive painting in Japan began only after the Second World War. Western realism was then already established, although it differed somewhat from its model. In the new situation, the immediate spur to the appearance of naive painting was the press, which introduced and popularised naive painting by the Frenchman Henri Rousseau, the American Grandma Moses, and others. Yet another reason must be taken into account: *Kiyoshi Yamashita* (1922—1971) attracted general attention and won great popularity as a naive painter. Though mentally retarded, he aroused the interest of the public in naive painting. Whereas abstract art, which found great currency in the international art world after the war, was not accepted by the people in general, the public wholeheartedly took to Yamashita's style of representation with its minute reproduction of objects.

Parallel with this phenomenon, during the sixties and seventies Japanese mass media printed a large number of coloured pictures in the style of naive painting which were distributed throughout the country, thus increasing the popularity of naive painting. The Sunday edition of the largest Japanese paper "Asahi Shimbun" carried pictures painted by *Jiro Takidaira* (1921) every week, while a weekly magazine "Shincho" published works by *Rokuro Taniuchi* (1921—1981) on the cover of each issue. Both publications had a very large circulation, so that naive painting gained general popularity in this way. The works of these two painters, Takidaira and Taniuchi, with their fresh and cheerful poetical sentiments, spread throughout the whole country, giving impetus to the flourishing of naive art.

Paintings for children are generally called "Dōga" in Japan. Executed in a crude and simple style, they are often confused with naive art. But Dōga are a kind of naive painting produced intentionally, so it seems appropriate to call this genre "quasi-naive." The works of Takidaira and Taniuchi, marked by the same characteristics as Dōga, are likewise often so termed. *Taiji Harada* (1940), who succeeded Takidaira and is still now painting for the Sunday edition of "Asahi Shimbun," may also be considered a quasi-naive, along with many illustrators of picture books for children. Their style aims at a childlike spontaneity, and may be described as a genre produced by fusing a childlike style with naive painting.

This kind of quasi-naive painting aside, *Suma Maruki* (1875—1956) and *Mine Klein*, who lives in New York, may be considered as orthodox naive painters of the postwar period. Both are women who turned to art in the latter half of their lives. Both have produced brilliant images in their works, using light colours. Judging from the fact that they have no connection with academic art techniques, they are orthodox and genuine naives. The subjects of their works are autobiographical stories and fantastic scenes, which entirely qualifies them as real naive painters. These two women, creating pictures independently for themselves, removed from the maintream of Japanese art, are real spontaneous naive painters comparable with the naives of Europe and American folk artists.

Thus in Japan, where there was no tradition of realism in the past, true spontaneous naive painting matured only after the Second World War. Compared with the history of naive art in Europe and America, this may seem a unique phenomenon. But if we consider the fact that the cultural structure of Japan today is coming to approximate that of the West, it is conceivable that more and more naive painters will appear, though still in smaller number than in the West.

Japan, like Western countries, has now entered a social stage where everything is artificially organised. In such an environment, people are keen to return to their native hearth which is, in their minds, beyond the realm of time and space. As this kind of consciousness seems to express itself through naive painting, the latter may be said to have great significance. Far from formal art ruled by authoritarianism, or modern art which is high-brow and difficult to understand, naive painting is rooted deeply in the minds of the people. Even when it is quasi-naive, it does not lose its value as long as it has the ability to soothe the uneasy consciousness of modern man. In consequence, great possibilities exist for the future of Japanese naive painting.

Ma. Dolores Barajas Palomo

NAIVE ART IN MEXICO

Mexican art history does not deal explicitly with naive art although among Mexican artists this aesthetic expression exists in singular form, displaying a specific feeling for life, colour and shape.

The discovery and significance of this kind of painting in Mexico is attributable both to the personal efforts of a number of artists, and to art critics who, in their intensive study of the phenomenon, succeeded in bringing many highly valuable works to public attention.

The rich history of Mexican painting in the 19th century includes an exceptional type of artistic expression whose forms and colours caused it to be designated "folk painting."

The word "folk" is not the only one defining such works; others are "naive" or "primitive."

In relation to academic art in Mexico, this trend is so important that it holds a unique place in the history of Mexican art. Consisting of a large number of works, differing in subject and quality, it is found in various parts of the provinces, the most outstanding being Muchoacan, Guanajuato, Durango, Puebla and Veracruz. Mexican folk art is rightfully said to represent the most profound expression of the Mexican spirit, to be the work of painters who denied and opposed academic art. A considerable number of these works are anonymous, proving in even greater measure that the artists were men of natural talent.

A typical feature of Mexican folk art is its familiar brilliant play of colours, wondrously vibrant and glowing. The picturesque composition of the works and the rich variety of half-tones and nuances owes much to that radiance and colour. Mexican market-places, overflowing with fruit, flowers and pottery, are a source of these forms and colours. From that vital energy, folk art emerged and grew.

In Mexican 19th-century painting, this folk or naive art is sometimes richer and more interesting in its themes than the formal art of academic painters, especially in depicting events from the life of the people. The artists were men of the people, belonging to them and painting for them.

Works by folk artists portray both historical events in Mexico in the 19th century and folk customs, depicted with patience and devotion.

City scenes are also present in these works but for the most part the artists are preoccupied with life on the farms and haciendas: work in the fields, livestock grazing on spacious pastures, sugar production, celebrations and moments of rejoicing in the lives of the hired hands and peasants. Other details of their lives are also portrayed — bullfighting, cockfighting, the taming of animals. All aspects of life were committed to canvas. Little was left out—even attacks on stage coaches, and cowboys herding cattle, inspired the painters. It was a typically Mexican world they showed, now lost in the mists of time or transformed under the impact of new conditions.

In folk painting, religious art was among the most extensive section. Altar paintings and frescoes reflected the faith and devotion of believers. Paintings were sometimes commissioned out of gratitude for divine aid in overcoming dangers, illness or other kinds of misfortune.

The forerunners of this religious painting are found in Mexico in the 17th century. The fact that it still exists today shows that it has not lost its relevance. Most works of this kind are simple in form and bear the recognisable hallmarks of folk art.

Altar paintings usually have two planes: one depicting the real life of the believer and the other representing the salvation scenes of miracles. The artist has plumbed his imagination to portray supernatural powers: miracles and God's intervention go beyond the bounds of logical reality and can be accepted only in terms of unquestioning faith.

Among the most outstanding folk or naive painters are Agustin Arrieta and Ernesto Icasa.

Agustin Arrieta (1802-1874), an Indian, was born in Tlaxcala. While still a youth he left for the town of Pueblo, where he was first recognised as a talented painter. Early works show him to have been an imaginative illustrator of allegories and mythological themes and reveal a certain discipline, suggesting that he may have had some artistic training. Later he switched to other subjects. Innovations introduced by him derive not only from his maturing as a painter but also from new value judgements about life. The teeming masses, family serenity in the homes of peasants and soldiers, the modest meals of farmers, the guilelessness of drunks, the loveliness of young girls — all these are parts of the mosaic of Mexican life as portrayed and interpreted by Arrieta's brush. The types of people he represents belong to certain social strata which nurture specific traditional customs. Equal attention is given to the various features of the environment: flowers, fruit, tools and ornaments in everyday use.

Ernesto Icasa (1866—1935), born in Mexico City, stands out for the number of his works, their quality and singularity. Icasa was a wage-labourer and was consequently well-acquainted with the life of peasants. His talent is exceptional, especially since there is no evidence of his having had any training in painting. A study of his entire opus reveals a strong streak of folklore influence. A careful observer and faithful interpreter of peasant ways, Icasa's name is a synonym for genuine folk, naive art.

This brief survey of folk art in Mexico stresses its generally recognised importance, in which the 19th century holds a place of special merit. Today, too, however, in the farthest corners of the country there are new artists, more or less known, who continue this type of art, among them *Camile Hernandez* and *Ezequiel Negrete*. Artistic imagination, aesthetic inspiration, a wide spectrum of bright colours — all features of Mexican art — have made for high artistic quality also in most of the folk paintings being produced today. Their discovery and the full recognition of their worth are only a question of time.

Nico van der Endt

NAIVE ART IN THE NETHERLANDS

It would not be an exaggeration to say that naive art has always existed but that its evaluation is a relatively modern phenomenon. The beginnings of such evaluation in the Netherlands are linked up with the oldest preserved naive painting. As far as I know, the painting dates from 1752 and it may therefore be assumed that a turning point occurred somewhere in the middle of the 18th century in evaluating the works of formerly unrecognised artists. Economic considerations certainly had a hand in this. The middle class, growing in strength, demonstrated a desire for decoration. Not in a position to pay well-known artists, they frequently had recourse to house painters or local and itinerant craftsmen. It was probably a house painter who produced the large, early naive paintings exhibited in the period furniture room of the Fries Scheepvaart Museum in Sneek. Also, it was the custom in Holland around 1800 to cover the walls not with wallpaper from floor to ceiling but with painted canvases. There were special workshops (for instance in Hoorn) engaged in this activity. It is possible, but not certain, that these works were personal in character. Some craftsman or house painter, finding himself with more free time than before, especially after retirement, may have become a naive artist, reviving his past and at the same time revealing his talent. This is a contemporary sociological phenomenon.

It is difficult to determine just what change in mentality gave impetus to early naive art. One thing is certain — that in the 18th century a development occurred that led to what was known as Romanticism. Jean-Jacques Rousseau, champion of the return to nature, inspired many romantics. The naive artist is a prime example of acceptance of the militant motto of the romantics: "Back to nature!" As an amateur, the naive artist is always natural and direct. From Romanticism on — with the abolition of guilds after the French Revolution — dilettantism and amateurism acquired a role in culture present to this very day. In the 19th century, naive art slowly took on a personal character. Not all preserved works were produced on commission. It is true of Holland, too, that only after modern art had proved the value of freedom of expression did people begin to respect in naive talents the specific features setting their art apart from academic works.

Just as in France the appearance of Henri Rousseau marks the end of early naive achievements, so can the same boundary line be drawn in Holland from the first pictures by *Sal Meijer* at the beginning of this century. His well-known "Cat in a Hatbox," which he painted in several versions, dates from 1909. With the exception of his works, not many naive paintings have been preserved from the first half of this century. Probably much work was done, because in 1941 an art critic wrote on the occasion of a naive art exhibition in the Town Museum of Amsterdam: "Attempts by talented men of the people are more in fashion than ever." Painters worthy of note from that period are the pastry-maker *Sipke Houtman* (1871—1945), who began to produce after retirement, and *Willem C. Ruysbroek* (1911—1961). Sipke Houtman's works are in the Town Museum in Amsterdam while Ruysbroek has an extremely interesting canvas in the International Museum of Naive Art of Anatol Jakovsky, from which it may be concluded that he was one of the most outstanding naive painters of Holland.

It was only in the sixties that more attention began to be paid to naive art. A large number of naive painters were discovered, thanks in substantial part to Dr Louis Gans, the art historian. In 1966, Dr Gans became the Chairman of the Albert Dorne Foundation, whose task it was to give impetus to amateur art and set up a collection of international naive art, known as the Albert Dorne Collection. The sponsor of this foundation was the "Famous Artists School," a commercial institution offering instruction and selling written lessons in drawing. The Albert Dorne Collection contains a hundred or so pictures by naive painters from all Europe, including some thirty works by Netherlands artists. In 1973, the Collection was taken over by the Clemens-Sels Museum in Neuss (Federal Republic of Germany). The generation of naive artists discovered by Dr Louis Gans (including *Pieter Hagoort, Leo Neervoort, Jentje van der Sloot)*, is almost gone today, but those men were exceptional, serving as examples for a definition of naive art, which was often mistakenly associated with technical imperfection. Their place is being taken by a younger generation of painters, better informed and searching for new roads in naive painting: *Ilona Schmit, Joop Plasmeijer* and *Gorki Bollar*. Now that naive art has rid itself of modishness, young talents can develop more freely. Clearly, however, the younger painters wish to transmit their spiritual development to their paintings, even if it means departing from naive art.

Naive art has always existed and will always exist, of that there is no doubt. It is characteristic, however, that in the new generation of the retired, there are almost no new talents. Is modern passivity in utilisation of free time, spent in looking at television, a danger to naive art?

Ernesto Cardenal

NAIVE ART IN NICARAGUA

Naive painting in Nicaragua appeared for the first time (as far as is known to us) with the works of *Salvadora Henriquez de Noguera*, a woman living in a little port on Lake Nicaragua. Her paintings were discovered around 1940 by the Nicaraguan poet José Coronel Urtecho. Salvadora would usually paint her own house, and with the paints that were left over she began to paint pictures on wood. She was a true naive artist: although there was not much detail in her works — since she used coarse brushes, not the fine ones for artists — there was a great deal of imagination and striking light-and-dark contrast effects achieved with just a few colours. Only seven of her paintings have survived. (I myself had two others, but these were lost when Somoza's army destroyed the settlement I had founded at Solentiname). Salvadora later began to go blind and eventually was unable to continue painting. She was a modest woman who never considered herself an artist; she was convinced that educated people who praised her work were really making fun of her.

The best known naive painter of Nicaragua is undoubtedly *Asilia Gillén*. She used to do embroidery which very much resembled naive paintings. This gave the writer Enrique Fernández Morales the idea that she might be able to paint, so he introduced her to the head of the art school in Managua, the painter Rodrigo Peñalba. When she came to the school, he took paints and brush from one of the pupils, handed them to her, and told her to paint. Recalling this much later, she recounted: "Never in my life have I felt more ashamed than that afternoon when I, at the age of sixty-three, out of curiosity, but facing the mocking smiles of young lads, sat down in the desk at the art school to do my first painting." She finished the painting at home for she never returned to the school. This is how Nicaragua's greatest naive painter, Asilia, began her career.

In his history of Nicaraguan painting, Jorge Eduardo Arellano wrote the following about Asilia: "In most of her paintings we encounter poetry and simplicity or, more precisely, a poetic simplicity which has an immense power of synthesis. It could be added that poetry and detail are the dominant elements in her pictures. Or that they combine fantasy and reality. She liked to paint the tropical landscapes of her country; in her attention to detail she was a real miniaturist. There were always some traces of embroidery in her paintings; she used her brush like a needle. When she had become famous and foreigners visiting Nicaragua were also scrambling to buy her works, she once complained that a buyer had carried off a picture showing a naked child standing before the door of a hut. The child's figure was painted in the greatest detail, but she was disturbed by the fact that it had gone out into the world naked — before she had had time to paint its clothes."

She liked to paint Las Isletas, an exquisite archipelago of innumerable islets covered with luxuriant tropical vegetation reflected in crystal-clear water, close to her native place of Granada. Though she painted other landscapes, the vegetation was always from these islands. In a painting of Paris which the French Ambassador in Nicaragua commissioned, giving her a postcard to copy, she put these delightful tropical isles in the Seine. She did the same when painting Washington, this time putting the islands in the Potomac River. She once told me she had spent her honeymoon on those islands, and had never visited them again, though their beauty had remained indelibly printed in her memory and found a place in many of her works.

The same town, Granada, was the birthplace of *Adela Vargas*, another woman who began painting late in life, encouraged by her son, the painter Alberto Icaza. A powerful imagination is apparent in her works, which Jorge Eduardo Arellano described as "glitteringly unreal, full of mystery and symbolic strength." He adds: "From the very start her subject-matter was varied — shining birds and flowers, mythical and religious scenes, whimsical subjects from the verses of Rubén Darío, folk tales and childhood memories — all presented with much skill and feeling."

Hilda Vogl, born in 1930, spent her childhood and youth on an estate. Later, the Somozan dictatorship drove her and her husband into exile, where she began to place her memories of village life on canvas. Her most frequent subject is a poor hamlet with cottages roofed with straw or palm-leaves, naked children, impoverished peasants amidst all the extravagant beauty of tropical vegetation. She presents this poverty not as something picturesque, but as social criticism. Now, after the victory of the revolution in Nicaragua, she paints other subjects as well: farming activities, the education of illiterate peasants, and so on.

June Beer, a mulatto, was born in 1933 on the Atlantic coast of Nicaragua. Here, on the Nicaraguan Caribbean, where the population is mainly black and English-speaking, she spent a large part of her life. Her paintings show the landscapes and life in this lovely region of the country. She now heads a naive painting studio which has been set up by the Ministry of Culture.

Manuel García, born in 1939 in the Indian settlement of Monimbó, began to learn painting at the art school in Managua, but was advised by the principal to follow the path of naive painting. He mainly paints scenes from peasant life and traditional festivities in the villages.

Julie Aguirre, born in 1953, married the young painter Holner Madrigal. One day, out of curiosity, she took up the paints and brushes her husband had left lying around, and tried to paint herself. Her husband, seeing the result, encouraged her to continue. "I painted many pictures to express my happiness," she once said. This was how she began her work as a naive artist. After her husband was killed by members of Somoza's National Guard in 1978, her canvases reflected her sorrow and the desire of the Nicaraguan people for freedom. Today, her paintings express the joy of the liberated nation.

Armando Mejía Godoy, born in 1946 in Somoto, a small place in northern Nicaragua, has lived in close contact with the countryside and villagers, being an agricultural technician by profession. Another of his interests is archaeological excavation. After meeting the naive painter *Manuel García*, in 1972 he too tried his hand at painting. In Somoto he established an art studio which gathered craftsmen and peasants of the region. His subjects are mostly places in the north of the country, the felling of trees by forestry companies, and the backwardness of that isolated region. His participation in the illegal struggles of the Sandinista Front led him into exile in Costa Rica, where his painting assumed an openly political character. After the victory of the revolution, he began painting the battles fought in the northern region, the entry of guerrillas into villages, and similar themes.

Mercedes Estrada de Graham, born in 1941, spent her childhood and youth in Nicaragua before going to live in Panama with her husband. She first took to painting pebbles found in rivers, and then turned to naive painting. Her early works were of the luxuriant jungles of Panama. Later she painted a series of historical pictures: the jungle with scenes and personalities from Panamanian history, Indians and Conquistadores, etc. According to her, the greatest influence on her work was exerted by Solentiname painting.

What, then, is Solentiname painting? Solentiname is an archipelago in Lake Nicaragua which until recently was almost completely cut off from other parts of the country, and inhabited by poor peasants. In 1966, I established a small community there where I spent twelve years. Soon after my arrival in that area, I noticed that some of the gourds used for drinking water, which are typical of Nicaraguan villages, were ornamented with engraved drawings; one of these showed a mermaid playing on a guitar. It occurred to me that the peasant who had done the ornamentation could certainly be a good painter as well, so I gave him paper and coloured crayons and he soon began doing fine drawings. Later on, when a young painter from Managua came there on a visit and gave him some paints, our peasant produced a magnificent naive painting. His name was *Eduardo*. Another peasant, watching him paint, also asked for some oils, and after him another, and yet another. And so the number of beautiful paintigs and good painters steadily grew. The pictures were then exhibited in the art school in Managua, and afterwards put on show and sold in many countries in Latin America, in the USA and in Europe. The peasants of Solentiname also made very lovely handcraft products which were sold in Managua and abroad. In 1977, many young men and women of Solentiname joined the armed struggle of the Sandinista National Liberation Front, and that was the end of our community, which the Somozan National Guard razed to the ground. Three young men of Solentiname, two of them naive painters, were killed in the fighting.

There were a great many painters, men and women, in Solentiname — about forty all told. Most prominent among them were: Eduardo, the first to begin, Marina, who achieved the greatest renown and earned the highest prices for her works, *Carlos García*, who lost one eye, *Alejandro Guevara*, a prominent guerrilla in the Sandinist ranks, and his mother *Olivia Silva* and sisters. Their styles differed widely, although they dealt with the same subjects: the lake and islands, and scenes from village life on those islands. Blue and green are the dominant colours; the blue of the lake and sky, and the green of tropical vegetation.

The peasant painter and guerrilla fighter *Alejandro Guevara* said the following about this painting: "All of us are bound to put the lake in our pictures, since it has many uses: man lives from the lake and the painter lives from the lake. The lake serves many purposes; it is the source of life, for people drink its water and eat its fish; they sail on the lake, their customs are connected with the lake, and, not to go on further, it is a place for recreation and meditation. A man sits on a rock and observes the lake, or sits in front of his house and gazes at it. When the lake appears in pictures it is because not one of those pictures would have come into existence were it not for the lake."

In the worst period of Somozan terror, after the destruction of our community, few painters in Solentiname engaged in art. Those who did could only paint in secret, hiding their pictures in the mountains, since the Somozan Guards destroyed them whenever they came upon them. Now, all the peasants who painted earlier have begun again, and been joined by others. Now they paint better than before.

After the victory of the revolution, I was appointed Minister of Culture. Since I have held this position, I have encouraged the work of naive painters in many places, as I did in Solentiname; in many places in Nicaragua naive painters are at work treating a variety of subjects in different styles. They paint the landscapes, which differ from region to region, illustrate episodes in the liberation struggle and the victory of the revolution, and depict traditional customs. All this — the start of the new naive painting of the new Nicaragua — is still in its initial phase as I write.

Aleksander Jackowski

NAIVE ART IN POLAND

Concepts ostensibly the same call forth different associations, different emotional reactions in each specific area of culture (as of language). The range of these reactions also depends on attendant manifestations and concepts. In the Polish language, "naivety" does not have a pleasant connotation. A naive person would be good-natured, an "honest Joe", but he would not know how to play the game, to get along in life: in other words, a fool of sorts.

In such a context, naivety in art arouses associations of the ineffectual, the unresourceful, of a person just like anyone else. This kind of naivety is easily discernible in many works by amateur folk sculptors in present-day Poland. But the phenomenon of interest to us cannot be equated with ineffectuality. If only every painter possessed the colour sense of *Nikifor*, the imagination of *Ociepka*, the precision of *Radke*! The form of creativity that goes by the name of naive art kindles our interest above all because it is

specific, because it is not like the rest, because it moulds a vision of the world independent of tradition, of influence, and even of models. Most of us live the truth of others, the knowledge of others, without even trying to check on them. One might say that we live on credit. But the naive artists are a law unto themselves; they paint and carve as the fancy takes them, in line with their inner reality. If there is an element of "naivety" in it, it is there in the sense of giving them the audacity to be themselves. Because the essence of the phenomenon lies precisely in the ability to express oneself, ones visions and experiences, without the influence of the environment, or of cultural influences. They are linked therefore by a similarity of solutions but not of the styles they are identified with (as is the case, for instance, of folk art). Each one of them is condemned to himself, to the hell or heaven inside him. They do not have the skill permitting them easily to seek out, to imitate and to paint in the frameworks of the various conventions. In any case, they do not search around themselves, they burrow. They burrow deep, going their own way. They do not choose their fate, they accept it because thus they can express themselves, and feel the need to do so. Each one of them has his own world, defined primarily by his individuality, the tenor of his imagination, his psychological and physical dispositions. Each one of them is different and it is this difference from others, from learned art that makes us see them out of time and often outside of space. We notice no mutual dependence and reciprocal influence among them, as is characteristic of history of art textbooks. A relationship to historical time is apparent only in details, in the requisites of recollection. Take, for instance, the "Flight into Egypt" of *Nikifor*. The Holy Family is carried along by a boat whose beak has the form of an ass's head. The sea, the sky, a blood-red setting sun, and in the clouds a pre-Second World War aeroplane. Then, in the work of *Edmund Monsiel*: a fantastic, terrible world of eyes, spying, commanding, overseeing. The eyes of God. And in this thicket, almost pulsing with eyes, there is only a trace of time present — the contours of an aeroplane in which the Secretary-General of the U. N., Dag Hammerskjöld, lost his life. Therefore, in writing about naive art we are not helped by chronology, affiliation, the traditional method of art history, based on the conception of linear or spiral development. If we scatter reproductions of the works of "official" art, we can reconstruct their chronological sequence by logical deduction. But reproductions of naive paintings can be mixed up interminably. With the exception of such "nests" as Hlebine in Yugoslavia, for instance, we cannot notice any connection among them because in essence they are outside fashion, artistic styles and time. The only thing noticeable is the echo of the cultural environment from which they spring, particularly if the milieu is a lively one, and if it differs from others. That is why groups of naive artists appearing on the soil of peasant cultures stand out so sharply.

No one is totally isolated from the world around him. From that world each takes the bricks of imagination, although he may construct with them a building unlike those of others. The naive appeal of paintings by *Gawłowa* draws our attention to the ancient folk culture: the religion, the legends of the saints and at the same time the habits of the mind — an inclination toward certain colours, closed compositions developed on the principle of symmetry, rhythmical use of elements, the application of plant ornaments. Gawłowa paints flat, without perspective. Also inspired by folk culture is the work of *Nikifor*, *Heródek*, *Szczypawka* and *Mucha*, although in their case it is only the point of departure, what I call the bricks of the imagination, because the decisive factors are their individualities, fantasy, type of talent, or the reasons why they create. For this purpose it suffices to compare Gawłowa, Szczypawka or Heródek on the one hand, and on the other Nikifor, Wnekowa or Mucha. The former speak of heaven, of goodness. Gawłowa began by painting her small, cold room in the blue colour of the sky, with angels singing the praises of the Madonna surrounded by flowers; Heródek carved in wood little angels which he then placed on stones in a brook. Both of them brought heaven down to earth. But while their world is linked with heaven, that of Mucha or Wnekowa takes our thoughts to hell, the punishment of sinners, the condemnation of evil, the warnings to a mankind descending into the whirlpool of the damned. Sometimes, as in the case of Nikifor, in their paintings they pass judgement on those who did them an injustice.

These and similar attitudes are also found in the work of men and women from urban environments. But the cultural sources of their works are not always recognisable, in any case not as readily as they are in folk culture. The stronger the part played by the imagination, the more the original source of the imagination itself is lost. Sometimes you have to know a man, see how he dresses, what his apartment is like, what kind of work he does, in order to recognise the sources of his art. Intuitively I felt the folk origins of the bouquets by *Wójtowiczowa*, but received confirmation that my intuition was right only after I had come to know her anxieties and restlessness, after I saw how she dressed. Paintings, blouses, dresses, dense bunches of flowers and colours, which on the paintings make an admirable impression — all of them belonged to the same world of a *horror vacui*.

In the case of *Rybkowski* (who like Michałowska began to paint toward the end of his life), creativity is associated with the past, with the atmosphere of childhood. In his works are the flora and fauna of fairy tales; forest creatures and insects behave like people; the world of Grimm's fairy tales and the world of reality are confronted in this kind of convention: "King Bambula II Attacks Vietnam," "The Peace Congress in the Jungle." However, *Michałowska* goes back to the first impulses of youth, to a kind of painting that she dreamed of her whole life long and that is associated with the personality of her beloved amateur painter, a Russian POW whom she took care of in hospital during the First World War. She creates worlds that do not exist, other planets, better ones, but even there she finds an evil that sullies the earth.

Wójtowiczowa paints flowers, cats and her own portrait. These gentle pictures with a sophisticated use of colour are painted by her to soothe her own restlessness and alleviate psychological stress. On the other hand *Teofil Ociepka* (like Monsiel) above all communicates what he considers to be most important. He indicates and warns. This he has been ordered to do by his friend who many years ago introduced him to the secrets of a mysterious science — theosophy. Ociepka never intended to be a painter. He became one in order to preach the truth, to reveal what was hidden from others, as though he were saying: "Look at what this world is like! Are you flying into outer space? Then I will show you what a man on Saturn is like, or a cow on the Moon." And he does. All this he knows from theosophical books. To the uninitiated, his work may seem purely surrealistic: an ear growing out of a torso, an eye below the knee, hands and feet strangely intertwined. This, explains Ociepka, demonstrates that there must be a God who has assigned an appropriate form and place to everything. Marxists say there is no God. If there were not, see what the world would look like . . .

It sometimes happens that motivations are susceptible to change while habits or the desire to create remains the same. As a rule, such a situation is subject to the influence of external factors, particularly the interest of collectors, meaning the business incentive. The creative act, fulfilling an inner need for expression, is transformed into a profession practised with greater or lesser satisfaction. Understandably, a show of interest can have a stimulating effect on the person who creates. That was the case with *Gawłowa* or *Zagajewski*. But when the number of commissions increases excessively, and the artist must face the fact that he cannot keep up with them, or feels fear that he will miss opportunities for sale, his creative urge may stagnate and he may (as actually happened in the case of *Ociepka*, *Korsakowa*, *Warczygłowa* or *Holesz*) start repeating his ideas and producing stereotypes in the absence of original impulses. Creativity then becomes a craft, a profession. It may be on a high level, as for instance, in the work of *Zenon Radke*. It may also happen that skill achieved while painting may generate a dilemma for the artist, initially considered naive (his having been able to express himself best by this method): for example, he already knows how to paint, say, landscapes "just like the real thing" and would like to advance in that direction. However, he would then no longer be thought of as a naive painter and purchasers would stop buying his work. *Maria Korsakowa* faced this dilemma. She made her decision — to continue in the naive vein she had perfected.

In considering the phenomenon known as naive art, we note two poles: authenticity and convention; authenticity as the complete association of man with his work, the fateful link of the artist with his form of expression, and convention as style, the accepted manner of painting. It is easily discernible that certain factors favour the former and others the latter creative posture. The demand for naives, especially when uncontrolled by the consciousness of the buyer, leads to their artificial multiplication. They become a tourist attraction, their work a sort of local souvenir. In Spoleto, a lovely Italian town where a famous festival is held every year "Festival dei due mondi." I saw a dozen local naive artists — hairdressers, photographers, café owners. Each had copied the other and so a local "naive style" took shape.

A local style forms where the work of a highly gifted artist becomes a model for others who have a sufficiently strong motive to engage in such creativity. Folk art came into being the same way. What this phenomenon is called is a matter of local tradition. In Poland, where folk art is a living and unbroken tradition, such phenomena are defined as modern folk art. We have new centres of painting on glass (Podhale, South Poland) artificially reactivated after a break of at least eighty years; we have centres of folk sculpture (Sierpce, Lukow, Paszyn, Laczyca, Radom). In the small town of Paszyn (near Nowy Sacz) there are about eighty people sculpting and over twenty women painting on glass. A priest in that area, Edward Nitka, made his contribution to this upsurge by helping the artistic efforts of people in this poor and neglected village and treating their works as a kind of prayer (the subject-matter is almost exclusively religious) and an uplifting of the kind of persons especially numerous in this locality of the handicapped: deaf mutes, epileptics and schizophrenics. The village has become famous at home and abroad.

In reply to the question of whether in Poland there are artistic centres similar to Hlebine and Kovačica in Yugoslavia, I would say — yes. The only difference is that we call this kind of creativity (in spite of its beautiful naive features) folk art. In our country it is precisely this kind of art that is the object of special concern and that holds a place in the cultural panorama of our people like the one held by the naives in Yugoslavia. It is an export article, but also a value we would like to preserve. This example shows how essential a role tradition plays in defining phenomena by the conditions of the country.

The existence in Poland of living folk traditions and of relics of the peasant economy of long ago has created a situation in which a group of artists rooted in the soil of the folk stand out strongly among the naives while at the same time there is a clear line running, on the map of conceptions, between the naive and the "folk." The difference lies in the attitude of the individual to the environment. In folk art, the individual represents a variant of creativity accepted by the milieu whereas the naives are outside of their milieu, they are isolated within it; they are different, and the story they tell is part of their personality, of their individual predisposition.

At the same time, the maintenance of a pure course in naive art is influenced by two other factors: the lack of stimulus from the outside, and from the inside. In Poland, the development of amateur creative activity is given much attention, being considered both an opportunity for man's fulfilment of his individuality and a bridge for his involvement in culture. Amateur art activity is for many people not only a pleasant hobby but also a refuge from the darker side of life, an end in itself, a joy unlike all others. Amateurism may therefore be called a kind of psychological hygiene, a factor of compensation for other lacks and shortcomings. On the whole, though, amateurs (and there are at least ten to twelve thousand amateur painters or sculptors in Poland) strive to be like other artists who are appreciated and respected. They want to be accepted by the public, by their milieu. This type of ambition is not productive of the best kind of creative attitude and combines with a disinclination, not to say scorn, for "naivety." Of course, an effective antidote would be a fashionable penchant for naive art, especially its most spectacular expression — a good market financially, although this does not exist in Poland. To put it more accurately, interest exists, but there are not many collectors or dealers. The initiated show an interest in genuine naive artists, but there is no market for naive souvenirs, no incentive for pseudo-naive artists to paint in styles bringing them benefits. Literally, there are only a few such persons. Among them is a Yugoslav who copies the work of the Hlebine school and three or four amateurs who deliberately work in the naive style, one of whom is already known on the international market (Jan Płaskociński).

In a situation, therefore, in which amateurs harbour ambitions and hold exhibitions, and in which there is every third year a national review of non-professional work in the fine arts when the best pieces are selected (at the last one, 27,000 works were registered), Poland has not been caught up in the fashion for pseudo-naive art. One of the reasons for this, I think, is the fact that in Poland lovers of naive art are above all artists, writers and others who know the secrets of art. They were the first to take note of the coquettish beauty of simplicity, primitiveness, naivety.

This began at a time when the European avant-garde had discovered African sculptures, masks from the shores of Australia, peasant art, and soon afterwards various manifestations of the so-called lower arts (drawings on barrack-room walls, in prison cells), as well as the work of the great naive artists. The motives of their interest differed. The unexpectedly discovered "heritage" shocked and entertained. Acknowledgement of belonging to these offshoots or branches was not only a gesture of recognition but a demonstrative rejection of the obedient, "fine" tradition of academic art of the 19th century. In Poland, interest centred on folk art, detected in the twenties of the last century, in the conviction that the people in distant mountain villages had preserved an ancient proto-Polish art still untouched by the influence of the Church and European civilisation. Folk art was especially significant during the struggle for independence so that even while the artistic avant-garde was fascinated by folk wood carvings (1910), sculptures and paintings on glass (they held a place of honour at the First Exhibition of Polish Expressionist), it saw in them not only values identical with its own artistic searchings, but also national Polish features.

At a time when interest was being aroused in the lower arts, grafitti, naive artists, and so on, in Russia, Germany and France, notice had not yet been taken of these phenomena in Poland, where folk art held the field. It was only at the beginning of the twenties, when Zygmunt Waliszewski, having returned from Georgia inspired by the work of Niko Pirosmanashvili, painted a number of canvases in the naive style, that other painters also "went naive" for a while: Tytus Czyzewski, Wacław Wasowicz, Tadeusz Makowski. The primitive outlook, as an element in the interpretation of the world, was also used by Leon Chwistek, painter, art theoretician, logician and aesthetician. But these attempts did not find a widespread response. The naive artists were not noticed, and if noticed were not taken seriously. In the spa of Krinjica, tens of thousands of people saw Nikifor painting on the stone fence surrounding the central hall of the spa. His souvenir paintings went for a song. Who could imagine then that in a dozen years collectors would be scrambling for them and that counterfeit paintings turned out by schooled artists, would be appearing on the market?

It was as late as 1931 that the paintings of Nikifor caught the eye of the painter Roman Turyn from Lwow. He and a few other artists were then buying the works of the master from Krinjica. One of them, Jerzy Wolff, in 1938 wrote an article on Nikifor in the then well-known art magazine "Arkady". Among the reproductions was one in colour faithfully conveying the artist's qualities. In a subsequent issue an article appeared about *Janeczko Franciszek*, a naive shepherd painter and epileptic. Young Warsaw painters began to concern themselves with him. Many new naive artists came on the scene, their works awakening interest: the drawings of *Pawlak*, the paintings of *Brańska* and *Lampartowa*, the sculptures of *Wowro* and *Kudła*. In 1937, a Warsaw evening paper organised the first amateur exhibition. Most of those participating in it were the unemployed, workers, craftsmen, shopkeepers, and pensioners. The works of naive artists were among the others on display but they failed to capture widespread interest.

Then came the war and occupation. Early in the fifties, interest was reawakened in self-taught creative work, in the art of amateurs, above all folk sculpture and painting. In Silesia, thanks to the efforts of Maria Żywirska, the work of certain miner-painters became well-known: *Paweł Wróbel, Stolarz, Bark*, and *Urbanek*. There then appeared an exceptional personality: *Teofil Ociepka* launched into fame by writers. Taken up first by intellectual circles, he later became widely known through exhibitions and publications. Nikifor and his career were the concern of Andrzej and Ela Banach, who saved him from being moved out of Krinjica (like other Ukrainians of the Lemkovje clan, he was to be resettled in the western regions of Poland). The Banachs put together a large collection of his works and, beginning in 1949, organised exhibitions first in Poland and later in France, Belgium, Holland, the USA and other countries. Two books about Nikifor popularised him further. A. Jackowski exhibited for the first time abroad (1956) a large selection of Nikifor's works, organised his Warsaw exhibition (1956) and later arranged a collective exhibition of the works of Nikifor, Kudła, Stolorz and Ociepka (1958), Głowacka (1967), and other Polish primitive artists in Yugoslavia (1959), and above all a large collective exhibition in the premises of the Warsaw *Zacheta* Salon under the heading of "Inni," meaning those who are different (1965). The press gave it good coverage and large numbers of people came. The Art Institute of the Polish Academy of Science collected documentation on the subject while the phenomenon of self-taught artists was explored by the Institute for Non-professional Art. Private collections came into being, above all the collection of Ludwig Zimmerer, now numbering almost 10,000 examples. Naive art was given official recognition. In spite of initial resistance, works of this art form began to be collected by museums (particularly ethnographic) and exhibitions were organised in the Federal Republic of Germany, Switzerland, France and England (1967—1970). A. Jackowski organised Polish sections at the I, II and III Triennials of Naive Art in Bratislava, in Zagreb (Naive Artists — 1973, 1977), and in Spoleto at the "Festival dei due mondi" (1972). Art dealers arranged exhibitions and sold naive and pseudo-naive works. Foreign tourists came to Poland in the hope of purchasing interesting pieces cheaply.

Does this however mean that naive art has won full recognition? I dare not say that it does. True, the exhibitions have been packed with visitors, the Inni exposition boasting no less a multitude than that claimed by the sensation of the year — the exhibition of Picasso's works. Despite this, the Cultural Administration and the Asso-ciation of Polish Artists, like those who look after the amateur movement (in the trade unions), regard the phenomenon of naive art without any special enthusiasm. And since it is on them, especially the Association of Artists, that exhibition policy depends, interest in naive art has effectively been extinguished. Nonetheless, in the public consciousness Nikifor has found place, having become the symbol of a brilliant dilettante. In the press definitions using his name began to appear: the Nikifor theatre, Nikifor literature, Nikifor economy. How many people now regret they once threw out his paintings? Do they regret the loss of the paintings? No, they regret the money they would be worth now. The naive artists have also become the subject of anecdotes. Quoted often is an alleged statement made by Ociepka in reply to a newspaperman's observation that dwarves did not exist. Astonished, Ociepka is cited as having said: "What do you mean they don't exist? And those tiny men in red caps underneath the mushrooms, who are they?" Even well-educated persons have found it hard to reconcile themselves to the fact that talent can reside in a beggar, an unlettered person, someone from the bottom of the social ladder. The Cracow press even carried a discussion of whether Nikifor was not perhaps the illegitimate son of a great painter from the end of the last century. It was established that at the time of Nikifor's birth in Krinjica, a famous Polish painter, Aleksander Gierymski, lived there. So, wrote the newsmen, he could be the father of Nikifor and the latter's gift of colour, the force of his talent, would then be understandable.

Thus we return to the beginning of our consideration. Naivety fascinates but is thought of as an anomaly difficult to explain. People accustomed to bourgeois order which is, as we know, independent of system, dream of a world of stable values, a comprehensible hierarchy, including studies, diplomas, environment and heritage. And where then do people like Nikifor, Ociepka, Monsiel fit in?

This is yet another reason making it worthwhile to study the work of the naive artists, which not only gives satisfaction and offers artistic experience but contributes to the destruction of the grooves and ruts along which thought moves, and opens the eyes to unknown truths.

Modest Morariu

NAIVE ART IN ROMANIA

As has happened elsewhere in the world, the so-called naive art has recently come to the fore in Romania and attracted wide public attention. Some aspects of earlier Romanian art, however, may well be considered as antecedents of naive art. First and foremost, there were instances of folk art which transcended the bounds of traditionalism and reached original stylistic solutions, evincing distinctive artistic personalities that are easily recognisable despite their anonymity. Some lesser known painters of the last century, labelled as "primitives," charm through the sentimental tones of their artless candour.

Elements of naive art can be found in 18th- and 19th-century rural church painting, primarily in the Maramures, Bucovina and North Oltenian regions. Complex political circumstances arising from the instability of Phanariot rule (the throne was purchased from the Turkish Sultan for a limited period of time) caused a gradual decay of court art, with its strictly theological subjects, which had been sponsored also by the native ruling princes and high dignitaries. The later builders of churches, much more modest in size and appearance, were townsmen or wealthy peasants, and the master-builders were themselves of the same stock. Having never been trained in a monastic school, and lacking a thorough grounding in the rigid theology, they gave freer rein to their creative imagination. This explains the inclusion of some folklore or local elements and the appearance of another type of vision — subjective and innocent, drawing its inspiration from everyday life and conveying an outlook on the world that is much more genuine, outspoken and undisguised.

A second possible antecedent of naive art in Romania would be some late 18th-century lay miniature paintings, illustrations of popular books. Thus, Nastase Negrule in "Alexandria" (The Book of Alexander) presents fabulous imagery with extraordinary freedom. He transposes the epic composition with its historical facts into the realm of the fairy tale, giving full play to his imagination and sensibility. Similar are Logothete Petrache's illustrations to Cornaro's "Erotokritos," in which the artist recomposed the subject-matter of an Italian-Greek sentimental exotic novel and expressed it plainly in the candid images of his time.

Finally, there was the flourishing art of icon-painting on glass in 18th- and 19th-century Transylvania. Though preserving the general structures of a Byzantine-style Orthodox iconography, it was given originality by a number of well-individualised artists who made bold innovations in subject and style, such as *Savu Moga*, *Matei Țimforea*, and *Ion Popp* of Făgăraș. Their departures might be translated into more up-to-date idioms as instances of naive art. They subtly infused the religious representations with a local outlook of the world, and thereby made their work more universal in scope; besides the rigidly circumscribed religious subjects, they drew on even more ancient sources, reminiscences of an ancestral spiritual stock, deeply rooted in folklore. Moreover, by virtue of a curious syncretism, the artists introduced additional decorative elements drawn from their own imagination, realistic details of social life, expressiveness in the types and figures, even breaking the rules by introducing historical characters. St Theodore is replaced by an anonymous artist with the likeness of Prince Michael the Brave; a Nativity is set in a local landscape and the birth is attended by a shepherd wearing peasant sandals and playing the pipe, while the Magi are clad in baroque robes; details of Transylvanian architecture are also represented here and there. The heterogenous elements used by the icon-makers find echoes in the work of Douanier Rousseau. There was thus good reason for the disapproval of the art of the icon-makers by some 19th-century Transylvanian priests on the grounds that some of the details misled the faithful.

Today this art is again blossoming in a non-clerical metamorphosis that is indisputably within the sphere of naive art. Such vitality, despite the present technological civilisation, is paradoxically explained as a sort of reaction to this development, attesting to the need to preserve a certain independence of the spirit, to prevent alienation and estrangement from one's origins. Resorting at times to old Byzantine patterns, borrowing something from professional art, now widely accessible, but producing elements from their own imagination, folk artists like *Ilarion Mureșanu* of Nicula, *Pop Mihai Sigheteanu* of Baia Mare, *Vasile Frunzete* of Rășinari, *Ghețu Petru* of Turda, *Alexandru* and *Mihai Cherecheș* of Cluj-Napoca, *Timotei Traian Tohăneanu* of the Monastery of Sîmbăta-de-Sus, developed a wide range of subject-matter, drawing their inspiration either from their actual surroundings or from history, but always filtered through their artistic individuality. These new "icon-makers" are perfectly integrated in the Romanian School of Naive Art, giving historical continuity to the phenomenon itself.

Nevertheless, such continuity could not have attained its present scope in Romania were it not for the generally favourable climate, the autonomous status gradually gained by naive art within the system of contemporary aesthetic values. Recognition followed the theoretical elucidation of the essence of naive art: the pioneer-work of Wilhelm Uhde in the first decade of this century, now fully crystallised thanks to the endeavours by art historians, critics and scholars such as Jean Cassou, Oto Bihalji-Merin, Pierre Courthion, Anatol Jakowsky, Nebojša Tomašević and many more, who have systematically studied the naive-art phenomenon. Their investigations and explanations on the one hand, and the spectacular, infectious affirmation of the so-called "Yugoslav miracle" on the other, were worldwide active incentives promoting naive art. Romania now has a vigorous naive art, which has made marked progress during the last decade. Numerous art historians and critics like Ion Frunzetti, Mihai Drușcu, Radu Bogdan, C. R. Constantinescu, Radu Ionescu, Adrian Petringenaru, have committed themselves to the cause of naive art, while Dumitru Dancu and Juliana Dancu are votaries of the traditional art of present-day "icon-makers". Prompted by a spirit of fellowship and solicitude, trained professional artists like sculptor Ion Vlasiu, and painters Ion Sălișteanu and Ion Pacea, have advocated the same cause. Following the example of the Yugoslav painter Krsto Hegedušić, Vasile Savonea, also a trained artist, is undoubtedly one of those who have done most to encourage naive art in Romania.

In 1964, the eminent art historian and critic Ion Frunzetti outlined a theoretical approach to naive art: "It is not the art of the world-weary, the blasé, mimicking naivety out of disgust for the 'refined' experiences of decadent art, but the natural, sincere expression of some feelings and ideas common to an entire nation; translated directly into its own language by people who live the life of the nation, such feelings are both persuasive and seductive."

The individual efforts of the supporters of naive art would have remained isolated and less effective had they not developed an administrative framework, in full agreement with the general principles of Romania's cultural policy to promote all forms of culture among the masses of the people. Naturally, this implies favourable conditions and possibilities of expression, and not bureaucratic interference and direction. In rural areas there were already a great many cultural centres (culture homes), and in the towns evening art schools and centres for the guidance of artistic creativity and for promoting art among the masses, but they operated more or less in isolation at their own narrow local level. Nevertheless, one third of all works exhibited in nationwide biennials of amateur artists in 1965 and 1976 were by naive artists, whose numbers are steadily increasing.

The periodical organisation, starting in 1976, of the national "Ode to Romania" festival, at village, town, district and national levels, offered nationwide opportunities for artistic affirmation to all amateur artists. The participants in the competition at national level included naive artists, who were thereby given a further chance to emerge from local isolation.

A significant landmark in the evolution of naive art was an exhibition by the fruit-grower *Ion Niță Nikodim* from the Apuseni Mountains, at the Writers' House in Bucharest in 1968. It was the first one-man show of a naive artist to gain wide public attention, in this way asserting the value of naive art.

Another noteworthy event confirming the rural environment as the cradle of naive art in Romania was the exhibition entitled "Peasant Painters and Sculptors" held in Bucharest in 1971. No less than one hundred and fifty works were exhibited there. It was followed by further group or one-man shows, smoothing the path towards the full acceptance of naive art with the "First National Salon of Naive Art in Romania" (1976), in Arad, displaying two hundred and seventy works by one hundred artists. This has become a traditional event.

All these events, supported by the critics, have helped to mould public taste and sensibility. Lovers of naive art have gathered collections, and some museums, like the Argeş District Museum, opened a special naive art gallery as early as 1969.

Statistically speaking, the first selective directory of the naive artists, drawn up by painter Vasile Savonea, identified (among the fourteen hundred amateurs participating in nationwide art exhibitions in the 1970—1980 period), one hundred and twenty artists who met the requirements for citizenship of the magic realm of naive art.

The rural environment is particularly fruitful; it could hardly be otherwise since the Romanian village, with its vigorous and lengthy folk-art traditions, offers the most propitious climate for the development of naive art. Besides the "icon-makers" listed before, or their prestigious doyen *Ion Niță Nicodim*, mention should be made of *Ion Stan Pătraş* of Săpînţa (Maramureş), whose name is linked to the "Merry Cemetery" (now a tourist attraction), celebrated for its brief epitaph-scenes, containing picturesque biographical data and moralising sentences painted on the crosses. No less important are *Ghiţă Mitrăchiţă* of Bîrca (Dolj), a chronicler of past and present rural life; the house painter *Alexandru Sava* of Poienari-Ulmi (Ilfoš), the creator of a strange dream world; *Petru Mihuţ* of Hălmagiu (Arad) and many more.

The urban milieu has contributed a number of artists of various occupations and trades: *Gheorghe Babeţ*, a locksmith of Timişoara, is one of the best; *Constantin Enăchescu* of Bîrlad is a retired printer; *Emil Pavelescu* is a driver in Bucharest; *Pavel Biro* of Arad is a retired agronomist; *Petru Vintilă*, Bucharest, is a writer; *Gheorghe Doja* is a locksmith in Lugoj; and *Petre Gheţu* is an office-worker in Turda.

Romanian naive art has won international recognition by participation in exhibitions organised abroad: the Naive Art Triennials of Bratislava (Czechoslovakia), 1969—1971, Zagreb (Yugoslavia) 1971—1973, the International Gatherings of Art and Culture in Lugano, 1973, Levallois Peret (Paris, 1975), and in international events in Italy (Milan, Viareggio). Several collections of the Institute for Ethnology and Dialectology of Bucharest toured Japan (1968), Italy (1971—1972), Denmark, Norway, Finland (1972), Czechoslovakia, Hungary (1974), Poland, West Germany, India, Egypt (1976), the United States, Mexico, Canada (1977), and Sweden (1978).

NAIVE ART IN SWITZERLAND

Great art is rare, whether from trained craftsmen or the self-taught we know as naive painters. Switzerland is no exception. In this small country of six million inhabitants, artists are few in number. And in comparison to figurative and abstract painters, naive artists are few. In the case of naive art, as in the case of all the other genres of modern art, recognition is generally slow in coming. One consequence is that the *aficionado* is unable to acquire the works of the most famous naive artists who are dead and whose works today command the highest market prices.

Looking into the past, there is the popular Appenzell school of folkloric painters, whose origins reach back into the 18th and 19th centuries. Centring on the villages of the region of that name in the German-speaking cantons of Switzerland, it is a school rooted in an old peasant tradition which from generation to generation has never varied in its course, that is, its choice of subject-matter. Mountain pastures and villages and shepherds keeping their flocks have come down to us in a style of painting which has undergone little change. The actual compositions are much alike: summer or winter landscapes rendered in great detail. Appenzell painters have been so true to the tradition of their forebears as to make it difficult sometimes to distinguish the work of one from that of another. Some of the names in this past are: *Johannes Müller*, born in 1806, a watchmaker and painter, and *Bartholomäus Lämmler*, born in 1809. In 1950, several of the latter's works were discovered at Brulisau, indicating that he once lived there. He is believed to have worked as a farmhand and to have been an alcoholic. Lämmler also made a name as a painter of peasant furniture, but few of these works are known to have survived. Most of his paintings date from between 1848 and 1854.

Christoph Sebastian Allgöwer, born in 1827, studied to be a lithographer and travelled in Germany and Austria. On his return, he settled in St Gall where he died in 1908. *Franz Anton Haim*, born in 1830, farmed with his brother. His painting was something quite separate from his farming, and he worked in a room whose walls he had painted over from floor to ceiling. Fragments of two wall paintings have survived on the outside walls of his house. They are of a cow and of a horse, and their date — 1872 — is still legible. *Anna Barbara Aemisegger-Giezendanner* was born in 1831. In 1873, her husband died in an accident, and she turned to weaving for a living and then to painting. In 1904, she died in the poorhouse at Hemberg. *Johann Jakob Heuscher* was born in 1843 and died 1881. *Johannes Baptist Zeller*, born in 1877, worked as a farm hand, bailiff and, later, a sawmill employee. He moved frequently until he settled finally in the Appenzell where he lived from his painting. Aside from painting on canvas, he decorated furniture with religious scenes and stylised bouquets.

Art history singles out a good number of portrait artists in Switzerland who are on the edge of naive art. Black predominates in the clothing in these 19th-century family portraits.

The excitement of naive art, in which interest grows from day to day, lies in its greater closeness to the general public, in contrast to abstract painting or the other extremes of art we have known in recent decades. Naive art brings a breath of freshness and relaxation into our world gripped by worries about its future and abandoned to rationalism and computer technology. Naive painters are still sometimes cast as outlaws but are becoming better known through their exhibitions, public relations and even television, to say nothing of the press, which maintains a constant interest in their work.

There is nothing we can define as typical in Swiss naive art, with the exception of the folkloric features of the Appenzell school. Each painter gives free rein to his imagination and fantasies. Frequent focuses are the mountains and lakes of the home regions of each. For example *Adolph Dietrich*, the Swiss Douanier Rousseau, painted numerous canvases of Lake Constance. When I knew him in Berlingen and was exhibiting his work, he was very much the peasant-worker of that region of Switzerland. His work was considered marginal, but appreciated nonetheless. Adolph Dietrich is "special" in Swiss naive art; he is certainly its master, and it is curious that this artist was virtually unknown during his lifetime in French-speaking Switzerland. This explains why almost all his canvases are to be found in German-speaking Switzerland, in private collections or in museums.

Other Swiss naive painters deserve mention: *Alfred Bordonzotti*, born in 1906 and died in Lausanne in 1973, was from Ticino and worked as a house painter. Injured at work, he afterwards dedicated himself entirely to his art, painting directly from life. *Jean Béral* was born in 1907 in Geneva but lived abroad most of his life. His world is one of imaginary landscapes, "paradises lost," a world into which man has made no incursions. *Helen Güdel*, born in 1936 in Zurich, belongs to the Henri Rousseau group. Her world is the farms of Berne and Appenzell. *Andreas Barth*, born in Basel in 1916, is a GSAMBA member and recipient of various state prizes. His works are in numerous collections. *Meieli-Holzer*, born in 1925, paints the landscapes of her home region in German-speaking Switzerland. *Maria Christen*, born in Stans in 1921, lives surrounded by cats and, one after the other, she paints their portraits. *Giuseppe de Checchi*, born in 1911 at Aguirre, in the Argentine province of Santa Fe, lives in Ticino. He is a former gardener and paints flowers and exotic gardens. *Elizabeth Hostettler*, born at Zofingen in 1921, has a preference for street scenes. *Alfred Peter*, born in 1890 at Aubonne, has lived in Paris for most of his life and has been called the Utrillo of naive art. He paints scenes of Montmartre and other parts of Paris. *Verena Broger*, born in 1943 at Thalwil, works in the Appenzell tradition. She often paints women in the costumes of earlier times,

and likes to work in crayon. *Albert Manser*, born in 1937 in the Appenzell, is one of Switzerland's best folkloric artists. *Jakob Binder*, born in 1928 at St Johannes, in Austria, is one of the most interesting Appenzell painters and lives in the region. *Henni Lüthi* was born in 1919 at Heiringen and died in 1982 in Berne. One of Switzerland's best women naive artists, she painted scenes of Berne and Paris and of England, and worked at the Curie Foundation in Paris. *Sibylle Neff*, born in 1929 at Appenzell, works in the style typical of the region. Other artists include: *Tamara Voltz* (born in 1898 in Berlin), *Güdel Ulrich* (born in 1931 in Berne), *Enrico Figini* (died in 1969), *Anton Bernhardsgrüter* (born in 1925 at Hohen). Failure to understand and hostility toward this genre have been receding over the last decade. New private collections have come into being, although museums continue, it must be said, to hesitate to enter the market for the better works of this current in modern art. Except for a few of the most famous names of French naive art, it is almost impossible to see naive art in the halls of Swiss museums. It is to be hoped that someday it will be possible to enjoy entire rooms devoted to naive art, as can be done in New York.

Julia Weissman

NAIVE ART IN THE UNITED STATES

Discernibly American in character, the work of untaught artists in the United States is frequently given the designation "folk art." And for reasons related to the country's history, the name clings to contemporary as well as antique paintings and sculpture that probably could just as well be called naive.

That part of North America where the nation was born, the Atlantic seaboard, was not invaded, as were other continents, by armies sent to conquer existing societies and pillage their wealth. It was instead settled by plain civilians whose dissident ideas or dissatisfactions drove them to forsake homelands whose bustling cities were rich with the imposing architecture, skilled craftsmanship and brilliant art of the Renaissance. These ordinary "folk" (to use the American vernacular) were for the most part urban-bred and as accustomed to buying as making their household needs and other wants.

If the settlers found the kind of freedom they craved, they also encountered behind bare and rocky shores an untamed wilderness of a sort most had probably never seen before in their lives. Further, they were severely limited in the furnishings, goods and even tools they could bring. These mundane facts were crucial determinants of the quantity, variety and individualistic quality of American folk art (of which representational art was an integral manifestation), for it meant the settlers and the pioneers who pushed westward had to recreate their households and re-establish community life from the ground up more or less literally, starting with clearing away stones and trees to make living space and building materials.

Removed from European exemplars by time and distance, early Americans were forced to rely on ingenuity abetted by memory and imagination. This had an uninhibiting effect, and much of what they made for daily use, crude though it may have been, was endowed with vigorous, unstudied originality and even humour in concept, design and style. These qualities, in the eyes of 20th-century admirers, so overrode the utilitarian purpose of the objects as to make them worthy of being displayed as uniquely American folk art, with the emphasis on the word art.

The term "folk art" generally suggests ethnically traditionalised craft methods, patterns and styles handed from one generation to the next. This is not quite the case with this area of American folk art. Though identifiable European influence and custom are certainly evident, even in portrait styles, the painted and carved furniture, houseware, ship carvings, gravestones, toys, pieced and appliqué quilts, woven coverlets, painted floor coverings, tinware and metalwork, decoys, etc. were dubbed folk art simply for having been made by ordinary individuals for their own use, pleasure or livelihood. Portraiture, sculpture and other areas of representational art have shared the designation because they were apt to be done by the very same artisans as part and parcel of their household chores or occupation, which may have been that of house- and sign-painter (like *Edward Hicks*), carpenter and cabinet-maker, wood- or stone-carver, metalworker or blacksmith (like *Henry Church*) or even labourer or farmer. Frequently they had been trained in their craft only by the doing of it and were, almost without exception, largely untutored in art.

Artisans who undertook portraits or sculpture or genre painting did so because there was a demand. Once settled and politically organised, the country prospered and there now was time for, and interest in, the niceties of the good life. With few trained artists of the calibre of a Copley or Stuart readily available, self-instructed craftsmen applied a confident will if not academic skill to meeting the desire of the comfortably and even modestly affluent to have themselves, their families, properties and important events eternalised on canvas or in wood or stone.

Known as limners (the word is said to derive from "limn," to draw) many artisan-artists found it necessary, in order to earn sufficient income, to travel from town to town as itinerant workmen. (There exists a myth, now disproved by research, that itinerant artists carried with them partially painted canvases which needed only the head of the sitter to be completed.) They evidently considered portraiture so much a part of their normal trade they seldom signed their works, and though research has uncovered the identity of some, others are known only by the general areas where they worked or the names of the families they painted, as, for example, the Freake Family Artist. There were professional female itinerants, too, among them *Mary Ann Willson*, who not only challenged convention by becoming a travelling artist but transgressed the morals of her time by maintaining without secrecy or show of shame a lesbian relationship. Another, *Deborah Goldsmith*, took to the road to support her ageing parents, and while temporarily residing, as many limners did, in the home of her sitters, married one of them.

Thus it became traditional, in a way, for the artisan to assume the role of artist, but as a paying profession it did not last beyond the third quarter of the century in which it flourished. Even when most in demand, the first half of the 1800s, limners were being rivalled by the new invention, the camera. As the popularity of photography grew and spread, so that of the limners waned and their practising number shrank. However, the creative drive being what it is, it seems unlikely that their kind, as evidenced by *Otto Krans* and *Henry Church*, disappeared altogether. If few works of the late 1800s survive, it probably was due to, in the words of Jean Lipman, the well-known collector of and writer on American folk art: "A decline in appreciation rather than creation." Tastes changed; the industrial revolution, rapid communication and travel were making the USA more sophisticated. Academic accuracy, popularised through inexpensive lithographs and printed reproductions, became fashionable. Chances are that much folk art — paintings and carvings along with outmoded household accoutrements, shop signs, etc., when not relegated to attics, barns and basements to moulder, were either lost when families or businesses moved, or were just thrown out.

Yet even as the tradition became extinct, appreciation of what it produced was awakening. And, just as early American crafts were progenitors of American naive art, so were they, in a circuitous way, its saviour. At the turn of the century an exhibition designed to salvage the skills and products of American craft customs found support in the American Federation of Arts. Major modern artists began to realise that early American non-academic art was as significant as the art of primitive societies which was then intriguing European artists breaking away from academic restraints. The first formal show of "Early American Art" was mounted by the Whitney Studio Club in New York City in 1924. Other similar and larger shows followed, and in 1932, with Holger Cahill as instigator, the Museum of Modern Art in New York held a major exhibition, "American Folk Art, The Art of The Common Man." By the fifties there were at least three museums devoted exclusively to American folk art, the core of their collections coming from influential private owners.

These first shows seemed to imply that the best of such art lay in the past (a view still held by some, and perhaps a pragmatic opinion, considering prices early American folk art brings today). However, possibly influenced by French interest in artists like Douanier Rousseau, perceptive American dealers in the thirties, among them Sidney Janis and Otto Kallier, were discovering that the USA had its share of very alive and remarkable naive artists, many of whom were from backgrounds not unlike the limners'. The works of several were honoured at the Museum of Modern Art in 1938, in a show entitled "Masters of Popular Painting: Modern Primitives of Europe and America." It was here that the art-going public saw *Joseph Pickett*, *Horace Pippin*, *John Kane* and *Morris Hirshfield*, among others.

It was evident that the spirit and vigour of the limner had by no means died. There was merely a shift in stimulus. Instead of need and demand, a different current of events made for an ambience in which untaught artists could flower.

Oddly, the American government played a considerable role. During the Great Depression of the thirties, it put into action several programmes to siphon off the fretfulness of both the unemployed and the unemployables. One of these was the Art Project. Under the aegis of the Works Progress Administration, professional artists and art teachers all over the country gave day and evening classes to anyone and everyone of any age who might be interested. The programme did much to encourage art as a desirable, even admirable, rather than queerly esoteric leisure activity. This tenet still endures, and it has become common for work done in "senior citizen" groups, adult education classes, museum outreach programmes, occupational therapy programmes of hospitals for the chronically ill and emotionally disturbed to be exhibited in museums, galleries and the lobbies of large buildings. Many a singular naive has been and continues to be discovered in such exhibitions.

While the social or occupational milieu of many of the "modern" untaught artists is similar to that of early folk artists, there *are* differences in the art — in style and in substance — that do relate the later ones to European naives. It may be said that these differences are to some degree due to societal changes as well as a personal impetus.

The works of the limner era have a bucolic calmness; there is little suggestion of social stress. The artists portray the people and the country at their best in peace and in war, content with the present, proud of themselves and the nation. In totality, there is a suggestion of abiding faith in the future, a pervasive optimism that has largely disappeared in our own times. Style, though a result of lack of training, was mannered by the desire to emulate as closely as possible the art conventions of the period. Rather than making a personal "statement," the artists worked to please a client or the public.

As for the 20th-century non-academic artists, even if they sought to sell their work, it was not their intention to become professional. Whatever the stimulant that initiated the activity, it was much more a matter of "art for art's sake." The works therefore have a different emotional quality — and effect. The artists are on the whole self-centred, dealing with their own lives, their own experiences, their own views, and so they reveal more of the interior *persona* than did the non-academic artists of former times.

True, there are still the pastoral painters such as *Grandma Moses, Clara McDonald Williamson* or *Mattie Lou O'Kelly*, who show us an American rural or small town past cleansed by memory. But side by side with them are those artists whose works reflect, in perhaps more easily understood terms than do the trained artists, the strains contemporary life inflicts upon the individual. These might be called the exhortationists, the visionaries, the commentators, such as former blue collar worker *Ralph Fasanella*, Baptist preacher *Fenster*, and *Minnie Evans*, a black woman limning with crayon strange visions of heaven and hell. A number of dealers and collectors (many of the latter themselves artists) are including the out-and-out mad, like *Ramirez*, in the spectrum of American folk or naive art. Possibly because of the insights modern psychology has given into the creative process, the works of today's folk artists, the visionaries and the emotionally disturbed seem to have elements that relate them to each other. On the whole, though aware of the world and its events, aware even of the trends in art, theirs is an intensely inner vision through which the surrounding culture is filtered.

Because it comprises so much of the folk art in major collections, there may be an impression that nearly all American folk art comes from east of the Mississippi River and is primarily Anglo-European in concept. There is, however, a body of American non-academic art that retains strong characteristics of different folk art traditions. There is that of the Roman Catholic *santeros* of Spanish origin in New Mexico, and the art of the American Indians.

The history of neither can be summarised in a paragraph, but it can be said that industrialisation and modern communications are altering those traditions as those people move more and more into the mainstream of American life.

The santero tradition goes back to when Mexico freed itself from Spain and ceased sending priests and sacred images to the tiny Spanish communities in the deserts north of the Rio Grande. Local artists undertook to replace the panoply of beloved saints so important to these communities. Untrained and often poor and uneducated, they painted retablos (wood panels) with homemade tinctures and carved bultos (painted and costumed figures). Isolated from contact with large churches, they, like the limners, relied on memory. When that faded, invention took over, so they frequently dressed their saints in the clothing of their own time. The santero was also an itinerant, travelling, and taking some of his pay in food and shelter.

The art of the American Indian is varied and widespread, each nation having its own tradition. Dictated by custom and ritual, the art can include wood carvings that speak of family and tribal history (like those of the Tlingit of the northwest), paintings on skins, clay figures, burial dolls, and, peculiar to the south-west, the "kachina" dolls. These last are typical of the effect commercialisation can have on a traditional art form. Kachinas play a special role in teaching children the roster of gods important in Hopi Indian lore, and as such have the same indefinable charm of fetish figures. But when created for the tourist trade, they are so academically sophisticated, they lose that magic quality. The same can be said for Eskimo art, which in its primitive form is rich in delightful, witty carvings on bone or walrus-tusk ivory related to their folk tales and folk ways. When the Eskimos turn their talents toward commercial sale, the work, though fine and dramatic, becomes too conscious an expression to be considered folk or naive art.

There is no doubt that those who have worked to win recognition for latter-day American folk or naive art have also, as many are aware, endangered it, through support of the very concept of naive art, by making it marketable. One can speculate about just how many "memory painters" of dubious ability and quality have been brought into the *rialto* of art because of the publicity given Grandma Moses — and the prices her paintings now bring.

And one wonders, too, whether the whole of society, permeated as it is by TV and other mass media, will become too homogenised to allow for real individualism. Still, creativity is a persistent human trait, and there has yet to be a society that has not spawned its rebels and eccentrics. Certainly, ever more American eccentric artists are being discovered to meet an ever-growing interest in their art.

Further, it will be interesting to see if the recent influx of peoples of other cultures into the United States will breed a new strain of American folk or naive art with underlays of Haitian, Latin American, Japanese, Chinese, Jamaican, Near Eastern and Vietnamese traditions.

Natalia Shkarovskaya

NAIVE ART IN THE USSR

Coexisting in the Soviet Union today are professional or "learned" art, and popular art of a folkloric category, which falls into three different types, one relating to the traditional arts and crafts and cottage industries, the second to naive art, and the third to the values of the learned visual and applied arts, with which it therefore has greater affinity than with popular imagery. All three types are in a constant dynamic interrelationship, with their more gifted representatives espousing what accords most with their own outlook.

For anyone attempting to compile or devise an encyclopaedia on visual folk art in the USSR, certain difficulties need to be overcome; one is how to present the various levels of national cultures and histories of the scores of ethnic units making up the USSR. Indeed, some, such as the minorities of the subarctic regions, Siberia, the Amur River Valley, and Kamchatka, entered the socialist stage from what was a semi-primitive period. Others, such as those in Central Asia who espoused Islam, had not progressed further than feudalism. Meanwhile, Russia and the Ukraine had inherited the Byzantine tradition and in their artistic development proceeded from definite religious and secular dicta. Finally, Lithuania, at one time part of a united kingdom with Poland, had been affected by West European influences, more specifically the baroque.

In the 18th century, when Peter the Great was Europeanising Russia, art divided into the two categories of learned professional art and popular art, the latter being long identified exclusively with peasant art. In both country and especially town an urge toward pictorial representation can be observed. We thus have in popular art such genres as portraiture, allegorical and mythological subjects, genre scenes, battle scenes, etc. There appear portraits of one or more subjects and landscapes of aristocratic estates and parks (drawn, however, not from the real thing but from ground plans), produced by serf painters, icon painters, and semi-artisans, whose manner was poles apart from that of the graduate of the Art Academy in St Peterburg. Meanwhile, in the urban areas, the woodcut and subsequently copperplate "lubok" broadsheet, gained ground, serving in its way as a vehicle introducing secular culture to the peasantry and urban lower-middle classes.

This style of the lubok broadsheet, constitutes a specific characteristic of pictorial folklore, of popular imagery. When assimilating and reinterpreting the formative principles of learned art, the folk artist employed the lubok style to present his subject-matter in an easily understandable, graphic manner that would be decorative, grotesquely conventional, and possess a purely national colour scheme.

When serfdom was abolished in Russia in 1861, the "third estate" appeared in the social and economic structure and a proletariat began to develop. The popular peasant culture and aesthetics mingled with those of the aristocracy and urban bourgeoisie and came to be expressed in such specific ways as the highly histrionic urban ballad about cruel, unrequited love and a lubok far removed from its 17th—18th century origins, being more of a lithograph based on these same ballads or on army and folk ditties.

At the beginning of the 20th century, Russia's professional artistic community, more specifically N. Goncharova, M. Larionov, P. Konchalovsky, and A. Shevchenko, to mention but four, were attracted to medieval Russian and Oriental art, seeking to assert thereby the undiluted character of everything Russian, especially in art, and isolate it from Western influences.

Moscow painters who formed groups with such exotic names as the "Knave of Diamonds" and the "Donkey's Tail" raved about such folk art objects as the signboard, lubok, icon, of course, of a primitive design, and hand-painted tray, and themselves produced works attempting to convey the pristine directness of folklore. From this point of view *Niko Pirosmanashvili*, better known as *Pirosmani*, the self-taught Georgian artist who had his own individual poetic style, was no primitive, even though he attracted early 20th-century avant-garde artists by his formal aspects. (Today art critics tend to single out artists who have broken through the boundaries of professional art and who express a bond with folklore, urban primitive art, and other fields).

The October 1917 Revolution fundamentally overhauled the view of the role that art played in the life of the masses and introduced a novel attitude to forms of art, whether of the peasantry or lower urban strata. At their very first exhibition, folk craftsmen and self-taught painters and sculptors of worker and peasant stock displayed an individual style and personalised attitude to the subject pictured. Art catalogues published in those years have preserved a few names; several works of art are extant which provide some notion of the mass scope of amateur art at the time.

The new socialist culture began to emerge right after the October Revolution. Ordinary people flocked to libraries and the free drama studios, art circles, and schools, specially organised for anyone who sought to learn.

The large Proletarskaya Kultura, or Proletcult (Proletarian Culture) organisation also played a certain role in promoting the creative arts of factory workers and organised art studios for them — even though its opinions and dicta were trenchantly criticised by the Communist Party at the time.

In those early years of the revolution, self-taught artists and professionals in Russia proper, in the Ukraine, and in the Transcaucasus frequently co-operated in painting stage scenery for popular theatres, adorning and embroidering banners and trade-union insignia, and providing the slogans, streamers, posters, and other decorations for parades and festivities on the great revolutionary holidays. Some took a hand in artistic and monumental propaganda, as it was called, decorating factory and farm clubs, "agit-prop" trains, steamers, and coaches that served as reading rooms and movie halls; these vehicles travelled all over the country in the years between 1918 and 1924. There were even urban agitprop tram trolleys. These picture galleries on wheels represented a pictorial language in a popular vernacular.

One could also mention some of the revolutionary monuments of the early 1920s modelled by workers and mounted in railway and factory yards, in town and village squares. These amateur sculptors had no special training, and no notion of the laws of modelling in the round, but they were inspired by high-minded ideals; their belief in the revolutionary slogan, in the social revolution, was pure and sincere, and it was this that they sought to express.

A characteristic highlight of those times were joint exhibitions of professional and amateur artists. One such exhibition, which had no hanging committee and which did not cost the exhibitors a kopek, was opened in the Winter Palace in Petrograd in 1919. A similar exhibition was organised in 1927 to mark the tenth anniversary of the revolution.

By the 1920s and 1930s, the amateur art movement was widespread, as is indicated by the many associations organised, such as the Society of Amateur Artists, the Izoram Young Workers Art Association, and the movement of worker-peasant correspondents who also tried their hands at drawing and painting, and who co-operated to produce wall newspapers for clubs, the Red Corner recreation rooms, and rural reading rooms, and sent their contributions to local and Moscow periodicals, such as the "Krestyanskaya Gazeta" (Peasant Gazette).

Subsequently, extra-mural courses were opened at the Krupskaya Central House of Popular Arts; in 1934 they were reorganised into the Extra-mural People's University of Art better known by its acronym, ZNUI, the Russian abbreviation of "Zaochny Narodny Universitet Iskusstv," and which over the years has been able to evolve definite methods for working with amateur artists.

Of the two hundred and fourteen collective-farm amateur artists from all over the Russian Federation who took part in a first exhibition of this kind in Moscow in 1934–1935, there were several fine self-taught painters (*Akbayev, Arkeryan, Utkin, Tochkin, Kile Pyachka* and others). This exhibition demonstrated that the artists had mastered the full range of visual arts whose means of expression they drew upon to reflect such current topical themes as the epic rescue of the Chelyuskin crew in the Arctic Ocean, transarctic flights, border guards, civil-war reminiscences, and the like. As most of the artists were of peasant stock, they addressed themselves overwhelmingly to peasant art and its traditions. Many elderly exhibitors preferred to copy classical painting, especially landscapes and portraits, but younger amateurs were more interested in contemporary subjects.

Of particular interest was the creative art of several representatives of the national minorities of Russia's subarctic regions, who at the time were studying at the Leningrad Institute for the Peoples of the North (*Lampai, Natuskin, Nikitin, Sirotkin, Terentieva, Pankov* and others).

Before the October Revolution, these ethnic units had reached but a semi-primitive phase of development, had no written alphabet, and followed pagan cults whose traditions, especially in the applied arts, derived from neolithic art and rock drawings. At the mentioned Institute, which trained political and cultural workers for these ethnic units, the creative bents of the students were noticed and two studios, one for sculpture, the other for painting, were organised for them. However, the students, conspicuous among whom was K. Pankov, were not obliged to follow academic tradition, but were merely taught to use the tools and supplies of the craft. Some of the works of the artists of the national minorities of the north were exhibited inside and outside the USSR.

In the 1920s attempts were made to evolve theories for the new phenomena observed in the artistic endeavour of the people. However, they were either vulgarly sociological or misrepresented the actual picture, thereby to prop up the numerous manifestos of the so-called *avant-garde*. No theory was developed for naive art, and only a few attempts were made to qualify it as purely intuitive, to link it with children's drawings and Oriental art, or to assess it from the angle of professional criteria. As a result, until the 1960s, exhibitions of amateur art displayed no naive paintings. The phenomenon was not understood and failed to be appreciated within the overall context of popular culture.

Present-day popular art reflects peasant primitive art and urban pictoral folklore, forms stably ensconced in the popular mentality, hence, the historically ordained multiplicity. Alongside of the propagandistic ardour of Soviet painting, there are genetic traits of the primitivist art of the past, which are to be observed in lubok features, a sentimentality, a romanticism, a harking back to the Itinerants, the Venetsiyanov school, and urban folklore. However, there is an appreciably enhanced individualised approach. There is far less digesting of borrowed motifs; on the other hand, the information area, by which we imply new ideas, images, subjects, etc., is far wider. Amateur artists, including naive artists, take lessons either at full-time courses or extra-murally, especially through ZNUI.

Tentatively we may single out two pertinent types. The first incorporates naive artists whose work is rooted in folkloric and peasant-art canon with its characteristic symbolism. The folkloric imagery has retained numerous features of primitive art, which it has traditionally carried forward, incorporating both poetic folklore and the primitivist features of icon painters and creators of luboks and sundry fantastic mouldings, carvings, etc. The extra-canonical aspect is responsible for the greatest number of truly naive artists, who seek to create in full accord with such characteristic features of this art as the disposition of subject-matter without fore-shortening, a reinterpretation of imagery, a childlike drawing, the application of such localised splashes of colour as a "blue hat," "red shirt," or the like, plus the urge for hyperbolised portrait symbols, such as "big-eyed," "big-nosed," "big-headed," or "beetle-browed" (*Aladashvili, Volkova, Zaznobin, Kazmina, Mazin, Jedziyev, Nikiforov, Primachenko, Chernyakhovsky*). We may also include in this category artists familiar with professional art, provided their compositional arrangements play up the naive for the simple reason that they have been able to remain within the context of their cultural background. These folk artists boldly undertake to paint or sculpt, drawing upon a mixture of spontaneous inborn artistic intuition and an acquired sum of knowledge from some source or sources, yet sincerely believe that they have achieved verisimilitude (*Ambartsumian, Bdeyan*). One may also place in this category some urban artists who, though influenced by professional art, nonetheless address themselves to non-extant folkoric aspects of peasant art (*Nalivaikene, Maradishvili, Murayev*). To sum up, one may say that the first type of naive artist is direct in his way of thinking and understanding of the world, and is little familiar with professional knacks. His development prefers to embrace a wider choice of subject-matter than to change means of expression (*Biciunene*). Though introducing new subjects and themes, he hardly modifies his manner. He is more of the real primitive, even though he has lost that enchanting purity of integrity in his means of expression.

The second type we take to refer to lay art, which we might call popular urban art, urban folklore, urban primitive art that is extra-canonical, personalised, and basically improvised. This is not a pure form, and there is still no clear theoretical concept of it. The type includes the artist and craftsman associated with the urban consumer. Yet there are many features which are attributive to naive art. The salient characteristic is the borderline between the primitive and amateur, on the one hand, and the professional on the other. For this artist, not only his own impression, but also the attainment of learned art, provides the point of departure, even the desired goal *(Bdeyan, Yelenok, Zarapishvili, Kondas, Kniukstaite, Milts, Riiner)*.

The background with its world outlook is responsible for the manner of artistic representation, implying the stiff hieratic posture and use of stereotype. There is a relative similarity and dissimilarity between peasant art and urban primitive art as there is between primitive and professional art. Peasant art also introduced many artistic concepts and structural elements that have left an imprint on urban pictorial folklore, i.e., the conventionalised representation, the ornamentalised stiffness of pattern and flatness, localised splashes of colour, and the lack of psychological or individualised features. In the past, many representatives of urban pictorial folklore were artisans and craftsmen *(Vishnik, Grigoriants, Pirosmanashvili, "Uncle Mitya," Kish, Shabatura)*, who had their own scale of artistic values to meet the demands of their clientele or the market generally (for portraits of merchants, signboards, the typically Ukrainian folk picture of Mamai the Cossack).

Artists oriented towards professionalism may only very tentatively be called naive. Possessing as they do a large store of information and knowledge, they usually lose directness and sincerity. More often than not, the artist of this category sketches from nature and attains some degree of mastery. Today, artists of the second type include some who evolve a certain degree of stereotyping, a conventionally panoramic presentation, which derives from copying postcards, photographs and reproductions. This no longer allows such work to be classified either in the urban pictorial folklore genre, or with naive art. It would be fair enough to exclude such artists as failing to possess the right type of popular imagery, yet because of the multiplicity of the phenomenon, we may introduce some of the more talented *(Gagua, Purigin, Smirnov, Khachaturian, Chernobrova, Ertuganov)*.

The day when an inner conviction and a straightforward sincerity of expression were the naive artist's primary virtues is past. For the naive artist in the USSR today — in most cases, at least — lack of knowledge is for many reasons out of the question. Though they still do not possess what O. Bihalji-Merin has termed the "virtuoso mask of jaded civilisation," they already eagerly seek to possess themselves of this civilisation's achievements *(Zhiltsov, Savinov, Zaznobin, Leonov, Selivanov)*.

As was noted earlier, the naive artist of today stands on a different rung, which relates to a further phase of development, an increased store of information, the taking of lessons either at full-time or extra-mural courses, and the creative assimilation of the specific features of learned art. It should be noted that an introduction to another, different system of artistic expression — through exhibitions, television, art journals — by no means always affects the depth of a person's psychological makeup, its roots. To sum up, the second type of artist should be understood today as a well-developed personality with intuitive qualities promoted through educational contacts, who has nevertheless been able to remain for the most part within the context of his cultural background and preserve an artless sincerity.

Our tentative attempt to introduce two categories of naive artists, with their own visual imagery, directness of acceptance and presentation, and extensive store of information, including even a minimum of study, is in its way an effort to indicate the different stages of development which do not depend on age or educational or intellectual levels. With each artist the personalised attitude is expressed differently, in accord with an inborn urge to convey pictorially one's opinions of one's environment.

This is well illustrated by the naive marine paintings from the island of Kiknu in the Baltic Sea — part of Estonia — discovered recently by M. Soosaar, a cameraman at the Tallinn Film Studios.

That artistic surrogate known as "kitsch" is intruding into various categories of naive art. Kitsch is not simply a lack of a definite world outlook and its related aesthetic taste; rather is it the aesthetic expression of a definite urban environment with its falsely romanticised understanding of life and the "good old times." It is this environment that attempts to reduce the ideal to its own level, as the result of which pictorial journeymanship appears, presenting not what comes of the mind, but what has been seen and has been cause for amazement, with this executed in the form of a likeness, a cheap imitation, creating the illusion that one is at last in possession of this cause for amazement.

The impact of urban folklore today is reflected for the most part in the art of the village, where a range of new, modern trends has emerged in which the impersonal and the traditional, such as ornamental designs and the symbolical aspect, are fused with what is purely personal and concrete. For the most part this is manifest in the hand-painted pattern, which is to be observed in many Ukrainian and Moldavian villages where the walls of cottages are embellished with hand-painted designs on both the inside and the outside. Themes include landscapes, scenes of hunters chasing deer, fêtes, couples in lover's lane, even some favourites from present-day animated cartoons and the launching of spaceships. Meanwhile, ornamental motifs and bouquets strive to imitate carpet and wall-paper designs; they are highly decorative and polychromatic, in a characteristically Ukrainian or Moldavian style, but are already devoid of semantic significance.

Despite the diversity of creative orientation, the two types of naive artists mentioned share common features, such as their sincere attitude to what is portrayed, their spatial arrangement, which is static and stiff, their combination of planes and actions, their multi-tiered composition, the static movement, the vibrant splashes of colour, and a lyrical affection for Nature. There is no psychological probing of individual portraiture. Often a naive painting is biographical, narrative, crammed with objects (*Varfolomeyeva, Ambartsumian, Mastaitene, Sergeyev, Stepanov, Rubashkin*). Still-lifes in which everything is symbol are more in the nature of signboards (*Volkova*). We also see a characteristic legend or inscription which displays an affinity with the lubok. Like popular art, naive art too displays a highly ornamentalised composition, and not infrequently reflects survivals of the peasant mentality and commune, the peasant "mir," with its cyclical shared tasks, such as ploughing, sowing and harvesting. (*Aladashvili, Lysenko, Varfolomeyeva*).

692

Amateur art in the Soviet Union enjoys rich opportunities as a socio-cultural phenomenon, as a movement with its own infra-structure, its own material, organisation, artistic and ideological principles geared to promoting realistic art. Among the thousands, there are, too, naive artists representative of a definite category of popular mentality. In recent years, thanks to exhibitions, publicity, and other measures, the attitude to the naive artist has drastically changed. We no longer have a situation in which a Rousseau or a Pirosmani would be overlooked — as is illustrated in part by this publication.

In my work to furnish the required material concerned with the USSR, I feel I must express my sincere gratitude to M. Aivazian of Yerevan, Armenia, B. Dapkunaite of Vilnius, Lithuania, I. Dzutsova of Tbilisi, Georgia, M. Millchick of Leningrad, K. Skalatsky of Poltava, Ukraine, M. Soosaar of Tallinn, Estonia, O. Chernykh of Moscow, and my husband and translator A. Shkarovsky-Raffe for their invaluable assistance.

Sheldon Williams

NAIVE ART IN VENEZUELA

Naive artists in Venezuela are known as "artistas del comun." They inhabit many and varied corners of their country; many live in scattered villages, and some are even forest dwellers. But near or far, they have remained virtually free from outside influences that might, as in other less fortunate countries, have commercialised them. There are those who live on the margin of civilisation, a kind of peasantry only just conscious of the most obvious aspects of modern progress. There are also those among them who aspire to the life of an artisan and make their way to small towns, even cities, still preserving within them the innocence of the villages they once knew. Only, in their case, what they paint is no longer before their eyes and needs to be drawn from their imaginations — a kind of compromise with truth, but nonetheless intriguing for all its enforced ambiguity.

Plainly, the situation in towns presents a more complex case. The artistas del comun who live there are, in a few instances, transformed into urban artists, but this transformation seems to imbue them with a special visionary magic so that they give their own naive version of 20th-century life. All these artists — and here we are talking about the best of them — have never received any tuition, but they have inherited a natural talent and the skills and understanding of generations without number — an intuition that needs no teacher.

There are artistas del comun to be found even in the capital, Caracas, and Maracaibo. *Victor Millán* is a good example. He is perhaps one of the most sophisticated of these artists, in both ideas and execution. Millán is a man who has sought for artistic answers to the problems set by geometry, construction and perspective — albeit discovering solutions of his own making and invention.

But more important than these two cities as a meeting place of Venezuelan naive artists outside the rural ambience is Petare, home of at least nine outstanding naives brought to light in the last twenty years.

To the east, beyond Barlovento, the population changes. Most of the inhabitants of this part of Venezuela are "mestizos" (people of mixed race), and it is in this area that *Gerardo "Aguilera" Andrade Silva*, a native of Barcelona (Venezuela) lives. Without doubt he is one of the strangest of all his country's autodidacts, an artist who has somehow managed to equate the past with the present, and one who uses sturdy pigment as if he was handling living flesh.

Western Venezuela (especially the provinces of Zulia and Falcón) carries the full weight of traditional and all-powerful Catholicism; it is as if its people were held in a tight grip whose nature they recognise but whose ubiquity they have never analysed, simply taken for granted. This is where *Salvador Valero* has his origins, a naive painter of exceptional strength, a unique figure among the artistas del comun; it is almost as if the towering authority of religious presence (whose splendid encouragement of the best in the arts of Europe vanished centuries ago) has invisibly invaded this naive artist's very personal inspirations and aided (or added to) his great and apparently limitless capabilities.

In the province of Cabimas, *Rafael Vargas* lives in peace with his simple evocations of his native El Lucero. Born in Pedregal (Falcón), in a way he is one of the closest of the artistas del comun to the spirit of European peasant art. The imagery may be different, but his natural ability to make the picture a pattern, together with his bright colours, give his works an unexpected European familiarity.

Placing these four artists — Victor Millán, Gerardo Aguilera Silva, Salvador Valero and Rafael Vargas — in the parts where they live and work emphasises how widespread in Venezuela is the extent of this natural naive artistic temperament, undisturbed by temperature, environment or social condition.

They have been picked out for the purposes of this introduction to the naive art of Venezuela and its naive artists to underline the amazing variety. This country has somehow produced a polyglot community very different to that experienced elsewhere, out of whose jumbled peasantry and assorted artisans a plentiful harvest of naive artists comes as no surprise — perhaps because it is a little off the world's beaten tracks, perhaps because Venezuela has retained at least a part of its untrammelled, pristine, original character, or perhaps because Indians, Spaniards and other visitors who have decided to remain, along with every sort of mestizo, have kept afloat a population of mixed bloods, all of them looking back upon long and permanent residence.

It is not difficult to find forty or more "pintores del comun" and "pintores populares" in Venezuela — all of whom, by world standards, would be considered of quality. Ten have been chosen for special consideration and illustration. But among those left out, take, for example the astonishing *Emerio Dario Lunar*, well-fleshed, and sitting there with a good head of hair and a large and carefully tended moustache; he could be posing for one of his own paintings. "Desnudo" would be a good choice, showing as it does, a full-frontal Ingres-type naked woman, big from her head to her toes, ample bosom, swelling hips, everything to match — and all rendered in subtle tones of orange pigment. Lunar, born in 1940 in Cabimas, could not be more different from *Rafael Vargas*, today also living in Cabimas, the black patternist whose life and work is to be discussed later.

And what about the lovely *Neke Alamo*? In a way, like Lunar, her personality and appearance are reflected in her paintings. The same humour in the twist of her mouth reoccurs in a neat picture she has painted with her customary eccentric defiance of perspective, which is called "La hora del café en el taller de Pedro."

In this bizarre composition, everyone (except for the two girls bringing in drinks and cakes) is sitting down painting pictures. A white man and two white girls are perched on red-draped stools with their backs towards us. On the same dais, between them and facing us, sprawls a black girl. All are naked.

Yet one of the artists in the picture is painting a large canvas of three fully-clothed girls arranged before a colonnade; the painter in the picture is seemingly unaware of the wild scene in front of him at the back of the café.

Lulu Peña of Barquisimeto was born about 1925. As a person and an artist she is in total contrast to those already mentioned. Her paintings are raw in execution, generally composed of thick and rough paint.

Apolinar is another oddity. Born in Guatire in 1929, as an artist he is a purveyor of a mixture of fantasy, close sometimes to Surrealism in appearance (though not in intention). "El Santo Oficio" is a folding picture in one half of which the Inquisitor sits in majesty backed by an explosion of light rays. His victim, in silhouette, stands small before him in the midst of large-scale clues to his guilt. The other half of this folding picture is packed with carefully painted and arranged butterflies.

The fierce and brilliant colours of the paintings of *José Arecio Perez* have their ferocity curbed in his painting of a house in the hills ("Avila Adentro"); they are almost burnt out in his strange picture of the female phoenix enthroned ("Alma da artista"), but burst into full panoply in his wonderful vision of the crowd watching a tightrope walker ("Los payasos en la cuerda").

As has already been suggested, religion plays a significant role in the work and lives of many Venezuelan naive painters, but just how far and how deep this factor can go in shaping the images of genuine naive artists is not always easy to perceive. However, *Esteban Mendoza* does not make his religious responses difficult to discover. Born in Carayaca in 1924, this is a painter whose pictures seem equally divided between folk tradition and religious subjects. These two themes are clearly evident in "El pájaro Guarandol" and "Cristo Vendra a la Tierra." In the first, a huge clown-figure carries an enormous bird into whose bill a young girl seeks to crowd a gigantic flower while behind her

a man levels a rifle. In the second, tiny black men try to drink blood from the wounds of the giant Christ, the central figure — a white one — holding aloft his pierced hands; the sky is blue, the earth is very, very green. Christ and the angels are pale and white and so is Judas, hanging from the branch of a tree, but most other things are red, including two big butterflies, the tree trunks and their foliage.

Of course there are those who include religious imagery more by chance than decision. *Baltazar Coa* invests the same *esprit* into "Fiesta en la Playa" as he does in "Procession" and "Carrera de Bicicletes." Each of these pictures has the same enthusiastic crowd, hundreds of rainbow-suited onlookers, in pictures where there is scarcely room for palm trees and lagoons, let alone sky, and where naive exuberance is as comfortable at a religious fiesta as it is on non-spiritual occasions.

By and large, all those who have been mentioned so far have been — with the possible exception of Lulu Peña — all vaguely recognisable as belonging (with strong or slight variations) to the kinds of naive art with which we are familiar in Europe, or at least those types of naive art which we have come to expect or accept: careful "realism" (however distorted and however much it violates the rules of trained academic art); exact "new" realism (with something of the same provisos listed above); eccentric figuration from the hands of autodidacts; peasant-style paintings usually the fruits of a long-standing tradition; highly decorative compositions which again feature easily recognisable subject-matter. But the case of *Antonio José Fernandez* presents yet another style of self-taught artist, not unknown in Europe, but, nevertheless, rare.

True enough, A. J. Fernandez does not restrict himself to painting pictures. Like many other Venezuelan naives, he fabricates figurines (like the young black man presenting a white girl with a bouquet in "Los Novios"), but these at least, roughly modelled though they may be, are clear-cut. His paintings are another matter. The colours, bright and/or sombre, are splashed on with a natural abandon so that the all-over effect is one of an unexpected expressionism, rich and — because of the pigment's lively and vibrant application — pulsing with arresting appeal.

The titles of his paintings match the visual impact. "El Incendio," with hurtling masses of red and yellow flame against which the poor local people have no defence, is a terrible visual warning of what one may expect from the mad actions of a "firebug" (pyromaniac). Even more dramatic is "Cuerpo de Destrucción," whose possible political overtones leave little to the imagination. This picture not only visualises the hysterical and apparently hopeless fight of people against the infliction of fire (there is plenty of fire present in the "Cuerpo de Destrucción" as well): here the forces of heavy arms and the military are the enemy.

All the artists mentioned here, in addition to those who have been specially selected for biographical and critical assessment, serve as a hint of some thirty or forty others, any one of whom could be singled out to confirm what should now be plain for all to see: Venezuela indeed has a rich treasury of fine self-taught artists, varied in style and manner, but virtually all blessed with that independence that should be the hallmark of every good naive.

NAIVE ART IN YUGOSLAVIA

Nebojša-Bato Tomašević

When they speak of Yugoslavia's naive art, people usually have in mind the village of Hlebine near the Drava River. In this extraordinary place amounting to a few muddy winding streets and one-story houses, a son, Ivan, was born to a poor peasant couple, Mate and Terezija Generalić, on 21 December, 1914.

At that time, virtually no one had even heard of the village of Hlebine, shrouded in the mists of the Drava plains. The Generalić family lived in an old house plastered over with mud and thatched with straw. "The two windows the house boasted looked out on a large pond complete with dipping geese and wallowing pigs, making an unbearable noise." The description is *Ivan Generalić's*, made after he had become famous, and it projects a typical picture of the peasant houses and barnyards in most of the Drava River area. Funerals, weddings, church processions, fairs, work in the fields, customs, beliefs and superstitions, nature in the various seasons of the year, all these together make up a mosaic of life as it has been lived on the land since time immemorial. In over half a century of painting, Generalić has presented this world, distilled from his own experience, better than have other naive painters. In the beginning, the world described was one of backbreaking farm labour, injustice and social themes; later it was a world without grinding machinery, the world of our childhood, undisturbed, left behind by us in the rush for jobs, money, fame, a world where there are no great secrets, where everything is as clear and as simple as in childhood dreams.

Looking back to a period fifty years ago, we can understand more easily how it has come about that Hlebine today, in a time of unrest generated by modern civilisation, symbolises an idyllic world in the process of disappearing under the impact of a new way of life, leaving little time for nature, peace and serenity of the soul.

"Together with other Croatian painters, Krsto Hegedušić founded the Zemlja (Earth) group in 1929. A special social and aesthetic programme bound together these artists who, at a time of alienation of art from the people, attempted to take root again in the real and the generally understandable world. That same year, the fifteen-year-old peasant boy Ivan Generalić made the acquaintance of the painter Hegedušić and from this meeting the Hlebine school came to grow in later years." (Oto Bihalji-Merin, "Naive Art in Yugoslavia", 1963).

Ivan Generalić himself states that Professor Krsto Hegedušić, after they met in Hlebine, gave him advice about his future work, telling him to paint things as he saw and felt them and not to copy anyone: "So, he took my early works to Zagreb and there I had my first exhibit as a guest of the 'Earth' Association of Artists in 1931." (Oto Bihalji-Merin).

In returning to the genesis of this art, we must recall the setting of the thirties: the Depression, unemployment, workers without money and peasants without land. Hlebine had the same social problems as the rest of the country. The social injustice, the burden of taxes imposed by the pre-war regime, were taken up as a theme by the peasant-painters *Ivan Generalić*, *Franjo Mraz* and *Mirko Virius*, three village lads, three comrades. Their first exhibition, supported and organised by progressive artists, students and workers, and attacked by the authorities and official critics, carried a message of dissatisfaction and refusal to be reconciled to the situation. These early works, watercolours, fashioned by an unskilled peasant hand, on themes such as the enforced auctioning off of a peasant's belongings for unpaid taxes, peasant rebellions, arrests and all the other things that made up life in the narrow village circle those men moved in and belonged to — are now part of history.

Somewhat later, during the war, Mirko Virius was arrested by the occupation forces and interned in the camp set up at the Zemun fairground near Belgrade; he was never heard of again. In the Second World War, this camp was the deathplace of sixty thousand people. Franjo Mraz was also arrested but managed to jump out of the truck taking him away and join the Partisans. After the war, he moved first to Zagreb and then to Belgrade, where he died in 1980. Of the famous threesome, only Ivan Generalić remained at the source he had come from, which provided the inspiration for his work. To his dead comrade he dedicated a painting showing Virius lying on his back on the ground, surrounded by flowers. He is being observed by a rooster, part of every Drava area household, who through Generalić's work became the most famous painted rooster in the world. Lighted candles burn red while to the left are Virius's camp mates weeping for their dead comrade. The whole is encircled by barbed wire outside of which the Sava River flows.

After the war, Generalić hit his stride, painting with great elan. It should be mentioned that the social climate in Yugoslavia favoured the development of naive art, which was heartily supported by the authorities, visitors to exhibitions, art critics and art lovers. Naive art galleries and museums were opened in Zagreb, Svetozarevo, Kovačica, Uzdin and Trebnje; meetings of Yugoslav and foreign naive artists were held. Among the most important of these were several biennials of world naive art held in Zagreb, organised by the Museum of Primitive Art in that city.

After Generalić came new painters. Major changes occurred in Yugoslav society, in both town and country, as a result of the war and revolution. Tremendous power was unleashed and even the semi-literate peasant easily found ways of expressing himself in painting and sculpture. The village, ancient stronghold of tradition and custom, began to change overnight and was no longer isolated as industrialisation and communications made rapid headway.

Streams of people, moved by the call of the times, made for the cities, desirous of adopting new ways while not yet quite ready to abandon the old ones. In this whirlpool, ordinary people from various parts of Yugoslavia, frequently only half literate, resorted to brush and colours, applied to glass, wood or other media. By-passing academic rules and institutions, with only the force of their talent, they portrayed a new world or, even more often, the old one from which they had come.

In Hlebine, Generalić swept others into creative activity. Under his influence, talented peasants took up the brush and acquired the technique of painting on glass: *Dragan Gaži, Franjo Filipović, Franjo Dolenec* and others. There are now about fifty naive painters in Hlebine.

There then appeared, a little further off but still in the same Hlebine area, another painter, somewhat mystic and very bold in his use of colour — *Ivan Večenaj*. Painting the inhabitants of his village of Gole, extending along the Yugoslav-Hungarian frontier with its ever-present border guards and observation posts, he invests everything he does with Biblical features. In the painting "Moses," says Večenaj: "There are no stone tablets and instead of the Ten Commandments I painted some birds. Every bird, by its colour, represents one commandment. The birds relating to God and parents are painted white; the raven is the sign of death and killing, the cause of many massacres and wars. The rooster is associated with the commandment: do not covet thy neighbour's wife. I have painted Moses on a hill and beneath him is the blood-red sea which closed over the Pharaoh and his army after the Israelites reached the other side. Black clouds hover over the earth. Behind Moses, Mount Sinai is visible, while the coming of the dawn is the sign of a better life in the Promised Land Moses never reached."

In a neighbouring village, Gornja Šuma, *Mijo Kovačić*, master of large compositions, transmits to glass with his brilliant technique the behaviour of people during events beyond their control and inexplicable to the peasant mind. For instance, his painting "Northern Lights" shows the fear felt by a peasant at this unusual phenomenon: "The old folks told me," says Kovačić, "that when this light used to appear, people would march in processions praying to God to take away the evil threatening them in this form. My peasants used to act the same way during eclipses of the sun, earthquakes, and even floods, which are frequent in this region."

Independently of Hlebine and Generalić's influence, in the village of Ključ near Varaždin, *Ivan Rabuzin* has with the passage of time created his own world, differing from the world of the Hlebine school. His sunny landscapes, light in colour and shadowless, are filled with gorgeous flowers, clouds of all forms floating lightly across the heavenly blue of the sky, above the rounded hills and dales. With his soft colours, Ivan Rabuzin, like Generalić, already well known in the world, has brought a new component to Yugoslav naive art — a lively optimism, as though he were eager to demonstrate that man's happiness lies above all in nature.

But before continuing this enumeration of naive painters and sculptors, who have sprung up like mushrooms after the rain the length and breadth of Yugoslavia, something must be said of the rich tradition of popular or folk art that cannot be ignored in any discussion of Yugoslav naive art. Naive artists, although for the most part unconsciously, still draw upon the underground springs of old folk art, now dry.

In the various parts of Yugoslavia, man has for centuries found ways of expressing in artistic form whatever he has found important and meaningful, natural and useful. The best evidence of this are the frescoes in some of the monasteries and churches, or the icons on wood and glass painted by men of the people. For these they used bright colours, shining gold, and strange and wondrous motifs. In Serbia, relatives and friends used to erect memorials on clearings along the roads, usually at places where their loved ones had met their fate, so that the weary traveller resting by the wayside could think of ancestors who had laid down their lives for freedom. A folk sculptor would often portray a man killed in ambush, chiselling him in stone with his hand resting on the weapon he had no opportunity to use because he was taken by surprise. In other regions, particularly in Bosnia and Herzegovina, the heretical medieval sect of the Bogumils, who had their stronghold there, or the local noblemen, or the one and the other, raised more than sixty thousand stone "eternal homes," sarcophagi with strange carvings of scenes and ornaments. Two hundred years ago, the Slovene peasant depicted events from real life or allegorical tales in paintings on bee-hives, intending in this way to indulge in humorous play at his own expense or that of friends. In Bosnia, Vojvodina, Slovenia, and some other areas, doors, windows and furniture were painted. Woodcarving was also a favourite pastime. In Vojvodina, along the roads and in the fields one can still see peasant carts painted with folklore motifs and drawn by powerful horses gay with decorations and ornamented bridles. Women possess veritable collections of distaffs, some carved with messages meant for young men, usually in symbols. Agricultural implements and other objects used in a peasant household, or intended as ornaments, bear the hallmarks of folk genius. All of this constitutes a rich spiritual and material tradition still present in certain forms in the Yugoslav countryside.

Fortunately, tradition in Yugoslavia is not yet forgotten. Industrial production has not gained the upper hand in all spheres of life. In spite of farming mechanisation, the peasant has not been divorced from nature. He still has the leisure time of long winter days and nights for meditation about life, youth, childhood, and the old ways lingering on in the villages. Also alive is the oral literature tradition, the feeling of collective living and the ties binding peasants. In some cases, patriarchal peasant life has been the precondition for a special kind of phenomenon: the emergence of peasant "schools" of painting in Hlebine, Kovačica, Uzdin and Oparić.

It would, however, be erroneous to seek an explanation for the flowering of naive art in Yugoslavia only in tradition and folklore, although these are, undoubtedly, directly present in the work of certain naive artists. Tradition, coupled with the need of the unlettered man to express himself artistically, plus talent and environment, make up an interwoven complex of circumstances favourable for the development of naive art.

A few more observations should be added to round out the picture of the circumstances that have provided fertile ground for the blooming of this kind of art. At an exhibition of Yugoslav naive art in Paris, André Malraux stated: "What they are doing is the depository of centuries, the good old days." In a statement to the Paris press, Salvador Dali said: "This painting is straight out of a fairy tale." The one who came closest to the truth was perhaps Jean Cassou who observed: "On their canvases they express the deepest and most essential reality of Yugoslavia. Whenever they speak of their country, the naive artists describe life, people, cities, villages, war . . ."

Far from Hlebine and in an entirely different region, hilly Šumadija, lies the village of Oparić. For over forty years now, the Dean of Serbian naive artists, the peasant *Janko Brašić*, has been painting there. Usually, these paintings are portraits of peasants he knows: "to show how they looked, these people I have spent my life with." The portraits, to which most of his fame may be attributed, comprise a fascinating gallery of psychological studies of peasants for he endeavours to record: "the good and the bad, skinflints, liars, brave men and cowards." He is also fond of portraying themes from Serbian history, battles between Serbs and Turks. A warrior by tradition, in his paintings he glorifies only battles in which the Serbs won. Under his influence, a number of other painters have appeared in his village and environs — *Marinković, Jovanović* and others, but with time they have found their own individual way of expressing themselves.

In the plains of Banat, some fifty kilometres from Belgrade, the Slovak village of Kovačica is synonymous in Yugoslavia and the outside world with a group of peasant painters. Among the first to start painting were the village miller *Martin Paluška* and his friends, the late *Jan Sokol*, and *Mihalj Bireš. Jan Knjazovic* and *Martin Jonaš*, both of whom have highly individual and distinctive styles, have taken the life and customs of the Slovaks for the subject-matter of their paintings.

Also in Banat is the village of Uzdin inhabited mostly by ethnic Romanians. There, more than twenty years ago, the late *Anujka Maran* began putting on canvas pictures of the national costumes and designs she wove. Soon a dozen or so peasant women followed her example, forming a group of Uzdin women peasant painters drawing their inspiration from Romanian folklore. Among the most outstanding are *Marija Balan, Florika Puja* and *Mariora Motorožesku*.

All the painters mentioned so far began working in the village and remained there, firmly bound to their environment. They consider themselves called upon to record how life was once lived. Part of the reason is nostalgia for a rural idyll and part is the inborn conservatism of the peasant. He knows that it is better for life to change and he himself enjoys the benefit of such change but still he regrets the disappearance of certain customs and the vanishing of the old ways. Thus he defends himself. "There are no betrothal ceremonies anymore," says one of them. "A young man and woman talk things over and all of a sudden she is living at his place." Then comes the official wedding, but in the old days a well-known ritual was involved, a ritual the villagers loved because they were all involved in it in various ways. A man's life and important landmarks in it were previously not a private affair but a matter concerning the whole village.

In Zagreb, Belgrade, Ljubljana and some other cities live naive painters, born and brought up in the countryside but caught up by circumstances in the migration from the village to the city characteristic of post-war Yugoslavia. Though they live in the city, at heart they remain peasants. They have come to realise some of the advantages of city life and to appreciate the greater comfort it offers, but in their minds they carry a vision of the village, usually dating from their childhood. The two intertwine and constitute a theme of their work.

A former postman, *Ivan Lacković*, is one such painter who idealises the village in his work. His soft, lyrical landscapes of the Drava area are a passionate ode to its tranquility, especially in the winter evenings when a life of undisturbed rural happiness is felt stirring under the white snow-covered roofs. Zagreb, where Lacković lives, is also the home of *Antun Bahunek*, who moved there before the war but retains in his paintings unbreakable ties with the world of his childhood, with nature, which not even long years in the hurly-burly of a city could erase from his consciousness. *Josip Generalić*, son of Ivan, who grew up in his village surrounded by the Drava landscapes, until a few years ago kept returning in his paintings to the village and its inexhaustible themes, to the events of his happy childhood. Recently, he has taken up subjects that have little in common with his native Hlebine. In one of his pictures, a man, having landed on the moon in a spaceship, takes a cow out to pasture.

One of the famous pre-war trio of Hlebine, *Franjo Mraz*, lived in Belgrade until not long ago. Although he spent many years on the asphalt of Belgrade, he was until his death concerned with the peasant's life, regarded by him not as a painter looking in from the outside but as a person who felt for him and had shared his work. In his works, one has the impression that the peasants are talking with the painter, their faces reflecting happiness or sadness. In Belgrade, after years of wandering and attempts to adjust to city life, *Čedo Spasić* and *Đorđe Dobrić*, both died prematurely of heart attacks. Also living in Belgrade for years now are the talented Serbian painters *Dušan Jevtović* and *Milosav Jovanović*. Deep in their souls somewhere, both of them stride over their native fields, carefree whistling kids with their hands in their pockets.

The same is the case with the colourist, *Milan Rašić*, from Svetozarevo, with *Pal Homonaj* of Novi Sad and the late *Đorđe Šijaković* of Skopje. Living in the cities, they either do not see the rush, noise and bustle, or the strength of their talent and peasant origins have enabled them to bring the world of green fields, the smell of grass and cherry trees in bloom, into their city dwellings.

Finally, there is a rather large group of painters whose work and life experience and its expression in painting are closely linked with cities, usually venerable architecture and with the subconscious, where reality and fantasy intermingle and everything is possible, as it is in dreams.

Perhaps the greatest and the purest dreamer of them all is *Matija Skurjeni* of Zaprešić near Zagreb. His trains travel in all directions, bearing our dreams. Although he worked for the railways many years, he travelled little. While he remained in place, seeing trains in and out of the Zagreb station, in his thoughts he went with them, following them and their passengers to their destinations. Thus he translated his wishes into dreams, almost the same thing for him. Perhaps his source of inspiration is traceable to this merging of the one and the other, this intermingling of dream and reality, giving his paintings the charm of the actual and the unreal at the same time.

Dragutin Jurak and *Branko Bahunek* also live in Zagreb. The first is a fantasist and the latter a painter of old Zagreb and life on the outskirts that no longer exist.

In Kranj there is *Boris Lavrič* and in Presečen *Franjo Klopotan* who travel to other worlds in their pictures. A retired mason from Belgrade, *Sava Sekulić*, and many others, have developed their naive vision of the world between the four walls of their city apartments, perhaps as an escape from the grey monotony of town to the enchanted world of the imagination.

The names of another five painters should be added to those above: *Ilija Bosilj, Emerik Feješ, Jože Tisnikar, Dragiša Bunjevački* and

Stepa Sirković. Why are they set apart and why do they come at the end? Because to do it differently would be difficult. Different in the themes they deal with, the power of their talent, the places where they reside, the lives they lead and their surroundings, together they provide a mosaic image of Yugoslav naive art, with all the elements and messages characterising that art and comprising its attributes and qualities.

In the prairie town of Šid in Srem, the peasant painter *Ilija Bosilj-Bašičević* died in 1972. After four years of grade school he tilled the land until sickness overcame him. Towards the end of his life, he was tied to his bed, paralysed. After a hard life of work and worry, Ilija Bosilj began painting when he was 63 years old. He had survived wars, come to know people, participated in many events. In his late-blooming painting, he dealt with apocalyptic themes, folk songs, history, Biblical stories, flying men, birds, animals with two faces. In a brief interval, and as the result of an inexplicable inner eruption, a new naive figuration sprang from this barely literate painter, opening previously unplumbed possibilities in naive art.

In the summer of 1969, in a suburb of Novi Sad, *Emerik Feješ*, buttonmaker and combmaker, died in his sixty-fifth year in a meagre setting differing radically from the luxury he created in his works. Feješ had begun to paint as he neared the half-century mark. His dream of travelling was never fulfilled so, afflicted by sciatica and asthma, he took trips the only way he could — with the help of the postcards he collected. These he painted and copied, adding squares, sections of streets and houses, or erasing things he did not like. The result was always a painting that differed completely from its model.

Apart from the buttons and combs made by him in his small flat, he left behind several hundred paintings on paper showing the rich façades and squares of well-known European and overseas cities.

Jože Tisnikar of Slovenj Gradec is employed in the autopsy room of a hospital and every day sees lifeless bodies on a slab in front of him. When he finishes his job, he starts thinking about the deceased's way of life. Then, in his painting, he brings him back to life again; the deceased no longer looks the way he did when alive for he has returned from the world of the dead from which only Tisnikar can retrieve him. Tisnikar's humanism does not permit him to reconcile himself to the fact of man's ceasing to exist altogether.

Dragiša Bunjevački of Novi Bečej, café musician, circus worker, a man without a home or the wherewithal of life, was in many ways an unusual phenomenon among Yugoslavia's naive artists.

In appearance and working method, he was by chance or intention similar to Douanier Rousseau. The small world of dreamers, to which Bunjevački also belonged, is equally the world of all dreamers since Rousseau. Among the circus performers and musicians he was most fond of painting is the eternally smiling, gentle and optimistic bearded figure of Bunjevački himself. Asked why he did not own a bed, he replied: "Why should I? The minute I purchased one, life would have passed." He died in 1983.

Stepa Sirković of the village of Drlup, nestling at the foot of Mount Kosmaj, not far from Belgrade, has been paralysed and immobile since childhood, and is physically underdeveloped. But all these shortcomings are made up for in his dreams. On all his canvases a person like him, only normally developed and grown, is the centre of various activities: he is waiting for his girlfriend under the blooming branches of a plum tree, he is driving a wedding coach with his bride beside him — young and beautiful. Is dreaming forbidden?

Finally, what do these five, and all the other naive painters in Yugoslavia, have in common? They share the urge and ability to express love, yearning, pain, happiness, suffering, daydreams or other moods in colour on glass or canvas.

Despite their local colour, in many cases, their work has a universal human quality. By their depiction of their way of life, their spontaneous, untutored portrayal of people, places, dreams and wishes, they unconsciously provide an answer to many questions people today ask themselves: where does happiness reside, what gives man's life value?

Among the naive sculptors a distinctive place is held by their doyen, *Petar Smajić*, better known for his early than for his later works, a man who has chiselled his bony countrymen in wood, in the form of slim, elongated figures. In Hlebine, *Mato Generalić*, brother of Ivan, and *Martin Hegedušić*, have for years been sculpting in wood, leaving painting to others.

In the village of Leskovac near Lazarevac, not far from Belgrade, the famous *Bogosav Živković* has engraved whole columns with reliefs of the people of his region and their legends: "Animal heads on human bodies, strange creatures resembling the initials of old Serbian manuscripts; male and female figures like those on the tombstones of village cemeteries or on roadside memorials." (Oto Bihalji-Merin, 1981). These, and others taken from the oral literature tradition, Serbian heroes remembered among the people for their feats, frequently overdimensioned like the figures on his columns, are among the subjects treated by this gifted chronicler and man of the people.

Not far from where Živković lives is the village of Jabučje where a father and son, *Dragiša* and *Milan Stanisavljević*, fetch the trunks of old oak trees submerged for years out of the Kolubara River flowing nearby. While in the water, the oak slowly blackens and becomes harder, offering father and son an even greater challenge.

The sculpture of Milan Stanisavljević is quite distinctive and cannot be associated with the work of any other sculptor in Yugoslavia, or any existing group or school. His carvings are original works of art based on the authentic village and on ancient philosophy, with strong remnants of the mythical. Patriarchal morals and religion are the groundwork for the powerful individuality of this artist. In the sculpture "Birth", Stanisavljević portrays a mother in the form of a large embryo, a large seed giving birth to a child. In place of her eye he has carved the head of the child, and from her mouth sprout its legs. "The mother dies and vanishes," says Stanisavljević, "while the child continues to regard the world through her eyes."

In contrast to his son, the father Dragiša Stanisavljević is more given to portraying the real outside world, using symbols depicting good and evil typical of this area. A woman who becomes pregnant without benefit of wedlock is always dubbed a sinner in the villages. For the sculptor to designate her as such, he introduces into his portrait of a woman elements symbolising sin and temptation, for instance, a snake.

Near the monastery of Manasija, in the village of Sladaji in Serbia, *Dragutin Aleksić* works in wood as the most suitable material for depicting the strenuous life of the peasant.

Đorđe Kreča from Bosnia was orphaned by the war, and spent his boyhood fleeing from the enemy or in a home for war orphans. Understandably, therefore, in his work he has turned to the theme of war: "I want to show generations to come," says Kreča, "the picture of wartime suffering in which I lost my parents and other relations. My sculptures therefore show heroes from folk songs, historic personalities and heroes from the last war." Some of Đorđe Kreča's sculp-

tures are as high as eleven metres, while others are reliefs telling war stories.

While naive painters are frequently strung together in groups or schools on the basis of region or a distinctive personality, the sculptors of Yugoslavia are for the most part strongly individualistic and rarely pattern themselves after others.

Finally, it should be added that among the growing number of artists working or attempting to work in this genre, there are, naturally, some who are purely imitative, who resort to stereotypes or succumb to commercialisation. However, there are also many younger naive artists who are bringing fresh elements to this form of artistic expression.

Generalić, Ivan: Woodcutter

Important Naive Art
Exhibitions, Museums and Galleries

IMPORTANT EXHIBITIONS OF THE WORK OF NAIVE ARTISTS IN THE WORLD

1886   Henri Rousseau exhibited publicly for the first time in the Salon des Indépendants, Paris
1904   Les primitifs français, Paris
1911   Henri Rousseau — retrospective exhibition in the Salon des Indépendants, Paris
1928   Les peintres du sacré coeur, Paris
1933   Un siècle de peintres naïfs, Paris
1937   Les maîtres populaires de la réalité, Paris, Zurich
1938   Masters of Popular Painting, New York, London
1941   Modern Primitieven, Stedelijk Museum, Amsterdam
1942   Primitifs du XXᵉ siècle, Paris
1947   Laienmalerei, Lübeck
1949   Moderne primitive Maler, Kunsthalle, Bern
1952   Maler des einfältigen Herzens, Museum am Ostwall, Dortmund
1953   Arbeit-Freizeit-Musse, Ruhrfestspiele, Kunsthalle, Recklinghausen
1954/55   Amerikanische Primitive, Museum am Ostwall, Dortmund
1958   La peinture naïve du Douanier Rousseau à nos jours, Knokke-le-Zoute
1961   Laienmalerei, Basel
      Das naive Bild der Welt, Baden-Baden, Frankfurt
1962   Naive Painters of Latin America, Durham, North Carolina
1963   The Naive Painting of Yugoslavia, Ermitage, Leningrad
      Laienkunst, Recklinghausen
1964   Le monde des naïfs, Musée national d'art moderne, Paris
      Les primitifs d'aujourd'hui, Galerie Charpentier, Paris
      Die Welt der naiven Malerei, Salzburg
      I Pittori Naifs, Rome
      De Lusthof der Naïeven, Rotterdam
      Naive Malerei, Oldenburg
1966   The First Triennial of Naive Art, Bratislava
      Rousseau et le monde naif, Tokyo
1968   Peintres naïves américains, Grand Palais de Champs-Elysées, Paris
1969   The Second Triennial of Naive Art, Bratislava
      Mostra internazionale dei pittori naifs, Lugano
      Kunst aus Haiti, Museum am Ostwall, Dortmund
1970   Naivi '70, Zagreb
1971   Werke und Werkstatt naiver Kunst, Kunsthalle, Recklinghausen
1972   The Third Triennial of Naive Art, Bratislava
      Naive Kunst aus sieben Ländern, Cologne
      Naive Kunst, Clemens-Sels-Museum, Neuss
      Festival dei due mondi, Spoleto
1973   Mostra internazionale dei pittori naifs, Lugano
      Naive Kunst aus Polen, Ruhrfestspielhaus, Recklinghausen
      Naiv Konst fran 20 lander, Sveagallerit, Stockholm
      Naivi '73, Zagreb
1974   Die Kunst der Naiven: Themen und Beziehungen, Haus der Kunst, Munich
      Rassegna internazionale dei naifs, La Grande Domenica, Milano
      De Grote Naïeven, Amsterdam
1975   Europäische naive Malerei, Kunstverein, Constance
      Das Bild der Naiven, Hoechst, Frankfurt
      Die Kunst der Naiven: Themen und Beziehungen, Kunsthaus, Zurich
1976   Naive Kunst, Lübeck
      Naive Kunst, Clemens-Sels-Museum, Neuss
1977   Naivi '77, Zagreb
1979/80   Naive Kunst und ihre Welt, Kunstverein, Düsseldorf
1981   Naive Kunst: Geschichte und Gegenwart, Kunsthistorisches Museum, Bielefeld
      Die Maler des heiligen Herzens, Charlotte, Galerie für naive Kunst, Munich

AFRICA

Important exhibitions of African naive art
1919   The Exhibition of Alphonse Lubaki, Brussels
1930   The Exhibition of Alphonse Lubaki and I. Djilatendo, Geneva
1965   The Oshogbo School, Goethe Institut, Lagos
1966   The First World Festival of Black Art, Dakar
1972   Contemporary African Art from the Collection of Ulli Beier, Prague
1974/77   Contemporary Folk Art in Ethiopia, Bielefeld (Wuppertal), Bonn and elsewhere
1974   Contemporary African Art, Chicago
      The Tingatinga Exhibition, Copenhagen
      Naive Art, Munich
1975   Painters from Dar-es-Salaam, Goethe Institut, Dar-es-Salaam, Naive Art, Zürich
1976   The Twin Seven Seven Exhibition, New York
1978   Masterpieces of Makonde, Düsseldorf
1979   Art from Africa, Berlin
1980   Art from Africa, Stockholm, Amsterdam
1980/81   Colonne Colon Kolo, Galerie Fred Jahn, Munich
1981   Art from Africa, London
1982   Painting on Glass from Dakar, Bayreuth
1983   Painting on Glass from Senegal, Mainz

ARGENTINA

Naive art is exhibited in the "El Taller" Gallery, Buenos Aires

AUSTRALIA

Galleries and other institutions where naive art is exhibited
Anvil Gallery, Kergunya, Victoria
Auckland Museum Gallery
Australian Gallery, Melbourne
Australian National Gallery, Canberra
Barry Sters Galleries, Sydney
Benalla Regional Gallery
Bloomfield Gallery, Sydney
Bonython Galleries, Adelaide, S.A.
Carnegie Collection, Victoria
Gallery A, Sydney
Gallery Art Naive, Melbourne
Johnstone Gallery, Sydney
National Collection, Canberra
National Gallery of South Australia
National Gallery of Western Australia
Queensland National Gallery
Realities Gallery, Melbourne
Shepparton Art Gallery
Swan Hill Regional Gallery
The Upstairs Gallery, Cairns, North Queensland
Toowoomba City Gallery
Wangaratta Council Collection
Wiregrass Gallery, Eltham, Victoria

AUSTRIA

Gallery exhibiting naive art
Galerie Autodidakt, Vienna

Important exhibitions of the work of naive artists in the country
1958   Discovered and Stimulated Talents, ÖGB, Vienna
1968   Galerie Autodidakt, Vienna
1969   Galerie Autodidakt, Vienna
1970   Galerie Autodidakt, Vienna

Abroad

1960 Lay Art in Austria, Recklinghausen
1971 Works and Workshops of Naive Art, Recklinghausen
1973 International Naive Art, Galerie Wolfgang Gurlitt, Munich
1974 Novotny Collection, Kunsthalle, Darmstadt
1975 Haus der Kunst, Munich and Kunsthaus, Zurich
1978 Kulturforum, Bonn
1979 Kulturgemeinde, Kelheim

BELGIUM

Galleries exhibiting the works of naive artists
Exclusively
Galerie de l'Art Naïf, Brussels
Galerie Dierickx, Brussels
Maison des arts spontanés, naïfs, folkloriques et marginaux, Brussels
Frequently
Galerie Tamara Pfeiffer, Brussels
Galerie l'Angle Algu, Brussels
Galerie Lorelei, Brussels
Galerie Louis Hutse, Brussels
Galerie Escalier, Brussels
Galerie Esschius, Begijnhofpoort, Diest
Galerie Alsput, St Pieter's Leeuw

Important exhibitions of the works of naive artists in the country
1958 Naive painting from Le Douanier Rousseau until today, Knok-ke-le-Zoute
1965 Belgian naive painters, Théâtre National, Centre Rogier, Brussels
     The same exhibition also in the Musée des Beaux-arts, Verviers
1969 Belgian naive painters in the context of the celebration of St. Martin, Tourinnes-la-Grosse
1970 Naive art from the province of Hainaut, Hôtel de Ville, Mons
1973 Naive painting, An Hyp Art Centre, Brussels
1976 Naive painting from Wallonia, Société Royale des Beaux-arts, Liège
1977 In homage to Léon Greffe, Palais des Beaux-arts, Charleroi
1978 Naive Art, Galerie CGER, Brussels
1978/79 Mobile exhibition of the CACEF: Naive art from Wallonia and from Brussels, Charleroi, Brussels, Liège
1979 International Exhibition of Naive Art, Centre du Rouge-Cloître, Brussels
     Brussels in the Eyes of Naive Artists, Kredietbank, Brussels
     The One Thousandth Anniversary of Brussels as Seen by Naive Artists, Hôtel Bedford, Brussels
1980 The Region of Liège in the Eyes of Naive Painters, Hôtel de Bocholt, Liège
     Ten Naive Painters from Wallonia, 'La Marotte' Association, Theu
1981 The Royal Dynasty in the Eyes of Naive Painters, Palais Royal, Brussels
     Christmas in Brussels, Hôtel de Ville, Brussels
1982 A Theatre in the Eyes of Naive Painters, Hôtel Bedford, Brussels
     Fifth Anniversary of the Founding of La Maison des Arts Spontanés et Naïfs; joint exhibition, Maison des Notaires, Brussels
1984 Holy Year in the Eyes of Naive Painters, Hôtel Bedford, Brussels
     Fifty Naive Painters, Galerie Alsput, Leeuw-Saint-Pierre

Abroad
1978 Naive Art from Wallonia, London, Glasgow, Edinburgh
1979 Mobile Exhibition of CACEF: naive art from Wallonia and Brussels, Laval (France)
1982 Belgian Naive Art, Laval (France)

BRAZIL

Exhibitions in the country
1945 Galeria Askenasy, Guanabara
1951 Galeria Bonino, Guanabara
1952 I, III, IV, V, VI, VII SNA
1953 Ministry of Education and Culture, Rio de Janeiro
1955 Salão de Cristo Negro, Guanabara
     Salão Artisanato, Rio de Janeiro
1955/56 V SNBA
1956 Galeria Dariano, Porto Alegre
     Brazilian Regions, Museum of Modern Art, São Paulo
1958 Museum of Modern Art, Bahia
1959 V BSP, IBNAP
     VIII, IX, XIV and XV SMBABH
     VII SNAM

1960 IX SNAM
1961 30 Years of Brazilian Painting, Galeria Macumaima, Guanabara
     Galeria Penguin, Guanabara
1962 Galeria Sabradinho, Guanabara
1962/66 X . XV SNAM
1962/64 XVII — XIX SMBABH
1963 Museum of Modern Art, São Paulo
     Galeria São Luis, São Paulo
     Museum of Modern Art, Bahia
     Brazilian Painting, Galeria Asteia, São Paulo
1964 Galeria Monmartre, Rio de Janeiro
     Galeria Relevo, Guanabara
1964/69 XII, XIII, and XIX SPAM
1965 Galeria Goeldi, Guanabara
     Brazilian Exhibition of Folk Art, Natal
     Petite Galerie, Rio de Janeiro
     Galeria Arte Hispanica, São Paulo
     Galeria Copacabana Palace, Rio de Janeiro
1966 XVI and XVIII SNAM
     April Salon, Museum of Modern Art, Rio de Janeiro
     Contemporary Brazilian Artists, Museum of Modern Art, Rio de Janeiro
     Galeria Actualidades, São Paulo
     Galeria Jotade, São Paulo
     Galeria Atrium, São Paulo
1967 Galeria Giro, Guanabara
     Galeria Goeldi, Guanabara
1968 Galeria Bonino, Guanabara
     Galeria l'Atelier, Rio de Janeiro
1969 Petite Galerie, Rio de Janeiro
     Galeria Tora, Rio de Janeiro
     Galeria Voltaire, Guanabara
     LXXIV SNBA
     Galeria Varanda, Rio de Janeiro
1970 LXXV SNBA
     'A' Galeria, São Paulo
1972 Petite Galerie, Rio de Janeiro
1975 Galeria Chico da Silva, Rio de Janeiro
     Galeria Ponto de Arte, Rio de Janeiro
1976 LXXXI SNBA
1977 Galeria Emy Bomfim, São Paulo

Exhibitions abroad in which naive artists from Brazil have participated
1946 Pan-American Union, Washington
1955 III Hispano-American Biennial, Barcelona
1965 Contemporary Brazilian Art — in various European cities
     Bienal Americana de Arte, Cordoba, Argentina
1966 Latin-American Art after Independence, in USA cities
     Twelve Brazilian Primitives, Moscow, Warsaw and Prague
     Festival of Brazilian Art, Philadelphia
1967 Galerie Delta, Amsterdam
     Galerie Debret, Paris
1968 Art Salon, Montevideo
1970 Brazilian Embassy, London
1971 Five Brazilian Painters, Elvaston Gallery, London
1972 Third Triennial of Naive Art, Bratislava
1973 Brazilian-American Cultural Institute, Washington, O'Hana Gallery, London
1976 Fortescue Swann Galleries, London
1979 Galerie Hamer, Amsterdam
     First International Exhibition of Naive Art in Britain, London
1978 Gallery of the Brazilian Embassy, London
     Maison de l'Amérique-Latine, Paris
1980 Festival of Colour, London
     The Round House, London
1982 RONA, London

CANADA

Important exhibitions of naive art
1974 A People's Art: Naive Art in Canada, National Gallery of Canada
1976 Saskatchewan Primitives, Mendel Art Gallery
1976 Folk Art of Nova Scotia, Art Gallery of Nova Scotia
1983 From the Heart, National Museum of Man, Canadian Centre for Folk Culture Studies, Ottawa, Ontario

Museum and galleries exhibiting naive art
Art Gallery of Nova Scotia, Halifax, Nova Scotia
National Gallery of Canada, Ottawa, Ontario
Musée du Québec, Québec City, Québec
National Museum of Man, Canadian Centre for Folk Culture Studies, Ottawa, Ontario

CUBA

Exhibition of Cuban naive artists
1963 Gallery UNEAC, Havana
1970 Art Salon '70, Havana
1971 Primitive Painters, Havana Gallery
1976 Eleven Cuban Primitive Painters, Jamaica Institute, Kingston
1978 International Exhibition of Naive Painting, Cultural Centre, Caracas, Venezuela

CZECHOSLOVAKIA

List of Czechoslovak galleries and museums exhibiting naive art
National Gallery, Prague
Ethnographic Museum, Prague
State Jewish Museum, Prague
Slovak National Gallery, Bratislava
Slovak National Museum, Bratislava
City Gallery, Bratislava
House of Arts, Brno
Ethnographic Institute of the Moravian Museum, Brno
County Museum, Brno
Arts Gallery, Litoměřice
South Bohemian Museum, České Budějovice
Gallery, Ostrov nad Ohří
Orlice Gallery, Rychnov nad Kněžnou
Museum, Mladá Bóleslav
Gallery, Havlíčkuv Brod
Museum, Netolice
Museum, Český Krumlov
Museum, Bakov nad Jizerou
Castle of Krásno, Valašské Meziříčí
Museum, Děčín
Museum, Bělá pod Bezdězem
East Slovakian Gallery, Košice
Tatra Gallery, Horný Smokovec
Kysuce Muzeum, Čadca
Orava Gallery, Dolný Kubín
District Gallery, Banská Bystrica
Agricultural Museum, Nitra

The most significant exhibitions of naive art in the Czechoslovak Socialist Republic

National exhibitions
1960 Exhibition of Amateur Artists in Slovakia, Bratislava
1962 Amateur Artists in Slovakia, Prague, Martin
1963 Naive Art in Czechoslovakia, Brno
1964 Naive Art in Czechoslovakia, Bratislava, Prague, Ostrava
1966 Naive Pictures, Prague
All-State Exhibition of Amateur Artists, Brno

International exhibitions
1966 1st Triennial of Insitic (Naive) Art, Bratislava
1969 2nd Triennial of Insitic (Naive) Art, Bratislava
1972 3rd Triennial of Insitic (Naive) Art, Bratislava

FRANCE

Principal museums in possession of works of naive artists
Paris: Galerie du Jeu de Paume et l'Orangerie (Rousseau)
 Musée National d'Art Moderne, Centre Georges Pompidou (Rousseau — Bombois — Vivin — Bauchant — Séraphine — Peyronnet...)
 Musée d'Art Moderne de la Ville de Paris (J. Eve — Ch. Pinçon)
 Musée du Louvre (Rousseau — Picasso's gift)
Grenoble: Musée de peinture et de sculpture (Bauchant — Bombois — Rimbert — Séraphine)
Laval: Musée du Vieux-Château — naive art collection (Rousseau — Rimbert — J. Eve — Bauchant — Lefranc)
Les Sables d'Olonne: Musée de l'Abbaye de Sainte-Croix (Jean-Jean Lefranc — Lallement — Pajot)
Lille: Musée d'Art Moderne de la Communauté Urbaine (Bauchant)
Limoges: Musée municipal (Baglione — Lascaux — Villoutreix)
Lyon: Musée des Beaux-Arts (Rodet)
Menton: Musée municipal (Bombois — Restivo — Tytgat)
Nantes: Musée des Beaux-Arts (Eve — Rondeau — Séraphine)
Nice: Musée A. Jakovsky (Bauchant — Crociani — Dêchelette — Fiorio)
Roanne: Musée Joseph Déchelette (Chabauty — Pincour)

Private museums in possession of works of naive artists
Vicq sur Yveline: Musée d'art naïf d'Ile de France (contemporary international naive art)
Gourdon (Alpes Maritimes): Château de Gourdon (Vivin — Lefranc — Séraphine — Fous — Bombois — Desnos — Rousseau...)

Important galleries exhibiting and selling the works of naive artists
Paris:
Galerie Antoinette, 7 Rue Jacob
Galerie Jeanne Bucher, 53 Rue de Seine
Galerie Mona Lisa, 32 Rue de Varenne
Galerie Naïfs et Primitifs, 9 Rue du Dragon
Galerie Naïf-Art, 19 Rue Mazarine
Galerie Dina Vierny, 36 Rue Jacob

Other parts of the country:
Galerie 17, 17 Rue de la Préfecture, Nice
Galerie Odile, Harel, 40 Av. Mercelin Maurel, Vence
Galerie La Tache, 5 Rue Jaubert, Aix-en-Provence
Galerie Mischkind, 7 Rue Jean-sans-peur, Lille

Most important exhibitions of the work of naive artists in the country
1911 Retrospective exhibitions of the works of Rousseau, Salon des Indépendants, Paris
1912 Exhibition of Rousseau's works, Galerie Berheim-Jeune, Paris
1923 Exhibition of Rousseau's Works, Galerie Rosenberg, Paris
1927 Exhibition of Naive Art in the Galerie Jeanne Bucher, Paris
1927 Exhibition of Naive Art in the Cabinet of M. Courteline, Galerie Bernheim-Jeune, Paris
1928 Les Primitifs Modernes, exhibition arranged by Wilhelm Uhde, Paris
1928 Les Peintres du Coeur-Sacré, Galerie des Quatres-Chemins, Paris
1929 Peintres populaires d'hier et d'aujourd'hui, Galerie Druet, Paris
1930 Exhibition of Naive Art, Galerie Bernheim, Paris
1933 A Century of Naive Painting, Galerie des Beaux-arts, Paris
1937 Les Maîtres Populaires de la Réalité, Paris
1940 Painters of Realism and Artists of Dreams, Galerie de Berri, Paris
1942 Primitives of the XX Century, Galerie Drouin, Paris
1950 Half a Century of Naive Art, Galerie Louise, Paris
1960 Naive Painting from le Douanier Rousseau to the Present Day, Maison de la pensée française, Paris
1964 The World of the Naive, Musée National d'Art Moderne, Paris
 Primitives of Today, Galerie Charpentier, Paris
1966 Introduction to a Museum of Naive Art — Henri Rousseau in Laval, Musée d'Art Moderne, Paris
 Retrospective Exhibition of the Works of J. Lefranc, Les Sables d'Olonne
1967 Exhibition for the Official Opening of the Musée d'art naïf, Laval
1974 The Wondrous World of the Naive Artists, Galerie Dina Vierny, Paris
1976 Exhibition of Naive Art, Galerie Antoinette, Paris
1980-81 Three Self-taught Artists Called Naive Artists, Grenoble

Important exhibitions of naive painters abroad in which French naive artists participated
1926 Exhibition of the Works of Henri Rousseau, Galerie Flechteim, Berlin
1932 Exhibition of the Works of Henri Rousseau, Kunsthalle, Basel
1937 Les maîtres populaires de la réalité, Kunsthaus, Zurich
1938 Masters of Popular Painting, Tooth Gallery, London
 Masters of Popular Painting, Museum of Modern Art, New York
1958 Naive Painting from le Douanier Rousseau to the Present Day, Knokke-le-Zoute
1961 Das naive Bild der Welt, Staatliche Kunsthalle, Baden-Baden
1964 Pittori Naifs, Palazzo Barberini, Rome
1964 Die Welt der naiven Malerei, Residenzgalerie, Salzburg
 Panorama international de la peinture naïve, Mission Culturelle, Rabat
1968 Il Mondo dei Naifs, Milan, Ferrara, Spoleto
1970 From Rousseau to the Present, Zagreb, Belgrade, Rijeka, Ljubljana
1972 Peinture Naïve, Galerie Isy Brachot, Brussels
1973 Naivi '73, Zagreb
1975 Die Kunst der Naiven, Haus der Kunst, Munich

EAST GERMANY
(GERMAN DEMOCRATIC REPUBLIC)

Museums exhibiting the works of naive artists
Staatliches Lindenau-Museum, Altenburg
Staatliches Museum für Volkskunst, Dresden
Haus der Heimat, Freital
Staatliche Galerie Moritzburg, Halle (an der Saale)
National-Galerie, Berlin

WEST GERMANY
(FEDERAL REPUBLIC OF GERMANY)

Museums, galleries and institutes possessing important collections of the works of naive artists
Staatliches Museum Preussischer Kulturbesitz, Berlin
Museum für deutsche Volkskunde, Berlin
Museum am Ostwall, Dortmund
Stadtgalerie, Frankfurt A. M.
Altonaer Museum, Hamburg
Clemens-Selss-Museum, Neuss
Vestisches Museum, Recklinghausen
Institut für Auslandsbeziehungen (IFA), Stuttgart

Museums possessing important works by naive artists
Städtische Kunstsammlungen, Bonn
Staedelsches Kunstinstitut, Frankfurt
Kunsthalle, Hamburg
Museum Sprengel, Hannover
Städtische Kunstsammlungen, Kassel
Stadtmuseum, Cologne
Stadtmuseum, Munich
Schleswig-Holsteinisches Landesmuseum, Schleswig

Important private collections
Charlotte (Lotta Zander), Munich
Dr. Volker Dallmeir, Hannover
Fa. Eisenmann, Böblingen
Dr. Matthias T. Engels,
Dr. Irmgard Feldhaus, Neuss
Hans Friedrich Geist, Lübeck
Karin Grochowiak, Kuppenheim
Egon Hasbecker, Heidelberg
Hans Holzinger, Munich
Prof. Rolf Italiaander, Museum für naive Kunst, Stade
Marianne und Heinz Kühn, Cologne-Dellbrück
Fritz Novotny, Frankfurt
Hans-Joachim i Christina Orth, Düsseldorf
Werner Böschel, Bielefeld-Bethel
Siegfried Poppe, Hamburg
Fred Stelzig, Besigheim
Alex Vömel, Düsseldorf
Elke i Werner Zimmer, Düsseldorf
Ludwig Zimmerer, Warsaw (Poland)

Important exhibitions of the works of German naive artists in the country
1954 Sinnvoles Laienschaffen, Ruhrfestspiele, Kunsthalle, Recklinghausen
1963 Laienkunst im Ruhrgebiet, Ruhrfestspiele, Rathaus, Recklinghausen
1964 Naive Malerei, Kunstverein, Oldenburg
1966 Carl Christian Thegen, Altonaer Museum, Hamburg
1969 Drei naive Künstler, Museum Folkwang, Essen
      Max Raffer, Sammlung Holzinger, Munich
      Adalbert Trillhaase, Clemens-Sels-Museum, Neuss
1971 Naive Kunst im Ruhrgebiet, Altonaer Museum, Hamburg
1972 Oluf Braren, Hochschule für bildende Künste, Hamburg
      Hundert Werke naiver Kunst, Schloss, Oberhausen
      Naive Künstler des Ruhrgebietes, Haus Weyand, Bochum
      Schiffe und Häfen (Wanderausstellung), Hamburg
1973 Vivan Ellis, Werkstatt Lydda, Bethel-Bielefeld
      Friedrich und Ludwig Gerlach, Kunsthalle, Recklinghausen
1974 Naive Malerei, Institut für Auslandsbeziehungen, Stuttgart
      Eduard Odenthal, Clemens-Sels-Museum, Neuss
      A. N. Tschistjakow, Kunsthalle, Bielefeld
      Josef Wittlich, Galerie Zimmer, Düsseldorf
1975 Jean Abels, Clemens-Sels-Museum, Neuss
      Minna Ennulat, Galerie Zimmer, Düsseldorf
      Erich Grams, Galerie Zimmer, Düsseldorf
      Eduard Odenthal, Charlotte, Galerie für naive Kunst, Munich
      Sonntagsmaler, Sammlung Eisenmann, Böblingen
1976 Erich Bödeker, Galerie Zimer, Düsseldorf
      Minna Ennulat, Charlotte, Galerie für naive Kunst, Munich
1977 Max Raffer — Ein Bauer malt Bilder, Werkstatt Lydda, Bethel-Bielefeld
      Max Raffer, Galerie Zimmer, Düsseldorf
1978 Emma Stern, Clemens-Sels-Museum, Neuss
      Adalbert Trillhaase, Galerie Zimmer, Düsseldorf
1980 Bilder von Max Raffer, Charlotte, Galerie für naive Kunst, Munich

Important group exhibitions in the Federal Republic of Germany of the works of German naive artists and naive artists of other countries
1947 Laienmalerei, Overbeck-Gesellschaft, Lübeck
1952 Maler des einfältigen Herzens, Museum am Ostwall, Dortmund
1953 Arbeit — Freizeit — Musse, Ruhrfestspiele, Kunsthalle, Recklinghausen

1954 Sinnvolles Laienschaffen, Ruhrfestspiele, Recklinghausen
1961 Das naive Bild der Welt, Staatliche Kunsthalle, Baden-Baden
      Das naive Bild der Welt, Kunstverein, Frankfurt
1963 Laienkunst im Ruhrgebiet, Ruhrfestspiele, Rathaus, Recklinghausen
1964 Naive Kunst (Bali-Jugoslawien-Ruhrgebiet), Mathildenhöhe, Darmstadt
1971 Werke und Werkstatt naiver Kunst, Ruhrfestspiele, Kunsthalle, Recklinghausen
1972 Naive Kunst, Clemens-Sels-Museum, Neuss
1973 Internationale naive Malerei, Galerie Guritt, Munich
1974 Die Kunst der Naiven, Galerie Zimmer, Düsseldorf
      Naive Kunst — Sammlung Novotny, Kunsthalle, Darmstadt
1975 Die Kunst der Naiven: Themen und Beziehungen, Haus der Kunst, Munich
      Meisterwerke naiver Malerei, Galerie Zimmer, Düsseldorf
      Das Bild der Naiven, Jahrhunderthalle, Frankfurt
      Europäische naive Malerei, Kunstverein, Constance
1976 Naive Kunst, Overbeck-Gesellschaft, Lübeck
      Naive Kunst, Clemens-Sels-Museum, Neuss
1979 Naive Kunst, Sammlung Novotny, Rastatt Kunsthalle, Kulturgemeinde Darmstadt Kelheim
1979/80 Naive Kunst und ihre Welt: Kunstverein, Düsseldorf
1981 Naive Kunst: Geschichte und Gegenwart, Kulturhistorisches Museum, Bielefeld
      Die Maler des heiligen Herzens, Charlotte, Galerie für naive Kunst, Munich

GREAT BRITAIN

Some exhibitions of English naive art in the country
1948 Mayor Gallery, London
1953 Beaux Arts Gallery, London
1959 Newlyn Gallery, Cornwall
1960 Gallery One, London
1962 Portal Gallery, London
1963 Arthur Jeffress Gallery, London
1964 Traverse Gallery, Edinburgh
1964 Crane Kalman Gallery, London
1967 International Naive Exhibition, Grosvenor Gallery, London
1968 The Spontaneous Eye, Grosvenor Gallery, London
1969 Portal Gallery, London
1970 Portal Gallery, London
1971 New Art Centre, London
      The Bluecoat Gallery, Liverpool
      The City Museum, Lancaster
1972 Northern Primitives, South London Art Gallery, London
      Portal Gallery, London
1973 New Art Centre, London
      Langton Gallery, London
1974 They Taught Themselves, Lantern Gallery, Manchester
1976 The Spontaneous Eye, Lantern Gallery, Manchester
      Portal Gallery, London
1977 Langton Gallery, London
      RONA (Register of Naive Artists) London's Naive Painters, Kensington Town Hall, London University, National Theatre, London.
1977/80 RONA exhibitions in London, Sheffield and Manchester
1978 Victor Waddington Gallery, London
      New Art Centre, London
1979 Northern Primitives, Artists Gallery, Leeds
      London's First International Exhibition of Naive Art, Hamiltons, London
1980 Wills Lane Gallery, St. Ives
1981 Chenil Art Gallery, London
      RONA, Ivory House, St. Katherine's Dock, London
      Camden Arts Centre, London

Some exhibitions of English naive art abroad and participation in international exhibitions
1962 UNESCO Expos, Monte Carlo and various towns in Italy
1963 Rudy Komon Gallery, Sydney
1967 Little Palace Gallery, Warsaw
1968 BWA Gallery, Katowice
1970 Bonython Gallery, Sydney
1972 Salon Contemporain, Paris
      Naivi '73, Zagreb
      Peinture Naïve Internationale, Paris
1974 Los Angeles Municipal Art Gallery, Los Angeles
1976 Galerie de Gueux, Paris
1979 XIV Grand Prix d'Art Contemporain International de Monte Carlo, Monaco
      Galerie '17', Nice
      International Naives, Galerie Pro Arte Kasper, Morges (Switzerland)
1980 XV Grand Prix International d'Art Contemporain de Monte Carlo, Monaco

GREECE

Important museums exhibiting naive art
Athens: Alexander Soutzosa Museum (National Art Gallery)
Folk Art Museum at Kidatinajion, Plaka
Lesbos: Theophilos Museum in Vareja (68 paintings by Theophilos Hatzimichail)

Private collection
Volos: The Private Collection of Kithos Makris

HAITI

Exhibitions of Haitian naive art abroad
1945 Centre d'Art — Havana
Haitian Popular Paintings — United Nations Club, Washington
1946 Paintings from Le Centre d'Art of Port-au-Prince — American British Centre, New York
1947 Breton organises exhibition of Hyppolite in Prague, Paris, Basel and Berlin
Peintres de l'Equateur, d'Haiti et Perou — UNESCO, Paris
Haitian Popular Paintings organised by the Centre d'Art of Port-au-Prince — American British Centre, New York
1948 Exhibition of Haitian Art — Pan-American Union, Washington
1949 Haitian Art — San Francisco & Los Angeles
1950 19 Haitian Artists — Stedelijk Museum, Amsterdam and European capitals
1951 Exhibition of Haitian Art — Caracas
1954 Haitian exhibition in Vienna & Caracas
1957 Haitian "Lay" Painters Exhibition — St James's Episcopal Church, New York
1961 Haitian Exhibition — St James's Episcopal Church, New York
1965 Haitian Artists, Hall University, New Jersey
1966 Touring exhibition of 50 Haitian artists organised by the Smithsonian Institute — American and Canadian Cities
1968/69 Popular Paintings from Haiti — Art Council Gallery, Cambridge; Art Gallery, Billingham; Mappin Art Gallery, Sheffield; Museum, Manchester; Arts Centre, Folkstone; Welsh Arts Council; Museum and Art Gallery, Doncaster; Hayward Gallery, London (The Kurt Bachmann Collection)
1969 Haitian Primitives, Anna Simond/Ann Wace exhibition of Haitian Art — London
Haitian Art, Davenport Municipal Art Gallery, Iowa
Haitian Art (Collection Kurt Bachmann, New York), Museum am Ostwall, Dortmund
1970 Haitian Art at the Portal Gallery, London
Peintres Naïfs d'Haïti — Mona Lisa Galerie, Paris
Naïfs d'Häiti et Voudou — Musée de Laval
Kunst aus Haiti — Museum am Ostwall, Dortmund
1972 Paintings from Haiti — Arthur Tooth & Son, London
1973 Haitian Art — American Hotel, New York
1974 The Naive Tradition/Haiti — The Flagg Tanning Corporation Collection, Milwaukee Art Centre
1977 Haitian Paintings and Sculpture — Sotheby Parke Bernet Ltd (the Kurt Bachmann Collection), New York
1978 Haitian Art — Brooklyn Museum, Brooklyn
1979 Kunst aus Haiti — Staatliche Kunsthalle, Berlin
1980 Haitian Paintings, Sotheby Parke Bernet Ltd — New York
Naïfs Haitiens — Galerie des Totem, Musée de l'Homme, Paris
Haïtiens — La Galerie des Lombards, Paris
1981 Haitian Painting — Central Falls Gallery, New York

HUNGARY

Museums and other institutions exhibiting the works of naive artists
Museum of Naive Artists, Kecskemét
Hungarian National Gallery, Department of Naive Art, Budapest
Institute of Folk Creativity, Department of Art, Budapest

Important exhibitions of the works of Hungarian naive artists in the country
1910 Exhibition of Kovács Mári, a peasant woman, Hotel Fekete Sas, Hódmezövásár
1910 Exhibition of Mokry Meszáros Dezsö, Art Hall, Budapest
1923 Exhibition of Benedek Péter, Art Hall, Budapest
1928 Exhibition of Benedek Péter, National Salon, Budapest
1934 Original Talent, I Exhibition, the National Salon, Budapest
1935 Original Talent, II Exhibition, Hall of Hungarian Original Talents, Budapest
1936 Three Painters, Three Sculptors, Hall of Hungarian Original Talents, Budapest
1964 Anniversary Exhibition of Benedek Péter, Kossuth Museum, Cegléd
1967 Exhibition of Hungarian Naive Artists, Museum in Székesfehérvár
1967 Retrospective Exhibition of Hyöry Elek, Nyiregyhaz

1968 Süli Andras — entire opus, Móra Ferenc Museum, Szeged
1970 Retrospective Exhibition of Györy Elek, Agricultural Museum, Budapest
1971 Exhibition of Balázs János, Center for General Education "Józef Attila", Salgótarjan
1972 Hungarian Naive Art in the XX Century, Hungarian National Gallery, Budapest. Exhibition presented also in other towns in Hungary
1976 Permanent Exhibition of Hungarian Naive Art in the Hungarian National Gallery, Department of Naive Art
1977 Museum of Hungarian Naive Artists, Kecskemét, I Exhibition. One-man and group shows have been held regularly since 1977.
1978 Artistic and Creative Therapy, Educational Center, Szentendre
1980 Agriculture in the Works of Naive Artists, Agricultural Museum, Budapest
1980 Founding of the Museum of Naive Artists in Kesckemét bringing together works from the Hungarian National Gallery and the Institute of Folk Creativity (Department of Art). A permanent exhibition has been established and occasionally special exhibitions are arranged of works by Hungarian naive artists.

Important exhibitions by Hungarian naive artists abroad
1929 Exhibition of Benedek Peter, Künstlerhaus, Vienna
1938 Hongaarsche Oertalenten, Esher Surrey Art Galleries, The Hague, The Netherlands
1972 Naive Malerei in Ungarn 1900—1971, Kunstmuseum, Winterthur, Switzerland
1972/73 Works by Hungarian Naive Artists from the III Triennial of Naive Artists in Bratislava were exhibited in Denmark, Finland, and Norway
1973 Naive Malerei in Ungarn, Donaueinkaufscentrum, Regensburg, Federal Republic of Germany
Arte Primitivo Hungaro en el siglo XX, Galería de la Habana, Cuba
1975 Hongaarse Naieven, Culturcentrum, Turnhout, Belgium
Art Naïf Hongrois, Musée des Beaux-Arts, Mons, Belgium
1976 Hungarian Naive Artists, Hotel Hilton, Athens, Greece

Hungarian naive artists have taken an outstanding part in various international exhibitions of naive art, such as the I, II, III Triennials in Bratislava and the Naivi '70 and '73 in Zagreb.

ITALY

Galleries exhibiting Italian and foreign naive works
Galleria Arno, Via della Vigna Nuova 73, Florence
Galleria La Feluca, Via Frattina 38, Rome
Generalic Gallery, Via Fontana 5, Milan
Art Gallery, Via Monte di Pietàl/a, Milan
Eskenaziarte, Via Massena 19, Turin

Important national and international exhibitions held in Italy
1968 Italian and French naive painters, Palazzo Barberini, Rome
1968 The World of Naives, Milan
1969 The World of Naives, Correggio (Reggio Emilia)
Czechoslovak Naive Artists, Reggio Emilia
1971 First Encounter with Primitives from 15 Countries, Prato
1973 Second Encounter with Primitives from 15 Countries, Galery Venezuela, Padova
Naive Artists in Rome, Palazzo Barberini, Rome
Award to Naive Artists from the Town of Cagliari
1974 Naive Artists, Galleria Sagittario, Pordenone
1974 Palm Sunday, Rotonda Besana, Milan
1980 IV International Biennial of Naive Artists, I Candidi Ente Fiera, Milan
The Luzzara National Exhibition annually since 1968, Reggio Emilia

Important exhibitions of naive artists abroad in which Italian naive artists participated
1964 De Lusthof der Naïeven, Rotterdam
1966 The First Triennial of Naive Art, Bratislava
1969 International Exhibition of Naive Art, Lugano
The Second Triennial of Naive Art, Bratislava
1970 Naivi '70, Zagreb
1971 Bucholz Gallery, Cologne
1972 The Third Triennial of Naive Art, Bratislava
Clemen-Sels Museum, Neuss
Simpson Art Gallery, New York
Municipal Art Museum, Los Angeles
Italian Naive Artists, Zagreb
1973 International Exihibition of Naive Art, Lugano
Naivi '73, Zagreb
Galerie am Rabeinstag, Vienna
Galerie Antoinette, Paris
1974 Haus der Kunst, Munich
Galerie Kasper, Morges

1975 The Italian Institute for Culture, Paris
Zapiecek Gallery, Warsaw
1976 Foyles Art Gallery, New York
International Exhibitions of Naive Art, Lugano
1977 Naivi '77, Zagreb
Palais de UNESCO, Paris
1981 Kulturhistorisches Museum, Bielefeld
1982 Le Génie des Naïfs, Grand Palais, Paris

ISRAEL

Galleries exhibiting the works of naive artists
Debel Gallery, Ein-Kerem, Jerusalem
Engel Gallery, Jerusalem
Goldman Gallery, Haifa

JAMAICA

Galleries and institutions exhibiting naive art:
Bolivar Gallery
Institute of the Art Gallery of Jamaica
National Gallery
Olympia International Art Centre, Kingston

Exhibitions of naive artists of Jamaica in the country
1938 St.George Exhibition, Kingston
1948 Anniversary Exhibition, Jamaica Institute
1966 Jamaica Institute
1977 Olympia International Art Centre, Kingston
Annual National Exhibition, Jamaica National Gallery
1978 Beginning Years: The Art of Jamaica 1922—1940
1979 Annual National Exhibition, Jamaica National Gallery
Intuitive Eye, Jamaica National Gallery
1980 Annual National Exhibition, Jamaica National Gallery

Abroad
1951 First Caribbean Exhibition, San Juan, Puerto Rico
1971 Three Decades of Jamaican Art, Commonwealth Institute, London
1972 Contemporary Caribbean Art, O. A. S. Art Gallery, Washington
1976 Eight Jamaican Primitives, Havana, Cuba
1978 Four Jamaican Primitives, Washington

THE NETHERLANDS

Museums exhibiting the works of naive artists
Permanent Exhibitions
Westfries Museum, Hoorn (collection of regional naives only, including Hagoort and Kaay)

Naive paintings in the Collections of
Stedelijk Museum, Amsterdam
Frans Hals Museum, Haarlem
Museum Boymans-van Beuningen, Rotterdam
Gemeentelijk Museum Het Princessehof, Leeuwarden

NICARAGUA

Works by naive artist are exhibited in
Casa "Fernando Gordillo" de la Asociación Sandinista de Trabajadores de la Cultura, Managua
Escuela Nacional de Bellas Artes, Managua
Galería Tague, Managua

POLAND

Collections of Polish naive art are found in the following museums:
State Ethnographic Museum, Warsaw
Ethnographic Museum, Cracow
Ethnographic Museum, Wrocław
Ethnographic Museum, Toruń (particularly representative of sculpture)
Regional Museum, Radom
Regional Museum, Nowy Sacz (Nikifor, Wnekova, sculptures from Pasin)
Ethnographic Museum, Poznań (Nikifor, Mroz)
Regional Museum, Siedlce (Korpa, Mucha)
Museum of the Kujawski and Dobrzynski Regions (Zagajewski)
Gornoslavski Museum, Bytom (in addition to paintings, also sculptures by miners)
National Museum, Kielce (local artists)
Regional Museum, Lublin
Zimmerer Collection, Warsaw, No. 28 Dabrowiecka Street

ROMANIA

Collections of the works of naive artists are in the following museums and galleries
The National Naive Art Salon of Arad (biennial)
The Inter-County Naive Art Salon of Piteşti (annual)
The Gallery of Naive Art at the Arges County Museum, Piteşti
The Naive Art Salon of Moldavia in Botoşani (annual)
The Naive Art Gallery at the Art Museum of Botoşani
The Naive Art Gallery of the Institute for Ethnologic and Dialectologic Research, Bucharest

A national exhibition of Naive Art is held biennially at the festival "Song of Romania."

THE SOVIET UNION

Museums and other institutions which exhibit folk, amateur and naive art
The Society of Folk Arts and Crafts, Vilnius, Lithuania
Archives of the folk arts and crafts methods centers in: Moscow, Vilnius, Tbilisi, Yerevan, Kiev, Tallin, Ulan-Ude, etc
Museum of Folk and Popular Amateur Art of the Russian Federation, Suzdal
Georgian Museum of Folk Arts and Crafts, Tbilisi
Armenian Folk Arts and Crafts Museum, Yerevan
Ukrainian State Museum of Popular Decorative Arts, Kiev
Poltava Art Gallery, Ukraine
Kihnu Island Museum of Ethnography, Estonia
Archives of ZNUI, People's Extra-mural University of Art, Moscow
Leningrad Museum of the Arctic and Antarctic
Kimri Ethnographical Museum near Kalinin
Rokishkas Ethnographical Museum, Lithuania
State History Museum, Moscow
Ciurlioni Art Gallery, Kaunas, Lithuania
Museum of Modern Art, Yerevan, Armenia
Zagorsk Toy Museum, near Moscow
Velek Ethnographical Museum near Archangel
Gori Ethnographical Museum, Georgia

Main exhibitions of naive art
1935 Show of collective farm amateur artists
1937 Show of amateur artists for 20th anniversary of October Revolution
1967 Show of amateur artists for October Revolution golden jubilee
1970 Lenin birth centennial: show of popular and amateur art
1970 ZNUI jubilee show, Moscow
1974 Glory of Labour, USSR show of amateur artists
1977 Show of last USSR Festival of popular amateur art for October Revolution 60th anniversary
1982 USSR show of amateur art for 17th Soviet Trade Union Congress, Moscow

SWITZERLAND

Museums containing works by naive artists
Kunsthaus, Zurich
Museum, Bern
Museum, Winterthur
Museum, Basel
Museum, Thun
Museum, Lugano

Important exhibitions of naive art in Switzerland
1969/73 Biennial of Naive Art, Museo Civico di Belle Arti, Lugano
1972 International Naive Artists. Musée de l'Athénée, Geneva
Naive Art from Hungary, Museum, Winterthur
1975 The Art of the Naive, Kunsthaus, Zurich
1976 Biennial of Naive Art, Museo Civico di Belle Arti, Lugano
1983 The World of the Naive, Musée de l'Athénée, (organised by the Galerie Pro Arte Kasper)

THE UNITED STATES OF AMERICA

Some museums and galleries exhibiting the works of naive artists
New York: The Museum of American Folk Art
The Museum of Modern Art
Brooklyn Museum
Phyllis Kind Gallery
Washburn Gallery
The New York Historical Association in Coopertown
Washington: National Museum of American Art, Smithsonian Institution
The Phillips Collection
National Gallery of Art

Bishop Hill: Bishop Hill State Historic Site
Hartford: The Connecticut Historical Society
Philadelphia: Philadelphia Museum of Art
Rockland: William A. Fransworth Library and Art Museum
Santa Fe, New Mexico: Museum of International Folk Art
Shelburne, Vermont: The Shelburne Museum
Springfield: Museum of Fine Arts
Williamsburg, Virginia: Abby Aldrich Rockefeller Folk Art Collection

VENEZUELA

Museums, galleries and other institutions exhibiting works of naive art
The Museum of Folk Art "Salvador Valero"
Galería "La otra banda"
Galería "Area de Noë"
Fine Arts Centre
National Gallery
Fine Arts Museum
Galería "Angel Boscan"
Galería Gaudi
Gallery of the House of Andres Bella
Galería "El Muro"
Exhibition Hall of Fondacomune
Galería Bellini
Galería "Viva Mexico"
Institute for Culture "Adres Eloy Blanco"
Ateneo de Caracas
Galería "22"
Museum of Modern Art
State Museum of Art
(all in Caracas)

YUGOSLAVIA

Museums of naive art
Gallery of Primitive Art, Zagreb (founded in 1952)
Gallery of Self-taught Artists, Svetozarevo (founded in 1960)

Galleries of naive art with collections
Gallery of Self-taught Painters, Trebnje (Slovenia)
Gallery of Original Art, Zlatar (Croatia)
The "Mirko Virius" Gallery, Zagreb
Gallery of Naive Art of Bosnia and Herzegovina, Sanski Most
Gallery of Naive Painters, Kovačica (Vojvodina)

Important colonies of naive art
Self-taught Artists' Camp, Trebnje (Slovenia)
Naive Artists' Gathering, Zlatar (Croatia)
The "Zilik" Winter Artists' Colony, Karlovac (Croatia)
Naive Sculptors' Colony, Ernestino (Croatia)
"Maytime Friendship on the Sana," Sanski Most (Bosnia and Herzegovina)

Important group exhibitions of Yugoslav naive art in the country
1952   Permanent Peasant Painters' Exhibition, Peasant Accord Hall, Zagreb
1955   The Village and Peasants in the Eyes of Peasants, Peasant Accord Hall, Zagreb
1957   Naive Art, Masarikova 4, Belgrade
       Yugoslav Naive Artists, Jakopič Pavilion, Ljubljana
       Naive Artists in Yugoslavia, Art Pavilion, Skopje
1957/58 Naive Artists of Yugoslavia, Art Pavilion, Zagreb
1960   Kovačica School, Gallery of Primitive Art, Zagreb
1961   Exhibition of Yugoslav Naive Artists, Gallery of Primitive Art, Zagreb
1962   First Quadrennial of the Naive Artists of Yugoslavia, "Nadežda Petrović" Gallery, Čačak
1966   Naive Art '66, Between the Ploča Gateways, Dubrovnik
1967   Profiles '67, Gallery of Primitive Art, Zagreb
1968   Profiles '68, Gallery of Primitive Art, Zagreb
From 1970 to 1979 Self-taught Artists' Salon, Self-taught Artists' Gallery, Svetozarevo (annually)
1970   Naives '70, The Naive Art of Yugoslavia, Gallery of Primitive Art, Zagreb; Cultural Centre, Belgrade
1970   Self-taught Artists' Gallery, Svetozarevo 1960—1970 (Exhibition of Self-taught Artists of Yugoslavia, organised for the celebration of the tenth anniversary of the Gallery's founding); Self-taught Artists' Gallery, Svetozarevo

From 1971 onwards Self-taught Artists' Salon, Self-taught Artists' Gallery, Trebnje (from 1971 to 1981 biennially, at present triennially)
1971   A Critical Retrospective of the "Zemlja" (Earth) School, Art Pavilion, Zagreb
1972   The Naive Art of Yugoslavia, Gallery, Hlebine
       Twenty Years of the Gallery of Primitive Art, Zagreb
1977   Naivi '77, The Naive Art of Yugoslavia, Gallery of Primitive Art, Zagreb
1979   Peasant and Worker-Painters and Sculptors Between the Wars, Gallery of Primitive Art, Zagreb
1981   Biennial of Yugoslav Self-taught Artists, Self-taught Artists' Gallery, Svetozarevo (biennially)
       The Hlebine Circle — fifty years of naive painting, Gallery of Primitive Art, Zagreb
1982   Thirty Years of the Gallery of Primitive Art, Gallery of Primitive Art, Zagreb
1983   Self-taught Art in Serbia (Exhibition celebrating the fiftieth anniversary of the appearance of naive art in Serbia), Self-taught Artists' Gallery, Svetozarevo; Slovenska Bistrica, Vukovar, Belgrade

Important international exhibitions of naive art in Yugoslavia
1970   From Rousseau to the Present, Gallery of Primitive Art, Zagreb, Belgrade, Rijeka, Ljubljana
       International Exhibition, Naivi '70, Art Pavilion, Zagreb
1973   International Exhibition, Naivi '73, Gallery of Primitive Art, Zagreb
       Arts and Crafts Museum, Ethnographic Museum, Zagreb; Gallery, Hlebine; Koprivnica
1977   International Exhibition, Naivi '77, Art Pavilion, Old Town Hall, Zagreb
1983   Foreign Naive Artists from the Collection of the Gallery of Primitive Art, Zagreb

Important exhibitions of Yugoslav naive art abroad
1959   Wystawa Prymitywów artystów jugoslawiánskich, Sala Záhety, Warsaw
       Wýstawa Lidoých primitivu Jugoslavie, Križove Chodbéstaromestskeé radnice, Prague
       Ivan Generalić, Palais des Beaux Arts, Brussels
1960   Generalić, Virius, Skurjeni, Galleria la nuova pesa, Roma
       Pintores populares Jugoslavos, Galeria Sistina, São Paulo
1961   Pintores populares de Jugoslavia, Galeria de arte Barcinski, Rio de Janeiro
       Contemporary Yugoslav Primitive Painters, The Arthur Jeffress Gallery, London
       Jugoslawische Malerei, Studio F, Ulm
       Das naive Bild der Welt, Staatliche Kunsthalle, Baden-Baden
       Das naive Bild der Welt, Historisches Museum, Frankfurt; Kunstverein, Hannover
       Jugoslawische naive Malerei, Museum am Ostwall, Dortmund
1962   Narodne hudožniki primitivisti Jugoslavije, Gosudarstveni Ermitaž, Lenjingrad; State Museum of Art, Moscow
1963   Jugoslawische Kunst der Naiven, Akademie der Künste, Vienna
1964   Sonntagsmaler aus Jugoslawien, Städtische Kunsthalle, Recklinghausen
       Naive Malerei in Jugoslawien, Kunsthaus, Hamburg
1966   Kunst der Naiven in Jugoslawien, Stadtmuseum, Munich
1968   Naïeve Kunst uit Joegoslavie, Bols Taverne, Amsterdam
       Arte naif de Yugoslavia, Museo de arte moderno, Mexico
1969   Yugoslav Naive Paintings and Sculpture, Williamsburg (USA)
1969   Yugoslav Naive Artists, Sveagalerie, Stockholm
       Yugoslav Naive Painting, "El Taller" Gallery, Buenos Aires
1970   Yugoslav Naive Paintings and Sculptures, in various cities in Canada and USA
1971   Naive Painters and Sculptors from Yugoslavia, Le Palais des Beaux Arts, Charleroi, Anvers, Ghent, Mons
1972   Naive Artists from Yugoslavia, 'De Vaart' Museum, Hilversum
1975   Naive Painters of Yugoslavia, Galerie 'Lafayette', Paris
1976   Premier Salon international d'art contemporain — Yougoslavie Peintres and sculptures naïfs, Grand Palais, Paris
       Naive Art in Yugoslavia, Camden Arts Centre, London and several towns in USA
       Naïeve kunst uit Joegoslavie 1930—1976, Frans Hals Museum, Haarlem
1983   Les naïfs yougoslave, Musée municipal, Cahors; Yugoslav Cultural and Information Centre, Paris

Yugoslav naive artists have taken part in all important international exhibitions.

Biographies of Contributors
with Key to Initials

OTO BIHALJI-MERIN was born in 1904 in Zemun, across the river from Belgrade. He studied painting and the history of art in Belgrade and Berlin. In 1928, together with his brother Pavle, he founded the publishing house of "Nolit" and edited the literary and political magazine "Nova literatura" (New Literature). While studying in Berlin, he wrote essays and art reviews and edited the magazine "Linkskurve" (Left Turn). In 1933, compelled to leave Berlin, he made his home in Paris and then Zurich. He was one of the founders of the Institute to Fight Fascism, with its headquarters in Paris. In 1938, he participated in organising the London exhibition "Twentieth-Century German Art", consisting of art works anathemized and labelled "perverted" by Hitler. Under the pen name of Peter Thoene, he wrote the book "Modern German Art." After the Second World War, released from a camp in Germany, he returned to Belgrade where he has lived ever since. During the World's Fair in Brussels in 1958, he was a member of the Committee for the exhibition "Fifty Years of Modern Art," and took part in organising the naive art exhibition in Knokke-le-Zoute in Belgium. He was also one of the organisers of the exhibition "The World of the Naive" (1964) held in the Museum of Boymans van Beuningen in Rotterdam and in the Museum of Modern Art in Paris, and wrote the foreword for the catalogue of the exhibition.

In 1964, the University of Vienna awarded him the Herder Prize for his efforts to promote understanding among nations through the medium of art. In the last twenty years, he has worked almost exclusively as an essayist in the field of art and social criticism.

Oto Bihalji-Merin was one of the leading organisers of the triennials of naive art in Bratislava and Zagreb and of the Exhibition of Constructivist Art in Nuremberg in 1969, where he was a founder of the Institute for Modern Art. In 1974—1975, he wrote a critical review of naive art of the world for the exhibition in the museums of Haus der Kunst in Munich and Kunsthaus in Zurich. In recent years, the following books by him have been published in the various Yugoslav languages and in Europe, America and Japan in many world languages: "Frescoes and Icons in Serbia and Macedonia," "Bogumil Sculpture" (with Alojz Benac), "Builders of Modern Thought," "Art Treasures in Yugoslavia" (prepared for publication and wrote the foreword), "The Adventure of Modern Art," "Masters of Naive Art" (in seven languages), "Henri Rousseau" (with Liza Bihalji), "Masks of the World," "The End of Art in the Age of Science?," "Unity of the World in the Vision of Art" and "Goya" (in four volumes). He is now working on the manuscript of "A Babylon of Styles or a Renaissance of Modern Art."

NEBOJŠA-BATO TOMAŠEVIĆ, born in 1929, comes from a Montenegrin family. As a child of thirteen he joined the forces of national insurrection in occupied Yugoslavia in the Second World War. After the war he continued his interrupted education and in 1952 graduated from the School of Journalism and Diplomacy. At the same time, he studied English language and literature at the University of Belgrade, continuing his studies from 1953 to 1955 at the University of Exeter, England.

Since 1963, he has been editor-in-chief of the monthly illustrated magazine "Yugoslav Review" published in five languages. Concerned primarily with the cultural heritage of Yugoslavia, he initiated the publication of several books in this field, to which he also contributed noteworthy articles. For almost two decades, he has focussed interest on the development of painting in Yugoslavia, popularising it in magazines and books.

He published the book "Yugoslav Naive Art" (1973), acclaimed as a singular documentation of the work of Yugoslavia's naive painters and sculptors printed in seven European countries. His book on Ivan Generalić ("The Magic Word of Ivan Generalić"), the world-famous Yugoslav naive painter, was published in eight countries and named a "book of the season" by American newspaper critics.

His book on the well-known Slovene painter Jože Tisnikar (1978), is a moving story of a great and original painter and dedicated chronicler of man's last moments on earth.

Tomašević's publication "Naive Painters of Yugoslavia" selects for treatment thirty-six of the country's best-known naive painters. It has been printed in the USA, Japan and six European countries.

Tomašević has also written two monographs on naive painting published in Romania. Between 1980 and 1983, he went to the People's Republic of China five times, studying Chinese naive painting for his new book on this subject.

ERNESTO CARDENAL, poet, priest, revolutionary and first Minister of Culture in the National Reconstruction Government of Nicaragua, was born in 1925 in Granada, Nicaragua. He studied literature, first in Managua, then in Mexico, and later in New York at Columbia University. His first collections of verse, published in the forties, are strong in their feeling for the history and political realities of Central America. After completing theological studies in Mexico, he moved to Colombia in 1961. Ordained in 1965, he left for the Archipelago of Solentiname, Nicaragua, where he set up a Christian commune that was at the same time a cell of the liberation movement. There, among the fishermen and peasants, thanks to his efforts, a school of naive painting developed, becoming highly esteemed in Nicaragua and abroad. As Minister of Culture, he established cultural centres, poetry workshops, and workshops for arts and crafts. In February 1982, the Nicaraguan Government awarded him its highest decoration for cultural achievement, "Rubén Dario."

GERT CLAUSSNITZER was born in 1935 in Dortmund and studied history of art at the Karl Marx University in Leipzig. Since 1959 he has been working as a reader in the Art Publications Enterprise in Dresden. An art critic for years, he has had articles published by various newspapers and broadcast over the radio network of the German Democratic Republic.

He has organised art exhibitions in Dresden. His published works include: "Peter August Böckstiegel, Graphics" (Dresden 1961), "Curt Querner" (Berlin 1970), "Naive Painting" (Leipzig 1977, second edition 1981), "Werner Witting" (Dresden 1978), "Wilhelm Dodel" (Dresden 1981), "Artists of Dresden" (Berlin 1983). He is the author of a number of scenarios for documentary films on art, including the film "Experienced Dreams" about the naive painter Theresa Walter-Visino, 1983.

JACQUES COLLARD, born in 1918, began his literary career with French adaptations of novels by English writers published under the pseudonym of Jean Laroche. Later he devoted himself to journalism. He became the head of the Press Bureau and the Public Relations Department in the General Government of what was then the Belgian Congo. Later he was Information Adviser to the government in Burundi.

Returning to Europe, he worked as a journalist and art critic, writing for several Belgian and foreign magazines and publishing a large number of books dedicated to cultural issues and particularly the fine arts. The best known of his books are: "Fifty Belgian Artists," "Six Belgian Graphic Artists," "Charles Counhaye," "The Man Himself," "Aubin Pasque or the Return of the Symbol."

Collard is a member of the Belgian section of the International Association of Art Critics.

MARÍA TERESA SOLÁ DE DANDOLO, born in 1929 in Buenos Aires, studied philosophy and theology and in 1976 also took a diploma in social psychology. Well-known as a poet and writer of short stories, she has also published translations from French and English as well as specialised works on psychology, and has also prepared cultural programmes for radio and television. Her art activities date from 1964, when she succeeded in persuading workers in factories and enterprises to join the Association of Friends of Museums. She is associated with the Museum of Fine Arts of the City of Buenos Aires and with the Chromos Art Gallery. In 1971, she organised an exhibition of Argentinian Artists in Chile, and of Chilean artists in Argentina. Since 1970, María Teresa Solá de Dandolo has been Director of the Carmen Waugh Gallery.

RUTH DEBEL was born in 1934 in Wiener Neustadt, Austria, and moved with her parents to Palestine in 1939. She studied art at the Sorbonne in Paris, where she took an interest in naive art, and obtained a degree from the Hebrew University in Jerusalem in 1957. In the late fifties and early sixties, she headed the Art Exchange Section in the Foreign Ministry and at the end of the sixties and beginning of the seventies was head of the Artists' Centre in Jerusalem and the Gallery of the Bezalel Academy. She discovered the naive painter, Gabriel Cohen, and helped him in his work. In 1973, she established her own gallery of contemporary Israeli art, in addition to her Debel Gallery, of which she is director.

NICO VAN DER ENDT, born in 1941, studied law and literature and has always showed a great interest in art, the reason for his wide-ranging travels. In 1969 he founded the Hamer Gallery in Amsterdam, and a year later organised an exhibition of works by Pieter Hagoort, winner of a first prize at the "Naives '70" exhibition held in Zagreb. He then decided to specialise in naive art and in 1976 organised the exhibition "Netherlands Naive Art" for the Frans Hals Museum in Haarlem. In 1979, he published a book on Dutch naive art in association with journalist Joop Bromet. Van der Endt was also the editor of the Netherlands Section of a number of foreign art publications. In "Guide Through the World of Naive Art," published in London, Van der Endt is the author of the section on the Netherlands.

JOHN FOWLER, born in 1942 in Great Britain, was educated in Australia and Latin America. Interested in the aboriginal society, he visited New Zealand in 1961 and travelled through Latin America in 1965. He spent seven years on the Pacific Islands of Vanua Vatu (New Hebrides), studying the life of the inhabitants and the traditional art of that archipelago and of the adjacent Solomon Islands. At the beginning of the seventies he spent two years on Bali and other Indonesian islands. He and his wife, Karen, took an interest in Balinese culture and persuaded the primitive painters of Bali to exhibit in the world's cities. After organising successful exhibitions of such works in London, New York, Dallas and Vancouver, they opened their own international gallery of naive art in Santa Monica, California. John Fowler is the author of a book on the art of Bali and a museum catalogue: "The Present and Past Art of the Australian Aborigines."

JOSÉ GÓMEZ-SICRE, born in 1916 in Matanzas on Cuba, studied at the University of Havana where he received a degree in political, economic and social sciences. He was an adviser for the organisation of a large exhibition of Cuban art in the Museum of Modern Art in New York in 1944. Between 1942 and 1945, he organised exhibitions of Cuban art abroad and participated in the preparation of national and foreign expositions in Havana. Between 1950 and 1962 he lectured on Latin American art in various countries, including West Germany, the Netherlands, Italy, Spain and Sweden. He has given a large number of lectures on Latin American cinematography on television in the USA.

He has published a great number of books in the field of painting.

He has done a number of documentary films on Latin American art and written the commentaries for them. Since 1976, he has been Director of the Museum of Contemporary Art of Latin America in Washington.

THOMAS GROCHOWIAK was born in 1914, the son of a miner. Self-taught in all fields, he has devoted himself to painting and art criticism and is a founder and director of museums, organiser of international exhibitions and commissioner of biennial expositions. In 1948 he formed the "Young Group West" of avant-garde painters and together with other members of the group exhibited in museums and modern art galleries in Amsterdam, Basel, Brussels and Paris. Since 1979, he has been President of the Association of German Artists. He has been director of municipal museums in Recklinghausen and Oberhausen and founded the Icon Museum in Recklinghausen. He has invested a great deal of devotion and energy in organising the well-known Ruhr Festival and encouraging the creative abilities of workers. A friend of many naive artists, and respected on the international scene as a connoisseur of art and expert in organising exhibitions, Grochowiak has taken a noteworthy part in many important international symposia and round tables of naive art. His book "German Naive Art" (1976) is considered a standard work. In 1972, he was given the title of Professor for his artistic work and promotion of artistic creativity in the Federal Republic of Germany and awarded the Grand Cross of Merit.

ALEKSANDER JACKOWSKI was born in 1920 in Warsaw, and studied sociology and history of art at the University there. It was then that he started his work as an art critic. He was one of the founders of the Institute of Art where, beginning in 1950, he headed the Folk Art Workshop and from 1964 on, the Workshop for the Study of the Non-Professional Arts. Since 1952 he has been editing the quarterly "Polish Naive Art". To date, he has organised a large number of exhibitions of naive art, among them "Polish Folk Art" in London in 1956; an exhibition of the paintings of Nikifor in 1956; "Polish Primitive Artists" in Belgrade,

Zagreb, Ljubljana and Maribor in 1959; "Different" in Warsaw in 1965; "Naive Art in Poland," Stuttgart 1967; "Art Naïf Polonais," Neuchâtel, 1967; "Primitive Art from Poland," London 1968; "Naifs della Polonia," Spoleto 1972; "Naive Kunst der Gegenwart aus Polen," Hamburg 1972; "Naive Art on the Occasion of the 30th Anniversary of the Polish People's Republic," Warsaw 1976; the Polish section of "Die Kunst der Naiven" in Munich 1974/75, in Zurich 1975, and at the I, II and III "Triennial of Insitic Art" in Bratislava 1966, 1969, 1972; the all-Polish "Triennial of Non-Professional Art" (Szczecin 1974, Wroclaw 1977, and 1980).

Among his published works are the books "Forty Thousand Years of Contemporary Art," Warsaw, 1962, 'The Art of the Polish People," Warsaw, 1969 (simultaneously printed in German, French, English and Russian) and over two hundred articles.

GEORGES KASPER, born in Geneva in 1907, worked as an archaeologist until 1940, when he opened his own art gallery. In 1946 he organised the first exhibition of French naive painters in Switzerland, and started the newspaper *Gazette pro Arte*. He set up a new gallery in Lausanne and organised in Switzerland the first exhibition of a number of important artists, among them Vasarely, Lucio Fontana, and Manzoni. In the last ten years he has worked mainly on organising exhibitions of naive art, among them "Art of the Naives" in Zurich (1975), "International Naives" in Geneva and a large exposition called the "World of the Naives" in Geneva in the summer of 1983, arranged by the Gallery pro Arte Kasper.

In 1970 he instituted the Swiss International Naive Painting Prize, and also founded the Henri Rousseau Group, numbering about forty of the most outstanding naive artists.

SUMIO KUWABARA was born in 1924. He completed his post-graduate studies at the Philology Faculty of the University of Tokyo in 1951 (Department of History of Art). He is the leading art critic of the papers "Tokyo Shimbun", "Asahi Shimbun", etc.

In 1977, he was appointed Professor at the Institute of Art and Design of the University of Tsukuba, and at present is Professor at the Musashino College of Art.

Works: "Japanese Self-portraits" (Nanbokusha), "Genealogy of American Painting" (Geijutsu shuppansha), "Treatise on Contemporary Japanese Painting" (Sansaisha).

Translations: Barbara Rose: "American Art Since 1900 — A Critical History" (Geijutsu shuppansha), Harold Rosenberg: "Art Works and Package" (Geijutsu shuppansha), Bernarda Shahn: "Ben Shahn" (Riburopooto).

THOMAS LACKEY was born in the United States and immigrated to Canada in 1969. He began his work with Canadian folk and naive art forms at the Dalhousie University Art Gallery in Halifax, Nova Scotia. With the assistance of the Canadian government, Mr Lackey spent two years travelling across Canada documenting both institutional and ephemeral collections of folk and naive art. Together with the director of the Dalhousie University Art Gallery, he helped to organise the first nationwide conference to deal with the problems of definition and identification of folk and naive art forms in Canada. At the end of the Dalhousie project, Mr Lackey spent a year collecting and recommending artifacts for purchase by the Canadian Centre for Folk Culture Studies of the National Museums of Canada. He served on the four-man advisory committee to the Centre during its organisation of the "From the Heart" exhibition of Canadian folk and naive art. Mr Lackey is currently employed by the Canadian government to write and produce films and exhibitions on aspects of Canadian history.

BIANCA McCULLOUGH was born in Munich but had her schooling in Vienna. Since 1949 she has lived in Australia, where she initially edited a fashion magazine. During the sixties, developing her interest in art, she began to work as a dealer in art works and was also for a time director of a gallery. From 1973 to 1979 she had her own art dealer's agency. The author of two books: "Australian Naive Artists" and "Alternatives," she also writes an art column for the newspaper "Southern Cross."

DINO MENOZZI was born in Reggio Emilia in 1933. Having graduated from college as a geometer, he began in 1958 to work on a professional and independent basis in films and did a number of documentaries that won praise and prizes at the most prestigious national and international film festivals. Among these are the films "One of Those Who Are Not" (1965), dedicated to the naive artist A. Ligabue, and "From Solitude to Community" (1967), devoted to the work of P. Ghizzardi, a naive painter from the Po Valley.

Given impulse by the works of Antonio Ligabue, Menozzi took a serious interest in the problems of naive artists. After a number of study trips to exhibitions of works by naive artists and useful contacts with the most highly qualified European critics and essayists, he gained the reputation of a genuine connoisseur of naive art. His book "La grafica naive," published in 1971, was the first serious study on naive artists in Italy. He was a member of the international organising committee of "Naivi 73" in Zagreb and founded the magazine "L'arte naive" in 1974, the first and for the moment the only Italian magazine devoted to naive art, of which he is the editor-in-chief.

IDA MIHÁLY graduated in 1952 from the Department of Philosophy of Budapest University, having specialised in the history of art of the medieval and modern periods. She was employed for eleven years in the Historical Museum in Budapest, and spent considerable time working in the Centre for Artistic and Historical Documentation. Since 1969 she has been an associate of the Hungarian National Gallery, where she founded and is now administrator of the Naive Art Collection. She is co-author of the book "Buda and Pest in the Middle Ages."

Specialised magazines have printed articles by Ida Mihály on the artistic work of Hungarian members of the Bauhaus. Her studies on Hungarian naive art are found in numerous journals.

Ida Mihály has also organised many exhibitions in Hungary and other countries and prepared catalogues, printed in various languages, describing the development and importance of Hungarian naive art and presenting its younger representatives.

MODEST MORARIU was born in 1929 in Chernovtsy, and studied at the University in Bucharest. A member of the Association of Writers and of the Association of Artists of the Socialist Republic of Romania, he is editor-in-chief of the Meridiane publishing house specialising in art books. He writes poetry (he has published three collections of poems), prose, essays and art criticism. His essays on art have been devoted to Goya, Toulouse-Lautrec and Le Douanier Rousseau. For the latter, he was awarded the prize of the Association of Artists in 1975.

He has translated about twenty works from French, among them books by Stendhal, Camus, Malraux ("Obsidian Head" — Award of the Association of Writers, 1977), and studies on the art of Marcel Brion, Henri Lhote, Jean Grenier and others.

FRITZ NOVOTNY was born in 1929 in Litoměřice on the Elbe, Czechoslovakia. After moving from Czechoslovakia to the Federal Republic of Germany he became a mason and then enrolled in the State Construction School in Darmstadt, becoming an engineer in 1948. That year he began working as a free-lance architect and later enrolled in the Higher Technical School in Darmstadt from which he graduated in 1954. Between 1958 and 1962 he taught architecture and spatial design at the School of Artistic Crafts in Offenbach on Main. There he established an architectural bureau together with another engineer, Arthur Mähner. The winner of many competitions, he has had a number of his buildings awarded prizes as "model buildings" in Hessen. He is also one of the founders of the Institute for Housing and the Environment in Darmstadt, and between 1974 and 1977 was President of the Federal Chamber of Architecture. He has published the books "Architecture without Politics" and "Naive Art" (1977, published by Modeln, Vienna-Munich-Zurich). He lives in Offenbach on Main.

DIMITRIOS PAPASTAMOS, born in Athens in 1923, studied classical archaeology, history of music and ancient Greek history at the University of Münster (Westphalia), where he also took his doctor's degree. After completing his studies he remained as a research associate at the same university, lecturing on the links between the art of antiquity and that of later periods from the Renaissance to Classicism.

Between 1970 and 1972 he was Director of the Department of Antiquities in the Greek Ministry of Culture and Science and in 1972 became Chief Curator of the National Art Gallery and Alexander Soutzos Museum.

Since 1949, Dimitrios Papastamos has published a large number of studies and essays on ancient, medieval and modern art in Greece.

ARSEN POHRIBNÝ was born in 1928 in Prešov, Czechoslovakia. He studied first in Brno and then between 1948 and 1952 at Karlovy University in Prague where he specialised in the history of art, ethnography and esthetics. Since 1952, he has been active as a writer and art critic. During the sixties, he did his post-graduate studies abroad. Since 1975 he has been a lecturer at the Higher School of Art in Darmstadt on the subjects of history of art and history of design.

Arsen Pohribný has been actively interested in naive art since 1959. In 1962—64 he was one of the organisers of the first big naive art exhibitions in Czechoslovakia. With co-author Stefan Tkáč he wrote a book "Naive Art in Czechoslovakia" (Artia, Prague, 1967). Since that time he has organised over seventy collective and one-man shows of naive art in Czechoslovakia, Italy, Switzerland and the Federal Republic of Germany. He has published also a collection of naive poetry "Bare Feet Tread the World" (Mlada Fronta, Prague, 1969).

TONY RUSSELL, born in Jamaica, is a well-known Latin-American photographer. Formerly the photographer for an official cultural institution in Jamaica, and for its cultural publication, "Jamaica Journal," he now lives in Trujillo, Venezuela. Continuing to photograph, he is rounding out his activities with audio-visual experiments at the Folk Art Museum of Salvador Valero. His works have been printed in many publications and his exhibitions widely recognised. Tony Russell is a member of the Association of Photographers in the Media of Communication (A. S. M. P.) and the founder and director of the Centre for Professional Photography (C. P. P.).

CHARLES SCHAETTEL, born in 1946, studied history of art and archaeology at the University in Dijon. He took a degree in history of art, and others in archaeology and history of music. In 1976, he was appointed curator of the Museum in Laval and did much to augment its collection. Special attention was paid to increasing the number of naive art works in the Museum of Vieux-Château, where fifteen years ago the first collection in France of naive art from various countries was founded. Charles Schaettel has organised exhibitions, prepared catalogues, written prefaces, and so on. His work in France and other European countries is notable for his efforts to make the Laval collection a witness to the history of the naive art movement.

GERHARD SCHOENBERNER, who lives in West Berlin, is a writer, critic and publicist, the author of many essays on art, literature and films. His international reputation is based on his books, exhibitions and films on modern historical subjects. The book "Yellow Star," published in several languages and also made into a film, won international acclaim.

As a lover and collector of naive art, Schoenberner has written on the naive painting of Yugoslavia, China, Africa and Nicaragua. Thanks to regular travels in Africa, he has also established contact with African art and its creators.

His collection of the works of African sign-painters was shown at major exhibitions: "Naive Art" (Munich 1974, Zurich 1975) and "The Art of Africa" (Berlin, Bremen, 1979; Stockholm, Erlangen, Amsterdam, Frankfurt/Main 1980; London 1981).

NATALIA SHKAROVSKAYA, art historian, critic and journalist, was born in Sverdlovsk, in the Urals region. She graduated in 1944 from the Department of Journalism at Moscow University, having specialised in subjects connected with culture and art. She has worked in radio, for newspapers, in publishing and in the Institute for Research in Arts and Crafts in Moscow. During the past twenty years she has been editor of the column on folk arts and crafts in the Moscow magazine "USSR Decorative Arts." As a collector and connoisseur of traditional folk toys and impressed by their primitive forms, she began to show a deep interest in naive creativity. With her husband, the translator G. J. A. Shkarovsky-Raffé, she owns a small collection of contemporary Soviet naive paintings. She was a member of the preparatory committees and juries for exhibitions of folk and amateur art of the Soviet Union held in Moscow in 1967, 1970, 1974, 1977 and was also a member of the international jury of the Triennial of Naive Art in Bratislava in 1972.

Her published works include the book "Amateur Art" (the Aurora Publishing House, Leningrad, 1975) and numerous articles, brochures and catalogues.

ANGELA TAMVAKI was born in Athens in 1945. She studied history and archaeology at the University of Athens and undertook postgraduate research at Oxford University, specialising in the Neolithic and Bronze Ages in the Aegean, and taking a particular interest in the representation of the human figure in Bronze Age art in Greece and Cyprus.

She has published a large number of articles on figurines of the Greek Neolithic and Bronze Ages in Greek and foreign archaeological journals. Since 1978 she has been working at the National Gallery in Athens, where she prepares Greek and foreign exhibitions and engages in research. In the last few years she has taken a special interest in contemporary Greek art and Greek folk and naive painting. The Agricultural Bank of Greece commissioned her to prepare its artistic calender on the subject "Village Life in Contemporary Greek Naive Painting", in connection with which she organised a large exhibition in 1983.

ŠTEFAN TKÁČ was born in 1931 in Hermanovci and now lives in Bratislava. As an art theoretician, he has devoted himself to the study of children's drawings and to folk and naive art. In 1960 he made the conceptual plans for a national exhibition, held in Bratislava, presenting a comprehensive picture of Slovak naive art. On his initiative, regular exhibitions were held in Dubnica of works by amateur artists and in Žilina by children. In 1965 he established the Department of Non-Professional Art in the Slovak National Gallery, and later the Cabinet of Naive Art in the same Gallery. At that time he was General Commissioner of the International Triennial of Naive Art in Bratislava (1966, 1969, 1972). He has written over 150 studies, prepared catalogues for one-man and collective shows, and published a number of books, among which are "Slovak Naive Art" (1966), "Naive Painters of Czechoslovakia" (in English, German and Czech, 1967), "World Naive Art." He also started the magazine "Insita" dedicated to naive art, the first publication of its kind in the world.

He is the author of a monograph on folk art in the publication "... Only Stone and Wood" (1977) and a monograph on the icons of southern and eastern Slovakia from the 16th to the 19th century.

JULIA WEISSMAN, born in El Paso, Texas, began her career as a copywriter and self-taught commercial artist in a local department store. She moved to New York several years ago. Now a free-lance writer with a strong interest in folk and naive art, she has been an art editor for a book publisher, editor of a knitting and crocheting magazine and of a newsletter on collecting art and antiques. She co-authored, with collector Herbert Hemphill, Jr., the book "Twentieth Century American Folk Art and Artists," a project she devised and for which she did the research, writing and securing of photographs. Among her other credits are researcher and ghostwriter for "Oriental Design in Needlepoint" for designer Eva Brent; ghostwriter of "Graffiti: Two Thousand Years of Wall Writing," using author Robert Reisner's notes; catalogues for the Museum of American Folk Art in New York City, and articles on American naive artists for its publication "The Clarion" as well as for other magazines; adviser for films on American naive artists for RM Productions of Munich and for Light-Saraf Folk Art Films of San Francisco.

Ms Weissman also lectures frequently on American folk art.

SHELDON WILLIAMS was born in 1919 in Cork, Republic of Ireland. He attended a number of higher art schools in England, Germany and France, among them the Central School of Arts and Crafts in London and the *Ecole des Beaux Arts* in Epinal. Williams has travelled in most European countries, the USA, Turkey, Tunisia, Kenya, Morocco, Haiti, Puerto Rico, the Virgin Islands and Brazil. Throughout the years of work and travel, he has regularly written art reviews and essays, and between 1960 and 1982 he has been author of a number of books, including the "The Human Situation" (published in three languages by Arthur Niggli, Switzerland), "Verlon" (published in two languages by Modern Masters), "Voodoo and the Art of Haiti" (published by Morland Lee), "A Background to Sfumato," "The Art of Haiti" (published by the Museum am Ostwall, Dortmund), "British Naive and Primitive Artists of the 20th Century" (together with Eric Lister, published by Astragal Books). He has participated in many international conferences dedicated to naive art and lectured on it on radio and television.

He himself paints (under the name of A. Oscar) and has exhibited his works in France, the Federal Republic of Germany, Austria, Spain, the Netherlands, Brazil, Canada and the USA.

LIST OF AUTHOR'S INITIALS

The lexicographical units were written by contributors to the Encyclopedia. This list enables readers to identify the authors of the individual units from the initials at the end of each. Unsigned texts were compiled from data gathered by editorial assistants.

A. D.	Aleksandar Demajo
A. J.	Aleksander Jackowski
A. P.	Arsen Pohribný
A. T.	Angela Tamvaki
B. McC.	Bianca McCullough
Ch. Sch.	Charles Schaettel
D. M.	Dino Menozzi
E. C.	Ernesto Cardenal
F. N.	Fritz Novotny
G. C.	Gert Claussnitzer
G. K.	Georges Kasper
G. Sch.	Gerhard Schoenberner
I. M.	Ida Mihály
J. C.	Jacques Collard
J. F.	John Fowler
J. G.-S.	José Gómez-Sicre
J. W.	Julia Weissman
M. Il.	Mirces Iliescu
M. L.	Mladen Lompar
M. T. S.	María Teresa Solá de Dandolo
N. E.	Nico van der Endt
N. Sh.	Natalia Shkarovskaya
N. T.	Nebojša-Bato Tomašević
O. B.-M.	Oto Bihalji-Merin
R. D.	Ruth Debel
S. K.	Sumio Kuwabara
S. T.	Štefan Tkáč
Sh. W.	Sheldon Williams
T. G.	Thomas Grochowiak
Th. L.	Thomas Lackey
T. R.	Tony Russell
V. M.	Victor Musgrave

Bibliography

GENERAL

BADER, Alfred: Wunderwelt des Wahns (under collaboration with) Jean Cocteau, Georg Schmidt, Hans Steck. — Köln : DuMont Schauberg Verlag, 1961.

BADER, Alfred & NAVRATIL, Leo : Zwischen Wahn und Wirklichkeit : Kunst : Psychose : Kreativität. — Luzern : Frankfurt/M : Bucher, 1976. — 299 S., XLVIII : ill.

BIHALJI-MERIN, Oto : El Arte naif : con 182 ilustraciones. — Barcelona : Madrid : Buenos Aires : Bogota : Caracas : Lisboa : Mexico-Montevideo : Quito : Rio de Janeiro: Labor, S. A., 1978. — 296 p. : ill.

_____ : Die Kunst der Naiven : Themen und Beziehungen. — München : Haus der Kunst, 1974; Zürich : Kunsthaus, 1975.

_____ : Les Maîtres de l'art naïf. — Bruxelles : La Connaissance, 1972. — 303 p. : ill.

_____ : Die Malerei der Naiven. — Köln : DuMont Schauberg, 1975. — 304 S. : ill.; [II izd.] ; Budapest : Gondolat, 1983.

_____ : Masters of Naive Art : A History and Worldwide Survey. — New York : St Louis : San Francisco : Toronto: McGraw-Hill Book Company, 1971. — 304 p. : ill.

_____ : Modern Primitives: Naive Painting from the Late Seventeenth Century to the Present Day : with 389 illustrations including 204 colour plates. — London : Thames and Hudson, 1971. — 304 p : Ill.; [reprinted] 1975, 1978.

_____ : Moderne Primitieven : naïeve schilderkunst van de late zeventiende eeuw tot heden met 389 illustraties waarvan 204 in kleur. — Amsterdam : Amsterdam Boek, 1976. — 303 p.

_____ : Mojstri naivne umetnosti : [zgodovina, sedanjost, perspektive]. — Ljubljana: Mladinska knjiga, 1972. — 312 str.

_____ : Le Monde des Naïfs. — Paris : Musée National D'Art Moderne, 1964.

_____ : Naivni umjetnici svijeta. — Zagreb: Mladost, 1972. — 304 str. : ill.

_____ : Naivni umetnici sveta : istorijski pregled : savremena kretanja : perspektive. — Beograd : Vuk Karadžić ; Ljubljana: Mladinska knjiga, 1971. — 304 str. : ill.

_____ : Das naive Bild der Welt. — Köln : DuMont Schauberg, 1959. — 304 S. : ill. ; Paris : Delpire, 1960, 1962 ; Milano : Saggiatore, 1960. ; London : Thames and Hudson, 1961. ; New York : Harry N. Abrams, 1961 ; Zürich : Wien : Frankfurt : Büchergilde Gutenberg, 1963 ; Stuttgart : Hamburg : Deutscher Bücherbund, 1963. ; Malmö : Allhems, 1964.

_____ : Die Naiven der Welt. — Stuttgart : Berlin (West) : Köln : Kohlhammer, 1971. — 312 S. : ill. ; Bruxelles : La Connaissance, 1971. ; New York : McGraw-Hill Books, 1971. ; London: Thames and Hudson, 1971.; Milano : Mondadori, 1972. ; Den Hag : Grade, 1972, ; [2. Auflage] Stuttgart : Berlin : Köln : Mainz : W. Kohlhammer, 1973.; [3. Auflage] München : Emil Vollmer Verlag ; Ljubljana : Mladinska knjiga, 1978.

_____ : Wahn oder Wirklichkeit. — München, 1980.

DIEMER, Karl : Über Sonntagsmaler oder wie naiv ist die moderne Kunst? : Bilder aus der Sammlung Eisenmann 1920 bis 1980. — Böblingen : Galerie Eisenmann im Hause Eisenmann KG, 1981. — 198 S. : ill.

EHLERS, Albert August : Sonntagsmaler. — Berlin, 1956.

ENGELS, M. T. : Naive Malerei. — Herrsching : Pawlak Verlag, 1977.

Europas neue Sonntagsmaler : 140 Preisträger des Wettbewerbs der Zeitschrift 'Wochenend'. — Frankfurt/M : 'Wochenend' : Heinrich Bauer Verlag, 1971. — 132 S. : ill.

FOURNY, Max : Das Buch der Naive Kunst. — Paris : Editions Hervas and Weber Geuf, 1982.

GOLDWATER, Robert J. : Primitivism in Modern Painting. — New York : London : Harper and Brothers, 1938.

GRAEBNER, Fr. : Das Weltbild der Primitiven. — München, 1924.

La Grande Domenica : Rassegna Internazionale dei Naifs organizzata da 'Grazia' con il patrocinio del Comune di Milano Ripartizione cultura 1 — 19 maggio 1974 / Prefazione di Anatole Jakovsky. — Milano : (Rotonda di via Besana) : Arnoldo Mondadori Editore, 1974. — 96 p. : ill.

GROCHOWIAK, Thomas & BIHALJI-MERIN, Oto : Werk und Werkstatt naiver Kunst. — Recklinghausen : Städtische Kunsthalle, 1971.

HAFTMANN, Werner : Malerei im 20. Jahrhundert : Band I und II. — München : Prestel-Verlag, 1957.

HANSEN, Hans Jürgen : Europas Volkskunst Hubmann — München, 1973.

HUBMANN, Hanns : Naive Maler : Garten der Träume — Garden of Dreams — Jardin des rêves. — München : F. Bruckmann, 1973, — 90 S. : ill.

Innocent Art / Edited by David Larkin. — London : Pan Books, 1974. — (47) plates : ill.

ITALIAANDER, Rolf: Spass und der Freud. — Hamburg, 1974.

JAKAB, Irene : Drawings and Paintings of Mental Patients ; Their Psychiatric and Artistic Analysis. — Budapest : Hungarian Academy of Sciences, 1956.

JAKOVSKY, Anatole : Ces peintres de la semaine des sept dimanches. — Milano : Giorgio Borletti, 1969. — 137 p.

_____ : Dämonen und Wunder : (Eine Darstellung der naiven Plastik). — Köln : Verlag M. DuMont Schauberg, 1963.

_____ : Naive Malerei. — Freiburg : Basel : Wien : Verlag Herder, 1976. — 61 S.

_____ : Naive Painting. — Oxford : Phaidon, 1979. — 104 p. : ill.

_____ : La peinture naïve. — Paris, 1947

_____ : La peinture naïve. — Paris : J. Damase, 1949.

_____ : Les Peintres naïfs. — Paris : La Bibliothèque des Arts, 1956.

_____ : Peintres naïfs : Lexicon of the World's Primitive Painters = Lexikon der Laienmaler aus aller Welt = Lexique des peintres naïfs du monde entier. — Wien-München : Schroll-Verlag, 1967. — 398 p.: ill. ; Paris : Moyer, 1976. — 351 p. : ill.

_____ : Les proverbes vus par les peintres naïfs. — Paris : Editions Max Forny, 1973. — 279 p.

_____ : Peintres naïfs : dictionnaire. — Bâle : Basiliuspresse, 1981.

KRUGMANN, Brigitte : Naive Malerei : Künstler, Werke, Tendenzen. — München: Keyser, 1980. — 160 S. : ill.

Die Kunst der Naiven : Themen und Beziehungen : Haus der Kunst München 1. November 1974 bis 12. Januar 1975 / Konzeption und Wissenschaftliche Bearbeitung der Ausstellung Oto Bihalji-Merin. —

München e V. : Ausstellungsleitung Haus der Kunst, 1975. — 561 S. : ill.

Kunstvolle Zeiten : 10 Jahre MD Volkskunst-Kalender. — München : Süddeutsche Klischee — Union, 1979. — 233 S. : ill.

LARKIN, David : L'arte naive. — Verona : Arnoldo Mondadori, 1976.

LOMMEL, Andreas : Vorgeschichte der Naturvölker. — Gutersloh : Bertelsmann, 1968.

De Lusthof der Naïeven : Katalog einer Ausstellung im Boymans van Beuningen-Museum. — Rotterdam, 1964.

MAHLOW, D. : Das naive Bild der Welt. — Baden-Baden, 1961.

Masters of Popular Painting : Modern Primitives of Europe and America. — New York : Museum of Modern Art, 1938.

Međunarodni susret naivne umjetnosti : »Naivi« '73 : 2. VI — 1. IX 1973. — Zagreb : Galerija primitivne umjetnosti. [1974]. — [507] s. : ill.

Međunarodni susret naivne umjetnosti »Naivi« '70. 1970, Zagreb — Hlebine = The international meeting of naive art Naivni '70. : Zagreb — Hlebine, July 18. — September 20. 1970. — Zagreb : Galerija primitivne umjetnosti, 1970. — 242 s., XLII s.: ill.

MEHRING, Walter : Verrufene Malerei. — Zürich, 1958.

NACENTA, Raymond : Les Naïfs. — Paris : Nouvelles Editions françaises, 1973. — 73 p., (47) t. : ill.

Naïeve schilders zien ons land /Introduction by W. A. Braasem. — Amsterdam : Uitgeverij Ploegsma, 1978. — 164 p. : ill.

I naifs : II Mostra Internazionale dei pittori naifs : Lugano, 31 agosto — 11 novembre 1973. — Lugano : Rassegna Internazionale delle Arti e della Cultura, 1973. — 153 p. : ill.

Naive Kunst : Geschichte und Gegenwart Ausstellungskatalog. — Bielefeld : Kunsthalle, 1981. — 158 S. : ill.

Naive Kunst der Seeleute : Kapitänsbilder und Galionsfiguren : 25. Ruhrfestspiele Recklinghausen : 9. Maj bis 27. Juni 1971. — Recklinghausen : Haus der Ruhrfestspiele in Recklingb usen, 1971. — 91 S. : ill.

»Naivi« '77 : Franc Klekawka : Leo Neervoort : Milan Stanisavljević : Međunarodni susret naivne umjetnosti = International meeting of naive art : 24. VII — 4. IX 1977. — Zagreb : Galerije grada Zagreba, 1977. — [20]str. s. : ill.

NAVRATIL, Leo : Schizophrenie und Kunst; Ein Beitrag zur Psychologie des Gestaltens. — München : Deutschaer Taschenbuch, 1965. — 144 S. : ill.

NOVOTNY, Fritz : Naive Kunst. — Wien : München : Zürich : Innsbruck : Fritz Molden, 1977. — 224 S. : ill.

Prinzhorn, Bildnerei der Geisteskranken. — Berlin — Heidelberg : New York, 1968.

READ, Herbert : Erziehung durch Kunst. — München : Droemer-Knaur, 1968.

SCHMIDT, Georg : Umgang mit Kunst. — Olten, 1966.

Schöpferische Freizeit : Künstlerisches Schaffen des arbeitenden Volkes. — Wien: Volksbuchverlag, [s. a.]. — 182 S. : ill.

TKÁČ, Štefan : Insitné umenie. — Bratislava : Slovenskà Nàrodnà Galéria, 1966. — 65 s. : ill.

Collection of reports and discussions contributed to the Ist and 2nd International Symposia on Naïve Art.

_____ : Insite Kunst der Welt. — Bratislava : Pallas Verlag, 1969. — 93 s. : ill.
UHDE, Wilhelm : Fünf primitive Meister. — Zürich : Atlantis Verlag, 1947. ; Lausanne, 1948.
_____ : Cinq maîtres primitifs. — Paris : Editions Palmes, 1949. — 139 p. : ill.
Werke und Werkstatt naiver Kunst : Ruhrfestspiele Recklinghausen 1971 / Vorwort Thomas Grochowiak & Oto Bihalji-Merin. — Recklinghausen : Städtische Kunsthalle, 1971. — [192] S. : ill.
ZIMMER, Elke : Meisterwerke Naiver Malerei : (Katalog). — Düsseldorf, 1975.
ZUCK, Rüdiger : Naive Malerei. — München — Wien, 1974.

MAGAZINE ARTICLES

Geist, Hans Friedrich : Laienmalerei. — Das Kunstwerk, IX, 1948.
_____ : Naive Kunst als Mode. — Werk 1961 No. 11, Seite 404.
Michailow, Nikola : Zur Begriffsbestimmung der Laienmalerei. — Zeitschrift für Kunst und Geschichte, No 5—6, 1935.
ROH, Franz: Das naive Bild der Welt. — Das Kunstwerk, IX, 1961.

SERIAL PUBLICATIONS

Art in America / ed. Jean Lipman. — (No 1, 1947 —). — New York (635 Madison) : Art in America, 1947.
L'Arte Naive : Rassegna semestrale / Dir. resp. Dino Menozzi. — (No 1, 1973—). — Milano (Via S. Fillippo, 14/B-Reggio Emilia 42100) : Tribunale di Reggio Emilia, 1973.
ISSN 0390-1319 = L'Arte Naive
Gazette Galerie Pro Arte. — Morges/Suisse (102, Grande Rue) : Galerie Pro Arte : G. et L. Kasper
Insita : Bulletin Insitného umenia = Bjoleten' insitnog iskustva = Bulletin de l'art insitie = Bulletin of insite art /Zostavil Štefan Tkáč. — (No 1, 1971 —). — Brno (Vytlačila Grafia 01): Obzor, 1971.

AFRICA

Afrika : Texte : Dokumente : Bilder / Herausgegeben von der Berliner Festspielen, Horizonte '79. — Berlin : Peter Hammer Verlag, 1979. — 203 S. : ill.
Colon : Das schwarze Bild vom weissen Mann : Katalog zur gleichnamigen Ausstellung / Herausgegeben von Jens Jahn. — München, 1983. — 320 S.
Colonne — Colon — Kolo : Katalog zur gleichnamigen Ausstellung / Herausgegeben von Fred Jahn. — München, 1980. — 73 S.
HECHT, Dorothea : Malerei in Äthiopien, in: Volkstümliche Malerei in Äthiopien heute : Katalog. — Wuppertal : Heydt—Museum, 1973.
LIPS, Julius : The Savage Hits Back. — New York, 1937/1966.
Moderne Kunst aus Afrika : 1. Festival der Weltkulturen : Ausstellung der Berliner Festspiele GmbH mit Unterstützung der Staatlichen Kunsthalle Berlin 24. Juni — 12. Avgust. — Berlin : Berliner Festspiele GmbH, 1979. — 196 S. : ill.
Neue Kunst in Afrika. — Mannheim : Bibliographisches Institut Ag, 1957. — 30 S. : ill.
Neue Kunst in Afrika : Das Buch zur Ausstellung / Konzept und Zusammenstellung des Katalogs Ulli Beier. — Berlin : Dietrich Reimer Verlag, 1980. — 145 S. : ill.
Peintres naïfs Tunisiens : Album / Text par Jellal Kesraoui. — Tunis, 1978. — 119 S.
Périer, Gaston-Denys : Regards sur l'art graphique indigène du Congo Belge. — Bruxelles, 1950.
SHORE, Herb & Megchelina : The Art of Makonde. — London, 1970.
STOUT, Anthony J. : Modern Makonde Sculpture. — Nairobi, 1966.
TEISEN, Merete : Tingatinga. — Kopenhagen : Nationalmuseum, 1974.
THIRY, Georges : A la recherche de la peinture nègre; Les peintres naïfs congolais Lubaki et Djilatendo. — (s. l.) : Editions Yellow Now, (s. a.). — 46 S.
WAHLMANN, Maude : Contemporary African Arts. — Chicago, 1974.

WILLETT, Frank : African Art. — London, 1971.
Wood Sculptures of the Makonde People : Album. — Laurenço Marques : Instituto de Investição Cientifica de Moçambique, 1963.

MAGAZINE ARTICLES

BEIER, Ulli: Ladenschilder und Legenden : Naive Malerei in Nigeria. — Tendenzen (München), 1966, Jg. 7, Nr. 37.
_____ : Middle Art : The Painting of War. — African Arts (London), February 1976, Jg. 9, Nr. 2.
_____ : Seven-Seven. — Black Orpheus (Ibadan), August 1967, Nr. 22.
Bela, Mwenze, Pilipili, Aroun. — Jeune Afrique (Paris), 1956, Jr. IX, Nr. 26
Contemporary African Folk Art : Barbershop Signs and Hairstyles. — African Arts (London), April 1975, Jg. VIII, Nr. 4.
Neue Kunst in Afrika. — Tendenzen (München) — I Sonderheft, 1967.
PRITCHETT, Jack : Nigerian Truck Art. — African Arts (London), February 1979, Jg. XII, Nr. 2.
SALMONS, Bill: Mammy Wata. — African Arts (London), 1977, Jg. X, Nr. 3.
Schwarzafrika : Kunst und Befreiung. — Tendenzen (München), Oktober-Dezember 1980, Jg. 21, Nr. 132
SZOMBATI-FABIAN, Ilona & FABIAN, Johannes : Art, History and Society : Popular Painting in Shaba, Zaire. — Studies in the Anthropology of Visual Communications (Philadelphia), 1976, Nr. 3.
_____ : Popular Art and Political Consciousness : Painting from Shaba, Zaire. — Ms. (Princeton/USA), 1978.
VOLLBACH, F. : Moderne abessinische Malerei. — Die Woche (Berlin), 1927, Jg. 29, Heft 14
WEMBAH-RASHID, I. A. R. : Tingatinga of Tanzania. — African Arts (London), April 1972, Jg. V, Nr. 4.

AUSTRALIA

McCULLOUGH, Bianca : Australian Naive Painters. — Melbourne : Hill of Content Publishing Company Pty, 1977. — 94 p. : ill.
The Past and Present Art of the Australian Aborigine : September 24, 1980 — January 4, 1981. — Pasadena: Pacific Asia Museum, 1980. — 57 p. : ill.

AUSTRIA

PRETZELL, Lothar : Laienmalerei aus Deutschland und Österreich : Katalog. — Berlin, 1979.

BELGIUM

'Art spontané et naïf'. — Bruxelles : Maison des arts S. R. N., 1980.
COLIN, Paul : 'La peinture belge depuis 1830'. — Bruxelles : Cahiers de Belgique, 1930.
DASNOY, Albert : Exégèse de la peinture naïve. — Bruxelles : Laconti, 1970. — 256 p. : ill.
FOURNY, Max : Les naïfs et le rêve. — Bruxelles, 1982.
SCHMITS, Georges : L'art naïf en Wallonie et à Bruxelles, Paris, Nathan. — Bruxelles: Labor, 1981.

BRAZIL

Dictionary of Naive Artists / written by Manuel Mujica Laivez. — Viscontea, 1966.
RODMAN, Selden : Popular Artists of Brazil. — Old Greenwich /Connecticut : The Devin-Adair Company, 1977. — 148 p. : ill.

CANADA

Arts Populaires du Québec. — Québec : Musée du Québec, 1975.
DE GROSBOIS, L., LAMOTHE, R. & NANTEL, L. : Les Patenteux du Québec. — Montréal : Parti-Pris, 1974.

Folk Art of Nova Scotia. — Halifax : Art Gallery of Nova Scotia, 1976.
Folk Painters of the Canadian West. — Ottawa : National Gallery of Canada, 1960.
From the Heart /edited by the National Museum of Man & Canadian Centre for Folk Culture Studies. — Toronto : McClelland and Stewart : National Museum of Man : National Museum of Canada, 1983.
HARPER, Russell J. : A People's Art : Primitive, Naive, Provincial and Folk Painting in Canada. — Toronto : Buffalo : University of Toronto Press, 1974. — 176 p. : ill.
LESSARD, M. & MARQUIS, H. : L'Art traditionnel au Québec. — Montréal : Les Editions de l'Homme, 1975.
Saskatchewan Primitives. — Saskatoon: Mendel Art Gallery, 1975.
SWINTON, George : Eskimo Sculpture = Sculpture esquimaude. — Toronto : Montreal : McClelland and Stewart, 1965. — 224 p. : ill.
TILNEY, Philip : Artifacts from the Canadian Centre for Folk Culture Studies Collection. — Ottawa : Canadian Centre for Folk Studies : National Museum of Man, 1973.

MAGAZINE ARTICLES

Grass Roots Art. — Artscanada, December 1969, No. 138-139.

CHINA

Bauernmalerei aus Huxian : Eine Ausstellung der Gesellschaft für deutsch-chinesische Freundschaft e. V. in Zusammenarbeit mit der Gesellschaft des chinesischen Volkes für Freundschaft mit dem Ausland in Peking und der Botschaft der Volksrepublik China in der Bundesrepublik Deutschland. — Frankfurt/M : Gesellschaft für deutsch-chinesische Freundschaft (GDCF) e. V., [1979]. — 143 S. : ill.
Peasant Paintings from Hu County, Shensi Province, China. — London : Arts Council of Great Britain, 1976. — 66 p. : ill.
A Picture of Chinese Farmers. — Shanghai : Fine Arts Publishing House, 1982.

CZECHOSLOVAKIA

BEER, Alois : Památnosti mého podomování. — Hradec Králové, 1978.
ČAPEK, Josef : Folk Painters = Maliři z lidu. — Praha, 1919.
_____ : Nejskromnějši umeni. — Praha : Čs. spisovatel, 1962.
DALLMEIER V. U. & ZIMMER, E. : Ondrej Šteberl. — Düsseldorf, 1974.
HELLER, Arthur : Guttman : Eine psychologische Studie. — Prag : Litevna, 1932.
HOFFMEISTER, Adolf : Predobrazy. — Praha, 1962.
HRABAL, Bohumil : Album deseti naivnich kreseb. — Olomouc, 1978.
KUKLA, A. O. : Marie Janku (katalog). — Polička, 1963.
KUNZ, L. : Naivni malba tri stoleti (katalog). — Brno, 1972.
Die naive Kunst : Katalog einer Ausstellung in Brno, 1963. / Texten von M. Mičko, Vl. Stanovský, Š. Tkáč, A. Pohribný, I. Zhoř und A. Kroupa — Brno, 1963.
NIKODEM, Viktor : Die primitive Natalia Schmidtová (Katalog). — Prag, 1946.
NOVOTNY, Fritz : Naive Kunst : Ein Reisebericht. — Wien ; München, 1977.
POHRIBNÝ, Arsen : Naifs Cecoslovacchi. — Reggio Emilia : Edizione Gruppo Naïf, 1969. — 24 p. : ill.
_____ : Naive Kunst aus der Tschechoslowakei : (Katalog). — Berlin, 1966.
POHRIBNÝ, Arsen und TKÁČ, Štefan : Die naive Kunst in der Tschechoslowakei. — Praha : Artia, 1967. — 199 s. : ill.
PRIŠUTOVA, Irena : Súčasnáludová plastika na Slovensku. — Bratislava, 1976.
TKÁČ, Štefan : Slovak Insitic (Naive) Art = Slovenske insitne umenie. — Bratislava, 1966.
ZIMMER, Elke : Ondrej Šteberl : (Katalog). — Düsseldorf, 1974.

MAGAZINE ARTICLES

Kovačevičová, Soňa: Lidové umenie a národná kúltúra. — Vytvarny Život, S. 122, 1963.

Mičko, Miroslav: Naivni umeni v Československu. — Výtvarná práce, Nr. 22-23, 1963.

'Naive Unschuld aus Paris'. — Der Spiegel, Hagrgang 1961, Nr. 52, Seite 60.

Pohribný, Arsen: A Time for Longing. — Universum Nr. 7, Prague 1969.

Pošová, Kateřina: Goulas, Rescuer of the Double Life of Josef Hlinomaz. — Film a diba Nr. 1, Prague 1973.

FRANCE

APOLLINAIRE, Guillaume : Chroniques d'art : 1902—1918. — Paris : Gallimard, 1960.

BAUCHANT, André : A. Bauchant : peintures : jeudi 13 mai 1976 (jusqu'au 12 juin 1976). — Paris : Kriegel : Sapiro, 1976. — 82 p. : ill.

BIHALJI-MERIN, Oto & Liza : Leben und Werk des Malers Henri Rousseau. — Dresden : Verlag der Kunst, 1971, 1973, — 256 S. : ill. ;
——— : Budapest : Corvina, 1973, — 162 S. : ill. ;
Köln : Du Mont Schauberg, 1976. — 194S. : ill.

BOURET, Jean : Henri Rousseau. — München : Bruckmann Verlag, 1963. — 267 p. : ill. ; Neuchâtel : Ides & Calendes, 1961.

CERTIGNY, Henry : La vérité sur le Douanier Rousseau. — Lausanne : Paris : La Bibliothèque des Arts, 1971. — 132 p. : ill.

COOPER, Douglas : Rousseau. — Paris : Les Editions Braun et Cie, 1951. — 76 p. : ill.

DEPOUILLY, Jacques : Enfants et primitifs. — Neuchâtel, 1964.

DUBUFFET, Jean : L'Art Brut. — Paris, 1964.

JAKOVSKY, Anatole : André Demonchy : peintre. — Verviers : L'association 'temps mêlés', 1962. — 43 p. : ill.
——— : Eros du dimanche. — Paris : J. J. Pauvert, 1964, — 243 p. : ill.
——— : Naive Malerei in Frankreich. — Zürich : Diogenes Verlag, 1957. — 170 S. : ill.

MORARIU, Modest : Douanier Rousseau. — Bucharest : Meridiane Publishing House, 1975. — 63 p. i ill.

L'opera completa di Rousseau il Doganiere / Presentazione di Giovani Artieri. — Milano : Rizzoli, 1969. — 127 p. : ill.

PERRUCHOT, Henri : Le Douanier Rousseau. — Paris : ed. Témoins du XXᵉ siècle, 1957. — 128 p. : ill.

ROUSSEAU, Henri : Henri Rousseau : Dichtung und Zeugnis. — Zürich : Verlag der Arche, 1958. — 108 S.
——— : Leben und Werk. — Dresden : Verlag der Kunst, 1971.

STABENOW, Cornelia : Die Urwaldbilder des Henri Rousseau : (Stilbildung und Verhältnis zum Gesamtwerk). — München : Universität, 1980. — Inaugural-Dissertation Universität, München.

UHDE, Wilhelm : Henri Rousseau. — Paris : Ed. Figuière, 1911. ; Berlin, 1923.
——— : Rousseau (Le Douanier). — Berlin: Alfred Scherz, 1948. — 82 S. : ill.

VALLIER, Dora : Henri Rousseau. — Köln : DuMont Schauberg, 1961. — 327 S. : ill.

MAGAZINE ARTICLES

Cassou, Jean : Les Maîtres Populaires de la Réalité. — Revue 'Art Vivant', Paris, Août—September 1937.

EAST GERMANY (GERMAN DEMOCRATIC REPUBLIC)

CLAUSSNITZER, Gert : Malerei der Naiven. — Leipzig : VEB E. A. Seemann, 1977.

WEST GERMANY (FEDERAL REPUBLIC OF GERMANY)

BUCHHOLZ, Ernst : Carl Christian Thegen: Katalog. — Hamburg, 1966.

DALLMEIER, Marija & Volker : Naivi Taide — Lasten Taide — Psykoosi ja Taide. — Lisalmi-Helsinki, 1973.

EHLERS, A., JASMUND, B. & KALIR, O. : Sontagsmaler. — Berlin, 1956.

ENGELS, M. T. : Adalbert Trillhaase als Zeichner. — Recklinghausen, 1979.

——— : Eduard Odenthal : Katalog. — Neuss, 1974.
——— : Erich Grams : Katalog. — Neuss, 1975.
——— : Jean Abels : Katalog. — Neuss, 1975.

FELDHAUS, Irmgard : Das Clemens — Sels — Museum. — Neuss, 1975.

GEIST, H. — Fr. : Carl Christian Thegen aus Oldesloe. — Kunst in Schleswig-Holstein, 1955.

GERLACH, Friedrich : Das Märchen vom Stein Unvermögen. — Baden-Baden, 1974.
——— : Die Strasse. — Baden-Baden, 1973.

GORSEN, Peter : Das Bild Pygmalions : Kunstsoziologische Essays. — Hamburg : Rowohlt, 1969.
——— : Friedrich Schröder-Sonnenstern : Eine Interpretation. — Frankfurt/M. : Heinrich von Sydow-Zirkwitz, 1962.
——— : Das Prinzip Obszön : Pornographie und Gesellschaft. — Hamburg : Rowohlt, 1969.

GROCHOWIAK, Thomas : Deutsche naive Kunst. — Recklinghausen : Verlag Aurel Bongers, 1974. — 306 S. : ill.
——— : Friedrich Gerlach : Katalog. — Zürich, 1968.
——— : Friedrich und Ludwig Gerlach : Katalog. — Recklinghausen, 1973.
——— : Naive Malerei aus Bundesrepublik Deutschland. — Stuttgart, 1974.
——— : Neun deutsche Naive : Katalog. — Bratislava, 1972.
——— : Vivian Ellis : Katalog. — Bonn, 1977/78.

HONISCH, D. : 3 naive Künstler. — Essen, 1969.

MICHEL, Peter : Die Staffelei im Hühnerhof : Naive Maler und ihre Welt. — Berlin: Der Kinderbuchverlag, 1981. — 78 S. : ill.

Naive and Outsider Painting from Germany and Painting by Gabriele Münter. — Chicago : Museum of Contemporary Art, 1983.

PÖSCHEL, Werner : A. N. Tschistjakow : Protokoll einer Entdeckung. — Bielefeld-Bethel, 1974.
——— : der Bauer und Krippenschnitzer Anton Woltering, Die Weihnachtskrippe. — Telgte, 1979.

PRETZELL, Lothar : Laienmalerei aus Deutschland und Österreich : Katalog. Berlin, 1979.

ROH, Juliane : Adalbert Trillhaase. — Recklinghausen : Verlag Aurel Bongers, 1968. — 68 S. : ill.

ROTH, Toni : Max Raffler. — München, 1969.

WEISNER, Ulrich : A. N. Tschistjakow : Katalog. — Bielefeld, 1974.

WIRTH, Günther : Deutsche Sonntagsmaler: Am Beispiel einer Sammlung. — Böblingen : Galerie Eisenmann im Hause Eisenmann KG, 1978. — 159 S. : ill.

ZIMMER, Elke : Minna Ennulat : Katalog. — Düsseldorf, 1975.
——— : Josef Wittlich : Katalog. — Düsseldorf, 1974.

ZIMMER, Elke & Werner : Erich Grams : Katalog. — Düsseldorf, 1975.

MAGAZINE ARTICLES

DALLMEIER, Volker : Erich Bödeker. — Art — Das Kunst Magazin, Erstausgabe, 1979.

ROH, Franz : Oluf Braren. — Das Kunstwerk, V/VI, 1927.

GREAT BRITAIN

AYRES, James : English Naive Painting : 1750—1900 / Preface by Andras Kalman. — London: Thames and Hudson, 1980. — 168 p. : ill.

BRADLEY, Helen : Miss Carter Came With Us. — London : Jonathan Cape Ltd, 1973. — 31 p. : ill.

Britain's First International Exhibition of Naive Art : for Hamiltons' / Assembled by Sheldon Williams. — London : Hamiltons, 1979. — 24 p. : ill.

CARRINGTON, Noel : Popular Art in Britain. — London : Penguin Books Ltd, 1945.

English Naive Paintings from the Collection of Mr & Mrs A. Kalman. — London : Crane Kalman Gallery.

FLETCHER, Geoffrey : Popular Art in England. — London : George G. Harrap and Co Ltd, 1962.

LISTER, Eric and WILLIAMS Sheldon : Twentieth-Century British Naive and Primitive Artists. — London : Astragal Books, 1977. — 192. p. : ill.

SCHREINER, Gérard A. : Scottie Wilson. — Bâle : Gérard A. Schreiner, 1979. — 135 p. : ill.

GREECE

MICHELE, Ephé : Effie Michelis. — Athenai, 1974. — 111 p. : ill.

HAITI

Art in Latin America Today : Haiti. — Washington, D. C. — 1959.

BRETON, André : Kunst aus Haiti : (Katalog). — Berlin, 1979.

BROWN, Karen McCarthy: The Vévé of Haitian Voudou : A Structural Analysis of Visual Imagery. — Ann Arbor : University Microfilms, 1975.

The Caribbean. New York, 1968.

COURLANDER, Harold : The Drum and the Hoe : The Life and Love of the Haitian People. — Los Angeles : Berkeley, 1960.

DEREN, Maya : Divine Horsemen : The Living Gods of Haiti. — New York, 1953.

DROT, Jean-Marie: Journal de voyage chez les peintres de la Fête et du Vaudou en Haïti. — Genève : D'Art Albert Skira, 1974. — 89 p. : ill.

Haiti : Black Peasants and Voodoo. — New York, 1960.

Haiti Singing. — New York, 1973.

Haitian Art: (Exhibition catalogue). — New York : The Brooklyn Museum of Art, 1978.

HERSKOVITS, Melville J. : Life in a Haitian Valley. 2. ed. — New York, 1971.

KLINGENDER, F. D.: Painters of Haiti. — London, 1947.

LEGER, Joseph N. : Haiti, Her History and Her Detractors. — Westport, Conn., 1970.

LEYBURN, James G. : The Haitian People. — 2. ed. — New Haven, Conn., 1966.

MARCELIN, Milo : Mythologie Vaudou : (Rite Arada) /Ilustrations par Hector Hyppolite. — Port-au-Prince, Haïti : Les Editions Haïtiennes, 1949.

MÉNDEZ, Fernandez Eugenio : Les primitif Haïtiens. — Port-au-Prince : Galerie Georges S. Nader, 1972. — 95 p. : ill.

METRAUX, Alfred : Haïti : La terre, les hommes et les dieux. — Neuchâtel, 1957.

The Miracle of Haïtian Art, New York, 1974.

MONTAS, Michèle : Haïti. — Papéété Tahiti, 1975.

Panorama de l'art haïtien. — Port-au-Prince, Haiti, 1956.

Renaissance in Haiti : Popular Painters in the Black Republic. — New York, 1948.

RIGAUD, Milo : La tradition vaudou et le vaudou haïtien : Son temple, ses mystères, sa magie. — Paris, 1953.

STEBICH, Ute : Kunst aus Haiti. — International Primary Art (IPA).

Le vaudou haïtien / Introduction by Michel Leiris. — Paris, 1977.

WILLIAMS, Sheldon : Voodoo and the Art of Haiti. — London : Morland.

MAGAZINE ARTICLES

ADLOW, Dorothy : Church Art in Haiti. — Collier's, 22 November 1952, p. 74—75.

ARQUIN, Florence : Contemporary Popular Art in Haiti. — Bulletin of the Pan American Union, January p. 10—20.

El arte Haitiano. — Mundo Hispánico, Año 12, No. 137, p. 59.

BRETON, André: Hector Hyppolite. — Der Surrealismus und die Malerei (Berlin), 1967, S. 313—317.

A Caribbean Chapter. — Americas XX, No. 10, September 1968, p. 8—15.

The Christ of the Haitian Primitives. — Harper's Bazaar, December 1950, p. 106—109, 175—177.

Church Art in Haiti. — Life, 22 December 1952, p. 64—65.

EFRON, Edith: The New Movement in Haiti. — Caribbean Quarterly, Vol. 4, p. 14—31.

GOLD, Herbert: The Arts in Haiti. — Mademoiselle, February 1955, p. 159, 201—207

713

Haiti — The Naive and the Knowing. — Art in America, 48, Autumn, 1960, p. 108—109.

LEIRIS, Michel : Martinique, Guadeloupe, Haiti (1950). — Das Auge des Ethnographen (Frankfurt/Main), 1978.

MILICKA, François: Castera Bazile est mort. — Conjonction (Port-au-Prince), April 1966, No. 101, p. 92.

MORVAN, Pierre : Aufbruch der Kunst, Haiti entdeckt sich selbst. — Du, No. 9, September 1958, S. 51.

Murals for Haiti from the Centre d'Art Jeep to the Miracle at Cana. — Art in America 39, December 1951, p. 189—204.

A Mural by Wilson Bigaud. — Magazine of Art 44, October 1951, p. 238—242.

PETERS, DeWitt C.: Haiti's Primitive Painters. — Harper's Bazaar, January 1947, p. 104—105, 153.

PRICE, Lucien : Hector Hyppolite est mort. — Conjonction (Port-au-Prince), August 1948, No. 16, p. 38.

RIGAUD, Odette Mennesson : Vaudou haïtien : Quelques notes sur ses reminiscence africaines. — Les Afro-Americains (Dakar), 1953.

RODMAN, Selden: Hector Hyppolite. — Magazine of Art 41, January 1948, p. 23—25.

The Serpent and the Cross. — Art News 47, September 1948, p. 38—41.

THOBY-MARCELIN, Philippe: La double vie d'Hector Hyppolite, artiste et prêtre vaudou. — Conjonction, 1948, No. 16, p. 40—44, No. 17, p. 37—41.

HUNGARY

BALÁZS, János : A Hungarian Gipsy Artist. — Budapest : Corvina Press, 1977. — 62 L.: ill.

BANNER, Zoltán : Csillagfaragók. Népi alkotók, naiv müvészek. — Bucureşti : Kriterion, 1972. — 108 L. : ill.

BÁLINT, Jenő : Magyar őstehetség, 1935.

———— : Magyar őstehetségek kiállitásának katalógusa. A Reggel 1934 augusztus 20. Különszáma

BÁNSZKI, Pál : Magyar Naiv Müvészek Muzeuma állandó kiállitásának katalogusa. — Kecskemét, 1978.

DOMOKOS, Moldován : Juli Dudás cronista naive di un epopèia contadina. — Roma : Carte Segrete, 1975.

F. MIHÁLY, Ida : L'art naïf Hongrois. Mons, 1975.

———— : Arte primitivo Húngaro en le siglo XX. — La Habana, 1973.

———— : La forma della vita nella pittura contadina. — Roma : Carte Segrete, 1975.

———— : Mezőgazdaság a naiv müvészetben. Budapest, 1980.

———— : Naive Malerei in Ungarn 1900—1971. — Kunstmuseum Winterthur, 1972.

F. MIHÁLY, Ida & BÁNSZKI, Pál : Magyar naiv müvészet a XX. században. — Budapest : Magyar Nemzeti Galéria, 1972.

KÁLLAI, Ernő : Egy ügyű piktorok. Uj Idök, 1936.

KERÉKGYÁRTO, István : A naiv müvészet esztétikuma. Művészet, junius 1979.

Sz. MURAKÖZI, Ágota : Magyarországi parasztfestők. Nyiregyháza : Jósa András Muzeum Evkönyve, 1968.

INDONESIA

BATESON, G. & MEAD, M. : Balinese Character. — New York, 1942.

COVARRUBIAS, Miguel : The Island of Bali. — New York, 1937.

GORIS, R. & DRONKERS, P. L. : Bali, Cults and Customs. — Government of Indonesia, [no date].

HOLT, Claire: Art in Indonesia. — New York, 1967.

RAMSEYER, Urs : The Art and Culture of Bali. — Oxford, 1977.

ISRAEL

DORON, Daniel : The Art of Shalom of Safed : Catalogue of the Exhibition in the Gallery of Israeli Art. — New York, 1966.

ZIMMER, Elke : Shalom von Safed : Katalog, 1973.

ITALY

BIGIARETTI, Libero : Orneore Metelli. — Ivrea : Ing. C. Olivetti, 1964.

BUCCARELLI, Palma : Orneore Metelli. — Roma : L'Indipendente, 1964.

CARLINO, Walter & MENOZZI, Dino : Catalogo Nazionale di grafica naive. — Reggio Emilia : A. G. E. — Grafica Editoriale, 1978. — 123 p. : ill.

CAVAZZINI, Gianni : Naifs parmensi. — Reggio Emilia : Edizione Gruppo Naif : Istituto delle Comunità, 1970. — 44 p. : ill.

COURTHION, Pierre : Orneore Metelli : Le peintre cordonnier (1872—1938). — Genève : Pierre Cailler, 1951.

DEGNI, Renato & CARLINO, Walter : Bernardo Pasotti. — Firenze : Il Candelaio, 1981. — 157. p. : ill.

DE GRADA, Raffaelle : Antonio Ligabue : Catalogo antologica di Gualtieri. — Reggio E. : Comune di Gualtieri, 1975.

DE MICHELI, Mario : Pietro Ghizzardi. — Parma : Gall. Steccata, 1975.

GHIZZARDI, Pietro : Omaggio a Pietro Ghizzardi. — Reggio Emilia : Age, 1971. — 90 p. : ill.

MACCARRONE, Pietro : Giuseppe Gagliano. — Milano : Il Dialogo, 1975.

MARGONARI, Renzo : Naifs. — Parma : La Nazionale, 1973.

MENOZZI, Dino : La grafica naive nella 1 Bassa Padana. — Reggio Emilia : Age, 1971. — 239 p. : ill.

———— : La sculptura naive. — Reggio Emilia : Age, 1973. — 67 p. : ill.

METELLI, Orneore : O. Metteli. — Roma : Stefano de Luca editore, 1973. — 93 p. : ill.

MICHELI, Mario de : I naifs Italiani. — Parma : Passera & Agosta Tota, 1972. — 391 p. : ill.

ORLICH, Lando : Pietro Ghizzardi. — Reggio Emilia : Age, 1975. — 374 p. : ill. gio Emilia : Age, 1975. — 374 p. : ill.

———— : Serafino Valla. — Reggio Emilia : : Serafino Valla. — Reggio Emilia : Age, 1972. — 58 p. : ill.

PUNGETTI, Alberta : Irene Invrea. — Reggio Emilia : Edizione gruppo Naif : Istituto delle Comunità, /s. a. /. — 45 p.

QUOREL, Vittore : Naifs. — Pordenone : Centro Iniziative Culturali, 1947.

VENTURI, Lionello : Il gusto dei primitivi. — Torino : G. Einaudi, 1972. 248 p. : ill.

VILLANI, Dino : La gente di Ghizzardi. — Verona : D'Arte Ghelfi, 1973.

ZAVATTINI, Cesare : Ligabue. — Parma : Franco Maria Bicci, 1973. 169 p. : ill.

ZAVATTINI, Cesare, DE MICHELI, Mario & MAZZACURATI, Marino : Ligabue. — Parma : Ricci, 1967.

JAPAN

Portfolio : Kiyoshi Yamashita, Nobel Publishing Inc., Tokyo, 1981, p. 200, 120 photos.

NETHERLANDS

BROMET, Joop : Nederlandse naïeve kunst. — Venlo : Van Spijk, 1979. — 151 p. p.

GANS, Louis : Naïeve kunst : aspecten van een randverschijnsel / L. Gans & W. P. H. Russelman. — Utrecht : Bruna, 1978. — 112. p. : ill.

Guide to the World of Naive Art : Dutch Section (Introduction by Nico van der Endt). — London : RONA-Guide, 1978.

Naïeve Schilders Zien Ons Land. — Amsterdam : Ploegsma, 1978.

VAN DER ENDT, Nico : Nederlandse Naïeve Kunst : exhibition-catalogue. — Haarlem: Frans Hals museum, 1976.

ZIMMER, Elke : Leonardus Neervoort : (Katalog). — Düsseldorf, 1977.

MAGAZINE ARTICLES

VAN DER ENDT, NICO : Naive Art in the Netherlands. — Art Investment Guide, Autumn, 1974, Weybridge, England

NICARAGUA

CARDENAL, Ernesto: Unser Land mit den Menschen die wir lieben : Gedichte [aus dem spanischen von Anneliese Schwarzer de Ruiz ; mit den Bildern aus Solentiname und dem neuen Nicaragua ; Nachwort von Paul Konrad Kurz]. — Wuppertal : Hammer, 1980. — 63 S. : ill.

POLAND

BANACH, Andrzej : Ociepka : malarz dnia siódmego. — Kraków, 1958.

———— : Nikifor. — Warszawa, 1982.

ENGELS, M. T. : Katarzyna Gawłowa. — Neuss, 1979

———— : Naive Plastik aus Polen. — Recklinghausen, 1979.

FLECKHAUS, Willi : Aus der Kunst des polnischen Volkes. — Frankfurt/M., 1979.

GRABOWSKI, Józef : Sztuka ludowa w Europie. — Warszawa : Arkady, 1978. — s. 342 : ill.

JACKOWSKI, Aleksander & JARNUSKIEWICZOVA, Jadwiga : Polnische Volkskunst. — Berlin : Henschel Verlag ; Warszawa : Arkady, 1968. — 476 S. : ill.

Malujemy . . . : Album sztuki Dziecka / zebral i opracowal Bolesław Zagota. — Warszawa : Nasza Ksiegarnia, 1961. — 79 s. : ill.

Naive Kunst aus Polen : 20. April bis 21. Mai 1967 / Vorwort Aleksander Jackowski. — Stuttgart : Württembergischer Kunstverein : Kunstgebäude am Schlossplatz, 1967. — 55 S. : ill.

Naive Kunst aus Polen : Skulpturen, Bilder, Reliefs : aus der Sammlung Orth : Kunsthalle Nürnberg in der Norishalle : 25. 10. 1980 bis 27. 1. 1981. /Vorwort Curt Heigel ; Einführung Hans Joachim Orth. — Nürnberg : Kunsthalle, 1980. — 110 S. : ill.

PIWOCKI, Ksawery : Dziwny świat współczesnych prymitywów. — Warszawa, 1975.

WITZ, Ignacy : Wielcy Malarze amatorzy. — Warszawa : Wydawnictwo związkowe, 163 s. : ill.

ZIMMER, Ludwig : Mit den 'Christussen im Elend', — Aus der Kunst des polnischen Volkes. — Frankfurt/M., 1979.

MAGAZINE ARTICLES

JACKOWSKI, Aleksander : Plastyka ieprofesjonalna. — Polska Sztuka Ludowa, 1974, nr. 4

———— : Pogranicze sztuki ludowej i naiwnej. — Polska Sztuka Ludowa, 1968, nr. 1/2

———— : Współczesna rzeźba zwana ludowa. — Polska Sztuka Ludowa, 1976, nr. 3/4

———— : Współczesne malarstwo ludowe i jego pogranicza. — Polska Sztuka Ludowa, 1977, nr. 4 ; 1978, nr. 1 i 2.

ROMANIA

Art plastique d'amateurs. — Bucureşti : Conseil de la culture et de l'éducation socialiste : Centre d'orientation de la création populaire et du mouvement artistique de masse, 1971. — 88 p. : ill.

CORNEA, Andrei : Primitivi picturii româneşti moderne. — Bucureşti : Meridiane, 1980. — 145 p. : ill.

IRIMIE, Cornel & FOCŞA, Marcela : Icônes sur verre de Roumanie. — Bucureşti : Meridiane, 1969. — 109 p. : ill.

———— : Romanian Icons Behind Glass. — Bucureşti : Meridiane, 1968. — 109 p. : ill.

———— : Rumänische Hinterglasikonen. — Bucureşti : Meridiane, 1968. — 109 p. : ill.

PETRESCU, Paul : Imaginea omului în arta popularà românească. — Bucureşti : Meridiane, 1969. — 146 p. : ill.

POP, Simion : Cimitirul vesel de la Sapînta. — Editura Sport-Turism, 1973.

SAVONEA, Vasile : Arta naiva în România. — Bucureşti : Meridiane, 1980. — 130 p. : ill.

THE SOVIET UNION

Agitacionno-massovoe iskusstvo pervyh let Oktjabrja. — Moskva : Iskusstvo, 1971.

ALPATOV, M. V. : Vseobšçaja istorija iskusstva : kn. I—III. — Moskva : (s. n.), 1954—1955.

AMIRANAŠVILI, Č. : Niko Pirosmanašvili. — Moskva : Sovetskij Hudožnik, 1967.

BEL'SKAJA, Tatjana Borisovna : Amateur Folk Painting : An Album. — Moskva : Sovetskij Hudožnik, 1980. 192 str. : ill.

_____ : Samodejatel'nye hudožniki. — Moskva : Sovetskij Hudožnik, 1981. — 116 str. : ill.

BILEC'KIJ, P. : Ukrain'skij portretnyj živopis XVII—XVIII st. — Kiev : Mistectvo, 1969.

BOLDYREVA, S. : Risunki detej doškol'nogo vozrasta, bol'nyh šizofreniej. — Moskva : Medicina, 1974.

GOR, G. : Neneckij hudožnik K. Pankov. — Leningrad : Sovetskij hudožnik, 1968.

Katerina Bilokur = Ekaterina Belokur / vstupnoe slovo Olesja Gončarova. — Kiev: Mistectvo, 1975. — 94 str. : ill.

Kunst der Volksschaffenden aus der Sowjetunion : im Haus der Ruhrfestspiele vom 22. Mai bis zum 10. Juli 1975. — Recklinghausen : Ruhrfestspiele, 1975. — 22 S. : ill.

KUZNECOV, E. : Pirosmani. — Moskva : Iskusstvo, 1975.

LIHAČEV, D. : Poètika drevnerusskoj literatury. — Moskva : Nauka, 1979.

LOGVINSKAJA, E. : Inter'er v russkoj živopisi. — Moskva : Iskusstvo, 1978.

LUNČARSKIJ, A. : Ob izobraziteľnom iskusstve. t. P. — Moskva : Sovetskij hudožnik, 1967.

MESTEČKIN, Grigorij Abramovič : Marija Prijmačenko : Al'bum na ukrainskom jazyke. — Kiev : Mistectvo, 1971. — 67 str. : ill.

OSTROVSKIJ, G. : Russkaja vyveska : Materialy k biografii. — Moskva : Panorama iskusstv — 78 : Sovetskij hudožnik, 1979.

PIROSMANAŠVILI, Niko : Niko Pirosmanašvili. — Moskva : Sovetskij hudožnik, 1967. — 94 str. : ill.

POMERACEV, N. : Russkaja derevjanaja skul'ptura = Russian wooden sculpture. — Moskva : Sovetskij hudožnik, 1967. — 132 str. : ill.

Sovremennyj literaturnyj process i fol'klor. — Moskva : Voprosy literatury, 1978, nojabr'.

ŠKAROVSKAJA, Natalija : Amateur Art. — Leningrad : Aurora Publishers, 1975. — 360 p. : ill.

_____ : Folk and Amateur Art : Rustic and Urban Traditional and Individual Applied and Representational Past and Present = Narodnoe iskusstvo i samodejatel'noe tvorčestvo : Krest'janskoe i gorodskoe tradicionoe i samodejatel'noe prikladnoe i izobraziteľnoe prošloe i sovremenoe ... — Moscow : VAAP-Inform, 1981. — 80 str. : ill.

_____ : Narodnoe samodejatel'noe iskusstvo. — Leningrad : Avrora, 1975.

TANANAEVA, L. : Sarmatskij portret. — Moskva : Nauka, 1977.

TUPITSIN, I. K. : Drawings by Soviet Children = Dessins d'enfants soviétiques = Zeichnungen sowjetischer Kinder. — Moscow : Foreign languages publishing house, 1957. — 96 p. : ill.

USPENSKIJ, B. : Poètika kompozicii. — Moskva : Iskusstvo, 1970.

VORONOV, V. : Krest'janskoe iskusstvo. — Moskva : Sovetskij hudožnik, 1972.

Vsesojuznaja vystavka proizvedenij samodejatel'nyh hudožnikov 'Slava trudu' : Živopis' : Skul'ptura : Grafika. — Moskva : Sovetskij hudožnik, 1974. — 147 str. : ill.

ZDANEVIČ, Kirill Mihajlovič : Niko Pirosmanašvili. — Moskva : Iskusstvo, 1964. — 127 str. : ill.

MAGAZINE ARTICLES

KAMENSKIJ, A. : Istoki stilja Pirosmani. — Dekorativnoe iskusstvo SSSR, 1981, nr. 3, str. 22—26.

SPAIN

VALLEJO-NAGERA, Juan Antonio : Naifs españoles contemporaneos. — Madrid, 1975.

SWEDEN

BLOMBERG, Erik : Naivister och realister. — Stockholm : Bokförlaget Aldus/Bonnier, 1962. — 110 p. : ill.

SWITZERLAND

BUCK, Hans : Adolf Dietrich als Zeichner / Geleitwort von Walter Hugelshofer. — Zürich : Stuttgart : Rotapfel-Verlag, 1964. — 107 S. : ill.

HANHART, Rudolf : Appenzeller Bauernmalerei = Appenzell Peasant Art. — Niggli : Teufen AR, 1970. — 132 S. : ill.

HOENN, Karl : Adolf Dietrich. — Frauenfeld-Leipzig : Huber & Co., 1942. — 108 S. 56 S. : ill.

KRISS-RETTENBECK, Lenz : Ex Voto. — Zürich, 1972.

THE UNITED STATES OF AMERICA

America's Arts and Skills / Introduction by Charles F. Montgomery. — New York : E. P. Dutton & Co., Inc, 1957. — 172 p. : ill.

American Folk Painters of Three Centuries / Editors Jean Lipman & Tom Armstrong. — New York : Hudson Hills Press, Inc. : Whitney Museum of American Art, 1980. — 233 p. : ill

American Naive Painting of the 18th and 19th Centuries : III Masterpieces from the Collection of Edgar William and Bernice Chrysler Garbisch. — New York : The American Federation of Arts, [1968—1970]. — 159 p. : ill.

American Primitive Paintings from the Collection of Edgar Williams and Bernice Chrysler Garbisch : Part 1. — Washington : National Gallery of Art : Smithsonian Institution, 1954. — 112 p. : ill.

BISHOP, Robert-Charles : American Folk Sculpture. — New York : Dutton, 1974. — 392 p. : ill.

FORD, Alice : Pictorial Folk Art : New England to California. — New York : Studio Publ., 1949.

HEMPHILL, Herbert W. Jr. & WEISSMAN, Julia : Twentieth-Century American Folk Art and Artists. — New York : E. P. Dutton & Co., Inc., 1974. — 237 p. : ill.

JANIS, Sidney : They Taught Themselves : American Primitive Painters of the 20th Century. — New York : Dial Press, 1942.

KALLIR, Otto : Grandma Moses. — Köln, 1975.

LIPMAN, Jean & WINCHESTER, Alice : The Flowering of American Folk Art 1775—1876. — London : Thames and Hudson, 1973. — 288 p. : ill.

_____ : Primitive Painters in America : 1750—1950. — New York : Dodd Mead & Co., 1950.

_____ : Primitive Painters in America : 1750—1950. — Freeport, N. Y. : Books for Libraries Press, 1971. — 182 p. : ill.

Morris Hirshfield / Testo di William Saroyan ; presentazione di Sidney Janis ; contributo critico di Oto Bihalji-Merin. — Parma : Franco Maria Ricci, 1975. — 141 p. : ill.

Morris Hirshfield / Text by William Saroyan ; introduction by Sidney Janis ; critical notes by Oto Bihalji-Merin. — Parma : Franco Maria Ricci, 1976. — 141 p. : ill.

MOSES, Grandma : Meine Lebensgeschichte. — Frankfurt/M. : Ullstein Taschenbuch Verlag, 1957. — 151 p. : ill.

OSBORNE, Duncan P. : Amanda de Leon — New York : Fine Arts Publishers, 1955. — 15 p : ill.

RODMAN, Selden : Horace Pippin. — New York : Quadrangle Press, 1947.

VENEZUELA

ANTONIO, Francisco da : El arte ingenuo en Venezuela. — Caracas : Huella, 1974. — 165 p. : ill.

YUGOSLAVIA

BIHALJI-MERIN, Oto : Ivan Generalić : Jugoslawische Pastorale. — Baden-Baden : Woldemar Klein, 1960. — 30 S. : ill.

_____ : Naive Art in Yugoslavia. — Beograd : Jugoslavija, 1959. — 144 p. : ill.

_____ : Naive Malerei aus Jugoslawien. — Hamburg : Kunsthaus, 1964.

_____ : Umetnost naivnih u Jugoslaviji. — Beograd : Jugoslavija, 1963. — 198 str. : ill.

_____ : Umetnost naivnih v Jugoslaviji. — Mladinska knjiga, 1965. — 202 str. : ill.

_____ : Die Kunst der Naiven in Jugoslawien. — Leipzig : VEB E. A. Seemann Verlag, 1966. — 198 str. : ill.

_____ : Die Kunst der Naiven in Jugoslawien. — München : Aries, 198 S. : ill.

_____ : Die Kunst der Naiven in Jugoslawien. — Beograd : Jugoslavija, 1966. — 202 S. : ill.

_____ : Naivné umenie v Jugoslávii. — Bratislava : Slovenské vydavateľstvo krásnej literatury ; Beograd : Jugoslavija, 1964. — 202 str. : ill.

_____ : Primitive Artists of Yugoslavia. — New York : McGraw-Hill Book Company; Beograd : Jugoslavija, 1964. — 202 p. : ill.

BIHALJI-MERIN, Oto & ŽIVKOVIĆ, Bogosav : Snovi i traume u drvetu. — Beograd : Jugoslavija, 1962; 1964. — 62 str. : ill.

_____ : Kollektiv-unbewusste Formen eines naiven Skulptors. — Baden-Baden : Woldemar Klein, 1962

_____ : Träume und Ängste aus Holz. — Belgrad : Jugoslawien, 1962.

_____ : The World of a Primitive Sculptor. — New York : Lyle Stuart ; Belgrade : Yugoslavia, 1963. — 40 p. : ill.

BOŠKOVIĆ, Miroslava & MAŠIREVIĆ, Milica : Samouki likovni umetnici u Srbiji / Introduction by Anatole Jakovsky. — Torino : Eskenaziarte, 1977. — 427 str. : ill.

CARRIERI, Raffaelle : Rabuzin / Introduction by Radoslav Putar. — Milano : Edizioni Tega, 1972. — 304 str. : ill.

CRNKOVIĆ, Vladimir : Gaži, Kovačić, Rabuzin : Grosse Meister der Naive in Jugoslawien = Veliki majstori naive u Jugoslaviji = The Great Masters of Naive Art in Yugoslavia = Grandi maestri dell'Arte naive in Jugoslavia. — Zagreb : Vladimir Crnković, 19. — 546 str. : ill.

_____ : Veliki majstori hrvatske naivne umjetnosti : Collection of Serigraphs. — Zagreb, 1975.

DIMITRIJEVIĆ, Kosta : Naiva u Jugoslaviji : mali leksikon slikara i vajara. — Beograd : Beogradski izdavačko grafički zavod, 1979. — 283 str.

GAMULIN, Grgo : I Pittori naifs della scuola di Hlebine. — Milano : Arnoldo Mondadori, 1974. — 237 p. : ill.:

_____ : Ivan Večenaj. — Zagreb : Spektar, 1975. — 126 str. : ill.

GENERALIĆ, Josip : Autobiografija / Introduction by Anatole Jakovsky, Mario de Micheli, Boris Keleman. — Zagreb : Spektar, 1971. — 115 str : ill.

GENERALIĆ, Ivan : Ivan Generalić / Text by Mića Bašićević, Anatole Jakovsky, Boris Keleman. — Zagreb : Spektar : Izdavački zavod Jugoslavenske akademije znanosti i umjetnosti, 1973. — 148 str. : ill.

_____ : Ivan Generalić / Texte Mića Bašićević, Anatole Jakovsky, Boris Keleman — Zagreb : Spektar : Verlag der Jugoslawischen Akademie, 1973. — 148 S. : ill.

_____ : Ivan Generalić / Textes Mića Bašićević, Anatole Jakovsky, Boris Keleman. — Zagreb : Spektar : L'institut d'édition de l'Académie yougoslave, 1973. — 146 p. : ill.

GRAKALIĆ, Marijan : Hrvatski naivni umjetnici i slovenski likovni samorastniki. — Zagreb : M. Grakalić, 1973. — str. 1—70

Hlebinski krug : pedeset godina naivnog slikarstva : Galerija Hlebine : Galerija Koprivnica 19. 9.—3. 10. 1981 : Galerija primitivne umjetnosti Zagreb 8. 10.—1. 11. 1981 / urednik Boris Keleman, Franjo Horvatić. — Zagreb : Galerija primitivne umjetnosti ; Koprivnica : RO Centar za kulturu, OOUR Muzej grada Koprivnice, 1981. — 58 str.

KELEMAN, Boris : Naivno slikarstvo u Jugoslaviji : paintings, drawings, 120 reproductions. — Zagreb : grafički zavod Hrvatske, 1977. — 112 str. : ill.

_____ : Naive Art. Paintings from Yugoslavia. — New York : Dutton Co., 1977.

_____ : Naive Art. Paintings from Yugoslavia. — Oxford : Phaidon Press, 1977. — 1—112 p.

_____ : Naive Malerei in Jugoslawien. — Wiesbaden : Ebeling Verlag, 1977.

_____ : La peinture naive yougoslave. — Zagreb : Galerije grada : Spektar : Stvarnost, 1969. — 121 p. : ill.

_____ : Yugoslav Naive Painting. — Zagreb : Galerije grada : Spektar : Stvarnost, 1969. — 120 p. : ill.

MAKAROVIĆ, Gorazd : Poslikane panjske končnice. — Ljubljana : Mladinska knjiga, 1962. — 138 str. : ill.

715

MALEKOVIĆ, Vladimir : Hrvatska izvorna umjetnost. — Zagreb : Grafički zavod Hrvatske, 1973. — 236 str. : ill.
_____ : Croatian Naive Art : Dictionary of Primal Artists. — Zagreb : Grafički zavod Hrvatske, 1974. — 296 p. : ill.
_____ : I Naifs Croati. — Novara : Istituto geografico de Agostini, 1975. — str. 1—303
_____ : Skurjeni. — Zagreb : Sveučilišna naklada Liber, (s. a.). — 127 str. : ill.
MIHAILOVIĆ, Milivoje : Seljaci slikari iz Kovačice. — Kovačica : Dom kulture, 1962. — 87 str. : ill.
_____ : Bauernmaler aus Kovačica. — Kovačica : Kulturhaus, 1962.
Monografija : Galerija samoukih likovnih umetnika 'Svetozarevo' u Svetozarevu edited by Milica Maširević i Miroslava Bošković. — Svetozarevo : Galerija samoukih umetnika 'Svetozarevo', 1979. — 111 str.: ill.
RABUZIN, Ivan : Rabuzin / Text by Vladimir Maleković. — Zagreb : Mladost, 1976. — 160 str. : ill.
Rabuzinov raj / Preface by Vigorelli Giancarlo. — Milano : Dino Tega, 1977. — 103 p. : ill.
TOMAŠEVIĆ, Nebojša : Ivan Generalić. — București : Editura Meridiane, 1982. — 86 p. : ill.
_____ : Ivan Generalić leven en werk. — Beograd : Jugoslovenska revija ; Antwerpen : Mercatorfonds N. V., 1976. — 223 p. : ill.
_____ : Ivan Generalić : Mein Leben meine Bilder. — Beograd : Jugoslovenska revija ; Königstein im Taunus : Karl Robert Langewiesche Nachfolger Hans Köster, 1976. — 223 S. : ill.
_____ : Magični svet Ivana Generalića. — Beograd : Jugoslovenska revija, 1976. — 223 str. : ill.
_____ : The Magic World of Ivan Generalić. — Beograd : Jugoslovenska revija ;

New York : Rizzoli International Publications, Inc., 1976. — 223 p. : ill.
_____ : Le monde magique d'Ivan Generalić. — Beograd : Jugoslovenska revija ; Paris : Fonds Mercator Antwerpen and Albin Michel, 1976. — 223 p. : ill.
_____ : Naivci o sebi : osamdeset naivnih slikara pričaju o svom radu. — Beograd : Jugoslovenska revija : »Borba«, 1973. — 388 str.
_____ : Joegoslavische Naïeve Kunst : Gesprekken met 84 Kunstenaars over zichzelf en hun werk. — Haarlem : Schuyt & Co CV, 1976. — 388 p. : ill.
_____ : Jugoslawische Naive : Künstler über sich selbst. — Königstein im Taunus: Karl Robert Langewiesche Nachfolger Hans Köster, 1974. — 389 S.
_____ : I naïf Jugoslavi : 84 pittori naïf parlano della loro vita e del loro lavoro. — Firenze : Editore Scala, 1974.
_____ : Yugoslav Naive Art : 80 Self-taught Artists Speak about Themselves and Their Work. — Belgrade : Review, 1973. — 387 p.
_____ L'art naïf Yougoslave : 80 peintres naïfs parlent d'eux mêmes et de leur travail. — Bruxelles ; Paris : Gulde Internationale de l'Art
_____ : Naivni slikari Jugoslavije. — Beograd : Jugoslovenska revija : Jugoslovenska knjiga, 1978. — 194 str. : ill.
_____ : Naive Maler Jugoslawiens. — Beograd : Jugoslovenska revija : Jugoslovenska knjiga ; Gütersloh : Bertelsmann Reinhard Mohn GmbH, 1978. — 194 S. : ill.
_____ : Naive Painters of Yugoslavia. — Beograd : Jugoslovenska revija : Jugoslovenska knjiga ; New York : The Two Continents Publishing Group, 1978. — 194 p. : ill.
_____ Peintres naïfs Yougoslaves . — Beograd : Jugoslovenska revija : Jugosloven-

ska knjiga ; Bruxelles : OYEZ, 1978. — 194 p. : ill.
_____ : Pictura naivă Iugoslavă. — București : Editura Meridiane, 1977. — 93 p. : ill.
_____ : Tisnikar : svet vaskrslih mrtvaca. — Beograd : Jugoslovenska revija : Vuk Karadžić, 1978. — 204 str. : ill.
_____ : Tisnikar . — Beograd : Jugoslovenska revija : Vuk Karadžić ; Königstein im Taunus : Karl Robert Langewiesche Nachfolger Hans Köster, 1978. — 204 S. : ill.
_____ : Tisnikar : Painter of Death . .— Beograd : Jugoslovenska revija : Vuk Karadžić ; London : Summerfield Press, 1978. — 204 p. : ill. ; Tokio : Conbunsha, 1979.
TRŠAR, Marjan : Jugoslovensko naivno slikarstvo. — Ljubljana : Prosvetni servis, 1971. — 59 str.
WINTERBERG, Ernst : Naive Malerei aus Jugoslawien. — Frankfurt/M., 1966. — 111 S. : ill.
ZIMMER, Elke : Emerik Feješ : Katalog. — Düsseldorf, 1975.
_____ : Ilija Bosilj : Katalog. — Düsseldorf, 1976.

Compiled by:
MIROSLAVA PIVIĆ, Editor of the Centre for International Exchange with the Library of the Yugoslav Bibliographical Institute
and
ALEKSANDAR MARINKOVIĆ, Librarian of the Centre for International Exchange with the Library of the Yugoslav Bibliographical Institute, Belgrade.

Acknowledgement

For their courteous generosity in sharing of information and transparencies the authors and the publisher wish to thank the following persons and institutions: Mr. José Gómez-Sicre, Prof. Thomas Grochowiak, Prof. Dipl. ing. Fritz Novotny and Mrs. Ruth Debel; Vestisches Museum, Recklinghausen; Schleswig-Holstein State Museum, Schleswig; Institute for Foreign Relations, Stuttgart; Charlotte, Gallery for Naive Art, Munich; Eisenmann K. G., Böblingen; Gottlieb-Keller Foundation, Bern; Gallery of Self-Taught Artists, Svetozarevo; Gallery of Primitive Art, Zagreb and Gallery of Self-Taught Artists, Trebnje.

716

List of Illustrations

143. Bollar, Gorki: *The Miraculous Draught*, 1978; acrylic on board, 40 × 50 cm; private collection, Amstelveen

143. Boiron, Rose: *The Muse of Alpilles*, Musée du Vieux Château, Laval; cliché Leportier

144. Bolognesi, Ferrucio: *Piazza Virgiliana*, 1974; oil on canvas, 45 × 40 cm; W. Carlino collection, Milan

145. Bombois, Camille: *Nude with Raised Arms*, 1925; oil on canvas, 81 × 60 cm; Musée National d'Art Moderne, Centre National d'Art et Culture Georges Pompidou, Paris

146. Bombois, Camille: *Self-portrait*, oil on canvas, 81 × 54 cm; private collection, Zurich

146. Bonnin, Maurice: *"Le Lapin Agile" Cabaret*, private collection, Paris

147. Borda Bortagaray, M. A.: *Morning in the Village*, 1980; oil on canvas, 90 × 70 cm

147. Bordonzotti, Alfred: *Landscape*

148. Borkowski, Mary: *The Crash*, 1968; needle painting, silk thread on silk, 40 × 98.75 cm; courtesy of Herbert Waide Hemphill, Jr., New York

149. Bos. I.: *A Summer Night's Dream*, 1982; oil on panel, 40 × 30 cm; property of the artist

149. Bottex, Jean-Baptiste: *Mary Magdalene and Jesus*, oil on hardboard; ex-collection Sheldon Williams, private collection, England

149. Borosné Endresz, Teréz: *Return*; painting on cloth, 75 × 101; property of the artist

149. Bouquet, André: *The Roofs of Gaillon*; oil on canvas, 46 × 55 cm; Musée du Vieux Château, Laval; cliché Leportier

150. Bourgeois, Jef: *The Actors of Toone Honouring the Manniken Pis*, oil on canvas, 100 × 70 cm; property of the artist

150. Boyadjian, Micheline: *The Easel*, oil on paper, 105 × 72 cm; private collection

151. Brachet, Lise: *The Path of Love*, 1981; gouache on paper, 63 × 63 cm; private collection

151. Bardley, Geoff: *The Library*; oil on hardboard; private collection, England

152. Brandes, Franz: *Miners' Choir Singing*, 1973; oil on canvas; Vestisches Museum, Recklinghausen

152. Brašić, Janko: *Portrait of a Mother*, 1935; oil on canvas, 54 × 48 cm; property of the artist

153. Braren, Oluf: *The Bride*, canvas, 168.5 × 48.5 cm; Schleswig-Holstein Staatliches Museum, Schleswig

154. Brašić, Janko: *Panic*, 1967; oil on canvas, 50 × 82 cm; Gallery of Self-taught Painters, Svetozarevo

154. Brašić, Janko: *A Fight in a Saloon*, 1960; oil on canvas, 50 × 65 cm; private collection

155. Brewster, John: *Portrait of Mr. James Eldridge*, 1795; oil on canvas, 135 × 101.25 cm; The Connecticut Historical Society, Hartford

155. Brewster, John: *Portrait of Mrs. James Eldridge*, Jr., 1795; oil on canvas, 135 × 101.25 cm; The Connecticut Historical Society, Hartford

156. Brice, Bruce: *"Shaft"*; acrylic on canvas, 61 × 76.2 cm; owned by the artist

156. Brown, Cleveland: *The Grunwick Strike*, oil on canvas; private collection, London

156. Brown, Cleveland: *The Spaghetti House Siege*, oil on canvas; private collection, London

158. Brown, Clinton: *A Son is Born*, 1978; oil on canvas board, 91.5 × 45.75 cm; Museum of Modern Art of Latin America (OAS), Washington D. C.

158. Brown, Everald: *Victory Dance*, 1976; oil on canvas board, 84 × 124.5 cm; Museum of Modern Art of Latin America (OAS), Washington D. C.

158. Buktenica, Eugen: *Boat Watchman*, 1972; oil on hardboard, 50 × 70 cm; property of the artist

159. Brown, Everald: *Ethiopian Apple*, courtesy of John Russel, Trujillo, Venezuela

159. Buktenica, Eugen: *Going to a Dance*, 1973; oil on hardboard, 50 × 70 cm; property of the artist

160. Bunjevački, Dragiša: *Honouring Rousseau*, 1971; oil on canvas, 63 × 51 cm; private collection, Belgrade

160. Bunjevački, Dragiša: *Self-portrait*, 1975; tempera on hardoard, 64 × 50 cm, private collection, Belgrade

161. Buryak, M. P.: *Gardeners Having Dinner*, 1973; gouache on paper, 61 × 86 cm;

property of the artist, near Pereslav-Khmelnitsky, the Ukraine

161. Byrne, Sam: *Block 10 Mine — Broken Hill*, enamel on board, 42 × 56 cm

C

167. Callins, Charles: *Honey Blossom Time*, oil on board, 70 × 90 cm

167. Calvo, Valerico Moral: *Buen Retiro Park*, oil on canvas; property of the artist

168. Calvo, Valerico Moral: *Recollection of History*, oil on canvas; property of the artist

169. Cameron, Barbara: *Outing on the Murray*, acrylic on canvas; 53 × 60 cm

169. Campuan, I Nyoman: *Ploughing the Rice Fields*, 1972; oil on canvas; Fowler-Mills Galleries collection, Santa Monica, USA

169. Cao Jinying: *The Whole Land Rejoices*, watercolour on paper, 100 × 40 cm; People's Art Gallery, Jin Shan

170. Cao Xiuwen: *Health Officer of the Brigade*, watercolour on paper, 70 × 50 cm; private collection, Belgrade

170. Carter, Bernard: *Waterway*, oil on canvas; private collection, London

170. Casimir, Laurent: *Cockfight*, oil on hardboard; Kurt Bachmann Collection, Costa Rica

171. Carabassa, Teresa: *Unforgettable Moment*, 1981; oil on canvas, 35 × 45 cm; private collection

172. Cedeño, José Antonio: *Baracoa*

173. Ceccarelli, Marino: *Umbrian Landscape*, 1964; oil on cardboard, 25 × 20 cm; private collection, Reggio Emilia

173. Chernyakhovsky, Ivan: *Chernyakhovsky the Uhlan*, c. 1950; oil on cardboard; S. Grigoryan collection, Kiev

173. Castain, Aimée: *View of Brousses*, oil on canvas, 110 × 132 cm; Musée du Vieux Château, Laval; cliché Leportier

174. Chernobrova, Susanna: *House with a Bush*, 1977; oil on cardboard, 15 × 15 cm, N. Shkarovskaya collection, Moscow

174. Chabauty, Malvine: *Landscape*, oil on canvas, 53 × 72.5 cm Musée de Roanne; photo Lucas

175. Chavarría, Julia: *Forest*, 1977; 37 × 56 cm; Ministry of Culture of Nicaragua, Managua

175. Chavannes, Etienne: *Market Day*, George Hurson collection, Cape Town

175. Checchi, Giuseppe de: *Jungle*, oil on canvas; private collection

176. Chen Mujun: *Ducks*, watercolour on paper, 50 × 50 cm; National Art Gallery, Husyen

177. Chereches, Alexandru: *A Rainmaker at Aruncuta*, 1976; oil on glass, 70 × 40 cm; private collection

178. Chesher, A. W.: *Steam Traction Engine*; oil on board; private collection, London

178. Chery, Jacques-Richard: *The Inauguration of la Citadelle*, oil on canvas; Morland Lee collection, England

178. Chick, Lorna: *South Wangeretta*, oil on canvas, 90 × 120 cm

179. Church, Henry: *Self-Portrait with Five Muses*, c. 1880, oil on wood pulp, 75.57 × 59.70 cm; Washburn Gallery, New York, collection of Samuel and Angela Rosenberg

180. Chvála, Josef: *St. Florian*; LITA, Bratislava

180. Cloes, Nicolas: *Vase with Flowers*, 1964; oil on panel, 32 × 41 cm; private collection

181. Coe, Clark: *Girl on a Pig*, 1910; polychromed wood, articulated, h. 92,5 cm; courtesy of Herbert Waide Hemphill, Jr., New York

182. Coelho, J. I. M.: *Man Releasing Birds*, oil on canvas, 80 × 110 cm; Charlotte, Galerie für naive Kunst, Munich

182. Coelho, J. I. M.: *The Gluttons*, oil on canvas, 58.5 × 80 cm; Charlotte, Galerie für naive Kunst, Munich

183. Cohen, Gabriel: *92 Days around the World* (first section of triptych), 1976; oil on canvas, 170 × 300 cm; Debel Gallery Collection, Jerusalem

183. Cohen, Gabriel: *Escapees from Hell*, 1979; oil on canvas, 60 × 70 cm; Debel Gallery Collection, Jerusalem

184. Colaço, Madeleine: *Candomblé Bay*, 1973; tapestry

184. Cole, Charles Frederic: *Winton Swamp*, watercolour, 50 × 70 cm

184. Cook, Beryl: *Chips*, oil on board; private collection, England

185. Convey, Tony: *Tallandoon Tin Mine*; oil on canvas, 15 × 20 cm

186. Cooper, Gladys: *The Cricket Match*; oil on wood panel, 60 × 75 cm; George Murray collection, Preston

186. Coulon, Berthe: *The Crowd*, 1968; oil on canvas, 108 × 80 cm; private collection

187. Coyle, Carlos Cortes: *Calling All Gods*, 1937; oil on canvas, 141.13 × 196.85 cm; in the collection of Berea College Art Department, Berea

187. Crepin, Benoit: *St. Joseph's Church, Martinique*; oil on canvas 40 × 52.5 cm; Musée du Vieux Château, Laval; cliché Leportier

188. Croix, Françoise de la: *Sunday in Ghent*, 1981; oil on unalite, 59 × 49 cm; private collection

188. Crociani, Emile: *Church in Vallauris*; Musée du Vieux Château, Laval; cliché Leportier

189. Crossley, Ralph: *The Fight of the World for Civilization Championship*; oil on board; collection Peter Silver, London

190. Csarejsné Hrabrovszki, Ilona: *Lunch at the "Red Dawn"*; oil on canvas, 65 × 77 cm; property of the artist

191. Csimin, József: *Weaving and Spinning*; oil on glass, 52 × 67 cm; Hungarian National Gallery, Budapest

191. Czene, Jánosné: *I Am not Selling the Colt*, 1980; oil on paper, 61.5 × 87 cm; property of the artist

D

195. Dafter, William: *Christmas*, 1971; oil on board, 42.5 × 56.25 cm; private collection, London

195. Daňko, Štefan: *Constantine the Great and St. Helen*, 1963; oil on canvas; LITA, Bratislava

196. Dapra, Regina: *Christmas Fair in Salzburg*, 1982; oil on canvas, 30 × 25 cm; private collection, West Germany

196. Davenport, Neil: *The Merry Widow*, 1981; oil on canvas, 35 × 45 cm; private collection

197. Davis, Vestie: *The Cyclone Roller Coaster*, 1970; oil on canvas, 70 × 76.2 cm; Sarah & Rebecca Bahm collection, New York

198. De Knibber, Jan: *Spacemen*, 1981; pastel, 64 × 49 cm; property of the artist

198. Déchelette, Louis-Auguste: *Les Arts, Lese-Arts, Lezards*; oil on canvas, 41 × 33 cm; Musée du Vieux Château, Laval; cliché Leportier

199. Delaporte, Roger: *St. Blaise Street and St. Germain Church*; oil on canvas, 73 × 60 cm; Musée du Vieux Château, Laval; cliché Leportier

199. Delattre, Louis: *Queen Victoria's Visit to the Church of St. Elizabeth in Ghent in 1843*

200. Delplace, Rupert: *The Road to Paradise*; oil on canvas, 80 × 60 cm; private collection, Brussels

200. Demonchy, André: *Train Passing Near Dormans*; oil on canvas, 61 × 50 cm; Musée du Vieux Château, Laval; cliché Leportier

200. Dempsey, Michael: *Couple in a Car*; oil on panel; private collection

201. Denda, Marko: *Beach in Igalo*, 1976; oil on canvas, 60 × 90 cm; property of the artist

202. Dennis, Margery: *Fern Forest*; oil on board, 55 × 45 cm

202. Deus, Wladomiro Souza de: *Slaughter*, 1975; oil on canvas, 70 × 99 cm; Gallery of Self-taught Painters, Trebnje, Yugoslavia

202. Dieckmann, Henry: *Public Urinal*, 35 × 30 cm; Vestisches Museum, Recklinghausen

203. Desnos, Ferdinand: *The Bridge of Artsor or "The Last Supper on the Seine;"* Musée National d'Art Moderne, Paris; © 1984, Copyright by A.D.A.G.P., Paris & COSMOPRESS, Geneva

203. Dévényi, Antal: *Pilisi Lake*, 1979; 35 × 50 cm; Hungarian National Gallery, Budapest

204. Dietrich, Adolf: *Porpoise*, oil on wood, 34.5 × 45 cm; collection of Prof. Fritz Novotny, Offenbach

205. Dietrich, Adolf: *In the Saloon*, 1924; oil on cardboard, 49 × 46.5 cm; Kunsthaus, Zurich

394. Lloyd, James: *Lamb;* watercolour on cardboard; private collection
395. Lloyd, James: *Feeding Time;* watercolour on cardboard; private collection
395. Löbel-Bock, Dorothea: *Iceskaters on the Lake,* 1966; oil on canvas, 50 × 50 cm; private collection, Berlin
396. Lohse, Frederico: *Manna from Heaven,* 1973
396. Lolishvili, Tenghiz: *Feasting,* 1973; watercolour, 32 × 52 cm; property of artist, Tbilisi, Georgian SSR
396. Lončarić, Dragica: *Raftsmen;* oil on canvas, 50 × 60 cm; property of the artist
397. López, Cándido: *Self-portrait,* c. 1859; oil on cardboard, 60 × 42 cm; Museo de Bellas Artes, Buenos Aires
398. López, Cándido: *Disembarkation,* 1891; oil on canvas, 48.5 × 152 cm; Museo de Bellas Artes, Buenos Aires
398. Loretian, Agavard: *An Armenian Church,* 1969; watercolour and pencil on paper, 35 × 47 cm; A. Shkarovsky-Raffe collection, Moscow
399. Lovak, Branko: *Milking Cows;* oil on glass, 55 × 60 cm; private collection, Belgrade
400. Lüthi, Hanny: *The Big Square in Winter;* oil on canvas © 1984, Copyright by A.D.A.G.P., Paris & COSMOPRESS, Geneva
400. Lubaki, Albert: *Leopard Devouring an Antelope,* watercolour, 29 × 41 cm; Galerie Dierickx, Brussels
400. Lubaki, Albert: *Woman Feeding Chickens;* watercolour, 29 × 41 cm; Galerie Dierickx, Brussels
401. Lysenko, Ivan Ivanovich: *Winter Festival in the Village of Drabovo,* 1976; oil on plywood, 42 × 52 cm; property of the artist, region of Cherkassy, the Ukraine

M

405. Maczó, Mihályné: *Threshing,* mosaic of coloured wheat seed, 58 × 85.5 cm; property of the artist
405. Maeder, Karl: *The National Park of Jungfernheide with Water Tower,* 1962; oil on wood panel, 56.5 × 63.5 cm; Institut für Auslandbeziehungen, Stuttgart
406. Magyar, Viktor: *Carnival;* oil on canvas, 60 × 50 cm; Gallery of Self-taught Artists, Trebnje
406. Mairena, Oscar: *Rural Festivity in Solentiname;* Ministry of Culture of Nicaragua, Managua
407. Ma Jali: *Drying Cotton,* watercolour on paper, 50 × 60 cm; Gallery of Folk Art, Husyen
407. Maldonado, Alex: *A Return of Christ in This Atomic Age;* oil on canvas, 35.72 × 61 cm; Ames Gallery, Bonnie Grossman, Berkley; photo Colin McRae
408. Maloney, Ellen: *Rangeville-Toowoomba;* oil on board, 90 × 120 cm
408. Mandeville, Anne: *Tree with Eggs;* private collection, Laval; cliché Leportier
409. Mandić, Petar: *Self-portrait,* 1973, oil on copperplate, 35 × 33.5 cm; Biškupić collection, Zagreb
409. Mandić, Petar: *Circumcision,* 1973; oil on canvas, 45 × 55 cm; Biškupić collection, Zagreb
410. Manoussaki, Athena: *A Tavern on a Greek Island;* oil on canvas, 45 × 30 cm;
410. Manso, Carlos: *Wedding,* 1979; oil on canvas, 40 × 60 cm; private collection
410. Maradishvili, Shalva: *A Georgian,* 1950s; oil on leather, 45 × 35 cm; The Museum of the Folk Arts of the Georgian SSR, Tbilisi
411. Maran, Anujka: *Red Horse,* 1964; oil on canvas, 45 × 66 cm; private collection, Belgrade
411. Maran, Anujka: *Procession,* 1964; oil on canvas, 80 × 100 cm; Gallery of Self-taught Painters, Svetozarevo
411. Marek, Jerzy: *Outing;* oil on panel; private collection, England
412. Marenco, Carlos: *Little Devils' Dance in Masaya;* Ministry of Culture of Nicaragua, Managua
412. Marín, Mario: *Procession of the Eucharist;* tempera on cardboard; Ministry of Culture of Nicaragua, Managua
413. Maringer, Lucien: *Confiscation,* 1971; oil on canvas, 100 × 90 cm; Galerie Racines, Brussels
413. Markakis, Antonis: *View of the Messara Plain;* oil on wood, 70.5 × 54; owned by C. Startakis, Heraklion, Crete

414. Marková, Cecilie: *Christ's Head,* 1963; oil on canvas
414. Marks, Rae: *Late Night Reading;* egg tempera, 90 × 60 cm
414. Markovits-Horváth, Antal: *King Matthew in Disguise,* 1932; woodcarving, h. 22 cm; Museum in the Rakos Palace, Budapest
415. Maruki, Suma: *The Cattle Dealer Comes to the Village,* 1945; oil on canvas, 92 × 73 cm
415. Maruki, Suma: *Animal Kingdom;* Kabusha International Ltd., Tokyo
416. Marx, Sophia: *Ball in Gürzenich*
416. Mason, Gwen: *The Intruder;* oil on board, 42 × 38 cm
417. Mastaitene, Marite: *The Shepherd,* 1980; oil on canvas
417. Matamoros, Ruperto Jay: *Bathing in the River;* courtesy of John Russell, Trujillo, Venezuela
418. Mavec-Tomljenović, Marica: *Iris and Her Pet,* 1981; oil on canvas, 70 × 50 cm
418. Maxime, Voyet: *Train Running through the Countryside,* oil on canvas, 52.5 × 71.4 cm; Musée du Vieux Château, Laval; cliché Leportier
418. Mayorga, Pablo: *Rural Homestead;* Ministry of Culture of Nicaragua, Managua
419. Mazin, Ignatii Andreievich: *Nursery,* 1932; painted carved wood, 6 × 26 × 2 cm; The Toy Museum, Zagorsk, near Moscow
419. Mazin, Ignatii Andreievich: *Working in the Old Days,* 1932; painted carved wood, 26 × 61 × 2 cm; The Toy Museum, Zagorsk, near Moscow
420. Mazin, Ignatii Andreievich: *Children Playing with Dolls in the Olden Times,* 1930s; tempera on wood; The Toys Museum, Zagorsk, near Moscow
420. Mazur, Frank: *The Wailing Wall,* 1972; unglazed terra-cotta, approximately 30.48 × 50.80 cm; courtesy of the artist, Brooklyn
421. McCarthy, Justin: *Ava Gardner,* 1944; oil on canvas, 40.64 × 30.48 cm; courtesy Herbert W. Hemphill, Jr., New York
421. McCarthy, Justin: *George Washington Crossing the Delaware,* c. 1963; oil on masonite, 70 × 122 cm
422. McClaren, Sydney: *Creative Imagination,* 1977; mixed media, 73.66 × 104.14 cm; courtesy Museum of Modern Art of Latin America (OAS), Washington D. C.
422. Mehkek, Martin: *The Servant;* oil on glass, 30 × 40 cm; private collection, Belgrade
423. Meijer, Sal: *Toren Dike in Amsterdam,* 1937; oil on canvas, 48 × 44 cm; Galerie Mokum collection, Amsterdam
424. Mejia, Godoy Armando: *Cockfight;* Ministry of Culture of Nicaragua, Managua
424. Mejo, Oscar de: *Women's Lib,* 1978; acrylic on canvas-board, 61 × 46 cm; private collection, New York
425. Meliashvili, Ivan: *The Poet Vazha Pshavela with Family,* 1979; oil on cardboard mounted on plywood, 58 × 61 cm; The Museum of the Folk Arts of the Georgian SSR, Tbilisi
425. Mentrup, Anna: *Windmill on a Pond*
426. Messinger, Menachem: *Birds* (detail)
426. Metelli, Orneore: *The Venus of Terni,* 1935; oil on cardboard, 69 × 48.5 cm; Aurelio de Felice collection, Terni
426. Metelli, Orneore: *Procession in Collescipoli,* 1938; oil on canvas, 64 × 93 cm; private collection, Terni
427. Metelli, Orneore: *Blessing Animals,* 1935, oil on canvas; private collection
428. Michałowska, Marta: *Portrait of Mother,* 1965; oil on chipboard, 52 × 36 cm; Aleksander Jackowski collection
428. Michelis, Effie: *Square in Heraklion,* 1967; casein on masonite, 73 × 100 cm
428. Middle Art: *The Manager in Charge,* oil on cardboard, 186.5 × 61 cm; Ulli Beier collection, Bayreuth
429. Middle Art: *Suffering Stages of Life,* oil on hardboard, 60 × 90 cm; collection Gunter Péus, Hamburg
430. Mihuț, Petru: *Making Jam,* 1975; oil on canvas, 40 × 70 cm; Institute for Ethnography and Dialectological Research, Bucharest
430. Millán, Carmen: *Women,* 1971; oil on canvas, 110 × 77.5 cm; permanent collection Museum of Modern Art of Latin America (OAS) Washington D. C.
431. Millán, Victor: *The Jungle,* 1972; oil on canvas, 107.5 × 140 cm; permanent collection

Museum of Modern Art of Latin America (OAS) Washington D. C.
431. Millán, Victor: *Adam and Eve,* 1974; oil on canvas, 162.5 × 118.75 cm
431. Miller, Anthony: *The Bedroom,* 1969; tinted drawing on cardboard; George Murray collection, Preston
432. Miller, Louisa: *Boy in Blue,* 1960—1965; oil on canvas, 151.13 × 60.96 cm; courtesy Viterbo College, La Crosse, Wisconsin
432. Milts, Elfrida Martsovna: *Bird Market on Trubnaya Place in Moscow,* 1973; gouache on paper, 50 × 70 cm; ZNUI collection, Moscow
433. Milojević, Dobrosav: *Goats around the Monastery,* 1973; oil on canvas, 59 × 49 cm; Gallery of Self-taught Painters, Svetozarevo
433. Mironova, Yelizaveta Fiodorovna: *The Cossack Mamai,* 1973; gouache on paper, 50 × 70 cm; property of the artist; Kiev, Ukrainian SSR
434. Mitrăchiță, Ghiță: *Peasant Wedding in Oltenia,* 1969; oil on canvas, 40 × 70 cm; Council for Socialist Culture and Education collection, Bucharest
435. Mitrakas, Yannis: *The Saints of the Underground,* 1983; egg tempera on wood, 30.5 × 15.6 cm; owned by Angela Tamvaki, Athens
435. Mitrakas, Yannis: *Lost Fatherland;* egg tempera on wood, 57.6 × 87.2 cm
435. Moke Art, P.: *Bandundu,* 1975; oil on canvas, 105 × 93 cm; Jochan R. Klicker collection, Berlin
436. Mokry-Mészáros, Dezsö: *Life on Alien Planet,* 1910; oil on cardboard, 26 × 32 cm; Hungarian National Gallery, Budapest
436. Mokry-Mészáros, Dezsö: *A Place to Stay;* oil on cardboard, 36.5 × 40 cm; Hungarian National Gallery, Budapest
437. Monsiel, Edmund: *God the Father,* 1956
437. Moore, Ross: *Desert Lake;* acrylic on canvas, 20 × 30 cm
438. Moraitis, Zapheiris: *Untitled;* casein on granite with mortar; left by the artist in a court in Chalkidike, Northern Greece
438. Morales, Elsa: *Waiting for a Happy Day;* courtesy of John Russell, Trujillo, Venezuela
439. Morgan, Gertrude: *Christ is the Head of this House;* crayon, coloured pencil and watercolour, courtesy of Herbert Waide Hemphill, Jr., New York
439. Moreno, Rafael: *Backyard in Marianao;* Collection of José Gómez-Sicre, Washington D. C., courtesy Museum of Modern Art of Latin America (OAS), Washington D. C., photo Angel Hurtado
440. Moses, Kivetoruk: *The Medicine Man and the "Cutter Bear,"* 1965; ink wash with colour on illustration board, 26.67 × 39.47 cm; courtesy Elgton of Aegstrom, Juneau, Alaska
440. Motoroẑesku, Mariora: *Carnival Time,* 1966; oil on canvas, 50 × 70 cm; private collection, Belgrade
441. Mraz, Franjo: *At the Well,* 1974; oil on glass, 50 × 65 cm; private collection, Belgrade
441. Mraz, Franjo: *Springtime;* oil on glass, 50 × 70 cm; property of the artist
442. Mucha, Szczepan: *Demons,* c. 1970; wood, 80 × 140 cm; Ludwig Zimmerer collection, Warsaw
443. Müller, Johannes: *Taking the Livestock to Highland Pastures,* c. 1860; oil on wood, 27.4 × 42.8 cm; private property
444. Murray, Andrew: *Daniel in the Lion's Den;* acrylic on canvas; private collection
444. Murayev, Mikhail Vladimirovich: *My Parents Drinking Tea,* 1950s; oil on cardboard, 30 × 40 cm; N. Shkarovskaya collection, Moscow
445. Musch, Jean Louis: *Never Again,* 1981; oil on glass, 45 × 55 cm; private collection
445. Mususa, Pungu: *Portraits of Ch. Hénault and J. M. Lahoye,* 1973; oil on canvas, 87 × 66 cm; Galerie Dierickx, Brussels

N

449. Nadera, Ida Bagus Made: *Village Scene,* 1930; chinese ink on paper; Puri Lukisan collection, Ubud, Bali
449. Nalivaikene-Yonelite, Jadviga: *Odessa Port in 1918,* 1965; oil on canvas, 130 × 112 cm; The State Art Museum of the Lithuanian SSR, Vilnius

502. Repnik, Anton: *People from the Poorhouse*, 1972; oil on canvas, 68 × 87 cm; owned by Nebojša-Bato Tomašević, Belgrade

502. Riec, Raymond: *Endymion's Slumber*, oil on canvas, 73 × 100 cm; Musée du Vieux Château, Laval; cliché Leportier

503. Řehák, Antonín: *Karlsbad* (View from the Pension Aleš) oil on canvas, 78 × 88.5 cm; Prof. Fritz Novotny collection, Offenbach

504. Rigas, Yorgos: *Threshing*; oil on canvas, 60 × 90 cm; owned by A. Tamvaki, Athens

504. Ristić, Petar: *The Pipe Player*; oil on glass, 50 × 50 cm; private collection, Belgrade

505. Riauba, Stasis: *Master Craftsman*, 1970; painted, carved wood; Archives of the Folk Arts Methods Centre of the Lithuanian SSR, Vilnius

505. Roda, I Nyoman: *Barong Landung*, 1979; oil on canvas; owned by the artist

506. Rodríguez. José: *The Kiss*; courtesy of John Russell, Trujillo, Venezuela

507. Rodríguez, Manases: *The Mad Woman*, 1971; oil on canvas, 60 × 62 cm

507. Roggeri, Toni: *St. Francis*, 1976; oil on canvas, 35 × 35 cm; private collection, Reggio Emilia

507. Roeder, John: *Bay with Islands*, c. 1948; oil on plywood, 50 × 72.7 cm; private collection, California

507. Roughsey, Dick: *Willy Long at Mushroom Gallery*; acrylic on canvas, 20 × 24 cm

509. Rousseau, Henri: *The Sleeping Gipsy*, 1897; oil on canvas, 129.5 × 200.7 cm; The Museum of Modern Art, New York, gift of Mrs. Simon Guggenheim

510. Rousseau, Henri: *Portrait of a Woman*, 1897; oil on canvas, 200 × 115 cm; Musée Jeu de Paume, Paris

510. Rousseau, Henri: *Child with Puppet*, 1903; oil on canvas, 101 × 81 cm; Kunstmuseum, Winterthur

511. Rousseau, Henri: *The Dream of Yadwiga*, 1910; oil on canvas, 204.5 × 298.5 cm; The Museum of Modern Art, New York, gift of Nelson A. Rockefeller

512. Rovesti, Bruno: *Hillside Village*, 1962; oil on hardboard, 23 × 27 cm; D. Menozzi collection, Reggio Emilia

512. Roy, Louis: *Clocktower in Rochelle*, oil on canvas, 46 × 55 cm; Musée de la Rochelle

512. Rubashkin, Samuil Jakovlevich: *Succoth*, 1974; oil on canvas, 80 × 121 cm; property of the artist's widow, I. Mesnyankina, Moscow

513. Ruan Zhangjun: *Water Bells*, watercolour on paper, 60 × 80 cm; Gallery of People's Art, Jin Shan

514. Ruggeri, Alfredo: *Small Town*

514. Rusewicz, Michał: *A Couple in Highland Clothes*, 1980; oil on chipboard, 58 × 60 cm; State Ethnographic Museum, Warsaw

514. Rzhevsky, Nikolai Alexeievich: *View of Courtyard and Lane*, 1973; oil on cardboard, 69 × 73 cm; ZNUI collection, Moscow

515. Rybkowski, Władysław: *Kingdom in the Jungle*, 1967; oil on plywood, 42 × 63 cm; Ludwig Zimmerer collection

S

519. Saldaña, Rafael: *St. Francis* (part of a triptych); oil on canvas, 2 panels 37 × 32 cm; 1 panel 45 × 32 cm

519. Samba, Wa Nbimba Nizinga: *The Artist Samba and the Siren*, 1978; oil on canvas, 109 × 120 cm; collection Galerie Dierickx, Brussels

520. Savakis, Yorgos: *Carnival at the Monument of Lyssicrates*, oil on canvas, 60 × 80 cm; private collection, Athens

520. Savić, Krsto: *The Swineherd*, 1960; tempera on paper, 31.5 × 51 cm; Gallery of Self-taught Painters, Svetozarevo

521. Savinov, Vasili Timofeievich: *Moujik (Beehive)*, early 20th century; painted carved wood; The State History Museum, Moscow

521. Savitsky, Jack: *The Miner's Week*, 1968; oil on board, 30.48 × 76.20 cm; courtesy of Mr. and Mrs. Elias Getz, Landsford, Pennsylvania, photo Eeva-Inkeri

522. Savu, Alexandru: *On the Sabar River*, 1975; oil on canvas, 40 × 70 cm; Collection of the Institute for Ethnographic and Dialectological Research

522. Scarborough, Joe: *Two Tram-Cars*; oil on canvas; private collection, London

523. Schaar, Monique: *Memory of a Journey*, 1979; oil on canvas, 55 × 100 cm; private collection, Brussels

524. Schepis, Angelo Armando Cassavia: *The Ball*; acrylic; photo Patrice Fury

524. Schilling, Heinrich: *Harbour*, 1960; oil on canvas, 32.5 × 41 cm; owned by the artist

524. Schmit, Ilona: *Church at Kloeting*, 1978; oil on canvas, 100 × 80 cm; private collection, Mijrecht

525. Schmidtová, Natalie: *Dreams of the South Seas*; oil on paper, 48.5 × 67.5 cm; Prof. Fritz Novotny collection, Offenbach

526. Schmitt, Hans: *Human Being and Sunflower*, 1969; wall relief, painted wood, height 78.5 cm

526. Schulz, Elfride-Maria: *In the Bedroom*, 1965; gouache, 52 × 75 cm; Vestisches Museum, Recklinghausen

526. Schumann, Günter: *The Chemie Leipzig Football Team*

527. Schumann, Günter: *Giraffe Named "Longlegged Emma"*

528. Schwartzenberg, Simon: *Paris. Place de la République*; oil on canvas, 81 × 73 cm; Prof. Fritz Novotny collection, Offenbach

528. Seemann, Fritz: *The Yellow Villa*, 1968; oil on cardboard, 60 × 50 cm; Vestisches Museum, Recklinghausen

529. Seifert, Max: *Threshing Wheat*, oil on canvas 56 × 72 cm; Vestisches Museum, Recklinghausen

529. Selivanov, Ivan Yegorovich: *Self-portrait*, 1972; oil on canvas, 71 × 55,5 cm; The Museum of Folk and Amateur Art of the Russian Federation, Suzdal

530. Serafini, Giuseppe: *Peasant*, 1973; special technique on cardboard, 50 × 70 cm; private collection, Florence

530. Séraphine, Louis: *Tree of Paradise*, c. 1929; oil on canvas, 229 × 195 cm; National Museum of Modern Art, Paris; ©1984, Copyright by A.D.A.G.P., Paris & COSMOPRESS, Geneva

531. Sergeyev, Grigori Sergeievich: *River Crossing in 1919*, 1977; oil on canvas, 48 × 70 cm; property of the artist, Kherson, the Ukraine

531. Sgro, Mercurio: *Going Downtown*; oil on canvas, 45 × 30 cm; private collection

532. Shalom of Safed: *Exodus*, 1966; acrylic on canvas, 52 × 91.4 cm; private collection, Daniel Doron, New York

532. Shen Dexian: *The Artificial Pearls*, watercolour on paper, 40 × 50 cm; Gallery of People's Art, Jin Shan

533. Šijaković, Djordje: *In Search of Happiness*; oil on board, 30 × 50 cm; property of the artist's widow

533. Šilhán, Václav: *Maya*, 1966; oil on canvas; LITA, Bratislava

534. Silva, Francisco Domingos da: *Intruder*

534. Silva, Marina: *The Cove*; Ministry of Culture of Nicaragua, Managua

535. Sirković, Stepa: *Wedding*, 1970; oil on canvas, 50 × 80 cm; Gallery of Self-taught Painters, Svetozarevo

535. Siváň, Štefan: *Flight into Egypt*, 1973; carved wood; owned by Ignac Kolčak, LITA, Bratislava

535. Skoulas, Alkiviadis: *Village Scene*, oil on novopan; 60 × 100 cm; property of C. Stavrekanis, Heraklion

536. Skurjeni, Matija: *Trains Passing*, 1970; oil on canvas, 55 × 70 cm; property of the artist

537. Skurjeni, Matija: *Animal Kingdom*, 1961; oil on canvas, 50 × 100 cm; Prof. Fritz Novotny collection, Offenbach

538. Sleep, Joseph: *Untitled*, c. 1976; oil on canvas, 60 × 74 cm; Dalhousie University Art Gallery, Halifax, Nova Scotia

538. Sloot, Jentje van der: *Hotel in Friesland*, c. 1962; oil on canvas, 80 × 90 cm; private collection, Amsterdam

539. Smajić, Petar: *My Family*, 1961; painted wood, h. 46.5 cm; Gallery of Primitive Art, Zagreb

540. Smirnov, Vladimir Borisovich: *Square*, 1973; watercolour and gouache on paper, 35 × 50 cm; N. Shkarovskaya collection, Moscow

540. Sobota, Józef: *Home Altars*, 1972—73; carved wood; Zimmerer collection, Warsaw

541. Sodang, Ida Bagus: *Women Bathing*, 1937; chinese ink on paper, 31.25 × 43.75 cm; Fowler-Mills Galleries Collection, Santa Monica, USA

541. Söhl, Manfred: *Two Sailors in St. Pauli*, 1970; oil on canvas, 30 × 24 cm; Vestisches Museum, Recklinghausen

542. Sokol, Ana: *Adam and Eve*, 1965; oil on canvas, 80 × 100 cm; private collection

542. Sokol, Jan: *The Funeral*, 1966; oil on canvas, 50 × 70 cm; Gallery of Self-taught Painters, Svetozarevo

543. Soomer, Jeanne de: *Football Game*, 1978; acrylic on panel; 40 × 50 cm; property of the artist

543. Soy, Ancent: *Kenyatta*, 1967; oil on cardboard; 50 × 35 cm; Rolf Jahrling collection, Weidingen

543. Sówka, Erwin: *The Queen of Sheba*, 1973; oil on canvas, 55.5 × 91 cm; Ludwig Zimmerer collection, Warsaw

544. Spasić, Čeda: *Gipsy Wedding*, oil on canvas, 80 × 100 cm; owned by the artist

544. Spatharis, E.: *The Hero Athanassios Diakos*, 1972; tempera, 99 × 69 cm; National Gallery, Athens

545. Spencer, Sam: *Charlie Conachor*, 1930; polychrome wood carving, 48.13 × 35 cm

545. Spielbichler, Franz: *The Ice-skating Rink*; oil on wood, 41 × 62 cm; Prof. Fritz Novotny collection, Offenbach

546. Stanisavljević, Dragiša: *Christ Crucified*, woodcarving, 150 × 60 cm

546. Staničić, Matija: *Woman with Flowers*, 1980; watercolour on paper, 100 × 70 cm; private collection, Belgrade

547. Stanisavljević, Dragiša: *Spacemen*; wood, h. 123 cm; owned by the artist

548. Stanisavljević, Milan: *The Wedding-Dirge*, 1967; wood, h. 210 cm; Ethnographic Museum, Belgrade

548. Stanisavljević, Milan: *Self-Creation*, 1977; oakwood, height 325 cm, width 110 cm; Hotel "Jugoslavija," Belgrade, property of the artist

549. Stapel, Rudolf: *Winter in Westphalia*, 1971; gouache, 31.5 × 41 cm; Institut für Auslandbeziehungen, Stuttgart

549. St. Brice, Robert: *Queen Erzulle*, 1957; courtesy of the Musée d'Art Haïtien du Collège St. Pierre, Port-au-Prince

550. Šteberl, Ondrej: *Šteberl Arrives in Heaven*, 1973; oil on canvas, 118 × 118 cm; private collection, Hannover

550. Šteberl, Ondrej: *The Couple*; oil on canvas, 53.4 × 34 cm; Prof. Fritz Novotny collection, Offenbach

551. Steinmann, Heinz: *Cape York Fantasy*; acrylic on board

552. Stepanov, Sergei Georgievich: *State Farm Woman Worker Ozhogin with Cucumber*, 1976; oil on cardboard, 70 × 50 cm; property of the artist, Orsk near Orenburg, Siberia

552. Stephane, Micius: *Scaring off Birds*; oil on board; Kurt Bachmann collection, Costa Rica

553. Stern, Emma: *Return from Work*, 1956; oil on canvas, 46 × 65 cm; Institut für Auslandbeziehungen, Stuttgart

553. Stevanović, Dobrivoje: *Fire in the Village*, 1981; oil on canvas, 50 × 70 cm; Gallery of Self-taught Painters, Svetozarevo

553. Stern, Emma: *Family Supper*, 1976; oil on canvas, 54 × 64 cm; Eisenmann collection, Böblingen

554. Stewart, Eric: *Legend of Everlasting Water*; oil on canvas, 45 × 75 cm

554. Stubbs, Douglas: *Farmer and Friends*; oil on board, 60 × 90 cm

554. Sturza, Gheorghe: *Wedding in the Country*, 1974; oil on cardboard, 70 × 40 cm; private collection

555. Su Junliang: *Drying Hot Peppers*, watercolour on paper, 50 × 80 cm; Gallery of People's Art, Husyen

556. Süli, András: *Family at Lunch*, 1935; oil on paper, 50 × 66 cm; Hungarian National Gallery, Budapest

556. Sutor, Edward: *Figure*, c. 1970; stone and wood, height 90 cm; Ludwig Zimmerer collection, Warsaw

556. Sullivan, Patrick J.: *Haunts in Totalitarian Woods*, 1939; oil on canvas, 50.80 × 70.7 cm; Sidney Janis Gallery, New York

557. Sund, Meike: *People of Gorinchen*, 1978; oil on canvas, 30 × 55 cm; private collection, Utrecht

557. Svoboda, Jakub: *An Old Gipsy Settlement*, 1903; oil on canvas

558. Szczypawka-Ptaszynska, Helena: *Sculpture*, c. 1960; polychrome wood, 10 × 60 cm; Ludwig Zimmerer collection

727

Artists According to Country

The artists marked with an asterisk are included in the biographical section.

AFRICA
see

ETHIOPIA
GHANA
KENYA
NIGERIA
SENEGAL
TANZANIA
TUNISIA
UGANDA
UPPER VOLTA
ZAIRE

ARGENTINA

Aguirre, Susana
* Borda Bortagaray, María Adelia
* Carabassa, Teresa
* Fernández, Marcelina
* Frías, Gato
* Fuentes, Gloria
* Ledesma, Valerio
* López, Cándido
* Manso, Carlos
* Sgro, Mercurio
* Sokol, Ana
* Szabó, Aniko
* Torrezapico, José

AUSTRALIA

Absalom, John
* Archer, Jimmy
* Bastin, Henry
* Blair, Oswald
* Byrne, Sam
* Callins, Charles
* Cameron, Barbara
* Chick, Lorna
* Cole, Charles Frederic
* Convey, Tony
Cook, James
Crooke, Diana
Daens, Mady
* Dennis, Margery
Deuchar, Seafield
Dilger, Stella
* Dorothy, Sister
* Fardoulys, James
* Fennel, Vera
* Fielding, David
Friend, Priscilla
* Graham, Anne
Hart, Pro
* Higgins, Roma

* Hirsch, Emma
* Jones, Dee
* Jones, Frances
Kele, S. W.
Kendall, George
* Lister, Mathilda
Litherland, Victor
Luders, Muriel
* Maloney, Ellen
* Marks, Rae
* Mason, Gwen
Minchin, Eric
* Moore, Ross
Morley, Sandra
Pickup, John
Pinkus, Lulu
Rathbone, George
Renner, Hilde
Rojahn, Beryl
* Roughsey, Dick
* Saldaña, Rafael
Schulz, Hugh
* Steinmann, Heinz
Steinmann, Evelyn
* Stewart, Eric
* Stubbs, Douglas
Todd, Milan
* Warren, Selby
* Watters, Max
* Yaxley, W. E.

AUSTRIA

* Dapra, Regina
Falzeder, Rupert
* Geyer, Rudolf
Knapp, Heinz
* Kratochwil, Siegfried
Muthspiel, Agnes
* Pachta, Josef
* Posz, Maria de
Satzer, Alexander
Schmidt, Oskar
* Spielbichler, Franz
Tham, Otto
* Vladimir (Bedeniković)

BELGIUM

Abeele, Albijn van den
Baivier, Adolphe
* Bastin, Mireille
* Batardy, Marie-Louise
Bellin, Léon
Bohet, Gabriel
* Bos I.
* Bourgeois, Jef
* Boyadjian, Micheline
* Brachet, Lise
Canpin, Joseph
Christiaens, Desiré

* Cloes, Nicolas
Collier, Adolphus
* Coulon, Berthe
Cremers, Jeanne
* Croix, Françoise de la
Damien, Théophile
* De Knibber, Jan
* Delattre, Louis
Delabois, Edmond
* Delplace, Rupert
Devalck, Jan
Driessche, Ernest van den
Eismann, Elke
* Faucq, Jean
* Ferdinand, Jean
Frison, Nadine
Funcken, Armand
Funcken, Françoise
Gabriel, Jean-Hubert
* Gérard, Françoise
* Greffe, Léon
Hacter, Luc van
Haro, Léopold
Hostier, Jean-Pierre
Howet, Jules
Joris, Ferdinand
* Ker Hove
* Lecossois, Victor
* Lefèvre, Pierre
Loffet, Josette
Machri
Malpas, Gilles Jean Nicolas
* Maringer, Lucien
Maximin, Incolle
Maxy
Mergeay, Jean Baptiste
Metsenaere, François de
* Musch, Jean-Louis
Nöel, Alfred
Ombraux, Maurice de
Paepen, Carolus
Palotay, Nicolette
Pedoux, Celeste
* Pepersack, Louise
Plancq, Lucien
Provost, Michel (Mikke)
Ruelle
* Sauter, Alois
* Schaar, Monique
* Soomer, Jeanne de
Thonon, Noëlle
Thumerel, Reine
Thurion, Guillaume
* Trebla
Tytgat, Edgar
* Wattyne, Jacques van de

BOLIVIA

* Baptista, Carmen
Favre, Indiana Reque Teram de

* Jordán, Armando
* Villazón, Vega Carmen

BRAZIL

"Alexandre Filho"
d'Amico, Fourpone Teresa
* Andrade, Moacir Couto de
* Andrade, Neuton Freitas de
* Auxiliadora, Maria Silva da
Barbosa, Antonio Silva da
Barbosa, Jose Silva da
Brennand, Francisco
"Calasans Neto"
Carvalho, Nair de
* Colaco, Madeleine
* Deus, Waldomiro Souza de
Dias, Antonio
* "Djanira" da Mota e Silva
* Elsa, Oliveira Souza de
Feitosa, Carlos Roberto Soares
* Freitas, Jose de
Gerson, Alves Souza de
* "Gilvan", Paulo
* Heil, Eli Malvina
* "Iaponi", Soares de Araujo
Iracema
* "Ivonaldo" Veloso de Melo
* Jesus, Isabel de
* "Juca" Ovídio Melo
Leal, Paolo Pedro
Lino, Mary
Luz, Edson Benicio da
Maia, Antonio
Milton, Ligia
"Miriam"
Morais, Crisaldo Assuncao de
* Pinto, José
Scaldaferri, Sante
* Schepis, Angelo Armando Cassavia
Segreccia, Vicente Roberto
* Silva, Francisco Domingo da
"Silvia" (de Leon Charleo)
Teixeira, Floriano Araujo de
* Teles, Ladario Ribeiro
Valentim, Rubem
Wladimir, Paulo
Xando, Niobe Nogeira
* "Zu Campos" Jesuino

CANADA

* Anonymous
Barker, Sydney H.
Bouchard, Simone Mary
Coates, Richard
* Gendron, Ernest
* Oad, Jan
* Picket, Sarah
* Sleep, Joseph
* Spencer, Sam
Steward, William N.
* Wyers, Jan

CHILE

Aciares, Julio
* "Arpilleras"
Bermúdez, M. Luisa
* Guevara, Luis Herrera
Inostroza, Marinero
* Lecaros, Juana Izquierdo
* Lohse, Frederico
Parra, Violeta
Pino, Alberto Jerez
San Martin, Fortunato

CHINA

* Cao Jinying
* Cao Xiuwen
* Chen Mujun
Dong Zhengyi
Feng Zhengxing
He Fangquan
Ji Fang
* Jiang Guohong
Jiao Caiyun
Liu Xuxu
* Ma Jali
* Ruan Zhangjun
* Shen Dexian
Sjao Chenzjan
* Su Junliang
* Tu Jianrong
* Wang Jinxi
* Wen Zhijiang
* Wu Shenggin
* Xia Zengqiang
* Xu Hengke
* Xue Deliang
* Zhang Fenying
* Zhong Dexiang
* Zhu Xi

CUBA

* Acevedo, F. I.
* Armas, Armando de
* Bermúdez, Mario
* Cedeno, José Antonio
* Duarte, Benjamín
* Iniguez, Silvio
* Matamoros, Ruperto Jay
* Moreno, Rafael
* Nuez, Gilberto de la
* Ortiz, Benito
* Rodriguez, José
Saurina, Alejandro
* Valdés, Simón

CYPRUS

* Kkassialos, Michail

CZECHOSLOVAKIA

* Beer, Alois
* Beneš, Alois
* Beránek, Václav
Chaba, Karel
Chlupač, V.
* Chwála, Josef
Černi, K.
* Daňko, Štefan
Filipová, Marie
Fulla, L.
Galando, M.
* Guttmann, Robert
* Halák, Petr
* Hlinomaz, Josef
* Hruška, Jan
Hubaček, Zigmunt
* Janků, Marie
* Jaurisová, Helena
* Jurovatý, Ladislav
Karasek, A.
* Kerák, Josef
Kemko, Josef
* Kochol, Ľudovit
Kolinska, J.
Komarek, V.

Kudera, Václav
* Lauko, Juraj
* Ličková, Anna
* Marková, Cecilie
Matoušek, V.
Michálek, F.
Musatov, Grigorij
* Pařik, Antonín
Pokorná, L.
* Procházková, Ludmila
* Řeha, Viktor
* Řehák, Antonín
* Schmidtová, Natalie
Sekal, Z.
* Šilhán, Václav
Šitalova, M.
* Siváň, Štefan
Srncova, Emma
* Šteberl, Ondrej
* Svoboda, Jakub
Vadura Billek, Alena
Valičkova, M.
* Viraghová, Zuzana
* Žák, Václav
* Zelenka, Horymír
Zemánková, Anna
Zrzavý, Jan

ETHIOPIA

* Anonymous
Tena, Solomon

FRANCE

Antigore, Baglione
Arcambot, Jean-Pierre
* Bauchant, André
Bell, Narcisse
* Benoit, Jacqueline
* Blondel, Emile
Boilauges, Ferdinand
* Boiron, Rose
* Bombois, Camille
* Bonnin, Maurice
* Bouquet, André
Bray, Ernest
* Castain, Aimée
Caillaud, Aristide
* Chabauty, Malvina
* Crepin, Benoit
* Crociani, Emile
* Déchelette, Louis-Auguste
* Delaporte, Roger
* Demonchy, André
Desir, Jean
* Desnos, Ferdinand
* Donati, Valentina
* Eve, Jean
* Favier, Cécile
* Favre, Marcel
* Ferrara, Daniel
* Fiorio, Serge
* Fortin, Edmond
* Fous, Jean
Freset, Georges
Furnier
* Grand-Mère Paris
Gratio, Sylviane
"Grim" (Maurice Grimaldi)
* Grossin, Fernande
* Guilleminot, René
* Guiraud, Jean-Baptiste
Guisol, Henri
* Hennin, Gaston
Hondry

* Jean-Jean, Léopold
Laforge, Adolphe
* Lagru, Dominique
Lamy, Marcel
Laplau, Gérard
Leclerc, Maurice
* Lefranc, Jules
Loirand, Maurice
* Mandeville, Anne
Masduraud, Robert
* Maxime Voyet
Molette, Jean
* Parade, Madeleine
Peyrade, Geneviève
* Peyronnet, Dominique
Pincon, Charles Lucien
Pincour, Marie
Rayb (Bussereau, Raymond)
* Riec, Raymond
* Rimbert, René
* Rousseau, Henri
* Roy, Louis
Salaun, André
Schubnel, Jean
* Schwartzenberg, Simon
Sénéchal, Marcel
* Séraphine
Simone le Moigne
* Trouillard, Henri
* Trovic, Jacques
* Van Der Steen, Germain
* Vieillard, Lucien
* Vivin, Louis

EAST GERMANY

(GERMAN DEMOCRATIC REPUBLIC)

Domschke, Marie
* Ebert, Albert
* Ehm, Ernst
Glöckner, Peter Michael
* Händel, Helene
Kaiser, Ernst
Kaiser, Johanna
* Klinger, Emil
* Mayerl, Willibald
Schadewitz, Sh. F.
Schönberg, Ewald
* Schumann, Günter
* Walther-Visino, Therese
* Weber, Rudolf Felix

WEST GERMANY

(FEDERAL REPUBLIC OF GERMANY)

* Abels, Jean
* Auer, Hildegard
* Balet, Jan
Bartens, Margarethe
Bauer, Elisabeth
* Becker, Hermann
Behr, Peter
* Bock, Ida
* Bödeker, Erich
* Brandes, Franz
* Braren, Oluf
Brucherseifer, Edmund
Byesse, Walter
* Dieckmann, Henry
Eilers, Michael
Eing, Ria
* Ellis, Vivian
Emhardt, Erna

Encke, Charlotte
* Ennulat, Minna
* Epple, Bruno
* Erkens, Sofia
Fabula (Waltraud, Freyberger)
Fehrie-Menrad, Klara
Fischer, Leonhard
* Frassa, Luise
* Garde, Silvia
* Gerlach, Friedrich
* Gerlach, Ludwig
* Goossens, Cornelius
* Grams, Erich
* Grimmeisen, Franz Josef
Guth, Gertraud
* Habeth, Maria
Hennecke, Dodo
Herbst, Renate
* Hertmann, Karl
* Hurm, Karl
* Kazmierczak, Karl Eduard
Kirchner, Margarethe
* Klekawka, Franz
Klose, Hermine
* Kloss, Maria
Koal
* Koehn, Hans
* Krauss, Gerlinde
* Kreitmeir, Lisa
* Kunert, Maja
Küster, Erich
Landsiedel-Eicken, Rosemarie
* Löbel-Bock, Dorothea
* Maeder, Karl
* Marx, Sophia
* Mentrup, Anna
Mis, Johann
Nix, Wilhelm
* Odenthal, Eduard
* Palleta, Karl Borro
* Paps (Waldemar Rusche)
* Raffler, Max
* Ramholz, Felix (Muche)
Rupp
S. Anita
Schächl, Michael
Schad, Klara
* Schilling, Heinrich
Schmidt, Adolf
* Schmitt, Hans
Schöller, Ernst
Schröder-Sonnenstern, Friedrich
* Schulz, Elfride-Maria
* Seemann, Fritz
* Seifert, Max
* Söhl, Manfred
* Stapel, Rudolf
Steen, Gerhard
* Stefula, Dorothea
* Stefula, György
* Stern, Emma
* Thegen, Carl Christian
Thewissen, Karl-Heinz
* Trillhaase, Adalbert
* Tschistjakow, Aleksej Nikolaewitsch
* Valerius, Max
* Voigt, Friederike
* Weert, Jan van
Weghaus, Heinrich
* Wimmer, Alfons
Wirschin, Josef
* Wittlich, Josef
Woltering, Anton

GHANA

Fabunmi, Adebisi
* Imperial, Falade

King Anthony
Prince Anthony

GREAT BRITAIN

* Abba, (Florence Abba Derbyshire)
* Allen, Elizabeth
* Allin, John
* Baird, Margaret
* Baring, Mark
Barker, Kenneth Dow
* Barker, Noel
Bates, Ralf
* Beckles, Gillian
* Bensted, John
Bond, Frances G.
Box, Eden
* Bradley, Geoff
Bradley, Helen
* Brown, Cleveland
Burne, Patrick
* Carter, Bernard
Carter, Jas
* Chesher, A. W.
* Cook, Beryl
* Cooper, Gladys
* Crossley, Ralph
* Dafter, William
* Davenport, Neil
Drakin, John
* Dempsey, Michael
Dodson, Tom
Gardham, Richard
Gill, Madge
* Goulding, Arthur
Haddelsey, Vincent
* Halsband, Gertrude
Harmer, Harry
* Hessing, Perle
* Holman, Betty
* Holzhandler, Dora
* Johnson, Taploe
* Korn, Halina
* Leman, Martin
* Lloyd, James
Lyon, Toby
* Marek, Jerzy
Maurer, Moshe
Maynard, Bill
* Miller, Anthony
Mitchell, Lewis
* Murray, Andrew
Newell, Wendy
Newman, Tom
O' Connor, Barry
* Oddie, Harry
O' Neil, Captain Michael
* Page, Derold
Parafimos, A. G.
* Pearce, Bryan
Perry, Henry
* Pic
* Pinder, George
Reardon, Laetitia
* Scarborough, Joe
Smith, Sam
Stockley, Henry
Taylor, Jack
Timaeus, Romaine
* Towers, William
* Wallis, Alfred
* Ware, Chris
Williams, Florence
Willcox, Ted
* Wilson, Scottie

Made, Ida Bagus
Mandra, I Nyoman
Meregeg, Anak Agung Gede
Mokoh, Ida Bagus
* Nadera, Ida Bagus Made
Ngendon, I
Oka, Cokorda
Pasek, I Dewa Kompiang
Patera, I
* Pugug, I Made
Radjin, I Wayan
Rai, Ida Bagus
* Roda, I Nyoman
Rundu, I Gusti Made
Soberat, Anak Agung Gede
* Sodang, Ida Bagus
Todjiwa, I Wayan
* Togog, Ida Bagus Made
Tombelos, I
* Widja, Ida Bagus Made

IRELAND

* Dixon, James
* O' Brien, Patricia

ISRAEL

* Cohen, Gabriel
Damari, Shoshana
Elnatan, Moshe
Geiger, Joseph Zvi
* Heber, Natan
Janiwer, Shlomo
* Lemberger, Shimshon
* Messinger, Menachem
Mizrahi, Moshe
Rubin, Reuven
* Shalom of Safed
Voscoboinic, Sarah
Zahavit, Jacobi

ITALY

* Alberino, Carmelina
* Allegretti, Ferdinando
* Andruszkiewics, Maria
* Benassi, Enrico
Benedettucci, Luigi
Berganton, Primo
Bini, Mauro
* Bolognesi, Ferruccio
Bortolami, Mario
Bragato, Gioacchino
Cadoni, Efisio
Caffi, Luciano
Capaccioni, Tonino
Cappuccio
* Ceccarelli, Marino
Ciancaleoni, Adele
Colibri, Bruno
Colombo, Mario
Dallos, Marinka
De Angelis, Luigi
* Di Girolamo, Giovanni
Di Terlizzi, Francesco
Ezechiele, Leandro
* Fereoli, Enrico
* Ferrari, Pierino
* Gagliano, Giuseppe
* Galeotti, Francesco
* Gentili, Aldo
* Ghizzardi, Pietro
Grande, Adriano
Imbrogno, Pietro
* Invrea, Irene

* Ligabue, Antonio
Lissia, Elena
Macca, Rodolfo
Maiolo, Francesco
Melis, Armando
* Metelli, Orneore
* Nasi, Rina
* Ordavo, Aldo
* Pagano, Luisa
Pardo, Amelia
* Pasotti, Bernardo
Pasqualini, Eo
Pau, Franco Corrado
Pecchini, Luciano
Pellegrin, Nino Luigi
Perra, Luigi
Pillitu, Luigi
* Ponzi Nello
Pomili, Giacomo
Prato, Lorenzo
Previ, Mario
* Roggeri, Toni
Rotunno, Graziolina
* Rovesti, Bruno
* Ruggeri, Alfredo
Sartori, Carlo
Savazzi, Gianfranco
* Serafini, Giuseppe
* Toniato, Udo
* Valla, Serafino
Verzelloni, Aldo
* Viva, Rosina

JAMAICA

* Brown, Clinton
* Brown, Everald
Burns, Ras
* Dunkley, John
* "Kapo" (Reynolds Mallica)
* McClaren, Sydney

JAPAN

Foussa, Itaya
Goseida, Horyu
* Harada, Taidji
Klein, Mine
* Maruki, Suma
Takidaire, Jiro
* Taniuchi, Rokurō
Takahashi, Yiuchi
Tokonami, Seji
* Yamashita, Kiyoshi
Yokohama, Shozaburo

KENYA

Msangi, K. Francis
Mwaniki, Louis
Oswaggo, Joel
* Soy, Ancent
Wanjau, Samwel

MEXICO

Arrieta, Augustín
* Hernández, Camila
Icasa, Ernesto
Negrete, Ezequiel

NETHERLANDS

* Alexandrine
* Bollar, Gorki

Breugel, Cornelis van den
Erfmann, Ferdinand
* Genk, Willem van
Gérard, Théa
Haar, Jaap Ter
* Hagoort, Pieter
* Hermans, Josephine
Houtman, Sipke Cornelis
* Jeuken, Johan
Kaay, Cornelis
Kuiper, Jannie
Loozen, Jacques
* Meijer, Sal
* Neervoort, Leo
* Noot, Gré
* Plasmeijer, Joop
Poelman, Willem
Ruysbroek, Willem Cornelis
Schepers, Petrus
* Schmit, Ilona
Slingerland, Adrianus
* Sloot, Jentje van der
Smits, Joop
* Sund, Meike
Vre, Stien de
Weert, Jan van
* Westerbroek, Willem
Wint, Rotmans J. K.
* Zomer, Anna

NEW ZEALAND

* Blumenfeld, Triska
Brown, Nigel

NICARAGUA

* Aguirre, Julia
Alemán, Emilio
Arana, Alonso
* Arana, Eduardo
* Arana, José
* Arellano, Rodolfo
* Beer, June
Chavarria, Chael
* Chavarría, Julia
* Faustino, José
* Fletes, Ignacio
* García, Carlos
* García, Manuel
* Graham, Mercedes Estrada de
* Guevara, Alejandro
Guevara, Esperanza
* Guevara, Gloria
* Guevara, Marita
* Guevara, Miriam
* Guillén, Asilia
* Hernández, Rolando
Henríquez, Salvadora
* Jimenez, Elba
Mairena, Julio
* Mairena, Oscar
* Marenco, Carlos
* Marín, Mario
* Mayorga, Pablo
* Mejía Godoy, Armando
* Ortega, Marina
Pineda, Elena
* Silva, Marina
Silva, Olivia
* Ubau, Yelba
Vargas, Adela
* Vogl, Hilda
* Ycaza, Adela Vargas de

NIGERIA

* Middle Art
* Olatunde, Asiru
* Rainbow Art
* Twins Seven Seven

PALAU

* Gibbons, W. Charles

PANAMA

* Lewis, Victor

POLAND

Adamczewska, Henryka
Albiczuk, Bazil
Bąk, Eugeniusz
Bąk, Stanisław
Bark
Błaszczak, Izydor
Boguszyński, Stefan
Brańska-Dzięciołowska, Zofia
Cąkala, Tadeusz
Centkowski, Jan
Centkowski, Teodor
Chelizon, Józef
Chojęta, Bronisław
Chwistek, Leon
Czajkowski, Feliks
Czyżewski, Tytus
Denkiewicz, Stanisław
Dobiasz, Stanisław
Duzynski, Stanisław
Dymurski, Piotr
Enri Hel (Helena Berlewi)
Gałek, Andrzej
* Gawłowa, Katarzyna
Głowacka, Felicija
* "Heródek"-Karol, Wójciak
Hess, Marian
Holsz, Ludwig
Iwańska, Władysława
Janeczko, Franciszek
Karulak, Stanisław
Kaznecki, Jan
Kołacz, Edward
* Korsak, Maria
Krajewski, Wincenty
* Krawczuk, Bronisław
Kudła, Leon
* Lada, Jan
Lamęcki, Jan
Lampart, Dorota
Lenczewska, Maria
Lipiec, Izydor
Maj, Wacław
Majcher, Bolesław
Makowski, Tadeusz
* Michałowska, Marta
Mickiewiczowa, Lucja
* Monsiel, Edmund
Mróz, Piotr
* Mucha, Szczepan
* Nikifor
* Ociepka, Teofil
Odrzywolski, Seweryn
Orlecki, Józef
Piłat, Józef
Plaskocinski, Jan
Płonkowa, Leokadia
Pluskowska, Felicija
* Radke, Zenon
Robakowska, Filomena
Rudnicki, Wacław

* Rusewicz, Michał
* Rybkowski, Władysław
Rysio, Wiktor
Rzepa, Izajasz
Ryszard, Sęk
Skoczylas, Jan
Skrętowicz, Zygmunt
Słominski, Aleksander
* Sobota, Józef
* Sówka, Erwin
Staniszewski, Jan
Stołorz, Paweł
Styka, Janina
Sułowski, Władysław
Surowiak, Bronisław
Suska, Bolesław
Suska, Wacław
* Sutor, Edward
* Szczypawka-Ptaszynska, Helena
Urbanek
Walczak, Władysław
Waliszewski, Zygmunt
* Warczygłowa, Zygmunt
Wasowicz, Waclaw
* Więcek, Ludwik
Wierchowski, Henryk
Wierzbicki, Stanisław
* Wnęk, Maria
* Wójtowicz, Maria
Wowro, Jedrzej
Wróbel, Pawel
Wydra, Adam
* Zagajewski, Stanisław
Zegadlo, Adam
Zegadlo, Henryk
Żeglinski, Mieczysław
Zywirska, Maria

PORTUGAL

* Coelho, José Isabelino Martins

ROMANIA

* Anonymous
Arvani
* Babeţ, Gheorghe
* Biró, Pavel
Bursan, Henia
* Cherecheş, Alexandru
Cijocaru, Mircea
Constantinescu, Maria
Cuircurescu, Traian
* Doja, Gheorghe
* Dumitrescu, Gheorghe
* Enăchescu, Constantin
Filip, Vasile
* Frunzete, Vasile
* Gheţu, Petre
* Grigorescu, Gheorghe Ion
Maric, Ion
* Mihuţ, Petru
* Mitrăchiţă, Ghită
Muresan, Ilarion
* Nicodim, Ion Niţă
* Pătraş, Ion Stan
* Pavelescu, Emil
Petrache, Logothete
* Petrescu, Simona
Pop Mihai Sigheteanu
Pop, Valentin
Popa, Toader
Purcariu, Matei
* Savu, Alexandru
Simonescu, Haralambie
* Sturza, Gheorghe

* Tohăneanu, Timotei Traian
Vaduva, Marin
* Vasilescu, Constantin
Vicol, Vasile
* Vintilă, Petru

SENEGAL

* Anonymous
Fall, Modou
Faye, Thierno
Lo, Boubacar
M' Bengue, Gora
Mor-Gueye
N' Gom, Alexis

SPAIN

Angulo, Domingo
Arrizabel, Luis
Balas, Fernando
"Boliche"
* Calvo, Walerico Moral
Carrascal, Isidro
Casanova, María Dolores
España, Argimiro
Ferrer, Vicente
Fuente, Tomás de la
Gómez, Manuela
Mallebrera, Higinio
Navarro, Andrés
Osorio, Felipe
Pérez Bueno, Vicente
Rivera Bagur, Miguel
Ruiz, Vicente
Sánchez, Manuel
Torre, Isidro de la
Uriarte, Domingo
* Vivancos, Miguel García

SWITZERLAND

Aemisegger-Giezendanner, A. B.
Alder, Jojannes
Allgöwer, Christoph Sebastian
* Appenzell Painting
"Avarni", Eugen (Avamitache)
Bareneo, Arnoldo
Barth, Andréas
* Béral, Jean
Bernasconi, Otto
Bernhardsgrütter, Anton
* Binder, Jakob
Bleiker, Heinrich
* Bordonzotti, Alfred
Broger, Verena
* Checchi, Giuseppe de
Christen, Maria G.
Dertig, Willi
* Dietrich, Adolf
Figini, Enrico
Frischknecht, Fritz
Georges, Joseph
Giezendanner, Babeli
Glass, Siggi
* Güdel, Helen
Güdel, Ulrich
* Haim, Franz Anton
Hefti-Stamm, Anja
Hermans, Josephine
* Heuscher, Johan Jakob
* Holzer, Meieli
* Hostettler, Elisabeth
Kaegi, Gertrud

733

* Lämmler, Bartholomäus
* Lüthi, Hanny
  Manser, Albert
* Müller, Johannes
* Neff, Sybille
  Palatini, Maria
* Peter, Alfred Ernest
  Saraceni, Ezilda
  Scheidegger, Ursula
  Schöttli, Emanuel
  Sollberger, Arthur
  Speiser, Gottlieb
  Staub, Anna
  Wells, Margot
  Zeller, Johann Baptist
  Zülle, Johannes

734

TANZANIA

  Mmatabwe, Adeusi
  Mpata, G. G. Simon
  Mruta, B. Hasim
  Tedo, Kasper Henrik
* Tingatinga, Eduardo Saidi
  Yakobo

TUNISIA

* Anonymous
  Chniter, Baghdadi
  Ghaddab, Mahrzia
  Guermassi, Amar
  Jtita, Ali
  Saâd, Hamadi Ben

UGANDA

* Katarikawe, Jak

USA

* Anonymous
* Aragón, José Rafael
* Arning, Eddie
* Black, Calvin
* Bochero, Peter
  Bond, Peter Mason
* Borkowski, Mary
  Brandley, John
* Brewster, John
* Brice, Bruce
  Brown, W. H.
  Castle, James
  Chamber, Thomas
* Church, Henry
* Coe, Clark
  Cordero, Helen
  Cox, W. A.
* Coyle, Carlos Cortes
  Darger, Henry
* Davis, Vestie
  Day, Frank Leveva
* Dinsmoor, S. P.
* Edmondson, William
* Evans, Minnie
* Fasanella, Ralph
* Felski, Albina
* Field, Erastus Salisbury
* Finster, Howard
* Fisher, Jonathan
* Fracarossi, Joseph
  Frost, J. O. J.
* Fryer, Flora
* Gatto, Victor Joseph

* Golding, William
  Goldsmith, Deborah
* Grandma Moses
* Hamblett, Theora
* Hampton, James
  Harley, Steve
* Hathaway, Rufus
  Hayes, G. A.
* Hicks, Edward
* Hirschfield, Morris
* Jones, Frank
* Kane, John
* Kasling, Charlie
* Klumpp, Gustav
* Krans, Olof
  Krans, Otto
* Lebduska, Lawrence
* Liebermann, Harry
  Litwak, Israel
  Lopez, José Dolores
* Maldonado, Alex
* Mazur, Frank
* McCarthy, Justin
* Mejo, Oscar de
* Miller, Louise
  Moran, Frank
* Morgan, Gertrude
  Morill, D.
* Moses, Kivetoruk
  Neusch, Erwin
* O' Kelly, Mattie Lou
* Palladino, Angela
  Park, Linton
* Pickett, Joseph
* Pierce, Elijah
  Pinney, Eunice
* Pippin, Horace
  Powel, H. M. T.
* Pressley, Daniel
  Prior, W. M.
  Raker, Colette
* Ramirez, Martin
  Rodia, Simon
* Roeder, John
* Savitsky, Jack
  Smith, Fred
  Stock, Joseph W.
  Stovall, Queena
* Sullivan, Patrick J.
* Tolson, Edgar
  Valentine, Kim
  Waele, Jeanine de
* Williamson, Clara McDonald
* Willson, Mary Ann
* Yoakum, Joseph
* Zeldis, Malcah

USSR

* Abaljaev, Ivan Mihajlovič
* Agapov, Mihail Mihajlovič
  Akbaev, Ishak
* Aladašvili, Aleksandr
* Ambarcumjan, Oganes
* Amirjan, Gerasim
* Andreev, Nikolaj Alekseevič
  Apojan, Grigor
  Arkerjan, Z.
  Arzumanov, Petr
  Babinets, Fedor
* Bdejan, Artjuša
* Bereznev, Aleksandr Dmitrievič
* Bičjunene, Monika
* Burjak, Marija Pantelejmonovna
* Černjahovskij, Ivan
* Černobrova, Suzanna
* Dikarskaja, Anna Petrovna

  Djadja Mitja
* Drungilas, Antanas
* Džalilov, Madžid
* Edziev, Soslanbek
  Ekaterina
* Elenok, Tat'jana Dmitrievna
* Ertuganov, Šamil'
* Gagua, Irina
  Galuško, Marija
* Gerlikene, Pjatronele
* Gluhovskaja, Galina Grigor'evna
* Grigorjanc, Karapet
  Gulian, Aram
* Hačaturjan, Gajane
* Helimiši, Hasan
* Jučuvene, Magdalena
  Kaidaš-Maškovskaja
* Kazmina, Marija Georgievna
  Kile, Pjačka
* Kiš, Elena
* Knjukštajte, Elena
  Komolov, Nikolaj
* Kondas, Paul
  Kopel, Martin
* Korovkin, Al'bert Nikolaevič
  Kosenko, Stepan
  Kotljarevska, Lija
  Kovaljčuk, Marija
  Kozlijastov, Pavel
  Krivickas, Blažejus
  Lampaj, P.
* Leonov, Pavel Petrovič
  Lolišvili, Tengiz
* Loretjan, Agavard
* Lysenko, Ivan Ivanovič
* Maradišvili, Šalva
* Mastajtene, Marite
* Mazin, Ignatij Andreevič
* Meliašvili, Ivan
* Milt's, El'frida Martsovna
* Mironova, Elizaveta, Fedorovna
  Mockus, Aleksas
* Muraev, Mihail Vladimirovič
* Nalivajkene, Jadviga
  Natuskin
* Nikiforov, Ivan Mihajlovič
  Očirov, Ciren Namžil
* Ol'šaneckaja, Lidija Vladimirovna
* Pankov, Konstantin Alekseevič
  Pičugin, Aleksej
* Pirosmanašvili, Nikolaj
* Plastinin, Vasilij Vasilievič
  Poležajeva, Aleksandra
  Potapov, Arkadij
* Prijmačenko, Marija Avksentievna
* Purygin, Leonid Anatol'evič
  Rijner, Val'ter
  Rimkus, Jaroslav
* Rjauba, Stasis
  Rubaškin, Samuil Jakovlevič
* Rževskij, Nikolaj Alekseevič
  Salo, Iljmar
  Sarčevic, Stanislav
* Savinov, Vasilij Timofeevič
  Sava, Stepan
* Selivanov, Ivan Egorovič
* Sergeev, Grigorij Sergeevič
* Smirnov, Vladimir Borisovič
  Sobačkova-Šostak, Ganna
* Stepanov, Sergej Georgievič
  Šabatura, Aleksandra Georgievna
  Šepka, Lionginas
* Terent'eva, M.
  Točkin
* Tret'jakov, Konstantin Ivanovič
* Tverdohvalov, Aleksandr Mihajlovič
* Utkin, M.
* Varfolomeeva, Efimija (Nina)

Ivanovna
* Vidrik, Georg
* Višnik, Aleksandr Dmitrievič
  Vizabaras, Jonas
* Volkova, Elena Andreevna
* Zakarjan, Gajk
* Zarapišvili, Emma
* Zaznobin, Vladimir Nikolaevič
* Žil'cov, Fedor Aleksandrovič
  Žukov, Nikolai

UPPER VOLTA

Kere, P.
* Rasmané, Nitiema

VENEZUELA

* "Aguilera", Silva Gerardo
* Alamo, Neke
* Alvarez, Andrés Antonio
  Alvarez, Juanita
  Apolinar
  Aranguren, Bernardino
  Baptista, Eusebio
  Boscán, Ali
  Carvallo, Feliciano
  Chávez, Isa de
  Chávez, Víctor de
  Coa, Baltazar
* Fagúndez Cruz, Amado
* Fernández, Antonio José
  Figueroa, Natividad
  García, Tulio
  Garlindo, Carlos
* Gómez, Crisanto
  Hernández, Mario Henrique
  Ilarreta, Hercilia
  Lunar, Emerio Darío
  Malu
  Méndez, Juan Ali
  Mendoza, Esteban
* Millán, Carmen
* Millán, Víctor
* Morales, Elsa
  Muñoz, Adán
  Navo, Homero
  Pena, Lulu
  Pérez, Eleutero
  Pérez, José Arecio
  Ramos, Luis
  Riojas, María Molleja de
  Rivas, Nicolás
* Rodríguez, Manases
  Sánchez, Julio César
* Valero, Salvador
  Vargas, Rafael
  Veraméndez, Dionisio
  Villagas, Luis

YUGOSLAVIA

* Bahunek, Antun
* Bahunek, Branko
* Balan, Marija
  Belić, Cvetin
  Belina, Drago
* Belković, Dragica
* Bireš, Mihalj
  Bobovac, Dragan
* Bogosav (Živković)
* Brašić, Janko
  Brusić-Kovačica, Marija
* Buktenica, Eugen
* Bunjevački, Dragiša

Čerimagić, Ragib
* Denda, Marko
* Djelošević, Gordana
* Dobrić, Djordje
* Doklean, Sofija
* Dolama, Anuca
  Dorešić, Vilma
  Dugina, Franjo
* Feješ, Emerik
* Filipović, Franjo
* Gazivoda, Predrag
* Gaži, Dragan
* Generalić, Ivan
* Generalić, Josip
* Generalić, Mato
  Generalić, Milan (Barberov)
* Grgec, Petar
* Halupova, Suzana
* Hegedušić, Martin
  Hegedušić-Janković, Nada
* Henc, Katarina
* Homonaj, Pal
* Husarik, Jan
* Ilija (Bosilj)
  Ivanec, Stjepan
  Jančić, Djuro
* Jevtović, Dušan
* Jonaš, Martin
  Jovanović, Petar
* Jovanović, Milosav
* Jurak, Dragutin
  Kec, Florika
* Kene (Ljubiša Jovanović)
* Klopotan, Franjo
* Knjazovic, Jan
* Kopričanec, Martin
* Košut, Tivadar
  Kovačević, Nikola
* Kovačić, Mijo
* Kreča, Djordje
  Kudeljnjak, Albina
  Kusanić, Andreja
* Lacković, Ivan
* Lavrič, Boris
* Lončarić, Dragica
* Lovak, Branko
* Magyar, Viktor
* Mandić, Petar
* Maran, Anujka
* Mavec-Tomljenović, Marica
* Mehkek, Martin
  Mihelič, Polde
* Milojević, Dobrosav
* Motorožesku, Mariora
* Mraz, Franjo
  Nap, Milan
* Naumovski, Vangel
* Nikčević, Milan
* Onč
u, Ana
* Paladin, Bruno
* Paluška, Martin
* Pečnik, Greta
* Petelinšek, Franciska
* Peternelj, Jože
* Peternelj, Konrad
* Petranović, Tomislav
* Pintarić, Josip
  Popov, Djordje
* Povolni, Mihalj
* Puja, Florika
* Puškarić-Petras, Mara
* Rabuzin, Ivan
* Rašić, Milan
* Repnik, Anton
* Ristić, Petar
* Savić, Krsto
* Šijaković, Djordje
* Sirković, Stepa

* Skurjeni, Matija
* Smajić, Petar
* Sokol, Jan
* Spasić, Čeda
* Staničić, Matija
* Stanisavljević, Dragiša
* Stanisavljević, Milan
* Stevanović, Dobrivoje
  Stojkov, Sava
  Stolnik, Slavko
* Tisnikar, Jože
* Topljak, Pero
* Večenaj, Ivan
  Večenaj, Stjepan
  Venjarski, Ondrej
* Vidović, Branko
  Virius, Branko
* Virius, Mirko
* Živanović, Slobodan
  Žunjić, Kosta

735

ZAIRE

* Djilatendo
* Kalume-Dikote
* Kiabelua, Alphonse
* Koyongonda, Louis
* Lubaki, Albert
* Moke Art
* Mususa, Pungu
  Pambu, Bodo
* Pili-Pili
* Samba, Wa Nbimba Nizinga
  Tschibumba